LEADERS
OF THE
INFORMATION AGE

EDITOR
David Weil

ASSOCIATE EDITORS
Mari Rich
Olivia Jane Smith

ASSISTANT EDITORS
Andrew I. Cavin
Martha A. Hostetter
Kate Stern

EDITORIAL ASSISTANT
Carolyn Ellis

PRODUCTION STAFF
Gray Young (Manager)
Jeremy K. Brown
Jennifer K. Peloso
Richard Joseph Stein

STAFF WRITERS
Denise Bonilla
Dimitri Cavalli
Kathleen D'Angelo
Peter G. Herman
Christopher Mari
Geoff Orens
Brian Solomon

The H.W. Wilson Company
New York • Dublin
2003

Library of Congress Cataloging-in-Publication Data

Leaders of the information age / editor, David Weil ; in-house editors, Mari Rich, Olivia Jane Smith, assistant editor, Martha Hostetter; staff contribitions Denise M. Bonilla ... [et al.].
     p. cm.
   ISBN 0-8242-0976-1
   1. Computer scientists—Biography. I. Weil, David. II. Bonilla, Denise M.

QA76.2.A2L43 2003
004'.0922—dc21
[B]

2003053542

PRINTED IN THE UNITED STATES OF AMERICA

TABLE OF CONTENTS

Preface

This book provides introductions to the lives and work of more than 200 of the pioneers of the modern Information Age—from Ramon Llull, who in the 14th century invented the Llullian machine, a mechanical device for manipulating logical propositions, to Seymour Cray, the designer of the world's first supercomputer.

As the scope and magnitude of human knowledge grew in the intervening centuries, mankind struggled to explain the physical and increasingly intricate world that was revealing itself. The complexity of science and mathematics grew with each year. (Imagine the difficulty of expressing in Roman numerals the distance between star systems or the small fraction of inches in the thickness of a plant cell.) As superstition and conjecture began to give way to empirical study and the scientific method, advances came with a flurry. Renaissance scholars thrust technology into the mainstream by encouraging the use of devices and machines to improve the quality of life. Telescopes, microscopes, clocks, and steam-driven looms were just a few such devices. The advancement of new and even more fantastic machines and ideas quickly followed. When Blaise Pascal designed and built a circular adding machine, in 1642, he came up with some of the foundations of calculus in the process. The ability to craft gears and miniature parts with precision and durability opened the way for complex thinking machines before the end of the 19th century. By the time Charles Babbage had created his Difference Engine—almost 500 years after Llull's era—there had been dozens of other devices invented to calculate, reckon, and keep accurate time.

With the proliferation of affordable electricity in the early 20th century, the possibilities and applications of timesaving devices challenged the imagination of tinkerers and dreamers alike. Thomas Edison probably never imagined, however, that his light bulb would lead to the creation of the vacuum tube or the Eccles-Jordan flip-flop, which were integral components of such early electrical digital computers as the ENIAC.

Computers appeared in universities, large businesses, and research facilities by the mid–20th century, and by the 1960s most people who had a bank account began to see their effects: monthly statements with up-to-date, accurate balances and checks processed in a matter of days rather than weeks. For the first time, information was becoming available to wider and more diverse segments of industry and society.

In the early 1970s most computers were still room-sized affairs run by several engineers, programmers, and data-input personnel. Microprocessors changed all that, and personal computers gradually became almost ubiquitous. By the end of the second millennium, the computer had made its presence known in almost every aspect of life—from mapping the human genome to space exploration, from medicine to music. Computers helped us develop products, design homes, open clogged arteries, operate our automobiles, and buy food in the supermarket. In the United States it is now virtually impossible to get through a day without interacting in some way with a computer.

The Information Age continues to unfold before us, and each subject profiled here has contributed in some way to its development. A few words about omissions in this volume: Many other names that were initially selected for this work are deserving of recognition for their contributions and accomplishments. Biographical information on them was scarce, however, if existent at all. To honor their successes, we have included them in the timeline and in references throughout the book.

I would like to thank the researchers, writers, and editors of the H. W. Wilson Company, including Denise Bonilla, Dimitri Cavalli, Andrew Cavin, Kathleen D'Angelo, Peter Herman, Martha Hostetter, Christopher Mari, Brian Solomon, Olivia Smith, Kate Stern, and Cliff Thompson, for all their efforts and skills. Thanks also go to Michael Schulze, Wilson's vice president for Editorial Services, for his belief in this project. A special thank you to Mari Rich, whose perseverance, talents, and good humor made this an enjoyable project, coast to coast. The H. W. Wilson production staff has my sincere gratitude as well. Thanks to the many librarians who have facilitated the research for this volume, including Christine Campbell and Charlotte Labbe of Fordham University, whose services were invaluable. I would like to pay tribute to Dr. Coleman Furr, the founder of Coleman College, for teaching me the concept of concinnity; my family, friends, and co-workers at the Computer Museum of America for their unflagging support; and my wife, Faye, and sons, Benjamin and Jonathan, who continually inspire me to keep up with them.

—David Weil
Del Mar, California
February 2003

List of Biographical Sketches

LEADERS

OF THE

INFORMATION AGE

Courtesy of Norman Abramson

Abramson, Norman

Apr. 1, 1932– Creator of ALOHANET

Today, the most common form of "surfing" is on the electronic pages of the World Wide Web. But when Norman Abramson—the designer of one of the earliest computer networks—went surfing, it was on actual waves. In fact, he moved to Hawaii, in 1968, out of a desire to surf the area's legendary swells. It was also there, at the University of Hawaii, that he embarked on a project to tie together seven computers on four different islands, resulting in the first modern data network—a predecessor to the Internet. This transmission system, which Abramson dubbed the ALOHANET in honor of his adopted state, formed the basis of the protocols used in the Ethernet, a popular type of local area network that communicates using radio signals as well as satellite and terrestrial radio links. During the high-tech boom of the 1990s, Abramson formed ALOHA Networks, a company that capitalizes on an updated version of the ALOHANET technology and promises to provide high-speed Internet access through highly efficient two-way satellite connections.

Norman Abramson was born in Boston, Massachusetts, on April 1, 1932. He attended Harvard University and received a degree in physics in 1953. He then left the East Coast behind for graduate school in California, first at the University of California at Los Angeles (UCLA), where he earned a master's degree in physics, in 1955, and then to Stanford University's legendary electrical engineering department, where he earned a Ph.D. in 1958. After graduating Abramson stayed to teach at Stanford until 1965, when he left to accept a series of visiting professorships at Berkeley, Harvard, and the Massachusetts Institute of Technology (MIT). A vacation to Hawaii during the late 1960s changed his life: Having fallen in love with the island's unmatched surfing, Abramson inquired at the University of Hawaii if they were hiring any electrical engineering professors. In 1968 he landed a job and moved to Hawaii, becoming a professor of electrical engineering, the first chair of the department of information and computer science, and the director of the ALOHA system project.

The ALOHA project aimed to connect four different Hawaiian islands via a computer network, a concept that had been gaining currency at the time. (The Department of Defense's ARPANET, a wide-area network, was also being developed in the 1960s.) Abramson and his team of engineers and graduate students designed the first wireless packet-switched network—the ALOHANET. It operated through radio waves rather than through telephone lines or conventional wires and sent information by breaking it into smaller units, called packets, which were then labeled with their source and destination and reassembled upon arrival. The ALOHANET was up and running by 1970, transmitting data at 9600 bits per second. (By comparison, early modems, called acoustic couplers because they used the tones of telephone equipment to send and receive messages, ran at a speed of 300 bits per second.)

The protocol Abramson designed for the ALOHANET was a radio-based data communications system. Users shared a single network pathway; if two or more packets were sent at the same time, they would sometimes collide, in which case the computer would be instructed to send the data from each of the packets again after a short pause. Later, Abramson developed Slotted ALOHA, which reduced the chance of collisions by dividing the channel into time slots and requiring that the user send only at the beginning of a time slot.

In 1971 the ALOHANET was connected to the ARPANET on the mainland, marking the first time another independent network was connected to the network of military, industrial, and academic sites. ALOHANET attracted the attention of a young engineer named Robert Metcalfe. After graduating from Harvard, in 1973, and before going to work at the Palo Alto Research Center (PARC), Metcalfe came to Hawaii to study the ALOHANET. During his three-month stay, he came up with an improvement on Abramson's protocol: instead of randomly sending out a packet of data, the transmitter would "listen" for any traffic on the network and send only if no other computers were sending packets. This reduced the chances of collisions and made communication smoother. Metcalfe went on to design the Ethernet at PARC, connecting two computers through radio frequency signals carried by a cable. The Ethernet has become the most popular type of local area network, and Metcalfe credits Abramson for much of its design.

From 1972 to 1987 Abramson served as an adviser to the United Nations for the use of satellite technology in developing countries, primarily in the cities of Budapest, Hungary; Jakarta, Indonesia; and Manila, in the Philippines. In 1996 Abramson left the University of Hawaii to found ALOHA Networks, a start-up based in San Francisco, California, and backed by venture capital. He founded the company to capitalize on his development of Spread ALOHA Multiple Access (SAMA) technology, which is used in the company's SkyDSL, a two-way satellite-based Internet access system. In the race to provide high-speed access to the millions of businesses and homes that are clamoring for it, Internet Service Providers (ISPs) have encountered problems with local telephone monopolies, who control the phone lines through which the ISPs would like to deliver access to their customers. Because of such challenges of infrastructure, Deborah Claymon noted in Red Herring (October 1998, on-line), "even the largest ISPs have been forced to limit expansion plans, especially globally." But Internet access via satellite—which would bypass the need to work with telephone lines—is widely considered to be prohibitively expensive; the cost of the so-called "uplink" connection to the satellite requires the use of either a costly one-to-one channel or the sharing of a single channel through multiple-access techniques. Abramson spent 10 years developing the SAMA, a protocol that allows multiple-user communication with a satellite in the most efficient, and therefore most cost-effective, way. SAMA is essentially a modernization of the ALOHA protocol, in which multiple computers used the same network path. ALOHA Networks plans to market satellite multiple-access networking equipment and service to large ISPs, who in turn will sell the high-speed access to their customers. As Claymon wrote, "by reaching skyward to satellites the company will enable ISPs to bypass local telephone carriers and serve geographically dispersed customers more cheaply." She cautioned that some experts are skeptical about the company's claims, arguing that satellite bandwidth costs four to ten times what terrestrial bandwidth costs. "There's no doubt that satellite bandwidth is expensive when used in the same wasteful way as terrestrial bandwidth," Abramson told Claymon in response to such doubts. And yet, he argued, terrestrial, wire-line Internet traffic typically uses only 1/1000 of the bandwidth available because it fails to take advantage of the "silences," the periods of inactivity typical of Internet use. Because of the high cost of satellite bandwidth, Abramson could not afford to squander any moments of bandwidth between transmissions, and so he developed SAMA to allow multiple users to access the satellite channel in a highly efficient manner. In Nerds 2.0.1 (on-line), the PBS history of computer communication, a writer compared Abramson's ALOHANET to a telephone party line; protocols help insure that users take turns accessing the network, just as polite people wait their turn to talk in a group. With the SAMA technology, Abramson created a method by which multiple users will be able to hold Internet "conversations," taking their turn accessing the bandwidth, one after the other, with virtually no silences in between.

For the development of his ALOHANET system, Norman Abramson was made a Fellow of the Institute of Electrical and Electronics Engineers (IEEE), in 1980, and received an IEEE Kobayashi Computers and Communications Award, in 1995. In August 1998 he was presented with the IEEE Information Theory Society Golden Jubilee Award for Technological Innovation for the invention of the first random-access communication protocol, including the SAMA technology.—M. A. H.

Suggested Reading: PBS Nerds 2.0.1 Web site; Red Herring (on-line) Oct. 1998

Aiken, Howard

Mar. 8, 1900–Mar. 14, 1973 Designer of the Harvard Mark I (a.k.a. the ASCC)

Howard Aiken was the designer of the first large-scale, automatic, general-purpose electromechanical computer. The Automatic Sequence Control Calculator (ASCC), more commonly known as the Mark I, was conceived by Aiken in the late 1930s and developed at International Business Machines (IBM) between 1938 and 1944 by the engineers Clair D. Lake, Benjamin M. Durfee, and Francis E. (Frank) Hamilton. A prototype of modern digital computers, the Mark I was a milestone in the history of computing because it convinced observers that large and complex calculating machines could function automatically. A professor at Harvard University, in Cambridge, Massachusetts, Aiken led the development of three other large calculating machines as well, and he is credited with estab-

Courtesy of the University of St. Andrews

Howard Aiken

lishing at Harvard the world's first degree program in what is now known as computer science.

Howard Hathaway Aiken was born on March 8 (some sources say March 9), 1900 in Hoboken, New Jersey, the son of Daniel H. Aiken and Margaret Emily (Mierisch) Aiken. His family later moved to Indianapolis, Indiana, where he was raised. In 1919 he graduated from the Arsenal Technical High School, and that same year he began undergraduate studies in electrical engineering at the University of Wisconsin. He also started working as an operating engineer for the Madison Gas and Electric Company, a job he kept until he earned his B.S. in 1923. Aiken then obtained a position with the Westinghouse Electrical Manufacturing Company. He left Westinghouse in 1931 to pursue graduate studies. He began his graduate work in physics at the University of Chicago, in Illinois, before transferring to Harvard University, where he received an M.S., in 1937, and a Ph.D., in 1939.

While working toward his master's degree, Aiken became dissatisfied with the available methods of computation, which he believed were impeding the development of the mathematically oriented sciences such as physics. In 1937, in a 23-page proposal for a large-scale calculating machine, he wrote, "There exist problems beyond our ability to solve, not because of theoretical difficulties, but because of insufficient means of mechanical computation," as quoted on the Computer Museum of America Web site. He began formulating the concept for a computing machine constructed by wiring together components of adding machines. He envisioned a device that could recognize and perform calculations using both positive and negative numbers, execute standard arithme-

tic operations, and perform operations in sequence.

A year earlier he had approached the heads of the Harvard physics department with his idea, but was informed that the university had a similar machine already—a remnant of the unfinished Analytic Engine, built by the 19th-century English mathematician Charles Babbage, which was stored in the Science Center attic. Taken to see the relic, Aiken recognized that he and Babbage had the same basic mechanism in mind, and he subsequently obtained a copy of Babbage's autobiography, *Passages from the Life of a Philosopher* (1864). Reading it, Aiken "felt that Babbage was addressing him personally from the past," as quoted by Martin Campbell-Kelly and William Aspray in *Computer: A History of the Information Machine* (1996). In Aiken's proposal and in his later writings regarding the Mark I, he frequently stressed Babbage's influence on his work.

After initially being turned away by the Monroe Calculating Machine Company, Aiken took the proposal to IBM, where Thomas J. Watson Sr., the company's president, agreed to fund and build the machine. Construction began at IBM's laboratory in Endicott, New York, in 1939, under the direction of the distinguished inventor and engineer Clair D. Lake. Assisting Lake were the engineers Francis E. (Frank) Hamilton and Benjamin M. Durfee. The cost was reportedly between $250,000 and $500,000, with some of the funding supplied by the U.S. Navy, which retained the machine for wartime use.

The completed Mark I stood 51 feet long, eight feet high, and two feet wide. It was composed of a series of basic calculating units, engineered to run in mechanical synchronism. They were lined up in a row along a 50-foot shaft, which was powered by a 5-horsepower electric motor, like "a nineteenth-century New England textile mill," according to Campbell-Kelly and Aspray. The machine weighed five tons and contained approximately 750,000 parts, including 500 miles of wire, 2,200 counter wheels, and three million wire connections.

The Mark I was electromechanical, built primarily from the same mechanical parts IBM used to construct its accounting machines. (The first fully electronic computer, ENIAC, was built a few years later, at the University of Pennsylvania, in Philadelphia.) In designing the Mark I, Aiken felt that vacuum tubes, which were widely used at the time in other electromechanical devices, were not reliable enough as electrical relays; he opted instead to use magnetized coils called solenoids. In addition to electromagnetically controlled relays and gears, the machine contained mechanical registers for storing numbers. Information was entered into the machine through long strips of paper tape or punched cards. Although a specially trained mathematician was needed to prepare the programs, the machine's operator did not need to possess any mathematical ability. The Mark I could solve three addition problems per second, but multiplication required about six seconds and division twice as long. It could also compute elementary, trigonometric, and hyperbolic functions, although these calculations took considerably longer. It could store up to 72 numbers and was accurate up to 23 decimal places.

The construction was completed at the Endicott facility in January 1943, but the machine was not demonstrated to members of the Harvard faculty until December of that year. It was then disassembled and relocated to Harvard, where it was housed in a large basement of the Physics Research Laboratory. By early spring 1944 the machine was fully operational, producing navigational and mathematical tables for the navy under the direction of Lt. Robert Campbell. Aiken himself had been only loosely involved in the development for some time. A reserve officer in the navy, he had been called to active duty in 1941 and stationed at the Naval Mine Warfare School, in Yorktown, Virginia. When Aiken returned to Harvard in 1944, he was placed in charge of the machine. "I guess I'm the only man in the world who was ever commanding officer of a computer," he quipped, as quoted by Campbell-Kelly and Aspray.

An official ceremony was held on August 7, 1944 for IBM to dedicate the computer to Harvard. A press release, however, prepared by the Harvard News Office in consultation with Aiken, failed to give proper credit to IBM and the engineers who worked on the computer. As the originator of the idea, Aiken considered himself to be the primary inventor, and he downplayed the construction expertise of the engineers and as neglected to mention that IBM had funded the project. When Watson saw the release, he was furious and almost boycotted the ceremony, but Aiken was able to persuade him to attend. Aiken apparently felt little compunction, however, and reportedly remarked, "The president of IBM can't tell the president of Harvard what to do," as quoted by J. A. N. Lee in the *International Biographical Dictionary of Computer Pioneers* (1995).

The new computer captured the imagination of the public, and the event was widely covered in the press. *American Weekly* heralded the arrival of "Harvard's Robot Super-Brain," while *Popular Science Weekly* announced, "Robot Mathematician Knows All the Answers," as quoted by Campbell-Kelly and Aspray. At the time, the speed of the machine was less impressive than the fact that it was fully automatic; once a program had been entered, the machine would run it through to completion, operating 24 hours a day, seven days a week. The Mark I was soon superceded by the greater speeds of electronic computers such as the ENIAC, but it remained valuable because it produced such reliable results and could function continuously, whereas electronic machines required periods of downtime. After the war, the machine continued to be used part-time by the navy. It remained in operation at Harvard University until 1959 and was

deployed by engineers and scientists on various problems associated with magnetic fields, optics, radar, and atomic physics.

Aiken's Mark I should not be confused with another machine, built in Great Britain by Thomas Kilburn and Frederic Calland Williams in the late 1940s. Known as the Manchester Mark 1, Kilburn's computer was entirely electronic and was the first computer to store data and programs in the same location.

With the assistance of Lt. Robert Campbell, Aiken authored the Manual of Operation of the Automatic Sequence Controlled Calculator, a 500-page guide explaining the method of coding instructions for the machine. Among the early computer luminaries to work with the Mark I was the programmer Grace Murray Hopper, who became the first person to "debug" a computer—when she discovered a malfunction in the Mark I that was caused by a moth crushed on a relay switch.

In 1947 Aiken became the director of Harvard's new computation laboratory. Recognizing the benefits to be gained from recording the development of this burgeoning area of study, he proposed to the United Nations Educational, Scientific, and Cultural Organization (UNESCO) the establishment of an "international bureau of computations," which would collect all available information regarding computing activities worldwide.

In 1947 Aiken's second calculation machine, the Mark II, was completed at the Harvard Corporation Laboratory. An entirely electronic computer containing some 13,000 electrical relays, the Mark II was 12 times faster than its predecessor and three times as large. It was shipped from Harvard to the Naval Proving Ground in Dahlgren, Virginia, where it was used by the navy in the fields of supersonics and aerodynamics. After it had completed a backlog of naval computations, the new computer was made available for use in industry and science. In 1949 Aiken introduced the Mark III, which was delivered two years later to the Naval Service Weapons Center in Dahlgren for testing. The Mark III, which contained more than 5,000 vacuum tubes and 2,000 relays, was the first large-scale computer to feature drum memory, meaning that information was stored on specially designed, rotating magnetic drums. In this way the Mark III was a direct predecessor of today's stored-program computers. The final version of the ASCC, the Mark IV, was constructed by Aiken in 1952 and featured an even more advanced magnetic memory system.

In addition to his work on these computers, Aiken inaugurated at Harvard University the world's first academic program in computer science, although it was not known by that name at the time. He established a course of studies leading to the master's degree (and eventually also the doctorate) that would prepare students with the mathematical and programming training necessary to work on the computers of the period. Among his students who became well known in the field were

Gerrit Blaauw, Frederick Brooks Jr., Kenneth Iverson, and Anthony Oettinger. Aiken left Harvard in 1961, when he was appointed professor of information technology at the University of Miami, in Florida.

Aiken published numerous articles on electronics and automatic data processing; some of these appeared in *The Annals of the Computation Laboratory of Harvard University*, of which he was the general editor. A detailed analysis of the Mark I, coauthored in 1946 by Aiken and Grace M. Hopper, appeared in *Electrical Engineering*, a publication of the American Institute of Electrical Engineers. Aiken was a member of the scientific research honor society Sigma Xi and the American Academy of Arts and Sciences, and he also served on the National Research Council, specializing in high-speed calculating machinery. Among his numerous awards were the Palmes de l'Académie Française in 1949, the Belgian officer's cross of the Order of the Crown in 1955, the Distinguished Public Service Award from the U.S. Navy in 1956, and a decoration from the U.S. Air Force for civilian service in 1957. The Institute of Electrical and Electronic Engineers (IEEE) honored him posthumously, in 1980, with its Computer Pioneer Award.

Aiken married Agnes Montgomery on January 7, 1943, and they had a daughter, Elizabeth. Aiken died on March 14, 1973 in St. Louis, Missouri, at the age of 73. The computer center at Harvard University, which Aiken directed for 15 years, now bears his name. Although Aiken is recognized as one of the foremost computer pioneers of his day, he was not as prescient about the future of computing as one might expect: he is famous for predicting, in 1947, that only six electronic digital computers would be needed to satisfy the computing needs of the entire United States.—A. I. C.

Suggested Reading: *Chronology of Digital Computing Machines* (on-line); *Computer* (on-line) Nov. 1996; Computer Museum of America Web site; *Computerworld* p182 Nov. 3, 1986; *Harvard University Gazette* (on-line) Apr. 9, 1998; *New York Times* p17 Aug. 7, 1944; Lee, J. A. N., ed. *International Biographical Dictionary of Computer Pioneers*, 1995; Campbell-Kelly, Martin and William Aspray. *Computer: A History of the Information Machine*, 1996

Alexanderson, Ernst F. W.

Jan. 25, 1878–May 14, 1975 Inventor of the high-frequency alternator for radio

Granted more than 340 patents over the course of five decades, Ernst F. W. Alexanderson was one of the most prolific geniuses of the electrical age. Along with Guglielmo Marconi, Lee de Forest, and Edwin H. Armstrong, he made integral contributions to the science of radio broadcasting. Worldwide fame came to him as a young man in 1906, when he revolutionized wireless telegraphy and telephony with his invention of the high-frequency alternator. Before this invention, communication via radio had been only through Morse code; Alexanderson's alternator allowed for the first transmission of the human voice by radio. In 1927 he enjoyed further acclaim for demonstrating the first home reception of television. During his 44 years of active service as an engineer for the General Electric Company (GE), he produced numerous inventions in such fields as railway electrification, motors and power transmission, telephone relays, and electric ship propulsion. From 1919 until 1924, in addition to carrying on his work for General Electric, he was chief engineer of the Radio Corporation of America (RCA). After his retirement Alexanderson served as an engineering consultant to both GE and RCA. In 1955 he received his 321st patent, for his invention of a color-television receiver for use with RCA's system of color broadcasting.

The son of Professor Aron M. and Amelie (von Heidenstam) Alexanderson, Ernst Fredrik Werner Alexanderson was born in Upsala, Sweden, on January 25, 1878. His father taught at the University of Upsala and later held the chair of classical languages at the University of Lund, where Ernst studied from 1896 to 1897 after graduating from Lund High School. Because of his aptitude for mechanics, young Alexanderson was sent in 1897 to the Royal Institute of Technology at Stockholm, from which he graduated as a mechanical and electrical engineer in 1900. He attended the Royal Technical Institute, in Berlin, Germany, for a year of postgraduate work and studied under Adolf K. H. Slaby, co-creator of the Slaby-Arco system of radio communication.

While in Berlin, Alexanderson read *Theory and Calculation of Alternating Current Phenomena* (1897) by Charles Steinmetz, GE's noted inventor and engineer, and was so impressed that he decided to go to America, where such men as Steinmetz and Thomas Alva Edison were working. He landed in New York City in 1901 and, after meeting Edison, went to visit Steinmetz, with whom he formed a close friendship.

Alexanderson began working as a draftsman for the C&C Electrical Company, in New Jersey; in February 1902 he was hired by GE, on the recommendation of Steinmetz. The next year he took the GE test engineering course, and in 1904 he became a member of the company's engineering staff, designing generators under the direction of Steinmetz.

When Alexanderson had first arrived in America, radio was limited in use because of the weak transmitters then available, which allowed only for the transmission of Morse code through low-frequency radio waves. In 1904 Reginald A. Fessenden, a pioneering radio experimenter, asked GE to build for him an alternator capable of producing alternating current (ac) of high frequency. Whereas the typical alternating generators of the time were capable of reaching only about 60 Hertz (Hz), Fessenden demanded that the new design be capable of reaching 100,000 Hz, or 100 kHz. Alexanderson was assigned to the task and, after constructing several models over the course of two years, he devised a practical alternator of the desired frequency, which was installed in Fessenden's laboratory in Brant Rock, Massachusetts. From this station on Christmas Eve, 1906, a radio program was broadcast that included a voice (Fessenden's) and a violin solo. It was the first broadcast of a human voice and marked the beginning of radio broadcasting as we know it today.

Alexanderson's work was immediately recognized as brilliant, and when he returned to Sweden on a visit, many industrialists there urged him to remain in his native land. However, his father predicted that the Old World was doomed to revolution and destruction and advised his son to settle in America. Alexanderson heeded the advice and became a naturalized citizen of the United States in 1908, several years before the advent of World War I.

Alexanderson soon improved his alternator, which led to the development of reliable transatlantic radio communication. In 1915 Guglielmo Marconi, known as the father of radio, came to see a demonstration of Alexanderson's 50-kilowatt alternator at the GE laboratories in Schenectady, New York; one of these alternators was subsequently installed at the Trans-Atlantic Marconi Company station in New Brunswick, New Jersey. During World War I a 200-kilowatt Alexanderson alternator installed at this same station was able to transmit to soldiers encamped in France and throughout the world. On October 20, 1918 the 200-kilowatt alternator transmitted an ultimatum of President Woodrow Wilson direct to Germany. By 1925 there were Alexanderson alternators installed in Sweden, Hawaii, England, and Poland, as well as in the United States. For Alexanderson's remarkable achievement, King Gustav V of Sweden decorated him with the Order of the North Star.

At the end of World War I, the British-Marconi Wireless Company renewed negotiations with GE for the exclusive use of the Alexanderson alternator. However, the United States government, realizing the huge potential of the invention, favored retention of control of the machine by a domestic company. As a result, GE and several other large American corporations organized RCA in 1919. Alexanderson was appointed chief engineer of this enterprise and spent the next five years dividing his time between GE and RCA. He relinquished his chief engineer's post at RCA in 1924 but remained as a consulting engineer with that firm until GE liquidated its holdings in RCA in 1932. (As late as 1955 several Alexanderson alternators were still in service in transoceanic radiotelegraph service. When modern shortwave transmitters and cables broke down during magnetic storms, or when sun spots were prevalent, the Alexanderson alternator at Rocky Point, New York, was then used to maintain contact with Europe and England.)

Alexanderson was inventive in almost every branch of radio technology. His tuned radio-frequency receiver system, patented in 1916, provided selective tuning to different frequencies and became one of the basic tools of modern radio broadcasting. Alexanderson's system soon came to dominate the radio industry, but only after an international legal wrangle in which selective tuning was attacked as unworkable. While on the witness stand during one of these trials, Alexanderson was confronted with the argument that no one in the court room had ever witnessed a demonstration of the system. As reported in the *New York Times* (October 25, 1952), the inventor called for a recess, sent out for materials, built a model in the court room, and successfully demonstrated the principle, all in the same day.

During World War I Alexanderson created the multiple-tuned antenna, the antistatic receiver, and the magnetic amplifier. In combination with the alternator and the multi-tuning system, the amplifier established the practicability of wireless transatlantic telephony; in 1919 the first two-way conversation took place between the Trans-Atlantic Marconi Company station in New Jersey and the steamship *George Washington*, 900 miles out at sea, with President Woodrow Wilson on board.

The magnetic amplifier was made obsolete by Alexanderson himself when he invented the highly important electronic modulator, which, by applying an improved vacuum tube to radio telephony, made possible the construction of powerful transmitters for high frequencies, another milestone in the history of radio. An unexpected and dramatic use of Alexanderson's inventions in radio was made in 1923 when his son, Verner, was kidnapped from in front of his Schenectady home. The six-year-old boy was missing until a caretaker at a lake resort notified the police after recognizing him and the kidnappers from a description broadcast by the radio station WGY.

Alexanderson is also known for his pioneering efforts in television as well as in the transmission of pictures by radio. On June 5, 1924 he transmitted the first facsimile message across the Atlantic, a reproduction of a handwritten greeting to his father. In 1927 he staged the first home reception of television at his own home in Schenectady, using high-frequency neon lamps and a perforated scanning disc. He gave the first public demonstration of television on January 13, 1928.

With the withdrawal of GE from the affairs of RCA in 1932, Alexanderson devoted himself at GE to the application of electronics to power supply. There he secured patents on such devices as the inverter—by which direct current (dc) was changed into ac through a mercury-arc rectifier—and single-phase motors for railway electrification. He also made important contributions to radiant-energy guiding systems for aircraft and boats and developed countless applications of vacuum tubes for power transmission.

Another electronic wonder with which the name of Alexanderson is associated is the amplidyne, an extremely sensitive and powerful system of amplification and automatic control that he designed in cooperation with other GE engineers. While the amplidyne was adapted to the firing of antiaircraft guns in World War II, it was originally designed for use in steel mills and other plants requiring delicate control of continuous manufacturing processes. Applications for the system are said to be practically limitless, since it can be extended to almost everything that moves under power.

Although he retired officially from his full-time position at GE on January 1, 1948, Alexanderson continued to work in the company's laboratories as a consulting engineer. In 1952 he renewed his association with RCA as a consultant and began working closely with that firm on the development of color television. His color-television receiver, used with the RCA system of color broadcasting, can also receive black-and-white programs. Alexanderson told the *New York Times* (February 12, 1955), "The novelty of my invention is in the method by which the color selection is accomplished."

While not as productive in his later years, Alexanderson continued to work on a number of projects and received a fair share of patents for such inventions as motor-control systems, electric motor-control apparatuses, and even a magnetic computer. He received his last patent, for an adjustable-speed motor-control system, at the age of 95 in 1973.

For his immense contributions, Alexanderson received the Gold Medal of the Institute of Radio Engineers (1919), the Order of Polonia Restituta (1924), the John Ericsson Medal (1928), the Edison Medal from the American Institute of Electrical Engineers (1944), the Cedergren Medal from the Royal Institute of Technology of Sweden (1945), and the Valdemar Poulsen Gold Medal and Royal Danish Medal (1946). He was awarded an honorary D.Sc. degree from Union College, in Schenectady, New York, in 1926 and an honorary Ph.D. degree from the University of Upsala, in Sweden, in 1938. He was a fellow of the Institute of Electrical Engineers and a member and past president of the Institute of Radio Engineers. He also held memberships in the Royal Swedish Academy and Sigma Xi. He was elected the first commodore of the Lake George Yacht Club and introduced there a shallow-draft type of Swedish-built boat used by North Sea pilots. As reported in *Popular Science* (July 1942), he liked to carry in his pocket many keys and a circular slide rule the size of a silver dollar.

Alexanderson was married to Edith B. Lewin on February 20, 1909. She died in 1912. On March 30, 1914 he married Gertrude Robert, who died in 1948. His third marriage was to Thyra Oxehufwud, in June 1949. He had four children: Amelie, Edith, Gertrude, and Verner. Alexanderson died at the age of 97 on May 14, 1975.—C. M.

Suggested Reading: *New York Times* VIII p12 Oct. 25 1942, p13 Jan. 25, 1945, p22 Feb. 12, 1955; *Popular Science* p89 July 1942; *National Cyclopædia of American Biography Current Volume A*, 1926; Benson, A. *Will To Succeed*, 1948; *Who's Who in America* 1954–55; *World Biography*, 1954; *American Men of Science*, 1955

Kathleen King Photography/Microsoft Corp.

Allen, Paul

Jan. 21, 1953– Co-founder of Microsoft

"I remember having pizza at Shakey's in Vancouver, Washington, in 1973," Paul Allen told Brent Schlender for *Fortune* (October 2, 1995), "and talking about the fact that eventually everyone is going to be on-line and have [electronic] access to newspapers and stuff." For Allen, who co-founded Microsoft in 1975 with his childhood friend Bill Gates, such prescience is not unusual. He and Gates shared a vision of computer software that proved to be well ahead of its time—their mantra was "a computer on every desktop and Microsoft software in every computer"—and together they laid the foundation for the software behemoth that Gates still runs.

Today, Allen continues to pursue the idea he was discussing at Shakey's back in 1973—a concept he later dubbed the "Wired World"—although he is no longer doing so at Microsoft. In 1983, after being diagnosed with cancer, Allen gave up his active role in Microsoft, where he had played the "idea man" to Gates's "doer." For several years afterward, he was involved in business ventures that did not pan out. Since 1990, he has invested at least $25 billion in more than 140 companies, which range from software, multimedia-content, communications, and electronic-entertainment firms to enterprises outside the orbit of high technology, such as the Seattle Seahawks football team. According to *Forbes*, in February 2003 Allen was considered the fourth-richest man in the world. (Gates was ranked first.) While he relinquished his seat on Microsoft's board in 2000, Allen remains a senior strategy advisor for Microsoft executives.

Allen's broad investment portfolio reflects his belief that no one can really predict where the next big idea will come from, and that whatever its source, he wants to be a part of its development. "The marriage of video technology, computer technology, and networking is . . . a sea change, where you try to ride the incredible wave that's coming," he told David Kirkpatrick for *Fortune* (July 11, 1994). "That's the core convergence of ideas for the information superhighway. So you say, 'We're getting a whole new medium here; what can we really do that people haven't thought about in their individual areas?' It's not just showing movies on demand," something at least one of his companies has explored. "What wholly new applications and user interfaces and products and services can you deliver?"

Paul Gardner Allen was born in Seattle, Washington, on January 21, 1953, and grew up in the suburb of Wedgwood with his younger sister, Jody. Both of his parents, Kenneth and Faye Allen, were librarians at the University of Washington. The Allens' home was packed with books, and as a youth, Allen was an avid reader. He loved science fiction, a passion he shared with Bill Gates. Allen's parents also tended to his cultural development by taking him to plays, concerts, and museums. He took lessons in classical guitar for a few years before turning his acoustic guitar into an electric one with a soldering kit and some wires. At about the same time, he discovered Jimi Hendrix; he has been a fan ever since.

Allen attended the Lakeside School, where, in about 1968, an organization of students' mothers arranged the installation of a teletype terminal that was connected to a remote mainframe computer. It wasn't long before some of the students became computer junkies; at the center of the group were the ninth-grader Paul Allen and the seventh-grader Bill Gates. Allen and Gates spent all their free time and a lot of their money exploring the machine's possibilities. Eventually some of the students were invited to work at a computer center in downtown Seattle. "We didn't have to pay for the time [as they

had had to do with the teletype machine] as long as we could find bugs in their system and report them," Gates told Schlender. "They brought us in like monkeys, but it was a godsend. . . . Paul and I got bonded together trying to figure out that machine."

Allen and Gates embarked on their first commercial venture, a company called Traf-O-Data, in 1971, the year Allen began his studies at Washington State University. They planned to computerize traffic-volume analysis, but they weren't sure exactly how to go about it. Then, in 1972, Intel introduced the 8008 microprocessor chip, and Allen recognized that the chip was powerful enough to have practical applications. With the help of an engineer, Allen and Gates designed and built a number of traffic-counting computers employing the chip, and they managed to sell them to several cities. "Even though Traf-O-Data wasn't a roaring success, it was seminal in preparing us to make Microsoft's first product a couple of years later," Allen told Schlender. "We were always interested in business. . . . We talked about being entrepreneurs. Obviously, it was on a smaller scale, because we were kids. Microprocessors were instantly attractive to us because you could build something for a fraction of the cost of conventional electronics."

In the summer of 1973, Allen and Gates worked to computerize hydroelectric dams at TRW in Vancouver, Washington. The following fall, Gates entered Harvard University, in Cambridge, Massachusetts. Allen meanwhile had grown bored with college, and midway through his junior year he dropped out. He moved to Boston, where he worked as a programmer for Honeywell. Allen continued to talk about his business ideas with Gates; Gates, however, seemed determined to pursue a degree.

The cover story of the January 1975 issue of *Popular Electronics* provided Allen with the ammunition he needed to change Gates's mind. The magazine told of the Altair 8800, to be manufactured by MITS, a company in Albuquerque, New Mexico. The Altair 8800, which would sell for about $400, would contain Intel's new 8080 microprocessor. In truth, the computer had few practical capabilities; its main attraction was that computer enthusiasts could buy and build their own personal computers. Yet Allen and Gates recognized that anyone who bought an Altair would want one essential component: software. Without a predetermined set of commands and operations, programming the Altair would be extremely difficult. "We realized that the revolution might happen without us," Gates recalled to Robert Slater in an interview for *Portraits in Silicon* (1987). "After we saw that article, there was no question of where our life would focus."

Allen and Gates, who had modified the computer language BASIC for use in their Traf-O-Data computers, wrote to MITS and proposed that they be hired to write a version of BASIC for the Altair. For a month, they worked day and night to produce a version of BASIC that would run on the Altair. While on the plane to Albuquerque, Allen made last-minute changes to the code. When he arrived, he loaded his version of BASIC into an Altair for the first time—he and Gates had written the code on a computer they had programmed to simulate the Altair—and typed "PRINT 2 + 2." The Altair answered, "4."

Allen and Gates sold their version of BASIC to MITS, but they also retained the right to sell it on their own. The Altair was a big seller, and other companies were quick to recognize that the market for personal microcomputers was huge. For their part, Gates and Allen recognized that each manufacturer would need a slightly different version of BASIC, and so, in June 1975, Gates dropped out of Harvard and joined Allen in Albuquerque, where they worked together as "Micro-Soft." "Our management style was a little loose in the beginning," Allen told Schlender. "We both took part in every decision, and it's hard to remember who did what. If there was a difference between our roles, I was probably the one always pushing a little bit in terms of new technology and new products, and Bill was more interested in doing negotiations and contracts and business deals."

For a couple of years, Allen and Gates were flooded with business as the market for microcomputers grew. MITS quickly faded from prominence, and other companies, such as Apple and Commodore, emerged. On January 1, 1979, the founding partners of Microsoft (the hyphen had been dropped from the name by that time) moved their operation, which by then consisted of 12 employees, to the Seattle suburb of Bellevue. The following year, a fortuitous turn of events helped secure Microsoft's place at the forefront of the computer industry. IBM, a leading manufacturer of office machines and computing equipment, was preparing to enter the personal-computer market, and contacted Gates about writing the operating system for its new computer. Gates, uncertain that his company would be able to meet IBM's deadline, referred the company to a competitor, Digital Research, but when a deal with that firm failed to materialize, IBM asked Microsoft to create the operating system. Gates and Allen agreed, but rather than develop a system from scratch, the duo hastily closed a deal with a company called Seattle Computer to buy their operating system, Q-DOS (an acronym for "quick and dirty operating system"). Microsoft's $50,000 purchase of Q-DOS has been called the "deal of the century." Allen and Gates modified and enhanced Q-DOS and sold the new version to IBM under the name Microsoft Disk Operating System, or MS-DOS. Allen and Gates also made several other important suggestions to IBM about how its computers should be designed.

The IBM PC came out in 1981; within a year it had come to dominate the market, and MS-DOS had become the preferred computer operating system. Microsoft's sales quadrupled in 1981, to $16 million, and continued to climb in the years that followed. According to Schlender, Microsoft's founders "create[d] more wealth than any business partners in the history of American capitalism." Allen's legacy persisted at Microsoft for the rest of the 1980s, even after his resignation, in 1983, as executive vice president of research and new product development. Company veterans have pointed out that Allen's contributions were crucial to the development of such successful products as Microsoft Word, Windows, and the Microsoft mouse.

Allen's cancer symptoms first showed up when he was on a business trip in Europe in 1982. "One day in Paris, I just felt really bad and decided I had to go back to the States," he told Schlender. A doctor in Seattle initially thought Allen had lymphoma; later, he informed Allen that his illness was Hodgkin's disease, a type of cancer with a relatively high cure rate. Two and a half months of radiation therapy limited Allen's involvement in the daily running of Microsoft. "Cancer therapy takes a lot out of you," Allen explained to Schlender, "but it was more than that. To be 30 years old and have that kind of shock—to face your mortality—really makes you feel like you should do some of the things that you haven't done."

Allen was advised that if the disease did not return in two years, he would be considered cured. "I took that time to step away from Microsoft and be closer to my family, and do some traveling and some other things I'd always wanted to do," Allen told Schlender. "After that two-year period, well, I just didn't want to go back to work. I went to Bill and said, 'I want to just do something different.'" Allen returned to Microsoft in 1990, serving on the company's board of directors for 10 years.

Allen's first project after Microsoft was not radically different; begun in 1985, it was another software company, called Asymetrix. Allen installed his college roommate, Bert Kolde, as president. According to Julie Pitta in *Forbes* (August 5, 1991), Allen started out by "pour[ing] money and three years of effort into . . . a combination spreadsheet and database using artificial intelligence, but scrapped the project because of technical obstacles."

In 1986 Allen set up Vulcan Ventures, an investment-research firm, and bought a stake in the growing Egghead retail software chain. In 1988, he indulged his enthusiasm for basketball by buying a National Basketball Association (NBA) franchise, the Portland Trailblazers. This, combined with the fact that Asymetrix had yet to release a product and that Allen had made few other inroads into high-tech investment, led some commentators to quip that Allen seemed more interested in watching his team play than in being a player in the software market. When Asymetrix at last released its first product, Toolbook, in 1990, some analysts questioned the software's relevance. Pitta described it as being similar to Macintosh's HyperCard, which had already been on the market for three years. Although Microsoft included Toolbook in its Windows software package for a while, the larger company discontinued the arrangement in order to develop its own version (to be called Visual Basic).

Thanks to his ownership of Microsoft stock, Allen was by this time a billionaire, despite the fact that Vulcan did not appear to be profitable. As Allen publicly pursued his interest in sports, rock music, and travel, the continued success of Bill Gates led many in the industry to conclude that Allen had passed his prime—or that he had never really had a prime, and that Gates had always been the brains behind Microsoft.

In 1992 Allen began taking aggressive steps, most notably by creating Interval Research. He felt that the computer industry was in "a fallow period," as he told John Heileman for the New Yorker (February 23–March 2, 1998), "where the last flurry of innovation was still being digested and you couldn't see where the next flurry was going to come from." Consequently, he decided to create the ultimate think tank in Silicon Valley—a research operation that would freely explore new possibilities in technology. He modeled Interval on the Palo Alto Research Center (PARC), a facility owned by Xerox. In the 1970s and early 1980s, PARC developed many of the concepts that have since become fundamentals of personal computing, including the graphical user interface and the WYSIWYG (an acronym for "What you see is what you get") word processor. Allen told Heileman that he was "blown away" by what he saw when he visited PARC in the early 1980s. "I said, 'We gotta have this on the PC, and this, and this—all of it!'"

Xerox, which was in the photocopying business, not the computing business, did not fully capitalize on the value of the groundbreaking research done at PARC. As David Liddle, a former PARC researcher, told Heileman, "If you already have a big, profitable business, it probably makes more sense to focus on feeding that bulldog instead of going into the new businesses your research points to." Taking inspiration from PARC, Allen decided to create a lab without a company. He put aside $100 million to support Interval for a 10-year period and hired Liddle as his head researcher. "I've been thinking for a number of years about creating the kind of organization that will take things far beyond where they are," Allen told John Markoff for the New York Times (March 31, 1992). "If you look down the road, what you see is the pervasiveness of high bandwidth data communications and completely inexpensive computing power. . . . If you combine those two things, there are many interesting things that you can do." In other words, the Wired World concept Allen had dreamed up two decades earlier was looking like a viable possibility.

Other important moves Allen made in 1992 include the founding of Starwave, a company through which he planned to package information electronically in CD-ROM or on-line formats for consumers. He also purchased shares in the on-line financial service Telescan, an electronic classified-ad service called SureFind, and America Online. In 1993 Allen invested in wireless data communication (Metricom), electric and electronic networking (Lone Wolf), business software (Harbinger-EDI Services), computer hardware (Cardinal Technologies), and a company developing a tiny computer screen a user could wear in a special pair of glasses (Virtual Vision).

In December 1993 Allen attracted widespread attention when he paid more than $300 million to buy 80 percent of Ticketmaster, the nationwide ticket broker. "I'm excited about the possibilities here," he told Paul Andrews for the Washington Post (December 5, 1993). One possibility that he mentioned was an interactive television channel that could market tickets in addition to showing music videos and giving biographical information about the artists. "There are a number of areas in sports, music, and entertainment where ticketing and related merchandise could be available on an information superhighway," he said. Ticketmaster, which so dominates the ticket-sales industry that some have described it as monopolistic, continued to perform well. Nevertheless, three years after his purchase, Allen swapped his stake in Ticketmaster for an 11 percent stake in Barry Diller's USA Network.

In 1994 Allen formed the Paul Allen Group to keep track of his technology and information investments, which then totaled about $800 million. By early 1998, Allen had spent nearly $1.6 billion following his "Wired World" investment strategy, the aim of which is to build what he calls the "Wired World's infrastructure." Along the way, he dropped some of his investments, among them Lone Wolf, Cardinal Technologies, and Virtual Vision. In addition, one of his most promising investments, a 24.9 percent stake in America Online, turned sour in 1994. Allen had pressured AOL to open its portal service to the whole World Wide Web rather than confine users to its own closed network. Although Steve Case, AOL's chief executive officer, would later move the company in that direction, at the time he wasn't appreciative of Allen's input. Worried that Allen was acquiring too large a stake in the company, he set up a "poison pill" shareholder plan to prevent Allen's ownership from growing and refused to seat Allen on the board of directors. Allen responded in 1994 by selling off his shares, for which he had paid $40 million, at a reported $100 million profit. Allen was later harshly criticized for the move, as the value of his discarded shares swelled to more than $30 billion by 2000.

Meanwhile, Allen's Interval Research was failing to produce results and was drawing criticism for its secretive policies. The lab's most visible project was Purple Moon, an innovative CD-ROM company that sought to open up the ostensibly male-oriented world of video gaming by designing games especially for young girls. Purple Moon eventually went bankrupt, however, and Allen closed Interval Research in early 2000, having failed to deliver any viable products. Allen explained his decision in an interview with David Kirkpatrick for *Fortune* (May 15, 2000): "Today you have to take ideas and turn them into products or Web sites very quickly. That's just reality. When we founded Interval we wanted to have substantial impact, spinning off startups and potentially changing the industry. We came from a very pure, high-minded place, but it always comes down to the particular ideas you have."

Since 1994 Allen's investments have brought more than 140 companies into his Wired World infrastructure, including CNET, DreamWorks SKG, Multimedia Asia Pacific, N2K Inc., NETSchools, and U.S. Satellite Broadcasting (USSB). Allen is the largest single shareholder in the entertainment company DreamWorks, in which he began investing in 1995. He also owns large shares of Oxygen Media, which produces TV and Internet content for women, the Internet retailer Priceline.com, and ZDTV, a channel dedicated entirely to computer technology. Perhaps the greatest success story of Allen's "older" ventures—those with which he stayed involved for more than a few years—was Starwave. Starwave, which runs the on-line services ESPNET SportsZone, *Mr. Showbiz*, and *Outside Online*, became one of the leading on-line content providers. Disney eventually bought the company from Allen in 1999 for more than $350 million.

Allen's most recent focus has been on the cable market, which, as he explained to Kirkpatrick, he considers essential for his vision of a Wired World communication network. "High-speed communication channels combined with computing power are a new platform," he said. "We have broadened our vision to include more aspects of the platform. If you can participate in that new infrastructure and build things on top of it, that's pretty exciting. Broadband cable is the base that I think has the best potential." In 1998 Allen purchased the cable entities Marcus Cable and Charter Communications for $2.8 billion and $4.5 billion, respectively. The combined company became his biggest investment yet, as well as the seventh-largest operator of cable services in the United States. The following year he invested another $1.65 billion in the telecommunications company RCN. Simultaneously, RCN announced a joint project with Vulcan Ventures, Allen's investment firm, to develop high-speed Internet portals for a number of residential areas. Throughout 1999 Allen purchased 12 more cable companies, and by 2000 he had paid nearly $15 billion for access to 6.2 million subscribers. He surprised many industry observers when, in November 1999, he held a public offering of stock for Charter Communications, his combined cable operation, raising an additional $3.5 million. The St. Louis–based cable entity has suffered financially in recent years, however, piling up $20 billion in debt and becoming the subject of an investigation by the Securities and Exchange Commission regarding accounting practices. By February 2003 Charter's stock had lost 90 percent of its value from

the previous year, effectively reducing Allen's investment to $420 million. Despite overall losses of an estimated $20 billion through many of these technology and communications ventures, Allen continues to forge ahead with his Wired World vision. His complex strategy often involves investments in a number of varied companies. "From the outside, if you're looking at our basket of companies, it may be difficult to find the common thread," he told Kirkpatrick, "but there is a thread there. We look for a company that is well positioned for the future, that has some synergies with other things that we are doing and has a management team we are excited about working with." Most recently, Vulcan has been exploring the "Mini-PC," a computer measuring 5" x 4" x 1.1" and weighing only one pound.

Allen has made numerous other investments and purchases, in addition to the Trailblazers, that are unconnected to his Wired World strategy. For many years he had been planning to build a museum to honor Jimi Hendrix. The idea expanded into the Experience Music Project (EMP), a music museum that opened in Seattle, in June 2000, and the EMP Foundation, which funds music and arts projects in the Pacific Northwest. Allen assumed all costs for construction of the EMP museum and its collection—estimated at more than $240 million—as a gift to the city of Seattle. His six additional philanthropic foundations, all of which bear his name, focus on such areas as community service, medical research, the visual and performing arts, and forest preservation. In 1997 Allen bought the Seattle Seahawks, a National Football League team, and contributed $130 of his own money for construction of a new $425-million, 72,000-seat stadium. Vulcan Northwest is the umbrella organization that oversees all of Allen's holdings.

Paul Allen is single and lives near Seattle, on an estate on Mercer Island, Lake Washington. His mother lives in a house on the grounds, as does Jody Patton, his sister (who also serves as Vulcan's chief executive officer), along with her husband and two children.—K. D.

Suggested Reading: *Details* p256+ Oct. 2000, with photos; *Forbes* p94+ Aug. 5, 1991, with photo, p186+ Nov. 15, 1999; *Fortune* p68+ July 11, 1994, with photos, p68+ Oct. 2, 1995, with photos, p249+ May 15, 2000; *New Yorker* p78+ Feb. 23–Mar. 2, 1998; *New York Times* D p1+ Mar. 31, 1992, with photo, III p1+ Oct. 29, 1995; *Rolling Stone* p53+ Dec. 1, 1994, with photos; *Washington Post* H p5 Dec. 5, 1993, with photo; Slater, Robert. *Portraits in Silicon* (1987)

Amdahl, Gene

Nov. 16, 1922– Designer of the first computer operating system

Gene Amdahl is one of the most important computer engineers of the post–World War II era. Working for IBM in the 1950s and 1960s, he designed the first operating system and introduced the concept of parallel processing, which allows a computer to perform numerous functions simultaneously, as opposed to one after another. He was one of the designers responsible for IBM's 360 computer line, the most commercially successful of its era. After leaving IBM, in 1970, he made several attempts at competing directly with the industry giant, starting up such companies as the Amdahl Corporation and, more recently, Commercial Data Servers. With the former company, Amdahl pioneered the idea of developing high-performance machines that mimicked those of IBM to the extent that they could use the same software, creating the first "IBM-compatible" computer. In the face of the personal computer revolution of the 1980s and 1990s, Amdahl remains a defender of larger, mainframe computers as a viable alternative.

Eugene Myron Amdahl was born November 16, 1922 in Flandreau, South Dakota, to Anton E. and Inga (Brendsel) Amdahl. His earliest experience with machines came from operating the equipment on his parents' farm. The family's home, however, did not receive electricity until Amdahl was in high school. He served during World War II, spending two years in the U.S. Navy. While in the service, Amdahl gained a knowledge of electronics that would serve him well later.

After the war, he attended South Dakota State University, where he earned a bachelor's degree in engineering physics in 1948. "I didn't know when I first entered college as a mechanical engineer in 1941 that I would end up in computers," Amdahl commented in *Computerworld* magazine (June 22, 1992). "I sort of thought my career in physics was like deciding to be a monk—in the sense that it would be a labor of love for the rest of my life." He continued his studies following graduation, earning a doctorate in theoretical physics from the University of Wisconsin in 1952. While pursuing his doctorate Amdahl became frustrated with the slide rule and the 10-digit desk calculator, tools he felt were inadequate for the study of atomic particles he had undertaken. "I decided there had to be a better way to do that," he recounted to Mark Blackburn for the *New York Times* (July 1, 1979), "so I invented a computer." The machine was dubbed the Wisconsin Integrally Synchronized Computer (WISC).

Amdahl began working for International Business Machines (IBM) in 1952 as a project manager at the corporation's Poughkeepsie, New York, office. One of his first projects was the IBM 704 computer, for which he was the chief design engineer. In 1954, Amdahl designed the first operating system, specifically for use in the 704. Intended to control all the operations performed by a computer, an operating system coordinates the many functions and elements that make up the computer, the most common example being Microsoft Windows. Personal computers, however, did not yet exist in 1954, and Amdahl's operating system was intended for the much larger computers of the day.

After his work on the 704, Amdahl contributed to the design of landmark IBM computers, such as the Datatron, the Stretch, and the IBM 7030, one of the first machines to employ the new transistor technology, first developed in 1947 by John Bardeen, Walter Brattain, and William Shockley of Bell Labs.

By 1956 Amdahl had become disenchanted with IBM and quit. "At IBM, I always wanted to do things the way I wanted to do them," Amdahl told *Computerworld* (June 22, 1992). "When I got put into top positions where I couldn't do that, that's when I would leave." He first went to work for the Ramo-Woolridge Corporation, in Los Angeles, California, as part of their computer research and development staff, and later in 1956 he became manager of systems design for Aeronutronic Inc., another Los Angeles company, where he worked until 1960. Amdahl then departed Aeronutronic and returned to IBM.

That was the beginning of a stellar 10-year run, during which Amdahl became one of the world's most renowned computer engineers, working for the world's leading computer manufacturer. Most notably, he was the head designer of IBM's System 360 series of mainframe computers, which was one of the most commercially successful lines produced up to that time and was largely responsible for IBM's continued dominance of the market. It was also during the 1960s that Amdahl introduced the concept of parallel processing, in which a number of compatible systems worked simultaneously on interrelated problems, or steps involved in one problem, instead of one processor tackling each problem or stop serially.

In 1969 Amdahl was appointed director of IBM's Advanced Computing Systems Laboratory in Menlo Park, California, where he was charged with designing the fastest large computer then technologically feasible. However, Amdahl soon came into conflict with company management over the direction that IBM should take to remain on the cutting edge of computer development. IBM, he explained, priced its large machines high in order to maintain a constant price/performance ratio throughout its whole line of products. Whatever benefit accrued from that policy in total revenues and profits, the effect as far as the large computers was concerned was a failure to attract enough customers to cover development expenses and show a profit. Failing to persuade IBM's administrators to change the pricing policy, he angrily decided to prove his point by forming a company of his own, and Amdahl left IBM for a second time, a decision that proved to be permanent. In 1970 he formed the Amdahl Corporation.

The goal of the Amdahl Corporation was to compete directly with IBM for the mainframe computer market. Many believed Amdahl was doomed to fail, as IBM then controlled 85 percent of the computer market in general and had an even bigger share of the market for large commercial machines. In order to compete, Amdahl used his knowledge of IBM's technology to help his new company produce computers that were faster than theirs, used the same software and peripheral equipment, and came at a lower price. Such a mainframe could be inserted directly into an IBM customer's computer center without the compatibility and programming problems that had been stymieing the other IBM challengers. Amdahl's ingenious marketing plan has endured, and by the late 20th century many companies were building PCs that were IBM-compatible, improving on models originally developed by IBM and selling them at competitive prices. The Amdahl Corporation sold its first computer, the Amdahl 470 V/6, to NASA in 1975. One-fourth the size of conventional mainframe computers of the time, the 470/V6 made use of solid-state devices known as large-scale integrated circuits, or simply LSIs. Into each LSI he packed 100 separate electronic circuits on a tiny semiconductor chip of silicon, and onto each chip he bonded an equally tiny molybden cooling stud, thereby obviating the necessity for the elaborate chilled-water plumbing system used by IBM. "In device technology at the logic level, Amdahl has gone the whole way," Norman S. Zimbel, a computer expert at Arthur D. Little Inc., commented, as quoted in *BusinessWeek* (March 10, 1973). Because of the risk of engineering oversights involved in cramming complex circuits onto a tiny chip, and the danger that those circuits might not work in an IBM computer environment, anyone less knowledgeable about the architecture of the IBM 360 would not have been able to carry off the bold innovation. As opposed to the six-by-24-foot panel then standard, the panel on which 470/V6's 42 printed circuit boards were mounted was only three-by-six feet. The machine was four times faster than the IBM 360 and sold for the same price, $3.5 million.

For several years, the Amdahl Corporation was highly competitive with IBM, and Gene Amdahl was hailed as the most successful computer entrepreneur in years. In fact, the IBM-Amdahl rivalry is often remembered as the first major instance of competition in the commercial computer industry. Between 1975 and 1977, Amdahl sold 55 computers. When IBM cut their prices in the first half of 1977, the Amdahl Corporation responded by cutting their own prices. In spite of the cut, Amdahl's profits reached $21.2 million, seven times more than his net from the previous year. In 1978, IBM introduced the 3033 processor, which was twice as fast as the 360 at one-third the price. Once again responding in kind, Amdahl introduced the V7, which was one-third faster than the 3033 at a price only 3 percent higher.

By 1979, however, IBM began to outdistance its upstart competitor. IBM introduced a new line of medium-sized computers, the Series E, and the mere rumor that it was developing a new line of large computers as well led many customers to begin leasing machines from Amdahl instead of buying them. Earlier, Amdahl had sold off large shares of his company to Fujitsu, Ltd., and other businesses in exchange for needed capital, reducing his own stake to 3.5 percent ownership. With the company barely breaking even, Amdahl resigned as chairman and left the Amdahl Corporation entirely in 1980.

Later that year Amdahl founded Trilogy Systems Corporation. This time, he sought to compete not only with IBM but also with his former, self-named company. His ultimate plan was to revolutionize the design of the semiconductor chips that powered mainframe computers, so that a single "superchip" would be able to perform all the functions that were then being done by 100 individual chips.

Amdahl's plans for Trilogy, however, were hampered by misfortune almost from the start. Torrential rain postponed the construction of the chip-manufacturing plant and then destroyed the first batch of chips by leaking into the air conditioning system and disturbing the controlled climate necessary for the chips' production. With one-third of the money that had been put up by his investors already spent, Amdahl did what he felt was necessary to keep his new company in business. Using the remainder of its start-up money, Trilogy acquired the Elxsi Corporation in 1985. However, the infusion of new talent and resources was not enough to halt the downward trend. The company never achieved a great level of success, and in 1987, while still chairman of Trilogy/Elxsi, Amdahl set out to establish a third computer manufacturer.

The new company was named Andor Systems, after the "and/or" logical switches employed in computer circuitry. With the PC revolution underway, the size of computers was generally decreasing, and Andor's goal was to compete with IBM's smaller mainframe machines. Amdahl sought to employ new technology that allowed the computer's central processing unit (CPU) to be built on a single circuit board, as opposed to the multiple boards used by IBM. The resulting mainframes would be more compact and not generate as much heat as competitors' products, relieving buyers of the expenses of extra space and special air conditioning.

However, Andor Systems proved even less successful than Trilogy had been. Due to faulty microchips, nearly two years passed before their first computers hit the market. In that time, IBM was able to produce its own smaller mainframe incorporating some of the technology Amdahl had planned on using. Andor was never able to recover from the delay in production, and by 1994 the company had gone bankrupt.

Amdahl's fourth and, as of 1999, last company is Commercial Data Servers (CDS), established in 1994. Amdahl has remained a defender of the mainframe system, in which a single large computer controls a group of subordinate terminals, and he started CDS in order to manufacture mainframes that were compatible with personal computers. For this purpose he also introduced a new processor of his own design. With the computer industry having moved away from mainframes, Amdahl's new company is targeting a market, for small mainframes, that other manufacturers may no longer be serving adequately.

Amdahl, who holds 30 patents, was cited in *Computerworld* (June 22, 1992) as one of "25 people that [the magazine] feels have made the greatest contributions in the field of information services." He was the recipient of the Computer Science Man of the Year Award from the Data Processing Management Association in 1976. In 1987, he was presented with the Eckert-Mauchly Award, named for the inventors of the large-scale, electronic, digital computer. The trade publication *Computer Weekly* gave Amdahl its Man of Achievement award in 1991. Additionally, he was named to the Information Processing Hall of Fame in 1985. Amdahl married Marian Quissell on June 23, 1946, and they have two daughters, Beth Delaine and Andrea Leigh, and a son, Carlton Gene, who also designs computers.

Though his business ventures over the years have struggled against more-established competitors, their fortunes have not diminished Amdahl's stature as a designer of revolutionary computer technology. At the age of 76, he continues to champion the cause of mainframe computers, while at the same time seeking to link the older technology with the PCs that have emerged as the dominant force in computing. "When people talk about the mainframe as being a dinosaur, I disagree," he declared in *Computerworld*. "The reason is that the investment in terms of equipment and mainframe software is very large. . . . It's not in the cards that they're going to be discarded or redone." As of this writing Amdahl remained actively involved in the computer industry, having recently worked to develop means to combat the "Y2K" computer dilemma that was expected to occur as computers worldwide, most of them programmed to recognize years that begin in "19," made the switch to 2000.—B.S.

Suggested Reading: *ACTS Corporation* (online); *Computerworld* S p11+ June 22, 1992; *Jones Telecommunication and Multimedia Encyclopedia* (on-line), 1999; *American Men and Women of Science 1998–99*, 1998; Spencer, Donald D. *The Timetable of Computers*, 1997; *Who's Who in America*, 1998

Andreessen, Marc and Clark, James H.

Andreessen, Marc
  (an-DREE-sin)
1971– Netscape co-founder

Clark, James H.
1944(?)– Netscape co-founder

When they teamed up to form the Netscape Communications Corporation, in 1994, James H. Clark and Marc Andreessen may have seemed, to some observers at least, to be an odd couple. Clark, then a 50-year-old millionaire, was the founder of the highly successful computer firm Silicon Graphics, from which he had recently resigned. Andreessen was a 23-year-old computer programmer, only a few months into his first full-time job. Andreessen, however, had been involved, while a college student, in the creation of Mosaic, a program that made the once-cumbersome retrieval of information from on-line sources much easier. Clark was impressed enough with the accomplishment to invest $4 million in seed money to start a joint venture.

In December 1994 Netscape unveiled Navigator, an Internet browser that revolutionized the use of computers. Millions of people around the world have downloaded the program for free and have been surfing the Net ever since. In addition, many companies now use Netscape software to create sites on the World Wide Web, which has become an important venue in which to do business. Since that time, several firms, including the software giant Microsoft, have introduced alternative browsers.

In 1998 Clark sold Netscape to America Online (AOL) for a reported $10 billion dollars, thereby creating an entity capable of competing with Microsoft. Since then Clark and Andreessen have dissolved their partnership, with Clark investing in a number of on-line projects and Andreessen founding Opsware Inc., a software company that aids in the automation and improvement of information technology (IT) systems.

James H. Clark was born in about 1944 in Plainview, Texas. He was suspended from high school "for antics such as sneaking in whiskey on a band trip," according to a reporter for *BusinessWeek* (December 18, 1995). He dropped out of school to join the navy, where he discovered that he had an aptitude for electronics. After completing his military service, Clark entered college. In 1974 he earned a master's degree in physics from Louisiana State University and a Ph.D. in computer science from the University of Utah three years later. Also in 1974, he was hired as an assistant professor at the University of California at Santa Cruz, and four years after that, he became an associate professor at Stanford University, in California.

While at Stanford, Clark worked with a team of six graduate students on the development of a set of microchips to enliven computer images. They were successful, but Clark could not persuade any of the computer companies that he approached that there was a large market for three-dimensional graphics. So, in 1982, he started his own firm, Silicon Graphics Inc., in Mountain View, California, taking the students along with him. The company manufactured a line of computer workstations that appealed, initially, to engineers and architects, who used the high-tech software to design aircraft, cars, and buildings. Then, the machines caught on with filmmakers and animators, who found them ideal for creating realistic special effects. Designers at Industrial Light & Magic, for example, used Silicon Graphics computers to create the dinosaurs in *Jurassic Park*, among other projects.

By the early 1990s Silicon Graphics had become a billion-dollar company and had expanded into chip development for the video-game and interactive-television markets. During the same period, Clark had begun to see his power wane as other executives in the firm took on senior roles, according to several reports. In 1994, after losing a fight over the company's future direction, Clark resigned as chairman. "I got tired of pushing against an immovable object," Clark told Alison L. Sprout for *Fortune* (July 10, 1995). "I felt like I wasn't having any influence."

Clark left Silicon Graphics a wealthy man, but uncertain of what he was going to do next. He toyed with the idea of creating a software company to help deliver interactive-television services. Then he became fascinated by the commercial possibilities of the Internet. He sent an e-mail note to Marc Andreessen, a recent graduate of the University of Illinois, who had helped to create Mosaic, the hottest software on the Net.

Andreessen had been interested in computers since childhood. At the age of eight or nine, he had taught himself the Basic programming language from a library book. He grew up in the small town of New Lisbon, Wisconsin, where he had been born in 1971. His father is a retired seed salesman; his mother works at Lands' End, the mail-order apparel company. In the sixth grade, Andreessen used the personal computer in his school's library to write his first program, which was designed to help him do his math homework; unfortunately, when the janitor turned the power off at the end of the day, the program was wiped out. By the seventh grade, Andreessen had persuaded his parents to buy him his own computer, so he could work at home. In high school he created a matchmaking program for lovelorn classmates.

After graduating from high school, Andreessen enrolled at the University of Illinois at Urbana-Champaign to study computer science. Once there, he discovered the Internet and immediately became fascinated by the wealth of information it offered. However, in the early 1990s, mastering Internet was difficult. It was primarily used by scientists and researchers who had to master a variety of computer codes and functions to navigate between sites. "Internet software was 10 years behind the hardware," Andreessen recalled to Rick Tetzeli for *Fortune* (December 9, 1996). "I realized that we could pull the software forward a few years."

In 1992 Andreessen was working part-time for about $6 an hour at the University of Illinois' National Center for Supercomputing Applications (NCSA). He approached an employee of the center, Eric Bina, and suggested that they work together on a program to create an easy-to-use interface to organize the retrieval of on-line material. Bina agreed, and along with several other programmers whom they brought in to help, the team completed the first version of their browser in about six weeks. In early 1993 the program, officially called NCSA Mosaic, was released, free of charge, on the Internet.

Mosaic was an instant hit. Thousands of copies were downloaded during the first year; users were delighted by the ability it gave them to browse interlinked text by simply clicking a mouse. Soon afterward, Andreessen earned his bachelor's degree, and headed to Silicon Valley, in California, to seek his fortune. He was hired by Enterprise Integration Technologies, a small firm that designed security software for the Internet. It was soon after he began working for Enterprise that he received James Clark's e-mail. "You may not know me, but I'm the founder of Silicon Graphics," Clark wrote. "I've resigned and intend to form a new company. Would you be interested in getting together to talk?"

Andreessen agreed. Several meetings followed, first at Clark's home and then on his yacht. The pair decided to create a firm that would improve on the Mosaic browser, by designing a "Mosaic killer," as Andreessen put it, that would offer users more speed, security, and sophisticated graphics than the original. As Alison Sprout wrote, "For Clark, the partnership was a chance to start over; for Andreessen, 23, it was a once-in-a-lifetime opportunity to form a company with a Silicon Valley legend." Clark invested $4 million of his own money to set up shop in Mountain View, California, and Andreessen recruited six other members of the original NCSA development team to work on the souped-up browser.

The new company was christened Mosaic Communications, a choice that sparked a legal battle with the University of Illinois, which claimed the rights to the Mosaic name. The university had licensed the responsibility for the commercial marketing of Mosaic technology to Spyglass Inc., an Illinois-based firm. The dispute was eventually settled out of court and Clark and Andreessen renamed their company Netscape Communications.

In December 1994 Netscape unveiled its browser, called the Navigator. Although individual users who wanted customer support from Netscape could pay for that service, most chose to simply download the program free of charge from the Internet. Businesses bought the browser outright. Within three months, an estimated 3 million copies had been distributed. "I'm astonished; I've never seen anything like it," Clark told Peter H. Lewis for the *New York Times* (March 1, 1995). One reason Netscape quickly established itself as the industry leader was its technological edge; among its innovations was a special encryption code that secured credit-card transactions on the Web. Other browsers, including Mosaic, lagged behind.

Setting the industry standard was one thing, but making money was another. Netscape's business plan was "essentially a reversal of the venerable marketing strategy of giving away safety razors to sell blades," as Peter Lewis noted. "Netscape is basically giving away the consumer versions of its program—the blade—in the hope of profitably selling and servicing the razors. The razors in this case include versions of the Navigator for companies that are operating sites on the World Wide Web." Netscape established fees ranging from $1,500 to $50,000 for server versions of Navigator, depending on the size of a company's home page and the range of services provided to its customers.

On August 9, 1995, Netscape made an initial public offering of 3.5 million shares, amounting to 10 percent of the company's stock. At that point, the firm had not made much of a profit, but investors purchased the shares in record numbers. The opening price was $28, but within minutes, it had soared to $74¼. "The perception is this is a unique company—that Netscape is going to be the Microsoft of the Internet," Roger McNamee, a financial analyst, was quoted as saying in *USA Today* (August 10, 1995). "And everybody wants to own the next Microsoft." As the first day of trading drew to a close, the price of the stock declined to $58 ¼. Even at that price, Netscape's market value was $2.3 billion—more than Bethlehem Steel, Wendy's, and Maytag, according to the *USA Today* article.

The stock offering was a windfall for Netscape's co-founders. Clark, who had taken no salary in his role as chairman, found himself in possession of stock worth more than $560 million. Andreessen's shares were valued at over $55 million—in addition to his reported $60,000 annual salary as senior vice president of technology. Their personal net worth, along with that of the other employees who owned company stock, continued to rise steadily along with Netscape's stock prices. In an interview for *Newsweek* (December 25, 1995–January 1, 1996), however, Clark remarked that with phenomenal success came increased pressure: "It makes you more visible. You're an abysmal failure if you fail."

The company in the best position to challenge Netscape was the software giant Microsoft. Its chairman, Bill Gates, appeared determined to make his company a major player on the Internet. Using Mosaic technology, which it licensed from NCSA, Microsoft developed its own browser, the Explorer, which debuted in the summer of 1995. Explorer could be downloaded for free and came bundled with Windows 95 software—a big advantage. "I'm totally paranoid about Microsoft—always have been, always will be," Clark was quoted as saying in *Business Week* (March 11, 1996).

Through the late 1990s Netscape remained by far the leading on-line browser. Because of its two-year head start, it retained a technological edge. It was the first browser to introduce Java, the programming language that animates Web pages, among other innovations. Andreessen pushed his employees to stay ahead of the pack. During a conversation with a reporter for *Fortune* (December 9, 1996), Eric Hahn, Netscape's chief technology officer and executive vice president, said, "Marc is on the aggressive side, especially when it comes to Microsoft. He always wants to announce products earlier than we do, his argument being that Microsoft is doing just that." Between 1995 and 1997 Netscape expanded its line to include intranet software, which runs inside corporate networks—another strategy that pits the firm squarely against Microsoft.

To manage Netscape's day-to-day affairs, Clark had hired James Barksdale as chief executive officer. Andreessen had a limited managerial role until July 1997, when he was named to a three-person executive committee as the head of product development. In October 1997 Andreesen's title became executive vice president of the products division. After Clark, as chairman, put his management team together, he turned much of his attention elsewhere. In June 1996 he launched another company—Healtheon, based in Palo Alto, California, which offers information services to help insurance companies and employers better manage the paperwork and bureaucracy associated with medical-benefit programs.

In 1998 Netscape stock took a tumble as a result of its heated competition with Microsoft, which was now quickly gaining ground on its competitor. In November 1998 Clark sold Netscape to America Online (AOL) for a reported $10 billion. In addition to Healtheon, Clark has also invested in such companies as Shutterfly, an on-line concern that prints digital pictures, Kibu, a site for teenage girls, and SmartPipes, a provider of advanced networking for Web businesses. He spends much of his free time sailing on his yacht or flying his airplane.

Andreesen joined AOL as the company's chief technical officer after the merger was completed in 1999. He left that same year, however, to form Loudcloud, Inc., which changed its name in August 2002 to Opsware, Inc. The company's focus was to provide IT automation software for server and application management. Their clients have included service providers and government agencies trying to increase the effectiveness of their IT departments while reducing costs. Like many start-up companies since the dot.com crash of 2000, Opsware has been struggling to maintain its market value. However, as of December 2002, the company had $65 million in cash on hand and hoped to see a profit by sometime in 2003.—C. M.

Suggested Reading: *BusinessWeek* (on-line) Sep. 27, 1999; *CNN.com* Nov. 30, 1998, May 4, 2000; Dec. 3, 2002; *Fortune* p140+ July 10, 1995, with photos, p136+ Dec. 9, 1996, with photos; *Newsweek* p32+ Dec. 25, 1995–Jan. 1, 1996, with photos; *Washington Post* H p1+ July 23, 1995, with photos

---

Andrews, Ernest Galen

Jan. 10, 1898–Oct. 13, 1980 Designer of electromechanical computers

E. G. Andrews was one of the leading designers of electromechanical computers between 1930 and 1945, a crucial stage in the development of computer technology. His work at Bell Laboratories in Murray Hill, New Jersey, provided many insights used by later computer engineers. In particular, Andrews was one of the first engineers to explore the use of binary code as a means of storing information. This binary format would become the basis of the digital electronic computers that came in the decades following those in which Andrews worked, and it is still used today in such encoding systems as EBCDIC and ASCII. Andrews also developed ways to reduce computers' errors in performing complex computational functions.

Ernest Galen Andrews spent his childhood in Topeka, Kansas, where he was born on January 10, 1898. With the outbreak of World War I, Andrews served in the U.S. Navy aboard the USS *Kansas* while he was still a teenager. After completing his military service, he attended William Jewell College in Liberty, Missouri, where he received a B.S. in mathematics in 1922. He accepted a position in the installation department of the Western Electric Company in Kansas City and was later transferred from that location to the company's office in Atlanta, Georgia, and subsequently to their New York City branch.

Bell Telephone Laboratories was formed in 1925 after breaking off from the engineering department of the Western Electric Company for the purpose of conducting research into telephone technology. Upon its creation, Andrews immediately joined Bell Labs, located in Murray Hill, New Jersey, and it was there that he would make his greatest contributions to the budding information age. Prior to his involvement with computational machines, which included early computers as well as other types of devices that performed calculations, he worked for many years on the installation and maintenance of switching equipment for the telephone system. In 1941, with the entrance of the United States into World War II, Andrews was put in charge of preparing manuals and training programs to instruct soldiers in using the relatively new radar technology.

By the late 1930s, the possibility of creating an electromechanical computing machine was considered a serious one. Purely mechanical computers, which were able to perform complex mathematical computations, had existed since Vannevar Bush's differential analyzer was invented in 1925. In 1937 Howard Aiken of Harvard University began to formulate the creation of a machine, partly mechanical and partly electronic, that would be more in line with the Analytical Engine, an advanced calculating device capable of performing advanced computations that had been proposed, but never completed, by the 19th-century mathematician Charles Babbage. While the technology to build such a device did not exist in Babbage's time, it did exist for Aiken, and his machine, which would come to be known as the Harvard Mark I, went into production in 1941.

At around the same time that Howard Aiken was proposing his ideas to Harvard University, George Stibitz, a Bell Labs scientist, was pitching his plan to construct a similar computer that would perform basic mathematical functions. Stibitz believed that dial-switching equipment, designed for coordinating telephone signals, could be used to execute these mathematical functions. He introduced the use of binary code in telephone switching equipment for this new purpose, and he initiated a project to test his ideas by building what he called the "Complex Computer." The Complex Computer project was headed by Bell engineer Samuel B. Williams, and E. G. Andrews was also heavily involved. The machine, which later came to be known as the BTL (Bell Telephone Laboratories) Model I, went into operation in January 1940. Designed to handle complex arithmetic operations using numbers with up to eight decimal places, it was demonstrated to the American Mathematical Society at Dartmouth College in the fall of 1940.

The BTL Model I was deemed a success, and Bell Telephone Laboratories became seriously interested in the possibilities electromechanical computer technology seemed to offer. Especially promising was the development of relay computers, which could be potentially used with telephone and other communication systems as a means of transferring calls. Electromechanical relay computers, those at Bell believed, would provide them with an automatic telephone switching system that could transmit digital data from one telephone to another. This would allow the telephone company to switch calls without human intervention, the elimination of which was becoming increasingly necessary as telephone service expanded at a staggering rate and operators were overwhelmed with more calls than they could handle. The need for doing away with human operators would also lower costs. The way such computerized relay systems would work is that numbers dialed from a telephone would be transmitted in the form of electronic impulses to a central point and then automatically directed through the correct circuit to their destination point, along with human voices translated electronically and sent over the telephone wire. Although work on such devices had been conducted by Bell Labs since its establishment, the new computer technology promised advancements well beyond anything accomplished previously.

After gaining useful experience developing early computer relay technology and as an assistant on the Complex Computer project, Andrews was called on to design Bell Labs's next series of computers, the BTL Models II and III. Starting with the BTL Model I, six versions of the Bell Telephone Laboratories large-scale electromechanical computer were eventually built, the first four of which were special-purpose military machines. In designing Models IV-VI, Andrews collaborated with fellow engineer Samuel B. Williams. One of the more important machines that Andrews helped design was the BTL Model IV, duplicates of which were constructed at a cost of $250,000 each for use by the National Aeronautics and Space Agency (NASA) as well as the U.S. Army. The NASA copy was housed at Langley Field in Virginia, while the army version was kept at the Aberdeen Proving Ground in Aberdeen, Maryland. Andrews, along with the engineers placed under his supervision, was responsible for many important concepts and features that went into the construction of the BTL computers. For example, the multiplier he included in the BTL Model III was capable of performing complex multiplications and storing the products, thus permitting many shortcuts in calculations. Models V and VI, which were also employed for civilian purposes, were innovative in that they featured floating point decimals, a major breakthrough that further improved the machines' calculating ability.

Perhaps the most groundbreaking feature of the BTL computers, and the one that represented Andrews's greatest contribution to the future of computer technology, was their use of binary language. A code involving combinations of zeroes and ones, binary was vastly superior to the coding systems that had preceded it. Andrews and his colleagues worked out a way to generate the binary-coded decimal-systems, which are used to encode numbers and other information, and the BTL computers became one of the first testing grounds for the language, which is the foundation of much existing computer technology. As the basis for the EBCDIC and ASCII systems, "languages" in which information is represented in the form of binary code, binary has continued to be relevant on into the 21st century.

Andrews contributed further to the advancement of computer technology through his participation in the Association for Computing Machinery (ACM), both as a founding member of the organization, in the 1950s, and, over the years, as an officer and as a member of many of its committees.

After World War II, Andrews was no longer as heavily involved with the BTL computers. He went on to work at planning and programming military communications systems based on computer technologies, first as a member of Bell Lab's military communications department and later as part of a study group in Bell's military systems engineering department. In working on such systems, Andrews made extensive use of his experience with relay computers.

Although the Bell electromechanical relay computers were slow compared to later electronic machines, they were reliable and accurate. Designed to repeatedly check their own calculations, they were well-equipped for correctly switching telephone calls. However, by 1950, the advent of fully electronic machines had begun to make electromechanical technology outmoded. Howard Aiken's Mark computers, the BTL models, and their like were eclipsed by electronic digital computers such as John Atanasoff's ABC and the ENIAC, designed by John Mauchly and J. Presper Eckert. These new machines relied not on mechanical parts but on vacuum tubes, and later on transistors, which were invented by the Bell Labs team of John Bardeen, Walter Brattain, and William Shockley and were more compact than their earlier counterparts.

Andrews retired from Bell Telephone Laboratories in June 1959, at the age of 61. He then joined Sanders Associates, in Nashua, New Hampshire, where he was named manager of preliminary design, a position he held until his second retirement, in 1969. He then developed an interest in cardiac biology, and, although he was unsuccessful in his attempts to make connections with scientists in that field, that interest, along with others in various areas of applied science and communications, continued up to his death, on October 13, 1980 in Hanover, New Hampshire, at the age of 82. Andrews held several patents throughout his life and also authored various articles pertaining to Bell Telephone Labs computing technology, including the early development of binary computers. His greatest scientific accomplishments, represented by his work with the Bell Labs computers, has proved to be a guiding influence for later designers.—B. S.

Suggested Reading: Cortada, James. *Historical Dictionary of Data Processing: Biographies*, 1987; Goldstine, Herman. *The Computer from Pascal to von Neumann*, 1972; Lee, J. A. N., ed. *International Biographical Dictionary of Computer Pioneers*, 1995

Antheil, George

July 8, 1900–Feb. 12, 1959 Composer and inventor of frequency hopping

The great experimental American composer George Antheil was once dubbed the "bad boy of music" for his ultra-modern and self-described cold, mechanical portraits of industrial America in the Jazz Age. Though Antheil's later works were considerably more romantic and traditional, it is due to these early compositions that a very important telecommunications technology was invented. While composing his early masterwork, *Ballet Mécanique*, he needed to find a way to keep 16 player pianos in time and used identical strips of punched tape to achieve this. At a Hollywood party in 1940, he met the actress Hedy Lamarr. With the war in Europe on their minds, Antheil and Lamarr began discussing a way to enable torpedoes to be controlled by radio without interference by enemy jamming devices. Together they invented frequency hopping, an idea based on Antheil's punched strips of paper, which would allow a torpedo to switch frequencies, seemingly at random, and thereby prevent its being jammed. In 1942 Antheil and Lamarr were awarded a patent for frequency hopping, but their idea was not used by the American military during World War II. Today, however, frequency hopping technology is used in cordless phones, cellular phones, and data transmission. It is effective in these systems because, in addition to being secure against interference, it uses the broadcast spectrum more efficiently than other techniques. Many experts believe that it will ultimately lead to unlimited frequencies being made available to broadcasters.

Georg Johann Carl Antheil was born on July 8, 1900 in Trenton, New Jersey, the son of Henry W. and Wilhelmina (Huse) Antheil. His father owned and managed a shoe store. Of German-Polish ancestry, Antheil added an "e" to his first name when he was a teen. In an autobiographical statement for *American Composers Today* (1949), Antheil described his youth and early musical education: "My childhood was like that of most American kids except that I exhibited a great love for music at an early age, studying the violin when I was five. The piano came much later, when I was ten. The study of harmony was begun in my twelfth year. My first serious teacher was Constantine von Sternberg, former pupil of Liszt. He was an old man, but devoted to my talent; he insisted upon a strict contrapuntal basis. Many persons believe, or have until recently believed, that I have had little theoretical training, but this is not so. I studied very intensively during those early adolescent years, and was able to write passable, and even musical, fugues when I was eighteen. Also sonata-allegro movements."

In 1917 Antheil graduated from Trenton High School, where he had edited the newspaper. During World War I he served in the aviation arm of the United States Signal Corps as a cadet. When the war ended, Antheil continued his studies with von Sternberg, but new styles of music began to influence him. He told Ewen: "At several Philadelphia Orchestra concerts I heard Stravinsky's *Petrushka*, which revolutionized all of my previous musical ideas. I commenced studying every piece of new music I could put my hands on. I left Sternberg in 1919, went to New York, and became a pupil of Ernest Bloch. It was while I was with Bloch that I composed my *First Symphony*. I wanted the symphony to express that part of America which I saw all around me: Trenton, the Delaware River, the people I knew, the sounds and emotions I felt."

After two years with Bloch, Antheil won a scholarship to attend the Music Settlement School (the forerunner of the Curtis Institute), in Philadelphia, Pennsylvania. He studied under George Boyle, improved his piano playing, and also gave lessons in elementary harmony. Hearing that the concert manager Martin H. Hanson was leaving for Europe and might need a concert pianist of the "fiery ultramodern variety," Antheil practiced the piano for 16 to 20 hours a day for 30 days and then sought an audition with Hanson. The audition was successful, and so in May 1922 he embarked on a European tour as a concert pianist. He soon acquired the reputation of being a "bad boy" of music, largely because of his insistence on playing the ultra-modern piano music of the era. For a while he settled in Berlin, where his *First Symphony* was introduced in December 1922 by the Berlin Philharmonic. The audience reacted politely to the symphony—said to be the first symphonic piece in which jazz was recognized—but the critics were hostile.

Realizing that he wanted to be a composer more than a concert pianist, Antheil soon devoted himself almost entirely to writing music. Abandoning his concert tours in 1923, he went to Paris and rented an apartment above Sylvia Beach's famous Shakespeare Bookshop at 12 rue de l'Odéon. There he wrote several of his early works, including his *Second Symphony* and *Ballet Méchanique*, as well as a great deal of chamber music. Playing the more fashionable Parisian salons, he soon became famous, and people flocked to see his concerts. On October 4, 1923, he introduced a group of piano pieces, "Mechanisms," "Airplane Sonata," and "Sonata Sauvage," at the Théâtre des Champs Elysées. As a result, rioting broke out, and overnight Antheil was famous in Paris as, in his own words, "an anti-expressive, anti-romantic, coldly mechanistic aesthetic."

In 1925 Antheil completed the *Ballet Mécanique*; scored for anvils, airplane propellers, electric bells, automobile horns, and 16 player pianos, it was described by its composer as a "mechanistic dance of life." "My idea was to warn the age in which I was living of the simultaneous beauty and danger of its own unconscious mechanistic philosophy."

Following the international success of his opera, *Transatlantic* (1930), a jazz-influenced saga about a presidential candidate and his obsession over a beautiful woman named Helena, Antheil landed in Hollywood. In 1936 he became a composer for both Paramount and Columbia studios. After writing the scores for *The Plainsman* (1936), Make Way for Tomorrow (1937), and *The Buccaneer* (1938), he wrote an article in the *American Scholar* (Summer 1937) in which he supported the idea that serious music could be written for film. In his autobiography *Bad Boy of Music* (1945), Antheil reiterated the need for good movie scores, because it is through background movie music that "the great larger public taste is being slowly but surely formed."

In 1940, at a Hollywood party, Antheil met the actress Hedy Lamarr, who, after leaving her native Austria, had risen to movie stardom as "the most beautiful girl in the world." What Antheil did not know about Lamarr was that she also had a keen understanding of technology. During her first marriage, to an Austrian arms manufacturer who had dealings with Nazi Germany, Lamarr overheard her husband and his clients discussing developing technologies. She recalled that her husband's clients were looking for ways to jam radio-controlled torpedoes so that they would either miss their targets or explode prematurely.

As the night wore on, Antheil and Lamarr began talking about how difficult it would be to defeat the Nazis. Lamarr suggested that if a torpedo could change frequencies—seemingly at random—it would be impossible for someone to find the right jamming frequency. Antheil thought this was an interesting idea and suggested that they work on it together. She agreed and was supposed to have scrawled her phone number in lipstick across the windshield of his car.

Antheil believed he had the solution to coordinating the change in frequencies between the radio and torpedo. While composing his *Ballet Mécanique*, he ran across the problem of keeping his 16 player pianos in time and synchronized them by using identical roles of punched tape. As Peter Y. Hong explained in an article for *Microwave Journal* (February 1999): "[Antheil] proposed controlling the frequencies for the transmitter and receiver with paper rolls like those controlling player pianos: The couple's design specified the use of rolls perforated with identical patterns to match the split-second hops in radio frequencies. The number of frequencies to be used, 88, matched the number of keys on a piano."

Antheil and Lamarr received their patent for a "Secret Communications System" in August 1942 and submitted their idea to the National Inventors Council, a wartime Commerce Department division designed to take ideas from the public. Unfortunately, no one in the U.S. government seemed particularly keen on their idea, partially because in their patent application they explained that their invention originated in player pianos. As quoted by the *World Press Review* (July 1997), Antheil recalled: "The brass hats in Washington who examined our invention could only focus on two words: player piano. I heard them all say: 'My God, how are we going to fit a player piano into a torpedo?'" As a result their patent lay dormant in the U.S. government's secret files for years. Their idea, better known today as frequency hopping, was revived in the late 1950s by the American military—after Antheil and Lamarr's patent ran out. Through the use of mainframe computers, the military was able to use frequency hopping to protect American communications from Soviet listeners during the Cuban Missile Crisis of 1962. In the subsequent decades, with the development of super-fast microchips and digital signal processors, frequency hopping became commercially viable. Cellular phones and wireless devices rely on discreet, or separate, signals, thus avoiding the problem of signal interference.

The honors conferred on Antheil include an award from the Société Académique, in Paris (1933), and the Bispham Memorial Award (1934). He held an honorary life membership with the Paris police for his work in criminal typing. He received Guggenheim fellowships for 1931 and 1932. In 1997 the Electric Frontier Foundation (EFF) awarded Hedy Lamarr and George Antheil its EFF Pioneer Award for their work in frequency hopping.

George Antheil married Boski (some sources say Elizabeth) Markus, a niece of the Austrian writer Arthur Schnitzler, on November 4, 1925. The couple had one child, Peter. George Antheil died on February 12, 1959.—C. M.

Suggested Reading: *Etude* p431 Aug. 1946, with illus.; *Microwave Journal* p70+ Feb. 1999; *Modern Music* p78+ Winter 1946; *Scientific American* p95 Apr. 1998; *World Press Review* p34+ July 1997; Antheil, George. *Bad Boy of Music*, 1945; Ewen, David, ed. *American Composers Today*, 1949; Howard, J. T. *Our American Music*, 1946; Thompson, O., ed. *International Cyclopedia of Music and Musicians*, 1949

Armstrong, Edwin Howard

Dec. 18, 1890–Jan. 31, 1954 Inventor and electrical engineer

Few inventors have contributed more to the development of radio and electronic communications than Edwin H. Armstrong, who in the early part of the 20th century created the circuits necessary for radio amplifiers and AM and FM broadcasting. His work has remained central to radio and television broadcasting, military communications, satellite and microwave transmissions, and cellular-phone technology. It has also found applications for space travel, providing radio control of remote-controlled probes as well as communications from Earth to astronauts in outer space. Along with Guglielmo Marconi and Lee de Forest, he is considered by many to be a father of radio.

Edwin Howard Armstrong was born in New York City, on December 18, 1890, the first child of John and Emily (Smith) Armstrong. John Armstrong worked in publishing and eventually became vice president of the American division of Oxford University Press; Emily Smith was a graduate of Hunter College and taught in New York City public schools for a decade before her marriage in 1888. When Edwin was 12 the family moved to a house in Yonkers, New York, that overlooked the Hudson River from a bluff.

As a child Armstrong was very interested in mechanics; by the age of 14 he was studying the work of Guglielmo Marconi in the field of wireless telegraphy. (Marconi had only a few years earlier sent the first wireless signal across the Atlantic Ocean.) Armstrong decided to become an inventor himself and filled his room with homemade wireless devices. Such wireless devices, then in their infancy, were extremely primitive mechanisms. As described in the *Dictionary of American Biography, Supplement Five, 1951–1955* (1977): "[Their] crude spark-gap transmitters produced electromagnetic wave signals so weak that sunlight washed them out through most daytime hours, while [their] iron-filing or magnetic receivers were cruder still, requiring tight earphones and quiet rooms to catch the faint Morse code signals that were all the early wireless was capable of transmitting."

Nevertheless, Armstrong yearned to know all he could about wireless telegraphy and, as a student at Yonkers High School, built a 125-foot antenna on his family's lawn in order to study it firsthand. He read all he could on the subject and learned how each new device worked—including the Audion tube (today known as a triode), a combined rectifier and amplifier used for transmitting radio waves, invented by Lee de Forest in 1906. After graduating from high school in 1910, he enrolled at the Columbia University engineering school, in New York City, where he studied under Michael Idvorsky Pupin, the inventor of the Pupin loading coil used in long-distance telegraphy. As an undergraduate in 1912, Armstrong realized that de Forest's Audion tube could be used as a highly sensitive radio receiver and, at higher amplifications, as an oscillator or transmitter. He built a new regenerative (or feedback) circuit that fed back part of the current at the plate to the grid, to boost incoming signals. When he tested this in his steeple room in Yonkers he found that signals from distant stations were coming in so loudly that he did not even need to use headphones to pick them up. In addition, he discovered that, when feedback was pushed to a high level, the feedback circuit acted as a transmitter as well. "Thus," as noted in the *Dictionary of American Biography* (1977), "this single circuit yielded not only the first radio amplifier but also the key to the continuous-wave transmitter that is still at the heart of all radio operations." With his new circuit Armstrong had made long-range radio broadcasts practical.

In 1913 Armstrong filed for a patent on his regenerative or feedback circuit. A year later de Forest filed an application for a patent that improved his Audion tube and embodied part of the same principle. A complex legal battle between the two men ensued that went on for some 18 years. In 1924 the legal tide turned against Armstrong; then, in 1933, he won in the court of appeals, only to have the U.S. Supreme Court reverse judgment in favor of de Forest in 1934. Though the patent rights ultimately went to de Forest, today most radio engineers agree that the honor of the invention belongs to Armstrong.

After receiving his bachelor's degree in electrical engineering in 1913, Armstrong stayed on at Columbia as an instructor and research assistant to Pupin. In 1917, after the United States entered World War I, he went to France as a captain. He later became a major in the U.S. Signal Corps, where he was assigned to detect enemy shortwave communications as well as aircraft; through this work his second great invention arose. The existing systems for detecting aircraft did so, as noted by Isaac Asimov in *Asimov's Biographical Dictionary of Science and Technology* (1982), "by the sound waves they emitted, but Armstrong believed it might be more sensitive and efficient to detect the electromagnetic waves set up by their ignition systems." Since such waves were too high in frequency to be picked up easily, he built a circuit (which he called a superheterodyne receiver) that lowered the frequency and amplified the resulting signal. Three months before the World War I armistice, he perfected the superheterodyne circuit, which today is the basic circuit for amplitude modulation (AM) in most radio receivers.

Armstrong returned to the United States with patents pending on this invention. Once again, the question of invention precedence came up, but the challenges to Armstrong's right to the patents were mostly groundless. He sold both his feedback and superheterodyne patents to major manufacturers, including Westinghouse Electric and Manufacturing Company and the Radio Corporation of America (RCA), but kept his royalty-earning licensing rights for the use of amateurs. During the 1920s, as the radio craze swept across America, earnings from these patents made him a millionaire. Though financially secure, he continued to work at Columbia as an instructor and researcher, drawing no salary. He married Marion MacInnis, a former secretary to the president of RCA, on December 1, 1923. They would later have a son and a daughter.

In 1921 Armstrong completed work on his superregenerative circuit, which had the distinction of earning more for him than any of his other inventions. The superregenerative circuit overcame his regenerative receiver's main flaw—its tendency to oscillate when the point of maximum amplification was reached. RCA bought the patent, though it initially earned the company no profit because the circuit did not work for broadcast receivers.

From the very start of his career, Armstrong had been interested in the problem of eliminating static. During the early days of radio, broadcasters used only AM to carry signals. As explained in the *Columbia Encyclopedia* (1993), "In an AM transmission the carrier wave is constant in frequency and varies in amplitude (strength) according to the sounds present in the microphone." The problem with this system, however, was that any electrical disturbances in the atmosphere—like storms or machinery—modulated the carrier wave and caused static to be picked up in the receiver. After working with Pupin on the static problem for a short time, Armstrong started to attack the problem on his own in 1924. The following year he proved to his own satisfaction that radio waves and static had the same electrical characteristics. In 1933 he and Pupin patented a method of broadcasting in which, according to the *Hutchinson Dictionary of Scientific Biography* (1994), "the transmitted signal is made to modulate the frequency of the carrier wave over a wide waveband. This method, called frequency modulation (FM), is unaffected by static and is capable of high-fidelity sound reproduction."

In 1935 Armstrong invited officials of RCA to his Columbia laboratories to observe his system of frequency modulation. During the demonstration a sound-reel recording was played that compared the reception of the old and new types of broadcasting during a thunderstorm. The FM recording boasted a program free of static, despite the fact that the FM station's broadcasting power was only 4 percent that of the larger AM station.

What impressed Armstrong and many observers about FM was the brilliant clarity of its reception. Faint musical passages came through perfectly; loud passages or sounds did not need to be turned down. A British journalist, after hearing FM reception for the first time, told his readers at home that the reproduction was "ghastly" in its reality. He half expected gurgling water to run out of the loudspeaker, and the scratching of a match seemed almost to burn his hand. During pauses in the programming it was impossible to tell whether the station was on or off the air.

For further experimentation Armstrong was given permission by RCA to set up an FM transmitter in its experimental broadcasting laboratory on the 85th floor of New York City's Empire State Building. RCA, however, was reluctant to promote FM. (In the Depression-ravaged 1930s, the radio industry had little interest in converting to an entirely new broadcasting system, despite its obvious benefits.) After RCA asked Armstrong to remove his apparatus to make way for television, he and his friend Carman R. Runyon, who ran an amateur radio station, worked together building an FM transmitter. The results were so successful that in 1936 Armstrong applied to the Federal Communications Commission (FCC) for a permit to erect a big FM station of his own.

Because television was seeking channels at the same time, the FCC delayed Armstrong's permit, and it was not until 1937 that he constructed his own station, W2XMN, a 40-kilowatt station equipped with a 400-foot tower and three 100-foot cross-arms perched high atop the Hudson River Palisades at Alpine, New Jersey. W2XMN could be heard clearly and steadily at distances of 100 miles; if Armstrong had not used his own money to rush construction of this station, it might have been years before the public ever heard of FM. The apparatus for the station was designed in the Hartley Research Laboratories at Columbia University.

The remainder of the equipment was constructed at the Radio Engineers' Laboratory, in Long Island City, New York, and at RCA in Camden, New Jersey. Armstrong gave much of the credit for the station to two of his assistants, John Bose and James Day.

Despite encountering opposition and general disinterest, Armstrong managed to set up more FM stations in Yonkers, New York; Hartford, Connecticut; and Paxton, Massachusetts. Soon Yankee Network Incorporated became interested and set up an experimental station on Mount Asnebumskit, in Massachusetts. By September 1940 there were 22 experimental stations licensed in the country, and many applications for FM commercial stations were pending. As the number of stations grew, radio manufacturers began building products to receive both AM and FM broadcasts. By 1939 such radios were available from the General Electric Company (GE) and the Stromberg-Carlson Company; other companies quickly followed suit.

In January 1940 Armstrong's associate Carman R. Runyon made a highly successful demonstration of FM's capabilities by broadcasting a program of music and speech over his FM station in Yonkers, New York. Armstrong's station, W2XMN in New Jersey, picked it up and relayed it to WIXOJ in Paxton, Massachusetts. From there the program was broadcast to an FM station at Mount Washington in New Hampshire, which reported absolutely clear reception. From there the signal was in turn rebroadcast by a standard shortwave station to a Yankee Network receiving outpost in Winchester, Massachusetts, and then sent by telephone wire to Boston, and finally back to Yonkers. This demonstration offered a solution to FM's major difficulty—limitation of range due to the curvature of the earth.

Despite the obvious advantages of FM over AM, it took a long time for it to catch on in the United States, where those with vested interests in AM put up a firm resistance. Television, which operated at the same frequencies as FM, also posed competition. On the status of Armstrong's outstanding work, *Fortune* (October 1939) reported: "While the duty of the FCC in making short-wave-band allocations was clearly to get television on the air as quickly as possible (the British having already beat the United States by a couple of years), the Commission's failure to understand Frequency Modulation and to place the proper estimate on its technological importance is just as deplorable as the industry's failure to push it. Instead of encouraging substantial capital outlays, which the development of this invention would cause, the Commission has acted as a deterrent by relegating Major Armstrong to an experimental corner of the ultra-short-wave spectrum. What FM needs at the present time above all things is an allocation that will put it on a commercial status and will at the same time be large enough to permit it to operate to full advantage. Of the many ultra-short-wave bands that have been allocated but are not actually in use, one band six megacycles wide would accommodate 30 FM stations, and through duplication get FM off to a start all over the country. Relieved of the heavy duties of policing its present restrictive wave lengths, the FCC might thus open a new era of democracy in the air."

In 1940 the FCC attempted to mediate a bitter fight between Armstrong and the television concerns. Testifying before the FCC, Armstrong requested that FM be granted full commercial licenses; that its then maximum power of 1,000 watts be raised to 50,000; that a band of frequencies from 41 to 44 megahertz (MHz) be allocated to FM stations; and that such provisions be granted immediately, since nearly 100 station applications from all over the country had recently been received. Because the first channel (Channel 1) on television's allocated bandwidth overlapped with Armstrong's demands, RCA opposed the measures, but it was at first dealt a setback. On May 20, 1940 the FCC took Channel 1 off the television band and allotted it to FM. The frequencies between 42 and 50 MHz were assigned to FM—enough for 40 FM channels—and commercial service was authorized to begin on January 1, 1941. After this victory Armstrong said he believed there was no longer any reason "why every city in the United States which can afford a radio station cannot have an FM station."

During World War II, FM radio slowly continued to expand in the United States, doubling from 18 fully operational stations in 1941 to 36 in 1942. By 1945 there were about 50 FM stations and at least 500,000 FM radio receivers in use. That year, however, Armstrong and FM received a heavy blow when the FCC moved it to a new, higher-frequency band in the name of protecting against a cycle of sunspots predicted to begin in 1948. (Sunspots can interfere with FM transmissions.) Meanwhile, television, which at the time still used FM for its audio, was nevertheless assigned the bandwidth vacated by FM. Restrictions were also put on FM's transmitting power, making the 50-plus transmitters then in existence, as well as the half-million radio receivers built since 1939, obsolete. Drained by these battles and by the long-term legal disputes with RCA and other companies over patent infringements, Armstrong found himself almost completely destitute by the early 1950s. On January 31, 1954, believing there was a conspiracy against him, he threw himself out of his apartment window in New York City, falling 13 floors to his death.

After his death Armstrong's widow carried on his legal battles, filing 21 patent-infringement suits and ultimately winning $10 million in damages. Another posthumous victory for Armstrong came in the late 1960s, when FM was finally recognized by the radio industry as a clearly superior system to AM. In addition to being used in military applications and televison and radio broadcasting, FM has spread even beyond Armstrong's wildest dreams: long-range FM transmissions have en-abled us to communicate with astronauts in space and on the moon as well as to control robot probes studying our solar system.

During his lifetime Edwin H. Armstrong received numerous awards for his achievements in radio, including the Institute of Radio Engineers Medal of Honor (1918), the Egleston Medal from Columbia University (1939), the Holley Medal from the American Society of Mechanical Engineers (1940), and the Franklin Medal from the Franklin Institute (1941). In 1945 he was honored for his contributions to the war effort with the U.S. Medal of Merit. After his death he was elected to the International Telecommunications Union in Geneva, where he joins such towering figures as Alexander Graham Bell and his old mentors Marconi and Pupin.—C. M.

Suggested Reading: *Christian Science Monitor* p3 Mar. 16, 1940; *Fortune* p86+ Oct. 1939; *Newsweek* p32+ Jan. 30, 1939, p30 Jan. 15, 1940, p30+ Apr. 1, 1940; *New York Herald Tribune* p11 Mar. 20 1940 , p7 Mar. 29, 1940, p20 May 21, 1940; *New York Times* X p12 Mar. 17, 1940, p46 Mar. 28, 1940, X p12 Oct. 20, 1940; *Popular Science* p59 Nov. 1940; *Saturday Evening Post* p18+ July 6, 1940; *Scholastic* p10 Apr. 15, 1940; *Science* p6 Nov. 15, 1935, p72 Jan. 27, 1939; *Scientific American* p3 Jan. 1936, p291 May 1939; *Time* p47+ July 31, 1939, p36 Apr. 1, 1940; *World Who's Who in Science*, 1968; *Dictionary of Scientific Biography*, 1970; *Dictionary of American Biography, Supplement Five, 1951–1955*, 1977; Asimov, Isaac. *Asimov's Biographical Dictionary of Science and Technology*, 1982; *Columbia Encyclopedia*, 1993; Porter, Roy. *Hutchinson Dictionary of Scientific Biography*, 1994

Ash, Roy

Oct. 20, 1918– Executive with Litton Industries and AM International

From the 1950s to the 1970s, Roy Ash helped shape the development of electronics, particularly what were then known as "business machines." Ranging from calculating devices, to photocopiers, to actual computers, these machines were the main products of the two multifaceted corporations helmed by Ash: Litton Industries and AM International. Ash was especially ambitious during his time with AM in the 1970s, attempting, albeit unsuccessfully, to bring the aging company's products up-to-date with modern technology. In addition to his business endeavors, Ash was also a high-ranking adviser to the administrations of U.S. presidents Nixon and Ford.

Roy Lawrence Ash was born on October 20, 1918 in Los Angeles, California, the son of Charles K. Ash, a hay and grain broker, and Fay E. (Dickinson) Ash. He had one brother, now deceased. Ash was raised Roman Catholic and grew up in Los Angeles, where he attended George Washington and Manual Arts High Schools, graduating in 1935. Unable to afford college tuition, he took a job in 1936 in the city cash collection department of the Bank of America National Trust and Savings Association in Los Angeles, California. He continued to work at the bank, where he was promoted into administrative positions, until he entered the army in 1942.

After completing training at the Officers Candidate School, Ash was selected to join the army air force's statistical control service, headed by Charles "Tex" Thornton, Ash's future business partner. The function of the service was to adapt modern management controls and techniques to the needs of the army air force. When the war ended, Ash chose not to follow Thornton to the Ford Motor Company like most of the others in the group, who became known as the Ford "Whiz Kids." Instead, after being discharged in 1945 with the rank of captain, he remained where the group had been based, at Harvard University, in Cambridge, Massachusetts. Ash entered the Harvard Graduate School of Business Administration, which accepted him despite his lack of an undergraduate degree. Completing the school's two-year course of studies in 18 months, he received an M.B.A. degree, in 1947, and was named a Baker scholar, the highest academic honor the school bestows.

From Harvard, Ash returned to the Bank of America as chief statistical control analyst at their headquarters in San Francisco, California. In 1949 he moved to the Hughes Aircraft Company, where as controller he worked closely with Thornton, who had left Ford to become operating chief at Hughes. At the time, Hughes Aircraft was developing into one of the nation's largest advanced-electronics companies. In 1953 Ash and Thornton left Hughes and organized their own company, known at first as the Electro-Dynamics Corporation. After raising $1.5 million from investors, the two men then bought Litton Industries, a small West Coast producer of microwave tubes with annual sales of $3 million, and their fledgling company took over the Litton name.

From the beginning, the development of Litton was planned so as to take advantage of the tremendous technological boom foreseen by Ash and Thornton. Selectively excluding enterprises not easily covered by its technological umbrella, it embarked on what was perhaps one of the most daring and successful courses of acquisition attempted in the 20th century. The dramatic growth began in 1958, when the company acquired the Monroe Calculating Machines Company, a well-known manufacturer of adding, billing, and other business machines, whose annual sales exceeded Litton's. The acquisition of Monroe gave Litton a foothold in the rapidly expanding business-machine field, and Litton Industries continued taking over one company after another at a staggering pace. By 1961, it had 25 mergers under its belt and was operating 48 plants in nine countries. Its yearly sales had climbed to $245 million, and its common stock, first offered to the public in 1955 at $10 per share, was worth $140 per share. Approximately 53 percent of the company's sales were military, and 47 percent were industrial and commercial, in diversified electronic and electrochemical lines, including communications equipment and systems.

The phenomenal growth of Litton was attributable, more than any other factor, to the complementary talents of Ash and Thornton. Thornton was the visionary with an extraordinary ability to predict with perfect timing the best opportunities for expansion, and Ash was the technical and financial wizard who made the operation work. Ash was little known outside the company, in which he held successively the positions of vice president, treasurer, and executive vice president, until 1961, when Thornton, then both president and board chairman, turned over the presidency to his lieutenant. As president, Ash became a frequent public spokesman for Litton. Beginning in 1960, he also served as president of Litton Systems, the company's military and defense contract subsidiary and one of its most important divisions.

With Ash as president, the fortunes of Litton Industries continued their dizzying upward climb. By 1965, sales had reached $914 million and the company was producing some 5,000 items, including credit cards, trading stamps, microwave ovens, submarines, the world's first automated cargo ship, one of NASA's first spacesuits, and the world's largest oil-drilling rig. Litton encompassed over 50 different enterprises by 1966. It was not a company in the old sense of that word, but rather, as Ash described it, "a management and technical concept formed to fit the times."

In 1966 Litton entered the magic circle of some 55 American companies whose annual gross sales totaled more than $1 billion, and its earnings were listed at approximately $50 million. With the number of Litton products increased to over 6,000, new groups of enterprises continued to form. For example, Litton became deeply involved in education, with divisions dealing with educational systems, instructional materials, and educational technology. The company contracted to run training programs for the Job Corps, and it entered the area of professional services with store design, computer preparation of income tax forms, and the conducting of broad economic studies. Litton also signed an unprecedented contract with the Greek government to develop the island of Crete and the western Peloponnesus, and it later negotiated a similar agreement with Portugal.

In May 1967 Ash participated in the American Bankers Association National Automation Conference in New York City. At the conference, Ash made what became known as the "One World" speech, in which he predicted that business and industrial organizations would eventually link all the nations of the world, and declared that "business organizations are the most efficient converters of the original resources of the world into useable goods and services." He would later further develop this thesis at a 1972 White House conference on world industry; he envisioned that "state capitalism may well be a form for world business in the world ahead," and that the communist nations of the world would switch to capitalist economic systems by around 1990, a prognostication that proved astonishingly accurate.

Litton suffered its first reversal in January 1968, when Ash and Thornton announced in a letter to shareholders that earnings would be substantially lower than expected. Soon afterward, it was announced that earnings for the quarter ending January 31, 1968 had fallen to $7.2 million, a drop of 56 percent from the previous year. Ash explained to interviewers at the time that much of the trouble was in the business machines division, which had been plagued by strikes at production plants, slow sales in office furniture, and delays in the introduction of several new business machines, including the Royfax 1700 photocopier and a new Royal portable electric typewriter. Ash also attributed Litton's difficulties to "certain earlier deficiencies of management personnel," thus arousing speculation that the drain of talented executives who trained at Litton and then moved on to other companies was beginning to hurt. For some time the company was known in the business world as "Litton University," and its former executives called themselves "Lidos" (Litton Industries Dropouts).

In December 1968 President-elect Richard M. Nixon announced that Ash would advise him on matters of "management and efficiency" during the transition to the new administration. Ash, now made an official assistant to the president, was also named chairman of the President's Advisory Council on Executive Organization. Ash stepped down as chairman in 1971 but continued to be a Nixon adviser.

In 1972 Ash departed Litton Industries to focus exclusively on his duties in the Nixon administration. The following year, he was made director of the Office of Management and Budget. He continued in this capacity through the Watergate scandal of 1974 and during the subsequent administration of President Gerald Ford. With the election of Democratic party candidate Jimmy Carter to the presidency in 1976, Ash, a long-standing Republican, left Washington for good.

Ash then returned to the private sector, this time taking the position of chief executive officer of Addressograph-Multigraph (AM) International, a long-time office machine manufacturer. Ash believed that the company was on a decline and worked to revitalize it. He set sweeping personnel changes in motion, and stressed more profitable products. Particularly, Ash wanted AM International to keep pace with the market for new technology and move to the cutting edge of computer development. One of his main objectives was to transform products that had previously been electromechanical into entirely electronic machines.

Unfortunately, Ash's attempts to bring AM into the modern computer era were disastrous, and the company began losing more and more money. Observers pointed out that Ash's long-range planning did not take into account the company's more immediate concerns, the result being that AM was not capable of achieving the goals its new CEO had set up. Specifically, the company's existing lines were not generating enough profit to finance the expansion Ash had initiated. In 1981, the board of directors asked Ash to step down from his position. He complied, thus ending his decades-long career in the electronics business.

Roy Ash has been described by journalists and associates as a "human computer," able to retain and discuss the minute details of his vast business enterprises. He married Lila Marie Hornbek on November 13, 1943, and they had five children: Loretta, James, Marilyn, Robert, and Charles. Since 1978, he has served as the director of the World Affairs Council of Los Angeles, where he and his wife currently reside.

One of the leading figures in the postwar commercial computer boom, Roy Ash was a pioneer in a business that had only recently expanded beyond its purely scientific and governmental origins. The new computing technology that was fast becoming a part of everyday life helped catapult Ash into a position of great prominence, as well as influence that extended to the highest echelons of business and government. While his plans for AM International proved unsuccessful, they represented the kind of forward-thinking business practices that would take the computer industry in revolutionary and unexpected directions in the decades to come. Ash once said that "an entrepreneur tends to bite off a little more that he can chew, hoping he'll quickly learn how to chew it."—B. S.

Suggested Reading: *Fortune* p47+ Feb. 27, 1978, p71+ Apr. 6, 1981; *Who's Who in America*, 1998

Atanasoff, John

Oct. 4, 1903–June 15, 1995 Inventor of the first electronic computer

The unsung inventor of the electronic computer, John V. Atanasoff, was not legally recognized for his pioneering work until an official court ruling in 1973 established that the machine he had built (the Atanasoff-Berry Computer, or ABC) almost 35 years earlier was the first to run completely on electricity, as opposed to early mechanical devices like Charles Babbage's Difference Engine or partially electrical machines like Howard Aiken's Mark I. For many years credit for the world's first electronic computer had been wrongfully attributed to John Mauchly and J. Presper Eckert, inventors of the ENIAC. However, the 1973 court decision invalidated the ENIAC's patent, deeming the concept to have been derived from Atanasoff's ideas. "After

Babbage, I was the one who turned computing into its present channels," Atanasoff once said, as quoted by Robert Slater in *Portraits in Silicon* (1987).

John Vincent Atanasoff Jr. was born on October 4, 1903 to John Atanasoff Sr. and Iva Lucena Purdy several miles west of Hamilton, New York. A Bulgarian immigrant, Atanasoff Sr. had originally been named Ivan Atanasov but underwent a name change while passing through Ellis Island in 1889. In addition to John, Atanasoff had nine children: Ethelyn, Margaret, Theodore, Avis, Raymond, Melva, Irving, and one who died in childhood. Shortly after John was born, the family moved to Florida, where Atanasoff worked as an electrical engineer.

John Atanasoff Jr. learned to read early on, and tried to learn everything he could, developing a keen interest and proficiency in electricity and mathematics. His father, who at the time was in charge of the electrical system of a phosphate mine, taught him he fundamentals of electricity. By the age of nine, Atanasoff Jr. was able to repair faulty wiring in the back-porch light of his family's Brewster home. A total fascination with his father's Dietzgen slide rule soon replaced the young Atanasoff's love of baseball. Shortly thereafter, he gained an interest in logarithms and trigonometric functions, and with the help of his mother, who was a math teacher, he was soon able to read a college algebra textbook. By the age of 10 he had added physics and chemistry to his personal studies, and began teaching the mathematics to himself when it became too difficult for his mother.

The family moved again to Old Chicora, Florida, where Atanasoff attended Mulberry High School and received his diploma in two years. While in high school he decided that he wanted to become a theoretical physicist. "The teachers found the easiest way to keep me entertained was to get good books in science and put them in front of me," he said, as quoted by Robert Slater. He entered the University of Florida in Gainesville in 1921 and graduated four years later with top honors and a B.S. in electrical engineering. He rejected a teaching fellowship at Harvard University in favor of one at Iowa State College, which he believed had better engineering and science departments.

While teaching two undergraduate classes at Iowa State, Atanasoff started working toward a master's degree in mathematics. During his first term he met Laura Meeks, a 25-year-old home-economics major from Oklahoma, at a meeting of the Dixie Club, a campus organization for southern students. He received his master's degree in June 1926 and married Meeks a few days later. Iowa State College immediately offered him a position as a mathematics teacher, which he accepted. A year later, the Atanasoffs' first child, Elsie, was born. In 1928 they moved to Madison, Wisconsin, where Atanasoff began doctoral work at the University of Wisconsin. Over the course of the next few years the couple would have two more children, Joanne and John.

While completing his doctoral thesis, "The Dielectric Constant of Helium," Atanasoff began working intensely with computers, spending hours on a Monroe calculator, one of the most advanced devices then available. It was at this time that he became interested in constructing a more efficient computing machine. He received his Ph.D. in theoretical physics in July 1930 and returned to Iowa State College determined to build just such a machine.

Atanasoff became an assistant professor of mathematics and physics at Iowa State in the fall of 1930. He began experimenting with vacuum tubes and radio and was soon promoted to associate professor. Examining the computational devices available at the time, Atanasoff classified them into two categories, analog and digital. The former refers to computers which operate with numbers represented by continuously variable physical quantities such as volts or rotations, while the latter refers to computers which operate with numbers expressed directly as digits. Attempting to develop a satisfactory calculator, he modified an existing IBM model, only to be reprimanded by IBM for tinkering with their product. Returning to the drawing board, Atanasoff decided to try to create something from wholly new. In 1936 he teamed with atomic physicist Glen Murphy to create a small analog calculator they called a Laplaciometer, intended for analyzing the geometry of surfaces. Atanasoff felt that a digital computer was closer to what a computer should be in terms of speed and accuracy but was unable to work out the logistics. Confronted with frustrating technical problems, he got into his Ford V8 one fateful night in the winter of 1937 and drove two hundred miles to an Illinois roadhouse. With the temperature at −20, a weary Atanasoff entered the establishment seeking warmth and rest. Attempting to unwind over a drink of bourbon, he finally began organizing ideas on the creation of his ideal computing machine. "I remember it perfectly as if it were yesterday," he commented in *Portraits in Silicon*. "Everything came together in that one night. . . . All of a sudden I realized that I had a power that I hadn't had before. . . . I had a power—I mean I could do things, I could move, and move with assurance."

Soon Atanasoff had formulated four key ideas which allowed for the invention of the electronic digital computer. The first idea was to use electronic elements such as vacuum tubes as the computer's driving force, contrary to the popular perception of the time in which electronics were seen as unreliable. Secondly, he would use the base-2 (i.e., binary) system as opposed to the more common base-10 system. Using a binary system, in which a circuit's "on" and "off" were represented by ones and zeroes, punch cards could hold a great deal more information. To this function he applied the term "memory," which is still used today. Thirdly, the computer would perform serial calculations, thereby enabling it to handle large numbers. And finally, Atanasoff envisioned his computer as having a memory device containing circuits which could regenerate electrical charge, so that memory would not be lost over time.

After reporting his ideas to Iowa State College, he received a $650 grant in March of 1939. Hiring graduate student Clifford E. Berry, the two men worked from 1939 to 1941 on developing what would become known as the Atanasoff-Berry Computer (ABC). A prototype was completed in November 1939 with a binary card punch reader for memory, making it the first computer to have separate memory and data processing units. It used 300 vacuum tubes for logic circuitry and capacitors for the automatic regeneration of memory. It was the first computer that could perform arithmetic electronically, as well as solve systems of linear algebraic equations. Numbers were stored on two eight-inch-diameter, 11-inch-long memory drums, each of which could hold 30 binary numbers of 50 binary digits. Output came in the form of an electric spark which produced burn spots on cards. (This proved to be a bad idea and eventually caused a destructive fire.) Base-10 punch cards were used for input, with the numbers being converted to binary by the computer. At top speed, it could perform an average of 3.75 calculations per second. However, Atanasoff and Berry found that the card puncher had a failure percentage of .001, which prevented the ABC from reliably performing certain operations.

In March 1941 Atanasoff and Berry received a grant from Research Corporation for $5,330, causing the college to take greater notice of Atanasoff's work. Atanasoff had to sign an agreement under which only Iowa State could apply for a patent for the ABC, and royalties would be split between himself and the school. Unfortunately, the college was unable to recognize the significance of Atanasoff's invention, and, fearing the machine was obsolete, failed to apply for a patent. Because of the agreement, Atanasoff could only stand by, unsuccessfully attempting to motivate the school to act.

In June 1941, John Mauchly, a physicist from Ursinus College in Pennsylvania, visited Atanasoff. The pair had met the previous December at the American Association for the Advancement of Science meeting at the University of Philadelphia. Discovering their common interest in computers, Atanasoff had described his own work to Mauchly and invited him to come to Iowa State to see the ABC. The two men discussed the ABC project extensively, and Mauchly took detailed notes on the computer and its construction. In September 1941, Mauchly contacted Atanasoff in an attempt to convince him to come to the University of Pennsylvania to build a similar calculating machine; but Atanasoff declined, wishing the ABC to remain under wraps until a patent application was filed.

However, with the beginning of the United States' involvement in World War II, Atanasoff drifted away from the development of the ABC. Two months prior to the completion of the ABC

prototype in 1939, Atanasoff had begun simultaneously working in a defense-related position for the Naval Ordnance Laboratory in Washington, D.C., and by the end of 1941 he was devoting the majority of his time to it, working primarily with mines and depth charges. He became chief of the acoustics division of the laboratory, earning far in excess of the $10,000 government salary cap that existed at the time.

Mauchly contacted Atanasoff in 1943 with the news that while working for the U.S. government, he and colleague J. Presper Eckert had developed a new method of computing which differed from Atanasoff's. Mauchly refused to explain any further concerning the computer which became known as ENIAC (Electronic Numerical Integrator and Computer), the first fully functional electronic digital computer. Years later, it would be established that Mauchly's assertion of the difference between the principle behind the ABC and ENIAC was not entirely true.

After the war, Atanasoff did not resume his work in computers. "I'd worked on computers for 12 years or so and under very hard circumstances," he explained, as quoted by Robert Slater. "I wanted a change of life." Atanasoff continued his work for the military, being presented with the Navy Civilian Service Award in 1945. He was later asked to construct a computer for the U.S. Navy but refused the $100,000 grant offered him in order to complete his work in the Naval Ordnance Lab Acoustics Division. In 1947 he participated in early atomic tests at the Bikini Atoll, having invented equipment for the detection and recording of underground seismic waves. At this time he also worked extensively on developing a phonetic alphabet based on binary language, which he hoped would help children learn to read.

Atanasoff returned for a visit to Iowa State in 1948, and was shocked to find that the ABC had been dismantled for parts by the school, which had not notified either of the inventors. It had been successfully tested in 1942, but never actually used. Around this time, the constant separation between Atanasoff and his family began to have a detrimental effect on his marriage. In 1949, he and his wife were divorced, with his wife moving with their three children to Denver, Colorado. That same year he married Alice Crosby, whom he had met while working in Washington during the war.

Atanasoff became chief scientist of the Army Field Forces in Fort Monroe, Virginia, in 1949, and returned to Washington the following year to direct the Navy Fuse Program at the Naval Ordnance Lab. He remained in that position for over a year before establishing the Ordnance Engineering Corporation in Rockville, Maryland, in 1952 with long-time friend and former student David Beecher. After five years the company was sold to the Aerojet General Corporation, with Atanasoff functioning as manager of its Atlantic division from 1957 to 1959 and vice president from 1959 to 1961, after which he left to start Cybernetics, a company that supplied scientific advice and material. The company was later taken over by his son John III.

In 1971 the Atanasoff-vs.-Mauchly controversy came to a head. Atanasoff had been approached 17 years earlier by an attorney representing IBM and was asked for help in disputing the patent for EN-IAC. Since the 1940s, Mauchly and Eckert had claimed credit for inventing the electronic computer and had patented the ENIAC as such. Atanasoff had been campaigning for years when the issue was revived due to a lawsuit filed by computer manufacturer Honeywell against the Sperry-Rand Company (which owned the ENIAC patent) alleging that Mauchly and Eckert had derived their ideas from Atanasoff's ABC. On October 19, 1973 Judge Earl E. Larson ruled in favor of Atanasoff, and the ENIAC patent was invalidated. However, the decision was announced in the midst of the Watergate scandal, and so received little publicity. Atanasoff's recognition as the true inventor of the electronic computer came very slowly over the next 20 years.

After the ruling, Atanasoff returned to Iowa State College (which had changed its name to Iowa State University in 1959) as guest of honor and grand marshal for a student-run festival, the largest in the nation. In October of 1983, on the 10th anniversary of Judge Larson's decision, Atanasoff was given a Distinguished Achievement Citation from the alumni association of Iowa State University. At the ceremony, a film created by the university entitled *From One John Vincent Atanasoff* was shown, relating the construction of the ABC. He was the subject of the book *Atanasoff: Forgotten Father of the Computer* (1988), by Clark Mollenhoff, and in 1990 he was awarded the National Medal of Technology by President George Bush. By this time he held a total of 32 patents, despite the fact that he never held a patent for the ABC.

At the age of 91, John Atanasoff suffered a fatal stroke on June 15, 1995, on his 200-acre farm near Monrovia, Maryland. He had been ill for quite some time, having had a previous stroke in 1975. He was survived by his wife Alice, son John Vincent III, daughters Elsie and Joanne, seven siblings, 10 grandchildren, and seven great-grandchildren. Though he is today recognized as one of the founding figures of the Information Age, he was not able to appreciate the importance of his work at the time. "If I had known the things I had in my machine," he said, as quoted by a reporter in the *Washington Post*, (June 19, 1995), "I would have kept going on it." Pieces of the Atanasoff-Berry Computer are now on display at the Smithsonian Institution.—B. S.

Suggested Reading: *Iowa State University* (online); *Changing Times* p100 Aug. 1990, with photo; *Virginia Polytechnic Institute Department of Computers* (on-line); *New York Times* A p11 June 17, 1995, with photo; *Washington Post* B p4 June 19, 1995; Slater, Robert. *Portraits in Silicon*, 1987

Atkinson, Bill

1951– Computer programmer; creator of HyperCard

The computer programmer Bill Atkinson is the creator of some of Apple Computer's most innovative designs. He worked on the groundbreaking user interface for the Apple Macintosh and wrote the original QuickDraw screen-display program. In 1983 he created MacPaint, a black-and-white painting program for the Macintosh that changed how users interacted with their computers. In 1987 he introduced HyperCard, a simple but powerful piece of software that let users create their own programs by employing a series of virtual "index cards." Long before the appearance of the World Wide Web, HyperCard popularized the idea of hypertext by allowing users to scroll through related virtual index cards via "clickable" buttons. HyperCard was eventually superceded by other hypertext programs, but the software retains a group of devoted followers, among them academic researchers and small-business owners, who insist that because of its simplicity it has yet to be improved upon. Atkinson, who left Apple in 1990 to found his own company, General Magic, is now a well-known nature photographer.

William Atkinson was born in 1951 and grew up in Los Gatos, California. He studied at the University of California, San Diego (UCSD), before entering the graduate program in neuroscience at the University of Washington in Seattle. There he had his first exposure to computers, which he used to analyze data from neuroscience studies. In 1977 (some sources say 1978) he was contacted by Jef Raskin, a computer scientist and former teacher of his at UCSD. Raskin, who had been hired by the newly formed Apple Computer, invited Atkinson to visit him there in California's Silicon Valley. Immersed in his studies, Atkinson at first declined the offer, but Raskin was persistent. "Airfare to the [San Francisco] bay area just showed up with a note saying just come down and look around with no obligation," Atkinson recalled, as quoted by David Read in *MacCentral Online* (June 21, 2001).

Atkinson flew out to meet Raskin, who introduced him to the company's employees—about 30 at that time—and to co-founder Steve Jobs, well-known for his ability to motivate people. "Jobs put a big sell on me," Atkinson told Greg Miller for the *Los Angeles Times* (January 5, 1998). "His argument, which hit home, was that I could influence how things come out, could be ahead of the curve. He said we had a chance to make a difference in the world." Atkinson was persuaded and left school, despite warnings from his professors. "Oh, what a great potential you had," one professor told him, as Atkinson recalled to Read.

In his new position Atkinson worked on some of the earliest software for the Apple II, Apple's easy-to-use personal computer, which became a major success. By appealing to ordinary people rather than computer experts, the Apple II turned the company from a small start-up into a serious business. Atkinson was responsible for adapting the UCSD version of the high-level programming language known as Pascal to the Apple II. He also led the development of the bold new screen display for the Lisa, the first personal computer with a graphical user interface (GUI, pronounced "gooey"). The unique features of the GUI—such as on-screen windows, graphical icons, files, and pull-down menus operated with the click of a mouse—were largely invented at Xerox Palo Alto Research Center (PARC), but it was Apple's application of these ideas that revolutionized the personal-computer industry. The Lisa, priced at $10,000, turned out to be a commercial failure, but Atkinson went on to create most of the GUI technology for Lisa's legendary successor, the Macintosh. After an initial period of poor sales, the Macintosh's popularity mushroomed; its user-friendly GUI became the new standard in PC screen display.

Atkinson also wrote the original QuickDraw program, which is the Macintosh's built-in method of presenting on-screen images. QuickDraw is not a drawing program for the user, but a screen-display system; it accepts instructions from the application that the computer is running and "draws" the corresponding graphics on the screen. QuickDraw provided a consistent interface for software developers to work with. It remained Apple's primary display system until 2000, when the company released Quartz, a new windowing system that utilizes Portable Document Format (PDF) as the basis of its imaging model.

In 1983 Atkinson introduced MacPaint, the original PC painting program. An image-editing program, MacPaint allowed users to create their own artwork on the computer screen by using the mouse. MacPaint utilized a bit-map display, in which the on-screen image is derived from a series of bits, or binary digits, which are either on or off. In monochromatic displays, such as that of the original Macintosh, each bit represents one pixel on the screen. The software, which was included free with the Macintosh from 1984 to 1988, was the first to bring computer art design to the average user, and, moreover, it helped popularize the mouse. "Atkinson can be seen as the man who made computing a 'right brain' activity," Bob Cotton and Richard Oliver remarked in *Understanding Hypermedia 2.000* (1997), as quoted by Hart Snider on the Scratch Video Web site. "People who had claimed to be totally uninterested by computers fell under the spell of the Macintosh when they played with MacPaint. Being able to create pictures on a computer shifted the whole idea of what computers were for."

Atkinson is arguably best known for HyperCard, the multimedia data-management program that he created in 1987. HyperCard made it possible for ordinary computer users to program their own customized applications. It was, according to Atkinson, as quoted by Peter H. Lewis for the *New York Times* (August 18, 1987), "an attempt to bridge the gap between the priesthood of programmers and the Macintosh mouse clickers." With HyperCard, information is stored in a series of "cards" that are arranged into "stacks." Each card may contain text, pictures, menus, sounds, and other features. The user is able to arrange the cards and determine the content; a basic example is using the program as an address book by entering the addresses on the appropriate cards. HyperCard's most notable feature is its ability to link cards to one another, using a method similar to hypertext linking on the World Wide Web. HyperCard employs a computer language called HyperTalk that allows the user to add "buttons" to a card, which when activated with a click of the mouse either cause another card to be displayed or launch an audio or visual feature.

Some computer purists insist that HyperCard is not a true form of hypertext—a term coined in 1965 by the computer guru Ted Nelson, who envisioned a method of linking texts together in a nonlinear fashion. Nelson's concept called for links to be embedded directly in a text, whereas in HyperCard they are included in the form of buttons, which must be manually altered when there are any changes in the text. Moreover, HyperCard was not the first program of its kind: beginning in the early 1980s, about a dozen hypertext-related systems had been developed, based on Nelson's ideas as well as those of the computer visionaries Vannevar Bush and Douglas Engelbart. Nevertheless, it was HyperCard, with its appealing format and easy-to-use programming language, that did the most to popularize the concept of creating ordered links between related pieces of information.

Apple, reportedly bowing to pressure from Atkinson, decided to include a free copy of HyperCard with every Macintosh it sold from 1987 to 1992, thus freeing the company from having to convince consumers to purchase software whose utility might not have been immediately apparent. Its popularity grew as users came to realize its potential, and Apple was able to raise the price tag of the software (when sold separately) from $49 to more than $200. As a programming platform, HyperCard appealed to professionals as well novice users. The video-game company Cyan Worlds used it to create such popular games as *Myst* and *Riven*.

As numerous similar programs—such as Super-Book, Plus, and ToolBook—began crowding the market, HyperCard receded into the background. In the mid-1990s HyperCard was passed off to Claris, an Apple software subsidiary. Apple eventually brought HyperCard back under its control, and the company continues to sell it through their Web site for $99. Apple, however, doesn't promote the software, and it has languished without any updates since 1998.

Despite the lack of support from Apple executives, HyperCard is still in use today. Academic researchers use it for creating index programs, teachers use it for educational purposes, and small businesses use it for such purposes as keeping inventory. The International HyperCard Users Group (iHug)—a collection of loyalists who operate an informational HyperCard Web site, publish a newsletter, and run HyperCard booths at computer conferences—has estimated that as of 2002 there were 10,000 HyperCard users worldwide. Among its more prominent applications is controlling part of the lighting system for the Petronas Towers, in Kuala Lumpur, Malaysia, currently the world's tallest buildings.

In an interview with Leander Kahney for *Wired* (August 14, 2002, on-line), Atkinson expressed regret that he had not applied his ideas for HyperCard during the formative years of the World Wide Web. If he had realized that cards could be linked not only within a single user's machine, but to cards on other people's machines through an integrated network, he could have created the first Internet browser. "I have realized over time that I missed the mark with HyperCard," Atkinson told Kahney. "I grew up in a box-centric culture at Apple. If I'd grown up in a network-centric culture, like Sun [Microsystems], HyperCard might have been the first Web browser. My blind spot at Apple prevented me from making [it happen]."

In 1990 Atkinson left Apple and founded a new company, General Magic, with two other former Apple employees, Andy Hertzfeld and Marc Porat. With Atkinson serving as chairman, the company set out to develop powerful new software for handheld computing devices. (Today these handheld computers are known as Personal Digital Assistants, or PDAs.) Atkinson worked on Magic Cap, an operating system for PDAs that became the interface for an early generation of communicators, such as Sony's MagicLink. Despite having such prominent partners and investors as Apple, Sony, Motorola, Phillips, and AT&T, the company failed to establish itself with a successful product in the PDA market. In the mid-1990s the emergence of the Internet undermined the networking technologies of General Magic, and the company lost its major backers before it could reshape its operating system and communications software for use on the Web.

In 1997 Atkinson left the beleaguered company. "The personal communicator didn't happen and wasn't going to happen," he confided to Greg Miller. "That's what disenchanted me. After 20 years of programming, I was also pretty burned out." Instead, he began to focus on his longtime hobby of photography, which had helped sustain him during his computer career. "Programming is left-brain intensive and requires intense concentration," he explained to Miller. "Photography was very relaxing and nourishing. It was the antidote to my programming stress."

Atkinson specializes in nature photography. Some of his favorite locations for shooting are the New England countryside; the Olympic Peninsula, in Washington; and the Smoky Mountains, in Tennessee. He works out of his Portola Valley home, in California, where he uses digital technology to process, enhance, and print his images; he sells them through his own personal Web site, which he established in 1997. Atkinson's wife, Sioux, whom he met at Apple, uses a HyperCard application of her own creation to handle the business inventory and accounting and keep track of the galleries that feature his pictures.

"I will not be a programmer ever again," Atkinson told Miller. "I still get a lot of e-mail from people thanking me for the work I did. But most of them are cheering for me, saying, 'Good for you, here's someone who got out of Silicon Valley before he had a heart attack.'"—A. I. C.

Suggested Reading: Bill Atkinson Web site; *Computerworld* p19 Nov. 4, 1987; *Los Angeles Times* D p3 Jan. 5, 1998; *MacCentral Online* June 21, 2001; *New York Times* C p7 Aug. 18, 1987; Scratch Video Web site; *Wired* (on-line) Aug. 14, 2002

Hulton Archive by Getty Images

Babbage, Charles

Dec. 26, 1792(?)–Oct. 18, 1871 Inventor of the Analytical Engine and the Difference Engine

A visionary who did not live long enough to see his ideas brought to fruition, the 19th-century thinker Charles Babbage is widely considered to be the father of the computer age. Babbage is credited as the first person to envision a machine that would be able to perform functions previously considered the exclusive province of the human intellect. Although Babbage spent years attempting to construct a mechanical computation device, due to a mixture of government impatience, his own overambitiousness, and the lack of adequate technology at the time, his plans were never fully realized, and the first stored-program, mechanical computer did not come into being until well into the 20th century, more than 50 years after his death.

Charles Babbage was born December 26, 1792 (some sources list 1791) in Teignmouth, Devonshire, in England, to Elizabeth Plumleigh (Teape) Babbage, and Benjamin Babbage Jr., a banker who was nicknamed "Old Five Percent." Charles's paternal grandfather, Benjamin Babbage Sr., had been mayor of the nearby town of Totnes. As the child of wealthy parents, Babbage received a private education, and he taught himself algebra. His scientific curiosity emerged at an early age; in his autobiography *Passages from the Life of a Philosopher* (1864), he recalled how, as a youth, he almost drowned while testing out a contraption he had designed for walking on water. In 1810 he entered Trinity College, at Cambridge University, and he soon discovered that his own knowledge of mathematics surpassed that of his professors. Concluding that mathematics in England had fallen behind European standards, he began to push for the reform of English methods for teaching math. With this goal in mind, he translated a book from French, *Differential and Integral Calculus*, and he advocated the abandonment of an outmoded form of Newtonian mathematical notation that was still in use in British schools. In 1812 Babbage joined with several fellow students to form the Analytic Society, and their efforts led to the introduction of continental European math notation in Britain.

In 1814 Babbage graduated first in his class from Peterhouse College and began writing what became a series of notable papers on applied mathematics for the journal *Philosophical Transactions*. That same year he married Georgiana Whitmore of Shropshire, and the couple later had three children: Benjamin Herschel, Henry Prevost, and Georgiana. (Babbage's wife died in August 1827, at the age of 35.) In 1816 Babbage became a fellow of the Royal Society, an organization he would later describe as "a collection of men who elect each other to office, and then dine together at the expense of this society to praise each other over wine and give each other medals" (*The History of Mathematics*). Babbage received an M.A. from Cambridge in 1817.

At around this time Babbage came up with the idea for a mechanized calculating machine that he called the Difference Engine, named after Sir Isaac Newton's method of successive differences, which the machine would use to make its calculations. The Difference Engine would be a special-purpose device, designed to produce logarithm tables for use in such fields as banking, navigation, engineering, architecture, and the military. Logarithm tables are charts that indicate the exponential values of numbers, and the errors humans inevitably made in tabulating them often threatened commerce as well as human safety. Babbage hoped his Difference Engine would eliminate such problems. The engine would be able to calculate the values

for logarithm tables using repeated addition and subtraction as opposed to multiplication and division, which had been used previously. The machine would add and subtract with the aid of trains of gear wheels and would also have an output device in the form of an attached printer. Unlike modern computers, however, the Difference Engine would require constant human intervention in order to perform its computations; for instance, it possessed a crank which had to be turned for the machine to operate.

Babbage constructed a small prototype model in 1822, and in July of that year he communicated his idea for the Difference Engine to the president of the Royal Society, Sir H. Davy. At around that time Babbage was awarded the Astronomical Society's first gold medal, and by the following year he had started working on a full-sized Difference Engine, with an initial grant of £1,500 from the British government. The proposed machine was so advanced that Babbage had to invent the special tools needed to construct it. He also had to develop his own form of notation for his construction plans, as the conventional mechanical blueprinting techniques of the day were inadequate for his purposes. For these reasons, the Difference Engine helped a great deal in advancing the British machine tool industry.

Extremely ambitious, Babbage continued to streamline his design, revising it almost constantly, while construction was in progress. By 1838 he had used up the grant money without achieving a finished product, and he began to finance the project himself. He also received assistance from Ada Augusta, also known as Lady Lovelace, the daughter of Romantic poet Lord Byron. In addition to financial support, Lovelace, a mathematician herself whom Babbage had met in 1833, also contributed what today would be considered "programs" for Babbage's engine. Later, a group of concerned friends succeeded in soliciting a grant of £3,000 from the Duke of Wellington, who was then prime-minister. However, in 1830, when Babbage insisted on moving the workshop in which the machine was being built to his home without providing a cash advance to his crew, Joseph Clement, a key engineer, walked off the project, thus bringing the construction of the Difference Engine to a halt.

Instead of causing him to scale down his plans, the collapse of the seven-year project seemed to add fuel to Babbage's ambitions. While the original Difference Engine was designed to handle numbers with up to six decimal places, Babbage now wanted a machine that could handle 20. This idea evolved into plans for a device that Babbage dubbed the Analytical Engine; it is this machine, even more so than the Difference Engine, that is considered the origin of the modern computer. Rather than performing one mathematical function at a time, the new machine would be able to do many computations simultaneously after receiving instructions in the form of hole-punched cards. Jacquard looms may have provided the kernel for this idea. They were "programmed" with large punched cards, which instructed the large looms to make specific designs in the fabric. The rough equivalent of modern computer programs, the cards were encoded with the numbers to be used in the computations as well as with the series of operations to be executed. The Analytical Engine would contain 1,000 columns of geared wheels, and each column would be able to process a number with up to 50 digits. It would also be equipped with special decision-making units similar in function to those found in computers. In short, the Analytical Engine would be capable of virtually any mathematical calculation, as Babbage explained to Prime Minister Lord Melbourne in 1834 in what proved to be a futile attempt to acquire more funding. After expending much time and money on Babbage without result, the British government was not ready to give him another chance.

With the project still in limbo and his private fortune dwindling, Babbage continued for eight years to apply for grant money. Prime Minister Robert Peel sarcastically suggested that Babbage program his machine to calculate the time at which it would actually be of any use. In 1842, after £17,000 in public grants, the British government officially pulled the plug on Babbage's work, which it deemed worthless. According to the *Virginia Polytechnic Institute* (on-line), in 1851 a disgruntled Babbage wrote, "Thus bad names are coined by worse men to destroy honest people, as the madness of innocent dogs arises from the cry of insanity raised by their villainous pursuers." The following year, he made one last unsuccessful petition to Prime Minister Benjamin Disraeli. Several historians have stated that Babbage's failure to complete the Difference and Analytical Engines resulted from his lack of political wiles and persuasive tact. In *Faster Than Thought*, B. V. Bowden wrote that Babbage "was frequently and almost notoriously incoherent when he spoke in public." Left without funding, Babbage gambled away what was left of his own savings and those of Lady Lovelace by mathematically handicapping horse races, a pursuit in which he met with failure yet again. Ironically, during Babbage's own lifetime a scaled-down version of the Difference Engine was successfully built by Swedish engineer Georg Scheutz using a description of Babbage's design featured in a magazine.

Charles Babbage's interests were amazingly far-reaching. They included probability, geophysics, astronomy, cryptanalysis (the deciphering of coded communications), ophthalmology, altimetry (the study of atmospheric pressure), and meteorology. An admirer of Babbage's work once called the inventor "a very interesting man, ardent, eager, and of almost indefinite intellectual activity, bold and frank in expressing all his opinions and feelings" (*IEEE Software* on-line, March 1995). Aside from his seminal contribution to the history of computers, perhaps his greatest accomplishment was in the field of business and finance. In 1832 he wrote *On the Economy of Manufactures*, which originated the concept of operational research, the scientific study of manufacturing processes. The book also contained plans for a primitive telephone and fax machine, and would later be cited by Karl Marx in *Das Kapital*. Babbage was among the first to apply higher mathematics to industrial and commercial problems.

In addition to calculating machines, Babbage is responsible for many useful and fascinating inventions. His research into railroad safety and efficiency was decades ahead of its time, and he developed the cowcatcher, a sloping attachment put on the front of locomotives to clear debris from the track. He was the first to propose uniform postal rates, as opposed to the earlier method of charging postage according to the distance a parcel traveled. He is also credited with being the originator of the speedometer, and the heliograph ophthalmoscope, a device used to view the interior of the eye. Additionally, Babbage composed the first reliable mortality tables for life insurance companies. He even tried his hand at politics as a Whig candidate but was unsuccessful in two runs for Parliament.

Enraptured by the technological advancements of his day, Babbage's passion for machines and statistics bordered on obsession. When attending the theater, he could not resist taking a look backstage to see how the set changes were accomplished. In *Passages from the Life of a Philosopher*, written prior to the modern era of electricity, he described his plans for constructing colored theatrical lights. His fascination with fire and heat once led him to bake himself in an oven at 265°F for several minutes as an experiment, and he was also lowered into Mt. Vesuvius to observe lava.

As a philosopher, Babbage attempted to reconcile his religious beliefs with his scientific devotion, most notably in his *Ninth Bridgewater Treatise* (1837). In that work he disputed the basis of the argument, set forth by eighteenth-century philosopher David Hume, that miracles cannot occur in a world governed by natural laws. Babbage based his personal theology on the concept of a mechanized universe; for example, just as he could theoretically program a computer to observe set guidelines and yet, in certain circumstances, stray from them, so could God "program" such irregularities—i.e., miracles—in the natural world. According to B. V. Bowden, Babbage also calculated the chances of human resurrection as one in one trillion.

Babbage cofounded the Royal Astronomical Society in 1820, the British Association in 1831, and the Statistical Society of London in 1834. With the Astronomical Society, Babbage served many functions over the years, namely those of secretary, vice president, foreign secretary, and council member. Babbage was the eleventh man to hold the Lucasian chair of mathematics at Cambridge University, which was once occupied by Sir Isaac Newton. Although Babbage served in the position from 1828 to 1839, he never delivered a lecture. Among Babbage's numerous written works are *Tables and Logarithms* (1827), *The Decline of Science in England*

(1830), *The Exposition of 1851* (1851), and his aforementioned autobiography. A member of Victorian Britain's elite, he was known for holding Saturday evening parties attended by 200 to 300 people, among them many of Europe's liberal intelligentsia.

Babbage is said to have harbored a hatred for music, particularly the street musicians who abounded in mid-19th-century London. Calculating that 25 percent of his concentration was eroded by "street nuisances," he pushed for the adoption of Babbage's Act, a law he proposed that would make it illegal to play music on the street. "Those whose minds are entirely unoccupied receive [street music] with satisfaction, as filling up the vacuum of time," he commented in 1864 in his *Observations of Street Nuisances*. His crusade made him an extremely unpopular man, causing neighbors to hang abusive signs in local shop windows and hire musicians to play outside his home. Offensive items such as dead cats were thrown at his house, and while on the street Babbage was often harassed and sometimes even stalked.

Babbage and his ideas were greatly underappreciated in the 19th century. Although he was offered the title of baronet, he refused, demanding instead life peerage, which was never granted. He gained the reputation of being a bitter old man, hateful of people in general, and was known as a "mathematical Timon," a reference to the misanthropic antihero of Shakespeare's *Timon of Athens*. The Charles Babbage Foundation (on-line) describes him as having a face "even sterner than Beethoven's." By 1861 he claimed to have never had a happy day in his life. On October 18, 1871 he died in his home on Dorset Street in London, a disappointed and disillusioned man who had spent the majority of his fortune on a dream he never realized. There was only one carriage, that of the Duchess of Somerset, in the burial procession that brought his body to Kensal Green Cemetery. No obituary was printed by the Royal Society, and the London *Times* ridiculed him posthumously. His brain was preserved for 37 years before being dissected, in 1908. An unfinished portion of the Difference Engine was kept in the King's College Museum from 1842 to 1862 and then was moved to the London Science Museum, where it is currently held. A small portion of an Analytical Engine constructed in 1879 by Henry Babbage, based on his father's blueprints, was recently auctioned off by the London Science Museum to Australia's Power House Museum for $300,000.

The information age owes much to the imagination of Charles Babbage, and by the 20th century his name commanded a great deal more respect than it did in his own time (in fact, a crater near the northern pole of the moon is named for him). He was among the first to consider science to be an essential part of culture and argue that national governments have an obligation to support scientific endeavor. As Babbage biographer J. A. N. Lee of Virginia Polytechnic University wrote of his subject, "with his harlequin curiosity about all things, with his wonderfully human sense of wonder, Babbage escapes pathos and attains greatness."—B. S.

Suggested Reading: *IEEE Software* (on-line). Mar. 1995; *Popular Mechanics* p99+ Mar. 1992, with photos; *University of Exeter* (on-line); *Charles Babbage Foundation* (on-line), with drawing; *Charles Babbage Institute Center for the History of Computing* (on-line), with photo; *Virginia Polytechnic Institute Department of Computers* (on-line); *Dictionary of Scientific Biography* vol. 1, 1970; *Larousse Biographical Dictionary*, 1994

Backus, John

Dec. 3, 1924– Inventor of the FORTRAN programming language

The invention of the computer language FORTRAN by John Backus in the mid 1950s was a key step toward bringing computers closer to the general public. The first high-level computer programming language, FORTRAN was able to convert standard mathematical formulas and expressions into the binary code used by computers, making it possible for someone to program a computer using such mathematical terms. Prior to FORTRAN, an in-depth knowledge of the actual functioning processes of computers was required in order to program the machines to execute even the simplest tasks. With Backus's innovation, for the first time, those outside the specialized field of computer engineering could program a computer.

John Warner Backus was born December 3, 1924 in Philadelphia, Pennsylvania, and spent some of his early years in Wilmington, Delaware. His father was a former chemist turned stockbroker who had grown wealthy in the post–World War I boom. In 1938, Backus entered The Hill School in Pottstown, Pennsylvania, but struggled, unable to apply himself to his studies and failing every year. As he recounted for Dennis Shasha and Cathy Lazere in *Out of Their Minds: The Lives and Discoveries of 15 Great Computer Scientists* (1998), "I hated studying. I was just goofing around. It had the delightful consequence that every year I went to summer school in New Hampshire where I spent the summer sailing and having a nice time." Backus finally graduated from The Hill School in 1942, and at the urging of his father he entered the University of Virginia, in Charlottesville, to study chemistry. However, he remained unmotivated, and by late in his second semester he was only attending one of his classes, an undemanding course in music appreciation. At the end of the term, the school administration officially ended his studies there.

Still unsure of the path he wanted to take, Backus joined the army in 1943 at the age of 19. He was soon promoted to corporal and put in charge of an antiaircraft crew at Fort Stewart, Georgia. His strong performance on a medical aptitude test led his superiors to send him to Haverford College, in southeastern Pennsylvania, to attend premed classes. As part of his training, he was assigned to an Atlantic City hospital neurosurgery ward where head wounds were treated. In a bizarre coincidence, while working at the hospital Backus himself was found to have a bone tumor in his skull and had to undergo surgery, resulting in a metal plate being fitted in his head. After serving his time in the army, Backus decided to enter medical school at Flower and Fifth Avenue Hospital (now New York Medical College), only to drop out after nine months, disillusioned by what he saw as a disproportionate emphasis on mindless memorization as opposed to individual thinking. At around that time, Backus discovered that the plate in his head fit improperly. After going to a hospital on Staten Island that specialized in plates and being dissatisfied with their design, Backus designed his own plate and had it implanted by doctors there.

Backus next rented an apartment in New York for 18 dollars a month. At that point, as he recalled for Shasha and Lazere, "I really didn't know what the hell I wanted to do with my life. I decided that what I wanted was a good hi fi set because I liked music. In those days, they didn't really exist so I went to a radio technicians' school. I had a very nice teacher—the first good teacher I ever had—and he asked me to cooperate with him and compute the characteristics of some circuits for a magazine. I remember doing relatively simple calculations to get a few points on a curve for an amplifier. It was laborious and tedious and horrible, but it got me interested in math. The fact that it had an application—that interested me."

Having at last found what he wanted to do, Backus enrolled at Columbia University, in New York City, to study math. When he was several months away from graduation, he took a tour of the International Business Machines (IBM) Computer Center, on Madison Avenue, where he saw the company's SSEC, or Selective Sequence Electronic Calculator, one of their early electronic computers. During the tour, he off-handedly said to the guide that he needed a job, and she told Backus that he should speak to the director. As Backus was quoted in *Out of their Minds*, "I said no, I couldn't. I looked sloppy and disheveled. But she insisted and so I did. I took a test and did ok." Meanwhile, he graduated from Columbia in 1949 with a B.S. in mathematics. Continuing his studies there, Backus earned a master's degree in mathematics the following year.

After graduate school, in 1950, Backus began working for IBM in the pure and applied science department as a programmer for the SSEC. He also worked on the revolutionary IBM 701 model computer, for which he developed the Speedcoding interpretive system. Speedcoding greatly facilitated the process of programming the 701 by allowing it to perform several advanced functions without the programmers having to use binary code. Backus also contributed to the design of the later 704 model.

In 1954, Backus moved to IBM's programming research department, of which he was named manager. At this time, he began developing the first truly "high-level" programming language, which would come to be known as Formula Translation, or simply FORTRAN. After working on the IBM 701 and 704, Backus was frustrated with the sheer complexity and painstaking nature of programming. In an interview with Leslie Goff for *Computerworld* (February 8, 1999), Backus explained bluntly the origin of the language: "It was pure laziness. Writing programs was a big drag. You had to have enormous detail and deal with things you shouldn't have to. So I wanted to make it easier."

Backus calculated that at least half to three-quarters of a computer's operating costs stemmed from testing and programming. He believed that if there were a language that would automate computer instruction codes, it would significantly reduce programming costs. At that time, computer programmers had to have an in-depth knowledge of binary code, the patterned sequences of zeroes and ones that are the basic "language" used by computers. Additionally, in order for computers to perform repetitive tasks, programmers had to feed the same instructions to the machines over and over again. The earliest attempt at an automated programming language had been the A-O compiler, developed by Grace Hopper of Remington Rand Inc. in 1952. However, Backus felt that the A-O compiler was slow, cumbersome, and difficult to use.

Backus's ideas were initially met with skepticism from IBM administrators, mostly due to the lukewarm response to the A-O compiler. However, with the confidence of Backus's supervisor Cuthbert Hurd, the project was allowed to develop. Backus recruited fellow IBM programmers Gene Amdahl, Irving Ziller, and Harlan Herrick to assist him. As he recounted to Leslie Goff, he recruited a team with "creativity, a lot of smarts and experience. We had a great variety of people: a physicist, a crystallographer, an English major." Over the course of two years, Backus and his team worked tirelessly on FORTRAN, keeping late hours and sometimes even sleeping during the day at the hotel across the street from IBM's offices so they could reserve computer time at night. By the summer of 1956, the prototype of FORTRAN was complete, and Backus spent the next few months testing it. The following year, the first commercial copies were introduced by IBM. One of the key innovations Backus introduced was the use of sets of instructions, which could be made to "loop," thus enabling computers to perform repetitive tasks without the necessity of writing repetitive instruction code. Backus's Formula Translation system was also the first high-level general-purpose computer code in that it used terminology understood by the programmer but not the computer, for example, and translated it into the binary code used by the computer. In developing FORTRAN, Backus and his team came up with several programming expressions that are still widely used nearly 50 years later. As a writer for *Software* magazine (March 1989) noted, these included "1. 'GO TO,' a branch instruction, 2. 'DO,' to set up an iteration, and 3. 'IF,' to execute instructions conditionally." FORTRAN was, and still is, most widely used in scientific and mathematical applications, and by 1959 most manufacturers of scientific computers had adopted it as their language of choice, making it the first language to be used on many different types of computers.

Backus joined IBM's T. J. Watson Research Center, in Yorktown Heights, New York, in 1959. During his years in that department, he worked on the computer languages ALGOL 58 and ALGOL 60 which, while not as groundbreaking as FORTRAN, are important milestones in the development of modern computer programming. While working to define ALGOL 58 in particular, Backus formulated a method of notation used to describe the syntax of a high-level computer programming language, and which is now known as BNF, or the Backus-Naur Form. (The technique was subsequently improved upon by fellow computer programmer Peter Naur to describe the syntax of ALGOL 60.)

John Backus was made an IBM fellow in 1963, and in that capacity he continued to conduct research at IBM's Yorktown Heights Center and also at their Research Center in San Jose, California. In the 1970s, he began delving further into the connections between pure mathematics and computer programming. He developed a functional programming language called FP, which puts forth a mathematical approach to programming and, along with FORTRAN and BNF, is considered one of his major contributions to the field. His work on FP during the 1970s and 1980s was the subject of his lecture when he won the prestigious ACM Turing Award, in 1977.

In addition to his IBM fellowship, Backus held a number of teaching positions, including an adjunct professorship of information sciences at the University of California, Santa Cruz, in 1974, and visiting professorships at the University of California, Berkeley, in 1980 and 1985. He retired from his fellowship in October 1991 but remained a consultant to the IBM Almaden Research Center as of 1999. Backus married Una Stannard in 1968, and they have two daughters, Karen and Paula. He currently resides in San Francisco.

In addition to his Turing Award, Backus received the National Medal of Science, in 1975; the Institute of Electrical and Electronics Engineers Computer Society Pioneer Award, in 1980; and the Harold Pender Award from the Moor school of Electrical Engineering at the University of Pennsylvania, in 1983. He is a member of the National Academy of Sciences and the National Academy of Engineers. In February 1994, he was recognized for his development of FORTRAN with the Charles Stark Draper Award, presented by the National Academy of Engineers. In the *International Biographical Dictionary of Computer Pioneers* (1995),

Backus is quoted as saying on that occasion, "I myself have had many failures and I've learned that if you are not failing a lot, you are probably not being as creative as you could be, you aren't stretching your imagination enough."

John Backus's FORTRAN is considered by many to mark the beginning of the computer software revolution, paving the way for the development of programming languages such as COBOL and BASIC. These languages went even further than FORTRAN in enabling non-computer experts to use computing technology, a trend that eventually led to the modern personal computer market, in which computers are accessible to the general public, with virtually no technical knowledge required to operate them. FORTRAN remains in wide use today in applications used for weather forecasting, analyzing nuclear explosions, and calculating large-scale fluid dynamics, to name a few examples. As of 1998, IBM was putting the finishing touches on FORTRAN 95, the latest of many updates to the language.—B.S.

Suggested Reading: *Computerworld* p87+ Feb. 8, 1999; *New York University Computer Science Department* (on-line); Lee, J. A. N., ed. *International Biographical Dictionary of Computer Pioneers*, 1995; Shasha, Dennis and Cathy Lazere. *Out of Their Minds: The Lives and Discoveries of 15 Great Computer Scientists*, 1995; *Who's Who in America*, 1998

Baldwin, Frank Stephen

Apr. 10, 1838–Apr. 8, 1925 Inventor of the Baldwin calculator

Frank Stephen Baldwin is best known for his invention of the Baldwin calculator, which he patented in 1875, and which became known—in a modified form—as the Monroe calculator, after he entered into a financial partnership with Jay Monroe in 1911. Baldwin made important changes to the mechanical calculator as it then existed, increasing its accuracy and usability and greatly reducing its size and weight, thus making it suitable for desktop use. The Monroe calculator was an essential tool for businesses throughout the United States until computer technology replaced it in the 1960s.

Frank Stephen Baldwin was born on April 10, 1838 in New Hartford, Connecticut. At the age of two he moved with his parents to Nunda, New York, and attended the state's first free school. He excelled in math, and after finishing his schooling in Nunda, Baldwin enrolled at Union College, in Schenectady, New York. When his father grew ill, he was forced to leave school before graduating, in order to take over the family architectural business. At the age of 27, Baldwin applied for his first patent, for a method of improving railroad cars. In 1860 he obtained a patent for a corn-planting machine that became a popular tool for farmers.

Baldwin moved to St. Louis in 1869 in order to manage Peck's Planing Mills, a lumber business. While there, he invented a metal lace latch used on shoes and boots. He began concentrating on calculating machines in the early 1870s, after repairing a primitive calculator known as the Thomas Machine for Peck's Planing Mills. In 1873 he applied for a patent for a four-function mechanical calculator that could perform addition, subtraction, multiplication, and division. According to some sources, shortly thereafter, the device was placed on exhibit at the Franklin Institute, in Philadelphia, Pennsylvania, and Baldwin won that city's John Scott Medal for the best invention of the year. The cost of mass manufacturing Baldwin's machine was prohibitively high in the mid-1870s, and over the next several decades he began a series of improvements on his invention. In 1890 he produced the Baldwin computing engine, and further modification in 1902 resulted in the Baldwin calculator, which measured 10 inches long, seven inches wide, and six inches deep; it sold for $250. Not until 1911, however, with the financial backing of Jay Monroe at the Western Electric Company of New York City, did Baldwin perfect his machine. He was awarded a patent in 1913 for what was called the Monroe calculator, even though Monroe's contribution to the invention had been purely monetary. The Monroe calculator began to sell widely throughout the United States.

Baldwin's innovations were the first major improvement upon mechanical calculator technology since Gottfried Leibniz invented a device based on nine stepped drums late in the 17th century. A stepped drum is a large, cylindrical gear that has a series of rows of varying numbers of cogs, or teeth, along its length, so that, depending on the number one wishes to enter, the drum can be moved back and forth to engage the corresponding number of cogs. Baldwin replaced the unwieldy drums with pinwheels, or variable-toothed gears, thus making the machines far smaller and appropriate for use in homes and businesses. The general idea, known as the Baldwin Principle, behind his machine was that the gears featured moveable teeth that could be manually engaged and disengaged by pulling a lever so that between zero and nine teeth protruded from the gear. One gear was used for each digit of a number, and the gears were lined up side by side on a single shaft. If one wished, for example, to add the number 75 to a sum, one pulled the lever in the tens column until the number seven registered and seven teeth projected from the gear; the same would be done for the five in the ones column. Once this was done, a different lever was pulled to rotate the whole group of gears along its common shaft, and the projecting teeth would engage the gear of the results register to increase it accordingly.

Just as Baldwin was developing his calculator in the United States, Willgodt T. Odhner, a Swede working in Russia independently from Baldwin, invented a similar calculating machine using vari-

able-toothed gears. In Europe such machines became known as Odhner machines, while in the United States they were called Baldwin machines. One of the early manufacturers of variable-toothed geared machines in the United States was the Brunsviga Company, which made its first prototype in 1885 and produced more than 20,000 machines by 1912. With the start of the Monroe Calculating Machine Company in 1911, sales of Baldwin's design began to increase dramatically. By the 1920s Monroe calculators were a common tool for many U.S. businesses, and few changes in Baldwin's essential design were made to four-function calculators until such mechanical calculators were made obsolete by computers. As Joel Shurkin wrote in *Engines of the Mind* (1996), "Essentially, the Monroe-Baldwin merger began the calculating-machine industry. . . . These machines . . . ran modern business until the invention of the electronic computer."

Baldwin died on April 8, 1925 in Morristown, New Jersey, after an operation. He was survived by his wife, four sons, and a daughter. Baldwin's other inventions include the anemometer, a device for measuring the speed and direction of wind; a passenger-counting step for street cars; and a device for recording and measuring four types of lumber simultaneously.—P. G. H.

Suggested Reading: *New York Times* V p23 Apr. 9, 1925; *The Office* p56+ July 1991; Shurkin, Joel. *Engines of the Mind*, 1996; Williams, Michael R. *History of Computing Technology*, 1997

Ballmer, Steven

Mar. 24, 1956– CEO of Microsoft

Since joining Microsoft in 1980, Steven Ballmer has held nearly every top management position, in such divisions as operations, operating systems development, and sales and support. In January 2000 he rose to replace Microsoft's co-founder Bill Gates as chief executive officer, thus assuming full management responsibility for the world's largest software company. Throughout his tenure at Microsoft, Ballmer has distinguished himself as an energetic and dedicated employee—and as Gates's right-hand man. He has been called "Gates's Number 2," or even "1.5." The two men, who met in 1974 as undergraduates at Harvard University, in Cambridge, Massachusetts, have remained close friends for nearly 30 years. Their unique business partnership has been described as being akin to a marriage, so close that each man is known to finish the other's sentences at times. Gates has dubbed this understanding of ideas "high-bandwidth communication," according to Mark Leibovich, writing for the *Washington Post* (December 31, 2000). As one Microsoft executive told John Markoff for the Montreal *Gazette* (January 15, 2000), "They're two

Courtesy of www.microsoft.com

Steven Ballmer

halves of the same person. Together they constitute the finest business executive in the world."

Despite their close working relationship, Ballmer and Gates exhibit vastly different character traits in their personal and professional lives. While Gates tends to be more quiet and reserved, Ballmer is loud and outspoken, a dedicated Microsoft cheerleader with a sharp sense of humor. He once ruptured his vocal cords from shouting at an annual meeting and required surgery to repair them. On another occasion, acting on a dare, he stripped to his boxers and swam across Lake Bill, a man-made lake on Microsoft's campus. When he applies such passion to his work, Ballmer is known to be an intense, focused, and demanding executive. While Gates is a consummate business strategist with an eye for how technology may shape the future, Ballmer excels at managing operations and bringing Gates's vision into being. He told Leibovich, "There are two ways to succeed in business. One is to have the big insights. The other is to take the big insights and make it happen." As a master of the latter, Ballmer is currently overseeing one of the most radical re-inventions of Microsoft in the company's history. In addition to changing the business model to allow greater control for senior executives, he has instituted a new corporate mission: "To enable people and businesses throughout the world to realize their full potential." To deliver on this mission, Microsoft has been actively expanding its line of products and services beyond its traditional Windows operating software. By most measures, Ballmer's success as CEO is clear. The company is currently worth around $280 billion, with reported revenues for the fiscal year ending June 30, 2002 of more than

$28 billion. In 2002, Ballmer was ranked 10th on *Forbes*'s 400 Richest Americans list and 15th on its World's Richest People list, with a net worth of $11.9 billion.

Steven Ballmer was born on March 24, 1956 in Detroit, Michigan, the oldest of two children. His father, a Swiss immigrant who came to the United States after serving as a translator in the Nuremberg war trials, worked as an accountant at the Ford Motor Company. (Ballmer's maternal grandfather was also an immigrant; arriving in America from Russia, he initially worked as an auto-parts dealer.) From Ballmer's early childhood, his father made clear the expectation that his son would attend the prestigious Harvard University. Ballmer grew up in Farmington Hills, a middle-class, Detroit suburb, where he attended a private high school and quickly proved himself a math virtuoso. Despite his academic gifts, he was a very shy child, who would occasionally hyperventilate before social events. "I was just so scared," he recalled to Leibovich. "So I wouldn't throw up, my mom would have to make me take short breaths."

Realizing his father's ambition, after high school Ballmer enrolled at Harvard, where he overcame his shyness by joining numerous campus activities. During his sophomore year he was introduced to his classmate Bill Gates when the two attended a double feature of the films *A Clockwork Orange* and *Singin' in the Rain*. Ballmer and Gates also lived near each other in Currier House, a dormitory that housed mostly math and science students. As Gates told Jeffrey Young for *Forbes* (January 27, 1997), "[Ballmer] was the opposite of me. I didn't go to classes much, wasn't involved in campus activities. Steve was involved in everything, knew everyone. Steve was the general manager of the football team, head of the lit[erary] magazine, ad manager of the *Crimson* [newspaper]. He got me to join the Fox Club, a men's club where you put on tuxedos, smoke cigars, drink too much, stand up on chairs and tell stories, play pool. Very old school." Another experience that solidified their friendship was when the two signed up for a graduate-level economics class together. Despite skipping nearly every lecture—Ballmer's excessive social obligations left him little time to attend classes—Ballmer and Gates received two of the highest grades in the class, after cramming all night for the final.

Despite their common interests, Ballmer and Gates initially had different career ambitions. While Ballmer was considering a career in government, Gates insisted he would return to Seattle, Washington, his hometown, to work as an attorney. However, in 1975 Gates dropped out of Harvard to start a computer software company, Micro-Soft, with his childhood friend Paul Allen. (The hyphen was later dropped from the firm's name.) Ballmer remained at Harvard, completing his bachelor's degree in applied mathematics and economics, in 1977.

Following college, Ballmer took a job as an assistant product manager with Proctor & Gamble, where he marketed such products as Coldsnap Freezer Dessert Makers and Duncan Hines cake mixes. He distinguished himself as an aggressive marketer, conceiving the concept of a horizontal brownie-mix box that would take up more space on grocery stores shelves, thus leaving less room for competitors' products. As one of his co-workers told Leibovich, "Steve was extremely intense, very personable and probably the smartest man I've ever met." Despite his talent for the job, Ballmer left Proctor & Gamble after two years to try his hand at screenwriting. He remained in Hollywood only briefly, before enrolling in 1979 at the Stanford University Graduate School of Business, where he excelled from the start. In his first year, he earned two $10,000 awards as the most promising first-year student, from the top-tier consulting firms Bain & Company and its rival, the Boston Consulting Group.

While choosing between summer jobs in consulting or investment banking following his first year at Stanford, Ballmer received a call from Gates, who was then in need of a business manager for his fledgling company. As Ballmer recalled to Young, the only thing he knew about Microsoft was that it was "a leading company in a growing industry I knew nothing about—I hadn't even used a personal computer then." Nevertheless, he flew to Seattle to meet with Gates and Allen, on the day before Gates was scheduled to leave for a Caribbean vacation. After some consideration, Ballmer agreed to join Microsoft if the terms were right; he reasoned that the opportunity would allow him to gain practical business experience that he could apply to his next job. Although Ballmer accepted a share offer of between five and 10 percent, based on the increase in sales after he arrived—meaning that he would be the only employee to own part of Microsoft, outside of Gates and Allen—Gates had to leave for his trip before an actual salary was agreed upon. As Gates recounted to Mark Whitaker for *Newsweek* (June 23, 1997), "I go off on this vacation and I have to negotiate the salary with Steve. So we were on this ship-to-shore radio phone, where I kept saying, 'Doo-Wah Doo-Wah! Over!' I think we started at $40,000. Everybody else on my vacation had been drinking and kept saying, 'Pay him whatever it takes! Get somebody to help you out! You look like you're really stressed out!' So I agreed to pay $50,000. Which, of course, turns out to be like 10 to the minus fifth portion of [his] compensation."

When Ballmer arrived at Microsoft in 1980, the company had fewer than 30 employees. His job as assistant to the president involved such duties as overseeing hiring, personnel, and finances. In one of his first acts, just weeks into the position, Ballmer approached Gates with a request to hire several more people. The appeal evolved into one of the friends' first and largest arguments. Although Gates had aggressive goals for the company, he was

resistant to take on debt. As Ballmer recalled to Whitaker, "Bill said, 'You're going to bankrupt this company! I did not ask you to come here to bankrupt this company! You are supposed to make my life more sane!' The first year, we had some pretty knockdown, drag-out [fights]. But they were effective in helping us learn how to work together." After thinking the request through, Gates gave Ballmer permission to hire more employees, as long as the company's revenue grew proportionally. The two agreed to exercise high standards in the company's hiring practices, to ensure the best quality of candidates, a move that Gates hoped would slow the process. Yet, the point soon became moot as Microsoft rapidly grew into the largest software company in the industry, and Ballmer was able to hire as many top-quality employees as he needed.

During his first year at Microsoft, Ballmer participated in another significant business sequence that helped determine the company's future: He was instrumental in securing from Tim Paterson, a Seattle programmer, the purchase of a rudimentary operating system that was to become Microsoft's core business. At the time International Business Machines (IBM), one of the world's largest manufacturers of office machines, had contacted Gates about devising an operating system for the personal computer it was then planning. Because Gates was uncertain that his programmers could develop the complex system by the established deadline, he recommended a competitor, Digital Research. However, IBM was unable to reach an agreement with the company and returned to Gates. In turn, Ballmer helped close negotiations for the purchase of Paterson's system—which Paterson had nicknamed Q-DOS (for "Quick and Dirty Operating System)—for only $50,000. Gates modified Paterson's program, added some new features, and sold it to IBM, under the name Microsoft Disk Operating System, or MS-DOS. Ballmer played a key role in negotiating the IBM deal, which ensured that MS-DOS would run on IBM's machines as well as on millions of IBM clones. (Gates had persuaded IBM to abandon its secret design specifications in favor of an open system for its personal computer, thereby allowing software developers to build software for the system more easily. About 100 companies, eager to be IBM-compatible, obtained licenses for MS-DOS, quickly making it the major operating system for personal computers.) With its place on the forefront of the computer industry firmly established, Microsoft's sales grew rapidly, mushrooming from $4 million in 1980 to more than $140 million in 1985.

In 1983 Ballmer shifted his role at Microsoft to oversee the operating-system platform-development operations. He was given the task less for his programming abilities than for his experience managing the company's IBM relationship. Realizing that businesses would soon require a better operating system than MS-DOS, IBM had set out to develop a powerful new operating system, known as OS/2, which would be capable of carrying out several functions simultaneously. In 1983 Ballmer successfully convinced IBM to let Microsoft collaborate on the development of OS/2; he failed, however, to persuade IBM to include a rudimentary Microsoft product, known as Windows, as an integral part of the new operating system. (Although the Windows launch was a year behind schedule when Ballmer took over the operating-systems team in 1983, he instituted measures to ensure its prompt release. Windows, first introduced in 1985, allowed IBM-compatible computers to be operated with a handheld mouse and onscreen symbols, rather than by typing in commands.) Nevertheless, Ballmer continued his support for IBM; as he later explained to Young, the management at Microsoft had put all "our wood behind the OS/2 arrow, [to] make OS/2 really great." In fact, in 1986, Ballmer and Gates offered IBM a 10 percent share of the company, in order to further secure the strong partnership that existed between the two concerns. IBM rejected the deal and introduced its OS/2 operating system in 1987, replacing MS-DOS in a new line of IBM personal computers called the PS/2.

As Ballmer began to realize the extent of IBM's competition, he and Gates decided to forge ahead with Microsoft's Windows product, in what he described to Young as a defensive act. "We hedged our bets; we had to," he said. "Independent of what I wanted for the part of the business I ran—[operating] systems—the applications group wanted to ship Excel and Word, and OS/2 was a long way off. The only way they could make any money was to have a Windows platform to ride on." Under Ballmer's direction, the operating-systems development group introduced two updated versions of Windows, in 1986 and 1988, before releasing Windows 3.0 in May 1990. This version was sophisticated enough to compete directly with OS/2 and even upstaged IBM's newest version of that system. Windows 3.0 became an instant success, with Microsoft selling an estimated one million copies per month. The rivalry between Microsoft and IBM heated up in 1991, when IBM announced plans to release OS/2 2.0 the following year, around the same time that Microsoft intended to introduce its competing Windows 3.1. By April 1993, however, Windows had become the most popular graphical operating system in the world, with more than 25 million licensed users; Microsoft had won a clear lead in the operating-systems market. Although some industry observers accused Microsoft of acting unethically by participating in the development of OS/2 and then using inside knowledge to create a more competitive product, Ballmer always insisted that the push to develop Windows had been an integral part of the company's business plan—to tie its software application programs to its own operating system.

In 1992 Gates reorganized the company's management structure, creating a three-member executive committee to fulfill duties that had previously been handled by one president. Along with Michael J. Maples and Francis J. Gaudette, Ballmer was promoted to serve as executive vice president, in the area of sales and support. Few were surprised by the appointment, in part because of Ballmer's close relationship with Gates but also because his skills seemed well suited for the job. A natural salesman, Ballmer has been credited with building Microsoft's sales force and developing the branding and pricing strategies that helped solidify and expand the company's dominance throughout the 1990s. In 1999 the group of three vice presidents was replaced by an executive committee of nine, though Ballmer remained in charge of worldwide sales and support. In 1998, Gates restructured the management team yet again, this time appointing Ballmer to serve as president (the first in six years), in control of all the company's day-to-day operations.

In one of his first moves as president, Ballmer created a new plan, which he named Vision Version 2, to better motivate and energize Microsoft employees. His goal was to encourage workers at all levels of the company to focus on consumers and to take a broader perspective in developing Microsoft's line of products and services. Replacing the old corporate mission to put a personal computer with Microsoft software on every desk in every home, Ballmer's new vision was to give "people the power to do anything they want, anywhere they want, and on any device," as Gates told Michael Moeller for *BusinessWeek* (May 17, 1999). Ballmer also took steps to lessen Microsoft's internal bureaucracy and move authority down the company ranks. He divided the company into eight separate divisions, arranged less by technology than by customers' needs. While in the past Gates and Ballmer had been involved in every decision, Vision Version 2 gave senior executives more control in managing their business and allocating how they would spend their budgets, as long as they met key goals for revenue, profitability, customer satisfaction, and industry leadership. As Robbie Bach, then head of the home and retail division, told Moeller about the new system, "[It] feels like I am running my own little company." While Ballmer acknowledged that the new system could require adjustments, he felt certain it was a step in the right direction. "Let's say this is V-2," he said. "We're gonna tune up. We'll have V-3 if we need to. We'll have V-4 if we need to. We're just gonna keep working it and working it and working it."

Another issue that demanded much of Ballmer's attention as president was Microsoft's task of defending itself in two broad antitrust suits. On May 19, 1998 the U.S. Justice Department and 20 state attorneys general filed suit against Microsoft, alleging that the company was engaged in anticompetitive business practices that were in violation of the Sherman Antitrust Act. One aspect under particular scrutiny was Microsoft's practice of bundling its Internet browser, Internet Explorer, within its Windows operating system and thus essentially distributing the browser for free. The trial, which began on October 19, 1998, garnered significant media attention as the largest antitrust case in a generation and the first such case in history to address the computer-software industry. Nearly two years after the initial filing, Microsoft was found guilty of violating the Sherman Antitrust Act and of having "maintained its monopoly power by anticompetitive means," according to U.S. District Judge Thomas Penfield Jackson's ruling. On June 7, 2000, Jackson ordered that Microsoft should be broken into two companies, though that decision was later reversed by the seven-judge federal appeals court. (The appeals court did, however, uphold Jackson's ruling that Microsoft had repeatedly violated the Sherman Antitrust Act.) Microsoft and the Justice Department ultimately settled the case, in November 2001, agreeing on a set of business restrictions to prohibit Microsoft's software monopoly; most provisions of the settlement were upheld the following year by U.S. District Judge Colleen Kollar-Kotelly.

Throughout the trial, Ballmer remained steadfast in his view that Microsoft had not thwarted competition and had instead acted vigorously and fairly in dealings with competitors. At one point in the case, he made headlines while defending Microsoft's practice of integrating Internet Explorer within Windows. He declared that, if customers found the practice to be valuable, then "the heck with [U.S. Attorney General] Janet Reno on this point," as quoted by Andrew Zajac for the *Chicago Tribune* (January 23, 2000). While Ballmer and Gates were disappointed by Judge Jackson's ruling against Microsoft—and acknowledged being "stunned" by his decision to break the company apart—they consistently predicted that the courts would ultimately find the company's actions to be lawful. Shortly after Judge Jackson's final ruling, in April 2000, Ballmer told a reporter for *Time* (April 17, 2000), "I would certainly not apologize for our actions. They were 100 percent legal, and they were 100 percent ethical. Our style, from time to time, took away from the sense of opportunity that we provide, and that's something we can work on. There is a difference in how you appeal to third parties if you're the biggest guy on the block than if you're one of the small scrappy guys. But are we still going to compete aggressively? You bet." Nevertheless, after the appeals process and the settlement agreement, Ballmer and Gates consented to comply with all new standards of conduct. As Ballmer explained to Jeff Moad, Peter Coffee, and Peter Galli for *eWeek* (November 18, 2002, on-line), "We have been very serious about compliance, and you should expect us to continue to be. . . . We understand we have new responsibilities of leadership not only because of the case but because of the way the whole industry looks at us. That doesn't mean we'll stop innovating in our core platform. The responsibility of leadership isn't to shut down; the responsibility of leadership is to drive forward—to understand, to anticipate and to work with the industry."

With the antitrust case at its height, on January 13, 2000, Gates announced that he would be stepping down as CEO of Microsoft and would assume the title of chief software architect. While Gates retained his role as chairman, Ballmer took over as CEO. Of the division of power today, Gates told Jay Greene for *BusinessWeek* (June 17, 2002), "Steve's the No. 1 guy, and I'm the No. 2 guy. . . . I have a strong voice, a strong recommendation, but Steve has to decide." On June 6, 2002, Ballmer issued a memo entitled "Realizing Potential" to Microsoft's 50,000 employees. In it he laid out a new corporate mission—"to enable people and businesses throughout the world to realize their full potential"—as well as the tools to achieve it. Ballmer's plan moved beyond Microsoft's technological capabilities to focus on how well the company handles relations with customers and with other companies in the technology industry. "The events of the last four years and the changes in our industry make this a good point to take stock of ourselves and our mission, to understand how others perceive us," Ballmer wrote, according to Steve Bodow for the *New York Times* (November 24, 2002). "Many of us feel a disconnect in the way we see ourselves and our mission and motives, and the way we are portrayed, and only we can change that." Ballmer also instituted a set of core values, which included honesty, integrity, and respect, that he expected all employees to practice; in fact, he made adoption of the values part of every employee's annual review.

Steve Ballmer resides on the eastern shore of Lake Washington, near Seattle, with his wife, Connie, and three sons. Once known for his excessive use of colorful language, Ballmer reportedly gave up cursing when he became a father. His feisty personality is also said to have mellowed some with age. Of his penchant for yelling, he told Bodow, "I do that much less frequently. As soon as I say, 'I'm not solving this problem; I'm helping somebody else solve this problem,' I change modes. If you put me where I think I'm supposed to figure out the answer, I'm as likely to be as much bull in the china shop as I ever was. It's not personal, I don't intend to hurt anybody. I just don't think I'm getting through to people. I get frustrated." In recent years, Ballmer has begun focusing more on his health: After years as a heavy eater, he began a regular exercise routine that has helped him shed more than 50 pounds. In one of his few extravagances, he often begins his mornings with an early basketball game, coached by a former coach for the Seattle SuperSonics.

Despite his wealth and success, Ballmer shows little sign of slowing down, particularly in his commitment to Microsoft. When asked about his motivation, he told Whitaker, "Pretty much the same thing that kept us going before we were worth whatever the number is today. A) it's [gratifying] to build stuff that people like, appreciate and changes the way they work and live. B) it's fun. Business is in part a game. You're seeing if you can outthink, outwit the other guy. It's a puzzle; it's a chess game. I mean, heck, I like playing chess."—K. D.

Suggested Reading: *BusinessWeek* p 106 May 17, 1999, with photo, p66 June 17, 2002, with photo; *Chicago Tribune* C p1 Jan 23, 2000, with photo; *Forbes* p86+ Jan. 27, 1997, with photo, p130 Mar. 5, 2001; *Fortune* p155+ Oct. 25, 1999; *New York Post* p58 July 26, 1998; *New York Times* D p1 Feb. 4, 1992, with photo, VI p72 Nov. 24, 2002, with photos; *Newsweek* p78+ June 23, 1997; *Time* p50 Aug. 3, 1998; *Washington Post* A p1 Dec. 31, 2000

Baran, Paul

Apr. 29, 1926– Developer of packet-switching theory

During the Cold War, many people feared that a first strike by the Soviet Union could cripple America's centralized defenses and prevent it from retaliating. Worried that such a scenario was possible, Paul Baran, a computer scientist involved in military research, devised a plan to create a distributed network of computers, capable of communicating with one another even if sections of the system were crippled or destroyed. Baran conceived of a digital communication system that could divide messages into smaller units, called packets, which could then be sent separately, by different routes, and reassembled at their destination. His store-and-forward technology allowed the messages to move smoothly from one switching station to another; the system was redundant, so that if any one path failed or was destroyed, the message could be sent through another path.

Even though Baran was never able to secure funding to build his distributed network, his work was incorporated into the first computer network, the ARPANET, which was developed under the auspices of the Department of Defense's Advanced Research Projects Agency (ARPA; also known as DARPA). Now regarded as the precursor to the Internet, the ARPANET was built through the work and inventions of many. "The process of technological development is like building a cathedral," Baran noted in *When Wizards Stay Up Late: The Origins of the Internet* (1996). "Over the course of several hundred years new people come along and each lays down a block on top of the old foundations, each saying, 'I built a cathedral.' . . . If you are not careful, you can con yourself into believing that you did the most important job."

The fact that military funding helped to propel the creation of the world's first Internet has led to the popular myth that the Internet was created specifically to withstand a nuclear attack. In fact, the ARPANET's creators were primarily interested in creating a nationwide network of computers to share data and resources. In his 1964 memorandum on distributed networks, Baran outlined the twofold nature of his ideas: "While highly survivable and reliable communications systems are of primary interest to those in the military concerned with automating command and control functions, the basic notions are also of interest to communications systems planners and designers having need to transmit digital data."

Paul Baran was born in Poland, on April 29, 1926 and emigrated with his parents to the United States when he was two years old. He was educated at Drexel University, in Philadelphia, Pennsylvania, where he received his B.S. in electrical engineering, in 1949. Ten years later he received a master's degree in engineering from the University of California, in Los Angeles. After graduating from Drexel, he worked for the Eckert Mauchly Computer Company for about a year. In 1950 he joined the staff at the Raymond Rosen Engineering Products Corporation, where he worked until 1954 (some sources say 1955). From 1955 to 1959 he worked in the systems group for the Hughes Aircraft Company.

At Hughes Baran worked as a design engineer for the Minuteman nuclear missile control system. Unlike the earlier Titan rockets, these rockets could be launched in a matter of minutes instead of hours. American military experts believed that the Minutemen were safer weapons; since they could be fueled and launched in a matter of minutes, there was less of a chance of them being hit on the ground during fueling. However, Baran and his associates at Hughes believed that this Minuteman system actually posed *more* of a threat than any other system ever built: one misunderstood order, one garbled message could have sent fleets of missiles into the air.

Realizing that the stop-gap measures being proposed at Hughes would not solve the problem of an accidental launch, Baran left the Hughes Company, in 1959, to work at the RAND Corporation. RAND, short for Research and Development, was a nonprofit think tank established after World War II for systems analysis. During this time Albert Wohlstetter, a noted strategist at RAND, was arguing that Soviet missiles had the ability to take out all American strategic air command bases surrounding the Soviet Union in a matter of minutes and then demand America's unconditional surrender. This theory, proclaimed in American newspapers and by John F. Kennedy during the 1960 presidential campaign, came to be known as America's "missile gap." Wohlstetter and his supporters asked the American military to give its nuclear systems a second-strike capacity—in essence the ability to endure a first strike and retaliate.

The argument for second-strike capacity was mostly psychological: Cold Warriors believed that—with both sides capable of destroying the other—neither side would be willing to fire first. However, in order to make a second-strike capacity system work, the communications, command, and control systems would have to be able to sustain a first strike. Baran believed that, as these systems existed in the early 1960s, a single nuclear weapon detonated at high altitude could wreak havoc with the ionosphere—the part of Earth's atmosphere in which gases are converted to charged particles—thus wiping out all radio communications for hours. He also realized that by knocking out any of AT&T's centralized switching stations, the entire system would collapse.

Baran became determined to create a communications system that could not only endure a first strike but could also send out a retaliatory attack. His idea was based on the model of the human brain, which can reconfigure itself to work, even if parts of it are destroyed. He wanted to develop a computer system with adaptive redundancy—a system with no central "brain" but a host of outlying branches, any of which could assume control in case sections of it were destroyed. Between 1960 and 1962 Baran outlined his plan at RAND and published it under the title *On Distributed Communications*, in 1964. According to that report, Baran believed that the United States should build a survivable "network of unmanned digital switches implementing a self-learning policy at each node so that overall traffic is effectively routed in a changing environment—without need for a central and possibly vulnerable control point." Because the data in this scenario would be constantly moving from node to node, Baran termed this "hot-potato" routing.

Baran developed a way to break digital traffic into "packets," which had their own routing information and were able to replicate themselves if part of the transmission was interrupted or broken. This new concept, called packet-switching, was just gaining currency in the 1960s. In 1961 the computer researcher Leonard Kleinrock published what is believed to be the first paper on packet-switching. In 1965 Donald Watts Davies of England's National Physics Laboratory independently developed a packet-switching theory, which he likened to old-style telegraph technology.

In telegraph systems, it was impractical to directly link all cities together, so switching centers were set up in such major cities as New York, Chicago, Detroit, and Los Angeles. A message going from Los Angeles to New York might be sent through a switching station in Chicago, for example. The message would then be recorded on paper—either by hand in the early days of the telegraph or later automatically, on perforated paper tape machines—before being transmitted down the line. This "store-and-forward" technology was the guiding principal behind Baran's and Davies's work. According to Martin Campbell-Kelly and William Aspray in *Computer: A History of the Information Machine* (1996): "Instead of having every computer connected to every other, store-and-forward technology would be used to route messages through the network; there would be a single 'backbone' communications line that connected the computers together, with other connections being added as the need arose." Sending messages in

packets also prevented the new digital communication lines from being overloaded. If any one of the packets became corrupted, that packet could be re-sent, rather than having to retransmit the whole message.

Baran also developed or enhanced prioritization, encryption, and roaming—innovations that have proved useful to Internet technology. However, packet-switching was his single most valuable contribution. As Campbell-Kelly and Aspray noted, "by enabling many users to share a communications line simultaneously, packet-switching did for telecommunications what time-sharing had done for computers."

Baran left RAND, in 1968, to form the Institute for the Future, a Silicon Valley–based research organization dedicated to forecasting technological and business trends. He led the institute until 1972 and went on to found a number of other companies, including Cable Data Associates, Packet Technologies, Metricom, and Interfax. Since 1992 he has been the founder and chairman of the board for Com21, a broadband supplier based in Milpitas, California; since 1997 he has also been a part of the President's Council at RAND. Baran is currently working to find better ways to use unused radio bandwidth for more efficient telecommunication. His honors include the Edwin H. Armstrong Award, from the Communications Society (1987); the Alexander Graham Bell Medal (1990); the Centennial 100 Award, from Drexel University (1992); and the Computer and Communications Foundation Award (1996). In October 1996 he, along with Vinton Cerf (co-inventor of TCP/IP) and Tim Berners-Lee (inventor of the World Wide Web), were presented with an award for their contributions to the Internet.

Paul Baran married Evelyn Murphy, an economist, in 1955. They have one son, David, a director of information technology at 20th Century Fox Home Entertainment.—C. M.

Suggested Reading: *Forbes ASAP* p106+ June 2, 1997; *New York Times* F p1 Oct. 12, 1999; *New York Times Book Review* p19 Sep. 8, 1996; RAND Corporation Web site; *Washington Post* F p17 Aug. 26, 1996; Campbell-Kelly, Martin and William Aspray. *Computer: A History of the Information Machine*, 1996; *American Men and Women of Science, 1998–99*, 1998

Courtesy of William A. Bardeen

Bardeen, John

May 23, 1908–Jan. 30, 1991 Co-inventor of the transistor

Before the pioneering work of John Bardeen, the field of electronics centered around a single device for the transmittal and amplification of electrical impulses: the vacuum tube. It was large and inefficient, and its size in particular limited the advancement of electronics beyond a certain point. In 1947 Bardeen, a theoretical physicist, joined with fellow physicists William Shockley and Walter H. Brattain to invent the transistor, a device that would eventually eclipse the vacuum tube and usher in a new age of electronics. Much smaller than vacuum tubes, transistors also possess a more rugged structure use less energy than their glass predecessors, and are also less expensive to produce. Yet they perform the same function: regulation of the flow of electricity. Bardeen was named one of the 100 most influential people of the 20th century by *Life* magazine and his accomplishments have had a tremendous impact on the development of computers. The first computer to use transistors was designed by engineer Seymour Cray in 1960. The transistor paved the way for the invention of the microchip, and thus it played an important role in the explosive development and use of microcomputers that took place in the last two decades of the 20th century.

John Bardeen was born in Madison, Wisconsin, on May 23, 1908. His father, Charles Russell Bardeen, had been the first graduate of the Johns Hopkins Medical School, and later became an anatomy professor and the dean of the medical school at the University of Wisconsin. Bardeen's mother, Althea (Harmer) Bardeen, studied Eastern art at the Pratt Institute in New York City and had been an interior designer in Chicago. John Bardeen's paternal grandfather was the author and educator Charles William Bardeen. Charles and Althea Bardeen also had, in addition to John, two older sons, Thomas and William, and a daughter, Helen. Althea Bardeen died in 1920, and Charles later married Ruth Hames, with whom he had another daughter, Anna.

John Bardeen attended an experimental elementary school, where he skipped from the third to the seventh grade. He went on to University High School and then transferred to Madison Central High School, where he graduated in 1923 at the age of 15. Throughout his youth he was a talented billiards player and champion swimmer, despite a hereditary illness that caused one of his hands to tremble.

While he was an undergraduate at the University of Wisconsin, Bardeen worked in the engineering department of the Western Electric Company (which later became the Bell Telephone Laboratories). In 1928 he earned a B.S. in electrical engineering from the University of Wisconsin, minoring in physics and mathematics. He then did his master's research, studying applied geophysics and radiation from antennas, and received an M.S. in electrical engineering from Wisconsin as well.

The following year, Bardeen obtained a job at the Gulf Research and Development Corporation in Pittsburgh, Pennsylvania, where he and his former research adviser Leo J. Peters worked on developing new methods of analyzing maps of gravitational and magnetic field strengths to aid in locating petroleum deposits. In 1933, after receiving a Proctor fellowship, he began his doctoral work at Princeton University in Princeton, New Jersey, studying mathematical physics with a focus on quantum theory applied to solids. He received his Ph.D. three years later, after completing his thesis on the attractive forces of electrons within metals. A year prior, he had accepted a postdoctoral research fellowship from Harvard University in Cambridge, Massachusetts, which he held until 1938, working on problems in electrical conduction and cohesion in metals.

After his fellowship came to an end, Bardeen continued his research on the behavior of electrons in metals as an assistant professor of physics at the University of Minnesota. The following year, in 1939, he published an important paper with colleague J. H. Van Vleck on the bonding of metallic electrons. During America's involvement in World War II, Bardeen worked for the Naval Ordnance Laboratory in Washington, D.C., as its principal theoretical physicist; he spent his four years of service studying the magnetic fields of ships.

After the conclusion of the war, Bardeen returned to Bell Telephone Laboratories, in Murray Hill, New Jersey, where he would do his most important work. He joined fellow researchers William Shockley and Walter H. Brattain in research on semiconductors—materials (such as silicon) whose ability to conduct electricity is intermediate, falling between that of insulators, such as rubber, and that of conductors, such as copper and other metals. Bardeen and his colleagues were trying to develop a semiconductor device that could both amplify and rectify electrical impulses. Shockley in particular had been looking into the possibility of such a device in which an external voltage could induce an electrical field that would influence the motion of electrons within the semiconductor itself (the transistor effect). All attempts at constructing such an invention had failed, until Bardeen, the team's theorist, suggested that the external voltage was being blocked by a layer of electrons trapped at the surface of the semiconductor.

Once the trio attained an understanding of the properties of semiconductor surfaces, they were able to build the first functioning transistors, at the end of 1947. The name for the device was an abbreviation of "transfer-resistor." Transistors were able to control electrical flow just like the earlier vacuum tubes, but they were a vast improvement in terms of efficiency and size, requiring approximately one-fiftieth the space and one-millionth the power needed by a vacuum tube. They contained fine-metal point-contacts called the emitter and collectors, and a third electrical contact called the base. The emitter and collectors were placed just 50 microns apart on a surface composed of the element germanium. Eventually, engineers were able to make transistors that were so tiny that they could be clustered together on minuscule silicon chips, allowing for the development of modern computers.

The invention of the transistor was not announced until June 1948, and it met with little media fanfare; the *New York Times*, for example, ran a four-paragraph article on the story on the next to last page. Its first major commercial application was in telephone-switching equipment, in 1952, the year in which the device was officially perfected. Transistors would later come to be used in portable radios and the miniaturized electronics used in space flight. "I knew the transistor was important," Bardeen once said, "But I never foresaw the revolution in electronics it would bring" (*Nobel Prize Winners*, 1987).

Bardeen left Bell Telephone Labs in 1951 and began working as a consultant to the Xerox Corporation in their research department in Rochester, New York. He split his time between that job and his duties at the University of Illinois at Urbana-Champaign, where he had accepted a dual appointment as professor of electrical engineering and professor of physics. There he began research on superconductivity, an area that had interested him since he was a graduate student. Superconductivity involves the properties of matter at extremely low temperatures; the field of research was spawned in 1911 by Dutch physicist Heike Kamerlingh Onnes, who discovered that certain metals lose all resistance to the flow of electric current at temperatures near absolute zero. Bardeen sought to explain why these metals became superconductive, and he theorized that superconductivity arose due to an interaction between electrons within an electric current and the atomic vibrations in the metal through which the current flowed.

In December 1956 Bardeen took a break from his research and traveled to Stockholm, Sweden to accept the Nobel Prize in Physics, along with Shockley and Brattain, in recognition of their invention of the transistor nine years earlier. The prize consisted of a diploma and gold medal, as well as $38,634, which was divided among the three winners.

After returning to Illinois, Bardeen, along with his research assistants Leon N. Cooper and J. Robert Schrieffer, developed an understanding of the tendency of free electrons in superconductors to flow in unison and thereby form a single "quantum state" that encompasses the entirety of the superconductive piece of metal. Bardeen's achievement in understanding superconductivity is widely seen as one of the most important developments of modern theoretical physics, profoundly affecting nearly every area of the field. In 1972 he was awarded another Nobel Prize in physics, which he shared with Cooper and Schrieffer. Bardeen thus became the first person to win two Nobel Prizes in the same field. In an ironic twist, Bardeen almost missed a champagne celebration in his honor the morning of the award ceremony due to a malfunction in his electronically controlled garage-door opener.

The Bardeen-Cooper-Schrieffer theory of superconductivity, also known as the BCS theory, has had widespread effects on technology, and Bardeen considered it to be his greatest contribution to science. The theory allowed for the development of new materials that withstand strong magnetic fields or become superconductive at low temperatures, thereby making possible the creation of relatively small and energy-efficient electromagnets of immense power. These magnets are used in the study of fusion, in high-energy particle accelerators; in frictionless high-speed trains that hover above their tracks; and in powerful, compact electric generators. The BCS theory also revolutionized procedures for medical diagnosis.

After developing the BCS theory in the mid-1950s, Bardeen served as a member of the President's Science Advisory Committee from 1959 to 1962. In 1975 he retired from teaching at the University of Illinois, and that same year he was named professor emeritus at the university, an honor he held for the remainder of his life. He served on the White House Science Council in 1981 and 1982.

Bardeen married Jane Maxwell on July 18, 1938. They had two sons, James and William, and a daughter, Elizabeth. In addition to the two Nobel Prizes, among the many awards Bardeen received throughout his life were the Stuart Ballantine Medal of the Franklin Institute, in 1952; the John Scott Award of the City of Philadelphia, in 1955; the National Medal of Science of the National Science

Foundation, in 1965; and the Presidential Medal of Freedom, presented by the United States government, in 1977. The recipient of 16 honorary degrees, Bardeen was honored the world over with such accolades as the Lomonosov Prize from the Soviet Academy of Sciences, in 1988, as well as with membership in the Royal Society of Great Britain, the Indian National Science Academy, and the Japan Academy. Additionally, he was a founding member of the Commission on Very Low Temperatures of the International Union of Pure and Applied Physics, on which he served from 1963 to 1972, and a member of the board of directors at Xerox from 1961 to 1974. He was the associate editor of the *Physical Review* for many years, and was also a member of the National Academy of Sciences, the American Academy of Arts, and the American Physical Society, of which he was a council member from 1954 to 1957, and president from 1968 to 1969. In his spare time, the soft-spoken Bardeen enjoyed traveling and playing golf. He once hit a hole-in-one in a golf tournament.

John Bardeen died of a heart attack on January 30, 1991 at Brigham and Women's Hospital in Boston, Massachusetts, at the age of 82. He had already been staying in the hospital as a patient when the attack took place. His death had been preceded by those of his two collaborators on the invention of the transistor, Walter Brattain having died in 1987 and William Shockley in 1989. Bardeen had continued publishing original scientific papers until the year of his death. As quoted in the *New York Times* (January 31, 1991), University of Illinois Vice Chancellor Robert Berdahl said of John Bardeen, "There are very few people who had a greater impact on the whole of the twentieth century."
—B. S.

Suggested Reading: *John Bardeen* (on-line) Dec. 5, 1995; *New York Times* B p9 Jan. 31, 1991, with photo; Spencer, Donald D. *The Timetable of Computers*, 1997; *Current Biography Yearbook*, 1957, 1991 (obit); *Nobel Prize Winners*, 1987; *Webster's American Biographies*, 1974

Barlow, John Perry

Oct. 3, 1947– Internet activist and co-founder of the Electronic Frontier Foundation

John Perry Barlow, a retired rancher, former songwriter for the Grateful Dead, and a registered Republican, became a champion of freedom of expression on the Internet only three years after he bought his first computer. While he enjoyed communicating with individuals around the world and having unlimited access to information, he eventually became concerned that the government could undermine constitutional freedoms in cyberspace. As a result, Barlow co-founded the Electronic Frontier Foundation (EFF), an organization that defends privacy and freedom of expression on the Internet.

John Perry Barlow was born on October 3, 1947 in Jackson Hole, Wyoming. He grew up on his family's ranch, near the small town of Pinefield. In an article published in the Harrisburg *Country Journal* (September/October 2000), Barlow wrote that his ancestors were "soldiers of the soil. Farmers, stock-growers, orchard men. Country folks. Hicks. Occasional lords, many peasants." In 1905 Barlow's grandfather had purchased land near the New Fork River, and it eventually became the family's 22,000-acre Bar Cross Ranch. John's father, Norman, owned the Bar Cross Ranch and Livestock Company and briefly served in the Wyoming state senate. "My parents had been married 20 years before I was born," John recalled to Steve Doughtery for *People* (December 4, 1995). "They had their own lives at the time. I was pretty much raised by the employees of the ranch."

Bart Nagel/Courtesy of www.eff.org/barlow

Barlow was considered a troublemaker by his family and teachers, and when he was 15, his father sent him to Fountain Valley, a prep school in Colorado Springs, Colorado, hoping the experience would instill discipline in him. At the school, Barlow became friends with Bob Weir, who helped found the rock band the Grateful Dead in 1965. "Oh, we got in a lot of trouble," Barlow told Doughtery. "I felt it really unfair when he got kicked out and I didn't."

In 1965 Barlow enrolled at Wesleyan University, in Middletown, Connecticut, majoring in comparative religion. "I started college intending to major in physics, but my reason for studying physics was a search for God," he explained to *Leaders of the Information Age*. "After finding the search for a passing grade in advanced calculus more difficult, I decided to look for God in areas where people claimed to have already found Him." Barlow graduated from Wesleyan with high honors in 1969.

After his graduation, Barlow spent a year traveling in Europe and India. When he returned to the United States, the Grateful Dead enlisted him as a songwriter. Barlow explained to *Leaders of the Information Age* that when Bob Weir "started writing songs for the Dead, he and the 'varsity' songwriter, Bob Hunter, had a hard time getting along. I had written poetry in college, and Hunter suggested that, since I knew how to tolerate Bobby [Weir], I should work with him. This was in 1970. We have continued writing together, on and off, until the present." Barlow estimated that he wrote between 30 and 40 songs for the Grateful Dead until the band broke up in 1995, when the lead vocalist and guitarist Jerry Garcia died. Among the many songs that Barlow wrote are "Cassidy," "Mexacali Blues," and "Estimated Prophet," which are favorites among many Deadheads, as the group's avid fans are known. He has also written songs for various other bands, including Bobby and the Midnights, a group Weir formed in the early 1980s. Over the years, Barlow used royalties from his songs to keep the family business afloat.

Barlow intended to settle in San Francisco, California, hoping to join the recording industry as a promoter. During his trip west, he stopped at his family's ranch in 1971 to visit his parents. At the time, Barlow's father, Norman, was seriously ill, having suffered a stroke in 1966, and the business was in financial disarray. John agreed to stay for six months at the ranch to work out the company's problems. Norman died in 1972, however, and John Barlow took over the company, managing it for the next 17 years. By 1987 the Bar Cross Ranch and Livestock Company had accumulated about $500,000 in debt. "With the greatest reluctance, I recognized that only selling off my birthright would spare it the indignity of eventually being seized by some remorseless tentacle of the Farm Credit System and being hawked on the courthouse steps, Barlow wrote in the Harrisburg *Country Journal*. "So, in June, after eighty-three years in the New Fork Valley and at least nine hundred years in agriculture, my family left the land."

Barlow purchased his first computer in 1987, to help him manage his finances. He had also heard that many Grateful Dead fans were communicating through the Whole Earth 'Lectronic Link (WELL), an early on-line bulletin-board service based in Sausalito, California. He explored the WELL himself and was completely captivated by what he discovered. "Inside the WELL was, it seemed, almost everything one might find going on in a small town," Barlow wrote for the *Guardian* (July 24, 1995). "I was delighted. I felt I had found the new locale of human community—never mind that the whole thing was being conducted in mere words from whom the bodies had been amputated."

In 1990 Barlow began using the word "cyberspace" to describe the virtual world in which computer users communicate and find information. William Gibson, the Canadian writer, had coined the word in his novel *Neuromancer* (1984). Barlow, however, helped popularized its use, and the term stuck when referring to the Internet as an actual place.

The same year, Barlow became concerned with possible government suppression of freedom of expression in cyberspace. In "A Not Terribly Brief History of the Electronic Frontier Foundation" (November 8, 1990), posted on the Electronic Frontier Foundation Web site, Barlow recalled that in April of that year FBI Special Agent Richard Baxter visited him at his home. Baxter, who normally investigated crimes involving the theft of livestock, interviewed Barlow for three hours. "He had been sent to find out if I might be a member of the Nu-Prometheus League, a dread band of info-terrorists (or maybe just a disaffected former Apple employee) who had stolen and wantonly distributed source code normally used in the Macintosh ROMs," he wrote. Barlow continued, "Agent Baxter's errand was complicated by a fairly complete unfamiliarity with computer technology. . . . I realized in the course of this interview that I was seeing, in microcosm, the entire law enforcement structure of the United States. Agent Baxter was hardly alone in his puzzlement about the legal, technical, and metaphorical nature of datacrime."

Barlow was also alarmed by "Operation Sundevil," a nationwide crackdown led by the U.S. Secret Service against several computer hackers around the country in 1990. He objected to the Secret Service's use of "levels of force and terror which would have been more appropriate to the apprehension of urban guerillas than barely postpubescent computer nerds," as he wrote in "A Not Terribly Brief History of the Electronic Frontier Foundation."

Barlow, fearing that the FBI's visit and the Secret Service's crackdown could be the first steps in the suppression of freedom of expression and privacy in cyberspace, posted a report of the FBI's visit on the WELL. Another subscriber, Mitch Kapor, read Barlow's account. Kapor, the founder of the Lotus Development Corporation and the author of Lotus 1-2-3, the company's popular spreadsheet program, had received a similar visit from FBI agents. Sharing Barlow's fears about the suppression of constitutional freedoms on the Internet, Kapor contacted Barlow and later visited him at his Wyoming home. The meeting between the two resulted in the creation of the Electronic Frontier Foundation (EFF), an activist organization dedicated to the protection of freedom of expression and privacy in cyberspace.

Kapor personally funded the EFF to get it off the ground. Barlow and Kapor also solicited the financial support of prominent members of the computer industry. Steve Wozniak, co-founder of Apple Computer, and John Gilmore, an executive at Sun Microsystems, were the first to donate large sums of money to the EFF. Other corporations followed suit, including IBM, Microsoft, Bell Atlantic, MCI, and the National Cable Television Association.

The EFF hired a staff, including a legal team and a press coordinator, and opened offices in New York City; San Francisco, California; Washington, D.C.; and Cambridge, Massachusetts. The organization sought to educate the public and raise awareness about computer privacy, and it lobbied policymakers on bills that affected the Internet. The EFF supported various lawsuits—they challenged, for instance, the Communications Decency Act (1996) as unconstitutional—and provided legal counsel to individuals who were charged with computer-related crimes. In a statement posted on its Web site, the EFF acknowledged that such problems as protecting intellectual-property rights, copyright infringement, and child pornography have to be addressed. However, the group warned that any laws enacted to combat these crimes should not undermine freedom of speech or stifle intellectual and artistic creativity. Such legislation would be ineffective in any case, the EFF pointed out, because the Internet transcends national and governmental borders.

Having retired from ranching, Barlow adopted a new role as a crusader for privacy and freedom in cyberspace. He frequently traveled the country, exchanging his views with other privacy activists at conferences, lecturing on the dangers of government intrusion, and lobbying public policymakers on Internet-related issues. Barlow began writing a regular column for *Wired* magazine, which he helped launch in 1993, and expressed his opinions in other publications, including the *New York Times*, as well.

On February 9, 1996 Barlow, who had become known in the press as the "cyberspace cowboy" and "poet laureate of the Internet," drew up *A Declaration of the Independence of Cyberspace*, which is available on the EFF's Web site. In it Barlow addressed the governments of the world directly. "Governments derive their just powers from the consent of the governed. You have neither solicited nor received ours. We did not invite you," he wrote. "Cyberspace does not lie within your borders. Do not think that you can build it, as though it were a public construction project. You cannot. It is an act of nature and it grows itself through our collective actions." Barlow continued, "Cyberspace consists of transactions, relationships, and thought itself, arrayed like standing waves in the web of our communications. Ours is a world that is both everywhere and nowhere, but it is not where bodies live." As a consequence, he argued, the laws of government regarding "property, expression, identity, movement, and context do not

apply to us. They are based on matter, [and] there is no matter here." Barlow's declaration was widely circulated throughout the Internet and received substantial praise from readers.

Although the EFF received considerable media attention, the organization seemed to run out of steam by the end of the decade. The first sign of trouble came late in 1994, when three top officials at the EFF resigned to form their own activist group, the Center for Democracy and Technology. In an article for the *Boston Globe* (December 29, 1994), Simson L. Garfinkel reported that the defectors and many other EFF members believed that the group had betrayed its own principles when it helped rewrite the Digital Telephony bill (1994) and then supported its passage. Garfinkel explained that the bill "requires the [telephone] companies [to] modify the nation's telephone system so calls can be more easily wiretapped by the Federal Bureau of Investigation and other law enforcement agencies." The EFF, which was instrumental in preventing the passage of an earlier version of the bill, supported the version it helped rewrite because its provisions did not apply to the Internet and on-line services. "I really think that what we did was far more worthy of praise than criticism, in the final analysis," Barlow told Garfinkel. "I am so dismayed about how much credibility EFF lost among people who didn't take the time to figure out what we did." Barlow argued that the rewritten bill was an acceptable compromise because some of its more restrictive provisions, such as requiring telephone companies to give law-enforcement agencies the ability to wiretap telephones remotely, were eliminated.

Many observers began raising questions about the EFF's independence, given that it received substantial corporate funding. "When I started writing about intellectual property, donations from Microsoft started drying up—from the company and its employees—even though I was not writing for the EFF," Barlow told Sandra Stewart for the *Industry Standard* (March 20, 2000). "One reason [the] EFF didn't deal with copyright for a long time is that it would have significantly cut into our funding." Stewart opined that the members of the EFF were also becoming bedfellows with the members of the political establishment in Washington, D.C. "We had an office down on K Street with the rest of the log rollers," Barlow admitted to her, referring to a prestigious thoroughfare in the Capital. "Marble floors, brass keys to the men's room and the whole catastrophe."

Despite the EFF's difficulties, Barlow has remained on the group's board of directors. He has taken clear positions on practically every controversy relating to the Internet. In a column for *Wired* (March 1994, on-line), Barlow opposed the application of copyright and "intellectual-property" laws to the Internet, arguing that such laws were designed to protect physical property, which did not exist in cyberspace. The self-described "cognitive dissident" also objected to the creation of an information superhighway, telling Spencer Reiss for the *American Spectator* (April 2001) that the idea would turn the Internet "into a massive, centrally administrated and planned government project, which it isn't."

More controversially, Barlow opposes the censorship of child pornography on the Internet as well. "The problem is that if you can regulate child pornography, you can regulate anything," he told Reiss. "Cyberspace is seamless. From a purely technical view, if you have a mechanism to regulate any aspect of it, then you can regulate all of it." Barlow explained further to *Leaders of the Information Age*: "I believe the crime is actually exploiting children, not in trafficking in images of such exploitation. We need to focus on the act, not the image."

Recently Barlow defended Napster, the on-line service that allows users to trade and download free music. "So-called intellectual property is very different from real property," he told Reiss. "When you take my horse I can't ride it anymore. But if you take my song I can still sing it, and the fact that both of us now know my song does not lessen its value. It may actually increase it." He continued, "I've been watching [this issue] for a long time, with Grateful Dead songs that I wrote quite a few years ago. We always gave those songs away every time we played them [in concert]. And all of our albums, bad as many of them were, went platinum."

In recent years Barlow has worked as a consultant on cyberspace issues for such companies as the Vanguard Group, the Global Business Network, and Digital Technology Partners. He has also served as an advisor for several new companies that conduct business through the Internet. In 1997 Barlow became a fellow of the Institute of Politics at Harvard University, in Cambridge, Massachusetts. In 1998 Harvard Law School named him a Berkman fellow.

John Perry Barlow's marriage, to Elaine Parker, ended in divorce in 1997. The pair had separated in 1992. He is the father of three daughters by that relationship. After his separation from Parker, he became engaged to Cynthia Horner, a vivacious and popular psychiatrist. In 1994, however, Horner died from a previously undiagnosed heart problem during a flight to New York City, where she shared an apartment with Barlow. Barlow delivered the eulogy at her funeral and eventually posted it on the Internet. In response, he received thousands of e-mails from people around the world expressing their sympathy.

When not traveling for work, Barlow divides his time between Pinedale, Wyoming; New York City's Chinatown; San Francisco; and cyberspace.—D. C.

Suggested Reading: *American Spectator* p24+ Apr. 2001, with photos; *Boston Globe* I p57 Dec. 29, 1994; *Country Journal* p32+ Sep./Oct. 2000, with photo; Electronic Frontier Foundation Web site *Guardian* p11 Jul. 24, 1995; *Industry Standard* (on-line) Mar. 20, 2000; *People* p23 Dec. 4, 1995

Baudot, Jean-Maurice-Émile
(baw-DOH)

1845–Mar. 28, 1903 Electrical engineer; inventor

The French engineer Jean-Maurice-Émile Baudot deserves recognition for his contributions to the development of electronic technology. Not immediately involved in the early development of actual computing machines in the way that Charles Babbage, the British inventor of the Analytical Engine, was, he nevertheless introduced innovations that remain to this day. Through his work on the electric telegraph, Baudot perfected the first machine to use a typewriter-like keyboard as an input device, as well as a unique communications code that replaced Morse code and is still in use, with a few contemporary modifications.

Jean-Maurice-Émile Baudot was born in 1845 in Magneux, a town in the Haute-Marne region of France. His professional career was linked to the communication industries from the beginning: he served on the staff of the local postal administration as a young man and later worked for the telephone administration, helping to regulate the application of the new technology in the late 1870s. Around the same time, Baudot began working as a telegraph engineer. Invented independently in 1837 by Sir Charles Wheatstone in England and Samuel Finley Morse in the United States, the telegraph was the world's first electric communication device. Because Morse's version was easier to make and use than Wheatstone's, it became the standard, and the code Samuel Morse formulated, composed of dots and dashes, took on his name and was the standard telegraph "language" for decades.

In 1874, however, Baudot perfected a new code that eventually supplanted Morse's as the most common telegraph language. Instead of the series of long and short signals that make up Morse code, in Baudot code each letter is composed of a five-unit combination of current-off and current-on signals of equal length. The signals could be transmitted in the form of a sequence of pulses and gaps, and subsequently decoded at the receiving end. This new format proved to be the more economical of the two, utilizing less power than Morse code due to the inclusion of current-off signals. Baudot provided 32 different combinations; this was enough for each letter of the Roman alphabet as well as some punctuation symbols and control commands for necessary mechanical functions. Among the system's drawbacks was that, despite its 32 combinations, it lacked enough to represent the numbers zero through nine.

In Baudot's time there was great interest in perfecting a printing telegraph, which could record its messages. Most ideas involved a wheel of some kind, which would have characters embossed around its outer edge. The problem was in finding a way to have telegraph signals spin the wheel in fixed increments, so that the correct characters faced the paper, and then to impress the character on to an ink tape placed over the paper. Several methods were introduced for controlling the wheel, but most of them were too slow or inefficient. In 1877 Baudot settled the issue by inventing the press telegraph, a device with printing capability. The machine recorded messages on a two-column paper tape, the design of which had been perfected earlier by the British telegraph inventor Sir Charles Wheatstone.

In addition to its recording function, Baudot's press telegraph was also the first machine to feature an input device in the form of a keyboard, which was inspired by the mechanical typewriter invented in 1869 by the American C. L. Sholes. This was a development from an earlier model Baudot had designed, which included a five-button keypad that required the operator to simultaneously push whichever keys were needed to form each character. Becoming aware of the much more user-friendly typewriter innovation, Baudot quickly adapted his machine before obtaining a patent for it. The press telegraph could transmit messages three to four times as quickly as the original telegraph and was soon installed on the crucial Paris–Rome line, which linked the two major European cities. In addition to the Paris–Rome line, Baudot helped install telegraphic lines from Paris to cities such as Vienna, Austria; Bern, Switzerland; Berlin, Germany; and London, England.

Baudot's last major invention was a distributor system, which could send up to eight messages simultaneously along the same telegraph line. Completed in 1894, it was known as a multiplex system, and represented a marked improvement from the slower serial systems in which messages had to be sent one after another.

Baudot died on March 28, 1903 in Sceaux, outside of Paris, at the age of 58. But his most successful invention, his telegraph code, survived him; by the middle of the 20th century, Baudot's code had become the standard format for telegraph communication. The code itself was modified over time to use seven or eight signals rather than five, allowing for more characters to be transmitted. Although Baudot's code remained in use long after his death, his press telegraph did not fare as well. Found to have numerous technical problems, including difficulties in synchronizing the transmitter and receiver, the machine was eventually abandoned in favor of later telegraph models.

An innovator in the field of communications technology, Baudot remains an essential contributor to the history of the Information Age—by its most basic definition. As a testament to his work's worth, by the 1930s his name had become a unit of measurement, abbreviated as "baud" and used to calculate increments of data transmission speed—one baud equals one bit per second. Baudot code is the forerunner of the more modern ASCII code. Using Baudot's original codes, a body known as Comité Consultatif International de Télégraphique et Téléphonique (CCITT), or the International Consultative Committee on Telephony and

Telegraphy, standardized character sets for use in telegraph and telephone messaging. In 1968, after four additional modifications to CCITT, a newer code was adopted as a world standard called American Standard Code for Information Interchange (ASCII).—C. M.

Suggested Reading: Cinemedia Web site; *Maxmon.com*; Spencer, David. *The Timetable of Computers*, 1997

Hulton Archive by Getty Images

Bell, Alexander Graham

Mar. 3, 1847–Aug. 2, 1922 Inventor

Though Alexander Graham Bell would have preferred to be remembered as a teacher and patron of the deaf, today he is best known as the developer of the telephone, a distinction that ranks him among the greatest inventors of all time. It is impossible to understate the importance of Bell's contribution, which began as an accident in 1875, while Bell was attempting to perfect the telegraph. His invention served as the starting point for the Information Age and helped set the stage for radio, television, satellite communications, and the Internet.

The second of three brothers, Alexander Bell was born on March 3, 1847 to Alexander Melville Bell and Eliza Symonds Bell in Edinburgh, Scotland. (In 1858, at the age of 11, Bell adopted the name Graham in tribute to his friend Alexander Graham.) Bell was born into a family devoted to the study of speech and elocution; both his father and paternal grandfather, also named Alexander Bell, had studied the mechanics of speech. Bell's father was a pioneer in the field of teaching speech to the deaf and had developed "Visible Speech," a teaching method that used drawings to display the action and position of the lips, tongue, and throat when forming sounds. Young Alexander had a great interest in phonetics, in part because his mother was deaf but also because his father taught this subject at Edinburgh University. Bell's father did little to encourage such studies; sources have indicated that he favored Alexander's outgoing older brother, Melville. Alexander's grades at Edinburgh Royal High School, where he studied formally for two years, suffered as a result of his almost paralyzing shyness.

In October 1862 Bell's paternal grandfather, Alexander Bell, asked that his grandson be sent to live with him in London, England, where he taught speech; he felt that young Alexander had been neglected at home and theorized that an extended visit would help him overcome his reclusiveness. As noted in *Library of North American Biographies*, Volume 3: Entrepreneurs and Inventors (1990), "Away from his demanding father, [Bell] felt freer. Instead of constantly having to prove himself, he at last could act however he wished. At home, his parents discouraged him from reading books for fun. But his grandfather loved to read novels and plays." With his grandfather, Bell read through Shakespeare's plays and other literary classics. When his father went to London to retrieve him, he was shocked by his son's transformation from shy to outgoing.

Having had a taste of the outside world, Bell did not remain in his parents' house for long. Although he had been mostly home-schooled and self-taught, he found a summer job in 1863 to teach music and elocution at Weston House Academy, a boarding school in Elgin, Scotland. While there he also received lessons in Greek and Latin. Though only 16 and younger than many of his pupils, Bell was respected by his students not only for his deft understanding of his subjects but also because of his confident carriage.

Bell enrolled at the University of Edinburgh in the fall of 1864 and the following year became a resident master at Weston House Academy, where he conducted his first sound experiments with vowel pitches and tuning forks. In 1866–67 he taught at Somersetshire College, in Bath. A year later he became his father's assistant and took charge of his father's research while the elder Bell was lecturing on Visible Speech in the United States. The stress of this work—compounded by the deaths of his brothers Edward and Melville from tuberculosis in 1867 and 1870, respectively—began to take its toll on him. To safeguard Bell's health, his parents moved the family to Brantford, in the Canadian province of Ontario, in August 1870.

In 1871 Bell traveled to Boston, Massachusetts, where he spent several weeks demonstrating the benefits of Visible Speech as a way of teaching speech to the deaf. He taught at the Boston School for Deaf Mutes; the Clarke School for the Deaf, also in Boston; and at the American Asylum for the Deaf, in Hartford, Connecticut. In the fall of 1872 he opened his School of Vocal Physiology, in Boston, where he trained teachers of the deaf in the methodology of Visible Speech. In 1873 Boston University appointed him as a professor of vocal physiology at its School of Oratory. Mabel Hubbard, a deaf pupil at Boston University, became his wife in 1877. (Her father, Gardiner Greene Hubbard, became one of his financial backers on the telephone.)

In the spring of 1874 Bell conducted acoustic experiments at the Massachusetts Institute of Technology, in Cambridge, Massachusetts. With the Boston ear specialist Clarence Blake, he experimented with the mechanics of the human ear as well as with a "phonautograph," a device that could translate sound vibrations into visible tracings. By the summer of 1874 he had formulated ideas for improving the telegraph and had noted his initial impressions for how such a machine would operate. Tom Standage, in his book *The Victorian Internet* (1998), described Bell's concept: "The idea of the harmonic telegraph was to use a series of reeds vibrating at different frequencies. Electrical signals produced by the reeds would be combined, sent down a telegraph wire, and then separated out again at the other end using an identical set of reeds, each of which would respond only to the signals generated by its counterpart. Morse telegraphy would then be possible by stopping and starting the vibration of each reed to make dots and dashes."

While Bell was familiar with acoustics, he knew very little about electrical engineering. But he met a young electrician and model maker, Thomas Watson, who was extremely interested in his idea. Starting in January 1875, Bell and Watson worked together nightly on their version of the harmonic telegraph. Less than two months later, they had produced results significant enough to receive financial backing from Thomas Sanders, a wealthy leather merchant, and Gardiner Greene Hubbard, Bell's future father-in-law. In June 1875, while testing the equipment, one of the reeds in their harmonic telegraph got stuck. Watson plucked it much harder than usual in order to free it, and Bell, who was listening at the other end, heard the reed twanging. Bell was stunned—this was a far more complex sound than the machine had been designed to transmit. He realized that with a few modifications the device could do more than just send multiple streams of telegraphy; it could transmit sounds, including human speech.

Bell and Watson spent, in addition to their normal working hours, almost every night trying to perfect the telephone, which Bell believed was a feat within reach. As Isaac Asimov wrote in *Asimov's Biographical Encyclopedia of Science and Technology* (1982): "It seemed to Bell that if the sound wave vibrations could be turned into a fluctuating electric current, that current could be reconverted into sound waves identical to the original at the other end of the circuit. In this way, sound could be carried across wires at the speed of light." Pushing himself to exhaustion, Bell grew weak, and he was forced to return to his parents home in Canada to recuperate. By September 1875 Bell was fully recovered; he wrote the specifications for the telephone and sent them to the U.S. Patent Office. He received his patent (No. 174,465) on March 7, 1876, three days before the first intelligible human speech was heard over the telephone.

The story of the first words transmitted via telephone is legendary. Watson and Bell had strung a wire from Bell's home laboratory to his bedroom. While Watson waited in the bedroom, Bell, who was making some final adjustments, accidentally spilled battery acid on his pants. He exclaimed: "Mr. Watson, come here. I want to see you." Watson had heard every word and hurried to the laboratory to tell Bell. (At the formal opening of the first transcontinental telephone line in 1915, Bell, in New York, repeated the same words to Watson, who was in San Francisco, California.) One of the most famous early public demonstrations occurred in June 1876 at the Centennial Exposition in Philadelphia, Pennsylvania. There, Bell presented his invention to the visiting Brazilian emperor, Pedro II, who dropped the instrument to exclaim, "It talks!" He also showed the telephone to Sir William Thompson, also known as Baron Kelvin, who was equally impressed.

After further refining the telephone to allow its use over a two-mile distance between Boston and Cambridgeport, Massachusetts, Bell, Watson, Hubbard, and Sanders formed the Bell Telephone Company in July 1877. The fledgling company had to fight off its share of lawsuits, one of the most famous coming from the Western Union Telegraph Company for patent infringement. A potentially damaging lawsuit was also filed by Elisha Gray, who had independently developed a similar device at about the same time as Bell and Watson were working on their telephone design. Gray had filed a caveat at the U.S. Patent Office the day Bell had filed for his patent. The caveat (a confidential declaration notifying the office that an inventor was intending to file a patent on an idea yet to be perfected) was for Gray's idea of a transmitter with a moving membrane attached to an electrically conductive rod immersed in an acidic solution. The patent-infringement case was so involved that it eventually went to the U.S. Supreme Court; after months of testimony, the court ruled in favor of Bell, declaring him the one and only inventor of the telephone.

Bell married Mabel Hubbard in 1877 and traveled to England, where they lived for the next year. Bell's invention—and the case surrounding its patent—made him internationally famous and extremely wealthy. In England he demonstrated his device for Queen Elizabeth. At just 30 years of age, he was one of the most highly respected inventors in the world. In 1880 he was honored with France's Volta Prize; he used the purse to establish the Volta Laboratory, a self-supporting experimental laboratory dedicated to scientific inventions. At Volta he developed the Graphophone in association with his cousin Chichester A. Bell and Charles Sumner Tainter. The Graphophone used an engraving stylus, wax cylinders, and controllable speeds to conveniently record sound. (The Graphophone's wax cylinders were used in Thomas Alva Edison's early phonograph; Edison returned the favor in 1886 when he improved telephone receivers by developing a mouthpiece containing carbon powder, which allowed for greater clarity.) In 1881 Bell used another of his inventions, an electromagnetic device called an induction balance, in an attempt to find a bullet lodged in the body of President James A. Garfield, who was slowly dying from an assassin's attack. Though the device worked perfectly, it could not locate the bullet because no one had thought to remove the president from the steel-springed mattress on which he was resting.

Bell became an American citizen in 1882, shortly after his telephone company expanded into the American Bell Telephone Company. Still, Bell had more interest in using his wealth to help the deaf and to fund scientific experiments than he had in his company. In 1883 he started a day school for deaf children at Scott Circle, in Washington, D.C. He later created the American Association to Promote the Teaching of Speech to the Deaf (known since 1956 as the Alexander Graham Bell Association for the Deaf) and directed funds to pay Annie Sullivan to teach Helen Keller, a blind, deaf, and mute girl, to communicate. (Years later, Keller dedicated her autobiography to Bell.) He also established the Volta Bureau, which was dedicated to studies of deafness.

With his father-in-law, Bell started the journal *Science* in 1883. He also helped found the National Geographic Society, which subsequently published its own magazine, *National Geographic*. Bell created the National Geographic Society to educate people about life in distant countries, especially those who did not have the means to see such lands for themselves. He served as its president from 1898 to 1903.

As the 20th century dawned, the American Telephone and Telegraph Company acquired the American Bell Telephone Company's business and property and emerged as the parent company of the Bell System, a group of corporations. Bell's own interests, however, turned to the possibility of flight as he endeavored to build a number of giant man-carrying kites. He had some success with the tetrahedral kite, which had four triangular sides that were as strong and rigid as they were light. With four young associates he formed the Aerial Experiment Association (AEA), which was overseen by Mabel Hubbard Bell, one of the first women to be an administrator of a nonprofit organization. In 1909 the group's plane, the Silver Dart, made the first flight of a heavier-than-air machine, in Canada.

For the remainder of his life Bell continued to investigate new areas of scientific study, including sonar detection, solar distillation, air conditioning, animal breeding, and hydrofoil crafts. In 1919 Bell and Casey Baldwin's HD-4, a hydrofoil sea craft weighing more than 10,000 pounds, set a world marine speed record of 70 miles per hour. Bell, however, never lingered on an area of interest long enough to see it to its completion. As noted in the *Encyclopaedia Britannica* (on-line): "The most cursory examination of his many notebooks shows marginal memos and jottings, often totally unrelated to the subject at hand—reminders of questions and ideas he wanted to investigate. It was impossible for him to carry each of his creative ideas through to a practical end. Many of his conceptions are only today seeing fruition; indeed, some undoubtedly have yet to be developed. The range of his inventive genius is represented only in part by the 18 patents granted in his name alone and the 12 he shared with his collaborators. These include 14 for the telephone and telegraph, 4 for the photophone, 1 for the phonograph, 5 for aerial vehicles, 4 for hydroairplanes, and 2 for a selenium cell."

In the summer of 1886 Bell began buying land on Cape Breton Island, in Nova Scotia, Canada, where he built his summer home because the surroundings reminded him of his native Scotland. Beinn Bhreagh, the family's Canadian outpost, was equipped with a research laboratory so that he would never be far from his work. Bell died there on August 2, 1922 from complications of diabetes. Alexander Graham Bell had two daughters—Elsie May and Marian (known as Daisy)—and two sons—Edward and Robert—both of whom died in infancy.—C. M.

Suggested Reading: *Alexander Graham Bell Family Papers at the Library of Congress* (on-line); *Encyclopaedia Britannica* (on-line); *Library of Congress Information Bulletin* p76+ Apr. 1999; *Who's Who in America*, 1920-21; *World Who's Who in Science*, 1968; *Dictionary of Scientific Biography* Vol. 1 1970; Asimov, Isaac. *Asimov's Biographical Encyclopedia of Science and Technology*, 1982; *Library of North American Biographies* Vol. 3: Entrepreneurs and Inventors, 1990; Standage, Tom. *The Victorian Internet*, 1998

Bell, Gordon

Aug. 19, 1934– Computer designer

During his time at the Digital Equipment Corporation (DEC), Gordon Bell designed the architecture for the PDP series, which included the first minicomputers. His work helped to revolutionize computing by making the machines smaller and more affordable, and therefore more accessible. Bell then took much of his architecture and adapted it to DEC's VAX series, a family of 32-bit computers that could be hooked up to personal workstations and a larger mainframe computer to create a network. Today, Bell continues to be an innovator, as a senior researcher at Microsoft, where he works on such projects as parallel processing and telecommuting.

Chester Gordon Bell was born in Kirksville, Missouri, on August 19, 1934, the son of Roy Chester Bell and the former Lola Dolph Gordon. Roy owned an electrical-contracting and appliance-repair business, and Gordon began working with him at the age of six, learning how to fix appliances and even wire houses. "I had grown up in a small town and had no idea what an engineer was, other than in my mind, and [I] decided I wanted to be one at about age 10," he explained to David K. Allison for the Smithsonian Institution Oral and Video Histories project (on-line). "I went straight from Kirksville, Missouri to [the Massachusetts Institute of Technology] against the recommendation of a college math teacher friend of my father's. He said, 'You don't want to go to MIT, you'll be competing with all these guys from eastern prep schools.

Courtesy of Gordon Bell

Why, they all have had calculus and all you've had is algebra.' I went anyway."

In 1956 Bell received a bachelor's degree in electrical engineering from MIT and followed it with a master's degree in the same field a year later. Bell disliked the situation many new engineers found themselves in at large employers, which he described to Allison as "a sea of desks butted together, where you looked at someone to your right and left and across your desk." Hoping to avoid such a position for a while longer, after leaving MIT Bell studied at the University of New South Wales, in Australia, on a Fulbright Scholarship. There he taught that university's first course in computer design. While there he met another Fulbright scholar, Gwendolyn Kay Druyer. Upon returning to the United States in 1959 the pair married. They later had two children: Brigham Roy and Laura Louise.

From 1959 to 1960 Bell worked as an engineer in the Speech Communication Laboratory at MIT. He left in 1960 to work in Maynard, Massachusetts, as a computer design manager for DEC, which had been started in 1957 by Kenneth Olsen, a former associate from MIT. Olsen decided to market his computers primarily to science and engineering buyers—those who wouldn't necessarily need the advanced peripherals and software that came with mainframe computers from such competitors as IBM and Sperry Rand, because they would be building and designing their own. DEC headquarters were lodged in a Civil War–era wool mill in which Olsen had partitioned semi-private offices, thereby avoiding the crowding Bell found so distasteful at other workplaces.

Bell joined DEC just in time to finish the design work and develop the software library on the PDP-1. PDP stood for Programmed Data Processor, a name that DEC, acting on the advice of the venture capital firm that had financed the work, chose to use instead of calling the machine a "computer." The firm reasoned that, in 1960, no one would believe that a fully functional computer could cost only $125,000 when most mainframes couldn't be built for less than a million. Not only was the PDP-1 a fraction of the price, but at 250 pounds, the machine was only a quarter of the weight of other computers on the market, most notably the TX-0 computer on which it was modeled. The TX-0, built by MIT's Lincoln Laboratory, was the world's first fully transistorized computer and like other mainframes of the day, it was incredibly large, taking up more than 9,000 square feet of floor space.

Bell was the architect of the PDP-4, an even smaller and less costly model that DEC unveiled in 1962. "One application I remember [for the PDP-4] was to control a Nabisco baking factory," Bell told Allison. "There was a lot of concern . . . because we might [have been] liable if the computer stopped or dumped flour into the river."

Bell next directed the development of DEC's first 12-bit minicomputer, the PDP-5, which was at the time the smallest computer ever built. In 1963 the machine was completed and delivered to the Atomic Energy Commission, for whom it was designed to gather data on nuclear reactors. Bell then worked on the hardware design for the PDP-6 as well as its software. This machine, which debuted in 1964, was primarily used for artificial-intelligence research and time-sharing.

DEC had success with these early PDP systems, but in 1965 they introduced a computer that would reshape the entire industry. The PDP-8 was the first successfully mass-produced minicomputer. This computer, which had been designed by Edson deCastro with Bell as the chief engineer, was half the size of the PDP-5 and four times faster. Built with integrated circuits—then an emerging technology—the PDP-8 cost far less to produce and sold at half the cost of other machines. It was able to perform a computation in as quickly as three-millionths of a second and could transfer data at up to eight million bits per second.

The PDP-8 helped to popularize computers outside traditional realms of use such as research and accounting. Several hundred PDP-8s were shipped the first year; between 30,000 and 40,000 were sold in the next decade. On college campuses and in university laboratories, students could now experience computing in a way that had not been possible in the mainframe era. In *Computer: A History of the Information Machine* (1996), Martin Campbell-Kelly and William Aspray noted: "Many of the users of PDP-8s became very attached to them, regarding them as their 'personal' computers. Some users developed games for the machines, [and] the experience of hands-on computing produced a strong computer hobbyist culture, not only among students and young technicians but also in the community of seasoned engineers."

In 1966 Bell became an associate professor at Carnegie-Mellon University, in Pittsburgh, Pennsylvania. "I can look back and say maybe I was burned out when I went to Carnegie Tech," he told Allison. "The DPD-6 begot the PDP-10, so that was going on nicely. The 5 and 8 were well established and growing . . . and so the company was doing well. I didn't see that I was essential to the company." Still, he remained at DEC as a consultant, and he was the primary architect of the PDP-11, a 64-bit computer put on the market in 1970. The PDP-11 became the most widely used minicomputer in the world by 1980, and over the next 20 years DEC produced four generations of the machines.

In 1972 Bell returned to DEC as vice president of engineering, while continuing to teach at Carnegie-Mellon University. "I was planning to take on a visiting professorship in Australia," he recalled to Allison, "but Ken [Olsen] said: 'Come back and run engineering. We've got so much going on and nobody can control it.'" Bell and his staff began working on the VAX-11, a 32-bit minicomputer based on the successful PDP-11 series. VAX, which stood for Virtual Address eXtension, gave users a great deal more working memory than any earlier minicomputer system. The first VAX-11 was released in 1977, and a year later, Bell developed a plan that called for the VAX system to be used throughout a customer's organization by wiring personal workstations to a departmental minicomputer. These minicomputers were then hooked up to larger computers through a network uplink. Sales of the VAX systems increased at a phenomenal rate, and by the mid 1980s they accounted for nearly all of the company's profits. Bell has said that DEC focused on VAX to the exclusion of the personal computer, thereby missing a major trend.

Bell and Olsen began to clash, and the work environment became stressful. In 1983 Bell, who had just suffered a heart attack, left DEC to form a new computer company, Encore Computer, with Kenneth Fisher and Henry Burkhardt. At Encore he helped build a 20-processor system called the Multimax. Bell left Encore in 1986 to become an assistant director of computer science for the National Science Foundation (NSF), in Washington, D.C. The NSF was then under the leadership of Eric Bloch, a scientist at International Business Machines (IBM). "His charter to me," Bell told Allison, "[was to] pull all these various parts of NSF that do computer research together and create the directorate for computing. We'll call it CISE for Computer and Information Science and Engineering." Bell continued, "That was a tremendously exciting thing to do. I loved it. . . . That was just a great time—to get the various divisions in place and to establish their direction and priorities." Bell is particularly proud of his role in establishing a separate networking division, independent and distinct from the supercomputer division, paving the way for the Internet as we now know it.

Today, Gordon Bell remains a professor of electrical engineering and computer science at Carnegie-Mellon University. He works as a consultant for the Bell-Mason Group, supplying expert advice to start-ups. In 1979 he co-founded the now-defunct Computer Museum, in Boston, Massachusetts, with his wife. (In 1999 he became a founding board member of the Computer History Museum, in Mountain View, California, which contains many of the artifacts from the earlier museum.)

In 1995 Bell became a senior researcher for the Microsoft Corporation, where he works on scalable network and platform architectures, also known as SNAP, as well as on a system called Telework, in which an individual might fully participate in a working environment from a remote location. Bell has been presented with a host of awards for his work over the years, perhaps most notably the National Medal of Technology, presented by President George Bush in 1991. He himself awards a $5,000 Gordon Bell Prize every year, to recognize outstanding achievement in high-performance computing.

Bell is the author or co-author of numerous well-regarded books, including *Computer Structures* (1971), *Designing Computers and Digital Systems* (1972), *Computer Engineering* (1978), *Computer Structure* (1982), and *High-Tech Ventures: The Guide for Entrepreneurial Success* (1991). He enjoys bicycling, skiing, scuba diving, and fishing. He currently resides in San Francisco.—C. M.

Suggested Reading: Microsoft Web site; *Research Technology Management*, p4+ May/June 1996; Smithsonian Institution Oral and Video Histories Web site; Campbell-Kelly, Martin and William Aspray. *Computer: A History of the Information Machine*, 1996

Berliner, Emile

May 20, 1851–Aug. 3, 1929 Inventor

Alexander Graham Bell invented the telephone and Thomas Alva Edison invented the phonograph, but it was the lesser-known Emile Berliner who perfected these devices and made them functioning parts of everyday society. Berliner's development of a microphone for a telephone receiver vastly improved sound quality in telephones, while his creation of the flat phonograph, or gramophone, facilitated easier and better sound recording. He was mostly self-taught and applied his keen analytic skills to study a problem and quickly find a solution. As Roger Burlingame observed in the *Dictionary of American Biography* (supplement 1, 1944), Berliner "is a brilliant example of an obscure amateur able solely by his own effort to lift himself into recognition as one of the foremost inventors of his time."

The son of a Talmudic scholar, Emile Berliner was born on May 20, 1851 in Hanover, Germany. He was the fourth of Samuel M. and Sarah (Friedman) Berliner's 11 children. He studied at the Samson School, in Wolfenbüttel, graduating in 1865. Though an average student, Berliner became interested in music as a child. After graduation he found work as an apprentice printer and later served as a clerk in a Hanover dry-goods shop.

In order to escape the growing Prussian militarism in Germany, Berliner emigrated to the United States in 1870 and settled in Washington, D.C., where he worked in a family friend's dry-goods store. After three years he moved to New York City and took odd jobs—teaching German, selling glue, and painting backgrounds for photographs—in order to study physics part time at the Cooper Institute (now Cooper Union), in New York City. He eventually found a position in Constantine Fahlberg's chemical laboratory, where he conducted his earliest research. (In 1879 Fahlberg accidentally discovered the first artificial sweetener—saccharin.) He also began to study acoustics and electricity through a physics book lent to him by a friend.

In 1876 two significant events occurred in Berliner's life: he applied for American citizenship and read about Alexander Graham Bell's first public demonstration of the telephone at the International Centennial Exposition, in Philadelphia. Berliner had already been experimenting in the field of electrical communication; after hearing about

Emile Berliner

Hulton Archive by Getty Images

Bell's telephone he did what many other inventors of the era had tried to do—he improved on it. Since he had never seen Bell's telephone, he was not influenced by his model and took a different approach to the transmitter. (Bell's telephone, while perfectly functional, had poor sound transmission.) Berliner returned to Washington and set up an electrical laboratory in his home. He discussed his research with a friend, Alvan S. Richards, who was the chief operator of the Washington fire-alarm telegraph office. Through his conversations with Richards, he discovered that the harder a telegraph key was depressed, the stronger the current that ran through the telegraph wires would be.

Berliner's insight led him to the development of an improved transmitter. Bell's transmitter relied on the voice itself, which, through magnetic induction, produced a weak and oscillating current. Berliner's carbon microphone transmitter, by contrast, imposed voice undulations onto an already-existing current, which was generated by a battery. This type of transmitter, which came to be known as a microphone, not only allowed for greater volume and clarity, but also increased the range of communication since it relied on an outside power source—the battery.

Without any assistance from legal counsel, Berliner wrote a caveat describing the principle behind his transmitter and filed it with the U.S. Patent and Trademark Office on April 14, 1877. He did not receive his patent until 1891, after a 15-year battle with Edison, who had filed a patent for his own mouthpiece just weeks after Berliner. According to Burlingame, Berliner's well-worded caveat enabled him to retain primacy on his invention; other sources claim that Edison was eventual-

ly awarded priority of patent. In any case, in 1878 Berliner sold his microphone patent to the new Bell Telephone Company (later the American Telephone and Telegraph Company) for $50,000 and began work at the company's offices in Boston, Massachusetts, as the chief instrument inspector. After spending a few years perfecting his transmitter by adding an induction-coil transformer, among other improvements, he returned to Washington with the intention of finding new challenges.

Berliner soon became interested in the phonograph. The original phonograph, which had been invented by Edison in the late 1870s, played wax cylinders by running a needle over a series of hills and valleys etched on the cylinder's face. Edison's cylinders had many problems, most notably that each cylinder had to be recorded individually: no mass reproduction of the cylinders was possible.

Berliner improved the phonograph by first using a flat disc, or record, that played and recorded by means of a needle that moved horizontally along a groove cut in the disc. Whereas Edison's needle had to be propelled across the cylinder, Berliner's needle followed the groove without the aid of an outside mechanism. Berliner also developed a mass duplicating system that allowed many records to be produced from a master disc, usually a nickel-plated copper cast. For a durable recording material he devised a shellac composition that was used until the late 1980s, when records were replaced by digital compact discs. Taken together, Berliner's innovations allowed inexpensive mass duplication and quality sound, forming the foundation of the recording industry for 100 years.

After patenting his gramophone, in 1887, Berliner established the Gramophone Company to manufacture and market it. In order to promote his machine he asked such popular opera singers as Enrico Caruso and Dame Nellie Melba to record for him. He also founded Germany's Deutsche Grammophon and Britain's Gramophone Company, Ltd. to promote his invention in Europe. In 1908 he adopted *His Master's Voice*, Francis Barraud's painting of a dog listening to a phonograph, as his company's official trademark. The Victor Talking Machine Company (later RCA) later bought out the Gramophone Company and adopted the trademark.

After the turn of the century Berliner turned his attention to the field of aeronautics. In 1908 he became the first inventor to perfect a lightweight revolving-cylinder internal-combustion motor for airplanes. Eleven years later he and his son, Henry A. Berliner, designed a helicopter that could rise and sustain itself in the air. In 1925 he returned to the study of acoustics and developed the first acoustic tiles and cells for concert halls and recording studios.

In addition to his scientific contributions, Berliner aided social causes. In 1901, after one of his daughters developed an illness that he believed was contracted from raw milk, he began to campaign for the compulsory pasteurization of milk and dairy products. This practice was eventually adopted by the United States government. In 1911 he established a fellowship to give qualified women the opportunity to conduct scientific research. From 1915 to 1921 he was president of the District of Columbia's Tuberculosis Association.

For his invention of the gramophone, Berliner was awarded the John Scott Award, given by the city of Philadelphia for useful inventions, and the Elliot Cresson Gold Medal from Philadelphia's Franklin Institute, a science museum.

Berliner married Cora Adler on October 26, 1881. The couple had six children: Herbert, Hannah, Edgar, Louise, Henry, and Alice. He died of a cerebral hemorrhage on August 3, 1929, at the age of 78.—C. M.

Suggested Reading: *Inventors Hall of Fame* (online); Asimov, Isaac. *Asimov's Biographical Encyclopedia of Science and Technology*, 1982; *Chambers Biographical Dictionary*, 1997; *Dictionary of American Biography*, Supplement 1, 1944

Berners-Lee, Tim

June 8, 1955– Creator of the World Wide Web

As creator of the World Wide Web, Tim Berners-Lee has had a tremendous impact on the daily lives of people across the planet—rivaling that of more-famous computer visionaries such as Steve Jobs or Bill Gates. During the 1980s, Berners-Lee imagined an easy way to exchange information across the Internet by using hypertext to link documents. To this end he developed HTML (HyperText Mark-up Language), which allows for such links; URL (Universal Resource Locator) addresses, which direct a browser to Internet documents; and HTTP (HyperText Transfer Protocol), the rules by which such documents are linked together. His invention brought a streamlined order to Internet cyberspace, allowing users all over the world to access information. The backbone of the Internet is formed by millions of networked computers, but it is the World Wide Web that allows users to click on a word or an image and access text, pictures, sounds, and software, in a seemingly endless abundance. Today, Berners-Lee works behind the scenes at the World Wide Web Consortium, which helps competing companies keep their software products in line with Web specifications, and which studies issues of security, intellectual property, and free speech in the on-line community. Through this work, he is able to assist the Web's growth and development far into the future. He believes the Web has the potential not only for individual expression, but for social change. In *Canadian Social Studies* (Winter 1997), Jack Dale quoted Berners-Lee's vision for the Web: "I would like to bring our friends and colleagues closer, in that by working on this knowledge together we can come to better understandings. If misunderstandings are the cause of many of the world's woes, then can we not work them out in cyberspace. And, having worked them out, we leave for those who follow a trail of our reasoning and assumptions for them to adopt, or correct."

Tim Berners-Lee was born in London, England, on June 8, 1955. His parents were computer scientists who met while working on the Ferranti Mark I, the world's first commercially sold computer. He received his high-school education at the Emanuel School in London between 1969 and 1973. Through his parents' guidance, he quickly learned to think in unusual ways—as a child he recalls playing games with imaginary numbers over breakfast. He soon developed his parents' interest in computers, initially playing with make-believe computers made from cardboard boxes and later, at Queen's College, at Oxford University, building his first real computer from an old television set and a leftover processor.

Berners-Lee studied physics at Oxford, which he considered to be a good compromise between electronics and mathematics. He graduated, with honors, in 1976 and immediately set out on a career in computing. Between 1976 and 1978 he worked at a large British telecommunications equipment manufacturer, Plessey Telecommunications Ltd., located in the town of Poole, in Dorset. There he worked on emerging bar-code technology as well as message relays and distributed transaction systems. He left Plessey in 1978 to work for D. G. Nash Ltd. in Ferndown, another town in Dorset, where he wrote software for a variety of computer applications, including typesetting and a multitasking operating system.

For the next year and a half, Berners-Lee worked as an independent computer consultant. From June until December 1980 he was a software engineer at CERN, the European Particle Physics Laboratory, in Geneva, Switzerland. During the course of his time there he had to learn the laboratory's complicated information system, a task that he felt his often forgetful brain could not handle. He decided to write a computer program to act as a sort of personal memory substitute, something that could store information and use random associations. He called the program "Enquire-Within-Upon-Everything," or "Enquire" for short. This system provided a number of easily accessible links between documents. Since the computer mouse had not yet been invented, the links were accessed by entering a number code. Today, such links are called hypertext and are accessed by clicking on an underlined or colored word, which then leads to a different location.

Hypertext was not Berners-Lee's invention. In 1945 Vannevar Bush, a computer pioneer, wrote an article for the *Atlantic Monthly* in which he described a theoretical electromechanical device called a memex, which would make and follow links between documents on microfiche. In the mid-1960s a computer scientist named Ted Nelson drew on Bush's work to develop a software framework called Xanadu; in the process he coined the word "hypertext." In 1968 Douglas Engelbart completed his prototype for an "oNLine System" (NLS), which linked documents through hypertext, allowed more than one person to work on a document, and gave users the ability to communicate on a system through e-mail. In order to manipulate all these functions, Engelbart invented the mouse.

While Enquire proved useful at CERN, Berners-Lee did not publish his work on it then, though it formed the rudimentary basis for the World Wide Web. He left CERN after his work as a consultant was finished and, in 1981, joined John Poole's Image Computer Systems Ltd., where he was in charge of technical design. He worked on graphics and communication software, firmware (programs essential to a computer's operation), and a general macro language, until 1984. In that year he returned to CERN, this time taking up a fellowship to work on distributed real time systems for scientific data acquisition and system control.

During this time at CERN, Berners-Lee began to conceive of a different type of Enquire system: Instead of limiting the links to documents on his own computer, why not link up all the computers of his colleagues at CERN, as well as those of CERN's associates in laboratories around the world? Almost 15 years old, the Internet had proven to be a reliable networking system, but it was still cumbersome to use. The question that burned in Berners-Lee's mind was how to simplify the exchange of information. As he told Robert Wright in *Time* (May 19, 1997): "In 1989, I thought, look, it would be so much easier if everybody asking me questions all the time could just read my database, and it would be so much nicer if I could find out what these guys are doing by just jumping into a similar database of information for them." Hypertext systems, at that time, had centralized databases that maintained all the links; this meant that a link would never be left "dangling"—i.e., that it would never point to a document or location that no longer existed. When Berners-Lee discussed decentralizing the system in order to create a global network, his associates brought up the difficulty of keeping track of all deleted links. Berners-Lee eventually realized that, in order for a hypertext system to be truly universal, it would have to become a bit less reliable, open to the occasional broken link.

When, in 1989, Berners-Lee first drafted a proposal for a global hypertext project, his bosses at CERN were skeptical; "This initial document," he told Wright, "didn't go down well." He pressed the issue, and eventually won approval to purchase a NeXT computer, which would act as the Web's first server. With a team of colleagues, he developed HyperText Mark-up Language (HTML), an easy-to-learn document coding system that allows users to click onto a link in a document's text and connect to another document. He also created an addressing plan that allowed each Web page to

have a specific location known as a universal resource locator, or URL. Finally, he completed work on HyperText Transfer Protocol, or HTTP, a system for linking these documents across the Internet. He then wrote the software for the first server (which would supply files and services) and the first Web client, a browser/editor program that would allow any computer user to view and navigate Web pages on their own computers, as well as create and post their own Web documents.

Berners-Lee's invention still needed a name. As he wrote in his book, *Weaving the Web* (1999), which is quoted on *Amazon.com*: "I thought of Mine of Information, or MOI, but *moi* in French means 'me,' and that was too egocentric. . . . The Information Mine (TIM) was even more egocentric!" He finally settled on World Wide Web, or WWW for short, even though his wife and colleagues complained that the abbreviation took longer to say than the actual name. In December 1990 the Web browser was running within CERN, and in the summer of 1991 it was running on the Internet at large, "instantly bringing order and clarity to the chaos that was cyberspace," according to Joshua Quittner in *Time* (March 29, 1999). Berners-Lee convinced CERN to waive any rights to the Web as intellectual property, so that the World Wide Web was made freely available to the public.

In the early years of the Web, Berners-Lee shaped the design as it formed, getting feedback from users and making refinements. He generally improved the specifications of URLs, HTTP, and HTML as the technology spread across the Internet. In the first five years, the number of Internet and Web users grew together at exponential rates, from 600,000 to 40 million, according to Quittner. "Berners-Lee's innovation," a *Technology Review* (July 1996) writer maintained, "was to apply the idea of hypertext to the growing reality of networked computers. His timing was just right."

Today the Internet is used by most people as an instantaneous mailing system or as a giant encyclopedia. Berners-Lee, however, had imagined the WWW to be a vehicle for the exchange of information: "less of a television channel and more of an interactive sea of shared knowledge," he has said, as quoted by Jack Dale. In the early days of the Web, a young computer scientist named Marc Andreessen wrote a Web browser, Mosaic, which was the first to combine text and images in one window. It became extremely popular because of this user-friendly multimedia interface, but it didn't have an editor component—like Berners-Lee's editor/browser program—so that Mosaic users couldn't create and post their own Web pages. By what Berners-Lee described to Wright as an "accident of fate," most of the first commercially successful Web programs have been browsers, and not editors. Since posting documents remains a more difficult task than Berners-Lee had envisioned, the majority of Internet users passively view the Web, rather than actively contribute to it.

When asked by an interviewer from *Technology Review* (July 1996) how the Web has departed from his original vision, Berners-Lee responded: "The original idea was that anybody would very easily be able to write documents that could be connected through hypertext links. What has surprised me is the way people have been prepared to put up with manually encoding text. HTML was never supposed to be something that you would see—it was intended to be something produced by an editor program. An analogy is with word processors. Computer users don't have to write in all kinds of codes to format their documents with fonts, margins, and so on. So it staggers me that people have actually put up with having to write HTML by hand. . . . URL syntax was never intended for human consumption. It was intended for a machine."

While many early Web developers—including Andreessen—became Internet entrepreneurs, Berners-Lee eventually chose an academic and administrative life. He left CERN in the early 1990s and spent research stints at various laboratories, including Xerox's Palo Alto Research Center (PARC), in California, and the Laboratory for Computer Science at the Massachusetts Institute of Technology (MIT), in Cambridge. In 1992 Berners-Lee met Michael Dertouzos, the director of the Laboratory for Computer Science, who had also dreamed of building a global information marketplace. "He was into the gigantic brain thing, building a network to store all the world's knowledge," Dertouzos recalled of his first meeting with Berners-Lee, in an interview with Simson L. Garfinkel for *Technology Review* (November/December 1998). "He did not quite see the commercial aspects at the time. But one thing was obvious: the intersection of our views." The pair convinced MIT and CERN to co-host a consortium to aid the development of the Web. Called the World Wide Web Consortium, or W3C, it was set up so that technology companies could pay a membership fee to get early access to the consortium's technology, and in turn could help to direct development of the Web. The consortium opened in October 1994 with Berners-Lee as the director. Though CERN backed out after two months, it was replaced by INRIA (the French National Institute for Research in Computer Science and Control). W3C members give advice to Berners-Lee, who in turn issues recommendations, which—though not legally binding— "carry a moral authority that is the closest thing the Internet has to law," according to Garfinkel. Thus, the founder of the Web still guides the development of his technology, making sure that competing technologies remain coordinated worldwide, and working to prevent the balkanization of the Web into many different fiefdoms. The consortium has hundreds of member companies, including Microsoft and Netscape, and has teams at MIT, INRIA in France, and at Keio University, in Japan.

Most recently, Berners-Lee and W3C have been developing software like P3P, the Platform for Privacy Preferences, which allows an Internet user to select the level of privacy he wants from companies interested in user information and preferences. They have also developed PICS, the Platform for Internet Content Selection, which allows a user to install filtering software that prevents children from viewing certain sites.

Since 1995 Tim Berners-Lee has received numerous awards for his development of the Web, including the Kilby Foundation's Young Inventor of the Year Award (1995), the IEEE Computer Society Wallace McDowell Award (1996), the 1998 Charles Babbage Award, and a 1998 MacArthur "genius" grant. In 1999 *Time* magazine named him one of the 100 greatest minds of the 20th century. The breathtaking growth of the Web has been "an incredibly good feeling," Berners-Lee told Wright, and "a lesson for all dreamers . . . that you can have a dream and it can come true."

He is married to Nancy Carlson, an American he met in Europe. He and his wife have two children.—C. M.

Suggested Reading: *Canadian Social Studies* p100+ Winter 1997; *Internet World* p58+ Jan. 1, 2000; *Newsweek* p134 Sep. 27, 1999; *New York Times* D p1 Dec. 18, 1995; *Technology Review* p32+ July 1996, p38+ Nov./Dec. 1998; Tim Berners-Lee Home Page; *Time* p64+ May 19, 1997, p153 Mar. 29, 1999

Berry, Clifford

Apr. 19, 1918–Oct. 30, 1963 Co-developer of electronic computing

When John V. Atanasoff built the world's first electronic digital computer in 1940, he did not do it alone. By his side throughout the planning and design process was a young graduate student by the name of Clifford Berry. Although often overshadowed by Atanasoff, Berry was an integral part of this crucial event in the history of computers. With Berry's assistance, Atanasoff was able to bring his dream to fruition, and he named his machine the Atanasoff-Berry Computer, or ABC. For many years Atanasoff and Berry went unrecognized as the codevelopers of fully-electronic computing, and Berry did not live to see the 1973 court decision which gave Atanasoff the proper credit for their landmark achievement, in place of John Mauchly and J. Presper Eckert, who had gotten the idea for their electronic computer, the ENIAC, from the ABC.

On April 19, 1918 Clifford Edward Berry was born in Gladbrook, Iowa, to Fred Gordon Berry and Grace (Strohm) Berry. He was the oldest of four children, the others being his brothers Keith and Frederick and sister Barbara. Fred Berry owned an electric appliance repair shop where his personal projects included the construction of the first radio in the town of Gladbrook. He taught his oldest son all about how the radio was made and how it worked, and young Clifford became enthralled with all things electric, experimenting with many of the things he found in his father's shop. Under his father's supervision, he was able to build his own radio at the age of 11.

Berry displayed remarkable academic aptitude as a child. Both his school principal and his second grade teacher wanted to move him a grade ahead, but his parents were apprehensive about such a measure. Gradually the principal was able to convince Fred and Grace Berry that their son needed more of a challenge, and Clifford was permitted to skip from third to fifth grade.

In 1929, the Berry family moved from Gladbrook to Marengo, another small Iowa town, where Berry's father had accepted a position as the manager of the Iowa Power Company's local office. Five years later, while Berry was in his sophomore year of high school, his father was shot and killed by an angry former employee whom he had recently fired. After the death of his father, Berry decided to attend Iowa State University after he finished high school. Fred Berry had always recommended that school to his son due to its outstanding College of Engineering, which he believed was perfectly suited to Clifford's intention of pursuing a degree in electrical engineering. The Berry family remained in Marengo until Clifford graduated high school; after Clifford was accepted into Iowa State, they moved to Ames, Iowa, where the university was located.

Berry continued to succeed in his scholastic endeavors throughout his undergraduate years, and in 1939, he received a B.A. in electrical engineering. At that point he made a personal connection that would have a defining effect on the course of his life and work. One of his electrical engineering professors, Harold Anderson, happened to be a close friend of John Atanasoff, a professor of physics and mathematics at Iowa State who was planning the construction of an electronic, digital, computing machine. Having been favorably impressed by Berry's academic performance, Anderson recommended him to Atanasoff, who was searching for a capable graduate student in electrical engineering to assist him in realizing his project. "Berry is a brilliant student, has a tremendous grasp of mechanical construction, and is well-grounded in electronics," Anderson told Atanasoff, as quoted in *The History of Computers* (online).

After being informed of Anderson's recommendation, Berry contacted Atanasoff to express his interest in the assistantship, and the two men met for the first time in the spring of 1939. Their initial meeting basically concerned the concepts that would be relevant, and the problems that they would face, in building Atanasoff's computer, which, if successful, would be the first of its kind. Up until this point, all computing machines were either entirely mechanical as in the case of Vannevar Bush's differential analyzer, or comprised of a mixture of mechanical and electrical components as with Howard Aiken's Mark I. What Atanasoff envisioned, in contrast, was a computer that would be entirely electronic and run on a digital system, as opposed to the then-standard analog system. It would also be the first computer to use vacuum tubes for electrical relays, and the first to process data using a binary number system which is still the predominant method at the end of the 20th century.

After meeting with him several times, Atanasoff decided that in addition to Berry's other qualifications, he "had vision and inventive skill" (*The History of Computers*). Berry was officially given the job as Atanasoff's assistant, and the two men immediately set to work constructing a prototype. They were able to complete an operating model in a relatively short time, spurred on by the need to have something to demonstrate to Iowa State College officials in order to obtain a research grant, which they would require to pursue the project any further than the prototype stage. By the end of 1939, Atanasoff and Berry were able to show their preliminary version of the computer to the Iowa State College Research Council, which judged the project worthy of a grant of $850. This money was to be used in the construction of a full-scale, computing machine capable of higher mathematical functions, such as solving extensive systems of equations.

After the Christmas holidays, Berry began working with Atanasoff to create a finished version of the computer. Construction took place in their basement laboratory at Iowa State, with both men suggesting ideas and improvements. The machine was well on its way to completion by 1940, and was named the Atanasoff-Berry Computer, cleverly shortened to ABC. Aware of the landmark importance of their invention, the two men sought to patent the device. With Berry's assistance, Atanasoff wrote a 35-page manuscript entitled "Computing Machines for the Solution of Large Systems of Linear Algebraic Equations," a copy of which was sent to Chicago patent lawyer Richard R. Trexler in an attempt to protect the ABC. However, due primarily to an abundance of bureaucratic red tape on the part of Iowa State, a patent was never acquired for the device. One of the consequences of this was that a colleague of Atanasoff's, John Mauchly, was able to incorporate elements he observed in the ABC into the computer he later invented with J. Presper Eckert, which was dubbed the ENIAC. For years Mauchly and Eckert were credited with having invented the first electronic digital computer, and it wasn't until 1973, 10 years after Berry's death, that a court decision overturned their claim and gave the credit to Atanasoff and Berry.

Work on the ABC continued until 1941, when the entrance of the United States into World War II brought it to an abrupt halt. Atanasoff departed from Iowa State University to work in a defense-related position at the U.S. Naval Ordnance Laboratory in Washington, D.C., leaving Berry to continue his graduate studies. In 1941 he received an M.S. in physics. On May 30 of the following year, Berry married Martha Jean Reed in Ames, Iowa. A fellow Iowa State graduate, Reed had been working as John Atanasoff's secretary when she and Berry met. The couple would go on to have two children, Carol and David.

Shortly after marrying, the couple left Iowa for Pasadena, California, where Berry had accepted a defense-related position with the Consolidated Engineering Corporation (CEC). He continued his education despite his relocation and new job, working towards a Ph.D. in physics, under a special arrangement with Iowa State University. He completed the Ph.D. in 1948 with a doctoral thesis entitled "The Effects of Initial Energies on Mass Spectra."

Berry remained with CEC, becoming chief physicist in 1949. Three years later, he became assistant director of research. In 1959 he was named director of engineering of the Analytical and Control Division, of which he also served as the technical director. After 22 years of employment, Berry left CEC in October 1963 for the Vacuum-Electronics Corporation in Plainview, New York, where he had accepted a position as manager of advanced development.

Berry was a prolific innovator and researcher in physics and electronics. Over the course of his life, he was issued 11 patents in various areas of electronics, as well as 19 in mass spectrometry. At the time of his death he had 13 additional patents still pending. He wrote articles for a wide range of scientific publications, among them *The Journal of Applied Physics*, *The Annual Review of Nuclear Science*, *The National Bureau of Standards*, and *Physics Review*. He also contributed a chapter to *McGraw-Hill's Process Instruments and Controls Handbook*. Among the numerous scientific and academic societies and organizations to which he belonged were Phi Kappa Phi, Pi Mu Epsilon, Sigma Xi, the American Physical Society, the American Vacuum Society, and the American Association for the Advancement of Science.

Clifford Berry died unexpectedly and somewhat mysteriously on October 30, 1963, shortly after arriving in New York; his family was preparing to join him there at the time. Although he did not live to see the court decision that gave proper recognition to his work with John Atanasoff, he has since gained the status of a trailblazer in computer technology.—B. S.

Suggested Reading: *The History of Computers* (on-line); Spencer, Donald D. *The Timetable of Computers*, 1997

Bezos, Jeff

(BAY-zoes)

Jan. 12, 1964– Founder of Amazon.com

In 1994 Jeff Bezos, an executive with the financial trading firm D. E. Shaw, in New York City, came across a study that reported that Internet usage was growing 2,300 percent every year. He concluded that conducting business through the Internet had a viable and profitable future. Bezos quit his job, which provided him with a six-figure income, and headed west to Seattle, Washington, to set up his new on-line business. The entrepreneur decided to sell books, reasoning that computers would make it easy for customers to browse through the 1.5 million titles available in English alone. No "brick-and-mortar" bookstore on Earth could hold that many titles; an on-line bookseller, however, could provide information about the book and obtain it within days for the customer. Operating from Bezos's garage, Amazon.com went on-line in July 1995. Although Bezos did not advertise his new venture, he got orders from customers in all 50 states in just the first month. The existence of a bookseller able to obtain virtually any book in print spread by word of mouth. Over the next few years, annual sales increased by astronomical proportions. As the chief executive officer of Amazon.com, Bezos also oversaw the company's ex-

Mario Tama/Getty Images

pansion into a super retailer, selling music, videos, DVDs, toys, software, tools, and kitchenware. Many observers have credited with Bezos with changing the way people shop and conduct business. Citing his achievements and role as an Internet pioneer, *Time* magazine in 1999 named Jeff Bezos its "Person of the Year."

Jeff Bezos was born Jeffrey Preston Jorgensen on January 12, 1964 in Albuquerque, New Mexico. His biological parents divorced about 18 months after he was born. For a short time Jeff and his mother, Jackie, lived with her parents. In 1966 Jackie met Miguel Bezos, a Cuban immigrant and a student at the University of Albuquerque. (The university was taken over by the College of Santa Fe in 1986.) Bezos legally adopted Jeff, who took his surname. After completing his education, the elder Bezos moved the family, which had grown to three children, to Houston, Texas, where he worked as a petroleum engineer for the Exxon Corporation.

Jeff Bezos showed early signs that he was a gifted child. At the age of three, he dismantled his crib with a screwdriver, in order to build himself a bed. During the summer months Bezos lived on his grandfather's ranch, in Cotulla, Texas. The young man performed odd jobs around the ranch, such as fixing windmills, laying pipes, and repairing pumps. Before retiring to the ranch, Jeff's grandfather, Lawrence Preston Gise, had worked on space technology and missile defense systems and was later appointed by the United States Congress to serve as the manager of the Atomic Energy Commission's operations office in Albuquerque. In an article for *Wired* (March 1999, on-line), Chip Bayers wrote, "His grandfather sparked and indulged Jeff's fascination with educational games and toys, assisting him with the Heathkits [a popular line of build-it-yourself electronic kits, which are no longer manufactured] and the other paraphernalia he constantly hauled home to the family garage." Growing up, Bezos remained fascinated by gadgets. "I think single- handedly we kept many Radio Shacks in business," his mother recalled to Bayers.

At age eight Bezos took a standardized test that confirmed his high intelligence. His parents enrolled him in a pilot program for gifted students at River Oaks Elementary School, in Houston, Texas. Each morning, Bezos traveled 20 miles from his home to the school. In an article for the *Washington Post* (September 3, 2000), Mark Leibovich wrote, "One of [Bezos's] early feats involved a teletype machine that could be connected to a mainframe computer by a modem. None of the teachers knew how to use a computer, but Jeff and a few other children figured out how to program it." Bezos caught the eye of Julie Ray, a local author, and in 1977 she published, *Turning on Bright Minds: A Parent Looks at Gifted Education in Texas*, a book that described a typical school day for him. To protect his identity, Ray changed his name to "Tim." (According to Bayers, the book was sold locally in Houston and cannot be purchased through Amazon.com.)

In 1978 Exxon transferred Miguel Bezos to the corporation's office in Miami, Florida. The family settled in the affluent Palmetto district, in Dade County. Jeff enrolled in Palmetto High School. Around this time Bezos was thinking seriously about becoming an astronaut. He envisioned himself running a space shuttle business that would ferry passengers from the earth into outer space.

Bezos graduated from high school, in 1982, as the class valedictorian. He was also one of three students in his graduating class who won the *Miami Herald's* Silver Knight Award, which recognized academic excellence. He spent the summer before he began college running his own business, which he set up with his then girlfriend, Uschi Werner. They established the Dream Institute, an educational summer camp for children. As Bayers explains, Dream was an acronym for Directed Reasoning Methods. The camp attracted six students, including Bezos's brother and sister, who paid $600 each. The curriculum ranged from such books as Robert Louis Stevenson's *Treasure Island* and Charles Dickens' *David Copperfield* to such science-fiction classics as Frank Herbert's *Dune* and Robert Heinlein's *Stranger in a Strange Land*. Bezos and Werner also gave lectures on such scientific topics as fossil fuels and space travels.

In the fall of 1982 Jeff Bezos began his undergraduate studies at Princeton University, in New Jersey. Determined to follow in the footsteps of Albert Einstein and Stephen Hawking, he set his sights on a career as a theoretical physicist. Bezos discovered quickly that he did not measure up to some of the other students in the class. "I looked around the room," Bezos told Bayers, "and it was clear to me that there were three people in the class who were much, much better at it than I was, and it was much, much easier for them. It was really sort of a startling insight that there were people whose brains were wired differently." Bezos switched to computer science and electrical engineering. In 1986 he graduated, summa cum laude, with a B.S. and Phi Beta Kappa membership.

Several prominent companies such as Intel, Bell Labs, and Andersen Consulting made generous offers to Bezos after he completed his education. Instead, he took a job with Fitel, a start-up company in New York City, that wanted to build a worldwide communications network for trading firms. Bezos left Fitel after two years because it failed to get off the ground. He then accepted a position with the Bankers Trust Corporation, where he developed software applications for the company's pension fund clients. Although he became a vice president within 10 months of his hiring, Bezos became disillusioned with the company's resistance to change. D. E. Shaw, a financial trading company that used the latest computer technology, hired him, in 1990. Bezos was impressed by the company's founder, David Shaw, who had earned a Ph.D. in computer science from Stanford University, in California. According to Leibovich, "many of the business practices Bezos later adopted at Amazon he learned from Shaw." D. E. Shaw promoted Bezos to senior vice president when he was 28 years old, making him one of the youngest people in the financial services sector to hold that position.

The increased popularity of the Internet prompted Bezos and David Shaw to look into possible on-line business opportunities around 1994. Although Bezos initially doubted the astronomical growth rates that were being reported in Internet usage, he ultimately concluded that the methodology used to calculate the rates was reasonable. Such a growth rate offered unlimited opportunities for selling products on-line, and Bezos decided that the time had come for him to start his own business. Although Shaw tried to get him to stay, Bezos left the company, in 1994, to pursue his dream and set up shop in what was still considered unchartered territory.

Bezos drew up a list of 20 products that could be sold through the Internet. He concluded that books were the ideal choice. "There are 1.5 million English-language books in print at any given time," he said to Karen Southwick for *Upside* (October 1996). "If you take all languages worldwide, it's about 3 million books active and in print. So when you're talking about a large number of titles like that, that's where computers really start to shine because of their sorting and organizing capabilities."

Bezos and his wife, Mackenzie, left New York City for Seattle, Washington, in 1995. Seattle offered Bezos a large pool of technically skilled workers and was also located near the largest book distribution center in the United States. To convey the venture's enormity, he named it after the Amazon, the world's largest river. To get Amazon.com off the ground, Bezos raised $1 million from investors and used $300,000 from his parents' and his own savings. The first two employees he hired were the engineers who helped him set up Amazon.com's Web site on the Internet. Bezos operated the company out of his garage, where he kept the three large computers that ran the site.

Amazon.com came on-line in July 1995. According to Leibovich, the company's sales in the first week totaled $12,438, and by the end of the month, Bezos had received orders from customers in all 50 states. By the end of the year, the bookseller posted $540,000 in sales. The massive number of titles offered undoubtedly attracted many customers to the site, and personal computers made browsing for and ordering books easy. Bezos also made customer service a top priority. "We may be the most customer-obsessed company ever to occupy planet Earth," he told Peter de Jonge for the *New York Times Magazine* (March 14,1999). "Making money on books was almost irrelevant, compared with establishing Amazon.com as the most trusted brand in this new space."

In 1996 Amazon.com's sales increased to $15.7 million. Although on-line shopping for various products had been available for more than a decade, Jeff Bezos helped popularize the method, which quickly became as common as a visit to a mall. Impressed by the phenomenal success of Amazon.com, many other companies began turning to the Internet to seek out new markets and attract customers. Such leading bookstore chains as Barnes and Noble and Borders also began selling books on-line.

Amazon.com began a phenomenal rate of growth that continued uninterrupted for the next few years, surprising many financial analysts. According to an article in the *Wall Street Journal* (November 29, 1999), the bookseller's sales totaled $147.5 million in 1997 and $610 million in 1998. To raise additional capital Amazon.com went public, in March 1997. According to Leibovich, the price of a share of stock in the company had risen an astounding 233 percent by the end of 1997. Starting in 1998, Bezos began selling other products in order to attract new customers, and by 2000, in addition to books, Amazon.com was selling CDs, videos, DVDs, toys, electronics, tools, lawn furniture, and kitchenware to tens of millions of customers in nearly every part of the world. In the company's promotional literature, "the world's largest bookstore" became known as simply "the world's largest store." In 1999 sales crossed the billion-dollar mark, a remarkable achievement given the fact that Bezos had started Amazon.com in his garage only four years earlier.

Although they were impressed with Amazon.com's progressive growth and annual sales, many financial analysts and journalists observed that the company failed to make a profit. In fact, as sales increased each year, they were matched by increased losses. According to Leibovich, despite reaping $1.6 billion in revenue in 1999, Amazon.com reported $719 million in losses the same year. Bezos has said repeatedly that letting the company lose money in the short term was part of his strategy to expand Amazon.com and ensure its future profitability. "Long-term profitability and building an important and lasting and sustained company is incredibly important to us," he explained to a reporter for *BusinessWeek* (May 31, 1999). "We just believe that, by investing now, we increase our chances of achieving those things."

Jeff Bezos reached what many consider the pinnacle of personal success, in 1999, when *Time* magazine named him Person of the Year. In an article for *Time* (December 27, 1999, on-line), Joshua Cooper Ramo, an editor at the magazine, explained why the coveted honor was presented to Bezos. "Every time a seismic shift takes place in our economy, there are people who feel the vibrations long before the rest of us do, vibrations so strong they demand action—action that can seem rash, even stupid," Ramo wrote. "Jeffrey Preston Bezos had that same experience when he first peered into the maze of connected computers called the World Wide Web and realized the future of retailing was glowing back at him."

The year 2000 brought unexpected problems for Amazon.com. Morale problems and a high turnover rate in the workforce plagued the on-line retailer. A report written by Ravi Suria, a financial analyst with Lehman Brothers, asserted that Amazon.com was operating with a "weak balance sheet, poor working capital management, and massive negative operating cashflow—the financial characteristics that have driven innumerable retailers to disaster through history," as quoted by Jane Martinson for the *Guardian* (June 27, 2000). The release of the report alarmed investors, and the price of company's stock fell from $106 in December 1999 to $41.50 in September 2000. Bezos dismissed the Lehman Brothers report as "pure, unadulterated hogwash," as quoted by Leibovich. To cut costs and make the company profitable, Bezos laid off 1,300 employees, 15 percent of Amazon.com's workforce, in February 2001. Bezos also stopped selling products that he deemed unprofitable and scaled back the company's inventory. In an article for the *Detroit News* (April 26, 2001), Allison Linn wrote that Amazon.com confirmed that it was being investigated by the Securities and Exchange Commission (SEC) for violating insider trading laws, but that Bezos denied any wrongdoing and said that he was cooperating with the authorities.

Jeff Bezos is married to the former Mackenzie Tuttle, whom he met while working for D. E. Shaw. They have one child and live in Seattle, Washington.—D. C.

Suggested Reading: *BusinessWeek* p137+ May 31, 1999, with photo; *Detroit News* p3 Apr. 26, 2001; *Guardian* II p2+ June 27, 2000; *New York Times Magazine* p6+ Mar. 14, 1999, with photos; *Time* (on-line) Dec. 27, 1999, with photos; *Upside* p29+ Oct. 1996, p76+ Sep. 1998; *Wall Street Journal* B p6 Feb. 2, 2001; *Washington Post* A p1+ Sep. 3, 2000, with photos; *Wired* (on-line) Mar. 1999

Bigelow, Julian

1913–Feb. 17, 2003 Cybernetics pioneer

As chief engineer on the Electronic Computer Project of the Institute for Advanced Studies (IAS), the American electrical engineer Julian Bigelow played a significant role in one of the defining moments of computer history. Completed in 1952, the IAS computer was to have a profound influence on the computer advances it preceded. Bigelow was hand-picked for the crucial position by the mathematician who had conceptualized the new machine, John von Neumann. As chief engineer, he contributed a great deal to the actual design of the IAS computer, a machine intended to perform scientific calculations at previously unattainable speeds. In addition, von Neumann intended for his computer to have certain self-regulating, or "cybernetic" qualities, which made Bigelow even more appropriate for the project. Prior to working at the IAS, he had been involved in military research during World War II, part of which focused on self-correcting computer technology that would minimize the need for constant human intervention; Bigelow had been a pioneer in the study of cybernetics.

Julian Himley Bigelow was born in 1913, and he developed an interest in automatic computing at the outbreak of World War II. He served in the Fire Control Division of the National Defense Research Committee (NDRC) as an engineer, where he conducted scientific research to aid the American war effort. During his tenure with the Fire Control Division, Bigelow worked as an assistant to his fellow engineer Norbert Wiener, mainly on projects involving automatic computing. He provided additional support on various projects through his involvement with the NDRC's Applied Mathematics Panel.

Chief among Bigelow's computing tasks was the construction of automated mechanisms for anti-aircraft artillery. When NDRC's chairman, Vannevar Bush—the inventor of the differential analyzer, the first fully functional mechanical computer—was confronted with the problem of building radar-controlled anti-aircraft guns, he tapped Wiener and Bigelow's expertise. Exploring ways to improve the gun-control mechanism, the two men promptly discovered the importance of a phenomenon known as feedback loops, by which past output can be used to predict future output. This complicated concept could be used, for example, to direct automatic artillery, steam engines, autopilots, and other self-steering machines. In such systems, a small part of the information output is returned to the central source as present input, in order to determine future output. Wiener and Bigelow figured that servomechanisms—devices that would automatically correct the performance of a machine—could use this radar feedback to control the movement of the gun, much as sensory feedback to the brain modified body movement in living creatures. Guided by continuously updated information (in the form of radar feedback) fed into the mechanism's central processor, the guns would be able to predict aircraft trajectories and make necessary adjustments automatically.

After successfully completing the self-controlled guns near the end of 1941, Wiener and Bigelow continued their research on automated computer technology. They approached the physiology expert Arturo Rosenblueth of the Instituto Nacional de Cardología in Mexico City to learn about the parallels between feedback loops in machines and sensory stimulation in humans. Together, Wiener, Bigelow, and Rosenblueth formulated a new model of nervous-system processes that unified human and machine, thus accounting for the relationship between sensory input and action in both. In 1943 the trio published their work under the title "Behavior, Purpose and Teleology" in the journal *Philosophy of Science*. The unifying theories presented in the article lay the foundation for an interdisciplinary study that would become known as cybernetics. (The term itself was coined by Wiener in 1948 from a Greek word meaning "steersman.") The study of automatic-control systems, both natural and artificial, cybernetics is a subsection of life science and computer science that has implications for such diverse disciplines as mathematics, anthropology, sociology, and psychology.

In March 1946 Bigelow was offered the position of chief engineer of John von Neumann's computer project at the Institute for Advanced Study (IAS) in Princeton, New Jersey. For his time, von Neumann was a true computer visionary. While pioneers such as John Atanasoff, John Mauchly, and J. Presper Eckert had used their engineering knowledge to make the electronic digital computer a reality, von Neumann remained more of a theorist. He was one of the few scientists able to grasp the full potential of computer technology, which he thought would revolutionize mathematics and experimentation in a number of scientific fields. He conceived of developing a fully automatic, digital, electronic, all-purpose calculating machine with a degree of autonomy not yet seen in contemporary machines, and in the mid-1940s von Neumann set out to build the fastest device yet invented: a stored-program computer with a logical control based memory system. The so-called Electronic Computer Project of the IAS was the embodiment of the ideas he had been working on for years. As Herman H. Goldstine—another notable engineer who was instrumental on the project—recalled in his book, *The Computer from Pascal to von Neumann* (1972), the program was "undoubtedly the most influential single undertaking in the history of the computer during this period."

The IAS had won a bidding war with other schools to host the project. In collaboration with both Princeton University, the nearby neighbor of IAS, and the electronics company RCA, von Neumann would be allowed to design and construct his scientific computer. While compiling his staff, he had first approached Eckert—the co-inventor of the first full-scale, general-purpose electronic computer, the ENIAC—to serve as his chief engineer. Eckert declined, however, choosing to enter the computer business rather than continue his academic research. It was then that Wiener, a friend of von Neumann's, suggested Bigelow for the project, largely because of the latter engineer's extensive background in the infant field of cybernetics. "He has a profound interest in automatic computing and control which is clearly a very important asset in this work," von Neumann said of Bigelow, in a memorandum on the project, as quoted by Goldstine.

In Bigelow's own words, the IAS computer project initially offered "few tangible assets," as quoted by David Ritchie for *The Computer Pioneers* (1986), other than its key engineers, von Neumann and Goldstine. Nevertheless, the prospects for the project quickly changed when von Neumann acquired the financial backing of the Atomic Energy Commission (AEC). As chief engineer, Bigelow was responsible for designing the stored-program digital computer that von Neumann envisioned. In essence, he had to determine whether von Neumann's ideas were workable given the existing technology. He also contributed to the circuitry design, allowing for the use of electrical components, and completed the actual physical design of the computer, as well as the design of the crucial arithmetic and controlling devices to be included within the machine.

In constructing the computer's physical design, Bigelow took a highly unorthodox approach. For example, in building the chassis, or the supporting frame, he avoided the popular practice of simply mounting all the tubes and components on flat metal sheets, which were stored in racks. Instead, he configured the device three-dimensionally so that all the parts were installed into a curved chassis. This arrangement provided more design options than the two-dimensional method, but also made such tasks as wiring and replacing faulty parts much more difficult. For this reason, his design was described by the computer historian Harry Wulforst, in his book *Breakthrough to the Computer Age* (1982), as being "as much a work of art as it was an engineering masterpiece."

One of Bigelow's guiding design philosophies was his belief that the IAS computer should operate asynchronously. In contrast to earlier machines, which all had allotted fixed amounts of time for the device to perform each action, Bigelow felt that his machine would operate more efficiently—and more quickly—if it conducted each action in its own time. In other words, when a given function was completed, a signal would be sent to the computer's mainframe, thereby instructing the next action to begin. Such a system, however, required that all information be stored in devices that could retain data over the passage of time. To accomplish this, Bigelow developed a reliable means of transferring the information through "positive latches." His asynchronous operating system was considered revolutionary in its time, making the IAS computer more self-regulating than anything that had yet been constructed.

From its inception, the IAS computer was intended to be a stored-program machine with memory. However, the mercury-based memory system that was initially installed provided only a 1,024-word capacity, and was unable to simultaneously hold both a program and the digital information for a problem. Additionally, the speed of input and output (I/O) to and from the memory was slower than Bigelow wanted. His team experimented with an I/O system involving pulley-driven wires, but this method proved unsuccessful because the wires had a tendency to snap. Bigelow began considering the use of magnetic drums, a method that had been pioneered by Atanasoff, but abandoned the idea in mid-1948. Around that time, he became aware of the cathode ray tube (CRT) invented by the British engineer F. C. Williams. While it was not the first such tube in existence, Williams's model was cheaper and more efficient than any of its predecessors. Interested in the possibility of using the tubes as the basis for the IAS computer's memory system, Bigelow traveled to Manchester, England, in the summer of 1948 to meet with Williams and to learn more about the device. Bigelow was impressed upon meeting Williams, whom he described as an excellent example of "the British 'string and sealing wax' inventive genius," as quoted by Ritchie, meaning that the British inventor had done the best possible work with the limited tools at his disposal.

While Bigelow was in Manchester, the IAS senior engineer James H. Pomerene began experimenting with the Williams CRT model. By the time Bigelow contacted the IAS three weeks later to inform his colleagues of his findings, Pomerene already managed to assemble a rudimentary Williams tube system. When Bigelow returned to Princeton, the decision was made to construct a parallel memory using Williams's device. Rather than use the traditional, but less reliable, mercury-based system, the IAS would instead employ CRTs, which were predecessors of Jay Forrester's breakthrough invention of random access memory (RAM) in the subsequent decade. The use of Williams's tubes solved the dual problems of increasing memory capacity while also speeding up the I/O system.

As an engineer Bigelow was widely known for his meticulous dedication—a quality, which combined with his continual exploration of new ideas, prolonged the IAS project into the early 1950s; the computer was ultimately completed in 1952. (Bigelow won a Guggenheim fellowship in 1950 and was replaced on the project by Pomerene, who had worked under him from the beginning. Pomerene supervised the modifications and updating of the IAS computer during Bigelow's absence.) The IAS computer was only the first machine constructed from von Neumann's theoretical template, and several modified copies were later made. One was used by the Air Force to track targets for nuclear weapons. The version built for the U.S. government's laboratory in Los Alamos, New Mexico, to be used for nuclear weapons–related calculations, was called MANIAC. The Rand Corporation named their version the JOHNNIAC, in honor of the machine's inventor John von Neumann. With its unique memory system, the model was capable of running 24 hours a day for two months at a time with only half a dozen errors, a remarkable feat in an era when the mean free time between failures (MFTBF) was measured in minutes, rather than hours or days. In 1952 Bigelow became a permanent member of the IAS.

Many of Bigelow's developments in programming and machine architecture during his years with the IAS have since had a major influence on the evolution of computer technology. For example, the instruction codes that Bigelow and his staff developed outlived the cruder instruction methods in use at the time and remained the standard for decades to come. His contribution to computer history may be best summarized by Goldstine, who wrote: "We were very fortunate indeed in having Julian H. Bigelow as our chief engineer during the formative stages of the [IAS] project. He had visionary ideas on circuitry and the intellectual toughness to force these ideas to fruition. Without his leadership it is doubtful that the computer would have been a reality."

Into his 80s, Bigelow flew planes and renovated them as an avocation. He and his wife, Elizabeth, had three children: Nicholas, Marc, and Alice. Bigelow died on February 17, 2003 in Princeton, New Jersey.—B. S., K. D.

Suggested Reading: Goldstine, Herman H. *The Computer from Pascal to von Neumann*, 1972; Wulforst, Harry. *Breakthrough to the Computer Age*, 1982; Shurkin, Joel. *Engines of the Mind*, 1984; Rheingold, Howard. *Tools for Thought*, 1985; Ritchie, David. *The Computer Pioneers*, 1986; Cortada, James. *Historical Dictionary of Data Processing: Biographies*, 1987

Binnig, Gerd

July 20, 1947– Co-creator of the scanning tunneling microscope

Gerd Binnig is best known for his collaboration with Heinrich Rohrer on the development of the world's first scanning tunnel microscope. Unlike a conventional microscope, which provides a direct, magnified image of an object, the scanning tunneling microscope uses a stylus that scans the surface of an object from a fixed distance. In recent years this microscope has become an extremely important research device that allows scientists to study surfaces atom by atom. It has also been very useful for the computer industry, since it allows for the development of extremely small electronic circuits. For their work, Binnig and Rohrer shared the 1986 Nobel Prize in Physics with Ernst Ruska, who developed the first electron microscope.

The German physicist Gerd Karl Binnig was born in Frankfurt, West Germany, on July 20, 1947 and lived in Frankfurt and the nearby city of Offenbach for the first 31 years of his life. He was the first of two sons born to Karl Franz Binnig, a machine engineer, and the former Ruth Bracke, a drafter. Young Gerd lived his childhood in the shadow of the World War II, playing in the ruins of bombed-out buildings. By the age of 10, Binnig had decided to be a physicist, though in his autobiographical statement for the Nobel Foundation, as archived on their Web site, he claimed that he did not know exactly what that entailed. He wrote, "While studying physics, I started to wonder whether I had really made the right choice. Especially theoretical physics seemed so technical, so relatively unphilosophical and unimaginative." During his childhood he spent more time playing music than studying physics. His mother had exposed him to classical music, and he took up the violin at 15. Meanwhile, his brother introduced him to popular music through the Rolling Stones and the Beatles. Discovering that he preferred that kind of music, he joined a band and even began writing songs. The collaborative effort of music-making proved instructive for him. He noted in his autobiographical statement, "In this way, I first learned how difficult teamwork can be, how much fun it is to be creative, and how unpredictable the reaction of an audience can be."

After receiving his secondary education at Rudolf Koch School, Binnig began his undergraduate studies at J. W. Goethe University, in Frankfurt am Main. While there he learned better to appreciate physics under the guidance of Dr. W. Martienssen and Dr. E. Hoenig. Martienssen impressed Binnig with his ability to understand and explain the scientific context of a problem, while Hoenig's gifted experimentation enabled the student to grasp concepts with which he had struggled in his earlier studies of physics.

After earning his bachelor's degree in 1973, Binnig pursued his doctorate in physics at the University of Frankfurt, where he studied superconductivity. Immediately after receiving his Ph.D. in 1978, Binnig became a staff member at the research laboratory of the International Business Machines Corporation (IBM) in Zürich, Switzerland. (Binnig credits his wife Lore Wagler with helping him to decide to join the Zürich facility.) There he began collaborating with Heinrich Rohrer on research into the surfaces of materials, around the same time Alan Shugart invented the floppy disk at IBM. The two investigators were drawn to the topic because of the challenging problems it posed; a thorough understanding of surfaces had so far proved virtually impossible to obtain. The source of the difficulty was that the arrangement of atoms on the surface of a solid was so different from the arrangement of atoms in the bulk; thus methods known at that time for exploring the latter were useless when it came to studying surfaces. Surfaces are of considerable interest, however, because it is on the surface that most interactions among materials take place.

In their attempts to probe the surfaces of materials, Binnig and Rohrer decided to try a variant of an effect of quantum mechanics known as tunneling. The effect, which was first verified experimentally by Ivar Giaever in 1960, is one of the many ways in which the so-called Heisenberg uncertainty principle (named for the German physicist Werner Heisenberg) makes itself felt. Richard Feynmann was good at explaining this principle in his

work on QED (quantum electrodynamics). According to that principle, it is impossible to measure the position and velocity of a subatomic particle simultaneously. As a consequence, the position of a particle, such as an electron, becomes "smeared out," or random and unpredictable, within a certain area: the particle behaves as a diffuse cloud of matter. Such a cloud can "tunnel," or diffuse, between two surfaces, even if they are not touching, in much the same way that water can seep through the ground from one puddle to another.

The tunneling effect was well known at the time Binnig and Rohrer began their collaboration and had been used to explore, albeit somewhat crudely, the nature of interfaces in "sandwiches," or layered materials (i.e., the physical and chemical reactions between different materials). What Binnig and Rohrer set out to accomplish was to make electrons tunnel through a vacuum, an idea that proved unexpectedly feasible. Their approach ultimately led to the development of a new instrument called the scanning tunneling microscope. The basic principle underlying this device involves scanning the surface of a solid in a vacuum with a sharp needle tip. A voltage is applied between the sample and the tip, and the distance between the two is kept small enough that electrons will tunnel from one to the other. The resulting flow of electrons is called a tunneling current. The amount of tunneling current has an exponential relationship with the distance between the sample and tip. Therefore, by sweeping the tip over the sample and measuring the current, a map of the surface can be produced at the atomic scale.

Binnig and Rohrer made their first successful test of the scanning tunneling microscope in the spring of 1981. Collaborating with two other IBM researchers, Christoph Gerber and Edmund Weibel, they resolved features only one atom high on the surface of calcium-iridiumtin ($CaIrSn_4$) crystals. A similar device had been built earlier, and independently, by the American physicist Russell Young at the United States National Bureau of Standards, using a somewhat different principle that yielded substantially lower resolution.

In developing the scanning tunneling microscope, the IBM team faced a formidable obstacle: they first had to eliminate all sources of vibrational noise. The vertical position of the scanning tip must be controllable to within a fraction of the diameter of an atom, owing to the sensitive dependence of the tunneling current on the distance between the sample surface and the tip. Street noises and even footsteps can jar the delicate operation of the instrument. Binnig and Rohrer initially attacked the problem by suspending the microscope with permanent magnets over a bowl of superconducting lead placed on a heavy stone table. They isolated the table itself from the laboratory building with inflated rubber tires. Piezoelectric materials, which contract or expand upon the application of voltages, were used to move the tip with great precision. Because of subsequent refinements, the scanning tunneling microscope now resolved vertical features as small as 0.1 angstrom (one hundred-billionth of a meter), or roughly one-tenth the diameter of a hydrogen atom. Lateral resolutions of two angstroms have resulted from scanning tips only a few atoms wide, and tips only one-atom wide are being developed. Since its perfection, the scanning tunneling microscope has become a standard tool in many research laboratories. The instrument is effective in a variety of environments besides the vacuum, including air, water, and cryogenic fluids. It has been employed to study a variety of materials other than inorganic substances, including virus particles.

In awarding half of the 1986 Nobel Prize in Physics to Binnig and Rohrer, the Royal Swedish Academy of Sciences declared, as quoted on the Nobel Foundation Web site, "It is evident that this technique is one of exceptional promise, and that we have so far seen only the beginning of its development. Many research groups in different areas of science are now using the scanning tunneling microscope. The study of surfaces is an important part of physics, with particular applications in semiconductor physics and microelectronics. In chemistry, also, surface reactions play an important part, for example, in connection with catalysis. It is also possible to fixate organic molecules on a surface and study their structures. Among other applications, this technique has been used in the study of DNA molecules." In recalling his emotions upon learning about the award, Binnig remarked, "It was beautiful and terrible at the same time," because while it signaled a great success, it also concluded "an exciting story of discovery."

Apart from research, Binnig's interests include skiing, soccer, tennis, golf, and sailing. A talented musician, he composes music, plays the violin and the guitar, and sings. Since 1986 he has been an IBM Fellow, the corporation's highest research position.

Binnig and Rohrer have shared other honors for their work in addition to the Nobel Prize. In 1984 they received the Hewlett-Packard Prize from the European Physical Society and the King Faisal International Prize in Science from the Saudi Arabian government for their efforts in scanning tunneling microscopy. Binnig was also the recipient of the Physics Prize of the German Physical Society, in 1982; the Elliot Cresson Medal from the Franklin Institute, in 1987; and the Minnie Rosen Award from Ross University, in 1988. In 1994 he and Rohrer were elected to the National Inventors Hall of Fame in Ohio.

In 1969 Binnig married Lore Wagler, a psychologist; they have a daughter, born in Switzerland in 1984, and a son, born in California in 1986.—C. M.

Suggested Reading: *New York Times* Oct. 16, 1986; Nobel Foundation Web site; Nobel Prize Internet Archive Web site; *R & D Magazine* p47+ June 1998; *Science* Nov. 14, 1986; *Science News* Oct. 25, 1986; *American Men and Women of Science, 1998–99*, 1998; *Larousse Dictionary of Scientists*, 1994

Bjerknes, Vilhelm
(BYERK-nes)

Mar. 14, 1862–Apr. 9, 1951 Creator of modern meteorology

If not for the work of Vilhelm Bjerknes, we might not know whether to grab an umbrella or an extra sweater as we leave our homes each morning. A Norwegian physicist and mathematician, Bjerknes developed theories and models that imposed sense upon what had previously appeared to be the chaotic, unpredictable patterns of weather. His work in the first quarter of the 20th century formed the foundation of modern meteorology—the study of atmospheric phenomena, especially the study of weather and weather forecasting. He is responsible for coining the term "front" and for describing the role of these air masses in weather formation. He believed that mathematical models could be used to predict weather patterns, but lacked the tools to perform such computations in a timely manner. Meteorology entered the computer age in 1952, when scientists made the first computer-aided weather forecasts, and entered the space age when Bjerknes's son, Jacob, then head of the meteorology department at the University of California, Los Angeles, advocated the use of photography from rockets to examine atmospheric weather patterns.

Vilhelm Frimann Koren Bjerknes was born on March 14, 1862 in Christiania, Norway, where his father, Carl Anton Bjerknes, taught at the University of Christiania as a lecturer in applied mathematics. His mother was the former Aletta Koren. Carl Anton had been raised in a poor farming family and lost his own father at age 12. He won scholarships to study in Norway and abroad and had become interested in mathematics and geophysics—the study of physical processes occurring on earth.

An early machine used for weather forecasting   Courtesy of the Computer Museum of America

After learning that a ball can move at a constant speed, without any external forces, through a frictionless fluid, Carl Anton embarked on a lifelong study of hydrodynamics, the branch of physics that examines the motions of fluids. Vilhelm acted as his father's research assistant when he was young and, when he was older, he documented the results of his father's research into hydrodynamic phenomena.

In 1880 Vilhelm Bjerknes enrolled at the University of Kristiania. (In 1877 the town of his birth had changed the spelling of its name from Christiania to Kristiania. In 1925 the town adopted its present name, Oslo.) Bjerknes graduated in 1888 with a master's degree in mathematics and physics. According to an article published on NASA's Earth Observatory Web site, he had by this time decided to make a break with his father, who was becoming increasingly reclusive and reluctant to publish his findings: "Young Vilhelm believed that continuing work with his father would be detrimental to his career, a tough decision for a son who was devoted to his father."

Soon after receiving his master's degree, Bjerknes won a state scholarship to study abroad. He first headed to Paris, then a hotbed of scientific activity. In 1890 he traveled to Bonn, Germany, where he became an assistant to the physicist Heinrich Hertz. For the next two years, Bjerknes and Hertz studied electromagnetic waves, measuring their length and velocity. Hertz's researched proved definitively that electricity can be transmitted in electromagnetic waves, which travel at the speed of light and possess many other properties of light. His experiments led to the development of the wireless telegraph and the radio.

In 1892 Bjerknes returned to Norway to complete a doctoral thesis on the work he had conducted with Hertz; he was awarded the doctoral degree later that same year and then embarked on what proved to be a lifelong teaching career. In the 1890s he taught mechanics and mathematics in Stockholm, Sweden, first at the School of Engineering and later at the University of Stockholm. During these years Bjerknes formulated a theory that synthesized hydrodynamics (having to do with liquids) and thermodynamics (having to do with heat); the theory, Bjerknes hoped, would enable the study of large-scale changes in the atmosphere and the oceans—that which today we casually call "weather."

In a 1904 paper Bjerknes advocated a system of weather prediction based on mathematical physics. Describing the mathematical process that has come to be known as "numerical weather prediction," Bjerknes set out to prove that, if scientists gather enough empirical information about the current state of the atmosphere, then they can use math formulas to predict future patterns. Until the advent of computers, such complex calculations could not be done quickly enough for weather prediction, but Bjerknes trusted that his theory of mathematical models for weather prediction would eventually prove feasible. On a visit to the United States in 1905, Bjerknes attracted the interest of the Carnegie Foundation, a philanthropic organization, which awarded him funds to pursue his research. He received grants from the foundation for the next 36 years.

In 1907 Bjerknes was appointed chair of applied mechanics and mathematical physics at the University of Kristiania, his alma mater. Five years later he was made chair of geophysics at the University of Leipzig, Germany, and given the directorship of the newly created Leipzig Geophysical Institute. During World War I he and a team of researchers set up a network of weather observation stations throughout Norway. The team included Bjerknes's son, Jacob, who had been born on November 2, 1897 and who would go on to become an esteemed meteorologist in his own right.

In 1917 Bjerknes accepted a position with a museum in Bergen (now part of the University of Bergen), in Norway, and founded the Bergen Geophysical Institute. Then 55 years old, Bjerknes began to assimilate his years of research and thinking about the mathematical model of weather forecasting. Working with Jacob and two other scientists, Bjerknes examined the findings from the various weather stations throughout Norway. He and his team concluded that the atmosphere is made up of discrete air masses with dissimilar features. They theorized that weather activity is concentrated in relatively narrow zones that form the boundaries between warm and cold air masses. They called these zones "fronts," borrowing the notion of World War I battle fronts. The "polar front theory," as it came to be known, is now a major part of modern weather forecasting. It helped to explain many phenomena, including cyclones, a type of storm that rotates around a center of low atmospheric pressure. In 1921 Vilhelm and Jacob Bjerknes co-published a paper describing the structure and evolution of cyclones.

In 1926 Vilhelm Bjerknes made his final move, back to his home town, now called Oslo. He remained an energetic teacher at the University of Oslo until 1932, when he retired. In an article published on the European Geophysical Society Web site, he was described as having "a rare ability to attract and inspire gifted students. . . . He was also efficient in making his . . . achievements known, not only to the scientific community, but to the politicians and the public as well." In May 1933 he was elected to Royal Society of London.

Jacob Bjerknes carried on his father's legacy as a professor of meteorology, first at the University of Bergen and later, in the United States, at the University of California. Among his major contributions to the science of meteorology was his advocacy of the use of rocket photography to aid in the examination of atmospheric weather patterns. Later, he helped to usher in the use of satellites for weather observation.

Bjerknes was the subject of *Appropriating the Weather: Vilhelm Bjerknes and the Construction of a Modern Meteorology* (1993), by Robert Marc Friedman. In it Friedman explains that modern meteorology has provided far greater benefits for mankind than simple sartorial guidance from our local newscast; he details, as well, the financial implications that accurate weather prediction has had for farmers, aviators, and others who depend on the forecast for their livelihood.—M. A. H.

Suggested Reading: European Geophysical Society Web site; NASA Earth Observatory Web site

Blankenbaker, John

Dec. 24, 1929– Electrical engineer; computer engineer; inventor

The personal computer is often associated with Steve Wozniak (creator of the Apple I) and International Business Machines (IBM), the company that introduced its enormously influential PC in the early 1980s. However, the distinction for introducing the first commercially available personal computer belongs to John Blankenbaker, who in 1971 developed a bread box–sized machine called the Kenbak-1. This system, which sold for $750, was primarily intended for educational purposes and was advertised as such. With a memory of only 256 bytes, the Kenbak-1 never became popular (only about 40 were ever sold), but the machine is considered by many to be the important first step toward the personal-computer revolution.

In a statement written for *Leaders of the Information Age*, John Blankenbaker discussed his life and his work: "After graduating from high school in 1946 at the age of 16, I enlisted for two years in the U.S. Navy as an electronics technician. I then entered Oregon State University in 1948 as a physics major. Every week we had to write a laboratory report in which the instructors wanted the computations done with logarithms which was an odious task. In February of 1949, I read a short story in a popular magazine about a new computing device that used only ones and zeroes. This was the essence of electro-mechanical relays which I thought that I understood. Fired by the thought I might construct a device on which I could do the computations for the reports, I undertook the design of a calculating machine.

"My first hurdle was to understand how to represent numbers using only ones and zeroes. It is an embarrassment to me now but it took several days to learn how to do this. Finally, I could convert decimal numbers to the binary format and I could do arithmetic in this format. I translated the paper ideas into a relay design which used a special purpose electro-mechanical device in the arithmetic unit.

"The system was not a stored program computer. I envisioned that the numbers would be selected from the memory bank by a rotary switch. The operation to be performed would be specified by a manually pushed button. After estimating the number of relays needed in a very modest memory, I saw that my financial resources were inadequate. With this realization, I lost interest in the project.

"Between my junior and senior years, I obtained a summer job at the National Bureau of Standards as it was then called [now the National Institute of Standards and Technology (NIST)]. Of the hundred students hired for the summer, I was fortunate to be one of the four assigned to the SEAC project, the Standards Eastern Automatic Computer. This was a working machine and it led me to a much better understanding of the use of electronics, the role of logic, and the importance of the stored program concept. My attempt to write a simple program was a failure but this did not discourage an interest in computers.

"On graduating from Oregon State University with B.S. degrees in physics and in mathematics, I applied and was accepted to a cooperative program at Hughes Aircraft Company and UCLA [University of California, Los Angeles]. The work at Hughes involved computers, both military and commercial. A supervisor said that each flipflop in the design added five hundred dollars to the cost of the computer. This was a motivation to design a computer with as few flipflops as possible. I realized that only one flipflop was necessary to have a general purpose computer, albeit a very slow processor. (Even this one flipflop could be eliminated.)

"The commercial computer on which I was working was canceled because the market seemed to be less than twenty machines. Even though I had designed the arithmetic unit for a large commercial computer, I had never used a computer except for the one program I had attempted on SEAC. I felt this was a serious problem when a computer, even though slow, could be built with only one flipflop. Already I was envisioning that a computer could be affordable for an individual. The most serious limitation preventing this was in the memories which were available. The logic and the processor were not the problem. This was my position in 1956 when I returned to school at MIT [Massachusetts Institute of Technology, in Cambridge]. (I had earned an M.S. degree from UCLA in physics.) The work there was in electrical engineering and my research was directed toward a novel way of filtering and predicting binary sequences of data. The result was an E.E. degree in 1959.

"The ideas lay dormant until 1970 when I was working for a company in the stock quotation business. After a top level management change, I resigned but the company granted that I had some cause for doing so and gave me a small termination grant. This seemed like the time to try for the development of a small computer, called the Kenbak-1, which could be afforded by a private individual. An objective of the design was that the computer would be an educational device. Speed was not important nor was the size of the memory which was MOS [metal oxide silicon] circulating registers with a total of 2,048 bits of storage. The logic was provided by small and medium scale (as defined in 1970) integrated circuits and was completed before the microprocessors were announced. The first unit was shipped about one year after the start.

"Marketing concentrated on the educational [sector]. In hindsight, more emphasis should have been given to the hobbyist market. Though it was well rated as an educational tool, the most enthusiastic comments came from experienced users of computers who recognized that the Kenbak-1 did act much like the big machines. After selling about 45 of the machines, the rights were sold to another company and Kenbak Corporation closed its doors.

The name, Kenbak, was derived from the name BlanKENBAKer and with the appeal of the similarity to Kodak both in format and in the objectives of making a product for the mass market.

"After Kenbak terminated operations, I worked for American Communication Systems (ACS) and developed a system for the analysis of four voice conversations into a stream of digital data plus the recreation of the voice. In a stint with Symbolics, I converted a wirewrap computer design into one that could be produced and maintained reliably. The designs from the Kenbak-1 to ACS to Symbolics ranged from simplicity of implementation to high performance to reliability of the finished product.

"Currently, I am interested in history and genealogy. I am publishing *Beyond Germanna*, a newsletter/journal which is now in its fourteenth year. I have written fourteen hundred pages for publishing on the Internet as a series of informative notes. Until recently, I have taught physics and mathematics at Lincoln University [in Lincoln University, Pennsylvania]."

By modern standards of personal computers, the Kenbak-1 was primitive: it had eight switches for input and eight lights for output, contained no microprocessor—Blankenbaker built his computer from standard integrated circuits—and had a memory of 256 bytes. It ran a hand-compiled assembly language—meaning that the translation from the assembly language to the machine language had to be entered manually—and could do some word processing.

Blankenbaker sold his machine for $750, hoping to entice buyers with its affordability. (The IBM PC, introduced 10 years later, sold for close to $3,000.) Unfortunately for Blankenbaker, the low price, as well as the small size of the machine, actually curbed sales. "I had found that individuals were very dubious," the inventor told *Computerworld* (November 3, 1983). "Most individuals regarded computers as giant, expensive machines. They couldn't believe that a relatively small machine at a reasonable price could exist that would allow some reasonable problems to be run." Having sold around four dozen machines after two years, Blankenbaker discontinued business. "I wasn't making any money," he told Clay Hathorn for *PreText Magazine* (on-line), adding that his venture was also undermined by a lack of foresight on his part. "I always felt like the computer [in general] couldn't get any better."

Blankenbaker went on to join the staff at Symbolics Inc., where he designed the first production version of the LM-1 artificial-intelligence system conceived at MIT. In 1983 he joined Quotron, and two years later he retired. In his retirement, Blankenbaker spends his time playing the stock market and researching 18th-century Virginians of German descent. His bimonthly journal, *Beyond Germanna*, looks at the Virginia Piedmont Germans. He also writes *Notes*, a history of Germanna, which he publishes on-line.

Though the Kenbak-1 was retired, Blankenbaker's machine has become more than a footnote in computer history. In 1986 the Computer Museum, which is now part of the Museum of Science in Boston, Massachusetts, recognized it as the first personal computer built and sold commercially. It has since been recognized as an important first step in the evolution of the PC and an important bridge between minicomputers and modern microcomputers.—C. M.

Suggested Reading: *Computerworld* p33 May 19, 1986, p173 Nov. 3, 1986; *Cox News Service* Aug. 7, 2001; Spencer, Donald D. *Timetable of Computers*, 1997

Bollée, Léon

1870–1913 Inventor of the calculer

In the late 19th century in France, Léon Bollée built one of the first mechanized calculating devices able to perform multiplication directly, as opposed to through repeated addition. Known as the *calculer*, his invention garnered him international attention at a young age. Bollée, however, soon turned his attentions to automobile design, another field then in its infancy, and the *calculer* was never successfully mass-produced. While the development of a commercially viable calculator of the kind envisioned by Bollée would fall to later inventors, his pioneering work paved the way for the creation of such a device, and the *calculer* remains an important contribution to the history of data processing.

Léon Bollée was born in 1870 in the French town of Le Mans. His family operated a metalworking foundry and Bollée was brought up learning the business. He demonstrated a knack for inventing early in life, when at the age of 13, in 1883, he designed, built, and patented a specially-crafted, buoyant bicycle made for use on water. The vehicle was actually employed years later by an adventure-seeker who used it to cross the English Channel.

In 1887, at the age of 17, Bollée designed a type of calculating machine which Bollée named a *calculer*, abbreviated from *machine à calculer* (calculating machine). Designed for the purpose of calculating the dimensions of bells produced at the foundry, the machine Bollée built was in a class with the Difference Engine designed by British mathematician Charles Babbage some 50 years earlier. An earlier predecessor of Bollée's device, and of Babbage's as well, was a mechanical calculating machine invented by the German philosopher Gottfried Leibniz in 1673. Leibniz's machine was the first to be capable of performing multiplication; however, much like Babbage's Difference Engine, it could do so only through repeated addition. The *calculer*, by comparison, could multiply two numbers directly, thanks to the inclusion of a device which stored multiplication tables. This is the first known example of a table hookup, a device which coordinates different multiplication tables. Apparently unknown to Bollée was the fact that his invention was not actually the first machine to perform direct multiplication and division; nine years earlier, in 1878, a man named Ramon Verea was issued a patent for what is actually the first such device.

Two years later, in 1889, Bollée displayed his device at the Paris Exhibition, the first of which was organized by Napoleon Bonaparte in 1801. It was at the 1801 Exhibition that the inventor Joseph Jacquard exhibited his mechanical weaving loom, one of the first machines to automate the process of making fabric and thus an important step towards the Industrial Revolution that took place later in the 19th century. Despite the significance of Jacquard's invention, he received a bronze medal in 1801, whereas Bollée was awarded a gold medal for the *calculer*. One possible explanation for the discrepancy is that the judges at the end of the 19th century were more attuned to the importance of mechanized technology than their early-19th-century counterparts had been.

The *calculer* had the overall appearance of a large wheel similar to those used in early-20th-century washing machines to wring water out of clothing. Containing many gears, it was extremely heavy, and it took two strong men to lift it. Its size and weight made it somewhat impractical to use, and thus only a few copies were ever made. One was put into use at the Bollée family foundry, and another was sent to the Belgian Ministry of Railroads. Bollée designed other calculating devices later, but none of them were ever built. One such example, described in papers found after his death, was a highly advanced calculating engine that would be capable of handling up to 27 orders of difference, far more than any other device then in existence. Bollée also worked on building smaller, more practical versions of his original machine.

Bollée's source of inspiration for the *calculer* remains unknown. It is possible, although unproven, that he had read the works of Babbage, or that he was familiar with the accomplishments of such other 19th-century inventors as Jacquard, Dorr Felt (who created the first key-driven calculator), and Herman Hollerith (who built an electromechanical statistical tabulating device in the 1880s). In later years Bollée continued to use his inventive skills, creating an early cash register, as well as a railroad ticket dispenser.

Bollée later abandoned his interest in industrial machines such as the *calculer* as he discovered his true passion in life: designing, building, and racing automobiles. In 1900 he set up a factory for building cars in Sablons, a city in the south of France. The development of automobiles was in its very early stages at the time, and Bollée made a name for himself as one of the first European manufacturers. In fact, he is best remembered today not for the *calculer*, but for establishing the automobile race track

Le Mans, which he named after his home town, and went on to become one of the world's most famous courses. He lent his own name to certain models of cars he produced shortly after the turn of the century; his racing cars in particular were known for their advanced, lightweight design. Towards the end of his life Bollée's business pursuits brought him into acquaintance with the Wright brothers, and certain parts that they used in their development of the first airplane which had its maiden flight in 1903, were manufactured by Bollée's auto company.

Bollée's work on the *calculer* would be later picked up by a Swiss engineer named Otto Steiger. Inspired by the inventions of both Bollée and Leibniz, Steiger in 1893 built a mechanical calculator that he named the Millionaire. Very similar to the *calculer*, the Millionaire was capable of direct multiplication, yet it was also less unweildy and thus easier to use. According to *The Timetable of Computers* (1997), the Millionaire was basically "an automated version of Gottfried Leibniz's machine." Unlike the *calculer*, Steiger's invention was successfully mass produced, and more than 4,500 were sold between 1894 and 1935, the year it was discontinued.

Léon Bollée died in 1913 at the age of 43. Although he spent the majority of his life building automobiles and running his family's foundry business, Bollée's early data-processing machines acted as a kind of stimulant for future inventions, and brought into focus the importance of that preceded his. Bollée led an eclectic life and he has been described as "a clever man [and] an interesting and creative inventor" (*Historical Dictionary of Data Processing*, 1987), as well as "an energetic and restless man" (*Bit by Bit*, 1984). The phenomenon of the mechanical calculator spread during the early twentieth century due to the work of men such as Steiger, Felt, and William Burroughs, and would eventually play a major role in the development of what are now known as computers.—B. S.

Suggested Reading: Computer Museum of America Web site; Augarten, Stan. *Bit by Bit*, 1984; Cortada, James. *Historical Dictionary of Data Processing: Biographies*, 1987; Spencer, Donald D. *The Timetable of Computers*, 1997

Boole, George

Nov. 2, 1815–Dec. 8, 1864 Logician; mathematician

The English mathematician and logician George Boole, in addition to being remembered as the father of modern symbolic logic, is responsible for inventing a form of algebra that has played a fundamental role in the development of computers. By applying mathematical ideas to the logic of reasoning, he created what is known as Boolean algebra, which uses a binary mathematics consisting of two states, denoted by the digits 1 and 0, and the logical operations of AND, OR, and NOT. Although Boole could not have foreseen the direction his creation would take, today Boolean algebra is important in the design and construction of electronic circuits and forms the basis of all modern computer architecture.

George Boole was born on November 2, 1815 at 34 Silver Street, in the industrial town of Lincoln, England. He grew up in a working-class household; his father, John, was a shoemaker, and his mother was a maid. Boole was a highly intelligent child who didn't mind showing off his gifts: on one occasion he disappeared from school and was later found in town spelling difficult words for an amused crowd of people, who were rewarding him with showers of pennies.

Despite his humble trade, Boole's father had a passion for science and an interest in optics and began teaching his son mathematics when the boy was still young. He also taught Boole how to build such devices as cameras, kaleidoscopes, and telescopes. (Some scholars suspect that Boole and his father may have even attempted to build a rudimentary calculating machine.) With the help of a tutor, the young Boole's studies soon included Latin, history, geography, and literature. He was aided in his studies by an excellent memory, which he described as "an arrangement of the mind for every fact and idea, which I can find at once, as if it were in a well-ordered set of drawers," as quoted by Eileen Harrison in her essay "George Boole—The Lincoln Genius," which is posted on Roger Parson's World of Lincolnshire Web site. Boole later taught himself Greek, French, German, and Italian. At the age of 14, he published in a local newspaper an English translation of an ancient Greek poem. The translation was so skillful that a local schoolmaster argued that an adolescent could not possibly have rendered such a mature composition.

As a teenager Boole considered joining the Anglican clergy. During his theological studies, however, his logical mind had trouble accepting certain religious doctrines, such as that of the Trinity, and he abandoned the pursuit. At about the same time, his father's cobbling business was failing, and Boole was compelled to enter the workforce to support his family, which included a sister and two younger brothers.

From the age of 16 Boole worked as an assistant teacher in village schools in West Riding, Yorkshire. When he was 20 he opened his own school in Lincoln. During his free time he studied higher mathematics, including Isaac Newton's three-volume *Principia Mathematica*. In 1839 Boole began contributing papers on differential equations and algebraic problems to the recently founded *Cambridge Mathematical Journal*; his first paper was "Researches on the Theory of Analytic Transformation." He also contributed articles on algebra and calculus to London's Royal Society, which subsequently awarded him a Royal Medal for his work.

During this time Boole began to apply his algebraic ideas to the field of logic. Although logic had traditionally been considered within the domain of philosophy, Boole argued in his pamphlet *Mathematical Analysis of Logic* (1847) that logic should henceforth be more closely allied to mathematics. The formal study of logic had begun with the teachings of the Greek philosopher Aristotle, who instituted the syllogisms and logical relationships that served as the starting point for logicians for centuries to come. Boole asserted that there was a deep similarity between the symbols of algebra and those of logical reasoning; in some sense, logic was a mathematics restricted to two quantities, 1 and 0. In this binary system, the 1 represents "thinkable" objects, or "the set of all objects being discussed," and 0 represents the empty set. Boole's work was influenced by the writings of the 17th-century German mathematician and philosopher Gottfried Wilhelm von Leibniz, who was the first to attempt such a system of logical symbolism. (In Leibniz's theological way of thinking, 1 denoted Being, or God, and 0 Not-Being or Nothingness) One of Boole's important insights was that symbols of operation could be separated from those of quantity and treated as distinct objects of calculation.

On the strength of that publication, in August 1849 Boole was granted a professorship in mathematics at Queen's College, in Cork, Ireland, even though he did not have a university degree. In 1850 Boole met Mary Everest, his future wife, while she was visiting her uncle, a professor at the college. (Mary's interest in science had been piqued by another uncle, the explorer Sir George Everest, for whom the world's tallest mountain is named.) During Mary's visit, Boole was asked to tutor her in the science of acoustics. When she returned home, they continued to correspond and developed a strong friendship, although he was 17 years her senior. When her father died, in 1855, Mary was left destitute. Boole proposed marriage, and the two were wed later that year. Mary began attending her husband's lectures at Queens College, and when this elicited the disapproval of the local women, Boole relocated his senior class to his own home.

Continuing his mathematical studies, Boole published *Studies in Logic and Probability* (1852). Two years later, he published what is considered by many to be his most important work, *An Investigation of the Laws of Thought on Which Are Founded the Mathematical Theories of Logic and Probabilities.* In it, Boole presented a finalized version of his theories on mathematical logic—what is now known as Boolean algebra. Boole based this algebra around the logical operations AND, OR, and NOT, as well as the operations in set theory of union, intersection, and complement. The system, based upon the binary mathematics of Leibniz, separates arguments into different classes of entities that can be processed according to the absence or presence of a given property. This allows for logical conclusions to be drawn from any proposition by a symbolic treatment of the premises, regardless of how many individual items are involved. A "truth table" is used to map out the various possible logical states of a syllogism.

In 1866, two years after Boole's death, the American logician Charles Sanders Peirce began two decades of work based on Boole's findings. As electricity began to come into popular use in the 1870s and 1880s, Peirce envisioned that Boole's logic could be used in the design of electronic circuitry. The level of technology available at the time was not yet up to the task, however, and it would not be until the 1930s that others, such as Claude Shannon, John Atanasoff, and Konrad Zuse, picked up where Peirce had left off. As a result of their work, Boole's binary algebra is today the key principle behind the function of digital computers. Computers are based on microchips that contain countless numbers of tiny electronic switches that operate according to Boole's idea of a two-value system, with 1 and 0 representing two states of electronic circuits, usually high and low voltage. Furthermore, microchips are designed to process this voltage information using Boole's logical operations of AND, OR, and NOT, which in computer science are known as logic gates.

Boole was elected to Britain's prestigious Royal Society in 1857. He was awarded honorary degrees from Dublin and Oxford Universities, and in 1958 he was made an honorary member of the Cambridge Philosophical Society. In 1859 he published *Treatise on Differential Equations* and the following year *Calculus of Finite Differences.* In all, Boole published more than 50 papers during his lifetime.

Boole's health began to deteriorate in middle age. He had developed an eyesight problem as a child, due to prodigious reading, and his vision was worsening steadily; he had also started to show signs of a hereditary lung disease. On November 24, 1864, he walked two miles through heavy rain from his home to the college to deliver a lecture. Boole gave the lecture in wet clothes and caught a cold. This cold subsequently became pneumonia, which infected his already diseased lungs. Unfortunately, Boole's wife may have inadvertently contributed to his illness; influenced by a popular 19th-century belief that the remedy for a disease should resemble the cause, she put her husband to bed and threw buckets of water on him in a misguided attempt to cure him. On December 8, 1864 George Boole died as a result of the lung infection, at the age of 49. Today, Queen's College (now renamed University College Cork) has a library and a mathematics scholarship named in Boole's honor. In 1967 a crater on the moon was named for him.—B. S.; C. M.

Suggested Reading: Kerry Redshaw's Pioneers Web site; Roger Parson's World of Lincolnshire Web site; Asimov, Isaac *Asimov's Biographical*

Dictionary of Science and Technology, 1982; Lee, J. A. N., ed. *International Biographical Dictionary of Computer Pioneers*, 1995; Spencer, Donald D. *The Timetable of Computers*, 1997

Kean Collection/Getty Images

Brady, Mathew B.

1823(?)–Jan. 15, 1896 Photographer

Mathew B. Brady helped popularize photography in the United States during the middle of the 19th century. After learning the craft from Samuel F. P. Morse, the inventor of the telegraph, Brady opened galleries in New York City and Washington, D.C. He took portraits of both ordinary people and some of the most prominent individuals at the time, including presidents, princes, generals, and authors. Brady preserved history through the photographic image, instead of through words. When the Civil War broke out, in 1861, he vowed to produce a photographic account, and assembled a team of photographers to help him. Brady and his photographers displayed their work in his two galleries and had the images published in many newspapers and magazines around the country. The graphic depictions of dead soldiers shocked many people, who had never experienced the horror of war. Although Mathew Brady was largely forgotten after the war, many other photographers and filmmakers followed in his footsteps.

Very little is known about Mathew Brady's early life. Several books about him estimate that he was born about 1823 in Warren Country, New York. His parents were Andrew and Julia Brady, about whom practically nothing has been written. In *Mathew Brady and the Image of History* (1997), Mary Pan-

zer theorized that Brady's photographic career had its genesis when he met the portrait artist William Page during a trip through upstate New York, where Brady was seeking treatment for a "violent inflammation of the eyes." In his book, *Mathew Brady: Historian with a Camera* (1955), James D. Horan writes that Page took an immediate interest in Brady and encouraged him to start drawing sketches.

In about 1839, Brady arrived in New York City with Page and found a job as a clerk with a local department store. At one point, he read a letter published in the city's *Observer* newspaper by Samuel F. B. Morse, who had already gained fame for inventing the telegraph. Writing from Paris, Morse described an early form of photography refined by the noted artist Louis Daguerre. Daguerre had recently impressed Parisians with an exhibition of his daguerreotypes, lifelike pictures produced with silver-coated copper plates. Morse learned the technique from Daguerre and had a camera built in Paris. Morse began to teach lessons in daguerreotypy to make extra money, and among his pupils was Mathew Brady, who was captivated by the new process. (The two had met through Page, who had opened a studio in New York City.)

The *New York City Directory* for 1843–44 identified Brady as a maker of jewelry cases. It is unclear when or if he had left his job as a department-store clerk. However, under Morse, Brady continued to study daguerreotypy and experimented with his own techniques for taking pictures. After he became skilled as a daguerreotypist, or photographer, Brady opened the Daguerrean Miniature Gallery, in New York City, in April 1844. Many other people also took up the new art, and competitions began to be organized. Brady won several medals at such competitions.

The press often published laudatory articles about Brady, and he eventually became known as one of the best daguerreotypists in the United States. His gallery became more successful, and he pursued other projects. In 1846 he photographed a number of criminals at a prison for use in a forthcoming essay on crime; the essay, The Rationale of Crime, authored by Marmaduke Sampson, was published in the fall of the same year, with engravings based on 19 of Brady's photographs.

In 1847 Brady opened a branch office in Washington, D.C. President James Polk and members of his cabinet were among the first subjects Brady photographed there. Two years later Brady took the first pictures of newly elected President Zachary Taylor and his cabinet. He sent engravings of the photographs to a friend, James Gordon Bennett, an editor of the New York City *Herald*. Bennett published the engravings in the *Herald*, making Taylor the first sitting president to have his picture published in a newspaper. Among other prominent Americans who were photographed by Brady were the authors Washington Irving and James Fenimore Cooper and three of the best-known political leaders in the country at the time, Daniel

Webster, Henry Clay, and John C. Calhoun. Several articles in the press celebrated Brady's ability to persuade subjects to be photographed. For example, *Frank Leslie's Illustrated Monthly* praised Brady's "urbanity of manners" and "untiring attention to the feelings and happiness of those with whom he comes in contact," as quoted by Panzer.

Panzer notes that in 1850, the *Photographic Art-Journal* advertised the book *The Gallery of Illustrious Americans*. Selling for $15, the gilt-bound volume featured a collection of Brady's photographs, lithographs by Francis D'Avignon, and essays by the minister and author Charles Edward Lester. In 1851 Brady and his new wife, Juliette Handy, spent 10 months in Europe, where Brady won a medal for his work at London's "Fair of All Nations." Brady's success as a photographer continued during the 1850s. His galleries earned him enough money to enjoy a lavish lifestyle, invest in real estate and railroads, and purchase stocks and bonds.

In January 1860 Brady opened the National Portrait Gallery, in New York City. The opening was celebrated with a lavish reception attended by invited guests, reporters, and many of the city's art lovers. "The new gallery was fitted-up in admirable taste and was richly and handsomely furnished," Roy Meredith wrote in his book *Mr. Lincoln's Cameraman: Mathew B. Brady* (1946). The subjects he photographed there included numerous prominent socialites, who, in their elaborate gowns, entered and exited his studio via a private entrance. In late February 1860 Abraham Lincoln, a former congressman and unsuccessful candidate for the U.S. Senate in 1858, visited New York City to deliver an antislavery speech at the Cooper Union. During his stay Lincoln visited the gallery to have himself photographed by Brady. The "immobilizer," or head clamp, on Brady's apparatus did not reach the head of the six-foot four-inch Lincoln, and its adjustment was only one of the problems facing the photographer. Lincoln looked haggard and worn, and his shirt and string tie were ill-fitting. "I had great trouble in making a natural picture," Brady recalled, as quoted by Meredith. "When I got him before the camera I asked him if I might not arrange his collar, and with that he began to pull it up. 'Ah,' said Lincoln, 'I see you want to shorten my neck.' 'That's just it,' I answered, and we both laughed."

In October 1860 Brady photographed Edward, Prince of Wales, and other members of the United Kingdom's royal family when they visited New York City. (The Duke of Newcastle, a member of the royal entourage, recalled Brady's success at London's Fair of all Nations nine years earlier and suggested to Brady that his triumph then had not escaped the eye of the prince.) The commission did much to raise the gallery's prestige, and after the royal visit Brady was inundated with new clients. Running on the newly formed Republican Party ballot, Lincoln was elected president in November 1860. In February 1861 Brady went to Washington to take the new president's picture on the day of his inauguration. One by one the Southern states responded to President Lincoln's election by seceding from the Union. The attack on Fort Sumter in Charleston, South Carolina, by Confederate troops on April 12, 1861, sparked the outbreak of the Civil War. In the first months of the war, Union soldiers, including several generals, flooded Brady's gallery in Washington, D.C. to have themselves photographed in their uniforms. Brady recognized the historical significance of photography, and he realized that he would have the groundbreaking opportunity to provide a photographic documentary of the battles of the war. Despite his wife's objections and the advice of friends, Brady took his work out of the studio and onto the battlefield. "I can only describe the destiny that overruled me by saying that, like Euphorion [a Greek poet], I felt I had to go. A spirit in my feet said, 'Go' and I went," he said, as quoted by Horan. To obtain permission to photograph the war, he went to see his friend, General Winfield Scott, who was then chief of the army. Scott, however, was on the verge of retirement and was no longer in a position to approve Brady's request. Brady later sought President Lincoln's approval, and the president agreed, on the condition that Brady finance the project himself—a burden that eventually lead to financial ruin.

In July 1861 Brady took his cumbersome equipment to Virginia to take pictures of the first major engagement of the Civil War, the first Battle of Bull Run. An article in *Humphrey's Journal* described the photographs of the battle as "the most curious and interesting we have ever seen. The grouping of entire regiments and divisions, within a space of a couple of feet square, present some of the most curious effects as yet produced in photography. Considering the circumstances under which they were taken, amidst the excitement, the rapid movements, and the smoke of the battlefield, there is nothing to compare with them in their powerful contrasts of light and shade," as quoted by Horan. (During the tumult of battle, Brady's wagon— laden with cameras, fragile plates, and darkroom supplies—was overturned.) Brady was nearly killed during the Seven Days Campaign, in late June 1862, when a cannon shell exploded just in front of his wagon. The constant fighting made it difficult for him to take pictures, but a few weeks later, he photographed scenes from a Union camp that are now among the famous images of the Civil War.

Brady and his team of photographers captured some of the most graphic images of the war at the Battle of Antietam, which was fought in Maryland, in September 1862. Alexander Gardner, one of the other photographers, took the most well-known photograph of the battle, showing a number of dead Confederate soldiers in front of a damaged church. In early July 1863 Brady and another of his photographers, Timothy O'Sullivan, were present during the climatic Battle of Gettysburg, in Pennsylvania. O'Sullivan took one of the most famous pictures of that battle, *A Harvest of Death*, which depicts dead soldiers strewn across a field. Brady displayed many of the pictures in his New York City gallery, and some were also published in *Harper's Weekly*. The photographs, displaying war ruins and dead bodies, horrified many people. In the *Atlantic Monthly*, the poet Oliver Wendell Holmes, Sr. wrote, "These terrible mementoes of one of the most sanguinary conflicts of the war, we owe to the enterprise of Mr. Brady of New York," as quoted by Horan. Although many photographers who worked for Brady took pictures during the Civil War, he received exclusive credit when they were published in newspapers and magazines, the captions reading, "Photographed By Brady." He adamantly refused to share credit with the others. (Alexander Gardner opened his own photography business in 1863.)

Because Brady was forced to finance the project himself, he ran up huge debts, and in September 1864 he sold one-half ownership of his Washington, D.C., gallery to its manager, James Gibson, for $10,000. In January 1865 Brady offered to sell his collection of portraits and Civil War photographs to the New York Historical Society. Although the society accepted the offer, agreeing that Brady's photographs had important historical value, the sale was never finalized. For several years he escaped bankruptcy by using his connections with the New York City Tammany Hall political machine headed by William "Boss" Tweed. In 1873, however, Brady was finally forced to declare bankruptcy, and in 1875 he closed his New York City gallery; lingering financial problems eventually forced the closure of the heavily mortgaged Washington, D.C., gallery, as well. (In 1875 Congress purchased his collection for $25,000, allowing Brady to pay some of his creditors.)

Brady spent his last years in obscurity, struggling to support his family and overcome alcoholism. His wife, Juliette Handy Brady, died on May 20, 1887 from a heart ailment. On April 16, 1895 Brady was struck by a carriage as he attempted to cross a street in New York City. Several months later, doctors confined him to a hospital bed after he developed a kidney ailment. Mathew B. Brady died on January 15, 1896 at Presbyterian Hospital, in New York City. Many newspapers in both New York City and Washington, D.C., published long obituaries, celebrating his achievements in photography and contributions to history.—D. C.

Suggested Reading: Meredith, Roy. *Mr. Lincoln's Cameraman*, 1946; Horan, James D. *Mathew Brady: Historian with a Camera*, 1955; Panzer, Mary. *Mathew Brady and the Image of History*, 1997

Brainerd, John Grist

Aug. 7, 1904–Feb. 1, 1988 Administrator of the ENIAC

The explosion of computer technology that took place in the middle of the 20th century was the product not only of imaginative and innovative scientists, but of determined and open-minded administrators as well. John G. Brainerd was such a person. Although Brainerd himself admitted his lack of sufficient knowledge or understanding of computer technology, his skill as an administrator made possible one of the defining developments of computer history: the Electronic Numerical Integrator and Computer, or ENIAC. The first large-scale, general-purpose electronic digital computer, the ENIAC was the brainchild of scientists John Mauchly and J. Presper Eckert, but it was Brainerd who decided to give the idea a chance, who helped negotiate a contract with the U.S. Army, and who eventually became supervisor of the entire project. Through his efforts, the ENIAC was allowed to become more than just a revolutionary idea.

John Grist Brainerd was born on August 7, 1904 in Philadelphia, Pennsylvania, the son of John Austin Brainerd and Mabel (Grist) Brainerd. He attended college at the University of Pennsylvania, while working as a part-time police reporter at the *Philadelphia North American*. In addition to his activities in his home state, Brainerd found time to take classes at the Massachusetts Institute of Technology (MIT), in Cambridge.

After receiving his B.S. from the University of Pennsylvania in 1925, Brainerd became a faculty member at the new Moore School of Electrical Engineering of the University of Pennsylvania. He went on to earn his Ph.D. at the Moore School in 1929. That same year, Brainerd established the University of Pennsylvania's first evening graduate school in electrical engineering.

In 1935 Brainerd received a Sc.D. from the University of Pennsylvania. That year, he began serving as acting state director for the Public Works Administration (PWA), a U.S. government agency that provided relief during the Great Depression. He served in this capacity until 1937, and also worked for the federal government on several scientific projects during the late 1930s and early 1940s. He was instrumental in the formation of technical organizations such as the IRE and IEEE, and in 1942 was named chairman of the division of physical sciences in the University of Pennsylvania's graduate school, a position he held for the next six years. While chairman, Brainerd instituted several new electrical engineering courses at the Moore School, and also coauthored two important engineering textbooks, *High Frequency Alternating Currents* (1931) and *Ultra-High Frequency Techniques* (1942). The latter book in particular was used to train engineers for radar development.

Brainerd's initial experience with computers came in the form of the Moore School's differential analyzer, a mechanical calculating device modeled after the original invented in 1925 by MIT professor Vannevar Bush. While attending a course at MIT on ultra-high-frequency techniques, Brainerd was approached by scientists from the MIT Radiation Laboratory (also known as the Rad Lab), who wanted to use the Moore School analyzer to solve problems their own version could not handle. Brainerd agreed to help, and was given 10 problems for the Moore School analyzer to work on. To accomplish the assignment, Brainerd assembled a group of electrical engineers, among them J. Presper Eckert, who would later become one of the coinventors of the ENIAC.

The chief contribution Brainerd made to the history of computers was his involvement with the ENIAC project. It was Brainerd who hired John Mauchly, the man who originally conceptualized the ENIAC, in the early 1940s. Mauchly's idea for a fully electronic computer first came to the attention of Herman Goldstine, a scientist and representative for the U.S. Army. Goldstine then brought it to Brainerd, who agreed with him that it was worth looking into. Although ENIAC was seen by some as either impractical or impossible, Brainerd believed in the idea of an electronic digital computer which was espoused by Mauchly, and later his partner J. Presper Eckert. Around the same time that the ideas of Mauchly and Eckert were making the rounds of the Moore School faculty, Brainerd received a tempting offer from the Rad Lab to join MIT along with the staff he had assembled to work with the analyzer. However, Brainerd declined the offer, deciding instead to stand by Mauchly's and Eckert's proposed electronic computer project.

With Brainerd's approval, Goldstine first brought the ENIAC idea before the U.S. Army's Ballistic Research Laboratory in Aberdeen, Maryland. The army responded with interest; they had previously been using Bush's differential analyzer to compute ballistic trajectories, but required a computing device that was even faster and more efficient. Goldstine reported that the ENIAC would be able to compute a trajectory in five minutes that would take the analyzer two hours to plot. With the army sufficiently intrigued, Goldstine asked Brainerd to come up with a document to clearly illustrate exactly what they had in mind. In April of 1943, Brainerd discussed the project with Eckert and Mauchly, who developed a proposal for the construction of the digital computing device at the Moore School. In addition to improved speed, Brainerd's ENIAC proposal also stressed the relative ease of detecting errors and making repairs. Together with Herman Goldstine, Brainerd advocated and took formal responsibility for the proposal. Their first meeting with the Ballistics Research Laboratory took place on April 9, 1943. Thanks in part to Brainerd's efforts, an agreement was reached in May and a contract for the construction of what would become the ENIAC was signed with the army by June 5.

As part of the University of Pennsylvania's agreement to the terms of the contract, Brainerd was appointed supervisor of the project, essentially gambling his entire career on the computer's success. Among his assigned duties was the maintenance of secrecy and security as ENIAC was a classified government project (at first known as Project PX). As one of his efforts, Brainerd placed posters all around the offices warning, "The enemy may be listening." While Brainerd's efforts did prevent a leak to the enemy, security on the ENIAC project was far from airtight, allowing British physicist Douglas Hartree to gain information on the machine and disseminate it among his nation's scientific community. Another of Brainerd's duties was the management of the project's $486,000 budget. "Considering the magnitude of the results," he later said, as quoted in the *International Biographical Dictionary of Computer Pioneers* (1995), "it was one of the cheapest research and development projects the government ever invested in."

Even before construction of the ENIAC was finished, Brainerd began to see the need to build a successor computer. In a 1944 letter to the Ballistics Lab, he stated that "progress of the work on ENIAC has led to some rather extensive discussions concerning the solution of problems of a type for which the ENIAC was not designed. . . . It is not feasible to increase the storage capacity of ENIAC . . . to the extent necessary . . . The problem requires an entirely new approach." (*Breakthrough to the Computer Age*, 1982). Brainerd's plea led to the allotment of a new budget for the construction of a second electronic computer, which would be known as the Electronic Discrete Variable Automatic Computer (EDVAC).

An unfortunate dispute arose in 1946 after the completion of the ENIAC involving Brainerd and the computer's two creators Eckert and Mauchly. Brainerd believed that the patent rights for the machine should go to the university, while the two inventors wanted to file for their own exclusive patent rights. To Brainerd, Eckert and Mauchly were in violation of academic ethics. As a result of the dispute, Brainerd resigned as supervisor of the abortive EDVAC project while Mauchly and Eckert left the Moore School to establish their own company. Many other engineers left the school as well, irreparably damaging the prestigious position the Moore School had occupied in the burgeoning field of computer development.

With the decline of the Moore School, Brainerd's involvement in computers came to an end. Although Brainerd would continue to be an important figure in the school's administration he devoted much of his time to curriculum revision, administration, and teaching, which was his greatest love. He became a force in the evolution of electrical engineering to what is now known as computer science and engineering, introducing the transmission of energy and information and the mathematics of magnetic and electric fields into the discipline. In 1953 he established the school's first academic program in systems engineering. Brainerd was promoted to full professor at the Moore School in 1954, and that same year he was also appointed director of the graduate division of physical sciences, of which he had previously been the chairman. He remained in both these positions until his retirement from the Moore School in 1970, at which point he was named University Professor of Engineering.

In 1959 Brainerd became a member of the Scientific Advisory Committee of the National Bureau of Standards (NBS). He was a member of this committee until 1965, and also worked with other scientific agencies throughout the remainder of the 1960s and into the 1970s. He was named Emeritus University Professor by the Moore School in 1975. Remaining active even after retirement, Brainerd served as president of the Society for the History of Technology and chairman of the Science and Arts Committee of the Franklin Institute until the end of his life, in addition to being a public speaker on energy and world food supply.

Brainerd, unlike many men of his time, had the vision to realize the importance of computing technology. However, he did not foresee the computer age as we know it today. He felt that the ENIAC could be used to solve differential equations, the results of which would then be published as function tables. These tables would then be made available to engineers as a reference tool. Looking at the computer more from the point of view of an administrator than that of a computer scientist, Brainerd did not envision the use of the computers to solve problems directly. He made a lasting contribution to computer history through his management skills, epitomizing an emerging generation of scientists in his time who were learning to coordinate and administrate activities, as opposed to conducting research or developing inventions alone as they had previously done. In a lecture delivered to the American Philosophical Society in 1991, Herman Goldstine said of Brainerd, "He combined a considerable interest in computation with substantial ability as a leader of men and a manager of affairs. . . . At all times it was a distinct pleasure for me to deal with this honest, kindly, and well-meaning gentleman. He undoubtedly deserves the credit for being the university's key man in the manifold relationships that were to be developed between it and Aberdeen" (*Computers at the University of Pennsylvania's Moore School, 1943–1946*, on-line).

Brainerd was married on September 6, 1930 to Carol Paxson, who died March 23, 1997, at the age of 91. The couple had no children. He died at the age of 83 on February 1, 1988 at Crosslands, a Quaker retirement community in Kennett Square, Pennsylvania. In public, Brainerd presented a reserved, quiet personality. His students sometimes regarded him as extremely demanding and overly strict. However, his friends and colleagues knew him for his sharp mind and dry sense of humor.—B. S.

Suggested Reading: *Computers at the University of Pennsylvania's Moore School, 1943–1946* (on-line), 1992; Cortada, James W. *Historical Dictionary of Data Processing: Biographies*, 1987; Lee, J. A. N., ed. *International Biographical Dictionary of Computer Pioneers*, 1995; Ritchie, David. *The Computer Pioneers*, 1986; Wulforst, Harry. *Breakthrough to the Computer Age*, 1982; *Who Was Who in America* vol. IX, 1985–1989

Courtesy of www.well.com/user/sbb/

Brand, Stewart

Dec. 14, 1938– Founder of The Whole Earth Catalog

Unlike many other environmentalists, the visionary Stewart Brand has long believed that computer technology, far from being at cross-purposes with the environmental movement, is the best way to foster the perspective necessary for ecological sensitivity. As he told Kellyn S. Betts for *E: The Environmental Magazine* (May/June 1996), "Computers have made for greater material and energy efficiency, less need for physical transport, more widespread intelligence basically throughout civilization and culture. All those things are good news for the environment." For Brand, unconstrained access to information and ideas has been a lifelong pursuit. In 1968 he founded *The Whole Earth Catalog*, a periodical source book dedicated to providing tools and information to those interested in environmentally sustainable lifestyles. He has been a vocal advocate for using computers to give people access to knowledge free from authoritarian control; he became involved with the computer-hacker community in the 1970s, and in the

1980s he organized one of the first on-line discussion networks. Brand has also earned a reputation for being a great predictor of technological trends. "Stewart has an extraordinarily acute sense of what's coming next," Mitch Kapor, co-founder of the Lotus Development Corporation, told David Stipp for *Fortune* (October 16, 1995). "If he thinks it's going to be important, I want to go along for the ride, even when I don't really comprehend what it's about."

Stewart Brand was born in Rockford, Illinois, on December 14, 1938, the son of Arthur Barnard, an advertising executive, and Julia (Morley) Brand. While still a teenager, he borrowed his parents' car for a road trip to northern California to pan for gold. From 1954 to 1956 Brand attended Phillips Exeter Academy, in Exeter, New Hampshire, and in 1960 he graduated from Stanford University, in California, with a degree in biology.

In 1960 Brand joined the U.S. Army. He qualified for the Airborne Division, served as an officer, and then worked for the Pentagon as a photojournalist. Two years later Brand left the military and developed an interest in hallucinogenic drugs. He fell in with the writer Ken Kesey and his friends, who were dubbed the Merry Pranksters. (Tom Wolfe, in his 1968 book *The Electric Kool-Aid Acid Test*, chronicles the group's experimentation with LSD.) Beginning in about 1963 he and a group of artists who dubbed themselves the USCO (the Us Company), created a series of multimedia installations using film, slides, video, special lighting, music, and other media. The titles of some of their shows were *America Needs Indians*, *War:God*, *Astronomia*, and *We Are All 1*. Around this time Brand also helped organize the widely publicized "Trips Festival," a countercultural gathering that attracted 10,000 people. In 1966 he began selling buttons that read "Why haven't we seen a photograph of the whole Earth yet?"; his hope was that such an image would help people think of Earth as a single integral unit rather than a conglomeration of separate parts. Some claim that the proliferation of Brand's button led NASA to develop photographs of the planet during the Apollo space program and that these pictures provided a solidifying image for the ecology movement in the late 1960s.

In 1968 Brand founded and edited *The Whole Earth Catalog*, which pictured Earth on the front cover and proclaimed on the title page, "We are as gods, and might as well get good at it." The catalog, which came out periodically, was a source book for environmental products and useful tools for self-sufficient living. It included articles on various related topics. It was enormously popular, even among some computer scientists, such as those at the Xerox Palo Alto Research Center (PARC), in California, the research team whose work led to the launching of the Internet. "The first book PARC owned was the *Whole Earth Catalog*," former PARC member Alan Kay said to Stipp. "It was a symbol of what we thought PC tools should be like. For instance, Stewart had discovered that people

only went to the parts of the catalogue with the things they liked. But he wanted them to read the whole thing. So he got a friend to write a novel about a VW bus with a soul, and on each page of the catalogue was one page of the novel. We thought that was one of the coolest ideas ever. It led to the PARC browsers, the predecessors of net browsers that use the serendipity of bringing up a lot of linked text." Despite the catalog's popularity, Brand capped his own salary at $36,000. In 1972 *The Last Whole Earth Catalog*, which had grown to 447 pages, won a National Book Award.

In 1972 Brand began hanging out with the researchers at PARC and wrote an article about computer hackers for *Rolling Stone* (December 7, 1972, on-line), in which he reflected on a computer game called "Spacewar" and concluded, "When computers become available to everybody, the hackers take over. We are all Computer Bums, all more empowered as individuals and as co-operators. That might enhance things . . . like the richness and rigor of spontaneous creation and of human interaction . . . of sentient interaction." Brand began to pursue seriously the idea that personal computers could be used to usher in an information revolution that was true to the antiauthoritarian vision of the hippies. In a special issue of *Time* (Spring 1995) he wrote, "The counterculture's scorn for centralized authority provided the philosophical foundations of not only the leaderless Internet but also the entire personal-computer revolution." He added, "Most of our generation scorned computers as the embodiment of centralized control. But a tiny contingent—later called 'hackers'—embraced computers and set about transforming then into tools of liberation. That turned out to be the true royal road to the future." In 1974 Brand published *II Cybernetic Frontiers*, which contains two essays: one is an expansion on his *Rolling Stone* article, and the other is an examination of the work of the anthropologist and psychologist Gregory Bateson. The book, Brand has said, contains the first usage of the term "personal computers" in print. A reviewer for *Choice* (November 1974) wrote of *II Cybernetic Frontiers*, "The book is a fascinating mixture of fact, legend, philosophy, and imagination."

In 1974 Brand founded *CoEvolution Quarterly*, a forward-looking environmental and general-interest magazine that he would edit and publish until 1985. (*CoEvolution Quarterly* continues to be published as *Whole Earth* magazine.) In 1976 Brand, once more looking to the future, edited *Space Colonies*, which dealt with the subject of colonizing space. From 1977 to 1979 Brand served as advisor to California governor Edmund G. Brown Jr. He edited the *Whole Earth Software Catalog*, a book of software reviews that received a $1.3 million advance and was first published in 1984. The venture failed, in 1985, when it became evident that it was impossible to keep up with evolving software technology in a book format. However, the advance money helped Brand, along with Larry Brilliant, to start the Whole Earth 'Lectronic Link, an on-line discussion network whose servers were based in the San Francisco Bay Area. The WELL, as it became known, soon earned a reputation for being a high-quality forum for intelligent discussion on an array of topics. The network received multiple awards, including a 1988 Community Journalism Award from the Media Alliance, a 1990 Best Online Publication Award from the Computer Press Association, and a 1994 Electronic Frontier Foundation Pioneer Award.

Brand in 1984 organized the "Hacker's Conference," which brought together leading computer scientists and was broadcast nationally: since 1986 it has been an annual event. In 1986 he was invited to be a visiting scientist at the Media Laboratory of the Massachusetts Institute of Technology (MIT), in Cambridge, an interdisciplinary research group that, as the group's Web site proclaims, "helped to create now-familiar areas such as digital video and multimedia." Brand wrote a book about his experience called *The Media Lab: Inventing the Future at MIT* (1987). Lawrence Hunter, reviewing the book for the *New York Times Book Review* (September 27, 1987), noted that "at times Mr. Brand seems overwhelmed by imminent utopia" and suggested that "the political and social implications must be vastly more complex than his brief discussions suggest." Taylor Horst, however, wrote for the *Christian Science Monitor* (September 29, 1987), "[The book] may seem to whisk readers through the ideas of those individuals contemplating, and ultimately shaping, the future of communications media. But readers will find themselves stopping and pondering. Indeed, this book requires and inspires thought."

In 1988 Brand co-founded the Global Business Network (GBN), a business-consulting group focusing on the environment. As the group's Web site explains, "GBN's cofounders were convinced that the business community—not government—was most likely to translate emerging opportunities into sustainable growth and a better future. The challenge: encouraging companies to question—and change—their mental maps, to embrace uncertainty, and to stop predicting the future based on the past." GBN's clients have included the Clinton administration, the Pentagon, AT&T, Lucent, IBM, Kodak, Monsanto, Disney/ABC, and Xerox. As one Xerox executive told Stipp, "We didn't want to be channelized into our normal ways of thinking about the future. At Xerox, we call ourselves the document company. But Stewart kept pushing us to consider what happens to the document company when the whole world is wired and people get most of their information on the Net." Among Brand's duties with GBN is running a book club, whose past offerings have ranged from *The Diamond Age*, a recent science-fiction novel, to Alexis de Tocqueville's *Democracy in America*.

In 1989 Brand won the Golden Gadfly Lifetime Achievement Award from Media Alliances and became a member of the Board of Trustees of the San-

ta Fe Institute, a nonprofit multidisciplinary research and education center. The following year he joined the board of directors of the Electronic Frontier Foundation (EFF), a defender of civil rights and responsibility in the usage of electronic media. In 1994, while continuing to work with GBN, Brand, published *How Buildings Learn: What Happens After They're Built*, in which he argues that the best architectural designs evolve slowly over time as occupants modify buildings to suit their own needs. New designs, Brand asserts, should seek to reflect this dynamic. At the time of the book's publication Brand himself lived in a converted tugboat he had purchased in 1982, and his office space was a rented shipping container. In *Library Journal* (May 1, 1994) Peter Kaufman wrote of *How Buildings Learn*, "Brand believes that architecture is most interesting in the way it changes over time. He is a close student of vernacular architecture and a staunch supporter of historic preservation. More than five years of nontraditional research in photo archives and at university seminars has produced a wonderful treasure trove leading to a whole new approach to design: letting buildings change to accommodate new uses and sensibilities." Brand wrote and presented a six-part series for British television based on the book; it aired in the summer of 1997.

In 1995 Brand co-founded, with the computer designer Danny Hillis, the Long Now Foundation, with the intention of fostering long-term responsibility for the world's well-being. The principle task of the Long Now Foundation is the building of a clock, designed by Hillis, which will keep time for the next 10,000 years. As Brand points out in a book he wrote about the project, *The Clock of the Long Now: Time and Responsibility* (1999), the project is not so different from his appeals for a picture of Earth in the 1960s: both are attempts to change people's perspectives and see the larger picture. "What with accelerating technology and the short-horizon perspective that goes with the burgeoning market economies (next quarter) and the spread-read of democracy (next election)," Brand writes, as quoted by Jon Carol for the *San Francisco Chronicle* (December 31, 2000), "we have a situation where steady but gradual environmental degradation escapes our notice. The slow, inexorable pace of ecological and climactic cycles and lag times bear no relation to the hasty cycles and lag times of human attention, decision and action." He continues, "Just as the Earth photographs (from space) gave us a sense of the big here, we need things that give people a sense of the Long Now."

In 1966 Brand married Lois Jennings, an Ottawa Indian; the couple divorced in 1973. In 1983 he married Patty Phelan; they still live on the converted tug, which is docked on the waterfront in Sausalito, California. Brand continues to embrace computer technology as a means to popular liberation. In the article he wrote for the special issue of *Time* Brand predicted, "Our generation proved in cyberspace that where self-reliance leads, resilience follows, and where generosity leads, prosperity follows. If that dynamic continues, and everything so far suggests that it will, then the information age will bear the distinctive mark of the countercultural '60s well into the new millennium."—P. G. H.

Suggested Reading: *Dr. Dobb's Journal* p93+ July 1999; *E: The Environmental Magazine* p10+ May/June 1996; *Fortune* p166 Aug. 28, 1995, p160+ Oct. 16, 1995; *Library Journal* p46+ Feb. 1, 1999; *Mother Earth News* p14+ Dec. 2000/Jan. 2001; *Rolling Stone* (on-line) Dec. 7, 1972; *San Francisco Chronicle* p8 Dec. 31, 2000; *Time* (Special Issue) p54+ Spring 1995; *Upside* p43+ Jan. 1997

Brattain, Walter

Feb. 10, 1902– Oct. 13, 1987 Co-inventor of the transistor

As one of the three men who contributed to the invention of the transistor in 1947, Walter Brattain played an integral role in one of the defining technological developments of the 20th century. Brattain was the experimental researcher on the team, which was also comprised of the physicists John Bardeen and William Shockley. The transistor revolutionized the field of electronics, replacing the bulky, inefficient vacuum tube, and it became the foundation for the vibrant growth in computer technology that took place over the next 50 years and continued on into the 21st century. By making the miniaturization of electronics feasible, transistors allowed for such innovations as portable radios, vastly enhanced telephone service and, perhaps most significantly, computers that were much smaller, more compact, and more energy efficient than the hulking machines that existed during the vacuum-tube–era. Without Brattain's research, the devotion that made possible the electronics and computer explosion of the late 20th century might not have been invented.

Walter Houser Brattain was born on February 10, 1902 in the city of Amoy, now Hsiamen, in southeastern China. His parents, Ross R. Brattain and Ottilie (Houser) Brattain, were both American citizens. Ross Brattain had been working in China as a teacher at a private boys school when Walter, the oldest of the Brattains' four children, was born. The family moved back to the United States shortly after Walter's birth, settling in Tonasket, Washington, where his father became a homesteader, cattle rancher, and flour miller. Brattain grew up on his parents' cattle ranch, where he grew to hate anything having to do with farming. "Following three horses and a harrow in the dust was what made a physicist out of me," he once commented (*Nobel Prize Winners*, 1987).

After making his way through the Tonasket public school system, Walter Brattain entered Whitman College in Walla Walla, Washington, in 1920. He majored in physics and mathematics, and received a B.S. in 1924. Two years later, he earned a master's degree in physics from the University of Oregon, in Eugene, followed three years after that by a Ph.D. in physics from the University of Minnesota, in Minneapolis. During the last year of his doctoral program, he worked at the United States National Bureau of Standards, where in addition to designing a portable, temperature-controlled oscillator with V. H. Heaton, Brattain looked for ways to improve the accuracy of time and vibration-frequency measurements (used in the study of sound and in radio technology.)

In 1929, Brattain joined the Bell Telephone Laboratories in New York as a research physicist. During his first seven years there, he conducted research in such areas as the effects of adsorbed films on electron emission from hot surfaces, electron collisions in mercury vapor, magnetometers, infrared phenomena, and frequency standards. In 1936 the course of Brattain's work was changed by the arrival at Bell Labs of William Shockley, a physicist involved in research on semiconductors. Shockley was interested in developing a device for electrical regulation and amplification that would replace the vacuum tube, which was the standard technology used at that time. Invented in 1907 by Lee DeForest, the vacuum tube was the first instrument created for the purpose of modulating electrical current, but nearly 30 years later it was seen as limiting the development of electronics. The vacuum tubes' bulb-like glass cases made them very fragile, they used up a great deal of space and energy, and they were expensive to manufacture as well. Shockley had the idea of creating a device that would perform the same functions as a vacuum tube without many of the earlier invention's drawbacks, and after coming to work at Bell he soon recruited Brattain as a research partner. Semiconductors—materials with properties of both excellent conductor of electricity, such as copper, and insulators, such as rubber, which conduct electricity poorly, were studied by Shockley and Brattain as the most likely building blocks for the new electrical relay device that Shockley envisioned.

In 1942 Brattain's and Shockley's research was interrupted by the World War II. Both men were sent to the Division of War Research at Columbia University, in New York City, and for the next three years their efforts were concentrated toward applying scientific methods to antisubmarine warfare. At the conclusion of the war, Brattain and Shockley returned to Bell, where they were joined in their research by theoretical physicist John Bardeen. Brattain's main function in the group was that of experimentalist, studying the properties of whatever materials were under investigation and testing early versions of the device. Shockley's theories provided the main impetus for the group's work; he believed that a current flowing through a semiconductor would be affected by an electric field created by an outside source, thus producing what he called a field-effect amplifier. The three men designed many experimental devices in attempts to achieve this effect, all of which failed.

Eventually, Bardeen figured out the main problem with failed devices. He suggested that a layer of electrons at the surface of the semiconductor prevented the electric field from entering it. This led Brattain and Bardeen, using Shockley's work as a theoretical basis, to undertake an extensive study of semiconductor surfaces. They discovered that the rectifying and amplifying properties of semiconductors occur at the surface as opposed to deep within the material. Armed with this new information, in December 1947 the two men constructed the first successful "transfer resistor," shortened to "transistor." It consisted of two closely spaced gold-film contacts mounted 50 microns apart on a block of germanium crystal, with a third terminal on the opposite side. An electrical signal applied to one of the gold contacts amplified the current flowing through the third terminal to produce what is known as "the transistor effect." The invention was officially announced the next year.

The transistor permitted a very small electrical current in one circuit to control a much larger current in another circuit, like the vacuum tube had done previously. However unlike vacuum tubes, transistors were compact, cheap to produce, and energy efficient, and for these reasons they quickly replaced their predecessors. Although the initial reaction to the new invention was somewhat less than enthusiastic, the world soon came around to comprehending its significance. The first commercial use of the transistor was by Bell Telephone itself; in 1952 the company employed the device in a "card translator," which rapidly selected routes for long distance calls. The first computer to use a transistor was the CDC 1604, designed in 1960 by Seymour Cray. Eventually, technology would reach a stage in which millions of transistors could be placed on a single silicon chip; these microchips formed the basis for the development of microcomputers, among them the personal computers that became ubiquitous during the 1980s and 1990s.

After the unveiling of the transistor, Brattain received a torrent of accolades. The University of Portland, in Oregon, conferred an honorary doctorate on Brattain in 1952. That same year he was a visiting lecturer at Harvard University, in Cambridge, Massachusetts, and shared the Stuart Ballantine Medal of the Franklin Institute, in Philadelphia, Pennsylvania, with John Bardeen. In 1955 Brattain, Bardeen, and Shockley were corecipients of the John Scott Medal, which came with a $1,000 prize. Also in 1955, Brattain received two additional honorary doctorates, from Union College and University in Schenectady, New York, and from Whitman College.

Brattain, Bardeen, and Shockley were awarded the Nobel Prize in Physics in 1956. The three men shared the $38,634 award presented in honor of their revolutionary work. Brattain and Bardeen in particular were recognized as the inventors of the transistor, while Shockley received credit as the father of the experimentation that led to the invention. The awarding committee in Stockholm, Sweden, had been influenced in their choice by the recommendation of Swedish telephonic expert Hakan Sterky. Brattain's Nobel lecture was entitled "Surface Properties of Semiconductors." In it he discussed the importance of surfaces, "where many of our most important and useful phenomena occur. In electronics, most if not all active circuit elements involve nonequilibrium phenomena occurring at surfaces," (*Nobel Prize Winners*, 1987). At the time the award was given, Brattain was the only one of the three men still on the staff at Bell; Bardeen had left in 1951 to join the faculty of the University of Illinois, in Chicago, and Shockley had departed four years after that to become the director of the Shockley Semiconductor Laboratory at Beckman Instruments Inc.

In 1957 Brattain was awarded his fourth honorary doctorate, from the University of Minnesota, and this was followed by similar degrees from Gustavus Adolphus College, in Minneapolis, in 1963, and Hartwick College, in Oneanta, New York, in 1964. In 1957 he was named chairman of the committee on semiconductors of the International Union of Pure and Applied Physics, a position he would hold for the next 12 years. He continued to do research on the surface properties of semiconductors, applying his findings not only to transistors but also to solar cells, which convert light into energy and are sensitive to surface electrical behavior. In 1962 he began teaching as a visiting lecturer at his alma mater, Whitman College. He became a member of the Defense Science Board in 1963, and a member of the advance board of the U.S. Naval Ordnance Testing Station in 1966; he left both positions in 1968. He retired from Bell Laboratories in 1967 upon reaching the mandatory retirement age of 65, and became an adjunct professor at Whitman College, where for the next five years he taught physics and studied the surface properties of living cells. Following his retirement from that post, in 1972, he held the title of overseer emeritus at Whitman College until his death. In 1976 he received the University of Oregon Distinguished Alumnus Award. He wrote extensively on solid-state physics throughout his life, and was granted several patents.

Brattain married his first wife, Keren Gilmore, a physical chemist, on July 5, 1935. Together they had a son, William Gilmore Brattain. Keren died in April 1957, and Brattain married Emma Jane Kirsch Miller on May 10 of the following year. He was a member of such academic and scientific organizations as the National Academy of Sciences, the Franklin Institute, the Inventors Hall of Fame (to which he was named in 1974), the American

Academy of Arts and Sciences, the Explorers Club, the Swedish Royal Academy, and the American Physical Society. He was known for his blunt, outspoken demeanor, and enjoyed reading, fishing, and golf.

Walter Brattain died on October 13, 1987 in Seattle, Washington, at the age of 85. He was cremated and inurned in Pomeroy, Washington. His contribution to the world is both multifaceted and extremely far-reaching, as the transistor made possible a myriad of technological advancements and new devices that became part of daily life for people across the globe. "It is a great satisfaction, to have done something in life and to have been recognized for it in this way," he stated when he was informed that he had won the Nobel Prize, as quoted in the *Bell Laboratories Record* (November 1956). "However, much of my good fortune comes from being in the right place, at the right time, and having the right sort of people to work with." All of these ingredients fell into place for Brattain and his colleagues and allowed them to develop one of the most important innovations of the 20th century, paving the way for the Information Age.—B. S.

Suggested Reading: *Bell Laboratories Record* p401+ Nov. 1956, with photos; *Current Biography Yearbook*, 1957, 1987; Asimov, Isaac. *Asimov's Biographical Encyclopedia of Science and Technology*, 1982; *American Men and Women of Science*, 13th ed., vol. 1, 1976; *Larousse Dictionary of Scientists*, 1994; *Nobel Prize Winners*, 1987; *Who Was Who in America 1985–89*, vol. 9; *World Who's Who in Science*, 1968

Courtesy of www.bricklin.com

Bricklin, Dan

July 16, 1951– Co-creator of the VisiCalc computer program

When Dan Bricklin and Bob Frankston's VisiCalc spreadsheet computer program was released in 1979, it proved so useful and reliable that it soon became indispensable to many businesses. The speed and accuracy of VisiCalc's calculations were so far superior to what most accountants could do with pencil and paper that businesses began buying personal computers just to use the software. VisiCalc nearly singlehandedly expanded the personal-computer market beyond hobbyists and made the new technology a necessity for offices.

Though Bricklin and Frankston did not reap huge financial profits from their spreadsheet program (partly because it was eventually surpassed by Lotus 1-2-3), they helped change the face of business by doing for accounting what word-processing programs had done for text—providing speed and accuracy in an easy-to-use application that aided in human problem solving.

Daniel Bricklin was born in Philadelphia, Pennsylvania, on July 16, 1951. He attended Solomon Schechter Day School, in Philadelphia, and began doing amateur computer programming in high school, including using the FORTRAN computer language in a science-fair project. In 1969 he began studying mathematics at the Massachusetts Institute of Technology (MIT), in Cambridge. In the middle of his junior year, he switched his major to computer science, mostly due to his work at MIT's Laboratory of Computer Science, where he wrote computer code that helped establish the computer language known as APL (a programming language). He also helped design an on-line calculator for the laboratory. Most importantly, the computer lab brought him together with fellow student and future collaborator, Bob Frankston.

Bricklin graduated from MIT with a bachelor's degree in electrical engineering and computer science in 1973. That same year he went to work for the Digital Equipment Corporation (DEC), where he wrote about a quarter of the company's first word-processing program, WPS-8, and developed programming for an interface between typesetters and newswire services. At DEC he also worked on computerized typesetting and learned about display screens and editing. He left DEC in 1976 to work as a senior systems programmer for the Fas-Fax Corporation, which built electronic cash registers. There he learned about microprocessor-based hardware designs and gained some knowledge of how to run a small business.

Bricklin left FasFax in 1977 in order to study business at the graduate level—which he and Frankston had discussed doing since their days at MIT. In the fall of 1977 he enrolled in the graduate program at Harvard University, in Cambridge, Massachusetts. However, he often found himself daydreaming in class: during a class in the spring of 1978, he had the idea that an electronic spreadsheet—a program that could work with numbers as easily as a word processor worked with text—would be of incredible value to businesses, allowing them to perform calculations much more easily than they could by hand. Having been a programmer at DEC, he realized that personal computers could be very powerful tools for businesses but that they were still used primarily by hobbyists to create computer games and other programs. What he needed to start his own business, Bricklin thought, was a simple, business-oriented computer program that could be used on personal computers. "The goal [of the program]," Bricklin has said, "was that it had to be better than the back of an envelope." He envisioned a program that would allow a user to insert and delete numbers as many times as desired and see an immediate change in the resulting calculations. Unlike the handwritten process, where every new calculation could provide an opportunity for a mistake, Bricklin's program would be error-free—and considerably more flexible.

Bricklin sought the assistance of a variety of people, including his Harvard professor, who was skeptical that Bricklin's program would be any more useful than the ones that ran on mainframe computers. Undaunted, Bricklin turned to Bob Frankston, who was working as a computer programmer. In Frankston's attic, the two wrote a spreadsheet program for the Apple II computer, with Bricklin laying out the fundamental design and documentation and Frankston doing the programming. They also contacted Dan Flystra, a Harvard alumnus who agreed to handle the marketing through his software-publishing company, Personal Software.

While Franklin proceeded with the programming, Bricklin continued to work on his MBA (which he earned in 1979), occasionally aiding Frankston with decision-making. Both agreed that the program should be as simple as possible, so that anyone—not just someone with programming knowledge—could use it. In the end, the program used only 25,000 bites of memory—large for personal computers at the time but negligible by today's standards. They named it VisiCalc, short for visible calculator, and started Software Arts to manufacture the product.

VisiCalc was launched in December 1979 and soon proved to be a success. In January 1979 a working version was shown to Apple Computer, which, though initially underwhelmed, eventually agreed to package it with its computers. Priced at $100, VisiCalc gave business people a reason to spend $3,000 on a personal computer. As sales skyrocketed, Bricklin and Frankston developed versions of the program for the Commodore PET, the Tandy TRS-80, and the Atari 800 personal computers.

VisiCalc did much to aid in the success of the fledgling personal-computer industry by proving that no technical training was needed to run a computer program. As Martin Campbell-Kelly and William Aspray remarked in *Computer: A History of the Information Machine* (1996), "The personal computer . . . offered some significant advantages that were not obvious at the outset. Because the personal computer was a stand-alone, self-contained system, changes to a financial model were displayed almost instantaneously compared with the minute or so it would have taken on a conventional computer. This fast response enabled a manager to explore a financial model with great flexibility, asking what later became known as 'what if?' questions." VisiCalc, as Campbell-Kelly and Aspray noted, was not only a breakthrough program, "but its users experienced for the first time the psychological freedom of having a machine of one's own, on one's desk, instead of having to accept the often mediocre take-it-or-leave-it services of a computer center. Moreover, at $3,000, including software, it was possible to buy an Apple II and VisiCalc out of a departmental, or even a personal, budget."

Bricklin and Frankston developed versions of VisiCalc for the new IBM PC and Hewlett-Packard computers, and by May 1981 they had sold more than 100,000 units. They soon increased sales to some 30,000 units per month, topping off in 1983 with more than half a million units sold. However, around this time Flystra's company—now called VisiCorp—sued for the rights to VisiCalc, alleging that Bricklin and Frankston had failed to improve or update it as promised. The ensuing legal battle took up much of the next two years, preventing anyone from updating VisiCalc and allowing sales to drop to a meager 2,500 units per month. Moreover, VisiCalc was encountering strong competition from a new spreadsheet program, Lotus 1-2-3, whose parent company, Lotus Software, bought Software Arts in 1985.

Bricklin served briefly as an advisor to Lotus before undertaking another business venture in late 1985. As president and founder of Software Garden, a company that he ran out of his home, Bricklin created "Dan Bricklin's Demo Program," a program that demonstrated and simulated other pieces of software. This $75 program allowed software creators to demonstrate their software even before it was finished. He also created "Dan Bricklin's PageGarden Program," which allowed for repetitive printing on laser printers.

In 1990, while still running Software Garden, Bricklin co-founded—with a group of software-industry veterans that included Bob Frankston—a new software company called the Slate Corporation. The company sought to develop software applications for pen computers; unfortunately, pen-based computers did not sell very well, and Slate shut down after four years. During the mid-1990s Bricklin produced a number of new software programs for Software Garden, including "Dan Bricklin's OverAll Viewer," which allowed users to display data visually, and "Dan Bricklin's Demo-It," a software-demonstration program designed for Microsoft Windows.

In 1995 Bricklin founded the Trellix Corporation, which produced Web site publishing technology and Web site creation tools. In early 2003 Trellix was acquired by Interland, of which Bricklin became chief technology officer.

Because Bricklin and Frankston did not copyright their VisiCalc spreadsheet program (software, at the time, was generally not considered important enough to copyright), they earned relatively modest sums from the revolution they helped to bring about. However, as Bricklin told the *Financial Times* (December 3, 1997), the creation is more important than any monetary gain: "When I turned 40, I didn't have to ask: 'What am I going to do with my life?' It really makes me feel good [to see the success of the spreadsheet]. If you are a child of the 1960s, you want to change the world."—C. M.

Suggested Reading: Bob Frankston Web site; Dan Bricklin Web site; *Financial Times* p18 Dec. 3, 1997; *Forbes* p84 July 28, 1997; *Fortune* p219 Aug. 4, 1997; *U.S. News and World Report* p126 Jan. 11, 1999; Campbell-Kelly, Martin and William Aspray, *Computer: A History of the Information Machine*, 1996; Shurkin, Joel. *Engines of the Mind*, 1996; Spencer, Donald D. *Dictionary of Computer Quotations*, 1997; Spencer, Donald D. *Timetable of Computers*, 1997; Spencer, Donald D. *Great Men and Women of Computing*, 1999

Brilliant, Larry

May 5, 1944– Co-founder of The WELL

At various times in his life Larry Brilliant has been a physician, an activist, a religious seeker in India, a leader of the drive to eradicate smallpox, a computer networking pioneer, and an Internet entrepreneur. Though Brilliant had little background in computers, his Network Technologies International (NETI) company launched in 1984 and eventually led to the founding of The WELL—sometimes written simply as The Well, despite being an acronym—an early on-line discussion network often credited with being one of the earliest and most influential computer communities. "I've worked with Black Panthers and Chicanos, with American Indians and East Indians," Brilliant told Daniel Goleman for the *San Francisco Chronicle* (August 24, 1986). "I'm used to dealing with all kinds of people. Everyone else at Network Technologies knows more about computers and business than I do, but I'm the catalyst that makes things work. Dealing with people and getting things done are carryovers from my past. They are generic skills that transfer as easily to stamping out smallpox as to starting a company." After forming NETI, Brilliant led a phone-card company and an Internet service company. During his ventures in the high-tech world, he also maintained his interests in medicine and public health through the Seva Foundation, a charitable organization he helped found in 1978.

Larry Brilliant was born in Detroit, Michigan, on May 5, 1944. After his father died of cancer while Brilliant was studying philosophy at the undergraduate level, he decided to attend medical school at Wayne State University, in Detroit. (Brilliant himself battled cancer of the parathyroid gland later in his life.) At Wayne State in the late 1960s, Brilliant founded a movement of fellow medical students to resist the draft. He earned his M.D., in 1969, and served his surgical internship at Presbyterian Hospital, in San Francisco, where he also became editor of the journal of the Medical Committee for Human Rights. That year he was married to his wife, Girija. In 1970, when a group of Native Americans affiliated with the American Indian Movement seized Alcatraz Island to protest abuses by the U.S. federal government, Brilliant joined them to help deliver a baby. (The baby was the child of John Trudell, the noted activist and poet.) As Brilliant told Harriet Rubin for *Fast Company* (October 2000, on-line), the infant was "the first Indian baby to be born on Indian- freed land in 200 years. [The mother] couldn't get a doctor to come out and deliver the baby. I agreed to go out there. I wound up living on Alcatraz for a couple of weeks, the only white person there."

Later in 1970, when a cyclone wreaked havoc on an island off Bangladesh, Brilliant went with a group called the Hog Farm commune to offer relief. Soon he met the guru Neem Karoli Baba and joined his ashram. When Neem Karoli Baba convinced him that he had a calling to fight the smallpox epidemic that was devastating India, Brilliant traveled to the United Nations offices to offer his services. "I had never seen a case of smallpox," Brilliant told Rubin. "I don't know how my guru knew that I could do this work. I had hair down the middle of my back, and I was wearing a white robe. Everybody in the United Nations was over 50 and wearing a business suit. I showed up at the United Nations office dressed as you would expect someone to be dressed in a monastery. I walked in and said, 'My mystic sent me to cure smallpox.' I was told to go home. I took the 17-hour bus ride back to the ashram and told Baba that I had failed. He said, 'Go back.' I did this two dozen times, making this trip back and forth. Slowly, the robe gave way to pants, then to a shirt, then to a tie, then to a haircut, and then to a résumé. I learned to look like a diplomat." In 1973 Brilliant became a medical officer for the World Health Organization (WHO), traveling through India as a head of the smallpox vaccination program. He left India in 1976, and in 1977 enrolled in the master's program in public health at the University of Michigan, in Ann Arbor, while continuing as a consultant for WHO. Having earned his master's, Brilliant worked as an assistant professor in public health at the university until 1980, at which time he resumed his position as medical officer with WHO for a year. In 1981 he became an assistant professor of epidemiology at the University of Michigan, a position he held until 1989.

In 1978 Brilliant, once again influenced by Neem Karoli Baba, helped found Seva—the name is derived from the Sanskrit word for service—an organization dedicated to providing health care for the poor, including performing eye operations to alleviate blindness. Brilliant told Rubin, "Seva started primarily as a spiritual organization. The work we did to alleviate blindness was a consequence of our spirituality. It was motivated by a desire to serve God by doing good." Bob Weir and Danny Rifkin of the Grateful Dead were early Seva board members.

After a helicopter on loan to Seva went down in the Himalayas, Brilliant organized an electronic meeting between parts manufacturers in the United States, the helicopter's owners, and Indian customs agents. This gave him the idea to start NETI, a company to sell computer conferencing systems. (Some sources report that the inspiration arose from the need to conference with a Seva board member living in Alaska.) Much of the start-up capital for NETI was the result of a serendipitous meeting in the 1970s, when Brilliant had befriended Steve Jobs, co-founder of Apple Computer. Jobs had convinced Brilliant to invest in his new company. "I tried to tell him that Apple was a terrible idea," Brilliant admitted to Rubin. "Why didn't he become the executive director of Seva and do some good? He kept saying, 'Computers are going to change the world. We're going to take away the power of the priestly class that runs these mainframes.' He wouldn't lead Seva, but he did give us money and computers. We were trying to do Steve a good turn, so we bought shares in Apple."

Brilliant gave five percent of NETI's stock options to Seva, which, as Goleman wrote, "set a startling new precedent in the business world. It is unheard of for a new company to give away part of itself to charity from the beginning. And yet Brilliant . . . felt it essential to 'tithe' his company by donating a percentage of its shares to charities." As Brilliant explained to Goleman, "I watched so many people who went into business saying they would give it away, then get rich and never give a thing. They keep saying, 'I'll do it when I get more.' And they never quite get that 'more.'" By the time NETI went public, on October 26, 1984, shares had risen from $1.25 to $3.25 each, which resulted in a $1.08 million endowment for Seva.

Unfortunately for Seva and Brilliant, NETI began to lose money and was sold, but not before it led to the formation of an innovative on-line discussion network known as the Whole Earth 'Lectric Link (WELL), in April 1985. Brilliant came up with the original idea based on his networking systems at NETI. Stewart Brand, the creator of *The Whole Earth Catalog*, agreed to run The WELL, while Brilliant financed it through NETI and supplied the main server computer and the needed software. The WELL started off as a forum primarily for the writers and readers of *The Whole Earth Catalog* and quickly expanded, earning a reputation for being a high-quality forum for intelligent discussion on an array of topics. In *CNET News* (April 7, 1999, on-line) Jim Hu wrote, "Many consider The Well to be the torchbearer of developing online communities centered around topics of interest." The network received multiple awards, including a 1988 Community Journalism Award from the Media Alliance, a 1990 Best Online Publication Award from the Computer Press Association, and a 1994 Electronic Frontier Foundation Pioneer Award. The WELL was acquired in April 1999 by the on-line magazine *Salon*.

In 1989 Brilliant found himself in the midst of yet another business venture when his younger brother asked him to start a "smart-card" business with him, which they called Brilliant Color Cards. Brilliant's smart cards allowed users to automatically pre-pay or bill phone calls to their bank accounts, and by 1994 Brilliant Color Cards had become the largest American producer of phone cards. Brilliant left the company, in April 1998, and assumed the post of chief executive officer for SoftNet Systems, a provider of broadband Internet services. Visitors to the SoftNet offices are welcomed by an eight-foot-tall statue of Ganesh, the Hindu god of wisdom. The statue carries its own set of communications tools: an ivory pen, a book, and a bird for sending messages. SoftNet provides broadband Internet service primarily to rural communities by working with small local cable companies. They began at a time when these areas were still mostly beyond the reach of the Internet revolution, and Brilliant felt he was doing these communities a service by making the Internet available to them. "We've got to be ruthless about equality of access in rural markets," Brilliant told Corey Grice for *CNET News* (July 15, 1999, on-line). However, a large-scale consolidation of cable companies—with 10 major companies controlling approximately 92 percent of the market—soon occurred, and Brilliant was forced to look toward other markets. In 1999 he acquired a subsidiary company, Intellicom, to provide satellite-based Internet service, aiming for untapped markets in Asia. SoftNet's stock shot up for a while before declining again in the latter half of 2000. On December 5, 2000 Brilliant resigned as CEO of SoftNet, retaining his position as chairman of the board. Not long after, he resigned from the board as well.

Brilliant, who has three children, has minimized his business involvements. He is a member of the International Epidemiology Association, the American Public Health Association, the New York Academy of Science, the American Association of World Health, and the Federation of American Scientists. He is chairman emeritus of the International Telecard Association and is active on the board of Camp Winnarainbow, a performing arts camp.—P. G. H.

Suggested Reading: *Byte* (on-line) June 1996; *CNET News* (on-line) Apr. 7, 1999, July 15, 1999; *Fast Company* (on-line) Oct. 2000; *Forbes* p74+ Feb. 21, 2000; *New York Times* I p1 May 28, 1994, C p11 May 31, 2000; *PR Newswire* p1 Apr. 24, 2000; *San Francisco Chronicle* p13 Aug. 24, 1986; *Telephony* p52+ Jan. 25, 1999

Bryce, James Ware

Sep. 5, 1880–1949 Chief scientist at IBM (1917–1948)

James Ware Bryce, the chief scientific director at International Business Machines (IBM) from 1917 to 1948, was known within the company as the "patron saint of engineering." He earned more than 400 patents for his designs and in 1936 was honored by the U.S. Patent and Trademark Office during its centennial celebration as one of the 10 greatest living inventors. He was one of the main innovators of punched-card technology—the process of punching a pattern of holes in a paper card to represent binary-coded data—which formed the basis of all early data-processing technology. Bryce was known to be both practical and innovative, working to improve existing products with established markets while monitoring new developments in electronics and data-storage media. Although his name is not widely known today, he greatly contributed to IBM's emergence as a leader of the Information Age in the early 20th century. According to a profile written after his death in IBM's *Think* magazine (April 1949), Bryce was "taciturn, humble, humane, dry-humored, straight-thinking, modest in his requirements, devoted to his family—and intensely proud of his ancestry."

James Ware Bryce was born on September 5, 1880 in New York City, to Scottish parents. As a teen, he attended public high school in New York and performed physics and chemistry experiments in a basement laboratory with his brother, Clarence. He was interested in all things modern, including gas engines, telephones, photographs, and—most of all—electricity.

Bryce studied mechanical engineering at New York's City College from 1897 to 1900. He left college before receiving a degree, believing that what he could not teach himself he would learn through practical experience. He first accepted a job as a draftsman and designer with D. H. Haywood.

Three years later, he teamed up with the inventor Wallace Christie and the Christie organization. Together, Bryce and Christie designed what is thought to have been the world's first front-wheel-drive automobile. It was a racing car that, when tested on Brighton Beach, in New York, exceeded 60 miles per hour—a speed that must have seemed astronomical in the early days of "horseless carriages" (as cars were called at the time). While with the Christie organization, Bryce also designed portable machinery for the navy.

In 1904 Bryce became the chief draftsman for Harry W. Goss, an engineer and patent designer with whom he would collaborate for the next 13 years and form the Goss & Bryce company. Bryce also became a valued consultant who was approached by manufacturers and investors to determine the feasibility and commercial value of projects. It was as a consultant with the Time Recording division of IBM that Bryce got to know that company's president, Thomas J. Watson. Watson recognized Bryce's talents and, in 1917, convinced him to become chief scientific director at IBM.

Bryce was first sent to IBM's plant in Endicott, New York, to study and improve the punched-card equipment. He helped increase their punched-card machine's speed and accuracy, but his greatest contribution was creating a flexible accounting machine that could add, subtract, multiply, and divide. During the 1920s he worked with Clair D. Lake on a new punched-card design with 80 columns, on which much more data could be stored. All IBM products were made compatible with this card, which, according to James Cortada's *Historical Dictionary of Data Processing: Biographies* (1987), accounted for 5 to 10 percent of all company revenue during the 1930s. Bryce also helped perfect the multiplying punch machine and a popular alphabetical accounting machine.

Bryce worked at IBM through the Depression years, when most U.S. companies were struggling and demand for expensive technology was low. Under Watson's guidance, IBM continued to manufacture and perfect its machinery through the lean years. After the passage of the 1935 Social Security Act, the company secured a government contract to maintain the employment records of 26 million people. According to IBM's Digital Archives Web site, this project was "the biggest accounting operation of all time" and proved so successful that other federal agencies soon placed orders for IBM machines.

For most of his time at IBM, Bryce focused his energies on products with proven technology and a ready market. At the same time, however, he was a voracious reader of scientific publications and kept abreast of new developments. Realizing the inadequacy of punched cards, which could be used only once, Bryce considered other means of recording data, including pencil marks, photographic film, and magnets. As early as 1937 Bryce was searching for ways to convert data into a magnetic medium—20 years before IBM announced the development of the first magnetic-disk storage computer, the 305 RAMAC. He also led research into electronics, including the potential of an electronic vacuum tube to perform calculations. (Calculating machines of the time used adding wheels, controlled electromechanically.) After World War II electric vacuum tubes formed the basis of IBM computers. The work Bryce directed and encouraged culminated in 1946 in the world's first full-sized digital computer: the Automatic Sequence Controlled Calculator, known as the Mark I. The result of a six-year collaboration between IBM and Harvard University, the Mark I was the first machine that could automatically execute long computations.

Bryce took part in many research projects with universities and scientific organizations. He served as the liaison between the U.S. Army and researchers at the University of Pennsylvania, in Philadelphia, where in 1946 the Electronic Numerical Integrator Analyzer and Computer, or ENIAC, was completed. Among other uses, the ENIAC was applied to scientific research and weather prediction. Bryce also took part in the construction of a wind tunnel at the California Institute of Technology, in Pasadena, and helped develop IBM products for automatically measuring and recording data in the wind tunnel.

Perhaps Bryce's name is less well known than some of his contemporaries because of his habit of working closely with many other talented inventors and engineers. In *Think* magazine he was described as a "friendly, fruitful" collaborator who would often conceive of an idea, explain it to others, and then delegate the work to his associates. "His main interest was in proving the idea practical, and whether they achieved this pneumatically, electro-mechanically, or electronically did not overly concern him."

Bryce operated IBM's patent department until 1948, by which point he had personally accumulated more than 400 patents and directed a staff that had secured hundreds more. A private man, he was known as a devoted father and husband. Outside of his work, he enjoyed reading history and biography and traveling to Scotland, the home of his ancestors. Bryce died in 1949, one year after his retirement.—M. A. H.

Suggested Reading: *Think* p30+ Apr. 1949; Cortada, James. *Historical Dictionary of Data Processing: Biographies*, 1987; *IBM's Early Computers*, 1986

Burks, Arthur W.

Oct. 13, 1915– Mathematician; philosopher; computer scientist

As one of the principal designers of three machines that shaped the future of computing, during the 1940s Arthur W. Burks made invaluable contributions to the Information Age. Burks worked on the Electronic Numerical Integrator and Computer (ENIAC), an early general-purpose electronic computer, as well as the Electronic Discrete Variable Automatic Calculator (EDVAC), the first computer built with stored-program capability. While working at the Institute for Advanced Study (IAS), at Princeton University, in New Jersey, he helped develop a computer whose architecture would become the standard for nearly three decades. Trained as a mathematician and philosopher, Burkes worked with many of the computer world's pioneering figures, including J. Presper Eckert, John Mauchly, and John von Neumann.

Arthur Walter Burks was born on October 13, 1915 in Duluth, Minnesota. In 1936 he earned a bachelor's degree in mathematics and physics from DePauw University, in Greencastle, Indiana. He received a master's degree, in 1937, and a doctorate in philosophy and logic, in 1941, from the University of Michigan. After receiving his Ph.D., Burks went to the Moore School of Electrical Engineering at the University of Pennsylvania, in Philadelphia, to take a class in electrical engineering. He did so well in the course that after finishing it, he was hired by the school as an instructor. During America's involvement in World War II, Burks researched mine-sweeping and radar antennas, among other projects. As part of the radar research, he was involved in the construction of a radar amplifier with a bandwidth greater than any that had yet been achieved.

Another Moore School project in which Burks participated was the development of the ENIAC. The ENIAC project had been planned and initiated in May 1943 by Burks's fellow Moore School faculty members Mauchly and Eckert. The proposed computer was to be made up completely of electronic parts; earlier computers were either a mixture of electronic and mechanical components, or completely mechanical in nature. Burks noted in David Ritchie's book *The Computer Pioneers* (1986) that the goal in designing the ENIAC "was to achieve, in a highly complex system, the greatest possible simplicity of design, construction, operation, and maintenance, in order to hold down both human and mechanical error."

Trained in mathematics, logic, and philosophy, Burks, who was named one of two senior engineers of the project, possessed a different educational background than the majority of his colleagues. His main responsibility was to make sure that all of the ENIAC's electronic circuits were logically correct and could function properly. Burks helped with the actual design of these circuits during the construction of the machine. He also kept the minutes of all meetings concerning the ENIAC and recorded many of the computer's technical specifications. In April 1945 Burks was assigned the task of writing up full reports on the new computer. Under his authority were Harry Huskey and Adele Goldstine, the wife of a U.S. Army engineer named Herman Goldstine; the pair wrote the first and only operating manual for the ENIAC, with Burks's supervision.

The completed ENIAC could do complicated calculations 10 times faster than the other equipment of the time and was used in plotting ballistics trajectories. In February 1946 Burks performed the earliest formal public demonstration of the ENIAC's capabilities. Before members of the press, he used the computer to execute several different computations, including a 5,000-number addition problem (completed in one second), a 500-number multiplication problem (also done in a second), the generation of various squares and cubes as well as a sine and cosine table, and the calculation of a trajectory for a cannon shell. "Just before I flipped the switch, I warned the journalists to look up from their notebooks," Burks recalled in the *Scientist* (August 21, 1995), "but most of the people were still writing when the results appeared."

While still in the process of building the ENIAC during the war years, the scientists at the Moore School began working on an even more advanced computer. Called EDVAC, the computer would be the first to be built with the capacity to store programs—a feature built into the ENIAC only later. Burks was appointed senior engineer of the EDVAC project when it began in the fall of 1944. During a large part of 1945, Burks's attention was focused on the EDVAC, while most of the rest of the staff continued to work on the ENIAC. Along with the mathematician John von Neumann and Herman Goldstine, Burks mapped out the mathematical and logical structure of the EDVAC, concentrating on flexibility of use, storage capacity, computing speed, sorting speed, and circuit design. According to James Cortada in the *Historical Dictionary of Data Processing: Biographies* (1987), Burks contributed much to the overall internal design of the computer, despite the fact that von Neumann later received most of the credit.

Burks left the Moore School in March 1946, after the ENIAC had been dedicated, to join the IAS. There he worked with von Neumann on the construction of a computer von Neumann had been conceptualizing for years. The first incarnation of these ideas, the IAS computer, as it was known, used a revolutionary form of memory involving cathode ray tubes and featured a unique three-dimensional interior architecture. It was the fastest machine yet built.

Also in 1946 Burks joined von Neumann and Herman Goldstine in writing "Preliminary Discussion of the Logical Design of an Electronic Computing Instrument," one of the most influential papers in computing history. A seminal work in engineering theory, this study was the first to explicitly describe not how any one specific electronic computer should be designed, but how all electronic computers in general should be designed, detailing the specifications for the logical structure and fundamental method of operation of all future machines. (The so-called "von Neumann model" became the standard template for computer design right up to the dawn of the personal computer in the early 1980s.) At about this time Burks also joined Adele Goldstine in assisting von Neumann and Herman Goldstine in developing the concept of the "flow diagram," a programming aid in which geometrical diagrams are used to logically express mathematical problems.

Burks joined the philosophy department of the University of Michigan, as an assistant professor in the fall of 1946. (He returned, however, to the IAS computer project during the summers of 1948 and 1949 on a temporary basis.) In addition, between 1948 and 1954, he was a computer consultant to the Burroughs Corporation, and he worked on the ORACLE computer at the Atomic Energy Installation, in Oak Ridge, Tennessee, from 1950 to 1951. He continued to teach at the University of Michigan while holding these other jobs, and the remainder of his career was devoted primarily to his work there as a professor of philosophy. After becoming an associate professor, in 1948, he founded a research group that studied the logic of computers. The group did research on various areas, including aspects of programming and automated technology.

In 1954 Burks attained the position of full professor at the University of Michigan. He was the cofounder of a doctoral program in computer and communication sciences there in 1956. When a department of computer and communication science was eventually established at the school, in 1967, Burks became the first chairman, a role he filled for four years. The University of Michigan named him the Henry Russel Lecturer for 1977–78, the greatest honor that institution can grant to one of its faculty. Toward the end of his teaching career, Burks was a visiting professor at various institutions, including Harvard University, in Cambridge, Massachusetts, and Stanford University, in California. In 1986 he retired from full-time teaching. Since then, he has been a professor emeritus of philosophy, electrical engineering, and computer science at the University of Michigan.

Burks received an honorary doctorate from DePauw University in 1973. He won the Institute of Electrical and Electronic Engineers (IEEE) Computer Pioneer Award in 1982. He has authored and co-authored several important works during the course of his career. In addition to the groundbreaking paper he wrote with von Neumann and Goldstine during their IAS days, Burks also collaborated with von Neumann on the book *Theory of Self-Reproducing Automata* (1966). Burks is the author of *Chance, Cause, Reason—An Inquiry into the Nature of Scientific Evidence* (1977), and he collaborated with his wife, Alice, on several works, including "The ENIAC: First General Purpose Electronic Computer," an article that appeared in the

Annals of the History of Computing (1981), and *The First Electronic Computer: The Atanasoff Story* (1988), which concerns John Atanasoff's invention of the Atanasoff-Berry Computer (ABC) in 1939. (There has been some controversy as to whether Atanasoff's machine or the ENIAC was the first fully electronic computer. In 1973, a court ruling invalidated the ENIAC's patent, deeming the concept to have been derived from Atanasoff's ideas.)

With his unique background and insight, Burks has had an important influence on the development of electronic computing technology. In his book *The Computer from Pascal to von Neumann* (1972), Burks's former colleague Herman Goldstine calls him "one of those rare people with a real understanding of mathematics, philosophy, and engineering and their interrelationships." Yet, much like many other early computer pioneers, Burks admits that, although he "understood and believed [the computer] would revolutionize science and engineering," as quoted in the *Scientist*, he never imagined the dramatic influence it would one day have on the entire world.—B. S.; C. M.

Suggested Reading: *Scientist* p3 Aug. 21, 1995, with photo; Goldstine, Herman. *The Computer from Pascal to von Neumann*, 1972; Ritchie, David. *The Computer Pioneers*, 1986; Cortada, James. *Historical Dictionary of Data Processing: Biographies*, 1987; Lee, J. A. N., ed. *International Biographical Dictionary of Computer Pioneers*, 1995

Burroughs, William Seward

Jan. 28, 1855–Sep. 15, 1898 Inventor; entrepreneur

The inventor William Seward Burroughs designed an adding machine in 1885 that provided for both the fast computation of smaller numbers and the printing capabilities needed by banks and other businesses for accounting purposes. While the new timesaving keyboards on Burroughs's machines were very similar to those found on the comptometers of Dorr E. Felt (who was granted a patent shortly before Burroughs), the printing function of Burroughs's machines made them particularly appealing to businesses. The American Arithmometer Company, which he founded to market his machines, was eventually renamed the Burroughs Adding Machine Company; it became one of the largest calculating-machine manufacturers in the United States. As Martin Campbell-Kelly and William Aspray wrote in *Computer: A History of the Information Machine* (1996), the success of the Burroughs Adding Machine Company and a handful of other office machine companies positioned the United States to become a leader in computer technology in the 20th century. "Powered by the fad for office rationalization," they wrote, "America was the first country in the world to adopt office machinery on a large scale. This early start enabled the United States to become the leading producer of information technology goods, a position it has sustained to present day. . . . There is thus an unbroken line of descent from the giant office-machine firms of the 1890s to the computer makers of today."

William Seward Burroughs was born on January 28, 1855 in Auburn, New York. After a fairly minimal education he began work as a clerk at the Cayuga County National Bank in Auburn, where he spent long hours adding sums. During his 20s his health failed; in 1882 he relocated to St. Louis, Missouri, to work as a mechanic. Always troubled by the number of errors he encountered at the bank, Burroughs soon decided to build an adding machine that would keep a printed record of its calculations.

While adding machines had been in existence since the 17th century, several problems needed to be solved before they could be useful to most bank clerks and other bookkeepers. Existing calculators required the manipulation of time-consuming mechanisms, making them useful only to those working with very large numbers. Until keyboard-equipped calculators replaced slower dial and lever mechanisms, those working with smaller numbers could still do calculations faster on paper. Additionally, no machine had combined calculating with printing, a feature that Burroughs knew would be helpful to the accounting processes of banks and other businesses.

The keyboard of Burroughs's adder consisted of several columns of nine keys. The two keys furthest to the right were designated as decimal places, a helpful feature for those calculating dollars and cents. Hitting one of the number keys caused a gear to turn a corresponding number of notches on its axis, which would cause the number to register in the total. For example, to add $51.20 to a sum one would hit, in any order, a "5" in the tens column, a "1" in the ones column, and a "2" in the one-tenths column, leaving the one-hundredths column untouched because there was no "zero" key. Since the keys could be punched in any order or all at once, sums could be added with great speed once a certain facility with the machine was reached. To print a total one simply pulled a lever.

On January 10, 1885 Burroughs applied for a U.S. patent. The initial design of his adder printed only the final results of the sums, and not the figures that were entered to create the total—this shortcoming was remedied before the patent was granted on August 21, 1888. With Thomas Metcalfe, R. M. Scruggs, and W. C. Metcalfe, Burroughs founded the American Arithmometer Company to market his calculators in 1886. The company sold just one product, Burroughs's printing adder, which sold for $475. The machine, however, proved quirky: Sums varied based on how vigorously one pulled the lever to execute the calculation, and few were able to work the machine correctly. Purportedly, one field agent for Burroughs was able to operate the machine so well that he refused to sell it, preferring to go around making bets on his accuracy. When Burroughs discovered that few besides himself could work the calculators, he went to his office and tossed 50 of the machines out the window onto the pavement, two floors below.

Burroughs corrected the problem by adding a dash pot—a liquid-filled piston to absorb the shock of vigorous movement—to the printing lever. On May 5, 1892 he received a patent for the modified calculator. Production and sales of the calculators increased each year, and in 1895 the American Arithmometer Company sold 284 machines. Soon, however, Burroughs's health faltered, and in 1898 he retired from the company. He died of tuberculosis on September 15, 1898 in Citronelle, Alabama.

The American Arithmometer Company sold 972 machines in 1900 and continued to grow, eventually adding various calculator models to its line and becoming the main manufacturer of calculators in the United States. In 1905 the company was renamed the Burroughs Adding Machine Company in Burroughs's honor. (The company became Burroughs Corporation and entered the nascent field of computers in the early 1950s.) The Burroughs Corporation had developed into the third-largest U.S. computer company by the mid-1980s; in 1986 the company merged with the Sperry Corporation to form Unisys.

William Seward Burroughs received the John Scott Medal of the Franklin Institute for his inventions in 1897. His grandson, also named William Seward Burroughs, was one of the leading and most controversial Beat writers of the 1950s.
—P. G. H.

Suggested Reading: *Dr. Dobb's Journal* p102 July 1998; Campbell-Kelly, Martin and William Aspray. *Computer: A History of the Information Machine*, 1996; Shurkin, Joel. *Engines of the Mind*, 1996

Bush, Vannevar

Mar. 11, 1890–June 28, 1974 Inventor of the first operative mechanical computer

Recognized for years as a computing pioneer, Vannevar Bush was the inventor of the first operative mechanical computer in 1925. However, even more relevant to the current state of computing, Bush was a major innovator of information science. He is credited as being the originator of the concept of what would one day become the World Wide Web. Bush theorized about a device called a memex, which possessed all the basic qualities of the Web, as it is known today. The developer of ideas that both set the Computer Age in motion in the early 20th century and opened the door for the information superhighway of the late 20th century, Vannevar Bush has had a profound impact on the evolution of modern computing.

Vannevar Bush descended from a line of seafaring whalers and traders. The son of Universalist minister Richard Perry Bush and Emma Linwood (Paine) Bush, he was born on March 11, 1890, in Everett, Massachusetts, and named after the clergyman who had married his parents. The family moved to Chelsea, Massachusetts, where the young Bush was raised and attended local public schools. As a child, he suffered through a succession of illnesses, but as he grew older he would spend a great deal of time sailing small boats in Boston Bay, and work as a cook on a fishing ship during summer vacations. Bush would also serve as the organ player at his father's church services.

Marie Hansen/Getty Images

After graduating high school in 1909, Bush attended Tufts University, where he received both his B.S. and M.S. degree in 1913. His master's thesis dealt with a report on the invention of a surveying device called the Profile Tracer, to be used to measure distances on uneven ground. Upon graduation, Bush took his first position with the test department of General Electric (GE). A year later, he left to work in the inspection department of the

U.S. Navy, also accepting a position as a mathematics instructor at Tufts. In addition to his jobs, Bush pursued graduate studies at both Harvard University, in Cambridge, Massachusetts, and the Massachusetts Institute of Technology (MIT), also in Cambridge; he received doctorates in engineering from both schools in 1916. Not long after, Tufts promoted him to assistant professor of electrical engineering.

When the United States entered World War I in 1917, Bush was selected by the U.S. Navy to develop antisubmarine technology at a laboratory in New London, Connecticut. After the conclusion of the First World War, Bush worked for the American Radio and Research Corporation from 1917 to 1922.. He returned to teaching in 1919 as an associate professor of electrical power transmission at MIT, and in 1923 he was promoted to full professor.

Between 1925 and 1930, Bush, with the help of several colleagues, designed and constructed the network analyzer at MIT. The network analyzer was a system for setting up miniature versions of large and important electronic networks. It was also at this time that Bush developed a prototype for his most significant invention, the differential analyzer. The first fully functioning computing machine (or analog computer), the differential analyzer was based on the concepts behind 19th century mathematician Charles Babbage's Difference Engine, which was never completed. Bush created the machine out of a frustration with the tremendously complicated and repetitive mathematics involved in his engineering work.

The analyzer was originally described as a "mathematical robot", and could solve complicated problems at speeds that were astonishing for the time. In recognition of this breakthrough, Bush was awarded the Levy Medal of the Franklin Institute in 1928, as well as the Lamme Medal of the American Institute of Electrical Engineers in 1935. A completed version of the device was built and patented by Bush in 1935. A revised version of the analyzer built by Bush in 1942 was used to solve problems in ballistics, acoustics, structures, and atomic physics during World War II. The longevity of the machine would lend to the invention of the electronic ABC of John Atanasoff and the ENIAC of John Mauchly and J. Presper Eckert.

In 1932 Bush was named vice president and dean of engineering at MIT. In this role he made a comprehensive study of the entire electrical engineering undergraduate curriculum in an attempt to improve teaching methods in the field. In 1939 Bush became president of the Carnegie Institution of Washington, one of the world's largest scientific foundations. "Dr. Bush is so eminently qualified for his new position and the post is of such great influence and opportunity in the field of science and human welfare that his colleagues at [the Massachusetts Institute of] Technology are unanimous in their approval of his selection," commented MIT president Karl T. Compton (*Current Biogra-*

phy Yearbook, 1940). During his tenure as president (which lasted until 1955), Bush attempted to closely coordinate the Institution's programs with other educational and research organizations.

With the outbreak of World War II, Bush became very vocal concerning what he perceived as the uncoordinated state of science in the United States and the need for the exploration of its potential as an asset in national defense. He proposed a general directive agency in the federal government and discussed the project with the National Advisory Committee for Aeronautics, or NACA (of which he was a member from 1938 to 1948 and chairman from 1939 to 1941). NACA set to work preparing a draft of a proposed National Defense Research Committee (NDRC) to be presented to Congress sometime in 1940. However, when Germany invaded France in May of that year, Bush decided there was no time to lose, and so appealed directly to the president himself.

One of the trustees of the Carnegie Institution, Frederic Delano, happened to be the uncle of Franklin Roosevelt. Through Delano, Bush managed to arrange a meeting with the president to discuss how civilian researchers might aid military mobilization. In less than a month the NDRC was established, with Bush as chairman; this committee eventually expanded into the Office of Scientific Research and Development (OSRD) in 1941, which put Bush in charge of the approximately 6,000 scientists involved in the war effort. Bush felt that one of the main objectives of the OSRD was maintaining the confidence of the military, who were notoriously distrustful of civilians when it came to observing security regulations. Succeeding in overcoming this obstacle, the OSRD developed more than 200 weapons and instruments of war, as well as making numerous advances in chemistry, physics, and medicine.

In addition to his work as chairman of OSRD, Vannevar Bush was an instrumental figure in the Manhattan Project, which was developing the atom bomb. Chief military-research advisor to President Roosevelt during the war, Bush was the administrator of the project in its initial stages, beginning in 1940. As part of his overall push for greater exploitation of scientific research in military defense, Bush strongly advocated the government's investment in research on the new weapon. He had originally been skeptical of the potential of nuclear fission, but was convinced by British research that in 1942 proved the possibility of setting off a chain reaction in which an initial nuclear fission would cause the fission of the surrounding nuclei. He also felt the need to develop the weapon before the Nazis inevitably did. Bush brought the idea to the attention of President Roosevelt, and then discussed financial backing with Vice President Henry Wallace. The pressure and magnitude of the project took its toll on Bush, however; after witnessing the first atomic test in New Mexico, Bush collapsed from nervous exhaustion, and required hospitalization. The project was initially under the administration of the OSRD, but had to eventually be transferred to the Army Corps of Engineers in order to make it easier to acquire funding. Aside from his work on the Manhattan Project, Bush also oversaw military wartime research in radar, biological weapons, amphibious vehicles, unusual methods of sabotage, and mass production of sulfa drugs and penicillin.

Toward the end of World War II, Bush became a motivating figure in the development of a permanent national science foundation to organize the scientific community in peacetime the way the OSRD had done during the war. He submitted a report to President Roosevelt entitled *Science: The Endless Frontier*, in which he argued for the creation of such a foundation. Influenced greatly by Bush, Senator H. Alexander Smith of New Jersey introduced a bill in February 1947 to establish such an entity. It was passed by both the Senate and House of Representatives, only to be vetoed by President Truman on the grounds that the proposed organization's administrators would not be properly responsible to government. Bush was named chairman, however, of a Research and Development Board established by the National Security Act in September 1947.

At the dawn of World War II, Bush had written "As We May Think," a visionary article on the burgeoning field of information science. Published in the *Atlantic Monthly* in 1945, the article would prove to be vastly influential. Perceiving the onset of an Information Age when knowledge would become prohibitively difficult to organize and access, Bush sought a way to ease the scientific and scholarly researcher of the future. Indeed, a veritable explosion of information was already occurring, a growing mountain of research confronting scholars and decision-makers in every field. In the article, Bush acknowledged the fact that the amount of information available had "extended far beyond our ability to make real use of the record." He felt that the greatest problem affecting research was information retrieval, which often led researchers to search for weeks for a single piece of material, as they waded through a maze of irrelevant information. According to Bush, this difficulty arose largely because of inadequate means of storing, organizing, and tagging data. As a solution, he proposed the invention of a machine he called a "memex." Instead of arranging information alphabetically, or through some other cumbersome means, the memex would connect bits of data on an interrelational basis, allowing for greater ease of accessibility. It would function by association, just as the human mind does naturally. A large part of this method would involve what are today called "links": connections leading from one piece of information directly to another related piece. Bush accurately predicted "wholly new forms of encyclopedias . . . ready-made with a mesh of associative trails running through them," as well as the sharing of linked information by individual reader-writers.

Bush envisioned the memex as a motorized machine which had nothing to do with computers. His original plan involved microfilm projectors and a motorized desk with levers and translucent screens. Despite the fact that Bush's original concept was more mechanical than computerized, many view his idea as the basis of hypertext, the database format used today on the World Wide Web and other online systems, and which operates on similar principles. Originally known only as a "founding father" of mechanical computing, in recent years, the legacy of Bush has been reevaluated, and he is now also referred to as the "father of hypertext."

In 1950 the U.S. government finally established the National Science Foundation, an organization of the type for which Bush had long lobbied. Bush himself was appointed director of the Foundation, a position he filled for three years before becoming a member of the organization's advisory committee. He continued in the latter capacity until 1955, when he once again returned to MIT, where he would remain until his retirement in 1971.

Among the numerous innovations developed by Bush were improvements in the design of vacuum tubes and four-engine bombers, and important studies on transient currents in machinery and dielectric phenomena. In addition to the differential analyzer, he invented the justifying typewriter, the rapid microfilm selector, and the cinema integraph. He was a member of such organizations as the American Academy of Arts and Sciences, the National Academy of Sciences, the American Institute of Electrical Engineers, and the American Physical Society. He was also a trustee of Tufts College and Johns Hopkins University, a lifetime member of the MIT Corporation, and a regent of the Smithsonian Institution. Additionally, Bush cofounded several businesses, including the American Appliance Company, an electronics manufacturer. The holder of honorary degrees from 20 universities and colleges, he was awarded the Medal of Merit by President Truman in 1948 and the National Medal of Science by President Johnson in 1964.

In addition to the numerous articles he contributed to scientific periodicals, Bush also authored several books, including *Principals of Electrical Engineering* (with W. H. Timbie) (1923), *Operational Circuit Analysis* (1929), *Endless Horizons* (1946), *Modern Arms and Free Men* (1949), and the autobiography *Pieces of the Action* (1970). When not involved in professional life, Bush enjoyed a variety of hobbies and diversions. He had an affinity for music and was an avid flute player. Oh his New Hampshire farm, Bush raised turkeys and built a feeding station bar for wild birds. Bush was also interested in photography and enjoyed the writings of Rudyard Kipling. Bush married Phoebe Davis on September 5, 1916 in Chelsea, Massachusetts. They had two sons, Richard Davis and John Hathaway. Vannevar Bush died on June 28, 1974.

Bush had a wiry frame, standing five feet 11 inches and weighing 150 pounds. He was known for his expressive eyes, sly grin, and sharp quick gestures. He had a gravelly voice, with a slight New England accent, and an unruly head of black hair. Among his trademark accessories were his wire-rimmed glasses and his pipe, which he carved himself. Many commented on his apparent resemblance to humorist Will Rogers. In *The Bulletin of the Atomic Scientists* (December 1992), Bush biographer G. Pascal Zachary describes the man as "tough, ambitious, and manly in a Teddy Roosevelt–sort of way."—B. S.

Suggested Reading: *Brown University Computer Graphics Group of the Graphics and Visualization Center* (on-line); *Bulletin of the Atomic Scientists* p24+ Dec. 1992, with photos; *Current Biography Yearbook* p129+ 1940, with photo, p80+ 1947, with photo, p456 1974 (obit); University of Arhus Deptartment of Computer Science Web site; Asimov, Isaac. *Asimov's Biographical Encyclopedia of Science and Technology* 2nd ed., 1982

Neel Mulller/Courtesy of uWink, Inc.

Bushnell, Nolan

1943– Video-game designer

By looking for a more interesting game than pinball or games of the three-tosses-for-a-quarter variety, Nolan Bushnell created a whole new way to entertain people. As a 29-year-old working in his garage, Bushnell developed the world's first commercially successful video game, *PONG*, an electronic version of ping pong. Players would manipulate dials in order to move electronic "paddles" on either side of the screen, trying to "avoid missing ball for high score." He established Atari Inc. with $500 dollars and began selling his coin-operated *PONG* machines to bars and amusement parks. After his first year in business, he sold more than 6,000 units. When Atari introduced a *Home PONG* version of the game in 1975, Sears sold 150,000 of them through their catalogue. Bushnell almost single-handedly created the video game market, giving consumers a new way to entertain themselves. He sold Atari in 1976 for $28 million and since that time has engaged in his share of good and bad business ventures. Today he is considered the "father of modern gaming" and sole architect of an industry that sells more than $5 billion in games annually.

Nolan Bushnell was born in 1943 in Clearfield, Utah, the son of a cement contractor. In an interview with Tenaya Scheinman of the Tech Museum of Innovation in San Jose, California, archived on their Web site, Bushnell claimed that his interest in creative ventures stretched back to his early childhood. "The spark was ignited in Mrs. Cook's third-grade class when I was assigned to do the unit on electricity and got to play with the science box," he noted. "And I put together this thing and showed the classmates. And I went home, set up the card table, found all the flashlights and batteries and pieces of wire and old stuff around the house and started tinkering, and never stopped."

Bushnell's father died when he was 15, and he became the man of the house, completing his father's outstanding cementing contracts, running his crew, and closing the business before returning to school in the fall. At 19, while attending the University of Utah (where he would earn a B.S. in electrical engineering), in Salt Lake City, he worked two jobs. During the day he sold advertising; at night he worked at an amusement park. The reason he wanted both jobs was simple: if he had a night job he would not spend the money he was earning during the day. He also thought working at an amusement park would be fun. As he told Scheinman of the Tech Museum, "I decided that the amusement park would be great. And it turned out that I had a knack for it. And even though it looked like there wasn't that much money to be earned, there was a lot of commission. And I found out that I could make a lot of money based on the commission, selling balls to knock down the bottles." He would later become a department manager at the amusement park, a position which he described as being like "an MBA, on-the-job training."

During his youth Bushnell absorbed a great deal about business and electronics. From his supervisor at the amusement park he learned something about business. From a man who lived down the street from him he learned about radios and electronics in general. From a professor at the University of Utah he learned about computer graphic design. After graduating from the university, he applied for work at the Walt Disney Company. When that opportunity failed to materialize, he began thinking about another interest—his love of games, in which he had indulged by playing tournament chess in college.

He eventually became aware of how boring most amusement park and bar games were, and, working out of his garage in the early 1970s, Bushnell developed *Computer Space*, the first computer video game. It was essentially a coin-operated version of a game that students at universities had been playing on mainframe computers since 1962. The instructions to Computer Space, however, were extremely complex and the game flopped, with most of Bushnell's backers taking whatever profits were left over. "To be successful, I had to come up with a game people already knew how to play," he recalled in *U.S. News and World Report* (December 27, 1999). "Something so simple that any drunk in any bar could play."

He emerged from his garage (and later his daughter's bedroom, which he had converted into a makeshift lab) with *PONG*, an electronic version of ping pong. He pooled his resources with a friend, and with $500 they formed Atari Inc. in 1972. They took the name of the company from the word for "check" from the Japanese game Go. The first *PONG* game—a black-and-white TV encased in a wooden cabinet—debuted at Andy Capp's Tavern in Sunnyvale, California, that same year. Initially, patrons of the bar were confused by the machine. When a quarter was deposited, a small dot of light moved back and forth across the screen between two rectangular paddles that players manipulated through a set of knobs. The rules, unlike *Computer Space*, were simple, and were even posted on the machine: "Avoid missing ball for high score." Two days after the machine arrived, *PONG* broke down from overuse and the milk container that was then serving as the coin box for the machine was bursting with quarters. The age of video games had begun.

By 1973 Atari had shipped more than 6,000 of these coin-operated machines. Bushnell himself made $1 million by 1974, by which time the company was employing 320 people. In an interview for *Playboy* (March 1974), Bushnell called his band "a closely knit group, interested in higher technology for games rather than bombs." His engineers soon began producing new games, including *PONG Doubles*, *Super PONG*, *Puppy PONG*, and *QuadraPong*, but their greatest triumph would come in 1975, when Atari produced a home version of *PONG*. At first Bushnell was concerned about the success of such an item, but he was soon convinced by many of his employees (a group that included a pair of young men named Steve Jobs and Steve Wozniak) that such an endeavor was profitable. In 1975 Sears ordered 150,000 *Home PONG* units for their catalogue; it went on to become the fastest-selling item in stock.

Just as he was beginning to achieve monumental success with Atari (the company had $100 million in sales by 1977) Bushnell sold the company to Warner Communications for $28 million. He explained his reasoning to Scheinman: "I was exhausted. Atari was an all-consuming entity. . . . So to sell the company was in some ways a relief." He stayed on as board chairman of the company until he was forced out in 1978. He remained with Atari long enough to see the video game craze sweep across the United States. In an interview for the *New York Times* (April 24, 1978), Bushnell explained to Judy Klemesrud why Americans were so enamored with video games. "They're fun," he noted simply, adding, "I think it's the first time people have been able to talk back to their television set, and make it do what they want it to do. It gives you a sense of control, whereas before all you could do was sit and switch channels."

Criticism of video games began early on. The U.S. Federal Trade Commission put forth a disclaimer in the fall of 1977 suggesting that video games damaged television sets. Though Bushnell conceded that some early games made by other manufacturers did damage sets, he noted that Atari's games had no such problems. Critics also believed that such video games as Atari's Outlaw promoted violence, since it involved guns. In his 1978 interview with the *New York Times*, Bushnell quickly dismissed such an idea. "Being raised in the 60s, I had some questions about that myself," he remarked. "But I believe one of the things these games do is provide a socially acceptable way of venting hostility and aggression. It's long been believed in taverns that coin-operated video games cut down the number of fights, because they give people a way of competing." Bushnell also pointed to some surprising medical benefits of video games, including how *PONG* helped stroke victims regain the use of paralyzed muscles and how people with crossed eyes or walleyes were advised to play video games to strengthen their weak eye muscles.

Atari continued to flourish after Bushnell's departure, with sales reaching a peak of $2 billion in 1982. At that point Atari was by far the dominant video-game producer, the youngest billion-dollar company in history, and one of Warner Communications' most profitable assets. However, competitors like Magnovox, Mattel, Bally, and Coleco soon began cutting into Atari's profits. Due to increased competition and irresponsible spending—games were recorded as sold when they were shipped to warehouses rather than when they were actually purchased by retailers—the company was losing more than $2 million a day by 1983. Though the company would continue to release games and game systems, it also began releasing home computers, beginning with the Atari 400 and Atari 800. This, however, did not stem the hemorrhaging of revenues. Atari was sold in 1984 to Jack Tramiel, who produced new video games and computers with little success. The company became Time-Warner Interactive in 1993 and merged with several more companies before its hardware and software rights were sold to the toy manufacturer Hasbro, Inc. for only $5 million. In 1999 Hasbro re-released many of Atari's classic video games for the home personal computer.

In the years since leaving Atari, Bushnell has become a relentless entrepreneur, founding 18 companies since 1978. One of the first companies he established was Pizza Time Theatre, a chain of Chuck E. Cheese theme restaurants that combined fast food, video games, and robot animals. Though the company boasted $99.3 million in revenues in under five years, the company went bankrupt in 1984. In 1983 he established Sente Technology, a company that produced advanced video games for arcades developed by former Atari engineers. Around the same time he established Androbot, a company that had hoped to make robots the next wave of family pets, but went through refinancing in 1984. By 1986 Bushnell had applied his ideas about robotics to toys in a new venture, Axlon Inc., which developed talking, microchip-driven stuffed animals like A. G. Bear. That same year, Bushnell planned to merge his company with that of Steve Wozniak's, the cofounder of Apple Computers, but the deal fell through. Axlon toys failed, even with an influx of money from the toy giant Hasbro, largely because consumers wanted a talking bear that spoke English, not the gibberish that Bushnell called "bear talk."

In 1988 Bushnell returned to the company he had established through an agreement made between his then present company, Axlon, and Atari. As part of the deal, Axlon would develop video games for the latter company. Though by this point the computer giant Nintendo controlled more than 70 percent of video-game sales in the United States, Atari boasted 20 percent and believed it could increase sales by rekindling the public's interest in the system that started it all, the Atari 2600. With more than 26 million units sold, of which, Bushnell told Lawrence M. Fisher in the *New York Times* (June 2, 1988), "probably half are in the closet," he said that his goal was "to get half of those dusted off and back in play." Unfortunately, this did not come to pass.

Throughout the 1990s Bushnell remained active as an entrepreneur, first in 1991 as chairman of Octus Inc., a company that sold electronic mail and fax machines for computer networks. In 1995, according to Rex Weiner in *Variety* (June 26, 1995), he reentered the restaurant business with a new venture called E2000, a more ambitious version of his Chuck E. Cheese franchise. Arguably Bushnell's most successful venture has been his umbrella company Catalyst Technologies, established in 1981. It serves as an "incubator facility" for a dozen start-up companies involved in advanced color television, toys, games, robotics, and electronic car navigation. He is also currently involved with Uwink.com. According to an entry in the *International Biographical Dictionary of Computer Pioneers* (1995), Bushnell once claimed, "Business is the greatest game of all. Lots of complexity and a minimum of rules. And you keep score with the

money." If that's the case, then Bushnell is a remarkable success: the video-game craze he started in 1972 with *PONG* generated more than $5.5 billion in sales in 1998 alone.

Nolan Bushnell lives in California with his second wife. He has eight children.—C. M.

Suggested Reading: *Applied-Design* (on-line); *BusinessWeek* p54 Feb. 28, 1983, p57+ Feb. 17, 1986; *History of Video Games* (on-line); *New York Times* Apr. 24, 1978, D p5 June 2, 1988, p37 Oct. 19, 1991; *Playboy* p175 Mar. 1974; Tech Museum Web site; *Time* p55 Jan. 14, 1985, p50 May 5, 1986; *U.S. News and World Report* p67 Dec. 27, 1999; *Variety* p6 June 26–July 9, 1995; *Wall Street Journal* p53 July 17, 1986; Lee, J. A. N., ed. *International Biographical Dictionary of Computer Pioneers*, 1995; Spencer, Donald D. *The Timetable of Computers*, 1997

Canion, Rod

Jan. 19, 1945– Co-founder of the Compaq Computer Corporation

As the co-founder of the Compaq Computer Corporation and the co-developer of the first IBM-compatible, portable personal computer, Rod Canion is one of the major innovators of modern computing. In 1981 Canion, along with his fellow Texas Instruments engineers James Harris and William Murto, had the idea that a portable personal computer that used the same architecture and software as an International Business Machines (IBM) personal computer could prove invaluable to a businessperson on the road. Compaq's immensely popular portable computers spawned a new computer industry and made the company one of the most popular manufactures of IBM personal computer (PC) clones.

Rod Canion was born Joseph R. Canion in Houston, Texas, on January 19, 1945. He studied electrical engineering at the University of Houston, from which he earned a bachelor's degree in science in 1966 and a master's degree in electrical engineering two years later. In 1968 he joined the staff at Texas Instruments, where he worked as an engineer until 1981.

Canion left Texas Instruments as a direct result of his conversation with James M. Harris and William H. Murto. Agreeing that it was feasible to build a portable computer, they formed the Compaq Computer Corporation in 1982. Originally, they each contributed $1,000 of their own funds to the venture, but their idea soon sparked interest and generated more than $30 million in venture capital.

In 1982 Compaq introduced the first portable clone of the IBM personal computer, a 28-pound machine that sold for between $3,000 and $4,000. During its first year of operation, the company set an American business record by generating revenues of $111 million and shipping more than 53,000 of its portable personal computers. Before long, Compaq became IBM's biggest competitor in the personal-computer market. "Compaq's machine appeals largely to professionals who have [IBM] equipment at the office and want one for the road," a journalist wrote for the *New York Times* (June 16, 1983). "It runs on virtually all the same programs. But the 9-inch screen is built in, and the keyboard folds up to create a machine the size of a bulky briefcase."

Compaq's initial success was due in part to the fact that IBM had published the technical specifications for its personal computer, believing that other companies would then be able to develop the technology needed to make the PC an industry standard. In its second year Compaq shipped 150,000 units and made a profit of $329 million; its prodigious sales helped the company raise $67 million during its initial public offering of stock.

By 1985 a slew of low-priced PC clones from Asia were gaining popularity in the United States. Canion refused to build a cheap model to keep competitive, arguing that cheaper machines would undermine Compaq's image as a quality alternative to IBM. The decision proved detrimental to the company in the short run, as it lost sales to foreign manufacturers, but by 1986 Compaq had rebounded; that year it made the Fortune 500 list of American companies, having accomplished the feat faster than any other business. Much of the success was owed to Compaq's new Deskpro 386, the first personal computer to use Intel's faster and more powerful 80386 microprocessor chip—which IBM had yet to install in its computers. The 386 helped the company become the second-largest seller of personal computers in the United States, just behind IBM. Such success was especially surprising considering that it came during an industry-wide slump in personal- computer sales. Mark Ivey wrote for *BusinessWeek* (June 26, 1989), "The 80386 machines have boosted Compaq's overall market share and have let it claim the title of industry leader—the company that incorporates the newest chips and other technical innovations first." By 1987 Compaq was a billion-dollar enterprise, known as a builder of some of the most reliable—and moderately priced—PCs on the market.

In October 1988 Compaq's first laptop computer, the 286/SLT, came to market. (Laptops differ from portables in that they have thin, fold-down screens.) The 286 became available well after laptops offered by such competitors as Toshiba, Zenith, and NEC, to which Compaq had lost substantial sales. The company had tried to build a laptop division as early as 1983, but the liquid-crystal display screens on the prototypes were substandard and hard to read. However, the 286's crisp new screen and fast operating speed helped Compaq quickly gain on the laptop competition and soon placed the company second only to Toshiba in laptop sales through dealers. By 1989 Compaq's overall revenues had reached more than $3 billion.

For his good stewardship of Compaq during the 1980s, Canion received a number of awards: he was named Houston's International Executive of the Year in 1988; received an "E" award, for excellence in exports, from President Ronald Reagan in 1988; and was selected as the CEO of the decade by the Financial News Net. Both the University of Houston and Southern Methodist University, in Dallas, Texas, presented him with awards for his business leadership.

In late 1991 sluggish European sales and a recession in the U.S. economy forced Canion to announce Compaq's first quarterly loss (more than $70 million), as well as layoffs of more than 1,400 employees. In October of that year, the company seemed to be moving ahead again, with the announcement of its Compaq Portable 486c computer, which it referred to as the "new generation of portables." However, by the end of the month the company's board of directors announced that Canion was being replaced by Eckhard Pfeiffer. Thomas C. Hayes wrote for the *New York Times* (July 22, 1992) that Canion had been dismissed because he "was not moving fast enough to reduce costs and speed development of new products." Two weeks later, James Harris, one of Compaq's original cofounders, who was then vice president of engineering, submitted his resignation to Compaq's board.

In mid-1992 Canion, who had negotiated a $3-million severance package and sold $10 million in Compaq stock, resurfaced with James Harris in a new business enterprise, the Insource Technology Corporation, a computer-management consulting firm. (The pair were unable to start a new manufacturing company because they had signed a non-compete agreement with Compaq.) Founded with $500,000 from each partner, Insource sought to provide executive-level assistance by experts in computer services, employee management, and business operations. Its chief focus was assisting in managing information and data resources. The company had three branches: financial solutions, technology solutions, and Internet solutions, each of which focused on the use of technology in business. One of the divisions of Insource Technology, for example, was the Insource Management Group (IMG), which specialized in health-care organizations. According to Paul Stranahan, writing for the *Jones Telecommunication and Multimedia Encyclopedia* (on-line), "In the highly competitive health care industry, IMG assists hospitals and insurance companies in reengineering their billing, record keeping, and management—all geared toward improving operations and profits."

After a short run in 1998 as chairman of GK Intelligent Systems, a software-development company, Canion became co–chief executive officer of Tricord Systems, in Plymouth, Minnesota, for which he helped develop new software. Founded in 1987, Tricord had found success in the early 1990s with a line of super servers (used to provide networking) based on Intel chips. Under Canion's guidance the company refocused its energies on the computer-storage market. Canion explained the company's goals in an interview with *Computerworld* (May 24, 1999): "The general area will be the storage-management arena. It will address the problem of adding storage to a network and managing it as one big pool."

In 1999 Canion invested seed capital in Questia Inc., a searchable on-line library of books and journals, and became the company's chairman of the board. He has continued to serve as co-CEO of Tricord Systems and as chairman of Insource Technology.

Rod Canion has been married twice. His first marriage ended in divorce in 1987; he remarried in 1988 to a Houston real-estate broker. He has two sons and three daughters from his two marriages.—C. M.

Suggested Reading: *Barron's* p14 Aug. 17, 1998; *BusinessWeek* p200 Apr. 18, 1986, Oct. 21, 1988, p145 June 26, 1989, p6 Aug. 7, 1995; *Computerworld* p29 May 24, 1999; *Forbes* p318 July 18, 1994; *Jones Telecommunication and Multimedia Encyclopedia* (on-line); *New York Times* D p1+ June 16, 1983, D p2 Dec. 28, 1987, D p1+ May 17, 1991, D p4 July 22, 1992, C p17 May 19, 1999; Spencer, Donald D. *The Timetable of Computers*, 1997

Courtesy of Xerox Corp., Xerox Historical Archives

Carlson, Chester Floyd

Feb. 8, 1906–Sep. 19, 1968 Inventor of xerography

The inventor Chester Floyd Carlson built a machine that has become so ubiquitous that it has spawned its own verb: to xerox. In the late 1930s, working out of a back-room laboratory in Astoria, Queens, Carlson developed the world's first photocopier—it could make duplicate copies without the messiness, expense, or lag time of existing methods. Today, it's impossible to imagine a school or office setting without a photocopier, which is usually called a xerox machine. Such machines rely on photoelectric phenomena to transfer an image from one sheet of paper to another; current models can make two copies a second, and sort, staple, and make double-side copies along the way. Carlson's invention gave rise to the Xerox Corporation, a multibillion-dollar industry that, through its Palo Alto Research Center (PARC), played a major role in creating early computing technology.

Born into poverty and a family plagued by illness, Carlson decided early on to become an inventor. "I had read of [Thomas] Edison and other successful inventors," he told A. Dinsdale in an interview for *Photographic Science and Engineering Magazine* (1963), archived on the Carlson Science and Engineering Library Web site, "and the idea of making an invention appealed to me as one of the few available means to accomplish a change in one's economic status, while at the same time bringing to focus my interest in technical things and making it possible to make a contribution to society as well." He was born on February 8, 1906 in Seattle, Washington, into a family beset by misfortune. His father, a barber, contracted tuberculosis when "Chet" was still a baby and later developed severe arthritis of the spine, rendering him a homebound invalid for the last 26 years of his life. Carlson described his father to Dinsdale as a "wreck of a man . . . wracked by coughing spells and defeated by the world" and recalled that "This, plus the resulting poverty and isolation, was to have a profound effect on my development." His mother also contracted tuberculosis and died when he was 17. The Carlson family moved from Seattle to various temporary homes in California, Arizona, and Mexico, and eventually settled in San Bernadino, California, where Carlson attended grammar and high school. With both his parents incapacitated, a teenaged Carlson took odd jobs in a printing shop and a chemical laboratory; by age 14 he had become his family's main source of income.

In explaining to Dinsdale how he came to be the inventor of xerography, Carlson recalled his youthful hobbies. "One of the first things I wanted was a typewriter—even when I was in grammar school," he said. "Then, when I was in high school I liked chemistry and I got the idea of publishing a little magazine for amateur chemists. I also worked for a printer in my spare time and he sold me an old printing press which he had discarded. . . . Then I started out to set my own type and print this little paper. . . . This experience did impress me with the difficulty of getting words into hard copy and this, in turn, started me thinking about duplicating processes. I started a little inventor's notebook and I would jot down ideas from time to time." After high school Carlson attended the nearby Riverside Junior College and, after three years as a part-time student, he transferred to the California Institute of Technology, in Pasadena. He graduated with a degree in physics in 1930—just as the country was sinking into the Depression. In debt and desperate for a job, he found employment as a research engineer at the Bell Telephone Laboratories in New York. He found the work dull, however, and obtained a transfer to the patent department, where he hoped he would be able to learn about the latest scientific developments.

In 1933 Carlson was laid off from Bell Telephone. He served a brief apprenticeship at a patent attorney's office and then accepted a better-paying job at the P. R. Mallory Company, a New York patent firm. He soon became a registered patent attorney, in charge of analyzing the viability of electronics proposals. A formal law degree was not required for this work, though in 1936 Carlson began attending evening law school courses at New York University, in New York City, and in 1939 he earned his degree. Carlson worked as a patent attorney at Mallory until 1945, by which time he had become head of the patent department.

As a patent attorney Carlson had to prepare many applications for the U.S. Patent and Trademark Office. He often needed to create multiple copies of documents, a laborious task that required extra typing and proofreading, expensive photographic copies, and, most onerous, tracing by hand. "Redrawing the copies took hours," an article about Carlson on the Lemelson-MIT Prize Program Web site recorded. "What's more, Carlson was nearsighted and had arthritis, which made his job even more difficult. He knew there had to be a better way."

In between his day job and law school, Carlson studied the available literature on copying processes in the New York Public Library. Knowing that several well-funded researchers were looking into photographic and chemical copying methods, Carlson decided to avoid these areas of inquiry. He came across an article about photoconductivity—a phenomenon discovered by the Hungarian physicist Paul Selenyi, by which the electrical conductivity of certain materials increases when they are exposed to light. In the proverbial flash of inspiration, he realized that a paper document—made up of dark and light areas—might be duplicated by exploiting photoconductivity. On October 18, 1937 he filed a preliminary patent application based on this theory and began research.

Carlson had married in 1935, and the couple lived in Jackson Heights, Queens, a suburb of New York City. For a while, Carlson ran experiments in his kitchen, once starting a fire over the gas range that filled the house with noxious fumes. After that, he rented a small room above a bar and beauty parlor in the nearby neighborhood of Astoria and, with the help of physicist Otto Kornei, a refugee from Hitler's Germany, he set up a makeshift laboratory.

Carlson and Kornei's first successful experiment came in the fall of 1938, when they wrote "10-22-38 ASTORIA" on a glass slide in India ink and then rubbed sulphur on a zinc surface with a handkerchief to give it a charge. They then laid the glass slide on this zinc surface and placed it under an incandescent lamp. After a short period, they removed the slide and sprinkled lycopodium powder (a common pharmaceutical powder made from spores of club mosses) on the surface. After blowing away the loose powder, what remained was a near-perfect duplicate. Thus, "10-22-38 ASTORIA" became the xerographic equivalent of Alexander Graham Bell's first telephone message: "Mr. Watson, come here. I need you." "Both of us repeated the experiment several times to convince ourselves that it was true," Carlson told Dinsdale, "then we made some permanent copies by transferring the powder images to wax paper and heating the sheets to melt the wax. Then we went out to lunch and to celebrate."

Though primitive, Carlson's technique worked. In fact, the most sophisticated photocopy machines today still rely on its two basic principles: materials with opposite electrical charges are attracted and certain materials become better conductors of electricity when exposed to light. In the typical xerox machine, a photoconductive surface is given a positive electrical charge. An image is then projected onto this surface, causing the electrical charge to drain away in exposed areas; the positive electrical charge remains in the dark areas marked by text or graphics. Negatively charged powder (now called toner) then coats the surface, adhering to the positively charged image area, thus making a viable image. The latent image is then attracted to positively charged paper, and heat is applied to create a permanent copy.

In 1940 the patent for Carlson's process—which he called electrophotography—was issued. Lacking the funds to develop the machine, he spent years making demonstrations for executives at IBM, Kodak, General Electric, RCA, and other large technology corporations. His assistant, Kornei, left to take a job at IBM, and Carlson began to think all his work had been in vain. Then in 1944, while on a business call to the Batelle Memorial Institute, a nonprofit research organization, Carlson mentioned that he held patents on a new duplication process. Officials there expressed interest and signed a royalty-sharing agreement with him, giving him 40 percent of any future profits from his invention. Batelle scientists made some improvements to the process, and then enlisted the Haloid Company of Rochester, New York, a firm that manufactured photographic products, to bring Carlson's idea to market.

On October 22, 1948—ten years to the day after Carlson's first successful experiment—the Haloid Company announced the world's first photocopier machine. According to Chip Holt in *Scientific American* (October 1996, on-line), it was "slow, dirty, hard to use," necessitating 14 different steps and 45 seconds to produce a single copy. The process clearly still needed a lot of fine tuning—and a catchy name. This was supplied by an Ohio State classics professor, who suggested "xerography": a combination of the Greek words "xerox" for "dry" and "graphos" for "writing," indicating that Carlson's copying process—unlike earlier photographic or chemical processes—required no liquids and no drying time. Convinced they had a valuable product, Haloid put millions into research, and in 1959 finally launched a greatly improved photocopier, the 914 model (so called because it could handle paper sizes up to nine inches by 14 inches. This machine and subsequent models became the basis of a multibillion-dollar industry. Within three years the net income of the company had increased tenfold; in 1961 Haloid renamed itself the Xerox Corporation in honor of this incredible boon.

"There were times when I felt impatient," Carlson confessed to Dinsdale in his 1963 interview. "You see, 15 years elapsed from the time I started working on xerography and the time the first piece of commercial equipment went on the market. And for exactly ten of those years I was working on my own, on my own limited resources." Carlson lived long enough to enjoy the fruits of his labor. He earned around $150 million from his invention, and gave away nearly $100 million to universities and laboratories around the country. There is, for example, a Chester F. Carlson Center for Imaging Science, at the Rochester Institute of Technology. He also remembered his assistant, Otto Kornei, and made him a gift of Xerox shares. In 1953, before most of the world had realized the value of Carlson's invention, the Franklin Institute, in Philadelphia, Pennsylvania, awarded him the Longstreth Medal, and in 1966 he was given the Horatio Alger Award. He died in 1968, at age 62, at a time when Xerox's annual revenues were approaching $1 billion.—M. A. H.

Suggested Reading: Carlson Science and Engineering Library Web site; Lemelson-MIT Prize Web site; *Scientific American* (on-line) Oct. 1996; Story of Xerography Web site; *Tribune India* (on-line) Dec. 4, 1999

Carlston, Doug

Apr. 30, 1947– Founder of Broderbund Software

As a software developer, Doug Carlston sought to create programs that would not only entertain, but educate as well. As founder and head of his family-owned company, Brøderbund Software Inc. (most often spelled simply as Broderbund), he maintained a fiscally sound and highly profitable company for 16 years—no small feat in an industry known for hostile takeovers and bankruptcy. Broderbund's most notable products include *Print Shop* (software for desktop publishing), *Where in the World is Carmen Sandiego?* (a mystery game that also teaches children geography), the Living Book Series (a collection of interactive CD-ROMs adapted from children's books), and *Myst* (an adventure game for teenagers). In 1998 Broderbund was named one of the 100 most influential companies by *PC Magazine Online*. Though no longer head of Broderbund—which has since merged with the Learning Company—Carlston continues to invest and work with other Internet-related companies looking for new markets to conquer.

Douglas Gene Carlston was born on April 30, 1947 in Boston, Massachusetts, the son of Charles Edwin Carlston, a theology professor from Dubuque, Iowa, and the former Alice Frances Swain. Doug's interest in computers began in the mid-1960s after he attended a summer engineering pro-

gram at Northwestern University, in Evanston, Illinois, as a junior in high school. The summer after his high-school graduation, he took a job sweeping up punch cards from the floor of a computer center in order to get free computer time. As an undergraduate he studied at Harvard University, in Cambridge, Massachusetts, where he also worked as a programmer at the university's computer laboratory. (During his time at Harvard he spent a year in Botswana teaching geography and mathematics.) After receiving his bachelor's degree, in social relations, in 1970, he took a year of postgraduate work at Johns Hopkins University, in Baltimore, Maryland. For a time after college he dabbled in writing, producing a few language texts for American Express and a book called *Beginning Swahili* (1970). Eventually he decided to study law and completed his juris doctor at Harvard, in 1975.

After completing his degree and passing the Illinois bar exam, Carlston worked for three years as an associate attorney for the firm Keck, Mahin & Cate, in Chicago, Illinois. In 1978 he moved to Newport, Maine, to become a founding partner in the firm Carlston & Hodson. While in Maine he wrote some simple game programs for his Radio Shack computer. Before long, three software publishers were selling his programs, and he was making more money from them than from his law practice. By 1979, Carlston became restless and decided to quit the law profession and head for Eugene, Oregon, where his younger brother, Gary, was then living. Somewhere in the Rockies his 1969 Chevrolet Impala's engine began bellowing smoke, and his windshield wipers broke down, but he managed to get into Eugene before the car completely died. As he told Edward Giltenan in a *Forbes* profile (April 27, 1992): "We started the company because I was stuck without a car and didn't have the money to buy a new one."

The brothers formed Broderbund Software Inc. with $7,000 in capital, mostly donated by family members. (The unusual name is a Scandinavian composite of the word "brotherhood.") The goal of the company was to sell Doug's software programs, which then included *Galactic Empire* and *Galactic Trader*, directly to software retailers. In 1981 Cathy Carlston joined her brothers in the family venture, serving as a vice president for the next eight years. Like many young software companies, Broderbund developed and marketed home-computer versions of popular arcade games. They also distributed software programs written by freelance programmers. Sometime in 1984, Doug and Gary noticed that schools were beginning to buy computers, but had very little in the way of educational software to use with them. They also realized that people would soon stop thinking of their personal computers as expensive playthings and would want to use them for something more productive. They decided to focus their energies on these two emerging software fields: education and personal productivity.

The product that put Broderbund on the map was *Print Shop*, which was released in 1984. *Print Shop* was software designed for aiding the fledgling desktop publishing business. According to Sonia Weiss in the *Jones Telecommunication and Multimedia Encyclopedia* (on-line) "the *Print Shop* titles offer easy-to-use, preconfigured layouts, type configurations and graphics that allow even the most graphically inept to create sophisticated looking greeting cards, posters, fliers and banners." The *Print Shop* was one of the earliest programs to bridge both business and personal software markets. It took advantage of the advances in printer output and graphics applications and the more powerful desktop computers that have now become an indispensable tool of modern life.

Even though software publishing does not generally require a great deal of capital, Carlston raised three million dollars between 1982 and 1984 from outside investors, on the off-chance that his company might need it. Luckily, the success of their programs was so great that this money was never used. The company followed *Print Shop* with another hit in 1985, this time in educational software: *Where in the World is Carmen Sandiego?* This interactive program, which was based on a game that the brothers had devised as children, sent players on the trail of a world-traveling spy named Carmen Sandiego and her associates. This game, which helped teach geography, marked the start of the genre of software now called "edutainment." *Carmen Sandiego* was a huge hit with children, par-

ents, and teachers. The game was so popular, in fact, that it resulted in several computer sequels, as well as a show on public television, a live-action movie, books, and puzzles. Broderbund sold 2.5 million copies of the *Carmen Sandiego* series over a seven-year period.

Broderbund's next great success was its Living Books Series, which consisted of CD-ROM adaptations of children's books. Carlston got the idea for the series after discovering that many members of his staff either had young children or were about to. This series—rich with graphics that combined with on-screen text—enabled children to bring an image to life with just a mouse click.

In his 1992 interview for *Forbes*, Carlston suggested that he wanted to create software games for teenagers as well; the result was *Myst* (1995), a hugely popular entertainment title targeted at ages 14 and older. Using more than 2,500 original 3-D graphics, an original soundtrack, and an hour of video, *Myst* centered around locating a family that had disappeared on a desert island. Players helped to find them by solving problems and looking for clues.

As a small independent business with conservative management, Broderbund was highly regarded in the software industry as a model for other companies to emulate. The Carlston family—and Doug in particular—were known as hands-on managers who made sure that a product had been completely developed and wasn't being rushed off to the stores. According to Sonia Weiss, Broderbund "always maintained complete control over its products and dealt with success. For many years, it survived on its cash flow alone, a tribute to the company's management as well as its ability to develop a small cadre of software titles that were not only initially successful but continued their success in the years to come, both on their own and as the basis for spin-offs and sequels."

Broderbund did, however, have occasional financial issues. In November 1991 several original investors wanted to cash out so the company was taken public. These investors eventually sold off about 36 percent of Broderbund's stock. Carlston sold none of his stock, and as a result he owned 23 percent of the company directly. (His brother and sister owned stock as well, although they had bowed out of management long before the public auction.) In 1994 Carlston attempted to form an alliance with Electronic Arts Inc., a video-game company, but after that company's stock share price dropped, he instead attempted a friendly takeover of Broderbund's rival, The Learning Company, in 1995. That deal, however, fell through, when The Learning Company accepted an all-cash transaction from SoftKey International, which had offered about $100 million more than Broderbund's $500 million bid.

In May 1996, after 16 years as the guiding force behind Broderbund, Carlston stepped down as chief executive, though he retained the position of chairman. Two years later, in June of 1998, Broderbund announced that it would merge with The Learning Company in a transaction estimated at $420 million. As reported in *GameSpot News* (on-line), Carlston cheered the finalization of the merger in September 1998: "Combining our award-winning titles with those of The Learning Company will give us exceptional strength in both domestic and international markets and provide great opportunities for the combined new company."

Today Doug Carlston serves on the boards of several Internet-related companies, as well as that of Public Radio International. He is a trustee of the Santa Fe Institute and an investor in IC Planet, an Internet start-up company that places professional-level independent contractors with businesses that need them. He is currently a member of the Long Now Foundation, an organization devoted to focusing humanity's collective creativity on the distant future.

Doug Carlston is also the author of *Applesoft Isn't Hard* (1984) and *Software People* (1985). He lives in California and has a daughter, Colleen Mara.—C. M.

Suggested Reading: *Forbes* p100+ Apr. 27, 1992; *IC Planet* (on-line); *Jones Telecommunication and Multimedia Encyclopedia* (on-line); *Long Now Foundation* (on-line); *Santa Fe Institute* (on-line)

Rountree/Getty Images

Case, Steve

Aug. 21, 1958– Former chairman of AOL Time Warner

Among cyberspace pioneers, few have done more to harness the vast potential of the Internet for ordinary personal computer users than has Steve Case. Having first encountered the world of personal computers in its infancy, when he was a marketing executive with PepsiCo during the early 1980s, Case has been a leading innovator in the rapid development of consumer applications for on-line services. He helped create, in 1985, the company that would later become known as America On-line, or AOL. (It's name at the time was Quantum Computer Services.) As the chief executive officer—and later the chairman—of Virginia-based AOL, Case adeptly turned the fast-growing company into the number-one Internet Service Provider (ISP). Not simply a means to access the Internet, however, AOL now also aims to provide subscribers with a sense of community, allowing them to communicate via on-line chat rooms, bulletin boards, e-mail, and instant messaging. The service helps users navigate the often daunting labyrinth of the World Wide Web, while enabling them to download software, shop by catalog, peruse news headlines and reference sources, and receive updates on travel information and upcoming concerts, among other things. Through a series of carefully managed acquisitions and strategic partnerships, Case was able to ward off larger predators such as Microsoft and pursue his own unique vision. Understanding the importance of interesting and useful content, for example, Case formed partnerships with several major content providers, including the *New York Times* and *BusinessWeek*. In perhaps his boldest move to date, Case engineered the acquisition of media giant Time Warner; completed in January 2001, it was the largest merger in U.S. history. The move put Case at the head of the world's largest media conglomerate and in charge of an unsurpassed roster of resources that includes film, broadcasting, music, books, and magazines. With 32 million subscribers to AOL's on-line service, Case is poised to see his dream—of making AOL Time Warner the largest, most respected, and most valued company in the world—become a reality.

[Since the writing of this article, AOL Time Warner has seen its fortunes take a dramatic turn for the worse. In the three years since the merger, the company's stock has fallen about 75 percent. In 2002, a year in which the Securities and Exchange Commission (SEC) and the Justice Department opened inquiries into AOL Time Warner's accounting practices, the company recorded an annual loss of nearly $100 billion—the largest annual loss ever in corporate history. Several top executives involved in orchestrating the merger have resigned under pressure, including Gerald Levin, the former chief executive officer of Time Warner, and Steve Case himself, who stepped down as chairman in May 2003. In September 2003 the company declared that it was removing the AOL from its corporate name. At the announcement of his resignation, Case—who remains a member of Time Warner's board of directors—remarked, as quoted by Ross Kerber in the *Boston Globe* (January 13, 2003), "I believed in America Online when we built it; I believed in AOL Time Warner when we created it; and I continue to believe in the great potential of this company and its people."]

Stephen McConnell Case was born on August 21, 1958 in Honolulu, Hawaii. He was the third of four children of a corporate lawyer and a schoolteacher. Steve Case's older sister, Carin, is a preschool teacher, and his younger brother, Jeff, is an insurance executive. With his older brother, Dan, now an investment banker, Steve Case shared a penchant for entrepreneurship. They worked as a team, expanding from typical childhood pursuits, such as operating a neighborhood juice stand and delivering newspapers, to running a mail-order and door-to-door sales business called Case Enterprises. The teenagers' company, which sold seeds and greeting cards, spawned the Aloha Sales Agency, whose sole product was a coupon-filled advertising circular.

As a student at Punahou School, a private, coed college-preparatory school in Honolulu, Case wrote album reviews for the school newspaper. Although it was not an income-generating activity, his foray into journalism placed him on record-label mailing lists, and he received free concert tickets and albums. After graduating from Punahou, Case enrolled at Williams College, in Williamstown, Massachusetts, where he studied political science because it seemed to be "the closest thing to marketing," as he quipped to a reporter for *BusinessWeek* (April 15, 1996). During his college career he ran the student entertainment committee, put on campus concerts, and founded a company that produced an album representing the best college bands. He also sang for two new-wave rock groups.

Upon his graduation in 1980, with a B.A. in political science, Case was hired by a marketing division of Proctor & Gamble, where he tried to revitalize sales of the Lilt home-permanent kit and to convince consumers of the value of Abound, a recently introduced wipe-on hair conditioner in the form of a towelette. "It was a disaster," Case remarked to the *BusinessWeek* reporter. In 1982 Case left Proctor & Gamble for the Wichita, Kansas–based Pepsi-Co, for whose Pizza Hut unit he had the enviable responsibility of managing new pizza development. For months at a time he would travel from city to city, sampling slices of pizza in search of exotic toppings. "I learned a lot about the big corporation experience, and that was good," he recalled in an interview with Kara Swisher for the *Washington Post* (August 27, 1995). "But a lot of it was about leveraging business and not about innovating. . . . It was all incremental rather than breaking new

The sluggish pace of corporate life allowed Case the time to develop a new hobby that would lead, serendipitously, to a more satisfying phase of his career. During his extended stints on the road, he began experimenting with a Kaypro CP/M personal computer, one of the earliest PCs on the market, and a modem, a device that converts digital computer signals to analog ones for sending and receiving transmissions over telephone lines. Through an early on-line subscription service called the Source, he spent his evenings perusing bulletin boards and chat services from his hotel rooms. "It was a very rudimentary setup," he told a reporter for the *Washington Post* (November 8, 1993). "It was all very painful and time-consuming, but I could glimpse the future. There was something magical about being able to dial out to the world from Wichita."

At a 1983 consumer-electronics show in Las Vegas, Case was introduced by his brother Dan, who was then an associate with the investment firm of Hambrecht & Quist, to the representatives of Control Video Corporation, a start-up firm in which Hambrecht & Quist had a small investment. Excited about the company's first product, a service that delivered Atari video games to personal computers, Case accepted a job with Control Video on the spot. The company soon ran into deep financial difficulties due to management problems and a collapsing market for its main product. "I arrived there just in time for the death of the video-game business," Case told Steve Lohr for the *New York Times* (August 14, 1995). After firing most of its management team, Control Video's board of directors installed as chief executive officer Jim Kimsey, a successful entrepreneur and restauranteur. Kimsey retained Case to scare up new venture capital, and the two of them, along with the company's product specialist, redefined Control Video's business plan.

Renamed Quantum Computer Services in 1985, the revamped company began offering on-line services for owners of Commodore personal computers. Two years later Case persuaded Apple Computer to allow Quantum to develop and provide on-line services for its proprietary operating system. The arrangement provided Quantum with enough clout to sign similar deals with the makers of Tandy computers and with the industry leader, International Business Machines (IBM). The enormous overhead costs that immediately accrued strained Quantum's resources to their limits. The $5 million in fresh capital that resulted from the deals with Apple, Tandy, and IBM was absorbed instantly, and venture-capital board members began calling for Case's removal. Kimsey stood by his protege, as he recalled to the *BusinessWeek* reporter. "I said, 'We have $5 million invested in this boy's education. Do you want to throw that out?'" They didn't, and Case redeemed himself by refraining from clinching any major deals for the next few years in order to shore up Quantum's existing customer base and increase the number of subscribers to its on-line services. In 1992, a year after Quantum became America Online, Kimsey moved into the chairman's position and named Case as his successor as chief executive officer (CEO). To raise capital for AOL's growth, the company announced an initial public offering of its stock, valued at $1.84 a share, in March 1992. The initial offering raised $66 million in new capital, which AOL needed desperately in order to catch up to the leaders in the on-line services industry, CompuServe and Prodigy. Case then launched an aggressive strategy for growth that involved rapid expansion of membership services, increased subscriber enrollment, and acquisitions and alliances with numerous companies that could help AOL get the job done.

Over the next several years, Case took the company on a multimillion-dollar buying spree. Through its November 1994 purchase of Advanced Network Services Inc. (ANS), which had been created by IBM and MCI Communications to build and manage the National Science Foundation's 12,000-mile-long fiber-optic "backbone" of the Internet, AOL began laying the groundwork for its ability to provide direct access to the Internet. The acquisition of BookLink Technologies Inc. the following month and, later, of Global Network Navigator provided AOL with "browsing" technology to allow its customers to find their way around the World Wide Web area of the Internet. Purchases of Redgate Communications, Medior, and Wide Area Information Servers, along with alliances with Broderbund Software and Novell, provided AOL with developers of CD-ROM technology to provide customers with graphics-filled companion disks to complement and interact with AOL's information and entertainment offerings. In February 1995 AOL formed a $100-million joint venture with the German media conglomerate Bertelsmann in order to expand abroad. Case announced a deal with AT&T's new Internet access business 13 months later.

The feverish pace of AOL's acquisitions was accompanied by an equally impressive growth spurt. In fiscal 1993 AOL earned $4.2 million on $40 million in revenues; a year later it earned $6.2 million on revenues of $104.4 million. By early 1994 AOL had 600,000 subscribers; in March 1995 membership surpassed the 2 million mark, and by August 1996 it had reached 6.3 million, making AOL the leading provider of on-line services.

The company's rapid expansion was not without occasional frustrations for customers, however. In the winter of 1993–94, subscribers began encountering busy signals, delayed access, slow data transmission, and other problems resulting from the strain on AOL's hardware capacity and telecommunications networks. At one point, in February 1994, the company rationed access to its services during peak hours. Case swiftly acknowledged the problems and took steps to remedy the situation by hiring new technical-support and cus-

tomer-service workers and by delaying the introduction of a new browser for the World Wide Web that would allow customers to move seamlessly between AOL's offerings and those found on the Internet. Still, problems persisted as membership continued to swell. Some users grumbled that the company should be called "America On Hold," and a Usenet newsgroup called alt.aol-sucks cropped up on the Internet. In the summer of 1996, AOL experienced a 19-hour power outage caused by technical difficulties arising from a maintenance installation procedure. Case promptly apologized for the inconvenience in an on-line memo to subscribers, noting that the outage was a reminder of how important AOL had become to many users. He also reported, in a memo of July 12, 1996, that the company had settled several class-action lawsuits filed in 1995 regarding AOL's billing practices. Some members had complained about AOL's practice of rounding up each logged-on session to the nearest minute rather than tallying a user's total monthly time. All members were given one free hour as part of the settlement. On October 29, 1996 AOL announced that it would charge a flat rate of $19.95 a month for unlimited access; previously, subscribers paid $9.95 for the first five hours and $2.95 for each additional hour.

While Case, who succeeded Kimsey as chairman of AOL in 1995, was struggling to manage his company's success, Microsoft—the behemoth that had single-handedly developed the operating system used by most of the world's personal computers—complicated his task by announcing in August 1995 that it was entering the on-line services market. Its new Windows 95 operating-system package would include instant access to its own proprietary network, which analysts estimated could attract between 9 million and 19 million subscribers in the first year alone. In addition to openly calling for Microsoft to separate the new Microsoft Network from the rest of the Windows 95 operating-system package, the three leading on-line providers—AOL, CompuServe, and Prodigy—urged the United States Justice Department to investigate the antitrust implications of the computer giant's attempt to move into the on-line services market via its existing domination of the personal-computer market. Case led the effort.

Case's openly antagonistic behavior toward Microsoft notwithstanding, he was, in a sense, grateful for its existence, as he explained in his interview with Steve Lohr: "Fear of Microsoft has helped this company enormously. Despite all our growth and the rise in our stock price, no one here is congratulating themselves. We're totally focused on the future." Indeed, in a maneuver that illustrates Case's ability to position his company favorably and continue to compete fiercely, AOL and Microsoft struck a mutually advantageous deal in March 1996, whereby AOL would include Microsoft's Internet Explorer browsing program in all software packages it would send to customers in the future while Microsoft would include access to

AOL's on-line services in upcoming versions of the Windows 95 system.

Throughout the latter half of the 1990s Case continued to expand the AOL empire through a series of acquisitions and strategic alliances, and in 1997 he announced a carefully orchestrated deal with CompuServe, a provider of on-line services to mostly small-business and professional users, and the large telecommunications company World-Com. In 1998 AOL acquired a beleaguered Netscape Communications for $4.2 billion worth of AOL stock. The deal included Netscape's Netcenter, a leading contender in full-service portals, which helped AOL tap into a new audience; whereas AOL is used predominantly in the evening and on weekends by teenagers and home users, Netcenter receives its heaviest traffic during the day from those in the corporate world who go on-line while at work. The acquisition also meant that AOL owned Netscape Communicator, the only alternative browser to Microsoft's Internet Explorer.

Case took AOL to new heights in January 2000, when he announced plans to merge with multibillion-dollar media company Time Warner. The $124 billion deal, completed after a year of negotiations, put Case, as chairman of the board of AOL Time Warner, at the head of a vast media empire of broadcasting, music, movies, and publishing assets. Time Warner has 70,000 employees worldwide, and under its corporate umbrella are such well-known names as CNN, HBO, TNT, Cartoon Network, TBS, *Time*, *People*, *Sports Illustrated*, Looney Tunes, and the Atlanta Braves. In addition to the 73 million subscribers to Time Warner cable systems, HBO, and Time Inc. magazines, the acquisition brought AOL coveted access to cable lines, which industry analysts predict will soon be the preferred method of transmission for all types of information—not just the Internet but movies, music, books, and shopping. Furthermore, Time Warner's media outlets provide an invaluable promotional venue for AOL. David Londoner, an expert on the entertainment industry, told *Fortune* (January 8, 2001) at the time that "this merger creates a media powerhouse that may well be impossible to duplicate." Other analysts would later praise Case for his prescience: he had used AOL stock, which was riding high during the dot.com frenzy, to acquire a stable "brick and mortar" company just months before Internet stocks began to tumble. The move appeared to help carry AOL through the drastic downturn in the technology market that followed. Although AOL stock fell as much as 51 percent over the next year, other Internet companies were hit even worse: Yahoo, for instance, at its lowest was down 86 percent; Amazon, at one point, had lost 83 percent of its value.

The unprecedented size of the AOL Time Warner deal drew careful scrutiny from the Federal Trade Commission (FTC). Although at first the merger did not seem to raise antitrust concerns—since AOL was an Internet company and Time

Warner a media company, the two didn't overlap—it soon became clear that the deal could have profound effects in both markets. It seemed to point, in fact, to the inevitable union of traditional media sources and new information technology. Among those to protest the merger were Microsoft and Disney. The latter was concerned that with AOL's control of Time Warner cable lines, they would restrict interactive TV (ITV) services offered by competitors. "I never had a problem with the merger," Disney chairman Michael Eisner told *Time* (December 25, 2000–Januray 1, 2001). "I have a problem with the fact that there might be a single entity that decides what intellectual property goes into the house." A cohort of companies that offered instant-messaging services soon charged that AOL was preventing any competitors' messages from penetrating AOL proprietary instant-messaging architecture. One insider reported to *Time* that by fall "the FTC was hitting us with a new issue every week." Eventually Case and Gerald Levin, the CEO of Time Warner, had to agree to FTC demands that the Time Warner cable pipes would be open to at least three competitors. Among those granted access was EarthLink, AOL's biggest rival. Furthermore, AOL pledged to continue investing in slower DSL service, which is carried over phone lines. The company refused, however, to grant FTC the right to regulate the placement of AOL Time Warner content—executives feared they would lose control over their own products.

In May 2000, while FTC deliberations were still going on, Case and Levin announced the new corporate structure: Case would serve as chairman, with Levin as CEO. Richard Parsons, of Time Warner, and Robert Pittman, of AOL, would act as co-chief operating officers. Levin, as it happens, was the head of HBO, Time Inc.'s cable TV network, back in 1980 when Case, then a young man just out of college, applied for a position there. According to Marc Gunther, even then Case was boldly predicting that "innovations in telecommunications (especially two-way cable systems) will result in our television sets (big screen, of course!) becoming an information line, newspaper, school, computer, referendum machine, and catalog." Case didn't get the position. His vision, however, has remained fairly consistent, and with the completed merger under his belt, he gained the resources to make it a reality. In a press release at the time of the closing, Case announced that "AOL Time Warner will lead the convergence of the media, entertainment, communications and Internet industries, and provide wide-ranging, innovative benefits for consumers. Our brands, services and technologies already touch hundreds of millions of people and, by closely integrating our assets, we will embed the AOL Time Warner experience more deeply into their everyday lives."

The merger further exacerbated already tense relations between AOL and Microsoft. The two companies had labored for months to work out a deal to include AOL in Microsoft's new operating system, Windows XP. The two couldn't come to an agreement however, and, in October 2001, Windows XP was released without AOL. The two also compete in the arena of instant messaging; AOL's large subscriber base—which includes a vast number of teenagers wanting to chat with friends online—guarantees it a strategic advantage.

During 2001 Case gradually withdrew from the daily operations of the business. "I don't get involved in day-to-day things," he told Shelley Emling for the *Atlanta Journal-Constitution* (November 9, 2001). "I don't try to meddle. I don't try to second-guess. My focus is on long term strategy." In November 2001 AOL Time Warner announced an initiative to create the "digital household"; through a partnership with Sony the company intends to engineer easy-to-use networking technologies that will meet all of a family's entertainment, information, and communication needs. AOL is also developing its brand of digital music, with the AOL Music Channel receiving 24 million individual visitors per month.

Removing himself from managerial issues also allowed Case to devote more time to philanthropy. Through the AOL Foundation and the Case Foundation, which he founded with his wife, Jean Villanueva, he supports organizations such as PowerUP, which works to establish computer centers for young people in inner cities and rural areas. AOL has also launched several community-minded Web sites, including helping.org, a philanthropy portal to facilitate on-line charity donations and connect volunteers with nonprofit groups, and GovernmentGuide, an on-line service that aims to put citizens in touch with government services and officials. On December 12, 2001 Case was selected by President George W. Bush to serve on the President's Council of Advisors on Science and Technology, a group of prominent industry executives and scientists who will advise the president on policy issues such as research and development and broadband incentives.

Despite a personal fortune estimated at $1.5 billion (in 2001), the unassuming Case is known for dressing casually (he wears khakis to work and once appeared in a Gap ad campaign for the pants). "Steve is very deceptive because he is so low-key, and he certainly does not fit anyone's stereotype of what a hard-driving [executive] should be like," Steven Rattner, an investment banker and AOL advisor, told Swisher. "But there is a quiet forcefulness to him." Case lives in a three-story house on a cul-de-sac in McLean, Virginia, with his second wife, Jean, the former vice president of corporate communications for AOL. The two were married in 1998 by the Reverend Billy Graham, after a highly publicized romance. Case's three children from his former marriage live nearby with his ex-wife, Joanne.—A. I. C.

Suggested Reading: *Atlanta Journal-Constitution* C p1 Nov. 9, 2001; *Boston Globe* C p1 Sep. 9, 1997; *BusinessWeek* p78+ Apr. 15, 1996; *Fortune* p70+ Feb. 7, 2000, p72+ Jan. 8, 2001, p92 July

23, 2001; *New York Times* III p10 Oct. 9, 1994, D p1+ Aug. 14, 1995; *Time* p58 Dec. 7, 1998, p138+ Dec. 25, 2000–Jan. 1, 2001; *USA Today* B p1 Aug. 16, 2001; *U.S. News and World Report* p14 July 9, 2001; *Wall Street Journal* A p1 Dec. 6, 2001, B p7 Dec. 12, 2001; *Washington Post* A p1+ Aug. 27, 1995, C p1:5 Sep. 9, 1997, E p1 Dec. 7, 2001

Caselli, Giovanni

1815–1891 Inventor of the pantelegraph facsimile machine

Though relatively unknown, Giovanni Caselli must be credited with not only inventing one of the earliest functioning facsimile machines, but also with the development of the first commercial fax company, which provided services in France in the 1860s. Caselli's device, the pantelegraph, used the existing telegraph technology of the era to send images, in addition to text messages across great distances, with the electrical current registering the differences between the light and dark spaces on the paper and relaying it to the receiving station. (The name pantelegraph is believed to be derived from combining telegraph and pantograph, an instrument comprised of four metal bars first used in the 18th century for copying geometric shapes.) Though the pantelegraph faded into obscurity, Caselli is credited with being one of the forefathers of the modern fax machine, along with such inventors as Alexander Bain, who came up with the initial concept, and Frederick Blakewell, who devised a rotating cylinder device that was the basis for fax machine technology up until the 1960s.

Giovanni Caselli was born in 1815 in the city of Siena in Tuscany, Italy. As a boy he studied science and literature, and in 1841 he began working as a tutor to the sons of the marquis of San Vitale, in Modena, Italy, then under ducal rule. He was exiled from Modena in 1849 after participating in demonstrations calling for the annexation of the duchy of Modena. (Modena was eventually annexed to Piedmont-Sardinia in 1860.) Caselli's next post was at the University of Florence, where he studied the telegraphic transmission of images.

In the mid-19th century the telegraph, as envisioned by the American inventor Samuel Morse, was not only a worldwide phenomenon but was fast becoming a worldwide necessity. As the only speedy way to communicate over long distances, it was used to conduct business, notify relatives of births and deaths, and even to distribute the descriptions of fugitives. The one thing it could not do, however, was send images. To this end, Bain and Blakewell, among other inventors, worked on developing machines that would use telegraph wires to send copies of images.

Though Bain never actually built such a machine, his patent design described a device that used a stylus and pendulum, which moved over a metal plate upon which was written a message in nonconductive ink; the pendulum electrically sensed light or dark areas on the message being sent. The receiving device's pendulum would then mark a chemically treated piece of paper whenever an electric charge—denoting a dark spot—was sent down the line. Blakewell used Bain's principle to build the first functional fax machine. The image to be transmitted on Blakewell's device was written with a nonconducting material on tinfoil, wrapped around a cylinder, and scanned with a stylus and pendulum similar to the ones in Bain's design. The cylinder rotated at a uniform rate, regulated by a clock mechanism, and was sent to another cylinder on the receiving end. The two cylinders on Blakewell's machine, however, were poorly synchronized, making transmission difficult.

With the money Caselli had saved during his time as a tutor, he began designing his pantelegraph. In 1856 he announced that he had developed a working prototype. The next year he traveled to Paris, where he received the aid and support of the noted inventor and engineer Paul Gustave Froment and completed an almost final version of the machine. Measuring more than two meters high and built of cast iron, the pantelegraph worked in a fashion similar to its predecessors. The user would write a message or draw an image on a sheet of tin. The tin was then placed on a curved metal plate and scanned with a needle. The telegraph signals that came through the receiving apparatus marked out the message in Prussian blue ink as the paper was immersed in potassium ferrocyanide. Caselli solved Blakewell's synchronization problem by developing needles that scanned at the same rate by means of two highly accurate clocks. The clocks set off the pendulum, which then set the needles in motion through an elaborate system of gears and pulleys.

The pantelegraph was warmly embraced by the scientific community in Paris; a Pantelegraphic Society quickly rose up to support its widespread use. Napoleon III, emperor of France, took an interest in the device. Long fascinated by mechanics and modern inventions, the emperor visited Caselli at Froment's workshop in May 1860 to see a demonstration of the machine. Impressed, Napoleon offered Caselli permission to use any telegraph lines in Paris he needed in order to continue his experiments. In November the emperor offered him telegraphic lines between Paris and Amiens so that the inventor could attempt an experiment bridging two cities.

Between 1860 and 1865 Caselli eliminated the final remaining fault in his machine by developing synchronized timers that did not depend on the current relayed by the telegraphic line, which proved too sensitive to atmospheric changes. In 1863 the French legislature approved measures to open an initial line between Paris and Marseille.

(Around the same time the British government approved the development of an experimental line between London and Liverpool for four months.)

The first commercial fax service opened for business in Paris, in 1865, transmitting text and images between major French cities for the next five years. Caselli was awarded the Cross of the Legion of Honor when a connection was opened between Paris and Lyons. The system transmitted nearly 5,000 faxes in its first year in operation. (Many of these perfectly legible faxes still exist in French museums today.) Caselli's device was quickly becoming a worldwide phenomenon; in 1861 King Victor-Emmanuel had sent an invitation to Caselli to demonstrate his machines at the Florence Exhibition, and the emperor of China sent emissaries to Paris to review the system, realizing the advantage such a device would have for Chinese text, which has thousands of ideograms. (Unfortunately, the negotiations between the inventor and the Chinese government dragged on for years and ultimately faltered.)

Caselli's pantelegraph had been developed at a time when governments around the world were investing heavily in traditional telegraph lines. Though initially interested in the idea, French authorities, worried that Caselli's service would pose too much competition with the regular telegraphic network, threatened heavy tariffs on fax dispatches. The Italian government proved to be prohibitively slow in developing their own fax lines. After its successful four-month testing of the experimental fax lines and the establishment of a pantelegraph company, the British government abandoned the project in the wake of the bank crisis of 1864.

In the public mind, the pantelegraph was exclusively used for images, even though it could send legible text messages. The Pantelegraphic Society promoting Caselli's device failed to emphasize the fact that it could also send text, so users did little more with it than send banking signatures or trademarks. By 1870 the French pantelegraph service was out of business.

Though Caselli continued to work as an inventor, his later devices—including a hydraulic press, an instrument to measure the speed of trains, and a torpedo that returned to its launching point if it missed its mark—never proved to be as commercially viable as the pantelegraph.

Giovanni Caselli died in Florence in 1891, his greatest invention long since having fallen into disuse. Some of his machines have been preserved at the Musée National des Techniques and have been demonstrated as recently as 1961, the centennial of the first tests. In 1982 Caselli's pantelegraph was also used at the Postal Museum in Riquewihr, France, where it worked six hours a day for several months.—C. M.

Suggested Reading: *History of Telegraphy* (on-line); *Invention of the Fax Machine* (on-line); Museo di Storia della Scienza Web site; Spencer, Donald D. *Timetable of Computers*, 1997

Courtesy of Vinton G. Cerf

Cerf, Vinton G.

June 23, 1943– Co-developer of TCP/IP

Amid all the hype over how the Internet is revolutionizing society, the story of how it came into existence has received surprisingly little attention. One of the key figures in its development is Vinton G. Cerf, currently the senior vice president of Internet architecture and technology at MCI WorldCom Inc. In December 1997, Cerf was awarded (along with his frequent collaborator, Robert Kahn) the U.S. National Medal of Technology for his pioneering work in the medium.

Although Cerf is often referred to as a father of the Internet, he is not entirely comfortable with the epithet. He would be the first to admit that many people made the information superhighway a reality. His specific contribution was in developing, back in the 1970s, the protocols that govern how local networks communicate with one another. The Internet is really a network of networks—a sprawling electronic realm composed of more than 100,000 local and national university, military, government, and corporate networks that often operate in different media (wires, radio, satellite). With Kahn, Cerf developed and refined the protocols that allow these electronic fiefdoms to communicate seamlessly with one another. These protocols go by the rather tongue-twisting acronym TCP/IP (Transmission Control Protocol/Internet Protocol). "The magic of the Internet is that all the computers in the world use this very simple protocol," a colleague of Cerf's at MCI told Katie Hafner for the *New York Times* (September 25, 1994). "And the magic of Vint Cerf is that he cajoled and negotiated and argued user communities into using it."

Indeed, sheer determination, diplomacy, and persuasion on Cerf's part have won him near-legendary status among "Internauts," as the pioneers of the medium are known. Ethernet inventor Robert Metcalfe told John Adam for the *Washingtonian* (November 1996) that Cerf should be recognized for, in addition to his technical contributions, "persevering with the Internet for 25 years, advancing it at every turn, and standing up to the forces of complacency and proprietariness." As an example of Cerf's diplomatic skills, one meeting in 1992 stands out. While a group of engineers was arguing over a particular design issue, Cerf, who is known for dressing in immaculate three-piece suits, took the podium and proceeded to perform a striptease. "I removed my coat, waistcoat, tie, and finally my dress shirt," he told Katie Hafner. Underneath, he was wearing a T-shirt that read "I P on Everything." The double meaning of the phrase was not lost on the audience, and in the ensuing laughter the tension that had made the debate seem unresolvable evaporated.

One of Cerf's motivations in developing the Internet was personal. He and his wife have been hearing-impaired since they were young. Though he wears a hearing aid, it is sometimes difficult for him to recognize voices over the phone, and when he lectures he often has to plunge into the audience like a talk-show host so that he can read the lips of those who have questions. The Internet has given him, his wife, and other hearing-impaired people another method of communicating. "E-mail has been vital to me for projects I have been involved in since about 1970," he told Katie Hafner. "I sometimes wonder whether this aspect of networking has kept me close to the field for the last 25 years."

The oldest of the three sons of Muriel and Vinton Thruston Cerf, Vinton Gray Cerf was born on June 23, 1943 in New Haven, Connecticut. A premature baby, he developed so "slowly and unevenly," as his mother told John Adam for the *Washingtonian*, that some people suspected he might be mentally impaired. His mother was one of the first to recognize that this was not the case. "One day as he was playing in the sandbox, I suddenly realized that what I was looking at was not mental retardation but a long attention span and quiet, self-contained maturity," she told Adam.

Cerf's ingenuity later became apparent in the way he handled his hearing problem, which was discovered when he was a child and worsened as he grew older. (He believes his condition might have been caused by too much oxygen while he was in an incubator as a baby.) He took lip-reading classes after school and eventually started using a hearing aid, but in certain places, such as noisy cafeterias and restaurants, neither lip-reading nor his hearing aid helped him much. Cerf tackled the challenge of communicating despite his hearing impairment the way an engineer might take on a design problem. "A typical strategy here is to dominate the conversation, not by doing all the talking, but by asking a lot of questions," he wrote in a paper entitled "Confession of a Hearing-Impaired Engineer." "In this way, the deaf listener will at least know what question the speaker is addressing, even if he cannot hear all of the response." There are, however, dangers in using this method. "In a group conversation, this can backfire embarrassingly if the question you ask is one which was just asked by someone else," he added. "A variation (equally embarrassing) is to enthusiastically suggest something just suggested."

Cerf grew up in the San Fernando Valley, in California. His father, who had fought in World War II as a captain in the navy, was a senior personnel executive at North American Aviation, an aerospace contractor that was eventually subsumed by Rockwell International. The young Cerf sometimes got to see rocket engines that were being tested at the company. "Imagine the effect on a kid who loved science fiction," he told John Adam. "You felt you were being confronted with the future right there, and you couldn't ignore it!" He also got a first look at computers, each of which, in those days—the 1950s and early 1960s—filled several rooms.

While his younger brothers played football and became presidents of the student bodies at their schools, Cerf was a bookworm. At Van Nuys High School, he was, in his own words, a "math freak." One of his best friends was Steve Crocker, who started the school's math club and later worked with Cerf on networking technology. The duo often re-created science experiments together and broke into the computer labs at the University of California, Los Angeles (UCLA), where Cerf had been taking calculus classes as a high-school senior. Cerf could be found in only two types of dress back in those days: either his ROTC uniform (he had joined ROTC to avoid gym class) or a jacket and tie and carrying a briefcase.

Cerf claims to have had two "oceanic experiences" while in high school. The first occurred in the spring of 1959, while he was walking past a building at his high school. He came to the realization that "the whole universe was hooked together," as he put it to Adam, and that he wanted to explore the connections. One year later, near the engineering building at UCLA, he had another such experience. "I got this very powerful sense of déjà vu, in that I knew I would be there again, I thought as a physicist," he told Adam. His premonition that he would end up at UCLA actually came true, in a modified form, seven years later, when he arrived there as a computer science student.

In the meantime, Cerf studied mathematics at Stanford University, in California. By the time he graduated, with a B.S. degree in math, in 1965, he had realized that math really wasn't for him, so he turned to an area that interested him more—computer science. "There was something amazingly enticing about programming," he told Katie Hafner and Matthew Lyon for their history of the Internet, *Where Wizards Stay Up Late* (1996). "You created your own universe and you were the master

of it. The computer would do anything you programmed it to do. It was this unbelievable sandbox in which every grain of sand was under your control." After graduating, he got a job as a programmer working on time-sharing systems for IBM in Los Angeles.

In 1967, after he realized he needed to add muscle to his computer education, Cerf enrolled in UCLA's graduate program in computer science. He initially worked with the professor Jerry Estrin, who had been awarded a contract with the Advanced Research Projects Agency, or ARPA, which was administered by the U.S. Department of Defense, to work on the "snuper computer," so called because it could observe the execution of programs running on other computers. After ARPA stopped funding the program, Cerf became involved, along with some 40 other students, in the work of another UCLA professor, Leonard Kleinrock, who had won an ARPA contract in fall 1968 to develop the Network Measurement Center. The center was to be responsible for performance testing and analysis of the ARPANET, the precursor to the Internet.

The ARPANET project was to connect computers at four sites (UCLA; the Stanford Research Institute; the University of California, Santa Barbara; and the University of Utah, in Salt Lake City) using a new technology called packet-switching. Packet-switching had been conceptualized in the 1960s by three computer scientists: Leonard Kleinrock when he had been at the Massachusetts Institute of Technology (MIT), in Cambridge; Paul Baran at the RAND Corporation; and Donald W. Davies at the National Physical Laboratory, in England. More efficient than circuit-switching, which is used by telephones, packet-switching technology involves breaking information into bits (or packets), which then take the fastest route to their destination, where they are reassembled. For example, if there were three nodes, A, B, and C, connected in a triangle, to get from A to B, the information could travel the direct route, A to B, or A to C and then to B, depending on which way was least congested. Moreover, like cars on a freeway, bits of information from other messages can travel on the same circuit at the same time. This is in contrast to circuit-switching, in which information moves from one point to another synchronously on a line dedicated solely to that connection.

Cerf was involved in the development of ARPANET's first node, at UCLA, and became the principal programmer of the Network Measurement Center. Through this work, Cerf became acquainted with Robert Kahn, who was the chief designer for the ARPANET at Bolt, Beranek & Newman (BBN), which had won the ARPA contract to build the IMP (Interface Message Processors) machines necessary to run the ARPANET. When all four of ARPANET's nodes were up, in December 1969, Kahn and Cerf devised various tests on the network to see how the system might crash and how efficiency might be improved.

Cerf finished his dissertation work in March 1972 and stayed on briefly at UCLA to help coordinate the first public demonstration of the ARPANET, in October 1972, at the International Conference on Computer Communication. The conference was a watershed in that it convinced many skeptics of the feasibility of packet-switching technology. At the conference, Cerf was made chairman of the International Network Working Group, which was composed of leaders of networking projects in other countries. One month later, he joined the faculty of Stanford University as professor of electrical engineering.

With the successful demonstration of packet-switching, many other countries stepped up their efforts to create their own national networks. Packet-switching networks employing radio or satellite transmission were also being developed. With each network having its own unique characteristics (with regard to interfaces, maximum packet sizes, and transmission rates, for example) optimized for its particular environment, a question arose: How could information originating in one network travel to another? A successful solution to this problem would have great military and commercial value. For instance, ships at sea or mobile units on land would be able to tap into land lines back in their home countries.

Kahn, who by then had left BBN and joined ARPA, broached the problem to Cerf. After many discussions, the two agreed that they wanted the "network of networks" to be open-ended—meaning that local networks with their own, specific rules would still be able to hook up to the larger network. The two came up with a solution that was initially sketched out on the back of an envelope in a San Francisco hotel in the spring of 1973. Computers called routers would be needed to serve as gateways standing between the networks. These routers would repackage the packets so that a foreign network would be able to recognize it. The entire network would also be governed by a minimum set of protocols called TCP/IP. These protocols dictate how information is organized and transported across the intervening networks and determine how computers communicate to ensure that all the bits of a transmission arrive at its destination intact and in order.

The definitive paper, "A Protocol for Packet Network Intercommunication," was published in a technical journal, *IEEE Transactions and Communications*, in May 1974. (Cerf's name appears first on the paper due to the luck of a coin toss; both he and Kahn collaborated "like two hands on a pen," as Cerf told Hafner and Lyon.) No copy of the original manuscript exists because it was not seen as a landmark document; however, TCP/IP would later become the basis for the Internet as it is now known.

Cerf continued to refine the Internet protocols, first from Stanford and then, in 1976, from the Defense Advanced Research Projects Agency (DARPA), the new name adopted by ARPA. (He says he left Stanford in part because his research time was being eaten up by administrative duties and the shepherding of students.) On November 22, 1977, another milestone in the history of the Internet was reached, when a moving van with a packet radio terminal in Menlo Park, California, successfully sent data via radio, land lines, and satellite on a 150,000-kilometer route that passed through Norway, England, and West Virginia to the University of Southern California Information Sciences Institute. The TCP/IP protocols were eventually adopted by ARPANET, in 1983.

Since then, Cerf has continued to develop the Internet from different positions within the private and public sectors. In 1982, realizing how difficult it would be to send his two children to college on his relatively meager government salary, Cerf left DARPA and joined MCI as a vice president of engineering, with a mandate to help the company develop a "digital post office." The result was MCI Mail, which has since become one of the largest e-mail systems in the country. In 1986, Cerf left MCI to help Kahn establish the Corporation for National Research Initiatives (CNRI), a nonprofit organization dedicated to researching technologies of information infrastructure. During his tenure there, he worked on a variety of projects, among them the development of digital libraries and gigabit networks as well as the founding of the Internet Society, a nonprofit, nongovernmental group that helps develop and maintain Internet standards. He served as president of the group from its 1992 founding to 1995; currently, he serves as a board member. While at CNRI, he also helped hook up MCI Mail to the Internet. Before, any commerce on the government-regulated Internet had to be of benefit to research. "We probably wouldn't have accepted a proposal from others, but Vint suggested it with such grace and charm," Stephen Wolff, a member of the Federal Research Internet Coordinating Council, told Adam for the *Washingtonian*. CNRI demonstrated the MCI Mail–Internet connection in June 1989, paving the way for other services, such as CompuServe, Sprint Telemail, AOL, and Prodigy to hook up as well.

In January 1994, Cerf returned to work for MCI, to set up NetworkMCI, the company's $20-billion project to combine voice, data, video, e-mail, and fax services in one pipeline. "There are people coming here just to spend a few years working with Vint Cerf," J. Robert Harcharik, MCI's general manager for data services, told Katie Hafner for the *New York Times* (September 25, 1994). His official title in the company, which merged with WorldCom to form MCI WorldCom in 1998, is senior vice president, Internet architecture and technology. Explaining his decision to return to the private sector, Cerf told Hafner, "After a lot of soul-searching, I concluded the right thing to do was go back into the private sector and take all I'd learned about information infrastructure and turn it into something people could use." He expects that he will collaborate with Kahn again sometime. "We have too many unexplored ideas between us," he told Adam.

Cerf is married to the former Sigrid L. Thorstenberg, an illustrator and interior designer, who lost most of her hearing when she was three. They married in September 1966, less than a year after they were introduced to each other by their mutual hearing-aid dealer. They have two children, David and Bennett.

Food and wine are two of Cerf's non-technology-related passions. "There are restaurateurs all over the world who hug Vint Cerf when they see him coming," Harcharik told Katie Hafner. Cerf is also an avid fan of science fiction and sometimes pens his own futuristic musings. He is currently a technical consultant for the science-fiction television series *Gene Roddenberry's Earth: Final Conflict* and has made a guest appearance on the show. Cerf also likes to write poetry, which, in its exacting detail, he has likened to writing computer code. He has even written a poem about the Internet that starts: "Like distant islands sundered by the sea, / We had no sense of community. / We lived and worked apart and rarely knew / That others searched with us for knowledge, too."

Since the 1970s, Cerf has encouraged deaf people to use e-mail. He also founded the Northern Virginia Resource Center for Deaf and Hard of Hearing Persons, in Fairfax, and he is a member of the board of trustees at Gallaudet University, a school for the deaf and hearing impaired in Washington, D.C. His wife has worked with the Smithsonian, WGBH, and the Folger Shakespeare Library to make works in various media accessible to the hearing-impaired.

For Cerf the ability to keep in touch with friends and family is one of the most important among the many advantages the Internet has provided. "More than anything," Cerf says, "I enjoy putting people together."—B. S.

Suggested Reading: *New York Times* III p4 Sept. 25, 1994, with photo; *Technology Review* p72+ May/June 1998, with photos; *Washingtonian* p66+ Nov. 1996, with photos; Hafner, Katie and Matthew Lyon. *Where Wizards Stay Up Late: The Origins of the Internet*, 1996

Clark, Wesley A.

Apr. 10, 1927– Computer designer; consultant

The computer designer and consultant Wesley A. Clark (who is not to be confused with the NATO general and presidential candidate, Wesley K. Clark) played key roles in the development of several noteworthy computers while working for Lincoln Laboratories at the Massachusetts Institute of Technology (MIT), in Cambridge, during the 1950s and early 1960s. With Kenneth Olsen, Clark designed the TX-0, the first computer built with transistors instead of the customary vacuum tubes. Clark followed that accomplishment with the development of the LINC, a small, reliable computer intended for biomedical research. Today, that computer is still an essential tool for biomedical researchers.

Wesley A. Clark was born on April 10, 1927 in New Haven, Connecticut. He eventually moved to Kinderhook, New York, a suburb of Albany, with his parents and two older sisters. Clark's father worked on a farm. His mother had been a teacher before she married. During the Depression, the Clark family moved to the Bay Area, in California, where his father managed a chain of stores.

In 1944 Clark enlisted in the U. S. Navy to serve in World War II. He was admitted to a two-year Reserve Officer Training Corps (ROTC) program at the University of Southern California, Los Angeles. In 1946 Clark was discharged from the navy before he could complete his degree. He then enrolled at the University of California, Berkeley (UC Berkeley), intending to continue with the ROTC program. Since Clark had gotten married the same year, he was ineligible for the ROTC because the program didn't admit married students. Although he originally intended to become a chemist, he became interested in physics, and in 1947 he earned a bachelor's degree in physics. Clark continued his education at UC Berkeley as a graduate student studying theoretical physics. One of his professors was J. Robert Oppenheimer [1904–67], the renowned physicist who played an important role in the development of the atomic bomb during World War II. Clark recalled to *Leaders of the Information Age* that UC Berkeley's physics department was quite famous, attracting over 300 graduate students. Clark, however, struggled with theoretical physics and withdrew from the program without receiving a master's degree.

In 1949 Clark got a job with the General Electric (GE) Atomic Energy Facilities, which operated a nuclear reactor, in Hanford, Washington. Clark explained to *Leaders of the Information Age* that both of his parents were employed at the Hanford reactor at the time and helped get him a job. Clark was a member of the Nuclear Reactor Dynamics Group, which performed the physics calculations—with desktop calculators—necessary to safely shut down the reactor. Although Hanford had analog computers, Clark never used them. He learned how computers worked by reading books and technical literature available in the facility's library. The Hanford reactor was eventually closed for safety reasons, and many employees who had worked there, including Clark, were subsequently checked for exposure to radiation.

The 1950 publication of Edmund C. Berkeley's article in *Scientific American* describing Simon, a primitive computer, further sparked Clark's interest in computers. At the time, computers were large machines that filled entire rooms, and Clark became intrigued by the idea of developing smaller models. In 1951 he was hired by the newly established Digital Computer Laboratory at MIT. He lectured on electrical engineering and learned to program MIT's Whirlwind, a high-speed computer that was built with funding from the U.S. Air Force to support defense projects. "One walked into [Whirlwind]," Clark recalled in a paper published in the book *A History of Personal Work Stations* (1988). "What now sits comfortably on a small desktop, in those days required an entire room for the control [console] alone. Programming for its small electrostatic memory (1,024 16-bit words on a good day) was a primitive affair carried out with the aid of heavily ruled coding forms on which to write out absolute-address instructions and octal numbers." Clark wrote a program that sorted a symbolic deck of playing cards for a training class on Whirlwind. "It's probably the only program I ever got right on the first try," he told *Leaders of the Information Age*.

Clark met Belmont Farley, a physicist who had joined the Digital Computer Laboratory to learn computer technology. In addition to Whirlwind, the laboratory also had the Memory Test Computer (MTC), which was built to provide a working computer to test the new ferrite core memory. "Belmont and I spent enormous numbers of hours interacting with MTC and with one another (he talked, I listened) as we tried out ideas, modified parameters, and studied displays of the simulated behavior of our strange little networks, grateful for such extensive access to such a powerful if not yet completely reliable machine," Clark recalled in his paper. "It was in these sessions that I began to learn from Belmont many of the basic attitudes toward computers that I hold firmly to this day: Computers are tools; convenience of use is the most important single design factor. Big computers are for big jobs; small computers, for small jobs."

In the mid 1950s MIT's Lincoln Laboratory, in Lexington, Massachusetts absorbed the Digital Computer Laboratory. Clark became a member of Lincoln's Advanced Computer Development Group and the leader of its logic design subgroup. Clark and Kenneth Olsen, a fellow member of the group, proposed that Lincoln build a revolutionary new computer, called the TX-1, that would have magnetic core memory and use transistors instead of vacuum tubes, which were gradually becoming obsolete. Lincoln's management rejected the project, thinking it too ambitious. Clark and Olsen, however, won approval for the construction of a much smaller and modest computer, the 18-bit, stored-program TX-0, that would serve as a precursor to a larger, more advanced computer, the TX-2. "The TX-0 was a demonstration to ourselves that we knew what we were doing," Clark recalled to *Leaders of the Information Age*. Built by Clark and Olsen, the TX-0 was the first transistorized computer, containing thousands of high-speed surface barrier transistors that cost about $80 each. Clark designed a light pen for the TX-0, which as he explained to *Leaders of the Information Age* "was the extension of a thing we were already using called a light gun." In her article for *Computerworld* (February 22, 1999, on-line), Leslie Goff observed that the TX-0's interactive features allowed users to enter data in real time and immediately produce results. "A simpler machine has probably not been built or used since," Clark told Goff. "Utter simplicity was the overriding goal. It would have to be a considered a RISC [reduced instruction set computer] machine in current terms because it was so primitively simple." The TX-0 was an outstanding success. Widely used for research, it helped train such students as Gordon Bell, Larry Roberts, and Ivan Sutherland, who all went on to make important contributions to the development of future computer technologies.

Clark and Olsen followed up the TX-0 with the 36-bit TX-2, which became operational in about 1958. Clark told *Leaders of the Information Age* that one of the TX-2's main features was multisequencing, a pre-cursor to time-sharing that allowed the computer to juggle different tasks. Clark noted that a time-sharing system accommodated different users whose programs were independent of one another, while his multi-sequencing system served multiple users who were working together on the same project. In 1957 Olsen left the Lincoln Laboratory to co-found the Digital Equipment Corporation (DEC), which became a leading manufacturer of computers.

Clark next designed the ARC-1 (Average Response Computer). Completed in 1958, the 18-bit ARC-1, which was about the size of two refrigerators turned on their sides, was similar in design to the TX-0. "Over the next several years the ARC served in a wide variety of studies, teaching researchers many new aspects of the neuroelectric behavior of the brain," Clark wrote in his paper. "It also confirmed my belief that there were indeed useful things that small digital computers could do in the laboratory." Clark also designed the 10-bit L-1, which he described in his paper as "an extremely simple stored-program computer of very limited capability."

At the first symposium of the Brain Research Institute at the University of California, Los Angeles (UCLA), in 1960, Clark told the audience, as quoted in his paper, "Stored-program computers like the TX-0 are beginning to appear in commercial form and there is reason to hope that these machines, or perhaps other general-purpose machines with a capability somewhere between that of the ARC and the TX-0, will find their way into the [medical-research] laboratory." For his next project at Lincoln, Clark set out to design a relatively small, low-cost machine that served this end. He decided that building the computer, which he named the LINC—partly as a play on the Lincoln Laboratory and partly for Laboratory Instrument Computer—should not cost more than $25,000, a low amount for computers at the time. In his book *Computing in the Middle Ages: A View From the Trenches, 1955–1983* (2002), Severo M. Ornstein, a hardware engineer and computer scientist who worked at Lincoln, recalled the LINC project. "That spring [in 1961] Wes disappeared from the lab for an extended period," Ornstein wrote. "When he returned he brought with him notebooks containing a preliminary design for a new small computer. A number of us gathered around to listen as he laid out the prospective design. We took notes furiously. Then he disappeared once more, leaving us to try to remember, ponder, and critique what he'd done, and to figure out how to program such a beast." Clark's colleagues offered their suggestions for the computer's modules and components, a number of which were incorporated in the final design. A team of about 20 engineers, programmers, and computer experts on the Lincoln Laboratory staff, including Clark, Ornstein, and Charles Molnar, began building the computer, which was completed in March 1962. "The demonstration prototype consisted of a set of four box-enclosed console modules, each connected by [20-foot] long cables to a common electronics cabinet now the size of only *one* refrigerator; this general configuration would be used in all subsequent 'academic' versions," Clark wrote in his paper. "One module, its box mostly empty, held a control panel that provided switches and register indicator lights . . . together with speed and audio control knobs and so forth. A second module held a [five-] inch CRT display adapted from a laboratory oscilloscope. A third module held the dual tape transport mechanics, while the fourth held a set of potentiometer knobs and jacks for analog input together with connectors for future input-output equipment. As an option for crowded laboratories, all modules could be removed from their boxes and mounted in standard equipment racks if desired."

In April 1962 Clark and several colleagues impressed the biomedical experts who attended the National Academy of Sciences Conference on Engineering and the Life Sciences, in Washington, D.C., by successfully demonstrating the new machine. The LINC was also demonstrated for Dr. Robert Livingston, the scientific director for both the National Institute of Neurological Diseases and Blindness and the National Institute of Mental Health (NIMH). In one of Livingston's laboratories, the LINC successfully performed its first scientific task, measuring the neuroelectric responses of a cat. "LINC was the first interactive machine that could be used in the laboratory to control experiments," Clark explained to *Leaders of the Information Age*. The computer's successful demonstrations caught the attention of officials at the National Institutes of Health (NIH) in Bethesda, Maryland, who were exploring the possible use of computers for biomedical research. Encouraged by the favorable reactions and the interest of a government agency, Clark and his colleagues planned to expand the LINC program, redesigning and up-grading the computer and building additional prototypes that would be tested at other biomedical research laboratories. "But it was not to be," Clark recalled in his paper. "Lincoln Laboratory management, sensing that there would be serious organizational difficulties in administering such a program within its established framework, firmly rejected both the expansion and 'wet' lab proposals. Instead, we were invited to find a more suitable home for any further work." By the end of 1962, however, the LINC team returned to MIT as part of its newly organized Center for Computer Technology and Research in the Biomedical Sciences, a multi-disciplinary and multi-institutional effort.

As members of the LINC Evaluation Program, Clark and his colleagues redesigned the LINC and built 16 machines. The NIH, NIMH, and NASA all provided substantial funding to support the program, and 12 laboratories around the country were chosen to test the machines. Most of the laboratories reported that the LINC greatly enhanced their research. Dr. Joseph Hind, a neurophysiologist with the University of Wisconsin, Madison, was so pleased with the LINC that he had his department order six additional machines. The LINC is widely considered to have opened the door for the extensive use of computers in biomedical research.

The LINC team continued to have its problems at MIT. "The nascent MIT Center, prospectively multi-institutional and multi-disciplinary, turned out to be irremediably multi-problematical as well and de-materialized," Clark wrote in his paper. "The result was that once again the peripatetic LINC team found itself in need of a more suitable home for its work." In 1964 the LINC team accepted an offer to move its operations to Washington University, in St. Louis, Missouri.

At Washington University, Clark taught computer science as a research professor and served as the associate director of the university's Computer Systems Laboratory, which housed the LINC team. In addition to his continuing work on the LINC, Clark participated in several other projects. He co-developed a patented method for open-loop broadcast transmission of computer software. As a consultant for DEC, Clark was the principal architect for the LINC-8, which was being manufactured for the commercial market. Clark also served as a computer-design consultant for both GE and National Transaction Networks.

In 1972 Clark left Washington University to return to Cambridge with his second wife, who had been admitted to the Harvard University Law School. Lincoln Laboratories rehired Clark as a consultant, but his contract wasn't renewed after it expired a few months later. "I'm the only person I know who has ever been fired by MIT for insubordination three times," Clark quipped to *Leaders of the Information Age*. From 1972 to 1982 Clark worked as a private design consultant, serving such noteworthy clients as the Xerox Palo Alto Research Center (PARC), in California; the Microbit Division of the Control Data Corporation; Merrill

Lynch; ITT; Advanced Technology Ventures; and Telenet. In 1982 Clark went to work for Sutherland, Sproull and Associates. Among his projects was the construction of a specialized keyboard and coding methods for the computer transcription of Chinese.

Clark's first marriage ended in divorce. In 1985 he and his second wife, Maxine Rockoff, founded Clark, Rockoff and Associates, a private consulting firm in New York City. The firm provided advice to clients on patent and litigation issues. Although he is semi-retired today, Clark still serves as a consultant to the Sun Microsystems Laboratories Asynchronous Systems Group.

From 1977 to1978 Clark served as the Sherman Fairchild Distinguished Scholar at the California Institute of Technology, in Pasadena. In 1981 he was honored with the Eckert-Mauchly Award for Computer Architecture. In 1984 Washington University awarded Clark an honorary doctorate.

Clark and Maxine Rockoff, an attorney, make their home in the New York City borough of Brooklyn. Clark is the father of four children, one of whom is a professor of computer science.—D. C.

Suggested Reading: *Computerworld* (on-line) Feb. 22, 1999; National Institute of Health Web site; *New York Times* III p12+ Aug. 19, 2001; Goldberg, Adele. ed. *A History of Personal Workstations*, 1988; Ornstein, Severo M. *Computing in the Middle Ages: A View from the Trenches: 1955–1983*, 2002

Hulton Archive by Getty Images

Clarke, Arthur C.

Dec. 16, 1917– Science-fiction writer; nonfiction writer

Arthur C. Clarke is best known for his many science-fiction novels. Working with the director Stanley Kubrick, he expanded one of his short stories into a screenplay for the film *2001: A Space Odyssey* (1968). Most critics consider *2001*, which follows the voyage of a doomed mission to investigate a mysterious alien object near the planet Jupiter, one of the greatest films of all time and the best science-fiction film ever made. Less known, however, are Clarke's contributions to science and communications. In 1945, while serving in the Royal Air Force and before attending college,

Clarke published a technical paper outlining a plan to place a network of communications satellites in space. The satellites would orbit the earth, transmitting radio signals around the planet. By the end of the next decade, Clarke's vision had become a reality as the United States, the Soviet Union, and other countries launched satellites into space that eventually transmitted telephone, radio, and television signals. The satellites have also been used for studying space, tracking weather patterns, and spying. As his reputation grew, Clarke became a frequent promoter of space exploration and technological innovations to improve people's lives. His fiction, nonfiction, articles, lectures, and talks inspired the imaginations of millions of people around the globe. In a lecture published in *Discover* (July 1985), Clarke wrote that "a future of infinite promise lies ahead of us in space. We may yet have a splendid and inspiring role to play, on a stage wider and more marvelous than ever dreamed of by any poet or dramatist."

Arthur Charles Clarke was born on December 16, 1917 in the small coastal town of Minehead, in England. His father, a farmer and postal worker, helped spark his interest in science. In an article published in the *New York Times Book Review* (March 7, 1983), Clarke recalled that his father gave him a card that came with a pack of cigarettes. The card had information about prehistoric animals, and young Arthur developed an immediate fascination with dinosaurs. He collected other cards about dinosaurs and also began making up adventure stories, which he told to his classmates at school.

During his teen years Clarke turned his attention upward. "In an earlier age I would probably have written stories about the sea," he wrote in the *New York Times Book Review*. "However, I was born at the time when men were first thinking seriously of escaping from their planetary cradle, and so my imagination was deflected into space." His imagination was also fueled by his discovery, in 1929, of *Amazing Stories*, a science-fiction magazine. The first issue he saw, from November 1928, depicted a spaceship exploring the planet Jupiter. During his school lunch hour, he went to the local store and bought all the science-fiction magazines he could find. At age 13, around the same time his father died, Clarke built his own telescope to explore the sky. He drew detailed maps of the moon based on his observations.

In 1930 Clarke discovered at his local library the book *Last and First Men* (1930), by W. Olaf Stapledon. In the *New York Times Book Review*, Clarke recalled that "the Stapledonian vistas of millions and hundreds of millions of years, the rise and fall of civilizations and entire races of men, changed my whole outlook on the universe and has influenced much of my writing ever since." Another book, *The Conquest of Space* (1931), by David Lasser, also influenced Clarke. Lasser discusses early rocket experiments and the possibilities of space travel, particularly of a trip to the moon.

Unable to afford college, Clarke went to work for the government at the Exchequer and Audit Department, in 1936. He also joined a science-fiction club called the British Interplanetary Society, whose members were often regarded as eccentrics.

During World War II, Clarke volunteered for military service, joining the Royal Air Force (RAF) in 1941. He operated radar systems and, as the war progressed, was placed in charge of a revolutionary new radar system, the Ground Controlled Approach (GCA) unit. The GCA enabled operators to guide approaching aircraft in landing safely. This system helped pilots who couldn't see during bad weather. While serving in the RAF, Clarke published his first science-fiction stories and technical papers. His military experience also sparked an interest in communications.

In 1945 Clarke published an article in *Wireless World*, a scientific journal. He theorized that "extra-terrestrial relays," or satellites, could be launched into space and remain in a fixed orbit about 25,000 miles above the earth. Such satellites, Clarke theorized, could transmit radio waves and thus make international communication much faster and easier. The notion of an artificial satellite was first suggested by Sir Isaac Newton, the 17th-century physicist and mathematician, who wrote in his book, *Philosophiae Naturalis Principia Mathematica* (1687), that an object shot at a sufficient velocity and height would enter an orbit around Earth. Nearly three centuries later, in 1957, the Soviet Union launched the world's first satellite—Sputnik—which circled the earth every 96 minutes and emitted a simple radio signal. The United States followed three months later with Explorer 1, which was used to detect space radiation.

Clarke's theory of a communications satellite network got closer to reality in December 1958, when NASA launched the Project SCORE satellite. During its 13-day elliptical orbit around Earth, SCORE successfully transmitted President Eisenhower's Christmas message—the first voice beamed in from space. In 1960 NASA launched Echo 1, a satellite in the form of an aluminum-coated Mylar balloon, which reflected radio waves back to earth and provided further viability of the radio transmission system. Over the next 10 years, both the United States and the Soviet Union launched many communications satellites into space, creating the global communications system that Clarke had sketched out in 1945. Although he is widely considered the "father of the communications satellite," Clarke never received any financial compensation for his idea, apart from the standard fee for publishing his article. In an interview with Marcia Gauger for *People* (December 20, 1982), Clarke noted that a lawyer had once told him that he "couldn't have obtained a patent in 1945 as the idea [for a communications satellite] was too farfetched," and that, even if he had, "it would have expired about the time the first communication satellite was launched." "So that," Clarke said, "was the end of my yacht." Clarke has frequently downplayed his contribution, saying that someone else would have eventually thought of the idea, and that the real credit belongs to the engineers who actually constructed the satellites.

After he was discharged from the RAF, Clarke enrolled at King's College, at the University of London. He graduated in 1948, receiving his B.Sc. degree with first-class honors, in physics and mathematics. In 1949 he became an assistant editor for the journal *Science Abstracts*. "All of the world's leading scientific journals passed over my desk, and I had to mark the ones that appeared important," he explained to Frank Houston for the online magazine *Salon* (March 7, 2000).

By 1950 Clarke had written many stories, articles, and his first book, and yet he still considered his writing to be "a pleasant and occasionally profitable hobby" rather than a profession, as he wrote in the *New York Times Book Review*. In his first book, *Interplanetary Flight: An Introduction to Astronautics* (1951), he detailed the scientific and mathematical concepts that would make space travel possible. In doing so, he made complex scientific ideas and concepts understandable to the average person—a skill that would serve him as both a nonfiction and fiction writer. *Interplanetary Flight* received favorable reviews.

Encouraged by this reception, Clarke in 1952 published *Exploration of Space*, an expansion of the ideas he had discussed in his first book. That year, *Exploration of Space* was a selection of the Book of the Month Club, thereby introducing Clarke's work to thousands of readers. In a review for the *New York Herald Tribune Book Review* (July 13, 1952), H. H. Holmes wrote that the book "is precisely calculated to bring our present knowledge of space travel before a whole new public which has hitherto known only the distortions of comics and television." With the commercial and critical success of his first two books, Clarke was encouraged to quit his job with *Scientific Abstracts* and become a full-time writer. His first two science-fiction novels, *Prelude to Space* (1951) and *The Sands of Mars* (1952), were also praised by most reviewers. Reviewing *Sands of Mars* for the *New York Times* (September 14, 1952), J. F. McComas remarked that the novel "[reads] like true history more than fiction."

Clarke was prolific, publishing books almost on a yearly basis. Although he continued to write nonfiction books about scientific topics and his new passion of undersea exploration, he focused on science fiction. His fifth novel, *Childhood's End* (1953), established him as one of the preeminent science-fiction authors in the world. In the novel, Clarke introduces the Overlords, an alien race that takes over the earth and abolishes disease, poverty, and other ills. The Overlords create a utopia for human beings, who gradually accept their rule after some resistance. As the plot unfolds, it becomes clear that the Overlords have other plans for humankind. Most critics consider *Childhood's End* to be Clarke's best novel.

In 1956 Clarke left the United Kingdom to become a permanent resident of the island nation of Sri Lanka (then Ceylon), in the Indian Ocean off the southeast coast of India. He had visited the nation previously to explore its underwater reefs, and was immediately captivated by the island's beauty. According to Andrew Robinson in the *Times Higher Education Supplement* (October 10, 1997), the nation's warm climate, endless opportunities to scuba dive, and the prospect of keeping a little distance between himself and his growing legion of fans also appealed to Clarke. Most Sri Lankans were happy to have him stay as a permanent guest, and the government granted him tax-free status in the 1970s. In 1979 Clarke was named chancellor of Moratuwa University, which subsequently opened the Arthur C. Clarke Centre for Modern Technology. Clarke lives in Colombo, Sri Lanka's capital, and his home is equipped with a satellite dish, television, VCR, fax machine, telephone, and a personal computer, all of which keep him in touch with the rest of the world.

In 1964 the director Stanley Kubrick, who won international acclaim for such films as *Paths of Glory* (1957), *Spartacus* (1960), and *Dr. Strangelove, Or: How I Stopped Worrying and Learned to Love the Bomb* (1964), approached Clarke about collaborating on a science-fiction film. After reading some of Clarke's fiction, Kubrick had become intrigued by Clarke's short story "The Sentinel" (1951). Clarke agreed to co-write a screenplay based on this story with Kubrick, and he also expanded the story into a novel. The film, *2001: A Space Odyssey*, was released in 1968, and the novel of the same name was also published that year. In *2001*, a mysterious black monolith is discovered on the moon. Scientists and government officials are completely baffled by the monolith's origin and purpose, but are certain that it was created and placed there by an alien intelligence. A far larger monolith is also detected in space, near the planet Jupiter. Eager for answers, the government dispatches a team of astronauts to investigate. As the spaceship Discovery approaches Jupiter, HAL 9000, the ship's interactive computer that talks and thinks like a human being, malfunctions, endangering the mission and even the lives of the crew.

The fact that the film, especially the ending, confused and puzzled many people did not detract from its popularity at the box office. Clarke and Kubrick shared an Academy Award for best adapted screenplay. In retrospect, both the book and film contributed to the image of Arthur C. Clarke as a prophet. He anticipated several technologically advanced tools that have since become a common part of people's everyday lives. In one scene, for example, a man uses a laptop computer that has an operating system similar to Windows. He uses the computer to read several electronic newspapers and to send electronic messages. In his interview with Gauger, Clarke said, "I am a hard-core science-fiction writer—I have seldom written anything that I thought could not happen."

2001 brought Clarke substantial media attention. In addition to writing books, he also became a vocal proponent of space exploration and technology. Clarke told Frank Houston that members of the Apollo 8 space capsule, which orbited the moon in December 1968, had confessed to Clarke that they were "tempted to radio back the discovery of a large black monolith" on the moon's dark side. In July 1969, Clarke provided commentary for CBS television during the moon landing.

Since then, Arthur C. Clarke has continued to write both fiction and nonfiction, publishing more than 80 books. He has also delivered lectures on different topics relating to space on many occasions. Clarke's novels include *Rendezvous with Rama* (1973), *The Fountains of Paradise* (1979), *2010: Space Odyssey II* (1982), *2061: Odyssey III* (1988), *Rama II* (1989), *The Garden of Rama* (1991), *The Hammer of God* (1993), *Rama Revealed* (1993) with Gentry Lee, and *3001: The Final Odyssey* (1997). In 1984 the director Peter Hyams adapted *2010* into a film of the same name. Although it wasn't proclaimed to be the visual masterpiece that *2001* had been, many of Clarke's fans were pleased that *2010* answered questions left unresolved in the previous film. (In one scene, there is a brief glimpse of a *Time* magazine cover, with illustrations of the president of the United States and the Soviet premier. The illustrations are actually modeled on Clarke and Kubrick.)

Clarke's nonfiction includes *The Challenge of a Spaceship* (1960), *Profiles of the Future* (1962), *The Promise of Space* (1968), *The View from Serendip* (1977), *Ascent to Orbit: The Technical Writings of Arthur C. Clarke* (1984), *How the World Was One* (1992), and *Greetings, Carbon-based Bipeds!* (1999).

During an interview for *U.S. News and World Report* (January 10, 1983), Clarke envisioned computers helping to educate a future generation of students and allowing more people to work from home. "I think one of the reasons I became a writer is that it takes me approximately 10 steps to get from my bedroom to my office," he said.

Over the decades, Arthur C. Clarke's work as an author and his contributions to science have been recognized many times. For his theory of communications satellites, he has been honored with the Aerospace Communications Award (1974) and a Marconi International Fellowship (1982). His fiction has earned him three Nebula Awards from the Science Fiction Writers of America (1972, 1974, and 1979), two Hugo Awards from the World Science Fiction Convention (1974 and 1980), and the John Campbell Award (1974). He is also the recipient of the Kalinga Award (1961) from UNESCO (United Nations Educational, Scientific and Cultural Organization) and the von Karman Award (1996) from the the the International Academy of Astronautics. Clarke was knighted by Queen Elizabeth II in 1998.

In recent years, Arthur C. Clarke has been confined to a wheelchair due to the progression of postpolio syndrome. His first marriage ended in divorce in 1964. He spends his time playing table tennis, answering the many e-mails he receives each day, and studying the data he receives from NASA and other space research centers.

In an interview with Tim McGirk, a reporter for London's *Independent* (January 23, 1994), Clarke said he had only two regrets in life: "I wish I could stay alive long enough to see man landing on Mars. And I'd like to be around when we make contact with extraterrestrials. But I've seen so much already."—D. C.

Suggested Reading: *Discover* p58+ July 1985, with illus., p68+ May 1997; *Independent* p12 Jan. 23, 1994, with photo; *Library Journal* p990 May 15, 1984; *New York Herald Tribune Book Review* p5 July 13, 1952; *New York Times Book Review* p14+ Mar. 7, 1983, with photos; *People* p87+ Dec. 20, 1982, with photos; *Salon* (on-line) Mar. 7, 2000; *Sunday Telegraph* p3+ Dec. 17, 2000; *Times Higher Education Supplement* p19+ Oct. 10, 1997; *U.S. News and World Report* p60 Jan. 10, 1983, with photos and illustrations; *Washington Post* C p1+ Nov. 16, 1982, with photos; McAleer, Neil. *Arthur C. Clarke: The Authorized Biography*, 1992

Cocke, John

May 30, 1925–July 16, 2002 Innovator of reduced instruction set computing (RISC)

As a member of the research and development team at International Business Machines (IBM) for more than 35 years, John Cocke greatly contributed to the development of computer architecture and instruction sets—and has numerous patents to prove it. During his tenure at IBM, Cocke advanced many of the company's innovative mainframe products, including the revolutionary System/360, for which he designed the instruction set. He is most famous for the development of reduced instruction set computing (RISC) in the 1970s, an innovation that boosted computer speed by simplifying instructions for frequently used functions. RISC architecture has been used in such IBM products as the Power PC computer and the AS/400 and RS/6000 servers. Today RISC is the basic architecture for most workstations.

John Cocke was born on May 30, 1925 (some sources say May 25, 1925) to an old Southern family in Charlotte, North Carolina. His father, Norman Cocke, was the chairman of the Duke Power Company and served on the Duke University endowment. Cocke was a poor student in his early childhood and needed a tutor in grammar school, but he was very adept at mechanics and managed to take apart his first bicycle in a matter of hours at age six, quite to his mother Mary's annoyance. He fared better in high school, where he proved himself to be very adept at physics and general science. He took those courses, however, to avoid taking Latin, and also enrolled in math, for which he felt he did not have to study.

Cocke's father took him to all of Duke's athletic competitions, and this early exposure to Duke led Cocke to enroll there for his undergraduate studies. At the university, in Durham, North Carolina, he studied mechanical engineering and earned his bachelor's degree, in 1946. As a college student during World War II, Cocke served in the U.S. Navy's V-12 program, a college training program classified under the U.S. Naval Reserve. He was called up for active service again in 1952, during the Korean War. Between 1946 and 1952 he worked at a number of jobs, including the Air Engineering Company from 1946 to 1949, where he served as a heating and air-conditioning engineer. From 1949 to 1950 he was an engineer at the General Electric Company's high-voltage laboratory. In 1954 he returned to Duke to study for his doctorate in mathematics; two years later he received his Ph.D. During his studies, he took a summer job in Florida at Patrick Air Force Base, where he designed a program that calculated (using a series of seemingly random numbers generated by a computer) the ideal number of aircrafts needed to deliver supplies to the Bahamas.

When Cocke was asked to join the IBM research division in 1956, he considered himself extremely lucky, because the company was at the forefront of computer technology at that time. In those early days he arrived at work late and stayed late, sometimes all night, mostly because those were the hours during which the computer was most available. Stories of Cocke's absentmindedness abound. Once a janitor found $4,000 in stock certificates in his wastebasket. Frequently, he needed to be reminded by accounting to pick up his paychecks.

Another story tells of how he would conceive a brilliant idea, run to the appropriate person's office to explain his idea, then in the middle of his explanation get another great idea and run to another person's office without having finished his first explanation. "I guess I was relatively absentminded," he explained to Anthony Brandt for *Forbes* (August 24, 1998). "But, you know, there are people more interested in science than in normal ways of life. And there were plenty of people around IBM who were just as bad."

One of Cocke's first assignments at IBM was the Stretch project, marketed as the IBM 7030, a machine designed to run several programs simultaneously using only a single central processing unit. The Stretch was IBM's first computer utilizing transistor electronics. The company lost a bid to build a high-performance decimal computer system for the Livermore Radiation Laboratory at the University of California in 1955. (The project instead went to IBM's competitor Univac, which was then the preeminent computer manufacturer.) The next year—the first year of Cocke's employment at the company—IBM inaugurated the Stretch project when it won a bid to build by 1960 a computer that was 100 times faster than existing computers.

Steven Dunwell headed the Stretch project and asked a number of IBM employees—including Gerrit Blaauw, Fred Brooks, Harwood Kolsky, and John Cocke—to contribute to the design. Blaauw and Brooks worked on the instruction set design; Cocke and Kolsky developed a simulator that helped their group explore organizational options. They envisioned new organization techniques which included "predecoding, memory operand prefetch, out-of-order execution, speculative execution based upon branch prediction, branch misprediction recovery, and precise interrupts," according to Professor Mark Smotherman of Clemson University. On his Web site, Smotherman went on to note, "In many ways, the Stretch organization of preprocessing the instruction stream to handle branches and memory loads as early as possible is a precursor of later high-end IBM mainframes (e.g., S/360 Model 91, S/370 Model 165, 3033, and 3090) as well as the IBM RS/6000 and PowerPC microprocessors."

Cocke and Kolsky developed five test programs for the simulator that established the computer's parameters, several dealing with scientific computations. Known as the Cocke-Kolsky simulator, it became a key component of the Stretch project. The instructions for the Stretch machine were to come through two processors: one that fetched, precoded, and partially completed the instruction stream, and another, arithmetic unit that completed the remainder of the instructions. Cocke also developed a "look-ahead" unit that was a combination of a completion buffer and a history buffer that would speed the machine's performance by allowing it to anticipate its next task while completing its initial task. (David do you find the preceding two paragraphs a little vague?)

Developers expected the Stretch machine to be 60 to 100 times faster than the IBM 704. As the 1960 deadline loomed, product planners set the machine's price at $13.5 million for the product version, known as the IBM 7030. Unfortunately, the machine's speed estimate was grossly exaggerated: Stretch was supposed to be eight times faster than an IBM 7090, which was itself eight times faster than the 704. After the Stretch was fully operational, however, the machine was discovered to be only four times faster than the 7090. Though it was faster than anything previously built, Thomas Watson Jr., then president of the company, and IBM's management were so embarrassed by the performance of the Stretch that they cut the price to $7.78 million. It was subsequently removed from sales brochures.

Though the machine was delivered late and was slower than expected, Stretch's innovations helped pave the way for a new line of IBM computers. Its state-of-the-art transistor design enabled the company to produce the first of the popular 7090 series in a little over a year from the time of the initial contract. Some of the computer organizational principles that had been developed for the Stretch machine—including multiprogramming, memory protection, the 8-bit byte, and generalized interrupts—made their way into the revolutionary IBM System/360, which debuted in 1964. The System/360 was the first family of computers that allowed a buyer to use interchangeable peripheral equipment and software. In an age of giant, one-size-fits-all mainframes, it was unique in that it gave customers the ability to upgrade parts of their hardware instead of buying a whole new system when their old one was outmoded. It also offered customers a choice of five processors and 19 various combinations of speed, memory, and power. The system's instruction set was designed by Fred Brooks's team, which included Cocke, Gene Amdahl, and Elaine Bone.

During the development of the System/360, IBM also asked Cocke to work on another project, which would eventually be known as the Advanced Computing Systems project. In IBM's highly secret research and development facility, the two projects were called Project X (System/360) and Project Y (the Advanced Computer Systems), respectively. While the goal of Project X was to provide a computer with 10 to 30 times the performance level of the Stretch machine, Project Y had the much more ambitious goal of producing a machine that was 100 times faster than the Stretch. Work on Project Y began in 1961 at the IBM Watson Research Center, in Yorktown Heights, New York, though it did not attain official status until November 1963 when it became part of Jack Bertram's Experimental Computers and Programming group in Yorktown.

Cocke took a major role in defining the instruction set, compiler technology, and circuit technology of Project Y. On direct orders from Thomas Watson Jr., the group set up a lab in California to build a computer "of the highest obtainable performance." The computer was designed to compete with machines like Control Data's CDC 6600 and the CDC 6800, which were cutting into IBM's sales to the scientific community. The IBM machine was to be equipped with 48-bit single precision and 96-bit double precision floating point arithmetic, capable of scientific computation in research laboratories.

Relocated to an old fruit warehouse in Sunnyvale, California, the group was renamed IBM Advanced Computing Systems, and Project Y became known as the ACS-1. Cocke, along with Frances Allen, was in charge of the compiler research; Herb Schorr headed the architecture team; and several dozen engineers joined the group from IBM's facilities in Poughkeepsie, New York, and San Jose, California. In 1965 there were 25 people working on the project; by 1968 there would be 200. As the project grew in scope, the group moved to a larger facility farther down the road.

The group was determined to build a machine that was 1,000 times better than the IBM 7090. They wanted the ACS-1 to have an optimizing compiler, cache memory, streamlined input/output channels to and from the cache, a new virtual memory operating system, fixed-head disks, and a new integrated circuitry design for the memory and processor. The project was expected to be shipped by 1968 but the target date was moved back to 1970. In about 1968 IBM management decided to convert the entire project to be compatible with the System/360, which eliminated Cocke's instruction set and other new features. At this point many members of the project left, and the ACS-1 project limped along as the ACS-360 project, under the supervision of Gene Amdahl. In 1969 the project was canceled, but many of its innovations made their way into other IBM projects, including Cocke's work on the central processing unit (CPU) organization, which was incorporated into the IBM RS/3600, 20 years later.

In the early 1970s, Cocke, with a team of 20 researchers, began developing his ideas for a reduced instruction set computer, also known as RISC. This architecture greatly boosted computer speed by employing streamlined machine instructions for often-used functions. By the 1970s, these architectures were becoming vastly complex as they attempted, according to IBM's Web site, "to directly support high-level language and operating system constructs in the machine instruction set." The IBM 801, the first RISC computer, was named for Building 801, where it originated. Its design was completed in 1974 and a working machine was finished in 1980.

With RISC, Cocke created a very different approach to systems architecture. By researching the frequency with which functions were being executed, he created a much simpler and faster instruction set. "I felt . . . that we should emphasize a simple instruction set . . . and forget the less frequent instructions. So just based on where we put our efforts in building the logic, we made a more effective machine," he explained to Anthony Brandt. This new, tightly integrated hardware and software system decreased the computer's complexity while providing stellar system and language performance.

Remarkably, IBM did not immediately take advantage of RISC architecture. The IBM System/360 and System/370 were doing so well that the company felt no need to change. In 1982 Sun Microsystems produced workstations for scientists using an architecture very similar to Cocke's RISC. Other companies soon followed suit, including Hewlett-Packard and the Digital Equipment Corporation. In 1986, when IBM did finally produce a RISC personal computer with the RT PC, it was the first such computer from a major computer manufacturer. RISC was also used in the development of IBM's Power PC, the AS/400, and the RS/6000 servers, and it remains the basic architecture for most workstations. When John Cocke retired from IBM in 1992, he held 22 patents, including one for the development of RISC. He served for three more years as a consultant to the company.

In addition to his position at IBM, Cocke was a visiting professor at the Massachusetts Institute of Technology (MIT), in Cambridge (1962), and at the Courant Institute of Math and Science at New York University, in New York City (1968–69). He received a number of awards, including the 1987 Alan Turing Award from the Association for Computing Machinery, the John E. Bertram Award from IBM in 1990, and the National Medal of Technology in 1991. In 1992 Cocke, along with Francis Carruboaur, Norman Kreitzer, and George Radin (all of IBM) were named Inventors of the Year for their work on RISC architecture. Two years later, the National Science Foundation presented him with the 1994 National Medal of Science for "his contributions to computer science in the theory and practice of high-performance computer systems." At that time, RISC machines were hailed as "the essential building blocks for today's high-performance parallel machines."

Despite all his accomplishments, John Cocke remained self-critical throughout his life. "I've always considered myself fantastically lazy," he told Anthony Brandt. "I hate arithmetic, for instance. No one should have to do it when you can design a machine that does."

In 1989 Cocke, a longtime bachelor, married Anne Holloway, who helped to rid him of some of his more eccentric habits, such as wearing the same clothes for a week or more. He also had the unusual habit of carrying on conversations lasting for months or even years on a variety of subjects. "He would start up a conversation with you on some detailed technical subject, plunging right in where he left off the last time he saw you a couple of months earlier," his old research associate Frances Allen recalled for the New York Times (July 19, 2002). "It was one of John's traits that took a little getting used to."

John Cocke died on July 16, 2002 in Valhalla, New York, after a long illness involving a series of strokes. He was survived by his wife, his niece, and three nephews.—C. M.

Suggested Reading: Association for Computing Machinery Web site; Clemson University Computer Science Department Web site; *Forbes* Aug. 24, 1998; The Franklin Institute Web site; IBM Research Web site; *New York Times* B p8 July 19, 2002

Courtesy of the National Human Genome Research Institute

Collins, Francis

Apr. 14, 1950– Director of the National Human Genome Research Institute

On June 26, 2000, President Bill Clinton announced the sequencing of the human genetic code—the 23 pairs of chromosomes containing 3 billion nucleotide bases that make up what has been described as the map of all human life. "Without a doubt, this is the most wondrous map ever produced by mankind," he said, as quoted by Tim Stevens in *Industry Week* (December 11, 2000, on-line). "It will revolutionize the diagnosis, prevention, and treatment of most, if not all, human disease." Standing on one side of Clinton during the announcement was Francis Collins, a medical geneticist and director of the National Human Genome Research Institute (NHGRI) at the National Institutes of Health (NIH) in Bethesda, Maryland. (On Clinton's other side was J. Craig Venter, president and chief scientific officer of the Celera Genomics Corporation, a private company that—in a

virtual tie with the government's NHGRI—completed its own draft of the human genome.)

Begun in 1990 under the directorship of Nobel laureate James D. Watson, who in 1953 discovered the chemical structure of deoxyribonucleic acid (DNA), the Human Genome Project is a government-sponsored genetic research initiative on an unprecedented scale. Collins described the project to Stephen Frazier for *CNN.com* (May 1999) as "more significant than splitting the atom or going to the moon," and even more audacious, since it is an "adventure into ourselves, to read our own blueprint." The project, which is due to conclude in 2005 after the final stages of sequencing, is ahead of schedule and under budget—an accomplishment that many attribute to Collins's skillful leadership.

Collins was put in charge of the Human Genome Project in 1993, after a decade as a physician and genetic researcher, during which time he helped to discover the gene responsible for cystic fibrosis, one of the most common and deadly genetic diseases. The discovery of the cystic-fibrosis gene in 1989 was an enormous achievement, but one tempered by the fact that it took years of laborious research, with Collins and his colleagues "feeling [their] way in the dark," as he described it to Peter Evans for the *BBC World Service* (January 30, 2001, on-line). In order to locate the genes responsible for thousands of other diseases, Collins realized then, scientists needed a better understanding of the totality of the human genetic makeup—in fact, they needed a map. Therefore, when asked to take over as director of the Human Genome Project—whose mandate is to locate and describe chemically each of the estimated 100,000 genes in the human genome—Collins felt a sense of calling. "The reason I got interested in genetics was because of my sense that it is involved in virtually every disease and it gives us a window to understand a long list of conditions that we currently describe but don't understand how they come about," he told Frazier. "I spent too many days in a clinic talking to families about diseases that I can't do anything for, not to be motivated to try to move us . . . into a better world."

The youngest of four boys, Francis Sellers Collins was born on April 14, 1950 in Staunton, Virginia. His parents, by his own account, were "wonderful, fascinating" people who instilled in him a love of learning and an interest in all areas of human endeavor. His father, who had a Ph.D. in English, earned his living by teaching at a local college and raising livestock on the family farm. He also collected folk music and, with his wife, an amateur playwright, staged plays at a theater that the couple had established on the farm. Francis Collins apparently inherited his mother's talent: at the age of seven, he wrote and directed his own version of *The Wizard of Oz*.

Collins's mother also played an unusually active role in her sons' education. Convinced that the local schools were inadequate, she taught her children at home. Collins's two oldest brothers, who are 18 and 16 years his senior, did not receive any formal education until they entered college, and Collins himself remained under his mother's tutelage until he entered the sixth grade. During an interview with Gina Kolata for the *New York Times* (November 30, 1993), he recalled how his mother and her pupils would cover a particular subject, such as etymology, for several days straight, and then begin a similarly intensive study of another subject, such as math. "It was a bit disorganized," he told Kolata. "I'm sure it would not have been deemed appropriate by today's standards." During his high-school years, Collins became hooked on chemistry, and he pursued his interest in that subject at the University of Virginia, in Charlottesville, which he entered at the age of 16. His fascination with chemistry and the other hard sciences was matched by his almost complete lack of interest in biology. "Somehow, I had the notion that life was chaotic and that whatever principles governed it were unpredictable," he told J. Madeleine Nash for *Time* (January 17, 1994, on-line). He received his B.S. degree, with highest honors, from the university, in 1970.

It was not until Collins enrolled in the doctoral program in physical chemistry at Yale University, in New Haven, Connecticut, that he became fully aware of the revolution then sweeping the biological sciences, which had been sparked by the discovery two decades before of the structure of DNA, the biological molecule responsible for all inherited traits. "I was completely blown away," he told Nash. As he pondered his future, he realized that a career in molecular biology would enable him to fulfill a need that was becoming increasingly important to him: improving the quality of human life. "When I asked myself what [physical chemistry] had done for anybody, the answer was, 'Not very much,'" he told John Carey in an interview for *BusinessWeek* (June 15, 1990).

All of Collins's concerns and interests seemed to point to medicine, and in 1974, after earning his M.S. and Ph.D. degrees at Yale, he enrolled at the University of North Carolina School of Medicine, in Chapel Hill. During his last year there he was introduced to human genetics. It seemed to be a perfect match; specializing in the study of human genes, especially those thought to cause life-threatening diseases, would both provide him with the intellectual challenges he craved and enable him to serve humankind. He received his M.D., with honors, from the university in 1977. Over the next several years, he completed both his internship and residency at North Carolina Memorial Hospital and served for three years as a fellow in human genetics and pediatrics at Yale University School of Medicine.

In 1984 Collins joined the staff of the University of Michigan Medical School, in Ann Arbor, as an assistant professor of internal medicine and human genetics. He soon began his rapid rise through the ranks of academe; within seven years he had

become a full professor in both disciplines. Meanwhile, he was also actively involved in laboratory research with the Howard Hughes Medical Institute, the largest biomedical research philanthropic organization in the United States. In 1992 alone the institute reportedly awarded him and seven other investigators research grants worth a total of $6.33 million.

Collins owes much of his success to his talent for tracking down disease genes that other scientists considered to be beyond reach. His first major discovery came in 1989, when he and his collaborators announced that they had found the gene that causes cystic fibrosis (CF). The most widespread life-threatening genetic disease in Europe and North America, CF compromises the ability of the lungs to fight off bacterial infections by causing the accumulation of sticky mucus in the organs. Collins also led the search, which ended in 1990, to locate the gene that causes neurofibromatosis, a disease of the nervous system characterized by the formation of grossly deformative tumors. (Neurofibromatosis was thought to be the disorder that afflicted Joseph Merrick, the so-called Elephant Man, and it is still sometimes erroneously called Elephant Man's disease.) In addition, he was a lead investigator in the Huntington's Disease Collaborative Research Group, which comprised six laboratories in the United States, England, and Wales; in 1993 the group discovered the gene that causes Huntington's disease, a neurodegenerative disorder that leads to loss of muscle control, dementia, and, eventually, death.

The discovery of the CF gene was especially dramatic, because it marked the first time that scientists succeeded in both isolating and describing the biochemical activity of a disease gene whose location at the start of the search had been completely unknown. At a news conference in August 1989 at which they announced their discovery, Collins and his fellow gene hunters compared their endeavor to a search for a broken faucet (the defect in the gene) in a house (the gene) in any of the fifty states (the chromosomes) in the United States (the human genome). "When we began our search seven years ago," Collins declared, as quoted in the *New York Times* (September 12, 1989), "we had no idea what state to look in. The house could have been anywhere between New York and San Francisco."

The combination of his scientific accomplishments, his leadership style, and his practical experience as a clinician made Collins an attractive candidate for the position of director of the Human Genome Project. Offered the position in 1992, he initially refused since he was hesitant to put aside his search for genes that cause disease. But, as he told Stevens, he eventually talked himself into it. "I thought to myself, 'Are you nuts? This is only going to happen once in history and your have a chance to lead this and you are saying no?'" As a condition of his acceptance of the job, Collins was permitted to create his own laboratory at NIH that would focus exclusively on the identification and understanding of genes that cause human disease, including breast and prostate cancer and adult-onset diabetes.

While some scientists have argued that an emphasis on searching for specific genes detracts from the overall effort to build the "infrastructure"—the maps and sequences—of the genome, Collins has consistently defended his position. "The reason the public pays and is excited—well, disease genes are at the top of the list," he told Leslie Roberts in an interview for Science (October 1, 1993). Once completed, the maps and sequenced DNA are expected to accelerate efforts to find cures for the some 4,000 diseases caused by mutations in single genes. Knowledge of certain genes that cause disease, including the gene responsible for CF, has already enabled better monitoring, earlier intervention, and more effective chemical therapies.

As director of the Human Genome Project, Collins sets policies and develops scientific, fiscal, and management strategies. One of his biggest challenges is coordinating all the activity between the 16 academic and research centers involved in the project while answering to the Department of Energy, which oversees the project, and the Wellcome Trust of London, which provides one-third of its financing. According to many observers, Collins has been skillful at encouraging the various scientific teams—many with competing agendas, all jostling for funding and recognition—to work together. Three years into his tenure, the preliminary goals of the project had already been accomplished: about 15,000 genetic markers had been mapped, giving researchers a rough guide around the human genome. But the more difficult task remained—the actual sequencing of tens of millions of pieces of code. To tackle this, Collins established pilot projects at individual laboratories in order to encourage the growth of the physical facilities and to test the management skills of the laboratory directors. Five laboratories—at Washington University, in St. Louis, Missouri; Baylor University, in Waco, Texas; Massachusetts Institute of Technology, in Cambridge; the U.S. Department of Energy; and the Sanger Center, in the United Kingdom—emerged as the frontrunners; now called the G5, they handle the burden of the sequencing load and, with the help of faster sequencing machines introduced in 1998, can be credited with completing the lion's share of the human genome. This reorganization of the project, which could have been enormously divisive, instead resulted in greater efficiency, lower costs, and—most important—imparted a sense of urgency and mission to those involved. "Francis has a manner of presenting things in a way that makes everybody feel good," George Weinstock, a Baylor University researcher, told Tim Stevens, adding that he can "make people feel that even if the decision that is being made is not necessarily the best one for them, it's certainly the best one for the project."

Collins's streamlining of the sequencing process paid off in May 1998, when the newly formed Celera Genomics company, headed up by the genetic researcher J. Craig Venter, announced their intention to sequence and complete the human genome in three years and, moreover, to become the "definitive source of genomic and related biological information," according to their Web site. Working under the slogan "Discovery Can't Wait" and using a company name that is Latin for "speed," the flamboyant Dr. Venter boasted that Celera Genomics would beat the government and be the first to complete the human genome. Fueled by Venter's showmanship, rumors began circulating that, perhaps, an assortment of academic centers was ill-suited to the industrial-scale task of decoding the genome. Collins mounted a vigorous response, encouraging the scientists working on the project to think of themselves as "factory managers" who needed to increase the production of code, as he told an interviewer for the Lasker Foundation (on-line). With funding and support concentrated on the most productive laboratories, the speed of the project increased dramatically. In April 1998, only 4 percent of the genetic information had been mapped, but, by June 2000, Collins could match the Celera company's claim to have a completed draft of about 90 percent of the human genome sequence. In the end, Collins told Frazier, the competition posed by Celera has "stirred the pot and gotten everybody really fired up to see how quickly one can go."

With the sequencing of the complete genome due to conclude in 2002, Collins is looking ahead to the implications of this massive storehouse of knowledge. He currently spends about half of his time addressing the ethical, social, and legal issues surrounding genetic research. Of great concern to Collins is the specter of discrimination based on genetic makeup. In testimony before the Senate Labor and Human Resources Committee, Collins argued that "Americans are still largely unprotected by federal law against insurance rate hikes based on genetic information and against unauthorized people or institutions having access to the genetic information contained in their medical records," as quoted by a reporter for Reuters (May 22, 1998, on-line). In public speeches and lobbying efforts, Collins is a strong voice calling for federal legislation to prevent all types of genetic discrimination.

As a devout Christian and empathetic physician, Collins agonizes over how genetic research will affect human behavior. Although Collins is "intensely uncomfortable with abortion as a solution to anything," as he told Tim Beardsley for Scientific American (February 1998, on-line), he acknowledges that abortion is a common outcome of prenatal screenings for genetic defects. "As a geneticist he honors a code of professional ethics that demands he hide from patients his own feelings of right and wrong," according to Nash. And yet, Nash related, Collins also gives regular talks on Huntington's disease (for which there is now a screening test), in which he shows slides of the folk singer Woody Guthrie, whom he calls "one of my heroes," and then explains that Guthrie died of Huntington's disease, leaving his audience to draw their own conclusions. "Predictive genetic testing of healthy individuals in the face of poor or uncertain preventative or therapeutic interventions raises many questions about benefits and risks," Collins testified before the House Science Committee on September 17, 1996, as quoted on the committee's Web site. Even as Collins carries out the genetic revolution, he refuses to downplay its dangers.

He is most outspoken about the potential legal status of genetic information. Courts are already beginning to define what kinds of genetic discoveries can be patented, and many predict that there will be pitched battles between public and private control of the human genome. Since the information charted in the genome is essentially raw material that in itself does not constitute a cure for a disease or even specific instructions for building, say, an arm or a leg, then Collins and others argue that it should remain in the public domain to facilitate further research. "We think of this as building the periodic table of the elements for human biology," Collins told Frazier. "Would it have been a good idea for the periodic table of the elements for chemistry to have intellectual property attached to it so that people couldn't work on it without signing some secrecy agreement or paying some royalty? . . . Would it have been good if hydrogen and neon and helium had all had licensing and royalty stipulations before you could go to the lab and do an experiment?"

Collins himself has worked hard to make the Genome Project's resources available to the public, including smaller institutions conducting their own research. Collins described to Frazier the overarching goal of the project as "putting the information into the hands of scientists all over the world, immediately so that they can try to figure out what it means." All sequencing information is made available within 24 hours in any of several on-line databases, and Collins is working to establish a public domain catalogue of subtle human genetic variations known as single nucleotide polymorphisms, or SNPs. Analysis of SNPs, pronounced "snips," can help track down single genes which on their own may play a small role in causing disease, but work together with other genes to cause such conditions as diabetes and hypertension.

Though clearly invigorated by the potential of genetic information to alleviate human suffering, Collins cautions that the real work for scientists lies ahead. The structural information—the order of the nucleotide bases—is only raw material; the challenge of understanding the instructions encoded in human DNA remains to be translated and interpreted. As Collins put it in his testimony to the House Science Committee, "having a complete dictionary of the English language at hand is necessary, but not sufficient, for understanding Shake-

speare's plays." This work will take decades and does not guarantee results. For example, there is still no cure for cystic fibrosis, though Collins's research team discovered the gene that causes it over ten years ago.

In his interview with Peter Evans, Collins described the study of proteins as the next big step in genetic research. In this field scientists will take the one-dimensional information, the DNA code, and try to figure out how it contributes to the development of a three-dimensional organism. Although it's a "mountain" of information, Collins told Evans, "it's going to be great stuff."

Collins is a deeply religious man who embraced the Christian faith in the late 1970s, after reading the works of C. S. Lewis, who argued that religious belief was not necessarily incompatible with rational thought. His religious convictions fuel his interest in curing diseases, but they have also led him to missionary work. Together with his daughter, Margaret, who is also a physician, Collins has twice traveled to Nigeria to volunteer at a missionary hospital. While there, Collins once treated a farmer who seemed to be suffering signs of imminent heart failure. In an emergency, do-or-die procedure, Collins plunged a needle deep into the man's chest to draw away the fluid that was apparently pressing on his heart. As he told Nash, the patient said to him, "I know you're wondering why you are here. I believe you were sent here just for me, because without you I would have died."

Collins is an elected member of the Institute of Medicine and the National Academy of Sciences. In December 2000 *Industry Week* magazine named both Collins and Venter as Technology Leaders of the Year; the election of Collins marked the first occasion when the award was given to someone in the public sector. Collins is divorced from his wife and has two grown daughters.—M. A. H.

Suggested Reading: *CNN.com* May 1999; *Industry Week* (on-line) Dec. 11, 2000; *New York Times* Nov. 30, 1993; *Scientific American* (on-line) Feb. 1998, with graph; *Time* (on-line) Jan. 17, 1994

Comrie, Leslie John

Aug. 15, 1893–Dec. 11, 1950 Astronomer; mathematician

Prior to the swift expansion in electronic computer technology in the years during and after World War II, advanced computing was accomplished by mechanical means. During the early decades of the 20th century, the potential applications of these computing machines were in the process of being defined. One of the most important of these uses was in the realm of scientific research, and the chief proponent of the computer as a scientific tool was British astronomer L. J. Comrie. During the 1920s and 1930s, Leslie John Comrie used electromechanical calculating devices to plot the orbit of the moon, and, in developing the methods to do so, he helped revolutionize computing in the scientific community. To this day, scientific research remains one of the most important applications of modern computers.

Leslie John Comrie was born August 15, 1893 in Pukekohe, New Zealand. As a child, he was a student at the Auckland Grammar School in Auckland, New Zealand. He attended University College in Auckland, graduating with a B.A. in chemistry in 1915 and completing an M.A. in the discipline a year later.

World War I was breaking out just as Comrie was beginning his career as a chemist. He enlisted in the military, serving in France as part of the New Zealand Expeditionary Force. After losing a leg, Comrie was discharged and sent home, and shortly after his return his professional career took a different path: instead of chemistry, Comrie turned to astronomy, which had always been a personal interest of his. In 1918, he was awarded a University Expeditionary Force scholarship in recognition of his service in the military, and he became a research student at St. John's College of Cambridge University in Great Britain. He took a particular interest in spherical astronomy, the study of the movement of celestial bodies in relation to Earth. While at St. John's College, he experimented with new computational techniques that would help him later in his career.

Comrie earned a Ph.D. in astronomy from Cambridge in 1923. Beginning in the fall of that year, he spent two semesters teaching mathematics and astronomy as an assistant professor at Swarthmore College in Swarthmore, Pennsylvania, following which he taught astronomy for an additional two semesters as an assistant professor at Northwestern University in Evanston, Illinois. He left teaching in 1925 to accept a post as deputy director of the Nautical Almanac for the British Navy in London.

During his years with the Nautical Almanac, Comrie applied and further developed his computational techniques. His first notable scientific achievement took place in 1928 and involved using early computing machines to predict the motion of the moon (his computations mapped out the lunar orbit through the year 1993). This was the first instance of computers being used for scientific research and resulted in Comrie's publication of the landmark paper Brown's Tables of the Motion of the Moon (1929). In 1931 he was promoted from deputy director to superintendent, and he proceeded to revamp the Almanac, updating its century-old methods of determining the movements of heavenly bodies. He also introduced the concept of the standard equinox, an important advancement in spherical astronomy that helped establish a single star map that could be used anywhere in the world at any time of the year. Most relevant to the history of the information age is the fact that Comrie became familiar with mechanical and electromechanical forms of computation while working at the Nautical Almanac, where he installed desk calculators and punched-card computing machines. Additionally, he devised the numerical methods necessary to apply these machines to astronomical study.

Comrie, who was known for his perfectionism and for his impatience with those who did not share the trait, left the Nautical Almanac in 1936, frustrated by the bureaucracy involved in working for the military. He founded the Scientific Computing Service, primarily for the purpose of using mechanical computation to create mathematical tables. With astronomical research in mind, Comrie developed many of the early techniques for programming computers to perform scientific calculations. He made extensive use of computing machines that were based on the work of Herman Hollerith, who at the beginning of the 20th century invented a machine to tabulate census information. Comrie's machine, like Hollerith's, operated through the use of punched cards containing information and instructions that the computers were able to understand. Such machines were the direct predecessors of the electronic computer.

The work done by the Scientific Computing Service had great impact on the scientific community worldwide, both by generating advanced mathematical tables and by inspiring the establishment of other organizations with similar goals. In the mid-1930s American scientists and mathematicians formed the Mathematical Tables Project (MTP) under the auspices of the Works Project Administration (WPA), part of President Franklin Delano Roosevelt's New Deal. An anecdote reported in the Annals of the History of Computing (1982) recounts how Comrie, upon hearing over the radio that the WPA was to be abolished, left home in a panic and headed for the nearest telegraph office, hopping on one leg because he had rushed out without putting on his artificial limb. Comrie wired President Roosevelt and implored him to save the MTP; although a connection has never been proven, shortly thereafter the MTP was made a part of the U.S. Department of Commerce's Bureau of Standards.

Comrie had a direct influence in making Great Britain aware of the potential of electronic computer technology. During World War II, Comrie learned of the electronic computers that were being developed, particularly in the United States, and in 1946 he journeyed to America to investigate the emerging technology. He acquired a copy of John von Neumann's "First Draft of a Report on the EDVAC," which contained the designs for an electronic computer capable of storing programs. Returning home, Comrie brought the report to the attention of British computer engineer Maurice V. Wilkes. Two years later Wilkes built the EDSAC, a full-scale electronic, stored-program computer.

During the 1940s, Comrie, then director of the Scientific Computing Service, developed one of his last innovations, which came to be known as the Comrie numerals. Designed to counteract the monotony of consulting mathematical tables, Comrie numerals are a numerical font in which numbers along the same line are alternately printed slightly higher and lower in relation to each other, giving the appearance of having been typed with a badly adjusted typewriter. This causes the reader to glance up and down as well as left to right, which reduces the number of errors that often result from boredom.

For his influential work Comrie was made a fellow of the Royal Society in 1950. Several months later, on December 11, Comrie died in London, England. His legacy is of great importance to both the information age and modern science as a whole; the *Dictionary of Scientific Biography*

(1971) states that L. J. Comrie "created computational science." The dictionary goes on to say that Comrie possessed "the clarity of mind, tenacity of purpose, scientific courage, and immense energy that enabled him . . . to obtain practical solutions to many problems that defied theoretical analysis." In 1933, during his tenure as superintendent of the Nautical Almanac, Comrie married Phyllis Betty. They had one son.—B. S.

Suggested Reading: *Performance Computing* (online) Jan. 1999; *Dictionary of Scientific Biography*, 1971; Lee, J. A. N., ed. *International Biographical Dictionary of Computer Pioneers*, 1995; Spencer, Donald D. *The Timetable of Computers*, 1997

Corbató, Fernando

July 1, 1926– Developer of the Compatible Time-Sharing System (CTSS)

During the 1950s the only computers that were available to ordinary users were immense and expensive machines that could be found only at large universities or in laboratories. These computers were slow and could serve only one user at a time. A single mistake would halt programming; if an error occurred, the user had to find it, fix it, and run the program all over again. Long lines at computer labs were common, and users were often left frustrated and discouraged. In order to make computers easier to use, Fernando Corbató of the Massachusetts Institute of Technology (MIT), in Cambridge, developed time-sharing, a concept that allowed a single computer to serve many users at the same time. As Corbató explained to Mary Brandel for *Computerworld* (March 29, 1999), "Time-sharing introduced the engineering constraint that the interactive needs of users [were] just as important as the efficiency of the equipment."

Fernando José Corbató was born on July 1, 1926 in Oakland, California. Corbató moved to Los Angeles in about 1931, after his father joined the faculty of the University of California at Los Angeles (UCLA). In an interview with Karen Frenkel for a publication of the Association for Computing Machinery titled *Communications of the ACM* (September 1991), Corbató recalled, "One of the more influential events in my life was World War II. I was in high school when Pearl Harbor occurred [on December 7, 1941]. One of the effects was that the most able-bodied men were drafted. To accommodate the number of high school students joining the work force, high schools went into double sessions. I discovered that by being clever I could take extra courses, so I completed high school in two years."

After his graduation Corbató enrolled at UCLA. During his first year a Navy recruiter approached Corbató, who was only 17 at the time, about joining

a new program that trained personnel to maintain electronic systems aboard battleships. "Since that seemed like a way to get further education and not just become canon fodder, I enlisted," he told Frenkel. After completing his training Corbató served aboard a destroyer as an electronic technician, helping to maintain radio, radar, sonar, depthfinder, and long-range navigation (LORAN) systems. Corbató believed that his military service was a valuable experience. "It was a fantastic education about what it takes to make big systems work, how to debug them, and how to look for trouble," he recalled to Frenkel. "It was a very deep background of anticipating things going wrong, trying to plan ahead and figuring out what went wrong."

After leaving the navy, Corbató decided against returning to UCLA and enrolled instead at the California Institute of Technology (Caltech), in Pasadena. He majored in physics and graduated in 1950 with a B.S. in physics.

Corbató pursued his graduate education in physics at MIT. Philip Morse, one of his professors, recognized that computers would eventually become important research tools and established MIT's Computation Center. He recruited Corbató as a research assistant. At first, Corbató and the other research assistants at the Center used punched-card machines for calculations. In 1951 Morse brought in the Whirlwind computer, which was based on a design for an aircraft simulator. The Whirlwind, one of the first digital computers, used vacuum tubes to store memory and was quite fast for its time. "It was a fantastic vehicle for learning about what a real computer might be able to do," Corbató told Frenkel. Many users, including Corbató, encountered difficulties with the machine, however. In an interview with Arthur Nordberg of the Charles Babbage Institute (April 18, 1989, transcript obtained by *Leaders of the Information Age*), Corbato recalled, "It meant you were working with difficult equipment, punch paper tape and all that, and we were facing all the growing pains of the industry. It was not an industry yet. The equipment was very erratic and difficult. The reliability was in error; the machine would crash every 20 minutes on the average." Corbató used the Whirlwind to conduct research on molecular physics and energy-band calculation. However, he eventually found that he was more interested in the computer itself than the problems it was meant to solve.

In 1956 Corbató received his doctorate in physics. He accepted an offer by Morse to help manage the Computation Center. Morse arranged with IBM to upgrade the center's equipment, and soon an IBM 704 computer replaced the Whirlwind. Over the next few years, IBM provided the center with increasingly more advanced computers.

In addition to his duties at the center, Corbató became an unofficial computer evangelist, encouraging people to learn how to use the machines as part of their work. "At first we had a hard time, but gradually we became more successful," he explained to Frenkel. "Then it became too successful in the sense that the machine was jammed from morning to night with jobs to run. It became so congested that we began finding new ways to use the machines more efficiently—to squeeze more out of the operating systems and to batch up the jobs on tapes." This crowded, chaotic environment often frustrated computer users.

In 1957 John McCarthy joined the faculty of MIT. After experiencing the difficulties of using the Computation Center, he began to think of a way to make computers more interactive and accessible to a greater number of users. In January 1959 he sent a memorandum to Morse describing the concept of "time-sharing," which would enable a computer to serve many users simultaneously, and explaining how the Center might begin to develop such a system.

Morse was impressed by McCarthy's ideas and encouraged those who worked at the Center to follow through on them. Both Corbató and his colleague Herbert Teager volunteered to build time-sharing systems. While Teager's proposed system included several innovative features, it required a new computer language and would have taken several years to complete. By contrast, Corbató preferred to immediately build a modest system that would demonstrate the benefits of time-sharing and serve as a model for more advanced systems in the future. As he began his work, Corbató encountered resistance from officials at IBM. "They were used to making money by selling mainframes and most of their customers were running factory-like computing centers," he explained to Frenkel. "The notion of optimizing people rather than the machines was just not on their minds."

Corbató and two assistants at MIT, Marjorie Mervin and Robert C. Daley, began their work on the Compatible Time-Sharing System (CTSS) in the spring of 1961. By November they had completed a prototype. In an article published in *Communications of the ACM* (September 1991), Corbató wrote, "The basic scheme used to run CTSS was simple. The supervisor program, which was always in main memory, would commutate among the user programs, running each in turn for a brief interval with the help of an interval timer." CTSS ran on an IBM 709 computer. The supervisor program used 5,000 bytes of memory, and 27,000 bytes were left to run other programs or jobs. CTSS managed four terminals, and stored data on magnetic tape. The following spring, Corbató and his team adapted CTSS to run on the more advanced IBM 7090, which MIT had obtained from the company. This upgraded system accommodated 16 terminals and boasted 64,000 bytes of memory. Soon many other universities, as well as the Woods Hole Oceanographic Institution, were making use of CTSS to provide computer access to more users.

In *Communications of the ACM*, Corbató discussed the ramifications of the new system: "One important consequence of developing CTSS was that for the first time, users had persistent on-line storage of programs and data. Suddenly the issues of privacy, protection, and backup of information had to be faced." He continued, "Another byproduct of the development was that because we operated terminals via modems, remote operation became the norm. Also, the new-found freedom of keeping information on-line in the central file system suddenly made it especially convenient for users to share and exchange information among themselves." He observed, however, "To our dismay, users who had been enduring several-hour waits between jobs run under batch processing were suddenly restless when response times were more than a second. . . . It seemed like the more we did, the more users wanted."

In 1962 Corbató became an associate professor in MIT's electrical engineering and computer science department. Corbató, Mervin, and Daley coauthored a paper, "An Experimental Time-Sharing System," which they presented at the annual meeting of the Spring Joint Computer Conference (SJCC) in 1962. The paper, which was obtained by *Leaders of the Information Age* from the Laboratory for Computer Science Web site, defined the concept of time-sharing, stressed why it was needed, and outlined the basic design for a time-sharing system.

Corbató invited more than 200 prominent individuals in the computer industry from around the world to visit MIT for several weeks to observe the system. Most of them were impressed and convinced that time-sharing could work. After the Cuban Missile Crisis of October 1962, the U.S. Department of Defense expressed interest in developing an effective time-sharing system. Corbató noted to Frenkel that many of the military's command-and-control systems failed to work properly during the crisis. The U.S. Department of Defense Advanced Research Projects Agency (ARPA; sometimes referred to as DARPA) allocated $3 million to establish Project Mac at MIT. As Corbató explained to Frenkel, the purpose of Project Mac, which was eventually renamed the Laboratory of Computer Science (LCS), "was to develop the next-generation time-sharing system that would be done 'right.'"

As the head of Project Mac, Corbató began work on the new time-sharing system, Multiplexed Information and Computing Service (Multics), in the summer of 1963. He sought assistance for the project from both IBM and the Digital Equipment Corporation (DEC), another prominent computer company. Unfortunately, both companies turned him down. However, Bell Telephone Laboratories and the computer department of General Electric supported the project, thinking that an ambitious time-sharing system would benefit their businesses.

Multics became available commercially in 1969. As Corbató wrote in *Communications of the ACM*, "Some of [Multics'] major strengths were the virtual memory system, the file system, the attention to security, the ability to do on-line configuration, and the information backup system for the file system." Corbató and his team experienced two setbacks. In 1969 Bell Telephone Laboratories withdrew its support from the project. As Corbató explained to Frenkel, the company's executives were "expecting this system to become the workhorse for computing at Bell Laboratories, so they expected commercial level quality." When their expectations were not satisfied, Bell Labs' executives opted to look elsewhere for a better system. In 1970 General Electric sold its computer department to Honeywell. "We had to keep reselling the ideas and the likelihood of success to people," Corbató explained to Frenkel. Although Multics sold well in Europe, it never became a commercial success in the United States.

Like CTSS, Multics was important because it served as a foundation for an even better system. Kenneth Thompson and Dennis Ritchie, the Bell Labs' computer scientists who worked on Multics, next developed Unix, an operating system that is still commonly used today in the United States. Corbató told Frenkel that Thompson "took the best of the ideas that he saw" in Multics and incorporated them into Unix. One major commercial advantage that Unix had over Multics was that it ran on standard, rather than specialized, hardware. Since Unix could run on almost any machine, consumers could adapt it to the systems they already owned.

Fernando Corbató continued to teach and conduct research at MIT until his retirement in 1996. He has co-authored two books, *The Compatible Time-Sharing System: A Programmer's Guide* and *Advanced Computer Programming: A Case Study of a Classroom Assembly Program*, both published in 1963. He has since authored and co-authored numerous scientific papers. Over the last few decades, Corbató's role in the successful development of time-sharing has been frequently recognized. He has been honored with the W. W. McDowell Award in 1966, the Harry Goode Memorial Award in 1982, the Computer Pioneer Award in 1982, the A. M. Turing Award in 1990, and the Computers and Communication Prize in 1998.—D. C.

Suggested Reading: Charles Babbage Institute, Oral History 162, "An interview with Fernando J. Corbató," conducted on April 18, 1989 and November 14, 1990 by Arthur J. Norberg; *Communications of the ACM* p80+ Sep. 1991, with photo; *Computerworld* p80 Mar. 29, 1999, with photo; Corbató Family Web site; Laboratory for Computer Science (LCS) Web site.

Couffignal, Louis

1902–1966 Developer of electronic-computing technology

Louis Couffignal was expected by many to be the man to lead his nation, France, into the computer age during the middle of the 20th century. He was to be the first Frenchman to construct an electronic computer, a feat that had been accomplished by the American inventors John Atanasoff, John Mauchly, and J. Presper Eckert. Unfortunately, Couffignal's project was never brought to fruition due to a variety of factors, ranging from administrative inefficiency; to shortage of funding; to governmental shortsightedness; to the mutability of a newly emerging industry. Despite the failure of Couffignal's project, he demonstrated the extraordinary vision in being the first in his nation to truly recognize the importance of computer technology.

Louis Couffignal was born in France in 1902. His professional career began with a position teaching mathematics and mechanics at the Ecole des Élèves Ingenieurs Mécaniciens, a French secondary school. A major debate was raging at the time as to whether or not calculators should be permitted in schools. With French scientific journals contending the issue, Couffignal, who had been working on his doctorate in mathematical sciences at the University of Paris, decided to write his thesis on the subject. Composed under the supervision of his academic advisor, M. d'Ocagne, Couffignal's paper represented the first time in the history of the University of Paris that such a topic had been undertaken as a thesis in mathematical sciences. Couffignal submitted his paper in March 1938, and d'Ocagne predicted it would have "consequences with a breadth and scope one could not yet assess," as quoted in the *International Biographical Dictionary of Computer Pioneers* (1995). Later the same year, Couffignal received his D.Sc. degree.

After receiving his doctorate, Couffignal pursued the position of chair of applied mathematics at the Conservatoire National des Arts et Métiers, but he was denied the job after being ranked second by the Académie des Sciences, which was in charge of the hiring. With war imminent in Europe, however, mathematics and scientific research gradually came to be in heavy demand by the French government. The process of mobilizing technical, industrial, and scientific resources was undertaken by an agency known as the Centre National de la Recherche Scientifique Appliquée (CNRSA). A study on the state of research in various technical fields was commissioned by CNRSA director Henri Laugier, and Couffignal was one of the people asked to help put the report together. In particular, his task was to comment on the application of math to scientific research. This would prove to be the first step in his life-long career as an administrator.

Couffignal became secretary of CNRSA's specialist committees, secretary-general of the CNRSA committee on inventions, and was later appointed director of the laboratory for calculation and mechanics in the Institut Poincaré. His assignment in this latter position was to oversee the laboratory, which was surrounded by other laboratories that housed calculating machines. This exposure to mechanical calculating technology sparked Couffignal's initial interest in the field. He began to consider the idea of designing and building his own computing device. One of Couffignal's main goals in the construction of his scientific computer was to reorganize bureaus using existing computers along rational scientific lines. For example, he believed his machine should be used to automate the accounting processes that were used for postal checks.

Couffignal's plans were temporarily put on hold due to the outbreak of World War II in 1939 and the occupation of France by the Nazis the following year. The very existence of the CNRSA, which had by that time become known simply as the CNRS (Centre National de la Recherche Scientifique), was in danger from the Vichy government that had been put in place during France's occupation by German forces. The organization did survive, albeit with some retooling. The Inventions Committee was disbanded due to what was perceived as a lack of results, and was replaced later by the Inventions and Patents Committee, with Couffignal once again serving as secretary general.

During this period, Couffignal was highly involved with France's scientific community, and he was able to familiarize himself with the state of scientific research in his country. His participation in many CNRS committees was helpful in this regard, and lent him a high enough profile in the necessary circles that he was appointed inspector general for technical education in France. He also wrote a book entitled *Histoire de la machine à calculer*, which garnered him the Binoux Prize from the Academie des Sciences, an honor traditionally awarded to historical or philosophic works.

With the war raging throughout Europe, Couffignal seized on an idea to get his mechanical calculator built. He was keenly aware of the government's willingness to fund military research. The Institut Poincaré's Statistical Lab had been given a grant of the previous year to construct a binary calculating machine, and was also working on an electronic computer. At the end of 1939, following the advice of General Desmazieres Couffignal turned his laboratory into a center for artillery calculations, per-

haps the most common application of early computer technology. He worked out a contract with the Outillage RBV Company to construct a computing device that would be made up of two already-existing machines—a Sanders-Octoplex 10-column accounting machine and a Monroe A-1-213 calculating machine—linked by an electromechanical connection.

Unfortunately, Couffignal's ambitions were once again impeded by the war, which gripped his entire continent. The fulfillment of his contract with Outillage RBV was delayed by the fact that the company's board of directors, made up mostly of Jews, was dissolved due to Nazi oppression. A new board was not organized until the beginning of 1942. However, by that time many of Outillage's machines had been seized by the advancing German forces, and the company found that it was going to be impossible to fulfill their two contracts to the Institut Poincaré Statistical Lab and CNRS, due to the unavailability of a Monroe machine.

The best suggestion the company could make was to combine the two contracts into a single project. For the total sum of both contracts, Outillage RBV could construct a Sanders-model machine and connect it to a binary calculator similar to a Monroe model. Couffignal supported the idea, and convinced the Institut Poincaré to put its original grant toward the new project. In exchange for allowing CNRS to use its grant money, the Statistical Lab would be given sole control of the machine two-thirds of the time.

The building of the Outillage computer was a start, but Couffignal continued to work towards his original goal of building his own device. A step toward this was taken in late 1944, when the CNRS proposed the creation of a subdivision called the Centre d'Études Supérieures en Mécanique (CEMA), which would focus on computing services. In preparation for the establishment of the CEMA, Couffignal was asked by the Mathematics Committee to compile a survey of all numerical function tables available in France. The inavailabilty of actual machines remained a major roadblock, however; Couffignal oversaw a plan to acquire computing machinery from Germany, but after news of the initiative spread, the CNRS was overwhelmed with requests for the machines from laboratories across France, to the point where they were simply unable to accommodate them all.

Over the next couple of years, through the end of World War II, a further restructuring took place within the CNRS in an attempt to take advantage of the burgeoning computer technology. A division called the Institut Blaise Pascal was formed as a result of Couffignal's influences. In 1946 he traveled to the United States to observe the first large-scale electronic computer, the ENIAC, in action. He also managed to obtain grants for the construction of his proposed computer, and by May of 1947 the CNRS was negotiating on a contract with the Logabax Company for the building of the machine. But the computer was never finished. Similar to the situation involving the British inventor Charles Babbage and his proposed Analytical Engine in the 19th century, mismanagement prolonged the project, which in turn caused the funding to dry up. There had been no regular supervision of the project's progress, thus preventing the CNRS from stopping it in time to avert a fiasco.

Several factors contributed to the eventual failure of the project. Couffignal himself was never able to recognize the potential of fully electronic computing, but instead insisted on interconnecting already existing electromechanical devices. Some historians attribute this seeming lack of vision to a certain insularity on the part of the French government and scientific community at the time. Couffignal demonstrated a lack of awareness of current developments in computing, which supports this idea. In articles published throughout his career, Couffignal discussed his efforts at building a computer that would be able to prove logic formulas, yet he neglected to even mention such crucial and relevant advances as the Gödel Theorem of 1931 or the Turing machine of 1936. However, it should be noted that Couffignal did make an important contribution to the development of computer memory systems by designing an electrostatic scheme for his machine that utilized neon lamps, based on the fact that a higher voltage is required to start them conducting than to keep them in that state (*A History of Computing Technology*, 1985).

Ironically, it was Couffignal who indirectly prevented his nation from fully capitalizing on the computing boom. While his original intention had been to bring France into the computer age, the failure of his computer project cost his country precious time while it was waiting for him to complete his machine. Apparently, Couffignal's project had been approved on the basis of his reputation rather than on any serious evaluation of the project itself. The result was that France was forced to turn to mass-produced computers made by foreign manufacturers.

The completion of the UNIVAC in the United States in 1951 marked the beginning of a shift away from scientific computers and toward more commercial ones, which did not bode well for Couffignal. In 1957 his post at the Insitut Blaise Pascal was abolished, and he found himself utterly pushed out of the field he had intended to revolutionize.

Louis Couffignal died in 1966 at the age of 64. Although his electronic computer was never realized, he was responsible for making France aware of the level of technology that existed during his time, in the same way that physicist Douglas Hartree spread the word in his native Britain. Couffignal's career was perhaps an example of reach exceeding grasp.—B. S.

Suggested Reading: Goldstine, Herman. *The Computer from Pascal to von Neumann*, 1972; Lee, J. A. N., ed. *International Biographical Dictionary of Computer Pioneers*, 1995; Williams, Michael R. *A History of Computing Technology*, 1985

Courtesy of Cray Inc.

Cray, Seymour

Sep. 28, 1925–Oct. 5, 1996 Electronic engineer; designer of the first supercomputer

Widely considered the "father of supercomputers," Seymour Cray developed technology that allowed for the construction of these fast and powerful computing machines, remaining a pioneer in his field for more than four decades before his death in 1996. Throughout his career Cray contributed to the founding of four separate supercomputer manufacturing companies, helping to shape the industry through his dedicated focus on supercomputing technology. By the late 1980s Cray had built approximately two-thirds of the world's supercomputers. Equipped with vast amounts of memory, Cray's machines contained hundreds of thousands of circuits packed tightly together to reduce reaction time and were capable of performing millions—and later, billions—of mathematical calculations per second. Allowing for technological and research developments that were once unimaginable, supercomputers have since been used by scientists for a wide range of purposes in virtually every branch of science and engineering. For example, they made possible reliable weather forecasting, aided in advanced engineering design for the creation of airplanes and automobiles to optimum aerodynamic specifications, and allowed the military to simulate nuclear detonations without having to test the actual devices. In addition, they have been used for oil exploration, drug research, and automobile crash simulation. While the supercomputer industry appeared in decline for much of the 1990s, as many defense and intelligence agencies could no longer afford such powerful and expensive machines, supercomputing has recently been revived, particularly in a number of large corporations where they are being used to manage information technology. They frequently handle tasks such as processing immense Web transaction volumes, measuring the risk of complex investment portfolios, and exploring large databases for sales patterns or indications of credit-card fraud. "[Cray is] one of the great Americans of the last half of the 20th century," Larry Smarr, a colleague at the National Center for Supercomputing Applications at the University of Illinois at Urbana-Champaign, told Kevin Maney for *USA Today* (September 1996, on-line). "It's hard to imagine what the world would be like today if it wasn't for Seymour."

Seymour Roger Cray was born on September 28, 1925 in Chippewa Falls, Wisconsin. His father worked as a civil engineer and eventually became the town engineer of Chippewa Falls, performing many departmental functions for the city and serving, for example, as plumbing inspector, electrical inspector, and building inspector, among others. "He certainly was a 'thing' oriented person instead of a human oriented person," Cray once said of his father in a rare interview with David Allison for a Smithsonian Institute oral history on computing (May 9, 1995, on-line). "The technical person as distinguished from the social person." As a child Cray was greatly interested in electronics and demonstrated his imaginative problem solving skills from an early age. His parents encouraged such hobbies and kept the family's basement stocked with radio gear and chemistry sets. As his sister, Carol (Cray) Kersten, recalled to Charles W. Breckenridge for *A Tribute to Seymour Cray: Supercomputing '96* (November 19, 1996, on-line), Cray once set up a Morse code connection between the siblings' bedrooms so they could communicate at night; when their father noticed the noise and instructed them to stop, the young Cray converted the clickers to lights so the children could continue their communications without causing a disturbance. As a high-school student, Cray passed many hours in the electrical engineering laboratories, working with such equipment as radios, electrical motors, and electric circuits. "I was one of those nerds before the name was popular," he told Allison. A true science enthusiast, he was also known to fill in and teach his high-school physics class when the teacher was absent. Cray graduated from Chippewa Falls High School in 1943, earning recognition as the school's top science student with the Bausch & Lomb Science Award.

After high school Cray was quickly drafted into the U.S. Army. As he recalled to Allison, his electronics work during World War II was limited. "Being reluctant to get into the service, I ended up in the infantry," he said. "In the infantry you don't have a lot of electronic equipment around. I did end up in a communication platoon so I carried around a walkie talkie and I pulled wires through the jungle and things like that." Cray arrived in Europe just after the Normandy invasion of June 1944

and later fought in the historic Battle of the Bulge, which lasted from December 1944 to January 1945. As part of the Allied forces he "tramped" his way through Germany to connect with the Russian forces. After Germany's surrender in 1945, Cray was sent to the Pacific theater, finishing his military duty in the Philippine Islands. "That was a real experience because I was in the middle of the jungle and I was supporting the Filipino Guerilla army who were routing out the remnants of the Japanese Navy," he explained. "It was, as you can imagine, an interesting experience to see these 17 and 18 year old Japanese kids coming out of the jungle after living on bananas for 2 or 3 years."

After the war Cray returned to the United States to resume his education. He attended the University of Minnesota, in Minneapolis, where he received a B.S. degree in electrical engineering in 1950. Just one year later, he earned a master's degree in applied mathematics, also from the University of Minnesota. Unsure of how to apply these degrees, Cray followed a professor's advice and took a position with Engineering Research Associates (ERA) in St. Paul, Minnesota, which was one of the earliest companies attempting to build general-purpose digital computers. At the time ERA was just one year old and was being sponsored by the U.S. Navy to develop cryptographic equipment. Cray described his early experiences with the company at a 1988 supercomputer conference in Orlando, Florida, as quoted by Gary H. Anthes for *Computerworld* (June 22, 1992): "I worked for about a week not knowing what I was doing, and then it occurred to me—none of these people knew what they were doing either. I realized in talking to the other people that the blind were leading the blind, and I was as good as anyone."

In one of his earliest assignments, Cray was instructed to build pulse transformers for a general-purpose computer. With a 10-inch circular slide rule—the largest that such instruments were then made—and a math course in Laplace transforms, which are used to solve differential equations, he felt confident that he could produce the calculations and the designs necessary for the project. Cray recounted in the speech: "I built a prototype and it worked, and Task 13 went into production, and I felt quite smug. Then one day I took a walk down to the glider factory [in which ERA housed its operations], and at the end of the line I found a much older engineer. I asked him what he was doing, and lo and behold, he was making pulse transformers, too. I told him how I had made pulse transformers using my Laplace transforms and my big 10-inch circular slide rule. He smiled and said, 'I know about Laplace transforms, and I know about circular slide rules, but I don't use either one of those. I use intuition.'" The experience had a profound effect on Cray, who began relying more on his own ingenuity in constructing his designs. In addition, as he conducted his own research into computers and their operation, he found that little information existed on the subject and was thus further inspired to pursue his own advancements in the field.

In 1951 Cray contributed to a project building 1100-series computers, which formed the basis for what later became the Universal Automatic Computer (UNIVAC), a series of mainframe computers designed for commercial use. Less than two years after joining ERA, Cray was named project engineer of the 1103 computer, which marked, as he described in his speech, "the beginning of serious computing." This machine featured new technology in its magnetic core memory. "My guiding principle was simplicity," he later told Allison. "I think there is an expression for that. Don't put anything in that isn't necessary." (This concept of the "reduced instruction set computing" [RISC]—a now popular design philosophy that calls for simplifying computer hardware to increase speed—is widely credited as an IBM invention from the 1970s; yet many industry observers have noted that Cray was applying RISC-type principles in his designs from the beginning, without giving his approach a name.)

When ERA was purchased by Remington Rand and later by Sperry (becoming the Sperry Rand Corporation, which developed the UNIVAC), the new company began phasing out Cray's projects, which were large-scale and very expensive, in favor of more commercially marketable products. In 1957 Cray opted to leave the company, as did William C. (Bill) Norris, who promptly formed the Control Data Corporation (CDC). Although Cray was not involved in the CDC's foundation, he joined the staff as an engineer and technician and took a lead role in shaping its objectives. He explained to Allison, "I had a clear idea of what I wanted to do which was to build large scientific computers. The rest of the half dozen or so founding people thought that they should go into commercial activities, like point of sale machines . . . and I said, 'No, no, no. I'm going to build large scientific computers.' And I proceeded to do that. So that's what happened to the company. We ended up building large scientific computers and quickly took over I would say, that particular market from the company we left." The company raised much of its $600,000 in start-up funds by selling company stock on the street corners of Minneapolis—a highly unconventional method of generating capital that no longer happens in business today. Cray invested $5,000 of his own money, which was a considerable sum for him at the time, representing most of his assets.

In one of his first projects at CDC, Cray launched construction of the Control Data 1604 computer, which was revolutionary at the time because it was the only large computer to use transistors in its design. Cray applied the individual transistors to amplify electrical impulses and miniaturize the computer's components, thus replacing the more bulky vacuum tubes of earlier designs. Their use also demonstrated the engineer's ingenuity: Faced with a limited budget and working to build the computer for the lowest cost, Cray learned that a local retail store was selling reject transistors at a low price. He purchased them all, ultimately exhausting the complete supply of reject transistors for transistor radios. As he recalled in his speech for the supercomputer convention in 1988, "I went back and tried to make a circuit out of these things. No two were alike, but never mind—I had to do it." Cray's efforts paid off and the 1604 computer was delivered to the Naval Post Graduate School in Monterey, California, in 1960.

Cray's overall methodology for designing and building computers was somewhat unique for his time. While many other engineers simply built upon earlier models, creating complex systems that would make each machine compatible with ones built before, Cray started every project with a fresh design. As he described to Allison, he would gather feedback—and complaints—from customers to determine how he could better design each new computer's architecture to meet their needs. "The blank sheet of paper is not a blank mind," he said. "I wanted to take advantage of all the things that I remembered and all the inputs I had gotten from people over a period of a few years to help me to decide what to make. But by the blank paper I mean that I liked to start over with the technical details, review all the things that the world offers at this point in time rather that to reuse things that were just used." While Cray's eagerness to experiment with new components in his machines did increase his risk of failure, this very tendency to explore exotic and unconventional materials led to some of his greatest contributions to computer history.

While Cray was proving himself an accomplished engineer, he had little patience for the corporate bureaucracy of working in an ever-growing company. In one frequently cited scenario, when Norris once requested that his eccentric engineer compose a five-year plan, Cray replied: "Five-year goal: Build the biggest computer in the world. One-year goal: Achieve one-fifth of the above," as quoted by John Markoff for the *New York Times* (October 7, 1996). As CDC gained more business, Cray also had little time to deal with the distractions of marketing and management activities. In about 1962 he persuaded Norris to let him move his laboratory to his hometown of Chippewa Falls—some 100 miles away from the company's Minneapolis headquarters. In his research and development facility there, Cray began work on the world's first commercially available supercomputer, the CDC 6600, which was introduced in August 1963. Due to its three-dimensional packaging and stripped-down internal design—what some experts view as the first true demonstration of RISC—the CDC 6600 computer was able to execute three million program instructions per second, making it the most powerful computer in the world, a distinction that the device held for the next several years. In addition, the 6600 featured a cooling system with Freon, similar to an air conditioner, as well as a more aesthetically pleasing exterior design. (Cray, who was reportedly a fan of the 1960s science-fiction television series *Star Trek*, was interested in improving the external architecture of computers. "Everything Seymour does is esthetically beautiful," Peter Gregory, a former executive at Cray Research told Russell Mitchell for *BusinessWeek* [April 30, 1990].) Only four years before, in 1959, IBM had unveiled its Stretch machine, the closest thing to a modern supercomputer at the time; nevertheless, Stretch was easily outmoded by the 6600, which ran three times faster. Frustrated at being surpassed by a relative newcomer to the industry, IBM president Thomas J. Watson Jr. remarked in 1963, as quoted by Donald D. Spencer in *The Timetable of Computers* (1997), "I understand that in the laboratory developing the 6600 there are only 34 people, including the janitor. I fail to understand why we have lost our industry leadership position by letting someone else offer the world's most powerful computer." In 1968 Cray furthered CDC's lead in scientific computing with the introduction of the CDC 7600, which was capable of handling 15 million instructions per second. This machine also featured blue glass doors to display the computer's insides. Cray promptly began work on another model, the CDC 8600, later that year. At the onset of this—his final project for CDC—Cray realized that he would need do much more than simply increase the speed of the new machine to achieve his performance goals. Instead, he sought to improve "parallelism," or the machine's ability to carry out several operations simultaneously, and designed the 8600 with four separate processors sharing the same memory.

Despite Cray's significant work on the 8600 computer, Norris put the project on hold in 1972 in favor of another engineer's design. Unwilling to accept the delay—and faced with an increasing perception there was little market for large scientific computers—Cray left CDC to found his own company, Cray Research Inc., where he could dedicate all his efforts toward building supercomputers. He explained his impulse to Allison: "I was willing to accept that perhaps the market would be small and so if I started a small company that was very dedicated to this one narrow area . . . , there would be an opportunity because I could see Control Data discontinuing all those efforts and pretty soon I'd be alone again in the marketplace. That pretty well happened." With his new company, Cray soon abandoned his work on the 8600 computer altogether in order to take advantage of a new technology known as the "integrated circuit," which was a collection of devices in one single microchip.

In 1976 he announced the creation of the Cray 1, a new supercomputer that surpassed the capabilities of any of its predecessors. Featuring integrated circuitry and new vector registry processing technology, the machine could execute up to 32 arithmetic operations at one time, at the speed of 240 million calculations per second; at one-fourth

the size of the CDC 7600, the Cray 1 could perform 10 times the amount of work. In addition, the device had more aesthetic appeal than any of Cray's earlier machines: it was constructed in the shape of a giant "C," with an extended base covered in padded vinyl that could serve as a bench. "This was my first opportunity to deal with the aesthetics," Cray explained to Allison, "go out of the way a bit, spend an extra 5 [percent] money perhaps to make something visually intriguing and so clearly this particular product was different than the rectangular boxes that were available from everyone else. I think it enhanced the early marketing opportunities for machine." Shortly after taking his young company public in 1976—raising $10 million in capital—Cray was able to sell the Cray 1 supercomputer to such scientific research centers as the Los Alamos National Laboratory and the National Center for Atmospheric Research for the cost of $8.8 million per machine.

By the late 1970s Cray had begun work on his next major project, the Cray 2. Although Cray Research was quickly growing into a $60 million company, Cray felt he was not suited to continue leading the management side of the business. In 1980 he relinquished all management duties to John A. Rollwagen, who became chief executive officer. Cray remained chairman of the company's board of directors until 1981, when Rollwagen took over that position as well. Although he still served as a consultant, Cray was largely free to work exclusively on designing the Cray 2 machine. He initially intended to increase the device's speed by using an ultra-fast semiconductor material known as gallium arsenide (GaAs) in his microchips. Yet, after extensive work with GaAs, Cray found that the expense and engineering problems associated with the material were too difficult to overcome; he returned to using silicon chips and completed the Cray 2 in 1985. The device, which sold for around $17 million, could perform 1.2 billion calculations per second—10 times the speed of the Cray 1. Its circuit cards were packed so densely that they were set inside a container of liquid fluorocarbon coolant, Flourinert, to remove excess heat. Throughout the 1980s the Cray 1 and 2 supercomputers were used widely by the defense industry to build sophisticated weapons systems and by the oil industry to locate mineral deposits.

Although the Cray 2 was a success, its delayed release had caused shifts within the company. To ensure that Cray Research was not becoming overly dependent on Cray himself, Rollwagen had authorized a second, competing project led by a Taiwanese computer designer, Steve S. Chen. The Cray X-MP, as it was called, was meant to be a faster, more powerful variation of the Cray 1. (The successful dual-processor system was completed in 1982 and functioned nearly three times as fast as the Cray 1.) The move launched a rivalry between Cray and Chen, as both men sought to develop the fastest supercomputing systems. When Cray began work on the Cray 3 in 1985, still hoping to incorporate gallium arsenide processing chips, Chen was simultaneously working on a project that competed directly with Cray's. (Rollwagen eliminated the Chen project in 1987.)

By 1989 Cray had spent more than $120 million developing his Cray 3 machine, but its completion was nowhere in sight. The delay was due in part to the use of GaAs, which was an extremely fragile material; few chips could actually survive the lengthy fabrication process. In addition, Cray intended to pack 1,024 chips into a package measuring only four inches by four inches by one-quarter inch, a delicate task that required the use of special robots for assembly. (The Cray 3 was designed to have 16 processors, thus requiring 208 of these packages.) With costs soaring, Rollwagen again turned to another designer, this time Lester T. Davis, a co-founder of Cray Research and a close friend of Cray's, to oversee the less risky endeavor of making evolutionary improvements to existing products at the company. The result, the Cray Y-MP, while based on silicon chips, was expected to perform near the same levels as the projected Cray 3. (The Cray Y-MP was succeeded by the C-90 model, which went on to compete directly with the Cray 3 in the early 1990s.) In 1989, faced with little other choice, Rollwagen and Cray decided to spin off Cray's research into a new company, Cray Computer Corporation (CCC), for which Cray would serve as the chief executive. In exchange for any future assets associated with the Cray 3 machine, Cray Research would retain 10 percent of the new company, which was located in Colorado Springs, Colorado.

Over the next three years, Cray continued working out the kinks of building a 16-processor, GaAs-based system; his work consumed more than $300 million of his young company's funds. The Cray 3, which was priced at $30 million, was finally set for release in 1991. However, when CCC postponed delivery of the machine in December of that year, the Lawrence Livermore National Laboratory, frustrated by the delay, canceled its order for the first Cray 3. While some analysts expected that another buyer in the defense or intelligence community would quickly step forward to place another order, none emerged. (This was due in part to Cray Research's success with its C-90 supercomputer; also selling for $30 million each, nine C-90s had been sold.) Additionally, the supercomputer industry had declined in importance during the early 1990s. By the time the Cray 3 was completed—capable of reaching clock speeds up to 500 megahertz, or 4 billion calculations per second—cheap and powerful shared-memory microprocessor chips had largely replaced the massive single-processor supercomputers in the computer market. These systems, which linked together hundreds or thousands of smaller processors to gain speed, were known as "massively parallel computers" and sold for less than $100,000, as compared to the multimillion-dollar price tag of the average Cray product.

Although Cray attempted to salvage his work on Cray 3 by initiating a partnership to develop smaller versions of the large machine—featuring for example four or eight processors rather than the traditional 16—these efforts failed. He also began work on the Cray 4, a machine that would have 64 processors and would be twice the speed of the Cray 3, but this project was never completed. In 1991 and 1992 CCC lost more than $100 million. Though the company's outlook brightened in 1994 with the announcement of a $4.2 million research contract from the National Security Agency, its finances continued to decline. When Cray was unable to raise $20 million for operating costs, CCC filed for bankruptcy in March 1995; the six-year-old company had never sold a computer. In a letter to his employees announcing the filing of Chapter 11 bankruptcy, Cray noted, as quoted by Markoff for the *New York Times* (March 25, 1995), "Our problem is basically one of timing. The business world, and our government are in a cost-cutting mode. They do not want to take any risks at the moment. Longer-term investment for the future is not popular." John R. Mashey, director of systems technology at Silicon Graphics (the company that eventually purchased Cray Research in 1996, before selling it to the Tera Computer Company in 2000) and a strong admirer of Cray's, described the defeat to Sarah Cohen for *Electronic News* (October 14, 1996): "Dating from the period when it became clear that CCC was unlikely to make it, I said, 'This is very painful. This is like watching your favorite quarterback, but his knees are gone and the 300-pound defensive tackles are fierce, and while he keeps getting up, it's agonizing to watch.'"

With CCC now out of business, Cray made one last-ditch effort, in 1996, to start a successful supercomputer company with the launch of SRC Computers Inc. He intended to dedicate the company's resources toward building competitive supercomputers for significantly lower cost. However, Cray's last dream was cut short by sudden tragedy. On September 22, 1996 he was involved in a serious car accident. He sustained a broken neck, broken ribs, and severe head trauma; after two weeks in the hospital, he died on October 5, 1996.

Cray married his first wife, Verene, shortly after his discharge from the army in 1946. They had two daughters and a son before divorcing in 1975. Cray married Geri Harrand in 1980. Throughout his lifetime, Cray was known as a withdrawn, reclusive genius who generally preferred to work alone, prompting James Conaway for the *Washington Post Magazine* (May 15, 1983) to dub him "the J. D. Salinger of CPUs." While his name became synonymous with high-performance computing, he avoided fame and publicity, often declining interviews, awards, and honors in order to keep focused on his projects. The awards he did accept included the W. W. McDowell Award from the American Foundation of Information Processing Societies (1968), the Harry H. Good Memorial Award (1972), and the MCI Information Technology Leadership

Award for Innovation (1994). While away from his professional pursuits, Cray enjoyed skiing, sailing, wind surfing, hiking, and tennis.

Cray's often eccentric behavior has become somewhat legendary, particularly among his colleagues and friends who began compiling their favorite "Seymour stories" shortly after his death. For example, Cray was known to tear down trees or dig tunnels in his yard to clear his mind. Rollwagen recounted another well-known and often-celebrated "Seymour" tale to James Cook for *Forbes* (September 12, 1983), recalling, "He used to make sailboats. He'd made a new sailboat every year. He built it in his basement, designed it and built it for himself. He'd take it out and sail it all summer and then burn it in the fall. He wanted to carry it from the point of conception all the way through a summer's worth of sailing. When he got all the ideas for what to do next year, he didn't want the boat to exist anymore. He'd burn it so it wouldn't be there to bother him the next year."

Rollwagen added, "He used to burn computers, too."—K. D.

Suggested Reading: *BusinessWeek* p80+ Apr. 30, 1990, with photo; *Computerworld* p38 June 22, 1992, with photo; *Electronic News* p1 Oct. 14, 1996; *Forbes* p108 Sep. 12, 1983; *New York Times* D p1 Feb. 21, 1992, with photo, D p3 Feb. 5, 1993, with photo, D p3 Aug. 18, 1994, 1 p37 Mar. 25, 1995, with photo, A p47 Oct. 7, 1996, with photo; *National Museum of American History, Smithsonian Institution: Seymour Cray Interview* (on-line) May 9, 1995; *USA Today* (on-line) Mar. 19, 1997; *Washington Post* B p6 Oct. 6, 1996, with photo, C p1 Oct. 7, 1996, with photo; *Washington Post Magazine* p8+ May 15, 1983, with photo; Murray, Charles. *The Supermen: The Story of Seymour Cray and the Technical Wizards Behind the Supercomputer*, 1997; Spencer, Donald D. *The Timetable of Computers*, 1997

Hulton Archive by Getty Images

Curie, Marie

Nov. 7, 1867–July 4, 1934 Pioneer of the science of radioactivity and radiology

It's possible to use the term pioneering to describe the legendary scientist Marie Curie without exaggeration, for any account of Curie's life and work must include a catalogue of groundbreaking firsts: She was the first woman to be granted a doctorate of science in Europe; she coined the term "radioactivity"; she became the first woman to win a Nobel Prize and the first person to win a second Nobel;

she was the first female professor at the famed Sorbonne, and she was the first woman to be laid to rest in France's national mausoleum for her own merits. At a time when few women contemplated careers at all, much less careers in the sciences, Curie made her way to the top of her field through her ambition, dogged determination, and her idealistic pursuit of scientific knowledge. Her research into the nature of radioactivity ushered in a new era of medical research and treatment, and led to a dramatic shift in our understanding of matter and energy. Throughout the 20th century and into the next, radioactivity has been used by doctors and scientists to track chemical changes and life processes; it has also been used to date ancient objects and archeological remains, and even to establish the age of the earth.

In a lecture to the Royal Swedish Academy, as reprinted on the Nobel e-Museum Web site, Nanny Fröman connects the fin de siècle discovery of radioactivity with the birth of modernism, and its radical undermining of a cherished world view. "Although admittedly the world did not decay, what nevertheless did was the classical, deterministic view of the world," she argued. "The radioactive decay, that heat is given off from an invisible and apparently inexhaustible source, that radioactive elements are transformed into new elements just as in the ancient dreams of alchemists of the possibility of making gold, all these things contravened the most entrenched principles of classical physics."

Marie Curie was born Maria Sklodowska on November 7, 1867 in Warsaw, Poland. At the time of her birth, Poland had lacked autonomy for almost a century, having been divided up by the occupying forces of Austria, Prussia, and czarist Russia. Warsaw was under the control of the Russian czar

Alexander II, and Maria, or Manya, as she was called, learned to be a Polish patriot from her parents, Bronislawa (Boguska) and Vladislav Sklodowski, both educators and intellectuals. Maria was the fifth child, and after her birth her mother quit her job as the head of a school, and the family relied on her father's ample salary as a teacher of mathematics and physics at a boys' high school. All this was to change before Maria reached adolescence.

Persecuted by his Russian supervisors because of his nationalist sentiments, Maria's father was forced into progressively lower academic posts, and eventually lost all of his savings in a bad investment. The Sklodowski family took in boarders to raise extra funds, and the oldest daughter, Zosia, contracted typhus from one of the boarders and died. Her death was soon followed by the death of the family matriarch, Bronislawa, after a five-year bout with tuberculosis. Ten-year-old Maria, her two remaining sisters, Bronya and Hela, and brother Józef drew closer together, bolstered by a father who read them great works of literature and shared with them his passion for scientific reason and experimentation. "I easily learned mathematics and physics," Curie remembered about her childhood, as quoted by Naomi Pasachoff on the Center for History of Physics Web site. "I found in this ready help from my father, who loved science. . . . Unhappily, he had no laboratory and could not perform experiments." Maria had a prodigious memory and earned a gold medal for academic excellence upon completion of her secondary education, in 1883. That same year, she suffered a collapse, which doctors attributed to overwork or "nervous" problems, but may have been acute depression brought on by her family's troubles. She recovered her strength after spending a year visiting family in the country.

Occupied Poland was a hostile environment for intellectual endeavor of any kind, but particularly for a young woman of nationalistic leanings. Speaking Polish was forbidden, as were laboratory instruction and university education for women. But Maria and her sister Bronya were able to study at the "Floating University," an illegal night school in which classes floated from one clandestine location to another, and students taught courses to each other and dreamed of Poland's eventual liberation. But Maria and Bronya longed to learn more, and hoped to study in what they regarded as the land of liberty—France. The two sisters made a pact: Maria would work as a tutor to help put her older sister through medical school in Paris, and as soon as she could Bronya would send for Maria and help to subsidize her education. For the next five years, Maria served as a private tutor for various Warsaw families, then as a governess for the children of an agriculturalist who ran a beet processing plant north of the city. Moved by the plight of a group of local peasant children, she gave them lessons when she was through with the agriculturist's children for the day. During this time she also embarked on a private course of study in sociology, literature, and the sciences, only gradually focusing on math and the physical sciences. In this effort she was aided by a correspondence course with her father and instruction by a local chemist.

In 1889 Maria returned to Warsaw. After a few more years of tutoring and with help from her family, she finally had enough money to travel to France and enroll at the University of Paris. Before she left, Maria convinced her cousin to smuggle her into the Museum of Industry and Agriculture, which was actually an underground training laboratory for Polish scientists. There, she embarked on a crash course in the principles of practical laboratory experimentation. Then, in 1891, at age 24, Maria set out for Paris, where she began to be called by the French name, Marie.

Marie enrolled at the Sorbonne, one of the University's famed colleges and a locus of European scientific thought. She soon discovered that—as she had feared—her math and science background were inadequate. She moved from her sister's house in the Paris suburbs to a student's garret in the Latin Quarter and began to catch up. By the summer of 1893, Marie had earned her master's degree in physics, graduating first in her class. The next year, she earned a second master's degree, in mathematics, this time graduating second.

Word of Marie's skills spread among the academic community. She was awarded a scholarship set aside for Polish students, and then commissioned by an industrial group to perform a study of the magnetic properties of different forms of steel. When she began searching for laboratory space, Marie was introduced to Pierre Curie, chief of the laboratory at the Paris Municipal School of Industrial Physics and Chemistry, where engineers were trained. Though a talented physicist who had done pioneering research on crystals and magnetism, Pierre was an outsider to academic circles and was only able to offer Marie the most rudimentary of laboratory spaces. In Marie, Pierre found someone not only of equal intellect but one who shared his idealism, his fervent belief in science as the path to human progress and freedom. Pierre and Marie became colleagues and friends, and their attachment soon turned romantic. Pierre, ten years her senior, convinced Marie to remain in Paris to pursue her doctorate, and eventually convinced her to become his wife. And yet, she hesitated, knowing that marriage to Pierre meant abandoning her country and her family. "Our work," Marie once wrote, as quoted by Pasachoff, "drew us closer and closer, until we were both convinced that neither of us could find a better life companion." On July 26, 1895 Marie and Pierre married in a simple civil ceremony, Marie having long abandoned her mother's Catholic faith in favor of agnosticism. With money from wedding gifts, the couple purchased bicycles and took a honeymoon tour through France.

Now a wife and soon to be a mother, Marie Curie had to learn to balance work and family. In the first few years of her marriage, she completed her research on the magnetic properties of steel and earned a certificate to teach science to young women, an occupation she would enjoy for many years to come. Then, in 1897, Curie gave birth to a daughter, Irène. Remarkably, given the social norms of the period, neither Pierre nor Marie considered the possibility of Marie abandoning her research to raise their child. "Such a renunciation would have been very painful to me," Pasachoff quoted Curie as saying, "and my husband would not even think of it." Pierre's father, a physician who had delivered Irène and who had been recently widowed, moved in with the family and became a full-time babysitter. Curie was then able to begin her doctoral studies.

At a time when no woman in the world had yet been awarded a doctorate in science, Curie's choice of subject was to prove historic. She had heard about two recent scientific developments. In 1895 the German physicist Wilhelm Roentgen had discovered a kind of ray that could travel through solid wood or flesh and yield photographs of living people's bones; he called these rays "X rays", with the "X" indicating the unknown. (In 1901, Roentgen became the first Nobel laureate in physics.) Then, in 1896, the French physicist Henri Becquerel happened upon the accidental discovery that uranium compounds emitted an impression on a photographic plate—even in the dark, and in spite of the plate's protective envelope. The effect wasn't caused by an external energy source such as light, as in the X rays, but instead it seemed to be an intrinsic property of the uranium itself. Most of the scientific community focused on the dramatic evidence of the X rays and ignored the weaker Becquerel rays. But Curie was interested in uranium rays as a subject for her dissertation, partially because, since there were few papers published on the subject, she could quickly get through the preliminary research and begin laboratory work. In an old storeroom on the Municipal School campus, Curie began to study the strange phenomenon of the uranium rays. She relied heavily on the electrometer, a device that had been invented some years before by her husband and his brother, Jacques, that enabled the measurement of extremely low voltages. After a rash of experiments, Curie confirmed Becquerel's observations that, whether uranium is in solid form or pulverized, wet or dry, exposed to light or heat, the electrical effects of uranium rays are constant. She also confirmed that substances with a higher proportion of uranium emitted more intense rays. Then, surpassing the work of Becquerel, Curie theorized that, because nothing she did altered the rays, they were the result of atomic properties of the element— something built into the structure of its atoms, rather than a product of a chemical reaction. At the time the atom was regarded as the most elementary particle, the word "atom" indicating something undivided, or altogether indivisible. Other scientists had discovered the existence of electrons around this time, casting some doubt on the atom's elementary structure, but no one had yet described the complex architecture or the potential energy inside of an atom. Curie wrote, as quoted in the *Dictionary of Scientific Biography* (1971), of the "tenacious property" of radioactivity, the term she coined to describe the phenomenon, which, she surmised, "must be an absolutely essential character of the material itself." The theory went so against the grain of scientific thought that Curie herself was not completely convinced of its truth and theorized that the Becquerel rays came from somewhere beside the atoms: perhaps the earth was bathed in rays, which some atoms absorbed and then re-radiated, for example. In the end, as Pasachoff argued, "Marie's real achievement was to cut through the complicated and obscure observations with a crystal-clear analysis of the set of conclusions that, however unexpected, were logically possible." Her theory about the atom would prove revolutionary, leading to the entirely new science of radioactivity and, through parallel work in other areas of physics, to the creation of the first useful picture of the structure of atoms.

In order to test her hypothesis, Curie went through all the known elements, checking to see if any would make air conduct electricity, or if uranium alone could do this. She eventually determined that thorium compounds also emitted Becquerel rays, and again theorized that the rays appeared to be emanating from the atoms themselves.

By this point Pierre had become so fascinated by his wife's work that he put aside his own research to lend a hand. Curie had the idea to study the natural ores that contain uranium and thorium. Working with samples obtained from geological museums, she eventually discovered that one such ore, pitchblende, was significantly more radioactive than uranium by itself. She hypothesized that the high radiation might be due to the presence of another, unknown element, and set about separating the various substances in the pitchblende ore while Pierre measured the amounts of radiation. The Curies identified two parts of the pitchblende that were particularly radioactive—one containing mostly bismuth, the other mostly barium. By the end of July 1898, they were ready to report their discovery to the French Academy of Sciences. The bismuth fraction was chemically almost identical to bismuth but, since it was also radioactive, they theorized, it had to be something new. This "something new," they surmised, was a substance hundreds of times more radioactive than uranium, a new element that they named polonium in honor of Curie's homeland. By December of that year, the pair had further proof of an additional, highly active substance in the barium portion, for which they suggested the name radium.

In order to convince the scientific community of the existence of these new elements and to have them added to the periodic table of elements, Marie and Pierre had to isolate them completely from the bismuth and barium with which they were mixed. This was arduous work because pitchblende is a complex mineral, a combination of up to 30 different elements. They worked as a team—Marie carrying out the chemical separations, and Pierre measuring after each step. Husband and wife worked side by side in the laboratory by day and studied their results at night. "Neither of us could foresee that in beginning this work we were to enter the path of a new science which we would follow for all our future," Curie later wrote, as quoted by Pasachoff. Because they had determined that the substances they were seeking constituted only about a one-millionth part of pitchblende, they had to treat very large quantities of the ore—black, foul-smelling stuff that Curie spent hours cooking in a huge cauldron, stirring with a heavy iron rod.

This period gave rise to romantic legends about the Curies, with the drafty old shed that served as their lab, the bubbling vats and flickering fires, and most of all the mysteriously glowing, radioactive substances providing all the elements of a scientific thriller. During her lifetime Curie perpetuated the image of herself and her husband as heroic scientists, struggling on their own—without any outside help—to get at the truth; the film *Madame Curie* (1943), starring Greer Garson and Walter Pidgeon, further solidified this legend. Recent scholarship has somewhat leavened this image. While it is true that science in general was underfunded by the French government during this time, from early on the Curies received substantial financial assistance from industrial sponsors, so that their work was not entirely independent. The Central Chemical Products Company, for example, supplied the Curies with chemical products and payed for laboratory staff; in exchange, the company took a share of the radium salts extracted and later made a handsome profit by selling them for medical uses. But, as Pasachoff argued, Curie's self-romanticizing made good public-relations sense and helped to win sympathy for scientific pursuit and raise funds for her continued research.

After three years of toiling in the "miserable old shed," as she frequently called it, Curie had isolated a decigram of pure radium chloride. She was never able to isolate polonium because, as we now know, that element has a short half-life, and quickly disintegrates; as Curie was working to isolate it, it disappeared before her eyes. The Curies freely shared their results with the scientific community and industry since neither believed that scientific pursuit should be motivated by the desire for financial gain. Had they patented their extraction processes, they would have amassed a fortune from the thriving industry based on radium that soon emerged.

If not riches than at least recognition and awards for the Curies's achievement came quickly. The public went crazy for radium: science-fiction novels depicted it as a magical elixir, capable of curing illness, powering machines, or destroying cities, and even the mainstream media waxed hyperbolic when describing the ethereal-looking, mysteriously glowing substance, which Curie had once described as "faint, fairy lights," as quoted by Pasachoff. When they began their work, the Curies evidently had little idea of the detrimental effects of the radiation to which they had constantly exposed themselves. Marie liked to have a little radium salt by her bed as a kind of night-light, and Pierre carried around a vial of it in his pocket to show friends. Both ascribed their increasingly poor health to long working hours in poor conditions; in fact, they were suffering from radiation poisoning. Even though they failed to recognize the dangers of radium to themselves, they came to understand that it could be used to damage human tissue, and could therefore be used as a therapeutic weapon against cancer and other diseases. Thanks to Pierre's research on the effects of radium on living organisms—research in which he and his wife were unwitting subjects—radium quickly became a miracle drug. Radium was far safer than surgery and more effective than other chemicals used at the time to combat disease. Factories began to produce radium en masse, and the price of the element soared.

The Curies had come out of their dark shed into international fame. Curie became the first woman to be appointed a lecturer at France's best teachers' training institution for women, and in 1903 she defended her doctoral thesis, "Researches on Radioactive Substances." The committee that awarded her the degree declared her work to be the greatest contribution to science ever made by doctoral research. In 1903 Pierre learned from a sympathetic member of the Nobel Prize nominating committee that he and Henri Becquerel had been chosen as candidates for the physics prize—but not Marie. In a firmly worded letter, Pierre responded that it would be a great injustice not to include her for consideration as well. That December, Becquerel and both of the Curies were jointly awarded the Nobel Prize in Physics, with the Curies's citation mentioning their collaborative work on the radiation phenomenon discovered by Becquerel. Too ill to travel to Stockholm for the awards ceremony, the couple benefitted from the prize money, which enabled them to hire a laboratory assistant. The French academic establishment also recognized their achievements—Pierre was given a teaching position at the Sorbonne, and as a condition of his acceptance insisted that the college build a laboratory for him and his wife. For the first time, Marie Curie was given a title—chief of laboratory—and a university salary.

In 1905 the Curies were able to make the trip to Stockholm to deliver the customary acceptance speech, but only Pierre was given the chance to speak. He carefully distinguished between his wife's independent accomplishments and their joint efforts, then went on to add a cautionary note about radium and scientific technology in general that—in light of the atom bomb—seems prophetic. Like other technology, Pierre said, radium might prove dangerous, "and here we must ask ourselves if humanity can benefit by knowing the secrets of nature . . . or if this knowledge will not be harmful to the world," as quoted by Pasachoff. He closed on an optimistic note: "I am one of those who believe with Nobel that mankind will derive more good than harm from the new discoveries."

The Curies' research stimulated other scientists to study radioactivity. In 1903 the English physicists Ernest Rutherford and Frederick Soddy proposed that radioactive emissions are produced by the disintegration of atomic nuclei. They argued that, in disintegrating, or losing their particles, atoms change—or transmute—from one element into another. Curie at first rejected this theory, since her research showed no evidence of the disintegration process, which in uranium, thorium, and radium is so slow as to be barely detectable. By 1906 she had accepted the Rutherford-Soddy theory as the most likely explanation for radioactivity and introduced the terms disintegration and transmutation to describe the radioactive process.

The Curies had a second daughter, Ève, born in 1904. They had become the First Family of Physics, pursued by journalists and obligated to attend many public engagements. The couple complained privately about the difficulty of working under these circumstances. To compound their chagrin, the university had yet to fulfill the promise of building them a new laboratory. Then, in April 1906, while crossing a Paris street, Pierre was struck down and instantly killed by a horse-drawn wagon. The news of the great scientist's death traveled around the world, and expressions of sympathy for Curie and her young daughters poured in by telegraph and mail. Encouraged by her family, she returned to the lab on the day after Pierre's death, although privately confessing to her diary of the pain of returning to a place "where I never thought I would have to live without you," as quoted on the American Association of University Women Web site. After refusing an offer from the French government for a state pension, Curie received another, surprising offer: to take up Pierre's academic position at the Sorbonne. By accepting, she became the first female professor to teach there, and a large crowd gathered on the day of her inaugural lecture to see how the famous widow, and the first woman professor, would fare. Curie began her lecture on the state of physics by repeating the last sentence that Pierre had spoken in his final lecture, thus making it clear that she would honor her husband's memory by continuing what had been their life work together.

It was not an easy course. Curie faced an almost immediate challenge from the Scottish scientist William Thomson Kelvin, who in the summer of 1906 put forth a claim that radium was not an element at all but a compound of lead and helium. Working with André Debierne, a laboratory assistant and longtime collaborator, Curie set out to defend her theory of radioactivity with an intensive program to identify and isolate radium. In 1910 she finally succeeded in isolating metallic radium; the pure, uncombined element could now be weighed, measured, and added to the periodic table, its existence indisputable. It was this final step that led to Curie's unprecedented second Nobel Prize, this time for chemistry. The citation attributed the award to her discovery of the elements radium and polonium and to the isolation and study of the "remarkable element" of radium. Curie was given the task of defining the international standard of radium, necessary both for research and for industrial and medical uses. The International Bureau of Weights and Measures then defined the unit of measure for radioactivity as a *curie* in honor of Marie and Pierre.

In 1910 Curie was persuaded to stand for the single vacant seat for a physicist in the French Academy of Sciences, the nation's most prestigious institution. Though Pierre had been elected to the Academy a year before his death, no woman had ever been included among its ranks. Her candidacy sparked an ugly controversy in France that involved sexism, racism, and outright slander. Having recently lost its fight against Alfred Dreyfus, a Jewish army officer who was falsely accused of treason, a conservative and anti-Semitic faction within France now turned their venom against Curie. Claims were made against her candidacy on the grounds that she was a Pole, a Jew (based only on her Jewish-sounding maiden name), and in any case as being a foreigner, not "truly" French. Her rival for the seat was 66-year old Edouard Branly, a scientist who had contributed to the wireless telegraph and who was Catholic, as opposed to the liberal and openly agnostic Curie. After months of invective, she was rejected from the Academy by two votes.

In 1911 Curie, Albert Einstein, and other prominent figures gathered in Brussels for the first international conference in physics, where discussions paved the way for a new physics combining relativity, quantum mechanics, and radioactivity. Meanwhile, the French press, now organized in their opposition to Curie and the liberal viewpoint she represented, obtained and published intimate (and possibly forged) letters between Curie and her friend and fellow physicist, Paul Langevin. Langevin, who was unhappily married, had been Curie's colleague and, in the years following Pierre's death, the two may have been lovers. When Curie returned to France, she discovered an angry mob in front of her home. In the press she was accused of having an affair with Langevin while Pierre was still alive, and thus of having driven Pierre to suicide, and of being a foreign and possibly Jewish home wrecker, bent on destroying the Langevins' good, Catholic marriage.

Under the strain of these attacks, and suffering from severe kidney problems, Curie retreated to a private clinic and then to the homes of friends, traveling only under her maiden name. Like many subsequent 20th-century scandals, the half-life of this one proved short. After a year Curie was welcomed back into France as the only double Nobel laureate and one of the most prominent scientists in the world. For her own part, Curie clearly hoped to move beyond the controversies of the past years. On December 13, 1912 she made her first laboratory notebook entry in 14 months, and she set to work on building the Radium Institute, a research and medical institution that, she hoped, would be a lasting tribute to her husband's memory. The Institute opened on the newly named Rue Pierre-Curie in August 1914, just as World War I broke out.

During the war most of the researchers at the Radium Institute were drafted, and Curie took her precious gram of radium, in a lead box, to Bordeaux, outside Paris, for safekeeping. As reports of the war-wounded filled the news, she realized that X-ray technology could save the lives of soldiers by helping surgeons locate bullets, shrapnel, and broken bones. After lobbying the French government for their support and raising funds among friends, she created a radiology service under the auspices of the Red Cross. As director of this service, Curie trained herself and her 18-year-old daughter, Irène, in everything from basic anatomy to how to change a tire on the vans in which they would drive the mobile X-ray units to the wounded in battle. By 1916 Curie had trained and mobilized a force of women to work in 200 stationary X-ray units and 20 mobile vans, which the soldiers dubbed "petite Curies." "The story of radiology in war offers a striking example of the unsuspected amplitude that the application of purely scientific discoveries can take under certain conditions," Curie later wrote about this work, as quoted by Pasachoff.

After the war Curie turned her full attention to the Radium Institute. Supported by the University of Paris and the Pasteur Institute, she envisioned the Institute as a center for the study of radioactivity and its uses in fighting human cancers. By the mid-1920s Curie understood all too well the dangers of working with radiation, having suffered from fatigue, cataracts, and other ailments for years. She participated in a commission to recommend lead screens and periodic blood testing for those who routinely worked with radioactive content. At the Institute, she was appointed director of basic research, while a colleague directed the division for research into medical applications of radioactivity. When an American journalist named Marie Meloney learned that Curie's most fervent wish was for a second gram of radium for her laboratory, she organized a Marie Curie Radium Campaign, which succeeded in raising the money to purchase it. Curie and her daughters came to the United States, in 1921, to personally accept the gift of radium from President Warren G. Harding. Curie returned, in 1929, just days before the stock market crash, to accept a second gift of radium for the benefit of a cancer therapy treatment center in Warsaw, directed by her sister Bronya. Though shy by

nature (she reportedly never overcame stage fright during her 30 years as a lecturer), Curie used all the weight of her two Nobel medals, 19 honorary degrees, and 15 academic medals to lobby for funds for the founding of international resources to support the medical uses of radium. In 1978 the Radium Institute was renamed the Curie Institute, and it remains an international center for research and radiotherapy treatment.

The romantic story of a husband-and-wife physicist team was repeated in a second generation. Curie's daughter Irène married Frédéric Joliot, and both worked as researchers at the Radium Institute. In 1934 the couple discovered artificial radioactivity by bombarding a stable element with nuclear projectiles, thus changing a normal element into a radioactive one. This discovery rendered Curie's painstaking procedures for isolating radioactive elements unnecessary, making radium much more available for science and medicine. Irène Joliot-Curie and Frédéric Joliot won the Nobel Prize in Physics for this discovery, in 1935, but Curie didn't live long enough to see it. On July 4, 1934 she succumbed to leukemia, almost certainly caused by radiation exposure. She was buried twice—first in the family cemetery outside Paris, then, more than 60 years later, she and Pierre were reinterred under the famous dome in the Panthéon, France's national mausoleum. Although the Panthéon contained one other woman, the wife of the chemist and politician Marcellin Berthelot, Curie was the first to be buried there on the strength of her own accomplishments. Without the discoveries of Madame Curie, modern medical diagnostics, physics, and perhaps even the mapping of the human genome would be decades away. Her scientific contributions, although often taken for granted, were the stepping stones to many of our modern-day technologies.—M. A. H.

Suggested Reading: Center for History of Physics Web site; Nobel e-Museum Web site; *Dictionary of Scientific Biography*, 1971; *Nobel Prize Winners*, 1987

Daguerre, Louis Jacques Mandé

(da-GAIR)

Nov. 18, 1789–July 10, 1851 Inventor of the daguerreotype

The 19th-century industrial and scientific revolutions were accompanied by a movement toward realistic representations in art, and during the first quarter of the 19th century, many individuals were at work trying to capture images from the real world through chemical and optical devices—rather than through an artist's eye and hand. They were frustrated that, even though artists could create a believable representation of a landscape or a person, they would still not be able to create a

Hulton Archive by Getty Images

Louis Jacques Mandé Daguerre

perfect mimetic image. A French painter and stage designer named Louis Daguerre was the first to create a commercially successful photographic process. His "daguerreotype" was introduced to the world in 1839, the same year that the term "photograph," or "light drawing," entered the English lexicon. Although there are many photographic techniques, most rely upon three basic steps: preparing a medium (usually glass, metal, or paper) to be sensitive to light; using a lens to form an image upon that medium; and making the medium insensitive to further exposure so that the image will be fixed for viewing. Daguerre perfected these three steps, and then successfully spread his "daguerreotypes" around the world, launching a craze for photography that has lasted well into the age of digital cameras and computer-generated art.

Louis Jacques Mandé Daguerre, known commonly as Louis Daguerre, was born on November 18, 1789 in Cormeilles, France, near Paris. Though his formal education was interrupted by the chaos of the French Revolution, his talent for drawing was noticed by his family, and he was apprenticed to an architect at an early age. This calling did not suit him, however, and in 1804 Daguerre moved to Paris, where he hoped to make a living painting portraits and landscapes. At age 16 he became an assistant stage designer at the Parisian *Théatre Ambigu-Comique*. There, his painted scenic designs became renowned for their realistic detail and lifelike perspective. Daguerre showcased his talents in dioramas—spectacles in which scenes were painted on enormous translucent screens and enlivened with changing light effects. Similar techniques had been used in peep shows and vaudeville before Daguerre, but he is generally credited with raising

them to the level of art. By 1825 Daguerre had become the proprietor of his own diorama theater, where spectators were entertained by elaborate historical, allegorical, and picturesque scenes, ingeniously lit to create the effects of day changing into night, or a clear day giving way to a storm, for example.

In order to create his lifelike paintings Daguerre employed the camera obscura—the ancestor of the photographic camera. The camera obscura technique was in widespread use among artists in the 18th century. The name, which is Latin for "dark chamber," refers to the process by which light is admitted into a darkened room (or a darkened box) through a single tiny hole (usually fitted with a lens), resulting in an inverted image of the scene outside the chamber being cast on the opposite wall. This technique was used to view eclipses (without having to look directly at the sun) and by artists, who traced the images cast by the camera obscura. Daguerre used a small box, its interior painted black, with an aperture and lens at one end and a screen at the other; it most likely contained a mirror to reflect the image, making it appear right side up on the screen.

Daguerre hoped to capture the image cast by a camera obscura, thus creating a facsimile of the real world that would be more precise than even his skilled hand could trace; in effect he hoped to let nature "draw itself." In 1826 he was introduced to Joseph Nicephore Niepce, an amateur inventor who had been experimenting with the camera obscura and light-sensitive media. Niepce is credited with taking the first successful photograph, using a camera obscura fitted with a pewter plate, which—after an eight-hour exposure time—produced an image of his courtyard. In 1829 Daguerre and Niepce formed a partnership to pool their efforts, but since Niepce's health rapidly deteriorated, Daguerre mainly carried on photographic experiments on his own.

Over the next few years, Daguerre tried to fix an image on a surface treated with light-sensitive chemicals; he called such experiments "heliography," meaning "sun writing." (In a pre-electricity era, photographers had to rely on natural light.) At first, Daguerre used kerosene fumes to develop the image; a (possibly apocryphal) story casts his discovery of mercury's usefulness as a happy accident. According to this story, Daguerre placed an exposed plate in his chemical cupboard and, days later, discovered that the latent image had developed. He eventually concluded that the plate had been exposed to mercury vapors from a broken thermometer that happened to be in the cupboard. Further experimentation showed that mercury vapor could quickly develop an image on a copper plate coated with silver salts, with a development time of about 30 minutes or less—far quicker than the eight hours needed in Niepce's process. By 1837 Daguerre had found a way to fix the image using a heated table salt solution.

Daguerre used his process to record familiar scenes in Paris, including the Louvre and Notre Dame. His most famous photograph was of a Paris boulevard, which appears deserted except for a man standing in the foreground. Since the exposure time lasted several minutes (from 15 to 30 depending on the intensity of light), anything that moved—including carriages and people—would not appear in the final image; the man in his Paris boulevard stopped to have his shoes shined, and thus may be the first person to ever have been photographed.

Now confident of his technique, Daguerre advertised and sought sponsors. A politician took notice and the French government purchased the rights to Daguerre's discovery and publicized his technique, "for the glory of endowing the world of science and of art with one of the most surprising discoveries that honor their native land," as quoted on the Daguerreian Society Web site. In exchange for the rights to his invention, Daguerre was awarded a lifetime pension, and, since Niepce had died in 1833, Niepce's son was awarded a pension for his father's contributions.

Daguerre's technique had its first public demonstration, in August 1839, at the Academy of Sciences. Crowds gathered to learn the secrets of the famous process, which soon became known as the daguerreotype. Eager not to be trumped by Daguerre, an Englishman named William Henry Fox Talbot rushed to announce that he, too, had developed a photographic process, which used paper made light-sensitive with salt and silver nitrate. Talbot's process created a negative image, which could then be used to create numerous copies, an advantage over the daguerreotype, which was a unique, irreproducible image.

In terms of aesthetics, however, the daguerreotype was clearly superior. While Talbot's process created grainy, unclear images, Daguerre's photographs—according to eye- witness accounts—possessed extraordinary clarity and beauty. Early reports of the daguerreotypes were ecstatic; the *Boston Daily Advertiser* (February 23, 1839) reported that the daguerreotype "reproduces the freshness of morning—the brilliancy of noon—the dim twilight and the dullness of a rainy day," and the *New Yorker* (December 14, 1839) declared that a daguerreotype exhibit displayed "a perfection never before attained by human ingenuity." (Both sources are archived on the Daguerreian Society Web site.) Daguerreotype images were seen as the barometers of truth, and daguerreotype portraits as the windows to the soul; one newspaper named itself the *Daguerreotype* in order to claim that it, too, was a instrument of honesty and truth.

Daguerre—being a man of the theater—knew something about self-promotion; after the public demonstration of his technique, he quickly manufactured a commercial camera and a 79-page manual explaining how to use it. "In a scene that we can easily relate to the release of Windows 95," Kenneth E. Nelson wrote in his history of daguerreotypes on the Daguerreian Society Web site, in reference to the popular Microsoft product, "everything remotely related to the making of daguerreotypes was whisked off the shelves of Parisian opticians and chemists within days of the announcement. France was caught in the grip of 'Daguerreotypomania." By the early 1840s a daguerreotype industry flourished in Europe and America. Millions of people who would never have been able to afford a painted portrait flocked to have their photographic portraits made, and tourists lined up to purchase photographic souvenirs of famous sites. After inventing the telegraph, Samuel Morse—like Daguerre a painter-turned-inventor—took a great interest in daguerreotypes and helped to introduce them to America.

In the years after 1839, various individuals improved upon Daguerre's technique, making the process more reliable and expedient. Nevertheless, by the 1850s cheaper forms of photography had supplanted daguerreotypes. During the Civil War, for example, tintypes and paper prints of soldiers became very popular. Today, a few artists have preserved the laborious daguerreotype technique, and an occasional art exhibit is seen by connoisseurs who relish the photographs' silvery quality and mirror-like sheen.

Daguerre was a member of the French Academy of Fine Arts and the Academy of St. Luke. He retired in 1840 and died of a heart attack on July 10, 1851, in Bry-sur-Marne, in France.—M. A. H.

Suggested Reading: Daguerreian Society Web site; *Digital Century* (on-line)

---

de Forest, Lee

Aug. 26, 1873–June 30, 1961 Inventor; radio pioneer

Lee de Forest, sometimes dubbed the "father of radio," held more than 300 patents; his best-known invention, however, is a triode vacuum tube he called the Audion, which was used in not only radio, but in moving pictures, television, radar, and early computers. The device remained in widespread use until the proliferation of the transistor and solid-state electronics in the 1950s.

Lee de Forest, one of three children, was born on August 26, 1873 in Council Bluffs, Iowa, to Reverend Henry Swift de Forest, a Congressional minister, and the former Anna Margaret Robbins, a choir leader and herself the daughter of a minister. Six years after de Forest was born, the family moved to Talladega, Alabama, where his father became head of Talladega College, founded to educate rural blacks. In the post-Reconstruction South, the members of the family were ostracized by their white neighbors, but de Forest and his siblings made friends with the area's black children, and by all accounts he had a happy childhood.

De Forest's parents wanted him to enter the ministry but his interests were geared more towards science than religion. He spent much of his youth inventing mechanical devices, including a miniature blast furnace and a working silver-plating apparatus; when he was 15 he proudly announced that he had discovered the secret of perpetual motion. Reverend de Forest still insisted that he study the classics in preparation for the ministry, and in 1891 de Forest entered Mt. Hermon Preparatory School. In 1893, however, determined to pursue his own course, de Forest enrolled in a three-year mechanical-engineering course at the Sheffield Scientific School of Yale University, in New Haven, Connecticut, then one of the few schools in America with a solid scientific program.

At Yale, de Forest was not known to socialize; he spent the majority of his time studying, reading books on electricity, and working on inventions. His greatest fascination during his undergraduate days was the fledgling field of wireless telegraphy, which was then being explored by Heinrich Rudolf Hertz, a German physicist who had demonstrated that rapid oscillations of electric current in a wire (which would later be called an antenna) could emit radio waves into the surrounding space, and Guglielmo Marconi, an Italian inventor who was developing a means to send traditional telegraph messages, using Morse code (an alphabet consisting of electronic signals), through the air via radio waves.

After de Forest received his bachelor's degree, in 1896, he commenced graduate work at Yale. When war broke out between the United States and Spain, in 1898, he enlisted in the army but was not called to action. After the war he returned to Yale to complete the research on his dissertation, "Reflection of Short Hertzian Waves from the Ends of Parallel Wires," which in 1899 earned him a Ph.D. This dissertation, according to most sources, was likely the first in the United States on the subject that would later become known as radio.

Leaving Yale, de Forest settled in Chicago, Illinois, where he began working as a laborer in the dynamo (generator) division of the Western Electric Company; he was later promoted to the telephone laboratory. There, he worked ceaselessly to develop an electrolytic detector of Hertzian waves—a device for detecting wireless signals. He discovered that he could use a telephone receiver as an indicating device in receiving such signals.

De Forest reportedly left the Western Electric Company for a time to live in Milwaukee, where he continued his research. He then returned to Chicago, where he obtained a job on the staff of an electrical magazine and another teaching at the Armour Institute (now the main building of the Illinois Institute of Technology). He continued working on his detector, which he called a "Sponder," until 1901, when he gave it its first successful long-distance test. Immediately, he and a partner, E. W. Smythe, began to patent and market the device. They set up a machine shop on the Jersey City,

New Jersey, waterfront and erected the first wireless station of its kind in that vicinity. In 1902 they obtained enough Wall Street capital to buy equipment and set up transmitting rooms, forming the De Forest Wireless Telegraph Company. In 1903 de Forest went to England to demonstrate his invention and while there communicated by wireless transmission from Wales to Ireland.

De Forest's work naturally interested the United States Army and Navy, and with their backing, he was able to compete with Marconi, who in 1901 had sent the first transatlantic radiotelegraph message, from England to Canada. To generate publicity, de Forest persuaded the Publishers' Press to let him report the 1903 International Yacht Races with his wireless in competition with Marconi operators, who were doing this for the Associated Press. De Forest's broadcast was a failure, but his equipment was later used by European reporters who were covering the Russo-Japanese War of 1904–05. Though he did not profit from these ventures, their publicity value was tremendous. De Forest was awarded a gold medal for his work at the St. Louis World's Fair, in 1904.

After a third voyage to the British Isles, in 1906, de Forest, never known for his business acumen, returned to find his company in financial shambles. The other directors urged him to resign, and—feeling forced out and facing continual patent problems—he took a severance package of a few hundred dollars and struck out on his own. He set up a laboratory in New York City and continued his research. His aim was to transmit actual human voices, instead of sending a series of Morse code dots and dashes through the air—a goal that would be made possible if he could develop an improved wireless detector.

To that end, de Forest started work on the Audion, his triode tube. It was a substantial improvement over the vacuum diode invented in 1904 by John Ambrose Fleming; because of the insertion of a third controlling electrode between the cathode and anode it was more sensitive to the reception of wireless signals than any other tube then in existence. In *Asimov's Biographical Encyclopedia of Science and Technology* (1982), Isaac Asimov describes how de Forest's Audion worked: "The stream of electrons moved from the filament to the plate at a rate that varied markedly with the charge placed on the grid. A varying but very weak electric potential on the grid could be converted into a similarly varying but much stronger electron flow in the filament-plate combination. In de Forest's hands Fleming's instrument became an amplifier as well as a rectifier." In 1906 de Forest applied for a patent on the device "for amplifying feeble electric currents." It wasn't until after 1912, however, when other scientists, including Edwin H. Armstrong, Fritz Löwenstein, and Irving Langmuir, began refining the device, that its use became widespread. De Forest had, despite his failure to fully realize his invention's potential, created the prototype of all electronic amplifiers. In 1907 he formed the De Forest Radio Telephone Company to promote his idea. By the end of that year, the U.S. Navy had ordered enough radiophone sets to equip its entire fleet.

De Forest married Nora Stanton Blatch, in 1908, and went with his bride to Paris to install a radio telephone transmitter on top of the Eiffel Tower. Back from his honeymoon, he built an aerial on top of the Metropolitan Life Insurance Building, in New York City, and shortly afterward installed microphones in the city's Metropolitan Opera House. On January 2, 1910—in the first radio broadcast of its kind—the voice of the opera star Enrico Caruso was transmitted. (The transmission was made possible by use of the scientist Reginald Fessenden's system of broadcasting voice, in combination with the Audion tube.)

Shortly before Caruso's historic performance, de Forest's company began, once again, to collapse. He moved to San Francisco to take a position as a research engineer for the Federal Telegraph Company. In 1912 he developed the idea of "cascading" a series of his Audion tubes to amplify high-frequency radio signals far beyond what could be achieved by increasing the voltage to a single tube. Not only did this have tremendous importance in radio broadcasting but in long-distance telephone service as well.

In 1914 de Forest refinanced his company with $50,000 he had received from the sale of his Audion tubes to the American Telephone and Telegraph Company. He returned to New York City, where he set up another laboratory and later mounted a transmitter at the World Tower Building, from which, beginning in 1916, regular radio broadcasts were given for the first time.

In 1917 de Forest sold further rights to his Audion tubes to the American Telephone and Telegraph Company (for a reported $390,000) and used the money for more experimental machinery. As radio developed, he found some success manufacturing tubes for the burgeoning industry, but he lacked enthusiasm for the work. Beginning in 1920 he sought to develop a practical way to record and reproduce sound for motion pictures, and to that end he developed a sound-on-film recording device he called the Phonofilm. In 1923 he presented the first sound motion picture in a theatre—the Rivoli in New York. Initially, movie producers weren't interested, and "talkies," as the films were known, did not catch on until after the 1927 debut of *The Jazz Singer*, which employed different technology than de Forest's.

Throughout his career de Forest had been plagued by lawsuits brought by other inventors over patent rights. He suffered years of expensive litigation with Edwin H. Armstrong, for example, until in 1934 his claim to the invention of the feedback and oscillating vacuum-tube circuits was upheld by the Supreme Court of the United States. That year saw an additional triumph; in 1934 he founded the Lee de Forest Laboratories, devoted chiefly to research and manufacture in the new field of radio diathermy, the use of high-frequency currents to heat human tissues, found highly beneficial in certain medical conditions. The United States Army and Navy used large numbers of de Forest Dynatherms in their medical facilities.

During World War II, de Forest worked for Bell Telephone Laboratories and involved himself in military research. He became interested in the development of "television torpedo planes," which he believed would provide the United States military forces with an inexpensive means of getting information by aerial surveys and which could also be used as robot bombers.

Despite recognition from learned societies, manufacturers, and scientists, de Forest failed to keep any of the fortunes he had made over the course of his life. In 1937 he filed a bankruptcy petition listing assets of $390 and liabilities of $104,000. Though de Forest never truly profited from his more than 300 patents, he was widely hailed by his contemporaries and many individuals supported him—unsuccessfully—for a Nobel Prize in Physics. He is considered by many historians to be the last of the individualistic inventors because, while he worked for a number of companies throughout his lifetime, his greatest achievements came as a freelance inventor.

De Forest was an outspoken critic of the commercialization of radio, which he believed had the potential to be a great cultural device. He remained an active inventor until the end of his life; some of his last projects include refinements on magnetic tape and work in thermoelectricity. At the age of 84 he received his last patent, for an automatic telephone-dialing device.

Lee de Forest died on June 30, 1961 in Hollywood, California. He had been married three times (some sources say four). His last wife, Marie Mosquini, an actress whom he married in 1930, donated his papers to the Foothill Electronics Museum, in Los Altos Hills, California, in 1969. During his lifetime, de Forest received many awards for his work, including the Medal of Honor from the Institute of Radio Engineers in 1915, the Edison Medal in 1946, and a Cross of the Legion of Honor from the French government. In 1950 de Forest published an autobiography, *The Father of Radio.*—C. M.

Suggested Reading: *New York Times* IX p12 Feb. 16 1941, IX p12 Mar. 30 1941; *Popular Electronics* p61+ Aug. 1996; *Radio News* p8+ Dec. 1940; Science Odyssey Web site; Asimov, Isaac. *Asimov's Biographical Encyclopedia of Science and Technology*, 1982

Courtesy of Dell Computer Corp.

Dell, Michael

Feb. 23, 1965– Founder and CEO of Dell Computer

When aspiring entrepreneurs in the computer industry are asked whose careers they would most like to emulate, a name that frequently pops up is that of Michael Dell, the founder of the Dell Computer Corporation At the age of only 19, he began assembling and selling personal computers out of his college dorm room. Like Microsoft's founder, William H. Gates, Dell dropped out of college to focus on his business full time. In his first year he sold $6 million worth of computers. Now, two decades later, his company's revenues have expanded to about $32 billion, making Dell the largest computer maker in the world.

In at least one category, Michael Dell, who turned 38 in 2003, has no equals: He has had the longest tenure as chief executive officer of any computer maker in the industry. He has succeeded primarily because he pioneered the simple concept of "direct selling" in the computer industry. Back in the mid-1980s, when he started his business, manufacturers sold an overwhelming majority of their personal computers (PCs) through dealers, such as CompUSA. Dell thought that relying on middlemen was unwise, not only because dealers' profits increase the cost of the computers to consumers, but also because dealers' stocks, even if vast, are necessarily limited and thus limit the choices available to buyers. Moreover, the computers would sit on dealers' shelves for days, or even weeks, before they were bought. Choosing direct selling as a better approach, Dell advertised heavily in computer trade magazines and established toll-free phone numbers that customers could call

to order computers. Each computer was made to a customer's exact specifications; it was assembled only after the order had been placed, and it was shipped within days. The advantages to both buyers and sellers seemed obvious to Dell: The price of the computers was lower, because dealers' markups were eliminated and because the least expensive available technology could immediately be incorporated in Dell's machines. In addition, the company's very method of conducting business amounted to instant market research (since customized orders signal consumer preferences). Dell perceived correctly that it would not take computer users long to become more savvy and more likely to understand the different components available.

When Dell was starting out, many businesspeople believed that buyers of expensive items like computers would not be willing to make a purchase before a hands-on inspection. As it turned out, corporations and government organizations—which comprise 90 percent of Dell's customers—have been quite willing to buy computers sight unseen. Though some of Dell's major rivals, including such giants as Compaq, International Business Machines (IBM), and Hewlett-Packard, have established direct-order services, Dell is the leader in direct sales of computers, and its annual revenues have continued to grow at a tremendous pace.

For Dell, the remarkable success of his company is the fulfillment of a childhood dream. He was born on February 23, 1965 in Houston, Texas, and as a child he used to look at gleaming corporate buildings that lined the Interstate 610 loop in that city and imagine that he would someday have a business in one of them. "I always knew I wanted to run a business someday," he told a reporter for *Fortune* (September 8, 1997). The young Dell proved to have keen business instincts. When he was 12 years old, he worked as a water boy and dishwasher at a Chinese restaurant and saved enough money to start a stamp collection. He subsequently made $2,000 by selling the stamps via mail order. By the time he was 16, he had saved enough to buy an Apple IIE computer. The computer helped him succeed in another business: selling subscriptions to the *Houston Post*. Reasoning that many new subscribers would most likely be people setting up new households—in particular, newlyweds—he obtained lists of marriage-license applicants from the local courthouse and other such lists. Then, using the computer, he sent out personalized letters with subscription offers. The approximately $17,000 he earned enabled him to buy his first BMW.

Dell's father, Alexander, an orthodontist, and his mother, Lorraine, a stockbroker for Paine Webber, wanted Michael (who is the second of their three sons) to become a doctor. When he entered the University of Texas, in Austin, in 1983, he obliged his parents by enrolling in premedical courses. But on the sly, he began a new business—selling computers. He had become something of an expert on computers, by taking his computer apart and examining its insides, and, during visits to local computer dealers, he often felt that his knowledge of computers outstripped that of the salespeople. Operating out of his dorm room, he bought remaindered IBM and IBM-clone computers from local dealers, upgraded them, and sold them both door-to-door and through mail order. When his parents found out what he was doing, they were angry and asked him to quit. A compromise was reached. Dell would put his business on hold until he finished the school year; if sales during his summer break were not good, he would return to college. Dell never returned: In the month that ended just before the fall term began, he sold $180,000 worth of PCs. He set up a shop called PCs Ltd., in Austin, and by the end of 1984 his sales had reached $6 million.

Dell soon realized that if he bought parts from suppliers directly and assembled the computers himself, he could sell the computers more cheaply. It would be a major undertaking, but Dell, in typical fashion, never hesitated. "It was obvious," he told Tom Richman for *Inc.* (January 1990), "from what I'd seen . . . that we'd have to learn how to do lots of things. I knew we'd have to get people, systems, executives. It was pretty clear to me." His first PC was the Turbo, a computer that used the Intel 8088 processor. By the end of his second year in business, Dell's sales had reached $34 million. In 1987, the company was renamed the Dell Computer Corporation, and in 1988, it went public and raised $30 million. By that time, *BusinessWeek* (February 2, 1987) and other prominent magazines had taken notice of the start-up computer maker and christened him "the hottest little computer maker in Texas." By the end of 1990, revenues and earnings had reached $546 million and $27 million, respectively, and a Dell plant was opened in Limerick, Ireland.

The success of Dell's "direct-business" model confounded critics who thought that fear of mail fraud and the inability to examine the computers in a showroom would make consumers reluctant to order computers via telephone and mail. To allay the fears some people still harbored regarding mail order, Dell beefed up his technical-support and service units. Beginning in 1987, Dell promised next-day, on-site service for problems that could not be handled over the phone, and the company gained a reputation for offering superlative technical support. At the end of 1992, Dell's sales had reached $2 billion, and Michael Dell became the youngest CEO to make the *Fortune* 500.

In 1993, after 14 consecutive quarters of rising profits, Dell Computer ran into some trouble. In May of that year, the company surprised the financial community with an announcement of a loss in the first quarter—the first quarterly loss it had ever incurred. Another loss followed in the second quarter. The losses occurred because Dell had grown too large too fast, causing serious strains in inventory management, accounting, and product

forecasting. As Dell explained to the the *Fortune* reporter, "One of the things that is confusing and almost intoxicating when you are growing a business is that you really have little way of determining what the problems are. You had different parts of the company believing they were making their plan, but when you rolled up the results of the company, you had a big problem. It was symptomatic of not understanding the relationship between costs and revenues and profits within the different lines of the business." One of the serious blunders Dell's company committed was underestimating the rapidly developing market for laptop computers. Caught with an outdated design that used the 386 Intel chip rather than the more advanced 486 chip, Dell eventually withdrew its line of laptops—a costly measure, since at the time, the laptop market was one of the fastest-growing segments of the computer market. Moreover, beginning in the early 1990s, Dell had deviated from its core "direct business" strategy by selling through stores like Wal-Mart and CompUSA.

During the rest of 1993, the company entered a period of retooling and cost cutting. Experienced managers much older than Dell himself were brought into the company. Dell named Mort Topfer, a former Motorola executive, vice chairman, and placed John Medica, who had designed Apple's Powerbook line of laptop computers, in charge of Dell's laptop division. The company began to focus less on growth, and the changes had a salutary effect. In the final two quarters of 1993, Dell returned to the black, thus holding its yearly loss to $36 million. In 1994, the company introduced the Latitude Series, an improved laptop-computer line, and abandoned retail sales altogether. Though the company lost some market share, it announced a healthy profit—$149 million—that year.

From 1995 to 1998 Dell's growth resumed its sizzling pace: Revenues grew at around 50 percent per year, and earnings, between 80 and 90 percent a year. By the end of 1997 (after 16 consecutive quarters of growth in revenues and earnings), Dell posted annual revenues of $12.33 billion, up 59 percent from those of the previous year, with earnings at $944 million, up 82 percent. Dell also expanded internationally. In 1996, for instance, the company set up a third assembly plant, in Penang, Malaysia. By 1998 Dell captured 5 percent of the worldwide market—virtually the same percentage as Hewlett-Packard—and trailed only Compaq (which had about 12 percent of the global share) and IBM (about nine percent). Midway through 1998, Lawrence M. Fisher reported in the *New York Times* (August 19, 1998), "Dell cited market research showing that it had moved into the number-one position in the United States in desktop computer sales, and the number-two place overall, behind Compaq Computer but ahead of IBM and Hewlett-Packard." In recognition of the strengths of Dell's business model, IBM, Compaq, and Hewlett-Packard each established their own mail-order businesses.

The Dell company has done particularly well in sales conducted over the Internet—an approach heavily pushed by Dell himself. The company, in fact, leads the world in Internet computer sales. The Internet removes the need for a human intermediary and is "the ultimate direct model," Dell noted to a reporter for *BusinessWeek* (April 7, 1997). Dell also entered the lucrative market for workstations and servers. "The first reason was that our corporate customers wanted one vendor for all products," he told Helen Thorpe for *Texas Monthly* (September 1997). "So if you had just desktops and notebooks, you were going to get in trouble with those accounts. The second problem was that our competitors had enormous profits in servers, and they were overcharging customers for servers and using those excess profits to compete with us in desktops and notebooks. So we said, 'We've got to put an end to this. We're going to go into the server market and take away the profit havens of our competitors.'"

In 1999 Dell grew by 48 percent, and in 2000 by 39 percent. The company was not immune to the general market downturn in 2001. It laid off 1,700 employees in February, the first major cut in the company's history. Nevertheless, Dell performed better than most, capturing 13 percent of the world PC market share and 23.6 percent of the U.S. market share, the largest since IBM in the 1980s. "Everyone else in the business is reeling from the combined effects of sagging demand and the scorched-earth price war Dell began this spring," Henry Norr wrote in the *San Francisco Chronicle* (September 10, 2001). "But Dell just keeps gaining ground, and I don't see anything on the horizon that's likely to slow it down."

Michael Dell owns about 13 percent of his company's stock. In 2001, for the third year in succession, he was the richest American under 40, with an estimated $16.3 billion. Dell could conceivably cash out and live comfortably for the rest of his life, but he hasn't seriously considered retiring any time soon. "I don't imagine many jobs that would be more fun than this," he told Helen Thorpe. "I mean, I don't really think of it as working. I think if you left the computer industry after having been in it for a long time, you'd be incredibly bored, and your brain would atrophy."

Dell and Susan Lieberman, a former commercial leasing agent, have been married since 1989. They have one daughter, and live in a $12 million home in the hills of Austin, Texas.—P. G. H.

Suggested Reading: *BusinessWeek* p71+ Feb. 2, 1987, with photo, p62+ Mar. 22, 1993, with photos, p132+ Apr. 7, 1997, with photo; *Canadian Business* p97+ Apr. 30, 2001; *Forbes* p82+ Oct. 12, 1992, with photo; *Forbes 400* p318+ Oct. 21, 1991, with photos; *Fortune* p117+ Sep. 18, 1995, with photos, p138 June 9, 1997, p76+ Sep. 8, 1997, with photo, p9+ Oct. 16, 2000; *Inc.* p43+ Jan. 1990, with photos; *New York Times* III p12 July 5, 1992, with photo, D p1+ May 28, 1993, with photo; *San Francisco Chronicle* E p1 Sep. 10, 2001; *Texas Monthly* p117+ Sep. 1997, with photo; *Wall Street Journal* A p1 July 2, 1993, B p1 Jan. 31, 1995

Dennard, Robert H.

Sep. 5, 1932– Inventor of DRAM (a.k.a. Dynamic RAM)

The celebrated IBM inventor Robert H. Dennard was inducted into the National Inventors Hall of Fame in Akron, Ohio, in 1997 for his invention of DRAM (dynamic random access memory; a.k.a. dynamic RAM). With this invention Dennard helped to significantly increase memory density by giving computers the ability to store each single bit of information as an electric charge in an electronic circuit known as a memory cell. DRAMs are used in most electronic devices and have become the industry's standard memory device. In 1996 alone, 2.5 billion units of DRAM were sold, making them the most manufactured object on the planet. Today, Dennard continues working at International Business Machines (IBM) to produce smaller and faster DRAM cells.

Robert Heath Dennard was born on September 5, 1932 in Terrell, Texas. His parents were Buford Leon Dennard and the former Loma Heath. He received his bachelor of science degree in electrical engineering from Southern Methodist University in 1954; two years later he received his master's degree in the same subject from the same institution. For the next two years he worked on his doctorate at the Carnegie Institute of Technology, at Carnegie Mellon University, in Pittsburgh, Pennsylvania.

In 1958, shortly after receiving his Ph.D., Dennard joined IBM's research division in Yorktown, New York, as a staff engineer. Some of his early work at IBM included studying new circuits and other devices used for logic and memory applications in the company's computers. He also aided in the development of advanced data communication techniques. In 1963 he transferred to the IBM Thomas J. Watson Research Center, also located in Yorktown, where he has worked on the development of microelectronics from its infancy. Though he has risen in rank from staff research member (1963 to 1971), to manager (1971 to 1979), to IBM fellow (1979 to the present), he remains dedicated to the task of producing better, smaller, and faster memory cells for computers.

In the 1960s Dennard was involved with the development of IBM's N-channel MOSFET (metal-oxide-semiconductor field effect transistor) devices. Field effect transistors (FETs) had been developed in the early 1960s at RCA laboratories and were considered to be effective replacements for bipolar memory chips, which ran at higher temperatures than field-effect transistors. Though field-effect transistors were slower than bipolar ones, such chips, including MOSFETs, could be made much smaller. Since they were smaller and ran cooler than bipolar chips, many more transistors could be packed onto a single chip. Such a tightening of circuit integration allowed manufacturers like IBM to construct the chips with thousands of components, thereby putting up to 20 layers on a single chip and increasing speeds tremendously. By the 1970s, FETs or MOSFETs were being used in computers. However, there were some limits to the degree to which a chip's circuitry could be minimized.

In "Electronics Design—Looking Forward . . . Looking Back," an article on IBM Research's Web site, the author noted the problems with miniaturization at that time: "For instance, no one had figured out how to reduce the number of tiny transistors in a memory cell. All early storage cells were static; the charge in the cell could be maintained with low amounts of power. But it took four to six transistors to make each cell static. This limited the ability to miniaturize the memory chip."

However, all this changed in 1966 when Robert Dennard attended a lecture on IBM's work in thin-film magnetic memory. The presentation was given by fellow IBM researchers who were using a very simple construct—"a piece of magnetic material and a couple of lines passing near it," as Dennard put it on the IBM Research Web site—to create a memory circuit. The simplicity of their design made Dennard rethink his own complex six-transistor arrangement for storage of a single bit.

"I went home that evening discouraged because their approach looked very simple compared to the complex six-transistor memory cell which my team was using for each bit of data," Dennard remarked to the IBM Press Office upon hearing of his election to the National Inventors Hall of Fame on June 18, 1997. "That evening I started exploring the possibility of storing data in a simpler way as a charge level on a capacitor. Within a few hours I had gotten the basic ideas for the creation of DRAM ironed out in my mind."

Dennard's dynamic random access memory developed from the idea that a single field effect transistor (FET) and data line could do the read and write a charge in a capacitor, thereby replacing multiple transistors. In DRAM technology each single bit of information is stored as an electrical charge in an electronic circuit known as a memory cell. Such technology also produces an increase in memory density. Within a year Dennard and IBM had been given a patent on this important technology, which is now the industry standard for memory. Today, DRAM cells power almost every conceivable electronic device in use. Computers were first treated to the power of DRAM in 1973 when two young engineers presented the details of a fully functioning but experimental 8,000-bit MOS-

FET memory that used Dennard's single-component design. Six years later, IBM presented the world's first 64K-bit DRAM chip, which also used Dennard's one-device cell design. (The first IBM PCs sold in the early 1980s with 64K of RAM, the first Apple MAC with 128K, and by 1985 most personal computers offered 640K as a standard configuration for DRAM.)

In the 1970s Dennard led a team that developed scaling theory—an orderly approach to addressing the problems that arose during attempt to construct smaller computer devices on silicon chips. His group researched methods of shrinking MOSFET even further, and in 1974 they published a seminal paper proving the reliability of their scaling theory. During the same decade Dennard also worked on yield models for integrated memory circuits and developed the theory for redundancy in DRAMs. Since the 1980s he has continued to work toward the miniaturization of devices and integrated circuits, producing MOS devices as small as sub-0.1-micron. Nevertheless, Dennard admits that there are limits to such endeavors. On the IBM Research Web site he noted, "I'm interested in finishing up this thing that I helped get started. And, as we're getting to the limits of this technology, the questions are even more interesting than they've been for a few years, because we're looking for ways around some of the problems." The difficulties to which he alluded include the lower performance, power, and density that result from the chips becoming too small to produce as much power as larger chips.

For his accomplishments, Robert H. Dennard has received numerous awards, including the Cledo Brunetti Award (1982), the 1988 National Medal of Technology presented by President Ronald Reagan, the Industrial Research Institute Achievement Award (1989), and the Harvey Prize from Technion in Israel (1990). From IBM he has been given six Outstanding Invention and Outstanding Contribution Awards, as well as two IBM Corporate Awards.—C. M.

Suggested Reading: IBM Research Web site; *American Men and Women of Science 1998–99*, 1998; Lee, J. A. N., ed. *International Biographical Dictionary of Computer Pioneers*, 1995

Dick, Albert Blake

Apr. 16, 1856–1934 Inventor of the mimeograph

Albert Blake Dick's mimeograph, a product that was ubiquitous in offices and schools for almost a century, is the grandfather of the numerous mechanical and electric duplicating devices available today. Anyone who has had contact with a mimeograph can usually recall the purple ink, dampness, and distinct chemical smell of its copies. Though these machines have, since the 1970s, been replaced by such devices as xerox machines, fax machines, and laser-jet printers, mimeographs were the first machines since the invention of the printing press that could generate multiple copies of the same document with ease.

Albert Blake Dick was born in Bureau County, Illinois, on April 16, 1856, the son of Adam Dick and the former Rebecca Wible. In 1863 the family relocated to Galesburg, Ohio, where young Albert attended public schools. At 16 he went to work for George W. Brown and Co., a local manufacturer of farm equipment. In 1879 he moved to Moline, Illinois, where he worked for the Deere and Mansur Co., a competitor of his former employer. Now an established businessman, he married Alice S. Mathews of Galesburg, in January 1881. (Dick married a second time, in June 1892. This marriage, to Mary Henrietta Mathews, also of Galesburg, took place in Geneva, Switzerland.)

Dick quickly earned enough money to become a partner in the Moline Lumber Company, and in 1883 he established his own Chicago-based lumber enterprise, which he called A. B. Dick and Co. In 1884 he incorporated the firm and became its president and treasurer. At the time handwritten copies of inventory sheets and order forms—all the paperwork needed to run a large company—had to be updated daily. Such handwritten copies were problematic for many reasons: there was much room for human error while copying, individual penmanship (and individual interpretations of that penmanship) varied wildly, and the entire process was far too time consuming. Dick speculated about possible ways to duplicate the necessary sheets without rewriting them by hand. In 1884 he started experimenting with wax wrapping paper, a file, and ink. He created a device he called an "automatic stencil," which employed a sheet of paper with a wax coating. The user could write a form letter on the waxed paper with a stylus, then apply ink to the surface by way of a handheld roller on a flat press, thereby permitting the duplication of hundreds of pages.

Hoping to improve on his invention, Dick contacted Thomas Alva Edison to acquire an electric pen, which he intended to incorporate into the mimeograph. Edison was intrigued by Dick's machine and helped him to refine it by providing not only the electric pen, but a device to coat the waxed stencil sheets. Edison invested financially in the enterprise, as well, and in 1887 the Edison-Dick Mimeograph became the first commercial machine of its type marketed.

Dick abandoned his lumber business to turn his full attention to perfecting and selling his invention. The mimeograph was improved over the years and adapted to typewriters and converted into a rotary device. As office machines became electrified in the late 19th and early 20th centuries, so did the mimeograph. By 1900 the A.B. Dick Co., as it is still known, was selling its duplicating machines throughout America; by the 1920s it was the preeminent supplier of such machines across the globe. By the 1930s the organization had grown

phenomenally: it employed 1,700 people and had its own marketing and sales departments. Dick himself led the company until his death, in 1934, by which time his machines could be found in most schools and offices in the United States.

After Dick's death the company was led by his son, Albert Blake Dick Jr., and later, Dick Jr.'s son, Albert Blake Dick III. The A. B. Dick Company maintained its edge in the duplication market until the 1970s, when other technologies came to the fore. The company is still in business, manufacturing and marketing equipment and supplies to the printing industry.—C. M.

Suggested Reading: A. B. Dick Company Web site

Diebold, John

June 8, 1926– Founder of the JD Consulting Group

John Diebold has been described as a high priest, evangelist, and prophet of the Information Age. If Diebold is more closely identified with automation than any other expert, it is not only because he was the first to use the term in its present meaning or that he has conceived of ingenious uses for the computer. His prominence stems more significantly from his vision of social transformation through automation and from his insistence on making people in industry, government, and education aware of the challenges he believes they must be prepared to face. In *Forbes* (August 15, 1966) he was described as "something of a controversial character with more than a little of the showman about him. . . . Diebold himself, if not a boastful man, has cultivated a brisk, authoritative manner that reinforces that image." Diebold is the founder, president, and chairman of the board of an international, multimillion dollar management-consultant firm, the JD Consulting Group (formerly the Diebold Group), whose assignments involve the future of some of the most influential companies in the United States and Europe as well as of the operations of entire governments.

John Theurer Diebold, the younger of the two sons of William Diebold, a lawyer, and Rose (Theurer) Diebold, was born in Weehawken, New Jersey, on June 8, 1926. His brother, William Diebold Jr., is a senior fellow emeritus at the Council of Foreign Relations. At local public schools—Alexander Hamilton Grammar School, Theodore Roosevelt Grammar School, and Weehawken High School—Diebold acquired a conventional academic training. The early educational forces that nourished his inquiring and creative inclinations came from the encouragement and understanding of his parents, who indulged his eagerness to keep a menagerie of pets, to collect and catalogue thousands of miscellaneous objects of historical and scientific interest, and to set up a research laboratory at home. They also often took him on educational trips, including a visit to Europe in 1937.

World War II was in full swing when Diebold graduated from high school and enrolled in Swarthmore College, in Swarthmore, Pennsylvania. As the war continued, he left college at the end of his freshman year to enter the United States Merchant Marine Academy, at King's Point, New York. Besides taking courses in shipping management and technical and industrial engineering, he served aboard the SS *Shooting Star* on convoy duty in the North Atlantic in 1944–45. He obtained a B.S. degree, with a regimental academic award, in late 1946, and upon his discharge from service, he returned to Swarthmore. His recreations at college included collecting rare books and horseback riding. In economics, his major subject, he achieved scholastic honors, and he also did well in political science and psychology, but meeting language requirements gave him so much trouble that he had to take a special course in German before qualifying for his B.A. degree, conferred in 1949.

During the next two years, as a graduate student at the Harvard Business School, in Cambridge, Massachusetts, Diebold found the subject that would inspire his lifework. In 1950 he was assigned to head a student group project, under the general direction of Professor Georges F. Doriot, to investigate automatic control mechanisms in manufacturing. As he explained to Jeffrey L. Cruikshank for Harvard's *New Business* magazine (Winter 2002), Diebold had become interested in this subject while serving in the Merchant Marines, where his ship's antiaircraft guns employed early self-correcting technology. "I kept thinking if we can build tools and if we have automatic antiaircraft firing control," he recalled, "why can't we have an automatic factory?" In the course of his research on the applications of electronic computers in factories, Diebold interviewed two leading pioneers of computer technology, John von Neumann and Norbert Wiener, and became interested in a complex concept that took him far beyond the group study.

The report that grew out of his research, "Making the Automotive Factory a Reality," became a starting point for Diebold's own pioneering work in automation. Awarded his master of business administration degree with distinction in 1951, he continued to amass and organize a wealth of information and observation, which he presented in 1952 in *Automation: The Advent of the Automatic Factory*. His authoritative, wide-ranging study included an exploration of the probable social and economic changes that would be brought about by automatic manufacturing and processing in the electronic age. As Diebold explained in the *Futurist* (May 28/June 1994), "When I wrote *Automation* over 40 years ago, I did not write it as an exercise in futurism. Instead, I wanted to tell people, particularly managers, that something so significant was brewing that it would change everything, that technologies such as computers and automation would

transform the way we do business. As we look back, that impact is easy to recognize, but at the time, it was very difficult."

Although Diebold is generally credited with coining the word *automation*, a simplified form of *automatization*, he has acknowledged its earlier use by D. S. Harder, an executive of the Ford Motor Company. As Wilbur Cross pointed out in his biography, *John Diebold: Breaking the Confines of the Possible* (1966), "Mr. Harder used the word to describe the use of machines for the automatic processing of parts, whereas the Diebold interpretation relates to the broad application of communications technology, ranging far afield from the factory and the assembly line." For Diebold, automation necessarily involves feedback and control: a machine not only does the work of man, but controls its own operations, such as correcting its mistakes.

Before his book was completed, Diebold had taken a position as a junior consultant with the management consultant firm of Griffenhagen & Associates at a beginning salary of $300 a month, considered rather meager for a graduate of the Harvard Business School. Soon he was transferred from the New York City office to Chicago, Illinois, to serve as personal assistant to E. O. Griffenhagen. Along with gaining practical experience in his consulting assignments, he came into contact with many leaders in business and industry, both nationally and internationally, who influenced his thinking. At the end of three years, however, he was ready for a change. "I left because the boss couldn't see any future in automation," he told Sidney Fields for the *New York Sunday News* (December 23, 1965). "So I started my own firm." (Some sources report that he was fired.)

With the help of his wife, the former Doris Hackett (whom he met at the Griffenhagen company and married on November 22, 1951), Diebold launched John Diebold & Associates, in 1954. For well over a year, using the family home in Weehawken as an office, the couple worked without capital to qualify themselves as experts in all aspects of automation. In 1954 Diebold also took part in the founding of the magazine *Automatic Controls*, to which he contributed a monthly column called "Feedback." Overcoming misconceptions about the word "automation" itself was among Diebold's early problems.

As the significance and inevitability of automation became apparent, several leading companies turned to Diebold for guidance. Diebold moved from Weehawken to an office in New York City, eventually setting up headquarters for the worldwide operations of the newly named Diebold Group. He later opened offices in Los Angeles, San Francisco, Washington, D.C., and Chicago and acquired control in 1957 of the firm that had once employed him, Griffenhagen & Associates. A few years later he merged Griffenhagen with L. J. Kroeger & Associates to form Griffenhagen-Kroeger Inc. Around the same time he took over a Philadelphia consulting firm specializing in marketing, Alderson Associates.

A study made in 1957 by a research branch of the Diebold Group showed that, when companies had been dissatisfied with their investments in computers, it was generally because businessmen handled conversion to automation as a technical, rather than a managerial, problem. Diebold's experts therefore offered planning for the future in all phases of management, but especially provided managerial techniques that facilitated the use of automatic equipment. Believing that a major company must be international in scope if it is to prosper, Diebold in 1958 formed two overseas partnerships: Urwick-Diebold, in England, and Berenschot-Diebold, in the Netherlands. A year or so later he became president of Diebold Europe, S.A., with subsidiaries in Frankfurt, Paris, and Milan. In 1964 he acquired Rothschild Freres as a partner in his management-consulting operations in France.

Diebold has often been called "the elder statesman of automation," and his position in the vanguard of proponents of the new technology was recognized in August 1960 when he was called to Capitol Hill to testify in hearings of the subcommittee on automation and energy resources of the Joint Economic Committee. Regarding automation as the country's "major economic tool" for increased productivity in factories and offices, he urged the formulation of a national policy to promote and make effective use of technological developments. At the hearing and afterwards, he repeatedly warned that, if the United States fell behind the Soviet Union and other countries in taking advantage of technological achievements in automation, it would lose its economic leadership. Diebold also frequently argued that the fear that automation would cause mass unemployment was largely unfounded. He did not deny that there would be some job displacement, but he insisted that automation would eventually create more and better jobs than it eliminated.

Job dislocation, Diebold asserted, was just one, and not the most important, of the many changes that must be prepared for in the new way of life that the machines were creating. "Today's machines," Diebold told a reporter for the *New York Times* (March 28, 1965), "deal with the very core of human society—with information and its communication and use." He predicted the birth of major industries that would provide, for example, the services of researchers, librarians, and teachers through central systems that would be analogous in some ways to those of the electric-utility industry—something not at all unlike the Internet. Information technology, he foresaw, would especially affect methods and products in publishing. Banking, too, he said would undergo enormous changes in the emergence of a cashless society, where buying and selling would involve only an immediate electronic transfer of money and credit.

Diebold served as a member of the advisory committee on manpower and automation to the U.S. secretary of labor in 1962. In 1963 he was a member of President John F. Kennedy's committee

for the Department of Labor's 50th anniversary and of the American delegation to the United Nations Conference on Science and Technology, for the benefit of less developed nations, in Geneva. He was active on behalf of the Institute for the Crippled and Disabled in New York and of the United Epilepsy Campaign. In keeping with his interest in educating for change in the world of automation, he served as chairman of the visiting committee of Clarkson College, in Omaha, Nebraska; was a member of the visiting committee on economics of Harvard University; and on the U.S. advisory committee of the European Institute for Business Administration.

Diebold issued a comprehensive statement of his views in *Beyond Automation* in 1964. When he founded his consulting firm in 1954, there were some 100 computers in the world. By the end of the next decade, the number of computers had increased to about 25,000. Among the clients that he served by 1966 were General Electric, International Business Machines, International Telephone and Telegraph Company, Radio Corporation of America, Westinghouse Electric, Xerox Corporation, and the American Hospital Association. He had also been retained for special assignments by the U.S. Department of Defense, the state of California, and the governments of Nepal, Indonesia, the Philippines, Jordan, and Venezuela.

To facilitate its entry into the areas of operating and manufacturing, John Diebold Inc. was made a holding company in January 1967. Diebold joined, in September 1967, with the Commercial Credits Company and a subsidiary of the Southern Pacific railroad, the Bankers Leasing Corporation, to form the Diebold Computer Leasing Company. The company captured a sizable part of the business for middlemen who bought computers from manufacturers and leased them to users. In 1968 Diebold started the Diebold Venture Capital Corporation, an investment company, but resigned as chairman in 1976 when Erik E. Bergstrom was nominated to direct the company.

In 1969 Diebold published *Man and the Computer: Technology as an Agent of Social Change*, a wide-ranging book that dealt with such subjects as educational technology, business responsibility, managerial training, pollution, the place of man in the universe, gene manipulation, and new developments in industry. L. J. Creek, in *Library Journal* (July 1969), stated, "Although the issues raised [in *Man and the Computer*] have a familiar ring, their seriousness deserves this additional attention." In the *Saturday Review* (July 19, 1969), C. W. Griffin wrote that in the book "a few crisp ideas stand out like cactus plants in a desert of profound banalities" and complained that "Diebold and other contemporary technocrats ostensibly see nothing wrong with the U.S. that can't be cured by more ingenious, efficient use of technology."

Eventually the John Diebold Group changed its name to the JD Consulting Group, and Diebold continued to serve as chairman of the board. He founded and served as chairman of the Diebold Institute for Public Policy Studies, a research foundation. In the mid-1990s, the Institute's "Infostructure" Project looked at how information-based technology could improve our society's health care and transportation systems. "Infostructure," as Diebold explained in the *Futurist* (May 28/June 1994), is short for "information-based infrastructure." "Information technologies," he continued, "offer many opportunities for improving the delivery of public services. Infostructure obliterates geographical limitations: We can now communicate with an individual anywhere on the globe."

In *Making the Future Work: Unleashing Our Powers of Innovation for the Decades Ahead* (1984), Diebold argues for greater privatization and less government involvement in social programs. "[Diebold] exhibits his considerable skill as a lateral thinker—one who can cut across disciplines and apply their lessons to complex issues," Gene R. Laczniak wrote of the book for *Library Journal* (November 1, 1984). In the *New York Times Book Review* (October 21, 1984) Robert Leckachman acknowledged that, in his previous work, Diebold had proven a reliable and prescient source. However, Leckachman expressed reservations about "[*Making the Future Work*'s] notion that information technology is the key to a new civilization. On this score, Mr. Diebold is singularly unpersuasive. . . . [Diebold's] is a world almost naïvely centered upon the self-interest of individuals, almost to the exclusion of the ties of community and social sympathy that define humane societies. His is a new era which I rather hope I do not live to experience."

With the goal of stimulating innovation and improving America's performance in international business competition, Diebold wrote *The Innovators: The Discoveries, Inventions, and Breakthroughs of Our Time* (1990). Sarojini Balachandran, in *Library Journal* (February 1, 1990), called it "a thoroughly readable narrative of modern technological breakthroughs." While George Winslow, in the *New York Times Book Review* (February 4, 1990), lamented that Diebold "rarely explains the technical jargon that riddles this book, and his uninspired prose fails to capture the drama and adventure of scientific discovery," he allowed that "*The Innovators* contains many useful insights into corporate strategies that nurture scientific creativity—skills that will play a key role in shaping the future of the American economy."

Diebold has served as the vice chairman of the board and chairman of the executive committee for the Academy of Educational Development (AED), a nonprofit organization dedicated to improving health and education in the United States and abroad. Among the professional organizations to which Diebold has belonged are the International Cybernetics Association, the Society for the History of Technology, the Systems and Procedures Association, the American Society for the Advancement of Management, the Commerce and Industry Association, and the Institute of Directors.

The U.S. Junior Chamber of Commerce chose Diebold as one of the country's Ten Outstanding Young Men of 1961, and in 1965 Rollins College, of Winter Park, Florida, awarded him an honorary doctor of laws degree. He has been decorated by the governments of Germany, Italy, and Jordan and was awarded the Legion of Honor by the government of France. He received the Distinguished Information Scientists Award from the Data Processing Management Association in 1980.

Diebold has a daughter, Joan, born in 1962, from his first marriage, which ended in divorce in 1975. He married Vanessa Vonderporten on June 12, 1982, and the couple has two children, Emma and John.

Diebold's views on technology have apparently changed little from when he summed up what might be called his own American dream in a speech at Columbia University in 1963: "Our task today is wisely to use our technology, our knowledge of history and our compassion, to make the age of automation a golden Periclean age in which a society based on the work of the machine—not human chattel—rises to the full heights of which the human spirit is capable."—P. G. H.

Suggested Reading: *Computerworld* p18 Feb. 25, 1991; *Forbes* p35 Aug. 15, 1966; *Futurist* p34+ May 28/June 1994; *National Observer* p8 Apr. 18, 1966; *New York Times* III p1+ Nov. 27, 1960, III p3 Mar. 28, 1965, p39 Oct. 23, 1976; Cross, Wilbur. *John Diebold: Breaking the Confines of the Possible*, 1966

Diffie, Whitfield

(DIFF-ee)

June 5, 1944– Mathematician; engineer; inventor; political activist

Although Internet commerce is common today, concerns remain that personal messages and online transactions can be intercepted, thus revealing credit-card numbers and other confidential information. As a student at the Massachusetts Institute of Technology (MIT), in Cambridge, during the 1960s, Whitfield Diffie wanted to protect his computer files from being accessed without his knowledge or consent; at the same time, he imagined a time when people would do business by communicating through their computers. However, in order for what he called a "paperless office" to become a reality, Diffie believed that all computer communications must be protected from improper third-party access, including access by the government. He tapped his childhood passion for cryptography, the process of disguising messages and information by turning them into code, as a means to secure computer communications. In 1975 Diffie and Martin Hellman, a professor of electrical engineering at Stanford University, in California, invented "public key cryptography," which successfully

Courtesy of Sun Microsystems Laboratories

Whitfield Diffie

provided security for communications between two computer users in different locations. Today, technology based on public key cryptography is used by telephone companies, Internet providers, computer manufacturers, banks, corporations, and government agencies to protect communications and data. Over the past 20 years, information security has blossomed into a billion-dollar industry. Speculating that advances in technology would threaten personal privacy, Diffie also became a political activist who strongly opposed attempts by the government to control the availability of encryption.

Whitfield Diffie was born on June 5, 1944 in Washington, D.C., and grew up in the New York City borough of Queens. His father, Bailey Diffie, was an author and college professor of Latin American history and Spanish, and his mother, Justine, conducted scholarly research on Madame de Sevigne, the 17th-century French woman of letters. Although he was raised in an academic household, Diffie was a poor elementary-school student and refused to read until he was 10 years old. When asked what he did as a child by Thomas Bass, who interviewed Diffie for *Omni* (Winter 1995), he replied, "The same thing I do as an adult. I mostly remember staring off into space." Diffie's fifth-grade teacher, Mary E. Collins, introduced him to cryptography, the process of protecting information and messages by converting them into a secret code that can be deciphered only by the person who has the appropriate key. "I found that I enjoyed unraveling secrets," he told Neal Thompson for the *Baltimore Sun* (December 31, 1998). As a youngster he read passionately on the subject of cryptography, and he also developed a passion for

mathematics, which he often studied on his own. In junior high school Diffie indulged in typical adolescent activities. "But I changed completely in high school," he recalled to Bass, "and the discussion groups of the Ethical Culture Society became the social and intellectual foundation of my life. I became a peacenik, marched for nuclear disarmament, sang folk songs in Washington Square Park. Wild parties became places where you sat around discussing the meaning of life."

Diffie enrolled at MIT in 1961. He initially expressed contempt for computers, thinking they were beneath his skills as a mathematician. A short time later, however, he began using MIT's computers for his own research and studies. Diffie became interested in computer privacy when he discovered how easy it was for anyone to access his computer files. "Whatever password I had on them, system programmers could always get at my files," he explained to Bass. "I saw the only way to control my files would be to encrypt them." Diffie graduated from MIT in 1965 with a B.S. in mathematics, and to avoid being drafted to fight in Vietnam he accepted a position with the Mitre Corporation in Beford, Massachusetts. Mitre developed command and control systems for the military, and Diffie worked as a computer programmer on Mathlab, an interactive tool for symbolic mathematics that eventually became Macsyma, a software program that is still used today.

Diffie's fascination with cryptography intensified after he read David Kahn's lengthy history of cryptography and espionage, *The Codebreakers* (1967). "It brought people out of the woodwork, and I certainly was one of them," Diffie told Steven Levy for *Wired* (May/June 1993, on-line). "I probably read it more carefully than anyone had ever read it. By the end of 1973, I was thinking about nothing else." In 1969 Diffie left the Mitre Corporation and found work with Stanford University's Artificial Intelligence Laboratory. He collaborated with John McCarthy, who made several contributions to the development of artificial intelligence. Diffie researched "proof of correctness of programs," which, as he described to Bass, "aspires to mathematically prove that the programs you write will always do what you want them to do."

In 1972 Larry Roberts, a Pentagon official, asked McCarthy to work for the Advanced Research Projects Agency (ARPA), which developed the network of military computers that became the foundation for the Internet. Roberts sought more effective ways to protect the network of computers from being tampered with or accessed by unauthorized users. Diffie, due to his interest in both cryptography and protecting his own computer files, volunteered his services. Several encryption programs existed at the time, but they were too slow, in his opinion. "I thought a serious cryptographic program should be able to encrypt a file as fast as you could copy it," Diffie told Bass.

As early as the 1970s, Diffie believed that computers would play a significant role in people's lives. He envisioned a world in which people shopped, conducted business, and exchanged personal messages through their computers. Diffie wanted to protect these computer communications and transactions from unauthorized access, especially by the government. (At the time, a series of political scandals collectively known as Watergate, which involved the attempts of the Nixon administration to collect damaging information on political opponents, was just unfolding.) By the spring of 1973 Diffie's research had come to be focused exclusively on cryptography, and he took an indefinite leave of absence from Stanford, where he was supposed to be working on proof of correctness. He traveled throughout the country to conduct library research and consult cryptography experts. Upon his return to Stanford, almost two years later, he met Martin Hellman, a professor of electrical engineering who dabbled in cryptography. (Diffie was referred to Hellman by Alan Konheim, a cryptography researcher at IBM in Yorktown Heights, New York.) Diffie and Hellman became friends and formed a partnership to explore effective ways to secure computer communications. In 1975 Diffie enrolled at Stanford University as a graduate student in electrical engineering and became Hellman's research assistant.

Diffie grappled with ensuring secure communications between users at different locations. One user could easily send someone an encrypted message, but the question remained as to how the intended recipient would be able to decipher the message and keep the key private. In May 1975 Diffie figured out a solution. He told Bass that in classical cryptography, "the cryptographic variable," or key, controls how text is transformed into "ciphertext," or code. To encrypt and decrypt messages, users had to have the same key, which is an enormous series of mathematical equations and algorithms. However, this system would be ineffective because it would be nearly impossible for users to share keys with one another. To communicate by a secure means and build a more efficient cryptographic system, Diffie proposed that users split the keys they generated in two pieces, which he called the public key and private key. "Imagine you want to send me a secure message," he explained to Bass. "You look up my public key in your phone book, plug into your machine, and encrypt a message for me in such a way that it can be read only with my private key. I generate the key pair and disseminate my public key as widely as possible, but I keep the private key to myself." Diffie called this system "public key cryptography," which provides a widely accessible cryptographic means to users and also ensures that messages are read only by the intended recipient. Hellman initially dismissed Diffie's two-part solution, but ultimately concluded that it was a revolutionary, yet practical, idea.

Diffie and Hellman soon encountered another problem. In the business world people needed to sign contracts, agreements, and other documents to make them legally binding, which seemed to be impossible in a paperless interaction. Additionally, in cyberspace it was easier for a person to use a false identity; security was required to ascertain and authenticate the identity of the user sending the communication. Diffie proposed adding a "digital signature" to encrypted messages. A digital signature belonging exclusively to the user would be the equivalent—and just as binding—as a regular signature on a paper document. When a user's system generates its own key, the system also generates its own digital signature to accompany outgoing messages.

Diffie and Hellman discussed how public key cryptography could protect communications in "Multi-User Cryptographic Techniques," which they presented to the National Computer Conference in New York City in 1976. The paper caught the eye of Ralph Merkle, a graduate student in computer science at the University of California at Berkeley. Merkle had some ideas about securing communications through random mathematical puzzles; he transferred to Stanford and worked with Diffie and Hellman to put the concept of public key cryptography into practice. In November 1976 Diffie and Hellman published "New Directions in Cryptography" in the *Institute of Electrical and Electronics Engineers (IEEE) Transactions of Information Theory.* "We stand today on the brink of a revolution in cryptography," they wrote, as quoted by Steven Levy for *Wired* (November 1994, on-line). This paper detailed how public key cryptography and digital signatures could be accomplished through complex mathematical algorithms. In 1980 Diffie, Hellman, and Merkle obtained a patent for their data encryption method, known as the "Diffie-Hellman key management system." The patented system served as the basis for many products that protect communications and "is a fundamental part of security and privacy infrastructure on the Internet today," as Chris Jones observed in *Wired News* (September 16, 1997, on-line). In 1985 Cylink purchased the patent, and licensed it to such companies as Intel, Cisco, AT&T, Motorola, and IBM. Other than $10,000 from Cylink for each of the three, Diffie, Hellman, and Merkle did not profit further from the invention. The patent expired in 1997, and the Diffie-Hellman key management system then became available to users in the public domain.

The Diffie-Hellman system served as the basis for more advanced public key cryptography systems. Based on Diffie and Hellman's work, three scientists at MIT—Ronald Rivest, Adi Shamir, and Leonard Adleman—decided to create on their own system. By May 1977, Rivest, Shamir, and Adleman had developed alternative ways to split keys and generate digital signatures. Their system, named "RSA," was more effective than the Diffie-Hellman system, and they secured it with a patent.

In his article for the *Proceedings of the IEEE* (May 1988), Diffie wrote that Rivest, Shamir and Adleman made "the single most spectacular contribution to public-key cryptography." By the mid-1980s, RSA Data Security Inc. was offering users public key encryption software for about $250.

As they were working on public key cryptography during the mid-1970s, Diffie and Hellman found themselves increasingly involved in politics. In 1975 they opposed the federal government's decision to adopt an IBM data encryption standard (DES), which would be used by banks and corporations to protect their secrets. "We thought its key was too small," Diffie told Bass. Additionally, Diffie alleged that the government was pushing IBM's system so it could easily access important secrets anytime. Diffie and Hellman also publicly clashed with the National Security Agency (NSA), over government control of encryption; the scientists felt that the if the government oversaw encryption that the privacy of computer users would be compromised.

Diffie never completed his graduate studies at Stanford University; instead, in 1978, he accepted a position as manager of secure systems research for Northern Telecom, a telecommunications company in Mountain View, California, where he worked on securing telephone lines. Although he designed a secure telephone system, it was never developed as a commercial product. However, as Levy noted for *Wired* (November 1994), part of Diffie's design "became the heart of an innovative product called PDSO, or packet data security overlay, used to provide end-to-end security between hosts on packet data networks." In 1991 Diffie joined Sun Microsystems in Palo Alto, California, as a distinguished engineer and advisor on computer and communications security. Two years later Diffie and Ashar Aziz secured a patent for a developing a method that provided secure communications between a mobile unit and a network.

In addition to his work for Sun Microsystems, Diffie has devoted more time to political activism during the past decade; he became known as a privacy advocate, and he testified before Congress and spoke at conferences. In 1993 he opposed the Clinton administration's proposal calling for a new federal encryption standard, which was known as the "key-escrow system." Diffie and many others observed that the key-escrow system required the placement of a "Clipper chip" in telephones and a "Capstone chip" in computers. Both the Clipper and Capstone chips provided users with tamper-resistant encryption. However, both chips provided a back door that made it easy for the government to decrypt telephone conversations, computer communications, and data. The effect of this new encryption standard "is very much like that of the little keyhole in the back of the combination locks used on the lockers of schoolchildren," Diffie told Ivars Peterson for *Science News* (June 19, 1993). "The children open the locks with the combinations, which is supposed to keep the other children

out, but the teachers can always look in the lockers by using the key." In his interview with Bass, Diffie suggested that the "government is obviously terrified about the proliferation of [encryption] products over which it has no control."

In *Privacy on the Line: The Politics of Wiretapping and Encryption* (1998), Diffie and Susan Landau wrote "If people are to enjoy the same effortless privacy in the future as they have in the past, the means to protect that privacy must be built into their communication systems." William G. Staples, in his review of the book for *Scientific American* (September–October 1998), observed, "This volume makes an important contribution to this scholarship by focusing on the intersection of new telecommunication technologies and government access to these electric channels. . . . Anyone interested in issues of technology, privacy and electronic communication will find it informative as well." The book won the Donald McGannon Award for Social and Ethical Relevance in Communications Policy Research and the IEEE-USA award for Distinguished Literary Contributions Furthering Public Understanding of the Profession.

Diffie has expressed displeasure that more people aren't more concerned with their privacy, telling Bass that "the vast majority of the world's communications is still uncrypted. Interception costs are dropping, meaning the need to protect telecommunication channels is rising, and at some point the situation will spark a vast range of products. But so far people still don't see the damage being done to them by insecure communications, so they keep postponing the decision to do something about it."

In his book *Crypto: How the Code Rebels Beat the Government—Saving Privacy in the Digital Age* (2001), Steven Levy profiled Diffie and celebrated him as a hero for co-inventing public key cryptography. Diffie's role in developing public key cryptography and securing communications has been recognized many times. He has been honored with the IEEE's Information Theory Society Best Paper Award (1979), the IEEE Donald E. Fink Award (1981), the Electronic Frontiers Foundation's Pioneer Award (1994), the National Computer Systems Security Award (1996), the Franklin Institute's Louis E. Levy Medal (1997) and the Association for Computing Machinery's first Paris Kanellakis Award. In 1992 the Swiss Federal Institute of Technology presented Diffie with an honorary doctorate in technical sciences.

Diffie is married to Mary Fischer, an Egyptologist. They live in Woodside, California.—D. C.

Selected Reading: *Baltimore Sun* A p1 Dec. 31, 1998; *Computerworld* p93 Sep. 9, 1996; *New York Times* A p26 Oct. 19, 1977, Aug. 19, 1995 (on-line); *New York Times Book Review* (on-line) Jan. 14, 2001; *Omni* p86+ Winter 1995; *Science News* p394+ Jun. 19, 1993; *Scientific American* p487 Sep.–Oct. 1998, *Wired* (on-line) May/June 1993, Nov. 1994; Levy, Steven. *How the Code*

Rebels Beat the Government—Saving Privacy in the Digital Age, 2000

Dijkstra, Edsger

May 11, 1930– Computer programmer; mathematician

Edsger Dijkstra first made his mark in the late 1950s and early 1960s by contributing to the development of the computer language ALGOL. His algorithms have helped computer programmers to simplify their programs and maximize their abilities, as with his "shortest-path algorithm," which enabled planners more efficiently to deploy communication networks. His "shortest spanning tree algorithm" helped the designers of the X1 computer to use the minimum amount of expensive copper wire. His "dining philosophers problem" inspired programmers to search for a means to facilitate the flow of information between the computer and its keyboard, as well as from program to program and network to network, without freezing up the system or denying some workstations access to information. By remarking that "GO TO [is] considered harmful," he prompted software designers to develop less complex programs which were also easier to use.

Edsger Wybe Dijkstra was born in Rotterdam in the Netherlands on May 11, 1930. He is the son of Douwe Wijibe Dijkstra, a chemist, and the former Brechtje Cornelia Kluyver, a mathematician. Since both of his parents were scientists, Dijkstra was exposed to scientific reasoning and expressed a great interest in the subject at an early age. His work on the shortest-path algorithm was partly influenced by his mother's philosophy on mathematics. As quoted by Dennis Shasha and Cathy Lazere in their book *Out of Their Minds: The Lives and Discoveries of 15 Great Computer Scientists* (1998), Dijkstra recalled, "I asked my mother whether mathematics was a difficult topic. She said to be sure to learn all the formulas and be sure you know them. The second thing to remember is if you need more than five lines to prove something, then you're on the wrong track."

Dijkstra was also fascinated by building things. As a young boy he became entranced with his older sister's Meccano set, which was similar to an American Erector set. Using the long metal strips with holes, he built a number of machines, including two cranes. One crane was built to retain its center of gravity directly above the fulcrum no matter how heavy the load became. The other was constructed so that the load would remain the same height from the ground despite a change in the distance between it and the crane's center.

When Dijkstra was 12 years old, during World War II, he enrolled in the Gymnasium Erasminium, an elite Dutch high school, where he acquired a classical education in Greek, Latin, French, German, physics, biology, chemistry, and mathematics. However, when food was scarce near the war's end, his family sent him out of the city. As he told Shasha and Lazere, "I traveled with a friend of a friend of my father's who still had a car. We drove to the country. There was no gasoline. The car has to run on methane. . . . The radiator broke. It was freezing. I was 14 and very weak—my heart couldn't manage more than 40 beats per minute."

In July of 1945, just after the war ended in Europe, Dijkstra rejoined his family. With the hardships of war behind him and feeling a new sense of political optimism, he considered studying law and serving his country as ambassador to the newly created United Nations. However, his father, after seeing how well he had scored on his final examinations in math, physics and chemistry, talked him out of such a career. Dijkstra enrolled at the University of Leiden and chose to study theoretical physics, figuring that "mathematics would look after itself." As a physics major at the university, he realized that many problems he encountered required extensive calculations. He therefore decided to take summer courses at Cambridge University in England, where he learned to program early computers in 1951. (Since the British had deciphered many German codes during the war with their calculating machines, England was considered to be the best place at that time to study programming.) In March 1952, just after earning his Candidaats degree from the University of Leiden, Dijkstra began working part-time at the Mathematical Center in Amsterdam, where he grew even more interested in the art of computer programming. Eager to complete his physics degree so he could better concentrate on programming, he earned his doctorate in 1956 and began to study programming more intensely. He received a Ph.D. in computing science from the Municipal University of Amsterdam in 1959 and continued working at the Mathematical Center as a programmer until 1962.

Computer programmers in the Netherlands in the 1950s faced a number of difficulties. First and most personally to Dijkstra, programming was not recognized as a real profession; when he applied for a marriage license in 1957 he thus had to say he was a "theoretical physicist." Second, before the creation of such computer programming languages as FORTRAN or LISP, programmers had to write programs to suit a particular computer. As a result, programming complexity was often sacrificed to accommodate a particular machine's design. But the hardware designers who worked with Dijkstra on the ARMAC machine at the Mathematical Center did the opposite; they built into the machine only those features which Dijkstra, as the programmer, deemed vital. "They would never include something in the machine unless I thought it was okay. I was to write down the functional specification that was the machine's reference manual. They referred to it as 'The Appalling Prose'—it was as rigorous as a legal document," he explained in *Out of Their Minds.*

In 1956, while still working for the Mathematical Center, Dijkstra was asked to demonstrate the ARMAC's computational abilities at the next International Mathematical Conference. It was for this demonstration that he devised the "shortest-path algorithm," a solution to the problem of finding the shortest route between two points on an imaginary railroad map. This relatively simple solution struck him one Saturday morning, while he and his wife were drinking coffee on the terrace of a café. Better known today as Dijkstra's algorithm, his solution was to form an expanding "core set" of cities between the city of origin, City S, and the destination city, City T. During the course of the entire algorithm, the user knows the minimum time between City S and every city in the core set. (For example, it takes no time to drive to City S since you are already there.) With every step, the user finds another city—City X—outside the core set that takes a shorter amount of time to reach than any other city. Since each route takes at least 0 minutes to drive, City X is linked to some city called Y in the core set. Driving to City X then takes the minimum amount of time to drive from Y to City S after the user adds the time to drive from Y to X. After adding X to the core set the user records the time computed so far. When City X is actually City T, the trip is concluded.

Dijkstra did not bother to publish his algorithmic solution, simply because he did not believe that such a solution would be valued by mathematicians, who were at that time more concerned with infinity and continuum. Since finite problems were considered inconsequential, it was not deemed mathematically important to conclude that any finite set has a minimum, as occurs in the shortest-path algorithm. Today, however, his algorithm is used to calculate, for example, airplane flight paths, road building, and communication networks. Dijkstra developed another algorithm, called the "shortest spanning tree algorithm," to aid ARMAC'S designers in determining the most efficient means of conveying electricity to essential circuits while using as little expensive copper wire as possible.

In the early 1960s Dijkstra was a principal contributor to the development of ALGOL, an early computer programming language that was considered a model of mathematical clarity. At the same time he began his innovative work on mutual exclusion and cooperating sequential processes. This work resulted from his designing of ARMAC's successors, the X1 and the X8. The machines themselves were large and bulky with a core storage cycle of only ten microseconds, a green button to turn the machine on, and a red button to shut it off. Dijkstra's software design, however, was revolutionary and his ideas have been incorporated into almost every memory board and processor since the IBM 360 Series released in 1964.

Dijkstra's ideas were in some ways very simple: he arranged for each component attached to the computer to perform its tasks one step at a time

while it informed the computer of its actions. Without this method, called communicating sequential processes, two processes may access the same information at the same time, thereby enabling one process to modify the information, which in turn causes the other to behave incorrectly. To avoid this occurrence, Dijkstra developed a means of synchronization he called mutual exclusion, whereby only one process has access to the information at a given time while it locks out the other. He used this idea specifically for the communication between a computer's keyboard and the computer itself. To facilitate the exchange of information between these two devices, he employed a buffer through which only one of them might read or write information at one time. His rationale was quoted in *Out of Their Minds*: "The cooperation of a number of units each with its own speed and clock—that was the given of the technology. What I wanted to do was arrange the cooperation in such a way that it would be independent of the relative speed ratios. I wanted to do this for safety's sake."

To achieve clean reasoning in communication among the various computer processes, Dijkstra employed the commands P and V. P stands for the Dutch word *passeren*, which means "to pass"; V stands for *vrijgeven*, which means "to give free." Both terms are still in use, even while English remains the dominant language in computer science. Nearly all modern processors use these operations in their hardware and memory boards as "test and set" instructions that will return either success— by temporarily locking the buffer—or failure, by preventing the use of a locked buffer.

In the fall of 1965, Dijkstra articulated his next computer engineering problem for his students at the Einhoven Technical University. Today called the "dining philosophers problem," it considers five philosophers sitting around a table, each with a bowl of rice in front of him and a single chopstick on either side of the bowl. The rules of the meal are simple: each philosopher must think for a while, eat for a while, and wait for a while. However, each must eat using two chopsticks and each can communicate only by raising and lowering his chopsticks. The problem is how all of the philosophers get a chance to eat. After all, they each need two chopsticks in order to eat, but if one of them uses two chopsticks it will deprive the philosophers seated to that person's left and right of a second chopstick. If anyone picks up two chopsticks, the others must wait; if they all take a chopstick deadlock occurs and none of them can eat. A "lack of fairness" could occur if one philosopher continues to eat and talk while the others wait. Such problems occur frequently in computer networks when, for example, computers on a local network share one modem wire. When all the users attempt to access the wire, the computers will freeze up. If one receives preference, others may never get access. A viable solution to this now classic dilemma was not proposed until 1975, when Michael Rabin, while on sabbatical at the Massachusetts Institute of Technology (MIT), in Cambridge, suggested using a random process to break through network gridlock; a computer can be programmed to wait a randomly determined amount of time after first receiving a "busy signal" before attempting to access the shared network a second time.

Dijkstra, in the meantime, became interested in working to eliminate the "GO TO" command in computer programs. After being unsatisfied with a demonstration of a procedure to eliminate existing GO TOs during a conference in Baden bei Wein, Austria, in 1964, Dijkstra spent the remainder of his evening developing programs that had no GO TO prompts at all. He argued that GO TO was a troublesome method, since it provided no means for a program to return to a job once it had begun working on another. As computer programs became more complex, GO TO commands became more and more confusing to follow. By the next morning Dijkstra was trying to impress upon his associates the benefits of his new style, noting that such a procedure would make programs even simpler. He also created a LOOP-EXIT command which would solve any structural problems that may result from the absence of a GO TO command. In March 1968 he published a famous article in *Communications of the ACM* in which he called GO TO "harmful" and said programmers should eliminate such procedures from their programs. Since that time, almost all programming textbooks have adopted his technique. For his work in advancing computer programming, he received the ACM Turing Award in 1972.

In 1973 Dijkstra left his teaching position at Eindhoven Technical University for a research position at the Burroughs Corporation in Nuenen in the Netherlands, where he advocated greater control and verifiability of programs, which turned out to be an unpopular notion. In 1984 he came to the United States after receiving a professorship at the University of Texas, in Austin, where he holds the Schlumberger Centennial Chair in Computer Science.

Dijkstra has received several notable awards for his work, including the AFIPS Harry Goode Memorial Award (1974) and an honorary doctorate from Queens University in Northern Ireland (1976). He continues to serve as editor of the journal *Acta Informatica* and is a distinguished fellow of the British Computer Society and the Royal Netherlands Academy of Arts and Sciences, as well as an honorary foreign member of the American Academy of Arts and Sciences.

Dijkstra married Maria Cornelia Debets on April 23, 1957; they have three children—Marcus Joost, Femke Elisabeth, and Rutger Michael.

In the *International Biographical Dictionary of Computer Scientists* (1995), the author of a profile of Dijkstra remarked that that the measure of the man could be seen in the influence he has had on his students. The author noted, "This influence has been caused by his particularly perceptive and brilliant mind, his intense desire to be professionally honest, a discipline that is unequaled, and a way with the pen (in both form and content) that others would kill to attain. His ability to make a decision on technical grounds and then to put it into practice is unrivaled. He seems to have been endowed with all the good qualities one would like to see in a scientist, and he has taken care to sharpen them."—C. M.

Suggested Reading: *Association for Computing Machinery* (on-line); *Mike Nussdorfer's Faculty Home Page at Kalamazoo College* (on-line); University of Texas Computer Science Department Web site; *American Men and Women of Science, 1998–99*, 1998; Lee, J. A. N., ed. *International Biographical Dictionary of Computer Pioneers*, 1995; Shasha, Dennis and Cathy Lazere. *Out of Their Minds: The Lives and Discoveries of 15 Great Computer Scientists*, 1998

Time Life Pictures/Getty Images

Eastman, George

July 12, 1854– Founder of the Eastman Kodak Company

When George Eastman, the founder of the Eastman Kodak Company, decided that the conservatory in his lush mansion in Rochester, New York, was too small, he proceeded to deal with it as he had dealt with nearly everything else in his life: by finding the best—although not necessarily the easiest—solution and pursuing it with thorough directness. He had the entire house cut in half, moved one side 10 feet away, expanded the room, and then rejoined the two halves. As a young man in the 1870s, when he set out to simplify the then-cumbersome process of photography, he employed the same meticulous determination. After several years of experimenting in his mother's kitchen, he perfected the mass production of a novel type of photographic plate and started a business to sell his new product. The first handheld camera followed not long after, as did the first flexible, rolled film and 35mm motion-picture film. In 1900 the company introduced the Brownie, a camera that even a child could operate and that cost only one dollar. In so doing, Eastman brought photography to average people of modest means and paved the way for the ascendance of the visual image as a primary means of communication—seen in movies, television, newspapers, magazines, advertising, and the Internet. Eastman expected the type of dedication from his employees that he always gave to his work, but he was also among the first to provide employees with cash bonuses, profit shares, and retirement plans. As a leading philanthropist he championed education and donated some $100 million to various causes over the course of his life.

The youngest of three children, George Eastman was born to Maria (Kilbourn) and George Washington Eastman on July 12, 1854 in Waterville, New York. When Eastman was five his father gave up his nursery business in order to establish the Eastman Commercial College, in Rochester, New York. He died shortly thereafter, leaving Eastman and his mother in a difficult financial position. When he was 14, Eastman left school to work and earn money for the family, which included two sisters, one of whom was disabled. He worked first as a messenger boy for an insurance company, earning three dollars a week, and a year later, became an office clerk for a different insurance company. Soon he greatly expanded his duties, even writing some policies for the firm. When not working Eastman studied accounting, hoping to secure a better-paying job, which he did in 1874, when he was hired as a junior clerk at the Rochester Savings Bank.

At the age of 24, Eastman, preparing to take a vacation to Santo Domingo, in the Dominican Republic, bought a camera so he could record the trip for his mother. He did not realize what an undertaking was in store for him. The camera itself was bulky and heavy, as were the tripod and the glass plates upon which the film was to be developed. Because photographs had to be taken and developed while the photographic solution was still wet, one had to spread collodion on a glass plate to serve as the emulsion, or light-sensitive coating, immediately before taking a picture. A portable dark room, including a tent, photographic chemicals, glass tanks, a plate holder, and other equipment had to be brought along. Eastman didn't go on the trip to Santo Domingo (although he would later travel and published two books of travel memoirs), but he never gave up on his newfound desire to, as he famously said, "make the camera as convenient as the pencil."

Determined to read everything available about photography, Eastman taught himself French and German. Finally, he read in an English journal about a relatively new photographic technique. A gelatine emulsion had been discovered that remained light-sensitive even when dry, thus allowing photographers a new freedom. For three years Eastman conducted experiments in his mother's kitchen late into the night until he discovered his own gelatin emulsion recipe, which he patented, in 1880, along with a machine for mass producing gelatine-coated plates. In April 1880 Eastman started his own business selling the plates, and the next year he quit his job to devote his full time to the business. Sometimes he did not sleep at all for five days at a time, so fervent was he about establishing himself. His success, however, was limited because there were still few photographers. Furthermore, some batches of plates he'd given to various dealers went bad, and the cost of providing new ones to customers nearly sent his business into bankruptcy. "Making good on those plates took our last dollar," said Eastman as quoted on the official Kodak Web site. "But what we had left was more important—reputation."

Though gelatine plates made photography more convenient than it had been, Eastman felt that the glass plates were still too unwieldy. In 1855 Frederick Scott Archer, a British inventor, had patented a method for replacing the glass backing with paper, but the technique never caught on. In 1884 Eastman incorporated his company, calling it the Eastman Dry Plate and Film Company, and started experimenting with using paper backing on his film. A year later he introduced the Eastman/Walker roller slide—developed with a colleague named William Walker—which consisted of a paper base upon which were layered a soluble gelatine beneath an insoluble gelatine emulsion. After exposure and development, the insoluble gelatine bearing the image could be stripped from the paper by dissolving the soluble gelatine layer, and then mounted on a sheet of clear gelatine and coated with a varnish.

Eastman's roller slide conveniently fit most existing cameras. However, it did not catch on, and Eastman decided to produce a simple-to-operate camera to use the film. Upon the introduction of the camera, in 1888, Eastman invented the brand name *Kodak*. " I devised the name myself," said Eastman, as quoted on the Kodak Web site. "The letter 'K' had been a favorite with me—it seems a strong, incisive sort of letter. It became a question of trying out a great number of combinations of letters that made words and ending with 'K.' The word 'Kodak' is the result." The Kodak camera included a 100-exposure supply of film and sold for $25, roughly 17 days salary for a general laborer in those days.

With the release of the new camera Eastman coined the slogan, "You push the button, we do the rest." Eastman was savvy about advertising his products and has been credited for ushering in the age of modern advertising. He was responsible for Kodak's widely recognized bright-yellow packaging and for the Kodak Girl posters that pictured fashionable women carrying Kodak cameras. He paid for advertisements in newspapers, magazines, displays, and billboards, and in 1897 London's Trafalgar Square was lit by an electric Kodak sign, one of the first such signs to be used in advertising.

In 1886 Eastman had employed a research scientist to pursue methods of producing flexible film that could be rolled up, and in 1889 the company introduced a transparent, flexible rolled film made of nitrocelluloid, an offering which also initiated a long, drawn-out lawsuit: In 1887 the Reverend Hannibal Goodwin had applied for a patent for nitrocelluloid rolled film, but it was not granted until 1898. Goodwin died two years later, and the company that had acquired the rights to his invention sued Eastman's company. Finally, in 1914 Eastman settled for $5 million.

In 1889 Thomas Edison asked Eastman to produce film for his newly invented movie camera, and in 1891 Eastman offered 35mm rolled film for that purpose. In 1909 Eastman convinced his international competitors to embrace the 35mm dimensions, still the standard today. In 1891 Eastman's company released the first daylight-loading camera, which allowed photographers to change film in the light. The following year the company changed its name to Eastman Kodak. In 1895 Eastman Kodak introduced a pocket camera that sold for five dollars. A folding pocket camera followed in 1898; its $2\frac{1}{4}$-by-$3\frac{1}{4}$-inch negative became a standard size for decades to come. In 1900 Eastman finally met his goal of making cameras available to nearly everyone when Kodak introduced the Brownie camera. Selling for one dollar, the camera was marketed to children and named after the popular cartoon characters known as Brownies created by Palmer Cox. The film sold for 15 cents a roll. (The company made additional profit, however, by developing the film into finished photos.)

Known for his fair treatment of workers, in 1898 Eastman began offering a cash reward to employees who made suggestions that proved helpful to the company. The next year he offered all of his employees cash bonuses drawn from his own personal funds. He then offered his employees a bonus salary awarded in proportion to yearly stock dividends. In 1919 Eastman donated one-third of his company stock, or $10 million, to his employees. He later provided retirement plans, life insurance, and disability benefits, all of which were novel for the time. In *George Eastman* (1996), Elizabeth Brayer wrote, as quoted on the Kodak Web site, "Mr. Eastman was a giant in his day. The social philosophy, which he practiced in building his company, was not only far in advance of the thinking during his lifetime, but it will be years before it is generally recognized and accepted."

Aside from his devotion to work, Eastman also dedicated himself passionately to his hobbies. An avid hunter and fisherman, he designed his own camping gear and always served as the camp cook. He devised a recipe book with ingredient listings as minutely accurate as his chemical formulas for Kodak. He loved music and often hosted concerts and musicales. His luxurious mansion in Rochester was equipped with an Aeolian organ, and he paid a performer to play for him twice a day.

In 1921 Eastman established the Eastman School of Music at the University of Rochester, which was one of his many acts of philanthropy. He was interested in improving dental treatment and donated millions to dental clinics around the world, but his main interest was in improving education. "The progress of the world depends almost entirely upon education," Eastman once said, as quoted on the Kodak Web site. Greatly impressed with employees he had hired out of the Massachusetts Institute of Technology (MIT), in Cambridge, he gave a series of anonymous gifts to the school, which amounted, over the course of several years, to $20 million. He helped develop a medical school and hospital at the University of Rochester, and in 1924 he gave a $30 million joint endowment to the African-American Hampton University, in Virginia, and the predominantly African-American Tuskegee Normal and Industrial Institute (now Tuskegee University), in Alabama. In total, Eastman gave approximately $100 million to charities in his lifetime.

Eastman's company continued to expand prodigiously throughout his life, which according to some, was partly the result of his somewhat ruthless business tactics—including industrial espionage and exertion of his near monopoly on film. "Eastman clearly used numerous patents he and his crew obtained to discourage rivals," wrote Joseph Losos in the *St. Louis Post-Dispatch* (August 11, 1996), "although he came to boast that his success was largely due to the 'difficulties of manufacture which have been surmounted by us in a larger degree than by anyone else.'"

Toward the end of his life, Eastman contracted a crippling spinal disease. On March 14, 1932 he invited a group of friends and colleagues to his mansion to witness the signing of his will. As they were exiting the house he shot himself in the heart, leaving a note that read, "To my friends: My work is done. Why wait?" Eastman died a bachelor and left his residual estate to the University of Rochester. In 1949 his mansion and archives were turned into a museum and research center, the George Eastman House, which is dedicated to documenting the history of photography.—P. G. H.

Suggested Reading: *American Enterprise* p80+ Sep./Oct. 1996; *Forbes* p400+ Nov. 30, 1998; *Guardian* I p30 June 3, 2000; *New York Times* E p6 May 22, 2000; *St. Louis Post-Dispatch* C p5 Aug. 11, 1996; *North American Biographies— Vol. 3: Entrepreneurs and Inventors*, 1990; *Hutchinson Dictionary of Scientific Biography*, 1999

Eckert, J. Presper

Apr. 9, 1919–June 3, 1995 Co-creator of the ENIAC and the UNIVAC

Conducting his research under the specter of World War II, J. Presper Eckert used the economic and military initiatives set in motion by the global conflict to develop technology that he hoped would eventually contribute to the betterment of humanity. Together with John Mauchly, Eckert built the Electronic Numerical Integrator and Computer (ENIAC), in 1945, ushering in the computer age. The ENIAC was the first fully functional, large-scale electronic digital computer. Inspired by Vannevar Bush's mechanical differential analyzer, which had been invented 20 years earlier, the ENIAC was able to work with mathematical problems of enormous complexity. It was 1,000 times faster than the major computer breakthrough that preceded it, Howard Aiken's Mark I. Although John Atanasoff is actually credited with having invented the electronic computer, his invention, the ABC, was never completed and was only a small-scale prototype model. Thus the ENIAC is widely viewed by computer historians as the first direct ancestor of the computer as we know it today. Furthermore, Eckert also helped design the UNIVAC, which was the first computer built in America for commercial use and is considered by many to mark the beginning of the modern computer boom.

John Presper Eckert Jr. was born in Philadelphia, Pennsylvania, on April 9, 1919, the son of J. Presper Eckert Sr. and Ethel M. (Hallowell) Eckert. Prior to college he attended the William Penn Charter School. He then entered the Moore School of Electrical Engineering at the University of Pennsylvania, in Philadelphia, and attained a bachelor's degree in 1941. Shortly after graduating, he joined the faculty of the Moore School, teaching various engineering and science courses in addition to conducting research in the design of radar range systems. Eckert was working as a researcher at the Moore School when the United States entered World War II, in 1941, an event that would profoundly effect the course of his professional career.

While a graduate student at the Moore School, Eckert met Dr. John Mauchly, who discussed with him the idea of constructing an electronic calculating machine. Both men found that they shared a common frustration. They had mastered mathematical theory, but were unable to practically apply most of it because of the problems inherent in performing the onerous calculations that were involved. "I always think of it as like having a nice larder or a pantry full of canned goods, and you don't have a can opener," Eckert explained to Peter Vogt in an interview for the Smithsonian Institute. Mauchly was looking for a partner to supervise the design and construction of an electronic computing device, which he hoped would be the answer to these frustrations, and he chose Eckert to fill the role. Mauchly composed a memorandum summarizing their ideas for the new computer and distributed it to the university administration and faculty to see if anyone was interested in their plans. The memo eventually came to the attention of Drs. Herman Goldstine and John Brainerd, who recommended putting together a formal proposal. Once the proposal was completed, in 1943, Goldstine and Brainerd presented the idea for the computer for the computer to the U.S. Army, pitching it as an electronic, digital version of Vannevar Bush's differential analyzer, which had operated on an analog system. "Mauchly and I were still finishing the appendices for the proposal, which weren't quite finished yet, putting a few drawings in and finishing it in the next room," Eckert said to Peter Vogt. "So we weren't in on the presentation; we were still finishing the paperwork when [Goldstine and Brainerd] made the presentation." The proposal was accepted the same day, and so in 1943, the same year that Eckert received his master's degree, he and Mauchly began working under a contract from the army's Ballistic Research Laboratory to develop their computer for use in compiling ballistics tables, which were needed for aiming heavy artillery.

The calculations required for aiming the guns had previously been accomplished through inefficient, painstakingly slow, and often error-plagued means, sometimes resulting in disaster. For the past several years, the army had been using the differential analyzer, but it was simply not fast enough. Eckert had attempted to speed it up by installing 400 vacuum tubes and thus making it partially electronic, but the best option for improving speed proved to be the construction of an entirely electronic device. Eckert and Mauchly believed that their invention would provide a way of performing the necessary calculations by an automatic method that went far beyond those employed by the mechanical calculators available at the time.

The result of their efforts was ENIAC which was completed at the end of 1945 with the help of 50 engineers, at a cost to the army of $500,000. It contained over 18,000 vacuum tubes that were connected to hundreds of electrical cables. Attached to the machine was a device that resembled an old-fashioned telephone switchboard, which was used for entering instructions into the computer. The ENIAC data was stored on punched cards, similar to those pioneered by 19th-century French weaver Joseph Jacquard and later employed by IBM-founder Herman Hollerith in his mechanical census tabulator. Weighing over 30 tons and covering a total of 233 square feet of floor space, the ENIAC was capable of completing in 30 seconds an artillery trajectory calculation that would take a person 20 hours to solve. It could perform 357 multiplications per second. A revolutionary innovation that enabled the computer to achieve such speed was the concept of subroutines, which allowed the computer to be programmed to perform an action repetitively instead of requiring the instruction to be re-entered for every repetition. "I've been told since then that [British inventor Charles] Babbage had some thoughts like this in his work, but I had not studied Babbage at the time," Eckert commented to Vogt. In addition to trajectory calculations, the new digital computer was also used to perform calculations used in nuclear physics, aerodynamics, and weather prediction; it was also used to process data for the Manhattan Project, which led to the development of the atomic bomb. The ENIAC was turned on for the first time in January 1946, and was housed at the University of Pennsylvania, in Philadelphia.

Eckert made several important contributions and modifications to the design of the computer. In response to the high failure rate of vacuum tubes, he ran them at a low voltage and employed hundreds of old-fashioned plugs instead of the brittle solder connections commonly used (as it was, the ENIAC still had 500,000 hand-soldered connections). By changing the arrangement of the plugs, the ENIAC could be "reprogrammed" to calculate solutions to a wide range of mathematical problems. Because the machine was programmed through the use of these external plugs, it did not truly store its own programs, a capability that is considered a defining characteristic of modern computers.

Although ENIAC was indeed a major breakthrough in computing, it came into being just as the potential of stored programs began to be discussed as a serious possibility by experts in the field. In fact, it is Eckert himself who is credited with being the first to use the word "program" in the sense in which it came to be used with regard to computers in the late 20th century. Eckert had been asked in 1946 to work on a stored-program computer called the EDVAC. Although the project eventually fell through, Eckert delivered a speech concerning the EDVAC at the Moore School in which he presented the modern concept of stored programming, stating, "We are simply going to use the memory to hold the information electronically and to feed those pieces of information which relate to programming from the memory into the control circuits in order to sequence the machine so that it will perform its various operations" (*IEEE Annals of the History of Computing*, Spring 1996).

Riding the success of the ENIAC, Eckert and Mauchly left the Moore School and established the Electronic Control Company in 1946. It was the first business created specifically for the construction of computers. In 1947 the company name was changed to the Eckert-Mauchly Computer Corporation, and Eckert became the vice president. In 1949 they designed the BINAC (Binary Automatic Computer), which stored data on magnetic tape instead of punched cards. One of the first operational stored-program computers, the BINAC actually consisted of two computers that worked simultaneously on the same calculations and then compared their results. The BINAC was used by the Northrop Aircraft Company, but on the whole it was found to be not reliable enough for routine service. The Eckert-Mauchly Computer Corporation

was sold to the Remington Rand Corporation in 1950, at which point Eckert became a director of engineering.

Before becoming a part of Remington Rand, the Eckert-Mauchly Corporation, under the guidance of its two founders, began work in 1948 on the Universal Automatic Computer, or UNIVAC. The machine was completed three years later. The UNIVAC I was the first American computer designed specifically for commercial use. It had magnetic tape memory and included the first main control console. It also contained 5,000 vacuum tubes and was able to store 1,000 12-decimal digit words, or units of data. There was an even an output mechanism, in the form of an electric typewriter. As a result of the tremendous success of the new device, the former Eckert-Mauchly Corporation became known as the UNIVAC Division of Remington Rand. The first U.S. government agency to make use of the machine was the Bureau of the Census. Shortly after the introduction of the UNIVAC, the company merged with the Sperry Corporation in 1955 and became known as Sperry Rand. Eckert remained with Sperry Rand as vice president in charge of engineering. The company would eventually merge with the Burroughs Corporation to form Unisys, a leading computer firm as of the late 20th century.

The ENIAC remained in use throughout the mergers and name changes, before being put out of service in 1955. Eight years later the UNIVAC I was retired, after more than 73,000 hours of continuous operation over 13 years, and it was given to the Smithsonian Institute. In 1964 J. Presper Eckert was given an honorary doctorate from the University of Pennsylvania. Four years later, President Lyndon B. Johnson presented Eckert with a medal for his work with computers. He worked for Unisys until his retirement in 1989, although he continued to be a consultant to the company afterwards.

Eckert's and Mauchly's work came under attack in 1973, when a Federal court ruled a critical patent of theirs to be invalid. The court stated that the concept of the ENIAC's design was actually derived by Mauchly from the work of John Atanasoff of Iowa State University, who had invented an electronic computer called the ABC in 1939. Although the ABC was never fully completed, and could not solve problems on the level of those completed by the much larger ENIAC, the ABC is now credited as being the original electronic digital computer, and not the ENIAC, as was previously believed. Eckert remained skeptical of Atanasoff's accomplishments, however: In a 1990 letter to a group of students, he criticized Atanasoff's work, claiming, "He never really got anything to work. He had no programming system. Mauchly and I achieved a complete workable computer system. Others had not" (*New York Times*, June 7, 1995).

Eckert married Hester Caldwell on October 28, 1944 at age 25. Together they had two children, John Presper III, and Christopher. Hester later died, and Eckert remarried in 1962. He and his second wife, Judith, had two children of their own, Laura and Gregory.

J. Presper Eckert died on June 3, 1995 in Bryn Mawr, Pennsylvania, at the age of 76. The cause of death was reported to be complications from leukemia. He was survived by his second wife of 33 years, as well as by his four adult children, and three grandchildren. Eckert's death was preceded by that of John Mauchly, who died in 1980. That same year, just prior to Mauchly's death, the two men had jointly received the IEEE Computer Society Pioneer Award. Eckert obtained 87 patents in his lifetime, the majority of them for his work on computers. His work on the ENIAC and the UNIVAC will always be remembered as his greatest achievements. While modern computers are light years beyond their 1940s predecessors, many of the elements that were a part of ENIAC and UNIVAC, chief among them the use of binary language, are still in use at the end of the 20th century. The introduction of electronics brought speed to the world of computers, a factor that remains a driving force in the development of new computing technology to this day.—B. S.

Suggested Reading: *Smithsonian Computer History* (on-line) Feb. 2, 1988; *IEEE Annals of the History of Computing* p51+ Spring 1996; *New York Times* B p12 June 7, 1995

Getty Images

Edison, Thomas Alva

Feb. 11, 1847–Oct. 18, 1931 Inventor

Thomas Alva Edison never wondered *whether* something could be done, only *how*. "Genius," he once said, as quoted in *Harper's Monthly* (1932), "is one percent inspiration, ninety-nine percent perspiration." His list of major inventions, including electric lighting, the phonograph, improved telegraph and telephone communications, and alkaline storage batteries, helped shape the 20th century. Edison received a record 1,093 patents from the U.S. government, including 150 for the telegraph, 34 for the telephone, 389 for electric light and power, 195 for the phonograph, and 141 for storage batteries. As Paul Gray wrote in *Time* (December 31, 1999): "He created the look and sound of contemporary life."

Before the American Revolution, Thomas Alva Edison's paternal ancestors lived in New Jersey as loyal British subjects. When war broke out they moved to Nova Scotia, Canada; later generations moved to Ontario and fought with the British against the United States during the War of 1812. Edison's mother, the former Nancy Elliot, was born in New York but during her youth moved with her family to Vienna, Canada, where she met her future husband, Samuel Edison Jr. In the 1830s Sam Edison, as he was known, was involved in a failed rebellion against British rule in Ontario, after which he fled with his wife to the United States. In 1839 the couple settled in Milan, Ohio.

The Edisons' seventh and youngest child, Thomas Alva Edison, was born on February 11, 1847 in Milan. The family soon moved to Port Huron, Michigan, where Sam had secured a position as lighthouse keeper and carpenter on the Fort Gratiot military compound. Despite the deaths of two of his sons and a daughter, as well as his lack of financial success, Sam maintained a cheerful disposition. The same could not be said for his wife who, devastated by her children's deaths, became sterner as the years passed, and never wore anything other than black. Young Thomas, known as Alva or Al by his family and intimates, took on his mother's sober disposition.

Edison was a sickly boy and, after a bout of scarlet fever, he began to lose his hearing. By the age of 12 he was completely deaf in one ear, and he was plagued by poor hearing in the working ear for the rest of his life. He regarded his hearing loss as a boon, because it allowed him to concentrate on research without distraction. (Edison himself believed that his hearing loss was accelerated when a man lifted him to safety by his ears as he was trying to jump aboard a train.) His poor hearing also encouraged his love of reading. As a boy, his favorite book was *The School of Natural Philosophy*, in which the author described scientific experiments he conducted in his makeshift basement laboratory.

Edison's great appetite for books was his main education. His formal education was limited to five years of sporadic attendance at the local public school. (Some sources say he attended school for as little as three months.) Bullied by his classmates and bored by the rote memorization then standard in the classroom, he was such a poor student that one of his teachers called him "addled" and unteachable. Upon hearing this, his irate mother—once a schoolteacher herself—took him out of school and taught him at home. As an adult, Edison remarked: "My mother was the making of me. She was so true, so sure of me, and I felt I had some one to live for, some one I must not disappoint," as quoted in Martin V. Melosi's *Thomas A. Edison and the Modernization of America* (1990) on the Library of Congress American Memory Web site.

Nancy Edison allowed her son's imagination to flourish and marveled at his interest in mechanical devices and chemistry. In order to buy supplies for his basement laboratory, Edison took a job selling newspapers and candy on the Grand Trunk Railroad, which ran from Port Huron to Detroit. At age 12 he was working 12-hour days, riding the train back and forth, reading books and napping when he wasn't hawking his wares. He did find time to conduct experiments in the baggage car, where he set up a laboratory and printing press. He founded the *Grand Trunk Express*, the first newspaper published aboard a train. When a fire broke out, he was forced to stop his experiments, but later in life he would recall his three years as a newspaper boy to be among his happiest.

In 1862 Edison saved a three-year-old's life by pulling him off a track before a boxcar could roll over him. The child's father, J. U. MacKenzie, was so grateful that he offered to teach Edison about telegraphy as a reward. This was a great opportunity for a young man interested in science; the telegraph, recently invented by Samuel Morse, was a booming technology that allowed for speedy communications over great distances by Morse code, a series of dots and dashes tapped out on a single-key keypad. Between 1863 and 1867 Edison moved across the country, from the Midwest to the South to New England, as a telegraph operator. Telegraph work also allowed him to stretch his scientific legs for the first time. As the technology grew more and more popular, telegraph wires were so overburdened that messages frequently had to be turned away, since only one message could be sent over a wire at any time. Edison began to study the problem and looked for ways to maximize wire use. He realized that if one message could travel in one direction, another could be sent in the opposite direction. In 1868 he perfected the duplex telegraph, which allowed two messages to travel at the same time. He took out seven patents for his improvements on the telegraph system and quickly found himself courted by a number of investors, who wanted him to pursue other ideas.

In 1869 Edison gave up his telegraph job to become a full-time inventor. His first invention, the electric vote recorder, received a patent in June 1869, but was a commercial flop because politicians were unwilling to use the machine. He swore never to waste time in the future inventing devices that no one wanted, and turned his attention once again to improving telegraphy. Over the next few years he organized two manufacturing shops, both in Newark, New Jersey, for building telegraph devices. He perfected the duplex telegraph, the automatic telegraph (which recorded messages through a chemical reaction brought about by electrical transmissions), and the quadruplex telegraph (which allowed four messages to be sent over a single wire). In addition to this work, he also invented an improved stock ticker, for which he received $40,000 dollars from Western Union. With this money he formed the Newark Telegraph Works to manufacture the stock tickers. He also developed an electric pen and autographic press copying system, in 1875.

Edison was now financially secure and involved with work he thoroughly enjoyed, but his personal life was changing. In 1871 his mother died. On Christmas Day that same year he married his 16-year-old employee, Mary Stilwell, with whom he would have three children: Marion Estelle (born 1873), Thomas Alva Jr. (born 1876), and William Leslie (born 1878). Though Edison loved his wife, he fought with her often, due in part to the fact that he was more devoted to his work than his family and preferred to sleep in the lab and spend time with his colleagues. Their relationship was further strained by Mary's poor health.

In 1876 Edison completed construction on a new laboratory for himself and a dozen employees in Menlo Park, New Jersey. The press dubbed the complex an "invention factory" after Edison bragged to a reporter that he and his employees planned to develop "a minor invention every ten days and a big thing every six months or so," as quoted in the *Library of North American Biographies, Volume 3: Entrepreneurs and Inventors* (1990). Edison's invention factory lived up to expectations. One of the first great inventions to emerge from Menlo Park came in 1877, while Edison was working on an underwater cable for the automatic telegraph. He discovered that the conductivity of carbon varied according to the pressure placed upon it. This enabled Edison to create what he called a "pressure relay," using carbon—rather than the magnets that had previously been used—to manipulate electric currents. He quickly understood that such a pressure relay would improve the quality of sound over a telephone, a device invented by Alexander Graham Bell only a year earlier. By the end of 1877 Edison had perfected the carbon-button transmitter, which is still in use in modern telephone speakers and microphones.

Edison's improvements to the "speaking tele-graph," or telephone, led to his conceptualization of the phonograph, also in 1877. Edison came to believe that telephone messages—human voices—could be transcribed, just as telegraph signals were recorded by the automatic telegraph. (The tele-phone was not yet considered as a tool of person-to-person communication, but instead as a way to relay messages.) A French inventor, Léon Scott, had theorized that a sound, if recorded, would pro-duce a unique shape, which might be readable by a sensitive instrument. Edison created his phono-graph by using a tinfoil-covered cylinder, a needle, and a diaphragm, or flexible disk, used to catch sound vibrations. Though primitive, this machine was able to record and play back a human voice; the first voice recorded was Edison's recital of "Mary Had a Little Lamb." Edison imagined that the phonograph could be used to record messages, which could then be sent by telegraphs, or tran-scribed as letters. He did not believe it should be used to record music, however. "I don't want it sold as an amusement," he remarked, as quoted by John Kehoe in *Biography* (November 1, 1997, on-line). "The phonograph is not a toy." Though the phonograph astonished its first listeners, which in-cluded the staff of *Scientific American*, and gar-nered international renown for its inventor, the product did not take off for another 10 years.

Setting the phonograph aside, Edison turned his attention to developing an electric light. Edison's study of electricity was an offshoot of work he did for a group of American scientists, who needed a sensitive instrument to detect tiny variations in the temperature of the Sun's corona during a solar eclipse, which occurred on July 29, 1878. Edison built a microtasimeter, a spectroscope attached to a microscope, which used a carbon button to ana-lyze light. Edison accompanied the scientists to the Rocky Mountains to observe the solar eclipse. Lat-er, the men began discussing electric arc lighting, an existing technology that, according to Victor Parachin in *Popular Electronics* (September 1998), "produced light by jumping a bright arc of electric-ity between two electrically charged rods." Arc lamps were not practical for everyday use since they burned too brightly and were very expensive, but they nonetheless generated great interest. Edi-son believed he could build a device similar to a microtasimeter to control the current and prevent the bulb from overheating.

With the backing of financiers (including the Vanderbilts and J. P. Morgan), Edison set out to build an inexpensive light source, capable of brightening a small room as well as a street. His leading trouble was coming up with a filament that had the ability to burn inside a vacuum. He experi-mented with platinum, chromium, nickel, osmi-um, boron, and silicon, among others, before dis-covering that a filament of carbonized thread could produce a long-lasting light source. Victor Parachin cited Edison's description of that discov-ery. "We built the lamp and turned on the current.

It lit up, and in the first breathless minutes we mea-sured its resistance quickly and found it was 275 ohms—all we wanted," Edison recalled. "We sat and looked and the lamp continued to burn, and the longer it burned the more fascinated we were. None of us could go to bed. . . . We sat and just watched it with anxiety growing into elation. It lasted about forty-five hours, and then I said, 'If it will burn that number of hours now, I know I can make it burn a hundred.'"

Edison didn't stop with the light bulb—he invented the entire system for sustaining electrical lights, from generators (co-created with Francis Upton), to switches, safety fuses, and junction box-es. Between 1881 and 1882 he designed the first power plant. He also established the companies to build and distribute the necessary parts for the sys-tem, including the Edison Electric Illuminating Company of New York, the Edison Machine Works, the Edison Lamp Works, and the Edison Electric Tube Company.

Edison's electric light was not without its com-petitors. The greatest challenge came from George Westinghouse, who argued that alternating current (AC) was better than the direct current (DC) pro-posed by Edison, which was unable to travel as far as AC could. Edison, in turn, complained that AC had the potential for accidental electrocution. In 1889 it was discovered that a device using an AC induction motor with a DC dynamo performed best, and after that AC became dominant. This did not lessen the significance of Edison's invention. As Victor Parachin remarked: "Edison's develop-ment of the electric light transformed the history of civilization. Because of his light bulb, daytime was lengthened—making it possible for people to enjoy evening leisure hours and to conduct business for more hours in a day. Electric light freed factories to operate two or more shifts, producing more goods. Edison's electric light bulb made the lives of people far more comfortable than those of previ-ous generations."

In January 1881 the first single-building electric lighting system was built for the New York printing firm of Hinds and Ketcham. The first commercial central-power system was established in Lower Manhattan in September 1882. Though the early systems were plagued with problems, Edison and his electric companies made a significant dent in the lighting market during the 1880s, challenging the dominance of gas lighting. In 1892 Edison left the electric business when his company merged with Thomson-Houston to become the General Electric Company (GE).

On August 9, 1884 Mary Edison died of a brain tumor after a bout of typhoid fever; she was 29. Edi-son was devastated by his wife's loss and troubled by the idea of raising three young children by him-self as a 37-year-old widower. Six months after Mary's death, he met 20-year-old Mina Miller through mutual friends. They married, on Febru-ary 24, 1886, and had three children: Madeleine (born 1888), Charles (born 1890), and Theodore (born 1898). Edison devoted himself to his new family and grew distant from the children from his first marriage.

Shortly before his second marriage, Edison had bought Glenmont, a mansion in West Orange, New Jersey. He built a sophisticated laboratory near Glenmont, and set out to perfect the phonograph he had abandoned years earlier. This new laboratory housed a library, machine shop, and phonograph and photograph departments as well as additional buildings for metallurgy, woodworking, and chemistry. His renewed interest in the phonograph was spurred by improvements made to it by other inventors, most notably Chichester Bell and Charles Sumner Tainter, who had created the Graphophone, which used a wax recording cylinder and a floating stylus. Adopting some of Bell and Tainter's improvements, Edison attempted to market his phonograph as a business dictation machine through the North American Phonograph Company. This attempt proved unsuccessful, and the company went bankrupt in 1894. Two years later Edison opened the National Phonograph Company and begrudgingly marketed phonographs for home entertainment purposes, including the recording of music. In this market the phonographs met with much greater success. By 1909 Edison switched from making cylinder phonographs to the more popular disc-playing machines.

Some of Edison's other ideas proved as impractical as the business dictation phonographs had been. For many years he was involved in unprofitable attempts to extract metal from ores in East Coast mines, and he tried, unsuccessfully, to promote the construction of concrete homes. However, such ideas were far outweighed by his many brilliant and useful inventions. While thinking about a way to popularize the phonograph by linking it to a zoetrope, a machine that created the illusion of motion by quickly flipping photographs in sequence, Edison envisioned a full-motion device, with synchronized sound. He entrusted the project to William K. L. Dickson, an Edison employee with an interest in photography. Dickson and Edison studied a number of European photographers who had experimented with recording full motion. They then attempted to build a cylinder-based device, which proved to be flawed. When Edison returned from a trip to Paris, in October 1889, Dickson surprised his boss with a new invention—celluloid-film strips that, when turned with a crank on a sprocket system, projected moving pictures. After some additional collaboration, Edison patented a motion-picture camera and a motion-picture peephole viewer, known respectively as the Kinetograph and the Kinetoscope. In one short film sequence shot in their laboratory, a man mimes a sneeze, accompanied by the sound of a sneeze recorded on an Edison phonograph. Unfortunately, the two men were unable to find a practical way to synchronize sound and motion, so they abandoned that idea, thus giving birth to the era of the silent movie.

By 1894 Kinetoscope parlors were opening in New York City and other metropolitan centers. By peering through a peephole, viewers could watch short films depicting circus performers, animals, and people performing everyday activities. Edison produced movies in a studio in West Orange that he dubbed "Black Maria." This building—the world's first motion-picture studio—was covered with tar paper, had a hole in the ceiling to allow sunlight to illuminate the stage, and was set on tracks, so that it could be moved to follow the sun. Other film companies began to rival Edison's invention with the development of screen-projector systems that allowed a large audience to see a film together. (Dickson was fired for assisting in the development of this kind of system.) In order to face his competition, Edison bought a film projector developed by Thomas Armat and Charles Francis Jenkins, renamed it the Vitascope, and marketed it as "Edison's latest marvel, the Vitascope." When it premiered in New York, in April 1896, it was highly praised.

Edison's later years were spent running his various businesses and trying to turn a profit from his long-standing investments in concrete and ore extraction. In 1899, however, he began work on one of his last and greatest inventions, alkaline storage batteries, which he developed while searching for a power source for the phonograph. (Most houses in the United States at this time still lacked electricity.) By 1909 Edison was supplying batteries for American submarines; three years later his friend, Henry Ford, asked him to build a battery for a self-starting motor in his Model T automobiles. Edison and Ford's friendship endured for the remainder of Edison's life; in October 1929 Ford staged an extravagant 50th-anniversary celebration of the electric light, which featured a nearly exact reproduction of Edison's old Menlo Park laboratory.

In 1911 Edison reorganized his various companies into Thomas A. Edison Inc., an organization more structured and diversified than his previous companies, but with the primary goal of maintaining the market viability of such Edison products as electric light, film, and recorded sound, rather than producing new inventions. During this period Edison became less and less involved with the day-to-day operations of his company, instead preferring to travel and dedicate himself to government commissions, including his membership, from 1915 to 1921, on the Naval Consulting Board. The board was the American government's attempt to bring science into its defense programs, which had grown considerably with the advent of World War I. In 1926 Edison stepped down as president of his company and turned the reins over to his son, Charles. As the 1920s came to a close, Edison's health worsened, though he continued to perform experiments at home. He was granted his last patent only a few months before he died, on October 18, 1931, at his estate. At the request of President Herbert Hoover, Americans dimmed their lights for one minute on the evening of Edison's funeral, October 21st, to commemorate the man who had laid the foundations for the modern world.—C. M.

Suggested Reading: *Biography* (on-line) Nov. 1997; Brief Edison Chronology (on-line); Library of Congress American Memory Web site; *Popular Electronics* p46+ Sep. 1998; *Time* p184+ Dec. 31, 1999; *Chambers Biographical Dictionary*, 1997; *Library of North American Biographies, Volume 3: Entrepreneurs and Inventors*, 1990

AFP/Getty Images

Einstein, Albert

Mar. 14, 1879–Apr. 18, 1955 Creator of special and general theories of relativity

The most famous scientist of the 20th century and one of the greatest of all time, Albert Einstein brought unique insights and an unsurpassed creative imagination to physics, which he revolutionized with his special and general theories of relativity. From an early age he had a sense of the world as a harmonious and understandable whole, "which stands before us like a great, eternal riddle." He believed, he said, "in Spinoza's God, who reveals himself in the harmony of all being." This "cosmic religious feeling" induced Einstein to try to describe nature with a mathematical system of great beauty and simplicity. The result was a scientific theory that forever changed the definitions of time, space, energy, and matter and laid the foundation for nearly all subsequent research in theoretical physics. Perhaps not since Isaac Newton has a scientist so fundamentally altered the world's view of the nature of the universe. "The world has changed far more in the past 100 years

than in any other century in history," the physicist Stephen Hawking wrote in *Time* (December 31, 1999). "The reason is not political or economic but technological—technologies that flowed directly from advances in basic science. Clearly, no scientist better represents those advances than Albert Einstein."

Albert Einstein was born in Ulm, Germany, on March 14, 1879, the son of Hermann and Pauline (Koch) Einstein. He grew up in Munich, where his father and uncle ran a small electrochemical plant. Einstein was a quiet, withdrawn child who was attracted to mathematics but otherwise disliked school because of its rote teaching and military-like discipline. During his undistinguished years at the Luitpold Gymnasium, in Munich, he read philosophy, mathematics, and popular science on his own and was deeply impressed by the idea of an orderly universe. Recalling his childhood, Einstein wrote in his brief autobiographical memoir *Albert Einstein, Philosopher-Scientist* (1949), "A wonder of . . . nature I experienced as a child of four or five years, when my father showed me a compass. That this needle behaved in such a determined way did not fit into the nature of events which could find a place in the unconscious world of concepts (effect connected with direct 'touch'). I can still remember—or at least I believe I can remember—that this experience made a deep and lasting impression upon me. Something deeply hidden had to be behind things."

When his father's business failed, in 1895, and the family moved to Milan, Italy, Einstein remained behind. But soon he quit school, feigning a nervous breakdown, and without having earned a diploma, he joined his family. The 16-year-old Einstein was struck by the atmosphere of freedom and culture he found in Italy. Although he had superior, largely self-taught mathematical and scientific knowledge and was precociously independent in his thinking, he had not chosen a career. At his father's urging to study for a technical occupation, needed to bolster the family's meager finances, he took the examination for entrance to the Swiss Federal Institute of Technology, in Zurich, which did not require a high-school diploma. Because he was unprepared, he failed; but the school's principal, who recognized Einstein's mathematical ability, sent the boy to finish high school in Aarau, 20 miles west of Zurich. Einstein flourished in Aarau, enjoying the close contact with teachers and the absence of militarism. He so resented his earlier experiences that he formally requested an end to his German citizenship, to which his father reluctantly assented. After a year's study in Aarau, he passed the examination for the Swiss Federal Institute in the summer of 1896.

In Zurich, Einstein studied physics, again paying more attention to his independent reading than to his courses. He had planned to teach at the Swiss Federal Institute, but after graduating in 1901 and becoming a Swiss citizen, he was not granted a teaching post at the school. Instead, he began teaching at the Winterthur Technical School, a high school, in 1901. In 1902 he went to work as a patent examiner in the Swiss Patent Office in Bern, a position he held for seven years. This was a happy and productive time for him. He had already published one paper, on capillarity (the effect on the surfaces of liquids in narrow tubes). Although his salary was barely enough to support him, his patent work was sufficiently undemanding to allow him the time and energy to pursue theoretical scientific investigations. His early papers dealt with intermolecular forces and applications of statistical thermodynamics. One of them, "A New Determination of Molecular Dimensions," was accepted as a doctoral dissertation, and the University of Zurich awarded him a Ph.D., in 1905.

It was also in 1905 that he published a small group of papers that not only established his powers as a theoretical physicist but also changed the face of physics. One of these papers, related to his early work, explained Brownian motion, the chaotic zigzagging of particles suspended in a liquid, which increases at higher temperatures. Einstein showed that particle motion, observable with a microscope, was caused by collisions with unseen molecules; moreover, he predicted that such observations would permit the calculation of the masses and numbers of molecules in a given volume. His prediction was confirmed by Jean Perrin a few years later. Einstein's accomplishment was particularly significant because the existence of molecules as anything but a convenient invention was much in dispute at the time, and his work gave atomic theory a major piece of corroborative evidence.

Another of the 1905 papers explained the photoelectric effect, the emission of electrons from a metal surface irradiated by ultraviolet rays or other electromagnetic radiation. In 1902 Philipp von Lenard had suggested that the electrons were knocked out by the impact of the light. He had also predicted that electrons ejected by a brighter light (one with a higher amplitude) should emerge at greater speeds, because the metal was being bombarded by more energy. His experiments showed that this was not the case, but no explanation was found. In 1900 Max Planck had tried to figure out how the radiation a heated object gives off (black body radiation) is related to its temperature. He made the radical proposal that the energy was not emitted continuously, but in discrete particles that came to be called quanta. The physical significance of a quantum was obscure, but its magnitude equaled a certain number (Planck's constant) multiplied by the frequency of the radiation.

Combining the insights of Lenard and Planck, Einstein revealed the precise mechanisms of the photoelectric effect, and relatedly, the dual particle-wave nature of light. A light energy particle is called a photon, the name given to a quantum of electromagnetic energy. Each photon's energy level is dependent on the frequency of the light, with energy increasing as frequency increases. A light source of a high amplitude (bright) and low frequency radiates many photons, each of which is relatively low-energy. A light source of a low amplitude and high frequency radiates fewer photons, each of which is relatively high-energy. Electrons ejected by a high-energy photon have a high kinetic energy; in other words, they move faster. No matter how many lower-frequency photons hit a piece of metal, the electrons emitted will not have as much kinetic energy as those emitted by higher-frequency photons. Einstein found that the electron's kinetic energy equaled the energy of the photon shone upon the metal, minus the amount of the energy required to dislodge the electron from its attachment to the metal. Light must have a dual nature: it could behave like a wave, as demonstrated by centuries of optical experimentation, but it could also behave like a particle, as in the photoelectric effect. This discovery later earned Einstein the Nobel Prize and helped launch the field of quantum physics that so troubled him later in life.

Einstein's view was to be confirmed experimentally many times, not only for light but for X rays and gamma rays. In 1924 Louis de Broglie proposed an additional step in the transformation of physics: that matter, such as electrons, also had wave properties. This idea, too, was experimentally confirmed and laid the groundwork for the field of quantum mechanics. Einstein's contributions to quantum theory also elucidated such phenomena as fluorescence and photoionization and explained puzzling variations of the specific heat of solids at different temperatures.

Einstein's third dramatic achievement in 1905 was his special theory of relativity, which applied to bodies moving at constant velocities. It gradually revolutionized all areas of physics. At the time, it was generally believed that light waves were transmitted through the "ether," a mysterious substance thought to fill the universe. Ether, however, eluded all experimental attempts to demonstrate it. An ingenious experiment in 1887 by Albert A. Michelson and Edward Morley failed to detect any difference between the velocity of light measured parallel to the motion of the earth through the supposed ether and its velocity measured at right angles to the motion. If ether carried the light as a disturbance, as air propagates sound waves, the ether velocity should add to or subtract from the apparent velocity of light, just as a river affects the velocity, relative to an observer on the shore, of a boat being rowed downstream or upstream. Although it is not certain whether Einstein was directly influenced by the Michelson-Morley results, his new theory was based on two universal assumptions that dispensed with the need for the ether: all laws of physics should appear the same to all freely moving observers; and light always travels through free space at the same velocity, regardless of the motion of its source.

The consequences of these assumptions changed ideas of space and time. Light always travels at the same speed and abides by the same physical laws for all observers. Therefore, to make the velocity of light the same for moving and stationary observers, moving clocks must run more slowly (because velocity equals distance divided by time). Even the meaning of the word *stationary* must be carefully considered. Motion or stillness must always be relative to some reference observer; an observer riding on a moving object is stationary relative to the object but may be moving relative to some other observer. Since the concept of absolute time is abandoned, simultaneity becomes relative. Two events that appear simultaneous to one observer may be separated in time to another. The prominent electrical engineer Charles Steinmetz, as quoted in *Light, Design and Application* (February 2000), noted that according to relativity "space and time do not exist in nature by themselves as empty space and empty time, but they only exist due to and as far as things and events occur in nature. . . . They are not fixed or invariable in their properties but depend upon the observer and the conditions of observation."

Furthermore, Einstein showed, no material object can travel faster than light. Relativistic effects, which are generally negligible at ordinary velocities, become significant only at the great speeds characteristic of atomic and subatomic particles. If an object were to move at the speed of light, to an outside observer its length would decrease to zero, time would stop, and its mass would be infinite.

Another discovery of 1905 was the equivalence of mass and energy. A mass (m) is a kind of frozen energy (E) related by the equation E=mc2, where c is the velocity of light. Thus, the emission of photons of light is paid for by a reduction in mass of the source. The loss of mass required to account for light emission is extremely small, generally undetectable by even the most sensitive chemical balance. However, relativity did provide the means for explaining otherwise incomprehensible features of atomic and nuclear physics. In the atomic bomb that was developed some 40 years later, physicists were able to calculate the expected energy release on the basis of the mass lost in the splitting of uranium nuclei.

After the publication of his 1905 papers, Einstein began to receive academic recognition. He became an associate professor of physics at the University of Zurich, in 1909, and a professor, first at the German University, in Prague, Czechoslovakia, in 1911, and then at the Federal Institute of Technology, in 1912. In 1914 he went to Germany as a professor at the University of Berlin and director of the Kaiser Wilhelm (now Max Planck) Institute for Physics. His German citizenship was restored, and he became a member of the Prussian Academy of Sciences. He did not support the German cause in World War I, however, advocating pacifism instead.

In 1915, after years of intensive effort, Einstein succeeded in developing his general theory of relativity, which went beyond the restrictions of the special theory of 1905 that motions be uniform and relative velocities constant. He now encompassed all kinds of motion and accelerations (varying velocities), and the previously prevailing theory of mechanics, founded by Isaac Newton in the 17th century, became only a special case useful at relatively slow speeds. Einstein also replaced many of Newton's concepts. He had been disturbed by such aspects of Newtonian mechanics as the coincidental equality of gravity and acceleration. "Although the theory of relativity fit well with the laws that govern electricity and magnetism," Hawking explained, "it wasn't compatible with Newton's laws of gravity. This law said that if you changed the distribution of matter in one region of space, the change in the gravitational field would be felt instantaneously everywhere else in the universe. Not only would this mean you could send signals faster than light (something that was forbidden by relativity), but it also required the Absolute or Universal Time that relativity had abolished in favor of personal or relativistic time."

Einstein performed what he called a "thought experiment." If a man in an elevator sitting on the earth's surface drops an apple, it falls to the floor at an accelerating pace of 9.8 meters per second per second. This would also be true in an imaginary location in space far away from any gravitational source if the elevator were propelled upward by some force at an acceleration of 9.8 meters per second per second. As a friend of Einstein's described the situation, the man in the elevator could not "tell whether he was in a gravitational field or subject to uniform acceleration."

Einstein's equivalence principle noted the coincidence between Newton's gravitational and inertial masses. He then extended the picture to light. If a light ray crossed the elevator horizontally while it was propelled upward, the ray would strike the far wall at a point closer to the floor than its point of entry because the elevator would have risen a little during the interval. To the man in the elevator, the light ray would obviously have been bent downward. To Einstein this meant that light rays are bent by gravitation in the everyday world if they pass close enough to a sufficiently massive body. "[Einstein] realized that the equivalence of gravity and acceleration could work if there was some give-and-take in the geometry of reality. What if space-time—an entity Einstein invented to incorporate the three familiar dimensions of space with a fourth dimension, time—was curved, and not flat, as had been assumed? His idea was that mass and energy would warp space-time in some manner. . . . Objects like apples or planets would try to move in straight lines through space-time, but their paths would appear to be bent by a gravitational field because space-time is curved."

Einstein's general theory replaced Newton's theory of gravitational attraction between bodies by a space- time mathematical description in which bodies influence the characteristics of space in their vicinity. According to this view, bodies do not attract each other; rather, each influences space-time geometry, which then guides the motion of bodies passing through. This eliminates the need for Newton's assertion of the instantaneous influence on other bodies of changes in gravitational fields. As Einstein's colleague, the American physicist J. A. Wheeler, explained, "Space tells matter how to move, and matter tells space how to curve." Einstein's work in this period was not confined to relativity theory. For example, in 1916 he introduced into quantum theory the idea of stimulated emission of radiation. In 1913 Niels Bohr had developed a model of the atom as a central nucleus (discovered some years earlier by Ernest Rutherford) surrounded by electrons restricted to certain orbits (energy levels) by quantum limitations. According to Bohr's model, atoms emitted radiation when the electrons were excited to higher energy levels and then fell back. The energy difference between levels equaled the energy in the photons absorbed or emitted. The return of excited electrons to lower energy levels was a random process. Einstein predicted that, under appropriate circumstances, electrons could be excited to a particular energy level and then triggered to cascade down simultaneously, a process that underlies the action of modern lasers.

Although the relativity theories were too radical to be greeted with immediate acceptance, they were supported by a series of confirmations. Among the first was an explanation of a peculiar wobble in the orbit of the planet Mercury that could not be fully accounted for by Newtonian mechanics. Then, in 1919, during observations of an eclipse, a star that should have been hidden behind the rim of the sun was visible, indicating that its light had been bent by the sun's gravitation. Universal fame came to Einstein after World War I, when the findings of the 1919 eclipse team were reported throughout the world and relativity became a household word.

In 1920 Einstein was appointed visiting professor at the University of Leiden. In Germany, however, Einstein also came under attack because of his opposition to the war and because his revolutionary theories were in disfavor with some German scientists, including a few who were anti-Semites. Some labeled Einstein's work "Jewish physics," calling it contrary to German standards. In the 1920s Einstein continued to espouse pacifism and actively supported the peace efforts of the League of Nations. He was also a spokesman for the Zionist cause and was instrumental in the establishment of the Hebrew University, in Jerusalem, in 1925.

Einstein received the 1921 Nobel Prize in Physics "for his services to theoretical physics, and especially for his discovery of the law of the photoelectric effect." "Einstein's law has become the basis of quantitative photochemistry in the same way as [Michael] Faraday's law is the basis of electrochemistry," said Svante Arrhenius of the Royal Swedish Academy of Sciences on presenting the award. Prior commitments to lecture in Japan prevented Einstein from attending the ceremonies, and he did not deliver his Nobel lecture until July 1923. He donated all of his prize money to charity.

As physicists were moving toward acceptance of the quantum theory, Einstein seemed to be moving away from its implications. In 1927 he expressed his unhappiness with the statistical interpretation of quantum mechanics advocated by Bohr and Max Born, which held that the principle of cause and effect does not apply to subatomic phenomena. Only the probabilities of events could be calculated. Einstein was convinced that statistics was nothing more than a tool and that a fundamental theory could not be statistical. As he expressed it, "God doesn't play dice" with the universe. Whereas proponents of the statistical interpretation rejected physical models for unobservable phenomena, Einstein thought a theory incomplete unless it could give "the real state of a physical system, something that objectively exists, and which can, in principle, be described in physical terms." His lifelong goal became a unified field theory that could derive quantum phenomena from a relativistic description of nature. In this he was unsuccessful. He engaged in many arguments about quantum mechanics with Bohr, but these tended only to strengthen Bohr's position.

When Hitler came to power, in 1933, Einstein was not in Germany, and he never returned. He became a professor of theoretical physics at the new Institute for Advanced Study, in Princeton, New Jersey. In 1940 he became an American citizen. He lived in Princeton for the rest of his life, formally retiring from the institute in 1945. As World War II approached, he renounced his earlier pacifism, feeling that only military force could stop Nazi Germany's expansion. He concluded that it was necessary "even to face battle" in order to "safeguard law and human dignity." In 1939, at the urging of several other refugee physicists, he wrote a letter to President Franklin D. Roosevelt warning that Germany might be developing an atomic bomb and urging support for American nuclear-fission research. Einstein himself played no part in the subsequent development, which led to the explosion of the world's first atomic bomb on July 16, 1945, in Alamogordo, New Mexico.

After World War II, horrified by the use of the atomic bomb against Japan and by the accelerating arms race, Einstein urged the abolition of war to ensure the survival of humanity. He was active in the movement for a world government. Shortly before he died, he signed what became known as the Russell Statement, drafted by Bertrand Russell, warning governments of the dangers of the hydrogen bomb and calling on them to renounce nuclear weapons. He championed the free expression of ideas and argued for the responsible use of science to make a better world.

Einstein's first wife was Mileva Maric, a fellow student at the Federal Institute of Technology in Zurich, whom he married in 1903, despite his parents' adamant opposition. They had one daughter and two sons. The marriage ended in divorce in 1919, after a five-year separation. In the same year, he married his cousin Elsa Einstein, a widow with two daughters. She died in 1936. Einstein's two favorite pastimes were music and sailing. He began to study the violin when he was six years old and continued throughout his life, often playing music with other physicists, including Max Planck, who was an accomplished pianist. Einstein found the serenity of sailing to be conducive to thinking about physics. In Princeton he became a local fixture, known as the world-famous scientist but also as the kindly, shy, gentle, and somewhat eccentric man down the street. He never gave up his quest for a unified theory of relativity, which would resolve what J. Madeleine Nash in *Time* (December 31, 1999) called "the conflict between two competing visions of the universe: the smooth continuum of space-time, where stars and planets reign, as described by [Einstein's] general theory of relativity, and the unseemly jitteriness of the submicroscopic quantum world, where particles hold sway." He held out against the opinions of most of his contemporaries, saying, as quoted by Nash, "I must seem like an ostrich who forever buries its head in the relativistic sand in order not to face the evil quanta." Since Einstein's day, physicists have observed that particles are capable of jumping from point A to point B, thus challenging Einstein's vision of continuous space and time.

Among Einstein's many honors was an invitation in 1952 to become the president of Israel; he declined. He received numerous awards in addition to the Nobel Prize, including the Copley Medal of the Royal Society of London (1925) and the Franklin Medal of the Franklin Institute, in Philadelphia, Pennsylvania (1935). He held honorary doctorates from many universities and was a member of all the leading scientific academies of the world. He died in Princeton of an aortic aneurysm, on April 18, 1955.—P. G. H.

Suggested Reading: *Christian Science Monitor* II p9 Jan. 30, 1951, p3 Mar. 16, 1953; *Christian Science Monitor Magazine* p5 Sep. 30, 1950; *Ladies' Home Journal* p47 Apr. 1951; *Life* p55 Mar. 29, 1953; *New York Herald Tribune* p1 Mar. 30, 1953; *New York Times* p27 Mar. 14, 1940, p37 Oct. 5, 1952; *Newsweek* p53+ Dec. 26, 1949; *Saturday Review of Literature* p9+ Nov. 26, 1949; *Time* p66+ Dec. 31, 1999, p83+ Dec. 31, 1999; Aichelburg, P. C., and R. U. Sexl, eds. *Albert Einstein: His Influence on Physics, Philosophy, and Politics*, 1979; Bernstein, J. *Einstein, 1973*; Clark, R. W. *Einstein: The Life and Times*, 1971; Friedman, A. J. *Einstein as Myth and Muse*, 1985; Hoffmann, B. *Albert Einstein, Creator and Rebel*, 1972; Infeld, L. *Albert Einstein, His Work and Its Influence on Our World*, 1950; Kuznetsov, B. *Einstein*, 1965; Schilpp, P. A. ed. *Albert Einstein, Philosopher-Scientist*, 1949; Seelig, C. *Albert Einstein: A Documentary Biography*, 1956

Ellison, Lawrence J.

1944– Chairman and CEO of Oracle

Lawrence J. Ellison is the chairman and chief executive officer of the Oracle Corporation, a Silicon Valley firm whose database systems keep track of the operations of such *Fortune* 500 businesses as American Airlines, Ford Motor, Sara Lee, and Pacific Bell, among others. Oracle is the world's second-largest software company, and Ellison has made no bones about the fact that he has long sought to overtake the first largest—the mighty Microsoft.

The thrice-divorced Ellison lives in a $40 million mansion built in the 16th-century imperial Japanese style and is as well known in California for his fondness of expensive cars, beautiful women, and exotic vacations as he is for his business acumen. His best friend, Steve Jobs, cofounder of Apple Computer, has called him the "outrageous CEO poster child." Ellison cites his preoccupation with the good life as one of the major reasons that Oracle nearly collapsed in 1990, when the total value of its stock plummeted from $3.8 billion to $700 million. "Oracle is run by adolescents, and that includes me," he said at the time. Since then, Ellison has kept a more careful eye on his business, and the new management team he hired has helped transform the company into a world leader in database systems.

Lawrence J. Ellison was born in New York City in 1944. His mother, Florence Spellman, was an unmarried teenager. When he was nine months old, she sent him off to be raised by her aunt and uncle, Lillian and Louis Ellison. Louis Ellison, a Russian immigrant whose difficult-to-pronounce original name was changed to reflect his American port of entry, Ellis Island, lost his real-estate business during the Depression and later went to work as an auditor for a public-housing agency. Lawrence Ellison has described his adoptive father as a bitter man who was hard to get along with. The family lived in a small walk-up apartment on Chicago's South Side. In high school young Ellison developed a reputation as a bright but lackadaisical student who often spoke his mind. "He was very intense, very opinionated," Rick Rosenfeld, an old friend, told Byran Burrough for *Vanity Fair* (June 1997). "Whatever he was talking about, he was loud about it. Larry just had an answer to every-thing. [Today,] he's the same guy I knew in high school."

After graduating from high school, Ellison en-rolled at the University of Illinois, where he ex-celled in science. Near the end of his second year, he learned that his adoptive mother had suddenly died. "I walked out [of school] and never went back," he told Burrough. "There was an incredible sense of loss. She was my sole support system growing up." He tried to resume his studies at the University of Chicago, but after a single semester he quit and headed to California. His father tried to discourage him by saying, among other things, "You'll never amount to anything." Ellison has told several interviewers that he has spent most of his adult life trying to prove his adoptive father wrong.

In California, Ellison discovered that the one marketable skill he had was his rudimentary knowledge of computer programming, which he had picked up in high school. His first job, in San Francisco, was working on a bank's computer sys-tem. He next moved on to several other computer-programming jobs in Silicon Valley; by the late 1960s he was earning enough money to buy his own home, as well as purchase an expensive sports car and a sailboat. Ellison's career took a pivotal turn in the early 1970s, when he began working at the Ampex Corporation. His job there was to help create large database systems, including one for the Central Intelligence Agency (CIA). That project's secret code name was Oracle, which Ellison later used for his own company.

Ellison started Oracle in 1977 with Bob Miner, who had been his boss at Ampex. Their first cus-tomer was the CIA, which paid them $50,000 to build a new database program. "We were very na-ïve," Ellison told Burrough. "There was this in-credibly long procurement process, just months and months. We were running out of money. I was living in a house in Woodside [in California] and building another. I couldn't make my mortgage payments." Just before the bank was about to fore-close on both of Ellison's houses, the money from the CIA came through. Soon afterward, Oracle got a database contract from the U.S. Air Force.

Meanwhile, Ellison had learned that Interna-tional Business Machines (IBM) was developing a new type of database program that was unusually efficient and useful for businesses. The program, called a relational database, used IBM's newly de-veloped programming language, dubbed SQL, to customize the organization of information. For ex-ample, a user would be able to retrieve the sales history of a product by region or customer, without having to sift through unnecessary data. Ellison and Miner immediately went to work using SQL to create a relational database for Oracle. They intro-duced a working prototype in 1979, two years be-fore IBM came out with its own version. Ellison hired an aggressive, young staff to sell it; the com-pany's sales motto was "growth at any cost."

Oracle quickly became one of the biggest suc-cess stories in Silicon Valley. Between 1981 and 1990 the firm made hundreds of millions of dol-lars, and Ellison "emerged as a swashbuckling CEO," as Rich Karlgaard wrote for Forbes (June 7, 1993), "capable of whipping his employees into the industry's most powerful sales force." Then, suddenly, in late 1990, Oracle's fortunes plummet-ed. The company's policy of recording revenues before they had actually been received was ques-tioned by auditors, who forced a reassessment of the firm's books. "In one quarter, Oracle lost $28.7 million, and within weeks the company's market cap fell from $3.7 billion to $700 million," Karlgaard reported. While many Wall Street ana-lysts were surprised by the crash, many of Oracle's customers weren't; they had reportedly become fed up with the firm's poor service and "buggy" new software. Ellison was blamed by many for the near collapse of Oracle, and he did not deny his respon-sibility. "Anyone who had any experience could have seen what happened coming a mile away," he remarked to Janice Maloney for Fortune (October 28, 1996). "I was clearly a completely inexperi-enced and incompetent CEO." Part of the problem, he told Burrough, was that "I was spending a little too much time in Hollywood, enjoying the new-ness of my celebrity."

Shaken by the experience, Ellison resolved to turn his company around. He hired a new manage-ment team to run Oracle's day-to-day operations, improve service and product quality, and cut costs. Ellison also set about reforming himself. "Two years ago, I thought only about getting to the next quarter," he explained to Karlgaard in 1993. "Now I get to spend time with customers, think about where the industry is today, where it's been, where it's going." Oracle made a strong comeback, win-ning back both clients and the confidence of Wall Street investors. In 1996 the company earned more than $600 million in profits from revenues exceed-ing $4 billion.

Meanwhile, at about the same time that Oracle's stock plummeted, Ellison was facing several per-sonal crises. He had had two serious accidents: in 1990 he broke his neck while bodysurfing in Ha-waii, and the following year his left elbow was smashed in a bicycle accident in California. While recuperating, he began to reevaluate his life, espe-cially the one thing that had always haunted him: the identity of his birth mother and why she had given him up. "I was confronting all sorts of things in my life and trying to order them and understand them," he told Burrough. "I had to understand my role in life. Who am I? Who is my family?" In 1991 he hired a private investigator, who located his birth mother, Florence Spellman, in New Haven, Connecticut. It took Ellison two weeks to muster the nerve to call her. That phone call lasted only five minutes, but the two began what would be-come a lengthy correspondence. Spellman had been unaware that Ellison had become a billion-aire. He eventually bought her a home in California and put his half-sister through college; he never learned what happened to his biological father. "It's all given me a better understanding of who I am," he told Burrough. "It's given me an ability to express my feelings I didn't have before. I no longer repress the feelings about my family. . . . The thing that I learned was that [the] family that raised me was my [real] family."

Once his company had resumed its upward trajectory, Ellison launched a campaign to win support for the network computer (NC). A stripped-down, easy-to-use, and relatively inexpensive (priced at about $500) computer, it would be attached by telephone or cable-TV wires to a network, where most information would be stored. No hard drive would be necessary and it would eschew the Windows operating system (making it a threat to Microsoft), but database systems provided by servers connected to a network would be needed (hence the advantage to Oracle). Ellison enlisted the aid of his Silicon Valley neighbors Sun Microsystems and Netscape in his drive to oust Microsoft from the top of the computing industry. Many industry analysts speculated that at least some of the motivation behind Ellison's campaign was the reported personal competition and animosity he feels toward Bill Gates, Microsoft's CEO. Gates, well known for his competitive verve, set his company on a course to compete directly with Oracle by hiring away some of its top engineers to develop database software.

Ellison had first conceived the idea for NCs in 1995, during a technology summit that was attended by President Bill Clinton. Ellison told Clinton that the industry knew how to make a computer that would retail for less than $500 and that there ought to be one on every child's desk in every school across the country. It wasn't until the media blitz associated with the introduction of Microsoft's Windows 95 operating system, however, that Ellison decided he was going to champion the NC publicly—as well as take on Bill Gates's company. Although there are many reports to the contrary, Ellison has said that his company's competition with Microsoft is purely a professional one. "I'm more interested in beating Microsoft than Bill Gates," he told a reporter for *Time* (May 12, 1997). "I obsess on the personal computer and the industry, and I would love to see the age of proprietary computers end."

What particularly rankled Ellison about Microsoft was its stranglehold on the personal-computer industry through its Windows-based operating system. In Ellison's view, the personal computer (PC) of today is too expensive and too complicated for most people, who really need it only for such tasks as word processing, sending and receiving E-mail, and surfing the Internet. "PCs should be more like pencils," he was quoted as saying in *Time*, by which he meant, as the author of the *Time* article pointed out, "cheap, user-friendly, and above all, ubiquitous."

Toward that end, Ellison considered mounting a takeover of Apple Computer in 1995, and rumors about his intentions were a hot topic within the industry for more than a year. An Apple-made NC "could well be a powerful lure for classrooms and businesses alike," Burrough predicted. However, Steve Jobs's return to Apple, first as a member of its board of directors and later as acting president of the company, apparently put a halt to Ellison's takeover plans. (In August 1997 Ellison was named to Apple's board, a post he resigned in 2002, citing a need to concentrate his attention on Oracle.)

As to Ellison's hope that the computing world would one day be dominated by network computers, that dream never came to fruition. When Sun Microsystems finally shipped its $699 Java Station NC in March 1998, the computer made little impact on the market. Part of the blame fell to NC visionaries like Ellison, who was accused of promising customers too much too soon. The Java was unable to do all that customers wanted, including run any programs that used a lot of memory. Additionally, just as network computers went to market, the average price of a personal computer was decreasing by as much as 40 percent.

Though Ellison had lost out to Microsoft regarding his network computers, he wasn't ready to give in to the computer-software giant. In July 1998 he testified before the United States Senate Committee on the Judiciary regarding Microsoft's alleged monopoly on desktop-computer operating systems and applications. "Microsoft is a monopoly," Ellison told the committee. "It controls 97 percent of the desktop operating system market and a near identical percentage in desktop applications—word processors, spread sheets, and presentation graphics. It is well-documented that Microsoft actively engages in anti-competitive tactics to protect and extend its monopoly into related markets." Though Microsoft was ultimately found guilty of violating the Sherman Anti-Trust Act in April 2000, an appeals court rejected the initial court's order for the software giant to break up. Following the dot.com and stock-market collapse in 2000, the U.S. Justice Department was hesitant to continue its costly lawsuit and agreed to a settlement with Microsoft in November 2001.

With the recession, Oracle's stock plummeted, despite favorable ratings of its software databases by customers. In 2002 Ellison split the company sales team into two groups, one to focus on the sale of applications software, the other on databases. In 2003 it was reported that Oracle continued to dominate the relational-database market, holding 39.4 percent of the market share (compared with 33.6 percent for IBM and 11.1 percent for Microsoft).

Larry Ellison has many interests beyond computers. He is a competitive sailor and has won several races with *Sayonara*, his 78-foot sailboat. He flies his own Italian fighter jet (which he bought only after the federal government frustrated his attempts to buy a Soviet MiG-29). He collects antique samurai swords, and he once pursued his interest in biochemistry and physics by spending a vacation doing lab work at Rockefeller University, in New York City. As Burrough noted, "his penchant for skirt-chasing is legend, and has landed him in legal trouble [for sexual harassment], while alienating some of the industry's leading female executives." In 1996 Ellison and the financier Michael Milken co-founded Knowledge Universe, which makes educational software for children and families.

Ellison has also involved himself in the emerging field of biotechnology, an interest he shares with his main competitor, Bill Gates. To that end he set up the Ellison Medical Foundation, a philanthropic institute dedicated to eradicating infectious diseases in the Third World and curing diseases for elderly people. He also has majority shares in Quark Biotech, which, according to its Web site, is "a pioneer in applied genomics-based

drug discovery and development." Ellison hopes that Quark Biotech will one day cure cancer. He told a reporter for *Fortune* (September 3, 2001) that "someone asked me once how much I would pay to cure cancer if I could. And I replied, 'Everything I've got.' What do you think is cooler: being the richest guy on earth or helping find the cure for cancer? What would you want to do? That's a pretty easy question. Let me nail the big C."—C. M.

Suggested Reading: *BusinessWeek* (on-line) Apr. 13, 1998, Mar. 21, 2003; *Computerworld* p35 June 18, 2001; *Fortune* p119+ Oct. 28, 1996, with photos, p144 Sep. 3, 2001; *Forbes ASAP* p71+ June 7, 1993, with photos; *New York Times* C p4 Sep. 21, 2002, C p4 Dec. 19, 2002; *San Jose Mercury News* July 31, 2002; *Time* p58+ May 12, 1997, with photos; *Vanity Fair* p146+ June 1997, with photos; United States Senate Committee on the Judiciary Web site

---

Engelbart, Douglas

Jan. 30, 1925– Personal-computing innovator

Douglas Engelbart has been called the "father of modern computing." While working at the Stanford Research Institute (SRI) in the 1960s, he developed many modern computing devices, including the mouse, hypertext, word processing, e-mail, teleconferencing, and windows. Though many at SRI scoffed at his ideas, seeing no practical use for them in an age when computers were confined to governmental and research facilities, several of Engelbart's associates eventually helped Xerox develop the Alto, the first modern personal computer, in 1973. Throughout most of his career, Engelbart's ideas have been either ridiculed or dismissed; it is only today, with the advent of the Internet, that he is receiving numerous accolades and awards. Still, Engelbart has consistently claimed that his dream of a personal computer, which would allow average people to make more-effective decisions, was never motivated by money or praise. "I made a conscious decision at the age of 25 that money would be secondary to what kind of contribution my work would make," he stated in an interview with *Forbes* (October 10, 1994). "Sometimes, though, I think I've overdone the pro bono idea. You get way out on the frontier and eventually you think, 'Maybe it's time to back out. Is it really necessary for me to be this cold and hungry?'" Engelbart is no longer cold or hungry; in 1997 he received the prestigious Lemelson-MIT Prize, which is worth $500,000.

The grandson of early Western pioneers, Douglas C. Engelbart was born in Portland, Oregon, on January 30, 1925. He grew up on a small farm during the Depression and graduated from high school in 1942. That fall he started working on his bachelor's degree at Oregon State College in Corvallis, majoring in electrical engineering. At the time, the

United States had just begun its involvement in World War II and the idea of a military career weighed on Engelbart's mind. As Engelbart told Jon Eklund in an interview (May 4, 1994) for the National Museum of American History at the Smithsonian Institution, as posted on their Web site, "I had heard about an exciting new technology in the military called RADAR and somehow there was a training you could go through to learn about RADAR and [I] didn't particularly have aspirations for any other military career so I figured I'd get ready for it by taking electrical engineering. I didn't have any career plans, but that was just coming out of the depression and my father had been dead since I was nine. So there wasn't much to orient me about a career, but I was interested in getting an education."

Through Engelbart's sophomore year of college, the U.S. military had a deferment plan for anyone majoring in electrical engineering. By 1944, however, the government revoked that privilege and Engelbart was drafted. He opted to go into the U.S. Navy, which at the time was testing enlistees who wanted to learn about RADAR. For the next year he worked through the navy's training program, learning not only RADAR but also SONAR, radios, and teletype transmission technology. As a navy technician, Engelbart absorbed a great deal about repairing and maintaining such equipment as antennas and amplifiers. He departed for the Philippines in 1945, just as the Japanese surrendered. Having missed the fighting, he was assigned to help with the demobilization effort, and while overseas he read Vannevar Bush's article "As We May Think" in the *Atlantic Monthly*. Bush's vision of a world in which computer-based tools bolstered the human intellect and aided in humanity's need to solve complex problems gave Engelbart new direction. In their book *Computer: A History of the Information Machine* (1996), Martin Campbell-Kelly and William Aspray quoted Engelbart's comments about the article's effect on him: "It just thrilled the hell out of me that people were thinking about something like that. . . . I wish I could have met him, but by the time I caught onto the work, he was already in a nursing home and wasn't available."

In the summer of 1946 Engelbart was discharged from the navy and returned to Oregon State University to finish his electrical engineering degree. He graduated with honors in 1948 and subsequently joined the staff of the National Advisory Committee for Aeronautics (NACA) at the Ames Laboratory in Mountain View, California, as an electrical engineer. NACA, the forerunner of the National Aeronautics and Space Administration (NASA), was involved with aeronautic research at the time, including motors and wind tunnels. Engelbart worked on 25,000-horsepower motors but had little real passion for his work. In December of 1950 he became engaged, and this shook him out of his complacency at NACA. He began wondering what he really wanted to do beyond having a steady job and getting married. As he began thinking more about his goals, he asked himself, "How can my career maximize my contribution to mankind?"

Engelbart spent the next couple of months considering what he wanted to do and searching for ideas at the local library. As he sat in his rented room in Los Altos, California, in early 1951, he had an epiphany. As he told Tia O'Brien for SiliconValley.com, "I thought, 'Damn, I never realized the world is so complicated. If we don't improve our ability to deal collectively with complex things, as the problems grow more urgent, we're in trouble.'" After reading about the development of the computer and considering it alongside the Vannevar Bush article he had read in the Philippines, Engelbart imagined computers working interactively with people through the use of a display screen— something that no computer had during this period. (He later claimed that this idea was heavily influenced by his work as a RADAR technician during the war.) He also imagined that the people sitting in front of these displays would be "flying around" in an information space where they could develop, organize, and work on their ideas, either alone or with other people, at great speeds.

Now that Engelbart had decided on the path to take, he returned to school, this time to the University of California, Berkeley. He received a master's degree in engineering in 1952 and followed it in 1955 with a Ph.D. in electrical engineering with a speciality in computers. Over the next year he taught as an assistant professor at the university and talked to anyone who would listen about his ideas for a personal computer. Friends told him that he would never become anything more than an assistant professor if he kept telling his peers— who were unwilling to accept such notions—about his ideas. He believed for a while that he could start his own business on the basis of the various patents he had developed through his doctoral work, but he soon realized that he could not make much headway without the financial backing of a research facility.

In 1957 Engelbart obtained a position at the Stanford Research Institute (now SRI International), in California, and worked on fundamental digital-drive phenomena, miniaturization scaling potential, and magnetic computer components. He received 12 additional patents for his work at SRI. The institute had enough confidence in his abilities to appoint him as the director of his own lab, the Augmentation Research Center, in 1959.

Over the next two years, Engelbart began formulating the theoretical framework to make his dream of a personal computer a reality. In an interview (July 1998) posted on the Association for Computing Machinery Web site, Engelbart remarked, "I had somehow become convinced that computers could make a huge difference in how humans do their thinking and everyday reasoning, handle their knowledge, and plan for the immediate and long-range future." In 1962 he completed a report entitled "Augmenting the Human Intellect," in which he explained how a computer could create a new medium that would give people the ability to develop, study, and rearrange their ideas. According to Engelbart's on-line biographical sketch for the Bootstrap Institute, his theoretical framework was "based on the assumption that complexity and urgency are increasing exponentially, and that the product of the two will soon challenge our organizations and institutions to change in quantum leaps rather than incremental steps."

At the Augmentation Research Center, Engelbart and his lab of 47 associates sought to develop the modern interactive working environment. To build "man-computer symbiosis," his group first had to invent instruments to create the tools that could serve humanity. One of the first things they developed was shared-screen teleconferencing via computers, which helped them more effectively to plan their work. They also developed on-line "journals" in which the various researchers' notes were brought together. Perhaps most important, he began working with Joseph Licklider, who was greatly interested in the development of interactive timesharing computers and had supported research toward this goal by heading the Information Processing Techniques Office (IPTO) at the U.S. Department of Defense Advanced Research Projects Agency (ARPA; also known as DARPA). Martin Campbell-Kelly and William Aspray wrote that "ARPA funds enabled Engelbart to build up a talented group of a dozen or so computer scientists and psychologists at SRI, where they began to develop what they called the 'electronic office'—a system that would integrate text and pictures in a way that was then unprecedented but is now commonly done on computers."

By 1967 SRI authorized Engelbart and his associates to start work on a computer networking project that entailed networking the Institute's 13 computers across the country. Engelbart was fascinated by the prospect of being able to study how a distributed community could do collaborative knowledge work. His computer was the second one tied into the ARPANET, which would soon develop into the Internet. He subsequently developed an on-line information center to aid in the researchers' work; it was called the ARPANET Network Information Center (NIC).

The results of this work in 1967–68 were astounding, especially when one considers how many of Engelbart's ideas have been incorporated into modern computing. In developing NLS (for oNLine System), he created many firsts, including the mouse, the concept of windows, word processing, mixed text-graphic files, structured document files, cross-file and display editing, electronic mail, and idea/outline processing. The group also produced hypermedia, hypertext, and groupware; the latter included a computer-supported meeting room and shared-screen teleconferencing. In December 1968 Engelbart's group provided a demonstration of their developments at the Fall Joint Computer Conference in a 90-minute multimedia session. As Engelbart used NLS to demonstrate their work, his associates linked up with him from their lab at SRI 30 miles away to show the benefits of on-screen video teleconferencing. He also demonstrated their mouse—then a wooden box with one large red button called an "X-Y Position Indicator for a Display System"—to show how someone could use a tool outside of a computer to move items inside of it. Later termed the "mother of all demos," as quoted by Tia O'Brien, spectators sat in awe as Engelbart, connected to the computer with a headset, mouse, and chord keyset (a five-keyed one-handed keyboard that allowed the user to work on the computer in shorthand), used the computer to plan a set of tasks that he wanted to do later. By using a primitive form of hypertext, he was able to work on a variety of tasks, including adding to, deleting from, and reorganizing a grocery list. When he began working with a colleague at SRI by teleconferencing, not only did they discuss a piece of text they were both working on, but they were also able to pass the computer controls and cursor back and forth, allowing each to make changes to the text. (Thirty years later, it is still difficult to find groupware that allows users to do as much as they did in that demo.)

Many who had witnessed the demonstration were extremely impressed, but according to Engelbart in his interview with Jon Eklund, "There would be people who'd come by and see demonstrations and say 'Wow.' But I began to realize over the following years that somehow it didn't connect with their perception of their own future. Y'know it's as if you'd gone to some laboratory and seen some people strap things on their backs that let them levitate and move around and 'Oh that's all very interesting but that has nothing to do with my own future.'" The sheer expense of computer equipment at the time also retarded the development of Engelbart's ideas—a minicomputer in the 1960s could cost up to $100,000. Computers also took up a large amount of space. Having a computer that would be appropriate for an individual—someone not associated with the government or scientific community—seemed, to most administrators, a waste of money.

What also prevented Engelbart from developing his computer was the fact that so many members of his staff had begun defecting to Xerox's Palo Alto Research Center (PARC), in California's Silicon Valley. In 1969 Xerox established PARC with the intent of developing the "office of the future." Lured by such claims and the millions of dollars Xerox was spending on research toward that goal, many members of Engelbart's team—including Robert Taylor, who had been head of IPTO at ARPA—changed companies in the hopes of developing this new technology further than SRI was willing to take it. One of the first concrete developments of their work was the Alto computer in 1973. The Alto had many features envisioned by Engelbart, including a mouse, icons, folders, and documents. It was also a network-capable computer and boasted a specially designed monitor, which could display an 8.5-by-11-inch sheet of "paper."

By the mid-1970s interactive computing had moved more in the direction of automating office work instead of augmenting human knowledge. Manufacturers wanted easy-to-use computers for offices and felt that, in an era of expensive mainframe computers, the idea of cheap personal computers seemed preposterous. This was clearly not the direction in which Engelbart wanted computing to go. Throughout the 1970s he was labeled a loose cannon or ignored outright for promoting NLS when, according to others in the business, it was clear that computing was moving in the direction of primarily automating tasks. Engelbart's lowest year was 1976, when his house burned down and SRI wanted to rescind completely funding for his laboratory and strip him of his directorship. He and his associates managed to convince the institute that they should auction NLS to a commercial market.

Engelbart stepped down from his directorship in 1977 and became a senior scientist at Tymeshare in Cupertino, California, after it bought the commercial rights to NLS. Tymeshare was a phone networking company that wanted the system for office automation. The company renamed the system Augment and developed it as a principal business line in a newly formed Office Automation Division. As the sole member of his original research team, Engelbart told Tia O'Brien, "I went and stayed and stayed [with Tymeshare and Augment] because that system represented a real outpost from where I thought we could go."

At Tymeshare Engelbart was allotted a very small research budget and a tiny cubicle in a low-rise office building. He had hoped to be doing what Steve Jobs at Apple Computer, located just a block away, was doing—helping to usher in the era of the personal computer. In the early 1980s Engelbart met Jobs, who demonstrated the Macintosh computer for the man who had invented many of its critical components. While Jobs boasted of the Macintosh's features, Engelbart looked on, stunned that the computer lacked what he considered to be the most important part of his system—networking. Without e-mail or access to other people's documents, the Mac was an extremely limited version of his vision.

In 1984 Tymeshare was bought by the McDonnell Douglas Corporation. Engelbart kept his position as a senior scientist and was now able to work on integrated information system architectures, and associated evolutionary strategies for the aerospace industry. Happily, this work proved to be an extension of Engelbart's work at SRI, but McDonnell Douglas was still unwilling to use his system for commercial applications. The company treated him "like a strange coding advisor," in his words, as quoted by O'Brien, as he attempted to convince management of the importance of having an internal computer network, similar to the modern Intranet used in many corporations today. "I showed them how it could change the way they did their design work and support for buyers," Engelbart explained to O'Brien. "Some people got excited. But then upper management canceled it. One guy said, 'IBM and Hewlett-Packard aren't using this sort of thing. I can't believe it's worth doing.'"

In the mid-1980s Engelbart was diagnosed with lymphoma and spent a number of years enduring chemotherapy treatments. He retired from research in 1989 after beating cancer. He and his daughter Christina subsequently formed the Bootstrap Institute, a think tank that seeks the best means to boost humanity's collective IQ, network collective brainpower, and improve the ways in which organizations conduct problem-solving. Bootstrap initially began in 1989 as an 18-month project at Stanford University to study collaborative knowledge development with an emphasis on Engelbart's lifelong fear that humanity's problems might become so complex that all of society could collapse under the burden. Engelbart's Bootstrap project has three major components: an open hyperdoc system (OHS); the means by which to develop associated work methods with successive OHS prototypes; and methods for in-house execution and the ongoing improvement of the project. The group also conducted a three-day management seminar for executives to display their strategy's framework.

Since 1990 Engelbart has been director of the Bootstrap Institute in Palo Alto, California. The office space for the institute was donated by Logitech, a company that in 1996 produced its 100 millionth mouse and gave the space to Engelbart's group in appreciation of his invention. The group has worked closely with governmental and industry heads in the hopes of implementing some applications of his work. Engelbart himself has continued as a visiting part-time scholar at Stanford, making speaking engagements and attending seminars. He is the author of 20 patents and 25 publications.

Though Douglas Engelbart's early accomplishments initially went unrecognized, he has more recently been recognized both for his innovative work and dedication to his vision. In 1986 he was presented with *PC Magazine*'s lifetime achievement award. In 1990 he won the ACM Software System Award, and a year later he received the Coors American Ingenuity Award, which was presented at the NAM Congress of American Industry in Washington, D.C. He also received the Institute for Electrical and Electronics Engineers Computer Pioneer Award in 1993. Since the beginning of the Internet's commercial growth in 1994 and 1995, Engelbart has been recognized for aiding the development of this new medium. In those years alone he won three substantive awards: the Price Waterhouse Lifetime Achievement Award (presented at the Computerworld-Smithsonian awards ceremony in Washington, D.C.), an honorary doctorate from his alma mater Oregon State University, and a fellowship from the American Academy of the Arts and Science. In 1997 he won the Lemelson-MIT Prize, which carries a stipend of $500,000—the largest award presented to an American inventor annually. For the 30th anniversary of the mouse, in December 1998, he was honored at a day-long symposium at Stanford University entitled Engelbart's Unfinished Revolution. In 1999 he was presented with the Benjamin Franklin Medal in Computer and Cognitive Science from the Franklin Institute, in Philadelphia, Pennsylvania.—C. M.; B. S.

Suggested Reading: Association of Computing Machinery Web site; *Bootstrap Institute* (on-line); *Buffalo News* A p9+ Dec. 12, 1998; *Computerworld* p72+ Jan. 18, 1999; *Electronic News* p88 Apr. 21, 1997; *Forbes* p130+ Oct. 10, 1994; *Lemelson-MIT Prize Program* (on-line); *Network World, Inc.* p67+ Oct. 3, 1994; *Newsweek* p8 Dec. 21, 1998; *Salon* (on-line) Dec. 15, 1998; *San Francisco Chronicle* Apr. 10, 1997; *Science* p537+ Apr. 25, 1997; *SiliconValley.com*; *Smithsonian Computer History* (on-line); *Time* p45+ Mar. 24, 1997; Campbell-Kelly, Martin, and William Aspray. *Computer: A History of the Information Machine*, 1996

Fairchild, George W.

May 6, 1854–Dec. 31, 1924 Founder of the International Time Recording Company

George W. Fairchild overcame a difficult childhood to become a prominent businessman and politician in upstate New York. After spending many years working as a printer, editor, newspaper owner, and corporate executive, Fairchild became an investor and director in 1896 of the Bundy Manufacturing Company, which made time clocks for factories and other businesses. In 1900 Fairchild established the International Time Recording

Company, which marketed the Bundy company's products. In 1911 the financier Charles R. Flint merged both companies with the Tabulating Machine Company and the Computing Scale Company to form the Computing-Tabulating-Recording Company (C-T-R), the precursor to the computer conglomerate internationally known today as IBM. Fairchild, however, never exercised much of a role with C-T-R beyond that of a figurehead, because at the time of its formation he was serving in the U.S. Congress. By the time Fairchild left Congress after the 1918 election to resume his business career, C-T-R was in the firm control of its president, Thomas J. Watson.

The second of nine children, George Winthrop Fairchild was born on May 6, 1854 in Oneonta, New York. One of his ancestors, Thomas Fairchild, had settled in Stratford, Connecticut in 1632. When he was 13, Fairchild was forced to leave school to help support his family after his father died. His first job was as a farm laborer, which paid him eight dollars a month. According to an obituary in the *Oneonta Star* (January 1, 1925), Fairchild was hired as apprentice printer by the *Oneonta Democrat*, a local newspaper, when he was 14 years old. Three years later, he completed his apprenticeship, earning the distinction of master printer. For the next five years, Fairchild worked as a printer in many different cities in the United States.

According to an obituary in the *New York Times* (January 1, 1925), in 1876 Fairchild assisted in the publication of *Trow's New York Directory*. Marking the start of his interest in politics, during the presidential campaign that year between the Democrat Samuel Tilden and the Republican Rutherford B. Hayes, who won in a disputed election, Fairchild printed a presidential chart. In the same year, Fairchild returned to Oneonta, where he was hired by the local *Herald and Democrat* newspaper as a compositor. He later served as the newspaper's foreman, printer, and editor. In 1882 Fairchild and Willard E. Yager, a lawyer and local community activist, purchased the newspaper and changed its name to the *Oneonta Herald*. In 1890 Yager gave up his interest in the newspaper to devote more time to his love of archeology, leaving Fairchild as the sole owner.

During the 1890s, George Fairchild gradually expanded his business interests. He served as the vice president of the Ostego Publishing Company and joined the Eckerson Printing Press Company, which manufactured an automatic printing press. In 1896 Fairchild invested in the Bundy Manufacturing Company, which made time recorders, and was later appointed its director. The company was co-founded, in 1889, in Binghamton, New York, by Willard and Harlow Bundy after they secured a patent for the design of a time clock that Willard had developed. The company, along with many competitors, was highly successful, as numerous factories and businesses purchased time clocks to improve efficiency by keeping track of their em-

ployees. In 1900 Fairchild set up the International Time Recording Company, which the IBM Web site describes as the "selling agency" of the Bundy Manufacturing Company. Fairchild became the president of the new company.

In 1906 George Fairchild entered politics, winning election to the U.S. House of Representatives as a Republican from the 34th district of New York. (He was re-elected five times.) In Congress, Fairchild served on the Merchant Marine and Fisheries Committee, the Foreign Affairs Committee, and the powerful Ways and Means Committee. In 1910 President William Howard Taft appointed Fairchild as a special representative to Mexico. Fairchild also served as the vice president of the International Peace Conference.

In 1911 the financier Charles Ranlett Flint (1850–1934) negotiated a consolidation of the International Time Recording Company, the Bundy Manufacturing Company, the Tabulating Machine Company, and the Computing Scale Company. Known as "the father of trusts," Flint enjoyed a long record of successfully consolidating companies within the same industry. By contrast, this four-way merger was Flint's first attempt to join companies that manufactured different, but related, products such as, in this case, time clocks, tabulating machines, and scales. The new company was named the Computing-Tabulating-Recording Company (C-T-R). Fairchild's political career prevented him from taking an active role with C-T-R. According to Robert Sobel in *IBM: Colossus in Transition* (1981), Fairchild agreed, however, to serve as a figurehead within the new company in order to satisfy local bankers and stockholders. Sobel wrote that Fairchild and Frank Kondolf, who became acting president of C-T-R, "showed little interest in developing new products, reinvigorating Computing Scale, or marketing the Hollerith tabulating machines to additional customers. No attempt was made to integrate operations, harmonize product lines, or eliminate overlaps. In this period C-T-R did little in the way of what today would be called research and development." In 1914 Flint hired Thomas J. Watson, a former salesman with the National Cash Register Company, to serve as C-T-R's general manager. Although Fairchild did not agree that he was the right candidate to exercise a leadership role, Watson became C-T-R's president in 1915.

In 1919 Fairchild left Congress after his term expired with the intention of devoting more time to his business interests. Although he planned to take a more active role with C-T-R, Watson had consolidated his power and, in effect, gained sole control of the company. Fairchild remained associated with C-T-R, however, serving as a vice president and chairman of the company's board of directors. Unlike Fairchild and Kondolf, Watson was committed to modernizing and expanding C-T-R. In 1924 Watson changed the name of the company to International Business Machines (IBM), which eventually became one of the leading manufacturers of computers.

Among his other business interests, George Fairchild founded the White Plains Development Company and was a vice president of the Guardian Trust Company. He also served on the boards of several firms. According to the *New York Times* (January 1, 1925), Fairchild suggested the project to Frank W. Woolworth, the founder of the F. W. Woolworth Company, that resulted in the 1913 construction of the Woolworth Building, one of New York City's first major skyscrapers.

In 1891 George Fairchild married Josephine Mills Sherman. After a long illness, George W. Fairchild died on December 31, 1924. An obituary in the *Oneonta Star* (January 1, 1925) recalled that his career "from small beginnings was marked by slow but steady progress to success and high standing in the larger world of business, statesmanship, and finance."

Fairchild's only son, Sherman M. Fairchild (1896–1971), went on to enjoy a successful career as an inventor and businessman, founding several notable companies, including the Fairchild Camera and Instrument Corporation, the Fairchild Engine and Airplane Corporation, and the Fairchild Recording Equipment Corporation.—D. C.

Suggested Reading: IBM Web site; *New York Times* p27 Jan. 1, 1925; *Oneonta Star* p1+ Jan. 1, 1925, with photo; O'Malley, Michael. *Keeping Watch: A History of American Time*, 1990; Sobel, Robert. *IBM: Colossus in Transition*, 1981

Chris Handros/Getty Images

Fanning, Shawn

1981– Internet software developer; founder of Napster

In 1999 the Internet software developer and Northeastern University student Shawn Fanning created Napster, a music-swapping software program that quickly became the focus of one of the most far-reaching controversies to date regarding the power of the Internet. Napster, a name that was Fanning's high-school alias, was an openly available "shareware" program that users could download onto their computers and then use to trade MP3 audio files with other users. (MP3, which is the acronym for Moving Picture Experts Group Audio Layer 3, or MPEG layer 3, is a program that compresses digitally recorded music into files that are 1/11 their normal size; the condensed size of MP3 files makes sending and downloading music on the Internet, as well as storing and playing CD-quality audio files on desktop machines, faster and easier.) Napster, acting as the electronic conduit for MP3 files, made it possible to disseminate music in a highly efficient and relatively easy manner, for free.

What began as underground software used mostly by college students, who are part of the music industry's core market and who often have access to high-speed Internet connections, mushroomed into a phenomenon that claimed 80 million users at its peak. The problem, however, was that most of those users were trading MP3 files of copyrighted music. In December 1999 the Recording Industry Association of America (RIAA) retaliated with a lawsuit against Napster for copyright infringement, on behalf of 18 record companies, including such major labels as Universal Music, BMG, Sony Music, Warner Music Group, and EMI. Napster supporters argued that the service posed no danger to CD sales, and probably even encouraged them, by exposing users to more music. Some musicians, such as Courtney Love, the lead singer of the rock group Hole, rallied behind Napster, arguing that it helped wrest control of music away from the big record labels; others, such as the heavy-metal band Metallica, voiced outrage that their songs were being illegally traded on an unprecedented scale.

For a time it looked as though Fanning's creation and the company he started to support it, Napster Inc., might radically transform the music industry, either by replacing the physical distribution of music—in the form of CDs—with its digital counterpart, or by circumventing record labels altogether by providing musicians with a more direct means of reaching listeners. Fanning appeared on the cover of *Time* magazine (October 2, 2000), and *PC Magazine* named him as its person of the year for 2000. The recording industry refused to relent, however, and in July 2001, Napster, beleaguered by a series of legal rulings, went off-line. After a failed attempt to revamp itself into a paid subscription service, Napster Inc., closed for good in September 2002. Although now defunct, Napster is credited with bringing peer-to-peer computing into the mainstream. (Peer-to-peer computing, or P2P, allows all users on the network to share their files with one another.) Numerous other popular file-sharing programs—such as KaZaA and Gnutella—have risen to take Napster's place.

Shawn Fanning was born in 1981 in Brockton, Massachusetts, into a household that already included eight children, one of whom was his mother, Colleen. When, at age 17, she became pregnant with Shawn, her father lent his support; Shawn's biological father did not. Colleen later married an ex-Marine who drove a delivery truck for a local bakery, and together they had four more children. "Money was always a pretty big issue," Fanning told Spencer Ante for *BusinessWeek* (May 1, 2000, on-line). "There was a lot of tension around that." Fanning's uncle John, Colleen's younger brother, became a mentor to Shawn, giving him $100 for each "A" he earned in school and nurturing his interest in computers. When Fanning was a sophomore in high school, his uncle bought him his first computer, eventually adding an Internet connection and paying for a new phone line. "I saw this as a way for him to work his way out of his situation," John Fanning told Ante. "He absorbed the stuff faster than anyone I've ever known." Shawn soon discovered Internet Relay Chat (IRC), an application that enabled him to talk to people all over the world and trade knowledge about the Internet. At about the same time, Fanning's mother and her husband had a falling out, and Shawn and his siblings were placed in a foster home temporarily; despite the turmoil, he maintained his interest in computers.

During summer vacations in high school, Fanning worked as an intern at his uncle John's computer-games company, NetGames, and learned about programming from Carnegie Mellon University students who worked alongside him. After he graduated from high school, Fanning, having failed to gain admittance to the computer-science program at Carnegie Mellon, enrolled at Northeastern University, in Boston, Massachusetts, where he was placed in junior- and senior-level courses as a freshman. Even so, he felt bored and looked elsewhere for stimulation. His roommates introduced him to MP3s, and soon he was downloading and collecting music files. Fanning's only previous programming experience had been in designing programs for the Unix platform, but with the encouragement of his uncle and the help of a Windows programming book, he began designing his own music application for the Internet. After working 16-hour days for several weeks, Fanning had the prototype for Napster. On June 1, 1999 he tested the software by giving it to 30 friends, asking them not to tell anyone about it; they broke their promise, and within days it was on the Internet and had been downloaded by perhaps as many as 15,000 people. "I think the point at which I realized it had serious potential was when download.com put us in the download spotlight," Fanning told Giancarlo Varanini for the on-line magazine *ZDNet* (March 1, 2000). "It was very early . . . and we started receiving a ton of downloads. The server became overloaded, and that's when I realized that this had a huge market." Fanning's uncle also recognized the software's potential, and he incorporated Napster Inc. on behalf of his nephew and quickly began to search for investors to develop the project. Later that summer, a fledgling company was in place in San Mateo, California, led by Eileen Richardson, a venture capitalist with 10 years of experience in the technology industry. Fanning left college to devote himself to Napster Inc., becoming part of an expanding group of young people who left or opted out of college in favor of joining Internet companies, as Shelley Donald Coolidge noted in the *Christian Science Monitor* (June 6, 2000). "That's why I ended up leaving school—because [refining the program] required so much time," Fanning told Varanini. "I figured I would regret not going full force with this idea. It seemed we could make something of it."

Fanning's concept for the software was elegant and surprisingly simple—what Bob Brand referred to in the *Newtown Bee* (March 10, 2000, on-line) as "a pure cyber-insight." The idea arose, Fanning has said, out of hearing his roommates complain about the difficulty of accessing MP3 files through the search engines available then, such as MP3.com and Scour.net. Napster software took advantage of MP3 technology by serving as a forum through which users could search a database of songs and artists, chat about their favorite music, and trade audio files—the Internet generation's version of making bootlegged cassette tapes. Rather than using a centralized warehouse server, the program used peer-to-peer networking that allowed users to share the music files using their own computers, which often meant fewer broken links and faster downloading time. Every user on the Napster network could access the MP3 files on the hard drives of other users simultaneously logged on to the system. The software operated on the share-and-share-alike principle; each time a user logged on to Napster, the software would automatically post to its database a list of the files the user had designated to be shared, making them freely available. Napster users could search the large, evolving database for the songs and artists they were looking for and download, or copy, them to their own computer.

The potential for thievery, however, caused a vigorous backlash from the music industry. Napster's technology made it much easier to distribute music electronically and thereby circumvent the need to purchase CDs, posing a major threat to record companies. Though some of the files traded through Napster's software were shared legally (many small bands without record labels made their songs available through the network), many trades were copyrighted versions of the latest hits from big-name stars. The fair-use doctrine of copyright law gives consumers the right to make copies of CDs for their personal use, but Napster made copying possible on a much greater scale. In December 1999 the RIAA sued Napster to stop the exchange of copyrighted material. Among the labels represented in the suit were Seagram's Universal Music, Bertelsmann's BMG, Sony's Sony Music, and AOL Time Warner's Warner Music Group and EMI Group. An RIAA press release, quoted by Janelle Brown in the on-line magazine *Salon* (February 3, 2000), equated Napster with "a giant online pirate bazaar: Users log onto Napster servers and make their previously personal MP3 collections available for download by other Napster users who are logged on at the same time. Napster provides its users with all the facilities and means to engage in massive copyright infringement." The company argued that it was not guilty of wrongdoing since it did not keep any of the illegal files on its servers. Eileen Richardson, Napster's interim CEO, told Brown: "Napster is like an ISP [Internet Service Provider], protected under the 1998 Digital Millennium Copyright Act. It isn't the company's fault that people use its service to exchange illegal files, just as it wouldn't be AOL's legal responsibility if terrorists used one of its private chat rooms to plan a bombing." The RIAA claimed that Napster was liable because the network provided an area of cyberspace for people to trade files illegally.

Fanning, himself an amateur musician, originally conceived of the Napster software as a way to create a virtual network among the many niche groups of music listeners. In testimony before the Senate Judiciary Committee on October 9, 2000, as quoted on the Napster Web site, Fanning said that he hoped to create "genuine opportunity for participation, interaction, and individual involvement by the [Napster] members sharing files." The company instated a New Artist Program, which gave music fans an opportunity to find independent music that they would not typically encounter on FM radio play-lists or MTV and that, in turn, offered independent artists a chance to share their music and tap into a community of listeners. Richardson told Brown that Napster worked as a music cooperative: "People are naturally passionate about music, naturally want to share it; artists naturally want to create and share their music and find their fans: That's what music is all about. Now we have the Internet—why can't we do some of that there?" The response from the music industry was skeptical at best. "We love the idea of using technology to build artist communities, but that's not what Napster is all about," Cary Sherman, RIAA's senior executive vice president and general counsel, told Varanini. Sherman told Amy Harmon for the *New York Times* (March 7, 2000, on-line), "There's an incredible disconnect out there between what is normal behavior in the physical world versus the on-line world. There are people who think nothing of downloading entire CD collections on Napster who wouldn't dream of shoplifting from Tower Records. There's just a massive

education program that's needed here for people to understand what goes into the creation of music."

In an injunction issued on July 26, 2000 by Marilyn Hall Patel, a Federal District Court judge, Napster was ordered to remove all links to music copyrighted by major record labels by midnight July 28, which would have effectively shut down its business. In the two-day interval between the injunction and the deadline, traffic at Napster's Web site increased 71 percent as users scrambled to make use of what they thought would be their final days of swapping music over the Internet; it was estimated that Napster logged on an average of 600,000 individual visitors each day. Then, on July 28, at Napster's request, the U.S. Court of Appeals for the Ninth Circuit granted a stay on the injunction, allowing Napster to continue operations until the case went to court. The federal appeals panel found, as expressed on its written order, that there were "substantial questions" concerning Patel's decision and issued a six-week formal appeals schedule.

Reactions to the controversy among the artistic community were mixed. "I couldn't believe it when I found out that this Napster was linking thousands of people to the new Notorious B.I.G. album, 'Born Again,' a week before it even hit the streets," the rap artist Sean Combs, also known as Puff Daddy and P. Diddy, told Varanini. "This album is a labor of love from Notorious BIG's friends to the man, his kids, the rest of his family. . . . BIG and every other artist Napster abuses deserve respect for what they give us." In April 2000 Metallica sued Napster (as well as three universities that had not banned its use) for copyright infringement. Representatives of the band later brought to Napster headquarters a list of 300,000 names of people who had downloaded Metallica's music without the band's permission, demanding that those users have their accounts shut down.

Other artists, however, welcomed the chance to be distributed to wider audiences through the Internet. The group They Might Be Giants released a recording in MP3 format only, and Courtney Love sought to end her recording deal with Geffen Records. "Love is among the musicians raising the revolutionary notion that the Internet may offer them a better shake than the labels, which they accuse of imposing burdensome contracts," Alec Foege wrote for the *New York Times* (June 11, 2000, online). Foege pointed out that most artists get only pennies from the sale of each of their CDs; the rest of the money goes into production, marketing, promotion, and the record company's coffers. Napster's supporters also included the investors who contributed millions in venture capital to the company. One venture capitalist, Stewart Alsop, said to Harmon, "Who's to say that because the music business is structured the way it is structured, that's the way it should always be structured? If I believe that the new model is a better way for artists to operate, that is a moral justification for feeling good about investing in Napster, even though technically what they're doing is facilitating illegal behavior."

Napster representatives compared the controversy to the early days of the VCR, when the movie industry tried to prevent Sony from selling its Betamax machine because it could be used to make illegal copies of videocassettes. Eventually the Supreme Court ruled in favor of Sony, arguing that, though the machines could be used for illegal copying, they could also be used for a legitimate purpose. In the end, the spread of VCRs resulted in enormous extra profits for the movie industry. At a hearing before the House of Representatives' Small Business Committee in Washington, D.C., one digital-entertainment analyst argued that the same could hold true for the new technology, and declared that it is "rash to assume that every time someone downloads an illegal music file, the recording industry has lost a sale," as quoted by Jeri Clausing for the *New York Times* (May 25, 2000, on-line). "When music is free, people will try a lot they wouldn't have otherwise. And while Napster may have enabled the worst climate for casual piracy ever, the music industry is growing. Total revenue is up, CD shipments are up. It's worth wondering whether free music and MP3 swapping have stimulated sales."

On October 31, 2000 Napster and the German media conglomerate Bertelsmann—whose subsidiary BMG was one of the five major record companies suing Napster—announced that they had struck a deal to pursue a joint business strategy. Bertelsmann began to extend a series of loans to Napster that would eventually total some $85 million, and Napster agreed to change course and remodel itself into a subscription-based service, charging users a fee and then distributing part of that fee as royalties to the record companies that allowed their music to appear on the site. As part of the deal, Bertelsmann received an option to buy a controlling stake in Napster. "This is a call for the industry to wake up," Thomas Middelhoff, chairman and chief executive of Bertelsmann, told Matt Richtel and David D. Kirkpatrick for the *New York Times* (November 1, 2000, on-line). Bertelsmann agreed to drop its suit against Napster once the new service was available. Middelhoff, expressing his enthusiasm for the technology's potential, urged other companies to follow suit. The deal came as no surprise to the many industry observers who had predicted that rather than alienate their best customers by trying to shut down Napster and similar enterprises, record companies would ultimately join forces with them and explore ways to profit from on-line music distribution.

By February 2001 Napster had about 58 million registered users, more than twice what it had the previous summer. Napster made an offer to settle the lawsuit with RIAA for about $1 billion, but the record industry refused. As Napster programmers worked to develop a viable subscription plan, Judge Patel issued a court ruling that required the company to remove all copyrighted material from its site in order to prevent any future copyright infringement. The injunction called for record labels to provide the titles, artists' names, and relevant file names of all songs that it wanted banned. Unable to comply with the court's demand, Napster went off-line in July 2001.

Napster appealed Patel's injunction, and a Ninth Circuit Court of Appeals lifted the order and allowed Napster to resume services. Napster, however, refrained from doing so, instead focusing on developing its legal subscription service, under the direction of a new CEO, Konrad Hilbers, a former executive of Bertelsmann's subsidiary BMG. The following May, Bertelsmann bid to acquire the troubled company for $8 million, and Napster declared bankruptcy to attempt a necessary restructuring. In the fall of 2002, a bankruptcy judge blocked the sale of Napster's assets to Bertelsmann, citing Hilbers's split loyalties. Napster, forced into liquidation, closed its doors for good on September 3, 2002.

The major record companies, meanwhile, attempted to tap into the large demand for downloadable MP3 music by launching their own subscription on-line music services. Sony and Universal joined to create Pressplay, and BMG, EMI, and Warner Music formed MusicNet. Their efforts were dwarfed, however, by the proliferation of on-line music sites offering free downloads using variations of the P2P technology that Fanning popularized. According to comScore Networks, as of September 2002 there were 8.2 million users of the file-sharing program KaZaA Media Desktop, and similar programs, such as Audiogalaxy Satellite, boasted about 3 million users. (Audiogalaxy has since been shut down.) The most successful system to arrive after Napster's decline has been Gnutella, an information distribution software that links together clusters of users into networks and operates, unlike Napster, with no central server.

Echoing the prevailing mood in Napster's heyday, Scott Rosenberg argued in *Salon* (February 3, 2000) that the CD will gradually vanish, just as the vinyl record and the shellac 78 did before it. "At some point, I think we will all wake up and accept that storing this stuff as discrete physical objects rather than data no longer makes any sense, except for collectors," he wrote. "Along with many new ways to catalog and access the music we love, we'll all gain a lot more shelf space. Meanwhile, the waves of change that are roiling the music world today will crash into the movie and TV industries next, as bandwidth improvements make the loose electronic redistribution of video as easy as audio has become today. It is no wonder the media behemoths are worried."

Fanning originally held a high-profile position during Napster's rise to fame, but later moved into the behind-the-scenes role of chief technology officer during the company's legal troubles. He left the company when it closed down in September 2002. Fanning, who lives in California, is currently collaborating with the filmmaker Alex Winter on a screenplay for a biopic about his life for MTV Original Movies. In 1998 Fanning's uncle John tracked down Shawn's biological father and facilitated a meeting between the two. "It was pretty strange," Shawn told Spencer Ante; he learned, he said, that his father runs a software company.—M. A. H., A. I. C.

Suggested Reading: *BusinessWeek* (on-line) May 1, 2000; *Fortune* p129+ Mar. 20, 2000; *Newsweek* (on-line) Mar. 27, 2000; *New York Times* A p1 Feb. 13, 2001, III p4 May 26, 2002, VI p13 July 28, 2002; *New York Times* (on-line) Mar. 7, 2000; *Salon* (on-line) Feb. 3, 2000, Feb. 4, 2000; *Time* (on-line) Mar. 27, 2000

Farnsworth, Philo Taylor

Aug. 16, 1906–Mar. 11, 1971 Inventor of electronic television

Philo Taylor Farnsworth first came up with the idea for sending pictures through the air while working in a field when he was 14, and by age 21 he had built a working electronic television system. Even though his invention has come to dominate modern life—with recent estimates that the average American watches up to 120 hours of television each month—his name is all but forgotten. An autodidact and natural inventor, Farnsworth latched on to the new science of the electron, which had been discovered in 1897, as a viable means of transmitting images through the air, and he did this while most of the world's great minds were focusing on mechanical, and not electronic, television systems. His genius eventually came up against the forces of corporate greed, and—after failing to earn money or recognition for his efforts—he came to regret ever having invented television.

Like Thomas Edison and Ben Franklin—American inventors he idealized—Philo Taylor Farnsworth came from a humble background and received little formal education. Farnsworth, known as Phil, was born on August 16, 1906 in the frontier town of Indian Creek, Utah, in a log cabin with no electricity or running water. He was the middle child in a large Mormon farming family that would eventually number nine children. He showed signs of genius early on, displaying an innate understanding of the mechanical tools used on the farm; at age three, as Matthew McCann Fenton wrote in *Biography* magazine (November 1997), "he astounded his father, Lewis, by drawing a detailed diagram of the inner workings of a steam locomotive." When he was 11 his family moved to a ranch in Idaho's Snake River Valley. To Farnsworth's delight, the ranch was equipped with electricity and a power generator, and he was soon inventing ways to make life easier, including motorizing the hand-cranked washing machine. In the attic of the new house, he discovered a treasure

trove of old scientific journals and technical magazines, and he eagerly read everything he could about physics, and in particular about the electron—the tiny particle that could move at the speed of light.

Much later in his life, Farnsworth appeared on a television game show as a mystery guest named Dr. X. In order to help the contestants guess his identity, he gave them the clue: "I invented electronic television . . . when I was 14 years old," he said, as quoted by a journalist for the *U.S. News and World Report* (August 17–24, 1998). The "eureka" moment for the 14-year-old Farnsworth came when he was cutting hay with a horse-drawn harvester. As he looked back over the horizontal rows he had just cut, he imagined electrons following the same path. If a viewing screen were divided into furrow-like rows, he theorized, then electricity could be used to create points of light and darkness along the row, thus "painting" a picture with light and shade that, to a human eye, would appear to be a solid image.

Farnsworth had heard that engineers in New York City, London, and Moscow were working on mechanical television systems, in which images were transmitted along a wire between two spinning disks. The two disks had rows of holes that picked up patterns of light at one end and then projected them at the other, the idea being that the changing patterns of shadow and light would resemble the black-and-white images of early movies. Although the concept generated interest in the scientific community, this system was crude, at best. "In ten years of research," Fenton wrote for *Biography*, "they had managed to create a blurry, shadowy image, about the size of a postage stamp." Farnsworth understood that the mechanical approach would never work—that the disks could never spin quickly enough to create a believable image. To work, he believed, television would have to transmit and receive pictures as electrical pulses through the airwaves, just as radios sent sound through radio waves.

Farnsworth approached one of the only people around him who might understand his idea—his high-school chemistry teacher, Justin Tolman. One afternoon after class Farnsworth spent hours making sketches and explaining his idea to Tolman for what he would later call an "image dissector," because it dissected images into smaller parts—light and dark areas—and then transmitted them as electrical impulses. The image dissector was basically a crude electronic television camera, based on the same principle as modern television cameras. Years later, those sketches, and Tolman's testimony, would prove crucial in the legal battles over who had been the first to invent television.

In 1923 Farnsworth's family moved again, to Provo, Utah, and Farnsworth enrolled—a few years early—at Brigham Young University. When his father died of pneumonia a year later (some accounts say two years later), he had to leave college to help support his brothers and sisters. He took a job delivering radios for a local furniture store and began a side business repairing radios. In 1926 he met two California businessmen who were passing through Salt Lake City, and he told them that he— and not the large corporations—knew how to build a workable television. George Everson and Les Gorrell must have been impressed, since they committed $6000, their life's savings, to the project, asking only that Farnsworth move to Los Angeles so that they could oversee his work. "Can you be ready to get married in three days?" his wife, Elma "Pem" (Gardner) Farnsworth, recalled as her husband's rather breathless marriage proposal, as quoted by Fenton. After Pem assented, Farnsworth spent all his savings on a beautiful engagement ring since, he told her, he didn't want her to be ashamed of it when they became rich. "You had to believe in him," Pem told Fenton. "His confidence in himself was amazing. He was the sort of person who inspired everyone around him."

The young couple moved within sight of Hollywood's searchlights, and set up a laboratory in their living room, staffed by Pem's brother, Cliff, and a few other engineers. Pem herself proved an able assistant, learning to make mechanical drawings and to use a precision spot welder. This was an era before ready-made electronic components, so the team had to blow their own glass to make tubes, and sculpt their own metal for components. In 1927 the Farnsworths relocated their laboratory to San Francisco; by now they had more financial backing, and events began to move quickly. In January of that year Farnsworth filed a patent application, and that September he made the first television broadcast. He painted a slide black and then scratched a straight line down its center; in another room Cliff Gardner dropped the slide between the image dissector and a hot lamp. A small line appeared on the viewing screen that, when Cliff turned the slide, was seen to move; according to Neil Postman in *Time* magazine (March 29, 1999), Farnsworth said: "There you are, electronic television." He next invited his financial backers to watch television, this time broadcasting a dollar sign as a message that they would get their money's worth. Early in 1928, he demonstrated the television for a group of journalists; although blurry, the 20 pictures per second were enough to convince the group that they were seeing motion. The *San Francisco Chronicle* ran the headline: "S.F. Man's Invention to Revolutionize Television," and the story was picked up nationwide.

The news reached the East Coast, where it came to the attention of Vladimir Zworykin, a Russian immigrant and electrical engineer who had spent years trying to build an all-electronic television. In 1923 he applied for a patent for a camera tube, and by 1925 he had patched together a crude system, but he had failed to produce a viable image, and his bosses at the Westinghouse corporation told him to work on something more productive. In 1929 David Sarnoff became president of the Radio Corporation of America (RCA); not wanting to be left behind in the radio age if televisions became a reality, he hired Zworykin and put him in charge of building an RCA television. In April 1930 Zworykin paid a visit to Farnsworth's laboratory. Nearly 20 years older than the young inventor, Zworykin had a Ph.D. and had worked with some of the world's best scientists, and yet he needed to follow the young inventor's lead. "Zworykin was in here just to find out anything he possibly could. And Phil was the other way around— 'Here's some ideas,'" Rom Rutherford, who worked in the Farnsworth lab, said on the PBS program *American Experience*, as archived on the PBS Web site. Pem Farnsworth told Evan I. Schwartz in an interview for *Technology Review* (2000) that her husband showed Zworykin everything, even building an image dissector in front of his guest. Zworykin believed that he had a better receiver, but he was impressed by Farnsworth's image dissector, and quickly sent a 700-word telegram back to his laboratory with a full description of how to build one. He imagined that RCA's television might be a hybrid of his and Farnsworth's designs.

Sarnoff had a different idea: RCA owned all the patents for manufacturing and operating radios, and he wanted to have the same advantage in any future television market. After Farnsworth's patent application for electronic television was approved, in 1930, Sarnoff himself traveled to San Francisco to meet the competition. Farnsworth was out of town, but one of his financial backers showed Sarnoff around the laboratory and had an engineer conduct a demonstration. The stock market had already crashed, and many of Farnsworth's backers were pressuring him to make a deal with a large corporation to bring his television to fruition. According to Schwartz, Sarnoff left the laboratory, saying that he planned to build a television without infringing on Farnsworth's patent, that "there was nothing here he needed." Even so, Sarnoff made an offer a few months later to buy Farnsworth's idea outright for $100,000, but Farnsworth refused him.

After that, the battle lines were drawn. In the words of Schwartz, "a portentous battle raged between a lone inventor and the indomitable mogul at the helm of the first electronic media-age monopoly." The fight would be played out in patent court. RCA had time and money on their side; some have even speculated that the company wanted to wait until the 1940s, when their radio patents expired, to introduce television to the public. RCA argued that Farnsworth's television was a copy of Zworykin's 1923 camera tube device (which had been granted a patent), but they could produce no evidence that Zworykin's model had ever worked. Farnsworth had little to back up his claim that he had first imagined the idea for electronic television when he was 14—that is, until his high-school teacher Justin Tolman, came forward to testify on his behalf. Tolman produced Farnsworth's original sketch; it was, according to Postman, "almost an exact replica of an Image Dissector."

As the court battles carried on, Farnsworth signed a deal with Philco, the nation's largest radio manufacturer, giving them the right to make televisions based on his plan. RCA got wind of this deal when they picked up Philco's test transmissions (the two companies' headquarters lay on opposite sides of the Delaware river), and threatened to cancel Philco's licensing arrangements with them. This would have crippled the radio company, and they were forced to break their deal with Farnsworth.

In 1932 Farnsworth was invited to give a public demonstration of his television at the Franklin Institute, in Philadelphia, Pennsylvania. Visitors to the science museum saw themselves appear on a television screen as they walked into the grand lobby, and for 75 cents they could watch a television show with dogs and dancing girls on a one-foot screen.

In July of 1935 the patent office finally issued its ruling: arguing that a machine based on Zworykin's design would produce meaningless shades of dark and light, they awarded priority of invention to Farnsworth. Now 29 years old, Farnsworth was the undisputed inventor of television. He began experimental transmissions from a television station outside Philadelphia; about 50 households, mostly headed by electronics hobbyists or engineers, picked up broadcasts of Baby Delores, a singing and dancing four-year-old, or Little Miss Television, an 11-year-old singer. In 1936 the Olympic Games in Munich, Germany, were broadcast using televisions that had been built under license to Farnsworth. In 1937 Farnsworth founded Farnsworth Television and Radio; he hoped to subsidize the commercialization of television by making and selling radios.

RCA countered these moves with a full-scale public-relations war. The company won the right to broadcast the 1939 New York World's Fair from their "television pavilion," and it stocked New York department stores with RCA televisions (by now RCA scientists had reverse engineered a working model based on Farnsworth's ideas, but had yet to pay him any licensing fees). The World's Fair event went down in history as the first television broadcast; and Sarnoff made headlines, claiming Zworykin as the father of television. "Now, ladies and gentlemen," Schwartz quoted Sarnoff as he announced at the fair, "we add sight to sound!"

Later that year, Farnsworth finally succeeded in extracting a $1-million licensing fee from RCA. Before televisions could really be marketed to the American public, however, World War II broke out, and the U.S. government suspended the manufacture of consumer electronic goods. Farnsworth's television technology was enlisted for use in radar and defense research. Exhausted from years of trying to promote his invention and fight court battles, Farnsworth retreated to a Maine estate, and became increasingly dependent on alcohol and sedatives. He suffered from depression, had a nervous breakdown, and briefly underwent shock therapy at a sanitarium.

In 1946 production of televisions resumed, but the very next year Farnsworth's key patents expired; "just a few months before TV began a sudden, rapid proliferation from just 6,000 sets in use nationwide to tens of millions by the mid-1950s," as Schwartz noted. RCA captured 80 percent of the market, and Farnsworth sold off his assets and got out of the television business.

In his later years Farnsworth made contributions to many scientific fields. He became interested in nuclear fusion as an energy source, and also contributed to the development of radar, the electron microscope, aircraft and rocket guidance systems, and incubators for newborns. When he died, on March 11, 1971 in Holladay, Utah, the *New York Times* obituary described him as one of the world's greatest mathematicians; in spite of this notice, his creation of television was largely unknown at the time of his death.

In the years since his death, Farnsworth has been slowly gaining recognition as the originator of electronic television. In 1983 a U.S. stamp was issued with his likeness. In 1984 he was inducted into the Inventors' Hall of Fame (Zworykin had been inducted seven years earlier). Farnsworth had lived long enough to see color television and the launching of the world's first commercial television satellite—which brought the Vietnam War into millions of Americans' living rooms—and yet he reportedly came to loath what he termed the "monster" that he had unleashed. His son, Kent, told Postman, "Throughout my childhood his reaction to television was 'There's nothing on it worthwhile, and we're not going to watch it in this household, and I don't want it in your intellectual diet.'"

Pem and Phil Farnsworth had three sons; two survived until adulthood and one of these—Philo, Jr.—became an inventor.—M. A. H.

Suggested Reading: *American Experience* Web site; *Biography* Nov. 1997; *Technology Review* p96+ Sep./Oct. 2000; *Time* Mar. 29, 1999; *U.S. News & World Report* p44+ Aug. 17–24, 1998; *Encyclopedia of Television*, 1997

Feigenbaum, Edward A.

Jan. 20, 1936– Computer scientist

The computer scientist Edward A. Feigenbaum helped bring artificial intelligence (AI) from the realm of science-fiction books and movies into the real world. In 1965 he helped create the world's first "expert system," Dendritic Algorithm (DENDRAL), a computer program that determined the chemical structure of molecules. To perform its task, Feigenbaum programmed DENDRAL with almost every fact known to chemists. This represented a major break from previous AI systems, which attempted to solve problems through reasoning alone. Feigenbaum argued that expert systems re-

Courtesy of Ed Feigenbaum

Edward A. Feigenbaum

quire specialized knowledge to perform tasks relating to disciplines such as chemistry, biology and physics. DENDRAL served as the model for many more expert systems that people use every day, such as personal computers, scanners, word processors and all types of interactive software. Feigenbaum hopes that the future will bring larger expert systems that will be able to think just like human beings.

Edward Albert Feigenbaum was born on January 20, 1936 in Weehauken, New Jersey. Edward's father, a Polish immigrant, died just before his first birthday. His mother eventually remarried, and Edward's stepfather helped spark his interest in science. In an interview with Dennis Shasha and Cathy Lazere for *Out of their Minds: The Lives and Discoveries of 15 Great Computer Scientists* (1995), Feigenbaum recalled, "Once a month, the shows at the Hayden Planetarium in New York City would change. My stepfather would take me to each new exhibit. Afterwards, we would explore one little part of the Museum of Natural History. Eventually, after all these months, we covered the whole thing. That's my first recollection of scientific things." His stepfather worked as an accountant and office manager in a small bakery. Young Edward found himself fascinated by the large Monroe calculator his stepfather used to keep the books. "There were large table models that weighed about twenty pounds or more with lots of wheels inside and motors with a big keyboard," he told Shasha and Lazere. "You'd punch in the numbers and you'd press big buttons that read 'plus' and 'multiply.' Then the wheels would turn and go clank, clank, clank. I was fascinated by what the Monroe could do for me—it could do all these complicated calculations that I would struggle to do by hand."

As he approached adulthood, Feigenbaum looked forward to a career in science. His parents, however, recommended that he take up electrical engineering, a more financially secure career path in the 1950s. In 1952 he enrolled at the Carnegie Institute of Technology (now Carnegie-Mellon University) in Pittsburgh, Pennsylvania. To broaden his knowledge, Feigenbaum took extra courses at Carnegie's Graduate School of Industrial Administration. In one of these classes, taught by James March, he was introduced to the concept of "game theory," whose principles were developed the previous decade by the Hungarian mathematician John von Neumann. Game theory involves the use of mathematics to select the best strategy that will maximize gains and minimize losses when a person has to make a decision; Feigenbaum believed that analytic principles and carefully constructed models could be applied to social areas. He was also influenced by Herbert Simon, another one of his professors at Carnegie. During the 1950s Simon and Allen Newell began thinking about how a computer could simulate human thinking. In January 1955 Simon told his students that he and Newell had invented a "thinking machine" that could solve mathematical problems on its own. The thinking machine was actually a computer program called the Logic Theorist, which ran on the IBM 701 machine. The Logic Theorist, as Shasha and Lazere explained, "attempted to discover proofs in the propositional logic of [Bertrand] Russell and [Alfred North] Whitehead's classic book *Principia Mathematica*." Simon and Newell programmed the Logic Theorist with many different "heuristics," basic rules for problem-solving. On the basis of these rules, the program could learn to solve problems in the same way human beings do. To help explain the concept of a thinking machine to his students, Simon gave them copies of the IBM 701 manual. After reading the manual in a single night, Feigenbaum was so impressed that he wanted a career that involved with working with computers.

Feigenbaum graduated from the Carnegie Institute of Technology in 1956 with a B.S. in Electrical Engineering. In order to learn computer programming, he took a summer job with IBM in New York, before he returned to school in the fall of 1956; the experience cemented his desire to work with computers. He then continued his studies as a doctoral student at Carnegie's School of Industrial Administration, earning his degree in 1960. In his doctoral thesis, part of which was researched at the National Physical Laboratory in the United Kingdom on a Fulbright scholarship, Feigenbaum applied the principles of cognitive psychology to computer programming, creating a program he called the Elementary Perceiver and Memorizer (EPAM). The program successfully mimicked a psychological experiment where people memorize two separate combinations of letters that formed gibberish words in a stimulus-response setting. (More advanced versions of EPAM are still used today.) Feigenbaum began his teaching career in 1960, joining the faculty of the School of Business Administration at the University of California, Berkeley, because the university did not have a computer-science department. But he continued to work with Herbert Simon on several computer-related projects, including updates of EPAM.

Most computer historians trace the development of artificial intelligence to the British mathematician and scientist Alan Turing, who is best remembered for breaking Germany's enigma code during World War II. In his paper, *Computing Machinery and Intelligence*, published in *Mind* (1950), Turing asked if machines could think, and he concluded that technology would eventually allow digital computers to imitate human thought processes. In 1963 Feigenbaum and Julian Feldman co-edited a series of articles and papers on AI in the book *Computers and Thought*. The book discussed the state of AI at the time. In the introduction, Feigenbaum observed that AI had been used for deductive tasks such as proving theorems and playing chess. He expressed hope that AI could develop to a level where it solve practical problems through empirical induction, making an informed guess on the basis of available information.

At nearby Stanford University, in Stanford, California, the university administration implemented plans to establish a computer-science department, which would include an artificial-intelligence laboratory. John McCarthy, who done some research in AI, was responsible for organizing the department and immediately recruited Feigenbaum. After teaching business administration for four years at Berkeley, Feigenbaum went to Stanford in 1965. In addition to teaching computer science, he was the director of the university's new Computer Center and also co-founded the Knowledge Systems Laboratory, which pioneered AI research.

Feigenbaum's ambition was to create "expert systems," which could solve problems in specialized areas such as chemistry and biology. He began searching for a task to explore empirical induction. Joshua Lederberg, the chairman of Stanford's genetics department and a 1958 Nobel Prize laureate in Physiology or Medicine, gave him an ideal task: Lederberg was working on a probe that would land on the planet Mars and search for any signs of life, especially precursor molecules. The probe would use a mass spectrometer to measure these molecules. Feigenbaum attempted to create an expert system that would determine the chemical structure of molecules. After working on the project for several months, he concluded that he needed help from a chemist to give the system knowledge about chemistry. Carl Djerrasi, a Stanford chemist who helped develop the birth-control pill, joined the project. Less than a year later, the three Stanford professors unveiled DENDRAL, the world's first expert system. To determine the chemical composition of molecules, DENDRAL used molecular formulas, data measured with a spectrometer and heuristic knowledge of organic chemistry.

In *Machines Who Think: A Personal Inquiry into the History and Prospects of Artificial Intelligence* (1979), Pamela McCorduck observed that DENDRAL was different from previous AI–based programs because it was programmed with specialized knowledge to solve specific problems. The reasoning behind other AI programs, as McCorduck wrote, was "that methods by which problems were solved were independent of the content of the problem itself." Although it was proclaimed a success, most researchers and scientists were unimpressed with DENDRAL because it contradicted conventional theories and assumptions about AI. However, within a few years, DENDRAL sparked a major revision in AI's principles and theories and became the model for other expert systems. Feigenbaum recalled to McCorduck that almost overnight "people beat a path to the DENDRAL door, trying to find out what kinds of knowledge representations we used, how we extracted the expertise from the experts, what do we know, and so on." Feigenbaum explained to Shasha and Lazere why expert systems needed specified knowledge by drawing an analogy. If someone had a heart attack, Feigenbaum asked if would be better if that person were rushed to the local hospital for treatment or the local university math department. "We rush that person over to the hospital where there are people trained in medicine," Feigenbaum said to Shasha and Lazere. "We don't rush them over to the math department where they are excellent reasoners. Right? Because reasoning doesn't make any difference. You need to know about medicine, not about reasoning." Although DENDRAL never made it to Mars, the program became an essential tool for Stanford chemists. As different university computers linked up in the late 1970s to form what became the Internet, chemists around the world were able to use DENDRAL as well.

In 1970 Feigenbaum completed work on "Meta-DENDRAL," which enabled the program to add to its own knowledge through induction. While specified knowledge was necessary for the program to solve chemistry problems, it also needed the ability to reason in order to acquire new knowledge by itself. If a chemical structure did not match anything in its programming, Meta-DENDRAL, based on the information it collected, was able to propose new rules and add to existing knowledge just as human chemists would. Unfortunately, having expert systems often proved to be a difficult challenge. Although most expert systems could solve specified problems, they failed to model the learning processes of human beings.

DENDRAL and Meta-DENDRAL served as models for other expert systems. In the 1970s a team of scientists developed Mycin, which helped doctors diagnose infectious diseases and recommend treatment. Feigenbaum continued his teaching and research at Stanford University, and several of his students eventually went into AI research. He became more visible as an evangelist for knowledge-based expert systems, aggressively promoting them during talks, conferences, and lectures. Feigenbaum also published many articles and several books on AI.

During the early 1980s Feigenbaum and several other scientists co-founded three start-up firms—Intellicorp, Teknowledge, and Design Power Inc.—in order to create an AI industry in the United States. Teknowledge received publicity when it designed an expert system for a French oil company. In *U. S. News & World Report* (December 5, 1983), Stanley N. Wellborn wrote that this system could "diagnose problems such as how to salvage a drill that gets stuck during drilling operations." During the 1980s expert systems gradually became part of everyday life. Hospitals were successfully using computers to diagnose diseases, and the computers' judgments were slightly more reliable than those of doctors. IBM unveiled a product called Epistle, a secretary-like program that scanned incoming mail and sorted out the more important pieces. A system called Prospector helped geologists find valuable deposits of oil and other minerals. Software programs, such as the popular word processors WordPerfect and Microsoft Word, are also types of expert systems based on Feigenbaum's ideas. In order for the spell check feature to work, the programs' designers had to include millions of correctly spelled words in their memories. By the 1990s computers could recognize human speech.

Despite the popularity of expert systems, the AI industry in the United States never became profitable. (Two of the three companies that Feigenbaum co-founded are still in business, but in radically different forms.) In 1983 Feigenbaum and Pamela McCorduck published *The Fifth Generation: Japan's Computer Challenge to the World*. In it, they attempted to sound the alarm that the United States was in danger of falling behind the Japanese in developing AI. (A short time before the book was published, Japan announced it would spending more than $1 billion to research and develop AI.) In order to remain competitive, Feigenbaum and McCorduck recommended that the United States create a "national laboratory" to promote AI. Although the Pentagon's Defense Advanced Research Projects Agency (DARPA) was sufficiently concerned that it asked Congress to allocate $500 million for AI research in the next decade, most AI firms in the United States went bankrupt. In an interview with Steve Cross, editor-in chief of the *Institute of Electrical and Electronics Engineers (IEEE) Expert* (December 1995), Feigenbaum attributed the success of Japanese companies in AI to their "staying power," explaining, "When they decide to get into an area—after much thrashing around with consensus building—then they are in that area for the long haul. They're willing to make a flow of investments over many years to bring that technology to fruition." Speaking to Bob Metcalfe for *Infoworld* (April 12, 1993), Feigenbaum suggested that American AI firms failed because they approached AI as a "business" instead of a research

effort that improved existing products and developed new expert systems to make people's lives easier.

Although AI failed as an industry, Feigenbaum believes that it succeeded as a research effort that made expert systems common. "I'm not interested in theoretical concepts," he told Daniel Lyons for *Forbes* (November 30, 1998). "I like to see my work used in the real world." Under Feigenbaum's supervision, his lab at Stanford is continuing AI research, hoping to complete a massive expert system that will be able to think like a human being by 2025. The process of programming every law, rule and specification, which number in the millions, into the expert system will take several decades.

From 1994 to 1997 Feigenbaum served as chief scientist for the U.S. Air Force. He was elected as a member of the National Academy of Engineering in 1986 and the American Academy of Arts and Sciences in 1991. He was named as a fellow to the American Association for Artificial Intelligence, the American College of Medical Informatics, the American Institute of Medical and Biological Engineering, and the American Association for the Advancement of Science. In 1991 he was the initial recipient of the Feigenbaum Medal, which was named in his honor by the World Congress of Expert Systems. In 1994 the Association for Computing Machinery (ACM) presented Feigenbaum and fellow computer scientist Raj Reddy with its highest honor, the A. M. Turing Award. In 1997 he was honored with the U.S. Air Force Exceptional Civilian Service Award.

Feigenbaum, who is married and has two children, lives in Palo Alto, California.—D. C.

Suggested Reading: *Communications of the Association for Computing Machinery* p97+ May 1996; *Forbes* p176+ Nov. 30, 1998, with photos; *Institute of Electrical and Electronics Engineers (IEEE) Expert* p8+ Dec. 1995, with photo; *U.S. News & World Report* p59+ Dec. 5, 1983, with photos; McCorduck, Pamela. *Machines Who Think: A Personal Inquiry into the History and Prospects of Artificial Intelligence*, 1979; Shasha, Dennis and Cathy Lazere. *Out of their Minds: The Lives and Discoveries of 15 Great Computer Scientists*, 1995

Felt, Dorr E.

Mar. 18, 1862–Aug. 7, 1930 Inventor of the comptometer

The development of calculating machines began in the late 19th century, with many scientists and inventors drawing their inspiration from the British mathematician Charles Babbage's Difference Engine, a machine that could compile mathematical tables, which Babbage, who is sometimes referred to as the father of modern computing, designed in the early 1820s. However, much like Babbage's proposed machine, the earliest calculating devices were impractically large and awkward to operate. It wasn't until 1885 that the American inventor Dorr E. Felt introduced the first office-sized, key-driven calculator. Dubbed the comptometer, Felt's invention was the first truly marketable mechanical calculator; its commercial version is generally regarded as having launched the business-machine industry. Felt's easy-to-use design is widely considered the forerunner of the modern calculator.

Dorr Eugene Felt was born on March 18, 1862 in Beloit, Wisconsin, where he spent most of his childhood, living and working on a Rock County farm. His parents, Eugene Kincaid and Elizabeth (Morris) Felt, raised him in the Baptist faith. Felt was educated in the public school system and ended his formal education after just one year of high school. At age 14 he began working at a local machine store, and at age 20 he ventured to Chicago, Illinois, where he labored on a maintenance crew for the Pullman Company. After a promotion to foreman, Felt left Pullman to become a sewing-machine salesman, but he quickly learned that he did not enjoy life on the road. Drawn back to work on machines, he took a position at Ostrander and Huke, a shop that used planing machines to cut various depths of metal. It was this experience that inspired some of Felt's original ideas for his calculating machine: He believed that many of the same mechanisms employed by the planing machine could be incorporated into the design of a calculating machine.

When Felt's work at Ostrander and Huke began to slow, he connected with A. B. Lawther, a businessman who was interested in an elevator invention that Felt had previously designed. Impressed with Felt's ideas, Lawther offered him a place to work in exchange for an interest in any resulting creations. In 1884, when Felt was just 22 years old, he began work on a crude design for a key-driven calculator. Unable to afford the costs of constructing a metal model, he instead built the prototype out of wood and an assortment of unusual parts, including meat skewers, elastic bands, string, and staples. As quoted by Michael R. Williams in *A History of Computing Technology* (1985), Felt once humbly described the machine's beginnings: "I went to the grocery store and bought a macaroni box to make a frame of. I went to the butcher and bought skewers to make the keys of, and to the hardware store and bought staples, and to the bookstore and bought rubber bands to use for springs. I went to work to make a calculating machine, expecting to have thousands in use in 90 days. I began on Thanksgiving Day, because it was a holiday, and worked that day, and Christmas and New Year's, but I didn't get it done in three days. It was a long time before I got it done." Felt's initial model was completed on January 1, 1885, and by the autumn of the following year, he had constructed a perfected metal model of the machine, which he called the comptometer.

The major innovation of the eight-column comptometer was that it could be operated through the use of push-button keys. At the time, calculating machines had no keys; rather, the numbers were entered by means of dials, switches, cranks, or other such comparatively clumsy devices. The keyboard of the comptometer, which resembled that of a typewriter, made Felt's machine a great deal easier to use. Much like today's calculators, the only requirement for entering a particular number or operation was for the key representing that operation to be pressed. (There was no room for error, however, because numbers were added with each press of the digit keys.) This essential element accelerated the calculating process beyond that used in any contemporary device. The keys, numbered 1 through 9 (there was no zero), were linked to springs, which in turn drove the device. The comptometer also featured a lever to clear the results, which were displayed in a group of 11 windows located below the keyboard. The key-driven method of Felt's operation was possible due to a complex "carry mechanism" that responded quickly when each key was pressed, performing its action before the key returned to its original position. This new level of speed initiated several technical problems of inertia and momentum that had not yet been faced by previous designers; Felt overcame them by using advanced engineering techniques that combined the strength of the parts with the machine's overall lightness.

The comptometer made computing technology accessible to the average consumer and was initially the only machine of its kind. Felt eventually bought out Lather's interest in his invention by borrowing $800 from his cousin, Chauncy W. Foster. (Felt had used some of this money to refine his design, replacing many of the original parts with custom-made pieces. On his first patent he actually credited the invention to both himself and Foster.) Because Felt anticipated a strong demand for his invention, he collaborated with Robert Tarrant, a Chicago machine-shop owner who provided him with work space and an investment of $5,000 for parts and materials. On November 28, 1887 the two men formed an equal partnership, and 14 months later they incorporated as the Felt & Tarrant Manufacturing Company, with Felt serving as president, a position he would hold until his death. By the 1890s the company was supplying comptometers to such clients as businesses, banks, accounting departments, and universities.

Despite the success of the comptometer, the instrument was shrouded in controversy during its earliest years of production. The Felt & Tarrant Manufacturing Co. might have enjoyed total domination of the mechanical-calculator market had it not been for William S. Burroughs (1857–1898), an ex-bank clerk from St. Louis who had also become an inventor. Although Felt is widely credited as the creator of the key-driven calculator, Burroughs developed a similar device known as the Adding and Listing Machine in 1884—the same year Felt was constructing his own design. Although Burroughs filed for a patent for his machine more than a year before Felt, Felt received his patent first (in 1887). The major difference between the two models was that in Burroughs's design the keys of the calculator were driven by a handle, while in Felt's comptometer the keys were driven by a spring. Burroughs's device also "listed" the figures onto a paper tape, making it one of the first machines to feature printing capabilities. Burroughs had rushed his product to the market, in 1887, only to learn of several defects that had to be corrected. Nevertheless, his device eventually became the chief rival to Felt's comptometer. The Felt comptometer and the Burroughs adding and listing machine were the two most widely used calculating machines in the world before World War I.

Competition heated up between Felt & Tarrant and the newly formed Burroughs Adding Machine Company. Felt hoped to beat his rival by combining the fast, key-driven design of his comptometer with a printing mechanism. On June 11, 1889 he patented the comptograph, one of the earliest printing desk calculators. This model, while it was key driven, required that a second, cumbersome lever be used to activate the printing device. Felt spent more than a decade working to improve upon this design so that the printing mechanism would also be key driven. (He did eventually release a key-set, two-motion system.) Although Felt was issued 13 new patents between 1889 and 1904 relating to various "lister machines"—indicating that he had made some notable enhancements to his original design—the comptograph was never able to compete with Burroughs's adding and listing machine. In 1902 Felt and Tarrant parted ways, with Tarrant taking all rights to the comptograph and Felt retaining all rights to the comptometer. The men formed two separate companies, and Tarrant continued selling the comptograph throughout Europe, where it had experienced some initial success. European sales quickly died off, however, with the start of World War I in 1914, and the Comptograph Company was eventually reabsorbed by Felt & Tarrant. The comptograph is often seen as a predecessor of the electronic printer, perhaps the most widely used accessory to the modern computer.

Throughout the early 20th century, Felt continued making improvements to his comptometer, and sales continued to climb. When the F-model comptometer was introduced in 1915, it featured an innovative error-detection and correction key, and sales exploded: More than 42,000 F-models were sold over the next five years—compared to just half that amount for all models of the previous 30 years. By 1920, the company employed more than 100 full-time salesmen. Nevertheless, Felt & Tarrant faced challenges within its market, particularly from Burroughs. Starting in 1911, as a number of Felt's original patents were beginning to expire, Burroughs sought to carve his own place in the comptometer market. (Just as Burroughs had

dominated the adder/lister market, Felt & Tarrant had maintained a significant stronghold on the comptometer.) Because Felt had dedicated so much of his energy over the previous decade to enhancing the comptograph, he had made few improvements to the comptometer since his original 1887 patent. In 1912 Burroughs was granted two patents for inventions that embellished aspects of Felt's expired patents and provided the foundation for his company's own line of calculators. When Burroughs released this calculator, the device was encased in a "shoebox" almost identical to that used in Felt's comptometer. Felt & Tarrant promptly filed a lawsuit alleging that the Burroughs Adding Machine Co. had violated Felt's patent on his metal case (a patent he had been granted in 1903, which was not due to expire for nearly a decade). While details of the court case are murky, it appears that Felt won the suit and that Burroughs was required to halt production on his calculator, and also to recall and destroy the models that had previously been distributed. Burroughs later issued a redesigned model of his product, and a healthy rivalry between the dueling calculator manufacturers continued until well into the 20th century.

In 1918, during the U.S.'s involvement in World War I, Felt served as a regional advisor (for Region 9) to the War Industries Board, representing Illinois, Indiana, and Iowa. He was appointed a member of the Employers Commission by Secretary of Labor William B. Wilson, and in 1919 he was sent to Great Britain to study British labor conditions and policies. That same year he held the presidency of the Illinois Manufacturers Association, and from 1920 to 1921 he was the director of the United States Chamber of Commerce. In addition, Felt was director of the Chicago Association of Commerce and a member of the executive committees of both the Illinois Taxpayers Alliance and the Legislative Voters League of America. He belonged to numerous clubs and societies, including the Chicago Public School League, the American Academy of Political and Social Science, the Academy of Political Science, the National Institute of Social Sciences, the Chicago Historical Society, the Union League, the Chicago Athletic Association, and the Western Society of Engineers.

Felt's fascination with computing machines never diminished; throughout his lifetime, he was widely known for his love of collecting, displaying, and lecturing on mechanical computing devices. The Felt & Tarrant Manufacturing Company boasted an extensive historical archive, which documented the development not only of Felt's own inventions, but of other calculating machines as well.

Dorr E. Felt married Agnes McNulty of Bellevue, Iowa, on January 15, 1891. The couple had four daughters: Virginia, Elizabeth, Constance, and Dorothea. Felt died of a stroke on August 7, 1930 in Chicago, having accumulated 46 domestic and 25 foreign patents throughout his life. At the time of his death, Felt's company was worth a reported

$3 million and employed 850 people. The J-model comptometer, the last "shoebox" version of Felt's original groundbreaking invention, was introduced in 1926 and remained in production for the next 40 years; several other versions were released after his death. In 1957 Felt & Tarrant became the Comptometer Corporation, and soon after it merged with the Victor Adding Machine Company to become the Victor Comptometer Corporation (1961–86). Felt's original string-and-macaroni-box prototype for the comptometer is on display at the Smithsonian Institute, in Washington, D.C.—K.D., B.S.

Suggested Reading: Spencer, Donald D. *The Timetable of Computers*, 1997; Williams, Michael R. *A History of Computing Technology*, 1985

Fessenden, Reginald Aubrey

Oct. 6, 1866–July 22, 1932 Radio pioneer

Reginald Aubrey Fessenden is second only to Thomas Alva Edison in the number of patents issued in his name—about 500—but his contributions to the development of radio are second to none. It has been argued that his contributions to the medium are even greater than those of Guglielmo Marconi—the man most often cited as the "father of radio." It was Fessenden who sent the first-ever wireless transmission of the human voice, on December 23, 1900. This remarkable achievement—known as wireless telephony—came about through his creation of amplitude modulation (better known by the acronym AM), a feat few in his era believed could be achieved because no one, including Marconi, believed that radio could be broadcast in continuous waves. Though Fessenden never received adequate compensation or recognition for his work, many historians credit him with developing both the protocols and the equipment upon which all modern wireless broadcasting is based.

Reginald Aubrey Fessenden was born in Milton, Quebec, Canada on October 6, 1866. He was the son of E. J. Fessenden, an Anglican minister with a small pastor in East Bolton, Quebec, and the former Clementina Trenholme. At the age of five Fessenden moved with his family to Fegus, a town in Ontario. The family moved again when he was nine, this time to Chippawa, near Niagara Falls. There he studied at the De Veaux Military College and displayed an exceptional aptitude for languages, music, and mathematics.

In 1876 Fessenden's uncle, Cortez Fessenden, a physics and mathematics teacher, was invited to watch the first Canadian demonstration of Alexander Graham Bell's telephone. Cortez was extremely interested in this new invention, but not nearly as much as his young nephew, who peppered him with questions about how the device worked. Fessenden, then 10 years old, was especially curious about why the device required wires to transmit voices. This interest would govern much of his experimental work for the rest of his life.

Fessenden next studied at Trinity College School, in Port Hope, Ontario, and at 14 he was awarded a scholarship to Bishop's College, in Lennoxville, Quebec. The scholarship provided him with a small income, as well as a year's worth of college credits, if he passed his classics exams. He did, but quickly grew tired of studying topics other than science. At age 18 he accepted a position as a teacher at the Whitney Institute, in Bermuda. Though he loved Bermuda and eventually made his retirement there, his great interest in science and inventions soon drew him back to North America. Long fascinated by Thomas Alva Edison, he kept a scrapbook devoted to the inventive genius. He also maintained a subscription to *Scientific American*, which he eagerly devoured. After a year of teaching, Fessenden traveled to New York to seek out his hero, hoping not only to meet Edison, but to obtain a job from him. Edison, busy in his lab, declined to meet his young admirer. Fortuitously, however, an instrument tester had just walked off the job and Fessenden quickly snatched up the position at Edison's Machine Works laboratory.

Fessenden's work at Edison's laboratory allowed him to display his innate aptitude for invention and experimentation. He quickly moved up to the position of chief tester, and in that capacity he impressed his superiors with his troubleshooting abilities in the field of electricity. He had a chance to display that talent at the mansion of J. Pierpont Morgan, the legendary financier. Like many rich men of his era, Morgan had a private generating plant on his property. One night the dynamo broke down, and Fessenden was sent to fix the problem. After restoring the power Fessenden was asked by Morgan to inspect the wiring. The wires then in use were bare, with no covering of any kind. Fessenden suggested to Morgan that he replace them with ones encased in rubber and galvanized tubing. Impressed with Fessenden's initiative and acumen, Edison promoted him to be his assistant.

At Edison's plant in New Jersey Fessenden experimented with generators and made improvements on his rubber insulation for electrical wiring. He was promoted to chief chemist of the facility; in this position he met some of the more notable minds of that generation, including Sir William Thomas (known as Lord Kelvin), who developed the temperature scale now named after him, and George Westinghouse, a prolific inventor who spearheaded the development of alternating currents. The idea that preoccupied Fessenden, however, was that of wireless voice transmission. Edison was dismissive of the proposal. "Fezzie, what do you say are man's chances of jumping over the moon? I think one is as likely as the other," he told Fessenden, as quoted by Charles Enman in the *Ottawa Citizen* (October 13, 1999).

In 1890 Fessenden left Edison's lab, after receiving an offer of employment from Westinghouse. At the Westinghouse Electric and Manufacturing Company, he became the supervising electrician for generators. There he designed new lead-in wires for electric light bulbs; Fessenden's wires were not made of expensive platinum, as had been called for in Edison's original design. This allowed Westinghouse's company to fulfill its contractual obligations to provide electric lighting to the entire Columbian Exposition in Chicago, Illinois. More important, Fessenden's design allowed electric light to be cheap enough for average people to install in their homes.

After a trip to England to study the steam engine turbine of Charles Parsons, Fessenden received an offer to teach electrical engineering at Purdue University, in Lafayette, Indiana. Westinghouse agreed to accept his resignation, provided Fessenden remained available to him for research. In the fall of 1892 Fessenden traveled to Indiana to begin his new academic life. He was given a free hand in purchasing all his needed equipment and encouraged in his experiments.

Much to the dismay of Purdue's administration and students, Fessenden left after just one year. He had received an offer from George Westinghouse, who invited Fessenden to head the newly endowed electrical-engineering department at the Western University of Pennsylvania, now the University of Pittsburgh. He agreed and there he conducted research on wireless telephony, as well as a host of other inventions, which he then patented. Most notable, perhaps, was his patent for micro-photography, which remains in use today not only in libraries as microfilm, but also in banks, which require mini-recordings of checks and other such important documents.

In 1896, just as Fessenden felt he was making headway in his wireless studies, the Italian scientist Guglielmo Marconi reported the successful transmission of radio waves. Discouraged by Marconi's success, Fessenden fell into a depression and was unable to make significant progress on his radio work. While sitting by a lakeside one day, he tossed stones into the water and was struck by an idea—could sound waves be continuous, moving out from a central point like ripples on a lake?

The idea that sound waves radiated continuously outward was a revolutionary one. Marconi dismissed it as a fraudulent concept; he believed instead that waves were generated by creating a spark, thereby instigating a whiplash effect. Marconi was concerned only with transmitting the dots and dashes of Morse code, short bursts of sound created by spark-gap transmitters. Fessenden quickly realized that such transmitters would be insufficient to transmit a human voice. He needed a transmitter that could produce a continuous wave of radio energy—something that would be possible only if the transmitter could produce 10,000 bursts of energy per second. In order to achieve this, Fessenden needed, according to Isaac

Asimov in *Asimov's Biographical Encyclopedia of Science and Technology* (1982), "to send out a continuous signal with the amplitude of the waves varied (or 'modulated') to make that variation follow the irregularities of sound waves. At the receiving station, these variations could be sorted out and reconverted into sound." Nothing like this existed at the time so he enlisted a pair of assistants to help build his transmitter and interrupter. Through their work they created amplitude modification, otherwise known as AM radio.

Through a happy accident Fessenden learned he was on the right track. While working one day one of the assistants accidentally jammed a Morse code key. The jammed key howled through the receiver, which was in another room with Fessenden. Upon hearing that continuous howl, Fessenden concluded that if such a sound could be transmitted for a sustained period, so could a human voice. He set out to develop a device that sent out very fast, high-frequency waves to carry such sounds. In order to do that, he needed money.

To secure funding, he demonstrated some telegraph equipment he had been developing to the U.S. Weather Bureau. Officials of the Bureau were impressed with his work and expressed an interest in the use of radio for weather reports. They hired Fessenden in 1900 at a salary of $3,000 a year, a significant sum in that era. He had three assistants by this time, who each received $1,200 a year. They conducted their research on Cobb Island, in the Potomac River. It was remote enough for privacy and allowed Frank Very, one of the assistants, to visit his sister, who lived in one of the few houses on the island.

Fessenden improved his interrupter by laboriously making almost microscopic incisions in a phonograph cylinder so that it would break the circuit 10,000 times per second. On December 23, 1900 he was ready to test his equipment by transmitting his voice through a primitive microphone to a receiving station about a mile away in Virginia. (He had convinced the Weather Bureau that their older generators were inefficient for weather reports and received funds generous enough to by a new one.) Awaiting a signal in Virginia was Alfred Thiessen, a Weather Bureau engineer who had become enamored with the idea of radio telephony. Fessenden tapped out Morse code to warn Thiessen that he was about to attempt voice communications, then leaned into the microphone and shouted: "One, two, three, four. Is it snowing where you are, Mr. Thiessen? If it is, telegraph back and let me know." Thiessen quickly responded that it was, in fact, snowing. Fessenden, although the fact is often overlooked, had beaten Marconi's famous 1901 transmission of Morse code from England to Newfoundland by almost a full year.

The Weather Bureau was pleased by Fessenden's successes, though they did not yet know about his unauthorized voice experiments. He and his associates had greatly expanded the distances covered by radio transmissions of all types and had built an improved detector, which greatly boosted the sensitivity of receivers. According to a biographical article posted on the Institute of Chemistry's web site at the Hebrew University of Jerusalem, "The [detector], which he called a liquid barreter, consisted of a silver-coated platinum wire immersed in a solution of nitric or sulfuric acid. The acid dissolved the silver, leaving a very fine contact between the acid and the platinum. A battery connected between the wire and the acid caused a current to flow in the detector. This current was soon interrupted by the formation of tiny gas bubbles over the platinum wireless waves, striking the detector, ruptured the bubbles, restoring current flow. This flow was proportional to the strength of the incoming waves. The device, therefore, besides being more sensitive than the coherer, could receive continually changing wireless waves, and could be useful in telephony as well as in telegraphy."

At the Weather Bureau's request, Fessenden and his associates moved their laboratory to North Carolina to begin experiments over a triangulated area of about a hundred miles, between Roanoke, Cape Hatteras, and the mainland. Shortly after arriving in North Carolina, the Weather Bureau's chief, Willis Moore, found out about Fessenden's forbidden radio telephony work and demanded that he either cease operations or sign over half of his telephony patents. Fessenden refused to give up his patent rights and even appealed to President Theodore Roosevelt for aid. Ultimately, he was forced to leave the Bureau, in August 1902. Experiments continued there without him with little success; the station was closed down, and the equipment auctioned.

Upon hearing of the inventor's plight, two millionaires from Pittsburgh approached Fessenden and suggested they form a company based on his inventions. The National Electric Signaling Company (NESCO) was formed shortly thereafter; Fessenden, as an employee, patented his inventions in the name of the company. NESCO immediately built two wireless stations with 400-foot antenna towers at Brant Rock, Massachusetts; they proved so successful that more stations were built in Washington, D.C.; Philadelphia; and New York. With these Fessenden extended the transmission range for wireless telegraph messages and set a record by sending a message to Alexandria, Egypt—6,000 miles away. Another important innovation came through a deal with the United Fruit Company, which allowed NESCO to establish wireless stations on their boats and at stations in Guatemala and in New Orleans.

By January 1906 the company had set up a receiving station in Scotland with equipment identical to that in Brant Rock. The success of the Morse code communications between Scotland and Brant Rock inspired Fessenden to improve his high-frequency alternator's resolution. He did so by building an umbrella antenna to clarify signals. In June 1906 NESCO built another station in Plym-

outh, about 11 miles from Brant Rock. The three stations were in continual communication. To further improve communications, Fessenden also discovered and exploited the heterodyne effect, which the Institute of Chemistry article described as "a received radio wave . . . combined with a wave of a frequency slightly different from the carrier wave. The intermediate frequency that is produced as a result is easier to amplify, and can then be demodulated to generate the original sound wave."

As Fessenden worked feverishly on his improvements, he began to better understand the impact of weather on broadcasting. He soon found that cold weather on long nights was good for broadcasts, while warm weather during the daytime made broadcasting next to impossible. In November an engineer at the Scottish station claimed to have overheard the voice of an engineer in Plymouth giving directions on running the dynamo while he was listening for telegraph signals. Fessenden checked the logs and saw that what his engineer had heard was accurate.

Despite a storm destroying the Scottish receiving tower on December 6 and the depressing news that Marconi had been given exclusive rights to build wireless stations in Fessenden's own native Canada, Fessenden decided to press on with a special wireless broadcast he had scheduled for Christmas Eve.

On December 24, 1906 at 9 p.m., operators on the boats of the United Fruit Company heard the familiar signal of C.Q., which meant "listen all stations." Fessenden had told them to be ready for something different on Christmas Eve but none of them had any idea of what it could be. What they heard was dumbfounding: Fessenden's own voice was coming through their headsets, followed by a recording of Handel's *Largo*, as well as the inventor's own violin performance of "O, Holy Night," which he ended by singing the last verse. He concluded his broadcast by wishing his listeners a Merry Christmas, thereby becoming the first person to transmit the human voice wirelessly across vast distances in real time.

Fessenden expected worldwide recognition for this monumental achievement but found himself embroiled in a variety of lawsuits and disputes instead. "He was ripped off by various companies," Ernest DeCoste, a senior curator at the National Museum of Science and Technology, told Carrier Buchanan for the *Ottawa Citizen* (July 31, 1991). "He wasn't a very practical man in terms of finance and organizing a business. But he was a superb inventor. He sort of had a one track mind."

Fessenden's association with NESCO broke down in 1912, following a dispute with the founders. Two years later the American Marconi Company infringed upon Fessenden's patents. A host of other companies, including General Electric, Westinghouse, and RCA, did the same. He spent years suing each one for patent infringement, and in 1928 he settled out of court for $500,000. The damage, however, was irreparable. Fessenden was never able to assert control over his inventions and never received the recognition he deserved for them during his lifetime.

In addition to his work in radio, Fessenden created a number of significant inventions, many of which are still in use today. To speed up operations around the NESCO plant, he created a signaling device that was fitted inside his employees' hard hats. This became the forerunner of the modern pager or beeper. After the sinking of the Titanic, in 1912, he used radio to bounce sound waves off icebergs and created an early form of radar. Another of his devices, the Fathometer, enabled explorers to measure ocean depths; the device was put to good use during World War I to detect enemy U-boats. Fessenden's other significant inventions include a voice-scrambler, tracer bullets, and the electric gyroscope. His passion, however, remained the transmission of sound, as demonstrated by his development of the World War I–era sonic oscillator, which allowed underwater communications for the first time via Morse code, between a ship and submarine.

After World War I Fessenden retired to Bermuda, where he reportedly developed a fascination for mysticism. He had married the former Helen May Trott in 1889; their marriage produced one son, Reginald Kenneley. Fessenden died in Bermuda, on July 22, 1932. According to *On the Shortwaves* (on-line), his tombstone reads, "His mind illuminated the past and the future and wrought greatly for the present." Also included on the stone is a line of Egyptian hieroglyphs, which translates as "I am yesterday and I know tomorrow."—C. M.

Suggested Reading: *On the Shortwaves* (on-line); *Ottawa Citizen*, A p4 July 31, 1991, D p3 Sep. 13, 1999; *QST* p49+ July 2001; *Washington Post* M p3 Dec. 17, 2000; Asimov, Isaac. *Asimov's Biographical Encyclopedia of Science and Technology*, 1982

Filo, David and Yang, Jerry

Yang, Jerry
1968– Co-founder of Yahoo!

Filo, David
1966– Co-founder of Yahoo!

Jerry Yang and David Filo are the co-founders of Yahoo! Inc., an Internet portal that is used by an estimated 237 million people around the world each month. As doctoral students in electrical engineering at Stanford University, in California, Yang and Filo spent their time surfing the World Wide Web instead of writing their dissertations. What eventually grew into Yahoo!, one of the best-known brands in the Internet world, began in 1994 as a simple list of the pair's favorite Web sites. Since finding sites was a difficult and tedious process at the time, many people found the list useful as a reference guide. Yang and Filo gradually expanded their list, adding sites suggested by people who e-mailed them. After the list became too long, they divided it into categories and subcategories. Believing that the burgeoning Internet offered commercial opportunities, in 1995 Yang and Filo turned their hobby into a business. Yahoo! soon added e-mail capabilities, chat rooms, news, message boards, and other features to attract customers. By 2000 the company's revenues had topped $1 billion.

Jerry Yang was born Chih-Yuan Yang in Taipei, Taiwan in 1968. His parents fled China during the reign of the brutal Communist dictator Mao Tse-Tung. Yang's father died when he was two years old. His mother, Lilly, supported Jerry and his younger brother, Ken, by teaching English and drama at a university in Taipei. Dismayed that Jerry and Ken would eventually be required to serve in the Taiwanese army, Lilly Yang decided to start a new a life with them in the United States. "It wasn't an easy decision for my mom," Jerry Yang told Brent Schlender for *Fortune* (March 6, 2000). "The ability to teach English wasn't exactly a skill that was in short supply in the U.S. So even though she had the language skills to get along here, she didn't have the slightest idea what she would do. She was really brave." In 1978 the Yang family, including Jerry's grandmother, settled in San Jose, California. Although they understood little English when they arrived, Jerry and Ken eventually picked up the language and excelled in school. "We got made fun of a lot at first," Yang recalled to Schlender. "I didn't even know who the faces were on the paper money. But when we had a math quiz in school I'd always blow everyone else away. And by our third year, my brother and I had gone from remedial English to advanced-placement English."

At Piedmont Hills High School, in San Jose, Yang was an excellent student and played tennis. In his senior year he was elected student-body president and named the class valedictorian. After graduating from high school, Yang enrolled at Stanford University, in California. After four years of study, in 1990 he was awarded both bachelor's and master's degrees in electrical engineering. Although he was courted by several recruiters, Yang believed that he wasn't ready to get a job and decided to stay at Stanford to pursue a doctorate.

One of five children, David Filo was born in 1966 in Wisconsin. Filo's father, Jerry, worked as an architect, and his mother, Carol, was an accountant. In a transcribed interview with Beverly Schuch for *CNN Pinnacle* (November 14, 1999), Filo described his parents as "hippie wannabees." After the Filos moved to Moss Bluff, Louisiana,

FILO and YANG

they lived in a commune with several other families. David became interested in computers as an undergraduate student at Tulane University, in New Orleans, Louisiana. In 1988 Filo graduated with a B.S. in computer engineering. He subsequently enrolled at Stanford University to pursue his graduate studies in electrical engineering.

Yang and Filo met at Stanford. Finding that they shared a passion for sports and a talent for mathematics and engineering, they became good friends. As part of an academic exchange program, they both lived in Kyoto, Japan, for six months. During the 1993–1994 academic year, the two doctoral students shared an office. "We both chose a Ph.D. program studying CAD [computer-aided design] software for semiconductors," Yang explained to Schlender. "In the late 1980s, that was where a lot of the startups were coming from. We both thought we'd rather be technical people at a small company than just another researcher at a big corporate lab. What happened was that before we finished up our Ph.Ds the CAD industry grew up, consolidated, and had become pretty much the province of two or three big companies. So in 1993 and 1994, even though we were trying to get through the last of our Ph.Ds in this narrow field, we were seriously asking each other what else is cool out there."

Disillusioned by the job prospects in their industry, Yang and Filo gradually lost interest in their doctoral studies. They found an amusing diversion in the Internet, which was still in its infancy. Since their faculty adviser was on sabbatical and could not monitor their progress, Yang and Filo spent countless hours surfing the World Wide Web instead of writing their dissertations. The lack of effective search engines made perusing the thousands of Web sites that were already running a tedious process. Searching for individual sites was akin to looking through thousands of randomly shelved books in a library without the benefit of a card catalogue. If users wanted to revisit a particular site that interested them, then they had to remember its exact address or Uniform Resource Locator (URL) code, which could be long and complicated. "We'd wander around the Net and find something interesting, and then I'd ask Jerry, 'Hey, where was that cool page we saw the other day,' and we could never remember where it was," Filo told Hal Plotkin for the San Jose *Metro* (April 11, 1996, on-line). "I mean, it could take us hours to just get back there, to find it."

Yang and Filo began compiling separate lists of their favorite Web sites. In January 1994, they began posting their combined lists on-line as a favor to their friends and fellow students. Yang and Filo called their directory "David and Jerry's Guide to the World Wide Web." After Filo decided that he preferred not to use his own name, the duo consulted the dictionary to a find a new label for the enterprise. Since they agreed that the first two words of the name would be "Yet Another," (acknowledging satirically the other lists they'd come across on the Web), Yang and Filo searched for a

word that began with the letters, "y" and "a" as an acronym. Filo reluctantly agreed to Yang's suggestion, Yahoo, for "Yet Another Hierarchical Officious Oracle." (The dictionary definition of the word as a boorish, crass, or stupid person is often cited by the media as a factor.) Filo admitted to Plotkin that, at first, he wasn't enthusiastic about the name. It eventually grew on him, however, and he told Plotkin that he was grateful that he and Yang had picked a name that "is so memorable and that conveys the sense of fun involved in all this, the sense of adventure. That is what really distinguishes our site. It is a place for adventures. A place to discover things."

With no publicity or money for advertising, Yahoo! (the exclamation point was added later) gradually spread through word of mouth. Each passing month, more and more people consulted Yahoo! to navigate their way through the Internet, which was growing at a phenomenal rate. Yang and Filo received hundreds of e-mails a day suggesting new sites for Yahoo! to add to its directory. In February 1994 Yang and Filo began dividing their many entries into categories and eventually subcategories "No one was as stupid as Jerry and I, doing this mundane work, going through hundreds of entries a day and categorizing them," Filo told Amy Harmon for the *Los Angeles Times* (April 10, 1995). "But we did enjoy it—we'd always rather be doing that than doing our [doctoral] research." Once linked on Yahoo!, many Web sites experienced a substantial increase in traffic. Some sites, especially those devoted to erotica, weren't pleased with the attention that Yahoo! brought them. "We'd list a site and the next day it would go down,"Yang recalled to David Plotnikoff for the *San Jose Mercury News* (March 31, 1995). "And they just die because they can't handle the traffic. People have asked for their sites to be un-listed on Yahoo because of the traffic a link can bring."

In May 1994 alone Yahoo! exceeded 100,000 total hits (referring to the number of times a site is visited). By the end of that year, the number of hits crossed the million mark. As Yahoo! expanded its directories and was used by more people, Yang and Filo were forced to devote their entire attention to running the site. The duo operated Yahoo! from their computer workstations at Stanford, which were part of a university-wide network and connected to the Internet. Concerned that the heavy traffic would overwhelm and possibly crash their network, the Stanford administration advised Yang and Filo to move Yahoo! onto an off-campus system.

The explosive growth of the Internet encouraged Yang and Filo (and many others) to explore commercial possibilities on-line. "In 1994 we heard about Netscape Communications being funded and how they were releasing [Netscape] Navigator [a Web browser] as a commercial product," Yang wrote in an article for *Forbes* (December 2, 1997). "It was amazing how many Internet startup ideas were being generated within a very close community of friends at school. And for a while, we were sitting there literally writing business plans for Internet-based businesses while on the side working on Yahoo!, thinking, 'That's never going to be a business.' So we [considered on-line] shopping malls. We did booksellers." Yang and Filo realized that they would have to abandon Yahoo! if they wanted to pursue other opportunities. "But finally we realized that if we stopped, then all those people using Yahoo! . . . wouldn't have anything," Yang wrote in his article. "We felt we were offering a service that people wanted. And that's what got us thinking about it as a business."

Unsure of how to turn their hobby into a business, Yang and Filo sought help. Yang persuaded Tim Brady, a friend who had graduated from Stanford and was attending the Harvard Business School, in Boston, to draw up a business plan for Yahoo! (Brady became Yahoo!'s third employee—after Yang and Filo—serving as a senior vice president for network and commerce services.) After incorporating Yahoo! in March 1995, Yang and Filo sought financing from venture capitalists. A month later, Mike Moritz, a partner with Sequoia Capital in Menlo Park, California, agreed to provide them with $1 million. In June Yang and Filo named Tim Koogle as Yahoo!'s president and chief executive officer. An experienced and successful executive, Koogle had previously served as the president of the Intermec Corporation, which earned more than $300 million in annual sales.

Yang and Filo believed that the best way for Yahoo! to generate revenue was to sell space on its many Web pages to commercial advertisers. Some longtime users, who considered the Internet an electronic paradise untouched by government regulation and corporate money, severely criticized the decision. "If we could do it without the ads, we certainly would," Yang told Julian Guthrie for the *San Francisco Examiner* (April 24, 1995). "Because we don't want to charge users, advertising is a necessity." The first advertisements ran on Yahoo! in August 1995.

The mid-1990s witnessed an incredible Internet boom. Many young entrepreneurs set up Web-based businesses to tap into the millions of people who were discovering the Internet, which was becoming as common a medium as television or radio. Many financial analysts and journalists hailed Yahoo! and its co-founders as leaders in the emerging on-line marketplace, predicting that it would reap substantial profits. On April 12, 1996 Yahoo! Inc. went public, with an initial public offering (IPO) price of $13 a share. The price closed at $33 a share, making one of the biggest gains in the history of the NASDAQ exchange. A month later, the company began an extensive marketing campaign to build consumer interest and introduced the tagline "Do you Yahoo!?"

As Yahoo! became a well-known brand name, Yang and Filo decided to withdraw from Stanford's doctoral program. (They shortly thereafter endowed a chair at the Stanford School of Engi-

neering, becoming the youngest people ever to do so.) With each of them holding the title of Chief Yahoo, they divided up their responsibilities at the company. Yang became the public face of Yahoo!, traveling around the world to promote the company and giving countless interviews to the media. Filo devoted himself to the company's technical issues and quickly established a reputation as a workaholic who often slept beneath his desk at the office.

Over the next few years, Yahoo! greatly expanded its services and operations. The company added such features as e-mail, chat rooms, message boards, clubs, interactive maps, on-line games, shopping, and more—all of which were offered free of charge to users. Filo and Yang signed deals with the Associated Press and the Reuters news agency to post their dispatches on the Yahoo! Web site. To remain competitive and boost revenues, Yahoo! acquired other on-line ventures, including broadcast.com and geocites.com. The firm soon went global, tapping into overseas markets by establishing subsidiaries in Italy, Germany, France, Japan, China, and Australia. Yahoo! currently serves users in a dozen languages.

During the late 1990s Yahoo! continued to grow, impressing financial analysts and investors. The company's annual revenues increased from about $70 million in 1997 to more than $200 million the following year. In 2000 Yahoo's revenues exceeded $1 billion. A strong economy, excellent revenues, and media hype caused Yahoo!'s stock price to reach a staggering high of $244 per share in April 1999. Yang and Filo, who owned a substantial amount of stock in Yahoo!, were both worth several billion dollars.

Yahoo!'s stock price began a sharp decline, however, later in 1999. In March 2000 the stock prices of many high-tech and Internet companies plunged by large margins. Since Yahoo! depended on many of these same companies for advertising, revenues began to drop. The press speculated that Yahoo! would founder.

To keep Yahoo! afloat, Yang and Filo decided that the company needed new leadership to guide it through tough times. In April 2001 Yang persuaded Terry Semel, a veteran executive with the entertainment conglomerate Warner Bros., to replace Tim Koogle as Yahoo!'s CEO. Semel cut operating costs by laying off more than 400 workers and sought more advertising from established *Fortune* 500 companies. He also announced that Yahoo! would start charging users fees for certain services such as extra e-mail storage, broadband access, on-line bill payment, and access to premium content. Semel's strategy worked, and in 2002 Yahoo!'s revenues increased to a healthy $953 million.

Yang is married to a woman he met during his 1992 stay in Japan. Of Filo, his college friend and business partner, he told Robert Reid for *Architects of the Web* (1997), "[We have] just a fantastic relationship, and I hope it's a lifelong one."—D. C.

Suggested Reading: *Business Week* p70+ June 2, 2003, with photos; *CNN Pinnacle* (on-line) Nov. 14, 1999; *Forbes* p50+ Dec. 12, 1997; *Fortune* F p79+ Mar. 6, 2000; *Los Angeles Times* D p1+ Apr. 10, 1995; *Newsweek* p58+ Feb. 24, 2003; *San Francisco Examiner* B p1+ Apr. 24, 1995; *San Jose Mercury News* C p1+ Mar. 31, 1995, with photos; S p39+ June 20, 2001; *Time* p30+ Nov. 1997, with photo; Yahoo! Inc. Web site

---

Flanders, Donald A.

Aug. 14, 1900–June 27, 1958 Mathematician

As a senior mathematician with the Argonne National Laboratory (ANL), in Lemont, Illinois, during the early 1950s, Donald A. Flanders played an important role in the development of three advanced digital computers, AVIDAC, ORACLE, and GEORGE. Consisting of 2,500 vacuum tubes, 8,000 resistors, and more than three miles of electrical wiring, AVIDAC filled an entire room and performed calculations in less than one second that would have taken weeks with an adding machine. ORACLE, which was built for the Oak Ridge National Laboratory, in Tennessee, was even faster. GEORGE, also built during Flanders's tenure at the ANL, was the facility's last "homemade" digital computer. In 1956 Flanders was promoted to the directorship of the ANL's Applied Mathematics Unit and remained in that position for the short time until his premature death in 1958.

Donald Alexander Flanders was born on August 14, 1900 in Pawtucket, Rhode Island. He was not the only accomplished sibling in the Flanders family; his brother Ernest achieved prominence as a telescope maker, and another brother, Ralph, served in the U.S. Senate from 1946 to 1959. In 1922 Donald Flanders graduated from Haverford College, in Pennsylvania, with a bachelor's degree in mathematics and minors in Greek and philosophy. He received a doctorate in mathematics from the University of Pennsylvania, in Philadelphia, in 1927. From 1927 to 1929 he served as a National Research Council fellow at Princeton University, in New Jersey.

In 1929 Flanders joined the faculty of New York University (NYU), in New York City, as an assistant professor in the mathematics department. His area of expertise was topology, the study of geometric figures unaltered by such deformations as twisting or stretching. Flanders, in a mission to recruit other talented mathematicians to NYU, sought out the advice of Oswald Veblen, a distinguished professor at Princeton, who brought him into contact with Richard Courant, a mathematician from Germany. Courant had left his country when the Nazis took power and was seeking employment at a university in the United States. In a letter to Courant, Veblen wrote that Flanders was eager to improve the quality of his department and noted, "I was quite impressed with his unselfish-

ness in the matter, because it was clear from the first that it would mean calling people in who outrank him in every respect, and he was under no illusions on the subject," as quoted in *Courant in Göttingen and New York: The Story of an Improbable Mathematician* (1976), by Constance Reid. (Courant joined NYU in 1934 and went on to enjoy a successful career as a mathematician in the United States.) In 1937 Flanders took a leave of absence to teach at the University of Copenhagen, in Denmark, for one year.

In 1943 Hans Bethe, a physicist with the Radiation Laboratory, in Cambridge, Massachusetts, was looking for mathematicians to work on the Manhattan Project, the secret government-sponsored research program that produced the atomic bomb during World War II. Among the people Bethe contacted was Courant, who then recommended Flanders. Flanders accepted Bethe's offer of work and relocated with his family to Los Alamos, New Mexico, where the bomb was being built. At first Flanders did not understand the full implications of the project. He recalled in his testimony to the Atomic Energy Commission (AEC) that it was explained to him only after his arrival at Los Alamos that the project "concerned the application of nuclear physics to the development of a super explosive," as quoted on the Ernest Flanders Family History Project Web site.

Flanders was initially unsure of how his mathematical knowledge would contribute to building the atomic bomb, a task he believed to be more suited to physicists. In fact, mathematicians were needed to perform the many complex calculations, including differential equations, instrumental to the development of the bomb. Working under Bethe, the head of the Theoretical Division at Los Alamos, Flanders ran the computing unit, which consisted primarily of some of the scientists' wives, who performed the repetitive—but required—calculations. The mechanical calculators they used frequently broke down, and IBM's punched card machines and, later, large computers were eventually installed instead. The Manhattan Project ultimately produced two atomic bombs that destroyed the cities of Hiroshima and Nagasaki, in Japan, and brought World War II to an end. Flanders remained at Los Alamos until September 1946.

Courant, who had become the chairman of NYU's mathematics department, wanted Flanders to return to the university and head up an advanced computing program there, but Flanders was reluctant. He wrote to Courant, as quoted by Constance Reid, "[When I am] at the university I am constantly oppressed by the feeling that I have gotten myself into a situation with which I am unable to cope, and I count the years until I can retire, hoping that I can at least get my children educated before I or the situation crack." After some gentle persuasion by Courant, however, Flanders accepted the offer. Working at NYU's newly established Institute of Mathematics and Mechanics, he conducted research on nonlinear equations.

In 1948 the Argonne National Laboratory (ANL), in Lemont, Illinois, hired Flanders as a senior mathematician. The next year Flanders; Norman Hilbury, the associate director of the laboratory; and Frank Hoyt, the head of the ANL's department of theoretical physics, pushed to have a digital computer built similar to the one then under construction at the Institute for Advanced Study (IAS), in Princeton. The ANL's computer would perform calculations relating to the design of nuclear reactors. Flanders thought up the name for AVIDAC, which stood for *Argonne's Version of the Institute's Digital Automatic Computer*. The ANL recruited J. C. Chu, a design engineer from the University of Pennsylvania, in Philadelphia, who had helped build ENIAC, the first electric digital computer. Chu and his team completed AVIDAC in 1951 at a cost of $250,000. "AVIDAC was actually four machines that filled a large laboratory room: an arithmetic unit, a memory unit, an input-output station, and a control section that electronically managed the operation," Jack M. Holl wrote in *Argonne National Laboratory, 1946–96* (1997). "The memory unit could store 1,024 twelve-digit decimal numbers on the inside face of 40 five-inch cathode ray tubes, which were similar to a modern computer screen."

AVIDAC could multiply two 12-digit numbers in a thousandth of a second and could solve in only 20 minutes problems that might have taken two mathematicians using an electric adding machine about three years. Holl wrote, "Amazing as [those statistics were] the most remarkable feature of AVIDAC was that it could be programmed to make 'decisions' about calculating sequence depending on the results it was generating. In effect, programmers could instruct AVIDAC how to solve complex equations and be assured that the computer would consistently solve the problem the correct way, every time, regardless of the values."

Alston Householder, director of the Oak Ridge National Laboratory, in Tennessee, also wanted a computer built for his facility, and he contracted the project to the ANL, because of the agency's success with AVIDAC. Chu organized a team, which included Flanders and engineers from the Oak Ridge facility, to build ORACLE (Oak Ridge Automatic Computer and Logical Engine). Costing about $350,000, ORACLE was completed in the summer of 1953. "The overall architecture was like the IAS machine. But the engineering design was different," Chu explained in an article for *A History of Computing in the Twentieth Century* (1980). "Much faster circuits were used, smaller cathode-ray tubes for memory—which was twice the size of the IAS memory. Magnetic tape [two inches] wide with 42 channels was provided as auxiliary memory." ORACLE was twice as fast as AVIDAC. In 1957 the ANL built its last digital computer, GEORGE, which replaced AVIDAC.

Flanders's many achievements at the Argonne National Laboratory were overshadowed, however, by controversy. Flanders was a friend of Alger Hiss, a former State Department official and president of the Carnegie Endowment for International Peace. In 1950 Hiss was convicted of perjury for lying to a grand jury about passing secret government documents to the Soviet Union during the 1930s. (Since the statute of limitations had run out, Hiss could not be prosecuted for espionage.) Although Hiss steadfastly maintained his innocence, his chief accuser, Whittaker Chambers, a senior editor at *Time* magazine, supplied microfilmed documents that backed up his charges that they had both spied for the Soviet Union. Flanders, who had known Hiss since 1931, believed he was innocent and stood by him. Flanders visited Hiss while he was serving a five-year prison sentence for perjury. The publicity over the Hiss case and allegations by Senator Joseph McCarthy that the American government was riddled with Communists helped create a climate of suspicion in the country during the early 1950s. (Senator Ralph Flanders, Donald's brother, publicly urged the Senate to censure McCarthy for his behavior.)

Concerned that he might be a Communist and a security risk, the AEC began investigating Donald Flanders in 1952. The investigation centered not only on Flanders's friendship with Hiss, but on his association with various left-wing organizations, including the Socialist Youth League and Progressive Citizens of America. (His family's involvement with such groups was also examined.) If the investigation concluded that Flanders was a security risk, the AEC could have revoked Flanders's security clearance and fired him from the ANL. In a letter to the AEC, Flanders wrote, "I can affirmatively say that I am a completely loyal and trustworthy citizen, else I would not contest the matter but would resign. I believe that my work, my character, my attachment to democracy, my scientific standing, discretion, and my professional value to the laboratory should serve to dissipate any question," as quoted on the Ernest Flanders Family History Project Web site.

Flanders also testified at hearings conducted by the AEC. During the hearings he adamantly denied that he and his wife, Sarah, were Communists. He clarified his political views, which he characterized as "left-of-center," and reaffirmed his loyalty to the United States government. Flanders also steadfastly continued to defend his friend Hiss, alleging that Whittaker Chambers had manufactured the evidence against him. The AEC investigation ultimately failed to uncover any evidence that Flanders was a security risk, and he continued working for the ANL. In 1956 he was promoted to the directorship of the facility's Applied Mathematics Division.

Donald Flanders had been suffering from ulcers and various other ailments, and on June 27, 1958 he committed suicide by taking an overdose of his prescribed medications. He left a suicide note for Sarah that read, "I can't bear to go back to the lab. There are many decisions to make, and I feel that I am not capable of making these decisions. I am worth more—in dollars—dead than alive," as quoted by a reporter for the *New York Times* (June 28, 1958). A week later, Sarah Flanders was killed in a car accident. The couple left behind four children: Peter, Stephen, Ellen, and Jane.—D. C.

Suggested Reading: Argonne National Laboratory Web site; Ernest Flanders Family History Project Web site; Los Alamos National Laboratory Web site; *New York Times* p38 June 28, 1958; Reid, Constance. *Courant in Göttingen and New York: The Story of an Improbable Mathematician*, 1976

Hulton Archive by Getty Images

Fleming, John Ambrose

Nov. 29, 1849–Apr. 18, 1945 Creator of the first electron tube

A leading electrical engineer of the late 19th and early 20th centuries, Sir John Ambrose Fleming worked for Thomas Edison to improve electric lighting and aided Guglielmo Marconi in the development of his wireless radiotelegraph. He is best known for building the first electron tube, a thermionic (which refers to the release of electrons by an incandescent material) valve that aided in the reception of radio signals. Fleming's tube, or diode as it is now known, was the forerunner for the triode—a three-element tube consisting of an anode, a cathode, and a controlling grid—which was an amplifier and therefore a cornerstone of early radio and television technology. Long since replaced by the cheaper and more durable transistor, Fleming's tube was an important step in the evolution of electronic devices and the invention from which all subsequent improvements have sprung.

The son of a parson, John Ambrose Fleming was born in Lancaster, Lancashire, England, on November 29, 1849. When he was four, his family moved to London, so his father could minister at Kentish Town. He studied at University College School and later at University College, both in London, graduating with a bachelor's degree in science in 1870. He worked as a clerk in a stockbrokers' firm for the next two years, and his schooling was sporadic, but from 1872 to 1874 he did some postgraduate work in South Kensington.

After leaving South Kensington, in 1874, Fleming taught science at Cheltenham College for the next three years, all the while saving money so he could continue his education. In 1877, after saving 400 pounds and passing the entrance exam, he began attending St. John's College, at Cambridge University, where he worked in the Cavendish Laboratory as an assistant. There he studied advanced mathematics and electricity under the noted scholar James Clerk Maxwell, who had written a famous work on magnetism and electricity. At the lab Fleming repeated the 100-year-old electrical experiments of Henry Cavendish, whose notes on the subject had then only just been uncovered.

In 1879 Fleming earned his doctoral degree and for the next year he served as the laboratory's demonstrator. In 1881 he left the laboratory to become a professor of physics and mathematics at University College, in Nottingham, but left that position after a year to become a consultant for the Edison Electric Light Company, in London, where he was responsible for improving electric generators and meters as well as incandescent lamps. In addition to becoming a consultant for Edison, he served as an engineer and adviser to the Swan and Ferranti electric lighting companies between 1882 and 1889. Over the years he would make many contributions to the improvement of transformers and to the field of photometry (the branch of science that deals with the measurement of light) in general.

During the early 1880s Fleming studied the Edison effect—the movement of electricity from a hot filament to a cold plate within an emptied light bulb. In *Engines of the Mind* (1996), Joel Shurkin noted the origins of this discovery: "When [Edison] stuck a plate of metal into one of his light bulbs, he was able to detect an electric current flowing through the vacuum from the filament to the metal plate when the bulb was turned on. Edison did not have a good idea of what to do with this discovery, but an Englishman, John Ambrose Fleming, did."

But Fleming did not, at least initially, know what do with the Edison effect. After repeating some of Edison's experiments in the late 1880s, he abandoned his work in favor of helping the Italian physicist Guglielmo Marconi on some of his experiments in wireless radiotelegraphy. He worked with Marconi steadily through the 1890s and aided him in designing the transmitter that Marconi successfully used to transmit across the Atlantic Ocean, in 1901. Upon completion of the transmitter, Fleming returned to his studies of the Edison effect, intending to produce a rectifier (a device for converting alternating current into direct current) that could replace the faulty detectors then used in radiotelegraphy.

What Fleming wound up doing, however, was combining the works of Edison and Marconi. He built a new lamp that had a metal cylinder surrounding the bulb's filament in a high vacuum, and the cylinder proved to be helpful in picking up weak radio signals. This was due to the fact that electrons had the ability to travel only when the plate was connected to the positive terminal of a generator, because then the plate attracted the negatively charged electrons. Isaac Asimov explained in *Asimov's Biographical Dictionary of Science and Technology* (1982): "This meant that in alternating current (where the charge on the plate was perpetually shifting from negative to positive, as the charge on the filament shifted from positive to negative) the current would pass only half the time, when the filament was negative and plate positive, and not the other half. Alternating current would enter the device but direct current would leave."

Fleming patented his invention in 1904, calling his device a "thermionic valve," since it was the electrical equivalent of a water supply valve that allows water to flow in only one direction. Although Fleming's valve was not very useful in that it could not amplify a radio signal, as Roy Porter noted in the *Hutchinson Dictionary of Scientific Biography* (1994), "it revolutionized the early science of radio." From Fleming's diode came the inspiration for Lee de Forest's triode, which added a third element to the tube—a control grid formed as a metal plate full of holes or a bent metal wire—allowing the tube to be more sensitive and, more importantly, to amplify radio signals. Though both the Fleming valve and the triode have long since been replaced by the transistor diode, Fleming's work helped to advance the science of radio and television and is considered by many to be an extremely valuable contribution to electronic engineering.

In 1885 John Ambrose Fleming joined the staff at University College, in London, as a professor of electrical technology, a position he held for four decades. After his retirement, in 1926, he remained active scientifically until his death. A highly successful teacher, he devised "Fleming's rules," a useful and popular mnemonic for the direction of motion, magnetic field, and current in electrical machines. From 1930 to 1945 he was president of the Television Society. He published more than 100 important scientific papers in his lifetime; he read his first, in 1874, at the Physical Society's inaugural meeting, and then, 65 years later, he read his last to the same group. He won numerous awards, including the Hughes Medal (1910), the Faraday Medal from the American Institute of Electrical Engineers (1928), and the Gold Medal from the Institute of Radio Engineers (1933). He was knighted in 1929.

Fleming was married twice but had no children. His first wife, Clara Ripley Pratt, died in 1917. In 1933, at age 84, he married Olive May Franks. He died at the age of 95 on April 18, 1945 in Sidmouth, Devon, England.—C. M.

Suggested Reading: Asimov, Isaac. *Asimov's Biographical Dictionary of Science and Technology*, 1982; *Cambridge Dictionary of Scientists*, 1996; *Chambers Biographical Dictionary*, 1997; *Dictionary of Scientific Biography*, 1972; *Larousse Dictionary of Scientists*, 1994

Flint, Charles R.

Jan. 24, 1850–Feb. 13, 1934 Financier

The financier and industrialist Charles R. Flint was the driving force behind the creation of new corporate trusts in the late 19th and early 20th century. Flint's experience as a trader during the 1870s led him to conclude that competition between companies that sold the same products wasted valuable resources. He argued that companies should merge in a trust (known then as "industrial consolidations"), working together from a common strategy and sharing profits. Flint's ideas laid the foundation for the modern corporation; he argued that consolidated companies should assign such diverse and important tasks as management, manufacturing, marketing, research, and legal affairs to the individual departments that employed the best qualified people, a practice many corporations follow today. Flint's most famous consolidation, the Computing-Tabulating-Recording Company (CTR), eventually became the corporate giant known today as IBM.

Charles Ranlett Flint was born on January 24, 1850 in Thomaston, Maine. In his autobiography, *Memories of an Active Life: Men, and Ships, and Sealing Wax* (1923), Flint wrote that he was "descended from Thomas Flint who came from Wales to the shipbuilding town of Salem [Massachusetts] in 1642." Through the succeeding generations, the Flints worked in the shipping industry, building, owning, and managing ships, and also serving as captains and mates. Charles Flint's father, Benjamin, was a builder and "owner-manager" of the many clipper ships that sailed from Thomaston.

Charles attended public school in Thomaston and later in the New York City borough of Brooklyn. He also studied at the Warren Johnson Boarding School, in Topsham, Maine. In 1868 he graduated from the Polytechnic Institute, in Brooklyn, earning the equivalent of a high-school degree. The elder Flint offered his son the opportunity to attend college, but he declined. Flint later had second thoughts about his decision, writing in his autobiography that "after years of experience I deeply regretted that I did not give the greater part of my time to the study of the English language and the classics; for a mastery over language is one of the most valuable possessions that a man can have."

After graduating and spending two months exploring the woods of Maine, Flint set out to look for an office position in New York City's shipbuilding industry. Lacking practical experience, he had difficulty finding a job and, without prospects in sight, eventually decided to go into business for himself. He had business cards printed that identified him as a dock clerk, a position that involved receiving, measuring, and delivering cargo from incoming ships. Flint found work as a clerk, earning $4 a week.

Flint later saw an opportunity for advancement when William R. Grace, an international trader, merchant, and shipping agent, opened an office in New York City. Flint introduced himself to Grace while the two men were aboard a ferry boat. He asked him for a job, offering to work for free until Grace decided whether his labor was worth anything. Grace agreed to these terms.

In 1871 Flint and Grace's father-in-law, Captain George W. Gilchrist, co-founded their own company, Gilchrist, Flint & Co., which shipped commodities. The business was so successful that, 10 months later, Gilchrist offered to release Flint from his partnership contract so that he could accept an invitation from Grace to organize a new shipping company, W. R. Grace & Co. Grace gave Flint 25 percent interest in the company, and later increased his share to 35 percent. The company traded extensively in Central and South America, and Flint became an expert on these regions. In 1877 he became the consul for Chile in New York City. He resigned from this position two years later, when a war broke out between Chile and Peru; Flint had financial interests in both countries and, during the war, shipped arms to both sides. He later served as consul general for Costa Rica and Nicaragua.

During the 1870s Flint's business dealings brought him into contact with manufacturers around the country. His experience and observations led him to conclude that fierce competition between companies wasted valuable resources and hurt profits. As a solution, Flint proposed a system of economic consolidation, whereby companies would join forces, work from a common strategy, and share the benefits. He recalled that he made his first public speech urging consolidation during the 1880s.

Flint made his initial effort at economic consolidation in the electric lighting industry. After purchasing a substantial amount of stock in the New York City–based United States Electric Lighting Company (U.S. Electric), which manufactured incandescent lights, he accepted an offer to become its president, in 1879. The era of electricity was just getting underway, and Flint foresaw immense potential profit, envisioning his company's lights illuminating private homes, businesses, and streets across the country. In order to showcase electricity, he had a wire laid in his apartment, dis-

playing what he claimed to be the first incandescent light in a New York home. "I put the bulb in a large globe which held American Beauty roses with gold fish swimming around their stems and around the electric light," he recalled in his autobiography. "The occasion of this display was a social event." Flint believed that the company needed to market a complete lighting system—rather than just incandescent lamps—to become successful. To research how such a system could be developed, he hired the best electrical experts he could find and secured the services of lawyers who specialized in patents.

Instead of having U.S. Electric develop its own lighting system, Flint explored the possibility of merging with a competitor who already had a viable system. He began talks with a representative from the Ohio-based Brush Electric Company, who proved hesitant to pursue a merger. However, the Brush representative told Flint that he would consider consolidation only if U.S. Electric obtained a lighting system similar to the one used by the Weston Electric Light Company, headed by the inventor Edward Weston. Flint immediately traveled to Weston's headquarters, in Newark, New Jersey, to discuss a merger. After some initial reluctance, Weston accepted Flint's offer, agreeing to a consolidation with U.S. Electric.

Despite his successful acquisition of Weston, Flint still faced stiff competition from several other electric lighting companies, including the one in Menlo Park, New Jersey, owned by Thomas Edison, who had made substantial contributions to incandescent lighting technology. "At this point, being in possession of all the facts," Flint recalled in *Memories of an Active Life*, "I clearly envisaged the possibility of bringing about a great electrical consolidation which would include light and power. I realized that if such a consolidation were not formed many millions of dollars would be lost as a result of patent litigation, wasted efforts, duplication of disbursements, and lack of standardization in manufacture." Flint successfully gathered the owners of all the major electric companies together to discuss consolidation. Edison, however, rejected Flint's offer. Flint quoted him as saying, "I will not merge my prestige as an electrician with that of any other." The failure of consolidation of the electric lighting industry resulted in costly litigation between the competitors. According to Flint, Edison filed many suits against U.S. Electric in an effort to control the industry by claiming exclusive credit for having invented incandescent lighting. Although Edison's suits were unsuccessful, Flint estimated that the litigation cost over $2 million. Disappointed by his failure to consolidate the industry, Flint then stepped down as president of U.S. Electric, which eventually merged with the Westinghouse Company, "thus centralizing the highest mechanical skill with a strong patent position," as he noted in his book.

Flint's first experience at consolidation taught him an important lesson: consolidations offers and negotiations should always be made by a disinterested intermediary, who could hope to earn the trust of all the parties involved. Since he handled the negotiations with the electricity companies himself, Flint believed the other companies were unwilling to trust him, assuming that he was acting in his own company's best interest, rather than the best interest of all parties.

Flint turned his attention to consolidating the crude rubber industry. He recalled that the companies that manufactured rubber boots and shoes were fiercely competitive. "Some of them, in order to survive, were turning out goods of attractive appearance but inferior quality," he wrote in his autobiography. "I told them that there was only one way to settle their industrial wars, and that this was for them to have an absolute identity of interest." As the years passed, the rubber companies became more open to the notion of consolidation. They began negotiating among themselves, but were unable to reach an agreement that satisfied all parties. The rubber companies then turned to Flint, who said he could consolidate them within 60 days. He insisted that the companies not discuss the consolidation with one another, believing that secrecy would ensure success. The companies agreed, and each provided Flint with detailed statements of intention, which he kept confidential. On the basis of those statements, Flint devised a plan for consolidation. The result was the United States Rubber Company (U.S. Rubber). Although two of the most important companies in the industry, the Boston Rubber Shoe Company and the Woonsocket Rubber Company, declined to join the consolidation, U.S. Rubber eventually absorbed both of them. "Steady profits and the elimination of speculation were among the happy results of this combination," Flint wrote.

Flint by now had developed a reputation as a trust builder, and was asked by many different companies to consolidate their industries. Over the next decades he successfully created 24 separate trusts, including the New York Belting and Packing Company, the American Woolen Company, the Clarksburg Coal Company, the Computing Scale Company, the International Time Recording Company, and the American Chicle Company, which manufactured chewing gum.

Flint helped to lay the foundation for modern corporations. "The consolidated corporation," he argued in his autobiography, "under a system of comparative accounting and comparative administration, subdivides its business so that each of its various departments is headed by a man who, through long experience and concentration, operates at the highest efficiency."

During the 1880s and 1890s trusts became increasingly unpopular with the public. Citing powerful monopolies such as Standard Oil, headed by John D. Rockefeller, and U.S. Steel, headed by Andrew Carnegie, opponents of trusts in both government and the press argued that they restrained trade and competition, hurt consumers, and exerted too much influence. In 1890 Congress enacted the Sherman Anti-Trust Act to fight "bad trusts." In 1896 William Jennings Bryan, the Democratic Party's candidate for president, campaigned against trusts, alleging that they were contrary to the public interest. (Bryan lost the election to the Republican William McKinley.) Despite the growing sentiment against trusts, Flint continued to defend them, arguing that they benefited the public. In 1900, U.S. Senator Mark Hanna, a leading Republican and one of President McKinley's closest advisors, asked Flint to defend industrial consolidations during the annual banquet of the Illinois Manufacturers Association, in Chicago. McKinley was up for re-election that year, once again facing Bryan, who frequently condemned trusts during the campaign. "A combination of labor is a trades union, a combination of intelligence a university, a combination of money a bank—a combination of labor, intelligence and money is an industrial consolidation—Work, Brains, and Money," Flint said in his speech, as quoted in his book. President McKinley had 500,000 copies of the speech distributed throughout the country. The Chicago press covered the speech and crowned Flint "The Father of Trusts," a label that stuck with him for the rest of his life. (McKinley defeated Bryan by a landslide.)

In 1911 Flint merged four early computing companies—the International Time Recording Company and the Computing Scale Company (both of which he controlled) with the Bundy Manufacturing Company and the Tabulating Machine Company. The Tabulating Machine Company had been established, in 1896, by inventor Herman Hollerith, who created punched-card controlled automatic calculating machines. According to Joel Shurkin in *Engines of the Mind* (1984), Flint's Computing Scale Company was in danger of going out of business by 1911, and Flint hoped to save the company by merging it with others. He made a generous offer to Hollerith, who at the time was in poor health. Hollerith agreed, and Flint created his most famous consolidation, the Computing-Tabulating-Recording Company (CTR). In his book, Flint explained that this merger differed from his previous efforts because he was "effecting a consolidation of allied interests, that is by consolidating the manufacturers of similar but not identical products."

In 1914 Flint made a decision that ensured CTR's long-term success. He hired Thomas J. Watson, a salesman from the National Cash Register Company, to serve as CTR's new general manager. Flint gave Watson complete freedom in running the company. In 1924 Watson changed the company's name to International Business Machines (IBM), which eventually became one of the leading manufacturers of computers. Watson served as IBM's chief executive officer until his death in 1956.

Charles Flint's business dealings brought him into contact with many prominent leaders, including Congressman and U.S. Secretary of State James G. Blaine, Senator Mark Hanna, President Theodore Roosevelt, King Leopold II of Belgium, among others. In 1906 Flint signed a contract with Orville and Wilbur Wright, the developers of the airplane, to represent their interests overseas. Flint himself became a pilot and was also famous for racing yachts.

Charles R. Flint died on February 13, 1934 in Washington, D.C., at age 84. He was survived by his wife, Charlotte Reeves Flint.—D. C.

Suggested Reading: *New York Times* p22 Feb. 14, 1934, with photo; Austrian, Geoffrey D. *Herman Hollerith: Forgotten Giant of Information Processing*, 1982; Cortada, James W. *Historical Dictionary of Data Processing*, 1987; Flint, Charles R. *Memories of an Active Life: Men, and Ships, and Sealing Wax*, 1923; Shurkin, Joel. *Engines of the Mind: A History of the Computer*, 1984

Courtesy of Steven Ovens

Flowers, Thomas H.

Dec. 22, 1905–Oct. 28, 1998 Designer of the Colossus computer

During the formative years of modern computer technology, while the United States had such breeding grounds as the Massachusetts Institute of Technology, the Moore School, and Bell Telephone Labs, Great Britain had Bletchley Park. Britain had been awakened to the potential of computers with the efforts of Douglas Rayner Hartree in

the mid-1930s, and Bletchley Park represented the cutting edge of British computer research in the 1940s. Thomas H. Flowers was one of the prominent British computer designers of the time, and was responsible for the construction in 1943 of the electronic computer known as Colossus. Built to decipher encrypted German codes during World War II, Colossus is believed by some to have been the first large-scale, fully electronic digital computer of any kind. However, Colossus was a special-purpose computer, whereas the ENIAC, invented three years later by Americans John Mauchly and J. Presper Eckert, was the world's first large-scale, general-purpose electronic computer. Due to the highly classified nature of the Colossus project, much about Flowers' work is unknown to this day.

Thomas Flowers began working at the British Post Office Communications Laboratories in 1930 and three years later, he received a Bachelor of Science degree from that same school. With the outbreak of World War II, Flowers became a staff member at the Bletchley Park Government Code and Cipher School while still working for the Post Office Labs.

Flowers had long recognized the potential for fully electronic data-processing equipment that would replace the electromechanical machines then in use. The idea first came to him while he was leading a Post Office Communications Lab research department at Dollis Hill in northwest London. The British post office differed from its American counterpart in that it handled both mail and telephone service, and Flowers's group was conducting research into telephone connections; these connections were electromechanical at the time, and errors were common. As early as 1930, Flowers began pushing to replace the electromechanical connections with electric vacuum tubes, a step he believed would help eliminate the problems. His opinion put him in the minority, mainly because vacuum tubes were much more fragile than the mechanized metal relays then in place. Flowers, however, would prove to be ahead of his time.

Flowers's interest in computers was sparked in part by an early prototype built by mathematician Max Newman and scientist Alan Turing in early 1943 for the purpose of cracking codes. His interest in vacuum tube technology led Flowers to theorize about building a reliable computing machine with entirely electronic components. He was convinced that such a device would outperform any of the mechanical ones in use at the time. Higher-ups at Bletchley Park were intrigued with the possibility of automating the process of deciphering Nazi codes, and saw Flowers's proposed computer as a means to do just that. Cracking the Enigma cipher codes were a vital element in winning the War. Both Britain and the United States had built electromechanical machines called "bombes" that emulated the code wheels of the Enigma machine and would run all day and night until they found a combination that worked. When that occurred, the machine would stop—and the cryptanalysts could read out the settings used for encrypting that message. Along with fellow engineer C. E. Wynn-Williams and several others, Flowers went to work on the project under a cloak of official secrecy, and in 11 months the team unveiled Heath Robinson, an electronic computer named for a British cartoonist famous for his drawings of whimsically complex machines.

The Heath Robinson was designed for the specific purpose of helping to break the German codes, and it contained five or six dozen vacuum tubes, as well as a tape recorder. The machine was housed in a makeshift wooden hut on the grounds of the Bletchley Park manor. As for the actual appearance of the computer, little is known, except that it was significantly more compact than Howard Aiken's massive Mark I at Harvard University, in Cambridge, Massachusetts. The Heath Robinson was able to read a maximum of 2,000 characters per second using a pair of synchronized photoelectric paper tape readers, which scanned loops of teleprinter tape. Because they were extremely long, the tapes had to be spooled on a large metal carriage with movable pulleys, referred to as a "bedstead." As for output, Heath Robinson possessed an early type of printer, which put out 15 characters, mostly numerical, per second. The computer contained an adder capable of performing binary calculations, thus giving it an edge in unscrambling codes in binary language, the system of zeroes and ones through which computer instructions are communicated. The use of binary would later become a defining characteristic of such general-purpose digital computers as the ENIAC and John Atanasoff's ABC.

The computer examined two streams of tape, one containing the German code, and the other a coded representation of what the British believed the German encryption device did to the message. By comparing the two tapes, the Heath Robinson was able to uncover clues as to the exact code that was being used in each case. Thus the machine did not actually crack the code itself, but rather it provided data that enabled the experts to do so.

Despite its importance as a technological milestone, the Heath Robinson had its share of problems. The paper tapes would often stretch or break, which generally led to inaccurate results, as both tapes had to matched up precisely. The computer also tended to overheat and if the problem was not dealt with in time, it actually caught fire. The circuitry had to be adjusted almost constantly, and the machine often shut down for no apparent reason. On one occasion, Allen Coombs, an engineer working on the project, complained to Flowers about a seemingly inexplicable malfunction. "Change the frequency," was what Flowers told him, and the machine worked after Coombs did so. "I still don't know why," Coombs later wrote in a memoir, "Nor, [Flowers] tells me, does he" (*The Computer Pioneers*, 1986).

The difficulties with the Heath Robinson threatened to bring an end to the entire project, but Flowers and the other engineers managed to bring the temperamental machine under control. When operating properly, the Heath Robinson aided the code-breakers immensely by eliminating a great deal of tedious manual labor. However, due to the various technical difficulties with which the engineers frequently had to grapple, it rarely reached its maximum speed of 2,000 characters per second, and its total output was not very large. Nevertheless, the Heath Robinson (along with several similar machines created soon after) proved that a high-speed electronic device could be an effective aid in cryptanalysis.

Flowers and his team worked with the machines almost nonstop, with only a few hours set aside each week for family and leisure. Time was of the essence due to the imperative need to decode the German messages as quickly as possible. Much of the time was also devoted to figuring out ways to eliminate the Heath Robinson's problems. Flowers came up with a way to avoid the malfunctions associated with punched-hole tape by replacing it with what he called a bit-stream generator, which would generate an electronic signal that took the place of actual tape. This would eliminate the necessity of preparing and installing the tape, and would make the remaining tape more reliable because it would not be hole-punched, and thus could not be damaged as easily. Although due to remaining doubts surrounding the capabilities of electronics his superiors at Bletchley Park were initially hesitant about Flowers's idea, his experience with vacuum tubes at the post office helped to reassure naysayers that the improvement would be feasible.

The incorporation of bit-stream generator marked the beginning of a process that would transform the modest Heath Robinson into the massive electronic giant known as Colossus. Many vacuum tubes were added as part of the enlargement, including a special set of tubes called thyratrons, which hold ionized gas under low pressure and respond a bit more slowly than regular vacuum tubes. Colossus contained 2400 tubes overall. "Ah, the warmth at 2 a.m. on a damp, cold English winter!" Flowers remarked, referring to the heat generated by the tubes (*International Biographical Dictionary of Computer Pioneers*, 1995). A general increase in electronic hardware was implemented, as well as the addition of electromechanical switches similar to the ones that were used by telephone operators. Alan M. Turing, one of Bletchley Park's senior scientists, was responsible for much of the design.

As long and wide as a small highway billboard and approximately one meter in height, Colossus was the largest computer ever constructed at Bletchley Park, and it was housed in a brick building near the manor house. While the Heath Robinson had electronic subsystems, the Colossus was run completely by electronic components. Overall, it represented a more finished product than the Heath Robinson, the design of which had involved a lot more improvisation. Colossus included a bedstead as its predecessor had, as well as a teleprinter about the size of a typewriter. Its face was covered with vacuum tubes and switches that were used to manually set up programs, and the entire machine had wires running all over it which connected the various switchboard attachments used to program the computer. Much like the Heath Robinson, Colossus did not actually decipher codes. Rather, it produced an intermediate text which would be read by an expert, who could then decode the message in question with relative ease.

Despite being a larger and faster version of the Heath Robinson, the first Colossus did not completely live up to Bletchley Park's expectations. While the designers originally hoped it would put out about 10,000 characters of data per second, its maximum speed turned out to be half of that. As a solution, Colossus was modified to accommodate parallel processing—that is, handling several different operations simultaneously. Five parallel processors were made for Colossus, and with the addition of shift registers that enabled the computer to read all five at the same time, Colossus was at last ready. The first model officially went into operation in December of 1943.

The British government was soon demanding more Colossi as the Germans began coming up with an increased number of codes, with even more sophisticated encryption. Flowers was shocked when in February 1944 he was informed of the order that a dozen more machines be up and running by June. As Flowers feared, the task proved impossible, however by the end of May Bletchley Park had a second Colossus operating in a limited capacity. This computer featured a significant improvement on the original, namely the ability to automatically alter its own program sequence. For instance, if it detected a possible pattern in the code, it was able to redirect its operations to specifically target the pattern. This ability to assess its own progress while performing a task and adjust accordingly would eventually become one of the defining features of digital computers.

The Colossi contributed immensely to the Allied victory in World War II, helping to decode Nazi intelligence leading up to and immediately following the Allied invasion of Normandy on June 6, 1944. When the European front of the war ended in 1945 and the threat to Britain was over, Bletchley Park's work on the Colossus project came to a halt, and the staff was dismissed. At the time, a total of 10 Colossi are thought to have been in existence. The fate of these machines after the war remains largely a mystery, information classified by the British government. It is generally believed that they were dismantled.

Thomas Flowers's contribution to computer technology following the war was minimal. With his responsibilities at Bletchley Park at an end, he traveled to the United States in the fall of 1945, where he visited sites that represented the apex of computer technology as it then stood: the Aberdeen Proving Ground, in Aberdeen, Maryland; Bell Telephone Laboratories, in New Jersey; the Massachusetts Institute of Technology (MIT) and Harvard University, in Cambridge, Massachusetts; and the Moore School of the University of Pennsylvania, in Philadelphia. He was careful not to divulge information about the Heath Robinson or the Colossus, the very existence of which remained unknown to most of the world until 1970.

In 1950 Flowers left the Post Office Communications Laboratories. He began working for ITT-England, where he would remain for the next 20 years. He received an honorary Doctor of Science degree from the University of Newcastle upon Tyne in 1977. On June 6, 1996, the 52nd anniversary of D-Day, Flowers attended the official activation of a rebuilt Colossus computer. On October 28, 1998, he died at the age of 92.

Flowers has been described as "a quiet genius," and "a modest bespectacled man with the air of a kindly but resolute schoolmaster" (*The Computer Pioneers*, 1986). Though built for a very specific, and thus limited, use, his creation was the first computer to be based entirely on electronic technology, and it set the stage for the general-purpose electronic machines that would be developed in America soon after. To a certain extent, official secrecy has prevented the Colossus from taking its rightful place among the landmark machines in computer history, however its importance is indeed great.—B. S.

Suggested Reading: Aspray, William. *Computing Before Computers*, 1990; Lee, J. A. N., ed. *International Biographical Dictionary of Computer Pioneers*, 1995; Ritchie, David. *The Computer Pioneers*, 1986; Shurkin, Joel. *Engines of the Mind*, 1984; Williams, Michael R. *A History of Computing Technology*, 1985

Forrester, Jay Wright

July 14, 1918– Creator of RAM

There are many different people responsible for the development of the computer, but had it not been for Jay W. Forrester, this revolutionary invention could never have become as widespread as it is today. Thanks to Forrester and his creation of core memory, also known as random access memory (RAM), today's computers are fast, compact, and practical. It was through his work that the computer began to take its steps from the bulky, gargantuan, and slow machines of the early computer age to the streamlined and efficient PCs of today. A true Renaissance man, Forrester is also responsible for the creation of the field known as systems dynamics, in which computers are used to predict patterns and changes in a myriad of social, cultural, ecological, and political areas. His work in this relatively new field has attracted its share of attention and controversy over the years.

Jay Wright Forrester was born on July 14, 1918 in the small Nebraska town of Climax, to Marmaduke and Ethel Pearl (Wright) Forrester. He grew up on his parents' cattle ranch and attended the town's single-room country school, where the young Forrester began his interest with electronics by conducting simple electrical experiments. By his senior year of high school, Forrester had used automobile parts to build a 12-volt wind-driven electrical system which he used to provide his family's ranch with electricity for the first time.

Originally, Forrester intended to enter the agricultural college of the University of Nebraska, but instead he opted for an electrical-engineering major a few months before his enrollment in the fall of 1935. In 1939 he graduated with the best record among the school's electrical-engineering students. In July of that year he started graduate studies at the Massachusetts Institute of Technology (MIT), in Cambridge, also working at the institute's High-Voltage Laboratory as a research assistant working with X-ray equipment. He switched over his research assistantship to the new Servomechanisms Laboratory in the 1940–41 school year, working under Gordon Brown. Forrester's master's degree work was put on hold during World War II when he became involved in military research, building electric and hydraulic servomechanisms for mounted guns and radar.

By the end of 1944, Forrester began thinking about leaving the Servomechanisms Lab and starting a business in automatic controls which was related to his previous military research. But in December, the U.S. Navy's Special Devices Center approached MIT to build an aircraft stability and control analyzer (ASCA) for testing the aerodynamics of new designs. Gordon Brown convinced Forrester to remain with MIT and take charge of the project. In 1945, shortly after accepting the job, Forrester finally received his master's degree in electrical engineering. His thesis, supervised by Gordon Brown, was entitled "Hydraulic Servomechanisms Developments."

The initial plan for the navy project was to construct an analog computer to simulate the performance of a manned aircraft. Forrester soon realized that analog technology was simply not going to be sufficient. The simulator required quick responses, but the analog device being planned was not nearly fast enough, lacking the real-time computing ability that was necessary. The answer was suggested to Forrester by Perry Crawford of the Special Devices Center. Crawford mentioned the possibility of digital computing, an area being explored by University of Pennsylvania scientists John von Neumann, J. Presper Eckert, and John Mauchly. Forrester traveled to Philadelphia, where he met with several of the engineers from the University of Pennsylvania's Moore School, then working on the groundbreaking ENIAC digital computer.

Convinced of the benefits of digital computing, Forrester returned to MIT and began work anew on his project in January of 1946. He was named director of MIT's new Digital Computer Laboratory, and the project soon became known as Whirlwind. Collaborating with Associate Director Robert R. Everett, Forrester began to envision the Whirlwind as a general-purpose computer with parallel processing, a feature which allowed for several functions to be performed at once. However, the inherent shortcomings of vacuum tubes and crystal diodes which plagued that era's computer engineers soon created problems for the Whirlwind.

Seeking to prolong the life of these electrical parts, Forrester began using silicon-free cathode material, thereby increasing the average longevity of the parts from 500 to 500,000 hours. He subsequently further increased their life span tenfold by installing a checking mechanism that could detect any malfunctioning components. Tirelessly dedicated, Forrester often gave the impression to his subordinates of being overly formal and distant, but there was no disputing his intuitive skill.

The frame for the Whirlwind, occupying 2,500 square feet of floor space, was erected in August of 1948. By the beginning of 1950, the machine was operational. It contained 4,000 vacuum tubes and was the fastest computer of the early 1950s, able to add two 16-bit numbers in two microseconds and multiply in 20 microseconds (in comparison, Howard Aiken's mechanical Mark I took a whole six seconds, which is 300,000 times longer). It was able to perform approximately 500,000 additions or 50,000 multiplications per second. Yet the Whirlwind still had its problems, systematically going down for several hours each day. Like all other first-generation electronic digital computers, the Whirlwind stored information in linear fashion in the form of coded digits, putting certain prohibitive limitations in terms of capacity on the memory system. Exacerbating the problem was the fact that the memory system was composed of storage tubes which lasted only a month and cost $1,000 to replace.

The need to improve the Whirlwind's memory storage led Jay Forrester to make his greatest contribution to the history of computers. "There was simply nothing that was suitable, and I had a project and a reputation that rested on our solving the problem," he stated in *Portraits in Silicon* (1987), "so it was very much a case of necessity being the mother of invention." In this case, the invention was the concept of three-dimensional storage, which would be more compact, with greater capacity, and a lower cost. Forrester mulled over the idea for several days. He took the Whirlwind's one-dimensional storage system and made it a two-dimensional one. The next step lay in elevating the system to a three-dimensional level. After a vacation on his father's ranch, Forrester returned with the solution.

He had been paging through the journal *Electrical Engineering* when he noticed an advertisement for a material known as Deltamax, which had been originally developed by the Germans during World War II for use in magnetic amplifiers in tanks. Seeing it as a possible catalyst for his three-dimensional system, Forrester obtained some of the material for his experiments. Running an electrical current through small rings of Deltamax, he was able to magnetize them and reverse them from one binary state to another. When the current was turned off, the rings remained in the same binary states, which was exactly the hoped-for outcome. However, the Deltamax itself was too slow and sensitive to serve Forrester's need, and so all he needed was to find a more suitable material. By this time, the U.S. Navy's original goal for the project had been overshadowed by the goal of creating a real-time computer.

In the next stage of development, Forrester replaced the Deltamax with magnetic ferrite. He strung the rings of ferrite, each about the size of a pencil-tip, onto a grid of wires, with each ring possessing its own coordinates. In this way, by energizing the appropriate pair of row and column wires on a certain grid, a binary digit could be read or written into the core memory. The ferrite cores were cheaper, faster, and easier to handle than the Deltamax. Perfected by the end of 1951, the new core system permitted information to be stored in three dimensions, and its magnetic cells were capable of both storing and switching.

The Whirlwind computer was equipped with magnetic core memory in the summer of 1953. As a result, the machine became twice as fast as before. Access to data and instructions was available in a few millionths of a second, and information could be stored for as long as was needed. Maintenance requirements were also drastically reduced. The Whirlwind thus became the first computer to operate in real-time—that is, to be capable of interacting directly with its operator instead of having to be extensively programmed over and over for each activity. The proliferation of computers, previously considered impractical and economically unjustifiable, now became a possibility due to this new invention, which would later become known as random-access memory, or RAM. Eventually, all digital computers switched over to RAM, and the earlier serial-type memory was phased out. RAM would remain the standard internal computer memory for almost 30 years.

While the Whirlwind had been undergoing its memory changes, there were many questions raised by the U.S. military as to whether or not the machine was still necessary. However, with the onset of the Cold War and the need to track the aircraft of a Soviet Union now in possession of atomic technology, the necessity of the Whirlwind ceased to be questioned. It became the center of the nation's air defense system, running simulations, aiming missiles, identifying unfriendly aircraft and predicting courses. Set up in 1958, this defense arrangement was named the Semi-Automatic Ground Environment System (SAGE) and was headed by Forrester. One of its most important assets was the AN/FSQ–7 computer, inspired by the Whirlwind and designed by Forrester and Robert Everett. The AN/FSQ-7 had a 32-bit memory and was the first computer to serve 100 users simultaneously. Another landmark development of SAGE worth mentioning was its use of computer monitors, invented to display tracked aircraft and provide a way of communicating more directly with the machine. This accessory remains a staple of the modern computer to this day. While the original Whirlwind was shut down in May of 1959, the SAGE program would remain in place for 25 years, not being scrapped until 1983.

Meanwhile, in 1956 Forrester became a professor at MIT's new Sloan School of Management. This marked the beginning of a whole new course of endeavor for him. At the Sloan School, he started to use computers to map out and analyze human social systems, leading to the establishment of the discipline now known as systems dynamics. A whole new application for computer technology, systems dynamics involves the use of computer simulations and projections to assess the difficulties and successes of social systems and corporate policies. By applying computer simulations to determine the implications of complex social systems, Forrester's methods emphasized empiricism and experimentalism in engineering as opposed to pure mathematics. One of Forrester's contributions to the new discipline he created was the development of the System Dynamics National Model for understanding fluctuations in the economy.

Among Forrester's numerous publications in the field of systems dynamics are *Industrial Dynamics* (1961), *Principles of Systems* (1968), and *Urban Dynamics* (1969). But the book for which he is most known is *World Dynamics* (1971). In this work he computer-analyzed global economics and the interrelationships among capital investment, natural resources, population, and pollution, to predict a worldwide depletion of resources, environmental disaster and mass starvation by the end of the 20th century.

World Dynamics produced a furor of controversy, with many critics disputing Forrester's extreme vision of impending doom. "Many of his formulas are simply educated guesses with no precise basis in research," remarked David C. Anderson in the *Wall Street Journal* (September 28, 1971). "Reducing human facets of life to mathematical formulas, however obvious, still oversimplifies them to some degree." Most of the book's predictions have not turned out to be accurate, and Forrester himself has since noted that he may have overemphasized certain aspects of his computer analysis (*National Review*, December 3, 1990). Despite his admission, however, he still maintains that the future scenario projected in *World Dynamics*, "is becoming more true every day."

In 1968 he received the Inventor of the Year Award from George Washington University. The Systems Management and Cybernetics Society presented him with an award for outstanding accomplishment in 1972, and 10 years later the IEEE Computer Society bestowed on him the prestigious Computer Pioneer Award. He has received numerous other accolades from countries such as Denmark, the United Kingdom, and Italy, and was inducted into the National Inventors Hall of Fame in 1979. He is also the recipient of eight honorary doctorates from universities around the world.

On July 27, 1946 Forrester married Susan Swett. The couple had four children: Judith, Nathan, Blair, and Ned Cromwell. Forrester and his wife currently live on their cattle ranch in Dunning, Nebraska. He has been described by computer historian Stan Augarten as "an extraordinarily capable, confident, though somewhat aloof man" (Bit by Bit, 1984).

Forrester became Germehausen Professor at the Sloan School of Management in 1972, and in 1989 became a professor emeritus and senior lecturer.

He remained the head of the System Dynamics Program at MIT until 1989. In recent years, his system dynamics work has become geared toward developing an improved educational framework in junior and senior high schools. He is also currently working on an extensive computer model of the U.S. economy called the National Model Project. In the *International Biographical Dictionary of Computer Pioneers* (1995), edited by J. A. N. Lee, Forrester comments, "The pioneering days in digital computers were exciting times. . . . However, the major challenges facing society will not be solved by still more technology. The next 100 years will be the age of social and economic discovery."
—B. S.

Suggested Reading: *National Review* p32+ Dec. 3, 1990; *Wall Street Journal* p18 Sep. 28, 1971; Augarten, Stan. *Bit by Bit*, 1984; Lee, J. A. N., ed. *International Biographical Dictionary of Computer Pioneers*, 1995; Slater, Robert. *Portraits in Silicon*, 1987

Frankston, Robert

June 14, 1949– Co-creator of the VisiCalc computer program

During the 1970s, when the first personal computers became available, consumers tended to view them as expensive toys with few practical benefits. Bob Frankston and Dan Bricklin helped changed that in 1979 with VisiCalc, the first spreadsheet program for personal computers, which eventually sold more than 800,000 copies. Although its features were simple, VisiCalc demonstrated how personal computers could benefit the workplace: accounting and other calculations that normally took days could be completed in a few hours. Users could also fix any mistakes with ease without having to start their work all over again. "For my money two guys named Bob Frankston and Dan Bricklin were the real fathers of the personal computer revolution," Joseph R. Garber wrote for *Forbes* (July 28, 1997). "Neither made big bucks. By turning hobbyists' playthings into workplace necessities, VisiCalc ultimately propelled the likes of Apple's Steve Jobs and Microsoft's Bill Gates onto the Forbes Four Hundred."

Robert Frankston was born on June 14, 1949 in the New York City borough of Brooklyn. His first experience with a computer was during junior high school. Frankston told *Leaders of the Information Age* that he grew interested in computers because they "were more fun than electric trains and more creative than modeling clay." In January 1963 he took a computer course at Hunter College, in New York City, where he learned how to use the IBM 1620 model. Frankston recalled to *Leaders*, "I was one of the few to understand it but only got a

chance to run FORTRAN I [a computer programming language] that computed leap years."

In the fall of 1963, Frankston enrolled in Stuyvesant High School, in New York City. "By my senior year at Stuyvesant, they were anticipating getting an IBM 1130," he told *Leaders*. "I took the first programming class at Stuyvesant and wound up helping to teach it, as well as find computers on which to run the class assignments." At the Courant Institute of New York University, Frankston also assisted in a minor capacity with efforts to provide time-sharing access to multiple users of the same computer, an IBM 6600.

After spending one year at the State University of New York (SUNY) in Stony Brook, Frankston transferred to the Massachusetts Institute of Technology (MIT), in Cambridge, in 1967. As an undergraduate he was one of the many students who contributed to the Multics Project, an effort to develop a more efficient time-sharing system. Professor Fernando J. Corbato, who ran the Multics Project, also supervised Frankston's undergraduate thesis, for which he developed a limited-access system for student computing. Frankston also co-founded the Student Information Processing Board (SIPB), which provided free computer access to students. He earned his B.S. degrees in computer science and mathematics from MIT in 1970 and remained at the school to pursue graduate work, receiving his M.S. and engineers degrees in computer science and electrical engineering in 1974. He continued to work on Multics and also wrote the programming language for the MicroMind computer, manufactured by the the the ECD Corporation.

While at MIT, Frankston had become friends with Dan Bricklin, an undergraduate who was also working on the Multics project. After completing his undergraduate studies, Bricklin enrolled in the Harvard Business School to pursue an MBA. In 1978 he had an idea for an "electronic spreadsheet," which would make calculations easier for PC users. Meanwhile, Frankston was working for White-Weld and Company (later named the Interactive Data Corporation), a Massachusetts-based investment-banking firm by which he had been hired while still in high school. He had continued to work in the computer-research division providing clients with on-line financial information from his dorm in Stony Brook—and later, from his apartment in Boston—by logging onto the company's computers. He had also worked on systems design and implementation and had developed other projects, such as an interactive computer-debugging system and an electronic-mail system. When he was contacted by Bricklin about the electronic- spreadsheet idea in 1978, Frankston was still with Interactive Data Corporation, but the idea soon came to occupy most of his energies. "The spreadsheet concept had been around for hundreds of years," Frankston explained to Janet Barron for *Byte* magazine (December 1989). "Companies used two to three rooms of blackboards or rolls of paper to do their production planning as rows and columns." Both Frankston and Bricklin believed that businesses would find this electronic spreadsheet a much more efficient means to keep financial records.

In a rented basement office in Cambridge, Frankston and Bricklin began working on the spreadsheet. Frankston wrote the actual program, and Bricklin tested it and fixed any problems. They decided to call their product VisiCalc, short for visible calculator. In January 1979 Frankston and Bricklin co-founded Software Arts to manufacture VisiCalc. To market and sell VisiCalc, Bricklin recruited Dan Fylstra, a friend from Harvard Business School who ran Personal Software. At the time, Personal Software was the leading seller and distributor of personal-computer software in the United States.

Frankston and Bricklin wrote VisiCalc to run on a 32-Kbyte Apple II computer. Because of the memory limitations of the Apple II (and other personal computers at the time), they had to decide which features to include with VisiCalc and which ones to leave out. Above all, Frankston believed that VisiCalc had to be fast and very easy to use. Detailing VisiCalc's features in *Byte* (December 1989), Tracy Robnett Licklider wrote that it "offered a small spreadsheet of only 254 rows by 63 columns, and its main menu was Spartan; it presented only a stark concatenation of its single-letter commands. On-line help, originally planned, had to be sacrificed to leave enough memory for spreadsheet data. The program offered only basic options for displaying cells."

During a meeting of the National Computer Conference in New York City in June 1979, Frankston and Bricklin for the first time publicly announced the creation of VisiCalc. Reaction from most of those who attended was less than enthusiastic. Frances X. Clines, a reporter who covered the conference for the *New York Times*, mentioned the name VisiCalc in his article without describing what the program was or did. Frankston and Bricklin, however, were actually pleased by the brief notice, because no other major newspapers or business publications were giving VisiCalc any attention.

Priced at $99, VisiCalc was released in October 1979. It sold slowly at first but eventually became a bestseller, as businesses realized its flexibility and time-saving capabilities. Frankston and Bricklin later adapted VisiCalc for computers manufactured by Atari, Commodore, Radio Shack and IBM. By 1985 the program had sold over 800,000 copies. In *Computerworld* (May 23, 1994, on-line) Steve Moore wrote that VisiCalc "did nothing less than spark a PC revolution among business users." In addition to widening the appeal of personal computers, VisiCalc also set the stage for more advanced electronic spreadsheets and other important applications such as WordPerfect, Microsoft Word, and e-mail systems that are used by many today.

Although it was a runaway bestseller and turned the personal computer into a necessary workplace tool, enthusiasm for VisiCalc declined in the early 1980s as more advanced electronic spreadsheets, especially Lotus 1-2-3, appeared on the market. In September 1983 Visicorp, Personal Software's successor, sued Software Arts, alleging that Frankston and Bricklin had violated their contractual obligations to keep VisiCalc updated. Software Arts countersued. The legal entanglements provided Lotus with an additional opportunity to capture the electronic-spreadsheet market. In the summer of 1984, both Visicorp and Software Arts reached a settlement. Visicorp went out of business, and Frankston and Bricklin sold Software Arts' assets to Lotus. As Frankston explained to *Leaders*, software programs were not patented at the time of VisiCalc's release, preventing him and Bricklin from amassing a fortune from their invention.

After the dissolution of Software Arts, Bob Frankston continued to work in the computer industry. In 1985 he joined Lotus Development, for which he created Lotus Express and a fax facility for Lotus Notes. In 1990 he moved to the Slate Corporation and worked on mobile and pen-based computer systems. In 1993 he went to work for Microsoft, where he helped promote the networking of personal computers, which at the time were, as he told *Leaders*, like "disconnected islands."

Frankston left Microsoft in 1998. He is currently pursuing other projects, such as utilizing IP infrastructure, which as he described on his Web site, is "a term I prefer to the Internet in order to focus on the underlying technology rather than the applications that use this infrastructure." Frankston told *Leaders* that he is "excited about exploring the world beyond the Web, where we have an infrastructure 1,000 times as large as the current Internet. And, of course, trying to implement it."

Frankston has received numerous awards and honors, including the William L. Stewart Award from MIT for co-founding the Student Information Processing Board as well as MIT's Industrial Achievement Award. He was named a fellow by the Association for Computing Machinery (ACM) and was granted a Software System Award by that organization. Frankston is a recipient of *PC Magazine*'s Lifetime Achievement Award and has been named to the Computer Hall of Fame.

Robert Frankston is married and lives with his family in Newton, Massachusetts.—D. C.

Suggested Reading: Bob Frankston Web site; *Byte* p324+ Dec. 1989, with photo; *Computerworld* (on-line) May 23, 1994; Dan Bricklin Web site; *Forbes* p84+ July 28, 1997

Courtesy of Gordon French

French, Gordon

Mar. 7, 1935– Co-founder of the Homebrew Computer Club

On March 5, 1975 Gordon French and Fred Moore convened the first meeting of the Homebrew Computer Club. About 20 people came to the meeting—which was held in French's garage in Menlo Park, California—to talk about computers and share information. Among the attendees were Steve Jobs,

who co-founded Apple Computer with Steve Wozniak, and Lee Felsenstein, who went on to enjoy a successful career as a computer designer. Over the months, the club gradually attracted more hobbyists, including a number of other people who would soon became famous in the computer industry, among them Adam Osborne, the founder of a personal-computer company bearing his name, and Tom Pitman, a developer of computer languages. Many computer historians view the first meeting of the Homebrew Computer Club as a milestone event in the development of personal computers.

The child of farmers, Gordon French was born on March 7, 1935 in Yakima, Washington. When he was 14, French and his mother moved to Portland, Oregon. French took courses at Portland State University, in Oregon, and Golden Gate University, in San Francisco, California.

In 1953 French joined the White Stag Manufacturing Company in Portland; his job was counting garment tags by hand. In 1958 he moved to San Francisco. "I wanted to write the great American novel," he explained to *Leaders of the Information Age*. French got a job with Remington Rand's UNIVAC (Universal Automatic Computer) division. After learning how to operate the UNIVAC by taking courses the company offered, French was given the task of sorting the machine's punched cards. "[The UNIVAC] was noisy," French recalled to *Leaders of the Information Age*. "It was big . . . but it worked."

In about 1964 French was hired by the Planning Research Corporation, where he helped program weapons and "snooper" systems. French told *Leaders of the Information Age* that it was "a fun company to work for." In the early 1970s he accepted a position as a software programmer with Fairchild Communications Equipment, which manufactured teletype machines with high-speed (1200-baud) modems.

During the early 1970s, two engineers helped French build his own computer, which consisted of an Intel 8008 microprocessor, a model 33 teletype, a modem, and a monitor. The computer could run a word processor and play games. "It was designed to take a document and transmit it over phones lines," he told *Leaders of the Information Age*.

In 1973 French spotted a sign for the People's Computer Company (PCC) in Menlo Park, California, where he was living at the time. Bob Albrecht and Dennis Allison had organized the PCC to make computers accessible to the ordinary person, by allowing users to rent time on the PDP-8, an early microcomputer. French eventually got to write a column under the pseudonym "Newett Awl" for the group's newsletter. Every Wednesday the PCC had a potluck dinner at which the main topic of conversation was, naturally, computers. The potluck dinners, despite their popularity, were eventually discontinued. French and Fred Moore, an antiwar activist and fellow computer enthusiast, decided that another forum was needed wherein hobbyists could share information. French agreed to provide his garage as a venue for the first meeting of the Homebrew Computer Club, as they called their new group. French gave Moore $5 to print handbills to advertise the venture. About 20 people showed up at the first meeting of the Homebrew Computer Club, which took place on March 5, 1975. French told *Leaders of the Information Age* that the meeting lasted about 90 minutes, and the participants spent most of the evening introducing themselves and then talking about their own computers and programs. When asked by *Leaders of the Information Age* why so many computer historians consider the first meeting of the club a milestone event, French observed that at the time, "Nobody had computers, but everybody wanted one." He admitted, "I didn't foresee everyone having more than one computer in their house." The Homebrew Computer Club attracted more members at its subsequent meetings. Many people who went on to enjoy successful careers in the computer industry attended the meetings. French later recalled that the Homebrew Computer Club had "the damned finest collection of engineers and technicians that you could possibly get under one roof," as quoted by Steven Levy in *Hackers: Heroes of the Computer Revolution* (1984).

French remained active in the computer industry, working in different capacities for several companies. In 1975 he joined Processor Technology, serving as the design engineer for the Sol computer, primarily designed by Felsenstein. Intended as a competitor to Apple, the Sol sold only several hundred units, and Processor Technology folded the next year. "None of us at Processor Technology knew how to grow," French told *Leaders of the Information Age*, explaining the venture's failure. He then joined IMSAI, which built an S-100 bus-type computer, as a technical advisor. In late 1976 French became the pilot-store manager and the head of products, selection, evaluations, and testing for Computer Shack, in Hayward, California. He also worked briefly for Microform Data Systems, Ames Research Center, Commodore Business Machines and EXIDY, which manufactured coin-operated arcade games. French helped build the EXIDY Sorcerer computer, characterized by software cartridges identical to those used in then-popular 8-track players. "It wasn't really a screaming success," he told *Leaders of the Information Age*. In 1977 French served as the operational manager for the first West Coast Computer Faire, which was organized by Jim Warren in San Francisco.

During the 1980s, Gordon French worked as a computer consultant. He also served as a distributor for the 3M diskette company and established his own company, Square One, which made "floppy armor," protective mailers for floppy diskettes.

Today, Gordon French lives in semi-retirement in Fremont, California, where he continues to work on freelance projects. He spends his time building steam locomotives that are large enough to ride on. He is the father of two sons.—D. C.

Suggested Reading: *Computer Shopper* p703+ Jan. 1992; *Contra Costa Times* D p8+ Apr. 2, 2000; *New York Times* III p1+ Mar. 26, 2000, with photo; Levy, Stephen. *Hackers: Heroes of the Computer Revolution*, 1984

Friedman, William Frederick

Sep. 24, 1891–Nov. 2, 1969 Cryptologist

William Frederick Friedman has been referred to as the "father of American cryptology." In the *Washington Post* (January 24, 1994), Ken Ringle observed that Friedman "led the evolution of cipher technology from pencils to machines." While cryptology had long been important to espionage, Friedman helped transform it from an art to a science by applying complex mathematics and incorporating electronic machinery. He worked as a cryptologist for the U.S. government in both world wars. In World War II he and his team cracked the Japanese government's secret code, which gave the Allied forces a distinct advantage in intelligence, helped bring the war to a swifter close, and saved thousands of lives. Cryptology has recently become important in the development of techniques to protect and encourage on-line commerce.

William Frederick Friedman was born in Kishinev, Russia, on September 24, 1891. His father, who was an interpreter for the post office and spoke eight languages, brought the family to Pittsburgh, Pennsylvania, in 1893. Upon graduating from high school, Friedman got a job at an iron mill, but enrolled at Cornell University in Ithaca, New York, in 1911. He earned a B.S. in genetics, and in 1914 he was hired by Colonel George Fabyan, a millionaire, to do genetics research on his farm, Riverbank, in Geneva, Illinois. Among other eccentricities, Fabyan had a pet gorilla and drove a carriage drawn by two zebras; he was also intent on proving that Shakespeare's works were actually composed by Sir Francis Bacon, which he believed would be revealed by decoding a secret message within the text of the play *Troilus and Cressida*. Soon Friedman was spending as much time as he could in the cryptology lab at Riverbank. "When it came to cryptology, something in me found an outlet," Friedman explained, as quoted by Sid Moody for the *Los Angeles Times* (October 28, 1990). "Just an inherent curiosity to know what people were trying to write that they didn't want other people to read." Friedman also found himself taken with one of the cryptology assistants, Elizabeth Smith, whom he married in 1917.

After the United States entered World War I in 1917, the American government, understaffed in the field of cryptology, began sending messages to Riverbank to be decoded. Friedman solved nearly all of them with relative ease, including one that had been encrypted with a book that he did not have. Friedman began training military officers in cryptology and eventually coined the term *cryptanalysis*—the process of analyzing a code without having the key—to differentiate it from *deciphering,* which is the more straightforward process of translating a message from code using a key. (Is it also important to differentiate cryptanalysis from cryptography. There are two types of cryptography: enciphering, in which each letter of a message is replaced with another letter or series of symbols, and encoding, in which syllables, words, or whole sentences are replaced according to some systematic method.)

Friedman, as director of the department of ciphers at Riverbank, published a series of papers known as the Riverbank Publications, beginning in 1917. They included: "A Method of Reconstructing the Primary Alphabet from a Single One of the Series of Secondary Alphabets" (1917); "An Introduction to Methods for the Solution of Ciphers" (1918); "Several Machine Ciphers and Methods for Their Solution" (1918); and "Synoptic Tables for the Star Cipher" (1918). Around the same time Friedman published a landmark article in cryptology, "The Index of Coincidence and its Applications in Cryptanalysis," which was one of the first texts to incorporate advanced mathematics, such as statistics, into cryptology. Still in print today, the paper, according to the *Historical Dictionary of Data Processing: Biographies* (1987), "opened the door to the use of computer-like technology in this field."

After World War I Friedman stayed on at Riverbank and continued his consulting work for the U.S. Army. On one occasion the army sent him a coded message that was considered virtually unbreakable, but he quickly managed to send a return message using an identical code. On the strength of this impressive feat and his earlier demonstrations of expertise in cryptology, Friedman was hired as the chief cryptanalyst for the U.S. War Department in 1921. Based on his recommendations, the military began to employ more mechanical and electronic means to encode and decode messages. In 1930 he was made the chief of the Signal Intelligence Service of the U.S. Army.

Friedman spent long hours aiding the evolution of more advanced cryptographic machines. At the time, most cryptographic machines used only a series of electronic rotors to encipher a message. Each rotor was shaped like a disk and had electrical contacts for 26 letters (when the Latin alphabet was used) arranged in a circle on either side. The contacts on one side of the rotor were wired in a mixed-up order to the other side, which caused a simple monoalphabetic substitution pattern that changed as the rotor rotated. The machines generally set a series of three or more rotors in tandem so that each letter in the original message would go through a series of substitutions. The German Enigma machine relied on such a mechanism, employing three rotors that rotated much like a speedometer, causing the next rotor to move once the preceding rotor had undergone a certain number of turns. Friedman presented a prototype of the SIGABA machines in 1935, after several years in development. (SIGABA was known in naval circles as the ECM–Mark Two.) The SIGABA used 15 rotors, and, instead of the speedometer-like mechanism used by the Enigma and many other machines, it incorporated a stepping maze, which allowed the rotors to spin in a much more random fashion. The SIGABA is the only cryptographic machine thought never to have been cracked during World War II.

In the 1930s the Japanese government began using its first rotor cryptographic machine, which was codenamed *Red* by the U.S. In an important victory for U.S. intelligence, in 1935–1936 Friedman and his team broke the Red machine code; after this success, Friedman's rank was elevated to lieutenant colonel. The Japanese initiated a greatly improved machine, the 97-shiki-O-bun Injiki, which the U.S. codenamed *Purple,* in the late 1930s. In 1940 Friedman and his team were assigned to crack the code. When the Japanese government announced to its upper-level embassies that it would now be using the Purple, it sent parallel messages on the Purple machine and, to the lesser consulates, on the Red machine. By comparing the messages sent by the Red and Purple machines, Friedman and his team were able to decode about 25 percent of the cipher within several weeks. Several months later it occurred to Harry Laurence Clark, one of the members of Friedman's team, that the Purple machine might be using telephone stepping switches rather than rotors for its scrambling mechanism, which would produce different patterns than the cryptologists were accustomed to seeing. Using only the encrypted Japanese messages as their guide, Friedman and his team began assembling a machine that employed stepping switches. Through trial and error, sophisticated mathematical analysis, and probably some intuition and luck, an American version of the Purple machine was able to successfully decode a message on September 25, 1940, more than a year in advance of the Japanese attack on Pearl Harbor on December 7, 1941. The combined efforts by the Army and Navy in cracking the Red and Purple machines was code-named *Operation Magic.*

Friedman maintained that no information deciphered by Operation Magic provided any clue to the date or location of a planned Japanese attack on Pearl Harbor, according to Frederick Allan Goerner in an article for the *San Francisco Chronicle* (December 1, 1991). However, in a 1957 secret report to the National Security Agency (NSA), Friedman, as quoted by Goerner, expressed puzzlement about why the U.S. had been so unprepared for the Pearl

Harbor attack. "U.S. war plans," Friedman wrote, as quoted by Goerner, "took into account the possibility that the Japanese might begin a war without a preceding declaration, that is by surprise attack, and although this possibility was placed first on a list of contingencies, with Pearl Harbor as the focal point for the attack, and although the war plans even envisioned that such an attack could come from aircraft flown from carriers, it is an almost inexplicable fact that all of this was forgotten by the end of the same year (1941)."

Though Operation Magic did little to prepare the U.S. for Pearl Harbor, it proved of inestimable importance later in World War II. According to a reporter for the London *Times* (July 15, 1998), the American Purple machines deciphered messages sent from Baron Oshima, a Japanese ambassador to Germany, from Berlin to Tokyo; these messages revealed the existence of Germany's new jet fighters, German troop strength in the Balkans, and aspects of Hitler's plans for Europe. Operation Magic also revealed Japanese military plans in the Pacific, which led to naval victories in the battles of the Coral Sea and Midway. These decisive victories changed the course of the war in the Pacific by drastically reducing the Japanese fleet and leading to the capture of Admiral Yamamoto Isoroku, Japan's Pacific commander. The American and Japanese versions of the Purple machine were so well matched that even after the war, the Japanese government refused to believe that the U.S. had copied the Purple machines by using only the encrypted messages; they insisted that a machine must have been captured. (A Japanese machine, abandoned later in Guam, had only two—of hundreds—wires that differed from the American copy.)

During and after World War II, Friedman held a number of different positions in the U.S. government. He was director of communications research for the Army Security Agency (1942–49); chief of the technical division of the Armed Forces Security Agency (1949–50); chief technical consultant to the NSA, which he helped found (1950–52); special assistant to the director of the NSA (1953–55); cryptologist at the U.S. Department of Defense (1947–55); and consultant to the U.S. Department of Defense (1955–69). His awards include the U.S. War Department's Exceptional Service Award (1944); the U.S. Medal of Merit (1946); the National Security Medal (1955); and a U.S. Congressional award (1956). In 1957 William and Elizebeth Friedman published *Shakespearean Ciphers Examined*, a book that discredited the cryptanalytic efforts that had provided the circumstances for their meeting. Friedman died in Washington, D. C., on November 2, 1969.—P. G. H.

Suggested Reading: *Los Angeles Times* p2 Oct. 28, 1990; *San Francisco Chronicle* p7 Dec. 1, 1991; London *Times* p23 July 15, 1998; *Washington Post* A p1 Jan. 24, 1994; Cortada, James W. *Historical Dictionary of Data Processing*, 1987

Courtesy of Microsoft

Gates, Bill

Oct. 28, 1955– Co-founder, chairman, and chief software architect of Microsoft

As the chairman and chief software architect of Microsoft, the world's leading software, services, and Internet-technologies firm, Bill Gates is the world's richest man, according to *Forbes* magazine, with a net worth of more than $40 billion. Gates co-founded Microsoft in 1975 (when he was just 19), and had risen to the status of billionaire by the age of 31, making him the youngest person ever to achieve membership in that exclusive club. The first maker of personal-computer (PC) software, Microsoft is now considered the most successful technology firm in history, with a worth of more than $280 billion and revenues for the fiscal year ending June 30, 2002, of $28.37 billion. Over the last decade, the company has generated an average annual sales growth of more than 30 percent and annual earnings growth of 37 percent—an astonishing feat for a publically traded corporation. Despite the recent economic slowdown, which has crippled many technology-related businesses, Microsoft has continued to experience solid growth, and the firm now employs more than 50,000 people in 78 countries and regions.

The key to Microsoft's phenomenal success has been its MS-DOS and Windows operating systems, the latter of which is now used in approximately 90 percent of all PCs worldwide. However, in recent years the company has expanded into other markets, providing products such as Internet technology, networking systems, software for small businesses, handheld devices, and cellular-phone technology. Microsoft's unprecedented dominance in the computer-software market has meant that Gates's original corporate mission—"to have a computer on every desk and in every home, all running Microsoft software"—has come close to being actualized.

Nevertheless, Microsoft's dominance came under fire in 1998, when the U.S. Department of Justice filed suit against the software giant for alleged antitrust violations. The company was accused of thwarting competition and engaging in aggressive business tactics to extend its monopoly on software. Despite the controversy that surrounded the antitrust case, and the company's sometimes uncertain future, Microsoft has continued to expand and develop its product line, most recently releasing its newest version of Windows, Windows XP, and an ambitious new brand of Web services known as Microsoft .Net (pronounced *dot-net*).

A born businessman as well as a technical wizard, Gates, according to a 1983 *People* magazine profile, "is to software what Edison was to the light bulb—part innovator, part entrepreneur, part salesman, and full-time genius." Elizabeth Corcoran noted for the *Washington Post* (December 3, 1995), "He has become a symbol of American supremacy in computer technology. Gates is the face that people use to humanize one of the world's fastest growing industries, a source of immense change in the way people work, study, play and fight. With his success, Gates has helped rekindle confidence in the American Dream: that someone with a good idea and an appetite for work can inspire an industry and become the richest guy around."

William Henry Gates 3d, the only son and the second-oldest of the three children of Mary (Maxwell) Gates and William Henry Gates Jr., was born on October 28, 1955 in Seattle, Washington. Nicknamed "Trey" (because of the 3d following his name), Gates grew up in a closely knit upper-middle-class family. His father was a partner in a prominent Seattle law firm; his mother was a teacher who later became a member of the University of Washington board of regents and the boards of several corporations. (Gates's mother died in 1994, at the age of 64.) His parents enrolled Gates, a bright and energetic child, at the Lakeside School, a private institution known for its rigorous academic standards.

In 1967 the Lakeside School Mothers Club used the proceeds from rummage sales to buy a digital training terminal that was linked by phone to a computer at a local computer company. As Gates's father told Richard Brandt for *BusinessWeek* (April 13, 1987), his son became hooked on it. "Completely engrossed," Gates and three likeminded friends (including Paul Allen, a co-founder of Microsoft) started the Lakeside Programming Group. They were soon cutting classes and hanging out at the school's computer center day and night. From the beginning, Gates saw the enormous potential of computers, and he even boasted to one of his teachers that computers would help make him a millionaire one day. One of the first programs he designed

was used to track class schedules for Lakeside School; Gates made sure that he could share classes with all of the prettiest girls. For a summer's work of arranging schedules, he earned $4,200.

Gates and his friends became so enamored of computers that they began rummaging through the trash bins at the nearby Computer Center Corporation (CCC), hunting for scraps of paper left by the programmers. "Paul [Allen] would hoist me up on the garbage cans," Gates recalled to Ed Zuckerman for *People* (August 20, 1990), "and I'd get the notes out with the coffee grounds on them and study the operating system." After searching for errors in the company's programs, the group produced a 300-page manual, *The Problem Report Book*, which earned them berths on the CCC payroll. Displaying his mischievous side, Gates learned how to cause an operating system to crash and then brought about the crash of Control Data Corporation's CYBERNET computer system. After a reprimand from the company, Gates temporarily gave up computers. As he recalled to Robert Slater in an interview for the book *Portraits in Silicon* (1987), an interest in computers was then "not a mainstream thing. I couldn't imagine spending the rest of my life at it." During his self-imposed leave of absence from computers, Gates spent his free time on such nontechnical pursuits as acting in the school play. (His English teacher has recalled that he once memorized in one reading a three-page soliloquy for a play.)

After a year's absence, finding himself unable to stay away from computers, Gates rejoined the programming group, which had begun taking on commercial jobs to help pay for computing time. In one such project, the group developed a new computerized payroll system for Lakeside School; in another they used a computer to count the holes punched in cards by the machines that monitor highway traffic. Because Gates was two years younger than the others, he was temporarily excluded from the group, but he was invited back when the would-be entrepreneurs discovered their inability to get along without him. Gates then became the group's unofficial head, and two years later, when the young computer enthusiasts formed a company called Traf-O-Data to sell the traffic-counting system to municipalities, the 14-year-old Gates was named its president. Within a year, Traf-O-Data had earned $20,000, but the firm's business fell off after customers learned that Gates and his friends were still high-school students.

Gates put his computer career on hold to work as a congressional page during the summer of 1972. That same summer he displayed the entrepreneurial instincts that would later make him so successful, when he and a friend bought 5,000 George S. McGovern–Thomas Eagleton presidential-campaign buttons for a nickel each after Eagleton was dumped from the Democratic ticket. They later turned a handsome profit by selling the buttons, which quickly became collector's items, for as much as $25 apiece. Returning home in the fall of 1972, Gates was offered a programmer's position by TRW, a large software firm in Vancouver, Washington, at an annual salary of $20,000. Then a high-school senior, Gates obtained permission to suspend his studies for a time in order to accept the position. Gates scored a perfect 800 on the mathematics portion of the Scholastic Aptitude Test (SAT), and in 1973 he graduated from the Lakeside School. He then enrolled at Harvard University, in Cambridge, Massachusetts, as a pre-law major, intending to become an attorney. As a freshman at Harvard, Gates reportedly got an *A* on an economics final exam without ever attending the class, simply by cramming the night before the test.

In January 1975 Paul Allen, then working as a programmer for Honeywell, read an article in *Popular Electronics* magazine about the world's first commercially available microcomputer, the Altair 8800, manufactured by MITS, a company in Albuquerque, New Mexico. Sold for less than $400, the computer was primitive by today's standards, as it contained just 256 bytes of memory (most computers today have from 128 megabytes to one gigabyte of memory), and it had no software. Allen showed Gates the article and urged his friend to join him in writing a program for the computer. "We realized that the revolution might happen without us," Gates told Robert Slater. "After we saw that article, there was no question of where our life would focus."

Gates and Allen set about adapting the computer language BASIC, used on large computers, to the Altair. They contacted Ed Roberts, the president of MITS, and told him they had finished the program, when, in fact, they had not even started. When Roberts expressed interest in seeing a demonstration, Gates and Allen began working day and night in Gates's dormitory room at Harvard. Speed was of the essence, since others were also trying to adapt BASIC to microcomputers. The biggest challenge the two men faced was fitting the ambitious program into the Altair's tiny memory. Because they had never seen an Altair or the 8080 microchip on which the machine was based, Gates and Allen devised their own simulator 8080 software on a computer at the Harvard Computer Center.

Gates then wrote a BASIC that would run on the simulator. "We just had this book that described the machine," Gates explained to Ed Zuckerman. "If we had read the book wrong, or the book was wrong, we were hosed." It was with those reservations in mind that Allen journeyed to MITS headquarters with a paper tape of the program to load into the Altair. Back in Cambridge, Gates waited nervously, aware that, if the program failed to work, he and his partner might not be given a second chance. Luckily, BASIC worked on the first try. "MITS didn't understand the importance of it," Gates told an interviewer for *People* (December 26, 1983). "Nobody did. But we knew that people in schools everywhere would have these computers." The BASIC that Gates and Allen wrote for the Altair became an industry standard that dominated the market for the next six years.

Despite objections from his parents, Gates dropped out of Harvard at the end of his sophomore year, in June 1975. He and Allen moved to Albuquerque, where they established a partnership called Microsoft to produce their BASIC program for MITS. MITS folded shortly after that, but Microsoft had, by that time, begun selling its programs to other fledgling hardware companies, including Apple and Commodore. Within 18 months of moving to Albuquerque, Gates and Allen had earnings of a few hundred thousand dollars. In 1977 the Tandy Corporation hired Microsoft to develop software for its popular Radio Shack computers, and in January 1979 Gates and Allen moved Microsoft's headquarters from Albuquerque to Bellevue, Washington, near Seattle.

Microsoft moved to the forefront of the burgeoning microcomputer industry in 1980, when IBM, one of the world's largest manufacturers of office machines, contacted Gates about devising an operating system for the personal computer it was then planning. Uncertain if his young company could develop the complex system IBM sought by the established deadline, Gates recommended a competitor, Digital Research. When IBM was unable to reach an agreement with that company, it returned to Gates, who paid a Seattle programmer named Tim Paterson $50,000 for the rights to a rudimentary system called Q-DOS, which stood for "quick and dirty operating system." Gates modified Paterson's program, added some new features, and sold it to IBM, under the name Microsoft Disk Operating System, or MS-DOS. Gates then persuaded IBM to abandon its secret design specifications in favor of an open system for its personal computer, thereby allowing software to be built for it more easily, since software developers would know how the operating system functioned. About 100 companies, eager to be IBM compatible, obtained licenses for MS-DOS, quickly making it the major operating system for personal computers.

Microsoft's staff grew from 15 in 1978 to 125 in 1981, and its sales mushroomed from $4 million in 1980 to $16 million just a year later. The success of MS-DOS led other computer companies to approach Microsoft for software, and Gates soon found himself developing programs for Apple's line of Macintosh computers and Radio Shack's Model 100. Meanwhile, in Japan, he unveiled the Microsoft Extended Basic (MSX) design, which standardized the construction of low-end home computers. In early 1983, when the Japanese electronics giants Sony, Matsushita, and NEC asked Microsoft to create customized versions of BASIC to run on their new lines of home computers, Gates asked the three firms to accept a standardized set of specifications for both software and hardware. Within four months, 18 other major Japanese electronics firms had agreed to go along. (MSX computers failed in the North American market, and export of the machines to the United States ended in 1984.)

Having set the standard for operating systems, in the mid-1980s Gates set about developing applications software—the programs that tell the computer how to perform specific tasks, such as financial analysis or word processing. In an interview with Stratford P. Sherman for *Fortune* (January 23, 1984), Gates admitted that he had "blundered" by concentrating too long on MS-DOS at the expense of applications, by far the largest share of the software business. Within a few years Microsoft had beaten out such competitors as VisiCorp, Micro-Pro, and Digital Research to become one of the leading applications-software firms in the United States.

Although Paul Allen was diagnosed with cancer in 1983, his disease went into remission, and he was able to return to Microsoft a year later as a vice president. His illness increased Gates's already staggering workload; between 1978 and 1984 he took a total of just six days of vacation. To ease his burden and at the same time bolster Microsoft's management, Gates began recruiting talented executives from other companies. In 1982 he hired James Towne from Tektronix, an electronic-instruments maker, to become president of Microsoft; Towne was succeeded by Jon Shirley, a former vice-president at the Tandy Corporation. Gates's ability to make the transition from creative genius to astute businessman, as well as his willingness to delegate authority, set him apart from most of the other young computer wizards. "Unlike some other pioneers of the industry, Bill Gates is still in control because he had the guts to give up some control," Esther Dyson, the publisher of *Release 1.0*, a software newsletter, told a reporter for *U.S. News and World Report* (July 21, 1986).

By 1983, 40 percent of all personal computers were running Microsoft software. The company's sales soared to more than $140 million in 1985, and in the following year its 1,200 employees moved into a new 29-acre corporate campus in Redmond, Washington, a Seattle suburb. While many other pioneers in the microcomputer industry grabbed quick profits and sold the companies they had founded, Gates clung tightly to Microsoft. By 1986 the company's pre-tax profits were running as high as 34 percent of revenues, meaning that its growth required no infusions of outside capital. Lotus and Ashton-Tate, two of Microsoft's chief competitors, went public in 1983, but Gates feared that taking Microsoft public would prove detrimental to the company. "The whole process looked like a pain," Gates told Bro Uttal for *Fortune* (July 21, 1986), "and an ongoing pain once you're public. People get confused because the stock price doesn't reflect your financial performance. And to have a stock trader call up the chief executive and ask him questions is uneconomic—the ball bearings shouldn't be asking the driver about the grease." Nonetheless, Gates, in an attempt to attract and retain top programmers and managers, began selling them shares and granting stock options, and in March 1986 he finally decided to take Microsoft public.

When Microsoft's initial stock offering went on sale on March 13, 1986, the price was $21 per share. Within days the shares were trading for $35.50, and, generally, prices have continued to rise ever since. Gates's 45 percent share of Microsoft made him a multimillionaire overnight, and when, in March 1987, the stock's price hit $90.75, he became a billionaire. Industry observers noted that he had made more money than anyone his age ever had, in any business enterprise. Unimpressed by the figures, Gates told Brian O'Reilly for *Fortune* (October 12, 1987), "The company is a high-tech stock, and high-tech stocks are volatile. The price is not a reflection of the contribution we're making."

Not content to sit back and rake in profits from his existing product lines, Gates forged ahead with a variety of innovations in what was becoming an increasingly competitive marketplace. Realizing that businesses would require a better operating system than MS-DOS if personal computers were to take on more complex tasks, Microsoft and IBM set out in 1985 to develop OS/2, a powerful system capable of carrying out several functions simultaneously. Introduced in late 1987, OS/2 replaced MS-DOS in a new line of IBM personal computers called the PS/2. In early 1989 Gates began devoting considerable energy to reducing Lotus's domination of the lucrative office-spreadsheet software market. (At that time, Lotus was Microsoft's largest competitor.) Used to analyze numerical data, spreadsheets had become indispensable for many business people. Sharply reducing the price of its Excel spreadsheet program in an attempt to undercut sales of the popular Lotus 1-2-3, Microsoft launched an aggressive advertising campaign aimed at its competitor.

Gates's next innovation was Windows 3.0, which allowed IBM-compatible PCs to be operated with a handheld mouse and on-screen symbols, rather than by typing in commands. The software was as simple to operate as Apple's Macintosh, and it sold at a fraction of the cost. Windows 3.0 went on the market on May 22, 1990; it was an instant success, with Microsoft soon selling an estimated one million copies per month. (By April 1993 Microsoft had reported more than 25 million licensed users, making Windows the most popular graphical operating system in the world.) Microsoft then undertook efforts to develop software for linking computers through a network, for recognizing handwriting, and for creating so-called multimedia computer systems that permitted users to mix sounds, video, graphics, speech, and text. The company also began trying to increase the popularity of optical discs as a means of storing encyclopedia sets and other large collections of information. In 1991 Microsoft launched its own computer-science research laboratory, known as Microsoft Research (MSR). More than a decade later, the 600-person think tank, with a budget of $4 billion for the current fiscal year, remains active in advancing some of the industry's most innovative research.

Disappointed at what it viewed as Microsoft's unwillingness to support OS/2, which had been billed as the future of operating systems, IBM announced plans in mid-1991 to introduce a new version of that system, OS/2 2.0, early in the following year, around the same time that Microsoft planned to introduce its new competing Windows 3.1 operating system. IBM further severed its ties with Microsoft in June 1991, when it signed a preliminary agreement with Apple to share several important technologies. The agreement was viewed by computer-industry analysts as an attempt by IBM and Apple to weaken Microsoft's ever-increasing power.

Microsoft found itself embroiled in two legal squabbles in the early 1990s. First, Apple Computer had filed a copyright suit against Microsoft in 1988, alleging that the Windows program violated Apple's user-interface copyrights on the operating system for its Macintosh line. Apple won a partial victory on March 6, 1991, when a federal judge declined to dismiss the suit. However, in May 1992 a U.S. District Court judge threw out the bulk of Apple's claims, rejecting the idea that the company had patent protection for the "look and feel" of its product. The case, which had been watched closely by industry analysts for any precedent-setting decision, was finally dismissed in 1993, and Microsoft continued its development of a graphics-oriented, consumer-friendly operating system.

Also in March 1991, Microsoft confirmed reports that it was being investigated by the Federal Trade Commission (FTC) for anticompetitive business practices, an investigation that centered around allegations that Microsoft used its superior position in operating-systems software to squelch competition in other areas, especially applications software. The FTC closed its investigation in 1993, but by that time both the U.S. Justice Department and the European Commission had begun their own inquiries into antitrust-related activities, after more than 10 companies—including Novell, Lotus, WordPerfect, and Borland, then the four largest software companies—had come forth with claims of Microsoft's predatory behavior. In 1994 Microsoft agreed to sign a consent decree with the Justice Department, indicating that it would halt certain business practices that had been under investigation. Most notably, Microsoft agreed to stop charging computer companies a licensing fee for installing the Windows operating system on all machines, even those sold without Windows. (In effect, this discouraged computer makers from installing a non-Windows system on any machine, since they would have to pay Microsoft the licensing fee regardless. This clause had been standard in Microsoft's licensing agreements.) While the consent decree signaled a clear win by the Justice Department, Microsoft officials did not appear to demonstrate any contrition. On August 21, 1995, the evening that U.S. District Judge Thomas Penfield Jackson approved the consent decree, Gates told CNN's Larry King, as quoted by David Streit-

feld for the *Washington Post* (June 8, 2000), "That whole thing really has no effect on Microsoft or how we work. . . . It's great to see it finally come to a close. Because there were a lot of years there where, you know, we were producing a lot of documents and what it comes down to is that there is nothing significant that we needed to change, and that just confirms the way we've viewed it all along."

Despite its legal troubles, by 1995 Microsoft was enjoying clear domination of the computer-software market. That August, the company launched the much-anticipated Windows 95, the newest version of its popular Windows software, amid a $1-billion marketing blitz. The product was designed to offer significant improvements upon earlier Windows versions by simplifying commands and reducing reliance on the outdated MS-DOS system, which often rendered the software awkward and slow. In addition, Windows 95 had more business applications, particularly for computers linked through a network; system administrators could access all computers in the "neighborhood" simply by clicking on a single icon. Windows 95 quickly became one of the most successful software products of all time, selling more than one million copies in the first four days alone. According to Microsoft's Web site, the software ultimately helped bring the PC into more than 250 million businesses, homes, and schools around the world.

Also in 1995 Microsoft announced plans to shift into the Internet services market. Although the company had been focused primarily on software development, Gates realized the enormous market associated with the Internet, which was rapidly becoming a strategic communications tool for businesses and individuals. In November Microsoft launched its own Web browser, Internet Explorer 2.0 for Windows 95, which would compete directly with Netscape's Navigator—then the dominant software for navigating the World Wide Web. (In a meeting earlier that year, executives from Microsoft had approached Netscape Communications Corporation with an alleged offer to split the Internet browser market. Netscape claimed that Microsoft had urged them not to make browsers compatible with Windows software because Microsoft wanted to control that market; in exchange, Microsoft would make an investment in Netscape and would provide the company with important technical information. When Netscape refused the offer—which government officials later viewed as an attempt at collusion in violation of antitrust laws—Microsoft allegedly began engaging in aggressive tactics to monopolize the Internet-browser market. This infamous meeting later became a central point in the Justice Department's case against Microsoft. Microsoft has always maintained that the meeting had been a routine encounter between competitors and that nothing illegal had transpired.)

In late 1995 Microsoft released its own Internet Service Provider (ISP), the Microsoft Network (MSN), enrolling more than 525,000 members in the first three months. This service would compete with other ISPs, such as American Online (AOL) and Yahoo. That December the company announced a joint venture with NBC to fund a 24-hour cable news channel known as MSNBC. The channel, which was launched in mid-1996, has become a premiere source for round-the-clock cable news, rivaling CNN and Fox News. Microsoft made even greater progress in its bid for Internet market domination on March 12, 1996, when AOL announced that it would feature Internet Explorer as its primary software for Web browsing. The news surprised many in the industry, since AOL had only the day prior reported a licensing agreement with Netscape Communications to feature Navigator as its Web browser. (AOL insisted that Navigator would still be offered as an option), but would not be integrated directly into the software packages that AOL sends to its millions of customers.) In exchange, Microsoft would distribute AOL's network-access software with all future versions of Windows 95. The deal helped solidify Microsoft's footing in the Internet-browser market—and also helped to dispel claims of monopolization, since AOL's software would now be featured alongside Microsoft's own competing MSN on-line service. In September 1997 Microsoft expanded its role in the Internet services market, launching Internet Explorer 4.0 in an effort to create further challenges for Netscape, whose share of the browser market was dwindling. Microsoft continued bundling Internet Explorer as part of its Windows software, thus essentially distributing the browser for free—a move that cut Netscape's dominance even further.

In late 1997 Microsoft's legal troubles returned when the Justice Department filed a motion in the Federal District Court, alleging that the company had violated the 1994 consent decree, specifically by forcing computer manufacturers to feature its Web browser as part of the licensing agreements for Windows. (Microsoft maintained that the Web browser was an integral part of Windows and thus could not be distributed separately.) With Microsoft scheduled to release an upgrade of Windows the following year, the Justice Department asked the court to halt the company's practice of tying the use of Windows with the use of Internet Explorer. In December 1997 Judge Jackson issued a preliminary injunction forcing Microsoft to separate its Windows software from its software for navigating the Web. However, a federal appeals court struck down the preliminary injunction on June 23, 1998, allowing Microsoft to release Windows 98, its newest version of Windows, with Internet Explorer intact. Windows 98 became available in stores on June 25, 1998, in more than 40 countries around the globe. The software was promoted as the first version of Windows to be designed specifically for consumers' needs, with improved speed, greater applications, and increased support. Although some critics found the product less revolutionary than its predecessor, Windows 95, had been, Windows 98 quickly became the newest standard for operating systems. By the late 1990s Microsoft had a market share for operating systems of more than 90 percent; in other words, Windows software was being installed on nine out of every 10 computers manufactured around the world.

The U.S. government remained determined to challenge Microsoft's growing software monopoly. On May 19, 1998 the Justice Department filed two broad antitrust suits against Microsoft, alleging that it was engaged in anticompetitive business practices that were in violation of the Sherman Antitrust Act. The suits accused Microsoft of, among other things, attempting to monopolize the market for Internet browsers by unlawfully integrating Internet Explorer with Windows and using illegal tactics to push Netscape out of the market; of discouraging Microsoft engineers from using Sun Microsystems's version of Java programming technology, which Microsoft considered a threat to Windows; of forcing personal-computer makers to have the Microsoft screen appear first when a user turns on the machine; and of demanding that ISPs and Web site operators distribute Internet Explorer in order to receive promotional space in Windows. The trial, which officially began on October 19, 1998, made headlines as the first effort to apply century-old antitrust laws to the rapidly evolving technology industry. (The Sherman Antitrust Act had been drafted in 1890.) Legal experts felt the case could establish a set of legal precedents for the technology industry, in the same way that the government's historic breakups of the Standard Oil Company in 1911 and AT&T in 1984 had created precedents for the oil and telecommunications industries. With the world's richest man associated with the case, media outlets around the world were eager to cover the trial closely.

Although Gates did not plan to testify or even appear in the courtroom, he did submit to a three-day taped pretrial deposition, parts of which were shown throughout the trial. Ultimately, these taped interviews generated the most controversy—and negative publicity—for Microsoft. In the footage presented, Gates appeared petulant, combative, and at times forgetful about his own e-mails or meetings; he showed little cooperation with the government's lead trial lawyer, David Boies. As Boies recalled to Joel Brinkley and Steve Lohr for the New York Times (June 9, 2000), in preparing for the interrogation he had expected to find Gates "a very effective witness." "I was expecting him to be articulate, passionate, tough, direct, intelligent and very, very knowledgeable about relating to the case," he said. However, when the two men met, Gates resisted answering many of the questions directly, instead offering largely mumbled, ill-informed, and obstructionist responses. Boies decided to exploit Gates's deposition as a trial strategy, telling Brinkley and Lohr, "The chairman of the company doesn't have any credible explanation for what they did, even though he was intimately involved. If he doesn't have an explanation, then how can you credit the explanations of his underlings?" In fact, the media publicity surrounding what came to be know as the "Gates Tape" at times overshadowed other aspects of the case. Gates later told Steven Levy for *Newsweek* (August 30, 1999) that he found the public response surprising. "I gave totally truthful answers," he said. "I have a great memory. When [Boies] would ask imprecise questions I would simply point out to him the imprecise nature of the question." Nevertheless, Gates did admit he could have handled the deposition differently. "If I'd known that the video was going to be shown . . . I would have helped [Boies] do his job more. Because I do come off as a bit pedantic when he does a bad job asking questions. Still, there is no law in this land about being a little rude in a deposition."

Throughout the 76 days of testimony, executives from some of the largest technology corporations, including IBM, AOL, Intel, Sun Microsystems, and Apple, testified before the court, describing how Microsoft had threatened to raise prices or withhold vital technical support and information if they did not meet the company's demands. The government presented much of its case through hundreds of internal Microsoft e-mails, which the company had been required to turn over to investigators. While the government claimed that these communications revealed a pattern of illegal behavior, Microsoft argued that they showed only the hard-nosed business tactics of a fiercely competitive firm. At one point the Microsoft legal team told the judge, "The antitrust laws are not a code of civility in American business," as quoted by Rajiv Chandrasekaran for the *Washington Post* (November 6, 1999). The Justice Department also attempted to show that Microsoft's anticompetitive practices had in fact hurt consumers by "stifling innovation" among computer-software manufacturers. Microsoft countered these claims, insisting that hundreds of new products are created every day for the computer industry. In addition, the firm asserted that the evolution of its own products had helped millions of consumers around the globe attain affordable access to computers. If it had been acting as a monopoly, Microsoft claimed, it would have charged at least 16 times more for its Windows software than its current prices.

Throughout its defense Microsoft maintained that it had not thwarted competition, and instead had acted vigorously and fairly in dealings with competitors. The company's view was that its direct competitors included most major technology-related concerns, regardless of whether or not those concerns sold computer software. With the rise of the Internet, Microsoft felt that it had to consider competition from Internet terminal devices, Linux (another operating system), and handheld devices (including cellular telephones) that could run computer software. Microsoft officials argued that in the near future, computers would run on free, open-source software and that customers would have the ability to access applications such as word processing over the Internet, thus making the Windows operating system obsolete. In this ultra-competitive environment, they argued, they were forced to deal with their opponents fiercely. More importantly, Microsoft representatives maintained that the core issue of the case—the company's bundling of Internet Explorer with Windows—was not really a matter of monopoly domination but rather of the firm's right to design software as it saw fit. "At the heart of this case," Gates told Walter Isaacson for *Time* (November 22, 1999), "is a principle that's pretty important: our right to add features to Windows. We have been taking things that people demand, whether it be adding a graphical interface of support for networking, and building it into the operating system. Doing that has been why the PC revolution has done so much for consumers." Of the restrictions the government sought, he added, "If we can't add functionality to Windows, there is no Windows! Let's face it. Without innovation, given the intense competition out there, Windows would become irrelevant."

When the main phase of the Microsoft trial came to a close on February 25, 1999, Judge Jackson urged the two sides to sit down to negotiations. Although talks continued through the summer, Microsoft rejected all proposed settlements, which ranged from a company breakup to severe restrictions on its behavior. On November 5, 1999, Judge Jackson issued his "findings of fact"—a legal ruling that lays the foundation for a final judgement—concluding that Microsoft had abused its dominance in the computer industry to thwart competition. The findings fell short of a conclusive decision as to whether the company's business practices had violated the Sherman Antitrust Act. "Microsoft has demonstrated that it will use its prodigious market power and immense profits to harm any firm that insists on pursuing initiatives that could intensify competition against one of Microsoft's core products," Judge Jackson wrote in the 207-page ruling, as quoted by Chandrasekaran. "The ultimate result is that some innovations that would truly benefit consumers never occur for the sole reason that they do not coincide with Microsoft's self-interest." While the ruling was clearly a blow to Microsoft, the company's executives remained committed to continuing their legal fight. "We respectfully disagree with a number of the court's findings and believe the American legal system ultimately will affirm that Microsoft's actions and innovations were fair and legal, and have brought tremendous benefits to millions of consumers," Gates noted in an official statement.

Upon issuing these findings of fact, Judge Jackson again urged negotiations. As he explained to Brinkley and Lohr, he had separated the findings from the final ruling in order to "encourage a settlement." To this end, he appointed Richard A. Posner, the chief judge for the Seventh U.S. Court of Appeals, in Chicago, to serve as mediator for voluntary negotiations. Despite four months of ongoing mediation, the settlement talks again failed, prompting Judge Jackson to resume his role in the case. On April 3, 2000 he issued his final ruling, finding that Microsoft had acted in violation of the Sherman Antitrust Act. He concluded that the company had "maintained its monopoly power by anticompetitive means," as quoted by the *Associated Press* (November 1, 2002), and had tried to monopolize the Internet browser market. In addition, Microsoft had broken other laws by "unlawfully tying its Web browser to its operating system" and could thus be sued under state anti-competition laws.

In late April the Justice Department and 17 states petitioned Judge Jackson to split Microsoft into two separate companies—one that would sell Windows and one that would distribute Microsoft's Office software applications, including its word-processing and spreadsheet programs. The Justice Department insisted that such a remedy was necessary to restore competition to the software industry and to encourage innovation. The government included a brief e-mail message from Gates, dated July 11, 1999, to support its claims that the antitrust case had not deterred Microsoft from continuing its monopolistic behavior: The memorandum accused Microsoft of plotting to harm companies that make handheld devices by designing its Office software to work less efficiently on these machines. "Neither mere conduct remedies like the earlier consent decree, nor this court's findings of fact and conclusions of law, will prevent unlawful conduct by Microsoft in the future or restore competition injured by it in the past," the government stated, as quoted by James V. Grimaldi for the *Washington Post* (April 29, 2000). Judge Jackson ordered the breakup of Microsoft into two separate companies on June 7, 2000, citing that the software firm had "proved untrustworthy in the past," as quoted by the *Associated Press*. Soon after, the U.S. Supreme Court rejected Microsoft's request to hear the case in appeals, sending it to a federal appeals court in Washington, D.C. More than a year later, the appeals court threw out Jackson's breakup order but nonetheless upheld his findings of Microsoft's antitrust violations.

The complex case was ultimately settled in November 2001—more than three and a half years after it began—when the Justice Department and Microsoft announced a settlement. This agreement gave computer makers increased flexibility in customizing icons and menu entries from Microsoft's Windows operating systems; prevented Microsoft from engaging in restrictive and discriminatory pricing agreements, or from retaliating against competitors; and required the company to provide some disclosures about its software code to promote competition. In addition, Microsoft agreed to the creation of a three-person technical committee to monitor the company's compliance with these terms. However, the settlement fell short of requiring that Microsoft acknowledge the antitrust violations that both Judge Jackson and the appeals court had found. It also did not restrict Microsoft's ability to enhance its primary product, the Windows operating system, with additional software that could extend its dominance into new software or products.

The settlement generated significant criticism from many in the industry, who felt that its terms failed to offer enough protection for both competitors and consumers, and could easily be evaded by a determined monopolistic giant. Nevertheless, U.S. Attorney General John Ashcroft asserted, as quoted by Stephen Labaton and Steve Lohr for the *New York Times* (November 3, 2001), "This settlement is the right result for consumers and for businesses, the right result for the economy and the right result for the government." Nine states did not accept the agreement and pushed ahead in a U.S. District Court for harsher remedies.

However, on November 1, 2002, U.S. District Judge Colleen Kollar-Kotelly approved most provisions of the original settlement and added some of her own. For example, Microsoft would be barred from not just retaliating against competitors but also threatening to retaliate, and computer makers would be given the freedom to choose which applications would launch when consumers start up Windows-based machines. The biggest change came in the enforcement of the settlement. Compliance would now be directed by independent Microsoft board members, who would be held accountable for any failures. Judge Kollar-Kotelly also retained jurisdiction of the case, so that she could act swiftly if she found Microsoft violating her decree. "It represents a fair resolution of this case," Gates said of the final ruling, to Joseph Menn and Jube Shiver Jr. for the *Los Angeles Times* (November 2, 2002). "I am personally committed to full compliance."

Throughout the duration of the antitrust trial, the market valuation of Microsoft's stock experienced increased fluctuations, particularly when Judge Jackson ordered a breakup of the company. However, the trial seemed to have little effect on Microsoft's day-to-day operations—or its sales and profits—with Gates consistently predicting that the courts would find his company's actions lawful. Generally, public confidence in Microsoft remained strong. In the case of the Windows 98 release, it appeared that the added publicity even resulted in increased sales. As Lawrence N. Mondry, an executive vice president for the computer chain CompUSA, told Steve Lohr for the *New York Times* (May 21, 1998), "The Government has created more demand for Windows 98 than could have ever been generated by a marketing program." On July 17, 1999 Microsoft made headlines as the first company in history to reach a market valuation of more than a half-trillion dollars, with the company's stock value totaling $507 billion. (Microsoft's stock lost 45 percent of its value over the next year, before climbing again in 2001. The company's current market valuation is over $280 billion.)

Despite his company's continued financial success, Gates suffered a personal toll as a result of the antitrust trial. As his father, William Gates Jr., explained to Levy, "It was in the press every single day. His own government, suing him, that's not [a] chocolate sundae! He was concerned, he was angry, he was distracted from things he'd rather be doing." On January 13, 2000 Gates announced that he would be stepping down as chief executive officer (CEO) of Microsoft and would assume the title of chief software architect. While he would retain his position as chairman, Steven Ballmer, the company president, would take over as CEO. Ballmer, a former college friend of Gates who joined Microsoft in 1980, had held nearly every top management position at the company and enjoyed a close working relationship with Gates. While it took both men several months to adjust to their new roles, they have continued to share a powerful partnership. Gates's move to oversee software development—and in turn to spend more time with the engineers creating Microsoft's products—has allowed him to capitalize on some of his greatest strengths, most notably his ability to foresee how emerging software technologies may shape the computer industry. His duties, which often include intense technical meetings with product-development groups, allow him to guide the company's overall technology vision. Craig Mundie, a chief technical officer at Microsoft, described Gates's role to Brent Schlender for *Fortune* (July 8, 2002): "Bill has three modes in meetings, which you might describe as listening, challenging, and coaching. He's gotten better at coaching in the past couple of years."

In recent years, Microsoft has significantly expanded its software mission. While the company is still committed to its Windows operating system, the product's development has paved the way for even greater software functions. While Windows Millennium Edition, released in 2000, offered users improved music, video, and home-networking services, it was still based on the Windows 95 design. However, in the most recent edition, Windows XP, released in 2001, Microsoft engineers removed all software coding associated with the archaic MS-DOS system, which had been the core of the company's operating systems for the previous 20 years. This project had been a matter of pride for Microsoft's software technicians for many years, since the MS-DOS–based systems were often criticized as inefficient, prone to crashes, and difficult to use. In fact, Microsoft had released a non-DOS operating system for businesses, known as Windows NT, in 1993. The consumer-friendly XP version was an extension of this NT system and provided enhanced performance, stability, security, and tech support for both business and home users.

The company's next innovation is the software-development project known within Microsoft as "Longhorn." More than simply another upgrade to Windows, Longhorn is being designed as a radical-ly new operating system. Microsoft engineers have started with a clean slate and are reevaluating the tools that compose an operating system, as well as the way in which users store data, share information, and interact with their machines. Because the company is overhauling its core operating system, it is also redesigning other software products and services to optimize efficiency, including MSN online, its server applications, and the Microsoft Office suite, which brings in nearly a third of the company's sales. Longhorn promises to make computers more customized than ever before. (For Microsoft it also poses a significant business risk, since many of the company's earlier products may be rendered obsolete.) Longhorn is slated for release in 2005.

In July 2000 Microsoft set forth an ambitious vision for a new software platform, known as Microsoft .Net. The brand includes a number of software technologies that can better connect people, information, systems, and devices over the Internet, through the use of integrated XML Web services. XML, short for Extensible Markup Language, is a standardized method for storing raw data so that it can be readily identifiable on another machine, or even through another software program. Using XML, software companies, corporate programmers, and Web designers could coordinate a vast array of revolutionary Web services. (For example, customers could use their PCs, digital cell phones, or even digital televisions, to consolidate one statement from all of their financial institutions, including unrelated banks, credit-card companies, and brokerages.) To ensure industry-wide compliance for storing and shipping data on the Web, Microsoft has joined the World Wide Web Consortium, a group that is developing XML standards. The move to work closely with its competitors—the consortium has the support of IBM, Sun, Oracle, Hewlett-Packard, Apple, and 400 other companies—is a significant shift for Microsoft. Another element of Microsoft's .Net strategy involves repackaging some of its core products, such as the Microsoft Office suite, to be sold as subscription-based services accessible over the Internet. The company has also begun releasing hardware that may eventually contribute to the overall .Net strategy, including cellular phones, handheld devices, set-top boxes (for interactive TV), the Tablet-PC, a notepad computer with digital-pen capabilities, and the Xbox, a device for computer gaming.

Gates is the author of two best-selling books, *The Road Ahead* (1995), in which he explores how new technologies will guide the future, and *Business @ the Speed of Thought* (1999), in which he shows how computer technology can help businesses better succeed in the digital economy. Gates has donated all proceeds from both books to nonprofit organizations assisting the use of technology in education. In 1992 Gates was awarded the National Medal of Technology by President George Bush. In December 1999 he was named Entrepreneur of the Millennium by *Entrepreneur* magazine.

In addition to software, Gates is interested in biotechnology and sits on the board of ICOS, a company specializing in protein-based and small-molecule therapeutics; he also invests in several other biotechnology companies.

In 1997 Bill and Melinda Gates, whom he married on January 1, 1994, moved into a $50-million, 45,000-square-foot compound built into the side of a hill on the shore of Lake Washington in suburban Seattle. The house includes a swimming pool, a trampoline, a 14,000-book library, a game room, a movie theater, underground parking, and a pavilion that seats 100 for dinner. In addition to spending time with his three young children, Gates often relaxes by playing tennis, golf, and bridge. Of his incredible success, he told Schlender, "You know, the notion that a kid who thought software was cool can end up creating a company with all these smart people whose software gets out to hundreds of millions of people, well, that's an amazing thing. I've had one of the luckiest situations ever. But I've also learned that only through focus can you do world-class things, no matter how capable you are."

Outside of his association with Microsoft, Gates may be best known for his extensive philanthropy. With his wife, he has endowed more than $24 billion to the Bill and Melinda Gates Foundation. Run mainly by Melinda, his father (who acts as CEO), and Patty Stonesifer (a former Microsoft executive who serves as president), the foundation donates roughly $1 billion each year to worthy causes. Since its creation in 1997, it has committed more than $2.5 billion to organizations working in global health, most notably distributing medicines and vaccines in developing countries and supporting research in HIV and AIDS. In addition, through the Gates Library Initiative, the foundation has provided more than $1.4 billion to bring computers, Internet access, and training to public libraries in low-income communities throughout the United States and Canada; Gates hopes to continue this initiative worldwide. The foundation has also given millions to community projects in the Pacific Northwest and to other special philanthropic interests. At the age of 48, Gates has given away more money than any philanthropist in history. He has vowed to give away the majority of his wealth—currently estimated at more than $40 billion—during his lifetime.—K. D.

Suggested Reading: *Entrepreneur* p14 Dec. 1999; *Forbes* p108+ Apr. 1 1991; *Fortune* p84+ Jan. 5 1987, p82+ June 18, 1990, p74+ July 11, 2001, with photos, p56+ July 8, 2002; *Los Angeles Times* 1 p1 Nov. 2, 2002, with photo; *Money* p66+ May 1, 2002; *New York Times* A p1 June 9, 2000, with photo, A p1 Nov. 3, 2001; *Newsweek* p40+ Aug. 30, 1999; *People* p37 Dec. 26, 1983; *Time* p62+ Apr. 16, 1984, p65+ Nov. 22, 1999; *Washington Post* A p1 Dec. 3, 1995, with photo, A p1 Oct. 19, 1998, with photo, E p1 July 17, 1999, A p1 Nov. 6, 1999, A p1 Apr. 29, 2000, A p1 June 8, 2000; Slater, Robert. *Portraits in Silicon* (1987)

Rich Frishman/Getty Images

Gibson, William

Mar. 17, 1948– Science-fiction writer

In 1984, when the science-fiction writer William Gibson published his first novel, *Neuromancer*, he launched a new genre called "cyberpunk" and introduced the world to the concept of "cyberspace." Cyberspace is intentionally a nebulous term, which accounts perhaps for its allure and its widespread usage. As Douglas Fetherling explained in *Saturday Night* (December 1994 / January 1995), "Cyberspace is taken to mean the data- and image-laden atmosphere that swirls around us all invisibly—like some huge ocean current in space or a great silent wind, stronger than any found in nature. Conversely, those who write about cyberspace with the ironic diction and heightened moral sensibility of a hard-boiled detective thriller are perforce the cyberpunks." Gibson himself, in *Neuromancer*, famously referred to cyberspace as a "consensual hallucination," and many commentators have understood cyberspace as an early vision of the Internet. In Gibson's fiction, governments have largely been replaced by vastly powerful corporations. Several years before the well-known software giant went public with its stock, Gibson's characters were inserting "microsofts" into their skulls in order to enter into "the matrix"—a term that Gibson used more than a decade before the popular movie of that name—to describe a sort of global computer network. So compelling and popular was Gibson's fictive universe that computer scientists and engineers scrambled to develop technologies that might resemble to a degree those which Gibson described in *Neuromancer* and subsequent novels, such as *Count Zero* (1986) and *Mona Lisa Overdrive* (1988). Gibson, however, has repeatedly maintained that, rather than offer predictions for the future, his books are meant to shed light on contemporary technology and the way it affects us. "I owe my reputation as an oracle to the Sunday supplement writers of the world," he told Brian D. Johnson for *Maclean's* (June 5, 1995). "I spend almost every interview saying [in a singsong cant], 'Science fiction is not really about the future. I'm not predicting anything. I just want you to watch CNN through a different lens.'"

William Ford Gibson was born on March 17, 1948 in Conway, South Carolina, to William Ford, a contractor, and Elizabeth "Otey" Gibson, a homemaker and volunteer librarian. He was raised in Wyethville, Virginia, a small town in the southwest of the state, near the Appalachian Mountains. Gibson described it as "A very backwater place, a detained backwater, by and large," to a writer for *Interview* (January 1989). "There was no library, and science fiction books were the only source I had for subversive information. It was a good escape, but I took some of it as a blueprint. It was as though I were hearing these lonely monsters from distant places."

When Gibson was six his father choked to death on a piece of steak. At the age of 16, upon his own request, Gibson was sent away to a boarding school in Arizona. His mother died two years later. In 1967 he was temporarily rejected for psychological reasons by the draft board for service in the Vietnam War. "I was such an odd duck," he told Johnson. "I'd been in Arizona and California, and I had inhaled, and it showed." Wanting to avoid further confrontations with the draft board, Gibson dropped out of high school and moved to Toronto, then the scene of an active counterculture. There, in 1972, he married Deborah Thompson. The couple settled in Vancouver, and in 1977 Gibson earned a bachelor's degree in English from the University of British Columbia.

While at the university Gibson took a course in science fiction. In lieu of a term paper, he submitted a short story and soon decided to pursue writing as a career. It was a precarious living at first, but one that enabled him to stay at home and care for his son, Graeme, and daughter, Claire, while his wife worked as a language teacher. His early stories included "Fragments of a Hologram Rose," "Johnny Mnemonic," and "Burning Chrome." By the early 1980s his dark vision of the future, a world of high-tech villainy, was drawing attention, and several of his short stories were published in *Omni* magazine.

Gibson came up with the idea of cyberspace while watching some teenagers playing a primitive video game in a Vancouver arcade. "Their posture seemed to indicate that they really, sincerely believed there was something behind the screen," he explained to Johnson. "I took that home and tried to come up with a name for it. I literally did sit down at a typewriter one night and go, 'Dataspace? Noooo. Infospace? Boring. Cyberspace? Hmmm. It's got sibilance. It sounds interesting.' What did

it mean? I had no clue. It was like an empty chocolate cup awaiting the whipped cream." (The word *cybernetics,* meaning the study of control systems in machines or biological entities, appeared as early as 1948.)

In 1984 Gibson published his first novel, *Neuromancer.* The antihero, Case, is described as tomorrow's computer hacker, a console cowboy, a data thief, and a cyberspace jockey. He is punished for his roguery with a nerve poison that prevents him from plugging into cyberspace. An enigmatic patron offers to help him to reenter cyberspace, in exchange for his services as an outlaw hacker and evader of electronic security systems. Accompanied by a biologically engineered female assassin, he ends up on a space station with two supercomputers, where he finds out that one computer, Wintermute, has hired him to help it dominate the other, Neuromancer.

Gibson mistakenly believed his work was too disturbing to appeal to a large audience. Both reviewers and audience proved him wrong. *Neuromancer* garnered some of science fiction's most prestigious honors, including a Hugo Award, a Philip K. Dick Award, and a Nebula Award—the first book to win all three. It was such a hit that Gerald Jonas started his review for the *New York Times Book Review* (November 24, 1985, on-line) by apologizing for not reviewing it earlier. He wrote, "What put me off, I think, was the title, which struck me as an ungainly play on words, hinting at some trendy hybrid of sword-and-sorcery fantasy and high-tech adventure, with perhaps a bit of heavy- breathing sex thrown in." He continued, "Now that I have read the book, I would like to cast a belated ballot for Mr. Gibson. The 21st-century world of *Neuromancer* is freshly imagined, compellingly detailed and chilling in its implications." In the *Washington Post Book World* (July 29, 1984), Charles Platt wrote, "The book's faults are glibness and a gimmicky use of farfetched gadgets. Gibson is no engineer, and doesn't even try to explain his pseudoscience. In visualizing the human impact of high technology, however, he is brilliantly perceptive. The resulting society is dehumanized and even repellent, but always derived from trends that are becoming apparent today."

Soon, articles about Gibson began to appear in such publications as *Time, Mondo 2000, People, Rolling Stone,* the *New York Times,* the *Wall Street Journal,* the *Village Voice,* and *USA Today.* Computer hackers everywhere looked to him as a guru. Artists such as the filmmaker Robert Longo and the musicians Donald Fagen and Billy Idol publicly expressed their admiration for him. To many, Gibson's book became not only a comment on technology, but a guide to future technologies—and this from a man who continued to write on an old typewriter and who hadn't logged on to the Internet or used e-mail until 1995. As he told Peter H. Lewis for the *New York Times* (May 22, 1995), he prefers to limit his impressions of technology and then expose himself "in large, homeopathic doses," because this allows him to better convey the shock and wonder of technology in his fiction. In 1991 MIT Press published a collection of essays entitled *Cyberspace: Essays from MIT Press*, in which leading computer scientists wrote about various software designs that might be used to create Gibson's "consensual virtual hallucination." "Gibson's world inspired the scientists at work on virtual reality. . . . But his ideas also influenced thinkers outside the cyberpunk loop," Steven Poole wrote in the London *Guardian* (October 3, 1996). Darren Wershler-Henry, a Gibson scholar, told Fetherling, "All these technological wizards and boffins and eggheads at various firms in Silicon Valley looked at this and said, 'Gee, that is a really good idea. Why don't we just build this?'"

Gibson's antiestablishment jockeys continued to hack their way through computer space in *Neuromancer*'s successful sequels, *Count Zero* and *Mona Lisa Overdrive*. In 1990 Gibson teamed with the science-fiction writer Bruce Sterling to publish a novel titled *The Difference Engine*. The book is based on the 19th-century inventor Charles Babbage, who is sometimes called the "father of modern computing." Among the colorful characters are "neo-Luddite anarchist criminals," according to David Porush in *American Book Review* (December 1991/January 1992). Their program "almost succeeds in seizing London during an apocalyptic collapse of the local environment, a foul atmospheric inversion at the height of summer that is made lethal by technology Gibson and Sterling have unleashed." Porush called the novel a "brilliant collaboration between . . . two luxurious and robust imaginations." Gibson's fiction continued to attract an enthusiastic, almost cultlike following. At a reading of his novel *Virtual Light*, in 1993, the audience included computer hackers who called themselves Voxers. The *New Yorker* (August 16, 1993) reported that one Voxer called Gibson the "Aesop of the computer age." Christopher Lehmann-Haupt, in the *New York Times* (August 29, 1993), called *Virtual Light* an absorbing thriller "driven by fascinating computer gimmicks . . . [including] a pair of glasses that enables the wearer to see the future cityscape of San Francisco as planned by a secret organization that is buying up real estate." Lehmann-Haupt faulted *Virtual Light*, however, for giving cyberspace short shrift: "Instead of a vision of what lies beyond modernity . . . we end up with . . . a futuristic version of *It Happened One Night*."

In 1995 Gibson's short story "Johnny Mnemonic" was made into a movie of the same title, starring Keanu Reeves. It did not fare well at the box office or in the critics' reviews. In 1996 he published *Idoru*. Set in the near future, the novel opens as Rez, of the Lo/Rez rock supergroup, announces that he intends to marry Rei Toe, an idoru, or Japanese virtual star that exists only as a series of separate media representations. Steven Poole, commenting on the novel, wrote, "Gibson's latest future no longer has the shocking power of a decade ago, but it is more cleverly politicized, and as fast, witty and lovingly painted as ever." Gibson's latest novel, *All Tomorrow's Parties*, was published in 1999 and shares characters with *Virtual Light* and *Idoru*.

Gibson lives in Vancouver with his wife. Though he has often discounted his own reputation as a futurist, he nonetheless occasionally offers predictions. For example, in an article called "Will We Plug Chips Into Our Brains?" in *Time* (June 19, 2000), he wrote, "Our hardware, I think is likely to turn into something like us a lot faster than we are likely to turn into something like our hardware. Our hardware is evolving at the speed of light, while we are still the product, for the most part, of unskilled labor."—P. G. H.

Suggested Reading: *American Book Review* Dec. 1991/Jan.1992; *Fantasy Review* July 1984; *Film Comment* Jan./Feb. 1990; London *Guardian* p12 Oct. 3, 1996; *Interview* p84 Jan. 1989; *Maclean's* p60+ June 5, 1995; *New York Times* Aug. 29, 1993; *New York Times Book Review* (on-line) Nov. 24, 1985, Aug. 29, 1993; *New Yorker* Aug. 16, 1993; *Saturday Night* p82+ Dec. 1994 / Jan. 1995; *Time* p84+ June 19, 2000; *Washington Post Book World* July 29, 1984; Barron, N. ed. *Anatomy of Wonder: A Critical Guide to Science Fiction*, 1987; *Contemporary Literary Criticism* 39, 1986; Gunn, J. ed. *The New Encyclopedia of Science Fiction*, 1988; *Twentieth-Century Science- Fiction Writers*, 1991

Gill, Stanley

1926–Apr. 5, 1975 Co-builder of the EDSAC

Stanley Gill was a mathematician who was involved in several important developments in the history of computing that took place in Great Britain in connection with the emergence of the electronic digital computer in the 1940s and 1950s. Most notably, he worked with Maurice Wilkes on the construction of the EDSAC, the first computer with the built-in capacity to store programs. Gill also helped to introduce the concept of subroutines, a key element in computer programming right up to the present day. Gill coauthored the landmark programming textbook *The Preparation of Programs for an Electronic Digital Computer* with Wilkes and David Wheeler in 1951, and also participated in the development of the Pilot ACE computer program with Alan Turing.

Stanley Gill was born in 1926. He attended St. John's College at Cambridge University, in England, in the mid-1940s. After graduating, he joined the British National Physics Laboratory's Mathematical Division in 1946. While at the National Physics Laboratory, he worked on the Pilot ACE computer, an early British attempt at building a machine that could store programs. The designer of the ACE and head of the project was the influential scientist Alan Turing.

Gill returned to Cambridge University in 1949 as a graduate student. In October of that year, he began working toward his Ph.D. as a research assistant under Maurice V. Wilkes at the university's mathematical laboratory. Wilkes later described Gill as having "a natural seriousness of manner" that helped him make an effective contribution to the work of the mathematics lab group (*Memoirs of a Computer Pioneer*, 1985).

The product of Wilkes's and Gill's collaboration was the Electronic Delay Storage Automatic Calculator (EDSAC), an electronic digital computer completed in 1949. Its design was inspired by the famous ENIAC, constructed three years earlier by the American engineers John Mauchly and J. Presper Eckert. However, the EDSAC was built with the unique capability to store programs, a capability eventually incorporated into the ENIAC as well. Instead of having to be rewired every time a new activity was to be performed, the EDSAC was able to draw on a memory that contained sets of instructions entered previously; the machine had the ability to translate its instructions from symbolic form into the computerized form it could understand. This ability would in the decades to come be considered one of the defining characteristics of computers.

In developing their stored-program device, Gill, Wilkes, and Wheeler, who was also a member of the group, worked out the concept of subroutines. Basically, a subroutine is a sequence of computer instructions that can be executed repeatedly, allowing the computer to automatically perform the same action for as many times as is necessary to execute a given task. A major use of the subroutine was the detection of errors within programs, thus rescuing programmers from the tedious and time-consuming efforts involved in hunting the errors down themselves. As Wilkes put it, he was afraid that "a good part of the remainder of my life was going to be spent in finding errors in . . . programs" (*Events in the History of Computing*). Eventually, Gill and his colleagues were able to compile subroutine libraries, which also became standard among computer programmers and which facilitated the reuse of previously written subroutines in many different programs.

One of the most important specific subroutines mapped out by Gill in the early 1950s involved a method of solving differential equations. Gill's small subroutine (containing only 66 orders, or lines of programming instructions) was a modification of what was known as the Runge-Kutta program, which was used to solve these difficult mathematical problems. Gill's innovative program design was a major step toward the fully automatic methods for solving these equations that would eventually be developed. Additionally, he created a type of subroutine called a "trace," that greatly improved on methods of detecting program errors. This subroutine printed the sequence of commands executed by the program, and thus was useful for picking up hidden flaws.

After the EDSAC project was successfully completed, Wilkes became interested in publishing the group's research. He was directed by a colleague to Addison-Wesley Press, a small publishing company based in Cambridge, Massachusetts. Wilkes, Gill, and the rest of the team prepared a preliminary draft, and Addison-Wesley agreed to publish it after making revisions. Concerned about the financial risk of printing a book on what was then an obscure topic, the company offered the Wilkes team the following terms: no royalties would be paid until 1,000 copies were sold, after which royalties would be 20 percent, lowered to 10 percent after the second 1,000 were sold. Gill, Wheeler, and Wilkes co-wrote the book, entitled *The Preparation of Programs for an Electronic Digital Computer*, and it was published in July 1951. To the relief of Addison-Wesley, sales reached the 1,000-mark in less than 15 months. Based primarily on the team's experience with the EDSAC, the book became the first widely read publication on the subject of computer programming.

At the end of 1951, Gill appeared in a short film produced by Wilkes as an accompaniment to a series of lectures he was giving on the EDSAC project. In the film, Gill, appropriately, played the role of a computer programmer. He demonstrated how programming code was entered into the EDSAC as well as the various steps involved in running the program and printing the results.

Gill wrote his doctoral thesis on the EDSAC project, and received his Ph.D. from Cambridge in 1952. Immediately after completing his degree, Gill participated in a group at the Massachusetts Institute of Technology (MIT) in Cambridge, Massachusetts, assembled for the purpose of designing a comprehensive programming system. David Wheeler and Maurice Wilkes also contributed to this group, which formulated the programming system known as the CS. Following his work at MIT, for the next three years Gill served as a Research Fellow at St. John's College at Cambridge. Between 1953 and 1954, Gill again spent time in the United States, working as an assistant professor of computer science at the University of Illinois. He was recommended for the post by his former research supervisor Maurice Wilkes, who was in contact with the head of the university's laboratory, J. P. Nash. In fact, Gill had been preceded at Illinois by his EDSAC collaborator David Wheeler.

In 1956 Gill became head of computing research at the computer department of Ferranti, a British company that built and sold commercial versions of the EDSAC. Gill held this position for nine years. In addition to his responsibilities at Ferranti, he also taught computer science at the University of London and the University of Manchester throughout the 1960s. Gill once again benefitted from his professional association with Maurice Wilkes in 1962, when he was appointed by the British Computer Society as the United Kingdom representative on the International Federation for Information Processing (IFIP) after Wilkes resigned from the position. Gill had accompanied Wilkes to several meetings of the IFIP Council, and was familiar with the organization. Gill also served as an adviser to Britain's Ministry of Technology from 1966 to 1970 and was president of the British Computer Society from 1967 to 1968.

Stanley Gill died on April 5, 1975 at the age of 49. His accomplishments in life helped to shape the development of computing in the United Kingdom. From his early work in the blossoming field of digital computing, to his later endeavors in the manufacturing of commercial machines, Gill's contributions to the history of the computer are great in number as well as importance.—B. S.

Suggested Reading: *Events in the History of Computing* (on-line) Nov. 26, 1997; Cortada, James. *Historical Dictionary of Data Processing: Biographies*, 1987; Nash, Steven, ed. *A History of Scientific Computing*, 1990; Wilkes, Maurice V. *Memoirs of a Computer Pioneer*, 1985

Goldstine, Herman Heine

Sep. 13, 1913– Administrator of the ENIAC and the IAS computer

The electronic-computer expert Herman H. Goldstine was a member of the U.S. Army's Ballistic Research Laboratory from 1941 to 1946 and an active member of the Institute for Advanced Study (IAS) in Princeton, New Jersey, from 1946 to 1957. During those years he was involved in the construction of two of the most important machines in computer history, the ENIAC and the IAS computer. In an administrative capacity, he participated in both early electronic computer projects. The mathematician, who had previously taught at the University of Chicago and the University of Michigan, served as a ballistics officer during World War II and afterward became a consultant for ordnance research at the Aberdeen Proving Ground and Los Alamos National Laboratory. As an observer for the United States at the United Nations Educational, Scientific and Cultural Organization (UNESCO) meetings in Paris in 1951, he took part in formulating plans for the establishment of an International Computation Center. After leaving Princeton, Goldstine worked for International Business Machines (IBM) until his retirement.

Born in Chicago on September 13, 1913, Herman Heine Goldstine was the only child of Isaac Oscar Goldstine, a lawyer, and Bessie (Lipsey) Goldstine. After he completed his secondary school education, at Chicago's Nicholas Senn High School, in 1929, he matriculated at the University of Chicago, where mathematics was his major subject. He remained at the University of Chicago for graduate courses after he received a B.S. degree in 1933; he earned a master of science degree in 1934 and a

Ph.D. degree in mathematics in 1936, submitting for the latter a dissertation entitled "Conditions for a Minimum of a Functional." As an undergraduate, in 1933 and 1934, respectively, he gained election to Phi Beta Kappa, the national scholastic honorary society, and to Sigma Xi, the national scientific honorary society.

For three years (1936–39) after he finished his postgraduate studies, Goldstine was employed as an instructor and research assistant at the University of Chicago. He then accepted an appointment as an instructor at the University of Michigan, where he soon advanced to assistant professor. At both universities he taught mathematics to undergraduate and graduate students. In 1942, sometime after the outbreak of World War II, Goldstine left his teaching job to become a ballistics officer in the Ordnance Department of the U. S. Army. In recognition of his services during the years 1942 to 1946, in the course of which he attained the rank of major, he was awarded the American Service Medal, the World War II Victory Medal, the Meritorious Service Unit Plaque, and the Army Commendation Medal.

In 1942 the U.S. Army appointed Goldstine military liaison to the Electronic Numerical Integrator and Computer (ENIAC) project. The brainchild of electrical engineers John Mauchly and J. Presper Eckert of the University of Pennsylvania, the ENIAC was the world's first full-scale general-purpose electronic digital computer. Mauchly's original idea for an electronic computer came to Goldstine's attention in 1942. Goldstine then met with John G. Brainerd, dean of the university's Moore School of Electrical Engineering, and the two men agreed that the concept was worth pursuing. With Brainerd's approval, Goldstine presented the idea to the U.S. Army's Ballistic Research Laboratory. After army higher-ups expressed interest in the possibility of backing the project, Goldstine was selected to represent army interests and ensure that negotiations with the university went smoothly. Along with Brainerd, Goldstine encouraged Mauchly and Eckert to write a formal proposal summing up their idea. Goldstine and Brainerd presented the proposal to the army in 1943, and it was instantly accepted. Construction of the computer was completed in 1945. The army used the device for several purposes, including the advancement of atomic-weapons technology.

In 1946 a bitter dispute over patent rights to the ENIAC erupted, with Eckert and Mauchly on one side and Goldstine and Brainerd on the other. While Eckert and Mauchly wanted to file for exclusive patent rights, Goldstine and Brainerd believed the rights should be held by the university. Eckert and Mauchly left the Moore School to start their own company, and afterward the school's prominence in the computer field steadily declined. Meanwhile, the feud continued; adding to the conflict was Goldstine's strong support of the claim that the mathematician John von Neumann (who had converted the ENIAC to a stored-program format) had invented the electronic stored-program computer concept. As a result of these disputes, both Mauchly and Eckert became permanently estranged from their former supervisor; until their deaths, in 1980 and 1995, respectively, they refused to speak with him or appear on any panel or at any function with him. Goldstine always claimed to have been open to a reconciliation; Joel Shurkin, who interviewed him for his book *Engines of the Mind* (1984), wrote that Goldstine seemed "puzzled and hurt" that the animosities had continued for so long.

In 1946 Goldstine left the Moore School to become a permanent member of the Institute for Advanced Study, in New Jersey, and assistant project director of the institute's electronic computer project. Conceived by Abraham Flexner, who envisioned a haven "where scholars and scientists may regard the world and its phenomena as their laboratory," the institute was established with the help of an initial gift of $5 million from Louis Bamberger and his sister, Felix Fuld. It opened in 1931 on the campus of Princeton University and in 1939 moved to quarters of its own at nearby Olden Farm. "Here, under one roof," Gertrude Samuels wrote for the *New York Times* (November 19, 1950), "is one of the most dramatic assemblages of intellectual power to be found anywhere in the world today."

The IAS computer project was headed by John von Neumann, who sought to realize many of the concepts regarding computers that he had formulated while working with the ENIAC. The computer was the fastest constructed up to that time, and it contained a memory capable of storing programs and certain self-regulating components that made it more automatic than any of its predecessors.

Aside from his administrative duties, Goldstine's function as assistant director of the IAS computer project was, in his words, "to conduct mathematical investigations into the numerical methods needed to operate high-speed, automatic computing devices; with particular reference to developing methods for handling the partial differential and integral equations of mathematical physics on electronic computing machines." The giant IAS computer—"a ceiling-high structure of wires and electronic tubes" that was designed by John von Neumann and built at the institute—made its public debut in June 1952. A revolutionary method of weather forecasting, in which the "mechanical brain" performed high-speed calculations based on as many as 50 variables governing the weather, was one of the first applications developed for the machine. Goldstine supervised tests of the forecasting method that were conducted during the summer of 1954.

In June 1952 the *New York Times* reported the beginning of a project in which the computer was to be used to make "a series of calculations designed to throw light on the impact of the nation's defense program on the economy." Other uses for the machine were the determination of strategy in games, the execution of calculations for use in ballistics, and the solution of specific problems in engineering.

In December 1951 UNESCO announced the launching of a program to establish an International Computation Center, where, at an operating cost of $100,000 per year, "some of man's electronic calculating brains" would be used for international purposes. Goldstine, who that year served as a United States observer at the UNESCO meeting in Paris and contributed to the drawing up of plans for the computation center, said, as reported by the *New York Herald-Tribune* (December 13, 1951), that "the core of the center is expected to be an electronic machine which might do 1,000 to 2,000 multiplications [per second]," far more than the ENIAC's 300 per second.

Goldstine became acting director of the IAS computer project in 1954. Three years later he left Princeton to join the computer manufacturing company IBM as director of its Mathematics Sciences Department. Throughout the 1960s he consulted on various IBM computer projects. He was the director of scientific development for the data processing division from 1965 to 1967 and a consultant to the director from 1967 to 1969. He retired from his full-time position in 1969 and was named an IBM Fellow.

Goldstine has written and edited several books on the subjects of mathematics and computing. Notable among them is *The Computer from Pascal to von Neumann* (1972), which is considered a definitive account of early computer history. In the book Goldstine emphasized John von Neumann's role in the development of the modern computer and discussed his own role in the 1940s and 1950s. His other books include *New and Full Moons 1001 B.C. to A.D. 1651* (1973), *A History of Numerical Analysis from the 16th Through the 19th Century* (1977), and *A History of the Calculus of Variations from the 17th Through the 19th Century* (1980). Goldstine edited *Mathematical Papers of John and James Bernoulli* (1988) and its German version, *Die Streitschriften von Jacob und Johann Bernoulli* (1991).

In addition, Goldstine has written a number of papers in his special fields of abstract spaces, calculus of variations, and numerical analysis. "A Multiplier Rule in Abstract Spaces" (1938), "Minimum Problems in the Functional Calculus" (1940), and "The Modular Space Determined by a Positive Function" (1942, with R. W. Barnard) are among the studies that he contributed to the *Bulletin of the American Mathematical Society*. For the *Duke Mathematical Journal*, he wrote "The Minima of Functionals with Associated Side Conditions" (1937), "Weakly Complete Banach Spaces" (1938), and "The Calculus of Variations in Abstract Spaces" (1942). In 1946 he collaborated with his wife on a paper titled "The Electronic Numerical Integrator and Computer." With von Neumann and Arthur Burks he wrote "Preliminary Discussion of the Logical Design of an Electronic Computing Instrument" in 1946, and in several succeeding published studies Goldstine and von Neumann analyzed the problems, theoretical and practical, involved in the building and use of the electronic computing machine.

Goldstine was a consultant for the Ballistics Research Laboratories at the Aberdeen Proving Ground beginning in 1947 and for the Los Alamos National Laboratory and the Ordnance Research No. I at the University of Chicago starting in 1948. Also in 1948 he was appointed chairman of a subpanel on the computing devices joint research and development board of the National Military Establishment.

Among Goldstine's many honors are the IEEE Computer Society Pioneer Award, in 1980, and the National Medal of Science, in 1985. He was inducted into the Information Processing Hall of Fame in 1985. He holds membership in the American Mathematical Society, the Mathematical Associa-

tion of America, and the Institute of Mathematical Statistics, and is a member of subcommittee A-I on computing centers of the last-named organization. He received honorary doctorates from the University of Lund, in Sweden; Amherst College, in Massachusetts; Adelphi University, in New York; and Rutgers University, in New Jersey.

On September 15, 1941 Goldstine married Adele Katz, who was also a mathematician. The couple had two children, Madlen and Jonathan. His first marriage ended with Adele Goldstine's death, in 1964. Goldstine currently lives in Philadelphia with his second wife, Ellen Watson, whom he married on January 8, 1966.—C. M.

Suggested Reading: *American Men of Science,* 1949; Cortada, James W. *Historical Dictionary of Data Processing: Biographies,* 1987; *Current Biography Yearbook 1952*; Lee, J. A. N., ed. *International Biographical Dictionary of Computer Pioneers,* 1995

Courtesy of Sun Microsystems

Gosling, James

May 19, 1956– Developer of the Java computer language

"I've always been interested in building things," the computer programmer James Gosling told John Markoff for the *New York Times* (September 25, 1995). The Canadian native created Java, the computer language that helped transform the Internet in the mid-1990s. Although Gosling and his fellow researchers at Sun Microsystems in Palo Alto, California, used Java (previously known as Oak) in the

early 1990s, they released it to the public in 1995. The new language impressed computer programmers and Web site designers because it conserved memory by building small programs that behaved as single larger one, and could be understood by any system. Such prominent companies as Intel, Microsoft, IBM, Netscape, and AT&T licensed the Java language for their own use. As the Internet exploded in the mid-1990s, Java helped eliminate the barriers between different computer systems and enhanced Web sites with graphics, images, and other interactive features.

James Gosling was born on May 19, 1956 in the Canadian province of Alberta. He grew up among farmers in the province's rural areas. As a child, he was fascinated by machines, as he recalled in an interview with Eric Nee for *Forbes* (July 7, 1997), "I loved to help [the farmers] fix combines and other equipment." He also enjoyed taking apart and reassembling old television sets to see how they worked. At age 14 Gosling discovered the computer center at the University of Calgary. "After that I was hooked," he told Nee. "I used to break in all the time to use the computers and read, read, read." Gosling became so skilled as a computer programmer that the university's physics department hired him about a year later to write software for a data processing system for satellites. "He could have gone into graduate school out of high school," Cliff Auger, the physics professor who supervised the project, told Brahm Eiley for the (Canada) *Financial Post* (June 1, 1997). "He did a lot of useful things for us back then." As a teenager, Gosling's dream was to work as a repairman for the Digital Equipment Corporation, then a leading computer manufacturer.

Gosling enrolled at the University of Calgary to study computer science. "Early on in university I figured that the choices for me were kind of limited," he recalled to Sandra Dillich for *Computing Canada* (June 12, 2000). "I could work for a bank, I could work for an oil company, I could work for the university or I could work a computer company. But the only computer jobs I had ever seen that looked even close to interesting were the guys who came around and repaired systems. So when I was like 18, 19, 20 years old my basic aspiration was to be a field engineer." Gosling graduated in 1977 with a Bachelor of Computer Science (B.Sc.) degree, but he concluded that his prospects for a job in Canada were limited. In 1978 he headed to Carnegie-Mellon University (CMU) in Pittsburgh, Pennsylvania, to pursue his doctoral studies in computer science.

During his years at CMU, Gosling wrote EMACs, tools that edited programs designed to run on the Unix operating system. EMACs were popular with computer programmers as text-editing devices and are still widely used today. Gosling's EMACs attracted the attention of Bill Joy, the computer scientist who co-founded Sun Microsystems in 1982, and Joy presented Gosling with a postdoctoral position. Gosling received his doctorate in computer science in 1983, but he declined Joy's offer and instead took a job with IBM, thinking this was a "safer" choice. (IBM was an established company, while Sun was just getting off the ground.) Gosling helped to build a new workstation, the PC/RT. But, disillusioned by the lack of support and encouragement for the project by the company's management, Gosling left IBM in 1984. "That one-and-one-half years was an education in how a company can really screw things up," he told Nee.

Gosling discovered that the job offer at Sun Microsystems was still open, and he joined the company at its headquarters in Palo Alto, California, in 1984. The focus of his work at Sun was developing computer languages. As Gosling explained to Eiley, "Languages and a strong visual component have been the pattern of my work from the beginning. I've always worked way down in the basement, doing something that no one ever sees but that helps to hold up the house." Among Gosling's early projects were the creation of a multiprocessor version of Unix, e-mail systems, several compilers (which allow programming languages to be read by the computer), and a text editor for WYSIWYG (What You See Is What You Get) software. Designed to work on Apple computers, WYSIWYG allowed users to print documents exactly as they appeared on the computer screen. WYSIWYG helped spark desk-top publishing.

Gosling spent about six years developing the Network Extensible Windowing System (NeWS) with David Rosenthal. NeWS enabled a computer to display a program that is running on another computer connected to the same network, and one of its best features was clear graphics. Gosling believed that NeWS would make an excellent alternative to Microsoft's Windows, which was beginning to dominate the industry. Sun's management, however, gave little support to NeWS, and failed to

market it. Although NeWS became popular with some computer programmers, it quickly faded into obscurity. Disappointed by what he considered Sun's professional incompetence, Gosling considered quitting several times.

Gosling wasn't the only Sun employee disillusioned with the company. A young programmer named Patrick Naughton was also displeased and in 1990 told Scott McNealy, Sun's chairman and CEO, that he was taking a position with NeXT Computer. "Before you go," McNealy told him, as quoted by David Bank for *Wired* (December 1995, on-line), "write up what you think Sun is doing wrong. Don't just lay out the problem. Give me a solution. Tell me what you would do if you were God." The next day Naughton sent an e-mail to McNealy, detailing what he considered Sun's problems and sketching out several recommendations, including: hiring an artist to spruce up the company's unattractive interfaces; developing one Windows technology, instead of several; adopting a single programming kit; and allowing Sun's programmers and engineers in Windows to work without interference from the management. McNealy was impressed with Naughton's e-mail and forwarded it to Sun's managers and programers, including Gosling, who concluded that Naughton's observations were correct. As he told Bank: "Somewhere along the line, we've lost touch with what it means to produce a quality product."

Naughton's e-mail sparked immediate reform at Sun Microsystems. The company's managers, engineers and programmers sat down together to exchange ideas. When the meeting ended at 4:30 in the morning the following day, the participants had agreed on new guiding principles for the company's projects. The projects would be geared to serving the needs of consumers, and a small team of programmers and engineers would work on projects in complete freedom and independent of the rest of the company. A fresh task was to build a new generation of machines that ordinary people could easily program and understand.

McNealy sanctioned the creation of the "Green project" in December 1990. Green was an elite team of eight programmers and engineers at Sun, and the team, which included Gosling and Naughton, who had been persuaded to stay on, worked secretly on projects at a location separate from the company's main offices. (According to Bank, Naughton insisted that they work secreted away in order to shield themselves from the watchful eyes of corporate executives, some of whom were notorious for discouraging innovative ideas.) McNealy allocated $500,000 to the group for the first year, and as the months passed, the Green team's ideas developed into concrete projects. The team decided that it was useless to create products in an effort to dislodge the dominance of the Microsoft Corporation in the computer industry. Instead, the team wanted to specialize in areas unchartered by Microsoft. As a long-term project, Gosling and his colleagues wanted to develop software that could run on any product that had a computer chip. "We wanted computers to go away," Naughton explained to Bank. "We thought the third wave of computing would be driven by consumer electronics. The hardware would come from Circuit City, and the software would come from Tower Records."

In the spring of 1991, at a Green team retreat in Lake Tahoe, California, Gosling proposed that they create a single remote-control device to power every household item that contained a computer chip. "With a little computer science, all of these things could be made to work together," Gosling explained, as quoted by Bank. The Green team agreed to develop a single, all-purpose remote control.

A short time later Gosling discovered how he would write the software for such devices. At a Doobie Brothers concert, he observed the wiring, speakers, and lights shooting back and forth. "I kept seeing imaginary packets flowing down the wires making everything happen," he recalled to Bank. "I'd been thinking a lot about making behavior flow through networks in a fairly narrow way. During the concert, I broke through on a pile of technical issues. I got a deep feeling about how far this could all go: weaving networks and computers into even fine details of everyday life." After several attempts, Gosling concluded that the C++ programming language was inadequate to write the software for the group's remote control. Although the language produced fast programs, they continually crashed. "I came to the conclusion that I needed a new programming language," he explained to Bank. Within a few months, Gosling completed the new language, Oak, which he named after a tree he saw from his office window. Based on many of NeWS's features, the new language "was always a tool for the job," Gosling told Lindsay Nicole for the London *Times* (December 10, 1997). "It's very grounded and realistic. It really solves developers' problems rather than exploring some sort of academic puzzle. It's like stainless steel, wood, or concrete."

The Green team decided that the remote-control device should interface with computers as well. In August 1992 they unveiled a prototype called *7 or StarSeven. Naughton explained to Bank that StarSeven was built with "hammer technology"—team members examined different products, such as a Sharp mini-television and a Gameboy, smashed them with a hammer, and took different pieces of each product to create the model. StarSeven resembled a small black box with a single antenna. It was battery-powered, lightweight, and slightly larger than the human hand. Users activated the device by simply touching the display screen. Bank wrote that StarSeven "opened to a cartoon world—no menus! A character named Duke, a molar-shaped imp with a big red nose, guided the user through the rooms of a cartoon house. You steered with your finger—no mouse!" People could use StarSeven to program a VCR to record a particular televi-

sion program or movie. McNealy and the rest of Sun's management were impressed with the product. "This is real breakthrough stuff," McNealy said in an e-mail to Sun employees, as quoted by Bank. "Don't fail me now. We need to sell this puppy hard, and there's tons of work to make it real." McNealy envisioned StarSeven making Sun Microsystems so popular that it could successfully challenge the dominance of such established corporations as Hewlett-Packard, IBM, Microsoft, and Apple Computers. In the end, however, few people expressed interest in the device, and Sun Microsystems was forced to shift strategies.

The effort to build StarSeven was not wasted. Sun's management saw the Oak language as a potential product. In an interview with Darryl K. Taft and Wylie Wong for *Computer Reseller News* (November 23, 1998), Gosling recalled that "we decided to see what we could do to turn [Oak] into a business." Sun began negotiations with Mitsubishi Electric and France Telecom to use interfaces created with Oak in their products. In 1992 Sun established a subsidiary, First Person Inc., to develop and market Oak for use in consumer electronic devices and appliances. Sun quickly discovered that there was little demand for Oak in the consumer electronics industry. Both Mitsubishi and France Telecom lost interest in the language. "Sun figured the cost of the chip, memory, and display device needed for Oak could be squeezed to about $50," Bank wrote, "but consumer electronics makers were used to paying nominal bucks for chips that made their products easier to use." Despite the setback, Sun did not give up on Oak. In the early 1990s, there was widespread discussion in the media and the computer industry about the emerging "information superhighway." At the time, this term was still associated with "interactive television" and not the Internet. Sun believed that Oak could play a key role in the development of interactive television. The company lobbied Time Warner in March 1993 for the contract to build "set-top boxes" that would make televisions interactive, but was unsuccessful. (This turned out to be a blessing in disguise—interactive television never lived up to the hype it received and attracted little consumer interest. First Person folded in 1994.)

Sun continued to search for markets for Oak. "After we realized that there wasn't a business in digital cable television, we had a group meeting at The Inn at Squaw Creek near Lake Tahoe. We had to figure out what to do with this technology, or what to do with the rest of our lives," Gosling explained to John Byous, in an essay posted on the Java Web site (May 23, 1998). An unexpected phenomenon created a viable market for Oak: In the early 1990s Internet usage increased by exponential proportions. More and more people were going on-line to search for information, conduct business, and communicate with others. Many companies also set up sites on the World Wide Web to reach potential customers. Bill Joy believed that Oak could aid the development of the Internet and make it easier for non-technical people to use. "The Internet was being transformed into exactly the network that we had been trying to convince the cable companies they ought to be building," Gosling told Byous. "All the stuff we wanted to do, in generalities, fit perfectly with the way applications were written, delivered, and used on the Internet. It was just an incredible accident."

Gosling adapted Oak for the Internet, and Patrick Naughton used it to develop an early Internet browser called "WebRunner." WebRunner was almost a copy of Mosaic, the first popular browser. In early 1995 Gosling and John Gage, the director of Sun's science office, demonstrated WebRunner at the Technology, Entertainment and Design Conference in Monterey, California. As Byous wrote, the demonstration "jolted a very influential audience off their seats, and they were delivering enthusiastic applause. And within this technology-entertainment crowd, word spread quickly." In January 1995 Sun changed the name of the language from Oak to the more commercially appealing Java. (WebRunner was renamed HotJava.) After using Java in-house for five years, Sun made it available to the public in March 1995. Computer users and programmers could download Java free of charge from Sun's Web site. By offering Java for free, Sun hoped that consumers would try it and create demand. Initially, only a handful of people downloaded the program, but several months later thousands were using it and seeking technical support from Sun. Java "programs are written in small packages of code, with each performing a very specific function," Shelley Knapp wrote for the Calgary Herald (May 28, 1998). "The packages, known as applets, are a fraction of the size of traditional software applications." One of Java's best features is that its applets could run on any system, breaking down barriers in cyberspace. Systems that were not compatible could now interact, share resources, and exchange information. Bank observed that Java's applets are written in an "intermediate language," meaning that different systems could interpret them despite the fact that users did not specifically program Java-based applications to work on a particular system.

The flood of favorable publicity for Java brought Sun Microsystems many prominent clients. Established corporations such as Netscape, Mitsubishi, Oracle, Toshiba, Intel, AT&T, Silicon Graphics, Adobe, and IBM all licensed Java from Sun before the end of 1995. Netscape used Java to update its popular Web browser, Netscape Navigator. Web site designers liked Java because it allowed them to add graphics and animation. In his article for the New York Times (September 25, 1995), John Markoff noted that Java also provided Web sites with real-time data updates. For example, Web sites devoted to sports could update players' statistics instantly during the game.

In 1996 Sun took several steps to help programmers and users understand Java and work out any bugs by selling Java "tool kits" and offering educational courses, several technical manuals, and a new magazine, JavaWorld. The same year Sun created a new division, JavaSoft, which assumed traditional responsibilities such as marketing, licensing, issuing updates, and providing technical assistance to users. In 1996 JavaSoft licensed the language to such industry giants as Apple Computers and Microsoft. Java's popularity grew through the late 1990s, and it became a popular course in university computer-science departments.

Gosling received substantial public acclaim for developing Java. Although he was eventually named a vice president at Sun, he shunned any corporate responsibilities and continued his research. "There are all kinds of research labs around the United States that are willing to pay you well to basically have fun, and if you accidentally do something interesting then, bingo, they're very happy," he told Ross Laver for Macleans (March 22, 1999). Gosling co-wrote several technical manuals on Java, including Java Application Programming Interface (1996), Java Language Specification (1996), Java Programming Language (1996), and Real-Time Specification for Java (2000). He also served as a spokesperson for Java, giving frequent talks at conferences.

In 1998 Java was at the center of a lawsuit Sun filed against Microsoft for breach of contract. Sun alleged that Microsoft was so fearful of Java that it developed a radically different version of the language (called J-Direct) for Windows that would be incompatible with the "pure" version widely distributed by Sun. Since Microsoft's Windows was used in most computers, Sun's original Java would be effectively frozen out of most systems. The same year, Microsoft's antitrust trial, which was initiated by the U. S. Department of Justice, began. Sun's executives, including Gosling, testified at the antitrust trial. An e-mail Gosling sent to Sun's executives in 1995 was introduced as evidence. Gosling had expressed doubts over the forthcoming licensing agreement with Microsoft, writing, "I just don't trust them. The planet is littered with companies that did deals with Microsoft expecting to win big but ended up getting totally screwed," as quoted by Elizabeth Wasserman for Computerworld (December 3, 1998, on-line). Gosling testified that Microsoft's actions were "analogous to adding to the English language words and phrases that cannot be understood by anyone else," as quoted by Ted Bridis for the Denver Post (December 3, 1998). In his own testimony, Microsoft chairman Bill Gates admitted he thought that Java could threaten his company but denied that he ever discouraged anyone from using it. Microsoft's lawyers countered that Sun intended to use Java to destroy Microsoft, citing several e-mails by Sun's executives that make critical comments about their competitor. (The court ultimately ruled that Microsoft had violated antitrust laws.)

Gosling has remained at Sun and continues to develop Java-related projects, including a new language, Jini, which would link different electrical devices. He is married, has two daughters, and lives in California.—D. C.

Suggested Reading: *BusinessWeek* p103+ May 20, 1996; *Calgary Herald* C p7 May 28, 1998; *Computer* p53+ June 1997, with illustrations; *Computer Reseller News* p133+ Nov. 23, 1998; *Computerworld* (on-line) Dec. 3, 1998; *Computing Canada* (on-line) June 12, 2000; *Denver Post* C p3 Dec. 3, 1998; *Financial Post* p7 Jan. 6, 1996, p53 June 1, 1997; *Forbes* p322+ July 7, 1997; James Gosling Home Page; Java Web site; *Macleans* p34 Mar. 22, 1999, with photo; *New York Times* D p1+ Sep. 25, 1995, with photos; Sun Microsystems Web site; *London Times* p17 Dec. 10, 1997; *Wall Street Journal* B p6 Dec. 11, 1998; *Wired* (on-line) Dec. 1995

Grant, George Barnard

1849–1917 Designer and manufacturer of calculating machines

Though today considered an obscure inventor, George Barnard Grant was celebrated in the 19th century as a designer and manufacturer of adding machines and calculators. Grant's work, which took its inspiration from the English inventor Charles Babbage's Difference Engine and Analytical Engine, greatly impressed visitors to the 1876 Centennial Exhibition who marveled at his machine's accuracy in calculating figures. For the next several decades, Grant continued to modify and improve his calculating machines in his own manufacturing plants. Though not widely known today, Grant's inventions helped to stimulate American participation in the Industrial Age and served as a springboard for later calculators, both mechanical and electronic.

George Barnard Grant was born in 1849 and raised in Maine. He received his advanced education at Harvard College, in Cambridge, Massachusetts, earning his bachelor of science degree, in 1873. As an undergraduate at Harvard, he read about the work of Charles Babbage, who early in the 19th century built a calculating machine that he called the Difference Engine. Constructed for the English government at a cost of £20,000, the Difference Engine calculated logarithmical and trigonometrical tables and printed the tables as fast as they were calculated. Babbage also designed, but was never able to build, a far more powerful machine, which he called the Analytical Engine. This machine, according to the 1878 *Appletons' Cyclopedia of Applied Mechanics* as reprinted on the University of Rochester Web site, "contains a hundred variables, or numbers susceptible of changing, and each of these numbers may consist of twenty-five figures. The distinctive characteristic of this machine is the introduction into it of the principle which Jacquard [the inventor of a loom that revolutionized the textile industry at the start

of the 19th century] devised for regulating by means of punched cards, the complicated patterns of brocaded stuff."

Grant's own experiments began in 1871, while he was still an undergraduate. He received his first patents, in 1872 and 1873, for a calculator and printer that were extensions of Babbage's work. He then proceeded to build a calculator that improved on the Arithmometer made by Charles Xavier Thomas de Colmar, which was then the most popular calculating machine in America. Grant's machine was a much simpler device with an upper cylinder controlled by a crank that moved a smaller shaft underneath it. The machine had a slide that allowed for eight different settings on the cylinder and carried eight figured rings that could set numbers up to eight digits. In order to add the numbers set on the rings to the number on the lower shaft, the operator turned the crank. Multiplication was somewhat more complicated; it is described by an example used in *Appletons' Cyclopedia of Applied Mechanics*: "To multiply 347 by 492, the three upper rings are set at 3, 4, and 7, respectively. The cylinder is then turned twice to multiply by the units figure of the multiplier. If now the slide is carried along one notch, where each ring will act on the next higher recording wheel, and turned 9 times, 347 will be multiplied by 90, and the product at the same time will be added to the product already scored. Another shift of the slide and four turns will complete the operation, and show the result, 170724 = (347 x 2) + (347 x 90) + (347 x 400), upon the recording wheels. A half-turn of the crank backward erases this result, bringing all the wheels to 0, ready for the next operation." Division on the machine was the opposite of multiplication, with the dividend on the wheels and the divisor on the rings. The result was then recorded on the upper wheels.

Grant displayed his first machine at the 1876 Centennial Exhibition, the same grand affair that displayed Alexander Graham Bell's telephone. Weighing more than 2000 pounds and measuring five feet high and eight feet long, Grant's calculating machine has the probable distinction of being the largest calculator ever built. As he worked on his calculating machines over the subsequent decades, they became more reliable and smaller. His most notable machines were the Barrel, also known as the Centennial, and the commercially successful Rack and Pinion, of which he sold 125. Grant won a number of awards for his calculating machines, including the Centennial Medal, the Scott Legacy and Medal of the Franklin Institute, and the gold Medal of the Massachusetts Charitable Mechanics' Association.

Because Babbage's work was little known in the United States, Grant's machines appeared to be totally new inventions and were highly praised. In an article detailing the functions of one of Grant's later calculating machines, the "grasshopper model," a writer for *Manufacturer and Builder* (September 1894) proclaimed: "It is no more necessary to argue the utility of the calculating machine than it is to prove that of the typewriter. Indeed, the two machines are similar in many respects, each doing well and easily work that can be done with the pen in a poor and difficult way, both effecting a saving of time, and neither being a strict necessity. The calculating machine bears the same relation to computation that the typewriter bears to correspondence."

Grant's most significant improvement to Babbage's work is that Grant's gears actually worked, whereas Babbage's did not. In fact, as an indirect result of working on his calculating machines for so many years, he became highly skilled as a mechanical engineer. In order to aid the development of his calculating machines, he began to manufacturer his own gears, establishing such companies as the Grant Gear Works, the Philadelphia Gear Works, and the Boston Gear Works. While not as widely remembered today for his contributions to the calculator, George Barnard Grant is remembered as father of the American gear-cutting industry.—C. M.

Suggested Reading: *Manufacturer and Builder* p195+ Sept. 1894; University of Rochester Web site; Cortada, James W. *Historical Dictionary of Data Processing: Biographies*, 1987

Grillet, René

(?)– Inventor of an adding machine

Though considerably less complicated than the adding machines created during the same period by Blaise Pascal and Samuel Morland, René Grillet's adding machine was a very useful addition to 17th-century society, when the only means available to record mathematical results were by using a quill and ink on paper. Grillet's machine was a pocket-sized precursor to modern electronic calculators, and allowed a user to add and subtract as easily as he could on paper. Though almost nothing is known about Grillet himself, his machine reflects not only his genius, but the ingenuity of 17th-century mechanical thinking.

There are no existing records of Grillet's birth or death, though it is known that he was a clockmaker for King Louis XIV of France. Some historians claim that he took an early calculating machine on a tour of county fairs around France. The only direct information scholars have about him comes from a short article he wrote, in 1678, for the *Journal des Scavans*, then one of the most respected scientific periodicals in France.

Because Grillet wanted to keep the workings of his machine a secret, he did not explain how it worked in the article, except to say that it brought together the technical achievements of Blaise Pascal's calculator, John Napier's bones (a set of graduated rods used for multiplication and division, based on logarithmic principles), and Petit's *cylindre arithmetique*, which were Napier's bones carved on a cylinder. The remainder of the article detailed how a reader could purchase one of Grillet's machines. The diagram accompanying the article did little to illustrate how Grillet's machine worked: it showed a box of 24 wheels set in the lid, each wheel consisted of four or five concentric circles; at the bottom of the box, a set of Napier's bones was carved on cylinders. Because none of the devices survived, the inner workings are unknown: up until the late 20th century historians did not know if Grillet's 24 wheels used a complex carry mechanism like Pascal's, a simple one like Morland's, or any carry mechanism at all. They believed it was very likely that the dials were turned by hand in order to store digits that would then have to be calculated mentally.

Historians learned more about Grillet's machine when they uncovered a manuscript by the 19th-century French mathematician, Michel Chasles, among the papers of the esteemed English inventor Charles Babbage. The 18-page handwritten manuscript, with four additional pages of diagrams, was misfiled under the name *Gaillet* for a century. The diagrams in the Chasles manuscript are practically identical to those in Grillet's 1678 paper and contain considerably more detailed information about the inner mechanisms of Grillet's machine than his original paper. According to this paper, Grillet's calculating machine was a very simple device, with no carry function; it was, in essence, a calculating substitute for pen and paper.

In order to perform an addition or subtraction, the operator would set up the first number on the top line of dials by turning the dials with a stylus, in a way similar to Morland's adding machine. (In all likelihood Grillet would have known about Morland and his work; Morland was a diplomat to the French court and a frequent visitor to France.) The second number would then be inserted into the middle line of dials. The user would then perform the operation mentally and turn the dials on the third line to show the answer. In *A History of Computing Technology* (1997), Michael A. Williams noted: "The lid would . . . have found its main use in adding up the partial products generated by the set of cylindrical Napier's bones, and the [Chasles] manuscript devotes several pages to a careful description of this process. After a brief mention of the fact that, when a wheel is rotated past the zero position, the operator must either add or subtract one from the adjacent wheel on the left, the subject is not mentioned further." Beyond that, the manuscript describes how an operator might use the device to divide, add, and subtract fractions, and to extract square and cube roots.

Grillet and Morland were contemporaries, and it is interesting to note how their machines compared. Grillet's machine, though simpler than Morland's, had some advantages over the latter's machine, not least of which was the ability to calculate numbers out to eight digits, whereas Morland's was limited to five. It was also better at multiplication than Morland's more complicated device. However, Morland's machine, because of its simple but effective carry function, allowed for less error, since computations were made by machine and not, as in the case of Grillet's machine, by human calculation.—C. M.

Suggested Reading: Cortada, James W. *Historical Dictionary of Data Processing: Biographies*, 1987

Courtesy of Intel Corp.

Grove, Andrew S.

Sep. 2, 1936– Chairman of Intel

"Every company reflects the personality of its leader," Richard Shaffer, a computer-industry analyst, told Robert Wrubel for *Financial World* (December 11, 1990). "Intel's culture is no exception. It is ruthless, intense, and disciplined. Just like Andy." Shaffer was referring to Andrew S. Grove, the chairman of the Intel Corporation, the Silicon Valley giant that makes nearly 90 percent of the microchips used worldwide to run personal computers (PCs). With net revenues of $26.8 billion in 2002, the company is one of the most profitable businesses on the planet. In addition to running PCs, Intel microprocessors power a huge array of devices—everything from traffic lights to calculators, medical equipment, and electronic toys. In recent years,

as sales of PCs have begun to decline while personal use of the Internet has exploded, Intel has developed alternative technologies that will allow more consumers to access the Internet through a variety of means, such as through hand-held Internet devices or the "servers" that maintain large on-line computing systems. While Grove helped to formulate the technology—the microchip—upon which his company is based, his genius has been in applying exacting management skills and tough business practices to create the efficient corporate environment responsible for Intel's success. Grove has written three books about his fiercely competitive style of management, including *Only the Paranoid Survive: How to Exploit the Crisis Points That Challenge Every Company and Career* (1996). In March 1998, Grove, who is a co-founder of Intel, resigned as president and chief operating officer, while retaining his position as chairman.

A Holocaust survivor, Grove fled his native Hungary in 1956 and arrived in the United States with a limited knowledge of English and about $20 in his pocket. His remarkable rise to a position of worldwide influence prompted *Time* magazine to name him its Man of the Year in 1997 and to call him "the person most responsible for the amazing growth in the power and the innovative potential of microchips."

Andrew Steven Grove was born András Gróf on September 2, 1936 in Budapest, Hungary. He is the son of George Gróf, who owned a small dairy business, and Maria Gróf, who worked as a bookkeeper. In 1940 he became seriously ill with scarlet fever during an epidemic that claimed the lives of many Budapest residents. A middle-ear infection that he suffered in the course of the disease left him with serious damage to his hearing. (He has since regained his hearing, thanks to a series of reconstructive operations.) By then, World War II was well underway, and the Holocaust had begun. In March 1944 German troops marched into Hungary and started to transport Jews to concentration camps and work camps. Grove's father was grabbed off the street and sent to a labor camp. Grove and his mother managed to obtain false identification papers, and they moved in with a Christian family, who risked their lives to shelter them. "I was eight years old, and I knew bad things were happening, but I don't remember the details," Grove told Joshua Cooper Ramo for *Time* (December 29, 1997–January 5, 1998). "My mother took me away. She explained to me that I would have a different name [András Malesevics], and that I cannot make a mistake, that I had to forget my [real] name and that I couldn't, if they said 'Write your name,' I couldn't write [the real one] down."

After the war Grove and his mother were reunited with his father, who returned from his ordeal as a forced laborer weakened from bouts of typhoid fever and pneumonia. The family's attempts to resume a normal life proved difficult, because obtaining food and fuel was a struggle in postwar Hungary. In addition, with the country having fallen under Communist rule, Grove faced prejudice for being the son of a "capitalist" as well as for being Jewish. Despite those obstacles, he was determined to realize his parents' dream that he go to college. After a youthful interest in journalism waned, he turned to science and became an outstanding chemistry student, with a special interest in the formation of molecules.

In 1956, when Grove was 20 and attending university classes, Hungary became the victim of an occupying power once again. This time it was the Soviet Union, whose Red Army stormed into Budapest to crush a budding political revolution and set up a puppet regime. Fearful that he would be arrested, like many other college students, Grove fled the capital and headed with a friend for the Austrian border. To their horror, they discovered that Red Army troops were moving in the same direction. They paid a smuggler to show them how to get through the countryside on little-used trails. After hours of walking, the two young men heard soldiers approaching—Soviet troops, they feared. Grove, who rarely talks about his early life, recalled to Ramo that he and his friend then heard a voice cry out in Hungarian, "Who is there?" Uncertain where they were or who was speaking, they did not reply. But the man called out again, and Grove mustered the courage to respond. "Where are we?" he asked. "Austria," the man replied. Grove and his friend were led to safety.

Several weeks later Grove boarded a rusty World War II–era troop ship filled with other refugees and sailed to the United States. The ship docked at the Brooklyn Navy Yard, in New York City. "We didn't see the Statue of Liberty or anything," Grove recalled to Brent Schlender for *Fortune* (July 10, 1995). "They immediately took us by bus to Camp Kilmer, New Jersey, which had been a POW camp during the war. We thought that all the propaganda was true, that America was just another drab, totalitarian state."

Not long after his arrival, he changed his name to Andrew Grove and moved in with an aunt and uncle in a small apartment in Brooklyn. He enrolled at the City College of New York, where he studied engineering. Although he read and spoke a little English, he was bewildered by words like *dangle* and *horizontal* that he heard in technical courses. "I had to go over each day's work again at night with a dictionary at my side," he told the *New York Times* in 1960, in an interview that recognized his position as class valedictorian. He earned a B.S. in chemical engineering with honors only three years after leaving Hungary.

Meanwhile, in 1958, Grove had married Eva, a fellow Hungarian refugee whom he had met while both were waiting tables at a summer resort. After he graduated from college, the couple moved to California, where Grove entered the Ph.D. program in chemical engineering at the University of California, Berkeley. He earned his doctorate in three years. His brilliance in his field had become well known, and he had his pick of jobs, including a po-

sition at the prestigious Bell Laboratories. But he opted to work for Fairchild Semiconductor, a start-up firm in the burgeoning computer field. One of the firm's top scientists, Robert Noyce, was an inventor of the integrated circuit, a breakthrough discovery that made it possible to put more than one transistor on a fragment of silicon, thus increasing the power and speed of computer operations. The head of research and development at Fairchild was Gordon E. Moore, a chemical engineer who was widely respected for his ability to solve tough technical problems.

At Fairchild Grove was part of a team that studied the use of silicon in transistors. The chips had been plagued by instabilities. After months of work, the team discovered why: The sodium used in the curing process had been "souring" the semiconductors and causing glitches. "The discovery solved a fundamental problem in materials science and set the stage for the semiconductor revolution," Ramo wrote. "Grove and his team won one of the industry's most prestigious awards for their work." Besides his talent for research, Grove had excellent organizational, communication, and leadership skills. That is why, when Noyce and Moore decided to leave Fairchild and start their own semiconductor firm, Grove was the first person they asked to go with them. He agreed "almost instantly," he has said. The company, which was founded in July 1968, was named Intel, a shortened version of "integrated electronics." It soon began churning out memory chips for mainframe computers.

"I was supposed to be the director of engineering, but there was so few of us that they made me director of operations," Grove told Schlender regarding his early days at Intel. In his managerial role, he quickly showed himself to be a "natural whip cracker," as Schlender put it. Indeed, in the very first years of Intel's existence, when he was head of factory production, Grove was determined to run a very tight ship. "Theoretician that he was, Grove had no truck with touchy-feely approaches to manufacturing that he believed were common elsewhere in the industry," Tim Jackson wrote in *Inside Intel: Andy Grove and the Rise of the World's Most Powerful Chip Company* (1997). "Instead, he wanted to be able to express Intel's production lines as a set of equations like those he delivered in his book *Physics and Technology of Semiconductor Devices* [1967]. To do this, he needed facts: statistics in huge quantities, regularly delivered. But this was 1971, not 1991. There was no company intranet, no spreadsheet software—not even desktop computers. The statistics that Grove demanded had to be collected and tabulated largely by hand—by people who were having problems enough just getting through the day, producing any output at all from the rudimentary designs and processes. . . . Most Intel engineers were lucky if they got home before midnight in time to see their families."

To ensure that he got the most out of his workers, Grove employed various tactics. One of them was to have all workers who arrived after 8:05 a.m. sign in late. In 1971 he sent a memo to all Intel employees reminding them that December 24 was a full working day. The "Scrooge memo," as it became known, generated resentment within the company, and many workers sent their memos back to Grove with nasty comments scrawled on them. "May you eat yellow snow," one of them read. In those early years at Intel, Grove wore a hearing aid that resembled headphones. The device seemed to fail at opportune moments—when Grove was being told something he didn't want to hear, for example. On other occasions, he would take the hearing aid off his head and thrust it onto his desk, as a pointed way of indicating that he would listen no more. Grove also kept his bosses on their toes. As Moore was quoted as saying in the *Fortune* article, "Andy always made it hard for me. I would be all excited that we were under budget or ahead of schedule on a product—and he'd ask why we couldn't do it faster and cheaper. He got very interested in the art of management, and that served us very well."

In spite of his hard-driving manner, many employees developed a grudging admiration for Grove, whose brilliance in solving problems and ability to complete difficult projects was apparent to all. He encouraged employees to set their own goals, and then made sure that they achieved them. "I learned more from him than anyone else I ever worked with before or since," his former secretary Sue McFarland told Tim Jackson. Grove made himself accessible for consultation to all employees—a practice he continues to this day. Throughout his years at Intel, he has worked in an open eight-foot-by-nine-foot cubicle rather than in an office. He also eats regularly in the company's cafeteria and insists that everyone call him Andy. Grove wrote about his vision of business management in *High Output Management* (1983). The book was well received, as was *One-on-One with Andy Grove: How to Manage Your Boss, Yourself and Your Coworkers* (1988), which was based in large part on text from his nationally syndicated business column.

Until the mid-1980s Intel's mission was to be the best and largest memory-chip manufacturer in the industry. Thus, when, in 1971, Intel engineers introduced the world's first microprocessor, called the 4004, which was powerful enough to run a small computer, Grove did not think of it as being part of the company's core business. "To me, the microprocessor, quite frankly, was sort of a commercially justifiable diversion from what we were doing, which was building memory chips . . . ," he told Stephen Frazier for the CNN program *Impact*. "So I didn't think very much of it at the time." Nevertheless, in the following years, Intel continued to make improvements in its microprocessors, which its creators predicted would one day be used in many devices besides computers, such as microwave ovens, cash machines, and cars. In 1972 the company introduced a second microprocessor, the 8008, and the idea that it could be used to run a small computer began to catch on in the industry. Intel introduced the 8086 in 1978, the 8088 in 1979, and the 80286 in 1982.

In the early 1980s Japanese memory-chip manufacturers began to present Intel with fierce competition. This crisis forced Grove (who by then had been named president and chief operating officer) to reassess the value of the microprocessor, and in 1985 he made a dramatic proposal to his colleagues: He suggested that Intel shift the focus of the company from memory chips to developing its microprocessor business. After persuading them to go along with his proposal, Grove shut down several plants and cut 6,000 employees from the payroll.

One key factor that aided Intel in its bid to become the premiere microprocessor manufacturer was that it had captured IBM as a client several years before. (IBM had selected Intel's 8088 microchip as the engine for its first generation of PCs.) "Plenty of companies have fumbled the IBM relationship," Shaffer told Wrubel. "Not Intel. Andy Grove capitalized on that like no other company except perhaps Microsoft."

Yet however important the Intel–IBM relationship proved to be, it alone cannot account for Intel's success; Grove's near-obsession with preserving his company's big lead in microchip technology was also a factor. To that end, until 1985 Grove refused to license the designs of new chips to other manufacturers, and he initiated expensive lawsuits against competitors, such as Advanced Micro Devices (AMD) and the Cyrix Corporation, for alleged copyright violations. "Grove focused Intel on microprocessors with a paranoia and manic competitiveness that informs much of what the company does today," Robert Hof wrote for *BusinessWeek* (January 16, 1995). By 1988, when Intel came out with the 80386SX (also known as the 386SX chip), the company had no formidable rivals, and the chip quickly became the industry standard.

Consumer awareness of Intel's chips has been heightened by the company's extremely successful "Intel inside" advertising campaign. By raising public awareness of the Intel name and asking PC manufacturers to label their machines with the company logo, the firm has persuaded the public to care about what powers their computers, and thereby dampen sales of PCs run by rival chips. However, that strategy backfired in 1994: After Intel released millions of flawed Pentium chips, consumers demanded replacements. At first, Grove resisted those demands, insisting that the glitch was so small that conventional PC users would not notice the difference. People who called the company to complain were told not to worry unless they had "some advanced astrophysics problems that weekend," as Ramo put it. Dissatisfied with that answer, several consumers complained about Intel to reporters, and before long, Grove had a public-relations disaster on his hands. Within a few days, he reversed his decision and set aside $475 million to replace the Pentiums on demand. It was "a difficult education" in consumer relations, Grove has since admitted.

Intel quickly recovered from the Pentium debacle, and sales resumed at their frenetic pace. The company had kept its profit margin, estimated to be between 40 and 60 percent, by selling, for top dollar, premium-quality chips that run top-of-the-line PCs. But in the late 1990s, Intel began to face a new challenge, one stemming from the sale of PCs priced at $1,000 or less. The low-end market exploded in 1997, and Grove positioned Intel to respond by making less expensive chips. "For us to walk away from a market whose size is going to be measured in tens of millions of units per year, maybe bigger, is inconceivable," Grove told Andy Reinhardt for *BusinessWeek* (December 22, 1997). While the cheaper chips threatened to affect Intel's huge profit margin, the company made up for the lower profits on individual sales by creating a higher volume of sales. In addition, Intel continued to produce high-speed processors—namely, the 450-megahertz to 1.33 gigahertz Pentium IIIs, and 1.40- to 2.80-gigahertz Pentium 4s, released in 2001. For the high-end server market, in 2000 Intel released the powerful 64-bit Itanium processor, which was intended to perform such tasks as hosting massive databases and high-volume processing, and the second-generation Itanium2 chip in 2001.

Throughout the late 1990s, Intel continued to show dramatic growth, with net revenues climbing from $26.3 billion in 1998 to $33.7 billion in 2000. This tremendous expansion was due in part to another shift in Intel's corporate focus, into the field of communications. While the company maintained its strong position in the microprocessing market, it also began branching out into other technologies, particularly those involving networking and Internet computing. Grove described the company's diversification to Bill Holstein for *U.S. News & World Report* (May 22, 2000), "For 15 years, the PC was the environment in which our products were used. Today, there is network computing and Internet computing. PCs are the dominant access device to this world of networked computing. But they are no longer as dominant as when they were a stand-alone tool. What is dominant today is a much broader configuration of factors that [are part of] a coherent network. We have to change along with the environment."

In the last several years, Intel has acquired a number of smaller communications businesses and has launched small start-up divisions within its own company. In addition they have released numerous chip technologies outside of the Pentium and Celeron microprocessors, many of which are designed for hand-held Internet devices. Of the long-term impact of this corporate shift, Grove told Holstein it may take up to five years for the company to determine its success in the new markets. "I can't look you in the eye and tell you we are mov-

ing at just the right speed, because how do I know?" In fact, as Intel expanded into different areas of business in 2000 and 2001, the company did experience setbacks in its core microprocessing business, including product shortages, delays, and other quality deficiencies. These setbacks, combined with lower volume sales and a technology recession, resulted in a sharp decline in the company's 2001 net revenues, which totaled over $26.5 billion.

In late 1994 Grove was diagnosed with prostate cancer. Faced with conflicting opinions about treatments from doctors, he decided to research the subject himself. He ultimately decided on undergoing a new procedure involving high-dose radiation, and the disease appears to be in remission. His health was not a factor in his decision, announced in March 1998, to step aside as Intel's president and CEO. Referring to Craig Barrett, who succeeded him in those positions, he told Lou Dobbs for *CNNfn.com* (March 26, 1998), "I am ready and Craig is ready. I have been CEO for 11 years. Intel has been around 30 years. I'm the third CEO, so I've had more than my average share of tenure."

Nevertheless, Grove has continued to play an active role in directing the future of Intel. While he no longer participates in many big-issue management decisions, Grove has remained involved in strategic discussions—particularly regarding the company's expansion into communications—offering his own ideas on issues and providing support for Barrett's decisions. As chairman of the board, Grove oversees corporate governance and has given the board more authority than his predecessor, Gordon Moore. Because of his stature in the industry as what John Heilemann for *Wired* (on-line, June 2001) called "Silicon Valley's elder statesman," Grove has had the opportunity to wield his influence nationally, speaking to Congress and to the news media on various topics affecting the technologies industry. In June 2002 he joined the Conference Board's Blue-Ribbon Commission on Public Trust and Private Enterprise, a 12-member panel dedicated to examining the ethical practices and governance issues confronting many American corporations, particularly following the recent rash of corporate scandals.

Throughout his career Grove has been the recipient of numerous honors and awards, including the Institute of Electrical and Electronic Engineers (IEEE) Engineering Leadership Recognition Award (1987), the American Engineering Association Medal of Achievement(1993), the Technology Leader of the Year award from *Industry Week* (1997), the CEO of the Year award from *CEO* magazine, and the IEEE Medal of Honor (2000). In 1998 he was named Distinguished Executive of the Year by the Academy of Management and was honored with the Lifetime Achievement Award from the Strategic Management Society in 2001. Grove is a fellow of the IEEE and a member of the National Academy of Engineering.

Grove enjoys skiing, biking, and sailing during his leisure time. He and his wife, Eva, are the parents of two grown daughters. He is a regular lecturer at Stanford University, in Stanford, California. One of his students told Ramo that attending Grove's seminars is "like learning from God." In *Swimming Across: A Memoir* (2001), he offers a rare reflection on his early life in Budapest and his escape to the United States.

In reflecting on his legacy—both at Intel and beyond—Grove recently told Heilemann: "I've had a fantastic life. . . . I was one of the world's experts in a field that was a cornerstone of the industry—I mean, how lucky can you get? And it's gone like that ever since. . . . I feel very fortunate to have had those opportunities and very satisfied with what I made of them. But I'm also very mindful that had I made a different choice—had I gone to a dif-

ferent university, or decided to work back east instead of here in the west, or if my timing had been off by just two years—the same me would not have accomplished nearly so much. Oh, I would have had a good career. But I did have certain lucky breaks in terms of timing that was not my merit." —K. D.

Suggested Reading: *BusinessWeek* p68+ Mar. 16, 1987, with photo, p88+ Apr. 29, 1991, with photo, p86+ June 1, 1992, with photo, p60+ Jan. 16, 1995, with photos, p70+ Dec. 22, 1997, with photos; *Financial World* p42+ Dec. 11, 1990, with photos; *Fortune* p88+ July 10, 1995, with photos, p168+ Oct. 15, 2001; *Time* p54+ Dec. 29, 1997–Jan. 5, 1998, with photos; *Wired* (on-line) June 2001; Jackson, Tim. *Inside Intel: Andy Grove and the Rise of the World's Most Powerful Chip Company*, 1997

Thomas D. McAvoy/Getty Images

Groves, Leslie R.

Aug. 17, 1896–July 13, 1970 Director of the Manhattan Project

Brigadier General Leslie R. Groves was the head of the Manhattan Project, the top-secret division of the U. S. War Department that directed the production of the atomic bomb. Groves, a shrewd, forceful, army engineer, took control of the project in September 1942, at the age of 45, and steered it to its successful—if horrific—conclusion on August 6, 1945, when the first atomic bomb was dropped on Japan. As the military head of the project, Groves was in charge of teams of prestigious scien-

tists at Columbia University, in New York City; the University of Chicago, in Illinois; and the University of California, Berkeley; as well as an armada of engineers: at its height the project employed nearly 125,000 personnel. Groves faced overwhelming obstacles: the complications of obtaining sufficient amounts of purified uranium and plutonium; the difficult logistics of maintaining fiercely tight wartime security standards; and the coordination of the parallel efforts of various labs and research centers located across the United States. Yet he succeeded in orchestrating the project with remarkable speed and control.

The son of Leslie Richard and Gwen (Griffith) Groves, Leslie Richard Groves was born on August 17, 1896, in the manse of the First Presbyterian Church in Albany, New York, where his father was a minister. While Leslie was still an infant, the Reverend Groves became an army chaplain, and consequently for a time the family lived at army posts across the country. At age 17 the young Groves entered the University of Washington, in Seattle, but after a year he transferred to the Massachusetts Institute of Technology (MIT), in Cambridge, where he studied engineering for two years. At the end of this time he received an appointment to the United States Military Academy, at West Point. Groves played second-string center on the football team, and in 1918 he graduated fourth in his class and was commissioned as a second lieutenant in the U. S. Army Corps of Engineers.

The 22-year-old lieutenant was first sent to the Engineer School at Camp A. A. Humphreys (now Fort Belvoir), Virginia. In June 1919 he was sent to France with the American Expeditionary Force for an observation tour; in September he returned to the Engineer School as a student officer. The following June he left the school again, this time to serve as the commander of a company in the Seventh Engineers. He recommenced his studies in February 1921, and in July he graduated, having completed both the basic and the civil engineering courses.

Over the next decade, Groves had several, successive appointments: he was stationed in San Francisco, California, with various engineering groups; he completed a tour of duty in Hawaii, with the Third Engineers; and he took assignments in Texas, Delaware, and Vermont. He was sent to Nicaragua for survey work on the proposed Nicaraguan interoceanic canal; Groves commanded a company from his regiment, and for his services he was awarded the Nicaraguan Medal of Merit.

Lieutenant Groves returned to the United States in 1931 and was assigned to the Office of the Chief of Engineers, in Washington, D.C. He was promoted to captain in October 1934. A year later he left Washington for Kansas to attend the Command and General Staff School at Fort Leavenworth, from which he graduated in June 1936. He then attended the Army War College, in Washington, D.C. After his graduation, in 1939, Groves remained in Washington for service in the Operations and Training Division of the War Department General Staff. In July 1940 he was promoted to major, and the following November he was raised to temporary colonel and made a special assistant to the quartermaster general. Groves was then assigned to the Office of the Chief of Engineers, where he assisted in the supervision of all military construction in the United States—work that cost $600 million dollars a month. During that time Groves supervised the construction of the huge Pentagon building across the Potomac River from Washington.

Groves' biggest assignment came in September 1942, when he was made head of what was known for purposes of secrecy as the Manhattan Engineer District, now called the Manhattan Project. For years such world-renowned scientists as Niels Bohr, Sir James Chadwick, Enrico Fermi, and E. O. Lawrence had been working on the problem of releasing the tremendous forces locked within the atom. Just before World War II began, the research in the field of atom fission was given immediate impetus by Lise Meitner, a scientist in Germany who discovered that a previously inexplicable phenomenon was actually an explosion of the atoms of metal uranium (a lustrous white metal that comes from the minerals pitchblende or carnotite). Meitner left Germany for neutral Sweden and there released the news of her astounding discovery. Both Allied and Nazi scientists realized to what ends this information would lead—and the race was on to turn atomic forces into a weapon of war.

Late in 1939, President Franklin D. Roosevelt appointed a commission to investigate the possible use of atomic energy for military purposes. Until then only small-scale research with navy funds had taken place. In two years' time the project was put under the direction of a group of eminent American scientists headed by Vannevar Bush and was turned over to a general policy group that included Henry A. Wallace, James B. Conant of Harvard, and Henry L. Stimson. British-American cooperation on the project was formally begun in October 1941. The following June it was decided to expand the work under the direction of the War Department; shortly thereafter Groves was called in to take charge.

"On the day I learned that I was to direct the project which ultimately produced the atomic bomb, I was probably the angriest officer in the United States Army," Groves later wrote, as quoted by Richard Rhodes in *The Making of the Atomic Bomb* (1988). "I was then a colonel in the Army Engineers, with most of the headaches of directing ten billion dollars' worth of military construction in the country behind me—for good, I hoped. I wanted to get out of Washington, and quickly." It was not to be, however. Groves' top superior, General Brehon B. Somervell, informed him that he could forget his ideas about duty overseas; he had been selected for a new and very important assignment. "Men like to recall, in later years, what they said at some important or possibly historic moment in their lives," Groves later wrote, as quoted by Rhodes. "I remember only too well what I said to General Somervell that day. I said, 'Oh.'"

Groves knew that the project he was to head was beset by a dismally low budget and littered with organizational obstacles. He had just completed the construction of the Pentagon; the budget for the Manhattan Project, by comparison, amounted to less than he had been spending in a week. Upon his briefing Groves learned that he was to be temporarily promoted to brigadier general; he also learned, however, that the state of the project was worse than he had feared.

By the time his promotion was made official, Groves had already solved some of the key problems facing the administration of the project, the first being the challenge of obtaining sufficient amounts of uranium ore. He arranged for the purchase of 1,250 tons of rich pitchblende—a chief source of uranium that, it had recently been discovered, was being stored in the open in 2,000 steel drums on New York City's Staten Island. He also succeeded in raising the priority status of the Manhattan Engineer District—a difficult task because the project was classed as experimental and could not compete with the army's more urgent needs. He acquired a 52,000-acre stretch of land in eastern Tennessee called Site X, the future location of the Clinton Laboratory at Oak Ridge. Rhodes quoted one of Groves' subordinates, Lieutenant Colonel Kenneth D. Nichols, as saying that Groves proved himself to be "one of the most capable individuals. . . . He had an ego second to none, he had tireless energy—he was a big man, a heavy man but he never seemed to tire. He had absolute confidence in his decisions and he was absolutely ruthless in how he approached a problem to get it done. But that was the beauty of working for him—that you never had to worry about the decisions being made or what it meant."

Groves was determined to ramp up the speed of the project. On October 5, 1942 he visited the Metallurgical Laboratory (Met Lab) at the University of Chicago, in Illinois, where a group of chemists was devising a method to extract plutonium from irradiated uranium. The technicians had been bogged down in a debate over cooling systems for months; Groves demanded a decision on the cooling system in one week's time. Groves left Chicago convinced that the plutonium process would ultimately be successful in producing a bomb, and history would prove him correct.

Groves was also instrumental in recruiting the theoretical physicist J. Robert Oppenheimer to be the director of a new top-secret lab—then still in the planning stages—where the bomb itself would be designed. Oppenheimer was in some ways an unlikely candidate. He had no experience directing a large group of people. He was a theoretician, but the lab he was to head would be focused on experimental and engineering concerns. The other project leaders were all Nobel Prize winners, and tended to look down on Oppenheimer, who was not. Perhaps the largest mark against him was that his former fiancée, wife, brother, and sister-in-law had all been former members of the Communist Party. Groves, however, had taken a liking to the gaunt, chain-smoking scientist, who could be at turns antagonistic and charming; through Groves' persistence, Oppenheimer was given the position.

Groves and Oppenheimer immediately set about choosing a location for the new lab. In November 1942 they settled on a remote desert plateau—Los Alamos, New Mexico. Construction soon began on the new desert community, which would eventually house more than 2,500 personnel. Oppenheimer succeeded in luring to Los Alamos a coterie of notable scientists that included four Nobel laureates and numerous European émigrés. This was all done under the strictest secrecy. Only those directly involved were informed of the project's mission; even Groves' wife had no idea of what her husband was doing. The obstacles facing Groves and Oppenheimer were daunting. In 1942 there was not yet enough uranium-235 (U-235) in existence to make a bomb. U-235 could be made only through an expensive, difficult, and time-consuming process of purifying natural uranium (U-238). It would be two years before enough U-235 was available; until then, Oppenheimer's team had to depend upon mathematics and their imaginations. In December 1942 physicists at the Met Lab under the direction of the Italian-born physicist Enrico Fermi achieved the world's first controlled fission chain-reaction. In doing so Fermi discovered that plutonium reacted much faster than uranium. Groves then ordered the construction of three huge plutonium-producing reactors in Hanford, Washington. (The U.S. government would spend decades attempting to mitigate the damage of 40 years of radioactive contamination released into the environment from this plant, as well as the detrimental health effects to people living nearby.)

In May 1945 Germany surrendered. The bomb preparations, however, proceeded as planned. Project Trinity—the code name for the top-secret test of the atomic bomb—came to fruition on July 16, 1945. The scientists at Los Alamos had succeeded in developing two bombs. One, nicknamed Little Boy, utilized U-235. It could not be given a full-scale test—there was only enough U-235 for the one bomb already made. The other bomb, Fat Man, used plutonium. Thanks to Groves' stewardship, enough plutonium had been produced to test one bomb and to produce another by August 1945.

Fat Man was successfully detonated atop a 100-foot-high steel tower in an isolated desert near the Los Alamos lab. "The first full-scale test was made of the implosion-type, atomic fission bomb," Groves wrote in his official report, as quoted by Martin Walker in the London *Guardian* (May 1, 1995). "For the first time in history there was a nuclear explosion. And what an explosion!" The explosion, Groves wrote, "far exceeded the most optimistic expectations and wildest hopes of the scientists." The report took five days to reach Potsdam, Germany, where President Harry S. Truman was meeting with British Prime Minister Winston Churchill and Soviet Premier Joseph Stalin to devise a surrender ultimatum for Japan. President Truman—hoping to secure the assistance of Russia in the ongoing war with Japan—noted in his diary, as quoted by Walker, that he "casually mentioned to Stalin that we had a new weapon of unusually destructive force."

According to the War Department release, those few who witnessed the monumental results of Project Trinity felt that they "had been present at the birth of a new age—the Age of Atomic Energy." They recognized as well their "profound responsibility to help in guiding into right channels the tremendous forces which had been unlocked for the first time in history." Several of the scientists involved argued strongly for a demonstrative rather than a military use of the bomb. Groves disagreed, however, and advised President Truman to proceed with plans to use the bomb on Japan. On August 6, 1945, an American B-29 dropped the first bomb—Little Boy—on Hiroshima, Japan, killing more than 92,000 people. The next day President Truman broke the news of the bombing to the American public, which thereby learned for the first time of the dreadful new weapon. A second bomb, this time made of plutonium, was dropped on Nagasaki, Japan, on August 9, claiming 40,000 lives. On August 14, Japan surrendered unconditionally.

A *New York Times* editorial, published on August 7, the day after Truman's announcement, commented that "a revolution in science and a revolution in warfare have occurred on the same day. . . . Civilization and humanity can now survive only if there is a revolution in mankind's political thinking." In the aftermath of the war, the subject of the development, use, and control of atomic energy was widely discussed by the public, press, scientists, the military, and national legislators. In October 1945 the Senate Committee on Atomic Energy was established. Groves appeared before the senate committee to state his belief that "this weapon must be kept under the control of the United States until all of the other nations of the world are as anxious for peace as we are."

In October Groves was promoted to brigadier general (permanent) and nominated as assistant to the army chief of engineers. He continued to serve as chief of the army's Special Weapons Project until 1947, when atomic energy affairs were turned over to the newly created civilian Atomic Energy Commission. He was promoted to lieutenant general (temporary) in January 1948. Groves retired from active duty a month later and became a vice president of the Sperry Rand Corporation, one of the prominent think tanks of the Cold War era, where he worked until 1961. He wrote a book about his experiences, *Now It Can Be Told: The Story of the Manhattan Project*, first published in 1962.

The War Department commended Groves for his performance in developing the bomb in such a short time, and for his organization of an airtight security system. Groves expressed his appreciation for the cooperation he received from scientists and technicians, contractors and industrialists, the American Federation of Labor, and the Congress of Industrial Organizations—members of which, he said, "in many cases buried jurisdictional difficulties of long standing so that work might be completed on schedule." Groves stated that some of the usual engineering procedures had to be abandoned in the course of production, but that progress was made "through determination and the willingness to take a chance." He received a Distinguished Service Medal for an achievement of "unfathomable importance to the future of the world." Groves died of heart disease, in Washington, D.C., on July 13, 1970 and was buried in the Arlington National Cemetery. His wife, Grace Hulbert (Wilson) Groves, whom he married on February 10, 1922, is buried with him.—A. I. C.

Suggested Reading: *Antioch Review* p482+ Fall 1995; *Bulletin of the Atomic Scientists* p32+ Dec. 1992; *Christian Science Monitor* p9 July 10, 1995; *Detroit News* A p11 July 9, 1995; (London) *Guardian* p20 Apr. 19, 1995, p10 May 1, 1995; *New York Herald Tribune* p6 Aug. 7, 1945, p9 Aug. 7, 1945; Cortada, James W. *Historical Dictionary of Data Processing: Biographies*, 1987; Kurzman, Dan. *Day of the Bomb; Countdown to Hiroshima*, 1986; Lawren, William. *The General and the Bomb*, 1988; Rhodes, Richard. *The Making of the Atomic Bomb*, 1986

Gutenberg, Johannes

1398(?)–Feb. 3, 1468(?) Inventor of the first moveable-type printing press

More than any other single event, the invention of the moveable-type printing press by Johannes Gutenberg in the mid-15th century can be said to be the origin of the Information Age. Gutenberg advanced existing technologies and combined them to make a printing press that, for the first time in European history, allowed for the mass reproduction of the written word. The printing press facilitated the spread of information throughout all levels of society, creating an explosion of knowledge and ideas that made the Renaissance possible and that served as the only basis for the large-scale transmission of information until the electronic age. Gutenberg's printing press was so functional one could argue that no significant changes in the technology were made until the 19th century.

The little that is known about Gutenberg's life comes primarily from documents of financial transactions. Johann Gensfleisch Zur Laden Zum Gutenberg was likely born in Mainz, Germany, between 1394 and 1399, the son of well-to-do parents of the patrician class. Gutenberg's knowledge of Latin, as evidenced by some of his later work, suggests that he may have attended university. He was trained in metalworking and served an apprenticeship as a goldsmith while living in Mainz. Around

Hulton Archive by Getty Images

1430 a struggle broke out between the patricians and the professional guilds in Mainz, and Gutenberg was forced to leave the city for Strassburg, which is now Strasbourg, France.

In Strassburg Gutenberg worked as a gem cutter and a teacher of crafts. He was also engaged in experiments, which he kept secret from his fellows, though he had borrowed money from several parties to finance the work. In 1438 several of the financiers, including Andreas Dritzehn, insisted that they be included in Gutenberg's project, and a five-year contract was drawn up. Though a clause had been inserted into the contract prohibiting the heirs of the men from assuming their roles in the company in the event of death, Dritzehn's heirs attempted to do just that when he died, later in 1438. Though Dritzehn's heirs lost the suit, it was revealed during the proceedings that Gutenberg had begun work on a printing press and that he had borrowed money from a carpenter named Conrad Saspach to perfect his press and bought substantial quantities of printing materials from a merchant named Hans Dünne, in 1436. Gutenberg's secret was now officially revealed.

It is unclear how Gutenberg occupied himself in the decade or so following the trial. In 1448 he returned to Mainz to borrow money from a relative. In 1450 he convinced Johann Fust to invest the significant sum of 800 guilders in his printing press. Two years later, Fust contributed another 800 guilders in order to become a partner in the printing enterprise. In 1455 Fust sued Gutenberg for lack of return on his investment, and the courts ordered Gutenberg to pay back the sum total of the two loans, plus interest. In November 1455 Gutenberg's printing offices and equipment were taken over by Fust and his son-in-law, Peter Schöffer, who had been Gutenberg's assistant during the years of the collaboration with Fust.

It is generally agreed that the printing of what is now known as the Gutenberg Bible, which contained two 42-line columns per page, was completed shortly before the trial of 1455. As such, it was the first time moveable type was used to print a manuscript in Europe. Moveable type consists of separate blocks of characters (the letters of the Latin alphabet, in Gutenberg's case) that can be arranged and rearranged to create passages of text that can be covered in ink to make repeated impressions on paper. In the 11th century, Pi Sheng, a Chinese blacksmith and alchemist, had made clay copies of Chinese characters that could be arranged on an iron plate and clamped in place—the first known use of moveable type. However, because there were approximately 50,000 Chinese characters, the systematization of printing proved too great a task, and printing did not become a widespread phenomenon in China at that time. Gutenberg probably knew nothing of Pi Sheng's work in China when he developed his own method of using moveable type.

Copies of manuscripts in Europe at the time were usually made by scribes, who copied the text by hand. Wood carvings of full pages of text were sometimes used to stamp multiple copies, though each page of text needed its own separate and elaborate carving, which made the process very expensive. Gutenberg's printing press featured four important innovations. First, he made copper molds that had the shapes of each letter stamped into them. The molds assured that the moveable metal letters would be of a precise size and shape and that new letters could be made quickly. Second, he developed a new metal alloy that melted at low temperatures and could be poured into the molds to make the moveable letters. Third, he made a new type of oil-based ink that resisted smudging and transferred crisp impressions from metal to paper. Finally, he built a press, based on the designs of wine and paper presses, that firmly applied the ink-covered metal letters to the paper. Though forms of these separate technologies already existed in Europe, they had never been combined in such a way as to make a moveable type printing press.

Gutenberg's technologies spread rapidly throughout Europe. According to some estimates, more books were produced in the 50 years following his invention than in the 1,000 years before it. The printing press helped disseminate knowledge to all levels of society. The classical works of the Greeks and the Romans that so greatly influenced the Renaissance would never have been as widely studied without the printing press. In *Lives and Legacies: Scientists, Mathematicians, and Inventors* (1999) it is noted that "Some scholars suggest that the Renaissance would have been stillborn without the invention of movable-type printing." Because the printing press drove down costs, members of the lower classes were now able to afford books, and consequently literacy and education spread. As Paul Gray wrote for *Time* (December 31, 1999), "Established hierarchies began to crumble. Books were the world's first mass-produced items. But most important of all, printing proved to be the greatest extension of human consciousness ever created." In the 16th century, when Martin Luther brought about the Protestant Reformation, which changed the face of Christianity and the intellectual climate of Europe, he propagated his ideas through numerous pamphlets produced on a printing press. The fact that Christian texts were for the first time made directly available to a larger sector of the populace created an environment ripe for the Reformation.

It is uncertain whether Gutenberg ever set up his own printing press after his equipment was seized by Fust. In 1457 a Psalter, or book of psalms, was completed that bore the names of Fust and Peter Schöffer. It is hypothesized that they would not have been able to complete the magnificent work, decorated with ornate, two-color letters and fine scroll borders, without the help of Gutenberg. Thus, the Psalter is often considered among Gutenberg's works. Others works attributed to Gutenberg include a Türkenkalender, a warning against the danger of a Turkish invasion after the fall of Constantinople, in 1453, printed in 1454; some letters of indulgence (purchased from the Church by devout Catholics to atone for their sins); some school grammars; and, in 1460, the *Catholicon*, a vast encyclopedia of more than 700 pages. In 1465 Gutenberg was given a pension of grain, wine, clothing, and a tax exemption by the archbishop of Mainz. The likely date of his death is February 3, 1468.—P. G. H.

Suggested Reading: *Economist* (on-line) Dec. 31, 1999; *Life* p132+ Fall 1997; *New York Times Magazine* p142+ Apr. 18, 1999; *Time* p158+ Dec. 31, 1999; Porter, Roy. ed. *Hutchinson Dictionary of Scientific Biography*, 1994; Simonis, Doris ed. *Lives and Legacies: Scientists, Mathematicians, and Inventors*, 1999

Hall, Robert

Dec. 25, 1919– Inventor of the semiconductor injection laser

During a long professional career in the research and development department of General Electric (GE), Robert Hall enjoyed several notable achievements, including his invention of an electron tube that is used today to operate microwave ovens. In 1962 he made one of his most important contributions to the Information Age when he invented the first semiconductor laser. Semiconductor lasers based on Hall's design are currently used in all CD players and CD-ROM units, all laser printers, some television remote controls, and most fiber-optic communications systems.

Robert Noel Hall was born on December 25, 1919 in New Haven, Connecticut, to Harry and Clara (Kommers) Hall. After earning a B.S. in physics in 1942 from the California Institute of Technology (Caltech), in Pasadena, he accepted a position with GE at the company's Research and Development Center, in Schenectady, New York. In that capacity, during World War II he designed systems that used continuous-wave magnetrons to jam enemy radar. (A magnetron is a type of electron tube that creates electromagnetic waves.) These magnetrons were later reengineered to be used in microwave ovens.

In 1946 Hall reenrolled at Caltech to study nuclear physics, and he earned a Ph.D. in 1948. He then returned to GE's lab in Schenectady, where he joined a team working on transistors, which had recently been invented at Bell Telephone Laboratories. A transistor is an electronic device used to control the flow of electricity. Composed of semiconductor materials, transistors are smaller and more efficient than vacuum tubes, which had previously been the primary means of building electrical circuits. (Semiconductors are materials, such as germanium and silicon, that conduct electricity with intermediary capability—not as well as conductors like copper and aluminum, but better than insulators like glass and rubber. The term is also used for electronic devices made from semiconductor materials.) Hall began working with germanium, a gray-white metalloid element that in the 1950s was the preferred choice for use in transistors. He developed a purification process that produced crystallized ingots of the purest germanium yet developed.

According to Hall's article "Early Transistor History at General Electric," which is available on the Classic Germanium Transistor Museum Web site, he made a "chance observation" while measuring the electrical properties of this germanium that led him to a discovery of alloyed "P-N junction" diodes. (A diode is a material that transmits an electrical current in one direction, but prevents the flow of current in the opposite direction.) The P-N junction diode is a result of adding impurities, in a process called doping, to semiconductor materials. Depending upon the type of impurities added, two electrically diverse types of semiconductor can be created—one that is rich in electrons (called N-type, for *negative*, because electrons have a negative charge) and one that is poor in electrons (called P-type, for *positive*). When these two types are placed in close contact, they form a P-N junction.

Hall's observation of the P-N junction diode led to the concept of a P-I-N rectifier. A rectifier converts alternating current (AC) into direct current (DC). Although in later developments the germanium in Hall's rectifier was replaced with silicon, his insight led to the creation of solid-state "thryistors," which are still used as rectifiers today in electric locomotives, high-voltage DC electrical transmission, and other applications.

The term *laser* was originally an acronym for Light Amplification by Stimulated Emission of Radiation. The first working laser, invented in 1960 by Theodore Maiman, was made using synthetic ruby. Other types of lasers had followed soon afterwards, including a uranium laser developed at International Business Machines (IBM) and a helium-neon laser created at Bell Laboratories. In 1962 Hall heard reports of intense, highly efficient infrared emission from gallium arsenide junctions, which led him to speculate that a semiconductor laser might be possible. Using a P-N junction semiconductor in gallium arsenide, Hall created a laser that produced coherent light in a highly efficient manner from a very compact source. Meanwhile, simultaneous developments of gallium-arsenide semiconductor lasers were taking place at IBM and at the Massachusetts Institute of Technology's Lincoln Lab. Hall explained in his on-line article that the courts acknowledge only one inventor, and patent officials deemed Hall to be first. His laser was patented in 1967.

During the 1970s Hall worked on various energy-related issues at GE, primarily solar cells and photovoltaics, the study of which relates to the voltage generated when radiant energy falls on the boundary between dissimilar substances—such as two different semiconductors. He eventually resumed working with germanium, which he has been credited with singlehandedly making "the cleanest material on earth," according to a profile for the "Inventor of the Week" section of the Lemelson-MIT Program Web site (December 1999). The substance thus became suitable, according to the site, "for use in electron-hole droplet experiments and in high-quality energy spectrometers for nuclear particle detectors."

Hall retired from GE in 1987, having earned 43 U.S. patents. He is the recipient of several honors and awards for his contributions to science, including the Institute of Electrical and Electronic Engineers (IEEE) David Sarnoff Award in 1963, the IEEE Jack A. Morton Award in 1976, and the Electrochemical Society Solid State Science and Technology Award in 1977. In 1989 he was awarded a fellowship from the Guglielmo Marconi International Fellowship Foundation, and in 1994 he was inducted into the National Inventors Hall of Fame, in Akron, Ohio. Since retiring he has worked as a consultant in various areas of semiconductor technology. He has also been involved in several educational and community activities, including tutoring the learning disabled and repairing tape recorders for the Library of Congress Talking Books Program.

Hall married Dora Siechert on August 2, 1941. They have two grown children, Richard and Elaine.—A. I. C.

Suggested Reading: Classic Germanium Transistor Museum Web site; Lemelson-MIT Program Web site

Hamming, Richard

Feb. 11, 1915–Jan. 7, 1998 Creator of Hamming codes

Early computers had a major flaw: they stopped working if there was a single error in any of their calculations or programming. Scientists and mathematicians spent many hours trying to find the error, correct it, and then reprogram the computer. While the problem was being fixed, important work that required a computer was often delayed. As a young mathematician working for Bell Telephone Laboratories, in New Jersey, Richard Hamming got tired of fixing the company's computers every time they broke down, and so he developed a program instructing computers to detect and correct their own errors. His innovation, which became known as Hamming Codes, made possible such technological breakthroughs as modems and communication satellites.

Richard Wesley Hamming was born on February 11, 1915 in Chicago, Illinois. He became interested in mathematics during his freshman year in high school. "I was a better mathematician than the teacher," Hamming boasted to Tekla S. Perry in an interview for the *IEEE Spectrum* (May 1993), published by the Institute of Electrical and Electronic Engineers. Hamming expected to study engineering in college, but his ambitions were derailed when the only scholarship he was offered came from the University of Chicago, which did not have an engineering department. As an undergraduate at the University of Chicago, Hamming majored in mathematics, receiving his B.S. in 1937. After his graduation Hamming continued his studies in mathematics. He received his M.A. from the University of Nebraska, in 1939, and his Ph.D. from the University of Illinois, in Urbana-Champaign, in 1942.

Hamming intended to pursue a teaching career. He joined the faculty of the University of Illinois, in 1942, and then began teaching at the University of Louisville, in Kentucky, in 1944. In 1945 a friend invited him to work on a top-secret project for the government in Los Alamos, New Mexico. He accepted the offer, believing that he was needed for the war effort. In Los Alamos, a team of scientists was working on the Manhattan Project, devoted to the development of the atomic bomb. Hamming was placed in charge of maintaining the large IBM computers that the scientists were using for their calculations. Although he had no experience working with computers, Hamming proved to be a quick learner at what he later described as being a "computer janitor."

During his time in Los Alamos, Hamming closely observed the renowned scientists who worked on the atomic bomb, including Edward Teller, Enrico Fermi, and J. Robert Oppenheimer. In a 1986 lecture at the Bell Communications Research Colloquium, as posted on the Digital Signal Processing Group's Home Page at Rice University, Hamming said, "I saw that although physically I was the same, they were different. And to put the thing bluntly, I was envious. I wanted to know why they were so different from me. . . . I became very interested in the difference between those who do and those who might have done." In order to become an truly great scientist, Hamming concluded, he would have to work on important problems.

During the months that followed the end of World War II, Hamming pondered the implications of the effort that produced the atomic bomb. He remained at Los Alamos for six months after the war's end, until most of the other scientists had left. "I wanted to figure out what had happened there, and why it had happened that way," he explained to Perry. Hamming recognized that computers would dramatically change the profession of science. As Perry put it, "Experiments were going to be possible with computers that were impossible in the laboratory." Hamming considered why scientists—rather than engineers—had designed the atomic bomb. He concluded that engineering schools at the time were not preparing students to work with the latest technological advances. "As an engineer," he told Perry, "I would have been the guy going down manholes instead of having the excitement of frontier research work." He concluded that he was fortunate to have studied mathematics instead of engineering.

In 1946 Hamming accepted a job with Bell Telephone Laboratories (Bell Labs), in New Jersey. He bonded with other young mathematicians at the company, in particular Claude E. Shannon, Donald P. Ling, and Brockway McMillan. The four men, who called themselves The Young Turks, were about the same age—30—and shared the experience of having been introduced to scientific research during World War II. They were also ambitious and determined to achieve. Their attitude, however, was not always appreciated by the Bell Labs management. "We were first-class troublemakers," Hamming recalled during his interview with Perry. "We did unconventional things in unconventional ways and still got valuable results. Thus management had to tolerate us and let us alone a lot of the time."

In 1947, in only his second year with Bell Labs, Hamming made his most famous contribution to computer science. Although he was hired to work on elasticity theory, because of his previous experience with computer maintenance Hamming was frequently asked to fix the company's computers when they stopped working due to an error in calculations. Samuel P. Morgan, who eulogized Hamming in the *Notices of the AMS* (September 1998), published by the American Mathematical Society, explained, "Data in digital systems are typically stored, transmitted, and processed in binary form as blocks of bits. If a single bit is in error, the message is garbled or the computation spoiled. In large-scale computers or telephone switching systems, an enormous number of computations must be performed without a single error in the end result." At the time, locating a single error in a calculation and then reprogramming the computer took many hours. Hamming hypothesized that, since computers could detect an error, they should be able to locate it and fix it as well. He devised a mathematical formula that instructed computers to locate and correct any errors, and then keep working. Through this process of parity checking, computers check the calculations for each block of data (or codes). If an error is discovered, then it is automatically replaced by the correct code. Hamming's development of error-detecting and automatic correcting formulas eventually became known as "Hamming Codes." In 1950 he detailed his ideas in a scientific paper published in the *Bell Labs Technical Journal*. Bell Labs used Hamming Codes in their computers and telephone systems. Eventually, Hamming Codes made modems and satellite communications possible, because these technologies require many calculations to function correctly. Hamming Codes freed computer scientists from laborious calculations—as Hamming (quoted by Morgan) said, "The purpose of computing is insight, not numbers."

In subsequent decades computer scientists developed more advanced error-correcting codes. In an interview with *Leaders of the Information Age*, Morgan observed that error- correcting codes "are essential to space travel, because they permit guidance computers to run reliably, and particularly because they permit low-power, low-error rate messaging over noisy deep-space channels."

As part of his work on error-correcting codes, Hamming also developed the "Hamming Distance," which identifies the number of different positions between two codes. For example, the Hamming Distance between the codes 1000 and 1011 is 2, because only two of the digits in each code are different. The Hamming Distance is used to identity and correct errors in data transmission. As Morgan explained to *Leaders of the Information Age*, "If the Hamming Distance to one of the codewords is less than the Hamming distance to each of the other codewords, the receiver replaces the received word by the closest codeword. This doesn't correct all possible errors, but it corrects most errors if the codewords are well separated in Hamming space."

After his breakthrough with error-correcting codes, Hamming received attention for his work at Bell Labs on digital filters, which are used to repair electronic signals and separate signals that have been combined. Hamming designed a new digital filter, the "Hamming Window," which he patented. Unlike previous digital filters, the Hamming Window allowed a user to examine a discreet part of a signal. This became an essential tool for digital engineers.

Hamming described his achievements at Bell Labs as the high points of his life, telling Perry: "The emotion at the point of technical breakthrough is better than wine, women, and song put together."

In later years Bell Labs offered Hamming several opportunities to be a manager at the company, but he always declined. He preferred to focus on his own research instead of being responsible for supervising others. "I knew in a sense that by avoiding management, I was not doing my duty by the organization," he admitted to Perry. "That is one of my biggest failures."

After 30 years working for Bell Labs, Hamming retired, in 1976, in accordance with his belief that scientists do their best work when they are young. In order to escape New Jersey's winters, he and his wife moved to Monterey, California, in 1977. Hamming became an adjunct professor at the Naval Postgraduate School the same year. "There is no school I know of in which the students are better selected and more likely to be worth the trouble," he noted to Perry. Though he had avoided a managerial role at Bell Labs, as a professor, Hamming enjoyed training and guiding young minds."If you don't work on important problems, it's not likely you'll do important work," he often told his students, as quoted by Morgan.

Richard Hamming also wrote nine books on such topics as computers, calculus, probability, coding and information theory, and digital filters. Three editions of his first book, *Numerical Methods for Scientists and Engineers* (1962), were published, and the book is still in print as a paperback. In discussing Hamming's *Digital Filters* (1977), which was also published in three editions, Morgan wrote that most of the literature on such technology is written in technical jargon. By contrast, Hamming avoids jargon and makes the complex mathematical concepts behind digital filters comprehensible to a general audience.

Richard Hamming has been honored with several prestigious awards and prizes. He has received the IEEE's Emmanuel Piore Prize (1949), the Association for Computing Machinery's Turing Prize (1968), the Harold Pender Prize (1981), and the Eduard Rheim Award for Achievement (1996). In 1986 the IEEE honored Hamming's achievements by establishing the Richard W. Hamming Medal; Hamming was the first recipient.

Richard Hamming retired from teaching in 1997. He died on January 7, 1998 of a heart attack.—D. C.

Suggested Reading: *IEEE Spectrum* p80+ May 1993, with photo; *New York Times* I p29 Jan. 11, 1998; *Notices of the AMS* p972+ Summer 1998, with photo

Hartree, Douglas R.

Mar. 27, 1897–Feb. 12, 1958 Campaigner for computer development in Great Britain

Douglas R. Hartree has been called "the father of modern British computing." His influence brought an initially hesitant Great Britain into the world of computers during the pivotal period of the mid-20th century. Spreading news of the spectacular technological advances taking place in the United States, Hartree, a physicist by profession, was a catalyst for the worldwide computer explosion. During visits to the United States in the 1930s, he came into contact with American engineer Vannevar Bush and the differential analyzer, a landmark mechanical computer invented by Bush. The analyzer was just what Hartree needed for making advanced differential calculations, and he managed to build one of his own, convincing his nation to support the construction of similar computers. He was among the first to apply the new technology to complex scientific computing, foreshadowing the supercomputer boom that would begin in the 1960s.

Douglas Rayner Hartree was born in Cambridge, England on March 27, 1897. His father, William Hartree, taught engineering at the University of Cambridge, and during his later years collaborated with his son on much of his research. Hartree's mother, Eva Rayner, was very active in public service and served for a time as mayor of Cambridge. As a child, Hartree attended St. Faith's School in Cambridge.

Staying close to home, Hartree entered Cambridge University in 1915. His studies were interrupted in 1916 by the outbreak of World War I, during which time his emerging mathematical skills were employed in military research. It was during this period that Hartree first became interested in numerical calculation. He joined an antiaircraft experimental group in the Munitions Inventions Department of the Ministry of Munitions. As a member of this group, he carried out ballistics calculations which were used to accurately position and operate anti-aircraft artillery. While working in this position, Hartree was exposed to complex mathematics, the kind that was necessary for working out all the possible variables that had to be considered in the operation of state-of-the-art machinery. After resuming his academic work at the end of the war, he received both his B.A. and M.A. in physics from Cambridge. He completed his Ph.D. in mathematics under R. H. Fowler in 1926. He also earned an M.S. from the University of Manchester.

On August 21, 1923 Hartree married Elaine Charlton; the couple would go on to have two sons (Oliver Penn and John Richard) and one daughter (Nesta Margaret). The year after marrying, he began serving as a research fellow at St. John's College at Cambridge. After three years there, he moved on to Christ's College, where he served in the same capacity for another two years. In 1929 Hartree became a professor of applied mathematics at the University of Manchester.

During the 1920s he began work in the area of differential mathematics, similar to the research he had done during the war. Differential mathematics is a form of calculus which deals with variables that depend on, and or vary with one another; these variables are known as functions. The main focus of differential mathematics is the study of the relationship between these functions and their rate of change.

Coming across logistical problems and complications inherent in solving differential equations, Hartree was interested to learn of the existence of an American device known as the differential analyzer that could aid him in his work. In America on summer holiday from the University of Manchester in 1933, he met the inventor of the analyzer, Vannevar Bush. As an electrical engineer working for the U.S. government, Bush had, in 1925, invented the analyzer, the first of the mechanical analog computers. Analog computers such as the differential analyzer operated with numbers represented by directly measurable quantities such as voltages or rotations. This distinguished them from the later electronic digital computers (including those of today), which represent numbers directly as digits.

After witnessing the analyzer in action and being trained by Bush in its operation, Hartree became instrumental in linking American and British scientists interested in the new technology. His first step was to build a copy of his own, which he accomplished with the help of his young assistant Arthur Porter. He constructed a miniature differential analyzer prototype using children's building supplies at a cost of £20. Hartree's machine worked as well as Bush's original, and Hartree was soon able to demonstrate its uses to the British government. In 1935, he built a full-scale version of the analyzer at the University of Manchester with the financial backing of businessman Sir Robert McDougall. The construction of the machine was performed by Metropolitan-Vickers Electrical Company, with Bush himself serving as a consultant.

Upon completion, scientists at the university were able to use the machine to study self-consistent fields, electrical surges on transmission lines, and radar pulses in the troposphere. With the aid of the device, Hartree succeeded in completing differential calculations. One of the most important and influential aspects of Hartree's work was that he investigated complex physical and engineering situations using computational methods, as opposed to experimentation and or observation. He was one of the first people to make serious mathematical calculations with a computer, thus exploring the potential of the new technology. This change in scientific approach demonstrated how scientists could benefit from the use of computers, encouraged others to develop the necessary technology, and foreshadowed the development of the electronic computer, which would initially be used primarily for such calculations.

Using computer technology, Hartree was able to make his greatest contribution to science, in the field of atomic wave theory. Developing powerful new methods of mathematical analysis, he was able to calculate the wave functions of polyelectronic atoms, which are neutral atoms with more than one electron. His new means of calculation allowed him to successfully apply the special approach he developed in 1928, called the "self-consistent field method." This method postulates that all electrons move in a separate field in relation to other electrons. The wave functions Hartree was able to uncover are of extreme importance to the calculation of macroscopic properties of matter, such as charge. Hartree's work in atomic wave theory encouraged physicists around the world to conduct similar research into other types of atoms. All the while, Hartree continued to work to maintain open lines of communication between English and American scientists.

Hartree switched in 1937 from teaching applied mathematics to theoretical physics. He once again aided in his nation's war effort when, during World War II, he became a member of the science research department of the Ministry of Supply. Much of his work at this time was in such crucial areas as ballistics calculations, atmospheric physics, and hydrodynamics. By this time, the influence of his work with the differential analyzer had begun to be noticeably felt, with four similar devices in existence in Britain by 1939. He helped to increase British technological awareness at the outset of the war, and personally instructed many of the nation's leading computer scientists, including Maurice Wilkes, who would go on to build the first British computer capable of storing programs, the EDSAC.

In 1945 Hartree helped establish the National Physical Laboratory (NPL) at Teddington, Middlesex. Similar to the U.S. National Bureau of Standards, the NPL was run by Sir Charles Darwin, grandson of the nineteenth-century evolutionary biologist, and eventually became a hub of computer technology development. As fully electronic digital computers began to take the place of mechanical analog computers after World War II, machines such as Bush's and Hartree's differential analyzers fell out of use. A desire to keep up with the progress of computer technology led Hartree to get involved with the ENIAC, the first large-scale electronic digital computer. In the summer of 1945, Hartree traveled to the University of Pennsylvania to see the ENIAC and was able to obtain access to information on its operation despite the fact that the ENIAC project was classified by the military.

In 1946 Hartree returned to Cambridge as a professor of mathematical physics, a position he would hold for the remainder of his life. He continued to work towards introducing computer development not only in scientific circles, but in governmental circles as well. Focusing his efforts on improving the effectiveness of computers in science, Hartree was somewhat unsure of the computer's potential as a commercial product: In 1950, he advised the Manchester manufacturer Ferranti not to build computers for commercial sale because he believed that the three electronic computer projects underway in England at the time would suffice to handle all of the nation's calculations.

Between April and July of 1946, Hartree was in the United States participating in the final work being done by John Mauchly and J. Presper Eckert on ENIAC. Several other British scientists also came to the University of Pennsylvania, where the ENIAC was being built; these scientists then returned home and developed machines of their own, such as Teddington's Automatic Computing Engine (ACE), Cambridge's Electronic Delay Storage Automatic Calculator (EDSAC), and the University of Manchester's Automatic Digital Machine (MADM). Just as he had been among the first in England to make use of the analog computer and popularize it among his colleagues in the 1930s, Hartree helped to introduce the digital computer in the United Kingdom in the late 1940s by influencing scientists such as those from Cambridge and

Manchester. By acting as a catalyst between interested parties on both sides of the Atlantic, Hartree once again helped bring the early far-flung world of computer science closer together.

His involvement in the American scientific and academic communities also continued. He was named acting chief of the Institute of Numerical Analysis of the U.S. Bureau of Standards at the University of California in 1948. In England, he lectured extensively on computers, and published many articles on the topic in such periodicals as *Nature*. Through his lectures, Hartree publicized American endeavors in computer technology, and pushed for the United Kingdom to follow the United States into the emerging territory of stored-program machines.

The differential analyzer he built, having been rendered obsolete by electronic technology, was brought from the University of Manchester to the National Physical Laboratory in 1948. In the early 1950s it was moved to the Cranfield Institute of Technology. It was returned to Manchester in 1965, where it was disassembled. The parts were then stored in crates until they were discovered by the Science Museum in 1974, at which time Roy Jordeson, a Manchester laboratory superintendent, was commissioned to reconstruct portions of the machine. The rebuilt portions were put on display in Manchester and London, and some engineers have proposed restoring the entire analyzer to working order.

Hartree authored several books over the course of his career in science. Chief among these is *Calculating Instruments and Machines* (1949). A copy of the book was sent by Hartree to his old friend and colleague Vannevar Bush, with the inscription "In recognition of all I owe to you in this field, in which my interest was first excited by your contributions" (*IEEE Annals of the History of Computing*, October–December 1996). His other works include *Textbook of Anti-Aircraft Gunnery* (1925), *Numerical Analysis* (1952), and *The Calculation of Atomic Structures* (1957). He also translated and revised the book *Atommechanik* by Max Born, which was published in 1927 as *The Mechanics of the Atom*.

Douglas Hartree died on February 12, 1958 in Cambridge. The British computer revolution he initiated led to the work of such pioneers as the aforementioned Wilkes, as well as Alan Turing, Andrew Booth, and Maxwell Newman. He was admired throughout his life for the clarity of his writings and lectures, as well as his tremendous generosity in sharing information with, and giving aid to, scientists throughout the world. By the time of his death, the growth of the computer industry was progressing on a worldwide scale. The work done by such visionaries as Hartree leading up to that era helped make possible the computerized global environment in which we now live.—B. S.

Suggested Reading: *IEEE Annals of the History of Computing* p5+ Oct.–Dec. 1996, with photos; Cortada, James W. *Historical Dictionary of Data Processing*, 1987; Goldstine, Herman. *The Computer from Pascal to von Neumann*, 1972; Shurkin, Joel. *Engines of the Mind*, 1984

Heart, Frank

1930(?)– ARPANET engineer

In 1969 a group of electrical engineers at Bolt, Beranek & Newman (BBN) began work on a historic government-sponsored project that would become the progenitor of today's Internet. The system, known as the ARPANET (Advanced Research Projects Agency Network), marked the first time that computers were linked, via telephone lines, for the purposes of sharing information across long distances. Frank Heart managed the team of BBN engineers who designed and built the computers that made the network possible. These machines, called Interface Message Processors (IMPs), used a newly developed packet-switching technology to transmit information between remote host computers. For his contributions to the ARPANET, Heart is widely hailed as a key innovator whose work helped change the face of communications.

Frank E. Heart was born in about 1930 and attended the Massachusetts Institute of Technology (MIT), in Cambridge, where he earned degrees in electrical engineering. He began his career at MIT's Lincoln Laboratory, which originated in 1951 as a federally funded research center in response to an Air Force request for the development of air-defense systems. When Heart became a laboratory research assistant, in the early 1950s, he worked mainly on a project known as Whirlwind, using the latest digital technologies (including the MIT Whirlwind computer, which had been constructed in the late 1940s) to create more effective radar systems. This project was the forerunner of SAGE (Semi-Automatic Ground Environment), a huge machine that involved a more complex approach to coordinating computers, radar, and telephone lines to produce advancements in radar tracking, air defense, systems reliability, and computer memory. SAGE was one of the first fully interactive real-time systems, capable of collecting data, interpreting it, and delivering output, all within a matter of a few seconds.

Heart remained at Lincoln for 15 years, amassing experience in the construction of computer communications systems. In 1967 Heart joined the research team at Bolt, Beranek & Newman (currently known as BBN Technologies), a private technologies company in Cambridge. By the following year he was supervising a group of BBN engineers who were then bidding on a contract with the Advanced Research Projects Agency (ARPA) of the United States Department of Defense. (ARPA, which later became known as DARPA, had been established in 1958 in response to the Soviet Union's successful launching of Sputnik, the world's first satellite.) ARPA was seeking to develop a system in which computers could serve as communications devices, with information being transferred across a network of linked sites. Though ARPA had concluded that computers were essential for national defense, the impetus for creating such a network was primarily to allow researchers to share information more easily and efficiently (using fewer computers, which were then quite expensive), thus providing general benefits for the military, as well as for the nation. The concept behind this network, which was to be called the ARPANET, originated with J. C. R. Licklider, who was the first head of the computer research program at ARPA, beginning in 1962. Licklider left the agency two years later, but by that time he had convinced others at ARPA, including Ivan Sutherland, Robert Taylor, and Lawrence G. Roberts, of the importance of the project. Many others played an important role in the ARPANET's design and development as well, including Leonard Kleinrock, Thomas Marill, Wes Clark, and Donald Davies, among others.

Roberts, who became the project manager of the ARPANET in late 1966, and was its principle architect, initially conceived of a system linking four sites, or "nodes": the University of California at Los Angeles (UCLA); the Stanford Research Institute, in California; the University of California at Santa Barbara; and the University of Utah, in Salt Lake City. Roberts outlined a one-year contract for the project's completion and sent out a request for proposals to about 140 potential contractors. Two of the largest computer companies at the time, IBM and Control Data Corporation, declined to bid on the project, believing that it had little potential.

Heart's team at BBN, in making their competitive bid, drafted a comprehensive proposal explaining their specific methods for delivering the project. As David C. Walden, one of the software developers who worked on the team, recalled in his preface to *Building the ARPANET: The Unpublished Source Documents of the First Computer Network*, (forthcoming), as posted on his personal Web site: "In retrospect, our approach to bidding on the [request for proposal] was very smart. We had decided to submit a fairly detailed design, including initial hardware designs, a software architecture and fairly detailed initial timing analysis, principles of system operation, and so forth as part of our bid. This level of detail helped us (I suspect) win the procurement. It also left us in a fairly advanced starting position at the beginning of the actual contract. This helped us finish in the specified one year, removed a lot of uncertainty from the beginning of the implementation period (we were sure we could do the design and development on

time), and enabled us to begin the actual development period with what was in effect a second design cycle."

On the merits of its 200-page proposal, BBN was awarded the ARPANET contract. Roberts's plan called for a system that would link computers at the four specified sites using ordinary dial-up telephone lines. Rather than have the host computers connected directly to each other, however, each host computer would be connected to the network via a small special-purpose computer, called an Interface Message Processor (IMP). The idea to use IMPs grew out of discussions that Roberts had with Wes Clark, who saw that it made more sense to establish connections between computers that would all speak the same language, and thus avoid the problems of trying to establish communications between machines that had incompatible operating systems and languages.

In order to transmit information efficiently, the ARPANET would use a routing system known as packet-switching, in which communications are broken down into individual pieces that can be transferred separately—down different directions and different paths, if necessary—and reassembled on the other end. The origins of the packet-switching concept are somewhat contested. Leonard Kleinrock published a paper on digital network communications in 1961 and a book, *Communication Nets*, in 1964, both of which concerned queuing theory, an aspect of packet-switching. Kleinrock's ideas had a significant influence on Roberts. Around the same time, both Donald Davies at the National Physical Laboratory, in Britain, and Paul Baran at the RAND Corporation, in the United States, although working independently, arrived at very similar theories about packet-switching. Roberts learned of these developments in 1967 and incorporated some of their insights into the final design. The term *packet-switching* was adopted from Davies' work.

It was BBN's job to find the best way to implement the packet-switching concept and design the IMPs. As Heart later explained in an interview with Dominic Gates for *PreText Magazine* (March/April 1998, on-line), the packet-switching system was one of the major characteristics distinguishing the ARPANET from all previous communications networks. "To my knowledge," he said, "that had never been [employed] before in any network that was really used by anybody." He continued, "Packet switching was certainly the single largest new idea. But the project developed many, many things that were new. I think a lot of the remote debugging, and remote management of the network, had not been done before in anything like the same way. The development of protocols to use the network hadn't been necessary ever before; so they were certainly new."

For the IMPs, Heart chose to use the Honeywell DDP-516, one of the most powerful minicomputers available (with 12K of memory), as the machine to modify. He told Gates, "It had a number of special interfaces, which BBN people designed and Honeywell built . . . into the machine. BBN at the time didn't have hardware construction capabilities; so it purchased the machine from Honeywell and convinced Honeywell to take our designs for special interfaces and implement them in the machines. That entire process was done in nine months." The IMPs functioned in a way that was similar to what would be called "routers" today. Heart explained to Gates, "Their job was to take messages from hosts, to break those up into pieces to get them to destinations, and to put them back together again." Ultimately, Heart's team, which included Bob Kahn, Severo Ornstein, Dave Walden, Bob Barker, Bernie Cosell, Will Crowther, and other key individuals, did a great deal more than build hardware and design appropriate software for their systems. "The specific contract was to build a four-node network, including those interface message processors, and to permit it to expand beyond that," Heart recalled to Gates. "Indeed our job was to decide what to use, to buy, to modify, to deliver, and to write the software for those machines. We had to [deal] with the phone company. We had to [deal with] all terminal equipment that connected the phone company to the computers. We also had to play a large role in the discussion with the hosts about the software in the host computers. So we really viewed ourselves as the systems engineers for the net. But we had a lot of ancillary responsibilities that were in some ways equally important; that is, if they hadn't been worked on, it wouldn't have run."

In early September 1969—after some last-minute refinements that required Ben Barker, a member of BBN's engineering team, to work 16-hour days adjusting the wiring within the modified Honeywell machine—Heart's team delivered the first IMP to Leonard Kleinrock's lab at UCLA, where it was successfully connected to the host computer, an SDS Sigma 7. The second IMP was delivered in October to the Stanford Research Institute (SRI), where the host computer was Douglas Engelbart's NLS (oN-Line System), an SDS-940 computer running a Genie operating system. On the first attempt to send a message from UCLA to SRI, the system crashed, but the second attempt proved a success.

By December of that year, ARPANET's four sites had been linked and were running efficiently. More computers were quickly added, and by April 1972 there were 23 sites functioning within the ARPANET system, including the Department of Defense, the National Science Foundation, NASA, and the Federal Reserve Board. The International Conference on Computer Communication, held in Washington, D.C., in October 1972, marked the first public demonstration of the network and resulted in even greater exposure for the project. ARPANET grew to connect more than 100 hosts until, in 1983, 45 sites were removed and placed on MILNET, an exclusive military network. ARPANET was eventually retired in the late 1980s, when it

was succeeded by NSFNET, a nation-wide network created by the National Science Foundation (NSF) to link its five regional supercomputing centers, as well as other existing computer networks, the whole of which had begun to be known as the Internet. NSFNET was originally intended to allow the U.S. research community to share information and resources, but in 1991 NSF opened the network to commercial use, and by 1995 NSFNET was officially dissolved and the Internet's network backbone was turned over to large commercial Internet providers (ISPs), such as MCI, Sprint, and UUNET.

Of his contributions to this significant technology and his role in developing the progenitor for the Internet, Heart told Gates, "I think it's quite amazing. There's probably nobody who was involved in the early '70s who had any clue what [ARPANET] would become. A number of people, including myself, knew it was moderately important. We knew we were doing something that was going to have an impact, certainly in science. But I don't think there was a single soul who was able to predict this explosion that took place."

Heart remained manager of the BBN team extending and refining ARPANET throughout the 1970s. He later became president of the Systems and Technologies Division before retiring from BBN, in 1995.

Frank Heart has been a member of the United States Air Force Scientific Advisory Board and a consultant for the Department of Health, Education and Welfare. In addition, he holds memberships in numerous professional societies and has directed many technical conference committees. In 2002 he was inducted into the Massachusetts Telecommunications Council's (MTC) Hall of Fame for "his key role in helping make the Internet a reality as leader of the BBN team that developed ARPANET," according to an MTC press release.—K. D.

Suggested Reading: *Boston Globe* A p85 Sep. 11, 1994, G p1 Sep. 19, 1999; *Computerworld* p101 Oct. 3, 1994, p103 Sep. 23, 1996; *Newsbytes* Sep. 12, 1994; *Newsweek* p56 Aug. 8, 1994; *PreText Magazine* (on-line) Mar./Apr. 1998

Helsingius, Johan

1961– Creator of remailing service

Finland native Johan Helsingius, who customarily sports a shaved head, earring, boots, and a scarf, does not look like the typical corporate executive. He currently serves, however, as the chief technology officer and senior vice president of KPNQwest, a Dutch-based telecommunications firm. In the early 1980s he helped to establish Europe's first commercial Internet Service Provider (ISP), and he set up the first network connections to the former Soviet Union. Helsingius is celebrated by computer users around the world as a champion of privacy and the freedom of expression on the Internet. He began anon.penet.fi, a "remailing" service, free of charge to the public, through which users could send and post anonymous messages on the Internet. He believed that anonymity allowed people to discuss sensitive topics, such as sexual abuse, more openly and report human-rights violations in repressive countries without the fear of government persecution. In the mid-1990s he found himself at the center of the debate over the regulation of the Internet's content, when law-enforcement officials demanded that he disclose the names of several of his users, who were accused of breaking the law. "I am definitely a believer in full freedom of expression," he told Volker Grassmuck for *IC Magazine* (December 1994, on-line). "However, stupid your point might be, I still support your need to say it."

Johan Mikael Helsingius was born in 1961 in Finland. He and his parents were among the country's Swedish-speaking minority, who make up about four percent of the nation's population. In an interview with Joshua Quittner for *Wired* (June 1994, on-line), Helsingius said that his experience allows him to relate to other members of minorities—racial, ethnic, religious, or sexual—who may have the need to "discuss things that are important to them without having to identify who they are." Helsingius learned to appreciate both privacy and freedom of expression by observing the political oppression in the former Soviet Union, which borders Finland. "If you actually owned a photocopier or even a typewriter there you would have to register it, and they would take samples of what your typewriter would put out so they could identify it later," he told Quittner. "That's something I find so appalling. The fact that you have to register every means of providing information to the public sort of parallels it—like saying you have to sign everything on the Net."

Exact details about Johan Helsingius's background in the computer industry are not widely known, and he did not respond to requests from *Leaders of the Information Age* for an interview. However, sources provide some information about his early life. He had reportedly been interested in computers since childhood, and he built the first computer he ever owned himself. Several sites on the Internet report that Helsingius was a student at the University of Helsinki during the late 1970s. In his article for *Communications Week International* (April 6, 1998, on-line), the reporter Kenneth Cukier wrote that Helsingius studied computer science, but dropped out of school to become a computer consultant and never earned a degree. Helsingius's profile on the KPNQwest Web site states that he has worked in information technology and networking for about 20 years and has founded and managed several companies.

Working with a team of other computer professionals, Helsingius played a major role in helping to set up EUNet, Europe's first ISP, in 1982. EUNet linked e-mail systems that were being used in Europe's universities and research institutions. At first, few people used EUNet, but that changed over the next two decades, and the company that operated it, EUNet International, became extremely successful as Europe's leading ISP provider.

In the late 1980s Helsingius offered Internet access in his homeland by founding EUNet Finland, a subsidiary of EUNet International. He is also credited with establishing the first Internet link to the former Soviet Union. This information outlet from the Soviet Union became important, in August 1991, when hard-line Communists in the military attempted to depose Premier Mikhael Gorbachev in a coup. Helsingius told Grassmuck that, during the coup, the Soviet military "cut off all traditional media, all telex lines went down, all phone lines went down, no information to any media came out of Russia, except on the nets where it was real-time reporting all the time. The information went back and forth. There was no way to stop the network, because if they tried to cut one line there was always a backup route somewhere, and information just kept flowing." In the early 1990s Helsingius founded Penetic, a company that helps Finnish businesses connect to the Internet. He was eventually made the director of marketing and product development of EUNet International, which was operating as a subsidiary of the multimedia firm Qwest Communications, based in Denver, Colorado. Helsingius's accomplishments and long career in computer networking brought him little public attention. His computer-related sideline, however, brought him international attention and made him the flash point of the debate over policing the Internet for inappropriate material.

In 1992, during a discussion with several other Internet professionals about creating a Finnish-language newsgroup, Helsingius engaged in a disagreement about whether users should include their proper names on all messages. Supporters of the requirement argued that it would hold all users accountable and verify the identity of who posted a particular message. "And I kept arguing that the Internet just doesn't work that way, and if somebody actually tries to enforce that, the Internet will always find a solution around it," he said to Grassmuck. To demonstrate his point, Helsingius set up anon.penet.fi, to prove that it was almost impossible to police the Internet. The service, which operated from a single computer in Helsingius's home in Helsinki, acted as a remailer, or an intermediary between the sender and the recipient. When a user sent a message to Helsingius's computer, it was stripped of its origin and assigned a code number. The remailer then forwarded the message to its intended destination. The remailer also automatically forwarded any anonymous responses to the message back to the sender. After using it for several weeks, many people e-mailed Helsingius, saying that his remailer was a valuable service. Helsingius kept it running, updating the software occasionally. Despite spending as much as $1,000 a month of his own money to keep the remailer running, Helsingius charged no fee for his service.

By 1994 tens of thousands of people around the world were using anon.penet.fi to send and post anonymous messages—a large number of which were directed to sexually oriented newsgroups. Helsingius, who was known in cyberspace as Julf, was the only one who could access the identity of every sender. When asked by Quittner how people would know if he ever read any of the messages that passed through his remailer, Helsingius replied, "You don't. There's absolutely no way I could guarantee to anyone, I mean really prove I'm not looking at the stuff. There's no way to prove it. People just have to trust me." In an interview with Michael Scott for the *Vancouver Sun* (April 10, 1993), Helsingius said, "Had I wanted to, I suppose I could watch the mails going in and out. But the volumes were just enormous—too enormous to do much with but marvel."

Helsingius believed that he was providing a public service by bringing the Internet to ordinary people and giving them a forum in which they could freely express themselves. In an interview with Charles Arthur for *New Scientist* (March 11, 1995), Helsingius said, "These servers enable safe discussion of sensitive issues, such as reporting violations of human rights. They are vital for support of freedom of expression. These servers are used by people all over the world who are under pressure or persecuted, or who want to discuss their personal problems and sufferings."

As use of anon.penet.fi increased during the mid-1990s, the service attracted controversy. As early as 1993, some disgruntled users attempted to sabotage the remailer by sending computer viruses and "worms" to destroy the software. Other users tried to shut down the remailer by "spamming" it— sending thousands of e-mails to overload the system—and Helsingius himself received death threats. As a precaution, he moved the computer that operated the remailer to a friend's business and then to an empty storefront, where it was hidden behind some potted plants.

Anon.penet.fi and other remailers eventually attracted the attention of law-enforcement agencies around the world. Timothy May, a computer consultant and cryptographer, explained to Arthur that law-enforcement officials feared that remailers could be "used for what I call the Four Horsemen of the Internet. That is—terrorism, child pornography, money laundering and drugs." Although he was committed to freedom of expression, Helsingius did keep an eye out for any troublemakers. As a safeguard, he equipped every message that passed through anon.penet.fi with a feature that allowed users to send him complaints. "I sent warnings to users who were causing problems; and of 18,000 users, only eight had their privileges closed off [as of April 1993]," he told Scott.

On several occasions Helsingius refused requests by law-enforcement agencies to disclose the identities of users who were being investigated for breaking the law. In early 1995 he became involved with a dispute with the Church of Scientology.

Representatives from the Church in the United States contacted Helsingius and asked him to reveal the identity of a particular user, who had allegedly taken documents from the Church's computers and posted them through anon.penet.fi in violation of United States copyright laws. Helsingius refused to cooperate, insisting that people who used his service had the right to privacy. In response, the Church filed a complaint with the authorities in Finland and asked them to investigate Helsingius's remailer. The Finnish police served Helsingius with a warrant, in February 1995, demanding that he reveal the name of the user sought by the Scientologists. Confronted by the possible confiscation of his computer, Helsingius disclosed the identity of the user to the police, who immediately forwarded the name to the Church's representatives in the United States. Many civil libertarians and Internet-privacy activists expressed concern over the legal actions taken against Helsingius, and he received hundreds of supportive e-mails. The Finnish police found no evidence that Helsingius himself had committed any crimes by simply serving as a conduit for the dissemination of material that was copyrighted only in the United States. To reduce the chances that anon.penet.fi would be used to illegally publish copyrighted material in the future, Helsingius limited the size of messages that could be sent through the remailer.

Helsingius's troubles with the Church of Scientology continued in 1996, when church officials sought the identity of another user who had allegedly posted dozens of copyrighted Scientology texts on the Internet through the remailer. "We are not opposing the existence of [Helsingius's] server," Helena Kobrin, a lawyer for the Church of Scientology, explained to Peter H. Lewis for the *New York Times* (September 6, 1996). "We have no opposition to there being anonymity for private, consensual communications. What we oppose is using anonymous servers for the purpose of permitting criminal or other unlawful acts. There has to be responsibility and accountability." This time, Helsingius refused to disclose the user's identity and fought the action in Finnish courts. In late August 1996, a judge in Helsinki ruled that Helsingius had to disclose the identity of the user to the Church of Scientology, arguing that Finland's telecommunications laws did not provide e-mails with the same level of privacy protection that postal mail and telephone calls enjoyed.

A few days before the ruling came down, a story in the London *Observer* newspaper alleged that anon.penet.fi served as a key link in an international pedophile chain, serving as one of the Internet's leading conduits for transmitting child pornography. The article labeled Helsingius himself as the middleman who handled 90 percent of all child pornography on the Internet. In reality, it was impossible for pornographic photos—or images of any kind—to travel through the remailer because it filtered them out and transmitted only text.

Dismayed by the court's ruling in the Scientology case and by the viciousness of the accusations in the *Observer* article, Helsingius shut down anon.penet.fi. on August 30, 1996. He posted a press release on the Penet Web site, stating, "I will close down the remailer for the time being because the legal issues governing the Internet in Finland are yet undefined. The legal protection of the users needs to be clarified. At the moment the privacy of Internet messages is judicially unclear. . . . I have also personally been a target because of the remailer. Unjustified accusations affect both my job and my private life."

Helsingius, considered a hero to many, remained active, participating in international forums about the laws and regulations affecting the Internet. In 1997 the Electronic Freedom Foundation honored him with a Pioneer Award for his commitment to freedom of expression and his role in bringing the Internet to Europe.

In 1998 Qwest Communications and KPN, a Dutch telecommunications firm, formed a new subsidiary, KPNQwest, to develop fiber-optic networks in Europe. Helsingius joined the new company, whose headquarters is in Amsterdam, as the senior vice president and chief technology officer.—D. C.

Suggested Reading: *Communications Week International* (on-line) Apr. 6, 1998; *Electronic Times* (on-line) Nov. 30, 1998; *IC Magazine* (online) Dec. 1994; KPNQwest Web site; *Los Angeles Times* A p1+ Aug. 31, 1996; *New Scientist* p14+ Mar. 11, 1995; *New York Times* D p2 Sep. 6, 1996; *Vancouver Sun* C p15 Apr. 10, 1993; *Wall Street Journal* A p7 July 17, 1995; *Wired* (on-line) June 1994

Hulton Archive by Getty Images

Hertz, Heinrich Rudolf

Feb. 22, 1857–Jan. 1, 1894 Radio pioneer

Heinrich Rudolf Hertz laid the foundations for radio communication by proving the existence of electromagnetic waves (of which radio waves are one type) and demonstrating that they travel through space at the speed of light. Though in Hertz's experiments the crude transmitter and receiver were never very far apart, the equipment he used provided the essential blueprint for later experiments in radio telemetry. The standard unit of wave frequency was subsequently named a hertz, equal to one cycle per second. (The modern computer runs at a speed measured in gigahertz—one billion cycles per second.)

Heinrich Rudolf Hertz was born in Hamburg, Germany, on February 22, 1857. His father was a prominent jurist and later a senator, and Hertz was raised in a cultured home and given a fine education. He entered the Johanneum Gymnasium, a private school in Herborn, Germany, at the age of 15. Three years later he went to Frankfurt to begin a career in engineering; in 1876 he began preparing at Dresden Polytechnic for the state engineering examination. A year of compulsory military service, from 1876 to 1877, convinced Hertz that he wanted to be a scientist rather than an engineer. He subsequently began studying mathematics at Munich University and then switched to physics. In 1878 Hertz went to Berlin to study under the distinguished physicist Hermann von Helmholtz. After earning his Ph.D., in 1880, he spent three years as Helmholtz's assistant. In 1883 he moved to Kiel, Germany, to become a lecturer in physics and two years later accepted a position as a professor of physics at Karlsruhe Technical College. In 1889 Hertz became a professor of physics at the University of Bonn.

At Karlsruhe Technical College Hertz began conducting experiments on electromagnetic radiation, which is energy that travels through space in the form of waves—such as light, radio waves, heat waves, and X rays. The Scottish physicist James Clerk Maxwell had, in 1864, predicted the existence of electromagnetic waves, and Hertz decided to test the theory that such waves existed and could indeed travel through air. In approximately 1888 Hertz, using two brass knobs, made an oscillator, a circuit used to generate pulses of high-frequency electric current. The current then passed over a tiny gap in the circuit, causing sparks to leap across at regular intervals. (At around this time Hertz also discovered that sparks could be produced more readily if the nodes at each end of the gap were irradiated with ultraviolet light, a phenomenon known as the Hertz effect.) If Maxwell's theory was correct, Hertz reasoned, the sparks should transmit electromagnetic waves through the air. Several yards away he set up a small receiver made primarily of looped wire, which also had a tiny gap. When Hertz threw the switch on his transmitter, the electromagnetic waves from the oscillator traveled through the air and induced a current in the receiver which, in turn, sent sparks across the gap. Hertz had succeeded in making the first practical demonstration of the existence of electromagnetic radiation.

In later experiments Hertz proved that all electromagnetic waves share properties previously only attributed to light: They travel at the same speed as light and can be reflected, refracted through a prism, polarized, and diffracted. Hertz never seized upon the possibilities of using radio waves for communication, leaving that for Guglielmo Marconi, Aleksandr Popov, and others. Beginning in 1890 he turned his attention to mechanics and laws of motion. Shortly after his ground-breaking experiment Hertz began to suffer from periodic toothaches, the beginning stages of a bone disease. He died of blood poisoning in Bonn on January 1, 1894. He left behind his wife and two daughters, Mathilde and Johanna.—P. G. H.

Suggested Reading: *American Scientist* p584 Nov. 1995; *Popular Electronics* p61+ Aug. 1996; Millar, David, et al., eds. *Cambridge Dictionary of Scientists*, 1996

Hewlett Packard/Getty Images

Hewlett, William R.

May 20, 1913–Jan. 12, 2001 Co-founder of Hewlett-Packard

One of the co-founders of the monolithic Hewlett-Packard computer company, William R. Hewlett helped initiate an unprecedented technology revolution over the latter half of the 20th century, focused in the region of California now known as Silicon Valley. Along with his partner, the late David Packard, Hewlett began manufacturing electronics out of a garage in 1939, unaware that the makeshift business partnership would become the multibillion-dollar corporation it is today. Known as the more reserved of the two, Hewlett helped develop many of the technologies that shaped the company's growth, while Packard maintained a more managerial role. Many of Hewlett's contributions centered on electronic instrumentation and calculating devices; the company did not enter the computer market until the 1960s. Today, Hewlett-Packard produces a full line of computer products and accessories, and is perhaps best known for its inkjet and laser printers. After decades of playing an active executive role in the company he started, Hewlett held the honorary title of director emeritus from 1987 until his death on January 12, 2001.

William Redington Hewlett was born on May 20, 1913 to Albion Walter Hewlett and Louise (Redington) Hewlett in Ann Arbor, Michigan. When he was three years old, Hewlett and his family moved to the San Francisco area; his father, a physician and a professor, had accepted a position at Stanford University Medical School. The elder Hewlett later became dean of the medical school before succumbing suddenly to a brain tumor in 1926. After his father's death, Hewlett, along with his mother, grandmother, and sisters, spent a year in Europe before returning to San Francisco, where he attended Lowell High School. Although he was a mediocre student—due to an undiagnosed learning disability—Hewlett was accepted to Stanford University, where he studied electrical engineering. At Stanford he befriended fellow undergraduate David Packard, and both young men developed a close student–mentor relationship with legendary engineering professor Fred Terman. Hewlett received his B.A. from Stanford in 1934 and promptly enrolled at the Massachusetts Institute of Technology (MIT), in Cambridge, where he earned his master's degree in electrical engineering in 1936. At the suggestion of Terman, he returned to Stanford in 1938 and received an advanced degree in engineering in 1939.

During his second stint at Stanford, Hewlett was reunited with Packard, who was earning an advanced engineering degree after several years at General Electric. In 1939 the two men formed a partnership, which they named the Hewlett-

Packard Company. (They decided the order of company name through a coin toss.) "We had a good education and there weren't a lot of jobs around," Hewlett recalled to Louis Kehoe and Geoffrey Owen for the *Financial Times* (July 3, 1992), "so (we thought) why not try to start a business." Hewlett-Packard's humble beginnings in a small garage behind Hewlett's Palo Alto home have since become the stuff of legend. The garage, which measured 12 feet by 18 feet, was located in back of Hewlett's rented cottage, which, in turn, sat behind the house in which Packard resided with his wife, Lucile. Working with loan of $538 from Terman, the duo began manufacturing electronic devices and were soon taking any job they could acquire. Their first product, a foul-line indicator for a bowling alley, met with a very small market. Some of the team's additional early projects included an automatic urinal flusher, a shock machine for losing weight, and an automatic lettuce thinner, designed to thin rows of plant seedlings. Hewlett and Packard, determined not to take on any major loans, opted instead to finance their company's growth through its earnings. However, to accomplish this type of goal, they first needed to create a commercially successful product.

The company's first such success was based on a design that Hewlett had developed while studying negative feedback in graduate school. Known as a resistance-capacitance audio oscillator, the device was designed to measure sound waves. Although such machines were already in existence, Hewlett's version worked much more efficiently and was much less expensive. (Although it was capable of tuning harmonicas, this remained only a minor selling point.) When Walt Disney purchased eight of the gadgets for use on his new film *Fantasia* (1940), Hewlett and Packard were finally on solid footing. The feedback principle that the oscillator employed inspired several more early products, such as a harmonic wave analyzer and a distortion analyzer. In 1940, with a net revenue of $34,000, three employees, and line of eight products, Hewlett and Packard moved their growing company out of the garage and into a rented building.

A watershed event in the history of computing, World War II also had a profound effect on the development of the fledgling company, which was then producing a wide array of electronic devices in the areas of radio, radar, sonar, and aviation. In fact, many of Hewlett-Packard's contracts were actually with the U.S. government in the area of defense. In 1941 Hewlett, who had a reserve commission, was called up to the army, leaving Packard to run the company in his absence. Hewlett became a member of the staff of the army's chief signal officer, and he also headed up the electronics section of the War Department's New Development Division. Immediately following the war, he was part of a special U.S. inspection team investigating Japan's technological capabilities.

Upon his return to Palo Alto, California, Hewlett discovered that the company had grown significantly in his absence: The number of employees had increased from 17 to more than 150, and the company's annual sales were over $2 million. "What the war did for us," Hewlett told Kehoe and Owen, "it made it evident that electronics could be applied in many provinces. So all of a sudden, you found it appearing all over. And we shared in this growth directly, because if you make something, you've got to measure it." Hewlett-Packard was incorporated in 1947, with Packard serving as president and Hewlett as vice president. (The hierarchy was established during the war years, when Packard had taken on more of a managerial role while Hewlett excelled for his engineering capabilities.) Hewlett-Packard signed with sales firms to market their products nationwide. As the company grew through the 1950s, expanding its product line to nearly 400 separate devices, Hewlett ascended to the board of directors of the Institute of Radio Engineers, now the Institute of Electrical and Electronics Engineers (IEEE). He was named IEEE president in 1954.

On November 6, 1957 Hewlett-Packard became a publicly traded company, with the common stock trading for $16 a share. In a notable move, Hewlett and Packard offered a stock grant to all employees at all levels of the company with just six months of service, and also made employees eligible for a stock-option program. This marked the first example of corporate profit sharing—a benefit that was later popularized among many firms in Silicon Valley. Hewlett-Packard's concern for its employees extended well beyond stock options—the two founders had a unique corporate philosophy, which emphasized openness, creativity, respect for the individual, and commitment to both customers and the community; this overall concept characterized the company from its inception and went on to have a strong influence on many corporations within the technology community. Avoiding large, formal offices and insisting on the use of first names, Hewlett and Packard advocated a humanistic approach that became known throughout the industry as "the HP Way." "We did not want to have a 'hire and fire' company," Hewlett told Kehoe and Owen. "Both Dave and I were products of the Great Depression. We had observed its effects on all sides, and of course it had a strong effect on us. It could not help but influence our decisions on how a company should be run." In 1962 Hewlett-Packard received its first listing on *Fortune* magazine's roster of the top 500 U.S. companies, entering at number 460. Two years later, Hewlett became president of the company. In 1969 he was given the additional role of chief executive officer (CEO) when David Packard left to become a deputy secretary of defense for the Nixon administration.

In the 1960s Hewlett-Packard made the jump from electronics to the computer market. Although the company had previously manufactured mostly electronic measuring instruments, it was now receiving requests for automatic devices—i. e., computers—to control and analyze the data from these instruments. "Dave and I didn't suddenly decide that we were going into the computer business," Hewlett told Joyce Gemperlein in a 1996 interview for the *San Jose Mercury News*, as posted on the Tech Museum Web site. "We'd been in business for half our careers, and so this was just an extension of what we'd been doing in the past, and a lot of these things just carried over." The first computer produced by Hewlett-Packard was the HP 2116A in 1966; it was the largest single mechanical package that the company had built to date. (That same year President Lyndon B. Johnson appointed Hewlett to serve on the nation's Science Advisory Committee, a position he retained until 1969.) Two years later Hewlett-Packard introduced the world's first desktop scientific calculator, the HP 9100A, with a pricetag of $4,900. They went one step further in 1972 with the introduction of the first handheld scientific calculator, the HP-35, based on Hewlett's own idea. This was the company's first consumer device; prior to the HP-35, Hewlett-Packard products were intended for academic and other professional scientific use. The realm of business computing was the next territory into which Hewlett-Packard ventured, with the HP 3000 minicomputer. By 1973 the company's small, general-purpose computer system had become the first commercially distributed data-processing system.

Hewlett-Packard continued to experience incredible growth in the 1970s, with the company expanding globally into Asia and Europe. Revenues in 1970 were $365 million, approached $1 billion by 1976, and increased to more than $2 billion by 1979. Hewlett resigned from his positions as president and CEO in 1977 and 1978, respectively, relinquishing the day-to-day operations to a new president and CEO, John Young. Hewlett then began serving as the chairman of Hewlett-Packard's executive committee. The company continued to expand its product line and in 1980 introduced its first personal computer, the HP-85. In 1983 Hewlett moved from chairman of the executive committee to chairman of the board of directors. The following year Hewlett-Packard began pioneering inkjet printing technology with the HP Thinkjet printer. The company also introduced the HP Laserjet printer, its most successful single product to date. In 1987 Hewlett was given the title of director emeritus of the board of directors, a position that he held until his death on January 12, 2001. In this role he remained highly active within the company in an unofficial capacity. His managerial days did not completely end in 1987, however; in the early 1990s, when the company's stock suddenly plummeted, Hewlett and Packard, both approaching 80, were called back on a temporary basis to resume management of day-to-day operations, to cut inefficiencies, to eliminate bureaucracy, and to set the company's growth back on course. Through the 1990s Hewlett-Packard made new inroads in the field of portable computing, expanded its sales in the personal computing market, and continued to advance its printing and imaging technology; the company's rate of growth remained around 20 percent for most of the decade.

The son of a medical professor, Hewlett maintained an interest in education and medicine throughout his professional life. He initiated Hewlett-Packard's entry into the medical technology business with the acquisition of the Massachusetts-based Sanborn Company in 1961. At the time Hewlett felt very strongly that the future of medical instrumentation would be in electronics. (This business eventually became part of Agilent Technologies, a company that separated from Hewlett-Packard in 2000.) Following the acquisition, Hewlett-Packard began producing cardiac-monitoring systems and soon became a pioneering force in this new market. Hewlett was also the chairman of the William and Flora Hewlett Foundation, an organization that he founded with his wife in 1966 "to promote the well-being of mankind," as quoted by Jack Schofield for the *Guardian* (January 15, 2001). Today the foundation has assets of more than $3 billion and contributes about $120 million annually to numerous causes aiding education, the arts, and the environment. Upon his death, Hewlett—who in 2000 was named the 26th richest American by *Forbes* magazine, with a personal fortune estimated at $9 billion—left most of his wealth to philanthropic endeavors (including his foundation), with one of the major beneficiaries being his alma mater, Stanford University.

Hewlett married Flora Lamson on August 10, 1939. The couple had two daughters, Eleanor and Mary, and three sons, Walter, James, and William, Jr. His oldest son, Walter, was elected to the Hewlett-Packard board of directors in 1987. Flora died in 1977, and Hewlett married Rosemary Bradford on May 24, 1978.

William Hewlett was awarded the prestigious National Medal of Honor by President Ronald Reagan in 1985. In addition to the National Medal of Honor, Hewlett was the recipient of 13 honorary degrees from institutions such as the University of California at Berkeley, Yale University, the University of Notre Dame, Dartmouth University, and Johns Hopkins University. He held life fellow memberships in the IEEE and the Franklin Institute. In 1992 he was inducted into the National Inventors Hall of Fame, and in 1995 Hewlett and Packard were presented with the Price Waterhouse Information Technology Leadership Award for Lifetime Achievement. Among Hewlett's numerous outside interests were skiing, mountain climbing, and fishing. He was also a part-time botanist and ran several cattle-ranching operations in California and Idaho. William Hewlett and David Packard remained close friends throughout the duration of their partnership, which ended with Packard's death in 1996.

HOERNI

Today, Hewlett-Packard is an international manufacturer of computation products, software, and systems used in numerous areas including business, science, and medicine. By 2000 the company had advanced up *Fortune*'s list of the top 500 U.S. corporations to number 13. The following year it reported estimated revenue of $45.2 billion, with approximately 88,000 employees, according to Hewlett-Packard's Web site. On May 3, 2002 Hewlett-Packard completed an historic merger with Compaq Computer Corporation, in what was the largest technology merger in history. Hewlett-Packard is still based in Palo Alto, California, where its two founders originated the phenomenon of start-up technology companies. Now known as "Silicon Valley," this area of California is widely considered the backbone of the American computer industry, home to such giants as Netscape, Oracle, and Yahoo!, and the garage where

Hewlett-Packard began is now a California state landmark. A pioneer in the realm of modern computer manufacturing, William Hewlett saw his company grow into one of the originators of the computer industry, a field in which it remains a major player. "I think we are in a strong position," Hewlett told Kehoe and Owen, on the status of the company in the early 1990s. "We've got a good work staff, we've got good management, and a good financial position. So unless we screw it up, I think we're in good shape."—B.S., K.D.

Suggested Reading: *Financial Times* p11 July 3, 1992, with photo; *Forbes* p182+ Apr. 30, 1990, with photos; *Fortune* p142 Mar. 14, 1988, with photo; *IEEE History Center: William Hewlett Interview* (on-line) Nov. 27, 1984; *Mercury News* B p1 Jan. 21, 2001, with photo; *Washington Post* B p7 Jan. 13, 2001

Hoerni, Jean A.

Sep. 26, 1924– Feb. 1997 Inventor of the planar process

Jean A. Hoerni significantly contributed to the development of the silicon-based integrated circuit through his invention of the planar process. Understanding that the bulky germanium-based chips that Jack Kilby had invented could not be successfully marketed, Hoerni sought to develop a process through which all of the chips' various components were embedded in a layer of silicon oxide, which protected the components and allowed for more secure connections between the chips and their wires. Hoerni's planar process—so named because all of the components were placed on a single plane, instead of in layers—allowed Robert Noyce to develop the first silicon-based chip in 1958. Hoerni's innovation has contributed to the success of a booming industry, as integrated circuits manufactured using his planar process are placed in more and more electronic products, including watches, televisions, cellular phones, computers, and cars.

Jean Amédée Hoerni was born in Geneva, Switzerland, on September 26, 1924, to Robert and Jeanne (Berthoud) Hoerni. He was educated at the University of Geneva where he received his bachelor of science degree in 1947 and his doctorate in physics in 1950. He received a second doctorate, also in physics, from Cambridge University in Great Britain in 1952. Shortly thereafter, Hoerni traveled to the United States hoping to start a career in research at the California Institute of Technology. (He became a naturalized American citizen in 1959.) While at the university his intelligence and skills as a researcher were noted by William Shockley, the electronics pioneer who would go on to win the Nobel Prize in Physics in 1956 for helping to develop the transistor. Shockley was starting

a new research facility—Shockley Transistor Laboratories, in Palo Alto, California—and he wanted Hoerni to join him in his research.

Though Shockley was a vastly intelligent researcher, he had little in the way of people skills and generated discord among his employees with his ruthless managerial style. According to Stan Augarten in his book *Bit by Bit* (1984), Shockley "held a somewhat conspiratorial view of the world. He posted a list of everyone's salaries, hoping to put an end to company secrets; he required his employees to rate one another regularly, a process that immediately degenerated into a popularity contest; and, after the lab's work ran into inexplicable delays that Shockley unaccountably blamed on sabotage, he ordered one of his employees to take a lie detector test. (The man passed.)" In addition, Shockley wanted his employees, including Hoerni, to concentrate their efforts on developing a four-layer germanium diode as a commercial product. This device was essentially a switch with a very weak "on" state and an extremely strong "off" state. Hoerni, Robert Noyce, and a number of their research associates believed they should be working to develop silicon transistors, but Shockley dismissed their ideas.

By the summer of 1957, about a year after the laboratory's founding, Shockley's prickly tactics caused eight of his employees—Hoerni, Noyce, Gordon Moore, Julius Blank, Victor Grinich, Eugene Kleiner, Jay Last, and Sheldon Roberts—to leave the company to found their own research laboratory. With $3,500 in backing from the Fairchild Camera and Instrument Corporation, a company based on Long Island, New York, the Fairchild Eight, as they would soon be called, founded Fairchild Semiconductor Corporation in the hopes of competing with Shockley and building the world's first commercially marketable silicon-based integrated circuits.

Fairchild Semiconductor planted the seeds for Silicon Valley, a freewheeling yet dedicated work environment in which employees strived to produce the best products. Like many entrepreneurs who followed the Fairchild Eight, the group dispensed with job titles (though Noyce was considered general manager because he was so well liked by everyone else) and were promised stock options—something that had never occurred before in American business. And like many of the Silicon Valley start-up companies that would follow them, the group at Fairchild Semiconductor had to build from scratch the equipment needed to create their silicon-integrated circuits.

They had their work cut out for them. In 1958 Jack Kilby, a young engineer at Texas Instruments, developed the first germanium-based integrated circuit by taking all the circuit elements (capacitors, transistors, and resistors), placing them on a thin, half-inch-long piece of germanium, and connecting all the components by tiny gold wires. While Kilby proved that an integrated circuit was theoretically possible, his germanium-based circuit was difficult to manufacture, primarily because the wires had to be hand-soldered onto the germanium and because the germanium itself would become too hot. His transistors could also short-circuit easily because the connecting wires tended to slip or break.

One morning in late 1958, at a time when he and his associates were stalled in their development of the silicon chip, Hoerni had a vision in the shower. He realized that in order to build this chip he needed to embed chemically the transistors' various parts into the silicon, thereby creating what would later be called the planar process. As Deborah Claymon noted in *Red Herring* magazine (on-line), "Mr. Hoerni's planar process, a means of fusing an insulating layer of silicon dioxide into the chip before the application of the conducting metal circuitry, turned out to be the breakthrough. With Mr. Hoerni's invention, Fairchild started a technological revolution and created an industry valued today at $140 billion."

Hoerni created a completely flat circuit, which, unlike Kilby's device, had no protruding parts. Almost completely covered in silicon dioxide, the chip was insulated in the same way that rubber casing protects electrical wiring. Though certain areas were left exposed in order to create contact points for the wires that would allow the chip to function, the wires in Hoerni's flat circuit were much less likely to slip. Also, by using the planar process, it was now unnecessary to attach the wires by hand. Fairchild Semiconductor patented the planar process once Hoerni had perfected it, and in 1959 Robert Noyce built the first functional silicon-based integrated circuit. Though lawsuits were filed between Texas Instruments and Fairchild Semiconductor to determine who actually invented the integrated circuit, history assigns Jack Kilby with credit for inventing the integrated circuit and Hoerni and Noyce for perfecting it in silicon and making it marketable.

Today we see the historical significance of such an invention, especially in light of the fact that everything from digital watches and washing machines to computers and automobiles function by use of some sort of integrated circuit. However, the Fairchild Eight did not view the silicon-based integrated circuit that way. As Jay Last told *Computerworld* (on-line), "The IC was not looked on as a big deal in those days. The focus was on making transistors. IC's did not look like earth-shaking inventions—they looked like obvious extensions of the technology if we could figure out how to make them."

In 1959, shortly after displaying the first IC, the 2N696, at Wescon 58 (North America's largest electronics convention) and receiving extraordinary interest in it, especially from the U.S. military, Fairchild Camera and Instrument bought out Fairchild Semiconductor and gave each of the eight founders $250,000 in stocks. The group stayed on, knowing that the device they had invented would arouse interest in the commercial market as soon as the chips' prices went down. However, they soon became dissatisfied with their positions because Fairchild's highly structured management style did not jibe with their more freewheeling work environment. Hoerni and three other founders left in 1961 to establish a new company, Amelco, which later became Teledyne Semiconductor. Others also left Fairchild to start their own companies, most notably Noyce and Moore, who went on to establish the Intel Corporation in 1968. According to several sources, more than 50 companies in Silicon Valley have their roots in the men who formed Fairchild Semiconductor.

Hoerni stayed at Teledyne in Mountain View, California, until 1963 and served as a freelance consultant in Silicon Valley until 1967. In that year he became founder and president of Intersil, a company in Cupertino, California. That company, now a part of General Electric, used the technology he pioneered to produce digital watches. Hoerni left Intersil in 1975 to return to consulting work in the Seattle, Washington, area, as well as in Hailey, Idaho. He was also on the board of directors at DEEPA Textiles, Inc.

Jean Hoerni was recognized for his pioneering work in 1966 when he received the John Scott Medal in the field of science from the city of Philadephia. He was also honored with the Longstreth Medal from the Franklin Institute (1969) and the SEMMY award from the semiconductor industry (1985). He died in February 1997 at the age of 72, leaving three children, Michael, Anne, and Susan.—C. M.

Suggested Reading: CNN Web site; *Computerworld* (on-line) March 8, 1999; IBM Web site; *Red Herring* (on-line) May 1997; Augarten, Stan. *Bit by Bit*, 1984

Hoff, Marcian E., Jr.

Oct. 28, 1937– Microchip pioneer

During the 1960s many people in the computer industry were convinced that a central processing unit (CPU)—a "computer on a chip," as it was then being called—would be feasible someday, when the necessary technology became available. Marcian E. Hoff Jr., a visionary electrical engineer better known by the nickname Ted, realized that it was possible to make a single-chip CPU with the technology then available. Aided by Stanley Mazor and Federico Faggin, Hoff worked from late 1969 to early 1971 to develop the device. The result was the Intel 4004 microprocessor—a chip the size of a child's fingernail but containing all the key elements of an entire computer. The microprocessor revolutionized computers, allowing smaller and more efficient machines to be manufactured, and it made Intel a major force in the market. Today such microprocessors are found not only in all computers, but in countless electronic products—including most automobiles and numerous medical devices.

Marcian Edward (Ted) Hoff Jr. was born on October 28, 1937 in Rochester, New York. He developed an interest in science at a very early age through his uncle, who was then studying chemical engineering and chemistry. In an interview with Rob Walker on March 3, 1995, for Stanford University's Silicon Genesis program, as posted on the school's official Web site, Hoff elaborated: "I loved the magic you could do with chemistry and pretty much decided to follow in that career until my uncle advised against it. He said that unless I went into chemical engineering, as opposed to chemistry, he thought the job market didn't look very good." When Hoff was 12 years old, his uncle presented him with a subscription to *Popular Science*. In one issue he came across an advertisement for an Allied Radio catalogue, which piqued his interest in electronics, and by the end of high school he was certain that he wanted to study that field in college. He attended Rensselaer Polytechnic Institute, in Troy, New York, and received his bachelor's degree in electrical engineering in 1958. During his summer vacations Hoff worked for the General Railway Signal Company and developed two patents. The first was for a circuit that detected trains through audio frequencies transmitted along the tracks, and his second was for a circuit that absorbed energy for protection against lightning.

Because he had never been "west of Niagra Falls," as he told Walker, Hoff decided to study for his graduate degrees at Stanford University, in California, in order to see another part of the country. He received a master's degree in 1959 and a Ph.D. in electrical engineering in 1962. He stayed on at Stanford to work with Professor Bernie Widrow, studying neural networks, computer systems in which processors are connected in a way suggestive of the neurons in the human brain. He also developed an interest in integrated circuits, small complexes of electronic components produced in or on a piece of material, such as silicon.

In early 1968 Hoff received a phone call from Robert Noyce, whom he had once met briefly. Noyce told Hoff that he and Gordon Moore were forming a new company called the Intel Corporation, a spin-off of Fairchild Semiconductor, and invited him to join the fledgling venture. Noyce and Moore believed that the semiconductor was the wave of the future and would, eventually, replace the magnetic-core memories then being used in large computers. Hoff accepted the job offer and was given a position as manager of applications research.

In April 1969 Busicom, a Japanese electronics company, asked Intel to develop custom chips for its new desktop printing calculator. A team of Japanese engineers, including Masatoshi Shima, came to the United States in June to show Intel engineers the details of their design. Hoff was assigned to act as a liaison for them and procure any equipment or supplies they might need. The Japanese design called for building 12 customized calculator chips, with separate chips for controlling the printer, keyboard, display unit, and other features. Upon looking over their designs, Hoff realized that it would be difficult to meet the budget set for the project. He suggested that Busicom simplify the calculator's functions and better utilize the read-only memory built into the device.

The Japanese engineers were initially reluctant to change their plans, but Noyce encouraged Hoff to continue his research into making the design more efficient. Soon Hoff realized he could make a very simple general-purpose computer by building a CPU that could not only run the calculator, but a variety of other products. He developed a simple instruction set with which he was able to prove that a user could do multiple scans and check for consistent results, while also maintaining a display and doing calculator arithmetic. He figured that his design would need just two chips (instead of 12) to make up the central processor, plus a timing chip, a read-only memory chip, and a read-write memory chip. Hoff was joined by Stan Mazor, who brought his programing and design skills to the project. In October 1969 Busicom officials, convinced by the argument that Intel's CPU would have applications beyond calculators, chose to use the new design.

As Hoff and Mazor further refined their design, they figured out how to combine the timing chip and the central processor, making a stand-alone 4-bit CPU. The new model worked with three chips: a random access memory (RAM) chip to store the data, a read-only memory (ROM), and several input/output (I/O) ports that would be able to interface with such other devices as a keyboard, lights, printer, and switches. In April 1970 an engineer named Federico Faggin came from Fairchild Semiconductor to aid the team with the design of the three major chips. At Fairchild, Faggin had developed silicon-gate technology, a process that made high-density, high-performance metallic oxide semiconductor integrated circuits. Faggin transferred Hoff's architectural designs into silicon and created the circuit design, logic, and layout for the chips. By March 1971 Intel had a working microprocessor to ship to Busicom.

Hoff, Mazor, and Faggin knew they had accomplished something of great importance and immediately began pitching ideas to Intel about putting the chips to use in products other than calculators. Initially, however, Intel managers were concerned that they would be unable to use the chips for their own purposes because they had signed the rights to the technology over to Busicom. Busicom, however, soon fell on hard financial times, and Intel was able to renegotiate the contract to get a non-exclusivity agreement from them. In November 1971 Intel began marketing the 4004 microprocessor, as it was called, to the general public, calling it a "microprogrammable computer on a chip" and touting it as having as much computing power as the Electronic Numerical Integrator and Computer (ENIAC), an early general-purpose electronic computer completed in 1946.

Hoff next worked on Intel's 8-bit processor, the 8008, which had been in development since December 1969, when the company signed a contract with Victor Poor of Computer Terminals Corporation (CTC). CTC wanted to develop a "glass Teletype"—in essence a computer terminal that used a cathode-ray tube for presenting information—using a processor designed by Intel. Hoff and the others developed the 8008 processor to fulfill Intel's contract with CTC, but the latter company was unable to use the product due to financial problems. However, Intel had retained the right to sell the product to other firms, and Seiko of Japan soon purchased the 8008. The 8008 microprocessor was the precursor to the 8080 microprocessor, which secured Intel as a major force in the computing industry.

After 14 years at Intel, including a stint in the company's telecommunications division, in 1983 Hoff accepted an offer from Atari to become a vice president of technology. He was fascinated by the variety of video games and home computers Atari was developing at that time. He considered the company's plans to build picture telephones and other revolutionary products an exciting opportunity. Hoff worked with Alan Kay to research and develop some of these newer ideas. He had, however, no inkling of the financial trouble the company was in when he joined. Atari had been selling products through distribution channels, and managers counted game sales and other items as sold as soon as they hit distributors' shelves. As a result of this reckless accounting, Atari continued to manufacture unwanted products, creating a massive surplus in unsold items. The company was eventually sold, and Hoff and Atari parted ways in 1984.

Hoff next joined Teklicon Inc. as a consultant, and he is now vice president and chief technologist there. Teklicon is an organization that provides technical expertise to companies or individuals who are entangled in patent litigation or prosecution. During his interview with Walker, Hoff noted that his company has made a significant contribution to the litigation process since "there's a limit to how much of the technology [lawyers] can follow because they have so many legal aspects that they have to worry about."

Ted Hoff is the recipient of a number of awards, including the Franklin Institute's Stuart Ballantine Medal, the Institute of Electrical and Electronic Engineers' Cledo Brunetti Award, and the Rensselaer Polytechnic Institute's Davies Medal. In 1980 he was named the first Intel Fellow, which gave him the highest technical ranking in the company. In 1996 he, Federico Faggin, and Stan Mazor were inducted into the National Inventors Hall of Fame, in Akron, Ohio. A year later, these three inventors, along with Masatoshi Shima, received the Kyoto Prize, an award presented yearly by the Inamori Foundation, in Japan, to recognize those who have made major advances in science, technology, and the arts.—C. M.

Suggested Reading: *Jones Telecommunications and Multimedia Encyclopedia* (on-line); PBS Web site; Stanford University Web site

---

Hollerith, Herman

Feb. 29, 1860–Nov. 17, 1929 Inventor of the Hollerith tabulator

Herman Hollerith is perceived by many computer historians as the father of information processing. His invention in the mid-1880s of an electromechanical statistical tabulating device is a landmark event in the history of the information age; the Hollerith tabulator is a direct forerunner of the programmable computers that would emerge in the early to mid 20th century. Hollerith was the first to successfully use punched cards as input for a computing machine, getting the idea from early-19th-century French inventor Joseph Jacquard, who had used cards in his automatic weaving loom. British mathematician Charles Babbage had also caught on to the punched cards concept for his Difference and Analytical Engines 50 years before Hollerith, but was unable to fully realize his ideas. However, unlike early-20th century machines such as Vannevar Bush's 1925 differential analyzer, the Hollerith tabulator was not a computer by the strictest definition, since it lacked certain defining elements such as memory capacity, and was non-programmable.

Herman Hollerith was born on February 29, 1860 in Buffalo, New York. He was the son of German immigrants George Hollerith and Franciska (Brunn) Hollerith. In 1875, at the age of 15, he enrolled in the City College of New York. He transferred to the Columbia University School of Mines, in New York City, and graduated with honors in 1879.

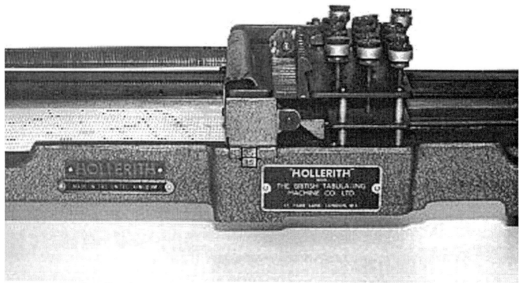

An example of Hollerith's tabulator

Upon graduation, Hollerith, then 19 years old, was hired as a statistician by the U.S. Census Bureau, where he worked as an assistant to his former teacher William Trowbridge. Simultaneously, he took college courses that he felt would aid him in such a position, including academic courses in geometry, physics, and surveying. Hollerith also took practical courses which required him to visit industrial sites and develop an understanding of their methods. His experience working on the 1880 U.S. census familiarized him with the kind of logistical difficulties he would later seek to eliminate by inventing an automatic statistical tabulator.

While employed at the Census Bureau, Hollerith came into contact with the renowned Dr. John Shaw Billings, head of the Bureau's Division of Vital Statistics and organizer of the New York Public Library. At the time, Hollerith was involved with Billings's daughter Kate. Billings is believed to have inspired Hollerith to build a mechanical statistic tabulator, casually suggesting the concept over dinner. Billings referred directly to the Jacquard loom as a possible model for the proposed machine. "He said to me, there ought to be a machine for doing the purely mechanical work of tabulating population and similar statistics," Hollerith is quoted as saying in G. D. Austrian's biography *Herman Hollerith: Forgotten Giant of Information Processing* (1982). "He thought of using cards with the description of the individual shown by notches punched in the edge."

Hollerith kept Billings's idea in mind, but he wouldn't get a chance to do anything about it for several years. He worked at the Massachusetts Institute of Technology (MIT), in Cambridge, during the 1882–83 school year as a mechanical engineering instructor. Following that position, he worked

for another year experimenting with the breaking systems of railroads in St. Louis, Missouri. While there, he came up with an electrical brake system, which was rejected in favor of a steam-powered one developed by Westinghouse. Finally, in 1884 Hollerith returned to Washington and became employed at the U.S. Patent Office. It was at this point that he began to seriously look into the creation of a mechanical tabulator.

With Jacquard's invention as his guide, Hollerith started to work on his own machine in the early 1880s. However, his original model used not cards but a single continuous paper feed with punched holes representing each element to be counted. The paper roll was fed into the machine and passed over a drum. Wherever a hole had been made in the tape, an electrical current was allowed to pass, completing a circuit; this in turn caused the corresponding counter to register a hit. "My idea was to use a strip of paper and punch the record for each individual in a line across the strip," he said (Austrian, *Herman Hollerith*). "Then I ran this strip over a drum and made contacts through a hole to operate the counters." He applied for a patent for the initial model in 1884.

The continuous paper strip Hollerith was using to store information presented problems, however, in that physical damage to any part of the tape affected the entire roll. Also, it was difficult to locate specific information or to go back and correct data. Referring once again to Joseph Jacquard, Hollerith solved these problems in 1886 by replacing the strip with separate pasteboard cards the size of dollar bills. In Austrian's book Hollerith is quoted on another source for the idea: "I was traveling West and I had a ticket with what I think was called a punch photograph . . . the conductor . . .

punched out a description of the individual, such as light hair, dark eyes, large nose, etc. So you see, I only made a punch photograph of each person." With the new design, brass rods would be pressed against the cards, and wherever there was a hole, the rod would be allowed to pass through into a cup of liquid mercury, thus completing the electric circuit and registering a hit on the counter. The cards could be ordered and stored in any manner desired, and could be corrected and replaced with relative ease.

One of the most attractive novelties of the Hollerith tabulating machine was that it was electric. The use of electricity was coming into widespread use at the time thanks to the pioneering work of Thomas A. Edison, and Hollerith was the first to apply it in this way. With electricity driving the tabulator, data could be compiled at a much faster and more efficient rate than a purely mechanical device employing a vast array of moving parts such as cogs and gears. Additionally, the hole-punch system is seen as a predecessor of binary language, introduced into computers by John Atanasoff in the 1940s and still in place today. Much like binary, which is based on a series of ones and zeroes, a hole could be considered to stand for a one and the absence of a hole for a zero.

Hollerith obtained a contract to test his machine at the Office of Registration in Baltimore, Maryland, in 1884. The machine was soon put to use by the state of New Jersey, followed by the city of New York. In 1885 Hollerith's machines were rented out to the U.S. Navy, and three years later by the Office of the Surgeon General in the U.S. Department of War. Acquiring the military and government as customers was very important to Hollerith, because he needed his invention to continue to be adequately funded and supported while he awaited the event for which he had designed the machine in the first place: the 1890 U.S. census.

By the late 19th century, census-taking in America had become a task of monumentally daunting proportions. The population was growing at an alarming rate; for example, in the 1880s the population grew by over 12 million, due to increased urbanization, a huge influx of immigrants, and a general increase in the birth of native citizens. At a cost of $5.8 million, the 1880 census was not completed for nine years; in fact the Census Bureau had begun making preparations for the 1890 census before the 1880 census was finished. With technology in the state that it was, the U.S. Census Bureau feared that the complexity and amount of tabulations required would soon reach a completely unmanageable scale, requiring them to run two censuses at once. More than a listing for bureaucrats or semantic curiosity, the census was (and is) required by the Constitution most notably as a means of assigning seats in the House of Representatives. Consequently, the Census Bureau was extremely concerned with developing a new way of obtaining and processing data.

In response to the problem, the Census Bureau held a competition to find the best new method to be used for the 1890 census. Hollerith entered with his tabulating machine, and won hands down. The Bureau tested entrants by having them transcribe and compile data taken from four sections of St. Louis, Missouri. Hollerith's two main competitors, William Hunt and Charles Pidgin, had designed systems which completed the transcription in six days and four days, respectively, while the Hollerith tabulator took only three days. The compilation was completed by both Hunt's and Pidgin's methods in approximately two days; the same procedure took Hollerith five and a half hours.

In the 1890 census, the Hollerith tabulator tallied the entire population count in just six weeks and saved the Bureau an estimated $5 million in manpower. Fifty-thousand people were employed in the collection and tabulation of data using the machines. A total of 235 questions were included, by far the most ever. To help the clerks punch the necessary holes in the cards, Hollerith developed a device he called the pantograph, which used a keyboard. The pantograph enabled each worker to process an average of 700 census forms per day. After this stage, the tabulators came into play, each counting an average of 2,500 families per day; the combined daily total of U.S. citizens counted by all the machines was over 6 million. All the census data was fully completed in two years. Through the experience gained in the census, Hollerith was able to make several modifications on his invention, including a means of cross-referencing information, as well as a mechanized card-feeding process and card sorter. "With these machines, the most complicated tables could be reproduced at no more expense than the most simple ones," Robert Porter, who headed the census, commented (Austrian, *Herman Hollerith*).

In addition to the $750,000 rental fee payed by the Census Bureau, the astounding performance of the machine brought Hollerith a great deal of notoriety. The machines were featured on the cover of the August 30, 1890 issue of *Scientific American*. Success also opened up quite a few new markets. Hollerith expanded into commercial industries, chiefly that of the ever burgeoning railroad, but also retailers and insurance firms. His machine was also used abroad, with nations around the world clamoring for the new technology to aid in conducting their own censuses. Canada, Norway, and Austria all made use of the machine in 1891. Russia purchased machines from Hollerith in 1897 to aid in conducting its first general census. The device was also used by Great Britain in 1911. Hollerith tabulators were once again utilized for the US census of 1900. With an even more dramatically expanding population than the last time, the Bureau was able to complete the population count in 19 months, instead of the eight years it would have taken just to compile the sex, birthplace, and occupation information without the tabulators.

On September 15, 1890, Herman Hollerith married Lucia Beverly Talcott. The couple went on to have six children: Lucia, Nannie, Virginia, Herman, Richard, and Charles. In 1896 Hollerith left the census bureau and went to New York, to establish the Tabulating Machine Company (TMC), which would rent out tabulating machines. When inventor James Powers developed an automatic hole-puncher for the Census Bureau in 1910, TMC sued for patent infringement, but eventually lost the suit when the case was appealed to the U.S. Supreme Court. Leasing machines from TMC was very expensive, requiring a lot of capital up front; much of the company's profit came from the sale of punched cards, which became known as Hollerith cards. In 1911, TMC merged with the Computing Scale Company and the International Time Recording Company to form the Computer-Tabulating-Recording Company (CTR). Hollerith remained with CTR as a consulting engineer until 1921; three years later, Thomas Watson Sr., the CEO, changed the name of the company to International Business Machines, later known simply as IBM. The Hollerith machine provided the main impetus for the early success of IBM, giving it the foundation on which to dominate the computer industry.

What was perhaps the most heinous and unfortunate misuse of the emerging technology of the early Computer Age occurred shortly after Hollerith's death and involved his tabulator. In the 1930s a German subsidiary of IBM, Deutsche Hollerith Maschinen Gesellschaft (DEHOMAG), constructed Hollerith machines for the Nazis. Using the device, the Nazis were able to establish a database and track essential variables which allowed them to coordinate and execute their ultimate plan of genocide now known as the Holocaust. With the aid of Hollerith's statistical tabulators, Hitler's Third Reich gained the capability to accumulate vast amounts of information regarding Jewish populations, and chart the progress of what would eventually amount to the systematic murder of over 11 million people. It is suspected that such a thoroughly orchestrated and all-encompassing program of wholesale slaughter would have been logistically impossible without the use of the Hollerith tabulators.

Herman Hollerith died on November 17, 1929, in Washington, D.C., at the age of 69. His work with tabulating machines led the way to later forms of data collection and information processing. In fact, his methods (including the use of punched cards) remained in wide use well into the 1960s and even lingered to a lesser extent up to the late 1970s. The code Hollerith used to record the census data on punched cards (called Hollerith code) is still in use today. IBM, the corporation his machine helped to launch, was the final word in the computer industry for more than 50 years and remains a giant in the business to this day.—B. S.

Suggested Reading: Austrian, G. D. *Herman Hollerith: Forgotten Giant of Information Processing*, 1982; Spencer, Donald D. *The Timetable of Computers*, 1997

Hopper, Grace

Dec. 9, 1906–1992 Computer-programming pioneer

Amid the numerous fathers of computing, Grace Hopper was one of the very few mothers. One of the key figures in 20th-century computer history, Hopper was involved in several defining moments in the development of computer technology. She is best remembered as a pioneer in the early stages of computer programming, having worked as a programmer for Howard Aiken's Mark computers as well as John Mauchly's and J. Presper Eckert's ENIAC, both landmarks in computing technology. Hopper also worked to make programming languages more accessible to those who were not mathematics experts. Her work in this area inspired the creation of COBOL, a computer language for use by businesses that became one of the most popular of its kind. She was instrumental in transforming 20th-century computer technology from enormous mountains of wires to simple, graceful, and effective words.

Grace Hopper was born Grace Brewster Murray on December 9, 1906 in New York City. She was the oldest of three children born to William Fletcher Murray and Mary Campbell Van Horne Murray. William Murray worked as an insurance broker, as had his father before him. One of her paternal great-grandfathers, Alexander Russell, had been a rear admiral in the U.S. Navy (a distinction she would later achieve herself), while her maternal grandfather, John Van Horne, was the senior civil engineer of New York City. It was her grandfather who first sparked Grace's interest in mathematics by bringing her with him on various surveying jobs. Her fascination with machines dated back to her childhood: at the age of seven, she dismantled several alarm clocks in the family's Wolfeboro, New Hampshire, summer home in order to see how they worked. As a child, Grace consistently excelled in school. Her home environment fostered her academic success, as she later explained in a profile for the Distinguished Women of Past and Present Web site: "My mother's very great interest in mathematics and my father's [interest], a house full of books, a constant interest in reading, and insatiable curiosity . . . these were a primary influence all the way along."

Cynthia Johnson/Getty Images

Grace Hopper

Grace displayed a remarkable aptitude for mathematics. When her father developed hardening of the arteries and had to have his legs amputated while Grace was in high school, she was driven to perform at an even higher level to raise his spirits. In addition to academic studies, she participated in basketball, field hockey, and water polo. In an age when women were not expected to pursue higher education, William Murray encouraged his daughters to go on to college and careers. Grace ascended through several private girls' schools before entering Vassar College in Poughkeepsie, New York, in 1923 at the age of 17. She graduated in 1928 with a B.A. in math and physics, and from there she went to Yale University, in New Haven, Connecticut, where she received a master's degree in mathematics in 1930. On June 15 of that year she married Vincent Foster Hopper, an English instructor, whom she had met in Wolfeboro, where both their families spent summers. After returning from her European honeymoon, she began teaching math at Vassar as an assistant while working towards her Ph.D. at Yale.

In 1934 Grace Murray Hopper earned her Ph.D. from Yale, with a doctoral thesis entitled "A New Criterion for Reducibility of Algebraic Equations." At that time, achieving a Ph.D. in mathematics in the United States was a rare accomplishment in itself, and for a woman it was practically unheard of. At Vassar, Hopper was promoted to instructor, and later to associate professor. She was awarded a faculty fellowship from Vassar in 1941 to study for a year at New York University's Courant Institute. After finishing the fellowship, she taught at Barnard College in 1943.

With the United States in the midst of World War II, Hopper decided to serve her country by joining the armed forces. She was initially turned down by the U.S. Naval Reserve for a number of reasons, including her age—36, which was too high—and her weight—105, which was too low. The navy also felt that she was more valuable in her role as a math teacher. However, Hopper took a leave of absence from Vassar and was eventually able to convince the navy to accept her. In December 1943 she was sworn into the U.S. Naval Reserve (USNR), and attended the USNR Midshipman's School for Women in Northampton, Massachusetts for the next six months. She graduated in 1944 at the top of her class, with the rank of lieutenant junior grade.

Hopper was assigned to the Bureau of Ships Computation Project at Harvard University in Cambridge, Massachusetts, working in the Cruft Laboratories under the supervision of renowned mathematician and computer designer Howard Aiken. She would be working with Aiken's invention the Mark I, an electromechanical machine that was the first programmable digital computer constructed in America. Her job would be to write computer codes, or programs, as they later became known. Her introduction to the historic Mark I was curt to say the least: "When I walked into the Mark I installation," she recalled in *Portraits in Silicon* (1987), "wonderful Commander Aiken waved a hand at the 51 feet of Mark I and said, 'That's a computing engine.'"

Hopper remembered Aiken as an extremely demanding supervisor. "If the work wasn't done, and it was dinner time, you stayed there," she remembered in *Portraits in Silicon*. "I slept nights on a desk to see if my program was going to get running." Aiken teamed Hopper up with two other programmers, Ensigns Robert Campbell and Richard Bloch. He also introduced her to the work of Charles Babbage, the groundbreaking 19th-century British mathematician whose unfulfilled legacy had inspired Aiken's own work. Together with Campbell and Richard, Hopper worked with the Mark I on several military applications, such as mine placement and calculating firing trajectories. Hopper was also given the task of writing an official operation manual for the massive computer. Programming was in its infancy, and human mistakes abounded. Hopper's *Manual of Operation for the Automatic Sequence Controlled Calculator* was the first book to set guidelines for avoiding such mistakes.

Grace Hopper and her husband Vincent divorced in 1945; that same year, Vincent Hopper was killed in the war. Deciding to remain in the navy after the war was over, Hopper sought a transfer from the reserves to the regular navy. Again, she was initially turned down because, at 40, she was over the age limit. Declining a position as full professor at Vassar, Hopper stayed at the Harvard computer lab, gaining the title of Research Fellow in Engineering and Applied Physics in 1946, the same year she was given the Naval Ordnance Development Award. Also that year, Hopper was promoted from junior grade lieutenant to full lieutenant while continuing her work at Harvard, programming both the Mark II and later the Mark III.

An interesting footnote of computer history involving Hopper occurred in 1947. While at Harvard working on the new Mark II computer, Hopper noticed the machine was malfunctioning, generating the wrong results. Investigating the problem, she discovered a dead moth caught in one of the electric relays. After removing the insect, she taped it in the logbook and one of the computer operators wrote next to it, "First actual bug found". Many computer historians believe the popular use of the term *bug* to mean a computer glitch can be traced back to this incident.

Hopper became interested in the potential application of computers to business while writing a Mark I program for the Prudential Life Insurance Company and in 1949, she left Harvard and accepted a position as a senior mathematician with the Eckert-Mauchly Corporation in Philadelphia. The company's founders, J. Presper Eckert and John Mauchly, had invented the first fully functional electronic computer the ENIAC, and the company was on the verge of developing the UNIVAC I, the first electronic computer for commercial use. Before working with the UNIVAC, however, Hopper was sent to Hawthorne, California, to train Northrup Aircraft personnel in the operation of the new BINAC, a computer intended for use on the Snark missile project.

Eckert-Mauchly was bought by Remington Rand in 1950 and subsequently merged into the Sperry Corporation, but Hopper remained with the business as a senior programmer. The U.S. Navy promoted her to lieutenant commander in 1952, the same year Sperry appointed her Systems Engineer and Director of Automatic Programming for their UNIVAC division. While in this position, Hopper made what many feel is her greatest contribution to computer history. Seeking a solution to the pervasive problem of human error in writing programs, she created a piece of software that could translate a set of programmer's instructions, written in symbolic language, into the binary language used by computers. She called the new type of program a "compiler," a term still in use today. The compiler eliminated the need for the programmer to write directly in complex computer language; for the first time, English language words could be incorporated to make things easier. Hopper explained the concept behind the compiler in *Portraits in Silicon*: "[A computer is] basically a symbolic manipulator. When it's doing numerical mathematics it is manipulating arithmetic symbols, and when it's doing data processing it's manipulating data processing symbols." The first compiler, created in 1952, was called A-0, marketed by Sperry under the name Math-matic. In 1957 she formulated an improved version for use with the UNIVAC, first called B-0 and later Flow-matic.

This version in particular was the first to make full use of English language words. Specifically, it was designed to translate a language words commonly used in business, such as billing and payroll. By 1958 Hopper had put together a manual for Flow-matic.

Flow-matic was essentially intended as the first computer language for businesses, just as the earlier language FORTRAN was designed for the scientific community. Soon after the release of Flow-matic, however, came a barrage of copycat languages, such as IBM's Commercial Translator and Honeywell's Fact. Unhappy with the idea of having several business languages instead of a single standard, a group of people within the computer industry, Hopper among them, set out in 1959 to create such a standard. After two meetings, one of them at the U.S. Department of Defense, the Committee on Data System Languages (CODASYL) was created to develop a common business programming language to be used on all automatic digital computers. The programming code they created was called the Common Business-Oriented Language, or COBOL. Although Hopper herself was only an advisor to the committee, Flow-matic, her brainchild, was cited as the direct inspiration for COBOL.

COBOL was created as a way of making programs easier to read, write, and understand. One important quality of the language was that, unlike all of the other business languages which existed at the time, COBOL was compatible with all types of computers. Also, COBOL used English syntax and terms, as opposed to the more mathematical structure of FORTRAN. In this way, COBOL can be seen as a forerunner of BASIC, an even more simplified programming language developed by John Kemeny and Thomas Kurtz five years later.

Hopper became a staff scientist of systems programming in the UNIVAC division in 1964. Reaching the legal limit of 20 years of reserve service, she retired from the navy in 1966 with the rank of commander. Seven months later, at the age of 60, she was called back (on a temporary basis which had to be renewed annually) to help standardize the high-level programming languages she had helped to create, and train the naval personnel to use them. In this capacity, she worked to standardize COBOL and implement it throughout the entire navy. She continued refining programming language techniques, keeping the navy on the cutting edge of computer technology. In 1969 the Data Processing Management Association named her as its first computer-sciences "Man of the Year." She retired from Sperry in 1971, and two years later was promoted to the rank of captain. Two years after that, she became the first American and the first woman to be made a Distinguished Fellow of the British Computer Society.

In 1982 Hopper became the oldest person in the navy, at age 75. The following year, she ascended to the rank of commodore in a special White House ceremony. In 1984 she became an advisor to the head of the Naval Data Automation Command. For many years, Hopper served as a public-relations ambassador, lecturing about computers on the navy's behalf all over the country. In many of her lectures she spoke out against the modern computer industry for what she felt was a general lack of standardization in areas such as programming languages and networks, which costs the government hundreds of millions of dollars a year in software and hardware in order to keep various parts of their systems compatible with each other. She also expressed concern regarding the onset of the information age. Specifically, Hopper was worried that with the vast amounts of information available to us today, people would become less critical of the nature of the content of that information.

Hopper received her final promotion, to rear admiral, from President Ronald Reagan in 1985, becoming the first woman to ever attain such a rank in the U.S. Navy. The nation's oldest military officer on active duty of the time, she retired from the navy for good in August of 1986 at the age of 79, at a ceremony held in Boston aboard the USS Constitution, the oldest U.S. naval vessel in existence.

Retirement from the navy did not mean retirement from professional life; weeks after the Constitution ceremony, Hopper accepted a position in public relations with the computer manufacturer Digital Equipment Corporation (DEC). Her duties for DEC included public relations appearances and educational lectures. In 1991 she was awarded the National Medal of Technology by President George Bush.

Grace Murray Hopper died in her sleep in Alexandria, Virginia, on New Year's Day, 1992 at the age of 85. She received a full naval funeral, and was buried on January 7 at Arlington National Cemetery. A true pioneer in the fields of computer programming and data processing, she was one of the most influential people in the history of computers. Known to her coworkers as "Amazing Grace," she always believed that her greatest contribution was in educating America's young people about computers.—B. S.

Suggested Reading: Yale University Web site; Distinguished Women of Past and Present Web site; *The History of Computing* (on-line); Slater, Robert. *Portraits in Silicon*, 1987

Hurd, Cuthbert C.

Apr. 5, 1911–May 22, 1996 IBM executive; mathematician

Cuthbert C. Hurd served as the director of the Applied Sciences Division of International Business Machines (IBM) during the 1950s. He directed the development of the IBM 701, an innovative machine that steered IBM onto the path of becoming a computer-industry giant. Also known as the "defense calculator," the IBM 701 was the first commercially successful general-purpose computer.

Cuthbert C. Hurd was born on April 5, 1911 in Estherville, Iowa, to Harland Corwin and the former Olive Grace Long. He studied at Drake University, in Des Moines, Iowa, graduating in 1932 with a B.A. in mathematics. He received a master's degree in mathematics in 1934 from Iowa State University, in Ames, and a Ph.D. in the subject from the University of Illinois in 1936. He completed postdoctoral work at Columbia University, in New York City, and the Massachusetts Institute of Technology (MIT), in Cambridge. He worked as a professor of math at Michigan State College until 1942 and served as a dean of Allegheny College, in Pennsylvania, from 1945 to 1947.

After working for a time as a mathematician at the Atomic Energy Commission laboratory in Oak Ridge, Tennessee, in 1949 Hurd joined IBM as the first director of the newly formed Applied Science Division. When the Korean War broke out in the early 1950s, Hurd and a colleague, James Birkenstock, were assigned to devise projects to assist in the war effort. They suggested that IBM design and

build a general-purpose computer used for high-speed calculations; they called the machine a "defense calculator," to appeal to IBM officials' sense of patriotism. Hurd believed that IBM should finance the project itself, instead of relying on government funds, so that the company would own the patents. IBM's CEO, Thomas J. Watson Sr., was reluctant. "Old man Watson didn't like the idea of going into a new industry when he was doing very well with the [punched-card] business," J. A. N. Lee, a professor of computer science, told Mary Brandel for *Computerworld* (February 1, 1999). However, Thomas J. Watson Jr., Watson's son, was convinced of the potential of the burgeoning field of computer electronics, and he successfully persuaded senior management that computers would not interfere with IBM's punched-card business.

IBM unveiled the new machine, the IBM 701, in 1952, after spending $3 million on its development. The 701, which had binary, fixed-point, single-address hardware, was the first large computer developed by IBM to utilize the vacuum tube. This made the machine easier to repair and adjust than IBM's Mark 1, built in 1944, which relied on electromechanical switches. The 701 executed 17,000 instructions per second—although the speed of the computer was limited by the speed of its memory. The machine was used primarily by government and research institutions, although the vacuum-tube design paved the way for such business applications as billing, payroll, and inventory control. The 701 was also one of the first machines to make successful use of magnetic tape to store information. Magnetic tape had been explored previously for its storage capacity, but it was fragile and prone to breakage during the rapid movements of machine computation. IBM solved this problem by designing magnetic tape drives that could read and write at fast enough speeds to be useful for reliable data processing. Their first high-speed magnetic tape drive was model 726, which could read and write at 100 bits per linear inch.

Hurd succeeded in convincing General Electric, the atomic research facility in Los Alamos, and approximately a dozen other organizations to purchase the 701, despite its price of $1 million. (It could be leased for $15,000 a month.) Fewer than 20 of the machines were made; the first one went to IBM's headquarters in New York. Others were sent to aircraft companies, research labs, and such governmental entities as the U.S. Department of Defense, the U.S. Weather Bureau, and the U.S. Navy.

Hurd also oversaw the development of the faster and more reliable successor to the 701, the IBM 704, completed in 1956. He directed the development of the 650 EDPM, which was IBM's first mass-produced computer. Hurd managed the group that created FORTRAN (FORmula TRANslation), a high-level programming language based on algebra, grammar, and syntax rules. FORTRAN, developed primarily by the IBM scientist John Backus, was a precursor of such high-level languages as COBOL, C, and C++. Hurd's other projects included the development of the IBM 7030 (also known as Stretch), which was IBM's first transistorized supercomputer, and the IBM 1710.

Hurd left IBM in 1962 to serve as chairman of the board of the Computer Usage Company, an independent software firm. He later served as chairman of Cuthbert Hurd Associates and the Picodyne Corporation, which specialized in educational software. In 1984 he co-founded Quintus Computer Systems, which focused on commercial applications for artificial intelligence.

Hurd died on May 22, 1996 at his home in Portola Valley, California. At that time he was the chief scientist for Northpoint Software Ventures, a developer of risk-management software. He was survived by his wife, Bettie; his son, Steven; and four daughters—Diana, Susan, Elizabeth, and Victoria.—A. I. C.

Suggested Reading: *Computerworld* p75 Feb. 1, 1999; *New York Times* p41 June 2, 1996; Lee, J. A. N., ed. *International Biographical Dictionary of Computer Pioneers*, 1995

Huskey, Harry Douglas

Jan. 19, 1916–1995 Developer of the SWAC

Playing major roles in the design and development of several early electronic digital computers, Harry Douglas Huskey was an important figure in the history of what is now known as the Information Age. He was involved in the ENIAC project, which produced the world's first fully functional, large-scale general-purpose electronic computer. He aided British computer designer Alan Turing with the Pilot ACE computer, eventually taking over the entire project himself. Perhaps most notably, Huskey was the driving force behind the construction in 1950 of the SWAC, a stored-program computer that bore a strong resemblance to the computers used today. His expertise was put to great use throughout the formative years of the modern computer, helping to move the technology rapidly forward.

Harry Douglas Huskey was born on January 19, 1916, to Cornelius and Myrtle (Cunningham) Huskey in Whittier, North Carolina. He received a B.S. in mathematics and physics from the University of Idaho in 1937 and then went to Ohio University and began working toward an M.S. in mathematics. He was a teaching assistant at Ohio University from 1938 to 1939, and then a teaching assistant at Ohio State University until 1942. He received his M.S. from Ohio University, in 1941, and was promoted to instructor at Ohio State University, where he earned a Ph.D. in mathematics in 1943.

By April 1944, Huskey had become a member of the faculty of the University of Pennsylvania, in Philadelphia, where he developed his interest in computers. At the university's Moore School of Electrical Engineering, work was being done on the first fully functional electronic digital computer. The machine was named the Electronic Numerical Integrator and Calculator, or ENIAC, and was being built by scientists John Mauchly and J. Presper Eckert. Although Huskey had arrived at the Moore School where the project was well underway, he contributed and learned all that he could, and this knowledge would serve him well in his extensive career as an engineer. Mauchly and Eckert assigned him the task of working with the input and output devices for the machine.

Huskey also cowrote a manual for the ENIAC with Adele Goldstine that was used by Army engineers at the Aberdeen Proving Grounds in Aberdeen, Maryland, and worked on the early logical designs for the EDVAC, a follow-up to the ENIAC. After the ENIAC was finished, there were many at the Moore School who believed that it was already obsolete due to the fact that it was not capable of storing programs, and it was for this reason that the EDVAC was proposed. The EDVAC would have a significantly larger amount of memory than the ENIAC, and would be a "speedier, simpler machine" (*Engines of the Mind*, 1984). Huskey's experience working on stored-program technology for the EDVAC would soon come into play in his design for the SWAC.

When Mauchly and Eckert left the Moore School in 1946, Huskey soon did the same, departing the University of Pennsylvania in June 1946 and moving in December to Great Britain, where he worked at the National Physical Laboratory (NPL) in Teddington, England, as a temporary principal science officer. At that time, the NPL was very much interested in computer technology, and had already begun pursuing research in that area. During his year with the NPL, Huskey worked with computer designer Alan M. Turing on Turing's ACE computer. In 1948 Huskey began work on a basic design and test model of the ACE, or Automatic Computing Engine, based on Turing's original design. Although some historians have mentioned that Turing was unhappy with Huskey's test model because he felt it undermined his own authority on the project, Huskey maintained that the British scientist bore no ill will toward him. "In all my relations with Turing, I found him helpful," he stated in *Computer Pioneers* (1995). "He did not 'boycott' the development of the ACE Test Assembly, nor did I feel that he resented my part in its beginnings." Whatever the case, Turing left the ACE project shortly thereafter.

After returning to the United States, Huskey took a position as head of the machine development lab with the National Bureau of Standards at the National Applied Mathematics Laboratory in Washington, D.C. It was there that he initiated the Standards Eastern Automatic Computer (SEAC) project, which was continued after his departure in 1948. This was followed by a job as assistant director of the Institute for Numerical Analysis (INA), part of the University of California at Los Angeles (UCLA) where Huskey worked from 1948 to 1954. While there, he constructed the Standards Western Automatic Computer (SWAC), an early digital machine of his own design.

Huskey's idea was to create a parallel-processing, stored-program computer with a high-speed electronic memory. The project was authorized by the INA in October 1948, and Huskey went to work the following January. He decided to use the fastest parallel operator available, that of the Whirlwind computer, originally built at the Massachusetts Institute of Technology, in Cambridge, in 1945. Completed in 1950, the SWAC was the fastest computer in the world at the time. Its organization and operating principles bore some resemblance to late-20th-century personal computers, despite its vastly different appearance. The SWAC was a stored-program computer, just like today's machines, and also like them it had an internal memory "clock" and arithmetic logic unit. It even featured a keyboard for input. It contained the equivalent of approximately 1,200 bytes of memory, and thus it could handle only one problem at a time. In 1952 the machine performed its most notable feat by completing in 13 minutes and 25 seconds a computation that would have taken a human being with a desk calculator approximately a century to finish.

Huskey was the technical director of Wayne University's Computation Laboratory from 1952 to 1953. In 1954, he went to the University of California, Berkeley, to teach electrical engineering, first as an associate professor (1954–58) and later as a full professor (1958–68). He became vice chairman of the electrical engineering department in 1966 and held that position for a year. Huskey then accepted a position at the University of California (UC) at Santa Cruz that he had been offered several years before, as a professor of information and computer science, a job he held until 1985. He was also director of the university's Computer Center from 1968 to 1977, and chairman of its Board of Information Science from 1976 to 1979 and from 1982 to 1983.

In addition to his work as computer designer, Huskey also acted as an adviser to many projects and organizations. He worked with the staff of the Bendix Corporation in designing the Bendix G-15 drum-memory minicomputer, a device whose design, which was inspired by that of the ACE computer, gave it great speed. This project began a long-term association with the company that eventually led Huskey to contribute to the logic design of their G-20 computer in the 1950s. He advised the United Nations on the role of the computer in India, China, Nigeria, and other developing countries, including computer education and the establishment of computer centers. Along these same lines, Huskey was the chairman of a committee established by the U.S. National Academy of Sciences to advise Brazil on data processing education. In the 1980s he was a member of the Advisory Panel of the Institutional Program on computers in the National Science Foundation, and he also worked with the Naval Research Advisory Committee. He was named professor emeritus at UC Santa Cruz in 1985 and held this title for the remainder of his life.

From 1960 to 1962, Huskey was the president of the prestigious Association for Computing Machinery (ACM), an organization that encouraged the spread of technical information regarding computer science. He was also an editor for publications put out by the Institute of Electrical and Electronic Engineers Computer Society (IEEE). He was a Fellow of the IEEE and of the British Computer Society, and published over 50 papers in the field of computer science. He was the recipient of the Distinguished Alumni Award at Idaho State University in 1978, and in 1980 he received the IEEE Computer Society Pioneer Award. In addition to the IEEE, he was also a member of the British Computer Society, the American Mathematical Society, the Association for Computing Machinery, and the American Federation of Information Processing Societies.

Huskey married his first wife, Velma Elizabeth Roeth, on January 2, 1939. They had four children: daughters Carolyn, Roxanne, and Linda, and son Harry Douglas Jr. Velma died in January of 1991 and Huskey remarried on September 10, 1994, to Nancy Grindstaff.

Harry Huskey died in 1995 at the age of 79. The G-15 computer he designed for the Bendix Corporation, and which had been in his personal possession for many years, is currently held by the Smithsonian Institution's National Museum of American History. The SWAC, Huskey's greatest individual achievement, was dismantled in 1967 after 17 years of service.—B. S.

Suggested Reading: Cortada, James W. *Historical Dictionary of Data Processing: Biographies*, 1987; Lee, J. A. N., ed. *International Biographical Dictionary of Computer Pioneers*, 1995; Shurkin, Joel. *Engines of the Mind*, 1984; *Larousse Dictionary of Scientists*, 1994; *World Who's Who in Science*, 1968

Jacquard, Joseph

July 7, 1752–Aug. 7, 1834 Inventor of a punched-card automated loom

At the turn of the 19th century, Joseph Jacquard, a French weaver, invented a mechanical loom that is considered one of the first important examples of automation, a process that characterized the Industrial Revolution and propelled innovation and technology well into the 20th century. The perfected Jacquard loom was designed to perform its actions while being guided by punched cards rather than human hands, making it the first machine to follow programmed instructions. Jacquard's work, particularly his use of punched cards, would later influence the British inventor Charles Babbage in the creation of his Analytical Engine, an early mechanical computing device that was the seed of the computer revolution of the 20th century, and for this reason Jacquard is an important figure in the early history of the information age.

Joseph-Marie Jacquard was born on July 7, 1752 in Lyon, France. He spent his early adulthood as a silk weaver, lime burner (heating the mineral substance for building and agricultural purposes), and maker of straw hats. In 1790 he began formulating his idea for an automatic loom. However, his plans had to be put on hold due to the French Revolution, which had begun the previous year and in which the country's citizens sought to overthrow the rule of the French monarchy. During the war, Jacquard joined the revolutionaries and fought to defend his native city of Lyon against the royal troops of King Louis XVI.

Through his experience as a weaver, Jacquard was well-acquainted with the difficulties involved in the textile manufacturing process as it existed in his day. In order to weave any kind of pattern in to a piece of cloth or fabric, a weaver was required to raise hundreds of specific vertical threads and manually pass a horizontal thread underneath them. An average piece of cloth might contain several hundred thousand threads, and raising just one wrong thread could ruin the entire pattern.

Jacquard's design for his mechanical loom was inspired by the work of an earlier French weaver, Basile Bouchon, who had built a semiautomatic loom more than 75 years earlier. Bouchon used a paper loop with rows of holes punched in it to aid the weaver in manipulating the threads; Jacquard took this concept a step further by using punched cards containing predefined instructions, which his loom was then able to follow without further human intervention. Although Bouchon's loom made weaving cheaper, easier, and faster, the response to his invention, similar to that evoked by Jacquard's loom years later, was disastrous. Weavers' assistants, whose jobs had in effect been eliminated, destroyed the looms; narrow-minded aristocrats and clergy suppressed them; and master weavers endeavored to buy them all in an attempt to protect their monopoly. The Bouchon loom wound up as an exhibit in the Paris Museum of Arts and Crafts, and it remained largely irrelevant until Jacquard began to update its design for use in the 19th century.

In 1801 Jacquard completed the first version of his mechanical loom, which was based on contemporary carpet-making looms. The Jacquard loom was able to create patterns on fabric using instructions given by an operator. Not only did the loom speed up the weaving process, increasing production and therefore potential sales, it was also able to execute more complex fabric designs than had ever been seen before. It was able to perform all weaving motions, and is credited with having woven the first figured patterns. By manipulating the individual threads, the device could weave highly detailed patterns, intricate work that was once the exclusive province of manual weavers. It could be used to create such fabrics as damask, brocade, and tapestry, and was later adapted so that it was able to knit patterned designs as well. However, the original Jacquard loom still required a human operator at all times to set the loom to carry out each step required in order to create the design. It would be four more years before Jacquard developed the punched-card method that made it possible for the loom to be "programmed."

Jacquard was summoned to Paris to take part in a national industrial technology exposition called the *Exposition Publique des Produits de l'Industrie Française*, organized by the French government, under Napoleon Bonaparte, in September 1801. Napoleon had been officially instated as the leader of France by the Treaty of Luneville earlier in the year, and he believed that a national exposition of industrial products would help to boost the nation's pride, as well as its confidence in its new ruler. The exposition was held in September in the courtyard of the Louvre, and Jacquard joined nearly 300 other exhibitors who had been called on to participate. Napoleon himself was present to inspect the various entries, and he witnessed a demonstration by Jacquard of his loom. In addition to being issued a patent, the invention was awarded one of 30 bronze medals given out at the event, with 12 gold medals going to such inventions as a canal lock mechanism and, in another example, to an impressive display of carpentry saws. While by the 20th century, it had become clear that Jacquard's loom was a key harbinger of industrialization and automation, it seemed that the exposition jury did not have a full understanding of its significance, commenting merely that it "replaces a worker in the weaving of brocades," (*The Napoleonic Expositions*, on-line).

In 1805 Jacquard designed and built a second loom that would prove to be the more important of the two. In this loom, punched cards controlled the weaving of the cloth, allowing any design or pattern to be woven into the fabric automatically, without the intervention of a human operator. The cards, mounted on a gear-driven belt, dictated the pattern of raised and depressed vertical threads so that the horizontal thread would pass through all the right places to create the desired pattern. Needles would be able to pull thread through the cards only where one of the holes had been made, and a single card could be used to guide approximately 1,200 needles. Using over 24,000 punched cards, Jacquard was able to use his invention to create a square rug with a self-portrait. In a later revision of the loom, Jacquard joined the punched cards to form an endless loop, which could be used to create a repeating pattern such as those found on carpets. Charles Babbage (at the suggestion of Lady Ada Lovelace) later proposed punched cards as a means of controlling and programming his early calculating machine, the Analytical Engine, which he began constructing in the 1830s. Punched cards were also used toward the end of the 19th century by the U. S. statistician Herman Hollerith as a means of entering data into his census machine.

Jacquard was shocked by the violently negative reception his invention initially received. The evaluation of the exposition jury in 1801, which noted the loom's potential for replacing workers, had foreshadowed the general public's reaction to the device. Silk weavers feared that the new mechanism would rob them of their livelihood, and hostility developed toward both the invention and its inventor. Looms that were under construction were burned by angry workers. The Conseil des Prud'hommes of Lyon dismantled a loom in the town square and sold its iron parts for scrap. Jacquard himself was physically attacked, on one occasion barely escaping with his life. In the five years following the introduction of Jacquard's first loom, the inventor received a total of six death threats.

High-ranking French officials proved to be more level-headed in their reaction to the loom than the country's citizenry had been. Recognizing Jacquard's creation as a machine that could give France a dramatic advantage over its major international competitor Great Britain, the government declared the loom public property in 1806. In recognition of his contribution to the nation, Jacquard was given an annual pension of 3,000 francs for the rest of his life, as well as royalties on each machine sold.

The Jacquard loom was eventually accepted by the public, who had gradually been won over by its usefulness and efficiency. Also, people were pleased to learn that the device actually created more jobs, employing even more men than before in order to efficiently operate the looms. By 1812 there were 11,000 looms being used throughout France. Jacquard was awarded a gold medal and the Cross of the Legion of Honor in 1819 in recognition of his tremendous contribution to the textile industry. During the following decade, use of his invention spread across the English Channel to Great Britain, and eventually it came to be used on a nearly worldwide scale.

The Jacquard loom brought about a revolution, particularly in men's and women's clothing. Previously, weaving colors and designs into fabric was extremely time-consuming, and therefore such fabrics were so costly that only the very wealthy could afford them. Jacquard's loom made it possible for detailed patterns to be cheaply produced, allowing those who were not well-to-do to own garments with such patterns, and even with intricate tapestries once reserved only for royal consumers.

On August 7, 1834 Joseph Jacquard died in the town of Oullins, just outside of Lyon. By the time of his death, his loom was used nearly universally in textile manufacturing. In addition to the influence his mechanical loom had on such early computer pioneers as Babbage and Hollerith, Jacquard's innovative punched cards were employed in several of the early mechanical and electromechanical computers of the 20th century, including Howard Aiken's Mark I and John Atanasoff's ABC. Jacquard's loom marked a crucial step in the development of methods of data entry and programming, development which eventually led to the completely electronic and digital formats that became the norm in the 20th century.—B. S.

Suggested Reading: *History of Computing* (on-line); *Moths to the Flame* (on-line) Sep. 27, 1996; Hellemans, Alexander and Brian Bunch. *The Timetables of Science*, 1991

Jevons, William Stanley

Sep. 1, 1835–Aug. 13, 1882 Inventor of the Logical Abacus

The economist and logician William Stanley Jevons was among the theorists who first treated logic as a branch of mathematics. In addition to writing several influential books on logic, Jevons designed an early logic machine, often referred to as the Logical Abacus or the Logical Piano. The reduction of logic to terms that could be entered into simple mathematical formulas contributed to an emerging discourse about mechanical rationality and gave Jevons the blueprint for his piano-shaped machine, which he completed in 1869. Though other logic machines had been built, Jevons's was the first that could perform logical operations faster than humans. The Logical Abacus is often cited as being an early precursor to the modern computer.

William Stanley Jevons was born in Liverpool, England, on September 1, 1835, the ninth of the 11 children of Thomas Jevons, an iron merchant and inventor, and Mary Anne (Roscoe), a poet well known in Unitarian circles. His mother died when he was 10, and his elder sister took her place as his caretaker. He was educated at the Mechanics Institute High School, in Liverpool. At the age of 15 he enrolled in college in London, where he pursued chemistry and mathematics. His father's iron firm went bankrupt, in 1848, after a railway crisis caused iron prices to fall dramatically. Jevons left school, in 1852, prior to graduation, to earn money for his family. He accepted a position as an assayer at the new mint in Sydney, Australia. The position made use of Jevons's knowledge of chemistry; as an assayer he was required to weigh, measure, and determine the purity of the coinage. He also studied meteorology and made weather reports, used by the government, from 1856 to 1858.

Jevons soon became interested in social and economic questions as well. In 1859 he returned to college to study mathematics, physics, and political economy. He often walked through the rundown sections of London, meditating on social conditions. "I began to think that I could and ought to do more than others. A vague desire and determination grew upon me," Jevons wrote in his *Letters and Journal* (1886), as quoted in the archives of the MacTutor History of Mathematics Web site. He felt that he wanted to be "powerfully good, that is to be good, not towards one, or a dozen, or a hundred, but towards a nation or the world." After earning his B.A. in 1860 and his M.A. in 1862, Jevons became a tutor at Owens College, in Manchester, England (now the University of Manchester). In 1867 he married Harriet Ann Taylor, daughter of the founder of the Manchester *Guardian*, with whom he had three children, including a son who became a well-known economist.

Jevons's first book on logic, *Pure Logic* (also titled *The Logic of Quality Apart From Quantity*), was published in 1864. It was influenced by George Boole, who in formulating Boolean Algebra had explored the connection between algebraic symbols and those used to represent logical terms. Jevons, though admitting his debt to Boole, also criticized him for over- complicating the mathematics of logic, positing instead his "substitution of similars." "When we examine carefully enough the way in which we reason," Jevons wrote in *Primer of Logic* (1876), as quoted in *The New Palgrave: A Dictionary of Economics* (1987) and posted on the University of Marburg Web site, "it will be found in every case to consist in putting one thing or term in place of another to which we know it to have an exact resemblance in some respect."

Having reduced the principles of logic down to basic elements, Jevons decided to design a machine that could solve logical puzzles mechanically. In 1869 he had a watchmaker build his Logical Abacus, which allowed users to compute logical problems containing up to four terms. The machine was demonstrated before the Royal Society in 1870, and Jevons was elected to the Fellowship of the Royal Society in 1872. He continued to expand his theory of logic in *The Principles of Science* (1874).

Jevons's writings on political economy include *General Mathematical Theory of Political Economy* (1862), *The Coal Question* (1865), and *The Theory of Political Economy* (1871). Among the important concepts he introduced to economists was his theory of marginal utility, which states that as the quantity of any commodity increases, its utility or benefit decreases proportionally.

Jevons remained at Owens College until 1876, first as lecturer in logic and political economy, then as professor of these subjects and also of mental and moral philosophy. He detested lecturing and in later years spoke in public as little as possible. From 1876 to 1880 he was professor of political economy at University College, and his reduced duties put less strain on his failing health and allowed him to dedicate more time to his writing. He died at the age of 47 by drowning, while swimming near Hastings, England, on August 13, 1882.—P. G. H.

Suggested Reading: *Studies in History and Philosophy of Science* p587+ Dec. 1999; Cortada, James W. *Historical Dictionary of Data Processing*, 1987; *The New Palgrave: A Dictionary of Economics*, 1987; Lee, J. A. N., ed. *International Biographical Dictionary of Computer Pioneers*, 1995

Jobs, Steven Paul

Feb. 24, 1955– Co-founder and CEO of Apple Computer; CEO of Pixar

"Part hustling opportunist and part technology visionary" is how Steve Lohr described the computer entrepreneur Steven Jobs for the *New York Times Magazine* (January 12, 1997). Jobs was only 21 years old when, in 1976, he co-founded Apple Computer with his friend Steve Wozniak. The following year, the company introduced the Apple II computer, the product that many consider to be most responsible for launching the personal-computer revolution. While Wozniak is remembered as the programming whiz, it was Jobs's entrepreneurial sense and willful self-confidence that turned Apple—then one of many upstarts just entering the business of personal computers—into a legend of computer history. Jobs was the chairman of Apple's board until 1985; after a bitter power struggle with the management, he left Apple and founded his own computer company, NeXT. At

Courtesy of Apple Computer

Steven Jobs

NeXT Jobs introduced the Cube, a powerful workstation computer that many acknowledged as a work of art, but that proved to be a resounding commercial failure. Jobs refocused the company on producing an operating system, and in 1996 Apple, desperate after a decade of falling sales, purchased NeXT for more than $400 million. Jobs was appointed as Apple's CEO in 1996 and helped to reverse the company's decline, revitalizing the firm with such new products as the stylish iMac computer and the iBook laptop, which redefined the aesthetics of personal computers. Jobs is also the CEO of Pixar Animation Studios, which he had purchased from Lucasfilm in 1986. In that role he oversaw the release of four of the most successful animated films of all time: *Toy Story* (1995), *A Bug's Life* (1998), *Toy Story 2* (1999), and *Monsters, Inc.* (2001). Known for his for messianic zeal, Jobs has been described as both a highly motivational leader and as a managerial terror whose temper often gets the upper hand. He is a perfectionist who demands a lot from his workers, but whose enthusiasm is contagious—those who work with him like to allude to the Steve Jobs "reality distortion field." "Being the richest man in the cemetery doesn't matter to me," Jobs once said of what motivates him. "Going to bed at night saying we've done something wonderful . . . that matters to me."

Steven Paul Jobs was born on February 24, 1955, in San Francisco, California. Shortly after his birth, he was adopted by Paul Jobs, a machinist whom Jobs remembers as "a genius with his hands," and Clara Jobs, an accountant. Early on, he displayed an interest in electronics and a strong will. A few days before beginning the ninth grade, he an-

nounced that he would not return to his old junior high school, because, he insisted, he wasn't learning anything there. His parents took his complaint seriously, and they moved from Mountain View, California, to nearby Los Altos, where Steven enrolled at Homestead High School. John McCollum, his electronics teacher at Homestead High, recalled to a *Time* (January 3, 1983) interviewer that Steven was "something of a loner" and "always had a different way of looking at things."

While in high school Steven attended lectures at the Hewlett-Packard (HP) electronics plant in Palo Alto. One day—at age 12, according to Steve Lohr—he boldly telephoned H-P's president, William R. Hewlett, and requested parts to build a frequency counter for a school project. Hewlett complied, and he was so impressed with Jobs that he offered him a summer job, too. In 1972 Jobs graduated from high school and entered Reed College, in Portland, Oregon. After one semester, he dropped out, but he hung around the campus for another year, taking classes in philosophy and immersing himself in the counterculture. He meditated, learned the I Ching, experimented with psychedelic drugs, and became a vegetarian.

Early in 1974 Jobs took a job at Atari, which had been founded in Sunnyvale, California, two years earlier by Nolan Bushnell, a pioneer in the electronic-arcade industry. One of the computer games Jobs worked on was *Breakout*, a game that involved bouncing a ball against a wall to break it down. Jobs asked a friend, Stephen Wozniak, then an employee at HP and a computer circuitry whiz, for help designing the game's hardware. Wozniak completed the job using so few integrated circuits that the duo earned a sizable bonus. Shortly thereafter Jobs left Atari, with the intention of returning later. With a shaved head and a backpack, he and a friend traveled to India in search of spiritual enlightenment. Upon his return to the United States, Jobs spent a short time working in an apple orchard in Oregon before returning to California.

Meanwhile, Wozniak had emerged as the resident genius of the Homebrew Computer Club, a group of young computer zealots in Palo Alto. Jobs began attending meetings in 1975, where he was exposed to some of the first assembly-required hobbyist computers, most notably the Altair 8800, built by Ed Roberts's company MITS. Wozniak was inspired by the Altair's technology, but Jobs was inspired by stories that MITS was being flooded with orders for the computer. When Wozniak showed Jobs a computer he had built using a Mostek 6502 computer chip, it occurred to Jobs that there was a real money-making opportunity available to them. Jobs, who was 21 at the time, suggested to Wozniak that they go into business together. At first reluctant to leave his job at H-P, Wozniak eventually agreed.

To acquire start-up funds, they sold Jobs's Volkswagen bus and Wozniak's H-P calculator for a total of about $1,500. They built a completed prototype, which consisted of a pre-assembled circuit board with built-in connections for a video interface and a keyboard, and showed it to Paul Terrell, the owner of the Byte Shop, the only local computer store. Terrell agreed to buy 100 computers at $500 each. To fill the order, Jobs turned the Palo Alto home of his parents, where he was then living, into an assembly line, building Wozniak's computer with the help of his sister, a couple of friends, and two teenagers who were proficient in Beginners All-purpose Symbolic Instruction Code (BASIC). Jobs christened the computer the Apple, in memory of his summer in the apple orchard, as well as a tribute to the Beatles, who had used the name for their record label. A few months later, the Apple I began selling to hobbyists and electronics enthusiasts for about $650.

In January 1977 Mike Markkula, a venture capitalist, invested $250,000 in the fledgling company. He split the ownership of the company three ways with Jobs and Wozniak, and set up a management team. The assembly line moved into a building in Cupertino, California. Meanwhile, Wozniak had been at work on an improved follow-up model, the Apple II. Unveiled at the West Coast Computer Faire in April 1977, the Apple II was designed to appeal not just to hobbyists, but to beginners and general users; it was the first personal computer with color graphics, and it came with a keyboard, a power supply, and an attractive case, all for $1,300. The user-friendly Apple II, dubbed "the Volkswagen of computers," was tremendously successful, and it set the standard in personal computers. Within three years, it earned the company $139 million—a growth in revenue of 700 percent. Fueled by its success, Apple went public in December 1980, offering 4.6 million shares at $22 per share. Within minutes, every share had been sold. At the end of the first day of trading, the stock closed at $29, thus bringing Apple's market value to $1.2 billion and the value of Jobs's 8.3 million shares to $239 million.

In 1980 Apple launched the Apple III, a more complex machine targeted for businesses. The attempt to enter the corporate market failed, however, as the first 14,000 Apple IIIs that were sold had to be recalled due to intermittent malfunctioning. In addition, Apple was now facing heavy competition from IBM, which had launched its own personal computer. By 1982 Apple had written off the Apple III—which meant that all revenues were still coming from its five-year-old line of Apple IIs.

Meanwhile, Jobs was at work on something new. Back in 1979, he had visited Xerox's Palo Alto Research Center (PARC), an advanced computing facility renowned for its pioneering technological creations. There Jobs was given a demonstration of Alto, a computer system that used a new screen display called a graphical user interface (GUI), consisting of icons, windows, menus, fonts, and a crisp display. Today GUIs are ubiquitous, but at the time, computer screens relied on the command-line interface, requiring the user to enter arcane commands using a keyboard. The Alto system, moreover, made extensive use of the now-familiar device called a mouse, used for moving a pointer around the computer screen. Jobs was stunned that Xerox hadn't yet released the technology commercially. "Why aren't you doing anything with this?" Jobs exclaimed, as quoted by Jeffrey Young in Forbes Greatest Technology Stories (1998). "This is the greatest thing! This is revolutionary!"

Back at Apple, Jobs agitated forcibly to incorporate a GUI and mouse into their next computer system, the Lisa, which was, however, by that time already well into development. After a major internal battle, Jobs succeeded in modifying the plans and recruiting several members of Xerox to oversee the additions, but his aggressive behavior had upset many at Apple, and Markkula tried to ease tensions by removing him from the project. Undeterred, Jobs organized a new project for a computer called the Macintosh (named by its original designer, Jef Raskin, who left Apple before the computer was completed). The Mac, as it came to be known, was to be a scaled-down version of the Lisa with a GUI and mouse, but would sell for much less. Considerable animosity developed between the two departments; Jobs housed his Mac group in a separate building, over which he flew a pirate flag. He drove his team fiercely, motivating them with such slogans as "The journey is the reward," and "It's better to be a pirate than join the navy."

The Lisa computer, released in 1983 after years of development, was a commercial failure. It was the first personal computer with a GUI and offered powerful features, but at $10,000 it cost more than most people could afford. Moreover, Jobs had undercut its success by announcing that within the year Apple would release a new version of the Lisa, albeit less powerful, but at a quarter of the cost.

When the Mac was unveiled early in 1984, there was tremendous enthusiasm in the computer world, and Jobs predicted sales of 750,000 in the first year. It soon became clear, however, that the computer had numerous shortcomings, and within a few months sales had trickled to 10,000 a month. Although it used the powerful new Motorola 68000 chip, the 128 KB (kilobytes) of memory was not enough to accommodate all the new features smoothly (Lisa offered a minimum memory of 512 KB), and it wasn't expandable. Better software was intended to compensate for this, but applications were slow to appear. Another mistake was designing the keyboard without cursor keys; Jobs thought the mouse made them unnecessary. The transition to three-inch floppy disks, from five-and-one-quarter inch ones, was a smart decision by Jobs that changed industry standards, but at the same time made the Mac incompatible with the Apple II drive, alienating millions of Apple II users.

Some of these drawbacks were later corrected, and by 1986 sales for the Mac had blossomed. Its successful use of a GUI changed the world of personal computers, leading Microsoft, for example, to develop its own similar operating system, Windows, for use on IBM's PC. Although the Mac never penetrated the lucrative corporate market, its ease of use made it a popular choice for homes and schools, and its powerful graphics ushered in the era of desktop publishing. Apple never commanded more than 16 percent of the worldwide PC market, but it retained a core of loyal users, and the Mac is remembered as a turning point in computer history.

By the time of the Mac's success, however, Jobs was no longer with the company. Slow sales of other Apple products and increased managerial infighting had vitiated the company. Jobs was feuding bitterly with then CEO John Sculley, a former Pepsi executive whom Jobs had recruited in 1983 to help run Apple. Jobs and Sculley vied for control of the company until late 1985, when the board sided with Sculley. Disillusioned and hurt, Jobs quit, selling nearly all of his estimated $200 million in Apple stock.

Shortly thereafter, using part of the money from the sale, Jobs launched his own company, NeXT Software, based in Redwood City, California. His goal for NeXT was to build a breakthrough computer that would revolutionize research and higher education, and his vision attracted an infusion of cash from outside investors, among them the Texas billionaire Ross Perot, who invested $20 million after seeing Jobs in a PBS documentary; from Stanford and Carnegie Mellon Universities; and from Canon, which invested $100 million in NeXT, for a 16.7 percent stake, in 1989.

Jobs was heavily invested in developing the NeXT computer, spending $100,000 to design the logo and hiring a West German industrial engineer to create a stylish casing for the machine. Jobs's team of computer experts, meanwhile, worked tirelessly to develop an innovative operating system. Called NeXTSTEP, it used object-oriented programming (OOP), another innovative technology Jobs had seen during his earlier visit to Xerox PARC. Unlike other operating systems, where programming was a line-by-line process, NeXTSTEP made it possible to program in chunks of data, designated as objects, thereby greatly reducing the amount of programming time required.

In October 1988, after much fanfare and several delays, the NeXT computer (known as the Cube) was introduced to the public. Positioned as a workstation for university researchers and scientists and housed in an elegant black magnesium case, the NeXT computer featured an array of hi-tech components, including an optical-disk drive that could hold 300 times more data than conventional floppy disks, a crisp video monitor, and compact disc–quality music. Although widely admired for its innovations, at $9,950, the NeXT Cube was several thousand dollars more than the workstations of such competitors as Sun Microsystems and Hewlett-Packard. In the three years following its debut, the company sold a meager 50,000 NeXT computers. (Apple, by comparison, was selling that many computers every week.)

In February 1993 Jobs stopped production of NeXT hardware, closed the company's highly automated factory in Fremont, California, and laid off more than half its workforce. He refocused the company solely on developing and promoting quality software programs. In 1994 NeXT negotiated deals in which DEC, Hewlett-Packard, and Sun Microsystems agreed to package NeXT software with their workstations. Their business helped NeXT emerge as an alternative to Microsoft, but NeXT was only that—an alternative, and never the standard. The following year NeXT changed direction yet again, and partnered with Microsoft to develop object-oriented technology for personal computers that used Microsoft's Windows NT and Windows 95 operating systems. In 1995 NeXT recorded its first annual profit in nine years.

Meanwhile, Jobs's other company, Pixar Animation Studios, was also having difficulty. Pixar, which Jobs had bought from the filmmaker George Lucas in 1986, first gained industry attention in 1988, when its computer-animated short film *Tin Toy* won an Oscar. But the company had not been a big moneymaker. Its prospects brightened when, on the strength of its innovative animation and Jobs's genius for seductive salesmanship, Pixar landed a deal with Disney to produce three computer-animated feature films. The marriage of Hollywood and Silicon Valley resulted in the production of *Toy Story*, the first feature-length movie made entirely with computer animation. Four years in the making, it was the work of 110 people (roughly one-sixth as many as Disney regularly employs to make an animated feature film). According to Edwin Catmull, a co-founder of Pixar, Jobs's persistence was crucial in the completion of the movie. "You need a lot more than vision—you need a stubbornness, tenacity, belief, and patience to stay the course," he told Lohr. "In Steve's case, he pushes right to the edge, to try to make the next big step forward. It's built into him." The first weekend after its release, in November 1995, *Toy Story* grossed $38 million, making it the top box-office draw. On November 29, 1995 Pixar went public at $22 a share. By the end of the day, Pixar stock was worth $39 a share, and Jobs, an 80 percent shareholder, was an instant billionaire.

Jobs made headlines again in December 1996, when Apple bought NeXT for more than $400 million, with the intention of developing NeXTSTEP into an operating system for Apple's next-generation Macintosh. Jobs was reappointed to Apple's board of directors and rehired as an adviser to Gilbert F. Amelio, who had just joined Apple as CEO and chairman. Apple was desperate: in Jobs's absence, the firm's share of the PC market had dwindled to 5.3 percent, and its reputation for innovation had plummeted. They urgently needed an updated operating system to replace MacOS. "We're hoping [Jobs] can show us where to go from here in emerging markets and technologies," Ellen Hancock, who was then Apple's chief technology officer, told a reporter. Jobs, for his part, declared to Lohr, "Joining Apple fulfills the spiritual reasons for starting NeXT."

Apple continued to lose money until mid-1997, when Gilbert Amelio resigned and the board made Jobs interim CEO. With Jobs at the helm, Apple's fortunes were reversed. He made the company profitable again by reducing the product lines and focusing on what the company does best: "The roots of Apple were to build computers for people, not for corporations," he told Michael Krantz for *Time* (October 18, 1999). "The world doesn't need another Dell or Compaq."

In August 1997, at the Macworld trade show in Boston, Massachusetts, Jobs announced that he had secured a controversial $150 million investment from Microsoft. John Markoff, writing for the *New York Times* (August 7, 1997), described the arrangement as "a stunning alliance that could alter the map of the computer industry and help insure the survival of Apple Computer Inc." Microsoft had a vested interest in Apple's survival, Markoff pointed out, because "Microsoft is . . . the largest seller of word-processing, spreadsheet, and other programs for Macintosh computers. The Macintosh market, in other words, is too big for Microsoft to lose." At the same time, Jobs told Macworld attendees (many of whom had booed upon hearing the news of the partnership), "We want to let go of this notion that for Apple to win, Microsoft has to lose." "We better treat Microsoft with a little gratitude," he added.

Jobs refreshed Apple with a host of new initiatives: he launched a bold and memorable ad campaign ("Think Different"), acquired PC clonemaker Power Computing, and began installing the G3 PowerPC chip in all Apple computers, which made its computers faster than pentium machines. In 1998 the PowerMac G3 became Apple's fastest-selling computer to date. Jobs followed that up with an exciting new approach to computer design—the iMac, a stylish, translucent, candy-colored desktop computer that was an instant sensation. Jobs gambled by releasing the iMac without the standard floppy-disk drive, but as he predicted, consumers were eager for an easy-to-use computer that was affordable, unintimidating, and could provide Internet access. More than 800,000 were sold after its debut in the last quarter of 1998, and sales reached two million by the end of 1999. The iBook, a laptop version of the iMac, followed soon afer. By early 2000 Jobs appeared to have done the impossible: Apple was now a strong and profitable company. In March 2000 Jobs became the permanent CEO.

Apple suffered in the second half of 2000, primarily as a result of the collapsing technology market. The Power Mac G4 Cube, a beautifully designed, powerful computer for which Jobs had high hopes, proved a bitter failure. Jobs predicted sales of 200,000 a quarter, but by March 2001 Apple was only selling 12,000 units a quarter. Like his earlier NeXT Cube, it was a work of art, but too expensive for the average consumer.

In 2001 Apple rebounded with several new applications intended to take advantage of the explosion of personal electronic devices: iTunes, iDVD, iPhoto, and iMovies (all of which were later released in a bundled software package called iLife). Apple also announced its first non-computer product in several years, the iPod, a small hard-drive–based MP3 player. In May 2001 Jobs startled the industry by announcing, at a time when other technology companies were practicing austerity, the opening of numerous retail stores across America, where the company would sell Apple computers and its new "digital lifestyle" products. The same spring, Apple unveiled Mac OS X (the *X* is pronounced *10*), the long-awaited revision of its Mac operating system. Unix-based and derived from the NeXT operating system, Mac OS X, also known as Jaguar, is a powerful, multi-tasking system with state-of-the-art user interface, intended to provide the foundation for future Mac products.

Meanwhile, Pixar continued to turn out highly successful animated features, such as *A Bug's Life* (1998) and *Toy Story 2* (1999), both of which were the top-grossing (worldwide) animated films in the year they were released. Pixar's most recent film, *Monsters, Inc.* (2001), had the largest opening weekend box office of any animated film in history. Pixar has three more films due out in the next few years: *Finding Nemo* (summer 2003), *The Incredibles* (2004), and *Cars* (2005).

Jobs has received several honors for his achievements. In 1985 President Ronald Reagan presented him with the National Medal of Technology. In 1987 he received the Jefferson Award for Public Service, and *Inc. Magazine* named him Entrepreneur of the Decade in 1989.

Jobs lives in Palo Alto, California, with his wife, Laurene, whom he met in 1989 after giving a talk to business students at Stanford University, where she was doing graduate work. Married in 1991, the couple have three children together. Jobs also has a grown daughter, Lisa, from an earlier relationship.

As for his own biological family, Jobs has a younger sister, whom he tracked down after discovering, when he was 27, that his biological parents had married and had another child after giving him up for adoption. Jobs's sister is the writer Mona Simpson, whose works include the novels *Anywhere But Here* and *The Lost Father*; her 1996 book, *A Regular Guy*, is about a Silicon Valley entrepreneur who bears a striking resemblance to Jobs. Simpson is "one of my best friends in the world," Jobs said during his 1997 interview with Lohr. "I call her and talk to her every couple of days." When Lohr asked him "what he wants to pass on to his children," Jobs responded, "Just to try to be as good a father to them as my father was to me. I think about that every day of my life." —A. I. C.

Suggested Reading: *Fortune* p48+ Oct. 9, 1989, with photos, p114+ Mar. 23, 1992, with photos, p71 Jan. 24, 2000; *New York Times* A p1 Nov.

30, 1995, I p19 Dec. 22, 1996, A p1+ Aug. 7, 1997, with photo; *New York Times Magazine* p14+ Jan. 12, 1997, with photos; *Rolling Stone* p73+ June 16, 1994, with photos; *Salon* (on-line) Jan. 5, 1999; *Time* p62+ Oct.18, 1999; *Wall Street Journal* A p1 May 25, 1993; Campbell-Kelly, Martin. *Computer: A History of the Information Machine*, 1996; Jager, Rama D. and Rafael Ortiz. *In the Company of Giants*, 1997; Young, Jeffrey. *Forbes Greatest Technology Stories*, 1998

Johnson, Reynold, B.

July 7, 1906–Sep. 15, 1998 Inventor of the first commercial magnetic disk drive

Although Reynold B. Johnson held more than 90 patents, including one for the pencil-sensing device that made possible the automated grading of standardized tests such as the SAT, his best-known contribution to the Information Age is the development of the first commercial magnetic disk drive. As manager of the IBM team that developed the Random Access Method of Accounting and Control (RAMAC), Johnson helped to usher in a new age of computer memory, one in which data files could be retrieved in a matter of milliseconds instead of minutes. Today's disk drives are vastly improved—the RAMAC occupied 300 cubic feet of space, weighed one ton, and stored just five megabytes of information, while IBM now makes drives as small as one inch in diameter and a few ounces in weight that can store up to 340 megabytes—yet all modern models are, in principle, identical to Johnson's original.

Reynold B. Johnson was born on July 7, 1906 near Dassel, Minnesota, to the Swedish immigrants John and Elizabeth Johnson. The ninth of ten children, Reynold was raised on the family farm with his seven sisters and two brothers. From an early age he showed a great aptitude for mechanics: one of his first creations was a submersible submarine, which he tested in a horse trough.

After graduating from Minnehaha Academy High School, in Minneapolis, Johnson studied at the University of Minnesota and in 1929 received a B.S. degree in science education. Upon his graduation he took a teaching position at Ironwood High School, on the Michigan Peninsula. While teaching math and science, Johnson became convinced that standardized testing was the key to improving students' education, and he began attempting to find a way to standardize his own tests and grading. He first experimented with perforated multiple-choice answer sheets on which students punched out their answers. The tests were then scored by way of an electrical contact system, which flashed lights when the correct hole had been punched by the student. Before he could market this idea, however, it struck him that he might be able to devise a simpler system—one in which the conductivity of pencil marks could be used as

a means to check for the correct answers instead. In 1932 Johnson completed an electromechanical grading device based on this simpler idea, but had trouble finding a patron for it. The next year, in the midst of the Depression, he lost his teaching position.

Though out of work and unable to sell his invention, Johnson's luck began to change when Professor Ben D. Wood, head of the Bureau of Education Research at Columbia University, in New York City, heard about the device. Wood was a believer in automated testing and had been working, unsuccessfully, with IBM to implement punched-card technology for that purpose at Columbia University. In the process he had befriended Thomas Watson Sr., the head of the company. Johnson sent his specifications and a model to Wood in 1934, and Wood was impressed enough to notify Watson. Johnson and his fiancée, Beatrice, were invited to New York City to discuss his work with IBM officials. Unfortunately, Watson was then away on vacation, so Johnson had to discuss his machine with junior IBM representatives who prematurely concluded that his concepts were not sound. Wood intervened once more on his behalf, and within a short time IBM not only bought Johnson's invention, but offered him a job as a senior researcher at their Endicott, New York, facilities. In 1937 the IBM 805 Test Scoring Machine was put on the market. Eventually, the process known as "mark-sensing" became an option on some IBM punched-card models, allowing both punched holes and pencil marks on one card.

Johnson worked at the IBM laboratories in Endicott from 1934 to 1951, amassing some 53 patents while there. He and his associates not only continued to improve on his test-scoring machines, but also developed hundreds of other inventions that led to improvements in the managing, punching, and reading of computer punched cards, then the main means of storing data. During World War II Johnson oversaw the military projects IBM had been asked to develop by the U.S. government. In the immediate postwar era, his work centered on wire-matrix printing and various card-retrieval systems.

In January 1952 Johnson moved his family to San Jose, California, where IBM had set up a new West Coast lab. The company offered him the opportunity to head the facility—the first applied-research laboratory in IBM's history—and to recruit a research staff whose sole purpose would be to find better and more efficient ways of retrieving data from computers' memories.

In the early 1950s mass computer-data storage was done either by punched-card files or by magnetic tape, but neither system had random access memory (RAM)—the ability to directly seek and access a particular piece of data. At the time state-of-the-art tape files could retrieve the correct data in a matter of minutes; Johnson's team wanted to reduce that retrieval time to a fraction of a second. His staff of 15 initially focused on a system consisting of a rotating drum, with a rapidly moving magnetic head inside that could read data from (or write data to) any track on its surface. They also studied the possibility of making a memory bank out of magnetic items, such as tape strips and wires. In early 1953 Johnson and his team read reports of a magnetic disk storage system designed and built by Jacob Rabinow of the National Bureau of Standards for the U. S. Army. Johnson became convinced that disks were the basis of a viable system, despite their having significant unsolved problems. He reasoned that although his rotating drum was simpler mechanically and could be developed for commercial use more quickly, disk drives had more potential for further refinements, including miniaturization and greater reliability as technologies improved over the years.

In June 1953 Johnson's staff completed the first working disk drive and began demonstrating it for interested parties in 1955. The first IBM 350 RAMAC shipped in 1956, to the Crown Zellerbach Corporation, then one of the largest paper mills in the country. The RAMAC, despite its physical size and limited memory by today's standards, met or exceeded all performance requirements requested by IBM management. Johnson's lab kept the evolution of disk storage as its primary focus for the next 30 years, but he and his colleagues also extended their research into analog-to-digital conversion projects, voice recognition, nonimpact printing, communications technology, and random access to image files. By 1962 the San Jose facility, which had started with a team of 15 people, now employed 3,000 and included onsite manufacturing facilities.

After being made an IBM fellow, in 1965, Johnson devoted himself to educational concepts, including a learning center through which he developed the present form of the videocassette. In 1971 he retired from IBM. With his wife, Beatrice, he then founded the Education Engineering Associates consulting firm, in Palo Alto, California, through which he continued to develop innovative educational devices, including a miniature phonograph that played inside a handheld reader, thereby supplementing textbooks and children's books with audio. (Fisher-Price's Talk to Me Books, which won several toy-industry awards, incorporated one of Johnson's devices.) In his later years, Johnson worked on a system to codify Chinese characters.

Johnson, a member of a number of professional societies, won a number of awards for his pioneering work, including the 1986 National Medal of Technology from President Ronald Reagan. He was also the recipient of the 1987 Computer Pioneer Award from the Institute of Electrical and Electronic Engineers (IEEE), the 1989 Magnetics Society Award for Information Storage, and the 1997 Founder's Gold Medal from the Educational Records Bureau. In 1991 the IEEE board of directors created the IEEE Reynold B. Johnson Information Storage Award, which is presented annually "for

outstanding contributions to the field of information storage, with emphasis in the area of computer storage."

Reynold B. Johnson died on September 15, 1998 in Palo Alto, at the age of 92. He was survived by his wife. The couple had three children: Philip, David, and Karen. (Karen died in 1991.) Johnson also had four grandchildren and two great-grandchildren. The farm on which he was born is still run by the family.—C. M.

Suggested Reading: Franklin Institute Online; Institute of Electrical and Electronics Engineers Web site; *New York Times* A p27 Sep. 18, 1998; Cortada, James W. *Historical Dictionary of Data Processing: Biographies*, 1987; *Memorial Tributes: National Academy of Engineering*, vol. 9, 2001

Peggy Reed/Courtesy of Anita Jones

Jones, Anita K.

Mar. 10, 1942– Computer scientist

In 1973 Anita K. Jones became one of the first women in the United States to receive a doctorate in computer science. She has taught at two prominent universities, edited two books, and published numerous papers and articles. Jones has worked as a programmer for IBM and co-founded her own software company, with her husband. A onetime member of the U.S. Air Force Scientific Advisory Board, Jones also served as the director of research and engineering in the U.S. Department of Defense during the first term of the Clinton Administration. "I see my life as a series of creeks running alongside one another," Jones told Joannie M. Schrof for the *American Society for Engineering Education (ASEE) Prism* (February 1999). "There's my national security work, my teaching life, my industry life, and my private time with my husband and in the garden. I just hop back and forth between the creeks."

Anita Katherine Jones was born on March 10, 1942 in Forth Worth, Texas. She grew up in Houston and had a close and supportive relationship with her parents. Anita's father, a petroleum engineer, taught her how to play chess, helped her with her with homework, and took her fishing. Her mother, who had trained as a ballerina, introduced her to the joys of art.

Instead of marrying and becoming a homemaker, as many women did at the time, Anita took her father's advice to "choose something to do in life that you love more than fishing," as she told Schrof. After considering careers in psychology and biology, she found herself fascinated by computer science, which was then a new discipline. Many colleges did not have computer science departments at the time. Jones told Schrof that computer science "was a whole new area then, and it was going to change the world. You would be able to build things that would do a piece of what human beings do."

Jones attended Rice University, in Houston. She majored in mathematics and took every computer science course the university offered. She graduated with her A.B., in 1964. To broaden her focus, she enrolled at the University of Texas, in Austin, to pursue a master's degree in English literature. Shortly before her graduation, in 1966, Jones took a course in FORTRAN, a computer programming language. When she graduated IBM hired her as a programmer, and she worked for the company in their Washington, D.C. and Boston offices.

In 1969 Jones left IBM to pursue a doctorate in computer science. After a brief stint at the Massachusetts Institute of Technology (MIT), in Cambridge, she transferred to Carnegie-Mellon University (CMU), in Pittsburgh, Pennsylvania. She became friendly with other computer science students and joined them in daily meetings of an unofficial club, "the brownie plate group." During lunch, they worked on problems from class, writing their notes and ideas on the cardboard used to serve brownies in the cafeteria. Jones also communicated with computer science students at other universities through ARPANET, an on-line network launched by government researchers in 1969 that served as the foundation of the Internet.

Jones's dissertation concerned the importance of security for computer networks. She received her doctorate, in 1973, and became an associate professor in CMU's computer science department. She served as a visiting scientist at MIT, in 1974, and the following year, she participated in the RAND Corporation's Summer Institute on Computer Security. In 1977 and 1978 Jones lectured on computer operating systems at Technische Universitat, in Munich, West Germany. In 1977 she edited *Perspectives on Computer Science*, which summarized the proceedings of the 10th-anniversary symposium of CMU's computer science department. In 1978 she co-edited the book *Foundations of Secure Computation*.

Jones's interest in military science and technology began, in 1979, when a colleague at CMU recruited her to join the U.S. Air Force Scientific Advisory Board. Although she knew little about military science, Jones saw the invitation as a valuable opportunity to learn about an important branch of knowledge that affected the real world. "I was 20 years younger than everyone else, and by learning from some of the brightest minds in the country, my understanding of technology issues expanded far beyond what I was even capable of comprehending before," she recalled to Schrof.

In 1977 Jones had married William Wulf, a fellow professor at CMU, and in 1981 they co-founded Tartan Laboratories, a software firm, based in Pittsburgh. Wulf served as president and CEO and Jones as vice president. In an interview with *Leaders of the Information Age*, Jones said, "The technology that Tartan was developing was the semi-automatic production of very highly optimizing compilers for a variety of languages and machines. Bill Wulf and his colleagues had developed some innovative and powerful techniques and representations for this purpose. We targeted general purpose languages (like C, Ada and Modula at the time) and general purpose machines." The company was successful, and in 1987 Wulf and Jones sold it to Texas Instruments. After working as a private consultant in Pittsburgh for about a year, in 1988 Jones and her husband accepted teaching positions at the University of Virginia, in Charlottesville. For the next five years, Jones served as chairwoman of the computer science department there.

On July 20, 1993 Jones, who was known to President Bill Clinton because of her advisory work, was sworn in as the director of research and engineering at the U.S. Department of Defense, the highest defense department job ever held by a woman. "The first week I took the job I read a graduate text on radar," Jones told Schrof. "And every week after that I learned something else that was new."

In her new position Jones was responsible for all of the defense department's science and technology programs, as well as its in-house laboratories and university research initiatives. She was faced almost immediately with the challenge of maintaining the United States' technological superiority despite a shrinking defense budget. Jones adamantly opposed efforts by Pentagon officials who wanted to drastically cut or even eliminate the science and technology funds. "Such cuts would have been a tragic mistake in the longer term," she told *Leaders of the Information Age*. Fortunately, the president, congress, and Secretary of Defense William Perry also opposed the cuts, and the budget remained mostly intact.

Jones was quoted on the San Diego Supercomputer Center Web site as saying, "I have one of the best jobs in the country that a scientist can have to influence science policy. . . . It is an honor to even hold this job. Every day brings surprises and opportunities to do things that matter." She had agreed, however, to serve only one presidential term, and she left the defense department, in 1997, to resume teaching at the University of Virginia and to write. (Jones continues to serve as a consultant to the Pentagon.)

Jones was named a fellow of the Association for Computing Machinery (ACM) in 1995, the Institute of Electrical and Electronics Engineers (IEEE) in 1996, and the American Academy of Arts and Sciences in 2000. She was also honored with the Department of Defense Award for Distinguished Public Service in 1996 and the Distinguished Service Award from the Computing Research Association in 1997. The U. S. Navy named a seamount in the Pacific Ocean after her, in 1997. Carnegie-Mellon University awarded her an honorary doctorate in science and technology in 1999.

Anita Jones and William Wulf live in the hills just outside of Charlottesville, Virginia. They have two grown children.—D. C.

Suggested Reading: *Aerospace America* p12+ July 1994; *American Society for Engineering Education (ASEE) Prism* p32+ Feb. 1999, with photos; Anita Jones's University of Virginia Home Page; *Government Executive* p123+ Aug. 1994; *Parallel Computing Research* (on-line) Apr. 1993

Josephson, Brian D.

Jan. 4, 1940– Nobel Prize–winning physicist; superconductor researcher

In 1973 the Welsh physicist Brian D. Josephson was awarded half of the Nobel Prize in Physics "for his theoretical predictions of the properties of a supercurrent through a tunnel barrier, in particular those phenomena which are generally known as the Josephson effects," according to the Nobel committee's citation. Discovery of the Josephson effects had a substantial impact on modern physics, and thus on the Information Age because devices using such effects may be used as computer circuitry elements with very high speed, but low power consumption.

Josephson's work was built on the foundation laid by the research of his fellow prize winners, Leo Esaki of Japan and Ivar Giaever of the United States, who had uncovered the tunneling process in solids and the tunneling of electrons through a sandwich of thin oxide and superconductive metal respectively. Josephson's work further advanced the understanding of tunneling in solids by predicting and proving new and unexpected phenomena—the so-called Josephson effects—in superconductors. The effects show that a supercurrent can flow through a barrier even when zero voltage is applied and that a fixed applied voltage would make a high frequency alternating current flow through a barrier with a microwave range frequency.

Brian David Josephson was born in Cardiff, Wales, to Abraham and Mimi Josephson. After completing his secondary education at the local high school, he entered Trinity College, Cambridge, where he received his bachelor's degree in physics, in 1960, and both a master's degree and a Ph.D., in 1964. From 1962 until 1969 he held a junior research fellowship at Trinity College.

Josephson first came to prominence as an undergraduate when, in 1960, he realized that researchers using the Mössbauer effect (named for Rudolf L. Mössbauer) to measure the gravitational red shift of gamma rays (which may be viewed as energetic particles of light) had ignored a major source of error in their experiments. Albert Einstein's general theory of relativity predicted that photons, such as gamma rays, would change their energy as they traveled in gravitational fields. Experimentalists were attempting to measure any change in the wavelength of gamma rays as they traveled up or down a tower. Josephson realized that differences as small as $1°C$ in the temperature of the gamma-ray source and of the detector could result in wavelength shifts as large as those they were trying to measure. Josephson's discovery caused experimentalists to repeat their measurements while controlling precisely the temperatures of their pieces of apparatus.

By 1962 Josephson had begun conducting research in superconductivity, a phenomenon in which materials, when they are cooled below a critical temperature, lose all resistance to the flow of electricity. Superconductivity arises from the ability of pairs of electrons in the superconductor to interact with each other by means of atomic vibrations (phonons) that they excite in the material. Working at the General Electric Company, Ivar Giaever had recently found that when an electrical contact was made between a superconducting material and a normal metal with a very thin insulating layer separating the two conductors, the electrical behavior of the contact provided a great deal of information about the properties of the superconductor. In 1962 Josephson calculated the behavior of such a junction between two superconductors. He found that current could flow through the insulator without any voltage difference between the two conductors (the DC Josephson effect), a totally unexpected result that was not in accordance with classical physical models. He also predicted that when a voltage was applied across the junction, an oscillating current would flow across the junction with a frequency dependent only on the applied voltage (the AC Josephson effect). Both effects were extremely sensitive to the magnetic field at the junction. These effects were soon observed and were found to behave as predicted by Josephson's theory. In fact, some experimentalists using Giaever's technique had already seen the effects but had discarded them as "noise."

Discovery of the Josephson effects had an immediate and major impact on modern physics. The frequency of the alternating current is dependent on the voltage across the junction and the ratio of the electronic charge to Max Planck's constant (a basic physical constant that determines the behavior of systems of atomic scale or smaller). The Josephson effects allowed a great increase in the precision with which this ratio (e/h) is known. They also permitted the creation of a new primary quantum standard for voltage, now used in many national standards laboratories, that is dependent on the Josephson effects. By putting two Josephson junctions in a loop, it became possible to develop sensors for magnetic fields that are extraordinarily sensitive. Such a construction, called a superconducting quantum interference device (SQUID), is the most sensitive detector of magnetic fields known and has been used for magnetic investigations of living organisms as well as for magnetic mapping and detection of subsurface objects. Similar sensitive detectors of extremely small voltage changes have been made by using Josephson-effects devices. Other Josephson-effects devices show promise for use as computer circuitry elements with extremely high speed and very low power consumption.

In the years following his discovery, Josephson investigated superconductivity and the critical phenomena that occur when systems are near to transition points, such as the critical point of water (where the distinction between fluid and gaseous phases disappears) and similar transitions between superconductivity and normal conductivity in systems that exhibit such transitions. In the late 1960s, he developed an interest in problems of mind and intelligence. He became a practitioner of transcendental meditation in the early 1970s, hoping to synthesize modern physics and mathematics with the mental theory of the spiritual leader Maharishi Mahesh Yogi, who was largely responsible for spreading transcendental meditation in the Western world. Josephson stopped his research in mainstream physics to devote himself to transcendental meditation and mental theory. Of this undertaking, he is quoted as saying in *Nobel Prize Winners* (1987), "I am taking a rather unconventional theoretical approach to the phenomenon of intelligence, in that I believe that the most basic concepts underlying intelligence were discovered in ancient times. In particular," he continued, "I am basing my research to a considerable extent on the formulations which have been given in numerous lectures by the Maharishi Mahesh Yogi. It is hoped that the usefulness and validity of these concepts can be confirmed by computer simulation."

From 1967 until 1972 Josephson served as an assistant director of research at Cambridge, and in 1969 he was appointed senior research fellow at the school. He held the post of reader in physics from 1972 until 1974, when he was made a professor of physics. He currently heads the Mind-Matter Unification Project of the Theory of Condensed Matter Group at the Cavendish Laboratory at Cambridge University. There he and his colleagues study possible connections between physics and studies of cognitive skills, parapsychology, homeopathy, and human-language acquisition, among other topics.

In addition to his Nobel Prize, Josephson's honors include the Science Award of the Research Corporation of America (1969) and the Hughes Medal of the Royal Society of London (1972). He has also received the Guthrie Medal (1972), the Elliott Cresson Medal (1972), the Holweck Medal (1973), the Faraday Medal (1982), and the Sir George Thompson Medal (1984). He has been a visiting professor at a number of institutions including the University of Illinois, in 1965; Cornell University, in New York City, in 1971; Maharishi European Research University, in Germany, in 1975; Wayne State University, in Michigan, in 1983; and the Indian Institution of Science, in Bangalore, in 1984. He is a fellow of the Royal Society of London and a foreign member of the American Institute of Electrical and Electronics Engineers and the American Academy of Arts and Sciences.

Josephson married Carol Anne Oliver in 1976; they have one daughter.—C. M.

Suggested Reading: Cambridge University Web site; Nobel e-Museum Web site; *Physics Today* Dec. 1973; *Science* Nov. 16, 1973; Cousins, Norman. *Nobel Prize Conversations*, 1985

Joy, William

1954– Co-founder of Sun Microsystems

William Joy, one of the founders of Sun Microsystems Inc., is renowned for developing new technologies in the field of computer networking. He was hailed as the "Edison of the Internet" in *Fortune* magazine for his role in creating Berkeley Software Distribution Unix (BSD), an early operating system. Joy designed BSD while a graduate student at the University of California, Berkeley, and distributed it in source code, which enabled other programmers to develop the technology on their own. This approach to software development has become known as the open-source philosophy, and Joy was one of its earliest advocates. In 1982 Joy helped found Silicon Valley–based Sun Microsystems; he now serves as Sun's chief scientist and corporate executive officer. The company has become an industry leader, today employing more than 40,000 people and providing half of the existing Internet server computers. Most notably, Joy led the creation and marketing of Sun's Java, a popular programming language that enables animation and other interactive features on World Wide Web pages. "I don't know anyone who has the same amount of knowledge [Joy] does," Mark Andreesen, chief technology officer at America Online, told Amy Rogers for *Computer Reseller News* (July 12, 1999). "He's probably the only guy in the industry who can design a microprocessor, design an operating system and write a programming language. He understands all of these things."

William Joy, known as Bill, was born in 1954 in Michigan, the eldest of three children. A precocious child, he started reading when he was three and entered kindergarten at four. He excelled in math and graduated from high school, at 15, having been voted North Farmington High's "most studious student." "In other words, I was a no-date nerd," Joy explained to Brent Schlender, in *Fortune* (February 15, 1999), as posted on the *Business 2.0* Web site. He studied electrical engineering at the University of Michigan, in Ann Arbor, earning a B.S.E.E., in 1975. He then received offers for graduate fellowships from Stanford University, in California; the California Institute of Technology, in Pasadena; and from the University of California, in Berkeley. Joy chose to attend Berkeley, although not for the reasons one might expect. "I went to Berkeley because it had the worst computer facilities of the three," he told Schlender. "I figured it would force me to be more ingenious."

Joy, indeed, proved ingenious: at Berkeley he led the development of BSD, a technology that played an integral part in the development of the Internet. The BSD project originated shortly after Joy arrived at Berkeley, when he and some colleagues in the computer science department began de-bugging the Unix operating system on their computer. They compiled the results of their work on a computer tape and offered copies to universities that owned similar machines at a price of $50 a copy to cover expenses. In 1976 Berkeley purchased a newer computer, called a VAX, and Joy and his colleagues developed a version of Unix to run on the new machine, which they then sold for $300. The VAX became popular at universities and research labs, fueling demands for the Berkeley team's improved version of Unix. It also attracted the attention of the U.S. Department of Defense Advanced Research Projects Agency (ARPA, also known as DARPA), which was then developing the ARPANET, the predecessor of the Internet. In 1978 Joy and his colleagues won a contract from ARPA to develop software to connect VAX machines with the emerging ARPANET network.

In 1980 Joy received his M.S. in electrical engineering and computer science from Berkeley. In 1982, while he was working toward his Ph.D., he received a visit from three Stanford University alumni—Vinod Khosla, Andreas Bechtolsheim, and Scott McNealy. Bechtolsheim had created a cheap but powerful desktop computer, which he called a Stanford University Network, or SUN, workstation. Khosla had recently graduated with an MBA, and had enlisted a fellow business school graduate, Scott McNealy. The three men planned to found a business to market the SUN workstations, and were looking for someone who had mastered the Unix operating system to join them. Joy—who was making slow progress toward his Ph.D. and feeling frustrated by the constraints that the university placed on his burgeoning Unix business—agreed to the venture, and Sun Microsystems was born. Joy's version of BSD was the foundation for the Sun operating system. (Sun later changed the name from BSD to Solaris). The company became a quick success; in spite of heavy competition, and in only six years, they reached annual revenues of $1 billion.

One of the most significant developments of Joy's career was his introduction of the immensely popular programming language, Java. Although Joy did not write Java, he oversaw its development and marketing strategy. In the mid-1980s, he assigned a group of programmers to develop a computer language, then called Oak; he hoped to use the language to network together various consumer-electronics equipment, including VCRs, microwaves, light switches, personal digital assistants (PDAs), and desktop computers. A market for this product failed to emerge, however, and the project languished. In the early 1990s the release of the World Wide Web led to a dramatic rise in Internet use, and it occurred to Joy that the Oak language was ideal for writing programs for Web pages. The Oak language was retooled and renamed Java.

Java is a relatively simple program that can be run across different platforms. It can be launched independently or embedded into Web documents, creating different kinds of animation or multimedia applications. According to Schlender, using Java a programmer can write "small, efficient programs that could be sent 'just in time' via the Web to run on just about any kind of computer. Today, Web retailers like Levi-Strauss use Java applications to take orders."

Joy not only pioneered the efforts that resulted in Java, he managed the business strategy as well. He forged a crucial partnership with Netscape, which licensed Java for incorporation into their browser. Mike Clary, a Sun vice president, told Alex Lash for the *Industry Standard* (June 21, 1999, on-line) that Joy succeeded because he was able to talk to Netscape representatives from "both the technical and business perspectives." He also negotiated deals to license Java to other major companies, including Oracle, Macromedia, and SGI. According to Kevin Kelly and Spencer Reiss in *Wired* (August 1998, on-line), a million programmers actively use the Java language, and, as of 1998, its popularity was still growing.

Joy's next major project at Sun was Jini (pronounced *GEE-nee*), a programming language that enables disparate electronic devices to communicate and share information across networks. Traditionally, adding a device, such as a printer or a digital camera, to a computer requires an installation process; a device that incorporates the Jini code is able to announce itself and become instantly accessible to other devices on the network. Kelly and Reiss commented on the ambitious reach of this new technology: "If [Sun programmers] succeed, Jini code will provide connections that will make today's information 'superhighways' look as confining as 19th-century railways," they wrote. Jini was released, in 1999, with great fanfare; Sun hired the San Francisco 49ers quarterback, Steve Young, to promote it, and Joy appeared on the cover of *Fortune* magazine. Jini never found a market, however, a failure generally attributed to the fact that it was overly complicated and required too much related software to work. "I wish we had sold more devices, but we didn't," Joy told Lee Gomes for the *Wall Street Journal* (June 4, 2001). "We take big swings. Sometimes they work and sometimes they don't."

In 2000 Joy published an article in *Wired*, "Why the Future Doesn't Need Us," in which he expressed his anxiety about the ethical pitfalls and potential dangers of technological progress—specifically in the fields of robotics, nanotechnology, and genetic engineering. Coming from one of the leading innovators of computing technology, such concerns surprised many. Joy traced his anxiety to a 1998 meeting with the computer scientist Ray Kurzweil, the inventor of a reading machine, among other technologies. Kurzweil gave him a copy of his soon-to-be-published book, *The Age of Spiritual Machines*, which heralds the advent of intelligent and self-replicating machines in the near future due to the exponentially accelerating pace of scientific discovery. Kurzweil was mostly optimistic about these developments, and it seemed to Joy that he had downplayed the unknown dangers involved, specifically the possibility that someday intelligent machines might overpower and even replace human beings. "In designing software and microprocessors, I have never had the feeling that I was designing an intelligent machine," Joy wrote in his article. "The software and hardware is so fragile and the capabilities of the machine to 'think' so clearly absent that, even as a possibility, this has always seemed very far in the future. But now, with the prospect of human-level computing power in about 30 years, a new idea suggests itself: that I may be working to create tools which will enable the construction of the technology that may replace our species. How do I feel about this? Very uncomfortable." Joy's warnings spawned a widespread media debate; some criticized Joy for being an alarmist, while others appreciated his efforts to stimulate discussion about the potential hazards of technology. Daniel Sarewitz, the director of Columbia University's Center For Science, Policy and Outcomes, told Tom Abate for the *San Francisco Chronicle* (September 23, 2001) that Joy's essay "made it possible to talk about the negative consequences of technology without being labeled a Luddite."

Joy's concerns have not deterred him from his work. One of his most recent projects was the software known as JXTA (pronounced *JUX-tah,* as in *juxtapose*). Like Jini, JXTA is designed to network together different electronic devices, but—according to many industry commentators—it improves upon its predecessor in many respects, particularly in its compactness and portability. Unveiled in April 2001, JXTA makes use of peer-to-peer technologies (made famous by on-line music-trading services, such as Napster) in which any computer can access the files of any other computer on a network. The JXTA language was released as open-source code in order to encourage programmers to create tools that allow individual users to share personal documents, music, photographs, or videos.

Joy has been honored many times for his achievements. In 1993 he was given the Lifetime Achievement Award of the USENIX Association. In 1997 President Clinton appointed him as cochairman of the Presidential Information Technology Advisory Committee. In 1999 he was a corecipient (with Andy Bechtolsheim) of the *Computerworld* Smithsonian Award for Innovation. For his work on Unix, he received the Association for Computing Machinery Grace Murray Hopper Award, given for outstanding work in computer science by individuals under the age of 30. In 2000 *Research and Development* magazine named Joy its "Scientist of the Year."

Joy has lived and worked in Aspen, Colorado, since 1991. He moved to Aspen from California in order to leave behind the day-to-day concerns of Sun's operations and to focus on research. He assembled a team of programmers and named his offices Aspen Smallworks. Scott McNealy, now the CEO of Sun, once offered a list of the top 10 reasons why he allowed Joy to move to Aspen, as quoted by Alex Lash. Among McNealy's reasons were: "Because Bill can live anywhere he wants" and "Mount Olympus was already booked."—A. I. C.

Suggested Reading: *Computer Reseller News* (on-line) July 12, 1999; *Computerworld* p13 Apr. 30, 2001; *Fortune* p84+ Feb. 15, 1999; *Industry Standard* (on-line) June 21, 1999; *Newsweek* p65 Sep. 24, 2001; *New York Times* C p9 Apr. 25, 2001; *Red Herring* (on-line) Oct. 1, 1995, Jan. 1, 1999; *Research and Development* S p3+ Nov. 2000; *San Francisco Chronicle* E p1 Sep. 23, 2001; *Upside* p34 June 2001; *Wall Street Journal* B p1 June 4, 2001; *Wired* (on- line) p128+ Aug. 1998, p238+ Apr. 2000

John Harding/Getty Images

Kahn, Philippe

Mar. 16, 1952– Founder of Borland International

After making history by writing the software for the first personal computer, in 1973, the French-born mathematician Philippe Kahn emigrated to California's Silicon Valley in 1982 to make his mark in the computer industry. Kahn built Borland International, as he called his company, from a small mail-order outlet to one of the world's leading software manufacturers in just a few years. Kahn's eccentricities, flamboyant style of competition, and bluntness brought him immense publicity and made him one of the computer industry's most colorful characters. In the 1990s Borland competed head-to-head against Microsoft, but mistakes in management by Kahn, combined with Microsoft's decision to drive smaller competitors from the market by giving away free software, nearly destroyed Borland. Defeated in the marketplace by the Microsoft juggernaut, Kahn left the company he founded. Instead of disappearing from public view, Kahn and his wife founded two new companies, Starfish Software and LightSurf Technologies, which promote the development of a wireless Internet.

Philippe Kahn was born on March 16, 1952 in Paris. During the 1930s his father had left Nazi Germany and settled in France. During World War II the elder Kahn served in the French Foreign Legion. Philippe's mother survived several Nazi death camps during the war. In an interview with G. Pascal Zachary for the *Wall Street Journal* (June 2, 1994), Kahn noted that his parents' wartime experiences caused them to pass along a sense of proportion to him, explaining that no "matter how hard things got for me, [my parents] had it much

tougher." After the war, his father worked as an aerospace engineer; he helped design the wings for the Concorde, the world's fastest commercial airplane. Philippe's mother enjoyed a career as a theatrical producer.

As a child Philippe attended boarding school in Zurich, Switzerland. In May 1968, when he was 16 years old, Philippe, who was deeply interested in philosophy, visited the Sorbonne, in Paris, and publically encountered Jean-Paul Sartre, the famous philosopher, existentialist, and author. In an interview with *Leaders of the Information Age*, Kahn recalled, "There was a long dialog between he and I that I believe was captured on tape. He was arguing existentialism, and I was putting forward more of a Zen look at things. They are actually not that far apart. It was fun and very disrespectful for a 16 year old. But I think that he and the whole audience enjoyed it." Kahn later enrolled at the University of Nice, in France, eventually earning a master's degree in mathematics. While pursuing postgraduate study, Kahn taught high-school mathematics in Grenoble, France, and then became a teaching assistant at the University of Grenoble. Bored with teaching, Kahn became involved with the fledgling computer industry in Europe during the early 1970s. He began working for Niklaus Wirth, who had developed the Pascal computer language, in Zurich.

The computers that existed at this time were large, mainframe systems, exclusively used by governments, the military, academic and scientific researchers, and corporations. However, technically savvy consumers could build their own personal computers by buying special kits. In 1973 Kahn wrote the software for the Micral, which is widely considered to be the world's first personal computer. "I was 21 and was handy with software (like a lot of kids today) and was asked to write some simple development tools for the Micral," he told *Leaders of the Information Age*. "I did. I have to confess that I really did it because I needed money for a new saxophone. Mine had been stolen." By the end of the decade, Apple, IBM, and other companies were selling personal computers. Kahn wrote video games for the Apple 2 computer. The games, which were sold in France, provided Kahn with samples of his work to impress potential employers in the computer industry.

In 1982 Kahn left France for the United States. He explained to William J. Cook for *U. S. News & World Report* (October 14, 1991), that while reading computer magazines, he noticed that "all the ads had ZIP codes in Silicon Valley." Kahn arrived in San Francisco, California, with only pocket money and a tourist visa, and began an unsuccessful search for a job as an engineer. His tourist visa expired, but he remained in the United States as an illegal alien, being careful to avoid agents from the Immigration and Naturalization Service (INS).

Because no one would hire him without a green card, Kahn established his own computer consulting business, MIT (for Market in Time), in 1983. "I noticed that if I had MIT initials in my letterhead, people would return my calls," he said to Cook. After the Massachusetts Institute of Technology, in Cambridge, threatened to sue him for trademark infringement, Kahn changed the name to Borland International Inc. Kahn explained to Cook that the name had been inspired in part by the American astronaut Frank Borman, who went into space as a member of the Gemini and Apollo missions during the late 1960s, and in part by a Celtic term for *deep forest.*

Kahn initially operated Borland from above an auto-repair shop, in Scotts Valley, California. The firm's first major product was a software program called Turbo Pascal. Kahn wrote the program, a fast adaptation of the Pascal language for the PC, himself. Since he didn't have money to advertise the product, Kahn convinced *Byte* magazine to run an ad for Turbo Pascal on credit. Selling for only $49.95, Turbo Pascal was far less expensive than other software programs at the time. The ad generated $150,000 in sales in just the first month. Thanks to its speed and low price, Turbo Pascal became popular with computer programmers and remained a best-seller for the next few years.

Kahn discovered that the secret of breaking into the software market and successfully competing against such established corporations as Microsoft, Lotus Development, and Ashton-Tate, was to sell consumers quality software at low prices. One of Borland's ads informed customers, "We're not greedy. We believe that it is better to sell hundreds of thousands of software programs at a reasonable price instead of a few at prices that would make Jesse James blush," as quoted by Janice Castro for *Time* (November 18, 1985). Kahn often received favorable attention in the media by denouncing his competitors as greedy. "The actual material of a program costs less than $5," he told Castro. "Most business programs cost between $300 and $500. This is kind of a rip-off. I'm trying to do things differently." Under Kahn's leadership, Borland also offered customers software upgrades at discounted prices. This practice eventually became common in the software industry.

Kahn developed such programs as Sidekick, an organizing tool for executives, and Turbo Gameworks, which offered chess and bridge. By 1985 Borland's annual sales reached $30 million. In September of that year, Borland acquired Analytica, a rival software firm. Kahn turned Analytica's Reflex, a database tool, into a best-seller by cutting its price from $495 to $99.95. He unveiled Turbo Lightning Library, an information system, for $99.95. The program included such innovative features as spell-check and a thesaurus. (In 1985 Kahn, who had lost his French accent by listening to talk radio, finally acquired a green card, which allowed him to work legally in the United States.)

Kahn's consumer-friendly business practices established a loyal following and market base for Borland. His low prices alarmed executives at Microsoft and Lotus. To remain competitive,

Microsoft offered $40 rebates for its own version of Pascal, and Lotus slashed the price of Spotlight, its counterpart to Sidekick, to $75.

The press often quoted Kahn making derogatory remarks about Microsoft's products and the corporate giant's chairman, Bill Gates. According to an article in *USA Today* (December 14, 1987), Microsoft employees began wearing "Delete Philippe" T-shirts and attached his picture to dartboards. Kahn claimed that he was frequently misquoted and that his comments were blown out of proportion, yet stories of the rivalry continued to appear with regularity.

Kahn's theatrics made him the P. T. Barnum of the computer industry and brought Borland frequent favorable publicity. Kahn commuted to work every day on his motorcycle and held corporate meetings in Chinese restaurants and aboard his sailboat. He gave lavish parties for his employees and dove into pools while wearing expensive tuxedos, but most often he wore loud Hawaiian shirts, which became his trademark. An accomplished musician, he often played his saxophone for reporters after concluding press conferences. On weekends, Kahn wore disguises and played the flute with the Turbo Jazz Band, which performed in local venues. His other passions included chess and martial arts.

In the early 1990s Kahn began referring to himself as the computer industry's "barbarian." He explained to Peter H. Lewis for the *New York Times* (August 18, 1991), "The Egyptians, Greeks, Romans and others were fascinated by those barbarians that represented the end of their own decadent worlds. Lean and efficient, that's what a barbarian is. . . . He is direct, trustworthy and disdains luxury or useless possessions." He concluded, "Borland qualifies as a barbarian technology-driven culture: We focus on essentials, substance over form, the things that really make a difference to our customers and our shareholders."

The 1990s looked promising for Borland International. In 1991 the software maker captured 75 percent of the database market when, for $439 million, it acquired Ashton-Tate Corporation, which—although plagued by financial problems—still dominated the database market with dBase, a popular application. Borland next unveiled several new products. By July 1992 the company's version of the C++ programming language had sold 700,000 copies. Borland issued its own spreadsheet program, Quattro Pro for Windows, to challenge the market domination of the popular Lotus 1-2-3 spreadsheet. A new database, Paradox for Windows, also appeared on the market. Borland's total revenues for 1992 were estimated at $500 million. Extensive profiles in the *New York Times*, *U.S. News & World Report*, *Forbes*, and many computer magazines lionized Kahn, and some reporters touted Borland as "the Microsoft for the 1990s."

Unfortunately, Borland failed to meet expectations, its fortunes souring almost overnight. The company's troubles had begun, in 1990, when Lotus sued Borland for copyright infringement. Lotus alleged that Quattro Pro copied many of the features of Lotus 1-2-3. Speaking to Lewis, Kahn acknowledged the similarities between the two programs, but said that "Lotus's attempt to copyright words, menus and sequences of events is like someone obtaining a copyright on the sequence in which gears are shifted in a car." Kahn added that since most people were already used to Lotus 1-2-3, they would not want to buy a spreadsheet that forced them to learn completely different features and options. In August 1992 Judge Robert E. Keeton of the Federal District Court in Boston, Massachusetts, ruled that Borland had violated copyright laws and ordered Quattro Pro withdrawn from the market. Several weeks later, Judge Keeton also ruled that a civil trial between Lotus and Borland would determine the amount of damages. The litigation continued for the next few years. In March 1995 a federal appellate court reversed Judge Keeton's decision, ruling that Borland had not violated copyright laws. In a letter to the editor published in the *Wall Street Journal* (March 24, 1995), Kahn wrote that the litigation "cost Borland and its shareholders millions of dollars, and probably robbed Borland of a bright future."

Other problems doomed Borland. Before it was removed from the market, Quattro Pro sold poorly. Additionally, Microsoft's own database, Access, reached the market before Paradox. While Borland sought to increase its market share with low prices, Microsoft sought to corner the market by giving away free software. (These practices forced many software manufacturers from the market and eventually attracted the scrutiny of the U.S. Department of Justice, which successfully sued Microsoft for violating anti-trust laws.)

Borland's acquisition of Ashton-Tate, in 1991, was plagued with problems. Zachary argued that Kahn failed to properly address Ashton-Tate's financial problems and chronic disorganization by installing proper management to oversee the transition. In one of his most controversial moves, Kahn authorized the spending of $100 million to build a new headquarters for Borland when the company was beginning to experience financial trouble. Both Borland's stock price and sales dramatically declined. By 1994 the company posted $220 million in total losses for the past three fiscal years.

Although Kahn vowed to turn Borland around, he faced growing criticism from financial analysts and Borland's own shareholders. Under pressure, Kahn stepped down, on January 11, 1995, as the CEO of the company he founded in 1983. Although Kahn continued to serve as Borland's chairman, Gary Wetsel, his replacement as CEO, became responsible for running the company's day-to-day operations. In a press release, Kahn said, "It has become clear that my continuing as president and CEO has become a distraction at a time when Borland needs to be fully focused on the challenges ahead of it," as quoted by Julie Pitta for the *Los Angeles Times* (January 12, 1995). Many observers attributed Borland's decline to Kahn's ambitious efforts to compete with Microsoft in nearly every product area. This ambition led Kahn to make several costly mistakes that eventually set the stage for Borland's downfall. In an interview with Bob Parks for *Wired* (October 2000, on-line), Kahn acknowledged that he wasn't always "perfect" when he ran Borland, but attributed the company's failures on Microsoft's business practices, saying that it "was basically giving away what Borland was trying to sell. It's hard to compete with a company like that." By the end of 1995, he also stepped down as Borland's chairman, severing his ties completely. Borland continued to develop and manufacture software. The company changed its name to Inprise, in 1998, and then to Borland Software, in 2000.

Although seemingly defeated by his software rival Bill Gates, Philippe Kahn did not fade away. In 1994, while he was still serving as Borland's CEO, he and his wife, Sonia Lee, started a new company called Starfish Software. The Starfish Web site explains that the company's founding vision is "Global synchronization and integration of wireless and wireline devices." Kahn wanted to develop the infrastructure to create a "wireless" Internet, linking it to cell phones, pagers, and personal organizers. To help clients make the transition to a wireless Internet, Starfish unveiled several software applications collectively marketed as the TrueSync Technology Platform. The patented applications, as described on the Starfish Web site, provide synchronization of wireless and "wireline" devices, allow users to access information anywhere, and promote the development of "ultra-thin" wireless devices. In 1997 Starfish released REX, an electronic organizer the size of a credit card. REX, from Rolodex Electronic Express, was capable of storing thousands of names, addresses, schedules, memos, and other information. Costing $100, REX ran for six months on the power of two watch-sized lithium batteries and connected to desktops by the slot normally used for modems. REX was not a success with consumers. Kahn explained to Parks that he had licensed REX to a New Jersey-based firm, Franklin Electronic Publishers, which did a poor job of marketing the product for Starfish. REX also failed to displace the popular electronic organizer, PalmPilot, which offered more features and had been on the market longer.

Despite the failure of REX, several companies, including Yahoo!, Excite, Motorola, and Hewlett-Packard, became Starfish's most prominent clients. Impressed with the company's TrueSync Technology, Motorola purchased Starfish Software, in 1998, running it as a subsidiary. Kahn continued to serve as Starfish's CEO.

In 1998 Kahn and Sonia Lee founded another company, LightSurf Technologies. "When building Starfish, and now LightSurf, we made sure that we focused on markets that are new, that are growing fast, and where there is an assurance of diversity," Kahn told Sean Donahue for the on-line magazine, *Salon* (September 27, 1999). "Wireless Internet is growing super fast because one of the most desired and popular devices in the world is the cell phone." Like Starfish, LightSurf focused on developing a wireless Internet. Kahn designed a small digital camera that could send images instantly and clearly through the Internet. He explained to Parks that inspiration for such a product came, in 1997, when his daughter was born. Kahn wanted to e-mail a picture of his newborn daughter to her grandmother but was unable to do so because he couldn't find a RJ11 jack in the hospital to hook up his digital camera. LightSurf licensed the technology to Motorola, which made it compatible with its line of Accompli cell phones, in December 2000. Selling for $500, Accompli is a combination digital camera and cell phone. After taking a picture, users can print out the image or send it instantly to a destination around the world. Kahn estimates that improvements in technology will eventually drive the price of the product down. In 2000 Kahn filed a lawsuit against Agfa-Gevaert Group, a Belgian company that had the term *e-photo* trademarked. He told Therese Poletti, a reporter for *Reuters* (March 28, 2000), as posted on the ZDNet Web site, that generic words with the letter *e* in front of them, such as *e-commerce, e- ticket,* or *e-photo* should not be trademarked because they have become part of the English language.

The passage of time has apparently mellowed the former Borland barbarian. Many observers note that Kahn displays more caution and maturity as the CEO of Starfish and LightSurf. Philippe Kahn is married to Sonia Lee, who also serves as his collaborator and business partner. Together they administer the Lee-Kahn Foundation, which they founded to support the arts and various educational initiatives and to promote conservation and the protection of endangered species. Kahn is the father of four children; his two oldest daughters are biotech engineers. He and his family live in Santa Cruz, California. In December 1995 *Byte* magazine named him one of the Top 20 Most Important People in the history of computers.—D. C.

Selected Reading: *BusinessWeek* p82+ Aug. 2, 1993, with photo; *Forbes* p159+ Apr 27, 1992, with photo; *Infoworld* p106 Sep. 6, 1993, with photo; Lee-Kahn Foundation Web site; LightSurf Technologies Web site; *Los Angeles Times* D p1 Jan. 12, 1995; *New York Times* F p9 Aug. 18, 1991, with photo, III p1+ July 26, 1992, with photos, D p1+ July 28, 1997; *Salon* (on-line) Sept. 27, 1999; Starfish Software Web site; *Time* p75+ Nov. 18, 1985, with photo; *U.S. News & World Report* p59+ Oct. 14, 1991, with photos; *USA Today* B p2 Dec. 14, 1987, with photos; *Wall Street Journal* A p1 June 2, 1994, A p14 Mar. 24, 1995; *Wired* (on-line) Oct. 2000

Kahn, Robert E.

Dec. 23 1938– Co-creator of the ARPANET and TCP/IP

The computer scientist Robert E. Kahn is one of the prime movers of the Internet. In the late 1960s Kahn realized that a packet-switching network could effectively transmit large amounts of data between computers. Along with fellow computer scientists Vinton Cerf, Lawrence Roberts, Paul Baran, and Leonard Kleinrock, Kahn built the ARPANET, the first network to successfully link computers around the country. Kahn and Cerf also developed the Transmission Control Protocol (TCP) and the Internet Protocol (IP), which together enable communication between different types of computers and networks; TCP/IP is the standard still in use today. Kahn actively promoted initiatives that led to the widespread expansion and eventual commercial use of the Internet during the early 1990s. Now chief executive officer of the nonprofit Corporation for National Research Initiatives (CNRI), Kahn is working to create a national digital library.

The son of a public-school administrator, Robert Elliott Kahn was born on December 23, 1938 in the New York City borough of Brooklyn. His father pushed Robert and his sister, Diana, to excel in school, and both children went on to earn doctoral degrees. "The joke in the family was if you got a 98 on the math test he would ask where the other two points were," Diana told John Adam for the *Institute of Electrical and Electronics Engineers (IEEE) Spectrum* (September 1996). In addition to playing sports and the piano, Robert became skilled at solving puzzles.

After high school Kahn embarked on a five-year engineering program, spending his first two years at Queens College and the last three at City College of New York. After considering industrial and chemical engineering, he decided on a career in electrical engineering.

During his summer vacations, Kahn worked at Bell Telephone Laboratories (Bell Labs), in the field of telephone traffic engineering. He learned the programming language FORTRAN and an assembly code for the mainframe computers and created simulations to study the call routing system. He recalled this work experience as beneficial, telling Adam: "We were into modeling and analysis tools that could apply to many things."

Kahn graduated from City College in 1960, earning a bachelor of electrical engineering (BEE) degree. With a fellowship from the National Science Foundation (NSF), he attended graduate school at Princeton University, in New Jersey, and continued working on a part-time basis for Bell Labs. For his doctoral dissertation, he explored the more effective use of bandwidth and sampling methods to convert analog to digital signals. His findings were later published in two of the IEEE's journals. Kahn received his Ph.D. in electrical engineering, in 1964.

In 1964 Kahn became an assistant professor at Massachusetts Institute of Technology (MIT), in Cambridge. He taught information theory, communications, and probability. Eager for some practical experience, he took a leave of absence from MIT, in 1966, to join Bolt, Beranek & Newman (BBN), a Cambridge-based company that conducted research in computing. He worked in the uncharted territory of computer networking; his tools, as he told Adam, were "pencil and paper and timesharing computers."

In his new position, Kahn became acquainted with Larry Roberts, the director of the U.S. Department of Defense's Advanced Research Projects Agency (ARPA), sometimes called DARPA, which was also researching computer networking. Since most computers at the time were large, expense mainframe systems, Roberts viewed networking as a viable economic solution that would allow computer users to exchange information and share their capacities and resources, including databases and applications.

In his article for *Scientific American* (October 1987), Kahn identified two necessary conditions for networking: an electronic link between computers and a common language, so that different computers can understand each other. Kahn and other computer scientists believed that the circuit-switching system used for telephone lines, in which each call is routed along a dedicated path, would be impractical for computer networking. In *Scientific American*, Kahn explained that "If circuit switching were applied to roads, and you wanted to drive, say, from New York to Washington, you would call the highway system and ask them to close one lane on the entire stretch of Interstate 95 to all other traffic. The result would be a lot of reserved but empty highway." Paul Baran, a computer scientist working for the RAND Corporation, also sought an alternative to circuit-switching; he pointed out that packet-switching along distributed networks would have clear security benefits over a centralized information location, which could be easily destroyed by enemy attack. During the 1960s, Baran, the UCLA professor Leonard Kleinrock, and Donald Davies at the National Physical Laboratory, in England, did independent work on packet-switching. Packet-switching involves breaking down messages into smaller units, or packets, for transmission. Each packet is marked with a header, containing its source and destination; packets then travel along different routes—whatever is available and most efficient—and are then reassembled when they reach their destination. Packet-switching allowed the transmission of more information between computers through telephone lines.

Roberts solicited proposals from the computer science community for a 19-node packet-switched network. In July 1968 Kahn, with the assistance of several colleagues, wrote BBN Technical Paper 1763, which outlined a plan for a packet-switched network and included Kahn's ideas for management of buffer space to hold incoming, unassembled messages. After reviewing the nearly two-meter stack of proposals he had received, Roberts awarded the ARPA contract to BBN, in December 1968. Kahn had planned to leave BBN at this point, but BBN's project manager, Frank Heart, persuaded him to stay with the company and oversee the implementation of the plan. In an April 1990 interview with Judy O'Neill for the Charles Babbage Institute, Kahn recalled, "It became very clear to me, shortly after we had gotten the award, the set of issues that were involved was very complicated relative to what you normally find in a typical engineering project. In fact, my being involved in it was actually far more important than I originally thought because I really played a key role in bringing it all together architecturally. It was a design role that was very essential to what was going on."

Kahn worked with a team of six computer scientists, including Severo Ornstein, who built the network's hardware, and Bill Crowther, who developed the software. The team selected Professor Kleinrock's UCLA laboratory as the site of the network's first node, which was installed on September 1, 1969. BBN then constructed nodes at the Stanford Research Institute (SRI), in Menlo Park, California; the University of California, Santa Barbara; and the University of Utah, in Salt Lake City. BBN constructed Interface Message Processors (IMPs) to link the nodes through dedicated, high-speed telephone lines. The IMPs broke down messages into 1,000-bit packets and added source and destination headings.

Back at Cambridge, Kahn worked—sometimes 23 hours a day—to fine-tune the network. At UCLA, a graduate student named Vinton Cerf joined the ARPANET project. As the months passed, Cerf's responsibilities increased, and he helped design the Network Control Protocol (NCP), which connected the host computers to the IMPs. By December 1969 four nodes of the ARPANET were operating. That month, Kahn traveled to California to assess the system's performance. As Cerf told Adam, "[Kahn] would ask for software to do something. I would program it overnight, and we would do the tests."

Through the process of trial and error, BBN gradually made improvements to the ARPANET. By the early 1970s there were more than 15 sites connected, and yet few people made practical use of this new technology. "If you did log on, it was rare that you could do anything useful," Kahn explained to Adam. Kahn believed—correctly, as it turned out—that nearly every aspect of life would eventually be transformed by networking capabilities. To generate interest in the ARPANET, Kahn spent over a year preparing a demonstration for the International Conference on Computer Communications, which was held in Washington, D.C., in October 1972. More than 1,000 computer scientists, journalists, and members of the business community attended the conference, where they witnessed many different pieces of hardware functioning together as one unit. By this time, the AR-PANET linked 29 nodes. Kahn described the demonstration as "the key event, in my view, that legitimized the whole notion of computer networking." According to Adam, ARPANET usage increased 67 percent during the month of the conference, and continued to grow.

Kahn left BBN in late 1972 to become the new director of the Information Processing Techniques Office (IPTO) at DARPA, formerly called ARPA. He continued work on a project initiated by Roberts to apply packet-switching to satellite communications and also began research on packet-switching for radio transmissions. DARPA was interested in both technologies for military use. A military commander aboard a ship or in the field could use such technology to access intelligence information from a central computerized database.

For Kahn and other computer scientists, the next logical step was linking computers, satellites, and radios into one, large network. At the time, the individual networks had incompatible formats and transmitted data at different speeds. Kahn enlisted his former colleague Vinton Cerf, who had joined the faculty of Stanford University, in California, to work on a plan for linking different networks. Through frequent telephone calls, e-mails, and visits, the two men hashed out their ideas; the discussions occasionally turned into heated arguments. "We just dove into it from first principles," Kahn recalled to Adam. "We generally build on each other's ideas to make progress."

By 1973 Kahn and Cerf had settled on a solution. They developed an idea for a Transmission Control Protocol (TCP). As Kahn explained in his article for *Communications of the Association of Computing Machinery (ACM)* (August 1994), TCP was an "internetwork architecture that would allow packet networks of different kinds to interconnect and machines to communicate across the set of interconnected networks." In effect, the TCP created a standardized envelope for enclosing packets that would be compatible with the different networks. Kahn and Cerf presented their ideas to the meeting of the International Network Working Group, at the University of Sussex, in Brighton, England. They also published their theory in *IEEE Transactions on Communications* (May 1974). "When Vint and I finished writing the paper, I was 100 percent sure when we hooked up the networks that it would work," Kahn said, as quoted by Adam. In the paper, Kahn and Cerf first used the word *Internet,* short for *Internetwork,* to describe the planned network of networks. Kahn allocated DARPA funding to build the TCP to three recipients—Cerf at Stanford University, Ray Tomlinson at BBN, and Peter Kirstein at University College, in London. Cerf and about a dozen of his graduate students worked on the project. In 1975, one of Cerf's students, Darryl Rubin, implemented the TCP prototype, successfully connecting the ARPANET with a radio network. BBN worked on connecting the ARPANET to the satellite network. Kahn insisted that BBN engi-

neers create a new IMP, as well as a separate satellite IMP (SIMP) and install a router between the networks, thus creating an enduring solution rather than the more improvised solution originally proposed.

In 1976 Kahn persuaded Cerf to join him at DARPA. The next year, the ARPANET, the radio network, and the satellite network were all connected with the TCP. On November 22, 1977 Cerf and his team tested its capabilities. Packets of information made a global journey, traveling from their source at mobile radio transmitters in Menlo Park, California; across the country to the ARPANET, in Virginia; via satellite to Norway and London; back via satellite to the United States; to the ARPANET again; and finally to a destination computer at UCLA's Information Sciences Institute (ISI). As Cerf recalled to Adam, "The packets took a 150,000-km round trip to go 650 km down the coast from San Francisco to Los Angeles. We didn't lose a bit." The success of the test forced a re-evaluation of networking. In a December 1992 interview with an *Omni* reporter, Kahn explained, "The historical approach to building networks was to have centralized control and management. But the Internet is the interconnection of these networks, owned and operated by different parties and encompassing different internal standards and conventions. The fact that the whole collection could be brought together and function under the Internet architecture was an important lesson."

In 1978 the TCP was split into two separate, but interrelated functions: the TCP, which breaks up messages into packets and then reassembles them, and the Internet Protocol (IP), which sends the packets to their destination. In 1980 the Department of Defense adopted a revised and updated version of TCP/IP as a standard. In 1983 the ARPANET replaced the antiquated NCP protocols with TCP/IP, ensuring that the new protocols would serve as the architecture for the Internet of the future.

Over the next several years, Kahn funded research projects that contributed to the Internet's development, including the building of large-scale integrated circuits and refining Unix, an operating system. He also initiated the Strategic Computing Program, a billion-dollar research project that supported the development of multiprocessor machines, large-scale databases, and knowledge-based systems.

Having grown disillusioned with bureaucratic infighting, Kahn left DARPA, in 1985, to form the nonprofit Corporation for National Research Initiatives (CNRI). He sought to develop what he coined the National Information Infrastructure (NII), which later became popularly known as the Information Superhighway. For this ambitious project, Kahn secured financial backing from such corporations as IBM, Digital Equipment, and Xerox, as well as support from government agencies, educational institutions, and research laboratories. "The highway system provides a means of interchange, linking cities and resources of this country. A high-speed network linking information resources, and the people using it, can do the same things for research and education, the economy, and social well-being in the twenty-first century," he told the *Omni* reporter.

Although more and more academics were using the Internet for research purposes, the federal government strictly prohibited using it for commercial purposes. Kahn believed that this regulation would inhibit the Internet's growth and discourage corporations from backing his efforts to build a nationwide network. In 1988 Kahn lobbied the government to change its policy, successfully persuading the Federal Networking Council to allow the connection of MCI's commercial e-mail system to the Internet. This decision opened the door to conducting business through the Internet. In 1989 Cerf, who was now with MCI, completed the connection of the company's e-mail to the Internet.

In 1990 Senator Al Gore of Tennessee introduced legislation to provide $1.75 billion to build an information superstructure in the form of gigabit networks, which would transfer huge amounts of data at high speeds, and link the nation's computers. (Although Gore clearly exaggerated when he took credit for "inventing" the Internet during the 2000 presidential campaign, he did play a major role in pushing its development.) That year, the National Science Foundation (NSF) allocated $15.8 million to CNRI to build five gigabit "test beds" across the country. Kahn also began research to create a national digital library that will put millions of books, articles, and other pieces of information at a computer user's fingertips.

Internet usage exploded during the 1990s. By the end of the decade, logging onto the Internet was as common as placing a telephone call or turning on a television set. Tens of millions of people around the world were on-line—communicating, conducting business, and sharing resources and information. Robert Kahn's role in facilitating this communications revolution has been recognized many times. In 1997 President Bill Clinton honored both Kahn and Cerf with the prestigious National Medal of Technology. Kahn has also received the Marconi Award, the Secretary of Defense's Civilian Service Award (twice), the Computerworld/Smithsonian Award, the President's Award and the Software Systems Award from the ACM, the Alexander Graham Bell Medal and Third Millennium Medal from the IEEE, and the National Academy of Engineering's Charles Stark Draper Prize.—D. C.

Suggested Reading: *Business Month* p30+ Apr. 1987, with photo; Charles Babbage Institute Web site; *Communications of the Association for Computing Machinery (ACM)* p15+ Aug. 1994, with illus.; Corporation for National Research Initiatives Web Site; *Current Biography* (on-line) Sep. 1998; *IEEE Spectrum* p57+ Sep. 1996, with photos; *New York Times* A p1 June 8, 1990, III p1 Sep. 2, 1990; *Omni* p83+ Dec. 1992, with photos and illus.; *Scientific American* p136+ Oct. 1987, with illus.; *American Men and Women of Science, 1998–1999*, 1998

Kapor, Mitchell D.

Nov. 1, 1950– Founder of the Lotus Development Corporation

Mitchell D. Kapor is the creator of Lotus 1-2-3, one of the most popular software applications of all time. When it hit the market in 1983, many corporations and small businesses around the country rushed to buy personal computers in order to use the program, an electronic spreadsheet that keeps financial records and can chart financial projections. The application was one of the first software packages; in addition to the spreadsheet, it offers word processing, data management, and the ability to create graphics on a single disk. Although the Lotus Development Corporation, which he co-founded in 1982, made Kapor a multi-millionaire, he preferred to focus on producing innovative programs that would simplify the use of personal computers and improve people's lives, rather than on the financial aspects of the business. At the height of his success, Mitch Kapor stunned the computer industry by leaving the company to devote himself to various projects. One of these was championing on-line privacy and freedom of expression in cyberspace; he co-founded the political activist group, the Electronic Frontier Foundation (EFF), in 1990. In recent years Kapor has worked to create a national information superhighway and has provided financial capital to several start-up companies.

Mitchell David Kapor was born on November 1, 1950 in the New York City borough of Brooklyn. He grew up in Freeport, a town on Long Island. A brilliant student, Kapor skipped the second grade. In an interview with Fred Bruning for *Newsday* (January 31, 1994), Kapor recalled that as a student at Freeport High School he lacked basic "social coping behaviors" and was often "a natural victim" for the other students. He served as the captain of the math club and scored 1,544 out of a possible 1,600 on the SAT exam.

In 1967 Kapor enrolled at Yale University, in New Haven, Connecticut. He took courses in linguistics, computer science, and psychology as part of an interdisciplinary major in the new field of cybernetics, the science of communication and control theory concerned mainly with the comparative study of such automatic control systems as the human brain or mechanical communications systems. As a student, Kapor developed an interest in

Courtesy of Mitchell Kapor

Mitchell D. Kapor

Eastern religions and joined WYBC-FM, the university's radio station, eventually serving as the music director and program director.

After his graduation, in 1971, Kapor found a job as a disc jockey for WHCN-FM, a progressive-rock radio station in Hartford, Connecticut. He later taught transcendental meditation in Fairfield, Iowa, and Cambridge, Massachusetts. In Cambridge Kapor began working as an entry-level programmer. In an interview with a writer for *Inc.* (June 1983), Kapor explained his disillusionment with programming: "I found the kinds of contortions you had to go through to get a mainframe computer to do anything seemed to me to be illogical, irrational, inefficient, and fundamentally uninteresting."

Still unsure of his career goals, Kapor returned to school, taking graduate courses at Campus Free College (later renamed Beacon College), in Boston. In 1978 he received his master's degree in counseling psychology. Kapor became a counselor at New England Memorial Hospital, in Stoneham, a town outside of Boston. He left the hospital a short time later, telling David E. Sanger for the *New York Times Magazine* (September 11, 1988), that the job was "the psychic equivalent of emptying bedpans."

In 1978 Kapor purchased the Apple II, one of the first personal computers on the market. "I got very excited about it," Kapor told the *Inc.* reporter. "A computer was something I could own, that would be under the user's control and was not some elaborate priesthood." Unlike the large mainframe systems that serve corporate interests, Kapor added, "personal computers most directly serve the individual user." He immediately began using it to write programs or applications in BASIC, a simple computer language.

To sharpen his business skills, Kapor pursued an MBA at the Sloan School of Business at the Massachusetts Institute of Technology (MIT), in Cambridge, in 1979. At MIT, Kapor discovered TROLL, a mainframe application that kept track of statistics and figures. Kapor and a friend named Eric Rosenfeld co-wrote Tiny Troll, a smaller version of the application in the BASIC computer language for the Apple II.

In Massachusetts Kapor met Bob Frankston and Dan Bricklin, who co-wrote VisiCalc, the first electronic spreadsheet. VisiCalc allowed users to keep financial records and make calculations with ease and more quickly than by hand. Frankston and Bricklin had signed an agreement with Dan Flystra, the owner of Personal Software Inc., based in Sunnyvale, California, to market VisiCalc. The program is often credited with helping to start the personal computer revolution in the late 1970s by giving people a practical reason to own one. Over the next several years, VisiCalc sold tens of thousands of copies. Frankston and Bricklin introduced Kapor to Flystra, who successfully persuaded him to leave the Sloan School, in 1980, to relocate to Sunnyvale and work for the company as a product manager. There Kapor saw an opportunity to make use of his Tiny Troll program. He divided it into separate applications, VisiPlot and VisiTrend, which he sold to the company (now renamed VisiCorp) for several million dollars, as reported by Darryl K. Taft for *Computer Reseller News* (November 16, 1997). Both programs were marketed as companions to VisiCalc and were commercially successful.

Kapor had an idea for an application that would combine the electronic spreadsheet with graphics. "It seems sort of obvious, if you look at the stand-alone productivity tools of spreadsheets or graphing programs, because of the overhead of having to swap and load and reload to sit around and wait while all this was going on," he told *Inc.* (June 1983). "So the notion of integration came out of observation: Wouldn't it be nice if we could reduce user frustration by putting together separate programs into a single multifunction application?" Kapor pitched the idea to Flystra, who was unwilling to pursue it. Around this time, Kapor also became disillusioned with living on the West Coast. He left VisiCorp and was given $1.2 million as a part of his separation agreement, as reported by David Sanger in the *New York Times Magazine*.

In 1982 Kapor used the royalties he received from VisiPlot and VisiTrend to co-found the Lotus Development Corporation with Jonathan Sachs. The word *lotus* means the state of perfect enlightenment in Hinduism. The company's first application, Lotus 1-2-3, was unveiled in January 1983. "Eighty percent of executive use of personal computers consists of four activities: financial analysis with an electronic spreadsheet, graphics production, data management, and word processing," Kapor explained to a writer for *Inc.* (February 1983). Priced at $495, Lotus 1-2-3 performed all four of these functions and consisted of a single disk. Like VisiCalc, 1-2-3 was easy to use, but the Lotus product was much quicker.

Lotus 1-2-3 became a runaway bestseller. Major corporations and small businesses purchased personal computers and the program to keep records, chart sales, and make financial projections. Favorable word of mouth and lavish reviews in computer magazines and other periodicals contributed to its popularity. In its first full year in business in 1983, the Lotus development Corporation reaped $53 million in total sales and $14.3 million in profits. The same year, the company went public to raise additional capital.

The 1-2-3 phenomenon continued in 1984. Lotus's sales tripled to $156 million. The popularity of 1-2-3 gradually drove its rival, VisiCalc, off the market. (Lotus Development acquired VisiCorp the next year.) Increased sales forced Lotus to expand. Within two years, what began as a two man operation grew into a powerful and successful corporation with over 1,000 employees.

Although impressed with the corporation's success, several analysts posited that Lotus had to come up with new products to remain competitive in the volatile software market over the long term and not depend exclusively on sales of Lotus 1-2-3. Kapor agreed with this line of reasoning and, in 1984, several new programs reached the market. Symphony was similar to Lotus 1-2-3, but had a feature that allowed a user to receive data through telephone lines and immediately incorporate it into financial calculations and projections. Symphony's use of split screens allowed a user to see the spreadsheet, graphics, and word-processing document at the same time. Lotus also marketed Jazz, the Apple version of Symphony, to people who owned the Macintosh (Mac) computer. Another innovative application, Signal, allowed a personal computer to receive stock information through FM radio signals.

In 1985 Lotus's sales increased to an impressive $256 million, but the corporation failed to meet expectations and struggled with several difficulties. Lotus recalled Symphony to fix a bug that destroyed data, and although it eventually enjoyed impressive sales, Symphony failed to displace the popularity of 1-2-3. Since few businesses at the time used Macs, Jazz generated little interest. Competition from rival software manufacturers, including Microsoft and Ashton-Tate, intensified. These problems, which received substantial attention in the press, caused Lotus's stock price to drop significantly in 1985, alarming shareholders and investors. Unlike VisiCorp, however, Lotus Development weathered these storms and remained a major player in the software industry.

In 1986 Mitch Kapor stunned the computer industry by announcing his resignation as the CEO of Lotus. He had become disillusioned by Lotus's success and substantial growth in four years. "I

never wanted to run a big company," he told Beppi Crosariol for the *Boston Globe* (June 6, 1995). "I didn't know that [until] I was running one." Kapor preferred working in a small company where he knew all of the employees by name and that explored innovative ideas regardless of their worth as potential products. Having come of age in the 1960s, he shunned the corporate culture, preferring to wear Hawaiian shirts to work instead of expensive suits. Kapor turned over management of Lotus to Jim Manzi, but remained with the company until 1987 to complete work on a new application, Lotus Agenda. "I fit a classic entrepreneurial pattern as a person who likes and is good at starting things and who should move on to a board role or an advisory role after the initial phase," Kapor explained to *Leaders of the Information Age.* "I wasn't successful in accomplishing any kind of graceful transition [with Lotus]. Since then I've learned a lot more."

Kapor remained active in the computer industry. In 1987 he and Peter B. Miller, a former executive at Lotus, co-founded a new company, ON Technology. "At Lotus, I was interested in building something large and successful," Kapor explained to Keith H. Hammonds for *Business Week* (May 30, 1988). "Here, I'm much more interested in accomplishing something important." Kapor added that ON's focus would be to develop products that would make computers more simple to use and more effective as a means of communications. ON would remain a small operation and market its products in joint ventures with other companies. Speaking to Hammonds, Kapor sketched out, in vague terms, a new software platform that would enhance the existing operating systems for computers. The platform, he explained, would have sophisticated database and communications tools that would perform different tasks. Kapor, however, abandoned the idea in 1989 after several hardware companies declined to pursue it. The next year, he severed his ties with ON Technology, which continues to remain in business as a software company. "With 20/20 hindsight, starting another software company after Lotus was a mistake," he admitted to Jim Impoco, a writer for *U.S. News & World Report* (November 29, 1993). "I felt like I had something to prove, which is not a good basis for starting a business."

In 1990 Kapor turned his attention to privacy and censorship by co-founding the Electronic Frontier Foundation (EFF) with John Perry Barlow, a retired Wyoming rancher and lyricist for the Grateful Dead Band. A political activist group, the EFF opposes attempts by the government to censor or restrict content on the Internet. In 1990 a group identifying itself as the NuPrometheus League sent part of the top-secret operating code for the Mac to many people, including Kapor, on disk. The code had been stolen from Apple, possibly by a disgruntled employee. In an interview with Ken Goffman, a contributor to *Wired* (August 5, 1990, on-line), Barlow recalled that he received a visit from an FBI agent investigating the theft. Barlow believed that he was suspected because he had attended a hackers conference in October 1989. He added that during the interview, the agent displayed complete ignorance of how computers worked. Kapor received a similar visit from the FBI. Both were also alarmed by Operation Sun Devil, an aggressive crackdown by the Secret Service on hacking. The effort involved many cases in which agents broke into homes with guns drawn, physically restrained family members, confiscated computer equipment, and arrested suspects—many of whom were still minors. "Some of these kids have done some things that are illegal and they should get busted," Kapor said to Willie Schatz for the *Washington Post* (July 11, 1990). "But the over-reactive level of law enforcement is out of scale with the crimes that have been actually been committed." Kapor and Barlow feared that these actions were the first steps in the federal government's suppression of the right to privacy and freedom of expression in cyberspace. To get the EFF off the ground, Kapor donated $1 million. The group also raised substantial sums of money from the major players in the computer industry, including such companies as Microsoft, Apple, Sun Microsystems, and IBM.

The EFF seeks to educate the public and raise awareness about privacy and threats to freedom of expression on the Internet. The group lobbies policymakers on bills such as the Communications Decency Act (1996) that affected the Internet. It also provides legal counsel to individuals who have been charged with computer-related crimes. (In 1992 and 1993 Kapor served as chairman of the Massachusetts Commission on Computer Technology and Law, which was set up to explore issues relating to computer-related crimes.)

Although the EFF's campaign received substantial attention and support, the organization found itself torn by internal strife in 1994. Many of the EFF's members were angered when it helped rewrite and supported passage of the Digital Telephony Act, which made it easier for law enforcement agencies to tap telephone lines. (The EFF supported the legislation because it did not apply to the Internet.) Three of the group's top officials resigned in protest. Other critics charged that the EFF was absorbed by the political establishment in Washington, D.C., and wondered if the organization's substantial corporate backing compromised its independence. By the end of the 1990s, the EFF lost ground to the American Civil Liberties Union (ACLU) and the Electronic Information Privacy Center, which both aggressively championed online privacy and freedom of expression. In response to the criticisms, the EFF closed its Washington, D.C. office and relocated its headquarters to San Francisco. Kapor left the EFF in 1995, but returned in 2001 as an adviser and financial supporter. The EFF remains active today, but is now one of many activist groups concerned with privacy and censorship.

During the 1990s Mitch Kapor became an evangelist for the development of the "information superhighway," which would make vast amounts of electronic resources accessible to ordinary citizens. In an interview with Martha Groves for the *Los Angeles Times* (May 18, 1994), Kapor said that he hoped that the information superhighway would be "a network that reaches out to include virtually everyone in the society and that is highly participatory, in which people are not simply passive recipients of prepackaged information, but are engaged in a wide variety of activities, from education to entertainment to recreation to commerce. A system which can help revitalize the democratic process by encouraging more citizen participation, a network which stimulates information entrepreneurship and innovation, something which really restores the balance of power in a way that puts more power in the hands of individuals and less power in large, centralized institutions." Kapor frequently testified at congressional committees and consulted with government officials in order to help influence the information superhighway's development. He was named to the National Research Council's Computer Science and Technology Board and the National Information Infrastructure Advisory Council. Noting how he never repeated the success he had with Lotus 1-2-3, Kapor described himself in an interview with John Burgess for the *Washington Post* (February 28, 1992), as "the Chubby Checker of the PC industry. I had a big hit a number of years ago, and now I do oldies shows."

From 1994 to 1996 Kapor worked as an adjunct professor at MIT's Media Lab, teaching courses on software design, the "digital community," and the relationship between democracy and the Internet. (In 1995 he watched as IBM acquired Lotus.)

Kapor's next venture was Kapor Enterprises Inc., which he established to manage his financial interests and investments. He used its resources to invest in several high-technology, start-up companies, including UUNET and RealNetworks. In an article for the *Wall Street Journal* (January 7, 1999), Ann Grimes and Stephanie N. Mehta wrote that Kapor's $500,000 investment in UUNET, an Internet service provider, yielded $150 million after it was sold to WorldCom Inc. Kapor invested $1 million in RealNetworks, resulting in a $75 million return. However, the technology company Go, which also received substantial support from Kapor, failed.

In 1997 he created the Mitchell Kapor Foundation. His home page explains that the foundation focuses "on the intersection of health and the environment, the social impact of information technology, and the removing [of] barriers to full participation and the workplace by historically disadvantaged groups."

In 1999 Kapor became a partner at Accel Partners, a venture-capital firm based in Palo Alto, California. Kapor's first two marriages ended in divorce. Now married for a third time, Kapor divides his time between San Francisco and Boston.—D. C.

Suggested Reading: *Boston Globe* p57 Dec. 29, 1994, p46 Jun. 6, 1995; *Business Week* p92 May 30, 1988, with photo, p82 Apr. 10, 1989; *Computer Reseller News* p63+ Nov. 11, 1997, with photo; Electronic Frontier Foundation Web site; *Inc.* p142 Feb. 1983, p114 Jun. 1983 *Los Angeles Times* D p9 May 18, 1994, with photo; Mitch Kapor home page; *New York Times* D p1 Feb. 13, 1984; *New York Times Magazine* p60+ Sep. 11, 1988, with photos; *Newsweek* p116+ July 2, 1990, with photos; *U.S. News & World Report* p88 Nov. 29, 1993; *Wall Street Journal* A p16 Jan. 7, 1999; *Washington Post* B p8 July 11, 1990, with photo, B p1 Feb. 28, 1992, with photo; *Wired* (on-line) Aug. 5, 1990

Kay, Alan

May 17, 1940– Inventor of the Dynabook

Alan Kay once remarked that "the best way to predict the future is to invent it," as quoted by Donald D. Spencer in the *Dictionary of Computer Quotations* (1997). And that's what he did with his Dynabook, the first computer envisioned for personal use. In the 1960s, when Kay's idea first crystallized, computers were large, time-sharing mainframes that often took up an entire room at a corporation or university, where they were used by highly trained specialists. Kay envisioned a computer that could be carried like a notebook and, in addition to displaying text, would also be able to generate pictures and sounds. Three decades later, sales of personal computers, virtually all of which could convey images as well as words, had skyrocketed, and portable notebook computers of the type Kay had imagined, while not as widely used as desktop PCs, had also become commonplace. In addition to helping pave the way for the revolution in personal computing, with the creation of Smalltalk, the first object-oriented computer-programming language, Kay helped to simplify computer languages so that even children could use them. Kay also helped to develop the modern computer workstation through his creation of an early user interface that incorporated overlapping windows, and he aided in the creation of the Ethernet, laser printing, and network client-servers.

Alan Kay was born in Springfield, Massachusetts, on May 17, 1940 and he spent the first few years of his life in Australia, where Kay's father, a physiologist, was from originally. With the growing threat of a Japanese invasion of Australia during World War II, the Kay family moved back to the United States, the native country of Kay's mother, a musician and artist. From 1945 to 1949, Kay and his parents lived in his maternal grandfather's farmhouse outside of Hadley, Massachusetts. At age three Kay was able to read and was showing signs of having an active interest in learning, and by age five he demonstrated the ability to question authority. In an interview with Dennis Shasha and

Cathy Lazere for their book *Out of Their Minds: The Lives and Discoveries of 15 Great Computer Scientists* (1998), Kay noted, "By the time I got to school, I had already read a couple hundred books. I knew in the first grade that they were lying to me because I had already been exposed to other points of view. School is basically about one point of view—the one the teacher has or the textbooks have. They don't like the idea of having different points of view, so it was a battle. Of course I would pipe up with my five-year-old voice."

Kay's innate intelligence did not protect him from embarrassing and awkward childhood experiences. After reading more than 400 books each year as a child, he became a "Quiz Kid" on a local radio station in upstate New York, but he didn't do well on the program because while he could retain facts, he was unable to think for himself, according to Frank Rose, who wrote an article about Kay for the *New York Times Magazine* (November 8, 1987). As Kay later recounted, his self-esteem at that age stemmed almost solely from his impression that he was smarter than everyone else, and when that impression was shattered, he lost all confidence in himself. It was a blow from which it took years for Kay to recover. "I was 27 and in grad school when I got my confidence back," he told Rose. "I got very excited by what was going on there [at the University of Utah, in Salt Lake City], and even more excited that somebody actually trusted me. But I never thought computer science was all that important. It was much easier than the stuff I really care about, like music."

Through his mother, Kay was exposed to music at a young age. Initially attracted to a career in music, he became a soprano soloist in the grade school choir and a solid guitar player. The tendency to question authority that Kay exhibited as a small child made for a stormy career as a student, and he was expelled from a junior high school and later Brooklyn Technical High School. In 1961, he was thrown out of Bethany College in West Virginia after protesting when a friend was expelled due to poor grades. Kay subsequently lived in Denver and worked as a music teacher, giving guitar lessons. Around this time he joined the U. S. Air Force and took a computer programming aptitude test, through which he discovered that he was specially gifted in that area, and was assigned to work on an IBM 1401 as a programmer.

Upon leaving the air force, Kay enrolled at the University of Colorado, in Boulder, where he majored in mathematics and molecular biology. After graduating in 1966, he entered a doctoral program at the University of Utah and studied electrical engineering, receiving his Ph.D. in 1969. While working toward his degree at Utah, he came into contact with a number of computer programs, including Simula (an object-oriented computer language that laid the framework for many current software methods used by high-performance computers) and Ivan Sutherland's Sketchpad (the first computer program that allowed the user to manipulate graphics). After studying each of these and thinking about them in terms of his biology background, Kay developed his "biological analogy" theory, which suggested that an ideal computer would act just like a living being, in that each component would be comparable to a cell; it would act in accord with other parts of the machine to complete a task but could also function self-sufficiently.

While visiting the Artificial Intelligence Laboratory at the Massachusetts Institute of Technology (MIT), in Cambridge, in the fall of 1968, Kay met Seymour Papert, who was then working on a new computer-programming language called LOGO. Papert and his associates were attempting something that had never been done before: they were showing children how to use computers by teaching them LOGO. From their school, the children were using large time-sharing terminals that were hooked up by phone line to a DEC mainframe at MIT. (Time-sharing, a method by which many terminals are connected to a single mainframe, allowed many users to work on one computer simultaneously.) The children input information through a keyboard and received output through a Teletype printer at each individual terminal. Up until this point, such activities had been confined to the ranks of highly knowledgeable programmers. By exposing children to an easy-to-learn language such as LOGO, Papert was attempting to bring programming, and computers in general, into the lives of everyday people.

This idea stunned Kay, who would subsequently devote his life to making computers accessible to all people, particularly children. Kay recalled Aldus Manutius, a 15th-century printer who, believing that books should be extremely portable, went out and measured his saddlebags to determine their ideal size. Kay wanted to do the same thing with a computer, so that children would be able to take it wherever they went. He envisioned a personal computer, no larger than a notebook, which he dubbed the Dynabook. Kay's idea represented a major creative leap in an era in which personal computers, much less portable ones, were virtually nonexistent. "A clear romantic vision has a marvelous ability to focus thought and will," Kay recalled, as quoted by Bob Johnstone in an issue of *Computing Japan* (October 1999). "Now it was easy to know what to do next. I built a cardboard model of [the Dynabook] to see what it would look like, and poured in lead pellets to see how light it would have to be (less than two pounds)." The model he made in 1968 looked very much like the laptop computer that became increasingly common during the 1980s and 1990s, except that it was flat instead of the clamshell design that its later counterparts took.

Beginning in 1969, Kay spent two years teaching at the Stanford Artificial Intelligence Laboratory, where he thought about his Dynabook concept and also began to develop the Smalltalk language. Using his biological analogy theory, Kay devised Smalltalk to mimic the way animal cells communicated with each other via impulses, or messages. In 1972 he joined the staff at Xerox's Palo Alto Research Center (also known as Xerox PARC), and there he began using Smalltalk for educational purposes, though the idea for such a language—the first of the object-oriented programming languages—would take more than a decade to catch on. At PARC Kay conducted a study in which children were exposed to computers and their reactions were noted. After analyzing the data, Kay came to the conclusion that children learned less through written words than they did through sounds and images. As a result, he and his colleagues developed a computer system that made ample use of graphics and animation and was geared specifically toward children, some of whom became so skilled in it that they developed their own programs with it.

While leading a research group at PARC, Kay also contributed to the development of the Ethernet, a type of local area network (LAN) in which computers are linked together and can share information; laser printing, which greatly improved the quality of information printed from a computer, so that it became comparable to the quality of documents printed at a print shop; and the client-server network model, in which many client computers—PC workstations, for example—are linked to a more powerful server computer that provides them with services, such as retrieving information from a database. However, throughout this period, Kay wanted most to develop his model of a laptop computer. Although the technology needed to build the Dynabook did not yet exist, the development of the flat-screen monitor at around this time further motivated Kay to produce his computer and caused him to see computing in a whole new light. In his interview with Frank Rose for the *New York Times Magazine*, Kay noted that upon seeing the flat-panel display, "That's when I realized that the computer was like paper, except with extensions into time and into other dimensions. Paper can hold the same kind of marks that computers can. But it's hard to have a piece of paper that can look at the marks and do what they say. All the newness of the computer comes from its *dynamic* qualities—that's why I called it the Dynabook. The computer is a new kind of medium—Gutenberg has come and we haven't recognized him yet."

Though initially given a blank check to develop new computer projects, Kay was unable to get enough funding from Xerox's management to develop the technology needed to build the Dynabook. Even more embarrassing for Xerox's management was that they not only ignored the developments being created by their own research team but also failed to copyright the Dynabook name. However, some of Kay's ideas—including windows, pull-down menus, and on-screen icons representing commands—made it from the drawing board, first into the GRID computer and later into the Apple Macintosh. GRID, the first serious portable computer, was created by two former PARC researchers, John Ellenby and Glenn Edens, in 1979. The computer contained a number of innovations that became commonly used in laptop computers, including a magnesium casing, a switching power supply, and a built-in modem. The GRID computer was also designed in a clamshell shape to protect the screen—an innovation the designers patented. They are paid royalties by portable computer manufacturers who utilize that design to this day.

Steve Jobs and Jeff Raskin of Apple Computer visited PARC in 1979 and realized that Kay's ideas were paving the way for the future of computing. Kay himself left PARC in 1983 and became an Apple Fellow in 1984, after working for a year at Atari, Inc. That same year, the Apple Macintosh, the world's first computer to incorporate a graphical user interface, was produced and became a commercial and critical success. Although the Macintosh introduced many of Kay's innovations to the public at large, more than a decade after he had envisioned the laptop computer, such a product was still not being manufactured in the United States.

This is not to say the laptop computer was not being developed elsewhere. In 1980 Ellenby and Edens took their design for the GRID computer to Japan, where flat-paneled screens were more widely used. After looking at a number of suppliers who had developed a variety of flat-screen designs, the duo settled on Toshiba's liquid crystal display (LCD screen). By 1989 Toshiba's laptop computer had become the top-selling model, with more than 40 percent of the European and Japanese markets and a quarter of the American market. Furthermore, Toshiba called their laptop by a name that Xerox had failed to copyright following the development of Kay's idea at PARC: the Dynabook. When Tetsuya Mizoguchi of Toshiba informed Kay that his company had designed the type of computer Kay had envisioned, he was delighted. By his own admission, Kay has always been more interested in developing ideas than actual products. As he told Frank Rose, "I'd be a lot richer if I wanted to get things out [on the market]." Laptops are still most widely used by businesspeople and not students, as Kay had imagined.

Beginning in the 1980s, Kay began to imagine "agent-based systems" in computers—small programs that perform specific tasks independently and that can often be customized for a particular use. Early examples of such agents, or "personal electronic servants," as Rose called them, can be found in the form of personalized start-up Web pages that have been programmed to search for and retrieve that information of greatest interest to a particular user and store it where the user can access it at his or her convenience. However, these are nothing like the type of agents Kay originally imagined, which would be able to recognize and adopt to changing circumstances and make decisions accordingly, without receiving additional instructions. While Kay was working at Apple in 1987, the company presented a video called *Knowledge Navigator,* in which it portrayed a fu-

turistic vision of a professor talking to his computer, which in turn manages his schedule, screens his telephone calls, and takes care of all his paperwork. Kay believes that such agents could even be trusted with the power to spend money, freeing an individual's personal time from mundane tasks, such as paying bills and shopping around for the best prices on consumer goods. However, as with the Dynabook, Kay's ideas about agents have proven to be many years ahead of their time. According to a writer for the *Economist* (June 15, 1996), "Describing such an agent was easy; creating one was not. An agent . . . would need to be able to recognize voices perfectly (including knowing who was speaking), to monitor and manage telephone calls, and to have a commonsense understanding of the world. All of these befuddle today's technology."

In 1996 Kay left Apple to join the staff of Walt Disney Imagineering Research and Development. His primary reason for switching companies was that he wanted to resume working directly on educating children about computers. Disney Imagineering was started by Walt Disney in 1952 with the intention of finding new ways to entertain and teach children, using methods ranging from theme parks to innovative educational tools. Today the company is a think tank for the larger Disney corporation, which is hoping to branch out into new forms of entertainment. In the late 1990s, Kay was working on creating a new software program for Disney called Squeak, which would give Disney's Web sites nearly instantaneous response times. Squeak is being designed specially for Disney's educational Web sites, which are rich with sounds and images that help children learn. As Kay remarked to Ronald Grover in an article in *BusinessWeek* (March 8, 1999), "Disney is a great place to try out new ideas because they know so much about kids, and they have the size and resources to put your ideas into practice."

Alan Kay lives in Brentwood, California, with his wife Bonnie MacBird, a screenwriter, director, and producer whom he married in 1983. He still enjoys music, including playing a pipe organ in a soundproof room in his basement. He frequently travels, particularly to teach at MIT, and has supervised an educational project called Vivarium, co-sponsored by MIT and the Center for Individualization in Los Angeles. Through Vivarium, elementary school students can use MIT's Media Lab software to, for instance, collect real data about their communities and share their findings with students in other schools, or simulate and study various ecosystems. He is a fellow of the Royal Society of the Arts, the National Academy of Engineering, and the American Academy of the Arts and Sciences. He has received many awards for his work, including the J. D. Warnier Prize and the ACM Software Systems Award.—C. M.

Suggested Reading: *BusinessWeek* p98 Dec. 1, 1986, p108+ Mar. 8, 1999; *Computing Japan* p17 Oct. 1999; *Economist* p76+ June 15, 1996; *Educom Review* p34+ Mar./Apr. 1999; *Hudson*

Valley Business Journal p19 Jan. 1, 1996; *New York Times Magazine* p56+ Nov. 8, 1987; *Virginia Tech Computer Science Department* (online); *American Men and Women of Science 1998–99*, 1998; Spencer, Donald D. *Dictionary of Computer Quotations*, 1997; Lee, J. A. N., ed. *International Biographical Dictionary of Computer Pioneers*, 1995; Shasha, Dennis and Cathy Lazere. *Out of Their Minds: The Lives and Discoveries of 15 Great Computer Scientists*, 1998; Spencer, Donald D. *The Timeline of Computers*, 1997

Kay, Andrew F.

1919– Founder of Kaypro

Andrew F. Kay's company, Kaypro, has come to symbolize the potential for both explosive growth and catastrophic failure in the volatile computer industry. When Kay introduced one of the first affordable portable computers, the Kaypro II, in 1982, it launched his company to the top of the industry. Eight years later, contending with a host of new competitors and ever-changing technology, the Kaypro Corporation went bankrupt amid scandal. Nevertheless, the Kaypro II remains one of the prototypical early personal computers, influential for its simple, functional, and cost-effective design.

Earlier in his career Kay started Non-Linear Systems (NLS), which developed and sold the first digital voltmeter (DVM), a device for measuring and digitally displaying a current. Owing to his role in creating this useful device, *Electronic Design* magazine in 1963 credited Kay and Dr. William Schockley, the inventor of the transistor, with starting the digital revolution. Though today few experts would be likely to place Kay on such exalted ground, he nevertheless remains an influential figure.

Andrew F. Kay was born in 1919, and in 1940 he received a B.S. from the Massachusetts Institute of Technology (MIT), in Cambridge. He began his career at a company called Bendix and then worked for two years at the Jet Propulsion Laboratory. He was then put in charge of test engineering at Jack and Heintz Co., owned by William Jack. Kay was subsequently made vice president of engineering at another of Jack's firms, Bill Jack Scientific Instrument Co. In 1952 he left to start NLS, in Del Mar, California.

Kay had come up with the idea for the DVM while at Jack and Heintz Co. after noticing that employees using analog voltmeters had trouble getting accurate readings and often destroyed the meters by overloading them with voltage. Kay's DVM tolerated overvoltage and featured a four-digit display for reading voltage. NLS sold the first DVM in April 1953 for $2,300 to the Naval Electronics Laboratory, and the devices were the staple of NLS's business for years to come.

In the 1960s Kay, influenced by management theorists such as A. H. Maslow, Rensis Likert, Frederick Herzberg, and Douglas McGregor, began experimenting with new business-management practices. He replaced his assembly lines with independent work groups that were responsible for making many of their own decisions and keeping their own financial records. Between 1960 and 1965 NLS's production increased by 30 percent and customer complaints about product quality dropped by 70 percent. However, in 1970 the aerospace industry, which provided most of NLS's customers, went into a slump and so, accordingly, did NLS.

NLS floundered for nearly a decade before Kay got an idea for a new product, in 1978. He noticed that his son-in-law, an architect, was having trouble transporting his Apple computer and wondered whether it might be possible to make a portable computer with the same basic features. He put together a research team financed by $1.5 million gleaned from a second mortgage on his house and his other properties and proceeded to develop the idea. The future looked bleak in 1981 when a computer company called Osborne introduced a portable computer before Kay's was ready for production. The Kaypro I portable computer soon followed but provided little competition for Osborne. Then, in June 1982, Kay unveiled the Kaypro II, which boasted a screen twice the size of Osborne's and with twice the memory capacity. The Kaypro II sold for $1,795 (IBM's unwieldy personal computers cost about $3,500 in those days) and became an immediate hit. While Osborne was driven out of business within 18 months of introducing its product, NLS's sales soared from $5.5 million in the 1982 fiscal year to approximately $75 million in 1983. Demand for the computers was so great that Kay was forced to erect a temporary tent near his headquarters, in Solana Beach, California, to house supplies and spare parts until a permanent warehouse could be built. By the end of 1983 NLS had changed its name to Kaypro and held the top place in sales among portable-computer manufacturers and the fourth place among makers of personal computers— behind IBM, Apple, and Radio Shack.

Kay's success was partly due to the fact that his overhead was low. Kaypros were made mostly from standard components that were decreasing dramatically in price at the time. He also set up a network of independent dealers so that he would not have to share profits with a distribution company. Kaypro was primarily family-run; Kay's wife, Mary, and his two sons, David and Allan, all held executive positions in the firm, and the family collectively owned approximately 75 percent of the company shares, though none earned more than $41,000 in salary in 1983. Kaypro's growth continued during the next couple of years, despite a securities violation class-action lawsuit filed against it by shareholders, who alleged that stock prices had been artificially inflated before a 1983 public

A Kaypro advertisement   Courtesy of the Computer Museum of America

offering. Beginning in 1987 Kaypro went into a steep decline. In 1987 and 1988 the company lost a combined $14 million. In 1988 Kay's son David, who was then the president of Kaypro, decided to leave the company amid rumors of family feuding. Kay denied the rumors. In *Inc.* (April 1990) he explained to Ellen Wojahn, "Now, we're supposedly an example of a 'troubled family business.' Well, there are managerial conflicts and differences of opinion in most companies that don't have family members, but in those circumstances, people look for other reasons. Where there's family, they figure that's reason enough. They don't look any further. It's like saying that if milk consumption is going up, and so is cancer, milk must cause cancer. It doesn't mean anything, but it makes a great headline." Kay continued, "When we ran into trouble, one sharp guy wrote a headline that said, 'Too many Kays, not enough pros.' He even had me believing it for a while. Then I realized something: if it hadn't been for the family and its cohesiveness, the company wouldn't have stayed together. . . . It was the family funds and the family relationships that held it together."

In order to get capital for business operations Kaypro was forced to borrow repeatedly from Kay's personal finances; he lent the company a total of $2.8 million in 1988 alone. In the 1989 fiscal year Kaypro lost $19.3 million and its sales decreased to $21.8 million (from $72.2 million in 1988). Kay hired a businessman named Roy Salisbury as CEO of Kaypro in February 1990, and on March 1 of that year the company declared bankruptcy. Kaypro "just became generally eclipsed by quicker-growing vendors like Compaq," George Thompson, a market analyst, told Kim Kowsky for the *Los Angeles Times* (February 22, 1990). "New

companies were able to come in with newer, more technologically advanced product lines, and they didn't have to worry about servicing older product lines." Kaypro was also forced to recall several products when it reportedly received bad computer chips from Malaysia, which caused negative publicity and even worse sales. Even Kay's makeshift storage tent came back to haunt him; Kaypro lost millions of dollars in computer parts that were presumably stolen from the tent.

In April 1990 Salisbury fired Kay, who nevertheless remained the board chairman of the company. Documents provided by Salisbury in the bankruptcy filing claimed that the company's accounting practices were so confused that no accurate financial records existed. He told Chris Kraul for the *Los Angeles Times* (June 19, 1990) that Kaypro and Kay were being investigated for possible violations by the Security and Exchange Commission, the Internal Revenue Service, and the San Diego County Sheriff's Department.

Kay regained control of the company in late June, after a U.S. bankruptcy judge appointed a Kay ally as the fifth board director. The newly configured board immediately fired Salisbury. In June 1992 a bankruptcy judge changed Kaypro's status from Chapter 11 bankruptcy, which protects a company from its creditors, to Chapter 7, which requires the liquidation of a company's assets to pay creditors. Kay himself was the company's largest creditor; he was owed $7.3 million by Kaypro.

In 1992 Kay and his brother founded Kay Computers, a personal-computer company. Kaypro continues to manufacture and sell computers, though it is no longer affiliated with Andrew Kay. Kay has in recent years suffered from health problems and still mourns the death of his beloved wife a few years ago. During his last interview, taped for the Computer Museum of America, in February 2000, Kay reiterated that education, especially reading, played an important role in his life. He strongly advocates studying vocabulary as the main component of a useful and productive education for children of all economic and ability levels.—P. G. H.

Suggested Reading: *BusinessWeek* p98+ Jan. 20, 1973; *Inc.* p81+ Apr. 1990; *International Management* p31 Apr. 1984; *Los Angeles Times* A p2 Feb. 22, 1990, A p2 June 21, 1990; *New York Times* III p4 Nov. 27, 1983, D p1 July 5, 1990; *San Francisco Chronicle* B p3 Mar. 3, 1990; *USA Today* B p2 Oct. 4, 1988; Osborne, Adam *Hypergrowth: The Rise and Fall of Osborne Computer Corporation*, 1984

Keck, Donald B.

Jan. 2, 1941– Physicist; co-inventor of optical fiber

The backbone of the modern telecommunications age is optical fiber, which was invented by Donald B. Keck, Peter C. Schultz, and Robert D. Maurer in 1970. Optical fiber is essential to all long-distance communications by phone or Internet, and it is vital to the cable-television industry as well. One look at the numbers tells the story: 25 million miles of optical fiber is installed in the United States alone, and 50 million more miles is in use across the rest of the world—enough to circle the Earth's equator thousands of times over.

Donald B. Keck submitted the following third-person account of his youth to *Leaders of the Information Age*: "Donald Bruce Keck was born in Lansing, Michigan, on January 2, 1941, the son of William G. Keck, a Ph.D. private consultant in geophysics specializing in groundwater hydrology, and Zelda D. Keck, a school teacher specializing in English and literature. His childhood was very typical of a boy growing up in mid-western America. He enjoyed the out-of-doors and collected his share of tadpoles and fireflies. A distinct advantage that he had was to grow up next door to his maternal grandparents.

"In particular, his grandfather was a jack-of-all-trades, having been a carpenter, deputy sheriff, mason, fireman and probably several [other] occupations during his career. Grandpa was always doing or building something interesting and valuable to learn. His father brought the technology dimension to him at an early age. Having been trained as a physicist and an electrical engineer he too was always creating some piece of high-technology equipment for his consulting business. A young mind couldn't help but be rapidly expanded by such an environment. Both these gentlemen shared the philosophy that one didn't have to buy something, they could simply build it. So

there were a great many home-built tools and gadgets around the two houses. One could not help but become interested in technology in such an environment. Growing up in the inventive environment as he did placed him in an excellent position for his later work.

"From the earliest age he was allowed free reign in the workshop. He was encouraged to take things apart to see how they worked. It was not long before he could fix most things around the house that broke down. His mother also greatly encouraged this because his father was often traveling for his consulting business. He would later lament that when he put a board on top of one of his roller skates and scooted around the basement being chased by his dog Skippy that he was only 40 years early in inventing the skateboard.

"His mother also kindled an interest in music by arranging for piano lessons starting in about the fourth grade. He would continue lessons for the next 6 years, stopping only as high school activities became too time consuming. He would later observe that he played more and greatly increased his repertoire after stopping the formal lessons. Later in his career he would teach himself to play the pipe organ and the folk guitar. This informal education with which he grew up probably contributed more to his later success than his formal schooling.

"While he was a quick learner and received good grades in the primary grades, his teachers would later suggest that he 'did not apply himself well' in junior and senior high school. Summers were the time of maximum fun. The family had a cottage on a mid-Michigan lake and summer water sports became a favorite past-time. As he grew older, water skiing became the favorite activity during these months. With time his skills increased with slalom and trick skis and eventually he learned to barefoot ski. During the final years of high school he and his friends would put on water ski shows on the Grand River in Lansing. He [once] placed second in the state of Michigan water ski tournament's slalom event. Upon entering college, however, he began to see the value of formal education, and did graduate from Michigan State University [in 1962] with honors. He attended Michigan State largely for financial reasons since it was only a short distance from his East Lansing home. He was able to ride his bicycle about two miles to the campus. In the winter this often became very uncomfortable if not treacherous. His graduate education was also obtained at Michigan State where he earned [his master's degree in 1964] and his Ph.D. in physics in 1967. It was during his senior year in college and during graduate studies that his interest in optics would manifest itself. His graduate thesis was in the field of molecular spectroscopy in the near infrared spectral region. A large part of this work included making improvements in the optics of the high resolution IR spectrometer that had been built in the Michigan State University physics laboratory many years earlier. Before finishing, he had doubled the resolution of the instrument. As is often the case, individual professors can have a great influence on a person's life. In addition to his father and grandfather, one noteworthy individual was his graduate electricity and magnetism professor, Alfred Leitner. He would later recall the day that Leitner showed the relationship between the dielectric constant and the magnetic permeability constant and the speed of light. It is best described as a theological experience, to see how God's world fit together so neatly. This further expanded his interest in optical physics and would ultimately lead him to his work on optical fibers."

Keck joined Corning Laboratories, in Corning, New York, in 1968 as a senior research scientist. He gave Leaders of the Information Age the following third-person account of his work there: "Upon graduation in 1967, there were many job opportunities. Several of these were in the area of semiconductors. The transistor had been invented about a decade previously and companies were frantically looking for scientists to expand this technology area. After Keck had interviewed with many companies and was about ready to take one of their offers, a scientist from Corning visited Michigan State. This scientist very much encouraged him to visit before making his employment decision. Upon visiting the Corning laboratory, he learned from Dr. Robert Maurer of the tremendous need to increase the transmission capacity of the telephone system. Maurer and a few others thought that sending telephone calls over beams of light would be the ultimate solution. But a conduit for the light beams had to be invented. Engineers were already hard at work on next generation coaxial cables. By increasing the size of the coaxial cable from about two cm to five cm they believed they could obtain a significant capacity increase. Systems in those days could transmit about 45 million bits of information per second over the existing coaxial cables. With the two-inch coaxial cables they believed this could be pushed to about 300 million bits of information per second. The promise of optical communication however would be several orders of magnitude higher. The laser had been invented in the early 1960s and was the logical light source for a communications system, but the transmission conduit did not exist that could reliably transport the laser beam over the large telecommunication distances without a too-severe loss of light. Sending laser beams through the atmosphere was unreliable due to severe weather limitations. Several systems were tested using hollow pipes with periodic lenses to refocus the laser beams. Unhappily vibrations on nearby roadways would vibrate the lenses and cause unacceptable noise in the telecommunication signals. Fiber optics had been invented in the 1950s but even for the very best optical fibers, laser beams could only be transmitted a meter or two before the light would be absorbed by the glass or scattered from the fiber and lost. It was to this problem that

Dr. Maurer introduced him. Dr. Keck was to be first full-time scientist assigned to work on a solution. Another young scientist, Dr. Peter Schultz, worked on the project, as well. This then was the Corning Incorporated team: Drs. Robert Maurer, Donald Keck, and Peter Schultz. The goal was to invent a fiber so transparent that at least 1 percent of the light incident on the fiber at one end would make it to the other end of a kilometer-long piece. Inputs from the telephone companies indicated that if that goal could be achieved, a viable optical-fiber telecommunication system could be made. The problem, however, was daunting. Light intensity is attenuated exponentially with distance. The very best fibers that anyone could make in 1968 had attenuation coefficients of about 1,000 dB/km. That is to say, if 10,000 trillion, trillion, trillion, trillion, trillion, trillion, trillion, trillion photons entered one end of the very best fibers, only one photon would emerge after traveling one kilometer. This number of photons would melt almost any material known to humankind. So the problem was to produce glass so clear that if only 100 photons entered the fiber, at least one would emerge a kilometer later. While a vast majority of the international effort was being spent on creating better coaxial cables, several other notable laboratories had programs in making more transparent optical fibers. All of these labs were following the approach of taking the very best optical glasses known at that time and trying to find purer chemicals from which to melt them.

"The Corning team took a 'contrarian' approach in three important aspects. If they merely duplicated the approach of others, they could only tie. They wanted to win. First, the team thought that simpler would be better—they selected fused silica as the glass with which to work. Fused silica, that is silicon dioxide or SiO_2, is what most people would think of as sand. However, rather than using sand and melting it, the team used a process called vapor deposition in which the silicon and oxygen are mixed together as chemicals and heated to form ultra-pure 'sand.' Second, a fiber consists of a core and a cladding glass. The refractive index of the core must be larger than that of the cladding in order to obtain confined guidance of the light beam. The obvious approach would be to use the ultra-pure fused silica as the core and then to find a lower index of refraction cladding material. Since that would be difficult and since the team knew both core and cladding material had to be ultra-pure they again took a contrarian approach. They purposely added an impurity to the vapor-deposited fused silica to ever so slightly raise the refractive index of the core glass. Ultra-pure fused silica was used as the cladding. By control of the 'impurity,' they could make sure it did not absorb light at the wavelengths they were trying to transmit. Third, most fibers are made by the 'rod-in-tube' process. This approach, however, allows lots of dirt and scattering centers to be trapped at the interface between the rod and the tube.

"Additionally, Keck's theoretical calculations suggested that the cladding thickness should be many times the wavelength of light being transmitted so that perturbations, dirt, and debris on the outside surface of the fiber did not [attenuate] the transmission. This meant the cladding should be at least 10 times the core diameter. Since the fiber-core diameter needed to be rather small (about four to five micrometers) this meant the cladding thickness needed to be 40 to 50 micrometers. The rod-in-tube process was generally only suitable to make large-core, thinly clad fibers—just the opposite of what was needed. A new process needed to be invented. Keck came up with the idea of depositing a thin layer of core glass on the inside of a thick-walled tube of pure fused-silica cladding glass. This did two things. It created an intimate interface between the core and cladding glasses, removing the scattering centers created by dirt and secondly it gave the proper size ratio between core and cladding glasses. He and Schultz learned to use the vapor-deposition process to deposit the core glass in the tube. The team would later find that the quality of the inside surface was most important and began using a fire-polishing technique to burn off debris and heal any voids created by the tube-fabrication process. Early in 1970, all the pieces of the process fell into place and a fiber was fabricated that met the magic 20 dB/km loss target.

"Late on a Friday afternoon, Keck decided to try one more measurement. After setting up the fiber on his laser attenuation measurement bench, he looked through the microscope to align the laser beam with the fiber core. As the laser spot fell upon the core, he was suddenly struck in the eye with a bright laser beam. This had never happened in any of the measurements made during the preceding two years. He knew something was very different. It took a few seconds for him to realize the laser light was traveling through the fiber to the far end, reflecting off the end surface, and traveling back through the fiber to his eye. He realized the loss must be very low. His measurement indicated a loss rate of 17 dB/km: the team had invented the process for making low-loss optical telecommunications fibers a reality.

"The team's result was published and presented at a conference dedicated primarily to microwave electronic telecommunications in the fall of 1970. It created quite a stir among the attendees. In a fairly short period of time, the work on microwave cables was terminated because of the promise of long-distance optical communications over fibers. Nevertheless, it took more than a decade to convince the telecommunications companies to abandon 'copper wire' in favor of optical fibers. While this was surprising to fairly young scientists like Keck and Schultz, in retrospect, it is to be expected with any technological revolution and underscores the patience and tenacity that inventors and their backers need to have in bringing new ideas to the market place."

Realizing they had a prototype for a very viable commercial product, the Corning team spent the next 10 years perfecting their invention by strengthening the fiber-optic cables so they could endure the wear and tear of field work, as well as streamlining the manufacturing process. The first large order for optical fiber came from the long-distance carrier MCI, but other carriers quickly followed suit. The first fiber wires were put down between cities to improve long-distance communications; by 1988 they were being laid across oceans. With the rise of Internet usage in the mid-1990s, the need for optical fiber increased, and the wire's load capacity kept up with the heightened demand. A single fiber is now able to carry 80,000 phone calls on just one infrared wavelength of light; the old copper wires could not carry even a tenth of that load.

As of 2002 more than 90 percent of all long-distance communications—either by phone or by Internet—is carried by Keck, Maurer, and Schultz's invention. In addition, the vast majority of cable television is carried by optical fiber. When asked if he was ever struck by the significance of his own invention—while making a long distance call, for example—Keck told *Leaders of the Information Age*: "I recall the first time I was consciously aware of the impact of optical fiber communications was while making a trans-Atlantic telephone call several years after our pioneering work. I had been familiar with the time delay and echoes that had been present in the coaxial cable systems for many years. On this particular call, the clarity was astonishing—it was just like calling next door. That made a tremendous impression on me." He continued, "Throughout history, by their very nature, people have been unable to predict the outcome of revolutionary advances. Similarly, the Corning Incorporated team did not predict the magnitude of their impact on the world. We are merely happy to have invented the critical element. It is somewhat sad that the vast majority of the public is unaware of these critical technological inventions and the people that have made them. It is no less difficult to strive to break technology records than it is to hit 73 home runs in a season, win several Olympic gold medals, or win an Oscar. The same dedication, training of the mind, discipline of behavior, and patient and persistent striving to accomplish your goal is required. Yet these technological advances that create a new and higher quality of life go relatively unnoticed and unrewarded in society. Organizations such as the National Inventors Hall of Fame and the National Medal of Science and Technology Foundation, and of course, the Nobel prize are attempting to change the public awareness—but alas we have a long way to go."

Donald Keck is the co-author of four books on optical fiber and holds 30 patents. In addition, he has contributed more than 85 articles to professional journals and was the editor of the *Journal of Lightwave Technology* from 1989 to 1994. He has received a host of awards for his work, including the Technical Achievement Award from the International Society of Optical Engineering (1981), the Industrial Research IR-100 Award (1981), the Engineering Materials Achievement Award from the American Society of Metals (1983), and the John Tyndall Award from the IEEE/Optical Society of America (1992). In 1993 he was elected to the National Inventors Hall of Fame and the National Academy of Engineering. Two years later he received the United States Department of Commerce American Innovator Award. In 2000 President Bill Clinton presented Keck, Maurer, and Schultz with the National Medal of Technology, one of the nation's highest honors.

Donald Keck married Ruth A. Moilanen on July 10, 1965. They live in Big Flats, New York and have two children, Lynn Ann and Brian William. They also have one granddaughter, Annika Clare Vaia. Keck says that his family is the most important thing in his life, but told *Leaders of the Information Age*, "I'm sure I've given them many instances to question this as I worked late in the lab or committed to some travel that took me from them. Nevertheless, life would be very much incomplete and without meaning were they not providing the raison d' être, the emotional support to persevere, and the sense of mutual pride in one anothers' accomplishments."

Keck remains devoted to music, and he and his wife participate in their church's choir. He enjoys woodworking and photography and keeps active by water and snow skiing. "Snorkeling in clear, warm Caribbean waters also ranks very high," he told *Leaders of the Information Age*.

Asked if there were times when he was sorry that he had helped make long-distance communication so easy or if he ever wished to simply shut off the phone and computer and go incommunicado, Keck gave a serious response. "It has been well documented by history that the gathering and sharing of knowledge has affected the quality of life on the planet. Nations with the highest capability for human dialogue have the highest gross domestic products," he told *Leaders of the Information Age*. "Whenever I think about the communications revolution the Corning Incorporated team has enabled, my most fervent hope is that fibers will very soon connect all the world's people and continue the knowledge sharing that will raise everyone's standard of living. The greatest chance for true world peace will come when information and ideas are shared by everyone. Optical fiber communications holds a great promise for humanity."

When asked to give some concrete examples of that promise, Keck stated, "The true mark of a technological revolution is when that piece of technology creates new applications and other technologies far beyond that for which it was originally intended. Such seems to be the case with low-loss optical-fiber technology. Many advances will yet occur in the telecommunications applications for which the fiber was invented. Today, individuals share information with one another. Tomorrow,

computers with millions of times higher information processing and transmission speeds will talk to each other. Huge information databases will be shared. Weather prediction models will become virtually perfect through the massive sharing of meteorological data. Doctors will be able to help one another make diagnoses of difficult medical conditions around the world with the help of digital-video images sent over the optical-fiber network instantaneously. Remote surgery will allow previously untreatable conditions to be handled routinely by a handful of specialists anywhere in the world. True ability to visually and orally communicate with anyone anytime and anyplace will become the norm. But there will be much more." He continued, "Fiber sensors could be imbedded in dams and bridges to detect the slightest change in stress and warn of impending failure. Fiber current sensors could be distributed along remote power lines to pinpoint any disruption in service. Fiber chemical sensors could surround land fills to warn of toxic seepage. Fiber structure-monitors could warn of imminent building collapse during an earthquake or other cataclysmic event. Wouldn't it have been nice to have the buildings of September 11th so equipped? Many lives could possibly have been saved. Fiber movement sensors could one day line all our roadways. These could warn motorists of accidents or stoppages ahead. They may also one day contribute to creating smart freeways that automatically guide cars along a hair—this strand of glass embedded beside the pavement. But it doesn't stop there." Keck concluded, "It is very probable that our homes will be equipped with biomedical monitoring devices that will analyze daily samples, perhaps by telemetering their data to a remote computer for help. This could warn us of changes in our state-of-health on a daily basis and automatically recommend treatment. While this field is just now developing and has a long way to go, it would not have existed without the invention of the optical fiber to act as a driving force. Truly, because of the invention of low-loss optical fiber, 'the world of the future will be full of light.'"—C. M.

Suggested Reading: Inventors Hall of Fame Web site; *Business Wire* (on-line) Nov. 13, 2000; *Charlotte Observer* D p3 Mar. 28, 2002; *Washington Post* H p1 Nov. 10, 1999

Kemeny, John

May 31, 1926–Dec. 26, 1992 Pioneer of time-sharing; co-author of the computer-programming language BASIC

John Kemeny co-authored the Beginners All-purpose Symbolic Instruction Code, a computer programming language better known as BASIC. Unprecedentedly easy-to-use, BASIC helped make programming—previously the exclusive province of specially trained mathematicians—an activity that could be pursued by individuals with relatively little computer experience. With BASIC, computer operators could use simple algebraic formulas and language commands consisting of English words, such as "input" and "go to," to write advanced programs. The language spread rapidly through the computer world, particularly after Bill Gates and Paul Allen, the founders of Microsoft, created a version for use on early personal computers (PCs) in the mid-1970s. Today BASIC remains one of the most popular programming languages available.

John George Kemeny was born on May 31, 1926 in Budapest, Hungary. His father was Tibor Kemeny, a commodities import-export broker, and his mother was Lucy (Fried) Kemeny. As a Jewish family, the Kemenys felt threatened by the rise to power of Germany's anti-Semitic Third Reich during the 1930s. When the Nazis marched into Vienna in early 1938, Tibor Kemeny, foreseeing worse things to come, left for the United States. A year and a half later, he sent for his wife, daughter, and 13-year-old John to join him. The three departed Budapest by train and sailed to the United States from Genoa, Italy. (John's grandfather, along with an aunt and uncle, remained and were killed in the Holocaust.)

Kemeny settled in New York City with his family and began attending George Washington High School. Although initially he could not speak English, he proved to be a quick study and graduated first in his class in just three years. He was offered a scholarship to study at Princeton University, in New Jersey, where he majored in mathematics and minored in philosophy.

In 1945, after obtaining American citizenship, Kemeny was drafted specifically to work on the Manhattan Project, the top-secret government program to develop an atomic bomb. He had completed just one year at Princeton. He was sent to the computing center at Los Alamos, New Mexico, where the bomb was being designed. There, under the supervision of John von Neumann, a mathematician and fellow Hungarian, Kemeny and his fellow team members worked long hours solving differential equations with IBM calculators to aid in the bomb's design. The work was grueling: some problems required two to three weeks to produce a single result because the calculators used punched cards that had to be moved by hand from machine to machine; the plug boards of the machines were manually rewired between calculations. When the calculations were finally printed out, they had to be checked by a human for errors, and if any were discovered, the entire process was repeated.

While at Los Alamos, Kemeny's interest in computers was piqued by one of von Neumann's lectures, in which the elder mathematician discussed the ENIAC (Electrical Numerical Integrator And Calculator), the first practical electronic digital computer, and the EDVAC (Electronic Discrete Variable Automatic Computer), an electronic, stored-program computer then being developed by John Mauchly and J. Presper Eckert.

Kemeny resumed his studies at Princeton University after the conclusion of World War II and earned his B.A., summa cum laude, in 1947. He began his graduate studies, and during the 1948–49 academic year he served as a research assistant to Albert Einstein, who was then working on advanced unified-field theory at the Institute for Advanced Study (IAS), in Princeton, New Jersey. Working three or four days a week, Kemeny spent most of the time doing calculations for Einstein. "The pleasant part of the job was that I was the person with whom Einstein could talk when he wanted to think out loud," Kemeny later recalled, as quoted by Robert Slater in *Portraits in Silicon* (1987). At one point Kemeny considered becoming a full-time staff member of the United World Federalists, a political organization that advocated global peace through disarmament, but Einstein, also a proponent of disarmament, persuaded him that political influence was best obtained by gaining preeminence in a given field and making a mark on the world, rather than simply joining a group.

In 1949 Kemeny received a Ph.D. in mathematics. He began teaching math and philosophy as an assistant professor at Princeton. In the summer of 1953, while moonlighting as a consultant at the RAND Corporation, a computer manufacturer, Kemeny had an opportunity to use the JOHNNIAC, a copy of a computer designed by von Neumann at IAS. As Kemeny later wrote in his book *Man and the Computer* (1972), as quoted by Jay Robert Hauben in the *International Biographical Dictionary of Computer Pioneers* (1995), he had great fun "learning to program a computer, even though the language used at that time was designed for machines and not for human beings."

In 1953 Kemeny joined the faculty of Dartmouth College, in Hanover, New Hampshire, as a full professor of mathematics. Two years later he was named chairman of the mathematics department, which he began to improve by hiring outstanding faculty and redesigning the curriculum. He initiated a program to introduce more advanced material into low-level classes, allowing beginning students to glimpse the exciting developments taking place on the frontiers of mathematics. He also set up a challenging undergraduate honors program and established Dartmouth's first doctoral program in math.

During Kemeny's first six years at Dartmouth, the school did not have its own computer. He and his colleagues were forced to travel 135 miles to the nearest computer center, which was at the Massachusetts Institute of Technology (MIT), in Cambridge. There Kemeny witnessed the arrival, in 1957, of the computer-programming language FORTRAN (derived from the phrase *formula translation*), designed by John Backus at International Business Machines (IBM). FORTRAN, the first high-level computer language, was a major improvement over both existing programming languages: assembly language and machine language. Machine language, also called machine code, consists of a series of binary digits, 1s and 0s, which the computer interprets as electronic instructions. Assembly language, more sophisticated than machine code, features some technical command words such as "add," which then must be translated into machine code. High-level languages, such as FORTRAN, are much closer to human language in that they use grammar and syntax rules, thus making it possible to operate a computer with rudimentary commands in the form of sentences. This was an inspiration to Kemeny, who thought that it made more sense to teach a computer to understand human language than to teach humans to learn the machine's obscure language. "All of a sudden access to computers by thousands of users became not only possible, but reasonable," Kemeny later wrote, as quoted by Hauben.

Dartmouth got its first computer, a Royal McBee LGP-30, in 1959. Kemeny helped in training undergraduates to use the LGP-30, and the aptitude demonstrated by many of these students greatly amazed the faculty. As the computing community grew, however, users found themselves competing for time to run their programs on a single central computer. Kemeny and a colleague, Thomas Kurtz, began working to solve the problem. Influenced by the work of MIT's John McCarthy and Joseph Licklider, they built a prototype time-sharing system that would link 60 remote terminals to a central General Electric 635 mainframe, thus serving the needs of numerous users simultaneously. Completed in 1964, the Dartmouth Time-Sharing System (DTSS) was one of the earliest systems of its kind, and its presence at the university ensured that even non-technical students at Dartmouth in the 1960s had far more experience working with computers than students elsewhere in the country.

DTSS made the development of high-level computer languages an absolute necessity. "We at Dartmouth envisaged the possibility of millions of people writing their own computer programs," Kemeny wrote, as quoted by Hauben. Kemeny had actually been at work on such a simplified code for years. In 1956 he and Kurtz had devised DARSIMCO (for Dartmouth simplified code), but it was overshadowed by the introduction of FORTRAN. In 1962, working with Sidney Marshall, a Dartmouth student, Kemeny wrote a language called DOPE (Dartmouth Oversimplified Programming

Experiment), which was an important precursor to BASIC, but like DARSIMCO was not a success.

Kemeny began writing a draft version of BASIC in 1963 and completed the work in spring 1964. Similar to FORTRAN, it used simple algebraic formulas and English words such as *input, print, go to,* and *end,* but BASIC was even easier for beginners to use, with about a 200-word vocabulary. BASIC enjoyed another significant advantage: it provided the programmer with an instant response to lines entered as input, making it easier to debug and modify programs. In order to encourage others to use the language, Kemeny and Kurtz wanted it placed in the public domain, and the program was made available free of charge.

BASIC spread rapidly, as did versions of DTSS, to other college campuses and government and military institutions. In 1965 General Electric adopted the language for use on its own time-sharing system. The biggest milestone for BASIC came in 1975, when Bill Gates and Paul Allen, two young programmers, compiled a version of the language to run on the Altair 8800, the first commercially successful PC, which was produced by a company known as Micro Instrumentation Telemetry Systems (MITS) run by Ed Roberts. Gates and Allen called their version MITS BASIC; it was the first product sold by their newly formed company, Micro-Soft. (The hyphen would later be dropped from the name.) BASIC also proved to be the subject of the first known major case of software piracy. While Microsoft's founders were trying to sell their version of BASIC, hobbyists began copying and illegally trading unauthorized versions, leading Gates to pen his now-famous and oft-quoted "Open Letter to Hobbyists" of February 3, 1976, in which he complained that rampant software piracy would prevent good software from ever being written.

Soon other programmers were developing versions of BASIC for use on computers from various manufacturers, such as Commodore and Atari. Steve Wozniak wrote a version of BASIC for the Apple computer. IBM licensed a Microsoft BASIC interpreter, which it included on its PCs. When Bill Gates later released the Disk Operating System (DOS), it came with a BASIC interpreter known as BASIC A; GW-BASIC, Quick BASIC, and Visual Basic followed. Variations of Kemeny's language would eventually run on almost every PC manufactured and serve as the basis for a myriad of applications. It became the standard for home and office computing and was widely adopted by schools for educational purposes; by the end of the 1980s, approximately 11 million school children had learned it.

Kemeny later regretted the decision not to copyright his invention. Although he was pleased with its popularity, the proliferation of differing versions led to difficulties in transferring programs from one computer to another. Moreover, some of the variations contained elements contradictory to BASIC's original design and purpose, leading Kemeny and Kurtz to derisively refer to them as "street BASICs." Kemeny and Kurtz decided in 1983 to engineer a new, improved version of the language, which they called True BASIC. Finished in 1985, True BASIC was more powerful than its predecessor and incorporated interactive graphics, formatting tools, and a window manager. It was designed to work on any computer without requiring modifications. The two creators established a company, True BASIC Inc., to oversee the new product, with Kemeny acting as chairman and Kurtz as vice chairman. True BASIC is still available and is widely used as a tool to introduce students to computer programming.

In 1970 Kemeny had become Dartmouth's 13th president. He held the position until 1981, during which time he instituted several progressive measures, including admitting women students for the first time in the college's history and crafting policies to encourage minorities to apply. A much-beloved figure on campus, he continued teaching on a part-time basis during his presidency and returned to full-time teaching when he stepped down from that post. He retired from Dartmouth in 1990, although he was known to say that his devotion to the institution was on a par with his devotion to his wife—total and undying.

In 1979 Kemeny was appointed by President Jimmy Carter as the chairman of the 12-member commission investigating the accident at the nuclear power station on Three Mile Island, on the Susquehanna River, south of Harrisburg, Pennsylvania. His investigation revealed unenforced regulations and found that the nuclear-power industry was not taking adequate safety precautions. According to Kemeny, the Nuclear Regulatory Commission (NRC) was to blame for being too lenient in their supervision of the industry. Although the investigating commission did not recommend a temporary halt on the construction of nuclear reactors, Kemeny later felt that it should have. The commission did, however, call for many changes in the methods of reactor construction and management.

Kemeny was the recipient of numerous honorary degrees and awards, including the Institute of Electrical and Electronic Engineers (IEEE) Computer Pioneer Medal in 1986, the American Federation of Information Processing Societies (AFIPS) Education Award in 1983, the New York Academy of Sciences Award in 1984, and the first Louis Robinson Lifetime Achievement Award in 1990. He was a trustee of the Foundation Center and the Carnegie Foundation for the Advancement of Teaching. He was an associate editor of the *Journal of Mathematical Analysis and Applications*, as well as a member of the American Mathematical Society, the American Philosophical Association, and the Association for Symbolic Logic. Kemeny wrote several well-regarded books on science and math, including *A Philosopher Looks at Science* (1959) and *Random Essays in Mathematics, Education, and Computers* (1964). He co-authored several oth-

ers, including *Introduction to Finite Mathematics* (1957), which sold more than 200,000 copies and was translated into several languages.

Kemeny married Jean Alexander on November 5, 1950. The two met when Alexander was a college freshman and Kemeny had just begun his assistant professorship at Princeton. "John and I were two cultures, two countries: a Yankee from Maine and a Jew from Budapest," she remarked in the *Dartmouth Alumni Magazine* (on-line). "But it worked." Together they had two children, Jennifer and Robert.

Kemeny was fond of science fiction, puzzles, and football; he disliked socializing and was said to enjoy the company of animals more than that of most humans. He died of a heart attack on December 26, 1992 at the Dartmouth-Hitchcock Medical Center, in Lebanon, New Hampshire.—A. I. C.

Suggested Reading: *Computerworld* p24 Jan. 11, 1993, with photo; *Current Biography Yearbook* p220+ 1971, with photo, p633 1993; Dartmouth Web site; *New York Times* I p40 Dec. 27, 1992, with photo; Slater, Robert. *Portraits in Silicon*, 1987

Kepler, Johannes

Dec. 27, 1571–Nov. 15, 1630 Astronomer; mathematician

Johannes Kepler permanently changed our view of the universe in discovering his three laws of planetary motion during the 16th and 17th centuries. He not only helped further the widely opposed views of Nicolaus Copernicus (who had postulated that the planets revolve around the sun in circular orbits), but improved on them by showing that planets have elliptical orbits that operate in accordance with certain mathematical principals. While Kepler was uncertain what underlying force accounted for planetary motion—he called it Holy Spirit Force, according to an article by James Burke in *Scientific American* (July 1998)—his works helped Isaac Newton to discover gravity. Kepler set new precedents in science by demanding a high degree of mathematical accuracy in his work and by realizing the importance of basing hypotheses closely on empirical evidence—even when that evidence ran contrary to expectations. A prolific worker, Kepler also greatly advanced the field of optics and helped form the basis of integral calculus.

Johannes Kepler was born into a family of modest means on December 27, 1571 in Weil der Stadt, Württemberg, Germany. His parents were Henry Kepler, a mercenary soldier, and Catherine Guldenmann, an innkeeper's daughter. Kepler was a sickly child; he suffered smallpox at the age of four, which left him with crippled hands and impaired vision. He lived with his grandparents from 1574 to 1576, after which his parents moved to Leonberg and entered Kepler in the Latin school

Hulton Archive by Getty Images

Johannes Kepler

the position. Among his tasks was calculating the orbits of the planets using precise data that Brahe had compiled during years of observation. Kepler started at the beginning: he wanted to figure out how the light from the stars and planets becomes visible to the eye. In 1604 he published *The Optical Part of Astronomy*, in which he discussed atmospheric refraction of light and offered a modern explanation of the workings of the eye and eyeglasses. He was the first to explain the way light enters the pupil of the eye, is bent by the lens, and focused onto the retina. Though eyeglasses had been in use for some time, Kepler was the first to make a distinction between near-sightedness and far-sightedness.

Upon examining Brahe's data on the orbit of Mars, Kepler noticed that it seemed to suggest a significant departure from the expected circular orbit of the planet as theorized by Copernicus. While Copernicus had made a radical break with orthodoxy in asserting that Earth was not the center of the universe, he nevertheless assumed, as did most everyone else, that the planets had perfectly circular orbits. Circular orbits were thought to be an expression of the perfection of God's creation, and to suggest otherwise was profoundly disturbing to many. Kepler, however, refused to disregard the empirical evidence he found in Brahe's data. "Kepler," as Paul G. Shotsberger noted in the *Mathematics Teacher* (November 2000), "had to overcome two thousand years of mistaken beliefs, pseudoscience, and downright superstition to derive his three laws of planetary motion." Kepler's first law, then, was that planets move in elliptical—rather than circular—orbits, as he asserted in *New Astronomy* (1609). By boldly stating his theory Kepler became, in the opinion of many, one of the first practitioners of modern science: developing theories to explain empirical evidence rather than bending empirical evidence to fit pre-conceived theories.

This did not mean, however, that Kepler's goals in applying his rigorous science were not profoundly religious. In fact, as a young man Kepler had wanted to become a theologian, but it was expected that graduates of Tübingen University would become school teachers or state functionaries. Kepler believed that scientific explorations was the best way to uncover the glory of God's creation, that "through my effort God is being celebrated in astronomy," as he wrote in his autobiographical notes, as quoted in *Old Worlds to New* (1993). Kepler's second law, also first published in *New Astronomy*, celebrated the wonderful symmetry of the universe. It noted and explained the phenomenon of the inconstant speeds of planetary orbits, wherein planets speed up when they are closer to the sun and slow down when they are further from it. Also known as the "area law," the second law states that planets cover equal areas of their orbital planes in equal amounts of time. For example, envision the orbit of Mars as an elliptical pie with the sun at its center; the path of Mars is

there. In 1584, shortly before his father abandoned the family entirely, Kepler enrolled in a Protestant monastery school in Adelberg and eventually won a ducal scholarship to the Lutheran Stift at the University of Tübingen, from which he received his M.A. in 1591. (The term *stift* refers to a monastery created by endowment.) There Kepler studied under Michael Maestlin, one of the leading astronomers of the time. Maestlin was one of the few believers in the Copernican theory that the planets orbit the sun (rather than the accepted belief that Earth was the center of the universe), but he did not teach the controversial theory to his students. He lent Kepler, however, a highly annotated version of Copernicus's *Six Books Concerning the Revolutions of the Heavenly Orbs* (1543), and Kepler became convinced of the truth of Copernicus's views.

In 1594 Kepler became a teacher of mathematics at the Protestant seminary in Graz, Austria; in his free time he continued to pursue his studies in astronomy. In 1596 he published his first work, *Cosmographic Mystery*, which attempted to find a mathematical correlation between the distances between the orbits of the planets and the five types of regular polyhedrons (objects that are identical on all sides, such as cubes). Though it was later proved that any connection was coincidental, the book impressed some of the scientists of the day, including the renowned Dutch astronomer Tycho Brahe. In 1600, Kepler was forced to leave Graz due to the widespread anti-Protestant sentiments of the Counter-Reformation, the period of Catholic revival that lasted from 1560 until 1648. He was invited to work with Brahe, who was serving as imperial mathematician, in Prague, to the Holy Roman Empire. In 1601, when Brahe died, Kepler inherited the outer edge or crust of the pie. Cut two wedges of equal area in different parts of the pie. In order for both slices to be of equal areas, the slice of the pie whose crust is closer to the center must have a longer section of crust than the slice whose crust is farther from the center. The first slice is wide and short, the second narrow and long. Therefore, even though the speed of a planet's orbit varies, the area of planar orbit covered remains constant.

In 1609, the year that Kepler's first two laws of planetary motion were published, Galileo Galilei built a telescope and noted the existence of some previously unknown stellar bodies, including the moons revolving around Jupiter. Kepler wrote a letter supporting Galileo's widely disputed discoveries, which was published as *Conversation with the Sidereal Messenger* (1610). Later that year, after obtaining his own telescope, Kepler published *Narration About Four Satellites of Jupiter Observed*. Both of these publications provided enormous support for Galileo, who wrote to Kepler, according to the Britannica Web site, "I thank you because you were the first one, and practically the only one, to have complete faith in my assertions."

In 1611, the same year Kepler published a work explaining the mechanics of the telescope entitled *Dioptrice*, his son Friedrich died of smallpox, and the next year his wife, Barbara Müller, whom he had married in 1597, died as well. (Some sources list her name as Barbara von Muhleck.) The couple had two other children, Susanna, born in 1602, and Ludwig, born in 1607. Kepler subsequently moved to the city of Linz, Austria to become the district mathematician, while retaining the position of imperial mathematician. He was remarried, in 1613, to Susanna Reuttinger, a widow with some degree of wealth. Susanna gave birth to seven children, five of whom died in childhood. In 1613 Kepler published a treatise, *Concerning the True Year in which the Son of God Assumed a Human Nature in the Uterus of the Blessed Virgin Mary*, in which he argued that Jesus Christ had actually been born in 4 B.C., five years earlier than first thought. (This is still accepted as the proper birth date of Jesus.)

In 1615 Kepler's mother was accused of being a witch, an offense punishable by death. Kepler vigorously defended her, traveling to various locales as needed, and in 1620 he succeeded in getting the charges against her dropped. She died the following year. Between the years 1617 and 1621 Kepler published the era's most influential textbook of astronomy, *Epitome of Copernican Astronomy*. The book introduced Copernican thought and included Kepler's own expanded theories of planetary motion. In the years to come no opponent of heliocentric astronomy could make an argument without considering Kepler's authoritative text. In *Harmony of the World* (1619) Kepler related the periodic revolutions of the planets and their distances from the sun to musical theory. In this work Kepler posited his third law, which stated that a planet's average distance from the sun is directly proportional to the time it takes it to complete a revolution (also

known as a period). Specifically, Kepler noted that the square of a planet's period is directly proportional to the cube of its average distance from the sun.

The Counter-Reformation and the Thirty Years' War, which raged from 1618 to 1648, had been causing disruptions throughout Europe, and repercussions were felt by Kepler in Linz. Because he was a government official, Kepler was exempted from a decree that forced all Protestants out the province, yet he suffered anti-Protestant persecution nonetheless. During this time he worked on the *Rudolphine Tables*, which—among other things—calculated the position of the planets at any date, past or future. In 1626 the printed manuscript of the *Tables* was burned during a peasant rebellion, and Kepler, fearing for his safety, left Linz. The *Rudolphine Tables* was published in 1627, but Kepler found himself jobless and without a salary.

Soon, however, Kepler found a new patron, the imperial general Albrecht von Wallenstein, who sent Kepler to Sagan, in Silesia, Austria, and asked in return for regular astrological readings. Though Kepler purportedly had little faith in astrology, he predicted that Wallenstein would encounter a tragedy in March 1634. (Wallenstein was, in fact, murdered on February 25, 1634.) Kepler had been trying to recover various debts owed to him, including a significant portion of his salary for the years he served as imperial mathematician. He was unable to collect most of his debts, and he found the frequent travel stressful and wearing. Kepler contracted a fever and died in Regensberg, Germany, on November 15, 1630. His book *Somnium*, published posthumously in 1634, described a fictional voyage to the moon. According to the Britannica Web site, Kepler's epitaph read, "I used to measure the heavens, now I shall measure the shadows of the earth. Although my soul was from heaven, the shadow of my body lies here."—P. G. H.

Suggested Reading: *Mathematics Teacher* p680+ Nov. 2000; *Scientific American* p116+ July 1998; Podell, Janet and Steven Anzovian. *Old Worlds to New*, 1993

Kettering, Charles F.

Aug. 29, 1876–Nov. 25, 1958 Former head of General Motors' Research Laboratories Division

Charles F. Kettering, the co-founder of the scientific research firm, Delco, and later head of General Motors' Research Laboratories Division, produced many inventions that changed ordinary people's lives. He made his greatest contributions to the improvement of automobiles. To start their early-model cars, drivers once had to crank their engines by hand, a cumbersome and potentially dangerous process. In 1911 Kettering invented a self-starter for automobiles that eliminated the hand-crank.

Leonard McCombe/Getty Images

Charles F. Kettering

His invention gave many more people access to cars and sparked a dramatic increase in auto sales. He also developed a high-compression engine that conserved fuel and a diesel engine that made steam locomotives obsolete. Having grown up on a farm himself, Kettering brought light and power to many farms and isolated rural areas with the portable electric generator he devised. "All the money and all the people in the world can't solve a problem unless someone knows how," he once said, as quoted by T. A. Boyd in the book, *Prophet of Progress: Selections from the Speeches of Charles F. Kettering* (1961). "Sometimes people tend to lean too heavily on facilities and forget that ideas are developed in the mind. . . . At any rate, when problems are solved, the solutions will be found to be simple. It is only the human brain that complicates problems."

Charles Franklin Kettering, nicknamed Boss, was born on August 29, 1876 on his parents' farm near Loudonville, Ohio. He was the fourth child of Jacob and Martha Hunter Kettering. "Now, I didn't know at the time that I was an underprivileged person because I had to drive the cows through the frosty grass and stand in a nice warm spot where a cow had lain to warm my feet," he once said about his childhood, as quoted by Stuart W. Leslie in his book, *Boss Kettering* (1983). "I thought that was wonderful. I walked three miles to the high school and I thought that was wonderful too." As a child Charles displayed the signs of genius that have distinguished many inventors; his family remembered him fixing his mother's sewing machine and dismantling farm machinery to see how it worked. He learned the principles of mechanics by watching his father build barns around the farm and observing the steam engine at the local mill.

Charles also showed great promise in the classroom. After passing an exam, Charles won a scholarship to Loudonville High School. He excelled in physics and mathematics. Fascinated by scientific experimentation, he helped his physics teacher, C. E. Budd, set up a physics laboratory at the school. He overcame his natural shyness to become an excellent public speaker and a strong debater—abilities he would draw upon later in life, as a much sought-after speaker.

After graduating from high school, in 1895, Kettering became a teacher at Bunker Hill, a one-room, rural school. According to Leslie, Kettering was a lively and pragmatic teacher. His science classes focused on agricultural topics, which directly interested many of his students. In the evenings, he taught electricity and magnetism to his advanced students. Although he supplemented his own education by reading books and science magazines at the local library, and enrolling in a summer course for teachers, he preferred knowledge acquired through experience and observation.

Kettering was forced to leave his teaching job two years later due to severe eye strain—a problem that had periodically affected him since childhood. After he recovered he taught at another school, in Mifflin, Ohio. In 1898 he enrolled at the engineering college of Ohio State University, in Columbus. He broadened his knowledge and helped pay for his education by getting a job at the university's power plant. Although he did well in his first year, focusing on the new science of electrical engineering, he had to take a leave of absence from the university after his eyesight went bad once again. "If my eyes won't let me finish my schooling, I hope the train runs off the track and kills me," he confessed to his landlady, as quoted by Leslie.

During a visit to Mifflin, Kettering found work with the Star Telephone Company. He began in the field, digging holes and stringing wires, but quickly rose to the position of foreman. He introduced many technological improvements to the still-primitive rural phone lines. For example, Leslie noted that Kettering installed the first "common-battery system in central Ohio over Thanksgiving, thus doing away with the magneto [magnetoelectric apparatus] at each customer's telephone."

After his eyesight recovered, two years later, Kettering returned to Ohio State University. He finally graduated, in 1904, at the age of 27, with a degree in electrical engineering. Instead of staying with the telephone company, Kettering accepted a lucrative offer from the National Cash Register Company (NCR), in Dayton, Ohio. Working as an "electrical inventor," Kettering created an accounting machine for banks, a credit system for department stores, and a low-cost printing register. His greatest invention for NCR was an electric cash register that eliminated the hand-crank. He built an electric motor that operated the register and was small enough to fit inside its case. Since the register did not open and close continuously, Kettering realized that its motor should provide only an immediate surge of power when needed, an insight that influenced his future inventions. He also patented his ideas as soon as he came up with them.

In 1909 Charles Kettering co-founded a company, the Dayton Engineering Laboratories Company, or Delco, with Edward Deeds, an NCR executive. Kettering continued his work at NCR, and moonlighted in the evenings on Delco projects out of a barn behind Deeds's home. (The partnership had begun when Deeds, who was building his own car, asked Kettering to help him with the electrical system.) The pair were a perfect match; Deeds handled the business end of Delco, while Kettering performed research. At his partner's urging, Kettering sought to develop a new ignition system for cars. According to Leslie, the "ignition system was, perhaps, the weakest link in the internal combustion engine system. A proper ignition system for such a variable, high-speed engine had frustrated inventors for decades." At the time, most cars relied on a series of dry-cell batteries that provided a shower of sparks that caused the engine to start. This ignition system was inefficient because it depleted the batteries—which could not be recharged—after a few hundred miles of driving. To develop a better ignition system, Kettering applied the same concept he had used to invent the electric cash register. Instead of a shower of sparks, his system provided one spark—at just the right moment—that was powerful enough to start the engine. This system significantly prolonged battery life. Kettering's ignition system drew the attention of the Cadillac Company, which, after a flawless demonstration of the ignition system in Deeds's barn, ordered 8,000 units. The fledgling Delco company did not have the facilities to manufacture them. On July 22, 1909, the Delco partners formally incorporated, and issued public stock in order to raise the capital needed to manufacture the ignition systems. Despite some initial technical flaws, the new ignition was a success. Kettering resigned from NCR in late 1909. By 1910 several automakers, including Cadillac, Stoddard-Dayton, Republic, and Speedwell, were installing Kettering's ignition system in their cars.

For his next project, Kettering went to work on inventing an electric self-starter for cars. At the time, people started their cars by turning a crank attached to the engine. Inventors and researchers in the automotive industry had tried, unsuccessfully, to develop a self-starter. Kettering focused on creating a comprehensive system, for starting, lighting, and ignition, rather than just an electric starter. After several months of research, he decided to use a generator small and light enough to fit into a car, but powerful enough to produce seven pounds of torque and 12 volts of power. Although it was sufficient to allow the car to drive, the generator did not produce enough power to start the engine. Therefore, Kettering attached a gearing mechanism to the generator that provided additional power at the moment when the engine was started.

He added a voltage regulator to the system that prevented the storage battery from being overloaded. According to Leslie, Kettering's "motor-generator" needed 12 volts to work, while the car's headlights needed only six volts. To supply the needed power for the complete system, he used four batteries that produced 24 volts when linked in a series. He also added a "parallel setup" to the system that ensured that the headlights used only the six volts they needed.

After several modifications and tests, Kettering's self-starter, which he immediately patented, was a success. By mid-1911 Cadillac was installing the self-starter in their new cars. "Not one man in a thousand imagined a year ago that the day was at hand when motor car engines would be started and cranked by electricity—many engineers declared that it could not be done—automobile manufacturers shook their heads, looked wise—and doubted," Kettering boasted in a promotional article for the *Saturday Evening Post*, as quoted by Leslie. His invention changed the automobile industry. A reporter for *U.S. News and World Report* (December 27, 1999) noted that, by the early 1920s, nearly every new car was equipped with Kettering's self-starter, including Ford's popular Model-T, and the number of cars sold annually reached 3.8 million in 1923.

In 1916 the United Motors Corporation, which became the General Motors Corporation in 1919, purchased Delco. Although Kettering had always shunned management responsibilities, he was named a vice president of General Motors. He also headed the corporation's Research Laboratories Division.

Over the next few decades, Kettering and his research team turned out a string of inventions and improvements to existing products, which eventually rivaled the number produced by the more well-known inventor Thomas Edison. During World War I, Kettering invented an "aerial torpedo," an early version of the guided missile. He also continued his automotive research, developing a quick-drying paint and a new finish that sped up auto production by days. His four-wheel brakes and "safety glass" improved auto safety, and his significant contributions to the development of the diesel engine resulted in the gradual replacement of steam-powered engines in locomotives during the 1930s. Many buses and heavy trucks also began using the diesel engine, which was powerful, reliable, and durable. Kettering's research lab also produced high-octane gasoline that greatly reduced engine knocks.

Kettering brought light and power to many farms and rural areas that did not have access to power lines by inventing a portable, engine-driven generator. Working with Thomas Midgley Jr., Kettering developed Freon, a chemical compound that eventually became widely used in refrigerators and air conditioners. Although Freon (a chlorofluorocarbons, or CFC) was identified as a leading cause of the depletion of the ozone layer several decades later, the compound was odorless and nontoxic to humans. Before Freon, many refrigerators used toxic and flammable chemicals such as methyl chloride, which could leak and cause fatal accidents.

Shortly before his retirement, in 1947, Charles Kettering made one of his greatest contributions to the automotive industry. In a paper submitted to the Society of Automotive Engineers (SAE), Kettering called for the development of a high-compression engine that would provide the same power, but run on less fuel. "Engines are all made out of metal and brains, and what we want to do is put in as much of the latter as possible," he wrote, as quoted by Leslie. "When that is done we get the most and cheapest power out of a pound of fuel." Kettering and his research team unveiled their high-compression engine during a meeting of the SAE, in June 1947. They tested the engine, which had six cylinders, on the Oldsmobile model. Observers were impressed by the fact that the car averaged 26.5 miles per gallon. Leslie noted that the standard Oldsmobile with its regular engine averaged only 18 miles per gallon. Kettering adamantly opposed General Motor's request to name the new engine after him. The company began selling cars with the V-8, high- compression engine within several years.

In 1927 Kettering established the Charles F. Kettering Foundation to support scientific research. Among the great puzzles of life he sought to solve was why grass is green. To pursue this puzzle, he established a study of photosynthesis at Antioch College, in Yellow Springs, Ohio. In 1947 Kettering and Alfred P. Sloan, the chairman of General Motors, co-founded the Sloan-Kettering Institute for Cancer Research, in New York City. Kettering hoped the institute would develop treatments for cancer, which had claimed the lives of many members of his family, including his wife, Olive, in 1946.

After his retirement, Kettering traveled the country, delivering speeches on a number of topics. In one address, Kettering said that he believed that "you can make human progress and scientific progress and get much better living conditions, better health, and better this and better that when you are willing to pay the price," as quoted by Boyd. Kettering added that the price of progress involves "long hours of hard work, disappointments, criticism, and often physical as well as mental discomforts. If you do not want to pay that price for human progress, then you pay a much greater price for standing still." In 1947 he co-wrote, with Allen Orth, *The American Battle for Abundance: A Story of Mass Production.*

During his life, Charles Kettering was honored with many awards. He received nearly 40 honorary degrees from universities and colleges around the country. In 1922 he was inducted into the Aeronautical Association of America's Hall of Fame. He also won the Franklin Institute's Franklin Gold Medal (1936), the Legion of Honor of France

(1937), Belgium's Officer of the Order of the Crown (1938), the American Manufacturers Association of America's Modern Pioneers Award (1940), the Society of Arts and Sciences' Thomas A. Edison Award (1945), the Ohio State Bar Association's Citizenship Award (1949), the New Jersey Patent Law Association's Jefferson Medal (1952), and the National Association of Power Engineers' Engineer of the Year Award (1954). A town in Ohio was renamed after Kettering to honor his contributions and achievements. In 1998 the General Motors Institute, in Flint, Michigan, changed its name to Kettering University.

Charles Kettering married the former Olive Williams in 1905. Their only chid, Eugene Williams Kettering, followed him into scientific research. Charles Kettering died on November 25, 1958 at his home in Loudonville, Ohio.—D. C.

Suggested Reading: *Current Biography* (on-line), 1951; *U.S. News and World Report* (on-line) Dec. 27, 1999; Boyd, T. A. ed. *Prophet of Progress: Selections from the Speeches of Charles F. Kettering*, 1961; Leslie, Stuart W. *Boss Kettering*, 1983

Kilburn, Tom

Aug. 11, 1921–Jan. 17, 2001 Co-designer of the Manchester Mark 1 and Atlas computers

During a 35-year career, Tom Kilburn helped design and produce the world's first stored-memory and virtual-memory paging computers, the Manchester Mark 1 and Atlas computers, respectively, thus commencing a technological revolution the effects of which were felt worldwide. At a time when England was advancing toward the forefront of the computer-science industry, Kilburn helped to establish the city of Manchester, where he was a professor and lecturer at Manchester University for more than 30 years, as a leading center for computer innovation. The impact of his contributions to science and engineering continues to be evident in computer technology today.

Tom Kilburn was born on August 11, 1921 in the town of Dewsbury, in Yorkshire, England, to John and Ivy Kilburn. He was educated at the Wheelwright Grammar school before continuing on to the Sidney Sussex College at Cambridge University, where he received a B.A. degree in 1942 and an M.A. degree in 1944. He had hoped to serve as a pilot in the Royal Air Force after receiving his undergraduate degree, but he was recruited by C. P. Snow to work on a secret project for World War II. He accepted Snow's offer and was ordered to report to the Telecommunications Research Establishment (TRE) in Malvern in 1942. Due to Kilburn's inexperience with radios and electronic equipment, before he began work he was instructed to take a crash course in electricity, magnetism, and electronics at City and Guilds in London. It was there that the young scientist first encountered F. C. (Freddie) Williams, his boss and future collaborator. In a 1992 interview with Joanne Allison posted on the University of Manchester's Web site, Kilburn commented on that initial meeting: "In effect [Williams] said, 'Oh, God, you don't know anything?' And I said, 'No.' That was the sort of relationship at the start. But of course by the time we left Malvern . . . the relationship was quite different."

It was not long before Kilburn began to distinguish himself at his new place of employment. As a key member of Williams's research group, Kilburn's innovative ideas and sharp grasp of engineering and electronic circuitry placed him in high favor with his boss. During his four years at Malvern, Kilburn worked intensely and made numerous contributions to the development of electronic radar in connection with the war effort. It was also during this period that Kilburn first learned of digital computing machines, and about mercury filled delay lines (lines in which sonic signals travel at a finite speed) used as serial storage devices, for the transference of data one bit at a time.

When Williams was appointed Chairman of Electrical Engineering at Manchester University in 1946, he invited Kilburn to join him there in order to work on an ambitious computer memory project. The duo's first breakthrough was the creation of a cathode-ray-tube storage system, which used what later became known as the "Williams tube" to store bits (binary digits) of information. In an interview with Christopher Riche Evans for *Pioneers of Computing*, Kilburn explained that the Williams tube proved to be far superior to the mercury-filled delay lines, which had been used previously, because it possessed immediate access capability, a type of main memory storage.

In 1947 Kilburn attended a series of lectures given by Alan M. Turing at the National Physical Laboratory (NPL), that focused on the specifics of Turing's design for the NPL's computer. Kilburn learned little from the lectures except the realization that he did not want to build a computing machine "like that," as he has been quoted as saying. According to Kilburn, however, it was around this time that he began formulating his own computer design. Later that same year, Kilburn published the news of the now-perfected cathode-ray-tube storage system he had developed with William, along with an outline of the design for his computer. The paper, "A Storage System for Use With Binary Digital Computing Machines," also served to justify to the management of TRE the extended sabbatical Kilburn had taken in order to work with Williams. Kilburn's paper was circulated widely, and it has been credited with influencing companies in both the U.S. and what was then the Soviet Union to adopt the cathode-ray-tube storage system for their computers.

In 1948 Kilburn and Williams were joined by G. C. Toothill, another former employee of the TRE, and by the middle of the year, a prototype machine had been constructed. The Manchester Mark 1, or the Baby Machine, as it was nicknamed, utilized the cathode-ray technology that Williams and Kilburn had developed earlier. The machine had a RAM (random access memory) of 32 locations or "words," and each word in turn consisted of 32 "bits," giving the Manchester Mark 1 a total memory count of 1024 bits. The RAM technology was based on the cathode-ray tube (CRT) which was used to store bits of information as charged areas on the screen's phosphor, which displayed a series of glowing dots on the computer screen. The CRT's electric beam could control this charge and then write a digit (1 or 0) and read it back to the user if given a demand.

The Manchester Mark 1, which consisted of CRTs and valves dating back to WWII, and which was large enough to fill a room, faltered on several trials, before successfully running its first program on June 21, 1948. The program, created by Kilburn, was entitled the Highest Factor Positive and took approximately 52 minutes to execute. Williams, who documented the program's run, wrote that the event "was the breakthrough and sparks flew in all directions" (Manchester University Department of Computer Science). The Manchester Mark 1 was the first computer that was truly able to store a program, and as such it represented a substantial leap in technology over all previous computers, which were able to perform calculations only after being programmed manually to do so. The "Baby" was also a fast and compact machine for its time, and it was considered inexpensive to produce because it could use existing CRT designs.

Later in 1948 the Manchester Mark 1 team was joined by two student researchers D. B. G Edwards and G. E. Thomas, and M. H. A (Max) Newman and Alan Turing lent their theoretical expertise to the project. At the same time, the new computer drew the attention of Sir Ben Lockspeiser, the chief scientist of the British government, and a governmental contract was drawn up with Ferranti Ltd. to manufacture a production version of the Manchester Mark 1.

In the years following its initial program run, the Mark 1 underwent continued retooling by Kilburn and his team, while Williams turned his interest to other engineering matters. The computer's programs were initially entered in binary language on a keyboard, and the output, also in binary, could be read on another CRT. In late 1948 Turing designed a primitive form of assembly language, which uses symbols translated by an assembler, instead of binary language, which uses a sequence of 0s and 1s. In addition Turing, along with Edwards and Thomas, developed a paper tape input and output system and a programming manual. In April 1949, the Manchester Mark 1, with two CRTs, had its memory enlarged to 128 40-bit words, and acquired additional memory through a magnetic drum attachment that could hold up to 1024 words. The machine was further enhanced when two index registers were added to the computer. After several years of research, an improved version was built, and in February 1951 a Ferranti Mark 1, the world's first commercially available digital computer, was installed at Manchester University.

By the early 1950s Kilburn had earned the respect of his peers and accolades from his alma mater. He was awarded a Ph.D. from Manchester University in 1948 for his work on the cathode-ray tube storage system, and in 1953 he was recognized for his research on the Manchester Mark 1 and Ferranti Mark 1 with a doctor of science degree. Kilburn became a lecturer at the university in 1949, a senior lecturer in 1951, a reader in electronics in 1955, and a professor of computer engineering in 1960. In 1964 Kilburn was made professor of computer science and he kept that title for the remainder of his years at Manchester University.

In 1956, with his career at Manchester well established, Kilburn began designing plans for a Mark 2 computer, which was nicknamed MEG for megacycle engine. Kilburn was chief architect on the project, which eventually evolved into his work on the Atlas project. The Atlas computer, which became operational in 1962, was the first machine to use both virtual memory (memory that appears to be on random access memory, or RAM, but is actually transferred from or to hard disk storage) and paging (a technique in which main memory is divided into segments called pages). It was designed as a multi-programmed system, to be run under the control of a monitor system, using programmed operators, or extra codes, which remained in either read-only or transformable main storage for extensibility. The Atlas's instruction execution was pipelined and it contained separate fixed and floating-point arithmetic units capable of approximately 200 kFLOPS.

Upon its unveiling, the Atlas computer became not only the first computer with a paged memory, but the most powerful computer in the world. Kilburn's work on the project influenced research on computer systems for years to come, and the Atlas served as a model for future developments in virtual memory paging and multi-programming. In 1965 Kilburn contributed further to the field of computing by assisting in the formation of a new department of computer science at Manchester University. The department was the first ever of its kind for a British university, and served as an prototype for other institutions worldwide.

Over the course of his 17-year professorship at Manchester, Kilburn received the McDowell Award in 1971, the John Player Award, BCS in 1973, and was proclaimed a Distinguished Fellow in 1974. He was awarded the Royal Medal in 1978, and the IEEE Computer Society Pioneer Award in 1980 for his paging computer design. In 1983 Kilburn was honored with the Eckert-Mauchly Award, which is given to individuals in recognition of their contributions to computer and digital systems architecture. Although he enjoyed a long, successful tenure as a professor and researcher,

Kilburn regards the initial program run of the Manchester Mark 1 as the defining moment in his career. As he recalled in his 1992 interview with Joanne Allison, "The most exciting time was June 1948 when the first machine worked. Without question. Nothing could ever compare with that."

Tom Kilburn married Irene Marsden in 1943 and had a son and a daughter. He retired from Manchester University in 1981. He died on January 17, 2001.—D. B.

Suggested Reading: *Biography* (on-line); Charles Babbage Institute Web site; *Chronology of Digital Computing Machines* (on-line); Manchester University Web site; Virginia Polytechnic Institute and State University Web site

Courtesy of Texas Instruments

Kilby, Jack St. Clair

Nov. 8, 1923– Co-creator of the microchip

As one of the co-creators of the integrated circuit, or microchip, Jack St. Clair Kilby is one of the most significant inventors in the history of computing, in that his invention has made an impact on virtually everyone who has ever used a modern electronic device. During a two-week plant vacation during the summer of 1958, Kilby, then a recent employee of the fledgling company Texas Instruments, solved a problem that had been plaguing engineers for years—how to make transistor circuits smaller, cheaper, and more durable. He discovered that a circuit could be made entirely of one material, and integrated onto a chip half the size of a paper clip. His innovation first helped to revolutionize the military and space industries by making machinery smaller and more reliable. In 1965 Kilby, along with Jerry D. Merryman and James H. Van Tassel, created a pocket calculator, which proved that integrated circuits could be useful in commercial products. And indeed they were: the microchip gave rise to a gamut of small electronic goods that have become ubiquitous in many parts of the world, including desktop, laptop, and hand-held computers, cellular phones, digital watches, "smart" household appliances such as washing machines and toasters, and interactive toys. On the other end of the spectrum, microchips are also in-dispensable in satellites, space probes, and sophis-ticated medical diagnostic equipment, including magnetic resonance cameras. For this revolution-ary invention, Kilby was awarded the 2000 Nobel Prize in Physics, along with Zhores I. Alferov and Herbert Kroemer, inventors of high speed microe-lectronic components. In a press release announc-ing the award, as published on the Nobel e-Museum Web site, the Nobel Committee noted, "Through [Kilby's] invention microelectronics has grown to become the basis of all modern technolo-gy."

Jack St. Clair Kilby was born in Jefferson City, Missouri, on November 8, 1923 to Hubert St. Clair Kilby and the former Vina Freitag. Kilby's father was an electrical engineer who sparked his son's interest in electricity at an early age. In 1927 Hu-bert Kilby moved his family to Salina, Kansas, after becoming president of the Kansas Power Compa-ny. In 1935 the family moved again, this time to Great Bend, Kansas, when the company transferred its offices to that city. During summers, Kilby ac-companied his father on visits to power plants throughout western Kansas, and helped him look for faulty equipment. In 1937 a major blizzard hit Kansas, and to stay in touch with distant power stations, Kilby's father began using a ham radio. Jack Kilby was fascinated and after studying in-tensely, became a fully licensed ham radio opera-tor. He began building his own radios, and by the time he entered high school, he knew he wanted to become an electrical engineer.

Kilby had his heart set on attending the Massa-chusetts Institute of Technology (MIT), in Cam-bridge, and took the school's entrance exam in June 1941. With a score of 500 needed to pass, he re-ceived a 497, and according to several sources he never completely recovered from the disappoint-ment. Kilby had not applied anywhere else, and had to scramble to gain admittance to the Universi-ty of Illinois, his parents' alma mater. Several months after he started college, the U.S. entered World War II, and Kilby served in the United States Army as a corporal for two years, from 1943 to 1945. He worked in a radio repair shop on a base in northeastern India, placing and maintaining transmitters used to communicate with personnel in the field. Following the war he returned to the University of Illinois, where he received a bache-lor's degree in electrical engineering in 1947. In 1950 he completed his master's degree in that field, this time studying at the University of Wisconsin.

In 1947 Kilby joined the Centralab division of Globe-Union Inc., in Milwaukee, Wisconsin, which specialized in developing parts for radios, televisions, and hearing aids. There he helped to design and develop ceramic-based, silk-screen cir-cuits and worked in the field of miniaturization, seeking new ways to manufacture smaller and more efficient electrical parts. During this era, the electronics industry as a whole had made great strides, particularly in that they had effectively eliminated the need for vacuum tubes, which were large, awkward, and fragile devices. Vacuum tubes also generated a lot of heat and used up a good deal of power. In 1947 Bell Laboratories had invented transistors, which gradually replaced vacuum tubes. In comparison to their predecessors, transis-tors were tiny, more durable, produced less heat, used less power, and generally lasted longer. With the onset of transistors, engineers began making more complex electronic circuits that could have hundreds or even thousands of components such as capacitors, transistors, diodes, and rectifiers. Unfortunately, engineers began to notice a problem when large numbers of components had to be con-nected by bits of wire in order to make circuits; be-cause each component had to be hand soldered to the next, there was always a chance that the con-nection could come apart. The more complex the circuit, the greater the number of components and connections it needed, and the more likely some-thing would go wrong with it. In addition, hand-soldering was an expensive and time-consuming endeavor. This problem— which effectively held back the entire electronics industry until Kilby made his breakthrough—became known in engi-neering circles as "the tyranny of numbers."

After paying Bell Laboratories a licensing fee, Centralab became one of the first firms to manufac-ture transistors. In 1952 the company sent Kilby to a 10-day transistor symposium at Bell Laborato-ries's headquarters in Murray Hill, New Jersey. When he returned to Centralab he began working to develop germanium transistors that could be used in hearing aids. Though germanium had been the initial choice of material for transistors, by 1958 engineers recognized that silicon, which was harder to work with but could withstand higher temperatures, was a better semiconductor. It was also more readily available than germanium, and thus less expensive. Kilby wanted to pursue re-search with silicon, but Centralab was hesitant to part with the germanium based electronics they had been producing. Unsatisfied with the direction his company was taking, Kilby left Centralab in 1958 for Texas Instruments Incorporated.

Based in Dallas, Texas Instruments was a young, cutting-edge company that manufactured transis-tors, resistors, capacitors, and semiconductors for commercial and military use. They had also built the first transistor radio, in 1954, as well as the first silicon transistor, and the company had several contracts with the U.S. government for producing the latter. Kilby was hired to work on the miniaturization of electronic components. One idea for miniaturizing circuits had come from the U.S. Army Signal Corps, whose idea was to make all components a standardized size and shape, with built-in wiring. The various modules could be snapped together to make circuits, so as to do away with the need for soldering wire connections. Micro-Modules, as the circuits were dubbed, were the focus of a major development initiative at Texas Instruments around the time Kilby was hired.

Kilby wasn't very satisfied with the Micro-Module; he felt a horizontal structure would be more efficient than the vertically stacked architecture of the Micro-Module prototype, and thought it would be more cost-effective to use only silicon, whereas the Micro-Module used germanium as well. Moreover, the Micro-Module, as an article on the Texas Instruments Web site stated, "didn't address the basic problem of large quantities of components in elaborate circuits." Rather than join Texas Instruments's Micro-Module program immediately, Kilby began trying to develop a viable alternative, using tubular components instead of the flat wafers used in the Micro-Module. He designed a version of a device known as an IF (intermediate frequency) amplifier, which was commonly used in radios, trying to incorporate the tubular components. After Kilby spent several months pursuing this idea and making models, a cost-analysis led him to conclude that his design would still require too much hand-labor.

This conclusion was reached just as Texas Instruments shut down for a two-week, company-wide vacation. As a new employee, Kilby had no vacation time pending and went to the deserted laboratories, where he reflected on his options. He realized that if he couldn't come up with a good idea before everyone returned from vacation, he would be assigned to the Micro-Module project, which he felt was not a worthy solution to the problem of miniaturizing and connecting circuits. In a 1976 article entitled "Invention of the IC [integrated circuit]," as quoted on the Texas Instruments Web site, Kilby wrote: "In my discouraged mood, I began to feel that the only thing a semiconductor house could make in a cost-effective way was a semiconductor. Further thought led me to the conclusion that semiconductors were all that were really required—that resistors and capacitors [passive devices], in particular, could be made from the same material as active devices [transistors]. I also realized that, since all of the components could be made of a single material, they could also be made in situ interconnected to form a complete circuit."

This notion, detailed in his lab notebook on July 24, 1958, would come to be known as the monolithic idea; if all circuit elements were made of the same material, everything, including the connections, could be included on the same chip, thus eliminating the need for wiring and increasing the potential number of components and the complexity of circuits. Kilby quickly sketched out a design

and showed it to his boss, Willis Adcock, when Adcock returned from vacation. He was impressed but somewhat apprehensive about whether or not a circuit made completely from semiconductors could work. He asked Kilby to first make a working resistor and capacitor out of separate pieces of silicon. Kilby did so, and incorporated them into a circuit called a phase-shift oscillator, a device that oscillates signals at a given rate. This first unit, assembled and demonstrated on August 28, 1958, proved that circuits using elements made only from semiconductors were viable. Adcock then gave the go-ahead for Kilby to build a completely integrated circuit on a chip, as Kilby had originally envisioned. That device, another phase-shift oscillator, contained two circuits on a small germanium chip. (Germanium was used because its properties were still better known than those of silicon). It was demonstrated before several Texas Instruments executives, including former chairman Mark Shepard, on September 12, 1958. What the executives saw was a chip about a half-inch long with protruding wires, glued to a glass slide. Kilby hooked the chip to a battery and an oscilloscope. When the power was turned on, the circuit oscillated at about 1.3 megacycles, creating a green sine wave across the screen of the oscilloscope. The world's first microchip worked.

Kilby and Texas Instruments filed for a patent for their "miniaturized electronic circuit" in February 1959. In March of that year, Mark Shepard announced the concept at a press conference in New York, declaring: "I consider this to be the most significant development by Texas Instruments since we divulged the commercial availability of the silicon transistor," as quoted on the Texas Instruments Web site. The company began offering their integrated circuits at the Institute of Radio Engineers Show for $450 a piece. Although the U.S. Air Force was quick to show interest in the IC, the electronics industry in general remained skeptical for some time; the Texas Instruments Web site, quoting from Kilby's writings, noted that the IC "provided much of the entertainment at major technical meetings over the next few years [following its introduction]." This resistance was due mostly to engineers' disbelief that effective capacitors and resistors could be made out of silicon. There was also a preconception that integrated circuits would be difficult to manufacture.

Unbeknownst to Kilby and Texas Instruments, Robert Noyce of Fairchild Semiconductor had invented a device similar to Kilby's integrated circuit, but with a key improvement, and applied for a patent in July 1959. Kilby's main concern had been integrating the various components on one chip, and in his rush to build a prototype, he had connected those components by hand with gold wire. Although he indicated in his patent application that hand-wiring would not be necessary in future versions of his chip, and had outlined other, more effective methods that could be used to interconnect the components, Noyce's patent application included a new chemical etching technique that simplified the manufacturing process and increased the chips' speed. The battle over the patent would last through much of the 1960s. In 1962 Texas Instruments filed a lawsuit against Noyce and Fairchild Semiconductor for patent interference. Two years later, Kilby and Texas Instruments received their patent for the miniaturized electronic circuits, though the case was not settled. Noyce also received his patent around the same time. A settlement was finally reached in 1969, when the U.S. Court of Customs and Patent Appeals ruled in favor of Noyce's invention. Texas Instruments and Fairchild had made a deal years earlier that enabled both companies to market the chip. Today, most historians credit Kilby for inventing and building the first working integrated circuit, and acknowledge Noyce for improving on the idea by solving the problem of interconnections. The two men, however, were not bitter towards each other; as Frederic Golden noted in *Time* (October 23, 2000): "The gentlemanly Kilby and the equally gentlemanly Noyce . . . were always content to call themselves co-inventors." Noyce died in 1990, and many have commented that were he alive, it is very possible he would have shared the Nobel Prize with Kilby.

Kilby's integrated circuit was first put to use in military applications. Texas Instruments began building the first computer to use silicon chips for the U.S. Air Force in 1961. A year later the microchip replaced the transistor in the Minuteman Missile, with each missile using 2500 integrated circuits for guidance control. The IC's use in the missiles increased the device's credibility, and the electronics industry began to take its presence seriously. Kilby was promoted to manager of engineering in Texas Instruments' semiconductor networks department in 1960. By 1962 he was in charge of the entire semiconductor networks department, overseeing the development of microchips for the Minuteman.

During the mid-1960s, the management at Texas Instruments wanted a "demonstration project" that would help speed the use of integrated circuits in the commercial market. Patrick E. Haggerty, then chairman of Texas Instruments, suggested to Kilby that he design a calculator as powerful as the bulky desktop models of the era, but which, by virtue of the microchip, would be small enough to fit in a pocket. In September 1965 Kilby spoke with two of his associates at Texas Instruments, Jerry D. Merryman and James H. Van Tassel, about building such a calculator. They knew that a year earlier, a Japanese company had introduced a desktop calculator that used transistors, but it was much larger and more expensive than what they had envisioned, weighing in at 55 pounds and costing around $2,500.

Over the next two years, Kilby, Merryman, and Van Tassel developed their pocket-sized calculator based on integrated circuits; their "miniature calculator" could perform the four basic functions—

addition, subtraction, multiplication, and division—and print results on a low-energy, thermal printer, invented by Kilby. Unveiled in 1967, the calculator ran on batteries, weighed 45 ounces, and measured about the size of a hand. Texas Instruments filed for a patent later that year and received it on June 25, 1974. The Smithsonian Institute accepted Texas Instruments' donation of the prototype in December 1975.

The calculator proved that Kilby's microchips were viable in commercial, mass-market products. By the late 1980s, more than 100 million pocket calculators were being purchased annually worldwide, in what had become a $1 billion industry. Another popular application that could not have existed without the microchip, the digital watch, was introduced in 1971, and millions of those products continue to be sold. Microchips opened up other new avenues of technology that had formerly been impossible due to the bulkiness of the electronic equipment. The microchip was used in a variety of deep space probes and in the onboard computers on manned flights to the moon. By the mid-1970s the modern computer industry began to hit its full stride, developing machines that were continually smaller, faster, less expensive, and more durable, and gradually giving rise to the desktop computer. Without the microchip, computer technology might not yet be available to the average consumer.

In 1968 Kilby became an assistant vice president at Texas Instruments, and in 1970 he was named the director of engineering and technology for their components group. In November of the latter year, he took a leave of absence from Texas Instruments in order to pursue other interests, though he remains on staff as a part time consultant. Since that time he has been a self-employed inventor, and he holds more than 60 patents obtained over the course of his career. Between 1975 and 1984 he devoted much of his time to an innovative solar energy project in which the processes of collecting and storing the energy were combined. Although the system proved commercially feasible and Texas Instruments acquired the rights to the idea, it was never marketed because a drop in oil prices decreased consumer interest in solar power. Between 1978 and 1985 Kilby served as a distinguished professor of electrical engineering at Texas A&M University. Now semiretired, he travels worldwide as a consultant for the electronics industry and the U.S. government. In 1998, in honor of the 40th anniversary of the invention of the microchip, Texas Instruments dedicated a research building in Kilby's honor.

In October 2000 the Nobel Committee awarded half of the Nobel Prize in Physics to Kilby, with the other half going jointly to Zhores I. Alferov and Herbert Kroemer for their contributions in the area of "semiconductor heterostructures used in high-speed- and opto-electronics." While many in the scientific community believe that a Nobel Prize for Kilby was long overdue, Kilby himself was much more modest about his accomplishments. "The integrated circuit didn't have much new physics in it," he said with a shrug to reporters at his front door, as quoted by Golden in *Time*. The Swedish Royal Academy, however, didn't see it that way: Kilby's invention has spawned an industry worth more than $230 billion worldwide and is the building block for nearly every electronic device on the planet. As quoted on the Texas Instruments Web site, a 1997 television program called Kilby, "one of the few people who can look around the globe and say to himself, 'I changed how the world functions.'"

In addition to the Nobel Prize, Jack Kilby has been the recipient of a variety of distinguished awards for his contributions to technology, including the National Medal of Science, presented in a ceremony at the White House in 1970. He has also received the Ballantine Medal from the Franklin Institute (1967), the Alumni Achievement Award from the University of Illinois (1974), and the Holley Medal (1982) from the American Society of Me-

chanical Engineers. He was inducted into the National Inventors Hall of Fame at the United States Patent Office in 1981, and is a fellow of the Institute of Electrical and Electronics Engineers (IEEE) and the National Academy of Engineering. He holds a number of honorary doctorates, including ones from the University of Miami (1982), the Rochester Institute of Technology (1986), the University of Illinois (1988), the University of Wisconsin (1990), and Yale University (1996).

On June 27, 1948, Jack St. Clair Kilby married Barbara Annegers; they have two daughters, Ann and Janet Lee.—C. M.

Suggested Reading: *Jones Telecommunications and Multimedia Encyclopedia* (on-line); Nobel e-Museum (on-line); *Science* p424+ Oct. 20, 2000; *Texas Instruments* (on-line); *Time* p78+ Oct. 23, 2000; Lee, J. A. N., ed. *International Biographical Dictionary of Computer Pioneers*, 1995; *Larousse Dictionary of Scientists*, 1994; *Timeline of Computers*, 1997; *Who's Who in America*, 1998; Slater, Robert. *Portraits in Silicon*, 1987

Kildall, Gary A.

May 19, 1942–July 11, 1994 Creator of CP/M, an early operating system

One of the great, unrecognized pioneers of the computer software revolution of the 1970s and 1980s was Gary A. Kildall, a computer programmer who created CP/M, the first popular operating system for personal computers. Like Bill Gates and other young entrepreneurs, Kildall established a company to market and distribute his software, which he customized to suit the needs of his customers. He was one of the few people who, early on, saw the potential in microcomputers and used his interest in this technology to generate a great fortune, not only for himself, but for an entire industry. Though later superceded by Microsoft's DOS program, Kildall's Control Program/Monitor, or CP/M, was a viable operating system, which controlled the way the central processing unit stored and retrieved information from the floppy-disk drive. In an article about Kildall's legacy posted on the California Digital Web site, Sol Libes wrote: "Every PC owner owes Gary a debt of gratitude. . . . Gary was the first person to interface a disk system to a microcomputer and create an operating system for it. He changed what had previously been a circuit designed for process control applications into a fully functional computer."

The son of a merchant marine-barge captain, Gary A. Kildall was born in Seattle, Washington, on May 19, 1942. His family owned and operated the Kildall Nautical School, in Seattle, a small college for the teaching of navigation that had been founded in the 1920s by Kildall's grandfather. Several members of the Kildall family worked in the

school, including Kildall himself, who taught there for a short time after high school.

Kildall's interest in mechanics began to emerge during high school, when he fixed cars and built machines that could be used to practice Morse code with a tape recorder, for example, or to operate a burglar alarm in an automobile. His main interest, however, lay in the field of mathematics. After graduating from high school he enrolled in the University of Washington. (Around this time he also married his high-school girlfriend, Dorothy McEwen, who would later become his business partner.) While pursuing his undergraduate studies, he became fascinated by computers and went on to earn a doctorate in computer science, in 1972.

During the late 1960s, between undergraduate and graduate school, Kildall joined the U.S. Naval Reserve. With the Vietnam War raging, the navy asked him to decide between serving in Vietnam or teaching at the Naval Postgraduate School, in Monterey, California. Kildall chose to teach, and began giving classes to naval personnel in computer programming. In Monterey Kildall learned about microchips—his introduction came by way of a note pinned onto a college bulletin board describing a $25 "microcomputer" for sale. It was an advertisement from a recent issue of the *Electronics News*, describing Intel's 4004 microprocessor (or "computer on a chip"), which had been designed by Ted Hoff. Kildall sent away for his microcomputer and began writing programs for it, including some arithmetic problems—suggested to him by his father—that could be used to calculate navigational triangles. He soon discovered that the Intel 4004 was a severely limited device, only able to handle data in four-bit chunks that were less than a character in size.

In early 1972 Kildall was invited to visit the Intel company to explore its nascent microcomputer division. Several mathematical routines he had created caught the attention of Intel managers, who invited him to work for them one day a week as a consultant. Working at Intel gave Kildall access to the company's quickly evolving technology, including the Sim-04, a prototype of a personal computer, and the faster 8008 and 8080 microprocessors. He wrote his first programming language, the Programming Language for Microcomputers (PL/M), to run on the 8008 chip.

A short time later Intel gave Kildall another early computer, the Intellec-8, which had just been upgraded to the 8080 processor and came with a display monitor and a high-speed tape reader. Kildall set up one of the world's first microcomputer stations in the back of his classroom at the Naval Postgraduate School, and he and his students began working on this system. Kildall quickly realized, however, that he would need a more efficient storage medium. As noted by Michael Swaine in *Dr. Dobb's Journal* (Spring 1997, on-line): "In the early '70s, paper tape was one of the standard storage media, along with the infamous punched card. Neither was very efficient, and the issue was particularly critical on microcomputer systems because the relatively slow microprocessors couldn't offset the inherent slowness of the mechanical process of punching holes in pieces of paper."

Around the time Kildall was working on his new computer system, IBM developed the floppy-disk drive. Based on the existing—and prohibitively expensive—technology of recording information with patterns of magnetization on large, rapidly spinning disks, the invention of floppy-disk drives made memory storage easier and more affordable. Kildall's personal computer now had ample memory, a microprocessor, and a display monitor, but it lacked a controller board to facilitate communication between the computer and the disk drive. At the time, such a device did not exist. For a while Kildall attempted to build one himself and then, in 1973, turned to a friend who had much more experience with hardware, John Torode, of the University of Washington.

Kildall and Torode began to work together, in spite of their shared belief that microprocessors would not have much appeal to a larger market. According to Swaine, they shared the opinion of most computer scientists at the time that microprocessors would be used mainly for "smart" consumer products, like blenders and carburetors. After Torode built a controller board, Kildall wrote the first disk operating system for a microcomputer, calling it the Control Program/Monitor (CP/M), or the Control Program for Microcomputers. The CP/M enabled him to control the way his central processor stored and retrieved information from his floppy-disk drive. Kildall offered to sell the software to Intel for $20,000, but the company passed. Undaunted, he decided to sell and distribute CP/M himself.

Initially Kildall placed an advertisement for CP/M in *Dr. Dobb's Journal*, an early microcomputer magazine, but once he received his discharge from the navy, in 1976, he established a corporation with his wife for designing and distributing his software. Their company, Intergalactic Digital Research Inc., later changed to the more familiar Digital Research Inc., or DRI, was at the forefront of the coming microcomputer, or personal computer, revolution. In 1977 Kildall's company struck a deal with an early microcomputer manufacturer to have them install CP/M on their machines. Other computer manufacturers quickly followed suit, and Kildall began rewriting CP/M to serve on different systems. Before long, CP/M was the industry standard.

Like many early computing companies, DRI had an unconventional, collegial atmosphere; Kildall himself was reputed to have roller-skated down halls and to have appeared in meetings wearing togas. While he was often frustrated by the day-to-day responsibilities of running a business, he loved to write programming code. As Michael Swaine noted: "[Kildall] improved CP/M, making it more portable. Certain features of the program were logically independent of the hardware, while others were intimately dependent on the exact features of the machine the program was running on. Gary shrewdly carved out the smallest possible set of machine-dependent elements, and made them easily field customizable. The result was that DRI could write one version of CP/M, and hardware vendors, field engineers, or whoever could customize it to their particular hardware configuration." By 1978 the computer languages FORTRAN, BASIC, Pascal, WordStar, and dBase, among others, were running on CP/M machines built by Commodore, Radio Shack, Apple, Zenith, and Sharp. According to Swaine, DRI boasted $6 million in sales in 1981, with at least 200,000 computers running CP/M in more than 3,000 hardware arrangements.

In 1980 IBM approached Kildall to develop a version of his CP/M program for their new personal computers. There are conflicting stories about what happened at the meeting between IBM and DRI: some say that Kildall didn't even attend, preferring to fly his airplane while his representatives worked out the details; others attest that Kildall's wife and attorney refused to sign an IBM non-disclosure agreement and wanted a high royalty on a program they refused to modify to suit IBM's needs. Kildall contended that he went to the meeting and left it believing that he had struck a deal with IBM. In any event, IBM also met with a small software company named Microsoft, whose owner, Bill Gates, agreed to sell to IBM his version of the BASIC software along with an operating system called DOS, which he had rushed out to purchase from the Seattle Computer Products company and quickly renamed MS-DOS. As much of a brilliant entrepreneur as a software maven, Gates offered IBM extremely favorable terms for the BASIC/DOS package.

IBM, as a result, sold personal computers that ran on either CP/M or MS-DOS. But, because of the differing licensing arrangements with DRI and Microsoft, they offered the operating programs at considerably different prices: IBM sold CP/M for $240 while pricing MS-DOS at $60. Although many believe that, at the time, CP/M was the far better product, the IBM computers with the cheaper MS-DOS program became immensely popular. Kildall continued to improve CP/M by introducing multi-tasking and multi-user versions. And, though CP/M remained an industry standard alongside MS-DOS throughout the 1980s, the different prices IBM had set for the software helped to insure DRI's eventual demise.

In 1983 DRI still had solid sales—in excess of $44 million—and employed 665 people. That year Kildall developed a Graphical User Interface (GUI), similar to the Macintosh GUI, called Graphical Environment Manager, or GEM, but his company did little to promote it. He also pioneered the development of CD-ROM software and contributed greatly to the interfacing of video disks and computers—precursors to today's interactive multimedia. In order to promote this work, he established a second company, called KnowledgeSet, in 1985. KnowledgeSet released a CD-ROM version of the

Grolier's Encyclopedia, an impressive product that demonstrated the potential of this new electronic storage medium.

DRI quickly lost ground after the Lotus company created its highly popular spreadsheet program, Lotus 1-2-3, to run exclusively on MS-DOS; after that the Microsoft software became the industry standard. In 1991 Kildall sold the company to Novell, which quickly discarded all DRI products. Kildall became a rich man from the sale and moved to a large, lakeside ranch in Austin, Texas. His philanthropic activities included funding efforts to help pediatric HIV/AIDS victims. After a fall, Kildall died from internal bleeding, on July 11, 1994, in Monterey, California. He was 52.

Gary A. Kildall and Dorothy McEwen Kildall were divorced in 1983. Kildall's second marriage also ended in divorce. He is survived by his two children, Scott and Kristin.—C. M.

Suggested Reading: California Digital Web site; *Dr. Dobb's Journal* (on-line) Spring 1997; *Jones Telecommunications and Multimedia Encyclopedia* (on-line); *New York Times* D p19 July 13, 1994; Cortada, James W. *Historical Dictionary of Data Processing: Biographies*, 1987; Spencer, Donald D. *Timetable of Computers*, 1997

Kircher, Athanasius and Schott, Gaspar

Kircher, Athanasius
May 2, 1602(?)–Nov. 28, 1680 Jesuit scholar

Schott, Gaspar
Feb. 5, 1608–May 22, 1666 Jesuit Scholar

In 17th-century Europe, at a time when the vast majority of the population was illiterate, some of the most learned individuals were members of religious orders. Of these orders, one of the most knowledgeable and widely traveled was the Society of Jesus, better known as the Jesuits. Athanasius Kircher and Gaspar Schott, two such learned Jesuits, conceived of and built a calculating device inspired by John Napier's "bones," which had been described in a 1617 treatise titled *Rabdologiae*. (Made of wood or ivory, the bones were printed with the numbers zero to nine and could be used for multiplication, division, square roots, and powers. They were soon in popular use throughout Europe.) Called an *organum mathematicum*, it proved too unwieldy for popular use; the book describing the device's operation was more than 850 pages long and required the user to memorize long passages of Latin poetry. Still, Kircher and Schott are well remembered for their mathematical studies and for their role in disseminating Napier's knowledge to their fellow Jesuits.

Various sources list Athanasius Kircher's birth date as either May 2, 1601 or 1602. He was born in Geisa, Thuringia, a small town on the northern bank of the Upper Rhone. The area was once known as Buchonia (or Buchavia) for its abundant beech trees. At that time the custom of adding one's birthplace to one's name was in vogue, so Kircher sometimes amended his name with the Latin epithets *Bucho* or *Fuldensis* (for Fulda, the capitol city). His given name, Athanasius, honored the saint on whose feast day he was born.

Kircher was the youngest son of Johannes Kircher of Mainz and the former Anna Gansek. The family included five other sons and three daughters. Johannes Kircher was an educated man who earned a doctorate in philosophy and theology without—as was the custom of the day—becoming a priest. All six of his sons, however, did enter the priesthood. (Many scholars have speculated that they did so only because the family was too poor to educate them otherwise.) Johannes Kircher had been named councillor and bailiff by Prince-Abbott Balthasar of Fulda, but after the abbot was expelled due to political upheaval, Kircher lost his political position and settled in Geisa.

Athanasius Kircher was educated at the Jesuit Gymnasium between 1614 and 1618 and studied Hebrew and Greek there. In October of 1618, he entered the Jesuit order and traveled to Paderborn, where he studied natural science, mathematics, and the humanities. His education was interrupted by the upheaval that ensued during the Thirty

Years' War (1618–48). In 1622 Christian of Brunswick, a Protestant military leader, forced the Jesuit college to close; Kircher fled first to Münster and Neuss before resuming his education at Cologne, where he studied philosophy. In 1623 he traveled to Koblenz, where he studied languages and the humanities and also taught Greek. He then moved on to Heiligenstadt, in Saxony, where he continued his studies and taught grammar.

Between 1625 and 1628, when he was ordained a priest, Kircher studied theology at Mainz. He continued to teach, to support himself. In 1627, while teaching philosophy at Würzburg University, he met his future pupil Gaspar Schott, who had recently entered the Society of Jesus. Schott was born on February 5, 1608 in Köningshofen, near Würzburg, Germany. Little has been written about Schott's family or early life; it is known that he had a childhood fascination with mechanics. (In one of his works, he recalled seeing a suction pump bursting at Paderborn, in 1620.)

After his ordination, Kircher remained in Mainz. There, he used a telescope for the first time, to study sunspots. Known for his scientific curiosity and acumen, he was asked by the Archbishop of Mainz to conduct surveying and mapping work on the territory reclaimed from the Protestants. He was exposed to professional medicine around this time and began a lifelong interest in it. (During an outbreak of the bubonic plague in Naples, in 1656, Kircher would study the blood and urine of victims under a primitive microscope and speculate that a living organism, "*contagium anamatum*," might be causing the disease.) In 1629 he spent a year in Speyer, where, after reading about the obelisks in Rome, he developed an interest in deciphering hieroglyphs.

In 1631, due to the continuing unrest of the Thirty Years' War, Kircher and Schott were forced to leave Würzburg for France. They settled first in Lyons, then at Avignon, where they were under papal protection. (Some scholars dispute that Schott accompanied his mentor to France, although most agree he did.) Schott ultimately arrived in Palermo, Sicily, where he would remain for the next two decades, not counting two years spent in Trapani, Sicily. He never lost contact with Kircher, who after continuing his interests in surveying, hieroglyphs, and astronomy in Avignon, was summoned by Holy Roman Emperor Ferdinand II to teach in Vienna. This displeased his patron, a Provencal senator named Nicholas Peiresc, who was greatly interested in the sciences. He arranged for Kircher to be called instead to Rome and given a professorship at the *Collegio Romano*, where he taught physics, mathematics, and languages.

Kircher remained in that post for eight years (some sources say six), then left to pursue independent studies. His work was highly valued by the elite—popes, princes, prelates, and emperors— each of whom vied for his attentions. With the freedom to conduct scientific inquires as he wished, he traveled to Malta to study volcanoes. (He witnessed the eruptions of Mts. Etna and Stromboli in the late 1630s.)

On his return to Naples, an earthquake destroyed the city of Euphemia. He decided to study such phenomenon firsthand by having himself lowered into the crater of Vesuvius in Naples. There, with the aid of an instrument called a pantometer, he determined the exact dimensions of the crater and its inner structure. The results of his studies became the foundation of his first major work, *Specula Melitensis Encyclia sive synagma novum instrumentorum physico-mathematicorum*, published for the Knights of Malta in 1638. (His fascination with the topic would culminate in the 1678 publication of *Mundus Subterraneus*, or the "Subterranean World," which covered not only volcanoes and earthquakes, but fossils, lizards, caves, and mountain springs, among other topics.)

After Kircher's return to Rome, he focused on maintaining and adding to the collection of antiquities, art, and natural specimens in a museum that had been founded with a donation by Alfonso Donmines, secretary of the Roman Senate, in 1650. (It eventually came to be known as Kircher's Museum.) The museum included stuffed animals given to Kircher by a number of rulers, portraits of ecclesiastical officials, and, among other oddities, what was believed to be the tail and rib bones of one of the legendary Sirens. The museum was considered a marvel for several centuries; its contents were divided, in 1913, between the *Museo Nazionale Romano*, the *Museo Nazionale de Castel Sant'Angelo*, and the *Museo Paleoetnografico del Collegio Romano*.

Kircher's remarkable museum reflected the breadth of his interests, which included everything from astronomy and optics to philosophy and theology. As an unofficial conduit for the exchange of information between far-flung groups of Jesuits, he studied and wrote about such diverse subjects as acoustics, philology, music theory, physics, chemistry, geography, geology, archeology, mathematics, and medicine. His works were so widely read that, in 1660, he was able to negotiate a handsome fee from a Dutch publisher in exchange for exclusive publishing rights. His list of notable patrons grew.

The scope of Kircher's work proved to be so extensive that he asked for Schott to be sent to Rome to aid him in his research. Schott left for Rome in 1651 (some sources say 1652) and spent the next few years collaborating with his mentor. While Kircher pressed ahead with his studies, Schott readied Kircher's papers, as well as work he was receiving from other Jesuits, for publication. Although still engaged in this editorial work, Schott returned to Germany in the summer of 1655 to teach mathematics and physics, first at Mainz and later at Würzburg. Over the next decade Schott produced 11 massive volumes, primarily summaries of works and experiments; the topics included hydraulics and pneumatics, air pumps, intravenous injections, and vacuums.

One of the most detailed entries in Schott's volumes is an explanation of Kircher's mathematical studies. In it Schott reports Kircher's algorithms and includes descriptions of several mechanical aids to calculation. (Kircher had undertaken the mathematical studies under the patronage of a technically inclined nobleman.) One such aid was a device called an organum mathematicum, or mathematical organ. Kircher and Schott had helped to spread the work of a Scottish mathematician named John Napier to their fellow Jesuits. Napier had invented an early calculating device called variously "Napier's bones" or "Napier's rods." The device could be used for multiplication, division, square roots, and powers, and hoping to expand its utility Schott built a more-complex version, as described by Kircher. It consisted of a box containing ten sets of bonelike tablets printed on cylinders, including sets for the calculation of arithmetic (similar to Napier's basic set), geometry, military fortifications, calendars, gnomics, spherics, planetary movements, the construction of earthworks, and the composition of music. Unfortunately, the mathematical organ proved unwieldy. As Michael R. Williams wrote in *A History of Computing Technology* (1997), "Although it was an interesting attempt at making [Napier's] bones easier to use, the system proved to be a failure. The parallelograms containing the digits to be added together span two adjacent bones, and the space required to mount the cylinders meant that these digits were widely separated. This led to a greater tendency to make mistakes and the device was soon abandoned."

Kircher had numerous triumphs in fields other than mathematics. In 1641 he published *Magnes sive de arte magnetica opus tripartitum*, a work that contained the sum knowledge of his era regarding electricity and magnetism. The volume contains the first use of the term electromagnetism. Additionally, Kircher's study of optical phenomenon paved the way for the development of the first projection device, a magic lantern. (The lantern itself has often been attributed to him, though most historians have concluded that it was actually the invention of Thomas Rasmussen Walgensten, a Danish mathematician.) Kircher was also deeply interested in outer space. Using telescopes he studied Jupiter and Saturn, and he was fascinated by comets and solar and lunar eclipses. (He believed, contrary to Church teaching, in life on other worlds, placed there by a benevolent and omnipotent God.) Kircher is also remembered as the inventor of a speaking tube for amplifying sound waves.

Schott, conversely, is said to have been more concerned with the dissemination of information than attempting any original investigation or experimentation. He was known for examining every side of an argument, but never expressing his own opinion on it. Famously, regarding a theory of the origin of underground springs, he argued that everyone involved was correct—that some springs were connected to the ocean, that others were a result of precipitation, and that still others were due to underground condensation. Still—he was considered one of the most learned men of his time, due to the fact that he was a remarkable editor who prepared and popularized the accounts of others for publication.

After returning to Germany, later in 1655, Schott longed for a return to Rome, the city he considered to be the center of intellectual life. German winters damaged his health, and he returned to Rome in 1661 for a brief visit. He tried unsuccessfully to secure a teaching position in that city. Now known primarily for a treatise containing the first description of a universal joint and a classification system for gear teeth, Schott died on May 22, 1666 in Germany.

Kircher died on November 28, 1680 in Rome, leaving behind 44 volumes of scholarly work. Though he contributed to a number of religious activities, including the restoration of churches, he was never allowed by Church officials to fulfill a lifelong dream to serve as a missionary in China. To console himself, he erected a sanctuary on the crest of Sabine Hill, near Rome. His heart was buried there, and the site still receives religious pilgrims.—C. M.

Suggested Reading: Galileo Project Web site; New Advent Web site; Asimov, Isaac. *Asimov's Biographical Encyclopedia of Science and Technology*, 1982; Williams, Michael R. *A History of Computing Technology*, 1997

Kleinrock, Leonard

June 13, 1934– Co-creator of the ARPANET

Although the Internet arose out of the work of many, Leonard Kleinrock's development of queueing and packet-switching theory—technologies that allow computers to speedily and efficiently transmit data over networks—was essential to the viability of computer networking. His research enabled the creation of the world's first computer network—the ARPANET, which was created by the United States Department of Defense Advanced Research Projects Agency (ARPA), sometimes called DARPA, and initiated at Kleinrock's UCLA (University of California at Los Angeles) laboratory, in October 1969. A renowned UCLA professor since 1963, Kleinrock has shared his networking expertise with his students, many of whom have made significant contributions to the networking field. Kleinrock also founded a branch of the National Research Council known as the Computer Science and Telecommunications Board (CSTB), through which he has campaigned for a standard and universally accessible information infrastructure to make use of future Internet and networking technologies. His company, Nomadix, which he founded in 1995, is developing technologies to satisfy the portable networking needs of the future.

Courtesy of Leonard Kleinrock

Leonard Kleinrock

Leonard Kleinrock was born in New York City on June 13, 1934. His interest in communications and engineering surfaced early, when, at the age of six, he found instructions for building a crystal radio in a comic book. He immediately set about acquiring the parts and, in his enthusiasm, even appropriated an earphone from a public telephone. As a student at the Bronx High School of Science, Kleinrock worked on any discarded radios he could find, while also taking courses in radio engineering. He graduated, in 1951, and his father, an immigrant from what is now called Ukraine, asked him to help support the family with a full-time job. Kleinrock worked as an electrical technician at a cousin's shop while attending night school at the City College of New York. In 1957 he graduated at the top of his class with a bachelor of electrical engineering degree, and then won a full graduate fellowship for the electrical engineering program at Massachusetts Institute of Technology (MIT), in Cambridge.

At MIT Kleinrock focused on the relatively unexplored area of data networks. He received his master's in electrical engineering, in 1959. In 1961 he published a paper on a mathematical tool called queuing theory. Queuing theory described the flow of data in a packet-switching network, an idea that gained currency during the 1960s. (Paul Baran, at the RAND Corporation, put forth a theory about packet-switching, also in 1961, and, in 1965, Donald Watts Davies, at the National Physical Laboratory, in England, did independent work on the topic). Kleinrock is thought to have been the first to make his ideas public. He theorized that data could be broken down and transmitted over a network in small packets rather than in a long, continuous

stream that would require a dedicated circuit. By breaking the data into packets, which were tagged with a destination, a return address, and sequencing information, data could be reassembled in its original form by the receiving computer. Thus, information could be sent quickly and efficiently between computers on a network without the need for a vast maze of communication lines. Kleinrock combined this idea with queueing theory, the notion that packets should be handled by networks on a first-come, first-serve basis. "Computers burst data," Kleinrock explained to Matt Welch for the *Zone News* (January 2000, on-line). "They transmit then they stop a while, while they're thinking or processing or whatever. And in those days data communication lines were really expensive. The idea was, don't dedicate a resource to somebody—when I was sitting there, scratching my head, that machine was idle, I'm not using it. You want to do it in dynamic fashion: whoever needs it gets it now. If you're not using it, let somebody else in."

Kleinrock received his Ph.D. from MIT, in 1963, and immediately joined the computer science department at UCLA. His dissertation was published as *Communication Nets: Stochastic Message Flow and Delay* (1964), but there was little scientific interest in his work at the time. "People were not thinking in those terms yet," Kleinrock told Welch. "They didn't recognize the need for computers to talk to each other." Then, in 1968, Kleinrock was approached by a former MIT colleague named Lawrence G. Roberts, who was then the director of ARPA. Roberts wanted to figure out a way for the various researchers associated with ARPA to share the resources of their specialized computers, and he had heard about Kleinrock's data networking theories. Although many of his ARPA colleagues were skeptical about using public funds to finance the unproven packet-switching technology, Roberts was able to persuade them of the utility of the project. As he told Florence Olsen for the *Chronicle of Higher Education* (February 18, 2000), "Because [Kleinrock] had done that work, I could stand up to those people."

Roberts asked Kleinrock to help write the specifications for the network, to be called the ARPANET. They contracted the computer company Bolt, Beranek & Newman (BBN) to build an Interface Message Processor (IMP), a computer that could translate data from local computers into a common network language. The IMP was then shipped to UCLA, in September 1969, where it was hoisted through an open window because it was too big to carry through the doors. By October Kleinrock and his team of graduate students were ready to connect to another computer located at Stanford University's Research Institute (SRI), in Northern California. The procedure was for a UCLA technician to type *log* on his computer keyboard, which would initiate the connection with the computer at SRI. Technicians at both sites were in contact by phone. The UCLA technician typed *l,* and the SRI technician acknowledged the transmission; *o* was typed and received. Then, when g was typed, the system crashed—an inauspicious beginning. The connection was successfully made on the second try, however, and, by December 1969, two other computers (at the University of California at Santa Barbara and the University of Utah in Salt Lake City) were added to the network. Kleinrock's team served as the ARPANET Measuring Center, testing the capabilities of the system, deliberately triggering network crashes and then finding ways to repair it. By mid-1970 10 computers were connected, and soon users were able to send e-mail over the network, greatly contributing to the network's growth.

In 1968 Kleinrock had co-founded a wireless communication company, the Linkabit Corporation. When he took time off from the company to work on the ARPANET, two of the executives that Kleinrock had hired eventually fired him and moved the company to San Diego, California, where it became the center of a profitable wireless communication industry. Kleinrock was one of the few UCLA computer science professors interested in using his technical expertise in the commercial realm, and he didn't let his experience with Linkabit deter him from further business ventures. In 1976 he founded Technology Transfer Institute, a producer of educational workshops, trade shows, and conferences on technology. He served as chair and CEO.

Kleinrock has written more than 200 scientific papers and six books, primarily on the subject of queueing systems. His *Queueing Systems: Theory* (1979) was a leading textbook in the field. Its companion, *Queueing Systems: Problems and Solutions* (1996), moves step-by-step through various queueing problems. As this reader-friendly approach suggests, Kleinrock has earned a reputation as a fine teacher. Describing his passion for teaching to Florence Olsen, he said, "You're working with young people—keeps you fresh, you have to stay sharp. You have no boss. You do research in any field you like. You travel a lot. The best minds in the world come to the university to lecture or visit. It's a prestigious job. The salary is not bad. If you work harder, you can get more. But it's the independence I really liked." One of Kleinrock's former graduate students, Vinton Cerf, helped design the language that allows most networks to communicate, called the TCP/IP protocol. In an interview with Welch, Cerf said, "Kleinrock is one of the best queueing theory experts in the world— and a phenomenal teacher. I took classes from him as a graduate student and his lectures were long on insight and mathematically sophisticated. He has a remarkable ability to find examples which are at once fun, compelling and easily understood."

In 1986 Kleinrock founded the Computer Science and Telecommunications Board (CSTB) of the National Research Council (NRC), a scientific advisory board. CSTB advises the federal government about computer and communication issues. Kleinrock chaired the committee that produced the CSTB's first report, *Towards a National Research Network,* which was presented to Senator Al Gore and led to the establishment of Gigabit Networking Alliance, a group committed to developing a single standard for high-speed data transmission in order to encourage networking compatibility between all computer operating systems. In 1994 CSTB produced a much-discussed report, *Realizing the Information Future: The Internet and Beyond,* and Kleinrock submitted testimony before the Subcommittee on Science, Space, and Technology of the U.S. House of Representatives. Once again, Kleinrock emphasized the importance of establishing a standardized, national information infrastructure.

In 1995 Kleinrock made another foray into the business world with Nomadix, a company dedicated to producing products for wireless computer networking. In July 2000 Nomadix received $17 million in venture capital investments, allowing it to pursue its vision of the future of computing. Kleinrock described this vision to Stephanie Sanborn for *InfoWorld* (October 4, 1999), "Your walls will be loaded with logic, processing, memory, cameras, microphones, speakers. . . . When I walk into a new environment, it should know that I have arrived. As I approach a desktop or laptop computer that's not being used, it will load my applications, my profile, my preferences, my environment. And, in fact, on my body I'll probably be wearing a network called a body LAN, which will connect all of the devices I carry around on my belt—maybe even connect my pacemaker if I had one. The Internet will be everywhere. It will be invisible. You will be able to interact with it using wonderful interfaces like speech and pointing. You won't have to think about it. It will be like electricity."

Kleinrock has received many awards and honors, including a Guggenheim Fellowship (1971); awards from UCLA for outstanding and distinguished teaching (1966, 1967, 1986); an Institute of Electrical and Electronics Engineers (IEEE) Fellowship (1973); an ORSA Lanchester Outstanding Research Prize (1976); the L. M. Ericsson Prize (1982); induction into the Computer Design Hall of Fame (1982); the Marconi International Fellowship Award (1986); and the INFORMS Presidents Award (1999). Kleinrock is married and has four children and five grandchildren.—P. G. H.

Suggested Reading: *Chronicle of Higher Education* A p53+ Feb. 18, 2000; *InfoWorld* p36 Oct. 4, 1999 *Los Angeles Times* p1 Oct. 11, 1999, p8 Oct. 25, 1999, B p4 Dec. 28, 1999; *USA Today* D p5 Sep. 1, 1999; *Zone News* (on-line) Jan. 2000

Knuth, Donald Ervin

Jan. 10, 1938– Author of The Art of Computer Programming; *developer of typesetting programs*

The first volume of Donald Ervin Knuth's seminal work, *The Art of Computer Programming*, was published in 1968; two other volumes followed, in 1969 and 1973. Although the three-book set has been called "an encyclopedic compendium" and "the Bible of programming," Knuth considers his work far from finished, and he has plans to write four more volumes. As quoted by Steve Ditlea in an article for *Technology Review* (September/October 1999), Knuth once quipped during a lecture, "Unfortunately, computer programming has grown over the years and so I've had to write a little more than I thought when I sketched it out." This growth is due, in part, to Knuth's own contributions to the field. During a hiatus from writing, he developed a pair of remarkable typesetting programs, TeX and Metafont, which are widely used by publishers of physics and mathematics books.

Donald Ervin Knuth was born in Milwaukee, Wisconsin, on January 10, 1938, the son of Ervin Henry Knuth and the former Louise Marie Bohning. Ervin Knuth, a teacher, was the first college graduate in his family. He was also an avid music lover who played the church organ on Sundays. (Donald Knuth inherited his father's love of music and has several instruments, including a pipe organ, in his home. Like his father, he regularly plays the organ at his church; in addition, he is an enthusiastic member of the choir.)

Knuth showed an early aptitude for math. In eighth grade he entered a contest sponsored by the George Ziegler Candy Company that required entrants to figure out how many words could be formed using the letters in the name Ziegler's Giant Bar, one of the firm's most popular confections. Knuth became obsessed by the challenge and worked on it constantly. To do so, he told Bruce Schechter for *Discover* (September 1984): "I feigned being sick to my stomach for a few days so I could stay home from school and work." He ultimately found more than 4,500 words—2,000 more than Ziegler's contest administrators had found. He won first prize—a toboggan for himself, a television set for his school, and a free Ziegler's Giant Bar for each of his classmates.

In high school Knuth continued to express a gift for computations, and he won honorable mention in the Westinghouse Science Talent Search. For the talent search he developed a new system of weights and measures called the potrzebie system. The term "potrzebie" was derived from a catchphrase often used in *Mad* magazine, a satiric publication widely read by adolescent boys. In Knuth's system a "potrzebie" was the thickness of one issue of *Mad*, a "Mad" was a unit made up of 48 parts, and a "whatmeworry" was the basic unit of power. (The motto of Alfred E. Newman, the magazine's fictional mascot, was "What, me worry?") In June 1957 *Mad* bought Knuth's winning paper for publication in an issue of their magazine.

Knuth planned on majoring in music at college. He had played the saxophone and later the tuba in his high-school band and had even arranged a medley of television theme songs for the group to perform. Upon receiving a physics scholarship from the Case Institute of Technology, in Cleveland, Ohio, however, he decided to major in that subject—even though he had very little interest in it. (After World War II, schools were encouraging anyone with an aptitude for science into the study of physics, then a burgeoning field.)

Knuth first came in contact with a computer, the IBM 650, during his freshman year at Case. He thought it was one of the greatest things he had ever seen. "I suppose it was natural for a person like me to fall in love with his first computer," he explained to Schechter. After spending some time dealing with the rigors of a physics major (including a mandatory welding class), he realized that the subject did not inspire him the way that the IBM 650 had. Knuth was quoted in *Out of Their Minds: The Lives and Discoveries of 15 Great Computer Scientists* (1995) as saying, "The manuals we got from IBM would show examples of programs and I knew I could do a heck of a lot better than that. So I thought I might have some talent." His experience with the Ziegler contest had shown him that he could think like a computer programmer—although at the time of his win he didn't even know the field existed. Paul Guenther, who taught freshman calculus, suggested that Knuth switch majors from physics to math. He did so and Guenther became his mentor.

Knuth longed to begin writing programs, and he got his chance in 1958. Case's basketball team, the Rough Riders, was having a terrible season. Knuth, then the team manager, created a computer program for the 650 that helped keep track of each player's statistics in 11 different categories, thus enabling the coach to see players' strong points and weaknesses and to decide who should play and who should be benched.

In 1960 Knuth received his bachelor's degree in mathematics from Case. In an unusual move, his teachers voted to simultaneously award him a master's degree. On June 24, 1961 he married his college girlfriend, Nancy Jill Carter. The couple moved so that Knuth could pursue a Ph.D. in pure mathematics at the California Institute of Technology (Caltech), in Pasadena. (Knuth received his doctoral degree in 1963.) Beginning in 1960 he served as a consultant for the Burroughs Corporation, then an office-machine manufacturer trying to break into the computer market. As a consultant, Knuth studied the firm's hardware, wrote software, and helped other employees better understand all aspects of the new machines.

As an employee of Burroughs, Knuth was approached by the textbook publisher Addison-Wesley to write a book on computer compilers. (Computer compilers are programs that change the programmers' typed text into executable instructions in a computer's native binary language.)

Knuth wrote the first draft of his book, in long-hand, between 1962 and 1966. The manuscript was 3,000 pages long. Knuth himself had little understanding of just how lengthy the book would be. As he told Steve Ditlea: "I was thinking it was one volume of maybe 600 pages. I just figured type in books was smaller than my handwriting. Then I typed up chapter one and by itself it was 450 pages. I sent it to the publisher and they said: 'Don, do you have any idea how long your book will be?'"

With the size of the manuscript now a major consideration, Addison-Wesley decided to publish the original manuscript in three volumes (1968, 1969, and 1973). The first volume was dedicated to Case's 650 computer, in appreciation for the "many pleasant evenings" Knuth had spent working on it. Since its publication *The Art of Computer Programming* has unarguably become the most important reference work on its topic available. As quoted by Steve Ditlea for the *New York Times* (August 10, 1996), in April 1995 Bill Gates of Microsoft wrote in a syndicated column: "If you think you're a really good programmer, or if you want to challenge your knowledge, read *The Art of Computer Programming* by Donald Knuth. It took incredible discipline, and several months, for me to read it. I studied 20 pages, put it away for a week and came back for another 20 pages. You should definitely send me a resume if you can read the whole thing."

Knuth, like Gates, understands how difficult his books are but has noted that the programming classifications he came up with almost 40 years ago still remain accurate. Steve Ditlea wrote in his *New York Times* piece about the continued relevance of *The Art of Computer Programming*: "Those programmers who do make it through Knuth's 650-plus-page tomes cite them like scripture."

Knuth was intent on writing four more volumes to complete his opus, but owing to the vast speed of changes being made in the field, he found himself struggling to keep up with his subject. In 1977 he got sidetracked while reviewing galleys for new editions of his original three volumes. "The galley proofs looked awful," he recalled to Schechter. "I felt like tearing them up." The printer had spaced the text badly, and this was especially noticeable in a book that mixed standard lettering with mathematical equations.

Since the earliest days of the printing press, books had been created by using bits of type locked together to form plates from which pages were printed. With the advent of photography, printers discovered that they could photograph an already printed page, cut and paste revisions into the text, and then take another photo of the page. Knuth felt that the revised edition would never look as good as the original—until he heard about digital printing, then an innovation in the industry. In such a process, the typeset page is created electronically out of a grid of black and white dots on a computer screen; the text page is then photographed and copied to a master plate for printing. Because the pro-cess was based in computing, Knuth was intrigued by its potential. He set out to write an automated book-designing program himself, which he estimated would take approximately four months. In reality, the task took three years to complete and another six years to perfect.

Knuth created two programs: Metafont for alphabet design, and TeX (pronounced Tek) for document design. Metafont allowed a designer to create an entire font on a computer screen and then instantly modify it. TeX gave typesetters the ability to take letters and symbols and space them as they wished on a page. Today, 90 percent of all mathematics and physics books are typeset with Knuth's two programs. This is due in large part to the fact that Knuth allowed the programs' source codes to be published openly in such books as *TeX and Metafont: New Directions* (1979), *TeXbook* (1984), *TeX: The Program* (1986), and *TeXware* (1986). In Ditlea's article for *Technology Review*, he quoted the reasoning Knuth espoused at a Stanford University lecture: "TeX is what we now call open-system software—anybody around the world can use it free of charge. Because of this, we had thousands of people around the world to help us find all the mistakes. I think it's probably the most reliable computer program of its size ever." In addition to making word spacing better, TeX and Metafont allow the user to improve poor choices for line breaks and eliminate one-word lines and strange spaces because, unlike other programs that pack the most words on a line, Knuth's program is computation-sensitive, meaning that it uses trial-and-error methodology to figure out the most attractive way a paragraph can be displayed.

Knuth realized that his study of typography was now occupying him full time; his hiatus from *The Art of Computer Programming* had lasted many years longer than he had originally intended. With the release of TeX 3.0, in 1990, he stated that he was done with the work and that others would have to carry on in his place. Since then, he has returned to writing the fourth volume of his master work, determined to have it complete by 2007, with volume five arriving sometime around 2010. He plans to write the final two volumes (on the theory of context-free language and compiler techniques) after that—if he remains healthy and his work stays relevant. Such an extended timetable doesn't bother Peter Gordon, his Addison-Wesley editor for the last 20 years. As Gordon told Ditlea for *Technology Review*: "Don has his own life plan and his own sense of timing. He's such a creative and gifted author, the best any editor can do is stay out of his way and let him follow his plan."

In 1992 Knuth took early retirement from Stanford University, where he had taught computer programming since 1968. He also taught at his alma mater Caltech, from 1963 to 1968. He has received a number of awards for his work, including a Guggenheim Foundation fellowship (1972–73), the Distinguished Alumni Award from Caltech (1978), the Priestly Award from Dickinson College

(1981), the Franklin Medal (1988), the J. D. Warnier Prize (1989), and the Harvey Prize from the Israel Institute of Technology (1995), among others. From the Institute of Electrical and Electronic Engineers (IEEE) he has received the W. Wallace McDowell Award (1980), the Computer Pioneer Award (1982), and the John von Neumann Medal (1995). Perhaps most notably, he was recipient of the National Medal of Science, presented by President Jimmy Carter in 1979, and more recently, in 1996 he was awarded the Kyoto Prize (the Japanese equivalent of the Nobel Prize).

Besides *The Art of Computer Programming*, Knuth has written several other books, not all of which are related to programming. *3:16 Bible Texts*

Illuminated, for example, analyzes several biblical passages in great detail; *Things a Computer Scientist Rarely Talks About* (2001) has as its theme the relation between science and faith.

Knuth lives in California with his wife. They have two children, John Martin and Jennifer Sierra.—C. M.

Suggested Reading: *Discover* p74+ Sep. 1984; Donald Knuth Home Page; *New York Times* (online) Aug. 10, 1996; *Technology Review* p66+ Sep./Oct. 1999; Shasha, Dennis and Cathy Lazere. *Out of Their Minds: The Lives and Discoveries of 15 Great Computer Scientists*, 1995

Kroemer, Herbert

Aug. 25, 1928– Nobel Prize–winning physicist; developer of semiconductor technologies

The theories of physicist and professor Dr. Herbert Kroemer have led to vast improvements in the performance of semiconductor transistors. The new type of transistor Kroemer devised, known as heterostructures, are used for high-speed computing, satellite communication, cell phone technology, and other applications. In 1963, along with Zhores Alferov, with whom he shares the 2000 Nobel Prize in Physics, Kroemer discovered a method for producing semiconductor-based lasers. Such lasers are the central component of fibre optics, the telecommunications technology that connects the Internet. Kroemer also pioneered the field of molecular beam epitaxy, the method for building multi-layered semiconductor chips. Since these discoveries, Kroemer's research has led to steady improvements in semiconductor technology and has pointed the way to future innovations.

Herbert Kroemer was born in Weiman, Germany, on August 25, 1928. He earned a doctorate from the University of Gottingen in Gottingen, Germany in 1952, writing his dissertation on the flow of electrons in transistors, the newly-invented building blocks of modern computers. After earning his doctorate, Kroemer worked at a laboratory in Germany and, in 1954, was hired by Radio Corporation of America (RCA) in Princeton, New Jersey.

One of the main contributions to information technology for which Kroemer received the Nobel came in 1957, when he figured out a way to improve the performance of semiconductor transistors and authored "Quasi-Electric and Quasi-Magnetic Fields in Non-Uniform semiconductors," a paper published by the Polytechnic Institute of Brooklyn Press. At the time, transistors were made from a single layer of semiconductor, usually silicon, which would not conduct electricity until voltage was applied; after voltage was applied, the transistors became conductive and electricity

could flow through. In this way, transistors could act as on/off switches to open and close a circuit, thus transmitting the binary code that is the basis of digital logic. However, there were inherent obstacles to the efficiency of current flow in the traditional transistor. As electrons flowed through semiconductor in one direction, "holes," or positively charged spaces left by the electrons, flowed in the opposite reaction, reducing the amplification of the current. Kroemer proposed the idea of using heterostructures—building a transistor from two layers of complementary semiconductors in such a way that the counterflow of holes was reduced or eliminated. The first layer might be made, for example, of gallium arsenide and the second from aluminum gallium arsenide, which would allow electrons to flow in one direction but prevent holes from crossing the boundary between layers. Eventually these heterostructured semiconductors were used to create high-speed transistors and the low-noise, high-frequency amplifiers used in satellite communications and cell phones.

Kroemer left RCA in 1957 to be a group leader for the German Philips Lab, where he stayed until 1959. He then took a position as Senior Scientist at Varian Associates, where he would stay until 1966. In 1963, three years after the invention of the laser, Kroemer devised a theory for using heterostructured semiconductors to make lasers. Nearly simultaneously, Alferov made a similar discovery in the Soviet Union. Lasers fire when electrons in a crystal or other material are stimulated into high energy states and then drop back down to lower energy states nearly simultaneously, emitting a high-energy pulse of light. The first lasers were made from expensive, specially made crystals. Kroemer showed that one could configure the layers of a heterostructured semiconductor so that electrons and holes were directed into a trap from which they could not flow out, causing the electrons to move into a high-energy state and emit light, just like a traditional laser. Kroemer published his findings in "A Proposed Class of Heterojunction Injection Lasers" in *Proceedings of the IEEE* (1963, vol. 51) and filed for a U.S. patent just one week after Alferov applied for a Soviet patent. These new lasers would eventually be the basis for fibre-optics communication, reading heads in CD players, optical data storage, and bar-code readers. However, whereas Alferov proceeded to explore and refine his discovery, Kroemer found no support for his invention at Varian Associates. "I was told that the new device could not possibly have any practical applications," Kroemer explained to Richard Fitzgerald for *Physics Today* (December 2000).

In 1966 Kroemer went to work in the New Phenomena section of the Semiconductor Research and Development team at Fairchild Semiconductor. He left Fairchild in 1968 to become a professor of electrical engineering at the University of Colorado at Boulder, where he stayed until 1976. That year Kroemer convinced members of the Electrical and Computer Engineering department at the University of California at Santa Barbara to hire him and expand the department into the field of semiconductor research, particularly heterostructure research. The university soon became the leader in that field, while Kroemer picked up the thread of his own research in molecular beam epitaxy, the method for growing heterostructured semiconductors. This sophisticated procedure, greatly furthered by Kroemer's research, is a way of depositing one layer of semiconductor upon another of different chemical composition while maintaining a high degree of purity.

More recently, Kroemer has continued to pursue his research in molecular beam epitaxy by experimenting with new materials that allow heterostructured semiconductors to be tailored to various functions. His research includes working with superconductor-semiconductor hybrid structures and figuring out the methods for producing ultra-high-frequency oscillators, which produce pulses of particular frequencies at regular intervals. In 1980 Kroemer gave an address called "Heterostructures for Everything," a prediction that has come true. As Fitzgerald remarked in *Physics Today* (December 2000), "Heterostructures have emerged as the basic building block of semiconductor devices."

Kroemer has received honorary doctorates from the Technical University of Aachen in Germany (1985) and the University of Lund in Sweden (1998). His awards include the J. J. Ebers Award from the Institute of Electrical and Electronics Engineers (IEEE) in 1973; the Jack A. Morton Award from the IEEE in 1986; the Senior Research Award from the American Society for Engineering Education (ASEE) in 1982; the Heinrich Welker Medal of the International Symposium on GaAs and Related Compounds in 1982; the Alexander von Humboldt Research Award in 1994, and membership in the National Academy of Engineering (1997). Kroemer continues to teach at the University of California at Santa Barbara. He married in 1950 and has five children.—P. G. H.

Suggested Reading: *Chemical and Engineering News* p6 Oct. 16, 2000; *New Scientist* p15 Oct. 21, 2000; *Physics Today* p17+ Dec. 2000; *Science* p424+ Oct. 2000; *Science News* p158 Oct. 14, 2000; *Washington Post* A p2 Oct. 11, 2000

Kurtz, Thomas E.

Feb. 22, 1928– Pioneer of time-sharing; co-author of the computer-programming language BASIC

In 1964 Thomas E. Kurtz and John G. Kemeny developed the Beginners All-purpose Symbolic Instruction Code (BASIC), a revolutionary computer-programming language that was easy to learn and use. As Kurtz noted in an open letter posted on the True Basic Institute Web site, "It turned out that easy-to-learn and use was also a good idea for faculty members, staff members, and everyone else." Kurtz continued, "The official [computer] languages . . . were designed for professionals. There were very few choices for students, teachers, and others who didn't want to dedicate their lives to programming. [BASIC] provided the solution and has played an important role in the field ever since." Indeed, today BASIC continues to be adapted and updated, not only by its inventors, but by computer users everywhere who understand it to be a cornerstone of computer programming.

Thomas Eugene Kurtz was born in Oak Park, Illinois, on February 22, 1928, the son of Oscar Kurtz and the former Helen Bell. He attended Knox College, in Galesburg, Illinois, and in 1950 he received his bachelor of arts degree. In 1956 he earned a Ph.D in mathematics from Princeton University, in New Jersey. (His first computing experience occurred not at Knox or Princeton, however, but during a summer session at the Institute for Numerical Analysis at the University of California at Los Angeles, in 1951.)

After receiving his Ph.D., Kurtz joined the mathematics department at Dartmouth College, in Hanover, New Hampshire, as an instructor. The department was then chaired by John G. Kemeny, a fellow Princeton graduate with an active interest in computing. In 1958 Kurtz became an assistant professor; a year later Dartmouth purchased an LGP-30 computer. Before this, those who needed access to a computer traveled more than 100 miles to the nearest computer center, which was at the Massachusetts Institute of Technology (MIT), in Cambridge. Kurtz was enthusiastic about the arrival of the new computer and became the first director of Dartmouth's new computing center.

As the center became more popular people encountered a problem typical of that era in computer history: long waits as many users vied for time to run their programs on a single central computer. Kurtz and Kemeny, both of whom believed strongly in the importance of making computers accessible to all, began working together to solve the problem. Influenced by the work of MIT's John McCarthy and Joseph Licklider, they built a prototype time-sharing system that would link 60 remote terminals to a central General Electric 635 mainframe, thus serving the needs of numerous users simultaneously. Completed in 1964, the Dartmouth Time-Sharing System (DTSS) was one of the earliest systems of its kind.

Now that even nontechnical students had access to the university's computer Kurtz and Kemeny realized that a simpler programming language was needed. Early computer programmers had been limited to assembly language and machine language. Machine language, also called machine code, consists of a series of binary digits, 1s and 0s, which the computer interprets as electronic instructions. Assembly language, more sophisticated than machine code, features some technical command words such as "add," which must subsequently be translated into machine code. Then, in 1957, a commercial version of FORTRAN, a high-level computer language developed by the IBM scientist John Backus, was released. FORTRAN was much closer to human language in that it used grammar and syntax rules, thus making it possible to operate a computer with rudimentary commands in the form of sentences. Inspired by Backus's work, Kurtz and Kemeny set out to develop a language that would use simple algebraic formulas and English words such as "input," "print," "go to," and "end." BASIC, as they named their 1964 invention, was even easier for beginners to use than FORTRAN. It used only about a 200-word vocabulary and enjoyed another significant advantage over its predecessor: it provided the programmer with an instant response to lines entered as input, making it easier to debug and modify programs. In order to encourage others to use the language, it was made available at no charge.

Because of this decision, BASIC was adapted and used by a wide variety of people, including two fledgling entrepreneurs named Bill Gates and Paul Allen, who developed a version of the language to run on the Altair 8800, the first commercially successful personal computer (PC). The program was the first product sold by their newly formed company, Micro-Soft. Soon other programmers were developing versions of BASIC for use on computers from various manufacturers, including Commodore and Atari. Steve Wozniak wrote a version of BASIC for the Apple computer. IBM licensed a Microsoft BASIC interpreter, which it included on its PCs. When Bill Gates later released the Disk Operating System (DOS), it came with a BASIC interpreter known as BASIC A; GW-BASIC, Quick BASIC, and Visual Basic followed. Varia-

tions of Kurtz and Kemeny's language would eventually run on almost every PC manufactured and serve as the basis for a myriad of applications. In subsequent years, BASIC would become the standard language of all home, office, and school computers, and it is bundled with almost every PC currently sold.

Kurtz and Kemeny eventually became dismayed by the proliferation of differing versions of BASIC, many of which contained platform-specific properties that led to difficulties in transferring programs from one computer to another. Kemeny and Kurtz decided, in 1983, to engineer a new, improved version of the language, which they called True BASIC. Finished in 1985, True BASIC was more powerful than its predecessor and incorporated interactive graphics, formatting tools, and a window manager. It was designed to work on any computer without requiring modifications. The two creators established a company, True BASIC Inc., to oversee the new product, with Kemeny acting as chairman and Kurtz as vice chairman. In October 1985 *Creative Computing* reviewed the new version and called it "well-designed and easier to use." True BASIC is still available and is widely used to introduce young students to programming.

Kurtz became a full professor at Dartmouth in 1966 and acted as director of the institution's computing center until 1975. He then assumed the directorship of the Office of Academic Computing. In 1979 he helped set up the first master's program in computing and information systems (CIS) at Dartmouth, which was funded in part by an IBM grant. In 1988, when the CIS program was terminated, he returned to teaching mathematics and computer science until his retirement, in 1993. A tribute on the CIS Alumni Web site includes the line, "We miss his animated conversations, especially when he was alone with his keyboard!"

Kurtz has served a key role on the committee that developed the American National Standards Institute (ANSI) guidelines for BASIC, as well as the committee concerned with international standards. He continues to act as vice chairman of True Basic Inc. and is the author or co-author of several books on programming.

Thomas E. Kurtz has been married twice. His first marriage, to Patricia Anne Barr, occurred on June 13, 1953 and ended in divorce in 1973. On June 10, 1974 he married Agnes Seelye Bixler. He has three children: Daniel Barr, Timothy David, and Beth Louise.—C. M.

Suggested Reading: *Byte* p 268+ Oct. 14, 1989; p 276 Sep. 1990; p 155+ Mar. 17, 1992; p 133+ Sep. 1985; *Creative Computing*, p 226+ Nov. 1984; p 54+ Oct. 1985

Courtesy of Kurzweil Technologies Inc.

Kurzweil, Raymond

Feb. 12, 1948– Futurist

By the end of the 21st century it will be possible to scan people's minds onto computers while preserving all aspects of their memories, personalities, emotional responses, and even spiritual beliefs. No longer dependent on their bodies for survival, people will therefore have achieved a certain immortality. This is one of the predictions of the inventor and futurist Raymond Kurzweil. Had he not invented so many pioneering technologies and been correct in so many of his predictions, such seemingly outrageous claims would probably be dismissed. However, because of his successful track record, his extensive knowledge of computer science, and his exacting methodology for forecasting technological change, both experts and others have taken his ideas quite seriously. By the mid-70s Kurzweil had already advanced the field of artificial intelligence (AI) through his inventions of an Optical Character Recognition (OCR) system that allowed computers to read print in any font; a scanner that allowed computers to commit the text to memory; and a text-to-speech synthesizer that enabled the computer to recite the text aloud. In 1976 the three technologies were combined into the Kurzweil Reading Machine, a device that enabled blind people to read books and documents of their choosing. In the last two decades Kurzweil refined these technologies and also produced the first convincing synthesizer of orchestral instruments, proving that the sublime sounds of a live orchestra could be digitized and reproduced. Kurzweil's first book on AI and its future, *The Age of Intelligent Machines*, appeared in 1990, and in 1999 he peered even farther into the future with *The Age of Spiri-*

tual Machines: When Computers Exceed Human Intelligence. Kurzweil was awarded the prestigious National Medal of Technology, presented by President Bill Clinton, on March 14, 2000.

Raymond Kurzweil was born on February 12, 1948 in New York City, the son of the composer Frederic Kurzweil. From an early age he knew that he wanted to be a scientist. He wrote his first software program when he was 12, and at age 13 he won an award for a database system he designed. When he was 16 Kurzweil designed a computer program that analyzed patterns in the compositional styles of various composers and then composed new works in those styles. The project won him first prize from among 65,000 applicants in the International Science Fair and inclusion among the 40 winners of the Westinghouse Science Talent Search; as a Westinghouse winner, he was invited to the White House to meet President Lyndon B. Johnson. Kurzweil was also invited to play one of his computer-composed pieces on Steve Allen's *I've Got a Secret* television game show.

Kurzweil entered the Massachusetts Institute of Technology (MIT), in Cambridge, when its computer science program was still in its infancy. The school offered only eight or nine computer- science classes and had only one computer, shared among all the students and faculty. After having taken all the computer science courses available, Kurzweil turned to creative writing in his sophomore year, studying under the writer Lillian Hellman. He soon earned the nickname "the Phantom" for his habit of missing classes in order to work on his own projects. One such project, begun in his sophomore year, was the Expert System for College Selection (SELECT), which used an extensive database to help match students to their ideal colleges. Using SELECT Kurzweil started a consulting company and regularly paid $1,000 per hour to access the only computer in New England powerful enough to run his program. He later sold SELECT to the publishing company Harcourt Brace World, for $100,000.

In 1970 Kurzweil earned a B.S. in computer science and literature from MIT. In 1974 he founded Kurzweil Computer Products (KCP) and began developing the first fully functional OCR system. Existing systems could recognize texts of a few select fonts, but by employing abstract pattern recognition software—similar to that which Kurzweil had designed for his music composition program—he and his team designed a system that could identify any font. Pattern recognition software enables computers to recognize abstract patterns in complex data (such as the various markings of letters on a page). This kind of activity is central to human thought processes but has proved challenging for machines. It was not until Kurzweil happened to be seated next to a blind person on a plane that he came up with the first practical application for his OCR system—a machine that could convert text to speech for blind people. In order to scan the selected print material into the machine, Kurzweil and his team designed the first CCD flatbed scanner (a Charge Coupled Device provides high-capacity memory storage); and in order to have the machine "read" the text they designed the first text-to-speech synthesizer. Kurzweil's Reading Machine was announced on January 13, 1976, and Walter Cronkite used it to deliver his signature sign-off, "And that's the way it was, January 13, 1976." The first Reading Machines sold for $50,000 and weighed 350 pounds.

In 1978 Kurzweil Computer Products introduced a commercial version of its OCR system, which was used by LexisNexis to build their on-line legal and news information databases. In 1980 Kurzweil sold KCP to the Xerox Corporation, which was interested in the scanning and OCR technologies. The OCR technology, renamed Text-Bridge by Xerox, continues to be a market leader. One of the first customers for Kurzweil's Reading Machine, in 1976, was the blind musician Stevie Wonder, and he and Kurzweil soon became friends. Wonder complained to Kurzweil that synthesized musical instruments, which he found useful for their accessibility and compositional flexibility, did not sound as good as the acoustic instruments upon which they were modeled. Kurzweil undertook the challenge to design electronic instruments that sounded like real instruments. In 1982 he founded Kurzweil Music Systems and Wonder joined him as a musical consultant. In 1984 the company came out with the Kurzweil 250, the first computer-based instrument—a keyboard—that could convincingly recreate the sounds of a grand piano, a guitar, a violin, and a range of other instruments. In blind tests many musicians were unable to tell the difference between the Kurzweil and the actual instruments. The Kurzweil 250 revolutionized the music industry; one is on display at the Smithsonian Institute, in Washington, D.C. In 1990 Kurzweil sold the company to the Korean musical instrument manufacturer Young Chang, which still sells keyboards under the Kurzweil name.

In the same year that he started Kurzweil Music Systems Kurzweil also founded Kurzweil Applied Intelligence, a company dedicated to developing an electronic speech- recognition system. Early systems responded to a limited vocabulary and required users to pause between words. In 1985 the company introduced VoiceMed, which allowed doctors to dictate medical reports into computers. The product, now called the Kurzweil Clinical Reporter, is used in 10 percent of U.S. emergency rooms. In 1987 Kurzweil Applied Intelligence introduced the first large-vocabulary computerized speech-recognition system. The company was sold in 1997.

Kurzweil's first book, *The Age of Intelligent Machines*, was published in 1990. It explored the philosophical and mathematical roots of AI and offered predictions for future technological innovations. Many of his predictions— including the creation of the World Wide Web, the winning of the world chess championship by a computer, and the widespread use of computer-guided weapons in warfare—have already proved accurate. During an interview with Glenn Rifkin for *Computerworld* (March 18, 1991), not long after the publication of *Intelligent Machines*, Kurzweil argued that computers would soon exceed human intelligence. "Once a computer can emulate essential human functionality," he said, "it can then combine that with the enormous superiority it is already displaying in its ability to remember billions or trillions of facts with extreme precision, to access that information at extremely high speed and to perform functions over and over again very quickly. If it can read a book, there's nothing to stop it from reading every book that's ever been published and all magazines and technical journals and from mastering all human knowledge. So once it reaches equality with human intelligence in some areas, it is necessarily going to be greatly superior to human intelligence in other areas." *The Age of Intelligent Machines* was named the most outstanding computer science book of 1990 by the Association of American Publishers.

In 1993, after curing himself of type 2 diabetes through a nutrition regimen, Kurzweil published *The 10% Solution for a Healthy Life, How to Eliminate Virtually All Risk of Heart Disease and Cancer*. In 1995 he founded Kurzweil Technologies, a software company that developed, among other things, Ray Kurzweil's Cybernetic Poet, a program that assists poets by suggesting rhymes, alliterations, and even authoring entire poems in the styles of various poets. In 1996 he founded Kurzweil Educational Systems, a developer of computer-based educational products (including a new generation of reading machines) designed to help people with reading disabilities and vision impairment. Kurzweil and his associates at Kurzweil Educational Systems received the Stevie Wonder "Product of the Year" Vision Award for the Kurzweil 1000 Reading System, in August 1998, after which the company was sold.

Kurzweil used one of his speech recognition systems to author much of his next book, *The Age of Spiritual Machines: When Computers Exceed Human Intelligence* (1999), which attempts to predict the course of computer technology and AI through 2099. By the end of the 21st century, Kurzweil asserts, it will be possible to scan people's brains into digital form and thus create a digital clone of a human being. A person's brain, thus computerized, will function as "software" that can be placed at will in a variety of different "hardware" systems, for example a perfectly engineered, humanoid body form. The distinction between humans and computers will blur, and people will have computers in their brains and bodies to supplement their own innate intellectual and physical capacities. In less than 50 years, he states, a potent form of virtual reality will be available by taking a pill consisting of billions of nanobots, or microscopic computers, that will attach to all the nerve fibers emanating from the sensory organs and, when activated, replace brain signals with computer-generated scenarios. Computers, Kurzweil claims, will also have spiritual capacities and will even pray, because the portions of our brains that control spirituality will be fully mapped.

Critical responses to *The Age of Spiritual Machines* varied widely. In *Library Journal* (December 1998) Joe J. Accardi wrote, "This superb work is a thoughtful melding of technology, philosophy, ethics, and humanism." Other critics, however, were unconvinced that computers can ever be as fully conscious as humans. In *Fortune* (February 1, 1999) Richard A. Shaffer wrote, "The reason computers don't yet have the intelligence of a child isn't that our electronic circuits aren't fast enough. Thought is more than the manipulation of symbols. Contrary to what Kurzweil envisions, the state of every atom inside a living skull will never be determined and programmed into a computer. But if this were possible, the effort would reveal no more of that brain's thoughts than a circuit diagram of a radio reveals about the music playing on it. The real reason we can't yet turn a machine into a mind: We don't know how. We never will." Oliver G. Selfridge, a pioneer in the AI field, wrote in *Psychology Today* (September/October 1999), "There is a vast gulf between a computer's cognitive skills, reasoning powers and problem-solving capabilities and those supposedly unique human qualities of common sense, having fun, seeking beauty, knowing right from wrong, and so on. Are these to be programmed in, or can the computer attain them by itself? How? Are they to be learned by example? From whom or what? This miraculous technology may be developed eventually, but, right now, it's unfair to make claims about the ease of such miracles without having performed at least one of them—which we haven't."

Also in 1999 Kurzweil founded Financial Accelerating Transactions—Kurzweil Adaptive Technologies (FAT KAT) and began developing software to analyze the stock market using algorithms based on evolutionary models. After the publication of *The Age of Spiritual Machines* Kurzweil became increasingly well known for his provocative ideas about future technologies, a subject he expounded in various interviews and articles. In *Time* (June 19, 2000), for example, he wrote about the melding of computers and humans. "By the second half of the 21st century, there will be no clear distinction between the two," Kurzweil wrote. "On the one hand, we will have biological brains greatly expanded through distributed nanobot-based implants. On the other, we will have fully nonbiological brains that are copies of human brains but vastly extended. And we will have a myriad of other varieties of intimate connection between human thinking and the technology it has fostered. Although some contemporary observers consider the prospect of merging with our technology disconcerting, I believe that by the time we get there, most of us will find it very natural to expand in this way our experiences, our minds and our possibilities." In an interview for *Technology Review* (January/February 2000) Kurzweil was asked whether he would be eager to have his own brain copied onto a hard drive. "It's a difficult question," he said. "You could scan my brain while I'm sleeping and recreate this new nonbiological Ray Kurzweil, which could come to me in the morning and say, 'Hey Ray, good news. We've successfully copied and reinstantiated your brain and body, we don't need your old brain and body anymore.' I might see some flaw in that philosophical perspective. I'll wish the new Ray well and I'll probably end up being jealous of him because he'll be able to succeed in endeavors I could only dream of, but I'm still here in my old biological body and brain. It's not clear how one gets over that divide to the other side—I haven't quite figured that out yet, but I do hope to see the era."

Kurzweil is married to Sonya R. Kurzweil, a child psychologist. The couple live in Massachusetts. Among Kurzweil's many awards and honors are the Governor's Award of Massachusetts, 1977; the Computer Science Award, presented by then-President Ronald Reagan, 1982; the Best of the New Generation Award from *Esquire* magazine, 1984; the White House Award for Entrepreneurial Excellence, 1986; the Inventor of the Year Award presented jointly by MIT, the Boston Museum of Science, and the Boston Patent Law Association, 1988; the Founders Award of MIT, 1989; the Engineer of the Year Award from *Design News*, 1990; Carnegie Mellon University's Dickson Prize, 1994; the Access Prize of the American Foundation for the Blind, 1995; and the President's Award from the Association on Higher Education and Disability (AHEAD), 1997. In 1986 he served as the Honorary Chairman for Innovation for the White House Conference on Small Business. He has also been awarded nine honorary doctorates.—P. G. H.

Suggested Reading: *Boston Globe* B p37 May 17, 1992; *Computerworld* p33 Mar. 10, 1986, p75+ Mar. 18, 1991; *Fortune* p124 Feb. 1, 1999, p252+ Oct. 9, 2000; *Futurist* p16+ Nov. 1999; *Microcomputer News* p18 June 17, 1976; *Technology Review* p80+ Jan./Feb. 2000; *Time* p82+ June 19, 2000, p102 Dec. 4, 2000; *USA Today* (on-line) Mar. 14, 2000; *Wall Street Journal* B p10 Feb. 26, 2001

Lake, Clair D.

1888–1958 Engineer; inventor

The engineer and inventor Clair D. Lake played a leading role in the development of the Harvard Mark I, the first large-scale, automatic, general-purpose, electromechanical computer. Also known as the Automatic Sequence Controlled Calculator (ASCC), it was the first machine that could execute long computations automatically. When it was unveiled to the public in August 1944, the *New York Times* (August 7, 1944) touted it as "an algebraic super-brain," and today many computer historians see it as one of the most important predecessors of the modern computer. A remarkable achievement in electromechanical engineering, the Mark I stood eight feet tall, 51 feet long, and weighed approximately five tons. Although the electronic computers that followed shortly thereafter were much faster, the Mark I could operate continuously for days, did not require periods of downtime and produced notably reliable results. The project was initiated in the late 1930s by the mathematician and Harvard professor Howard Aiken, inspired by Charles Babbage's work on computational devices a century earlier. When Aiken brought his proposal to International Business Machines (IBM) in 1937, the project was placed under the direction of Lake, assisted by the engineers Francis E. (Frank) Hamilton and Benjamin M. Durfee—and marked IBM's first foray into the computer business.

Clair D. Lake was born in 1888. He was one of IBM's senior engineers and inventors in the 1930s, having designed IBM's first printing tabulator in 1919 and patented the rectangular hole in the punched cards used by the company's machines. He had come to IBM (at that time known as the Computing-Tabulating-Recording Company, or C-T-R) in 1915 from the automotive field. His "credentials were based on performance, not education," J. A. N. Lee noted in the *International Biographical Dictionary of Computer Pioneers* (1995), referring to the fact that Lake, after eighth grade, had attended a manual training school rather than a traditional high school.

Aiken was a Ph.D. student at Harvard University, in Cambridge, Massachusetts. The idea for the machine had grown out of his frustration, when working towards his master's degree in physics, with the long sequences of tedious and error-prone calculations that his mathematical derivations frequently required. "There exist problems beyond our ability to solve, not because of theoretical difficulties, but because of insufficient means of mechanical computation," Aiken wrote in his proposal, as quoted on the Computer Museum of America Web site. Aiken fortuitously discovered the writings of the 19th-century British inventor Charles Babbage, whose work on such computational devices as the Difference Engine and the Analytical Engine inspired Aiken to devise his own calculating machine. Aiken surmised that it would be possible to assemble a collection of commercial desk calculators into one machine, a super-calculator that could perform long sequences of tabulations. He soon came to the conclusion, however, that to build the computer he wanted, simple mathematical functions would not be sufficient, since the features required for scientific calculating were different from those of common accounting machines. Aiken's proposal called for a machine that would be able to compute both positive and negative numbers, to perform trigonometric functions, and to operate automatically once set in operation.

Lake and his team constructed the Mark I to meet Aiken's specifications. The computer was electromechanical and made use of the basic mechanical components used in IBMs accounting machines. In addition to magnetized coils and electromagnetically controlled relays and gears, the Mark I contained mechanical registers for storing numbers. The machine was constructed out of switches, relays, rotating shafts, and clutches—in total it had about 750,000 different parts, 1,000 ball bearings, 500 miles of wire, and was driven by a five-horsepower electric motor. When it was operating, it was described as making the sound of a "roomful of ladies knitting," as quoted by Martin Campbell-Kelly and William Aspray in *Computer: A History of the Information Machine* (1996). Programs were entered using punched data cards and long strips of paper tape about three inches wide. Although a specially trained mathematician was needed to prepare the programs, the machine's operator did not need to possess any mathematical ability.

Like Babbage's Difference Engine, the Mark I was engineered to calculate the elements of navigational and mathematical tables. It could solve an addition problem in less than a second, but it required about six seconds for multiplication and twice as long for division. The machine could also execute elementary, trigonometric, and hyperbolic functions by consulting logarithmic and other functional tables that were either built into the system's hardware library or entered as programs. The results of such computations were accurate up to 23 decimal places.

Construction of the Mark I began at IBM's Endicott Laboratory in New York in 1939 and was completed, after several delays, in 1943. The cost was reportedly between $250,000 and $500,000. As World War II progressed, the U.S. Navy took an interest in the project, and offered financial backing under the heading of "strategic wartime work." After the initial development phase, Aiken's role was primarily that of a consultant. A naval reserve officer, he was called to active duty in May 1941, after which he was largely uninvolved in the details of design and engineering. (The Harvard Mark I is not related to another computer of the same name, built in Great Britain by Tom Kilburn in the late 1940s. Known as the Manchester Mark 1, Kilburn's computer was entirely electronic and the first computer to store data and programs in the same location.)

At the completion ceremony in August 1944, when IBM presented the computer to Harvard University, Aiken issued a press release that failed to give proper credit to the IBM engineers who had spent years on the project. As Aiken was responsible for the idea behind the machine, he considered himself the primary inventor. However, as Bernard Cohen wrote in *Howard Aiken: A Portrait of a Computer Pioneer*, as quoted by Lawrence Hunter for the *New York Times Book Review* (September 12, 1999), "Without [the engineers'] experience and inventive skill, Aiken's ideas would never have been translated into a working device." Aiken also neglected to mention that IBM had funded the project. Thomas J. Watson Sr., the founder and CEO of IBM, piqued at the insult, reportedly told Aiken, as quoted by *Computerworld* (November 3, 1986): "You can't put IBM on as a postscript. I think about IBM as you Harvard fellows do about your university."

Although the Harvard Mark I was not particularly fast, even according to the standards of its day, it was the first fully automatic analytic computer to become entirely operational. It convinced others in the field that large-scale calculating machines were possible and practical, and inspired such early computer pioneers as Grace Murray Hopper. It also carried a certain symbolic importance in the blossoming computer era—such as that attached to it by the leading British computer expert L. C. Comrie, who memorably dubbed the machine "Babbage's Dream Come True."—A. I. C.

Suggested Reading: *Computerworld* p182 Nov. 3, 1986; *New York Times* p17 Aug. 7, 1944; *New York Times Book Review* p38 Sep. 12, 1999; Lee, J. A. N., ed. *International Biographical Dictionary of Computer Pioneers*, 1995; Campbell-Kelly, Martin and William Aspray. *Computer: A History of the Information Machine*, 1996

Hulton Archive by Getty Images

Lamarr, Hedy

Nov. 9, 1913–Jan. 19, 2000 Actress; originator of frequency hopping

Most people remember Hedy Lamarr as one of the most beautiful and glamorous actresses in Hollywood, a screen siren second to none in the 1930s and '40s. Initially notorious for appearing naked in a 1933 Czech film, she was dubbed by the media "the most beautiful girl in the world" after appearing in such Hollywood pictures as *Algiers* (1938), *The Strange Woman* (1946), and *Samson and Deli-*

lah (1949). What few people know about Lamarr is that she helped develop an idea during World War II that impacts information technology to this day. During her first marriage, to the Austrian arms manufacturer Fritz Mandl, she was privy to information about Nazi weaponry, including their military's ability to jam radio-controlled torpedoes. After leaving Mandl and coming to the United States, she came in contact with George Antheil, an avant-garde composer. At a party one night they began discussing the possibility of quickly switching a torpedo's frequency to prevent jamming. Though their invention was never used during World War II, it later served the United States during the 1962 Cuban Missile Crisis. Today frequency hopping, as the technique is commonly called, is used in most high-speed communications, including cellular phones and other wireless devices. In 1977 Lamarr and Antheil were recognized by the Electric Frontier Foundation, an influential lobby, for their contributions to modern telecommunications.

Hedy Lamarr was born Hedwig Eva Maria Kiesler in Vienna, Austria, on November 9, 1913, the daughter of a wealthy banker and a concert pianist. During her youth she was educated by private tutors and studied at elite private schools in Vienna. She also studied acting with the noted Austrian director Max Reinhardt, in Vienna, who while watching her read lines one day, pronounced her to be "the most beautiful girl in the world." This idea was seconded by Louis B. Mayer, one of the founders of Metro-Goldwyn-Mayer (MGM) movie studio, a few years later and widely repeated by the press.

In 1931 she began appearing in German and Czech films, the best-known of which is the 1933 picture *Extase* (*Ecstacy*), in which she appears nude. The film caused a sensation in Europe, where it made the rounds at the film festivals, but controversy followed it, and it was denounced by Pope Pius XI. Male viewers flocked to see it, however, a situation which so enraged Fritz Mandl that he attempted to buy up as many copies as possible. As Richard Severo noted in the *New York Times* (January 20, 2000): "[Mandl] explained that it was not so much because his wife could be seen nude, but because of the look on her face during the sex scenes." (According to legend, that look was contrived by the director sticking pins in Lamarr's posterior.) Mandl's obsession with his wife soon extended to their everyday life; he rarely allowed her to leave his side and ordered the house servants to spy on her. She was forced to endure endless business dinners during which armaments were the central topic of conversation. Distressed that her husband had business dealings with the fascist governments in Germany and Italy, she learned a great deal about the Axis war machine during these dinners. After four years with Mandl, she made her escape by excusing herself from dinner one night, drugging her maid with sleeping pills, and crawling out her bathroom window.

The actress made her way to London, England, where she met Mayer for the first time. The prudish studio head knew her from *Extase* and believed that she could be a star in "more wholesome" American movies. He offered her a $500-a-week contract and suggested she change her name from Hedwig Keisler to Hedy Lamarr, in tribute to the late silent-film star Barbara La Marr, whom he greatly admired. Lamarr arrived by ship in New York, in 1937; *Extase* had arrived three years earlier and, while not seen by the majority of Americans, it greatly impressed those who had viewed it. Intent on making a name for herself as a serious actress, she refused requests from reporters—who met her ship at the dock—to show her knees.

Co-starring Charles Boyer, Lamarr's first American film, *Algiers*, was hugely successful, even though her command of the English language was somewhat faulty. Columbia University undergraduates voted her their dream "desert island" girl in a poll; she was equally popular with women, many of whom copied her hairstyle (parted down the middle). She even influenced comic books: the original rendition of the *Batman* villain known as the Catwoman was based on Lamarr.

Lamarr starred opposite some of the biggest male stars of the era, including Robert Taylor, in *Lady of the Tropics* (1939); Spencer Tracy, in *I Take This Woman* (1940) and *Tortilla Flat* (1942); Clark Gable, in *Comrade X* (1940); and James Stewart, in the *Ziegfield Girl* (1941) and *Come Live With Me* (1941). Many of Lamarr's roles painted her solely as a seductive beauty, leaving her little room to display her acting ability. "Any girl can be glamorous," she once remarked, as cited by the *German-Hollywood Connection* (on-line). "All you have to do is stand still and look stupid." Although critics of that era often found her talents lacking, she did occasionally receive good reviews, particularly in films such as *Ziegfield Girl* and *H. M. Pulham, Esq.*

(1942), in which she played an independent career woman.

At one Hollywood dinner party, in 1940, at the home of the actress Janet Gaynor, Lamarr met George Antheil. They began discussing how difficult it would be for the Allies to stop the Nazi war machine, a topic about which Lamarr was familiar—thanks to the frequent dinner conversations between Mandl and his fascist clients. She recalled that the Nazis were attempting to find ways to jam radio-controlled torpedoes to cause them to explode early or miss their targets. She knew the Allies needed to build a countermeasure device that would protect torpedoes from attempts to jam them, and she believed that a device could be built that sent radio signals over quickly changing frequencies, thereby preventing an enemy from finding the right frequency to jam the torpedo. She realized the signal would have to be picked up by a receiver inside the torpedo that could switch frequencies to match those of the transmitter, but she lacked the technical know-how to build such a device.

Antheil was intrigued by Lamarr's idea and suggested that they work together. She agreed and reportedly made the flamboyant gesture of scrawling her phone number in lipstick on his car's windshield. An extremely experimental composer, Antheil had once scored a composition for four xylophones, 16 player pianos, two airplane propellers, four bass drums, and a siren. In order to keep the player pianos in time, he used punched tape to synchronize them and felt that such an approach could also effectively synchronize the transmitter and receiver for the torpedo-control system. He and Lamarr worked out a system in which two rolls of paper, with identical patterns of random holes, were used. One would be placed in the transmitter on the submarine; the other in the receiver on the torpedo itself. (They used 88 frequencies, matching the number of keys on a piano.) On August 11, 1942 Lamarr and Antheil received their patent—No. 2,292,387—for a "Secret Communications System."

They sent their idea to the National Inventors Council, a wartime Commerce Department division that had been created to evaluate ideas from the public, and offered it to the U.S. government free of charge. Government officials, however, felt they had no use for what they believed would be a cumbersome device. In the paperwork for their patent, Lamarr and Antheil had explained that the rolls of paper would be similar to those found in a player piano. Antheil later recalled (as quoted in the *World Press Review* in July 1997): "The brass hats in Washington who examined our invention could only focus on two words: player piano. I heard them all say: 'My God, how are we going to fit a player piano in a torpedo?'"

Lamarr was told that she could better serve her adopted country by encouraging people to buy war bonds. She eventually sold millions of dollars worth of the bonds at rallies where she claimed to be "just a gold digger for Uncle Sam." She also continued to make movies; two of her most notable came in the postwar period: *The Strange Woman* (1946), which many critics have called her finest performance, and *Samson and Delilah* (1949), a Cecil B. De Mille epic featuring Lamarr as the biblical seductress. In the 1950s she starred in such films as the *Copper Canyon* (1950), with Ray Milland; *My Favorite Spy* (1951), with Bob Hope; and *The Face That Launched a Thousand Ships* (1953), in which she portrayed Helen of Troy. After her last starring role, in the 1957 film *The Female Animal*, Lamarr retired from acting.

Lamarr and Antheil's invention languished in the government's files for almost two decades, and their patent eventually expired. When early computer processors made synchronizing the hopping sequence more viable, in the late 1950s, the U.S. military began to use the technology. During the 1962 Cuban Missile Crisis, the United States Armed Forces used frequency hopping in conjunction with mainframe computers to protect their communications from the Soviet Union. As communications expanded in the subsequent decades, frequency hopping was used in satellite communications systems to secure communication links worldwide. In the 1990s frequency hopping began to be used in the commercial arena. As explained by Peter Y. Hong in *Microwave Journal* (February 1999): "Interest in frequency hopping grew because it is one way to enable multiple users to share a single radio frequency—an important task as more and more pagers, cellular phones, and other devices crowd the limited airwave space."

Little was heard from Lamarr after her retirement from the film industry; she made some appearances on television programs, but was mainly in the news in her later years because of brushes with the court system. In 1965 she was arrested on shoplifting charges in a Los Angeles department store, but was later acquitted. (She sued the store, but the lawsuit was subsequently dismissed.) A year later she published a revealing autobiography, *Ecstasy and Me: My Life as a Woman*, which detailed her sex life in graphic detail, and she sued her ghostwriters and publisher for misrepresentation. In the 1970s she made headlines again by suing the director Mel Brooks for using a character named "Hedley Lamarr" in his comic film *Blazing Saddles*; the case was eventually settled.

By the early 1990s she was living in south Florida off a Screen Actors Guild pension. In 1991 she was again arrested, for shoplifting a few dollars' worth of merchandise from a drug store; she was placed on a one-year probation. During this period she was reportedly legally blind and rarely ventured out alone. In March 1997 she and George Antheil (who died in 1959) were finally formally acknowledged for their development of frequency hopping with an Electronic Frontier Foundation Pioneer Award. Lamarr's only public comment on the award, as reported by *Scientific American* (April 1998), was "It's about time."

Hedy Lamarr died on January 19, 2000 in Orlando, Florida. Married and divorced six times, she had two children, Anthony and Denise, with her third husband, John Loder, a British actor she had wed in 1943. Lamarr also had one adopted son, James.—C. M.

Selected Reading: *German-Hollywood Connection* (on-line); Internet Movie Database Web site; *Microwave Journal* p70+ Feb. 1999; *New York Times* B p15 Jan. 20, 2000; *People* p107 Feb. 7, 2000; *Scientific American* p95 Apr. 1998; *Vanity Fair* p414 Apr. 1999; *World Press Review* p34+ July 1997

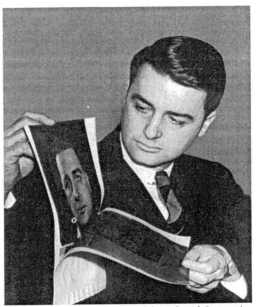

Courtesy of the Polaroid Corporation

Land, Edwin H.

May 7, 1909–Mar. 1, 1991 Founder of the Polaroid Corporation

Edwin H. Land, who founded and led the Polaroid Corporation for more than 40 years, was a creative visionary as well as a down-to-earth pragmatic. He was a scientist, inventor, businessman, philanthropist, and educator, whose work resulted in a wide variety of products and processes. His invention of the light-polarizing plastic named Polaroid led to such products as polarized sun glasses, equipment for 3-D movies, antiglare products, liquid crystal displays (LCDs), and photography filters. However, of Land's 530 patents, the ones pertaining to instant, one-step photography brought him international renown. After five years of experimenting, Land and the Polaroid Corporation introduced the first instant camera, in 1948. Through a complex process involving exploding pods of developing chemicals, the new machine produced a finished, sepia-toned picture in just 60 seconds. It took Land and his associates another 12 years to master instant color photography.

During the years of Land's tenure, the Polaroid Corporation exemplified its founder's best characteristics: inventiveness, tenacity, hard work, and the ability to communicate. Working out of a private laboratory adjacent to his office at Polaroid, Land pioneered such innovations as infrared polarizers, heat-stable filters, infrared night goggles, and optical systems for high-altitude surveillance. As the guiding spirit of Polaroid from 1937 until his retirement, in 1980, Land saw the company's sales climb from $142,000 to more than $1 billion, its stock quoted on the New York Stock Exchange, and its inclusion as one of *Fortune*'s 500 companies. From his retirement to his death in 1991, he was the director and chief researcher for the Rowland Institute for Science, where researchers have worked on a wide range of subjects related to color vision, including the development of microscopic laser "tweezer" beams.

Edwin Herbert Land was born in Bridgeport, Connecticut, on May 7, 1909, the son of Harry M. Land, a successful scrap-metal dealer, and Martha F. Land. Young Edwin had a great interest in physics and photography, which his mother encouraged, and slept with a copy of R. W. Wood's *Physical Optics* (1905) under his pillow. In an interview with Philip Taubman of *Time* (June 26, 1972), he recalled how he was particularly interested in photography. "To a child," he said, "a photograph gives a permanent thing that is both outside himself and part of himself." The first picture that he developed as a child was of the family's French poodle, which was constantly running away. But the photograph made a difference: "There I had him. He couldn't get away."

At Norwich Academy, in Norwich, Connecticut, Land achieved a nearly perfect academic record, showing a special aptitude for physics, and was a member of the debating team and the track team. Graduating from the academy in 1926, he entered Harvard University, where he continued the research and experiments begun in his home laboratory, on polarization phenomena that led to his contributions to optics and his first inventions.

When Land began his experiments, the only available light polarizers were fragile and expensive crystals, despite widespread recognition that a synthetic polarizer would have many and various scientific applications. Inspired by contemporary interest in a "plane polarizer"—a substance that would transmit light waves in a straight line instead of around all the planes of an axis—Land left Harvard to pursue his research. He took a small apartment on West 55th Street, in New York City, spending his time doing library research and, with the help of a friend at Columbia University, using the university's research labs. He formulated a possible solution—orienting many small crystals of iodoquinine sulfate in a synthetic sheet—and set out

to solve the associated problems. "In my then youthful innocence," he has recalled in a discussion of his work, "it seemed to me that these problems could be solved in a rather short time, perhaps in a few months." A year and a half later Land returned to Harvard, and after further work in a laboratory there, presented his ideas in a paper, "A New Polarizer for Light in the Form of an Extensive Synthetic Sheet," at a colloquium of the physics department in 1932.

Instead of remaining at Harvard to graduate, Land joined George Wheelwright III, a Harvard physics instructor, in setting up the Land-Wheelwright Laboratories in Boston, Massachusetts, in 1932. At first their partnership was a consulting firm not exclusively concerned with Land's polarizer, but by 1934 the company was manufacturing the Polaroid J-sheet, as the first polarizer was called, for commercial uses. The Land polarizer quickly became popular because it had many attractive features: it was thin, inexpensive, and could be easily cut to any size or shape. Land also developed other sheet polarizers, which introduced substances besides crystals and which quickly became useful in colloid chemistry and other fields of science. They also had commercial applications: Eastman Kodak began using polarized filters in its cameras in 1935, and the American Optical Company began marketing polarized sunglasses in 1936. Polarizers for automobile headlights, to reduce glare and make night driving safer, had been one of Land's early objectives in his research. But auto manufacturers declined to make use of them, because, according to *Time* (June 26, 1972), "polarizing sheets deteriorated when exposed to heat." Today, however, such polarizers have found use in new applications, including screens to reduce the glare from computer screens and other visual-display units.

Separating from Wheelwright in 1937, Land founded the Polaroid Corporation in Cambridge, Massachusetts, with the financial backing of a number of Wall Street businessmen, including W. Averell Harriman and Lewis Strauss. Although the hoped-for application of headlight polarizers did not materialize, Polaroid prospered during World War II. Together with his research associates, Land invented a number of weapons improvements, including optical elements for use in infrared night-vision instruments and an optical sighting mechanism. He served as a consultant to the Navy on guided missiles and to the National Defense Research Council and participated in a project to create computerized thermal homing heads for 1,000-pound bombs. The Polaroid Corporation produced filters for goggles, gunsights, periscopes, range finders, aerial cameras, and the Norden bombsight.

Unlike many companies bound to wartime contracts, Polaroid did not suffer a prolonged decline with the end of hostilities. The return of peace encouraged Land to carry to fruition an idea that had preoccupied him since 1943. On vacation in New

Mexico that year he took a picture of his three-year-old daughter, who then asked him why she could not see the picture right away. Pondering her question as he walked around Santa Fe for an hour, he envisioned a camera and film that would produce an immediate photograph. Many years later he referred to that event when explaining "cumulative creativity" in an interview for *Life* (October 27, 1972): "All that we at Polaroid had learned about making polarizers and plastics, and the properties of viscous liquids, and the preparation of microscopic crystals . . . was preparation for that day in which I suddenly knew how to make a one-step photographic process."

In February 1947 Land demonstrated his revolutionary process with a working model of his camera at the American Optical Society. Polaroid's product first reached the market at Christmas in 1948—Model 95, which weighed about four pounds and made sepia-toned prints. Although the Polaroid Land Camera, as it was called, underwent many refinements since its inception, its main principles held for some time. The photosensitive element used was a silver halide emulsion. A full-size negative was exposed when the picture was snapped, and it was brought into contact with a positive print sheet. Rollers through which the sheet was drawn ruptured a pod of developing reagent and spread it evenly across the surface. The jellied compound developed the negative and positive prints simultaneously, and the photo was finished—a minute afterward in the early models, a few seconds in later ones. The first Land camera, in addition to making the first practical use of "dry" processing, incorporated an "exposure value system" that simplified the calculation of aperture and shutter speed to the single adjustment of a dial and has since become a standard feature on many cameras.

An immediate commercial success that brought sales of about $5 million in its first year, the Land Camera, as a writer for *American Photography* commented in March 1949, "has certainly opened up new opportunities for photographers which many of them have not been slow to embrace." Although some professional photographers were said to dismiss the new camera as a high-priced toy, it soon found many applications in science, industry, the military, and medicine. It was adapted to X rays, and more sophisticated models became available for use in aerial photography, real estate photography, and commercial and press photography. Black-and-white film replaced the sepia prints in 1950, and faster developing film was introduced in 1955.

Another idea of Land's, the Vectograph, became especially lucrative for Polaroid in the early 1950s, with the sudden and immense popularity of 3-D movies. The Vectograph, which Land and the Czech scientist Joseph Mahler had conceived of in 1937, is an image rendered in terms of the percentage of polarization, rather than in dyes. It could then superimpose two images on a single sheet of film, thereby rendering a stereoscopic picture. In collaboration with Mahler, who joined the Polaroid laboratories in 1940, Land used the Vectograph in the process of making stereoscopic pictures to obtain a three-dimensional image. Vectographs were used during the war, most notably in a survey of the French coast prior to the Normandy Invasion by Allied forces on D-Day (June 6, 1944). They were also later used in X-ray work, as well as during the 3-D movie fad of the 1950s. (Polaroid manufactured about 100 million of the special polarized glasses for viewing such movies.) Today vectography is still used by the American military in aerial photography as well as satellite reconnaissance.

With the introduction, in 1963, of color film for Land cameras, the inventor achieved a goal toward which he had been working for many years. Also important was the related outcome of Land's extensive experiments in color perception, which led him to challenge the classical theory of color vision—that the color perceived depends on the relative amounts of blue, green, and red light reaching the eye. He proposed, ultimately, what he called the retinex theory. The experiments, carried out by Land and his collaborators during the 1950s, were described in Land's article in the May 1959 issue of *Scientific American*. He demonstrated what he believed were inconsistencies in the generally accepted theory, coming to the conclusion that color perception cannot be described in terms of an analysis of wavelengths of light.

To explain how a person sees the same colors or hues under different conditions of illumination, Land suggested that several hypothetical retinal-cortical mechanisms (retinexes) interpret color through their comparative interaction. Although not all scientists agreed that Land's theory was preferable, the experiments themselves were striking in conception. "Land's major contribution," Joseph J. Sheppard Jr. wrote in his *Human Color Perception* (1968), "has been to demonstrate the astonishing extent to which the human visual system is able to make adjustments in order to perceive object colors of all hues, even though the visual system receives incomplete color information."

The continual improvement of the Land camera through the 1960s and 1970s, together with the introduction of less expensive models, assured Polaroid's commercial appeal under Land's direction. The low-priced Swinger took small black-and-white instant photographs and retailed for about $20 when introduced in 1965. It was an immediate success that brought Polaroid into competition with the Instamatic of Eastman Kodak. Other models soon followed, and in 1969 an inexpensive camera that took color prints, the Colorpack II, also sold well.

Polaroid's sophisticated SX-70 camera, which went on sale in late 1972, required almost a decade to develop because of the technological innovations incorporated into its elaborate design. In previous Polaroid cameras a layer of paper had to be peeled away from the picture, but in the "no-garbage" SX-70, 17 layers of chemical compounds were built into the single sheet that became the finished photo. The self-developing print was ejected from the camera instantly after exposure and was gradually processed within minutes as an "opacifier" shielded the chemicals from light. The 26-ounce, four-by-seven-inch SX-70 was so small that Land had to equip it with an optical system using a series of precision mirrors. The battery that powered the camera was built into the film pack rather than into the camera.

Five new plants to manufacture and assemble the components of the SX-70 cost Polaroid $250 million out of the $500 million spent on the entire project. Previously the company had bought its film and camera components from other firms. Although Polaroid invested $20 million in advertising, it sold only about 700,000 SX-70 cameras during the first year they were marketed, instead of the several million it expected to sell. Land later said in an interview for *Forbes* (June 1, 1975) that several small problems for the customer, one of them with focusing, affected the sales and that in introducing the SX-70, the company "did underestimate how infinitely important a small amount of instruction is." Even though its initial low sales disturbed Polaroid's hitherto virtually unqualified record of success, the SX-70 eventually became a best-seller.

Another of Land's long-cherished objectives, an instant-movie-camera system, which he introduced in 1977, never proved itself in the marketplace. Polavision consisted of a handheld camera and a viewer, which together had a list price of $675, and a two-minute-40-second film cartridge, costing $9.95. It provided no sound. An unfavorable market for home movies and competition from videotape cameras (which boasted long-playing, compact, and recordable magnetic tapes with sound) forced Polaroid to write off its entire Polavision inventory as of September 1979.

In early March 1980 Land, who had retired as his company's president in May 1975, announced that he would step aside as chief executive officer, turning that position over to William J. McCune Jr., his successor as president. For the next two years he continued to serve as chairman of the board as well as the company's director of research. After leaving Polaroid, in 1982, he devoted most of his time to scientific experiments at the Rowland Institute for Science in Cambridge, Massachusetts, a nonprofit center for basic research that he had founded in 1981. There he continued his research on color vision and oversaw the development of laser "tweezer" beams for manipulating microscopic organisms. He remained the institute's director and chief researcher until his death on March 1, 1991 in Cambridge, Massachusetts.

Edwin H. Land was a recipient of the Presidential Medal of Freedom (1963), the National Medal of Science (1967), and the National Medal of Technology (1988). Among his some 30 other medals and awards are the Rumford Medal of the

American Academy of Arts and Sciences (1945) and the Potts Medal of the Franklin Institute (1956). He held honorary doctoral degrees from Harvard, Yale, Columbia, and many other universities and colleges. Elected to the National Inventors Hall of Fame, in 1977, Land also belonged to the Optical Society of America, the American Academy of Arts and Sciences, of which he was once president, and several other learned societies. From 1956 to his death he was a fellow and visiting institute professor at the Massachusetts Institute of Technology. Land also taught at Harvard, where he was William James lecturer in Psychology from 1966–67 and Morris Loeb lecturer in physics, in 1974.

Married in 1929, Land and his wife, the former Helen (Terre) Maislen of Hartford, had two daughters, Jennifer and Valerie. Throughout his life Land avoided publicity and was often reported to be reclusive, although he belonged to many clubs. In *Time* he was described as looking "every inch the scientific genius," but when the *Forbes* interviewer asked him how he saw himself, Land replied, "I suppose that I am first of all an artistic person. I'm interested in love and affection and sharing and making beauty part of everyday life. And if I'm lucky enough to be able to earn my living by contributing to a warmer and richer world, then I feel that it is awfully good luck. And if I use all of my scientific, professional abilities in doing that, I think that makes for a good life."—C. M.

Suggested Reading: *Across the Board* p10 July–Aug. 1996; *Forbes* p34+ June 15, 1969, with photos, p48+ June 1, 1975, with photo; *Fortune* p66+ Apr. 7, 1980, with photos; *MIT Tech Talk* (on-line) Mar. 6, 1991; New York Times p57 Apr. 26, 1972, with photo; Polaroid Corporation Web Site; Rowland Institute for Science Web site; Tech Directions p16 Apr. 2000; *Time* p80+ June 26, 1972, with photo; *American Men and Women of Science*, 1979; Heyn, Ernest V. *Fire of Genius*, 1976

Langmuir, Irving

Jan. 31, 1881–Aug. 16, 1957 Nobel Prize–winning chemist; inventor

While Irving Langmuir may be best remembered for winning a 1932 Nobel Prize in Chemistry, he also made several notable contributions to the Information Age. The holder of more than 60 patents, he developed the gas-filled light bulb (which burned brighter and cleaner than its vacuum-based predecessor), as well as a high-vacuum radio tube, which served as the basis for radio transmissions until the development of the transistor.

Irving Langmuir was born in the New York City borough of Brooklyn, to Charles Langmuir and the former Sadie Comings. He was the third of four sons. His paternal grandfather was a minister who

Hans Kopf/Getty Images

Irving Langmuir

had emigrated from Scotland to Canada and later settled in Connecticut. Charles Langmuir, an insurance executive, had started as a clerk at the age of 14; he had made and lost a fortune by middle age. Sadie had long-standing roots in America and could trace her ancestors back to the *Mayflower*. The Langmuirs encouraged their children to look at life seriously and to record their observations in detailed diaries.

Langmuir did not enjoy his early public-school education in Brooklyn, and it has been theorized that he learned a great deal more in his parents' basement, where he and his older brother Arthur (who also went on to a career in chemistry) set up a workshop. In 1892 the family moved to Paris so Charles Langmuir could attend to his business interests there. Langmuir was sent to a boarding school on the outskirts of the city, and his brother helped him set up a makeshift laboratory next to his bedroom. Encouraged by one of his teachers, Langmuir taught himself logarithms and trigonometry. His mother proudly wrote to a friend of her 13-year-old son's intelligence, as quoted in a 1950 edition of *Current Biography*, "Irving's brain is working like an engine all the time, and it is wonderful to hear him talk with Herbert [another brother] on scientific subjects." At about this time Langmuir took up mountain climbing, and the sport became a lifelong passion.

The family stayed three years in Paris; on their return to the United States they settled in Philadelphia, where Langmuir studied at the prestigious Chestnut Hill Academy. He then attended the Pratt Institute, in Brooklyn, and in 1899 he received his bachelor's degree.

Entering Columbia University, in New York City, for postgraduate work, Langmuir enrolled in the School of Mines. As quoted in *Nobel Prize Winners* (1987), he explained, "The course was strong in chemistry. It had more physics than the chemical course, and more mathematics than the course in physics—and I wanted all three." In 1903 he received a metallurgical engineering degree and then went to Germany for graduate study at the University of Göttingen under the physical chemist Walther Nernst. At Göttingen Langmuir's research focused on the dissociation of various gases in contact with a glowing platinum wire, a topic closely related to his future industrial research in electric lighting. He was awarded a Ph.D. from Göttingen in 1906, after writing his dissertation on the actions of gasses while cooling.

Having been trained in both chemistry and mathematical physics, Langmuir now faced a choice. Should he begin his career in the high-paying field of commercial chemistry, as his elder brother Arthur had done, or should he devote his life to basic research? Choosing the latter, he returned to America and for three years served as an instructor in chemistry at the Stevens Institute of Technology, in Hoboken, New Jersey. His years at the Stevens Institute were unhappy ones. He found teaching rudimentary chemistry to apathetic students unsatisfying and bemoaned the endless piles of assignments waiting to be graded. Perhaps most dispiriting, he found little time to pursue his own research there.

Langmuir resigned from Stevens in the summer of 1909 and went to work at the research laboratory of the General Electric Company (GE), in Schenectady, New York. The General Electric laboratory, then under the direction of Willis R. Whitney, represented a new concept of industrial research. The electrical industry had initially capitalized on knowledge gathered by academic scientists in the 19th century. In that first decade of the new century, GE executives decided that the company itself should contribute to the advancement of scientific knowledge. Whitney, who had been recruited from the faculty of the Massachusetts Institute of Technology (MIT), in Cambridge, encouraged Langmuir to develop his own research program. "When I joined the laboratory," Langmuir said, as quoted in *Nobel Prize Winners* (1987), "I found that there was more academic freedom than I had ever encountered in any university." This freedom, paired with the laboratory's superb research facilities, provided Langmuir with challenging and important missions for the rest of his professional life.

His first major contributions to science were based on his doctoral research into the characteristics of filaments burned in various gases. Three years after joining GE, Langmuir challenged the notion, then common among lamp engineers, that a perfect vacuum would make a perfect lamp. He showed instead that a light bulb filled with nitrogen was stronger and brighter than any made to that date. The simple and efficient new bulb used less energy, which amounted to an aggregate consumer savings of $1 million per day in electric bills. (General Electric's profits from Langmuir's new bulb exceeded $58,000,000 in 1939 alone.)

Langmuir's interest in vacuum phenomena led to his 1916 invention of the high-vacuum mercury pump. In his book *Crucibles* (1930), Bernard Jaffe called it "the most perfect vacuum pump in existence." One hundred times more powerful than any previous pump, it enabled Langmuir to create the low pressures needed to manufacture the high-vacuum transmitting tubes then used in radio. His studies of the flow of electrons in high vacuums and gases also led to the development of a number of other electronic devices. Around this time Langmuir tested a strip of tungsten coated with thoria (an oxide of thorium) for its electron-emitting powers; he discovered that the filament behaved best if coated with a layer of thoria only one molecule thick. This finding led him to investigate surface phenomena, the molecular activity occurring in a thin film, or surface. In this virtually two-dimensional world he studied absorption and the surface tension and behavior of thin films on liquids and solids. Absorption—the power of certain materials to retain other molecules on their surfaces—had been investigated in the 19th century by the Scottish chemist James Dewar and by the American physicist Josiah Willard Gibbs, but a comprehensive and successful theory had not yet been proposed. Using insights gained from atomic theory, Langmuir described the chemical behavior of surfaces in terms of individual atoms and molecules assuming definite positions as if they were pieces on a chessboard. During World War I, when his research on surface chemistry was interrupted, Langmuir worked on submarine-detecting devices for the United States Navy.

After the war Langmuir became interested in atomic structure. His contributions to atomic theory stem from his fascination with the boundary between chemistry and physics. Langmuir advanced a theory describing chemical valence (the measurement of the differential tendency of atoms to combine) as the effect of electrons filling up electron "shells," or orbits, surrounding the atomic nuclei.

In 1923 Langmuir began a nine-year investigation of the properties of electronic discharges in gases. He coined the term "plasma" for the ionized gas he observed when he used extremely powerful alternating currents during his experiments. He also developed the concept of electron temperature, as well as a method of measuring both electron temperature and ion density with a special electrode, now called the Langmuir probe. The field of controlled thermonuclear fusion depends on the basic theories of plasma first reported by Langmuir.

After 15 years of experimentation with atomic hydrogen, in 1927 Langmuir developed the atomic hydrogen torch, a device able to weld metals that melt only at very intense temperatures. This invention was an extension of his work studying hydrogen at high temperatures, where he first observed that atoms disassociated, recombined, and caused a tremendous increase in heat conduction.

Langmuir received the 1932 Nobel Prize in Chemistry "for his outstanding discoveries and investigations within the field of surface chemistry," according the Nobel e-Museum Web site. His contributions to the chemistry of surface processes were of great importance in many technical fields: in biology, for the study of complex viruses; in chemistry, for the study of giant molecules; and in optics, for the study of the transmission of light. The same year that he received the Nobel Prize, Langmuir was named associate director of the GE laboratory.

From 1938 into his retirement years Langmuir devoted himself to studying the natural world, especially the atmosphere. He studied such phenomena as windrows, which are regular patterns of seaweed on the windblown surface of the sea, and cloud nucleation, which is the formation of liquid particles of various sizes in the air. During World War II he helped produce a smoke-making machine that was used to shield troops and ships from enemy observation. He also studied methods for preventing the formation of ice on airplanes. During the winter of 1945–46 Langmuir and Vincent Schaefer, a fellow GE chemist, conducted additional studies regarding the formation of ice on aircrafts and during this time they began to consider artificial snow and rainmaking. At a weather station on Mount Washington in New Hampshire, the duo seeded the super-cold air with dry ice and vaporized silver iodide in the hopes of sparking a chain reaction that would create snowflakes. The results of their experiments created violent thunderstorms when conditions were optimal. They continued these weather-control and rainmaking experiments in New Mexico in July 1949 as members of Project Cirrus, which worked under the joint cooperation of the Army Signal Corps, the Office of Naval Research, and GE.

In 1912 Langmuir married Marion Mersereau, with whom he shared interests in mountain climbing, sailing, aviation, and classical music. They adopted a son, Kenneth, and a daughter, Barbara. Much in demand as a lecturer, Langmuir enjoyed sharing his views on the philosophy of science and on the interrelationship of science and society. Langmuir died on August 16, 1957, at Woods Hole, Massachusetts.

In addition to the Nobel Prize, Langmuir received many other honors, including the Hughes Medal of the Royal Society of London (1918), the Rumford Medal of the American Academy of Arts and Sciences (1920), the Nichols Medal (1920) and Willard Gibbs Medal (1930) of the American Chemical Society, the Franklin Medal of the Franklin Institute (1934), and the Faraday Medal of the Institution of Electrical Engineers in London (1944). He was elected to the National Academy of Sciences and the Royal Society of London and served as president of the American Chemical Society (1929) and the American Association for the Advancement of Science (1941). He was the recipient of 15 honorary degrees. Mount Langmuir, in Alaska, is named for him, as is a residential college at the State University of New York at Stony Brook.—C. M.

Suggested Reading: *Current Biography Yearbook*, 1950; Great Chemists, 1961; Rosenfeld, A. *The Quintessence of Irving Langmuir*, 1966; Westervelt, V. *The Incredible Man of Science*, 1968; *Dictionary of Scientific Biography*, vol. 8, 1973; *Biographical Memoirs of the National Academy of Sciences*, vol. 45, 1974

Lebedev, S. A.

Nov. 2, 1902–July 3, 1974 Developer of the MESM

The Russian academician S. A. Lebedev was a pioneer in the field of digital computing, and he is generally considered to be the founder of the Soviet Union's computer industry. He is most well known for developing the first electronic digital stored-program computer in continental Europe, the MESM. (The full name translates in English to the Small Electronic Calculating Machine.) As the director of the Institute of Precise Mechanics and Computer Technology from 1953 to 1974, he oversaw the development of more than a dozen digital computers, including the BESM, BESM-2, M-20, M-40, M-50, and BESM-6. His book, *Stability of Parallel Work of Electrical Systems*, co-authored with A. S. Gdanov, was influential within the Soviet Union and reprinted in many other countries.

Sergei Alekseevich (sometimes spelled Alexseevich) Lebedev was born on November 2, 1902, in Nizhniy Novgorod (formerly Gorky), Russia. His was reportedly a disciplined but happy youth, and he excelled at swimming, chess, and science. When he was a child he once rigged a homemade electrical doorbell to his house. Lebedev graduated from the Moscow Higher Technical College (MHTC), in 1928, with a degree in electrical engineering. In 1934 he started teaching at MHTC and became a junior researcher at the V. I. Lenin All-Union Electrical Engineering Institute (known as the VEI), one of the Soviet Union's most prestigious scientific research institutions.

During World War II, known in Russia as the Great Patriotic War, Lebedev developed a method for stabilizing tank units that made it possible for soldiers to aim and shoot from a moving tank. Lebedev's wife, Alisa, once recalled, according to an article on the Web site of the International Charity Foundation for History and Development of Computer Science and Technique (ICFCST), that in the first months of the war, when Moscow was without electricity, Lebedev worked at night in the bathroom by the light of a gas burner. He was given prowess and patriotism awards for this work.

In May 1946 Lebedev, whose background was in high-voltage technology and power transmission, became the director of the Institute of Energy of the Ukrainian Academy of Science, in Kiev. Planning the country's power systems required complex calculations. Lebedev and his colleagues thus began to take an interest in digital computing. They debated the advantages and disadvantages of such concepts as floating-point arithmetic, word length, and different command-address structures. (Now commonly used in the computer industry, the floating-point system represents real numbers in scientific notation.) In late 1948 construction began on the MESM, and floating-point representation was discarded in favor of a simpler 17-bit fixed-point representation. Lebedev discussed the creation of the MESM in a 1957 address to the Coordination Council of the Academy of Science of the Union of Soviet Socialist Republics, as quoted on the ICFCST Web site: "I began to deal with high-speed electronic computers toward the end of 1948. From 1948 to 1949, I had elaborated the basic principles of building similar computers. Taking into account the great significance of the computer in economic development and also the absence in the Soviet Union of any kind of experience in the realm of computer construction and operation, I decided to create as quickly as possible a small electronic computer, with which we would be able to investigate the basic principles of computer building, examine strategies for the solving of certain associated problems and get experience in computer operation. In this connection, initially it was planned to create a working model of the machine and then develop it into a small electronic computer. To prevent a delay in the work, it was necessary to make a memory bank on flip-flop cells which, however, had limited memory capacity. The development of the basic elements was completed in 1948. . . . The general components of the machine and the principal circuit diagrams for its units were completed by the end of 1949 and by the end of 1950, the final adjustments on the working model were finished. After that, it was successfully demonstrated before a commission."

The work was not without problems. According to some reports when the MESM was tested for the first time, it generated so much heat that a portion of the laboratory's ceiling had to be knocked out for ventilation. At the time of the machine's completion, there were only two similar computers in operation. The Small-Scale Experimental Machine (SSEM), also known as the Manchester Baby, had been designed by Tom Kilburn and F. C. Williams; finished in June 1948, it was the world's first stored-program electronic digital computer. The Electronic Delay Storage Automatic Computer (EDSAC) was built at Cambridge University by Maurice Wilkes and completed in 1949. The MESM differed from these two machines, however, in that they both employed a sequential operational arithmetic unit, while the MESM worked on parallel arithmetic units. From 1951 to 1953, the

MESM was used to solve important problems in such areas as thermonuclear engineering, rocketry, space flights, and long-distance electrical transmission.

In 1950 Lebedev moved to Moscow, where he became the director of the newly established Institute of Precise Mechanics and Computer Technology. There he developed a successor to the MESM, the BESM. (The full name translates to the High-speed Electronic Calculating Machine.) The new machine included a larger memory, facilities to support subroutines, hardware to perform rounding, and a teletypewriter as an input device. Over the following years Lebedev developed 15 high-performance computers in all, including the

BESM-2 (1956), M-20 (1958), M-40 and M-50 (1959), and the BESM-6 (1965)—each of which was at the forefront of computer technology in the Soviet Union.

Lebedev, reportedly a mild-mannered and modest man, remained the director of the Institute until his death, on July 3, 1974. In 1996 the Institute for Electrical and Electronic Engineers (IEEE) honored him posthumously with its Computer Pioneer Award.—A. I. C.

Suggested Reading: International Charity Foundation for History and Development of Computer Science and Technique Web site; Moscow Economic School Web site

---

Lehmer, Derrick Henry

Feb. 23, 1905–May 22, 1991 Mathematician; inventor; professor.

A mathematician who became intensely interested in number theory and in finding prime numbers through mechanical means, Derrick Henry Lehmer stands credited with being one of the first individuals to use computer technology in order to explore complex theoretical number problems. His first foray into the construction of a calculating machine resulted in a primitive number sieve, hastily constructed with bicycle chains but capable of processing 3,000 numbers per second. Lehmer improved on his invention in 1932 with a photoelectric sieve that processed 5,000 numbers per second and was unveiled at the World's Fair in Chicago, Illinois, that same year. Thirty years later, Lehmer improved on his device again, to the point where it could process 1 million numbers per second with few or no malfunctions, making this new machine, the Delay Line Sieve (DLS-127), one of the most reliable number-sorting devices ever created. Lehmer was also instrumental in having number sieves incorporated into the ENIAC computer built by John Mauchly and John Presper Eckert in 1946, making Lehmer one of the earliest researchers to combine mathematical theory and computers. He was also a vocal proponent of the dissemination of computer information, and held one of the first conferences on computers in 1945.

The son of a noted mathematics professor, Derrick N. Lehmer, and a poet, Eunice Mitchell, Derrick Henry Lehmer was born on February 23, 1905 in Berkeley, California. One of the couple's five children, Lehmer was educated in public schools in Berkeley before entering the University of California (UC) at Berkeley in 1923. His father's longstanding interest in mathematics had an impact on Lehmer, and he studied number theory and computation in school, graduating with an A.B. degree in mathematics, in 1927.

While he was an undergraduate, Lehmer began to exhibit an interest in finding a mechanized way of solving linear congruence relations—such as x=y(m). The problem that Lehmer sought to solve, was to find integer values of x (y or m) such that x-y is a multiple of m. In 1926 he began to construct his first number-sieve computer in the students' workshop, LeConte Hall, at the university. It was a primitive mechanism, which consisted of 19 separately looped bicycle chains; the number of links in each chain was a prime number, up to number 67. Small prime numbers were represented by composite chains with nonprime numbers of links; thus, chains with 22, 25, 26, 27, 49, and 64 links represented the prime numbers 11, 5, 13, 3, 7, and 2 respectively. The chains hung in loops from sprockets on a common shaft driven by a motor. A counter was used to indicate how many links had passed the top position. Every chain, both prime and composite, had a zero position, or link, which was red. Each prime chain also had a pin that was attached at the zero position, while the composite chains had several pins, one at each multiple of the prime that divided the length of the chain. Lehmer described the arrangement as such: "Whenever a link provided with a pin arrives at the top of the shaft a small spring with a tungsten point is lifted by the projecting pin. This breaks for the moment the electric contact between the spring and a brass bar running parallel to the shaft. By means of a relay in the circuit, the motor is shut off and the machine stops itself. When several chains are provided with springs the machine will not stop unless all the springs are lifted, so that every time the machine stops it means that a number satisfying all the imposed conditions has appeared. This number can be read directly by means of a revolution counter connected to the shaft. The shaft revolves at 300 rpm so that the machine canvases 3,000 numbers per minute. When all chains are provided with springs a 'solution' occurs once in several hours, during which time the machine runs without any attention" (*Computer Pioneers*, 1995).

During the next year, Lehmer attended the University of Chicago in order to take courses with the many noted math professors employed there at the time. In 1928 he headed off to graduate school at Brown University, in Providence, Rhode Island, where he received his M.Sc. degree in 1929 and his Ph.D. the following year. His doctoral thesis, "An Extended Theory of Lucas' Functions," was sent to E. T. Bell at the California Institute of Technology for review, and Lehmer was given a research fellowship there from 1930 to 1931, followed by one at Stanford University in Palo Alto, California from 1931 to 1932.

During 1932 Lehmer decided to build a much faster sieve, using gears with different numbers of teeth that would be driven by a common gear. His description of the machine explained how it improved on his previous sieve: "There are 30 driven gears, all driven at the same linear speed of about 1,700 meters per minute by a single driving gear. The 30 driven gears correspond to 30 modules and have for numbers of teeth convenient multiples of every prime number less than 127. The largest gear has 128 teeth and the smallest 67 teeth. At the base of each tooth, on each driven gear, holes are drilled at a constant distance from the periphery of the gear, this distance being the same for all gears. These holes are about 2 millimeters in diameter and correspond to the numbers 0, 1, 2, . . ., p-1 modulo p. If x is to be restricted to a set of s numbers modulo p the holes corresponding to these numbers are left open, while other holes are stopped with wooden pins. The gears are mounted parallel to one another and a common line of tangency so that if a beam of light from an incandescent lamp shines through a hole in any gear it is transmitted or blotted out by the next gear. If the driving gear is rotated (from some zero position) until x teeth have turned past and if x satisfies the conditions imposed by all the modules, then there will be an alignment of open holes and the beam of light will traverse the system of gears," (Computer Pioneers, 1995). Lehmer's new device, dubbed a "photoelectric sieve," was able to process 5,000 numbers per second, making it, in Lehmer's eyes, "the first high-speed computer." The device was first exhibited just prior to its major debut, at the Mathematics Exhibit at the Chicago World's Fair, during the summer of 1932.

The number sieves that Lehmer constructed were not intended to be general purpose calculating machines, but were conceived instead as special-purpose devices designed to carry out the one specific task of finding prime numbers. The sieves were considered to be parallel computers, which are often compared to the human brain because they could carry out several different operations, or "chains of thought," simultaneously.

Lehmer left for the east coast once again after receiving a Princeton Institute Fellowship for the Institute for Advanced Study from 1933 to 1934. He taught briefly at the Stanford Summer School, in California, before leaving in 1934 to teach mathematics at Lehigh University in Bethlehem, Pennsylvania, where he stayed until 1940, taking a leave of absence from 1938 to 1939 in order to visit Cambridge and Manchester Universities in England on a Guggenheim Fellowship. Lehmer left the east coast permanently in 1940 in order to take a position as an assistant professor of mathematics at the University of California at Berkeley. In 1945 Lehmer accepted an appointment at the Ballistic Research Laboratory of the Aberdeen Proving Ground, in Aberdeen, Maryland, which was then financing the construction of the ENIAC computer at the University of Pennsylvania in Philadelphia. Lehmer was on hand to witness the building of this machine, the first general-purpose electronic computer, and he posed the question of whether the ENIAC could be used to perform the sieve process. The team of researchers, which included John Mauchly and John Presper Eckert were able to incorporate a sieve into the machine, and sieve programs were later implemented in a variety of general-purpose computers, including the SWAC and the IBM-7094. Lehmer was also very interested in the dissemination of material regarding the workings of the ENIAC, as well as computing in general. In 1945 he helped plan and carry out one of the earliest conferences involving computers on the topic of computing equipment, which was held at the Massachusetts Institute of Technology and Harvard University, both located in Cambridge, Massachusetts.

At the end of World War II, Lehmer returned to his post at UC Berkeley. By the early 1950s, he was again at work on his sieves, this time joining up with Paul Morton of Berkeley's electrical engineering department, who had previously assisted in the construction of the CALDIC (California Digital Computer), a general-purpose magnetic drum computer. The pair began by attempting to build electronic counters (counters used to measure frequency and time interval), but abandoned the project after running into problems with reliability. They then built a delay line version using electrical delay lines from Navy surplus. Over the years, Lehmer experimented with his electronic sieve again and again, making improvements on it and eventually baptizing it with the formal name of Delay Line Sieve (DLS-127). It was a solid-state machine which was constructed entirely at Berkeley with the help of both the mathematics and electrical engineering departments. In 1965 Lehmer watched as his DLS-127 became fully operational, capable of processing a million numbers per second. For 10 years, the sieve operated in this manner, unassisted, 24 hours a day, with few problems occurring.

Lehmer left UC Berkeley in 1950 after refusing to take part in the oaths of loyalty to the U.S. government which were being mandated by the University as Senator Joseph McCarthy's campaign against communist sympathizers gained speed. Lehmer took a position as the director of the Institute for Numerical Analysis of the National Bureau of Standards located at the University of California at Los Angeles, and remained there until 1953. During his tenure there, Lehmer witnessed the debut of the SWAC (National Bureau of Standards Western Automatic Computer), the first stored-program computer to arrive on the west coast. The computer was just becoming operational at the time he accepted his post, and Lehmer used the machine to explore the application of a Fermat theorem in theoretical number conjectures. One of Lehmer's former colleagues from Berkeley, Raphael Robinson, used the SWAC instruction documentation to write a program that would enable the SWAC to use the Lucas test for primality to search for Mersenne prime numbers. The program, mailed from Berkeley to Los Angeles, was immediately punched into the SWAC, and ran without error, verifying the known results and discovering two new prime numbers, 2^{521}-1 and 2^{607}-1.

In 1954 the practice of the loyalty oath was repealed by UC Berkeley, and Lehmer returned to the institution as chairman of the mathematics depart-

ment. He remained in this position until 1957, also serving as vice chairman of the computer-science department from 1969 to 1970. In 1972 he retired from the university, becoming a professor emeritus.

Derrick Henry Lehmer passed away in Berkeley, California on May 22, 1991 at the age of 86. He published over 181 papers during his lifetime and received a great number of awards and honors. In addition to his Guggenheim Fellowship, Lehmer was awarded the Fulbright Lectureship from Australia in 1959, and served as vice president of the American Mathematical Society (1953–54) and the American Association for the Advancement of Science (1955–56). He married Emma Trotskaya, a fellow mathematician who assisted Lehmer in much of his research, in 1928, and the couple had two children, Donald and Laura.—D. B.

Suggested Reading: Goldstine, Herman H. *The Computer From Pascal to von Neumann*, 1972; Ritchie, David. *The Computer Pioneers*, 1986

Hulton Archive by Getty Images

Leibniz, Gottfried Wilhelm von

July 1, 1646–Nov. 14, 1716 Inventor of the Stepped Reckoner and a developer of calculus

Gottfried Wilhelm von Leibniz, in addition to making many important contributions to 17th-century science, mathematics, and philosophy, built one of the earliest mechanical calculators, called the Stepped Reckoner, in the early 1670s. The device, which could perform the four basic arithmetic operations, greatly influenced the development of

mechanical calculators throughout much of the 18th and 19th centuries. Leibniz is also credited with being the first person to have successfully described a binary, or base-two, arithmetic system, using only the digits 1 and 0. Leibniz's system was eventually developed by later mathematicians into a comprehensive binary mathematics, which is today the fundamental principle behind the operation of digital computers.

Gottfried Wilhelm von Leibniz (sometimes spelled Leibnitz) was born on July 1, 1646 in Leipzig, Germany, into an educated and affluent family. His father, Friedrich, was a professor of moral philosophy at the University of Leipzig. His mother, Katherina Schmuck, Friedrich's third wife, also came from an academic family. Leibniz had a sister, a half-brother, and a half-sister.

A precocious child, Leibniz was a consummate reader from an early age. His teachers attempted to limit his reading to books considered suitable to his years, but upon Friedrich's death, in 1652, a relative arranged for the boy, then six years old, to be given unhindered access to his father's library. Leibniz subsequently began educating himself with a wide range of classical, scholastic, and patristic writings. By the time he was eight years old he had taught himself Latin, and by age 14 he had learned Greek.

In 1661, when he was 15, Leibniz entered the University of Leipzig to study law. He soon became acquainted with the important scientific works of such writers as Francis Bacon, Galileo Galilei, and Johannes Kepler. In 1663 Leibniz completed his bachelor's degree, and the following year he earned a master's degree in law. In 1666 he finished his dissertation for a doctorate of law, but the university refused to confer the degree, reportedly because he was considered too young for such advancement. Leibniz instead brought his work to the University of Altdorf, in Nuremberg, where he was awarded a doctorate in 1666. That same year Leibniz wrote his first mathematical paper.

The university offered Leibniz a professorship, but he declined. He worked briefly as a secretary for the Rosicrucian Society, an order of alchemists in Nuremberg, before accepting a governmental position in Frankfurt, Germany, in the employ of Baron Johann Christian von Boineburg. He was also an advisor to the Archbishop Elector of Mainz, Germany, Johann Philipp von Schönborn, in whose service he worked on legal problems and anonymously drafted several papers on matters of religion and politics. During this period Leibniz made many important contacts both in Germany and abroad, and he began a prolific correspondence that would continue throughout his lifetime. (Today, more than 15,000 of his letters survive.) His position also entailed a fair amount of travel, and, as he was continuously seeking to broaden his knowledge of the natural sciences, on his visits to various cities he always sought out the leading mathematicians and scientists of the day. In 1672, while living in Paris on a diplomatic mission, he formed a lasting friendship with Christiaan (spelled in some sources as Christian) Huygens, the Dutch physicist and astronomer. In London the following year he made the acquaintance of several notable English scientists, including Robert Boyle and Robert Hooke. Meanwhile, he continued to study physics and math, particularly the works of French mathematicians René Descartes and Blaise Pascal. In 1673 the Royal Society of London accepted him as a member.

Leibniz had begun examining methods of mechanical calculation as early as 1671, having been influenced by reading about the Pascaline, a mechanical adding device built by Pascal in 1642. The Pascaline was housed in a rectangular brass box, about one foot in length. It displayed eight figures and could perform addition and subtraction using a series of gears with interlocking teeth.

Leibniz, like Pascal before him, believed that the development of automatic devices would spare individuals from the drudgery (and likelihood of error) involved in performing long calculations by hand. He once remarked, as quoted in an article on the Maxfield and Montrose Interactive Web site, "It is unworthy of excellent men to lose hours like slaves in the labor of calculation which could be safely relegated to anyone else if machines were used." Leibniz wanted to build a device that surpassed Pascal's by including multiplication and division. The machine he developed, called a Stepped Reckoner, accomplished this by using a stepped-drum mechanism, also known as the Leibniz Wheel, which was a long cylinder with nine bar-shaped teeth of increasing lengths running parallel to the cylinder's axis. When the drum was rotated using a crank, an adjacent toothed gear was turned from between zero and nine positions. The device contained eight of these gear sets, one for each digit. It also employed a primitive carrying function.

Leibniz worked on his calculating machine while living in Paris in 1672 and demonstrated an incomplete prototype at the Royal Society in London in 1673. Some members of the group, including Robert Hooke, were harshly critical of the machine's utility and suggested possible alterations. Leibniz applied himself to improving the design, but he soon became engaged in other intellectual pursuits, and he gave his designs to a clockmaker in Paris, France, who completed the work on a final version in 1674. No other models of the Stepped Reckoner were ever made, and the final version was apparently lost in a university attic for the next 200 years. Nevertheless, Leibniz's stepped-drum design was innovative for the time, and it served as the basis for many of the mechanical calculators developed over the next two centuries. The basic design was not improved upon until the 1870s when the Swedish engineer Willgodt Odhner built a calculator that employed a pinwheel mechanism instead of the stepped drum.

During the 1670s Leibniz made his most important contribution to mathematics—his invention of calculus, the branch of math that treats questions involving rates of change, the value of functions, the slope of curves, and the area bounded by curves. This discovery was marred, however, by a bitter dispute between Leibniz and the English mathematician Isaac Newton over which of the two was the true originator of the revolutionary mathematics. Newton had made important discoveries in the field as early as 1665, but had refrained from publishing his results. Leibniz began working on his version in the early 1670s and published his first paper on differential calculus, in 1684, and on integral calculus, in 1686. Newton, who suggested that Leibniz had stolen his methods, finally published his first account, in 1687. The Royal Society eventually undertook an investigation into the matter, and declared formally for Newton in 1713. This failed to resolve the controversy, however, which had by that time resulted in a detrimental rift between the scientific communities of England and Germany. The dispute between the two men was not decided conclusively during their lifetimes, but historians today believe that each arrived at his own version independently. It is Leibniz's system of notation, which he first used in 1675, that has been adopted as the standard.

In 1676 Leibniz left Paris and moved to Hanover (in present-day Germany), where he accepted a position as a librarian in the court of the Duke of Brunswick. He resided primarily in Hanover for the rest of his life, although he continued to travel extensively throughout Europe, meeting with important scientists, philosophers, and dignitaries. He kept up his immense correspondence, wrote tracts on history and philosophy as well as science and math, and was charged by the duke with performing a large amount of genealogical research for the Brunswick family.

In 1679 Leibniz formulated what is generally considered to be the first binary mathematics, a system of numeric representation that includes only two digits, 1s and 0s. Leibniz ascribed metaphysical value to the digits: 1 was equated with Being, or God, and 0 was equated with Nothingness. The entire created universe, he surmised, could be reduced to a mixture of these two elements and therefore expressed in a binary numeral system. These ideas had their roots in Leibniz's mathematical paper of 1666, *Dissertatio de arte combinatoria* (Dissertation on the Combinatorial Art), wherein he made his first attempt at devising a system of logical symbolism. Leibniz believed that such a system would make reasoning more precise, by reducing thought to a set of symbols that could then be manipulated and solved like a mathematical equation.

Leibniz's binary arithmetic remained largely a philosophical curiosity until the 19th century, when it was developed by the English mathematician George Boole into what is known as Boolean algebra. Boole's binary algebra is today the key principle behind the function of digital computers, as computers relay information in a series of 1s and 0s (called bits, which is short for binary digits). Additionally, electronic circuits are designed according to the binary system, with 1 and 0 representing two states of digital circuits, usually high and low voltage.

Throughout his life Leibniz remained active in political and intellectual affairs. He was, among other things, a strong promoter of scientific societies. In 1700 he persuaded Frederick I of Prussia to found the Prussian Academy of Sciences, in Berlin. The group's aim was to create an international community of scholars who would share their ideas freely, and Leibniz was named the academy's first president. His later years were largely occupied with his philosophical writings (in addition to his mathematical dispute with Newton). In 1710 he published *Théodicée*, a work that attempted to reconcile the existence of evil in a world created by a good God. His best-known philosophical doctrine was likely his theory of monads—simple, indivisible, immaterial entities, infinite in number, that constitute the fundamental substance of reality and whose nature is to perceive and reflect that reality.

When the Duke of Brunswick, Ernst August, died in 1698 and was succeed by Georg Ludwig, Leibniz's position at the court was essentially ended, although Ludwig urged him to complete his history of the house of Brunswick. Leibniz was fortunate to find other sources of patronage, and in his various posts he continued to advocate for religious and political reforms. In 1712 Peter the Great of Russia appointed him imperial privy councilor, and he served in Vienna until 1714. He returned to Hanover in 1714 and, learning that Georg Ludwig had departed for London to assume the throne of England as George I, applied for a position in George's court. The king, however, refused to employ him until he had finished his genealogy of the house of Brunswick. Leibniz, never married and sick with gout, struggled for two years to complete the work. He died on November 14, 1716.—A. I. C.

Suggested Reading: Maxfield and Montrose Interactive Web site; *X-Number World of Calculators* (on-line); Williams, Michael R. *A History of Computing Technology*, 1997

Lerner, Sandra and Bosack, Leonard

Lerner, Sandra
July 14, 1955– Co-founder of Cisco Systems; founder of Urban Decay

Bosack, Leonard
1951(?)– Co-founder of Cisco System; founder of XKL

The story of the founding of Cisco Systems, which in March 2000 passed Microsoft to become the world's most valuable company, worth $200 billion, is a Silicon Valley legend, part love story and part cautionary tale. During the 1980s Leonard Bosack and Sandra Lerner, graduate school sweethearts at Stanford University, figured out a way to send messages to each other across different computer platforms. The combination of hardware and software they developed and marketed, which came to be known as a router, forwards packets of data from one computer network to another. Routers helped usher in a new age of communications and formed the backbone of the Internet; recent estimates suggest that 80 percent of the Internet's infrastructure is made up of Cisco routers. Cisco is a juggernaut company—the world's biggest manufacturer of computer networking equipment—the switches and routers tell the millions of words, ideas, and images exchanged over the Internet where to go, and how to get there.

Sandra Lerner, known as Sandy, was born in Phoenix, Arizona, on July 14, 1955. Her parents were artistic; her mother worked as a window dresser for clothing stores, and her father was a painter. Following her parents' divorce when she was four, Lerner was sent to live with her aunt and uncle on a ranch in California, while her younger brother stayed with their mother. Lerner remembers spending a lot of time alone as a girl, taking care of animals and doing chores around the ranch. At age nine she joined the 4-H agricultural club, an experience that gave her confidence and the ability to speak in front of a group, as Lerner recalled in an interview with Linton Weeks for the *Washington Post* posted on the *Augusta Chronicle Online*. Lerner was a rebellious child: she refused to pledge allegiance to the American flag in grade school and, at a precocious 13, protested the war in Vietnam. After graduating from high school, at age 16, Lerner took a job at a bank—a rude cultural awakening for the spirited girl brought up on a ranch. "The president would make us kneel on the floor, so he could check the length of our skirts," Lerner told Weeks. After a year of this work, Lerner fled to college, to California State University, at Chico, and graduated in two years. She then enrolled at Claremont College, in Claremont, California, to study econometrics, a discipline that uses statistics to analyze economic conditions. At Claremont Lerner first saw a computer station, an experience that she described to Weeks as "religious." In 1977 she transferred to another graduate program, at Stanford University, in California, the Mecca of early computing, and changed her major to computational mathematics. There, Lerner fell in with a group of what she described to Weeks as "very hard-core computer nerds." The only woman among a group of men, Lerner was initiated into the joys of staying up late and tinkering with computers. Out of all the "nerds," Lerner found herself attracted to Leonard Bosack, a computer science student who—unlike some of the others—possessed some social skills. "Len's clothes were clean, he bathed, and he knew how to use silverware," Lerner recalled to a *Forbes* (August 25, 1997) reporter. "That was enough. I was enchanted."

Leonard Bosack, called Len by his friends, was the less visible half of Cisco Systems. He was born in about 1951. He belonged to one of the first computer clubs, which was founded by high-school students in a barn in the small town of Hopewell, New Jersey, in 1966. The club members called themselves the R.E.S.I.S.T.O.R.S. (Radically Emphatic Students Interested in Science, Technology, and Other Research Subjects). Members, who were frustrated by the poor technology offerings at their schools, met through the 1960s and 1970s and taught each other how to program computers.

Bosack enrolled in the graduate computer science program at Stanford. In 1980, while still in graduate school, Lerner and Bosack were married. A 1995 *Fortune* reporter characterized the young couple as polar opposites; Bosack was a "somewhat philosophical, nonconfrontational, 'big think' kind of scientist," and Lerner was a "flamboyant, highly confrontational" individual. Bosack and Lerner graduated, in 1981, Bosack with a computer science degree and Lerner with a degree in computational mathematics. Both stayed on at Stanford to work. Lerner ran the computer system at the business school, and Bosack, in a building 500 yards away, maintained the computers for the computer science department. In the early 1980s there were 5,000 mostly incompatible computers around campus, running on different software, a situation that Lerner described to Weeks as "complete bedlam." In order to communicate with each other, Lerner and Bosack ran cables between their two buildings and then connected the two separate networks with rudimentary hardware switches. This made it possible to connect different kinds of computer platforms, and to "shovel bits of infor-

mation faster and better than anything else," as Lerner told Weeks. It was an updated and improved version of the Interface Message Processor (IMP) used for the different nodes in the ARPA-NET, a wide area network (WAN) created in the 1960s that was the precursor to the Internet. Soon these routers, as they came to be called, brought all of Stanford's different networks together, thus creating one unified network. According to the PBS *Nerds 2.0.1* Web site, word quickly traveled through the computing community about this development, and other universities and research centers asked Stanford if they could purchase routers. Bosack and Lerner went to Stanford officials with a proposition to start building and selling their routers, but were turned down. So, they founded their own company.

A caveat to this widely reported story is offered by Tom Rindfleisch, the director of the Lane Medical Library at Stanford and former director of the SUMEX-AIM Project at Stanford, the first nongovernmental node of the ARPANET. In "A Perspective on the Origin of Cisco Systems," published on the Stanford Medical Informatics Web site, Rindfleisch noted that a Stanford professor named Bill Yeager initiated an effort, in 1980, to build a network router and Terminal Interface Processor (TIP). Such early router systems were disseminated widely at Stanford. "Thus, by the time Bosack had access to the router source code in 1985, multiple-protocol routers were a relatively mature technology," Rindfleish wrote. "The software was licensed by Bosack and Lerner on behalf of Cisco Systems in 1986. . . . Yeager is named in the agreement document as the principal developer/inventor. . . . Bosack's and Lerner's contributions lay in the important (and risky) realization that this technology could be made into a commercial venture—and credit for that should not be denied."

In the living room of their home, with the help of "borrowed" Stanford equipment and several credit cards, Lerner and Bosack founded cisco systems, in 1984. It was named in honor of San Francisco, but the company's lower-case "c" and "s" have metamorphosed to upper case over time. With the help of friends and volunteers, their home soon became a busy center of building, testing, manufacturing, and shipping network routers. They developed a high-performance and reasonably affordable router, which enabled different network systems to be connected. Once this was in place, they created software for the router, based on an open-communication, or highly intercompatible, protocol. Cisco sold its first router in 1986. Most of the early clients were fellow computer scientists, who had heard about the new technology through the ARPANET. In the late 1980s Cisco came out with devices to connect wide area networks (WANs) with local area networks (LANs), called internetworking devices. These devices became the standard way of sending information in smaller pieces, or packets, across the Internet. Today, a router stores and forwards electronic messages between networks by first determining all possible paths to the destination address and then picking the most expedient route. Such developments fueled the market for networking, and, in turn, the market for Cisco's products increased dramatically. From 1984 to 1990 Lerner and Bosack grew Cisco into a $500 million company. It wasn't just the universities and computer scientist communities that were interested in the new technology, either. "We suspected that Procter and Gamble in Des Moines was going to want to talk to Procter and Gamble in San Francisco," Lerner told Julie Pitta in an interview for *Forbes* (March 16, 1992) that is posted on the Washington and Lee University Web site.

Most accounts of Cisco's success ascribe the technological savvy to Bosack and the entrepreneurial spirit to Lerner; Bosack was the main visionary behind Cisco's networking technology, and Lerner acted as the company's business manager and driving force. "Some credit Cisco's success to the eccentric founders," noted Matt Marshall in the *Mercury News*, as posted on *Silicon Valley.com* (March 28, 2000). The two founders set a target of $500,000 for each sales employee, an ambitious figure in what was then still a small industry.

In the early years of Cisco, short of cash and struggling to keep up with orders, Bosack and Lerner approached Silicon Valley venture capitalists for backing, but were repeatedly refused until, in 1987, they met Don Valentine of Sequoia Capital. "At that point I think we were—Cisco was doing, I think, a quarter million, maybe $350,000 a month without a professional sales staff and without an official conventionally recognized marketing campaign," Bosack is quoted as saying on *Nerds 2.0.1*. "And so I think just for the novelty of it, the folks at Sequoia listened to us." Valentine, a powerful figure with a reputation for maintaining strict control over the companies he funded, gave Cisco $2.3 million and hired an experienced management and sales team, including John Morgridge as CEO. Bosack became the company's chief scientist and Lerner became director of customer service under Morgridge. The sudden transformation of Cisco from an ad hoc company made up of former graduate students and friends to a corporate firm managed hierarchically created some friction, particularly between Morgridge and Lerner. In 1990 Cisco made a successful public offering in the stock market but, as a result of their differences, Morgridge asked Lerner to leave. (Lacking the benefit of professional legal advice, Lerner and Bosack had effectively handed over control of the company to Morgridge as part of their deal with Sequoia.) When Bosack learned that Lerner had been fired, he left the company in protest. The couple departed with between $80 to $100 million each in Cisco stocks.

During their tumultuous years at Cisco, Lerner and Bosack grew apart. "Len and I didn't talk," Lerner recalled to Weeks. "Our conversations had nothing to do with each other." The couple is now separated, although they remain close and have pooled much of their money into a trust, Ampersand Capital, which supports a variety of charities and projects. According to Julie Pitta, by 1992 Lerner and Bosack had given away 70 percent of their fortune.

Since 1990 Lerner has been an animal-rights activist; the founder of a grunge-themed cosmetics company, Urban Decay; a major supporter of Janeites (Jane Austen scholars); and an all-around wealthy eccentric. According to Marshall, when *Forbes* ran a story on Silicon Valley wealth, in 1997, the magazine's editors asked Lerner for a photograph. She sent one of herself, posed nude on horseback.

Linton Weeks described Lerner as having purple-tinged hair, blue nail polish, and "bruise-blue" shadow above and below her eyes. She founded Urban Decay, in 1996, with the motto "Does Pink Make You Puke?" The company markets cosmetics inspired by contemporary urban life, with such product names as Asphyxia, Gash, Radium, Roach, Storm Drain, Spare Chain, and Toxin. Lerner has amassed a collection of novels by Austen's contemporaries, 19th-century women writers who have not received nearly the notice that Austen has. In 1992 she purchased a country estate in Chawton, England, down the road from where Austen wrote, and established the Centre for the Study of Early English Women's Writing. Lerner lives on an 800-acre farm, nestled in Virginia's Blue Ridge Mountains, where she raises organic produce with horse-drawn wagons, and experiments with the latest computer technology.

Leonard Bosack's pet cause is "alternative technology." He has funded academic researchers who are looking for signs of extraterrestrial intelligence and has also given money to the Search for Extra-Terrestrial Intelligence (SETI) Institute. During the 1990s, Bosack founded the XKL engineering company, in Redmond, Washington. The company focuses on improving networking architecture.

—M .A. H.

Suggested Reading: *Augusta Chronicle Online*; *Forbes* p136+ Mar. 16, 1992, p58+ Aug. 25, 1997; *Los Angeles Times* p10+ Mar. 1, 1998; PBS *Nerds 2.0.1* Web site; Stanford Medical Informatics Web site

Licklider, Joseph C. R.

Mar. 11, 1915–June 26, 1990 Pioneer of computer networking

Though the computer scientist Joseph C. R. Licklider is not well known, those who are aware of his contributions to computer networking (which ultimately led to the Internet) and other areas acknowledge his seminal role in originating modern computing. As quoted in the on-line Netbook *Netizens: On the History and Impact of Usenet and the Internet*, by Michael and Ronda Hauben, one colleague said of him, "I think most of the significant advances in computer technology, especially in the systems part of computer science were simply extrapolations of Licklider's vision. They were not really new visions of their own. So he's really the father of it all." Harold Jackson, in the London *Guardian* (July 27, 2000), stated that Licklider "has probably had as great an impact on his age as Einstein." While director of the U.S. Department of Defense's Advance Research Projects Agency (ARPA) from 1962 to 1964, Licklider fostered his vision of what he whimsically termed the "Intergalactic Computer Network," which he hoped would allow people of common interests to share information and ideas via computer networking. Licklider filtered millions of dollars into creating computer-science programs in universities around the country, and helped instill those programs with his dream of the Intergalactic Network. He did this at a time when most in the computer industry assumed that giant mainframe computers would continue to be specialized machines, useful primarily for calculating complex mathematical problems. A network of university computing centers, called ARPANET, was launched in 1969 and is generally credited with being the precursor to the Internet. According to a writer in *Science* (September 3, 1999), Licklider's phrase "Intergalactic Computer Network" was the inspiration for the current designation: the Internet. Trained initially in psychology, Licklider brought a unique perspective to computer science that always took into consideration how users might interact more intuitively with computers. In *Technology Review* (January/February 2000) M. Mitchell Waldrop wrote that Licklider "laid the foundations for time-sharing, point-and-click interfaces, graphics and the Internet—virtually all of modern computing." While Licklider was perhaps the first to conceptualize many of the innovations we associate with modern computing, and while he set up several top-notch university programs that pursued many of his ideas, it took time for technology to catch up with him, and the actual implementation of his vision was mostly done by others.

Joseph Carl Robnett Licklider, known to friends as "Lick," was born in St. Louis, Missouri, on March 11, 1915. He was a playful and curious child, who took an immediate interest in all things technological. At 15 he bought his first car, a junker that he soon fixed up. For years afterward he maintained that he would never buy a car for more than $50 because, with a little tinkering, he could make anything run. Licklider entered Washington University, in St. Louis, in the 1930s and graduated in 1937 with a triple-major in math, psychology, and physics. He earned a master's degree from the university in 1938. He then earned his Ph.D. from the University of Rochester, in New York, and for his dissertation mapped out frequency responses on the auditory cortex of the brain. At Swarthmore College, in Swarthmore, Pennsylvania, he worked as a research associate and studied Gestalt psychology, the school of psychology that provided the foundation for the modern study of perception. In 1943 he joined the Psycho-Acoustics Laboratory at Harvard University in Cambridge, Massachusetts. The lab was conducting an Air Force–funded study on acoustics in an attempt to help Air Force men function better amid the din of jet engines. Licklider invented "clipped speech," a way of altering a radio transmission so that consonants were stressed over vowels, which increased the clarity of speech and made it possible to understand radio communications in noisy situations. After the war Licklider's work with the Acoustics Lab ended, but he stayed at Harvard, teaching and researching physiological psychology.

In 1950 Licklider became an associate professor at the Massachusetts Institute of Technology (MIT), in Cambridge, where he helped set up a psychology section within the electrical engineering department and also taught some electrical engineering classes. He headed the "human factors" team of an Air Force project to create a computer-based missile defense system against the Soviet Union. While working on this project, Licklider had the opportunity to use one of the first computers—named Whirlwind—that was not organized through batch-processing. With batch-processing, users took turns running their programs on a central computer, and because each program was run to completion before the next batch could be run, users were unable to access computers as problems arose. Whirlwind attempted to respond to each user on a command-per-command basis, thus facilitating a more interactive relationship between user and computer. This system intrigued Licklider and alerted him to the possibilities of computer-assisted thought. He began to track his own thinking process, and noticed that much of his time was spent dealing with details that were necessary but peripheral to his central aims. The realization further sparked his interest in human-computer interaction. "From my point of view, a lot hinged on a little study I had made on how I would spend my time," Licklider once explained, as quoted in an entry in the *International Biographical Dictionary of Computer Pioneers* (1995). "It showed that almost all my time was spent on algorithmic things that were no fun, but they were all necessary for the few heuristic things that seemed so important. I had this little picture in my mind about how we were going to get people and computers really thinking together."

In 1957 Licklider left MIT and accepted the position of vice president in charge of psychoacoustics, engineering psychology, and information systems at the consulting firm Bolt, Beranek & Newman (BBN). He also continued to expand his ideas about computer-assisted thought and, in 1960, published a prophetic paper called "Man-Computer Symbiosis." In the paper, as quoted by Michael and Ronda Hauben, Licklider foresaw that, in this new relationship, people would "set the goals, formulate the hypotheses, determine the criteria, and perform the evaluations," while computers would "do the routinizable work that must be done to prepare the way for insights and decisions in technical and scientific thinking." Licklider also had a vision of connecting computers together in order to share information between people. As Waldrop related, Licklider postulated "thinking centers," much like on-line libraries, and foresaw "a network of such centers, connected to one another by wide-band communications lines and to individual users by leased-wire services."

Though Licklider was content at BBN, when he received an offer in 1962 to direct a division of ARPA, he could not refuse the chance to help foster the vision he had elaborated in "Man-Computer Symbiosis." ARPA was founded in 1958—largely as a response to the Soviet Union's launch of the Sputnik satellite, the first to orbit the earth—to encourage cutting-edge technology and communications research. Licklider was given approximately $10 million in funding to direct the newly formed Information Processing Techniques Office (IPTO), and he immediately gave money to several universities to create computer science programs and do research in time- sharing and other areas. Participating schools included MIT; Stanford University, in Stanford, California; the University of California at Berkeley; the University of California at Los Angeles; and Carnegie Tech (now Carnegie-Mellon University), in Pittsburgh, Pennsylvania. Larry Roberts, a successor of Licklider's at ARPA, told the Haubens that Licklider's university programs "form the basis for the progress the United States has made in the computer field. That production of people started with Lick, when he started the IPTO program and started the big university programs. . . . The people from those programs are in large part the leaders throughout the industry."

In addition to funding university research, Licklider encouraged communication between computer scientists and continually advanced his idea of computer networking. In April of 1963 he sent a memo to various researchers affiliated with his IPTO program entitled, rather lightheartedly, "Members and Affiliates of the Intergalactic Computer Network." In it he wrote, as quoted by Waldrop, "If such a network as I envisage nebulously could be brought into operation, we would have at least four large computers, perhaps six or eight small computers, and a great assortment of disc files and magnetic tape units—not to mention the remote consoles and teletype stations—all churn-

ing away." Licklider's idea of an Intergalactic Computer Network ran counter to most thinking about the role of computers; it was generally thought that computers would be sold mainly to those who needed them for complex mathematical formulations, rather than for communications and shared multitasking. Even though much of what he hoped to achieve was beyond the reach of current technology, he used his infectious enthusiasm to promote his vision to his colleagues.

Because it was customary for most ARPA directors to hold their posts for only a couple of years, Licklider left ARPA in 1964 and became manager of information sciences, systems, and applications at the Thomas J. Watson Center of IBM. In 1965 he published *Libraries of the Future*, a study of how technology might affect information sciences. After Licklider left ARPA, the agency continued to follow his vision of networking, particularly under the tutelage of the director Robert W. Taylor, with whom Licklider authored "The Computer as Communication Device" in 1968, a year before the ARPANET was launched. In this paper the two men wrote, as quoted by the Haubens, "We believe that we are entering into a technological age, in which we will be able to interact with the richness of living information—not merely in the passive way that we have become accustomed to using books and libraries, but as active participants in an ongoing process."

In 1968 Licklider returned to MIT to head Project MAC (short for both Multiple Access Computer and Machine- Aided Cognition), a laboratory that he had helped found while at ARPA. The lab had been responsible for major advances in time-sharing technology. Licklider also taught electrical engineering classes. Apart from a return to ARPA (1974–75), he remained a professor there until his death. Licklider's second stint as director of ARPA's IPTO was less successful because his research was limited to only that which had direct relevance to the military, and he found it difficult to work within those constraints. In 1986 he retired from MIT, remaining associated with the university as a professor emeritus. Hundreds showed up to express their appreciation of Licklider and his work during his retirement ceremony. David Burmaster, an assistant of Licklider's at Project MAC, who had felt enormous admiration for him, explained to Waldrop, "I'd felt I was the only one, that somehow Lick and I had this mystical bond. Yet during that evening I saw that Lick had had this amazing relationship with—a hundred? Two hundred? I'm not sure even how to count them. And everybody he touched felt that he was their hero, and that he had been an extraordinarily important person in their life."

Licklider died in Arlington, Massachusetts, on June 26, 1990, from complications arising from a severe asthma attack. He is survived by his wife, Louise; his son, Tracy; and his daughter, Linda Smith. His awards include the Franklin V. Taylor Award from the Society of Engineering Psychologists (1957) and the Common Wealth Award for Distinguished Service (1990). He was a member of the National Academy of Science, the Acoustic Society of America, the Academy of Arts and Sciences, and the Association for Computing Machinery.—P. G. H.

Suggested Reading: *Denver Post* A p36 Oct. 29, 2000; London *Guardian* p21 July 27, 2000; *Los Angeles Times* p8 Oct. 25, 1999; *Science* p1478 Sep. 3, 1999; *Technology Review* p66+ Jan./Feb. 2000; *U.S. News and World Report* p67 Dec. 27, 1999; Lee, J. A. N., ed. *International Biographical Dictionary of Computer Pioneers*, 1995

Llull, Ramon

1232(?)–1315(?) Inventor of the Llullian logic machine

"Many of the fundamental ideas in artificial intelligence have an ancient heritage," Clark Glymour, Kenneth M. Ford, and Patrick J. Hayes wrote for *AI* magazine (Summer 1998). "Some of the most fundamental, surely, are that thinking is a computational process, that computational processes involve combining symbols, that computation can be made mechanical, and that the mathematics of computation involves combinatorics. All of these ideas have their origin, so far as we know, in the work of an eccentric 13th century Spanish genius, Ramon [Llull]." The poet, theologian, and inventor Ramon Llull (also spelled Lull) invented the Llullian machine, a mechanical device for manipulating logical propositions, while searching for a way to convince unbelievers to convert to Christianity. Llull's machines and his writing on the logical foundations of Christianity in *Ars Magna* (c. 1274) greatly influenced other thinkers, including fellow Spaniard Juan Luis Vives, a 15th-century philosopher, and Gottfried Wilhelm Leibniz, a 17th-century German logician and mathematician, who developed and improved upon Llull's logical methodology. The first to translate logical thought into a mechanical system, Llull helped pave the way for later discoveries in mathematics and computing.

Ramon Llull was born in either 1232 or 1233 (sources differ) on the island of Majorca, now a part of Spain, only about three years after the island had been taken from the Muslims by King James of Aragon. As a reward for fighting in the campaign of 1229, his father had received extensive property on the island and had settled there. At about the age of 14 Llull joined the king's mainland court in Spain as a page, returning to Majorca with the crown prince in 1256. During the years at court, he had cultivated the vernacular art of the troubadour, a form of love poetry popular at the time, writing mostly in the Romance language Catalan. By his own admission, Llull was, in keeping with the spirit of troubadour poetry, something of a woman-

izer. In 1257 his marriage to Blanca Picany was arranged by the king, but neither marriage nor children put a stop to his love affairs.

By all accounts, Llull, shortly after his marriage, had a vision that abruptly changed his life view, though accounts differ as to what precisely sparked the vision. Some say that Llull had been courting a certain woman who finally allowed him into her chambers, revealing to him her diseased, withered breasts. Llull took the gruesome experience as a sign from God to change his ways. It is also commonly held that Llull, while writing a love poem, had repeated visions of Christ in agony on the Cross. In any case, in about 1263 he underwent a radical conversion, leaving behind his wife and children to devote himself to Christianity.

From his conversion onward Llull devoted his life to self-discipline, to grandiose literary and evangelical projects, and to converting Muslims to Christianity. For about nine years he lived among Cistercian monks, studying theology, philosophy, and Arabic. He bought a Moorish slave to tutor him in Arabic and instruct him in the Islamic faith. After making a mendicant pilgrimage to Santiago de Compostela, Rome, and the Holy Land, he went to Mount Randa in Majorca to meditate and to write. The first of his many voluminous works, *The Book of Contemplation* (1272), written at least partly in Arabic, is a theological and devotional encyclopedia of almost a million words.

Llull's chief project, the conversion of Muslims by rational persuasion and preaching rather than by force, was also beginning to take shape. He had a mystical vision on Mount Randa in which he saw all the divine attributes of God reflected in the wonders of the universe, and it occurred to him that the main obstacle to gaining converts to Christianity was the difficulty in recognizing and understanding the vast array of God's attributes. Thus he began his masterpiece, the *Ars Magna* (The Great Art), which includes *Arbor Scientae* (The Tree of Knowledge), and *Liber de Ascensu et Descensu Intellectus* (The Book of the Ascent and Descent of the Intellect). Primarily, the *Ars Magna* was a work of apologetics, or a logical defense of Christianity; it consisted of complex combinatory diagrams and made use of a mechanical system for manipulating logical symbols. These mechanical systems, or Llullian machines, were complex devices; the basic element consisted of a central spindle upon which wood or stone discs could be rotated. The outer rim of each disc was divided into sections bearing Latin letters that might correspond, for example, to the attributes of God. A Llullian machine consisted of two or more discs that could be rotated to make various combinations that might be used to aid in positing a logical defense of Christianity. As Llull's influence spread, his combinatorial system was incorporated and improved upon for purposes other than Christian apologetics.

For the rest of his life Llull remained a dedicated Christian missionary while also continuing to write religious tracts, poetry, and novels. His novel

Blanquerna (c. 1283), a monument of Catalan literature, is a chivalric romance in which reasonable arguments replace weapons in righting wrongs and building a quixotic utopia. After he has remade the political order, the hero reorganizes the Church, from the local monastery to the College of Cardinals; then, resigning from the papacy, he becomes a hermit. In this fantastic, harmonious vision of reason and nature in action, of poverty and holy joy, Llull, according to some scholars, expresses the spirit of St. Francis of Assisi (he joined the Third Order of Franciscans in 1295) as does no other European author.

After visits to popes and to the King of France urging missionary crusades into Africa, Llull wrote in Paris another important Catalan prose work, *Felix* or *Libre de Meravelles* (1286). It treats encyclopedically all the marvels of the universe, from God to Hell, including plants, metals, beasts, and man. The section on beasts is perhaps the most interesting because of the folkloric tales, in which the animals tell tales of human actions and draw moral conclusions from them.

Later in life, Llull traveled to Majorca, Rome, Cyprus, and Armenia and undertook a series of missionary trips to North Africa, including Tunis, after each of which he was banished from the areas. In 1311 he attended the Council of Vienna to urge the establishment of missionary language schools and of a unified crusading order of knights. In 1314 Llull, now more than 80 years old, returned to Tunis, where he spent the last year of his life preaching and translating. According to a likely legend, he was finally stoned to death in 1315 or 1316 by an angry mob in North Africa. He received a martyr's burial in Majorca, where he has ever since been the object of a pious and patriotic cult. Despite Dominican opposition, he was at last officially beatified and bears the title Doctor Illuminatus.—P. G. H.

Suggested Reading: *AI Magazine* p136 Summer 1998; *Art Journal* (on-line) Fall 1997; *New York Times* (on-line) Sept. 29, 1985; Peers, E. A. *Ramon Lull*, 1969

Lovelace, Ada King

Dec. 10, 1815–Nov. 27, 1852 Computing pioneer; mathematician; science writer

When Charles Babbage introduced his Difference Engine and Analytical Engine in the mid-19th century, not many people cared. Augusta Ada King, also known as Lady Lovelace, was one of the few people able to perceive the potential of Babbage's inventions to spawn a technological revolution. The only legitimate child of the British Romantic poet Lord Byron, Lady Lovelace became Babbage's adviser, collaborator, and confidante, supporting his work financially, intellectually, and emotionally. Her notes on Babbage's Difference Engine and his proposed (but never completed) Analytical Engine are the clearest glimpses we have into the concepts behind these machines, which were important precursors to modern computers. Although her work in programming is a matter of some dispute, she is known to have collaborated with Babbage on early programs for the Difference Engine, placing her among the first—if not *the* first—computer programmers. Her life was plagued by drug and gambling addictions and was cut short by cancer at the age of 36. Had she lived, she may have helped Babbage to initiate the computer age a full century early.

Augusta Ada Byron was born on December 10, 1815 in the English town of Piccadilly, in the county of Middlesex (now part of London). Her mother was Anna Isabella Millbanke, and her father was George Gordon Noel Byron, better known by his aristocratic title, Lord Byron. Her parents, who had been married a year at the time of her birth, were ill-matched. Byron was a well-known poet, a major

Hulton Archive by Getty Images

figure of the Romantic Movement in English literature. He was a highly passionate and somewhat eccentric man. In contrast, Anna Millbanke was conservative and puritanical. When it was revealed that Byron had been having an affair with his married half-sister, Augusta Leigh, Millbanke left Byron and took their five-week-old daughter with her. Young Augusta's name was changed to Ada in order to avoid association with her aunt, for whom she had been named. Lord Byron fled the scandal.

He never saw his daughter again, but several of his letters show his affection for her and his deep regret at missing her childhood. She is mentioned fondly in several of his poems, including "Childe Harold's Pilgrimage." At the time of his death, in 1824 at the age of 36, Ada was only eight years old.

Anna Millbanke felt disgraced by her husband's scandalous affair and sought to detach young Ada from any connection to her father. Concerned that the outspoken child would turn out as nonconformist as Lord Byron himself, she attempted to curb her. Ada was administered a daily dose of a laudanum-laced tincture, which produced a "calming" effect. It also produced an addiction, which would be joined by other addictions later in her life.

Ada's mother was an accomplished mathematician (whimsically known in some circles as "the Princess of Parallelograms"), and she encouraged Ada when she began to display an aptitude for math as a child. She was educated at home by governesses and tutors specially selected by her mother. (Once Ada tried to elope with one of them.) At 15 she was introduced by her mother to the renowned Scottish mathematician Mary Fairfax Somerville. The two attended geography lectures together at the University of London in 1830. Afterwards, they kept up a correspondence regarding matters of mathematics.

As an adolescent Ada lost her ability to walk for approximately three years due to a vague illness, which some believe to have been psychosomatic in nature. During those years she excelled in her studies, learning all she could of mathematics as well as becoming an adept linguist and musician. In addition to her personal mathematical study, she was aided by the prominent mathematician Augustus de Morgan, who was also a mentor to the brilliant logician George Boole.

Ada was a member of the Bluestockings, a loosely knit group of women who engaged in intellectual pursuits in private settings. They would often invite men of learning to their meetings or visit museums and the homes of prominent scientists. It was at one of these gatherings—at a dinner party in the home of Mary Somerville, in June 1833—that Ada first met the mathematician and inventor Charles Babbage, who invited her and her mother to his studio for a demonstration of his calculating machine, a prototype of the Difference Engine.

Two weeks later Ada, her mother, and several other women, including Mary Somerville, went to see Babbage's invention. The large wood-and-brass machine could calculate all forms of arithmetic operations. It had toothed gears and wheels and was run by a series of manually operated cranks. Babbage also spoke of another, more advanced machine that he was planning called the Analytical Engine, which would receive input in the form of punched cards, store this information in a kind of "memory" section, and output results through a printing-press attachment.

Fascinated by the Difference Engine prototype, and even more so by Babbage's plans for the Analytical Engine, Ada was the only one in the group to fully grasp the ramifications of what he had created. "While the rest of the party [merely] gazed at this beautiful instrument," the wife of Augustus de Morgan, also present, wrote, as quoted by Howard Rheingold in *Tools for Thought* (1985), "Miss Byron, young as she was, understood its workings and saw the great beauty of the invention." Babbage was impressed with her understanding of his work, and a friendship between the two began that would continue for the rest of Ada's life.

In 1835 Ada Byron met Lord William King through Mary Somerville. Later that year, at the age of 19, she married him. They moved to the country and eventually had a daughter and two sons. The first child, Byron Noel, was born in 1836, and the second, Anne Isabella, in 1837. The following year, King gained the title of earl of Lovelace, making Ada the countess of Lovelace, or Lady Lovelace, as she was more commonly known. She bore her final child, Ralph Gordon, in 1839. Her marriage to King was basically a happy one; King supported his wife in all her intellectual endeavors.

Lovelace and Babbage began corresponding by mail in 1836. Lovelace supported and defended Babbage's often maligned work throughout their association, and once wrote to him, "I am working very hard for you, like the Devil in fact (which perhaps I am.)," as quoted by Betty Toole in *Ada, The Enchantress of Numbers* (1992). Much of the mathematical work she was doing at this time was recorded in a notebook which frequently passed back and forth between her and Babbage. (The book is now lost.)

In 1840 Babbage delivered a lecture on his computing engines at the University of Turin, in Italy. The Italian mathematician (and future prime minister of Italy) Luigi Menabrea wrote a paper in 1842 detailing the Difference and Analytical Engines as they had been presented by Babbage at the lecture. Lovelace decided in 1843 to translate the paper from French to English. When Babbage read the translation, he suggested that she add some notes of her own. The result was that Lovelace's notes were three times longer than Menabrea's paper, and far more significant. It is this work for which she is most known. These notes were the first complete description of Charles Babbage's invention.

Describing the functions and purpose of the Difference Engine, the notes explain Babbage's work more thoroughly than even Babbage himself had done. Lovelace outlined the basic concepts of computer programming and described the essential elements required for any programming language, including the coding of various symbols into numerical data. She stressed that the Analytical Engine would be capable of being programmed and explained how it would solve problems considered impossible at the time. Referring to the punched cards that derived from the French weaver Joseph-Marie Jacquard's automatic loom, Lovelace remarked in her notes, "We may say most aptly that the Analytical Engine weaves algebraic patterns just as the Jacquard loom weaves flowers and leaves," as quoted on the Lady Lovelace Web site offered through Yale University, in New Haven, Connecticut. Her notes included descriptions of how computers would be able to analyze and organize data, and she predicted the general-purpose computer of the next century. She even mentioned the possibility of using computers to produce graphics and music. While she described the engine's capacity to store information, she also refuted the possibility of artificial intelligence, emphasizing that a computer cannot reason for itself and can only do that which it has been instructed to do.

Although their relationship was decidedly amicable, some friction developed between Lovelace and Babbage during the final revisions of her notes. The Countess began to lose patience with the eccentric inventor, particularly because of his carelessness and impracticality. She felt that his general abrasiveness of personality prevented Babbage from being fully trusted and supported by potential backers. Babbage closely oversaw most of Lady Lovelace's work on the notes, which led to further conflicts of interest. "I am much annoyed at your having altered my Note," she wrote to him on one occasion, as quoted on the Ada Home Web site. "You know I am always willing to make any required alterations myself, but that I cannot endure another person to meddle with my sentences." Once the paper was published (under the title "Observations on Mr. Babbage's Analytical Engine"), their friendship resumed its playful, even flirtatious tone, with Babbage in his letters often referring to his young associate as "the Enchantress of Numbers." Because of the social constraints against women publishing, Lovelace signed her manuscript with only her initials, A. A. L.

Lovelace's contribution to programming is a matter of some dispute. Some sources cite her as the first programmer, because of her suggestions to Babbage and her proposed mathematical instructions for the theoretical Analytical Engine. Other sources claim that she was more of an assistant to Babbage, reworking programs that Babbage had already written. In either case, she was a crucial part of the development process in this extremely early stage of computer programming. Some of the programming methods she helped develop include subroutines, loops, and jumps, all of which would be rediscovered by pioneering 20th-century programmers, such as Stanley Gill. It is also believed that Lovelace prophetically favored the use of the binary system for digital computing instead of the decimal system. Lovelace's awareness of the fantastic possibilities inherent in computer technology is demonstrated in a letter to Babbage in which she famously mused, "No one knows what power lies yet undeveloped in that wiry system of mine."

Throughout their relationship, the Countess of Lovelace helped stabilize the tempestuous Babbage. She encouraged him to continue his work despite his periodical lack of motivation. She coaxed him to develop ideas for his Analytical Engine by discussing the subject with him in depth. "[She] seems to understand it better than I do, and is far, far better at explaining it," he once commented, as quoted by Rheingold. Lovelace also funded Babbage's project to a certain degree, particularly after the British government ceased to do so.

By the age of 29, after giving birth to three children and working diligently on her programming theories for several years, Lady Lovelace began to decline physically and mentally. She began to suffer from respiratory and digestive ailments, for which doctors of the time often prescribed hazardous combinations of brandy, wine, beer, opium, and morphine. Soon she became addicted to these substances, in addition to the laudanum she had been taking since childhood, and she began experiencing delusional visions. She thought that her mind was directly in touch with the mind of God, and she developed personality disorders which led her to believe that she could understand the universe and was God's prophet. In a letter from this period, she wrote, as quoted on the Pioneers Web site (www.kerryr.net/pioneers), "That brain of mine is something more than mortal, as time will show."

Eventually, Lovelace was able to overcome her addictions through sheer willpower, but another all-consuming compulsion soon overtook her. Lovelace had always had an affinity for gambling, but following her recovery from drug and alcohol addiction, it developed into an obsession. She often sent her servants, or even Babbage, to place her bets, because it was unacceptable for a woman to do so. Together with Babbage, who was deeply in debt and desperate for funding, she attempted to use the Difference Engine to calculate formulas for betting on horses. Rheingold referred to their scheme as "a curious mixture of vice, high intellectual adventure, and bizarre entrepreneurship." The result was disaster. While Babbage narrowly escaped bankruptcy, Ada had to pawn her husband's family jewels to pay off her debts. It is not clear how much her husband knew of her betting scheme, but he and Babbage worked frantically to fend off her creditors and salvage what they could of her reputation. Squabbling led to estrangement between Ada and her mother and strained the previously tranquil Lovelace marriage.

It is believed that in her final years, free from the influence of her mother, Lady Lovelace was able to embrace the memory of the father she had never known and come to terms with her identity as his daughter. On November 27, 1852 she died of uterine cancer. She was 36, the same age that her father had been when he died. Although she had never known her father, she requested to be buried next to him in the Byron family crypt, in Nottinghamshire. She had intended to leave an inheritance to Babbage to aid him in completing his engines, but her mother prevented this wish from being carried out.

The work of Lady Lovelace remained in obscurity until the middle of the 20th century, when the field of computer science began to take shape. Today, there is a computer language developed by the U.S. Department of Defense called ADA, in her honor. Without Ada's support and assistance, Babbage was never able to complete the Difference Engine or the Analytical Engine, and her concepts were not put into practice for almost 100 years.
—B. S.

Suggested Reading: Babbage Pages Web site; Biographies of Women Mathematicians Web site; Rheingold, Howard. *Tools for Thought*, 1985; Toole, Betty. *Ada, The Enchantress of Numbers*, 1992

Ludgate, Percy E.

Aug. 2, 1883–Oct. 16, 1922 Creator of an analytical engine

In 1909 Percy Ludgate, an Irish accountant, sketched a design for an "analytical engine," or primitive computer, that could solve mathematical problems. Although Ludgate never actually built such a machine, his design detailed how an analytical engine could store and retrieve data, just as modern computers save programs and documents on floppy disks and hard drives. Also like a modern computer, Ludgate's machine had to be programmed to operate; it worked by reading the equivalent of punched cards. A person would enter data into the engine by using one keyboard, and a second keyboard would enable a user to instruct, or "program," the machine with additional mathematical formulas, which it could remember. Ludgate imagined that his analytical engine would be no larger than a modern desktop computer and would be powered by an electric motor.

Percy Edwin Ludgate was born on August 2, 1883 in the village of Skibbereen, in County Cork, Ireland, and grew up in Dublin. In an article for the *Computer Journal* (January 1971), Brian Randell writes that, while little is know about Ludgate's life, he is thought to have attended the North Strand Parish School and studied accounting at the Rathmines College of Commerce, in Dublin. The Corporation of Accountants awarded Ludgate a gold medal after he passed his final exam with distinction. He later joined the accounting firm of Kevons and Son. One of Ludgate's co-workers, E. Dunne, told Randell that the young accountant "possessed the characteristics one usually associates with genius. . . . Like all men of his stature he was humble, courteous, patient and popular, and his early death closed a career that was full of promise for the future."

It is believed that Ludgate designed his analytical engine in his spare time. He published the results of his research in the *Scientific Proceedings of the Royal Dublin Society* (April 1909), as repub-

lished in the book, *The Origins of Digital Computers: Selected Papers* (1975), edited by Randell. Ludgate began by noting that his paper was "the result of about six years' work, undertaken by me with the object of designing machinery capable of performing calculations, however intricate or laborious, without the immediate guidance of the human intellect."

Ludgate's engine was to be about the size of a desktop computer, measuring 26 inches long, 24 inches wide, and 20 inches high. It was supposed to perform such basic calculations as addition, subtraction, multiplication, and division. He imagined that two keyboards would run the engine; one keyboard would have 10 numbered keys, from zero to nine, that would enter numbers into the engine, and the other keyboard would instruct the engine to perform mathematical functions in order to solve specific problems. According to Ludgate, the engine would have the ability to "remember" a mathematical formula after it was entered into the machine by the user.

The analytical engine worked like a punched-card machine, reading perforated holes on a paper. Each combination of holes would represent different formulas and instructions. Ludgate noted that the perforated paper tape could program the engine to perform "an indefinite number of calculations, provided that they are all of one type or kind (i.e. algebraically identical)."

Ludgate explained that an "Analytical Machine must have some means of storing the numerical data of the problem to be solved, and the figures produced at each successive step of the work (together with the proper algebraical signs); and, lastly, a means of recording the result or results." He designed an elaborate mechanism for the storage of such data, and claimed that the engine would have the capacity to store 192 variables, of 20 digits each. In his published paper, he borrowed terminology from weaving to describe the storage and calculation system. In weaving, different colors of yarn are passed back and forth on spindle-shaped devices, called shuttles, to create a woven pattern. Ludgate imagined that his machine would have two connected compartments, which he termed shuttle-boxes. Each shuttle-box would have shuttles equipped with a set of sliding metal rods—one rod for the sign of the figure (positive or negative), and other rods to represent each of the 20 decimal digits comprising a number. According to Ludgate's plan, the shuttle-box could be rotated to access any given number. He also noted that more shuttles could be added to the engine to increase its storage capacity; Randell suggested that "one could perhaps claim that this was the forerunner of the modern replaceable disk!"

To multiply two variables, for example, a user would type the numbers into a keyboard; the two variables would then be inscribed, separately, in shuttles in each of the two shuttle-boxes. When the engine was directed to multiply the variables, the shuttle-boxes would rotate until the two shuttles that hold the variables face one another. The sliding rods would then move out, and the variables would be converted into logarithms of Ludgate's invention.

Ludgate's analytical engine also had a mechanism that enabled it to print calculations. In general, the inventor strove to make his machine accessible, noting, "It must be clearly understood that the machine is designed to be quite automatic in its action, so that a person almost entirely ignorant of mathematics could use it, in some respects, as successfully as the ablest mathematician."

After working on his project for some time, Percy Ludgate discovered that the mathematician Charles Babbage had also designed an analytical engine, though he hadn't completed a working model at the time of his death, in 1872. Ludgate stressed that his work "was not based on Babbage's results— indeed, until after the completion of the first design of my machine, I had no knowledge of his prior efforts in the same direction." However, Ludgate noted that Babbage's work influenced the advanced stages of his research. Despite some similarities, there are several notable differences between Babbage's and Ludgate's analytical engines, in particular their methods for storing figures and performing calculations. Randell argued that 'all three main components of [Ludgate's] analytical engine, the store, the arithmetic unit and the sequencing mechanism show evidence of considerable ingenuity and originality."

Percy Ludgate probably would have remained obscure if Brian Randell, a computer-science professor at the University of Newcastle upon Tyne, in England, had not discovered his papers while conducting research on Charles Babbage. Randell learned what he could about Ludgate's life by tracking down his niece and a former colleague. In addition to the paper on his analytical engine, Ludgate published only one other paper, in 1914, about Charles Babbage's analytical engine. As an accountant during World War I, Ludgate played a major role in helping to organize the distribution of oats to feed the horses in the Army's cavalry divisions. There is no evidence to suggest that Ludgate ever attempted to build the analytical engine he had designed. After contracting pneumonia while on vacation, he died in Dublin, on October 16, 1922. He never married. The research papers and drawings of his engine, which he mentioned in his first published paper, have vanished.—D. C.

Suggested Reading: *Annals of the History of Computing* p327+ Oct. 1982, with photo and illus.; *Computer Journal* p317+ Jan. 1971, with photo; Randell, Brian, ed., *Origins of Digital Computers: Selected Papers*, 1975; Lee, J. A. N., ed. *International Biographical Dictionary of Computer Pioneers*, 1995

Mandelbrot, Benoit

Nov. 20, 1924– Developer of fractal theory

"Science would be ruined," the Polish-born mathematician Benoit Mandelbrot once wrote, "if (like sports) it were to put competition above everything else, and if it were to clarify the rules of competition by withdrawing entirely into narrowly defined specialities. The rare scholars who are nomads-by-choice are essential to the intellectual welfare of the settled disciplines." A nomad-by-choice since the early 1950s, Mandelbrot has contributed to fields as diverse as linguistics, economics, physiology, and physics. His greatest interdisciplinary contribution is fractal geometry, one of the most important developments in 20th-century mathematics. The behavior of earthquakes, the patterns of the weather, and the distribution of galaxies in space are a few of the irregular, even chaotic phenomena that have begun to yield the secrets of their structures to the new geometry.

Mandelbrot's unifying theme is the concept of scaling, which refers to patterns whose large-scale irregularities are echoed in their finer details. Its companion concept, fractal dimension, measures the degree of irregularity, and the related ability to fill space, of those patterns. Mandelbrot spent much of his time during the 1960s and 1970s collecting curves and other geometric patterns that

Courtesy of Benoit Mandelbrot

mathematicians had once considered to be "pathological" and showing them to be virtual blueprints of many natural objects. In so doing, he went beyond the limits of older theories of shape such as

Euclidean geometry, which describes the natural world in terms of one-dimensional lines, two-dimensional surfaces, and such three-dimensional objects as spheres and cones.

Scientists following Mandelbrot's lead have begun to theorize about previously poorly understood phenomena whose shapes are related to their behavior. Mathematicians have found the most complex orderly object yet known in their field in the form of the Mandelbrot set, invented by Mandelbrot in 1979 and later named in his honor. More recently, Hollywood filmmakers have made use of fractals in computer graphics to create alien planets for their blockbuster movies. From 1958 to 1993 Mandelbrot worked at International Business Machines (IBM), where he became IBM fellow in 1974. In 1993 he joined Yale University, in New Haven, Connecticut, where he is now Sterling Professor of Mathematical Sciences. He remains at IBM as Emeritus. In 1985 he was awarded the Barnard Medal for Meritorious Service to Science, given by recommendation of the National Academy of Sciences once every five years to those persons whose contributions to the discipline are "beneficial to the human race." His major awards have included the Wolf Foundation Prize for Physics in 1993 and the Japan Prize for Science and Technology in 2003.

Benoit Mandelbrot was born in Warsaw, Poland, on November 20, 1924 to Charles Mandelbrot, a clothing manufacturer, and Bella (Lurie) Mandelbrot, a physician. He learned very early that "some people live by and for the production of new mathematics" through the example of his uncle, Szolem Mandelbrojt, a leader in mathematical analysis. Tutored by another uncle, Loterman Mandelbrot, because his mother was "afraid of epidemics" and kept him at home when he should have been attending the first and second grades, Benoit began reading books and studying maps before he had mastered the entire alphabet. A precocious chess player, he was a champion in his age group, but he retired from the game in 1936 at the age of eleven, when his family moved to Paris.

At the outbreak of World War II the Mandelbrot family moved again, this time to Tulle, near Clermont-Ferrand in central France. Mandelbrot told Anthony Barcellos, who interviewed him for *Mathematical People: Profiles and Interviews* (1985), that in 1942, after he completed the curriculum at the Lycée Edmond Perrier in Tulle, "poverty and the wish to keep away from big cities to maximize the chances of survival" forced him to dispense with higher education. "For a while, I was moving around with a younger brother," he told Barcellos, "toting around a few obsolete books and learning things my way, guessing a number of things myself, doing nothing in any rational or even half-reasonable fashion, and acquiring a great deal of independence and self-confidence."

When Paris was liberated in 1944, Mandelbrot took the grueling entrance exams at France's leading science schools, the École Normale Supérieure

and the École Polytechnique, achieving scores that placed him near the top of his class in both schools. His success had little to do with any profound knowledge of analytical mathematical techniques, for he had little training in them. As he explained to Barcellos, "Faced with some complicated integral, I instantly related it to a familiar shape; usually it was exactly the shape that had motivated this integral. I knew an army of shapes I'd encountered once in some book or in some problem, and remembered forever, with their properties and peculiarities. . . . Everybody else took an exam in algebra and complicated integrals, and I managed to take an exam in translation into geometry and thinking in terms of geometric shapes."

After two days at the École Normale, where geometry was out of favor, Mandelbrot switched to the École Polytechnique. Freed from a requirement to concentrate and compete in any single subject area, he read widely and voraciously and soaked up classical music "like a big dry sponge." In 1947, after receiving his degree from the École Polytechnique, he left for the California Institute of Technology, in Pasadena, where he completed the requirements for a Master of Science degree in aeronautics in 1948 and for a professional degree in aeronautics before returning to France. After serving for a year in the French air force, he enrolled at the University of Paris to work towards his Ph.D. degree.

Mandelbrot's doctoral thesis, "Mathematical Theory of Games of Communication," was inspired in part by a book review that he once had fished out of Szolem Mandelbrojt's wastepaper basket. It explained away Zipf's law, which rules word frequencies in all languages and in the discourse of all speakers. In explicating Zipf's law, Mandelbrot made his first use of the concept of scaling, devising lexicographic trees, each of whose branches, with their sub-branchings, replicated the entire tree on a smaller scale. The trees indicated the richness of a particular vocabulary or discourse by assigning probabilities to words corresponding to certain branch tips. In the second part of the two-part thesis Mandelbrot discussed thermodynamics. Some scholars remarked on the oddity of the combination, but Mandelbrot was granted his Ph.D. in 1952.

In an era of increasing specialization, Mandelbrot's interdisciplinary instincts were held in suspicion by academics, and well-meaning friends warned him to "settle down" if he wished to develop a successful career. He won a temporary reprieve from that impasse when the distinguished mathematician John von Neumann sponsored him for a fellowship to the Institute of Advanced Study in Princeton, New Jersey, for the academic year 1953–54. There he met Henry McKean Jr., who introduced him to one of his major tools, the concept of Hausdorff-Besicovitch dimension. McKean had used that concept to study shapes traced by the frantic and fantastically irregular motion of fine particles suspended in a fluid, known as Brownian motion. Since a particle's motion takes it all over the two-dimensional surface of the liquid, its trail becomes two-dimensional from a Hausdorff-Besicovitch perspective, though from other mathematical perspectives it remains a one-dimensional line.

That fact was a revelation to Mandelbrot. Even topology, which mathematicians had used since the 19th century to study objects that changed position by moving, stretching, or being twisted, would not have recognized any fundamental dimensional difference between the path of a Brownian particle and a regular line. Mandelbrot later showed that the Hausdorff-Besicovitch dimension, which he adopted on the spot, was an almost ubiquitous tool and a special example of the wider notion of fractal dimension. After his year in Princeton, Mandelbrot returned for three years to Europe, first to Geneva, Switzerland, and then to France, where he taught mathematics at the University of Lille and the École Polytechnique and continued an association that he had begun in 1949 at the Centre National de la Recherche Scientifique (National Center for Scientific Research) in Paris.

Returning to the United States, Mandelbrot began a long association with IBM as a faculty adviser in the summer of 1958, and, after staying on as a consultant, he pursued his developing interest in economic topics. His first major conceptual breakthrough came in 1961, when IBM asked him to analyze errors caused by random noise clustering in telephone circuits—noise that the company's engineers originally thought was caused by men working somewhere in the system with screwdrivers.

Characteristically, the behavior of the noise reminded Mandelbrot of a shape—a diagram of the zero-crossings of Brownian motion, a dustlike pattern of points with a dimension between zero and one. Mandelbrot realized that the noise could not have been caused by workmen because it came in bursts made up of increasingly smaller bursts. Furthermore, it was intimately linked with the strength of the telephone signals being sent. Mandelbrot saved IBM from a major waste of corporate resources by having its early noise-correcting projects called off. He and an IBM associate, Jay Berger, published "A new model for the clustering of errors on telephone circuits" in 1963, basing their model on what is now known as a "Cantor fractal dust," which can be made in its simplest form by taking a line segment and removing the middle third, then removing the middle thirds of the resulting two-line segments, and repeating the process ad infinitum. The infinite "dust" thus generated, as randomized by Berger and Mandelbrot, accounted for the pattern of noise that clung to the telephone signals.

"The full strength of scaling assumptions," as Mandelbrot put it, became clear in the early 1960s when he applied them to the wild fluctuations of stock market prices. His model helped to disprove a then-accepted method of anticipating optimum buying times and succeeded in modeling market changes on a dizzying range of time scales. Mandelbrot was able to account almost exactly for the statistical distribution of the changes in daily cotton prices over a five-year period, for fluctuations in those prices on a monthly basis, and finally for often violent price changes, involving recessions and depressions, over almost a century. Not known for his false modesty, Mandelbrot has written, "I know of no other comparably successful prediction in economics." He also hastens to say that the prediction is only statistical in nature.

Although the regular practitioners of the disciplines Mandelbrot encroached upon still viewed him as "a stranger who (for reasons unknown) was wandering in and out," Mandelbrot told Barcellos, "Luckily the striking (and often shocking) news I was bringing could not pass unnoticed. . . . I became very popular in many diverse departments as a visiting professor, but no major university wanted a permanent professor with such unpredictable interests." Mandelbrot became associated with Harvard University, in Cambridge, Massachusetts, as a visiting professor of economics and a research fellow in psychology, from 1962 to 1963, and a visiting professor of applied mathematics and a staff member of the Joint Committee on Biomedical Computer Science, from 1962 to 1964.

Exchanges of ideas with his colleagues at Harvard made it clear to Mandelbrot that his scaling assumptions could be applied wholesale to the mysteries of turbulence—the violent disruptions in fluid flow and the atmosphere that are visible in waterfalls and hurricanes and are all too familiar to airline passengers who experience sudden series of bumps during flights. He prepared for his investigation by listening to amplified recordings of turbulence and by studying photographs and drawings of turbulence stretching back to the drawing known as "The Deluge" in the notebooks of Leonardo da Vinci. He concluded that one ought to study geometrically the intuitive notion that turbulence could be considered as "the superposition of eddies of many diverse sizes."

Mandelbrot next integrated a number of theories about the phenomenon, many aspects of which had baffled scientists since the 19th century. One theory, put forward by Lewis Fry Richardson, held that turbulent areas form when a disturbance sets off a cascade of eddies in a fluid. Mandelbrot demonstrated that such cascades "curdle" into precise fractal shapes whose dimension is greater than two. That these shapes were fractals implied a greater likelihood of intense—and, in some instances, dangerous—pockets of turbulence than had previously been realized. Mandelbrot later extended the curdling concept to the formation of galaxies. One property of fractals is that their density decreases as they grow larger. Pointing out that galactic clusters are distributed over a fractal whose dimension is less than two, Mandelbrot showed that the density of matter in the universe decreases as the volume of space increases.

Despite his wide-ranging achievements, Mandelbrot found himself in the mid-1960s still having to delete prefaces explaining the increasing unity of his insights in order to have his papers published in reputable journals. He sought and, in 1967 found, a natural and concrete representation of his ideas in the form of coastlines, and in a paper published that year asked what has become his most famous question, "How long is the coast of Britain?" His answer was that it depends on the length of the ruler used to measure the coastline and its numberless promontories and bays, which can be found on all scales down to the molecular level. An extremely long ruler would fail to measure many small inlets and tiny nooks and crannies. As increasingly short rulers were selected, the coastline's measured length would grow and become infinitely long. The speed at which the coastline's length increases and becomes infinite as the ruler shrinks yields its fractal dimension. In 1973, using an algorithm supplied by Mandelbrot, Sigmund Handelman of IBM was able to make computer-generated images of coastlines that resembled those of New Zealand and the islands of the Aegean. "After seeing the coastline pictures," Mandelbrot has recalled, "everyone agreed with me that fractals were part of the stuff of nature."

That agreement led to a wider appreciation of the mathematical "monsters" that Mandelbrot had consulted and adapted in developing his models. In modeling coastlines, for instance, he had made use of the Koch snowflake, which was invented by Helge von Koch in the early years of the 20th century. The snowflake begins with an equilateral triangle on each of whose sides is centered an equilateral triangle one-third the size of the first, to form a Star of David. On the sides of the triangles that form the points of the star, triangles one third *their* size are centered. Repeated until the curve starts to resemble a snowflake, the process is continued ad infinitum, so that the curve's perimeter quickly becomes infinitely long and so detailed that no straight line can be drawn to touch it at only one point. That fact caused one of von Koch's colleagues to turn away "in fright and horror" when he first saw the snowflake. Between 1875 and 1925 an entire "gallery" of such monsters was created by mathematicians in an outburst that paralleled the development of atonal music and cubist painting in the arts and that was intended to prove that mathematicians could create figures totally divorced from nature.

The physicist Freeman J. Dyson has noted that Mandelbrot's triumph consists in his demonstration that "nature has played a joke on the mathematicians," since their pathological structures "turn out to be inherent in natural objects all around us." After the success of the computer-generated coastlines, Mandelbrot collaborated more and more with IBM colleagues such as Richard Voss to generate pictures of his algorithms. He also began to work on developing fractal landscapes because of their potential to drive home the persuasive power of his theory.

The fact that immensely detailed fractal shapes could be generated from relatively brief equations, and the fact that so many of them suggest snails, jellyfish, and other forms of life, led Mandelbrot to suspect that much of nature is created by the repetition of simple steps. The fact that a small change in the dimension of a fractal can drastically alter its shape suggested to Mandelbrot a possible way of modeling the manner in which a relatively small amount of genetic material can give rise to complex structures such as the lung and brain, and to entire organisms. By using fractals he was able to account for the biological sleight of hand that allows the blood vessels to fill every part of the human body while taking up only five percent of its volume. Such insights led to Mandelbrot's appointment to an unpaid visiting professorship in physiology at the Albert Einstein College of Medicine, in New York City, in 1970, a year in which he also served as a visiting professor of engineering at Yale.

Mandelbrot saw "a golden opportunity" to integrate his interests before the public when he was asked to give a talk at the Collège de France in Paris in January 1973. Unlike the prefaces he had been forced to leave unpublished over the years, the talk, he told Anthony Barcellos, "was received with much praise and no hostility at all," bringing home to him the fact that his "years in the wilderness were about to end." While consulting his son's Latin dictionary soon afterwards, he coined the word "fractal" from the Latin for broken and irregular. Mandelbrot's work *Les objets fractals: forme, hasard et dimension* was published by Flammarion in Paris in 1975. A revised English version, *Fractals: Form, Chance, and Dimension* (1977), was followed by the full-scale "fractal manifesto," *The Fractal Geometry of Nature* (1982). By that time, Mandelbrot and Voss's computer imagery had become spectacular, generating realistic lunar landscapes and earthlike planets, as well as islands and unearthly mountain ranges. Fractals, used by special effects teams, started appearing in motion pictures like *Star Trek II: the Wrath of Khan* (1982) and *Return of the Jedi* (1983).

In 1979 Mandelbrot began to investigate so-called self-inverse fractals and then self-squared fractals, which led him back to the work of Gaston Julia, whom he had encountered years before while studying at the École Polytechnique. During World War I, Gaston Julia wrote a monumental paper referred to in Mandelbrot's school days as "the celebrated prize essay." Julia described a set that grows from a simple "mathematical seed," a number on which a certain operation is performed. In one example, the number is squared and a constant such as "one" is added to it to yield a new number, which then becomes the mathematical seed. The process is repeated indefinitely and the mathematical seeds at the heart of it are the "complex numbers"—two-part numbers involving the square root of negative one.

The result, as illustrated in Mandelbrot's computer graphics, is that "basins of attraction," appearing on the computer screen as colorful pools, form in the plane defined by the complex numbers. In the example in which the mathematical seed is squared, for instance, the general equation that defines Mandelbrot's procedure has two solutions, or roots. Many of the mathematical seeds, when used in the general equation, converge toward one of the roots at a certain rate. Each seed is assigned a color whose shade indicates the rate at which it converges toward a root. In this way, shade by shade, color by color, the basins of attraction form. "The result is like a glowing tapestry," Ivar Peterson observed in *Science News* (February 28, 1987). "And right on the convoluted boundary [of the tapestry] lie points that lead to no root." Mandelbrot named such boundaries "Julia sets." They were fractals so fantastic in shape that Mandelbrot dubbed his favorites "mathematical dragons." He created entire families of dragons and other Julia sets by allowing the constant added to his mathematical seeds to vary.

Further investigations led Mandelbrot to discover the set now named in his honor, which is the most complex orderly object in mathematics, with an entire Julia set associated with every one of its infinite points. The Mandelbrot set and the Julia set have since become objects of systematic study by mathematicians and computer scientists in a number of countries. Computer microscopes have discovered that, unlike self-similar fractals such as the Koch curve, the Mandelbrot set, characterized at first glance by a kind of rounded, upside-down heart shape bonded to a circular shape, reveals entire baroque landscapes of new and chimerical shapes in addition to the original one when its least detail is magnified.

Ideas that developed from the Mandelbrot set have been found to provide a good description of what happens in dynamic systems such as the human heart when they break their normal rhythm and race out of control. Together with the rest of the fractals, it has exerted a powerful influence on science. In some areas of physics, in which the shape of a system, either in real space or so-called "phase space," accounts for much of its behavior, fractals have become crucial. In meteorology the shape of large cloud systems, and therefore the pattern, intensity, and timing of the rain that falls from them, have been found to be fractal, as is the pattern in which rainwater seeps through the soil.

Benoit Mandelbrot has received numerous additional award for his work, including a Guggenheim fellowship, in 1968; IBM's Research Division Award, in 1983; and IBM's Corporate Award, in 1984. After being given the Barnard Medal for Meritorious Service to Science in 1985, he received the Franklin Medal for Signal and Eminent Service in Science from the Franklin Institute of Philadelphia in 1986. In 1988 he won the Charles Proteus Steinmetz Medal; that same year he won the Alexander von Humbolt Prize, the Science for Art Prize, and

the Harvey Prize of the Technion-Israel Insitute of Technology. He won the Nevada Prize, in 1991; the Honda Prize, in 1994; the Medal of the City of Paris, in 1996; and the Lewis Fry Richardson Medal, in 1999. He received the Sven Berggren and Proctor Prizes in 2002. In 1982 he became a fellow of the American Academy of Arts and Sciences and in 1987 a member of the National Academy of Sciences.

Benoit Mandelbrot married the scientist Aliette Mandelbrot on November 5, 1955, and they have two sons, Laurent and Didier, and one grandson. His most recent books include "La Geometria della Natura" (1987), "Fractals and Scaling in Finance: Discontinuity, Concentration, Risk" (1997), "Multifractuals and l/f Noise: Wild Self-Affinity in Physics" (1999), and "Gaussian Fractals" (1999). Although the isolation in which he worked for so many years has been dispelled by the growing popularity of fractals, Mandelbrot still insisted as of a 1985 interview, "I don't belong to any of the groups, and my work flies against the natural tendency of everything to divide itself into pieces."—C. M.

Suggested Reading: *New York Times Magazine* p64+ Dec. 8, 1985; *Omni* p64+ Feb. 1984; *The World & I* p162+ Feb 1987; *American Men and Women of Science 1998–99*, 1998; Gleick, James. *Chaos: Making a New Science*, 1987; Albers, Donald J., and G. L. Alexanderson. *Mathematical People: Profiles and Interviews*, 1985

Marconi, Guglielmo

Apr. 25, 1874–July 20, 1937 Pioneer of radio telegraphy

During the 1890s and early 1900s, the Italian electrical engineer and inventor Guglielmo Marconi perfected the technology that made wireless radio a practical means of communication. Before Marconi, the only means of rapid long-distance communication—the telegraph and the telephone—depended upon a vast network of wire cables; communication was therefore limited to those connected to the network, and constrained by the cost of building the necessary infrastructure. Marconi's development of wireless telegraphy provided a way to send traditional telegraph messages, using Morse code (an alphabet consisting of electronic signals), through the air via radio waves. (Wireless telephony, the transmission of electronic signals to replicate the sound of the human voice, was developed separately by Canadian inventor Reginald Fessenden between 1900 and 1906.) In 1895 Marconi transmitted his first radio signal across a distance of approximately 1.5 miles. In 1899 he sent the first wireless signal across the English Channel, and in 1901 he sent the first transatlantic radiotelegraph message, from England to Canada.

Hulton Archive by Getty Images

Guglielmo Marconi

Guglielmo Marconi was born in Bologna on April 25, 1874, the second son of Giuseppe Marconi, a landowner, and his second wife, an Irish woman named Annie Jameson. Between the ages of three and six, Marconi lived with his mother and older brother in England. Upon his return to Italy, his English was better than his Italian; he was therefore tutored privately in Bologna and Florence before entering a technical school in Livorno. By the age of 20, he had developed a strong interest in the physical sciences, especially electricity, and had studied the work of James Clerk Maxwell, Heinrich Hertz, Edouard Branly, Oliver Lodge, and Augusto Righi, who was a friend and neighbor of the Marconis.

Radio technology had its origins in the discoveries made by Maxwell, a Scottish physicist, who had predicted the existence of electromagnetic waves, or radio waves, in the 1860s. In the late 1880s, Hertz, a German physicist, demonstrated that rapid oscillations of electric current in a wire (which would later be called an antenna) could emit radio waves into the surrounding space. The machine he used was dubbed a Hertzian oscillator, and radio waves were known for a time as Hertzian waves. (Today radio frequencies are measured in hertz, abbreviated Hz, which refers to cycles per second.) Marconi's involvement with wireless telegraphy began in 1894, while on an alpine vacation, when he read a description of Hertz's demonstration. Although Hertz had failed to explore the ramifications of his discovery, Marconi realized that these radio waves could be used to transmit signals through the air—and hence communicate at a distance without the use of wires.

After applying to the University of Bologna, Marconi failed the entrance exams, and his mother asked Righi (who taught at the school) if her son could use their laboratory facilities. Righi consented, allowing Marconi to begin a series of telegraphy experiments. Marconi built a simple radio transmitter, using a Hertzian oscillator and an induction coil (to increase voltages), which he combined with a Morse key to send the Morse code. For his receiver, he used a coherer, which is a glass tube filled with loose metal filings, that was able to detect Hertzian waves. One of Marconi's first improvements upon his system was modifying the coherer. When a strong electrical spark went off, even at a considerable distance, the filings would cohere and allow a current to flow. The coherer could be attached to an electric doorbell, which the current would cause to ring. There was a problem, however, in that once the filings had cohered, they remained that way, thus making any further detection of signals impossible. Marconi therefore added a mechanical device that tapped the coherer after each signal in order to loosen up the metal filings for the next signal. He named his device, aptly, a tapper. Soon Marconi had succeeded in using his transmitter to ring an electric bell attached to a receiver across the lawn of his father's estate near Bologna. By mid-1895 Marconi had figured out how to further amplify a transmitter signal by grounding the oscillator and connecting a metal plate or cylinder to a vertical antenna far above the ground, creating a rudimentary radio tower. In this way, he was able to send a signal about 1.5 miles.

Marconi tried unsuccessfully to interest the Italian government in his invention. He then traveled to England, where he hoped to secure funding for research and eventually develop a commercially viable product. His visit to the country began unfavorably when suspicious customs officials smashed his wireless apparatus, but after rebuilding it, he was able to attract the attention of British entrepreneurs and government officials. A cousin, Henry Jameson Davis, introduced Marconi to Sir William Preece, the engineer-in-chief of the post office, who helped Marconi obtain the first patent ever granted for radiotelegraphy, in 1896. After making a few improvements to his system, Marconi sent a message almost two miles in September of that year. When the Italian government called upon him to serve three years of military service, he was fortunate to secure a nominal assignment as a naval student at the Italian embassy in London, allowing him to continue his work. In May 1897 Marconi sent messages across the Bristol Channel, a distance of almost nine miles. That July, he and a small group of investors formed the Wireless Telegraph and Signal Company to install wireless telegraph systems in lighthouses along the English coast. (In 1900 the firm was renamed Marconi's Wireless Telegraph Company, Ltd.) In September 1899 Marconi equipped two U.S. ships with radio transmitters so they could transmit messages about the progress of the America's Cup yacht race to newspapers in New York City, an achievement that created a sensation in the U.S. and led to the formation of the American Marconi Company.

In the course of his work, Marconi found that the range of transmission was proportional to the number and length of antennas used. To send a message 28 miles across the English Channel, he used a battery of antennas each 150 feet high. In 1900, applying the discoveries of Karl Ferdinand Braun, Marconi added a condenser and tuning coils to his transmitter, giving the signal more energy. The condenser magnified the effect of the oscillations produced by the sparking apparatus, and the coils induced the antenna to oscillate precisely to the period of the enhanced oscillations. These two circuits were now tuned to one another, preventing destructive interference and minimizing signal diminution. At the same time, he improved signal reception by adding tuning coils to the receiver, so that the receiving antenna passed on to the coherer only tuned oscillations identical to those transmitted. This allowed various radio towers to transmit without interfering with one another, while also enabling the receiver to be tuned to the chosen signal. In April 1900 Marconi filed patent No. 7777 for Improvements in Apparatus for Wireless Telegraphy, now a famous part of radio history, securing a virtual monopoly by enabling multiple stations to transmit at different frequencies without interference. (In 1943 the U.S. Supreme Court overturned patent No. 7777, ruling that Nikola Tesla, Sir Oliver Lodge, and John Stone had also contributed to the development of the patented technologies.)

By the end of 1900 Marconi had successfully transmitted messages as far as 150 miles. In January 1901 he established wireless contact between points 186 miles apart along the English coast. For various broadcasts, Marconi employed the novel technique of floating antennas upon kites and balloons to increase the range of transmission. Then, toward the end of 1901, Marconi enjoyed his greatest achievement. At the time many experts believed that the curvature of the earth would inhibit the transmission of radio signals further than about 200 miles. It was assumed that a signal would travel in a straight line out into space. Marconi proved his contemporaries wrong in 1901 when he received a signal at a station in St. John's, Newfoundland, on the eastern coast of Canada, that had traveled 2,100 miles across the Atlantic Ocean from Cornwall, England. The event was highly publicized worldwide, making Marconi's a household name.

A host of other achievements followed. In 1902, while on board the U.S. liner *Philadelphia*, Marconi found that the radio transmissions he received at night had traveled as much as three times farther than those he received during the day. He was the first to take note of this phenomenon, which is attributed to the ionization of the atmosphere during the hours of sunlight. In 1905 he patented a horizontal directional aerial. In 1907 he opened the first transatlantic commercial wireless service. In 1910 Marconi, stationed in Buenos Aires, Argentina, received radio transmissions that had originated more than 6,000 miles away, in Ireland.

Marconi's radio transmitters became required equipment on all seagoing ships during this period, saving many lives, including the 705 passengers on the *Titanic* who were rescued from lifeboats in 1912, after a nearby vessel received a distress signal from the sinking ship. Also in 1912, Marconi patented an improved "timed spark" system for generating continuous transmission waves. During World War I Marconi served in the Italian army as a lieutenant and later a captain, before becoming a commander of the Italian navy. He also directed the telegraphy program of the Italian armed forces. In 1919 Marconi was named Italian plenipotentiary delegate to the Paris Peace Conference, signing for Italy the peace treaties with Austria and Bulgaria.

It was during his tenure in the Italian military that Marconi first began to experiment with signals of shorter wavelength. He observed that shorter wavelengths permitted the use of reflectors around the aerial transmitter, which focused the signal and reduced the risk of transmissions being intercepted by enemies. After the war, in 1921, Marconi converted his steam yacht, the Elettra, into a home, laboratory, and office, and began an intensive study of shortwave telegraphy. In 1923 he received a shortwave signal sent from a one-kilowatt transmitter 1,400 miles away in Poldhu, Cornwall. The signals were significantly louder than those that had been sent from Caernarfon, in Wales, using a wavelength several hundred times greater and using 100 times the power. Marconi's focused, shortwave transmissions have become the basis for most modern long-distance broadcasting systems today. By 1927 Marconi's company had established an international network of commercial shortwave telegraph links. In 1931 Marconi began to study the transmission of microwaves, and by the following year he established the first microwave radiotelephone link—between the Pope's palace at Castel Gandolfo and Vatican City. In 1934 Marconi demonstrated the utility of microwave telegraphy for navigation at sea.

Marconi received numerous international honors and awards during his lifetime. In 1909 Marconi and Karl Braun shared the Nobel Prize in Physics, in recognition of their contributions to the development of wireless telegraphy. Hans Hildebrand of the Royal Swedish Academy of Sciences, noting the theoretical work of Michael Faraday, Hertz, and others who preceded Marconi, pointed out that Marconi's first success was gained as a result of his ability to shape current technologies into a practical, usable system. Marconi's other awards included the Franklin Medal of the Franklin Institute and the Albert Medal of the Royal Society of Arts in London. In Italy he received the hereditary title of Marchese, an appointment to the Senate in 1929, and the Grand Cross of the Order of the Crown of Italy.

Marconi married the Irish-born Beatrice O'Brien in 1905; they had three children. The marriage was annulled in 1924, and three years later he married Countess Maria Bezzi-Scali, with whom he had one daughter. Marconi died in Rome on July 20, 1937.—P. G. H.

Suggested Reading: *Audio* p20+ Aug. 1995; *Life: The Millennium Supplement* p104 Fall 1997, with photo; *Tech Directions* p58 Mar. 1999; *Voice and Data* (on-line) 1999; de Boinod, B. L., and Collier, D. M. *Marconi: Master of Space*, 1935; Dunlap, O. E. *Marconi: The Man and His Wireless*, 1937; Coe, D. *Marconi: Pioneer of Radio*, 1943; Marconi, D. *My Father Marconi*, 1962; Gunston, D. *Marconi, Father of Radio*, 1965; Clayton, H. *Atlantic Bridgehead*, 1968; Jolly, W. P. *Marconi*, 1972

Marquand, Allan

Dec. 10, 1853–Sep. 24, 1924 Archaeologist; professor

Allan Marquand is best remembered for his distinguished career as a professor of art and archaeology at Princeton University, in New Jersey. A renowned scholar, during the early part of 20th century he wrote many books on art history, including eight volumes devoted to the Della Robbias, a Renaissance-era family of sculptors and artists, and also helped found the university's Museum of Art. Less known, however, is Marquand's contribution to the development of data processing. In 1877 one of Marquand's professors at Johns Hopkins University, in Baltimore, Maryland, introduced him to the "logical machines" built by the British mathematician W. Stanley Jevons. Logical machines were early computers, encased in wooden boxes and operated mechanically through a system of rods, ropes, pins, and a keyboard. Borrowing heavily from Jevons's designs, Marquand built two machines of his own, and in 1885 he designed, but never built, a logic machine powered by electricity, a revolutionary development in its time.

The son of a prominent banker, Allan Marquand was born on December 10, 1853 in New York City. His father, Henry Gurdon Marquand, was one of the chief benefactors and co-founders of the Metropolitan Museum of Art, in New York City. The younger Marquand studied at New Jersey's Princeton University, where in 1874 he graduated second in his class and served as the class president and Latin salutatorian. According to Alexander Leitch's book *A Princeton Companion* (1978), Marquand was both an excellent student and an accomplished athlete. In addition to being a gymnast, he was also a member of the track team and president of Princeton's boating club.

After his graduation Marquand studied theology at the Princeton Seminary for three years and then briefly at the Union Theological Seminary, in New York City. In 1877 he went to Germany to study at the University of Berlin. When he returned to the United States a year later, Marquand enrolled at Johns Hopkins University, to pursue a Ph.D. in philosophy, which he earned in 1880. In 1881 he joined the faculty of Princeton University, lecturing in logic and tutoring in Latin.

While at Johns Hopkins, Marquand had taken a course with Professor Charles S. Peirce, who introduced him to "logical machines," which are widely considered to be the precursor to the modern computer. Peirce was an admirer and correspondent of the British mathematician W. Stanley Jevons (1836–64), who in 1877 had constructed a mechanical device to teach Boolean logic in concrete terms to his students at Owens College (now the University of Manchester) in the United Kingdom. (The British mathematician George Boole (1815–64) explained how logic could be presented in algebraic forms. When combined with binary numbering systems, Boolean logic, as it is called in honor of its developer, forms the basis for the operation of most digital computers today.)

In 1881, the year he began lecturing at Princeton, Marquand constructed his own logical machine, which displayed logical syllogisms. The machine was composed of six interconnected wheels. The three wheels in the back of the machine were of ascending size—one, two, and four inches in diameter. Three one-inch wheels on the front of the machine contained cards that displayed different syllogisms. Turning the crank eight times produced seven variations of the original syllogism and then restored the original one. Marquand admitted that his machine was "somewhat similar to the well-known machine of Prof. Jevons," as quoted by George H. Buck and Stephen M. Hunka in an article for the *IEEE Annals of the History of Computing* (1999). The only advantage of Marquand's machine was that it could solve Boolean expressions of up to 10 terms—six more than Jevons's.

Buck and Hunka speculated, however, that Marquand's original logical machine did not work as anticipated, because during the winter of 1882, Marquand had C. G. Rockwood, a fellow professor at Princeton, build a new machine. The second machine, which is still on display at the university, could solve expressions of only four terms. It displayed Boolean expressions with a system of pointers activated by a series of rods, springs, and cords. The pointers remained in one of two positions, horizontal or vertical. A horizontal pointer indicated that a particular letter is a binary 1, and the vertical pointer represented 0. Like Jevons's machine, Marquand's was activated by manipulating its keys. (It required only half of the 20 keys on Jevon's design, though, making it simpler to operate.) The 1, or "restoration key," readied the machine to solve a problem by raising all of the pointers horizontally to the left. The 0, or "destruction key," caused the pointers to rotate downward in a vertical position. The letter keys were connected to strings that, when pressed, rotated either two vertical or two horizontal rods. The rods held pins that engaged catch releases on certain pointers, causing them to drop to the vertical position. Spiral strings on the rods returned them to their original position when the keys were released. Although both Jevons's and Marquand's machines simplified complex Boolean expressions, both were limited in the number of terms that could be displayed. As quoted by Buck and Hunka, Peirce said, "I do not think there would be any great difficulty in constructing a machine which should work the logic of relations with a large number of terms."

In 1885 Marquand, perhaps inspired by his mentor, Peirce, sketched out a diagram for a logic machine powered by electricity. "Even though Marquand does not appear to have had the electromechanical logical machine constructed, the idea nevertheless represents a natural progression from mechanical digital computing to electrical," Buck and Hunka observed. "Indeed, had Marquand's ideas become more widely known in his time, then the development of electronic digital computing might well have occurred before the 20th century."

Despite his achievements with the design of logical machines, Allan Marquand won the most acclaim as an archaeologist and professor of art history. (According to Leitch, James McCosh, the president of Princeton, had urged Marquand in 1882 to begin teaching art history after "detecting an unorthodox . . . bent in [his] teaching of philosophy.") A year later, Marquand became the first professor to hold a chair in art and archaeology, which was endowed by his uncle. Marquand published many books, including *Greek Architecture* (1909) and an eight-volume set on the Della Robbia family, whose members were renowned sculptors and ceramists during the Renaissance in Florence. In 1885 he helped found the Archaeological Institute of America, and he served as the associate editor of the group's publication, the *American Journal of Archaeology*.

Over the ensuing decades Marquand supervised the expansion of Princeton's art and archaeology department, often paying for such expenses as new books himself. In 1910 he relinquished his chair so the department could hire an additional professor, in effect, working for free. By 1922 Marquand presided over a faculty of 13 professors, who taught more than 800 students. Marquand also became the first director of Princeton's art museum and often made important gifts to its collection.

Allan Marquand married Eleanor Cross in 1896. The couple had four children. Marquand died at Presbyterian Hospital in New York City on September 24, 1924, after a long illness. An editorial in the *New York Times* (September 26, 1924) observed that Marquand "leaves an enduring monument of a twofold sort—his own profound and mature scholarship as represented in his writings, and the organized structure of higher education in the history of art which he conceived and promoted."

His work with logical machines is not mentioned.—D. C.

Suggested Reading: *IEEE Annals of the History of Computing* p21+ vol. 21, no. 4, 1999; *New York Times* p23 Sep. 25, 1924, p20 Sep. 26, 1924; Leitch, Alexander. *A Princeton Companion,* 1978; Peirce, C. S., ed. *Studies in Logic,* 1883

Martin, James

1933– Information-technology consultant; business leader; author

The author of more than 100 computer textbooks, the information-technology consultant and business leader James Martin has been called "the guru of the Information Age." He is widely recognized as one of the most influential authorities on the social and commercial impact of computer technology. In his well-known book, the Pulitzer Prize–nominated *The Wired Society* (1978), Martin formulated a number of predictions about how computers would revolutionize peoples' lives; these progressive ideas about technology, many of which have since been actualized, helped secure his reputation as a leading computing futurist. Martin's most recent book, *After the Internet: Alien Intelligence* (2000), continues this exploration of the frontiers of computer technology. In addition to writing books, Martin has been involved in the foundation of several management and technology consulting companies. He currently serves as chairman emeritus for Headstrong, an international consulting leader that he started in 1981 as James Martin Associates. Martin was inducted into the Computer Hall of Fame in 1997.

James Martin was born in England in 1933. He earned his M.A. and D.Litt. degrees from Oxford University before obtaining a D.Sc. (equivalent to a Ph.D.) from the University of Salford in England. In 1959 he began working for the International Business Machines Corporation (IBM) and later the IBM Systems Research Institute, where he remained for the next 19 years. Since that time he has founded or co-founded several successful technology businesses, including KnowledgeWare (formerly Database Design Inc.), James Martin Insight, James Martin Investments Ltd., Graphnet, and Computer Channel Inc. (For the latter two companies, he also served as chairman.) In 1981 Martin started his own technology consulting business, James Martin Associates, which later became James Martin & Co. and, most recently, Headstrong.

Martin began writing computer books in the 1960s, publishing several programming and software textbooks, including *Programming Real-Time Computer Systems* (1965), *Design of Real-Time Computer Systems* (1967), *Telecommunications and the Computer* (1969), *Teleprocessing Network Organization* (1970), *Systems Analysis for*

Data Transmission (1972), The Design of Man-Computer Dialogues (1973), Security, Accuracy, and Privacy in Computer Systems (1973), Computer Data-Base Organization (1975), Principles of Data-Based Management (1976), and Communications Satellite Systems (1978). While he first explored the subject of futurism in his 1970 book The Computerized Society: An Appraisal of the Impact of Computers on Society over the Next Fifteen Years (with Adrian R. D. Norman), Martin made his most notable predictions regarding computers in The Wired Society (1978). In this work he presented a clear picture of how he thought technological advances would affect society in the coming decades. Martin's expectations included a world "wired to provide instant mail, invisible money transactions, information on demand, and all sorts of electronic marvels," according to Daniel La Rossa for Library Journal (May 15, 1978). While Martin did consider potential infringements on privacy and other abuses, his book was generally optimistic about the opportunities for progress, which included everything from significant benefits—the Internet, e-commerce, telecommuting, a world networked by personal computers, and breakthroughs in the distribution of medical care around the globe—to the more mundane, such as a husband having use of a car telephone to contact his wife at home. La Rossa noted, "Even those who find themselves dismayed by the book's title will be enthralled by this glimpse of things to come." The Wired Society became an instant classic among computer books and was nominated for the Pulitzer Prize.

Over the last two decades, Martin has continued publishing computer-related textbooks at an astonishing rate. To date, he has more than 100 titles to his name, achieving the record for the most textbooks written by one individual. Some of his most important books include Managing the Data Base Environment (1980), Program Design Which Is Provably Correct: A Quantum Leap in Software (1982), Application Development without Programmers (1982), Software Maintenance: The Problems and Its Solutions (1983) with Carma L. McClure, An Information Systems Manifesto (1984), A Breakthrough in Making Computers Friendly: The Macintosh Computer (1985) with Joe Leben and Jim Arnold, and Technology's Crucible: An Exploration of the Explosive Impact of Technology on Society during the Next Four Decades (1987). Martin is also closely associated with the technology system known as computer-aided software-engineering technology—or CASE—which was introduced in 1984 to revolutionize companies' systems development processes and to increase effectiveness and productivity. Martin is often credited as the father of CASE. CASE ultimately proved a disappointment, however, because only some aspects of the personal computer–based hardware and software technology met the standards it initially promised. In 1990 Martin introduced Rapid Application Development (RAD), a

second system that combined CASE tools with information engineering methodologies and other management techniques to improve a company's development and speed of applications.

Martin's most recent books, Cybercorp: The New Business Revolution (1996) and After the Internet: Alien Intelligence (2000), have addressed new aspects of computer technology's impact on both society and corporate interests. In Cybercorp, he outlined a new business model for corporations aiming to compete in the technological age. As Martin described in a 1995 interview for Computerworld (October 9, 1995), a cybercorp is "a corporation designed for cyberspace." He noted, "The cybercorp has to be designed for real time, with electronic sensors and the ability to quickly respond to changing events worldwide. It needs different software from the software that is common today. And it needs a lot of management and decision-making assistance. The cybercorp is likely to be virtual: virtual operations, virtual offices and so on." Nevertheless, Martin insisted that creating a cybercorp required a great deal more than simply moving a company on-line. He explained to Vivian Pospisll for Industry Week (September 16, 1996), "[Cybercorp] is not about building Web pages or establishing a presence on the Internet. It is about deep structural changes that are necessary for the age of network-centric computing and the new business opportunities that they bring." Martin foresaw the rise of cybercorps as an evolution in the corporate world, one that would dramatically alter the structure of commerce and business around the globe. Within the new business model companies would have to reevaluate many aspects of operations—everything from productivity and distribution to marketing and intercorporate relations—while significantly increasing the role of information systems.

In After the Internet: Alien Intelligence, Martin presented even more predictions about how the next generation of computers would revolutionize society in the 21st century. Rather than classifying computer technology as "artificial intelligence," he referred to it as "alien intelligence"—a description signifying that computers are not artificial but are instead non-human, or alien. He envisioned that computers would soon be assigned to tackle tasks well beyond human capabilities. "Right now, in one profession after another the machines are outperforming humans in critical tasks," he told Mike Wendland for the Detroit Free Press (August 8, 2001). "In the future, humans won't stand a chance against machines in certain areas." His projections included the emergence of powerful neuro-computers that could produce "cyber-thought;" implanted devices that would allow real-time control in medicine; behavioral monitoring devices to aid in the identification of potential criminals or terrorists; and image-processing computer cameras that would allow individuals to open doors, make purchases, start their cars, and log onto their computers through simple facial identification. According to Martin, these and other advances in alien intelligence have the potential to dramatically improve the quality of life around the globe, bringing about what he called "planetary correctness." While such enhanced, self-programming machines could threaten to develop beyond human control, Martin concluded that the probable advantages outweighed the risks. "For the immediate future, developments in alien intelligence will bring great benefits to society," he told Wendland. "We are perhaps two decades from the time when we will need to worry about machines being difficult to control."

One of the world's best-attended lecturers, Martin often shares his business and technological track-record with high-level executives and technology-oriented groups. He spends much of his time on the road visiting companies to explore numerous management and technology issues first-hand, and he convenes more than 40 one-, three-, or five-day lectures each year on such topics as technology, leadership, industry trends, finance, human resources, telecommunications, management, and health care. As he explained to Joanna Mancey for *Computer Business Review* (September 1, 1997), "You can't be on top of things if you just read books, you have to be out in the real world. We do everything from meeting the top management right down to writing the code." He continued, "We are concerned with getting real results. There are lots of examples where we have made big profits for companies. There are no failures." Martin is also chairman of the Internet-based education company, *WatchIT.com*, which produces advanced-level courses on information technology.

Martin is a lifetime fellow of the Association of Computer Programmers and Analysts. He served as an advisor to the British government during a restructuring of its telecommunications system, and he has served on the software Scientific Advisory Board to the U.S. Department of Defense. He currently holds the James Martin Chair of Computing at Oxford University. When he is not writing, consulting, or lecturing, Martin enjoys ballroom dancing, photography, and filmmaking. Of his commitment to the computer industry, he once told Patricia Keefe for *Computerworld* (June 22, 1992), "I'm not ready to slow down. I look at [the Welsh mathematician and philosopher] Bertrand Russell when he was 90, and I hope than when I'm 90, or at least 80, they'll pull my wheelchair out of the stage and I'll give a seminar. I have tended to talk about the future all my life. People look at you like you are mad. I change subject material constantly. Change is mandated in the computer industry. You can become obsolete very fast."

James Martin owns and resides on Agar's Island, a small, private island of Bermuda.—K. D.

Suggested Reading: *Accounting Review* p225+ Jan. 1975; *Business & Society Review* p82 Winter 1978–1979; *Computer Business Review* Sep. 1, 1997; *Computerworld* p43 June 11, 1984, p118 Sep. 22, 1986, with photo, p27 Jan. 2, 1990, p7 June 22, 1992, with photo, p83 May 31, 1993, with photo, p41 Oct. 9, 1995, with photo, p62 Sep. 30, 2002; *Detroit Free Press* Aug. 8, 2001; *Government Computer News* p32 Jan. 16, 1987; *Information Systems Management* p93+ Winter 1998

Mataré, Herbert F.

Sep. 12, 1912– Physicist and developer of the transitron

The invention of the transistor, a device made from semiconductor material that can amplify and switch off an electronic signal, is widely credited with transforming the electronics industry during the 20th century. The transistor gradually phased out vacuum tubes, allowing the construction of smaller and less-expensive radios, televisions, and computers. In 1956 three physicists—William Shockley (1910–89), John Bardeen (1908–91), and Walter H. Brattain (1902–87)—shared the Nobel Prize in Physics for their contributions to the development of the transistor in the previous decade at Bell Telephone Laboratories, in Murray Hill, New Jersey. Less known, however, is the work of two German physicists, Herbert F. Mataré and Heinrich Welker, who developed a similar device, the transistron, at a Westinghouse Corporation laboratory in Paris, France, after World War II. If the war had not disrupted their research, it is possible that both Mataré and Welker might have unveiled

their transistor long before the physicists at Bell Labs.

Herbert Franz Mataré was born on September 12, 1912 in Aachen, Germany. Mataré's father, Josef, studied geometry, painting, and sculpture in Berlin and Munich and was well known as a portrait artist. A good mathematician, Mataré's mother, Paula, taught school before she married. As a child Mataré developed a passion for science and the emerging field of radio communications. "This started in my early youth, at 10, because I was attracted by the fact that I could hear good music, using earphones," he explained to *Leaders of the Information Age*. "I remember that I listened early on to compositions by Liszt, Beethoven, Mozart, [and others]. At the same time I was fascinated by the fact that I could put together a detector receiver and capture many German and Austrian radio stations. In addition, I admired technical and scientific people and was attracted by mathematics as a tool." At age 11 Mataré built a radio receiver with lead-sulfide crystals and "cat whiskers," tiny metal wires that are moved by hand around the crystal to pick up radio signals.

Courtesy of Herbert F. Mataré

Herbert F. Mataré

Mataré wanted to work as an engineer for one of the major companies in Germany that manufactured radio tubes. His mother, however, insisted that he study engineering and earn a degree before going to work. Mataré enrolled at the University of Geneva, in Switzerland, where he often visited the Geneva home of his uncle, Dr. Franz Mataré, a German delegate to the League of Nations, and his family. Herbert Mataré studied physics, mathematics, and chemistry, and earned a B.S. in 1933. (The same year the Nazi Party, led by Adolf Hitler, seized power in Germany and established a dictatorship that brutally suppressed all opposition and persecuted the Jewish population and other groups.)

After receiving his undergraduate degree, Mataré returned to Germany, where he pursued a master's degree in technical physics at the Aachen University of Technology. Mataré soon caught the attention of the Gestapo, the Nazis' secret police. "Someone in the neighborhood must have denounced me as an enemy of the government because I talked too freely, as my whole family was very critical, especially [because] we had many Jewish friends," he told *Leaders of the Information Age.* "This led to a house search of my student rooms and a police summons [to appear for interrogation]." In 1936 Mataré taught physics and electronics as an assistant professor at the Aachen University of Technology and received an M.S. three years later.

In 1939 Mataré joined Telefunken, one of Germany's most prominent scientific-research laboratories, in Berlin. The Gestapo once again questioned Mataré, as now he was considered an enemy of the Third Reich. Mataré explained to *Leaders of the Information Age* that he was saved from being sent to a concentration camp only because his scientific expertise was needed by the Nazis. On September 1, 1939 Germany invaded Poland and World War II broke out. The demands of the war effort forced Mataré and his colleagues at Telefunken to devote their research to the improvement of radar technology. "We did research on ultra high-frequency rectifiers, aiming at the development of an effective crystal mixer as a duodiode or three-electrode crystal, based on the advances that had been made in crystal rectifiers over the past two decades," Mataré wrote in a letter to the editor published in *Physics Today* (February 1998). "Early on, the director of research, Horst Rothe, gave us the task of comparing electronic noise measurements for vacuum mixer diodes and crystal rectifiers. We also studied the compensation of the oscillator noise through the use of duodiodes in push/pull microwave mixers and the improvement of the signal/noise ratio through the crystal mixers with crystals such as silicon, silicon carbide, lead sulfide, and germanium." Since the crystal or semiconductor material Mataré and his colleagues used was inhomogeneous, their tests failed to result in the desired oscillator noise compensation. In 1942 Mataré and his colleagues published the results of their research in a German scientific journal. The same year, the Technical University in Berlin awarded Mataré a doctorate in physics on the basis of his dissertation, "Noise Behavior of Diodes and Detectors in Mixer Stages of cm-wave Receivers." (In 1950 Mataré earned his second doctorate, this one in solid-state physics, from the École Normale Supérieure in Paris.)

In 1943 Allied bombing attacks on Berlin forced Mataré and his colleagues to relocate to a new laboratory in Leubus, part of Silesia. The scientists managed to obtain better-quality crystal material from two sources: Dr. Karl Seiler, a physicist at Breslau University, in Breslau, Germany, who produced silicon diodes by evaporating silicon layers on carbon substrates, and Dr. Heinrich Welker (1912–81), a scientist at the Institute of Physical Chemistry, in Munich. In 1944 the scientists abandoned the laboratory in Silesia, leaving their equipment and papers behind, to escape the advancing Soviet army. After building a new laboratory in Thuringia, Mataré and his colleagues resumed their research. The lack of sufficient technical support, which they had previously enjoyed, contributed to their difficulties. "During the work in Thuringia our base material was highly doped [with foreign substances] since purification methods were not yet sufficiently sophisticated," Mataré wrote in an unpublished paper, "The Lesser Known History of the Crystal Amplifier," which he shared with *Leaders of the Information Age.* "Therefore, all attempts to achieve equal diode characteristics, so necessary for noise compensation and efforts to influence the space charge with the second whisker were unsuccessful." Mataré's inability to overcome the problem of barrier-layer interference frustrated his research. "Barrier layer is the word for the actual, small area on the semiconductor crystal, where rectification takes place, the open conduction [of the electrical current] in one direction and the blocking of the current for the other polarization," he explained to *Leaders of the Information Age*. "In the case of two whiskers, two point contacts, you can have interference, when the barriers are close to each other. So, if one side is positively biased, it can inject holes, missing electrons, into the reverse, negative, biased side. When I tested double diodes in 1944 and used germanium, I noticed this effect. I had to discard these crystals and take silicon in order to get two equal characteristics for the mixer."

The end of the war in Europe in the first months of 1945 forced Mataré and his colleagues to abandon their research. "The advancing U.S. Army closed all research laboratories," Mataré recalled in his paper, "and we all were lucky to be free to rejoin our families. From Thuringia I returned to Kassel, where my family resided."

Mataré's reputation as an opponent of the Nazis benefitted him during the post-war Allied occupation of Germany. In 1946 the U.S. Army hired him to teach physics, mathematics, and chemistry at the newly established Wabern University, where American soldiers took college-level courses for credit. After Wabern University closed, Mataré rejoined the faculty of the Aachen University of Technology as an assistant professor of electronics and physics.

In 1946 American, British, and French representatives of technical-information agencies visited Mataré to inquire about his wartime research. A short time later he accepted an invitation to build a semiconductor diode plant in Paris, France, for the Westinghouse Corporation, which was under contract with the French government's Ministry of Post, Telephone, and Telegraph (PTT). Westinghouse also hired Heinrich Welker for the project. Welker built the factory's Bridgman crystal furnace, which he used to produce the pencil-thin germanium rods that were cut for use in the semiconductor diodes. Mataré installed the production lines for building and testing the diodes. "Dr. Heinrich Welker was a highly gifted theoretical physicist from the Sommerfeld school in Munich," Mataré recalled to *Leaders of the Information Age*. "He had started the germanium crystal studies in Munich during the war. He was responsible for the crystal growth at Westinghouse after 1946. His practical capabilities did not match his theoretical knowledge. We worked fine together—we even often discussed his main interest, superconductivity."

At Westinghouse Mataré resumed his research into the crystal amplifier. Recalling his previous insights with barrier-layer interference, he tested the crystal material using two whiskers. "I noticed in these tests that the interaction between the two whiskers was much more pronounced for larger size crystals," he wrote in his paper. "I suggested

to Welker that a larger graphite crucible be used [to grow larger crystals]. For a larger bulk to surface ratio the crystals proved to be much better suited for the injection tests and amplification." Although they made substantial progress, the scientists' inability to obtain highly purified germanium in postwar Europe often frustrated their work. "With the larger size crystals, we were able to now consistently obtain amplification," Mataré wrote. "We took the time to make sure that these measurements were reproducible which meant that we had to grow large size crystals with the only Bridgman furnace available."

In 1948 Mataré and Welker unveiled the transistron, a three-electrode crystal that successfully amplified an electric signal. The French PTT minister brought the device to the attention of the French press, which hailed Mataré and Welker as the "fathers of the transistron." In 1949 Mataré published a survey of his and Welker's work in a German scientific journal. Mataré also proposed, as he recalled in his paper, "a number of circuit applications of the transistron, and I also proposed and made a phototransistron, using the first Westinghouse transistrons but adding a lens."

In the United States, a team of Bell Telephone Laboratories physicists comprised of Shockley, Bardeen, and Brattain, pursued similar research with the aim of developing a semiconductor amplifier, which later became known as the "transistor." Unlike their counterparts in Europe, the American physicists benefitted from the availability of highly purified semiconductor material. In 1945 Shockley outlined the design for a semiconductor amplifier, which was later called a field-effect transistor, but he was unable to build a successful prototype. Shockley instructed Bardeen and Brattain to investigate why his invention failed to work as planned. In December 1947 Bardeen discovered that a barrier of electrons on the semiconductor's surface was blocking the electrical signal. Without consulting Shockley, Bardeen and Brattain solved the problem by developing the point-contact transistor, which successfully amplified an electrical signal and was able to switch it off. Outraged that he wasn't consulted and determined to preserve his standing in the scientific community, Shockley designed the junction transistor. In 1956 Shockley, Bardeen, and Brattain were awarded the Nobel Prize for Physics for their work on semiconductors and their discovery of the "transistor effect."

In 1948 Bell Labs publicly unveiled the transistor, which generated little interest at the time, and applied for patents for both the point-contact transistor and the junction transistor from the U.S. government. The same year, Mataré and Welker applied for a patent for their transistron from the French government. They also applied for a U.S. patent, but their application was delayed because of conflict with Bell patents. Michael Riordan, the author of the book *Crystal Fire: The Invention of the Transistor and the Birth of the Information Age* (1997), told John Markoff for the *New York Times*

(February 24, 2003), "There were ongoing worries about the Paris group at Bell Labs." In 1950 Shockley and Brattain visited Mataré and Welker at their laboratory in Paris. "Dr. Shockley was astonished that our transistrons worked fine in telephone repeaters," Mataré told *Leaders of the Information Age*. "In fact, he talked over the phone with colleagues at the university in Algiers via transistorized repeaters."

Despite the favorable press attention they received, Mataré and Welker were unable to obtain any additional financial support for their research. In 1952 the two physicists decided to leave Westinghouse and pursue other ventures. After concluding that there was no market for the transistron, Westinghouse eventually closed the Paris laboratory. Welker returned to Munich, where he conducted semiconductor research for the Siemens Corporation. Mataré accepted an offer from New England Industries, in New York City, to establish a transistor-manufacturing subsidiary in what was then West Germany. At the time, New England Industries had assets in German marks that it could not covert into U.S. dollars because West German laws prohibited the export of capital and so decided to invest its German holdings in a new subsidiary, which Mataré called the Intermetall Corporation. Intermetall's laboratories grew silicon crystals and other compound crystals. Based in Düsseldorf, the subsidiary began producing transistors and germanium diodes. In 1953 Intermetall unveiled a prototype of the first-ever transistor radio with earphones at a trade show in Düsseldorf. "It was received very well," Mataré recalled to Markoff. "People were amazed by its [small] size." The same year, after West German laws on the export of capital changed, New England instructed Mataré to sell Intermetall. The subsidiary was sold to the Clevite Corporation, which also acquired the Shockley Transistor Corporation.

In 1953 Herbert Mataré immigrated to the United States. There, he went to work for the U.S. Army Signal Corps Laboratories, in Fort Monmouth, New Jersey. He continued his research into crystal properties and crystal-growth methods and began systematic measurements on grain boundaries in polycrystals. In 1956 Mataré joined the General Telephone & Electronics Co. (GTE) in the New York City borough of Queens. "My main research at [GTE] in New York was concerned with the creation of new devices using semiconductors," he told *Leaders of the Information Age*. "We studied cyclotron resonance in germanium at low temperatures, a kind of variant of the MASER [microwave amplification by stimulated emission of radiation] scheme." In 1959 Mataré went back to West Germany, where he served as the director of research in the semiconductor department for the Tekade company, in Nuremberg. After returning to the United States, Mataré worked in research capacities for several companies, including Bendix Research Laboratories in Southfield, Michigan; Lear Siegler in Santa Monica, California; the Douglas

Aircraft Company (which later became McDonnell-Douglas); and the North American Rockwell Company. Mataré currently serves as the president of International Solid State Electronics Consultants (ISSEC), a professional consulting group that he founded in 1970. He has also taught at several universities. At age 91, Mataré remains a working scientific consultant. "Currently I am advising only the Pyron-Company in La Jolla, California, which is active in building new solar electric power plants, especially in view of the future hydrogen technology," he told *Leaders of the Information Age*.

As of September 2003, Herbert Mataré holds 84 patents. He has published more than 100 technical papers and several books, including *Defect Electronics in Semiconductors* (1971), *Conscientious Evolution* (1978), *Energy, Facts, and Future* (1989), and *Bioethics: The Ethics of Evolution and Graphic Interference* (1999). Mataré has also self-published his autobiography in German, *Erlebnisse eines Deutschen Physikers und Ingenieurs von 1912 bis zum Ende des Jahrhunderts*, which is translated as "Experiences of a German Physicist and Engineer from 1912 until the End of the Century." In his upcoming book, "The Silicon Revolution," the Belgian historian Armand Van Dormael will bring further attention to Matare's and Welker's development of the transistron.

In 1939 Herbert Matare married the former Ursula Krenzien. After her death, in 1983 Mataré married Elisabeth Walbert. Mataré has two children, Felicitas and Vitus, from his first marriage, and a son, Victor, from his second marriage. Mataré divides his time between Malibu, California, and Düsseldorf, Germany.—D. C.

Suggested Reading: *IEEE Spectrum* p10 Oct. 1998; *New York Times* C p1+ Feb. 24, 2003, with photo; *Physics Today* p97+ Feb. 1998; Riordan, Michael. *Crystal Fire: The Invention of the Transistor and the Birth of the Information Age*, 1997

Mauchly, John William

Aug. 30, 1907–Jan. 9, 1980 Co-creator of the ENIAC and the UNIVAC

For most of his life, John William Mauchly, inventor and professor of physics, remained a largely dismissed figure in the field of computing. His various contributions to technology include work on the ENIAC, the world's first completely electronic computer, and UNIVAC, the world's fastest electronic computer at the time it was built and the first created as a commercial, general-purpose machine. Mauchly was also responsible for the design of an improved version of the ENIAC, known as the EDVAC, and of the BINAC, the first stored-program, electronic digital computer to operate in the United States. Yet, despite their ingenuity,

Mauchly's machines were often overlooked by mass society and by other inventors, who viewed his vision of a commercial computer industry as fanciful. In addition, towards the end of his life, Mauchly was stripped of all credit for his ENIAC machine, which the courts ruled was based on another scientist's work. Despite lacking recognition for much of his own career, in recent years Mauchly's keen insight into the future of computers has been recognized for its true merit.

John William Mauchly was born on August 30, 1907, to Sebastian J. and Rachel Mauchly in Cincinnati, Ohio. When Mauchly's was six years old, his father received an appointment as a physicist at the prestigious Carnegie Institute of Washington, D.C., and the family relocated to Chevy Chase, Maryland. Mauchly expressed an eager interest in the sciences from a young age, expressing a deep curiosity towards electricity and calculating machines. While he was still in elementary school, Mauchly installed electric doorbells on neighbor's houses in order to earn money. A playful boy, he was not always motivated by thoughts of money; he once created an electric trigger that he placed on the stairs of his home, so that when his mother came up the stairs to see if he was sleeping, his reading light would turn off, turning on again when she returned down the stairs.

Mauchly led a comfortable life as an upper-middle class student at the highly regarded McKinley Technical High School in Washington, D.C., where, in addition to his recreational long walks and tennis matches, he would conduct mechanical experiments. When he dismantled an adding machine, the experience sparked a continuing curiosity about calculating machines. He entered Johns Hopkins University in Baltimore, Maryland, in 1925, with the intention of studying electrical engineering, but he soon complained to his father about courses such as the general engineering course, which provided a theoretical approach to engineering that the young Mauchly did not approve of. By the end of his sophomore year at college, Mauchly began to feel bored with engineering, and in 1927 he took advantage of a special provision in school policy which gave exceptional students the choice of enrolling directly into a Ph.D. program even if they hadn't finished their undergraduate studies. Without a bachelor's degree, he transferred into the more appealing graduate physics program of Johns Hopkins, specializing in molecular spectroscopy. He received his doctorate in physics in 1932, and the following year accepted an offer to become head of the physics department at Ursinus College in Collegeville, Pennsylvania. Mauchly had tried to obtain a position at a larger, more prestigious school, but his chosen field of study, molecular spectroscopy, was not particularly popular at the time among such institutions of higher learning, and as it was the height of the depression, jobs were scarce.

Despite lacking materials he had become accustomed to using at Johns Hopkins, Mauchly began to perform research on calculating energy levels, and hoping to improve weather prediction, he eventually turned to meteorology. In particular, he wanted to prove, through statistics, that following a solar flare, a phenomenon in the climate would occur within a specific time frame. Mauchly hired a group of graduate students from the mathematics department, and had them calculate an enormous amount of data on office adding machines, but soon realized the necessity of a computer for such operations. Mauchly had always been interested in creating a faster calculating machine, and he continued with his experiments, viewing electronics as the key component. He had wanted to use vacuum tubes, but because of their high cost, settled for gas tubes instead. However, he never ceased in his quest to find the valued vacuum tubes, even borrowing them from student's radios. He built several devices during this time period, including a gas-tube counter that could count 500 times a second. However, due to his lack of financial resources, his vision of building a computer out of electronic components, was out of the question.

In late 1940, Mauchly wrote a letter to one of his students, in which he expressed the desire to become the first individual to build an electronic computing device that would "have the answer as fast as the buttons can be depressed." Soon after, Mauchly attended a conference at the University of Pennsylvania, at which he presented a paper detailing the use of computers in handling weather statistics. It was at this lecture that Mauchly met John Atanasoff, who invited Mauchly to come see his ABC computer in Iowa. When he returned from the excursion in June 1941, he told others that he had been disillusioned with Atanasoff's creation. In particular, Mauchly said that he was shocked to find that the ABC was not automatic and that it could not be programmed, each step being dictated by an operator who controlled various buttons. Mauchly said he was also dismayed at what he viewed as Atanasoff's improper use of vacuum tubes, which he felt could have been better incorporated into the ABC and improved existing computing technology tremendously.

After his return from Iowa, Mauchly learned that he had been accepted into the Moore School of Engineering's Emergency Science and Management Defense Training course located at the University of Pennsylvania. In order to expand his knowledge of electronics, he decided to take the course.

It was at Moore, in a program consisting of no more than 20 students, that Mauchly met his future partner, J. Presper Eckert. At the time, Eckert was a 22-year-old master's student, 12 years Mauchly's junior, who shared Mauchly's enthusiasm for building an electronic vacuum tube computer. In September 1941, Mauchly wrote to John Atanasoff saying that he had ideas for a computer which were nothing like Atanasoff's machine, and that he wanted to "make exploratory tests of some of my different ideas with the hope of getting something very speedy, not too costly, etc." He asked Atanasoff for his approval to include some of the features of the ABC into his own computer, a move that his second wife Kathleen later said was intended to draw Atanasoff to the Moore School, where they could work on the computer together. Atanasoff, however, expressed no interest in sharing ideas and declined his offer.

Upon finishing the course, Mauchly was asked to stay on at Moore as an instructor. It was during these first few months in 1942, working for Moore, that he learned of the school's contractual work for the Ballistics Research Laboratory (BRL). It was the height of World War II, and the Allies were having difficulty fighting in North Africa because their firing tables were inaccurate, and as a result their artillerymen could not function. The U.S. Army Ordnance Department was regularly receiving requests for new ballistics tables, and the calculations required to prepare these tables were enormous. The best available equipment at the time, the differential analyzer, was not performing accurately enough for such precise work, and with the fate of the war hanging in the balance, Mauchly used the intensity of the moment to his advantage. Mauchly suggested to the school that they build an electric high-speed vacuum tube computer where numbers could travel, through the use of electric pulses, from one column to another. Reaction to Mauchly's suggestion was far from enthusiastic. While Eckert firmly supported Mauchly, others questioned the reliability of vacuum tubes, known to burn out easily, and predicted that the machine, if it worked at all, would probably cease running after five minutes of use. Mauchly and Eckert persisted in their attempts to sway the school to undertake the project, and asserted that even if the machine ran only five minutes out of every hour, it would still be faster than any machine created to date. Mauchly's vision was that his machine would be able to perform 1,000 multiplications per second and solve problems in one to two minutes, a rate of 15 to 30 times faster than the differential analyzer.

In August 1942 Mauchly wrote a five-page memo to the school titled "The Use of High-Speed Vacuum Tube Devices for Calculating," in which he exalted the importance of utilizing electronics to increase calculating speed. After some more lengthy debates, the U.S. Army Ordnance approved the project and supplied $400,000 in funds for the highly secretive endeavor, which the Moore School would only refer to as the PX Project. Mauchly, in formulating his ideas for the first electronic digital computer, conceived not only the technology to build the equipment, but also foresaw the vital use such a machine would have for ballistics, and for his initial interest, meteorology.

The creation of the computer, called the Electrical Numerical Integrator and Computer (ENIAC), was a daunting task. While the largest electronic

equipment at the time contained 200 vacuum tubes, the ENIAC would require over 17,000 tubes. Furthermore, Mauchly and Eckert wanted the machine to be simple. They did not want the computer to use the binary system, which would take programmers longer to convert results to binary digits. A central component of the machine was the accumulator, or adding unit. A number would be transferred from one accumulator to another and would serve as storage for ten digits (the longest number the ENIAC could handle was one that was 20 digits long). The computer's read-only storage could hold up to 300 numbers, the same number as a modern computer's read-only memory. Data for the machine's calculations was input in the form of IBM cards at the rate of 125 cards per minute, and its output occurred at a rate of 100 cards a minute.

Progress was slow on the ENIAC; by April 1944 only the two accumulators and the cycling unit had been built. The results of premature tests on these components were encouraging to Mauchly and Eckert, however, and they began to formulate ideas for an improved ENIAC that would possess an increased storage. What began as mere brainstorming turned into reality when, in the fall of 1944, the BRL agreed to fund the new computer, which was given the title Electric Discrete Variable Automatic Computer (EDVAC). The plan for the EDVAC was that it would be a stored-program machine (capable of storing 1,000 words) that would use mercury delay lines to hold data. The delay lines worked on a simple premise; bits would circulate as ultrasonic pulses in a column of mercury, and when each bit got to the end of the mercury column, it became an electrical signal that could be read. These lines could then have the capacity of storing hundreds of words each, a vast improvement over the ENIAC. This new the EDVAC, and it was Mauchly and Eckert's major contribution to the project.

During this time, the noted mathematician John von Neumann began to take an interest in both the ENIAC and the EDVAC, and Mauchly and Eckert feared a rivalry for authorship of the plans. The university did not have a patent policy at the time, so the pair, sensing that their computer could have significant commercial value, wrote a letter to the school informing them that they were going to take out a patent on the ENIAC.

The machine was intended for use in the war effort, but as it took a considerable amount of time to complete, it was not ready by the war's end in May 1945. The team of 50 men and women (women were employed as programmers only) were lead by Chief Engineer Eckert into a tireless effort to speed up progress on the ENIAC. Mauchly was said to have immersed himself into the building of the computer with such effort that he often went for several days without sleep, refusing even to leave the office.

In addition to time constraints, there were a great many problems involved with using such a large number of vacuum tubes in one machine, one of the most significant being their reliability. Eckert solved this problem by running the vacuum tubes under their intended voltage, thereby making them last longer. But there were other interferences, including mice who would get into the machine and then proceed to eat the wires, requiring the team of researchers to perform experiments with the vermin to determine which type of wire would be "mouse-proof." There were still more kinks in the system, but von Neumann pushed to have the machine ready for use with H-bomb development, and so the historic first tests of the ENIAC were conducted in front of scientists from Los Alamos on December 10, 1945.

The ENIAC was formally unveiled to the public on February 16, 1946—an 80-foot-long, eight-foot-high, three-foot-deep hulk of metal and wire weighing 30 tons and consisting of 40 panels, 10,000 capacitors, 6,000 switches, and 17,468 vacuum tubes. The computer's first task, a highly complex problem that would have taken any of the other calculating machines of the day nearly 40 hours to complete, took the ENIAC only 20 seconds to finish. Despite its massive size and potential power, the unveiling of the ENIAC drew little media attention, and few reporters even chose to run the event as a story. Only years later would the world take note of the true significance of the machine as the world's first all-electronic computer.

By the spring of 1946, the University of Pennsylvania began to realize the potential of the ENIAC, and they demanded that Mauchly and Eckert give up their rights to the patents on their machines. When the pair refused, the university told them they were either to allow the university rights over all future patents or else cease work for the school. Mauchly and Eckert resigned from the University of Pennsylvania in March 1946, before completion of the EDVAC could be realized, claiming they were fired by the university over the patent disputes. Their departure had a significant impact on all future production of the EDVAC, and the machine was not completed until 1951. The ENIAC, meanwhile, continued to garner attention at the university, and was at the center of a great number of projects. In addition to its initial purpose of creating firing tables, the computer helped in the study of random numbers, cosmic rays, and Mauchly's first interest, weather prediction.

After leaving the university, Mauchly and Eckert struck out on their own by founding a firm called Electronic Control Corporation (ECC) in Philadelphia. The purpose of the company was to design and construct the EDVAC–like machines, and their first business come from the Federal Bureau of the Census. Ironically, the summer after they left the University of Pennsylvania, the duo returned there to teach a six-week course, Theory and Techniques for Design of Electronic Digital Computers. The course was a major turning point in computer history, serving as a forum for the exchange of ideas among scientists, and was a critical step in the transfer of technological information to other organizations both within the U.S. and also abroad.

Due to struggling finances, Mauchly and Eckert undertook a contract with Northrop Corporation in California to build a computer called the Binary Automatic Computer (BINAC). The BINAC was intended to be constructed as a small computer that could help the air force in a project related to long-range guided missiles, and eventually progress toward a machine that could be placed in planes during flight. Mauchly and Eckert completed the BINAC in August 1949, further enhancing their financial troubles by going nearly $200,000 over budget and absorbing the loss themselves. The machine was a tremendous success, however, becoming the first operating stored-program electronic digital computer in the U.S. It was also one of the smallest computers at the time, a "tiny" five-foot-tall, four-foot-long, and one-foot-wide piece of equipment that served as a crucial safety back-up for planes. However, the researchers had expressed little interest in their work on this project, focusing almost exclusively on their machine for the Census Bureau.

Still firm believers in the commercial possibilities of computers, Mauchly and Eckert worked for several years to develop a Universal Automatic Computer which they called UNIVAC. The UNIVAC possessed a highly advanced form of stored data, that stored both data and instructions side by side. In addition, the instructions were held on a magnetic tape (which was capable of holding millions of characters) rather than the previously used punch cards, of which the UNIVAC would have required tens of thousands to operate. The UNIVAC was also smaller in size than the ENIAC, measuring 14.5 feet by 7.5 feet by 9 feet, and containing only 5,000 vacuum tubes. It was a much faster machine as well, producing 2.5 million electronic pulses per second, a vast improvement over the ENIAC's 100,000 pulses per second.

This machine could be utilized for a diverse collection of commercial applications, and Mauchly successfully obtained a considerable amount of interest in his design from outside companies and government agencies other than the Census Bureau. In 1949, however, ECC's chief investor died in a plane crash, leaving Mauchly and Eckert in serious financial destitution. Forced to realize their limitations, the pair accepted an offer to sell their business and come work for Remington Rand, which later merged with the Sperry Corporation to become Sperry Rand. The two inventors continued to work on UNIVAC in their new company, and while they foresaw the potential impact their machine could have on computing, initial interest was lukewarm. The press, as they had with the ENIAC, downplayed the importance of such a computer, and *BusinessWeek* stated that "The UNIVAC is not the kind of machine that every office could use." Even some fellow scientists failed to see the long-term uses of a computing machine such as UNIVAC. Mark I inventor Howard Aiken once commented that Eckert and Mauchly were on the wrong track with their commercial vision for computers, and that there would "never be enough work for more than one or two computers." Despite the critics, during the years of completion, from 1951 to 1953, UNIVAC would become a highly marketable product, eventually selling 46 units (despite their hefty price tag which stayed in the neighborhood of hundreds of thousands of dollars), in the process becoming the world's first commercially produced electronic digital computer.

Mauchly remained with Sperry-Rand as director of UNIVAC applications research until 1959 when he and Eckert parted company after a nearly 18-year partnership. Mauchly went on to form his own computer consulting firm called Mauchly Associates, which eventually developed the Critical Path Method (CPM) that computers used to schedule jobs and resources for the planning and construction of large facilities, such as hotels. In 1968 Mauchly started another company, Dynatrend, which was a systems consulting company that began by performing weather forecasts, but ultimately moved into the arena of predicting stock market trends.

In 1973 the original controversy over the ENIAC's patent rights, and the role of John Atanasoff in its conception, moved into the courts. Mauchly and Eckert had been granted a patent for the ENIAC in 1947, and gave patent rights to Sperry-Rand in 1950 when they joined the company. After 1964 Sperry began to receive royalties from various firms building computers (Mauchly and Eckert each received $300,000 of this money). In 1971, however, Honeywell refused to pay royalties and were promptly sued by Sperry. Honeywell countersued, insisting that the ENIAC was the result of Atanasoff's ABC and not Mauchly and Eckert's original design. On October 19, 1973, a judge ruled that the original patents obtained by Mauchly and Eckert were invalid, and that Mauchly had formed the concept for the ENIAC from John Vincent Atanasoff. Mauchly was livid over the decision, protesting for many years afterward that his design had been original, and that he had been building such electronic equipment for years before he had even met Atanasoff. The ruling remained however, and he lost all official credit for his work. In 1974 Mauchly acquired an infection from which he never fully recovered. He died during heart surgery in Abington, Pennsylvania on January 9, 1980.

John William Mauchly was married to Kathlene McNulty, a former programmer from the ENIAC project, for over 30 years at the time of his death. McNulty was his second wife, his first wife Mary having drowned during a weekend at the New Jersey shore in 1946. As of 1995, Mauchly was survived by his wife, seven children, 17 grandchildren and two great grandchildren. During his career, Mauchly was the recipient of several honors and awards, including the Howard N. Potts Medal of the Franklin Institute (1949), the John Scott Award (1961), the Modern Pioneer Award of NAM (1965), and the Emanual R. Piore Award of IEEE (1978).

While Mauchly may not have received proper recognition of his work during his lifetime, the influence of his computer designs will remain evident for many generations to come. During the anniversary of the ENIAC's unveiling in 1996, Mauchly's contributions and the impact of the ENIAC was heavily lauded by the crowd gathered in Philadelphia. Gwen Bell, director of collections for the Computer Museum in Boston, Massachusetts, was quoted by the *New York Times* (February 19, 1996) as saying that "the ENIAC was the catalyst for a lot of things. It certainly has a legitimate claim for being the starting point for the computer age."—D. B.

Suggested Reading: *Annals of the History of Computing* (on-line); *New York Times* D p3 Feb. 19, 1996, with photo; *University of Pennsylvania Library Exhibitions* (on-line); *Virginia Polytechnic Institute and State University, Computer Science* (on-line); Lee, J. A. N., ed. *International Biographical Dictionary of Computer Pioneers*, 1995; *Dictionary of Scientific Biography*, vol 13, 1976; *Larousse Dictionary of Scientists*, vol 1, 1994; Slater, Robert. *Portraits in Silicon*, 1987

Maurer, Robert D.

July 20, 1924– Physicist; co-inventor of telecommunications optical fibers

The invention of optical fiber in 1970 helped pave the way for the explosive growth in telecommunications that has taken place over the last quarter century. When the scientists Robert D. Maurer, Peter C. Schultz, and Donald B. Keck made their discovery at Corning Glass Works, they could not have foreseen the extensive applications for their find, which now include long-distance telephone calls, Internet usage, and even cable television. Ultimately, optical fiber technology has enhanced the speed and efficiency by which all telecommunications signals are transmitted across long distances. Today, more than 90 percent of all long-distance communication in the U.S. is carried via optical fiber, on more than 145 million miles of cable.

Robert D. Maurer was born on July 20, 1924 in Arkadelphia, Arkansas, the eldest of John and Josephine Maurer's three sons. (Some sources list his mother's name as Elizabeth.) John spent his career in the U.S. Army, and by the time Robert was born, he was stationed at a college in Arkadelphia, a small, close-knit town with a about 5,000 residents. Maurer's family was distinctly lower-middle class—as were most of their neighbors—and life throughout his childhood remained relatively simple. As he recalled to Kathy L. Woodard for the *American Ceramic Society Bulletin* (August

2000), his early years were spent mostly at school or at the nearby river, where children swam or caught turtles and snakes. Later, he enjoyed such activities as playing tennis or constructing model airplanes. "I had a fairly good time of it [in school]; studied, but not very hard," he told Woodard. "I was mostly interested in technical things and by the time I was in high school, I knew I wanted to have a technical job. Chemistry was always an interest."

Maurer was interested in attending college and decided to enlist in the U.S. Army Reserves to help offset the costs. He entered the University of Arkansas in 1943, but within months was called up by the Army in preparation for the escalating war in Europe. During the first part of his service, he was stationed in Huntsville, Texas, where he was able to attend pre-engineering classes at a state college through the Army's specialized training program. Maurer's division, the 99th, was sent to Europe late in 1944; he saw combat on the German border, as well as in Belgium and France. While on combat patrol, he stepped on a land mine and was severely wounded. He was returned to the U.S., where he recovered in a hospital for 20 months before receiving an honorable discharge from military service in 1946. (Maurer was later awarded the Purple Heart in recognition of his combat wounds.)

Maurer returned to the University of Arkansas in 1946. He initially registered for a program in chemical engineering, but he realized that his true interest was physics. He graduated with a B.S. in physics in 1948 and enrolled at the Massachusetts Institute of Technology (MIT), in Cambridge, in pursuit of a Ph.D. During the summers, Maurer obtained research fellowships that allowed him to work in a low-temperature laboratory, where he conducted work on his thesis about the nature of liquid helium. He graduated in the winter of 1951 with a Ph.D. in physics; after earning his degree, he remained at MIT to continue his research. In 1952 Maurer accepted a position at the Corning Glass Works, in Corning, New York, in part because of his interest in materials and condensed matter. "Corning appealed to me because glass seemed like such an interesting topic, and I didn't know much about it," he told Woodard. "And I liked the idea of a smaller town."

In his initial work at Corning, Maurer sought to develop new applications for glass. Some of his projects included making ultrasonic delay lines of glass, which were then being used as components of radar, and studying heat transfer during glass formation in order to better understand its structure. He would later apply such work on the nature of glass to his development of optical fiber. With a team of other researchers, he began working on glass-ceramics—then a growing field within the industry—studying various processes that were occurring inside different types of glass. Since his days at MIT, during which he had been influenced by Professor Melvin Herlin, Maurer had adopted a unique research philosophy: he conducted experiments based on his initial ideas, then used the experimental data to further develop his research. He applied this philosophy to his work on glass-ceramics: "You get the data, and then figure out what is going on," he told Woodard. In 1963 he was appointed the manager of the applied physics department at Corning, but he remained active in the day-to-day technical work. At that time many researchers in his field were working on glass lasers. (The first working laser had been built in 1960, by Theodore Maiman of Hughes Research Laboratories.) With existing research showing that optical frequencies were billions of times faster than those of electrical frequencies, Maurer began exploring the field of optical waveguides. "I was interested in all aspects of optics," he recalled, "but found it more interesting to see that wave-measured light gave you certain kinds of patterns."

Around 1966 one of Corning's scientists, Dr. William Shaver, began contacting labs abroad to see what type of research was being done on telecommunications. At that time telephone communications were transmitted via a copper cable system, in which the thick copper wires could handle only two dozen simultaneous phone calls each. As engineers tried to increase the frequency of the electrical waves carrying the signal—in the hopes of sending more information through the wires—they found that the signal would deteriorate into static. Attempts to increase bandwidth, therefore, required expensive devices to be installed every few thousand feet to boost the signal. Laying additional copper wires into the ground did not seem a plausible solution either, as city streets were often stuffed with communication cables, electrical wires, steam pipes, water pipes, and subways. As engineers explored the limitations of the copper system, they began to realize that new technologies would likely be needed to support future telecommunications traffic.

Shaver, who was then in Great Britain, contacted that country's national office for communications and learned that a British scientist at the Standard Telecommunications Lab, Charles Kao, had theorized that optical fibers could provide an efficient, high-volume transmission for telecommunications. With this information, Maurer began compiling a team of researchers to explore the possibilities of optical technology; he soon recruited two young scientists, Peter C. Schultz and Donald B. Keck, to assist on the project. Maurer's team was essentially trying to steer light through a fiber. Existing fiber technology had an attenuation of 1,000 decibels per kilometer (dB/km), which meant that there were significant losses in the signal as it traveled over a distance of one kilometer; the goal for Maurer's team was to achieve practical fibers at 20 dB/km. "This was an approximate number arrived at by taking the power of conventional laser at the time, the sensitivity of the detector and arriving at the fact that you could stand to lose 99 percent of your light between the laser and detector," Maurer explained to Woodard. "Then you had to go at least a kilometer if you were going to use it for long distance communication to make it practical." Applying his usual research philosophy, Maurer led his team of researchers in exploring different types of glass, using trial and error to establish conditions such as temperature and composition. He arrived at the appropriate attenuation factor only after making several fibers and then examining the problems inherent in each formulation.

In 1970, after three years of research, Maurer, Schultz, and Keck developed optical fibers that achieved their criteria, losing only 20 dB/km. To do so they created a unique glass-in-glass fiber that was one million times more transparent than the clearest known glass. In the core, where the light would be carried, they used a thin silica glass fused with titanium atoms; the impurity helped prevent the glass from absorbing light. Strands of this glass were so thin that a few dozen could fit inside a human hair. The outer glass was composed of an ultrapure "cladding" glass that would keep the light in, ensuring that the smallest amount of information was lost. This outer layer also served as a type of cylindrical mirror: As light traveled through the tube it ricocheted off the cladding glass and back into the core, thus enhancing the transmission of information. The team named their discovery "optical waveguide fibers" and spent much of the next decade strengthening and refining both the fiber and the process. In 1972, for example, they created a new fused-silica fiber, with a touch of germanium impurities, that produced even lower optical losses of only four decibels per kilometer.

Although the invention of optical fiber would dramatically alter the field of telecommunications, it took seven years for it to be used in an operating telephone. "There was a long period of time trying to get people up to speed with this technology," Maurer explained to Woodard. Today, optical fiber is used to carry more than 90 percent of long-distance phone calls in the U.S. More than 140 million miles of the wire have been installed around the world, even across oceans. Through the optical system, one fiber can carry up to 80,000 telephone calls using just one infrared wavelength of light—or, what it would take bundles of copper wire to accommodate. In short, a single fiber can deliver more than 400 billion bits of voice, data, and video traffic per second, according to the *Business Wire* (February 23, 2000). In addition, many people believe that Internet technology could not exist in its present form without the discovery of the Corning scientists. Maurer told Woodard his invention has surpassed even his own expectations; yet, his greatest sense of accomplishment is not in his contributions to the Internet: "I take a lot more satisfaction in the improvement of our general communication infrastructure and how that is used by everyone to keep our economy going," he said. "That's my major impact in terms of ceramics, without question."

Maurer remained at Corning for the duration of his career, remaining manager of applied physics research until 1978, when he became a research fellow. He retired in 1989, although he continued to consult and contribute to notable projects for several years beyond that. In the years leading up to his retirement, Maurer was forced to dedicate much of his time to defending the patent and technology for optical fiber—which he owned jointly with Schultz—in court. He told Woodard, "There was an awful lot of testimony that I had to go through, and trials up to the time I retired. But the patent was always upheld and even in settlements, the validity of the patent was recognized. That was probably the most stressful and time-consuming part of my career."

For his achievements in developing optical fiber, Maurer has received numerous honors, including the George W. Morey Award from the American Ceramic Society (1976), the first Prize for Industrial Physics from the American Institute of Physics (1978), the Morris N. Liebmann Award from the Institute of Electrical & Electronics Engineers (IEEE, 1979), the L. M. Ericcson International Prize for Telecommunications from the Swedish Academy of Engineering (1979), the Industrial Research Institute Achievement Award (1986), the John Tyndall Award from the IEEE/Optical Society of America (1987), a Naval Research Laboratory Citation (1989), the International Prize for New Materials from the American Physics Society (APS, 1989), a Distinguished Alumni Award from the University of Arkansas (1994), the first American Innovator Award from the U.S. Department of Commerce (1995), and the 1999 Charles Stark Draper Prize from the National Academy of Engineering (NAE), which he shared with Kao and John B. MacChesney. In announcing this award, which included a cash prize of $500,000, NAE President William A. Wulf announced: "The NAE is proud to honor these visionaries for the development of one of the most revolutionary inventions the world has ever seen. Communication as we now know it, including the Internet, would not exist without fiber optics. Innovations such as videoconferencing, electronic commerce, and high-quality, long-distance telephone service are a direct result of the work of these engineers." The following year, Maurer was awarded the National Medal of Technology—the nation's highest honor for technological achievement—along with his fellow researchers Schultz and Keck; the trio was inducted into the National Inventors Hall of Fame in 1993. Maurer, who was elected to the National Academy of Engineering in 1979, is also a fellow in the American Ceramics Society, IEEE, and the APS. He holds 16 patents and has written or contributed to more than 50 technical papers.

Robert D. Maurer currently resides in Painted Post, New York, with his wife of more than 50 years, Barbara. The couple has three adult children—Robert, James, and Janet—and several grandchildren.—K. D.

Suggested Reading: *American Ceramic Society Bulletin* p50+ Aug. 2000, with photos; *Business Wire* Feb. 23, 2000; Inventors Hall of Fame Web site; *Washington Post* H p1 Nov. 10, 1999

Mazor, Stanley

Oct. 22, 1941– Inventor of the single-chip microprocessor

When Stanley Mazor joined the computer chip manufacturer Intel to develop a calculator for a Japanese firm, he did not expect permanently to alter computing by helping to invent the first single-chip microprocessor. As a member of a team headed by Marcian E. Hoff, who is better known as Ted, and later joined by Federico Faggin, Mazor helped to design and build the 4004 microprocessor, a chip the size of a child's fingernail that equaled the computing power of the ENIAC, the first electronic computer, which filled a room. Though Hoff designed the chip's basic architecture, Mazor contributed greatly to the software used by the chip, which was essentially a tiny computer, as well as to the details of the design. Faggin implemented the chip's design in silicon, thus transforming an elegant idea into an actual working product. The group's achievement in successfully compressing over 2000 transistors onto a single chip revolutionized the computer industry and began an evolution in technology that has continued into the 21st century. By 2000 engineers were able to compress millions of transistors onto chips to produce faster and more powerful computing. The single-chip microprocessor put Intel at the forefront of the microcomputer revolution, since such chips are found in everything from computers, to gas station pumps, to medical equipment, and the company has remained there since; as of 1999, Intel was the leading manufacturer of microprocessing chips. In 1997, Mazor, along with Hoff and Faggin, was inducted into the Inventors Hall of Fame, joining the ranks of Thomas Edison, Alexander Graham Bell, and the Wright brothers.

Stanley Mazor was born on October 22, 1941 in Chicago, Illinois. He attended San Francisco State University from 1960 to 1963 and received a degree in mathematics and computer programming. He impressed professors and fellow students at the university when he programmed the campus IBM 1620 computer. In 1964 he joined the staff at Fairchild Semiconductor as a programmer but he soon switched to a job as a designer in their digital research department. While at Fairchild, Mazor was awarded a patent for the Symbol computer. He left the company in 1969.

That same year Mazor joined the staff of Intel, then a year-old spin-off company of Fairchild, which had been established by Robert Noyce and Gordon Moore in 1968. Mazor was assigned to work with Ted Hoff, then the manager of applications research. Since April 1969 Hoff had been as-

signed to develop a family of chips for a Japanese calculator company called Busicom. The Busicom engineers had designed a high-end scientific calculator that would perform trigonometrical and other advanced mathematical functions, using 12 individual chips. Each chip would be responsible for a separate function, such as keyboard scanning, printer control, and display control. Such a design, Hoff soon realized, would be costly to produce, and he sought to find a simpler way to create the product the Busicom engineers had envisioned. He felt that some of their ideas—including using read-only memory to customize the calculator—were quite good, but he believed that they could make better use of the memory. However, the Japanese engineers were not interested in changing their designs. Robert Noyce encouraged Hoff to continue working on a redesign, which he did, developing the first "computer on a chip." He replaced the 12-chip design with a simpler two-chip design featuring a universal central processing unit (CPU) that performed most of the calculator's functions. The Japanese engineers, however, rejected Hoff's design.

Encouraged by Noyce and others at Intel, Hoff continued to work on the design with the help of Mazor, who refined the specifics of Hoff's approach and developed the chip's logic design and software. The finished design included a central processor with a timing chip; a read-only memory chip, which contained the calculator's general programming instructions; and a read-write memory, which allowed users to save their results or instructions for complex calculations. Hoff and Mazor soon realized that in addition to calculators, their computer on a chip had other possible applications as well. In October 1969 the management of Busicom came to Intel from Japan to consider the two possible designs and eventually decided on the Hoff-Mazor chip, which Intel would later promote as the 4004 microprocessor.

Hoff and Mazor simplified their design further by figuring out how to combine the timing chip and the central processor, creating a stand-alone central processing unit capable of digesting four bits of information at a time. As a result this new central processing unit worked with three additional chips instead of four: a read-only memory (ROM), a random access memory (RAM) chip to store data, and a number of input/output ports that could interface with a keyboard, lights, printer, and switches. In April 1970 Federico Faggin joined Hoff and Mazor's team and he also helped to design the three chips. Faggin had previously worked at Fairchild Semiconductor developing silicon-gate technology, a process by which high-density, high-performance, metallic-oxide-semiconductor integrated circuits were made. (In an integrated circuit, all elements of the circuit are contained on one chip, rather than having separate devices wired together.) The group then transferred Hoff's architectural designs and Faggin's advanced chips into silicon. They finalized the logic functions, circuit design, and layout of the chips and by March 1971 had a working microprocessor, which was immediately shipped to Busicom.

Hoff, Mazor, and Faggin believed they had done something important with this invention and began suggesting to Intel's management other uses for the CPU chip. The management, however, was fearful of using the chips in other devices because Busicom owned the rights to the technology. After producing a small number of calculators Busicom got into economic trouble, which enabled Intel to renegotiate the contract. In exchange for approximately $60,000, Intel was granted the right to produce and market the CPU chip. In November 1971 Intel placed an ad in *Electronics News* promoting the 4004 microprocessor: "Announcing a new era of integrated electronics . . . a microprogrammable computer on a chip." The ad went on to claim, fairly accurately, that the chip had as much power as the ENIAC, the first electronic computer, which ran using more than 1200 vacuum tubes and took up 3000 cubic feet when it was completed in 1946. The 4004, in contrast, was one-eighth of an inch wide by one-sixth of an inch long and contained 2,300 metallic-oxide-semiconductor transistor. As of early in the 21st century, 64-bit microprocessor chips remain similar in design to the 4004, although they have many more transistors—more than 5.5 million in some chips, enabling such processors to perform hundreds of millions of calculations per second.

Electronics consumers were shocked by Intel's ad, most believing that the 4004 was another four-bit slice and nothing more. Mazor attended a Fall Joint Computer Conference in 1971, and many customers with whom he came into contact aired complaints about the advertisement, claiming the 4004 couldn't possibly do what Intel said it did. After Mazor showed them the data sheet most doubters were satisfied, though still amazed.

Hoff, Mazor, and Faggin subsequently worked on developing a new eight-bit processor, which could handle twice as much information at a time as the 4-bit 4004. Intel had signed a contract to develop such a chip with Victor Poor of Computer Terminals Corporation (CTC) in late 1969. Initially CTC wanted to develop a glass teletype, which was basically a computer terminal that used a cathode-ray tube screen to present the output, instead of a paper printout. Poor's first contact at Intel was Mazor, who proposed that the whole processor be compressed into a single chip. The 8008 was officially launched in early 1970, but it soon became clear that CTC was having financial troubles and would be unable to use the microprocessor. As a result of a clause in the contract, Intel was able to licence the product to other companies, which it did, including Seiko of Japan. In addition to processing more information than the 4004, the 8008 had an interrupt capacity its predecessor lacked, enabling it to stop what it was doing and start on a new task, and later return to the point at which it stopped the original task.

The 8008 microprocessor was the precursor to the 8080 microprocessor, which became the first chip used in a personal computer, the Altair, and thus greatly advanced Intel's standing in the computer industry. The 8080 was developed because Faggin wanted to add an n-channel process to the 8008, and the team soon realized that such an addition would require an entirely new layout. Since Hoff had been hearing complaints from customers about the lack of processing power and the difficulties with the interrupt capacity, in the 8008, they decided to also repair those problems. The resulting chip was a harbinger of the personal-computing revolution. In a 1995 interview for the Silicon Genesis project at Stanford University, in California, Hoff told Rob Walker, "And so, really Stan and Federico and I all contributed to what ultimately became the 8080. And I consider that [to be] the first microprocessor that really had performance comparable to a minicomputer and I still think of it as one of the first really successful microprocessors."

After working on the 8080, Mazor, the software designer of the team, turned to writing Computer-Aided Design—better known as CAD—modeling programs for Intel. From 1977 to 1983 he taught at Intel's Technical Training group and also at Stanford University and Santa Clara University, both in California, and overseas in China, South Africa, and Stockholm. In 1984 he founded Silicon Compiler Systems and in 1988 he formed another start-up, Synopsys; both were CAD software companies. While working at Synopsis he wrote *A Guide to VHDL* (1993) about a computer language used to design and program microprocessor chips using VHDL CAD tools. He has also written more than 50 articles on Large Scale Integration (LSI), which refers to chips that have more than 1000 active components and which were used widely in computer memories around the early 1970s.

As of the late 1990s, Stanley Mazor served as training director at BEA Systems. In 1995 he presented "A History of the Microcomputer" at the Institute of Electrical and Electronics Engineers Proceedings. A year later, he, Hoff, and Faggin were inducted into the Inventors Hall of Fame in Akron, Ohio, for their development of the microprocessor. Mazor has also received the Outstanding American Innovator Award and was a co-recipient of the Kyoto Prize, awarded annually by the Inawari Foundation of Japan, in 1997.—C.M.

Suggested Reading: *Business Journal Serving San Jose and Silicon Valley* p12 July 8, 1996; *BusinessWeek* (on-line) Dec. 9, 1996; *Information Week* p12 July 8, 1996; *Michael Cole's Home Page on University of Waterloo's Mathematics Department* (on-line); *National Inventors Hall of Fame* (on-line); *San Francisco State University Computer Science Department* (on-line); *Stanford University History of Science and Technology* (on-line); Ceruzzi, Paul E. *A History of Modern Computing*, 1998; Spencer, Donald D. *The Timetable of Computers*, 1997

Courtesy of John McCarthy

McCarthy, John

Sep. 4, 1927– Pioneer in the field of artificial intelligence

John McCarthy has been widely credited with inventing the term artificial intelligence, and for more than 50 years he has been conducting groundbreaking research in the field. Artificial intelligence—also known as AI—is the science of creating machines, especially computer programs, that can think or reason for themselves on some level. The field has utility in computer gaming, speech recognition, and commerce, among other applications. McCarthy is also the inventor of the LISP programming language, still the most widely recognized AI language today.

John McCarthy was born on September 4, 1927 in Boston, Massachusetts. His father was of Irish-Catholic descent and worked as a fisherman, carpenter, and union organizer; his mother was of Lithuanian-Jewish descent and worked as a journalist for the Federated Press wire service and later as a social worker. The family relocated frequently and lived at various times in New York and Los Angeles. Both parents were members of the Communist Party. In an interview with Dennis Shasha and Cathy Lazere for the book *Out of Their Minds* (1998), McCarthy noted that his parents' political leanings helped to focus his interest on science from an early age. "There was a great confidence in technology as being simply good for humanity. I remember when I was a child reading a book called *100,000 Whys*—a popular Soviet technology book written by M. Ilin in the early 1930s. I don't recall seeing any American books of that character."

In 1943 McCarthy graduated from Belmont High School, in Los Angeles. As a junior he perused a course catalog from the California Institute of Technology (Caltech) to discover which calculus texts were used by freshman and sophomores there; he then purchased the volumes and worked through the exercises. This allowed him to skip his first two years of mathematics courses when he was admitted to Caltech after high school. In 1948 he received a B.S. That same year he attended the Hixon Symposium on Cerebral Mechanisms in Behavior at Caltech. There he met John von Neumann, the celebrated computer designer and mathematician, who was delivering a paper at the symposium about self-replicating automata—essentially machines with the ability to create duplicates of themselves.

From 1950 to 1951 McCarthy was a Proctor fellow at Princeton University, in New Jersey. He earned his doctoral degree, in 1951, and was hired by Princeton as a Higgins research instructor in mathematics. While at Princeton he began to formulate some early theories about cognitive qualities in machines, and he approached von Neumann, who encouraged him to write up his ideas.

In the summer of 1952, a graduate student at Princeton named Jerry Rayna made a suggestion to McCarthy: why not publish a volume of papers by people who had a similar interest in machine intelligence? McCarthy asked for Claude Shannon's input on the project. Shannon was at the forefront of information theory, a scientific study of the communications process, and an early proponent of AI. The elder scientist disliked what he considered flashy nomenclature, however. He suggested calling the volume *Automata Studies*, a general term that did not attract the more specific papers McCarthy had been looking for; very few of the submitted papers concerned intelligence in machines.

Undeterred, in 1955 McCarthy started organizing a conference on the subject at Dartmouth College, in New Hampshire. (He had just joined the mathematics department as an assistant professor there, following a brief period of teaching at Stanford University, in California.) Determined to attract the attendees he wanted, he told Shasha and Lazere, "I wanted to nail the flag to the mast and used the term *artificial intelligence* to make clear to the participants what we were talking about." Helping to organize the conference were Shannon; Marvin Minsky, a cognitive psychologist and mathematician then at Harvard; and an IBM computer designer named Nat Rochester. Also attending the workshop were Alan Newell and Herbert Simon, who had just developed the Logic Theorist, an early problem-solving program, as well as the Information Processing Language (IPL), which they used with a computer chess game.

The conference, held in 1956, is generally considered to mark the birth of artificial intelligence as a unique study within computer science, and many of the participants went on to make great contributions to the field. Newell and Simon, for instance, formulated the idea for what they termed "list structure," which realized the importance of lists in symbolic processing. (By way of example— If X happens, then Y and Z will follow.)

McCarthy joined the staff of the Massachusetts Institute of Technology (MIT), in Cambridge, as an assistant professor of communication science, in 1958. There, he and Minsky established the first artificial-intelligence laboratory. McCarthy soon created LISP, short for "list-processing language," in response to his dissatisfaction with the ability of FLPL to handle the applications he needed. (FLPL was the first attempt to add symbolic formulations to the parameters of FORTRAN, the high-level programming language created in 1956 by John Backus at IBM.) LISP was developed on an IBM 704 computer, a large mainframe of the period.

While IPL was once described by its creators as a language that grew more complex over time, McCarthy described LISP as a language that simplified over time. Using LISP, items were grouped inside of parentheses to reflect either the importance of the order of the words, as in (*Mary saw Jane*) or to show that no order was necessary, as in (*dogs, cats, elephants*). LISP has had a remarkably long run: it has remained the standard AI language for more than four decades. Many of its functions, such as conditional expression and recursion, were adapted into ALGOL, C, and Pascal.

McCarthy never anticipated LISP's longevity, merely viewing the language as a means to an end. His main focus remained on developing an intelligent machine. "If you want the computer to have general intelligence, the outer structure has to be common sense, knowledge and reasoning," he once remarked, as quoted by Donald D. Spencer in the *Dictionary of Computer Quotations* (1997). He outlined his theories in a seminal 1959 paper titled "Programs with Common Sense," explaining that such sense was the ability to "deduce for [the machine's self] a sufficiently wide class of immediate consequences of anything it is told and what it already knows." The example he used to illustrate this point was that of a man, sitting at his desk, who would know that he required his car in order to get to the airport.

In 1962 McCarthy left MIT to return to Stanford University as a professor of computer science. A year later he founded an AI laboratory at the school. (He served as the lab's director from 1965 to 1980.) There he worked to expand on his already impressive body of AI work by suggesting a type of logic called situational calculus. Shasha and Lazere explained, "A *situation* represents a state of the world. When an agent acts, a new situation results. What action the agent then takes depends on what he knows about a situation." In the 1970s McCarthy proposed the circumscription method of non-monotonic reasoning. Non-monotonic reasoning supposes that gaining new information will not cause one to retract an original conclusion, unless the new information contradicts the old. For exam-

ple, if one heard barking outside of the window, one would reasonably assume the presence of a dog. If one looked out the window and saw a small, furry animal, one would reasonably assume that it was a dog—unless told otherwise (if, for example, the animal was a cat, and the barking was coming from a neighbor's television set). One would generally, however, circumscribe the ability to bark to a dog.

In addition to his contributions to the field of artificial intelligence, McCarthy was responsible for strides in the concept of time-sharing (in which one computer can be used by several people from remote locations). His most recent work, aside from the continued formalization of common-sense knowledge and reasoning, includes the development of a new programming language called Elephant 2000, which would never forget any event in its history.

McCarthy has sometimes expressed frustration at the slow speed of progress in the field of AI. He writes on his home page, "[Computer] chess programs now play at grandmaster level, but they do it with limited intellectual mechanisms compared to those used by a human chess player, substituting large amounts of computation for understanding. . . . Unfortunately, the competitive and commercial aspects of making computers play chess have taken precedence over using chess as a scientific domain. It is as if the geneticists after 1910 had organized fruit fly races and concentrated their efforts on breeding fruit flies that could win these races."

John McCarthy has been widely celebrated for his achievements. He was the recipient of the 1971 Alan M. Turing Award from the Association for Computing Machinery, the 1985 Research Excellence Award from the International Joint Conference on Artificial Intelligence, the 1988 Kyoto Prize from the Inamori Foundation in Japan, and the 1990 National Medal of Science. He is a member of the National Academy of Sciences and a fellow of the American Association for Artificial Intelligence, among other organizations.—C. M.

Suggested Reading: John McCarthy's Home Page; Lee, J. A. N., ed. *International Biographical Dictionary of Computer Pioneers*, 1995; Spencer, Donald D. *Dictionary of Computer Quotations*, 1997; Spencer, Donald D. *Timetable of Computers*, 1997; Shasha, Dennis and Cathy Lazere. *Out of Their Minds*, 1998

Courtesy of Sun Microsystems

McNealy, Scott

Nov. 13, 1954– Chairman, CEO, and co-founder of Sun Microsystems

Scott McNealy wanted to avoid the exhausting corporate lifestyle that had been so hard on his father, hoping instead to become the owner of a small machine shop. Then, in 1982, while he was working as the director of manufacturing at a factory, he received a telephone call that changed his plan: a former classmate at Stanford University's Graduate School of Business invited him to become a founding partner in a computer company. He agreed, although at the time he knew so little about computers that he could not identify a disk drive. The company, Sun Microsystems Inc., which designs workstations that link computers electronically, was immediately successful, with sales of $9 million in 1983. In an industry dominated by giants, especially Microsoft Corporation, Sun became known as a scrappy start-up with a catchy slogan, "The Network Is the Computer." That vision of enhanced connectivity, under McNealy's guiding hand, has propelled Sun into the upper echelon of the technology industry; today the company employs over 40,000 people and provides half of the existing Internet server computers. Sun established itself early on, building powerful workstations that appealed to scientists and engineers, among others. Its influence grew substantially in May 1995, when the company launched Java, a software language that added a new vitality to World Wide Web sites by providing animation, music, narration, and interactivity. Sun's success has been attributed in large measure to McNealy, who has served as its chief executive officer since 1984. "There are two things I think about Scott,"

Lawrence J. Ellison, the chief executive officer of Oracle Systems, a rival computer company, was quoted as saying in *BusinessWeek* (January 22, 1996). "One is passionate leadership, and the other is rigorous financial management. And that's uncommon to find in one person. Usually, the financial guys aren't so outspokenly passionate, and all leaders are not detail-oriented."

Scott G. McNealy was born on November 13, 1954 in Columbus, Indiana, to Marmalee Doris (Noffke) McNealy and Raymond William McNealy, Jr., a business executive who became vice chairman of American Motors Corporation (AMC) in 1962. He grew up in Bloomfield Hills, a suburb of Detroit, with his siblings—Raymond William III, Barry, and Susan—and he attended Cranbrook Kingswood School, a preparatory school near his home. As a teenager, McNealy was an avid sportsman, excelling in tennis, ice hockey, and golf. He was also interested in business, and he liked to spend evenings debating various corporate strategies for increasing AMC's sales with his father. The company had trouble competing against the larger American car makers and, in 1987, it was purchased by the Chrysler Corporation. "[McNealy] says he saw how AMC was marginalized because it never had sufficient market share," Robert D. Hof wrote in his profile of McNealy for *Business Week* (January 22, 1996), "and he has vowed to make sure that doesn't happen to his company."

McNealy enrolled at Harvard University, in Cambridge, Massachusetts, which awarded him a B.A. degree in economics in 1976. After his initial attempts to get into a graduate business school failed, he took a job as a factory foreman at a Rockwell International Corporation plant in Ashtabula, Ohio. Anticipating a labor strike, the company mandated double shifts to increase its production of truck hoods. After two months of working 14-hour days, McNealy contracted hepatitis and spent six weeks in the hospital. Shortly thereafter, on his third try, he won admission to Stanford University's Graduate School of Business, in Stanford, California. One of only a few students at the school to concentrate on manufacturing courses, he often cut classes that he felt wouldn't help him find a job. "I minimized hours per grade point," he joked to Robert Hof.

After receiving his MBA degree from Stanford, in 1980, McNealy went to work at the FMC Corporation, a tank manufacturer in Chicago. Ten months later he resigned. "FMC put me on a strategy team, and I wanted to be a plant manager," he explained, as quoted in *Fortune* (May 23, 1988). "I wanted to make something." In 1981 he was hired as director of manufacturing at Onyx Systems, a microcomputer maker in San Jose, California. His first assignment was to improve quality control, which he accomplished by seeking employees' input about production problems and then encouraging them to iron things out for themselves. "Without exerting authority, Scott turned the place around in two months," Doug Broyles, McNealy's boss at Onyx, told Jonathan B. Levine for *Business Week* (July 24, 1989). By that point in his life, McNealy had vowed not to become a lifelong workaholic, as his father had been, and he dreamed about striking out on his own. "I wanted to run a machine shop. . . , my own little business with 40 or 50 people," he told Charles R. Day, Jr., who profiled McNealy for *Industry Week* (December 5, 1994). "If it all worked out, I figured my kids would run it someday, and I'd get out when I was 45 or 50 years old and play golf." McNealy's plan for the future took another course in 1982, when he got a telephone call from a former Stanford classmate, Vinod Khosla, an engineer, who was planning to start a computer company along with another Stanford alumnus, Andreas V. Bechtolsheim, a product designer, and William N. Joy, a software programmer who had studied at the University of California at Berkeley. Khosla invited McNealy to join the venture and assume control of manufacturing. McNealy immediately agreed, although his knowledge of computers at that time was limited. "Ten months before I started, I didn't know what a [computer] disk drive was," he admitted to Charles Day. "I couldn't explain the concept of an operating system."

The four men founded Sun Microsystems Inc., in Mountain View, California, and set out to fill a need in the marketplace for specially designed computer workstations. From the outset, as Jonathan Levine noted, Sun's concept of computing has been "linking powerful microcomputers in high-speed networks, rather than having many workers share a minicomputer or mainframe." Sun's workstations were an instant success with demanding technical customers, including scientists and engineers, and in only a year's time, the company generated $9 million in sales; that figure jumped to $39 million in 1984.

McNealy's vaunted manufacturing skills allowed the company to keep up with what Robert Hof called the "wild demand" for its products, but Sun was fast outgrowing its facilities and needed cash to expand. In 1984 McNealy asked one of Sun's corporate customers, J. Philip Samper, then an executive vice president of Eastman Kodak Company, for help. Impressed by McNealy's business acumen, Samper approved a $20-million investment from Kodak in the new computer company, on the condition that McNealy be named its president. At about the same time, Vinod Khosla, Sun's first chief executive officer, left the firm, and the board of directors appointed McNealy president on a temporary basis. A few months later, as the company's fortunes soared, he was officially named president and chief executive officer.

Sun's engineers had designed the company's workstations to operate with a programming language called Unix, which was originally developed by AT&T's Bell Labs. Unlike the operating systems created by Microsoft and Apple Computer, the Unix system is an open, nonproprietary system that does not force users to stay with only one brand of equipment. As Andrew Pollack explained in the *New York Times* (January 7, 1988), "Customers bought Sun's machines because of their power, because of their ability to connect with other machines in networks, and because of the Unix operating system. Customers realized that if someone else came out with a more powerful Unix machine, they could switch and still use their software. While that helps Sun sell machines, it also keeps pressure on Sun to update its machines. Sun can lose customers much more easily than a company with a proprietary operating system." Sun's success in selling machines based on Unix technology impressed executives at AT&T, who were interested in expanding into the computer business. In October 1987 McNealy announced that AT&T and Sun had signed a cooperative technology development agreement to design a new version of Unix. Three months later, the two companies reached a second agreement, allowing AT&T to purchase 20 percent of Sun's stock. "All this understandably alarmed the other companies that sell Unix-based computers," Kathleen K. Wiegner wrote in an article about Sun for *Forbes* (June 27, 1988), "particularly when they heard Sun's salesmen were suggesting to customers that Sun would now have the inside track on future Unix developments." According to Wiegner, one firm, Hewlett-Packard Co., asked to be included on the AT&T/Sun development team but was turned down.

Deciding it was time to take action against the brash new company, seven of Sun's competitors, including Hewlett-Packard, International Business Machines (IBM), and Digital Equipment Corporation, announced in May 1998 that they were setting up a nonprofit organization called Open Software Foundation (OSF) to develop their own version of Unix. In response, McNealy publicly mocked the foundation, declaring that the initials OSF really stood for "Oppose Sun Forever." Although the consortium ultimately met with "more setbacks than successes," as one business writer put it, Hewlett-Packard and IBM beefed up their workstation divisions and began to cut into Sun's core business.

In 1989 Sun's fourth-quarter earnings declined, representing the first quarterly loss in the company's seven-year history. Market analysts expressed concern that the explosive growth at Sun, which had racked up nearly $2 billion in sales in the fiscal year 1989, had become too much for McNealy alone to handle. The departures of Bernard J. Lacroute, the company's executive vice president, and Joseph Graziano, the chief financial officer, compounded those concerns. "There has been a growing uneasiness [about Sun]," Richard Shaffer, the editor of the Technologic Computer Letter, told Lawrence M. Fisher of the *New York Times* (June 2, 1989). "I hope this is not the first sign of the story everybody has been waiting for, which is that Sun is about to crash and burn." McNealy attributed Sun's earnings decline to glitches in a new management information system, difficulties caused by the introduction of five new products, and insufficient supplies of some component parts.

One of McNealy's first steps aimed at improving Sun's financial performance was to streamline the company's internal organization. In the product-development department, for example, seven technical teams had been competing against each other for projects. While the intense competition bred an aggressiveness that had often given Sun an edge in the industry, by the late 1980s the strategy had backfired, for when one group needed another's help to complete a large assignment, a cooperative spirit was often lacking. McNealy combined the seven units into two, thus doubling his share of the management workload by taking on direct responsibility for both engineering and manufacturing. He also imposed tighter hiring and cost controls throughout the company, except in sales and customer service. At the same time, he was careful to preserve the employee freedom that had been one of Sun's hallmarks; indeed, one of the company's early mottoes was "To ask is to seek denial." In just a year's time, productivity and sales improved, and the value of the company's stock more than doubled, from $14 to $37 a share.

In the early 1990s Sun continued to expand its workstation business, and despite fierce competition, the company retained its position as the number-one seller of the units, both domestically and internationally. By 1994, however, growth had become difficult to sustain, and revenues had started to fall. Having anticipated a drop-off in workstation sales as early as 1991, McNealy had tried to break into the mainstream office and personal computer market by encouraging Sun's engineers to adapt the company's Unix-based operating system, Solaris, for smaller machines. "So far, the strategy has flopped," Joan E. Rigdon wrote in the *Wall Street Journal* (May 10, 1994). "In three years, Sun has sold only 20,000 to 25,000 copies of the PC version of Solaris, compared with sales of more than a million a month for Windows. Its Windows emulation software, called Wabi, doesn't yet work very well, Sun executives concede."

The greatest obstacle to Sun's move into the personal computer market was the Microsoft Corporation. Like many other computer firms, Sun found it almost impossible to compete against Microsoft's proprietary grip on the basic operating system that runs millions of personal computers. In July 1994 Microsoft and the United States Justice Department came to an agreement on an antitrust consent decree that ended some of the company's licensing practices but did little to alter the company's operating-system dominance. McNealy, like many others in the computer industry, protested the terms of the settlement. In an editorial for the *Wall Street Journal* (July 27, 1994), he wrote, "Imagine, if you will, that the English language is not in the public domain, but owned by a single company, which requires everyone who speaks or writes in the language to pay a right-to-use fee. [Microsoft's] DOS and Windows are the native language of the great majority of the world's personal computers. Switching to a different technology now is at least as difficult as learning a new spoken language. This means one company has a virtual lock on a language that is now as critical to the world economy as the written and spoken language. . . . U.S. law simply has not kept up with the pace of technology. In the wake of this settlement, it is time for Congress to take a fresh look at whether our antitrust laws are adequate to meet the novel challenges of the information age."

In the mid-1990s the introduction of the World Wide Web and the resulting spike in Internet usage shook up the entire computing industry and changed the fortunes of Sun. Sun was primed to take advantage of this technological revolution due to the built-in networking capabilities of its computers. As early as 1996, over a third of all World Wide Web servers were Sun machines. Robert Hof noted at the time that "as companies adopt Internet standards for internal networks, they are turning to Sun. . . . And thanks to the new UltraSparc chip, Sun's workstations are once again on the leading edge."

Sun bolstered its advantage in May 1995 when it unveiled Java, a new programming language for the Internet that Philip Elmer-Dewitt of *Time* (January 22, 1996) called "the hottest thing in cyberspace. More than 100,000 copies have been downloaded by software developers eager to try out the new language, which promises to make sending programs across a computer network as easy as sending e-mail or pictures." By accessing Java applications (called "applets"), computer users can make the text and graphics of a Web site come alive with sound, animation, or other visual effects. Applets also create text interaction, so that someone who has accessed a statistical table, for example, can adjust the numbers and ask for a new result. One of Java's many technological marvels is that it is compatible with Sun's Unix and Apple's Macintosh systems as well as Microsoft's Windows 95. McNealy was so delighted by the idea of bypassing Windows that he decided to make Java's Internet accessibility free. "We're not going to make any money on Java, but that's all right," he explained to Rick Boyd-Merritt in a conversation for *OEM* magazine (September 1995). "We'll make money selling servers and desktops and network-management software. We just want the world to be free from having to write to Windows."

Philip Elmer-Dewitt observed that, "with Java, data and programs—the twin staples of computing—don't have to be stored on your computer anymore. They can reside anywhere on the Internet, called up by whoever needs them, whenever they need them." McNealy has envisioned a time in the not-too-distant future when people will buy stripped-down personal computers that merely serve as vehicles to reach the "brains" of the Internet, fulfilling the corporate slogan Sun has held for years: "The Network Is the Computer." This sea change in the industry—if it indeed takes place as

McNealy hopes—would represent a serious threat to Microsoft's preeminent position in the personal computer market, from ownership of the DOS operating system to the software that supports it. Microsoft chairman William H. Gates reluctantly agreed in December 1995 to license Java from Sun (as did several other companies, including IBM and Netscape). The value of Java was not lost on industry, either, and by 1995 major companies such as Ford Motor were relying on Sun systems in their operations.

The company continued to prosper under McNealy's leadership, hiring 10,000 new employees in 2000. That year saw Sun's server revenues increase by 42 percent—when the server market as a whole grew only 7 percent. At the height of the technology boom, in September 2000, Sun was valued at a remarkable $210 billion. Even then, however, McNealy began to discern signs of economic trouble. To respond, Sun cut $40 million from its sales, marketing, and overhead expenses in the last quarter of 2000, followed by an even greater reduction of $247 million in the first quarter of 2001. Sun's business in servers was hurt when, following the collapse of the Internet economy, the market was flooded with billions of dollars worth of previously used Sun hardware as defunct technology companies unloaded their inventories. In July 2001 Sun posted its first loss since 1989.

McNealy has hopes that the recently released Sun Fire 15K server—dubbed Starcat—will reverse the tide. The new system offers a simple, unified server platform, in contrast to the amalgam of Windows NT, Unix, Linux, and other platforms that competitors offer.

Although Sun received a $20-million settlement in its own case against Microsoft, McNealy has voiced his discontent with the Department of Justice's proposed settlement in the Microsoft antitrust case—under which Microsoft will not be required to pay any damages. McNealy has asserted that the government acted prematurely when it announced in September 2001 that it would not seek to break up the company. "They gave away the bazooka and walked in with a spoon," McNealy told Don Clark in the *Wall Street Journal* (November 5, 2001). "We have a convicted monopolist, and we give them a wet kiss." Although the settlement is intended to encourage makers of personal computers to incorporate software programs in their machines that compete with Microsoft products, McNealy believes that there are too many loopholes that will preserve Microsoft's monopolistic power. Some critics, however, detect a certain irony in the fact that McNealy—a staunch defender of free-market capitalism—should go after Microsoft so vehemently. "Everybody calls me a crybaby," McNealy told Clark. "But I'm not crying for me; I'll do just fine." He does admit, however, that the decision will mean more years of struggle—and some unfortunate consequences for his personal life. "I can't retire now," he said. "I have young kids, and I'm not going to see them as much. I can't leave the world to anarchy."

McNealy lives in Palo Alto, California, with his wife, Susan, and their three sons.—A. I. C.

Suggested Reading: *BusinessWeek* p68+ July 24, 1989, p66+ Jan. 22, 1996; *Computer Reseller News* p149 Nov. 16, 1998, p14+ Oct. 1, 2001, p18 Oct. 1, 2001; *Denver Post* C p1 Mar. 5, 2001; *Forbes* p82+ Jan. 22, 2001; *Fortune* p86+ May 28, 2001; *Industry Week* p13+ Dec. 5, 1994; *Newsweek* p44+ Feb. 5, 1996; *New York Times* D p1+ Jan. 29, 1996; *Wall Street Journal* A p30 Oct. 5, 1988, A p14 Nov. 5, 2001; *Wired* (on-line) p128+ Aug. 1998

Courtesy of Firaxis Games

Meier, Sid

(MY-er)

Feb. 24, 1954– Video-game designer

Sid Meier is one of the best-known video-game designers in the computer industry. In 1982 he and Bill Stealey co-founded MicroProse Software Inc., to develop and market games for personal computers. Borrowing from many of his childhood interests, Meier created such well-received and popular combat games as *Silent Service* (1985), *F-15 Strike Eagle* (1985), *F-19 Stealth Fighter* (1987), *Gunship* (1987), and *Red Storm Rising* (1988). Unlike the hundreds of other titles that were on the market at the time, Meier's games were simulations with actual storylines that required players to consider different factors and develop strategies in order to win. By the late 1980s MicroProse had expanded into one of the most successful computer game companies in the industry. Meier became so highly regarded as a designer that he became something of a brand name; the titles of many of the games he developed featured his name, including *Sid Meier's Pirates!* (1987), *Sid Meier's Covert Action* (1990), and *Sid Meier's Railroad Tycoon* (1990). In 1991 Meier released *Sid Meier's Civilization*, a simulation that had players plan and build an entire civilization through the span of thousands of years. Selling more than one million copies, *Civilization* was of the most popular games of the early 1990s. In 1996 Meier co-founded another software company, Firaxis Games, and continued to enjoy commercial success and critical acclaim with such titles as *Sid Meier's Gettysburg* (1997), *Sid Meier's Alpha Centauri* (1999), *Sid Meier's Antietam!* (1999), *Sid Meier's Civilization III* (2001), and *Sid Meier's SimGolf* (2002). Sometimes called the Father of Computer Gaming, Meier continues to develop games that he hopes will thrill, challenge, and entertain players. "With the potential of on-line gaming, I really believe that in the next 10 years computer gaming will make incredible leaps and offer new possibilities that even the leaders in the industry have not envisioned," Meier told a contributor to *PC Games* (January 25, 1999, on-line). "It should be a very exciting and interesting place to be."

Sidney K. Meier was born on February 24, 1954 in Detroit, Michigan. As a child he enjoyed playing board games and reading about history, airplanes, submarines, and pirates. In college Meier studied computer programming. After completing his education, in the mid-1970s, he went to work as a systems analyst for the General Instrument Corporation, an electronics manufacturer.

The first computer Meier purchased was the Atari 800, which reached the market in 1979. "I had really held off on getting a personal computer because they were all very hardware oriented," he explained to Terry Coleman for an article posted on the GameSpot Web site. "But the Atari 800 came out, and it was finally a computer that didn't have switches and paper tape—you could actually program it—so I got into making some games on it."

Meier became acquainted with Bill Stealey, a former air force pilot and flight instructor who worked at General Instrument in business development. During a business convention in Las Vegas, Nevada, Meier and Stealey amused themselves by playing Red Baron, a coin-operated, arcade game in which a player assumed the role of a fighter pilot in World War I. Stealey, who had logged thousands of flight hours during his military career, did not understand how Meier consistently got higher scores than him. After observing the game, Meier figured out how the enemy planes were programmed to attack and adjusted his playing strategy accordingly. "As a pilot, that hurt my pride [that Meier got higher scores]," Stealey recalled to Brian Steiner for the North Carolina *Charlotte Observer* (June 29, 1997), "so when he said that the game wasn't very good and he could make a better one, I bet him that he couldn't and told him if he made a better game, I'd sell it."

Meier took Stealey up on his bet and spent four months writing *Hellcat Ace*, a game that simulated air combat over the Pacific Ocean during World War II. Meier incorporated Stealey's suggestions, such as having the bullets slope downward as they actually do when they are fired from an aircraft, to improve the game and make it as realistic as possible. In 1982 Meier and Stealey each invested $1,500 of their own money to set up a company, based in Hunt Valley, Maryland, to market the game. Meier served as the creative force, writing and developing the games. Stealey was responsible for the business end of MicroProse, as they called the enterprise, selling and marketing its products. Unsure if their venture would succeed, Meier and Stealey kept their day jobs with General Instrument. MircoProse's first game, *Hellcat Ace*, and its instructions, which were created with an Epson printer, were packed in clear plastic sandwich bags they bought at the supermarket. Stealey demonstrated the game at one local computer store, which ordered 100 copies. With no money to advertise *Hellcat Ace* in computer magazines, Stealey devised a ruse to generate interest in the game. "One of [Stealey's] favorite tricks was to call game stores, posing as a customer, and ask for *Hellcat Ace*," Frank Maley wrote for *Business North Carolina* (June 1997). "When the clerk replied that his store didn't carry it, Stealey would throw a fit. Later he would call back, making sure to get a different clerk. After several months of this, he would call and offer to sell the game to the store manager, who by then had been sucked into the bogus hype."

Stealey's efforts were successful, and by early 1984, *Hellcat Ace* had generated more than $200,000 in revenue for MicroProse Software. Meier and Stealey used the profits to gradually expand the fledgling company, hiring additional game designers and programmers to convert games to run on the different computer systems that were on the market at the time. That same year, Meier and Stealey left General Instrument to devote themselves to MicroProse full-time.

In 1984 MicroProse introduced Meier's game *Solo Flight*, in which players simulated flying a single-engine private plane. The airplane features retractable landing gear, brakes, three-position flaps, and other realistic features. According to a survey in *Inc.* (December 1989), MicroProse posted $1.7 million in sales in 1984.

In 1985 Meier wrote *NATO Division Commander*, which simulated war in Europe between the military forces of the U.S.-led North Atlantic Treaty Organization (NATO) and the Soviet-led Warsaw Pact during the Cold War. Meier attempted to make *NATO Division Commander* as sophisticated and diversified as some of the board games he had played as a child. He found, however, that this made the game too complex for people to enjoy. He explained to Coleman, "You lose the scope of the map [on the computer], the ability to take in everything at once. It's fun to have a [computer] opponent there all the time . . . , but I'm not sure those games are dramatically more fun on a computer than they are on paper."

Meier incorporated the lessons he learned from *NATO Division Commander* for his next three war games: *Crusade in Europe* (1985), *Decision in the Desert* (1985), and *Conflict in Vietnam* (1986), which he co-wrote with Ed Bever. MicroProse marketed the three games as the *Command Series* trilogy. *Crusade in Europe*, which featured General (and future President) Dwight Eisenhower on the cover of the box, was set in 1944–45, as Allied forces fought to liberate Europe from the Nazis. *Decision in the Desert* recreated the military campaign in North Africa in 1942–43, with British troops under the command of Field Marshall Bernard Montgomery fighting the Germans, who were led by Field Marshall Erwin Rommel. *Conflict in Vietnam* simulated five key events in Southeast Asia, including the 1954 Vietnamese defeat of the French at Dien Bien Phu and the 1970 U.S. invasion of Cambodia. Meier and Bever simplified the three games, making them easier for players to learn and more enjoyable than *NATO Division Commander*.

In 1985 Meier released *Silent Service*, a submarine simulation set in the Pacific theater during World War II, and *F-15 Strike Eagle*, which allowed players to fly combat missions in different hot spots around the world. Both games became immediate best-sellers and helped establish MicroProse as an important player in the computer-game industry. In 1987 a government agency in what was then West Germany restricted the sale of *Silent Service*, alleging that it corrupted the morals of young people by glorifying war. However, the agency lifted the ban a year later. By the end of 1988, *Silent Service* had sold more than 400,000 copies, making it the most popular submarine simulation of the time. *F-15 Strike Eagle* received a major boost in April 1986, when President Ronald Reagan ordered an air strike against Libya, whose leader Muammar Al-Qaffadi was accused of sponsoring terrorism, because attacking Libya was one of the game's missions. *F-15 Strike Eagle* went on to sell more than one million copies. MicroProse released sequels to both games, *Silent Service II* (1990), *F-15 Strike Eagle II* (1989) and *F-15 Strike Eagle III* (1993), which all featured improved graphics and different scenarios.

In 1987 Meier returned with the role-playing adventure *Sid Meier's Pirates!*, which was the first game that included his name in the title. The same year he worked with other MicroProse programmers to develop *F-19 Stealth Fighter*, a combat flight simulator with a technologically advanced aircraft that could avoid radar detection, and *Gunship*, in which the player flew an AH-64A Apache helicopter on missions. Both games, which offered improved 3-D graphics, posted impressive sales for MicroProse. In 1989 the Software Publishers Association (SPA) named *F-19 Stealth Fighter* the best simulation of the year. In 1988 MicroProse licensed Tom Clancy's best-selling techno-thriller

Red Storm Rising (1986), and Meier helped adapt it into a submarine simulation of the same name.

What began in 1982 as a two-man operation with no venture capital had expanded into one of the most successful firms in the software industry, employing hundreds of people by the end of the decade. According to *Inc.* (December 1989), MicroProse Software recorded more than $16 million in sales in 1988, and Stealey publicly boasted that revenues could exceed $100 million by 1990. According to Kurt Kleiner in an article for the *Baltimore Business Journal* (September 5, 1988), Stealey, in 1988, unveiled his plans to continue MicroProse's growth by expanding its business in the international market, publishing and distributing software developed by other companies, and branching into the arcade-game market.

During the 1990s, Sid Meier shifted his attention away from war games to more advanced simulations. In 1990 Meier and Bruce Shelley introduced *Sid Meier's Railroad Tycoon*, in which players and computer-generated opponents compete to build a profitable railroad conglomerate in the United States and Europe during the 19th century. "[For] *Railroad Tycoon* . . . I got the idea of taking multiple simple systems and having them work together to create an interesting complexity," Meier told Coleman. "There was operating the railroad, playing the stock market, building track. It was like different things that individually are pretty simple and easy to understand and easy to get into, that when they interact, create an interesting kind of complexity."

In 1991 Meier and Shelley collaborated on *Sid Meier's Civilization*, in which players oversee the development of an entire civilization through the span of thousands of years, from a small band of settlers with little or no technology to a technologically superior world power that has the ability and resources to colonize other planets. "*Civilization* may, in fact, be the most open-ended and flexible computer game ever designed," Keith Ferrell wrote in his review for *Compute!* (January 1992). "Each step along the pathway to a fully functioning, happy, and healthy, well-managed civilization can lead in several directions. Decisions made early in the game can generate consequences that stretch across centuries. There is no right or wrong way to play the game." Players had to decide whether to use resources to strengthen their armed forces or to build museums and other cultural centers. They could expand their empires by conquering other nations or pursue peaceful policies. Depending on the decisions players made, a single simulation could take days, weeks, or even longer to complete. In fact, some players found themselves addicted to the game, spending countless hours monitoring the progress of their civilizations. Many observers asserted that the game represented an important milestone in Sid Meier's career as a game designer. *Sid Meier's Civilization* generated substantial attention in computer magazines and the general media and went on to sell more than one million copies. "I knew we had something special [in the game] that I really enjoyed playing, but I had no idea it would be as big of a hit as it's been," Meier told Mike Smith for the Games Domain Web site. "It's amazing that ten years later people are still having fun with [*Civilization*]."

Despite Meier's success, MicroProse began experiencing several problems in the early 1990s. In 1991 the company's plans to branch into arcade games failed, costing them $6 million. Delays in the shipping of several new games also hurt revenues. The national recession of 1991–92, which impacted the entire computer industry, slowed MicroProse's growth as well. Although the company went public in 1991 to raise additional capital, MicroProse continued to rack up debt. In 1993 the company was purchased by Spectrum HoloByte Inc., the California-based video-game maker, and Stealey left.

Meier remained at MicroProse after Stealey's departure. For his next project, Meier developed *CPU Bach* (1993), an application that created classical music in the style of the German composer Johann Sebastian Bach (1685–1750). "I like Bach's music," Meier told Coleman. "Bach has a bunch of sons, and one of them was not as responsible as the others, and he lost about a third of Bach's music. That's always been an incredible frustration [for me]. . . . So my motivation [in developing *CPU Bach*] was to find a way to get more Bach music." Meier also explained to Coleman that he felt the need to change direction because the success of *Sid Meier's Civilization* "created this big wave of pressure of 'what's Sid going to do next?' I really sensed a danger that I didn't want to get into this 'topping myself every time' phenomenon. I saw mental illness down that road."

Meier's next projects included *Sid Meier's Colonization* (1994), a scaled-down version of *Civilization* that focused on the early history of the United States; *Sid Meier's Civilization II*, an upgraded version of his earlier game; and *Magic: The Gathering* (1997), an adaptation of the popular fantasy card game.

In 1996 Sid Meier left MicroProse, which had failed to reverse its slide after being acquired by Spectrum HoloByte. Meier then co-founded a new company, Firaxis Games, with Jeff Briggs and Brian Reynolds, two game designers he had worked with at MicroProse. Briggs became president of Firaxis, which is based in Hunt Valley, Maryland, and Meier served as the chairman and director of creative development. Firaxis remained small, hiring only a handful of employees, and signed agreements with other companies to publish, market, and sell the games it developed.

For his first game at Firaxis Meier returned to war simulations. *Sid Meier's Gettysburg* was released in 1997. In it players could command either the Union or Confederate armies to recreate the decisive Battle of Gettysburg, which helped turn the tide of the Civil War in favor of the Union in 1863.

The game was a commercial hit for Firaxis and was recognized with Wargame of the Year awards in 1997 from *Computer Gaming World* magazine, *Computer Games and Strategy Plus* magazine, the Gamespot Web site, and the Gaming Nexus Web site.

In 1999 Meier enjoyed success with *Sid Meier's Alpha Centauri*. The game borrowed from the concepts behind *Civilization* and involved building intergalactic empires by exploring space, developing advanced technologies, colonizing and conquering planets, and forming alliances with other empires. *PC Gamer* magazine recognized *Alpha Centauri* as the Turn-Based Strategy Game of the Year, in 1999. The same year, Firaxis released a follow-up to *Gettysburg*, *Sid Meier's Antietam!*, a recreation of one of the bloodiest battles of the Civil War.

In 1999 Meier and a team of designers at Firaxis began work on the third entry of the *Civilization* series. *Civilization III*, which featured more-detailed art, animations and sound, reached the market in 2001. In 2002 Meier tapped his passion for golf to create *Sid Meier's SimGolf*. Unlike other golf games on the market, *SimGolf* allowed players to design their own golf courses, which they then managed in hopes of building them into top resorts and attracting professional tournaments.

Sid Meier's wife, Susan, works at Firaxis in an employee-support capacity. They have a teenage son. In 1999 Sid Meier was the second person inducted into the Academy of Interactive Arts and Sciences Hall of Fame. (The first was Shigeru Miyamoto of Nintendo.) In 2002 the state of Maryland recognized Meier with a governor's citation for his leadership and contributions to the game industry.—D. C.

Suggested Reading: *Baltimore Business Journal* p2+ Sep. 5, 1988; *Business North Carolina* (online) June 1997; *Compute!* p86+ Jan. 1992; Firaxis Games Web site; Games Domain Web site; GameSpot Web site; *PC Games* (on-line) Jan. 25, 1999; *Washington Post* Business p1+ Feb. 15, 1993, with photos, E p1+ Dec. 10, 2001, with photo

---

Mensch, William D., Jr.

1945– Microprocessor pioneer; founder of the Western Design Center

In the early 1970s William D. Mensch Jr. helped design the 6502 microprocessor, a revolutionary chip used in many of the affordable personal computers introduced shortly thereafter by Apple, Commodore, and Atari, among others. By the end of the 1990s, more than two billion 6502 chips had been sold, and Michael S. Malone wrote for *Forbes* (June 1, 1998), "The list of Mensch's original 6502-based products reads like the roster of the high tech Hall of Fame." Mensch went on to design numerous additional chips, which are often called the "brains" of the computer, leading several journalists to dubb him the "brains behind the brains." In 1978 Mensch set up the Western Design Center (WDC), an intellectual-property company that licenses his designs for microprocessors and other computer technology. Mensch's microprocessors have been used to improve the performance of countless electronic items, including household appliances, automobile dashboards, audio and video equipment, manufacturing robots, and cell phones.

The fourth of eight children, William D. Mensch Jr. was born in 1945 and grew up on his family's dairy farm in Bucks County, Pennsylvania. "I remember that we didn't have a lot of things," he recalled to a reporter for the Temple University *Conwell Society News* (Winter 1994). "I called it pleasant poverty. I didn't know that we were poor." As a child Mensch was fascinated by a generator his father had purchased to serve as an auxiliary power source for the farm. "He put the old generator in the shed," Mensch told the *Conwell Society News* reporter. "My dad had the generator rigged where the tractor was always parked. He would usually take the conveyor belt that was primarily used to move hay into the silo, and place it on the generator during a power failure to provide electricity. It was fun—we couldn't wait for the power to go out!"

Mensch didn't plan to attend college after graduating from high school. His parents had dropped out of school during 10th grade, a sister had quit after her elementary-school years, and a brother had dropped out during high school. In his senior year, however, Mensch did well on an equivalency exam of the Scholastic Aptitude Test (SAT). Much to his shock, his guidance counselor recommended that he consider college. Acting on that advice, in 1963 Mensch enrolled at Temple University, in Philadelphia, becoming the first member of his family to attend an institute of higher education. He didn't like English or history, so Mensch took courses in electronic-engineering technology.

During his sophomore year in college, Mensch worked at his aunt's general store. One frequent customer was a man who worked at Bell Laboratories, one of the most prominent scientific-research centers in the United States. At the time, Mensch was still undecided about his major. Mensch's aunt believed that her customer could give him some valuable advice about choosing the right career path. "When this man arrived, she introduced me to him as a Temple University student with an interest in electronics and looking for some guidance," Mensch told the *Conwell Society News* reporter. "His response was simply—get into computers. And he left. I never saw him again. And that was in 1965! I looked at my aunt and asked her, 'What's a computer? How can he suggest that I get into this field, and simply walk away? What did it mean?'"

In 1966 Mensch received his Associate of Electrical Engineering Technology (AEET) degree from Temple University. In 1967 he went to work as an electronic technician for Philco-Ford, an electronics researcher and manufacturer in Blue Bell, Pennsylvania. Among his responsibilities were providing support to Philco-Ford's semiconductor design group and testing the early prototypes of the company's solid-state alternators and high-frequency radio components. Mensch also analyzed and redesigned the clock system for the United Aircraft Corporation's solid-state jet-engine control system.

In 1968 Mensch enrolled as an undergraduate student at Villanova University, in Pennsylvania. A year later he transferred to the University of Arizona in Tucson and left the employ of Philco-Ford. In 1971 Mensch graduated with high distinction, earning a degree in electrical engineering.

In 1971 Mensch joined the Motorola Corporation, in Mesa, Arizona, as a design engineer. He designed and implemented Motorola's negative-channel metal-oxide semiconductor (NMOS), positive-channel metal-oxide semiconductor (PMOS), and complementary metal oxide semiconductor (CMOS) standard cell libraries. Mensch was part of the engineering team that designed Motorola's eight-bit 6800 microprocessor, the 6820 programmable interface adapter (PIA), the 6860 modem, and the 6840 timer, among other products. "Motorola had a budget that would allow us to get any tool we needed when we needed it," Mensch said, as quoted by a writer for the *Microprocessor Report* (December 26, 1991), "and supported us very well as engineers." The Motorola 6800 reached the market in 1974 and provided an alternative to the Intel 8080, which was then the most widely-used microprocessor. The Motorola 6800 was installed in several minicomputers, including the Altair 680, and used in several automotive and video-game applications. For his work on microprocessors and related circuitry at Motorola, Mensch became the joint holder of eight patents.

In August 1974 some of Motorola's design engineers, including Mensch and Chuck Peddle, decided to join MOS Technology, the world's largest manufacturer of calculator chips, in Norristown, Pennsylvania. There Mensch co-designed two microprocessors, the NMOS 6501 and the NMOS 6502, which reached the market in 1975. Although the architecture of both microprocessors was similar to that of the Motorola 6800, the 6501 and 6502 included several enhancements. Michael Slater explained in an article for the *Microprocessor Report* (July 11, 1994), "The primary difference [is] that the 6502 has two 8-bit index registers and one accumulator—a generally more useful configuration than the 6800's odd arrangement of two accumulators and one 16-bit index register." In November 1975 Motorola sued MOS Technologies. According to the terms of the out-of-court settlement that the two companies reached, MOS Technologies agreed to withdraw the 6501 from the market, but could keep selling the 6502.

At the time Intel and Motorola were charging hundreds of dollars each for samples of their microprocessors. In order to attract interest, MOS Technologies offered samples of the 6502 for $25. The 6502's low cost, architecture, and quality made it a popular choice for the various brands of home computers that came on the market in the late 1970s and early 1980s. The 6502 caught the attention of Steve Wozniak, who had co-founded Apple Computer with Steve Jobs. Wozniak installed the 6502 in the company's first product, the Apple I, which was nothing more than a circuit board sold as a computer kit to hobbyists. In 1977 Wozniak and Jobs unveiled their revolutionary Apple II personal computer, which also contained the 6502. Unlike its predecessor, the Apple II included a case, keyboard, and color display. The machine's look and relatively low price made it appealing to many ordinary people who wanted to experiment with a home computer. The Apple II quickly became a bestseller and turned Apple Computer into a major player in the emerging home-computer industry.

In 1976 Jack Tramiel, the founder and owner of Commodore Business Machines, acquired MOS Technologies to ensure that his company, which manufactured electric calculators, had a reliable and continuous supplier of low-cost chips. Peddle, one of the designers of the 6502, persuaded Tramiel that home computers had a profitable future and that the 6502 could serve as the engine for them. Intrigued by Peddle's ideas, Tramiel decided to branch into home computers, and in 1977 he introduced the 6502-based Commodore PET. To attract consumer interest, Tramiel promoted the machine with extensive advertising and drastically cut its price. The 6502 also powered the Commodore VIC-20, which sold over one million units, and the Commodore 64, which became the best-selling computer of its time.

In addition to Apple and Commodore machines, the 6502 was installed in Atari 400 and Atari 800 home computers, which reached the market in 1979. Versions of the 6502 powered the extremely popular Atari 2600 video game console and the best-selling Rockwell 2400-baud modem. In 1985 the Japanese-based Nintendo Corporation introduced the Nintendo Entertainment System (NES), which used the 6502 chip, in the United States. The NES enjoyed impressive sales and helped revitalize the then-struggling video-game industry.

The success of the 6502 forced Intel and Motorola to cut the cost of their own microprocessors, which facilitated the production of more advanced personal computers. The price wars declared by Commodore's Jack Tramiel and Philippe Kahn, the chief executive officer of Borland International, a software manufacturer, resulted in lower costs for both personal computers and software.

In 1977 Mensch left MOS Technologies, where his work had resulted in two more joint patents for microprocessors and related circuitry. After a brief stint as a staff consultant with Integrated Circuit Engineering (ICE), in Scottsdale, Arizona, in 1978 Mensch founded his own company, the Western Design Center (WDC). "I wanted to have total flexibility to do what I wanted to do, and the only way to do that was to have less people and less materials and focus on creativity," he explained to Jane Magruder for the *Arizona Business Gazette* (July 4, 1996). "As much as I wanted to make money, I wanted to be creative more. I wanted to change the world." Mensch's first client was Jack Tramiel, who contracted the WDC to design a low-power CMOS calculator chip. After successfully completing the chip, Mensch severed his ties to Commodore and turned his attention to other projects.

Mensch wanted to build an eight-bit, low-power CMOS version of the 6502, to be named the 65C02. He approached several companies to finance the project, but they all turned him down. He pressed forward, however, exclusively relying on the WDC's resources to design and build the chip, which he unveiled in 1982. "The 65C02 instruction enhancement has actually 29 instruction opcodes [machine language commands] added to the original 6502 instruction set," he told Selby Bateman for *Compute!* (Fall/Winter 1986). "Those new opcodes are meant to enhance the capabilities in the controls marketplace and also for some of the high-level language applications." Mensch licensed the 65C02 to such companies as GTE, Rockwell, and Synertek, which manufactured the chips and sold them. When the 65C02 reached the market, Commodore filed suit, alleging the theft of trade secrets. The WDC settled the case with Commodore, which received the rights to the 65C02 for internal use at half the standard licensing fee. Apple Computer licensed the 65C02 for its Apple IIc machine, which was a bestseller, and chips based on the 65C02 were installed in many electronic items—from toasters to medical devices. Mensch followed up the 65C02 with the 16-bit 65C816, which was installed in the Apple IIgs and the Super Nintendo game system, which both did well with consumers.

The Western Design Center remains in business today as an intellectual-property company that licenses its patented designs to other companies. Mensch's work at the WDC has resulted in 12 more patents, giving him a total of 22. "We have no intention to have a factory of our own [to mass produce our products]," Mensch told Bateman. "It would be a bit foolhardy to think that I'm going to raise a half-billion dollars to get a factory and then fund it with design. I don't think that'll work. My strategy, then, is to work with [other] factories and license them on my microprocessors, and as a result have a favorable situation where I can buy [silicon] wafers. And that's what I'm doing."

Mensch has pursued several charitable endeavors, many related to education. He donated $220,000, for example, to Temple University's College of Engineering and Architecture to establish a scholarship fund for students who wish to pursue careers in medical electronics, and he contributed

$240,000 to the University of Notre Dame, in South Bend, Indiana, for graduate fellowships and summer stipends. He has also established the William D. Mensch Jr. Scholarship at Xavier College Preparatory, in Phoenix, Arizona.

Mensch has five children. He currently lives with his wife, Dianne, in Mesa, Arizona.—D. C.

Suggested Reading: *Arizona Business Gazette* p13 July 4, 1996, with photo; *Commodore World* (on-line) Jan. 1996; *Compute!* (on-line) Fall/Winter 1986, with photo; *Conwell Society News* p3+ Winter 1994, with photo; *Forbes* p66+ June 1, 1998; *Microprocessor Report* p13+ Dec. 16, 1991, p10+ July 11, 1994; Western Design Center Web site

---

Metcalfe, Robert M.

Apr. 7, 1946– Inventor of the Ethernet and founder of the 3Com Corporation

In 1973, when Robert M. Metcalfe, a telecommunications expert, invented the Ethernet—the industry-standard method for speedily connecting computers within a local area network (LAN)—he wasn't content to wait for his invention to catch on. He actively promoted his work and in 1979 founded 3Com Corporation, now a multibillion-dollar concern, as a marketing vehicle for Ethernet-related products. Metcalfe's message was that allowing computers to communicate with one another made them more powerful and useful and that the value of a network grows exponentially with each additional user. This idea became known as Metcalfe's Law. Today most personal computers come with an Ethernet port already installed. In the early 1990s Metcalfe moved on to journalism, where he continued to exert his influence on the computer world with an opinionated column in *InfoWorld*, a magazine for which he also served as publisher.

Robert Metcalfe was born in the New York City borough of Brooklyn, on April 7, 1946. His father was an engineering technician in the aerospace industry. His mother was a riveter. Metcalfe told Joyce Gemperlein and Trevor Getsla for the *San Jose Mercury News* (on-line) that his grandmother was his greatest mentor. She was part of a commission to reduce organized crime in the New York City harbor area, and, as Metcalfe said, "This woman was constantly surrounded by really tough people, mafiosi. And she was as tough as nails." Metcalfe emulated his grandmother's bravado. One night, when he was in fourth grade, Metcalfe had a book report due but hadn't read a book. Choosing one of his father's engineering textbooks off the shelf, he wrote a vague report. To make up for this weak attempt, he inserted a bold statement at the end: he promised to go to the Massachusetts Institute of Technology (MIT), in Cambridge, and earn a degree in electrical engineering. (Nobody in Met-

calfe's family had ever gone to college.) Eight years later Metcalfe graduated second in his class at Bay Shore High School, and in 1964 he enrolled in MIT's electrical-engineering program. At MIT he took a full course load, worked as a computer programmer, and was captain of the tennis team. He graduated in 1969 with bachelor's degrees in electrical engineering and business management.

After MIT Metcalfe attended Harvard University, also in Cambridge, to study applied mathematics. He received his master's degree, in 1970, and began working towards his doctorate in computer science. It was at about this time that Metcalfe got his first experience with computer networking. Harvard wouldn't give him the responsibility of connecting the school to the new ARPANET, a long-distance computer network funded by the U.S. government and the forerunner to today's Internet, so he went to work for MIT and helped build the hardware to connect their computers to the ARPANET.

In 1972 two setbacks gave Metcalfe his first real taste of failure. First, he was chosen by MIT to demonstrate the ARPANET to executives at AT&T, using some of the hardware he'd helped design. During the demonstration the system, which had never before crashed, did so. To Metcalfe's surprise and dismay, the executives seemed to enjoy his failure. Metcalfe explained to Scott Kirsner for *Wired* (November 1998) that it was a formative experience for him. "I saw that there are people who will connive against innovation," he said. "They're hostile to it. And that has shaped my behavior ever since." Next, after inviting his relatives to his graduation, Metcalfe discovered that his Harvard doctoral dissertation on the ARPANET had been rejected. He had already accepted a position at Xerox's Palo Alto Research Center (PARC) and was worried that he would lose the job. Despite his failed dissertation, he was given the job.

Researchers at PARC were beginning to develop early personal computers, and they wanted Metcalfe to figure out how to connect them on a network to a new ultrafast laser printer. Meanwhile, Metcalfe had become familiar with AlohaNet, a networking technique developed at the University of Hawaii. He found that the basic ideas behind AlohaNet were good, but he identified potential problems with the system. These insights served a dual purpose: Metcalfe used his analysis of AlohaNet as part of a revised dissertation and also applied his knowledge to developing a new system at PARC. In 1973 he received his Ph.D. from Harvard, and the same year he developed the Ethernet.

Metcalfe named his technology after ether, the invisible medium scientists had hypothesized must be present everywhere in the universe to allow electromagnetic waves to be transmitted. Though the theory had long been proven incorrect, Metcalfe thought the concept was still a good metaphor for his invention. As he told George Leonard for *Esquire* (December 1985), "We use coaxial cable or fiber optics or any passive medium *as if* it were ether." Through the Ethernet, computers on a network check to make sure that lines aren't busy before transmitting data. And the busier the network is, the longer the computers wait before attempting to send data again. The result is fast and efficient networking that allows large numbers of computers to communicate simultaneously.

On November 11, 1973 the Ethernet ran for the first time. Metcalfe's technology enabled PARC employees to communicate almost instantaneously, to share software, and to connect to such central components as printers. It also meant that the computers on the network would collectively have the capabilities of larger, more expensive systems based on central mainframe computers. The Ethernet also worked at an incredible speed—up to three megabits of information per second.

Today, computers sharing an Ethernet can transmit more than a gigabit of data per second. Part of the reason for the advancement is that after inventing the Ethernet, Metcalfe worked prodigiously to promote it and entice other companies to embrace compatible technologies. After hooking several hundred computers together at PARC and receiving four patents for his Ethernet inventions, Metcalfe began thinking about starting his own company. "For the next two years," Metcalfe told Leonard, "I spent a lot of time having breakfast, lunch, and dinner with every venture capitalist and entrepreneur I could find and just asking them how to do it." Gregarious and outspoken, Metcalfe was a natural entrepreneur. He succeeded in getting three major companies (Digital Equipment, Intel, and Xerox) to back his Ethernet technology, and in 1979 he founded 3Com.

The three "Coms" of Metcalfe's corporation stood for computers, communication, and compatibility. He planned to sell the software and hardware to make the Ethernet run, but it wasn't until 1981 that Metcalfe succeeded in raising $1.1 million in venture capital to get the company operating fully. Metcalfe served in many capacities at 3Com, including CEO, president, chairman of the board, and division general manager. He says the hardest thing he ever did, and ultimately the most rewarding, came in 1982. "The board of directors of a company that I had founded, a board that I had recruited, person by person, informed me that I was no longer going to be chief executive of my company," Metcalfe told Gemperlein and Getsla. "And I did not quit my job. I stayed and became the head of sales and marketing." Metcalfe found he was quite a talented salesman. In 1982 3Com had no income, but by 1984 his sales pitches were bringing in $1 million per month. By 1990 Metcalfe felt he was ready to resume his old post as 3Com's CEO. The job went, however, to a quiet, but capable engineer, Eric Benhamou. At that point, Metcalfe undertook a dramatic change. He left 3Com, sold his stake in the company, and moved back East.

Metcalfe, his wife (the writer Robyn Shotwell Metcalfe), and their two children moved onto Kelmscott Farm, a 150-acre property in Maine. Robyn, an avid conservationist, was interested in the preservation of rare domestic animal breeds, and the family acquired 250 Cotswold sheep, Nigerian dwarf goats, and Gloucestershire Old Spots pigs. Metcalfe told Anthony B. Perkins for *Red Herring* (November 1994), "[My children are] going to roll around in the dirt and be farm kids." Metcalfe, however, continued to work away from the farm. From 1991 to 1992 he was a fellow in the computer laboratory at Cambridge University, in England. Upon his return he wrote articles for such magazines as *Computerworld*, *Communications Week*, and *Technology Review*. Then, in 1993, he became vice president of technology for the International Data Group and the publisher and columnist of its affiliated magazine, *InfoWorld*. Though Metcalfe was no longer inventing new technologies or heading *Fortune* 500 corporations, his new role as a journalist gave him continued influence over the computer industry. As quoted in *Wired*, a Digital Equipment executive said of Metcalfe, "He's got a lot more sway as a columnist than he would have as head of one of the three big suppliers of networking equipment. People listen to him, and they respect him. He has an opportunity now to be influential over the direction of technology, rather than the direction of one company's [bottom line]."

Metcalfe developed into one of the most outspoken journalists in the computer world. In his columns, he introduced new technologies and had no problem criticizing huge corporations like Microsoft, which he accused of monopolistic practices long before a lawsuit was brought against it. Describing his column to Perkins, he said, "My favorite thing to do is explain things that are being hyped, because the people who are hyping things don't do a good job at explaining them, because they are generally busy lying about them." In 1995 Metcalfe received his first journalism award, the Public Understanding of Science Award from the San Francisco Exploratorium. He was also elected to the American Academy of Arts and Sciences that year. But Metcalfe's most noted antic of 1995 was predicting in his *InfoWorld* column that the Internet would soon collapse. The following year, when his prediction never materialized, he literally ate his words at a meeting of Internet service providers. He tore his column into little pieces, dropped them into a blender with some water, hit the on button, and ate the mixture with a spoon in front of the audience.

From 1975 to 1983 Metcalfe was an associate professor of electrical engineering at Stanford University, in Stanford, California. Throughout his career he has won numerous awards and honors for his work. In 1980 he received the Grace Murray Hopper Award from the Association for Computing Machinery (ACM). Then, in 1988 he received the Alexander Graham Bell Medal from the Institute of Electrical and Electronics Engineers (IEEE).

In 1996 he won the IEEE Medal of Honor. That year he also became chairman of the Association for Computing Machinery 50th anniversary conference. In 1998 he helped organize Vortex, a telecommunications conference, and Agenda 99, a high-tech conference sponsored by the International Data Group. Also in 1998, he received an Industry Legend Award from the Computer & Communications Industry Association and an MCI Information Technology Leadership Award for Innovation from the Computerworld Smithsonian Awards Program.

On September 22, 2000 Metcalfe wrote his last column for *InfoWorld*. Ever in search of new challenges, in 2001 he joined Polaris Partners, a venture-capital firm.—P. G. H.

Suggested Reading: *Computerworld* p96 June 21, 1999, with photo; *Esquire* p399+ Dec. 1985; *Red Herring* Nov. 1994; *San Jose Mercury News* (online); *Wired* Nov. 1998

Metropolis, Nicholas C.

June 11, 1915–Oct. 17, 1999 Developer of the Mathematical Numerical Integrator and Computer (MANIAC)

The computer scientist and physicist Nicholas C. Metropolis was involved in electronic computing from the time of its invention. While working in the Los Alamos Laboratory on the Manhattan Project (the United States' endeavor to build the first atomic bomb), he used the Electronic Numerical Integrator and Computer (ENIAC), the world's first electronic computer. The ENIAC, which filled an area the size of a large room, astounded the scientific community in 1945 by successfully completing complex calculations crucial to the development of the atomic bomb.

At the Los Alamos Laboratory, Metropolis oversaw the building of the lab's own electronic computer, the Mathematical Numerical Integrator and Computer (MANIAC), completed in 1952. Metropolis also developed several important algorithms, or problem-solving procedures, that have found wide applications in computing and other fields.

Nicholas Constantine Metropolis was born on June 11, 1915 in Chicago, Illinois. He earned his B.S. (1937) and his Ph.D. (1941) in chemical physics from the University of Chicago, where he worked with the physicists Enrico Fermi and Edward Teller on the first nuclear reactors. After earning his Ph.D. he became a research associate at the school. In 1943 he moved to Los Alamos, New Mexico, after being recruited by J. Robert Oppenheimer to join the Manhattan Project. Metropolis was charged with developing equations for the states of materials at high temperatures, pressures, and densities. He and Richard Feynman, the Nobel Prize–winning physicist with whom he worked, were forced for these purposes to use slow and er-

ror-prone electromechanical calculators; as a result, they became adept at repairing the machines. Metropolis was relieved from having to use the calculators when John von Neumann, the mathematical consultant on the project, arranged for him to do calculations involving thermonuclear reactions as a test of the newly developed the ENIAC. After several months, in 1945, the ENIAC successfully completed Metropolis's highly classified calculations, thus contributing to the creation of the atomic bomb. "It is sad to observe, Metropolis wrote in a chapter of *A History of Scientific Computing* (1990), "that a war seems to be essential to encourage and stimulate developments such as the computer."

After the war Metropolis returned to the University of Chicago to teach and do research. In 1948 he went back to the Los Alamos Laboratory to lead research efforts in mathematical computing. "We had learned about the slow and arduous methods of desk calculators, then the primitive adaptations to electromechanical devices; finally, the dawn of electronic computing was emerging. Even scientists thought they were dreaming. Many of us were anxious to explore some of the new directions as we returned to peacetime academia." Metropolis helped to develop the Monte Carlo Method, an algorithm that can be applied in such fields as weapons design, mathematical economy, and operations research. (Fermi, von Neumann, and Stanislaw Ulam also contributed to the method.) In 1949 Metropolis and Ulam made the first Monte Carlo calculations using the ENIAC.

At the Los Alamos Laboratory, Metropolis was put in charge of overseeing a computer-building project to meet the lab's research needs. The new computer, which Metropolis dubbed the MANIAC, incorporated an innovative, new memory circuit and ran its first problem in March 1952. (Metropolis has said that he hoped, in vain, that the name would end the fad for acronyms in the scientific community.) The MANIAC was subsequently used to solve research problems in physics, chemistry, biology, and mathematics.

In 1953 Metropolis authored a paper with Arianna Rosenbluth, Marshall Rosenbluth, Augusta Teller, and Edward Teller that outlined a new algorithm, called the Metropolis algorithm. It has been cited by various sources as being one of the 20th century's most influential algorithms in the development and practice of science and engineering.

Metropolis next oversaw the building of MANIAC II, after which, in 1957, he went back to the University of Chicago and founded the Institute for Computer Research. Nandor L. Balazs noted in *Physics Today* (September 2000, on-line) that during this time, "Perhaps his least known, though extremely important, achievement was the invention of online data processing in scientific experimentation. He designed and built—with a soldering iron in his hands—a computer that was coupled to the Navy cyclotron. This computer could receive and analyze data while an experiment was running, allowing the experimenters to modify their experiments during their allotted time."

Metropolis stayed at the University of Chicago until 1965, when he again returned to Los Alamos, where he stayed for the rest of his career. There he developed methods of parallel computing, or the simultaneous performance of two or more tasks on a computer. Later in his career he collaborated with the mathematician Gian-Carlo Rota to advance ideas in several fields of mathematics. In 1980 he was named a senior fellow of the Los Alamos Laboratory, and in 1987 he became the first Los Alamos employee to be given emeritus status. His other honors include the Institute of Electrical and Electronic Engineers Computer Society Com-

puter Pioneer Award and fellowships from the American Physics Society and the American Academy of Arts and Sciences. Several years before his death he established the Nicholas C. Metropolis Mathematics Foundation, dedicated to supporting young mathematics and computational-science students. On October 17, 1999 Metropolis died in a nursing home in Los Alamos. He was survived by his son, two daughters, and two sisters.—P. G. H.

Suggested Reading: *New York Times* A p14 Oct. 23, 1999; *Physics Today* (on-line) Sep. 2000; Nash, Stephen G., ed. *A History of Scientific Computing*, 1990; Shirkin, Joel. *Engines of the Mind*, 1996

Miner, Jay

May 31, 1932–June 20, 1994 Developer of the Amiga computer

Jay Miner, often called "the father of the Amiga," was a significant figure in the world of early microcomputers. When it was released, in 1985, the Amiga was considered revolutionary. It included a graphical interface, stereo sound, and a full range of colors—in an era when most computers used command prompt lines, emitted only uninspired beeps, and featured simple green or amber display screens. Though it was soon overshadowed by increasingly sophisticated machines, there are still Amiga fans who maintain their old units, trade software and new operating systems on-line, and scoff at the idea of ever buying an Apple or IBM.

Jay Glenn Miner was born in Prescott, Arizona, on May 31, 1932. He grew up in southern California, and attended San Diego State University. During the Korean War he served in the U.S. Coast Guard and studied for six months at the Coast Guard's Electronics Technical School, in Groton, Connecticut. He then worked for three years in the Coast Guard's North Atlantic Weather Patrol, fixing radios and radar equipment.

During his time in Groton, Miner met Caroline Poplawski, whom he married in 1952. The couple returned to California when Miner completed his tour of duty. He then continued his education, receiving an electrical-engineering degree from the University of California at Berkeley, in 1958. Shortly after graduation he taught himself transistor-circuit design and logic design. "It was easy in those days," Miner jokingly told an interviewer for *Amiga User International* (June 1998), "to learn enough out of one book to become [an] expert."

In 1964 Miner was hired by General Micro Electronics, a spinoff of Fairchild Semiconductor. At General Micro he designed metal oxide semiconductor (MOS) chips for the world's first MOS calculator, which contained 23 custom chips. For the next decade he worked on calculator chips for a variety of companies, as well as designing some of

the world's first digital voltmeters and wristwatches.

In 1974 Miner joined the Atari Corporation, a company founded by Nolan Bushnell. Atari had attained some success with a coin-operated video game called Pong. Simple by today's standards, the game required a player to hit a virtual ball to an opponent, as in table tennis. Miner was hired as a chip designer and worked on the Atari 2600 home video-game system, which became a national phenomenon, selling millions of units in the late 1970s and early 1980s. Riding high on the 2600's success, Bushnell decided to move his company into the burgeoning home-computer market and asked Miner to design the chip sets. In 1977 Miner began to direct work on the architecture and chip design for the Atari 400 and 800 home computers. The 400 debuted in 1979 and proved remarkably popular. However, Miner told the *Amiga User International* interviewer, "[Atari executives] made a decision to write off all of the development costs in that first year [of] production. This allowed them to show just enough profit that year to not quite trigger the bonus payment they promised to the engineers and programmers." Miner, already bothered by the bonus situation, was angered when Bushnell vetoed his plans to develop a powerful 16-bit computer system to compete with Apple. Along with many other engineers and programmers, Miner left Atari. (He accused the company of producing only "junk cartridges" after the mass defection and blamed Atari officials, in large part, for the crash the video-game market suffered a few years later.) Miner joined the staff of Zimast, a microchip company that developed chips for cardiac pacemakers.

In 1982 Larry Caplin, an ex-colleague from Atari who had left to form the video-game company Activision, asked Miner to help him with yet another start-up. Caplin originally planned to call the venture Hi Toro, but changed the name to Amiga. The initial plan called for Caplin to program the games and Miner, while still employed at Zimast, to design the chips. Caplin, although he had written the business plan, found offices, gotten financial backing, and hired a CEO, soon became impatient with the slow pace of establishing the business and pulled out of the deal. Miner quit Zimast to take his place as chief engineer at Amiga.

Although Miner would have preferred to be working on a general-purpose computer rather than a gaming station, the project's financial backers felt differently. Trying to satisfy both goals, Miner believed he could develop a game system that would be expandable into a full computer system, and over the next two years he developed a machine with the housing of a video-game station and the motherboard of a computer.

Miner brought his dog, Mitchy, to work everyday. "That set the tone for the whole atmosphere of the place," he told Mike Nelson for *Amiga User International* (September 1992). "It was more than just companionship with Mitchy—the fact that she was there meant that the other people wouldn't be too critical of some of those we hired, who were quite frankly weird. There were guys coming to work in purple tights and pink bunny slippers. [One engineer] looked like your average off the street homeless hippy." (Eventually, Mitchy's paw print was molded into the top cover of the first model Amiga, along with the signatures of the design team.)

Despite Miner's design successes and Amiga's appealing work environment, the company was losing money because all of its capital was tied up in development costs. By 1984 it was evident that Amiga would have to be sold. Commodore, then an industry leader, made the purchase, and the development team, headed by Miner, transferred to that company. Somewhat ironically, Commodore executives decided to develop the Amiga as a high-performing computer because the video-game market had by this time begun to nosedive.

Miner was delighted with his official new mission. "I've always wanted to do a machine with the graphics of a good flight simulator," Miner told Susan Chira for the *New York Times* (August 29, 1984). "[The Amiga's] ability to do high-speed animation still excites me the most. It opens up all sorts of educational opportunities." The Amiga 1000 debuted in mid-1985, "a date of biblical proportions to the Amiga faithful," according to John Stebbins, writing for the *Ottawa Citizen* (February 10, 1997). Unlike other computers of the day, the Amiga had a multitasking operating system that enabled it to run a variety of programs simultaneously. Its 16-bit chips allowed it to have stereo sound (when most computers just beeped), two playfields instead of one, and 4,096 colors instead of the 500 that were then the norm. Industry analysts were enthralled. "It's just exceptional," Tim Barajin from Creative Strategies International told Chira. "It's a Mac with color graphics built in." Barbara Isgar of Paine Webber enthused, "What I have seen of the machine leads me to think it's exciting enough that the entire industry is going to have to take notice."

Despite such predictions, the Amiga fared poorly. In its first year, it sold fewer units than the Apple Macintosh, even though, at $1,300, the Amiga was more of a value. Many blamed Commodore for preventing the Amiga from reaching its potential audience, citing the fact that for almost a full year the machine wasn't advertised at all. When they did advertise, Commodore executives marketed the Amiga as an expensive toy, as opposed to a fully viable computer capable of either home or office use. (Many of the Amigas still in use today are employed by filmmakers to create inexpensive computer-graphic effects for such television shows as *Babylon 5* and *Star Trek*.) In addition, Commodore never developed a full line of software for the machine, which further hampered sales. Despite this, the company did continue to produce new Amigas, including the A500, A500+, A600, and A1200. These machines were priced lower, and although they included fewer expansion options than the original Amiga 1000, they were more attractive to some consumers.

Still, in 1994 Commodore filed for bankruptcy and liquidated its assets. Amiga changed hands several times and has been owned by QuickPak and Escom, among others. In March 1997 Amiga was purchased by Gateway and established as a subsidiary, Amiga International. The division immediately announced that it would be developing a new, improved operating system. Although there have been numerous product announcements since then, firing the hopes of the Amiga's avid fans, little has actually been released into the marketplace. Olin Wread commented on the brand's possible future for *ExtemeTech* (January 23, 2003, on-line): "[It is] likely the Amiga will continue to be a geek toy treasured by hard-core users. With sufficient market presence and continued public resentment towards Microsoft and avoidance of Apple, the platform may live another day."

Jay Miner spent the last years of his career at a biotechnology company called Ventritex, working on chips for an implantable defibrillator. He suffered from kidney disease for several years and underwent regular dialysis. In 1990 his sister, Joyce Beers, donated a kidney to him, and Miner lived for four years after that. On June 20, 1994, around the time of the Commodore liquidation, he died of heart failure brought on by the complications of his kidney disease. The Internet is now host to scores of Amiga users' groups and impassioned tributes to Miner's work.—C. M.

Suggested Reading: *Amiga User International* June 1988, Sep. 1992; *ExtremeTech* (on-line) Nov. 7, 2002; *New York Times* D p1 Aug. 29, 1984; (London) *Observer* S p8 Apr. 3, 1994; *Ottawa Citizen* A p10 Feb. 10, 1997

Minor, Halsey

1965– Former chairman and CEO of CNET: The Computer Network

"Halsey Minor's sort of the Ted Turner of the Internet," Sky Dayton, the founder of EarthLink Network Inc., told Tom McNichol for *Salon* (March 13, 1998). "He's got a big dream and isn't afraid to take risks. He's building a lot of things at once. He knows what he wants, and isn't shy about going out and getting it."

The comparison between the two entrepreneurs goes beyond personal styles. Just as Turner succeeded in spinning his original TBS Superstation into a host of cable stations—CNN, Headline News, TNT, and the Cartoon Network, among others—Minor parlayed his first on-line computer magazine, *CNET.com*, and television show, *CNET Central*, into a new-media company responsible for 11 Web sites and four cable television shows, each with computer-oriented programming. In creating CNET: The Computer Network, a company that provides both Internet-based services and television programming, all with computer- and technology-oriented content, Minor achieved one of his long-stated goals. "On-line is very much like TV," he told a reporter in 1995, the year CNET launched both *CNET Central* and *CNET.com*. "It includes all the same things—the talent issues and production elements are all the same, and they're both ratings-based." Minor stepped down as CEO and chairman of CNET in 2000 and is now on the board of Grand Central Communications, a Web-services company.

Halsey McLean Minor, who was born in Charlottesville, Virginia, in 1965, has been obsessed with computers since his youth. When it was time for him to go to boarding school—a family tradition for two generations—he told his father and grandfather that he did not want to attend their alma mater, Episcopal High School in Washington, D.C., because the school did not have the proper computer facilities to meet his needs. Instead, he attended the Woodberry Forest School in Orange, Virginia, which had a microcomputer lab. "I was kind of a closet nerd," Minor admitted to McNichol. "I played football, but I'd lock myself away in the computer room and program for hours. I loved reading all the computer magazines."

Minor attended the University of Virginia (UVA) and chose anthropology as his major—although he remained obsessed with computers. "I nearly lost a girlfriend in college because I used to spend Saturday and Sunday nights on the couch reading all the computer magazines," Minor recalled to McNichol. Demonstrating an entrepreneurial streak, he started a company called the Rental Network, which distributed a series of databases that provided customers with information on how to locate apartments for rent around the immediate UVA vicinity. "I had to drive around to each of these kiosks and load the database by hand three times a week," he told Paul Schindler of

CMPnet (September 1997). "I thought, 'Wouldn't it be great if all these things were actually connected?' At the time, I didn't even know the Internet existed."

When he graduated from college, in 1987, Minor was hired by Merrill Lynch Capital Markets in New York City, where he began an investment-banking training course. "I [had] started a company. That impressed Merrill Lynch enough that they overlooked the fact that I worked in anthropology," he told Schindler. At Merrill Lynch, Minor got to know his fellow employee Jeff Bezos. The two convinced the brokerage firm's management to develop their idea of designing a program that would deliver news and vital information to its employees electronically. Merrill Lynch gave the idea the go-ahead, but after a few months, the company, under pressure to cut costs, was forced to cancel the project. Minor was devastated. Bezos left the firm and went on to launch an on-line bookstore, which has since evolved into the hugely successful company Amazon.com.

Minor joined Russell Reynolds Associates, the world's largest executive-search firm, as Reynolds's executive assistant. Reynolds told Minor that if he stayed in the position for two years, he would help Minor develop a new business plan. "One day [Halsey] came in with a stack of PC magazines, $279 worth, that was three feet tall," Reynolds recalled to Saul Hansell of the *New York Times* (June 15, 1998). "Halsey said, 'Get it: People are spending money on this stuff.'" Minor's opportunity to begin a new company did not materialize, however, and he decided to pursue his plan without Reynolds's help. In 1992, "after a year of living off money from friends and credit cards," as Hansell put it, Minor was finally in business for himself. He called his company CNET: The Computer Network and established its headquarters in San Francisco, California.

In founding CNET: The Computer Network, Minor's ambition was to create a company that would integrate television programming with Internet-based services. The main focus of the firm was to be its Web sites, but because so much of the so-called new media at that time consisted of on-line versions of print magazines, Minor knew he had to come up with a strategy to compete with these entities, which already had established built-in audiences. The idea he came up with was to launch a television network that would provide computer- and technology-oriented programming, with the ultimate goal of raising viewers' awareness of his company's Web sites. "I never believed that I could compete against [the computer magazine publisher] Ziff-Davis and all these guys without TV programming," he said to Nikki C. Goth for *Red Herring* (on-line). "But with TV, I could reach more people than they reached through their magazines."

With an infusion of a substantial amount of cash from Paul Allen, the Microsoft co-founder turned billionaire investor, Minor more or less achieved this goal in 1995—"more or less" because he did not actually establish a cable network but rather developed a cable television show. The program, *CNET Central*, debuted on USA Network in April of that year, and in June, CNET launched *CNET.com*, an on-line publication that, like its magazine counterparts, offered users reviews of new computer products and columns by industry insiders, but, unlike them, could be updated continually. *CNET Central*, which has been variously described as "the *Entertainment Tonight* of computing" and "a sort of MTV for computer lovers," went on to build a sizable audience, and was joined by three more television shows developed by CNET: *The Web*, *The New Edge*, and *TV.com*. Similarly, CNET has since established 10 other Web sites, including Computers.com, Shareware.com, and News.com.

When Snap! Online, Minor's Web portal, was introduced in 1997, industry observers dismissed it as too costly and as having been introduced too late to cash in on the portal market. Minor was undeterred; knowing that he needed a well-known Internet company to advertise on his Web portal, Minor called Russell Pillar, a friend from his Merrill Lynch days who was then chief executive of the on-line service Prodigy. Minor wanted Prodigy not only to advertise its services on Snap! but also to make the portal Prodigy's primary search engine. Pillar, however, chose a competitor, Excite. "My ears still ring," Pillar told Hansell of his decision. "Halsey likes to win at all costs."

By early 1998, Snap!, though considered technically excellent, was attracting only a fraction of the number of visitors the leading portals did. Stock market analysts began to wonder if perhaps CNET, which had yet to break even, would end up as a noble failure. In April, CNET's stock fell considerably, and this came on the heels of multiple quarter losses in the previous fiscal year. CNET was at a crossroads. It was then that Minor pulled a much-needed rabbit out of his hat.

On June 15, Minor announced that NBC had purchased the option to buy a controlling stake in Snap! and had acquired a small percentage of CNET as a whole. In exchange, the network giant agreed to advertise Snap! extensively on NBC stations. When news of the deal hit Wall Street, CNET stock surged to an all-time high. Minor had managed not only to save his fledgling and cost-inefficient portal service, but also to make CNET a bundle of money. Yet while most analysts hailed the move as a milestone for CNET, some focused on one aspect of the deal whereby Minor could lose control of his brainchild if NBC exercised its option to buy 60 percent of Snap! The possibility of a future buyout prompted Vernon Keenan of Zona Research to suggest to *CMPnet* (June 23, 1998) that "Halsey Minor is grimacing all the way to the bank," because, *CMPnet* observed, "in saving Snap!, he may have lost it." For his part, Minor felt he had had no choice but to agree to the deal. He was losing too much money. As he told Hansell,

"Ultimately, we said we would rather own 40 percent of No. 1 than 50 percent of No. 3."

On June 19, 1998, four days after the NBC deal was announced, Minor delivered the final keynote speech at the annual PC Expo held in New York City. During the speech, Minor seemed highly optimistic. He was quoted by Lev Grossman for *Time.com* (June 19, 1998) as saying, "Commerce on the Internet is about to go supersonic. . . . The medium is the market." He had reason to be optimistic—in 1998 CNET was one of the few profitable Internet companies.

Moreover, Snap! ultimately proved to be a worthwhile undertaking, in part because Minor concentrated on setting up a series of Web sites designed to link to CNET. Among them were Download.com for software purchases and Shopper.com for price comparisons on tech products. Minor claimed the latter Web site would help transform the Internet into a "leveler and democratizer," with his company leading the charge. CNET also began charging for click-throughs by vendors who were interested in checking out how their products were rated. All of these investments and changes impressed Wall Street, and in 1999 the company was named to the Nasdaq 100.

In March 2000 Minor stepped down as CEO of CNET. While he remained the company's chairman, he wanted to devote more time to new projects and had grown tired of dealing with day-to-day personnel matters. That November he stepped down as CNET chairman as well, to work on developing a new venture, 12 Entrepreneuring. The company was founded in February 2000, with Eric Greenberg, formerly of Scient. The pair considered their new firm to be an "incubator" for Web start-ups, including Grand Central Networks, a Web-services software maker, and iBuilding, a Web-services company with a focus on real estate. In order to finance the company, Minor and Greenberg raised $30 million from investors, as well as $137 million from blue-chip companies such as Goldman Sachs and Merrill Lynch. The new company invested more than $10 million in Grand Central and iBuilding. By summer 2000, 12 Entrepreneuring raised another $100 million from notable names in the new-media world, including the Netscape co-founder Marc Andreessen, the eBay founder Pierre Omidyar, and the Gateway founder Ted Waitt.

Despite its big-name backing, 12 Entrepreneuring was soon in trouble. After months and months of backroom fighting, the board forced Greenberg out as co-CEO, leaving Minor in charge. Andreessen, upset by the way Greenberg had been ousted and doubtful of the company's fiscal responsibility, abruptly resigned from the board. Stories began emerging about reckless spending that included extravagant offices and executive salaries of up to $500,000. In February 2001 the company was forced to shut its New York office.

Robert C. Conway, an investor, told Linda Himelstein for *BusinessWeek* (November 26, 2001), "They aren't losing money because the market's bad. They are losing money because they're wasting it." Conway and other investors wanted their money back, pointing out such excessive expenditures as $13 million in new office furniture and equipment and $45 million in an office-lease commitment for 60,000 square feet.

Minor, who had sunk some $22 million into 12 Entrepreneuring, asked for a truce and tried to ease worries. The investors, led by Conway, suggested that the company close and return its assets to them. After several months of haggling and conces-sions, including the closing of iBuilding and the firing of half of the employees, the board decided to dissolve the company. Grand Central Communications remained in operation. Despite the imbroglio, Halsey Minor was named the 27th-richest person under 40 by *Forbes Magazine* in late 2002. As of mid-2003 he remains on the board of Grand Central Communications.—C. M.

Suggested Reading: *Advertising Age* p48 Sept. 23, 1996, with photos; *Brandweek* p22+ Mar. 23, 1998, with photos; *New York Times* (on-line) June 15, 1998, with photos; *Salon* (on-line) p1+ Mar. 1998; *Time* (on-line) June 19, 1998; *Variety* p35 Mar. 27, 1995

Minsky, Marvin

Aug. 9, 1927– Artificial-intelligence researcher

For Marvin Minsky, a pioneer in the field of artificial intelligence, the human mind is no more than an immensely complex thinking machine whose powers, in principle, could be replicated by computer technology. A major obstacle to such a breakthrough, Minsky believes, has been the lack of adequate "theories about how thinking works." Minsky advances such a theory in his book *The Society of Mind* (1987), in which he proposes that "you can build a mind from many little parts, each mindless by itself," and proceeds to explain his belief that the human mind works according to that principle. As early as 1951 Minsky built a "learning machine" from 400 vacuum tubes and other "mindless" parts. Called the Snarc, the machine learned to find its way through the maze of its own circuitry and distinguished itself as being among the first—if not the very first—electronic learning machines ever constructed. In 1956 Minsky and his colleague John McCarthy, who coined the phrase "artificial intelligence" that year, organized the Dartmouth Summer Research Project in Artificial Intelligence—a major landmark in the history of that field. Minsky, in *The Society of Mind*, defined "artificial intelligence" as "the field of research concerned with making machines do things that people consider to require intelligence."

During his 40 years on the faculty of the Massachusetts Institute of Technology (MIT), in Cambridge, where he has been Donner Professor of Science (1974 to 1989) and Toshiba Professor of Media Arts and Sciences since 1990, Minsky published several pioneering books, and he was cofounder and later director of MIT's Artificial Intelligence Laboratory. His 1961 essay "Steps toward Artificial Intelligence," one of the conceptual cornerstones of the field, is included in E. A. Feigenbaum and J. Feldman's *Computers and Thought* (1964). Minsky's work has been integral to the establishment of the scientific foundations of several esoteric areas in addition to artificial intelligence, including the mathematical theory of computation, as well as the areas of robotics, computer vision, and telepresence. His myriad research interests also include musical cognition and physical optics.

Marvin Lee Minsky was born in New York City on August 9, 1927. His father, Henry Minsky, an eye surgeon as well as a musician and a painter, was for a time director of the ophthalmology department at Mount Sinai Hospital in Manhattan, and his mother, Fannie Reiser, was active in the Zionist cause. Marvin's older sister Charlotte became an architect and a painter, while his younger sister Ruth became a genetics counselor. On the basis of an intelligence test administered when he was five, Minsky was selected to attend a private school for gifted children in Manhattan. After a short time, however, his family's move from Manhattan to the Riverdale area of the Bronx necessitated a transfer to a public school. In an interview with Jeremy Bernstein for the *New Yorker* (December 14, 1981), Minsky recalled that he was "physically terrorized" at the school by bullies, and that a teacher wanted him to repeat the third grade because of his poor handwriting. Consequently, Minsky's parents transferred him to the Fieldston School, a progressive, private institution, where he soon developed an interest in electronics and chemistry that led him to enroll in the Bronx High School of Science in 1941. He remembered his classmates there as "people you could discuss your most elaborate ideas with and nobody would be condescending." His hyperactivity, which caused concern in some of the adults whom he encountered in the outside world, did not pose any problem for him at the school.

Although Minsky was comfortable at Bronx Science, his parents sent him to the more prestigious Phillips Academy in Andover, Massachusetts, for his senior year to enhance his academic prospects. But after graduating from the academy in June 1945, Minsky interrupted his formal education to enlist in the U.S. Navy, with the understanding that he would be placed in a naval electronics school. At the Great Lakes Naval Training Center, north of Chicago, Illinois, Minsky trained with about 120 regular recruits, most of whom seemed rather alien to him. "They provided my first—and, essentially, my last—contact with nonacademic people," he told Bernstein. Among the 40 recruits enrolled in the electronics program, however, Minsky did find a few kindred minds, including a musician named David Fuller, who praised a piano concerto that Minsky had drafted and who tried unsuccessfully to persuade him to complete it. Everything about Minsky's term of enlistment, which he finished in Jacksonville, Florida, in 1946, seemed to him "very unrealistic." For example, he held the base record for shooting down "planes" on an antiaircraft simulator as a result of having memorized the training tape.

In September 1946 Minsky entered Harvard University, in Cambridge, Massachusetts, where he encountered a much broader spectrum of people whose ideas he found congenial. He began exploring what he felt were the three key areas of science: genetics, physics, and the nature of intelligence. The latter subject seemed to him "hopelessly profound," and for a time he could hardly think of anything else worth pursuing. His interests did, however, extend to a variety of other subjects. Nominally a physics major, he also studied psychology, sociology, mathematics, neurology, and musical composition, the latter of which he pursued under the guidance of Irving Fine. Minsky's interest in neurology led to laboratory work involving the manipulation of the claws of crayfish, which in turn engendered in him an enduring curiosity about robotic instrumentation. (In 1967 he would invent the Serpentine Hydraulic Robotic Arm, a predecessor of modern robotic arms.) His work in that area eventually culminated in his editing of the book *Robotics* (1985), which was described by a critic for *Voice of Youth Advocates* (October 1985) as "a well-organized, easy to read, and definitive analysis."

For all his varied interests, Minsky was, by his own account, "almost pathologically uninterested in how minds work" until he came across the theories of B. F. Skinner, the behavioral psychologist. Minsky thought that Skinner's theories were "terrible," he told Bernstein, "because they were an attempt to fit curves to behavior without any internal ideas." He felt that it was worthwhile to search for a better scientific explanation for Skinner's success in conditioning animal behavior, and he began to frequent Harvard's psychology laboratory in the basement of Memorial Hall. There he found behaviorists and physiological psychologists, none of whom seemed to have a complete understanding of human psychology. Minsky told Bernstein that he "couldn't fathom how these people could live down there arguing about personalities, with . . . no real theories of what was happening deep inside the mind," so he "tried to make one up." The result was a model of a "stochastic neural network" in the brain, which examined the role of probability in determining neural response. Minsky's theory developed alongside the similar ideas of Donald Hebb, a Canadian. The two men were unaware of each other's work, and Hebb became the one to present the idea to the public, in *The Organization of Behavior* (1949), which Minsky described as "a seminal book."

In the meantime, Minsky had decided to write a thesis that would compensate for his fairly low grade-point average. Since Harvard had no provisions for undergraduate theses in physics, he switched his major to mathematics in his last semester and wrote an original thesis of a problem in topology concerning "fixed points of functions on spheres." The thesis impressed the mathematician Andrew Gleason, then a junior fellow at Harvard, who advised Minsky to work for a Ph.D. degree at Princeton University, in New Jersey. After receiving his B.A. degree from Harvard in 1950, Minsky enrolled at Princeton, located in New Jersey, where he turned his attention to building the electronic learning machine that became known as the Snarc (for Stochastic Neural-Analog Reinforcement Computer), in collaboration with Dean Edmonds, a physics student who was "a whiz at electronics." With funding from the Office of Naval Research and facilities provided by Harvard, Minsky and Edmonds were able to simulate electronically various components of memory, including neurons, synapses, and "storage" sites. According to Minsky's description, the machine "was composed of forty agents, each connected to several others, through a 'reward' system that, when activated after each success, made each agent more likely to rearouse the same recipients at later times." In that way, the machine learned to trace a path through a maze. "But," Minsky recalled in his postscript to *The Society of Mind*, "its limitations convinced me that a more versatile 'thinking machine' would have to exploit many other principles."

One such principle became the focus of Minsky's doctoral dissertation, "Neural Nets and the Brain Model Problem," in which he postulated that a second memory could enable a learning machine to predict the results of its behavior based on past actions. Minsky placed that idea in the context of how the nervous system might learn and submitted the resulting dissertation to the mathematics department at Princeton in 1954. A. W. Tucker, one of the members of his dissertation committee, had expressed misgivings to the computer pioneer John von Neumann about whether the thesis "should really be called mathematics," to which von Neumann reportedly replied, "Well, if it isn't now, it will be someday—let's encourage it." Armed with his Ph.D. degree, Minsky was further encouraged by a three-year junior fellowship at Harvard. "It was a welcome opportunity for me," Minsky has recalled, "because I was trying to make general theories about intelligence—in men or machines— and I did not fit into any department or profession." As a junior fellow from 1954 to 1957, Minsky developed a high-resolution optical microscope and an electromagnetic micromanipulator, and he patented scanning microscopes. Even more important for Minsky's future was the 1956 Dartmouth Conference on Artificial Intelligence, during which he worked out geometric theorems that he believed could be proved by a computer. In 1959 a computer proved a theorem in geometry for the first time, using a program written by Herbert Gelernter, who based his work on Minsky's experience at the Dartmouth conference.

In 1958 Minsky became an assistant professor of mathematics at the Massachusetts Institute of Technology, in Cambridge, on the staff of MIT's Lincoln Laboratory. He was joined at MIT by John McCarthy in 1959, and that year they founded the MIT Artificial Intelligence Project. Minsky described their collaboration in the postscript to *The Society of Mind*: "We agreed that the most critical problem was of how minds do common-sense reasoning. McCarthy was more concerned with establishing logical and mathematical foundations for reasoning, while I was more involved with theories of how we actually reason using pattern recognition and analogy. . . . Our laboratory had an atmosphere that combined mathematical power with engineering adventure; this led not only to new theories of computation, but also to developing some of the very first automatic robots." The project became the Artificial Intelligence Laboratory in 1964, when Minsky assumed the directorship after three years as associate professor of electrical engineering. Finding that he did not enjoy the administrative and grant-seeking tasks, he went back to teaching in the electrical engineering department as a professor in 1973. The next year he was promoted to Donner Professor of Science in the department of electrical engineering and computer science, a title he held until 1989. In 1990 he became the Toshiba Professor of Media Arts and Sciences, and he remained in that position as of 2000.

In the meantime, Minsky continued his pioneering work in the field of artificial intelligence. In addition to *The Society of Mind* and *Robotics,* Minsky has written *Computation: Finite and Infinite Machines* (1967), edited *Semantic Information Processing* (1968), and coauthored *Perceptrons: An Introduction to Computational Geometry* (1969) with the South African scholar and mathematician Seymour Papert. Minsky believes that scientists should resist the "publishing imperative" and limit their published writings to only those that are important.

Minsky considers *Perceptrons* to be one of the more important works in its field. He and Papert—who arrived at MIT in 1963, after having studied child development with Jean Piaget in Geneva, Switzerland—collaborated on a variety of projects, in such areas as human perception, child psychology, and creating new mathematical techniques. The Perceptron of which they wrote was a machine billed as being capable of recognizing patterns and weighing evidence. Invented by Frank Rosenblatt in 1959, the Perceptron consisted of photocells linked to an apparatus for analyzing whatever the photocells "saw," such as a letter of the alphabet. In their book, Minsky and Papert provided mathematical proof of the machine's shortcomings and of the limits of its effectiveness. Minsky and Papert also constructed a robot called Builder, which erected towers using children's building blocks in accordance with the skills that children themselves develop, such as eye-hand coordination. According to Minsky and Papert, so simple an act as filling a pail with sand could involve thousands, perhaps millions of little processes, and yet seems to proceed "so automatically that we regard it as 'ordinary common sense.'" In 1972 the pair completed work on a computer programming language for children, called Logo.

Ordinary common sense is more complex and more effective, according to Minsky, than the "expert" knowledge used, for example, in chess-playing computer programs. Common sense requires many different types of knowledge and skills, whereas expertise involves larger amounts of knowledge based on only a few types of skills. But most computer scientists in the early 1970s were still trying to explain artificial intelligence according to principles of mathematical logic. Minsky expounded a new theory of reasoning by analogy in his 1974 essay "A Framework for the Representation of Knowledge," which later appeared in *The Psychology of Computer Vision* (1985), edited by P. H. Winston. "I suggested representing common-sense knowledge not in terms of separate facts of sentences, but in much larger units called 'frames,'" Minsky recalled. "The idea was to represent each kind of experience in terms of a stereotype structure that includes additional knowledge about how to remember and use it." The essay had a major influence on research over the next few years. Minsky expanded his theory to include "frame-arrays," which he described as families of frames, each having access to memory details stored in one another's terminals. The interaction among frames and frame-arrays results in a more accurate representation of knowledge.

Minsky's idea that knowledge and meaning exist solely in the interactions, or connections, among parts of the brain (such as frame-arrays) is central to his conception of the mind as a machine. For Minsky, the mind is composed of parts or processes, called agents, that congregate along what he calls "knowledge lines," or "K-lines." He views a K-line as "a wirelike structure that attaches itself to whichever mental agents are active when you solve a problem or have a good idea." The K-line thus becomes the mechanism of learning as well as the basic filament of memory. The K-lines themselves grow within a framework of level-bands that correspond to a certain range along a continuum from the abstract to the particular. As K-lines grow, they connect to one another to form "societies" of memory and knowledge. The societies themselves exist at different levels of detail and call one another into play when confronted with a problem. In learning to drive a truck, one might well activate the knowledge societies needed to drive a car. Minsky concludes that "we can imagine an endless sequence of such societies, in which each new one learns to exploit the last." He proposes that "this is how our minds develop in infancy—as sequences of layers of societies."

The Society of Mind was published in 1987 to an admiring but skeptical public. Minsky was praised for his ambitious treatment of so complex a subject as the nature of intelligence and for describing his highly technical speculations in lay terminology. But the idea that knowledge consists of societies exploiting each other's expertise independently of a governing homunculus—or "little person," a miniature self inside the mind—disturbed some people. As Paul Hoffman wrote in *Discover* (September 1987), "Biologists claim that Minsky has slighted the contributions of their discipline. . . . Humanists are grumbling about his mechanistic treatment of the role of emotions and his dismissal of consciousness and self-awareness as convenient illusions." According to Minsky, however, these are not merely convenient illusions, but necessary myths. If we stopped believing in a consciousness that is somehow larger than the sum of its parts, he has explained, we would have to cease believing in free will. And without a concept of free will, our notions of responsibility, guilt, blame, shame, credit, virtue, and reward would no longer have any basis. "No matter that the physical world provides no room for freedom of will," Minsky observed. "That concept is essential to our models of the mental realm. Too much of our psychology is based on it for us to ever give it up. We're virtually forced to maintain that belief, even though we know it's false."

Minsky provides a way out of the dilemma by instructing his readers to think differently "about the natures of the brain-machines that manufacture thoughts." In response to the question, "Are minds machines?" Minsky has said, "Of that, I've raised no doubt at all but have only asked, *what kind of machines?* And though most people still consider it degrading to be regarded as machines, I hope [to]. . . make them entertain, instead, the thought of how wonderful it is to be machines with such marvelous powers." Christopher Lehmann-Haupt, reviewing *The Society of Mind* in the *New York Times* (February 16, 1987), noted that some people would find the idea that human intelligence could be artificially simulated "a terrible prospect to contemplate" but added that "Minsky would respond that if the comparison of the human mind to a machine seems so invidious, it is only because we understand as little about machines as we do about intelligence." Minsky's relentless curiosity has gone a long way toward rectifying this dearth of understanding, and in the view of Paul Hoffman, *The Society of Mind* seems to be the only book that "even tries to offer a comprehensive explanation of how the mind works."

Although Minsky pursued the principle of artificial intelligence, according to which computers mimic psychological processes, such as learning, he had long been skeptical of the concept that computers could mimic the biological processes of the brain's circuitry. He has since modified his views on that subject. Attending a meeting of the International Conference on Neural Networks in San Diego, California, in July 1988, he predicted that over the next two decades scientists might well discover that the human brain consists of a society of neural networks that could be electronically simulated.

After the publication of *The Society of Mind*, Minsky was approached by his friend Harry Harrison, a noted science fiction author. Harrison told Minsky that he believed the ideas expressed in Minsky's book could reach a wider audience if Minsky wrote a novel about artificial intelligence. According to Minsky, he did not have the credentials to write a work of fiction, but Harrison suggested that they co-author the book, with Harrison writing the narrative and Minsky supplying the technical background. The duo decided that the main character would be a "mathematical super-hacker of the future who would build the first AI [Artificial Intelligence] with a human-like mind," according to Minsky's Web site. Over the next couple of years, the pair added a plot device in which the brain of the main character Brian is severely damaged by a bullet. As Minsky wrote on his Web site, "This let us explain the computational part of the theory [from *The Society of the Mind*] in the context of repairing Brian's brain, while also explaining [the theory's] psychological aspects in the context of reconstructing his childhood memories." The book, entitled *The Turing Option*, was published in 1992 and received mixed notices, including the following from *Kirkus Reviews* (June 15, 1992): "Cliched, melodramatic, and thuddingly plotted—but, still, this novel by a Grand Old Man of sf [science fiction] and the world's leading expert on artificial intelligence contains some of the best extrapolation on the nature and creation of AI ever offered in fiction."

Over the years, Minsky has lent his expertise to various professional societies, and he was a founder of the business firm of General Turtle Inc. In the early 1970s he and Seymour Papert founded Logo Computer Systems Inc., which they later turned over to a Canadian friend. In the early 1980s Minsky established Thinking Machines Corporation, which he financed with the help of the former CBS chairman William S. Paley. Among other affiliations, Minsky is a member of the Institute of Electrical and Electronic Engineers. He has served as an adviser to NASA, the National Dance Institute, and the L-5 Society, which advocates the exploration and colonization of outer space. In 1970 Minsky received the Turing Award from the Association for Computing Machinery. During 1981–82 he was president of the American Association of Artificial Intelligence. From MIT, he received the Killian

Award in 1989. More recently, he has been the recipient of the Japan Prize from the Japanese Science and Technology Foundation, in 1990, the Excellence Award from the International Joint Conference on Artificial Intelligence Research in 1991, and the Joseph Priestley Award from Dickinson College in 1995.

Marvin Minsky has been described by Steven Levy, author of *Hackers* (1984) as "an elfish man with twinkling eyes behind thick glasses, a starkly bald head, and an omnipresent turtleneck sweater." On July 30, 1952, he married Gloria Anna Rudisch, a pediatrician. They have three grown children, the twins Juliana and Henry, and an older daughter Margaret, a graduate of MIT who has studied astronautics and designed educational programs for home computers. The Minsky home, in Brookline, Massachusetts, was described by Jeremy Bernstein as "a sprawling house" containing computer equipment, medical supplies, and an assortment of musical articles including a brass alpenhorn, three pianos, two organs, a Moog synthesizer, and a jukebox. In his spare time, Minsky enjoys composing and improvising music.—C. M.

Suggested Reading: *Discover* p84+ Sep. 1987; *Kirkus Reviews* June 15, 1992; Marvin Minsky Web site; *New Yorker* p50+ Dec. 14, 1981

Courtesy of Moog Archives

Moog, Robert

1934– Inventor of the Moog music synthesizer

Robert Moog created the modular Moog synthesizer in the 1960s, giving musicians and composers a nearly unlimited array of possible sounds and textures. By the mid-1970s the synthesizer (sometimes referred to as the synth) had become an important element in the sound of many rock, jazz, and dance acts. Particularly popular was Moog's Minimoog synthesizer, released in 1970, which revolutionized the synthesizer with its portability and ease of use. Suddenly more artists were able to work with keyboards, bringing the Minimoog to studios, concerts, and rehearsals. Known for its lush, heavy tone, the Minimoog is considered by many synthesizer experts to be among the greatest analog synths. It is still used by many electronica and rock artists. In fact, while the arrival of digital synthesizers in 1975 slowly shifted focus away from analog synths, there has been a recent revival of interest in the older technology, which many believe offers a warmer sound than most digital keyboards. "There are some things that digital synthesizers can do better than analog," Moog told J. Munnshe for *Amazing Sounds* (on-line), "and there are some things that analog can do better than digital. It's possible to make a digital model of an 'ideal' analog circuit, but it still sounds digital, because there is none of the characteristic analog warmth and richness of sound that comes from the little technical variations and imperfections of analog circuits. Digital instruments are fine for a lot of things, like sample playback, programmability, precision, and relatively low price. But soundwise, I think we're talking about the difference between, say, a plastic guitar and a wood guitar."

Robert Moog (rhymes with "vogue") was born in 1934 and raised in Flushing, in the New York City borough of Queens. As a child he received daily piano lessons from his mother, who wanted him to be a concert pianist and often punished him when he failed to practice. Moog developed an interest in electronics through his father, who was an amateur radio hobbyist. In his teenage years Moog became fascinated with the theremin. (Invented in the 1920s by Leon Theremin, it is one of the earliest electronic musical instruments. It creates a high-pitched, warbling sound and was commonly heard in horror and science-fiction movies and television shows of the 1940s and '50s.) Moog built his first theremin at the age of 15 (some sources say 14) after reading an article on how to build the instrument in the hobby magazine *Radio and TV News*. "Theremin's original designs are elegant, ingenious and effective," he told Frank Houston for *Salon* (April 25, 2000, on-line). "As electronics goes, the theremin is very simple. But there are so many subtleties hidden in the details of the design. It's like a great sonnet, or a painting, or a speech, that is perfectly done on more than one level." Moog also studied the schematics of the Hammond, Baldwin, and Wurlitzer Organs—but his expertise did not make him many friends in high school. "I was the class brain," he recalled to Houston. "I knew I was smarter than they were, so they felt compelled to beat me up periodically to keep me in my place."

After graduating from high school, Moog entered an engineering program offered cooperatively by Queens College and Columbia University's engineering school, in New York City. In 1954 he formed the R. A. Moog Company and began selling custom-made theremins, which he built with his father. Walter Sear, a New York sales representative who sold tubas, assisted in the marketing. Moog also began to experiment with electronic circuitry to create and modulate sounds, and in 1956 he designed a circuit for the Clavivox keyboard synthesizer, developed by the inventor and composer Raymond Scott. In 1955 the first modern synthesizer had been created by RCA. The instrument filled an entire room and had no keyboard for an interface. Instead, engineers had to feed it binary codes on a paper roll, while an oscillator generated a sound wave of the programmed timbre, pitch, and volume.

Although Moog played piano in a four-piece dance band in the 1950s, his primary focus was electronics. "We were pretty bad," he recalled of his band to Munnshe. "I really don't think I could have made a living as a musician. It's not in me. Designing electronic stuff is my calling." To that end, Moog enrolled in the doctoral engineering program at Cornell University, in Ithaca, New York, in about 1957. After an article he wrote about build-it-yourself theremin kits was published in *Electronics World* in January 1961, Moog began selling the kits himself; from 1961 to 1963 he sold some 1,000 kits out of his three-room apartment. At a New York State School Music Association convention in early 1963, Moog met Herbert Deutsch, a composer who taught music at Hofstra University, in Long Island, New York. After the two discussed the need for new electronic instruments, Moog decided to create a portable guitar amplifier and set up a shop in Trumansburg, New York. "I had no concept of synthesizers or electronic music at all," Moog wrote (with Connor Freff Cochran) as quoted in *Vintage Synthesizers* by Mark Vail and excerpted on *Synthmuseum.com*. "It was just me and a couple of people in a storefront, designing a portable, battery-operated musical instrument amplifier kit—which never did go into production, because it was way overpriced."

Nonetheless, when Deutsch traveled to see Moog, he was impressed by Moog's work and decided to collaborate with him. The two spent weeks designing what would become a modular analog synthesizer. Moog's synth consisted of a series of modules—each of which controlled a specific component of a sound wave—that could be wired together by the user to create a vast array of sounds. The essential components of sound waves are frequency (pitch), amplitude (volume), and harmonic content (timbre). They can be electronically reproduced, respectively, by oscillators, am-

plifiers, and filters, each of which Moog housed in a separate module. Because natural musical sounds fluctuate continuously in these three categories, Moog needed a way to control the fluctuations. His method was known as voltage control; by regulating the amount of voltage going to the oscillators, amplifiers, and filters, Moog was able to manipulate pitch, volume, and timbre. Although modular Moogs were custom built, each consisted of a small keyboard that was dwarfed by a stack of modules of various sizes above it. In September 1964 Moog was invited to display his circuits at an Audio Engineering Society (AES) convention, where he received his first orders for the synthesizer.

Moog worked part-time on his synthesizers until the summer of 1965, when he finally completed his doctoral dissertation at Cornell University. That summer he developed a custom modular synthesizer for the classical composer John Cage. Soon he had hired some half-dozen employees at his shop. However, as Moog wrote for *Vintage Synthesizers*, "From the point of view of competence, we were never a business. Never. We got some of the elements in place, but none of the controls or forecasting or planning that go with a well-run business. We just never had it. We were always in the red. We had no capital. None. Zero! And yet, we managed to keep stumbling along."

In addition to having help from Deutsch, Moog was also assisted with his synthesizer designs by the composer Walter (later Wendy) Carlos. The earliest synthesizers lacked accuracy in reproducing pitch, a weakness that was corrected before making them available to a larger commercial market. The modular Moog was the first synthesizer to use attack-decay-sustain-release envelopes (ADSR), sets of parameters that control a sound's onset and fade. Like many of his designs, it would become a standard component on later synthesizers. In 1968 Moog patented a voltage-controlled lowpass filter for his synthesizer; it came to be known as the Moog Filter and was capable of creating horn, string, and voice timbres. Moog's synthesizers became popular not only for their innovation but because of their relatively modest price tags. Whereas RCA's synthesizer sold for $100,000, Moog's sold for $11,000. "It had a tremendous impact on many people and brought electronic music to many composers, both popular and academic," Jeffrey Hass, the director of the University of Indiana's Center for Electronic and Computer Music, told Houston for the *New York Times* (December 16, 1999).

The first use of the Moog on a pop record was on *Zodiac: Cosmic Sounds* (1967), a psychedelic album recorded by various artists. The first mainstream rock group to use the Moog was the Monkees, who debuted the instrument on "Star Collector," from their album *Pisces, Aquarius, Capricorn, and Jones Ltd.* (1967). In 1968 the composer Wendy Carlos released *Switched-On Bach*, which consisted of Moog performances of several works by the 18th-century classical composer J. S. Bach. Shortly before the album was released, Moog had caused a stir by playing an excerpt at an AES convention in New York. "I could feel it in the air," Moog wrote for *Vintage Synthesizers*. "They were jumping out of their skins. These technical people were involved in so much flim-flam, so much shoddy, opportunistic stuff, and here was something that was just impeccably done and had obvious musical content and was totally innovative. The tape got a standing ovation." *Switched-on Bach* went on to sell more than a million copies and appeared on the *Billboard* classical charts for almost five years, boosting Moog's sales in the process. The Canadian pianist and Bach interpreter Glenn Gould said, as quoted by Houston for *Salon* (on-line), that Carlos's version of Bach's fourth "Brandenburg Concerto" was "the finest performance of any of the Brandenburgs—live, canned, intuited—that I've ever heard."

Following the success of *Switched-on Bach*, various easy-listening and lounge artists began using the Moog, and several record companies quickly released Moog-related albums. (Moog has dismissed most of this music as mediocre and opportunistic.) More widely heard were pieces by the composer Eric Siday, who used the Moog to record music for advertisements, and the Beatles, who used the Moog on their song "Because" on the album *Abbey Road* (1969). The instrument was also used to eerie effect by Wendy Carlos in the soundtrack to the film *The Clockwork Orange* (1971). Mother Mallard, the first all-keyboard group, became Moog's house band, putting on concerts at the Moog factory and releasing albums that are hailed today as visionary.

In 1970 Moog launched the portable Minimoog. Keith Emerson was one of the first to record the instrument, on Emerson, Lake, and Palmer's eponymous debut album that year. (Emerson also lugged the massive modular Moog on stage with him for live shows.) Later the Minimoog was made famous by such progressive-rock bands as Yes, Rush, and Pink Floyd, who relied heavily on the keyboard to achieve their complex, psychedelic sounds. Compact, and with a minimum of sound-generating devices, the Minimoog did not require users to have any special knowledge of engineering or electronics. "It was really the advent of the Minimoog that saw synthesizers take off," Doug Keislar, an editor with the *Computer Music Journal*, told Houston for *Salon*. "The Minimoog showed that there was a significant market for portable, cheaper synthesizers." In addition to being used in progressive rock, the Minimoog was utilized by Donna Summers, for her hit single "I feel Love" (1977), and the German experimental rock group Kraftwerk, on *Trans Europe Express* (1977).

By 1969 R. A. Moog Inc. had 42 employees and was turning out two or three modular systems a week. The company fell behind on orders through 1969 and into the first half of 1970. However, in 1970 things suddenly changed, despite the arrival

of the Minimoog. "The market became saturated," Moog wrote for *Vintage Synthesizers*. "The guys who'd jumped on doing their Moog records hadn't had hits, so they'd dumped their synthesizers. . . . We [also] had competition—ARP—and their product had the appeal of stable oscillators and no patch chords." A general recession, which caused music producers to cut budgets, did not help matters, and soon Moog was having trouble finding stores to sell his synthesizers. The situation was compounded by his lack of business skills. "I suddenly found myself in a growing business and I didn't know how to run it," Moog told Houston for *Salon*. "I didn't know anything at all about business back then. I didn't know what a balance sheet was. I didn't know what cash flow was. So the business survived as long as it grew, but as soon as a contraction occurred, I ran out of money."

In 1971 Moog sold his company to Bill Waytena, who specialized in reviving financially troubled firms and then reselling them. Under Waytena's guidance the name of the company changed to Moog/Musonics, and later, to Moog Music Inc. Moog remained as president. The company was relocated to Buffalo, New York—in a reportedly smelly, damp, and unpleasant former gelatin factory, where it would stay until 1974. In 1973 Moog Music was sold to Norlin Music Inc., which at the time was the largest manufacturer of musical instruments in the United States. Under Norlin, Moog also designed guitar effects, guitar amplifiers, and small electronic devices. The last Moog synthesizer that Moog helped develop for the company was the Micromoog, in 1975. In 1976 the company released the Polymoog synthesizer, designed by the company's new head of synthesizer design, David Luce. Moog told Houston for *Salon* that "reliability-wise it was a disaster." Moog believed Luce was given control over synthesizer design rather than himself because of his social skills. "Luce liked to go out and drink and socialize with the Norlin brass," he told Houston, "and I didn't, or maybe couldn't."

By the time Moog's contract with Norlin ended, in 1977, he was president in name only, and he decided not to extend the contract. Norlin Music eventually went bankrupt in the early 1980s, after which Moog Music was sold in a leveraged buyout deal. The Moog name was sold to a succession of companies, each of which eventually went out of business.

In June 1978 Moog moved to North Carolina, where he founded Big Briar Inc. to design and build electronic musical equipment, including a transistorized version of the theremin. In addition, from 1984 to 1988 he worked as a full-time consultant and vice-president of new product research for Kurzweil Music Systems. In the late 1980s he collaborated with the composer Jon Eaton to build the Multiple-Touch-Sensitive Keyboard, which allowed users to manipulate sounds by moving their fingers around on the keys. (The keyboard was not designed for mass production.) In the early 1990s Moog taught several courses at the University of North Carolina, in Asheville. He quit to build theremins after demand for the instruments began to increase. In addition, he collaborated on the design for the Van Koevering Interactive Piano, which looks like a concert piano but is run by a computer and is equipped with a 120-watt amplifier and a half-dozen stereo speakers. A laptop-sized screen takes the place of sheet music, and the computer can transcribe any composition. Among its 128 different sounds is a digitally sampled Steinway grand piano. Part of the reason Moog helped create the instrument was to encourage the social aspect of music-making. "There has been a very long trend away from music as a social activity," Moog told Houston for the *New York Times*. "Before the radio and the electric phonograph, people made their own music, for themselves and for each other. What I see now is that, more and more, we're all in our own little boxes, using the fruits of technology to make or listen to music in isolation."

In March 2000 Moog was officially awarded the Moog trademark, after nearly 30 years, and Big Briar changed its name to Moog Music Inc. Moog continues to sell a redesigned Minimoog Voyager as well as Moogerfoogers—analog effects modules. He also designs custom analog instruments for academic and experimental musicians. Moog Music

Inc. is currently the world's leading manufacturer of theremins—larger than all of its competitors combined. In 1997 Moog released a theremin called the Ethervox that featured a Music Instrument Digital Interface (MIDI).

In 2001 Moog was awarded the Polar Music Prize for his design of the Minimoog. The following year he was awarded a technical Grammy Award for outstanding technical significance to the recording field. He was enshrined on the Rock Walk, which opened in Los Angeles, California, in 1985 and features the hand prints of famous musicians. In his spare time Moog enjoys gardening, hiking, and reading. In recent years several rock and electronica musicians have made use of analog synthesizers, among them Stereolab, the Orb, Mouse on Mars, the Shamen, Radiohead, and Boards of Canada. "He's viewed like a God," the musician Pamelia Kurstin told Richard Leiby for the *Washington Post* (April 15, 2000). "Everybody knows who he is, especially in Europe. He's a superstar."—G. O.

Suggested Reading: *Amazing Sounds* (on-line); Associated Press Feb. 1, 1992; *electronicmusic.com*; *New York Times* G p9 Dec. 16, 1999; *Salon* (on-line) Apr. 25, 2000; Synthmuseum Web site; *Washington Post* C p5 Apr. 15, 2000

Moore, Charles H.

1938– Developer of the Forth computer language

The programmer Charles H. Moore is known for developing the Forth computer language. While attending college during the late 1950s, he began working part time as a programmer for an observatory that tracked satellites. Moore was often frustrated by the fact that because computers were scarce, their use was limited by administrators, who needed to accommodate as many people as possible. Writing a program was a time-consuming process that required the mastery of different tools such as interpreters, compilers, assemblers, and supervisors. Moore developed Forth to aid in the effort. In 1971 he used Forth to control a 30-foot telescope at the Kitt Peak National Observatory (KPNO) in Tucson, Arizona. A fellow programmer named Elizabeth Rather found that the language's simple, interactive qualities reduced her work load. Recognizing Forth's commercial potential, Moore and Rather set up a company in 1973. "Today [Forth] is accepted as a world-class programming language," Moore wrote in his paper "Forth—The Early Years," as posted on the Color-Forth Web site. "That it has achieved this without industry, university or government support, is a tribute to its efficiency, reliability, and versatility."

Charles H. Moore was born in 1938 in McKeesport, Pennsylvania, which is near Pittsburgh. He grew up in Flint, Michigan. His father was a divisional manager who sold mutual funds for Investors Diversified Services, and his mother was a homemaker. An excellent student, in 1956 Moore was the valedictorian of his graduating class at Central High School, in Flint. He then earned a National Merit scholarship to attend the Massachusetts Institute of Technology (MIT) in Cambridge.

On October 4, 1957, during Moore's sophomore year at MIT, the Soviet Union launched the Sputnik satellite into orbit, bringing mankind into the space age. On January 31, 1958 the United States launched the Explorer 1. Moore got a part-time job with the Smithsonian Astrophysical Observatory (SAO) at Harvard University, in Cambridge, Massachusetts. "SAO was responsible for optical tracking of satellites [with its telescope]," Moore recalled in his paper. "Caught off-guard by Sputnik, they hired undergraduates to compute predictions with Frieden desk calculators." Moore taught himself the FORTRAN II computer language from a manual given to him by John Gaustad, a Harvard student who was working at the SAO, and wrote his first program, Ephemeris 4, on MIT's IBM EDPM 704 computer. The program, which computed predictions of the orbital path of satellites, was so successful that it eliminated Moore's job. In his paper, Moore wrote that he remained at the SAO, working with the mathematician "George Veis to apply his method of least-squares fitting to determine orbital elements, station position and ultimately the shape of [the] Earth . . ." (Devised in the early 19th century, least-squares is a method of drawing a curve through a set of points representing statistical data.) "Of course," Moore added, "this part-time job was at least 40 hours, and, yes, my grades went to hell." As an undergraduate, Moore learned the LISP programming language from John McCarthy, the MIT professor of communications who devised it. (McCarthy, who later joined the faculty of Stanford University, in California, is a pioneer in the field of artificial intelligence.)

During the late 1950s, the only computers that were available were large mainframe systems that ran programs written on punch cards. Since the computers could run only one program at a time, a laborious process, their use was often limited to accommodate as many people as possible. In order to make the most efficient use of his Ephemeris 4 program, Moore recalled in "Forth—The Early Years" that he "wrote this simple interpreter [a program that runs other programs] to read input cards and control the program. It also directed calculations. The five orbital elements each had an empirical equation to account for atmospheric drag and the non-spherical Earth. Thus I could compose different equations for the several satellites without re-compiling [the program]." The ideas behind the interpreter for the Ephemeris 4 program helped lay the foundations for the eventual development of the Forth language.

In 1960 Moore graduated from MIT with a B.S. in physics. The following year, he enrolled at Stanford University as a graduate student in mathematics. Moore broadened his knowledge of programming, learning the ALGOL language for the university's Burroughs B5500 computer. He found work as a programmer with the Stanford Linear Accelerator Center (SLAC), a research laboratory. Although it was intended to be a part-time job, the position took up a lot of Moore's time and he left Stanford University in 1963 without receiving a degree; he worked at SLAC for two more years. There, Moore wrote Transport, a program in ALGOL that optimized beam steering for SLAC's electron accelerator. In 1964 he wrote another program, Curve, in ALGOL. In his paper, Moore explained that Curve, a precursor to Forth, was "a general-purpose non-linear differential-corrections data-fitting program." To control Curve, Moore enhanced the interpreter he wrote for Ephemeris 4.

In 1965 Moore moved to New York City, where he worked as a freelance programmer with the languages FORTRAN and ALGOL, among others. The computer world was quickly changing. The emergence of minicomputers with terminals was gradually making mainframes and punch cards obsolete. Moore upgraded his interpreter to accommodate character input through teletype terminals and

manage output. For one of his clients, Realtime Services Inc. (RSI), Moore wrote a FORTRAN-ALGOL translator that supported a time-sharing service and created file-editing utilities.

In 1968 Moore was hired by Mohasco Industries Inc., a major home-furnishings company in Amsterdam, New York. Moore took advantage of the company's IBM 1130 minicomputer with a 2250 graphic display. The machine featured a 16-bit central processing unit (CPU); 8,000 bytes of Random Access Memory (RAM); keyboard; disk drive; printer; and a FORTRAN compiler. Moore created a graphics program by adding a cross-assembler to his interpreter to generate code for the 2250. "The system was a great success," he wrote in his paper. "It could draw animated 3-D images when IBM could barely draw static 2-D." Moore wanted to call his interpreter "Fourth," representing software that would be used for the "fourth-generation" of computers. However, he was forced to shorten the name to "Forth" because the operating system limited the names of files to only five characters.

Moore developed Forth in response to his frustration with the programming environment of the time. In an unpublished book he wrote in 1970, as quoted by Elizabeth D. Rather, Donald R. Colburn, and Moore in their paper "The Evolution of Forth," as posted on the Forth Inc. Web site, Moore explained: "The software provided with large computers supplies a hierarchy of languages: the assembler defines the language for describing the compiler and supervisor; the supervisor the language for job control; the compiler the language for application programs; the application program the language for its input. The user may not know, or know of, all these languages: but they are there. They stand between him and his computer, imposing their restrictions on what he can do and what it will cost. And cost it does, for this vast hierarchy of languages requires a huge investment of man and machine time to produce, and an equally large effort to maintain. The cost of documenting these programs and of reading the documentation is enormous. And after all this effort the programs are still full of bugs, awkward to use and satisfying to no one." Forth reflected Moore's philosophy that programmers could write high-quality programs with less time and effort. Forth replaced this vast hierarchy of languages, as Rather, Conklin, and Moore explained, with "a single layer, requiring only two elements: a programmer-to-Forth interface, consisting of minimal documentation . . . and the Forth-machine interface, consisting of the program itself." In "Forth—The Early Years," Moore called Forth a simple, natural computer language. "Forth is a text-based language that is essentially context-free," he wrote. "It combines 'words' separated by spaces to construct new words."

While at Mohasco, Moore wrote a program that generated reports for the company and Spacewar, a video game. He also simplified the performance of a chess program he wrote in ALGOL by converting it into Forth. In 1970 the company leased a UN-

IVAC 1108 to establish a network of leased lines for an order-entry system. Moore noted in "Forth—The Early Years" that since the corporate software he had to use was in the COBOL language, he installed "a Forth system on the 1108 that interfaced with COBOL modules to do the transaction processing." An economic downturn forced Mohasco's management to cancel the 1108, however, and Moore resigned in protest.

In 1971 Moore was hired by the National Radio Astronomy Observatory (NRAO), working most of the year at its headquarters in Charlottesville, Virginia. During the summer he and his wife lived in Tucson, Arizona, near the NRAO's Kitt Peak National Observatory (KPNO), which operated a 30-foot radio telescope. There, Moore was placed in charge of developing a system on the observatory's two computers to control the telescope. Although the observatory's computers were programmed in FORTRAN, Moore used Forth to create a program that performed such tasks as pointing and tracking the telescope, collecting data and storing it on magnetic tape, and supporting an interactive graphics terminal that allowed astronomers to analyze previously collected data. Moore's system, which was the first implementation of his completed version of Forth, was a success and impressed his superiors at the NRAO. "The Forth story has the making of a morality play," Moore reflected in his paper. "Persistent young programmer struggles against indifference to discover Truth and save his suffering comrades."

In 1971 the NRAO hired Elizabeth Rather, a systems analyst at the University of Arizona in Tucson, on a part-time basis to help maintain the telescope's control system while Moore was living in Virginia. At first, Rather was displeased that the system was programmed in an unknown and undocumented language. She considered reprogramming the entire system in FORTRAN, but lacked the time and money to do so. Instead, Rather decided to learn Forth and document it. After working with the language for a few months, she eventually grew to appreciate it, finding that Forth greatly reduced the amount of time she needed to perform tasks.

Rather left her job at the university to work at the NRAO full time, and in 1972 she wrote the first Forth manual. A year later, Moore and Rather installed a new system, which ran from a single, disk-based PDP-11 computer, to control the telescope. "This was a multi-user system, supporting four terminals in addition to the tasks controlling the telescope and taking data," Rather, Colburn, and Moore wrote. "It was so successful that the control portions of it were still in use in 1991." Many observatories around the world began asking for the software, and in 1976, the International Astronomical Union adopted Forth as a standard language for computer systems.

In 1973, after completing the updated system, Moore and Rather co-founded a company, Forth Inc., with Edward Conklin, the former head of the Tucson division of the NRAO, to explore commercial uses of the language. The gradual shift from large mainframe systems to minicomputers created increased opportunities. Many programmers began using Forth to create applications. In an article for *Byte* (August 1980), Gregg Williams wrote that Forth software operated the computer-controlled cameras that were used to film the spaceship sequences in the science fiction feature *Battle Beyond the Stars* (1980). Williams also noted that Allen Test Products of Kalamazoo, Michigan, had used Forth to develop "an ignition analyzer for use in service stations and automobile repair shops that analyses the behavior of automobile ignition systems and displays both diagnostic and corrective information." According to Williams, a single computer using Forth at the Cedar-Sinai Medical Center in Los Angeles, California, managed 32 terminals, stored patient information from an optical reader into a database, and analyzed blood samples and heart behavior in "real time" as a patient exercised on a treadmill. The aerospace industry also began using Forth to control satellites.

In 1982 Moore left Forth Inc. to start a new company, Novix Inc. He developed the first Forth microprocessor, the Novix NC4000, which was marketed by Harris Semiconductor as the RTX2000. Moore told *Leaders of the Information Age* that Novix folded in 1984, however, "after being unable to raise enough capital for its ambitions."

From 1985 to 1995 Moore worked at a venture called Computer Cowboys, designing computer chips and circuit boards, including the Forth microprocessors ShBoom, MuP21, and F21. After leaving Computer Cowboys, in 1996 Moore founded the iTv Corporation to design and market Internet applications such as Web browsers and e-mail systems. In 2000 iTv ceased operations after it was unable to raise the necessary capital to market its products. In 2001 Moore returned to Computer Cowboys, where he developed ColorForth, an enhanced version of Forth. Moore told *Leaders of the Information Age* that he is currently working on the design of a new Forth chip.

Elizabeth Rather serves as the chief executive officer (CEO) of Forth Inc., which is based in Hawthorne, California. Although the company is small, it serves many noteworthy clients, including the Ford Motor Company and the General Electric Corporation. Today Forth continues to maintain a loyal following with many programmers.

Charles Moore holds 10 patents for developing Forth-based microprocessors and applications. Moore and his wife, Min, a spinner and weaver, are the parents of one son, Eric. They make their home in Sierra City, California.—D. C.

Suggested Reading: *Byte* p8+ Aug. 1980; ColorForth Web site; *Computer Language* p121+ July 1989; *Computer Shopper* p598+ April 1997; *Dr. Dobb's Journal of Software Tools* (on-line) June 1992; *Electronic Design* p97+ Nov. 22, 1999; Forth Inc. Web site

Courtesy of Intel Corporation

Moore, Gordon E.

Jan. 3, 1929– Co-founder of Intel

In 1965, when gigantic mainframe computers cost more than a million dollars and were kept in their own hypercooled wings of buildings, Gordon E. Moore issued a prediction that the silicon microchip would change the face of computing by bringing complex electronic applications to the general populace. The silicon microchip was made of a tiny wafer of pure silicon that acted as a semiconductor—halfway between a conductor and an insulator—and was used to make up intricate electric circuits. In what later became known as Moore's Law, he postulated that the power and complexity of silicon chips would double every year for 10 years—with proportionate decreases in cost. At that time, few people realized that silicon chips would eventually become the "brains" of most of the world's computers. Three years later, Moore co-founded Intel, now the world's leader in silicon-chip microprocessors and went on to not only make his prediction come true but to have it become the standard by which the entire computer industry paces itself. Brian O'Reilly wrote in *Fortune* (April 26, 1999), "With his impressive scientific mind and quiet determination, [Moore] probably did as much as anybody to develop the semiconductor, the microprocessor, and the entire personal computer revolution."

Moore was born not far from Silicon Valley in the little town of Pescadero, California, on January 3, 1929. His father was the deputy sheriff, and his mother's family owned the town's only general store. Growing up, Moore was less interested in technology than chemistry. A neighboring child got a chemistry set for Christmas one year, and the two of them played with it together. "In those days," Moore told Jill Wolfson and Teo Cervantes for the *San Jose Mercury News* on-line, "you got really neat chemicals in the chemistry set. You could make explosives and a variety of things." Later, Moore got his own home lab and learned how to make nitroglycerin. He enrolled at the University of California at Berkeley (becoming the first one in his family to go to college) and in 1950 he received his B.S. in chemistry. In 1954 he earned a Ph.D. from the California Institute of Technology, in Pasadena.

Moore's first job out of school was in the Applied Physics Laboratory at Johns Hopkins University, in Baltimore, Maryland, where he studied the properties of light. But Moore wasn't content with the job. As he told Cervantes and Wolfson, "I was more of an engineer than a scientist in that having some practical outcome from what I did was important. With my chemistry set, I had to get a good explosion at the end or I wasn't happy." His search for a new job ended when one of the three inventors of the transistor, Dr. William Shockley of Bell Laboratories, found Moore while looking for a chemist to help him produce silicon transistors. According to Moore Shockley was a great inventor but an ineffective manager. After about a year, Moore and a co-worker named Robert Noyce led a sort of mutiny. In 1957 they convinced six other employees to leave and start a new company called Fairchild Semiconductor.

Later christened The Fairchild Eight, the group knew they wanted to find a way to mass produce silicon transistors that could be used in a variety of applications; they didn't know, however, that they were spawning what would become a $100-billion business. In a characteristically humble way, Moore maintains that his groundbreaking start-up company was, in many respects, an accident. He told Robert Lenzner for *Fortune* (September 11, 1995), "The accidental entrepreneur like me has to fall into the opportunity or be pushed into it. Things have to line up right. Then the entrepreneurial spirit eventually catches on." Certainly the entrepreneurial spirit caught on in Silicon Valley after Moore helped set the stage; It is estimated that Fairchild Semiconductor itself spawned at least 150 spin-offs. After concentrating on silicon transistors, in the early 1960s the company started to make integrated circuits. In this process, complete electronic circuits, including interconnecting wiring, were built on single silicon chips, or microchips. Part of Moore's genius was to realize these chips could be the building blocks for all sorts of electronics applications, and in 1965 he issued Moore's Law.

But management problems were brewing at Fairchild Semiconductor's parent company, Fairchild Camera and Instrument Corporation, which had gone through two CEOs in a six-month period. Additionally, Moore was beginning to resent what he felt was a lack of freedom to develop new technologies. Once again, Moore joined Noyce, and in

1968 the pair formed Intel, with $2.5 million from Arthur Rock, a noted venture capitalist. As executive vice president, Moore planned to continue refining the integrated circuits he had started making at Fairchild Semiconductor and to produce them on a large scale. Part of the problem in producing integrated circuits, however, was that it was easier to build one after it was known what specific task it would be performing. "The problem," Moore told W. Wayt Gibbs for *Scientific American* (September 1997), "was that when you defined complex integrated circuits, they tended to be unique—you know, used once in a computer system or something. And we saw semiconductor memory as an opportunity to make something complex and sell it for all kinds of digital applications."

The start-up years of Intel were busy, but productive and lucrative. Often the staff mounted spontaneous parties to celebrate milestones in the development process of new products. In an article for *Daedalus* (Spring 1996) describing these early years, Moore wrote, "By the time we outgrew this facility, the tiles in the ceiling were peppered with the imprints of all these champagne corks." Early applications of Intel's chips included automating a chicken house and replacing police dogs with mechanical marijuana-sniffers. The chips were also used to analyze blood. Then, in 1969, the groundwork was laid for one of the biggest advances in the history of computing.

Busicom, a Japanese manufacturer of calculators, was looking for a company to supply its chips. They had already come up with a technical plan that would require 13 complex circuits to perform the necessary calculations. Intel was still so small that manufacturing the chips didn't seem feasible. Then a young engineer named Ted Hoff came up with the idea of using just one central computer chip, in combination with specific programs and memory storage to perform all the necessary calculations. Intel made what seemed a very bold proposal to Busicom—essentially asking the established company to disregard its own engineering research and try using Intel's one-chip method. To Moore's surprise, executives at Busicom agreed. What Intel had designed by combining an integrated circuit with built-in programming and memory storage was the first microprocessor, or central processing unit (CPU), which would later become the main component of every personal computer in the world.

Because Busicom had agreed to fund some of the research for the microprocessors, they also owned the rights to them, and Intel could not sell them to anyone else. When Busicom pressured Intel to sell the chips for less money, however, Intel cannily agreed—on the condition that they be granted permission to sell the chips for other applications. Later, when Busicom ran into financial difficulties, Intel gave them back the $65,000 they'd been given for research in exchange for full rights to the microprocessor. In so doing, Intel secured their role as the leader of the computer industry. As Moore told Gibbs, "So the Japanese initially owned all the rights to microprocessors, but sold them for 65 grand. In retrospect, it was kind of like the purchase of Manhattan [from Native Americans for $24]."

Throughout the 1970s Intel continued to successfully develop its microprocessors, and in the first half of 1974, for example, the company's before-tax profit was more than 40 percent. Moore became the chief executive officer of Intel in 1975. Then, in 1979, a leading computer company, IBM, chose one of Intel's processors to run its first personal computer—inaugurating an entirely new use for microprocessors. Previously, most microprocessors had built-in programs to perform specific functions that could not be altered. The personal computer had a user-programmable memory, so that the computer could serve a wide variety of functions—as chosen by the user.

Intel did have competition, however. In the mid-1980s mass production of microprocessors in Japan drove down prices so drastically that from 1984 to 1986 Intel's staff was reduced by more than 30 percent. Intel responded to the challenge with another innovation: the Intel386 chip. This was a milestone because the 386 crowded 275,000 transistors onto one chip, thus producing the fastest, most advanced microprocessor to date. In the beginning, Intel had struggled to put 2,000 transistors on a chip, but, true to Moore's Law, the numbers had doubled nearly every year

In 1987 Moore gave up his CEO post at Intel but remained a chairman of the company. Though he gradually reduced his role during the 1990s, he continued to work at Intel, in the same cubicle he had been using from early on. In 1993 Intel came out with its Pentium processor, which had 3.1 million transistors. In 1997 (the year of Pentium II, with 7.5 million transistors) Moore was named chairman emeritus.

Meanwhile, Moore had been indulging other interests. In 1990 he had joined the board of directors of an environmental organization called Conservation International (CI), which focuses on providing incentives to corporations and governments to protect and preserve wilderness areas and biodiversity. Long before his involvement with CI, Moore had been an enthusiastic outdoorsman. When their two boys, Kenneth and Steven, were young, he and his wife, Betty, would park next to northern Californian rivers and take turns fishing while the other watched the children. By 1998 Moore had donated $35 million to CI. Moore was also a benefactor of the Search for Extraterrestrial Intelligence (SETI), a nonprofit group dedicated to scientific research, education, and public outreach. Moore was quoted in *Forbes* (October 13, 1997) as saying, "I can hardly think of a more profound question to ask than, 'Are we alone in the universe?'"

Thanks in large part to Moore's contributions, we on earth are not alone, at least insofar as we are connected by vast, international computer networks. Moore has received many awards for his work: among these are a 1984 Institute of Electrical and Electronic Engineers (IEEE) Computer Society Pioneer Medal, a 1985 Medal for the Advancement of Research from the American Society of Metals, a 1988 Founder's Award from the National Academy of Engineering, and a 1990 National Medal of Technology, presented by President George Bush. Moore has been a director of numerous companies, including Varian Associates, Gilead Sciences Inc., and Transamerica Corporation. He is currently retired from Intel and frequently travels the world looking for perfect fishing spots with his wife. In 2000 the couple created the Gordon and Betty Moore Foundation, which funds ambitious environmental and educational projects aimed at improving the quality of life for future generations.—P. G. H.

Suggested Reading: *Computerworld* p67+ Aug. 5, 1996; *Forbes* p162+ Sep. 11, 1995, with photos; *Fortune* p166+ Apr. 26, 1999, with photos; *Scientific American* (on-line) Sep. 1997

Morland, Samuel

1625–Dec. 30, 1695 Inventor of mechanical calculators

The 17th-century English diplomat Sir Samuel Morland invented three mechanical calculators: a trigonometrical calculating machine, an adding machine, and a mechanical version of John Napier's "multiplying bones"—a set of graduated rods that could be used to multiply and divide using logarithms. While not the first mechanical calculators invented, they were the first to be commercially marketed in Europe. His trigonometrical calculating machine was considered a vast improvement over any other machine then available for calculating navigation at sea. His adding machine was a pocket-sized mechanical forerunner of contemporary electronic calculators. His multiplying machine proved to be complementary to his adding machine; when combined they allowed for addition, subtraction, multiplication, and division. Though Morland's machines were considered more of a curiosity in his day than practical, everyday devices, they are significant for providing a bridge from earlier mechanical devices, such as Napier's bones, to modern electronic calculators.

Samuel Morland was born in 1625 in Sulhamstead Bannister, Berkshire, England, the son of Thomas Morland, the rector of Sulhamstead Bannister. He was educated at Winchester College from 1639 to 1644, and then at Magdalene College, part of Cambridge University. Though he hailed from a religious family, he earned his bachelor of arts in mathematics, instead of theology, from Magdalene in 1648. In 1649 he became a fellow of the college and continued his education there, receiving his master's degree, in 1652. While studying for his postgraduate degree, he became good friends with Samuel Pepys, from whose diary historians have uncovered information about Morland's personal life.

After leaving Cambridge, in 1653, Morland became deeply immersed in the political turmoil surrounding Oliver Cromwell's overthrow of King Charles II and the establishment of the English Commonwealth. As a Cromwell supporter, Morland found favor in the Commonwealth government and joined the diplomatic staff of ambassador Bulstrode Whitelocke. Their first diplomatic mission was to Sweden, in 1653, where they arranged a commercial treaty between England and Queen Christina's court. As a great supporter of the sciences, the Swedish queen frequently brought esteemed scientists and philosophers to her court to discuss their work and present their inventions and findings. In 1652 the inventor Blaise Pascal had sent the queen a copy of his adding machine, which she kept on display to show visiting officials; historians believe it is very likely that she would have shown the machine to Morland as a visiting ambassador.

A year after returning from Sweden, Morland was again sent by the Commonwealth government on a goodwill mission, this time to the court of the duke of Savoy, in Italy. On his return from Italy he stopped in Paris, France, to perform some diplomatic services with the court of Louis XIV. While his diplomatic mission was not much of a success, he established contacts with scientists and scholars in both the French court and the French scientific community. After Morland married his first wife, Susanne de Milleville, the daughter of Daniel Milleville, the Baron of Boissay, in 1657, his association with France was further solidified. Over the next several years he and his wife made a number of trips to France and very likely became acquainted with René Grillet, the clockmaker to Louis XIV and inventor of his own calculating machine.

Morland's relationship with the Cromwell government deteriorated after he became aware of a plot to assassinate Charles II and his brother. After warning Charles of the plot against him, he began working as a spy for the monarchy, hoping to achieve its restoration. After the restoration of the king, charges were brought against Morland for having worked with Cromwell, but he received a full pardon in 1660, and later that same year, he was knighted by Charles II and made a baronet. Though he never received the financial help he wanted from the king, he was provided with a pension—enough of an income to focus his energies on the building of mechanical devices.

Morland's trigonometry machine, less than a foot long on each side, was made of brass and coated with silver on its front surface. It combined a ruler with two simple gears turned by two handles on the lower right- and left-hand sides of the machine; the handle on the left turned the machine's large central circle, while the one on the right moved the horizontal bar across the center of the large circle up and down across the face. The two arms of the sector were arranged so that one was locked to the central disc, and the other could move around the rotation of the central wheel. The disc and the face of the instrument were marked in such a manner as to measure hours, minutes, and degrees, or to show the directions of a compass. As Michael A. Williams noted in *A History of Computing Technology* (1997): "This device, because of its mechanical settings, had obvious advantages over the elementary sector when being used for navigational calculations at sea. In addition, the mechanical settings would often allow much finer readings from the scales than were possible when using a simple pair of dividers to transfer readings from one scale to the next."

Morland's adding machine was designed to add English money and was composed of eight dials that were moved by a simple stylus. (The non-decimal dials for farthings, pence, and shillings were on the lower half of the device, thereby allowing the upper part to be used for adding decimal numbers up to five places.) As Williams explained: "If it was desired to add four pounds to a sum already registered on the machine, you simply put the stylus into the hole at the position marked four on the dial corresponding to the units digit of the pounds register (upper right-hand dial) and then rotated it in a clockwise direction until the stylus was at the top of the dial. The result of the operation could be seen through the small window at the 12 o'clock position on each dial." However, since there was no carry instrument on the machine, Morland built several auxiliary dials above each of the major dials, so that every time a major dial moved from 9 to 0, a tooth inside the machine would advance the carry dial. Williams goes on to note: "Morland's adding machine was . . . both simple in construction and reliable in operation as long as the operator remembered to add the carries forward at the end of the normal adding operation." Morland advertised the pocket-sized device in the London *Gazette*, on April 16, 1668, though few were actually sold.

Morland's final calculating machine, a mechanical version of Napier's bones, was a flat, brass dish with a hinged, perforated gate and circular discs carved with numbers. This was mounted on semicircular pins. The discs themselves were circular versions of Napier's bones, the numbers set around the edge of a disc instead of a straight line. (In total the machine had 30 discs for standard multiplication, plus five more for finding square and cube roots.) Williams detailed how the machine worked: "To find the single-digit products of a given number, for example, 1234, the disks representing these digits would be removed from the upper pins and placed over the semi-circular pins on the lower portion of the instrument. The hinged gate would then be lowered over the disks, and the key would be turned until the small pointer indicated that the proper multiple would be showing

through the windows in the hinged gate. The act of turning the key would, through an elementary rack-and-pinion mechanism, rotate the disks under the gate and move the pointer along the product indicator. The digits of the required product could then be found by adding together the pairs of digits showing through each gate window."

In 1671 Morland built a speaking trumpet that he claimed would allow a conversation to be conducted over a distance of three-quarters of a mile. He also invented the diagonal and balance barometer. But his central preoccupation was in the field of hydrostatics. In the 17th century many scientists were interested in developing mechanical ways to raise water. Morland's invention was comprised of a cistern from which air was expelled by a charge of gunpowder, causing water to rise to fill the vacuum thus produced. In the London *Gazette* of July 30, 1681, as quoted in the *Dictionary of Scientific Biography* (1974), the author described a demonstration near Windsor castle, during which Morland brought the water—tinted with a vat of red wine to make it more visible—up in a continuous stream at the rate of 60 barrels an hour, "with the strength of eight men." In 1681, recognizing his success, the king proclaimed him to be "Master of Mechanicks."

Sir Samuel Morland married at least four times. He married his second wife, Carola Harnett, on October 26, 1670. After she died, in 1676, he married Anne Fielding on November 16, 1676. She died in 1680, and he married Mary Aylip, on February 1, 1687. He was survived by only one of his children, Samuel, who became the family's second and final baronet. Morland went blind in the last three years of his life and died on December 30, 1695, in Hammersmith, where he had retired.—C. M.

Suggested Reading: *Dictionary of Scientific Biography*, 1974; Cortada, James W. *Historical Dictionary of Data Processing: Biographies*, 1987; Williams, Michael A. *A History of Computing Technology*, 1997

Morse, Samuel F. B.

Apr. 27, 1791–Apr. 2, 1872 Pioneer of the electric telegraph and inventor of Morse code

Samuel Morse was the developer of the first widely adopted electric telegraph and the inventor of Morse code. The telegraph, developed by Morse in the 1830s, allowed people to communicate with unprecedented speed over long distances by sending electric signals through wire cables. These signals were sent in Morse code, an alphabetic system wherein letters are represented by dots and dashes, corresponding to short and long bursts of electric current. A telegraph operator dispatched these bursts of current using an apparatus with a tapping key, and the currents were registered on the receiving end by a mechanically operated pen, marking

Time Life Pictures/Getty Images

Samuel F. B. Morse

dots and dashes on a tickertape. Morse organized the building of the first telegraph line in the U.S., in the 1840s; over the next few decades, the network of telegraph wires expanded rapidly, both in the U.S. and in countries across the globe. Morse's telegraph brought about a revolution in communication, paving the way for the late-19th-century inventions of the telephone and radio.

Samuel Finley Breese Morse was born on April 27, 1791 in Charlestown, Massachusetts (now a part of Boston), the eldest of three sons of Jedidiah Morse, a Congregational pastor, and his wife, Elizabeth Ann Breese. As a student, first at Phillips Academy, in Andover, and then at Yale College (now Yale University), in New Haven, Connecticut, Morse was only moderately interested in his academic curriculum. The emerging science of electricity, however, did capture his imagination. He also took up painting at this time, specializing in miniature portraits.

After graduating from Yale, in 1810, Morse worked briefly as a clerk for a Boston book publisher before persuading his reluctant parents to send him to England to study art. In London Morse absorbed the prevailing English style of painting, which included the romantic portrayal of historical and legendary events and personalities. When the War of 1812 broke out between Great Britain and the United States, Morse remained in England, but the conflict stirred his American patriotism. After returning to America in 1815 he found that the English style of painting had fallen from favor, and to support himself he returned to portrait painting. For the next ten years he worked as a painter in New York, New England, and South Carolina, slowly building his reputation. In 1825 he

settled in New York City, where he became the founder and first president of the National Academy of Design. He staged two unsuccessful campaigns to become mayor of New York City. Meanwhile, he nurtured an interest in inventions, taking out three patents for water pumps in 1817 with his brother Sidney.

In 1832, while returning from three years of artistic study in Europe, Morse had an encounter that inspired him to build his first electric telegraph. Traveling aboard a sailing ship called the *Sully*, Morse overheard one of the passengers, Dr. Charles Jackson, discussing the principles of electromagnetism, a field which had recently been pioneered by such scientists as Hans Christian Oersted and Michael Faraday. One of the other passengers wondered aloud how fast and how far electricity could travel along a wire, and Dr. Jackson explained that scientists believed that electricity could travel through any length of wire almost instantaneously. Morse was captivated by the idea. According to Tom Standage in his book *The Victorian Internet* (1998), Morse is reputed to have remarked: "If the presence of electricity can be made visible in any desired part of the circuit, I see no reason why intelligence might not be instantaneously transmitted by electricity to any distance." Morse spent the rest of the ocean voyage sketching out plans for his electric telegraph.

Morse was not the first to conceive of using electricity to convey information through wires. The first telegraph had been built in 1774, but it was a primitive machine that required 26 separate wires, one for each letter of the alphabet. Subsequent models, although made to use fewer wires, were equally impractical. Morse apparently believed, however, that his proposal was the first of its kind, and it is likely that his lack of awareness about the difficulties of building such a device helped bolster his determination. He intended to build his telegraph using a single wire.

Since he assumed that the electronics would pose little difficulty, Morse turned his attention first to the practical problem of how communication would take place. He realized that an efficient signaling code was necessary. He soon arrived at the idea of using long and short bursts of current, a two-signal approach that would eventually evolve into the series of dots and dashes now known as Morse code. In his initial scheme Morse ascribed a pattern of long and short bursts to correspond to each of the digits from zero to nine. A message to be sent would first have to be converted into numbers using a codebook, and then similarly translated back into words at the receiving end.

Morse spent the next several years designing and building his electric telegraph, although much of his time was still devoted to painting, as well as teaching art at New York University (NYU), in New York City. One of the early obstacles he faced was sending a signal over long distances. Morse was not alone; a contemporary in England, William Cooke, who was independently building an electric telegraph of his own, had encountered the same problem. Unbeknownst to both men, Joseph Henry, an American physicist, had conducted several experiments in 1830 demonstrating how to send an electric current for more than a mile through wire to activate an electromagnet and ring a bell. The key to sending current over long distances, he discovered, was to employ a row of attached batteries, rather than a single large battery. Morse learned of Henry's experiment only later, through Leonard Gale, a professor of science at NYU. Morse partnered with Gale and together they adopted Henry's design, which allowed them to send a message first through 200 feet of wire, then through 1,000 feet, and finally through 10 miles of wire arranged on wheels in an NYU lecture hall. Gale and Morse soon acquired a third partner, Alfred Vail, who had witnessed one of the duo's demonstrations. In exchange for a share of the patent rights, Vail, who had mechanical skills and access to his family's New Jersey ironworks, helped construct improved instrumentation for Morse's telegraph. Morse unveiled his first full prototype in 1837.

Vail and Gale made several important contributions to Morse's project. They helped him revise the transmitting apparatus, which was overly complicated, into a simple system using a tapping key operated by hand. Moreover, they worked with Morse to replace his numbered code with an alphabetic system wherein each letter was denoted by a series of dots and dashes. The most commonly used letters were given the shortest counterparts in code; the letter "e," for example, was represented by a single dot. This alphabetic system made Morse's codebooks unnecessary, as a message could be easily "sound read" by an operator familiar with the code. At an exhibition of his telegraph in 1838, Morse transmitted an impressive 10 words per minute using the new code.

Believing that he now had a marketable device, Morse traveled to Washington, D.C., in 1838 to demonstrate his telegraph to government officials and persuade them to build a telegraph line. Congress was unreceptive to the idea, although Morse succeeded in acquiring a congressman as an additional partner. Morse then traveled to Europe to organize the construction of a telegraph line there, but again met with resistance. When he returned to the United States he found that his partners had grown anxious that their investments would fail to yield a profit. Now becoming desperate, Morse returned to Washington, D.C., in December 1842 to demonstrate his telegraph once again to Congress; this time he strung wires between two committee rooms in the Capitol and sent messages back and forth. Congress, by a slim vote, allotted him $30,000 to build an experimental telegraph line, the first in the United States, between Baltimore, Maryland and Washington, D.C., a distance of about 40 miles.

Construction of the Washington-Baltimore line was completed in May 1844. On May 24 Morse officially opened the line by transmitting a quote from the Bible: "What hath God wrought?" Although the newspapers praised Morse's invention, the public initially had little use for the device. It was viewed as a novelty item; curious citizens came to see it, but they did not use it to communicate. Instead they gathered to watch chess games played between opponents in each city. Morse and his partners despaired that the line was not being utilized to its full potential. Soon, however, the line was made to serve other purposes: to confirm deaths in families, to transmit the descriptions of wanted criminals, and to relay information between merchants. Morse returned to Congress, citing these examples and others, to urge that the line be extended to New York. If more cities were connected, he argued, the line would be immanently more useful.

His attempts at gaining further government support proved futile, however, and he instead turned to private enterprise. He made deals with several companies to use his patented technology. One of the first, the Magnetic Telegraph Company, was formed in May 1845. Soon lines were being built to such cities as Philadelphia, Pennsylvania; Boston; and Buffalo, New York. As more and more cities were connected, the utility of the system increased. The network began to grow at dizzying speeds, with lines of wire stretching westward across the United States, commonly following the routes of railroad tracks. By 1854 approximately 23,000 miles of telegraph wire had been laid in the U.S. In the mid-1860s the first transatlantic cable was laid, connecting the United States and Europe. Meanwhile, development had kept apace abroad, with lines of wire stretching from England to India. By 1875 there were, according to some accounts, more than 650,000 miles of wire worldwide, including more than 30,000 miles of underwater cable. The radical increase in the speed of communication led to many changes in the way people lived and worked. "Time itself is telegraphed out of existence," declared the London *Daily Telegraph*, a newspaper whose name was chosen to convey a sense of rapid, up-to-date delivery of news, as quoted by Tom Standage.

Morse and his partners, having applied for a patent in 1844, were almost immediately besieged by lawsuits from rival inventors. The series of legal battles lasted a decade, ending in 1854 when the United States Supreme Court established Morse's rights as inventor of the telegraph. The profits from his invention made Morse a wealthy man. Although he wasn't the sole inventor of the telegraph or the single-handed designer of Morse code, he arguably did more than anyone else to popularize the technology, leading to the wide acceptance and rapid development of the telegraph network both in the U.S. and abroad.

The telegraph remained the only means of rapid long-distance communication until the 1870s, when the telephone was developed. Soon after, wireless radio technologies began to appear, and in the face of these two improvements to communication, use of the telegraph faded. Morse's fame, accordingly, has waned, although he is still remembered in conjunction with Morse code, in particular the internationally recognized Morse code signal for help, SOS. (The term SOS, incidentally, is not an acronym. It was reportedly chosen because the Morse codes for the letter S [three dots] and O [three dashes] were considered easy to remember and recognize.)

In 1818, when Morse was 27, he married 19-year-old Lucretia Pickering Walker, from Concord, New Hampshire, with whom he had three children. Lucretia died from an illness in 1825, leaving Morse to raise the children. In 1847 Morse purchased a country home, Locust Grove, on 100 acres outside of Poughkeepsie, New York. He spent his summers there with his large family of children and grandchildren, returning each winter to his home in New York City. In 1848 he married a cousin, Sarah Elizabeth Griswold, with whom he four children.

In his old age Morse became a philanthropist, donating generously to Vassar College, which he helped found, in Poughkeepsie, and to Yale. He also contributed to churches, religious organizations, and temperance societies. He died of pneumonia on April 2, 1872 in New York City.—C. M.

Suggested Reading: Locust Grove Web site; Asimov, Isaac. *Asimov's Biographical Encyclopedia of Science and Technology*, 1982; Standage, Tom. *The Victorian Internet*, 1998; Simonis, Doris. *Lives and Legacies: Scientists, Mathematicians, and Inventors*, 1999

the scientific community. The 18th-century French astronomer Pierre Simon Laplace famously said of Napier that he had doubled the lifetime of astronomers, by reducing their labors by half. Napier was also the inventor of an early calculating device known as "Napier's bones" or "Napier's rods."

John Napier was born in 1550 in Merchiston Castle, near Edinburgh, Scotland, the son of Sir Archibald Napier and Janet Bothwell, the daughter of an Edinburgh burgess. Napier's family was landed Scottish aristocracy, his father being the Seventh Laird of Merchiston; they were also staunch Calvinists and supporters of the Protestant Reformation. As a young child Napier was tutored at home, but in 1563, when he was 13, he went to study at St. Salvatore's College, part of St. Andrew's University. Although Napier did not earn a degree in his three years there, he did study theology, a subject which would engage him greatly later in life. After his time at St. Andrew's, his uncle Adam Bothwell, the bishop of Orkney, suggested that he study on the European continent for a period, as was commonplace for members of the nobility at that time.

Though it is unclear if Napier followed Bothwell's advice, it is known that Napier was in Scotland by 1571 and the following year married Elizabeth Stirling, with whom he would later have a son and daughter. At his family's suggestion he built a castle at Gartnes, which was completed in 1574. After his wife died, in 1579, he married Agnes Chisholm, with whom he had 10 children. He lived at Gartnes until his father's death, in 1608, after which he moved to Merchiston Castle to become the Eighth Laird of Merchiston.

Beginning about the time of his first marriage, Napier became deeply involved in the political and social changes occurring in Scotland, which at the time was experiencing religious strife between

Time Life Pictures/Getty Images

Napier, John

1550–Apr. 4, 1617 Mathematician; inventor

The 16th-century Scottish mathematician and author John Napier is remembered chiefly as the inventor of logarithms—a method of mathematical calculation that allows multiplication and division problems to be simplified into subsets involving addition and subtraction. At a time when mathematical calculation had to be done by hand, logarithms were an enormous labor-saving device. Napier published his tables of logarithms in 1614, after which they were enthusiastically adopted by

Catholics and Protestants. Still a devoted Calvinist, Napier took up the Protestant cause in his first published literary work, *A Plaine Discovery of the Whole Revelation of Saint John* (1593). In that work Napier denounced the Catholic Church and offered an interpretation of the writings of St. John suggesting that the Pope was the Antichrist. The book, which was one of the first interpretations of Scripture published in Scotland, was translated into German, French, and Dutch, earning Napier a considerable reputation in Protestant circles as a scholar and theologian.

Napier was so concerned about conflicts with the Catholic Church and the European monarchs who supported it that he spent a great deal of time developing weapons to protect Scotland from a possible invasion by Philip II of Spain. Among the weapons he designed were heavy artillery, armored war chariots, submarines, and a burning mirror originally attributed to the Greek inventor Archimedes. Though none of these designs were ever implemented, they garnered Napier a reputation among the aristocracy for having a keen scientific mind. Amongst the local commoners, however, Napier's intelligence appears to have incited rumors that he was in league with the devil and practiced sorcerery.

Napier, who acquired the nickname "the Marvelous Merchiston," also developed a number of methods to improve his crops and livestock, including a way to improve the fertilizing properties of manure using common salt. In 1597 he created and received an exclusive patent for a hydraulic screw and revolving axle that removed water from flooded coal pits. However, his greatest interest was in the field of astronomy, an occupation that led to the development of his lasting achievement—logarithms. Napier began working on logarithms (a word that derives from the Greek words *logos*, meaning expression or ratio, and *arithmos*, for number) in about 1590, when he realized that numbers could be written in exponential form. The numeral 100, for example, can be written as 10 to the power of two, or 10^2. Napier ascertained that rather than multiplying two numbers, such as 100 x 100, it would be possible to rewrite the numbers in exponential form, 10^2 x 10^2 and simply add the exponents. In this example 2 + 2 = 4, and 10^4 = 10,000. In this way a simple addition problem replaces a complicated multiplication problem.

For this method of calculation to be useful, Napier had to compile tables showing the logarithms of different numbers. A person wishing to solve a mathematical problem could then consult one of these tables for the appropriate logarithms to be used. Completing these tables proved a formidable task that took several years, and in 1614 Napier published his results, *Mirifici logarithmorum canonis descriptio* (Description of the Marvelous Canon of Logarithms). In addition to the tables, the work contains an explanation of logarithms and their uses. Napier also described his motivation, as quoted in a biographical article posted in the Mac-Tutor History of Mathematics section of the University of St. Andrews Web site: "Seeing there is nothing (right well-beloved Students of the Mathematics) that is so troublesome to mathematical practice, nor that doth more molest and hinder calculators, than the multiplications, divisions, square and cubical extractions of great numbers, which besides the tedious expense of time are for the most part subject to many slippery errors, I began therefore to consider in my mind by what certain and ready art I might remove those hindrances. And having thought upon many things to this purpose, I found at length some excellent brief rules to be treated of (perhaps) hereafter. But amongst all, none more profitable than this which together with the hard and tedious multiplications, divisions, and extractions of roots, doth also cast away from the work itself even the very numbers themselves that are to be multiplied, divided and resolved into roots, and putteth other numbers in their place which perform as much as they can do, only by addition and subtraction, division by two or division by three."

The work had a stunning impact on the scientific community of the day, arguably comparable to the advent of electronic computers in the 20th century. Logarithms, like computers, relieved scientists of the time-consuming drudgery of long calculations. Napier also outlined the use of decimal notation. Though the decimal point had been developed earlier, Napier's use established it as standard notation to separate a whole number from a fractional part. In 1616 the English mathematician Henry Briggs journeyed to Edinburgh to discuss the logarithm tables with Napier. The two men collaborated on improvements to the tables, including the decision to use base 10 and log 1 = 0, which have now become standard. (Incidentally, Justus Byrgius, a Swiss watchmaker and mathematician and contemporary of Napier, independently developed a system of logarithms, the results of which were first published in 1620.)

Napier also devised a set of calculating rods, the use of which he explained in a treatise published in 1617 titled *Rabdologiae*. The rods, which were made of wood and sometimes ivory—leading to the appellation "Napier's bones"—were printed with the numbers zero to nine and could be used for multiplication, division, square roots, and powers. Napier's bones were soon in popular use throughout Europe and contributed to the mathematician's international reputation.

Suffering from severe gout and strained by overwork, John Napier died on April 4, 1617. Briggs carried on some of his work, including the development of certain trigonometric relations known today as Napier's anthologies. *Mirifici logarithmorum canonis constructio* (Construction of the Marvelous Canon of Logarithms), in which Napier offered further explanation of logarithms, was published posthumously by his son Robert Napier in 1619.—C. M.

Suggested Reading: *Mathematics in School* p32+ Sep. 1998, p9+ Nov. 2000; University of St. Andrews Web site; *Dictionary of Scientific Biography*, 1974; Asimov, Isaac. *Asimov's Biographical Encyclopedia of Science and Technology*, 1982; Lee, J. A. N., ed. *International Biographical Dictionary of Computer Pioneers*, 1995

Naur, Peter

Oct. 25, 1928– Co-developer of the Backus-Naur Format

The Danish scientist Peter Naur was one of the principal designers of the early versions of ALGOL (short for Algorithmic Language). The first universal programming language, ALGOL is now considered to be a milestone in the development of today's complex computer languages. In 1966 Naur, in another notable achievement, reportedly coined the word datalogy to describe the study of data and data processing, and later in the decade the University of Copenhagen created a professorship in the field expressly for him. Naur is perhaps best known, however, for the Backus-Naur Format, a system of formal notation to describe the syntax of a programming language.

Peter Naur was born in Frederiksberg, Denmark, on October 25, 1928. While in high school, he developed an interest in astronomy. In 1947 he entered Copenhagen University and received an astronomy degree, in 1949. His first experience with computers came while he was working at the university observatory on calculating the orbits of minor planets and comets. Between 1950 and 1951 he was a research assistant at King's College, part of Cambridge University, in England. While there, he helped design an astronomy program for the Electronic Delay Storage Automatic Computer (EDSAC), an early stored-program machine. He next traveled to the United States, where he visited a number of observatories and laboratories, including the Yerkes Observatory at the University of Chicago, in Illinois, and the International Business Machines Corporation (IBM) Thomas Watson Laboratory, in Yorktown Heights, New York. At the IBM laboratory he was exposed to cutting-edge computer technology, further peaking his interest in how the machines could aid astronomers in their calculations.

From 1953 to 1959 Naur was a scientific assistant at the Copenhagen Observatory. He earned his Ph.D. in astronomy from Copenhagen University, in 1957. During this time he was also asked to aid the designers of the DASK machine, Denmark's first computer, which was being built by an independent company called Regnecentralen. In 1959 he joined the staff of Regnecentralen, where he specialized in designing high-level computer languages. In that capacity he became involved in developing ALGOL, a highly adaptable programming language used in scientific and mathematical applications. Naur became the first editor of the *ALGOL Bulletin* and was one of the 13 members of the international team that in 1960 produced the final design of ALGOL 60. Between 1960 and 1967 Naur helped produce increasingly sophisticated versions of ALGOL.

John Warner Backus, who had earlier developed the high-level computer language FORTRAN, was also involved in ALGOL's development. Backus had introduced the idea for a precise grammar to describe computer languages in a report at an UNESCO conference on ALGOL 58. (He had originally hit upon the idea after reading the work of the mathematician Emil Post.) Naur read the report and modified the system for ALGOL 60. His modifications were almost unanimously accepted, and Backus-Naur Form (BNF), as it came to be called, began to be widely used in the programming community. The system's rules were elegant and easy to understand; for example, angle brackets were used to surround category names, and a break bar signified "or."

During the 1960s Naur became increasingly interested in what he termed datalogy—the study of data and data processing. In 1969 the University of Copenhagen created a professorship in the field for him. That same decade he toured a number of Danish schools as a lecturer and also traveled to the United States to lecture at the University of North Carolina and the University of Pennsylvania. He was active in the International Federation of Information Processing, as well as numerous ALGOL–related committees. In 1968 Naur co-edited the first NATO Software Engineering Conference report.

Since 1960 Naur has co-edited the Danish computer journal *Nordisk Tidskrift for Informationsbehalding*, more commonly know as *BIT*. On October 25, 1988, a special issue of *BIT* was devoted to Naur in honor of his 60th birthday.

Since 1966 Naur has served as the president of the Danish Society of Datalogy. A prolific writer, he has produced more than 150 published articles and a number of books. These include: *Concise Survey of Computer Methods* (1974); *Programming Languages, Natural Languages, and Mathematics* (1975); and *Computing: A Human Activity* (1992). Naur has received the 1963 G. A. Hagemanns Gold Medal and the 1966 Rosenhjaer Prize. In 1986 he received the Pioneer Award from the Institute of Electrical and Electronic Engineers (IEEE) Computer Society.

Naur is an aficionado of classical music. He has been married several times and has four children: Jesper, Thorkil, Birgitte, and Barbara.—C. M.

Suggested Reading: Cortada, James W. *Historical Dictionary of Data Processing: Biographies*, 1987; Nash, Stephen G. *A History of Scientific Computing*, 1990; Spencer, Donald D. *Timetable of Computers*, 1997

Brian W. Smith/Getty Images

Negroponte, Nicholas

1943– Director of the MIT Media Laboratory

Nicholas Negroponte, heralded as a new-media guru and prophet of the Information Age, is the co-founder and director of the Media Laboratory at the Massachusetts Institute of Technology (MIT), in Cambridge. Since the mid-1980s Negroponte and his team of researchers have focused on the future of multimedia and sought to transform traditional conceptions of newspapers, cinema, television, and music. Negroponte is the author of a best-selling book, *Being Digital* (1995), a utopian celebration of the future of digital technology, now translated into 40 languages. In 1995 *Wired* magazine called him the "most wired man we know (and that's saying a lot)." Negroponte was a monthly columnist for *Wired* from 1993 to 1998, and he is still well known for his enthusiasm about the future of computing; in interviews and essays he frequently offers grand predictions about what the future will hold. In a recent article for *Time* (June 19, 2000), for example, he predicts that "the dominant user of the Net in the future will not be people at all. It will be machines talking to one another in ways we cannot imagine. . . . Today you may have one or two dozen wireless devices (radio, cell phone, TV, pager, car key, a gaggle of remote-control units). Tomorrow, you will probably have thousands of them." He envisions a future in which not only will refrigerators and medicine cabinets be able to know their own contents, but "all these inanimate objects will be able to talk to one another and pass messages among themselves." He continued, "Computers are coming out of the box. Our grandchildren will look back at the personal computer as a quaint artifact, as common tomorrow as an ice chest is today."

Negroponte was born on New York City's Upper East Side, in 1943. The son of a Greek shipowner, he studied architecture at MIT in the 1960s. He became interested in computer design in graduate school, where his thesis advisor was Steve Coons, a professor of mechanical engineering who was working on the mathematics that would make computer graphics a reality. Negroponte joined the faculty of MIT in 1966, and in the following years he spent time as a visiting professor at Yale University, in New Haven, Connecticut, and at the University of California at Berkeley. In 1968 he founded MIT's Architecture Machine Group, his first organized attempt to develop new insight into the way humans and computers interface. He was interested in creating computers that would assist and eventually replace the architect. He wrote two books, *The Architecture Machine* (1968) and *Soft Architecture Machines* (1975). One of the successful projects developed by the Architecture Machine Group was the creation of a virtual tour of Aspen, Colorado, in 1978. Using photographs of every street in Aspen, Negroponte and his team developed a computerized video experience that allowed the user to "drive" through the city, stop at various locations, and even converse with the computerized inhabitants. The work generated some publicity and funding, most notably from the Pentagon.

Negroponte's interest in the human-computer interface led him to found the Media Lab at MIT. He conceived the idea for the Lab, which he modeled after MIT's successful Artificial Intelligence Lab, in 1979. Negroponte began rasing money and by the mid-1980s the Lab was operational. It moved into its current location, a $45-million building designed by the architect I. M. Pei, in 1985. In an interview with Thomas A. Bass for *Wired* (1995), Negroponte discussed the original goal of the Media Lab as an attempt to unite three "rings"—computers, broadcasting, and publishing: "The original idea for the Media Lab was very simple. You would pull the audiovisual richness out of the broadcast-entertainment ring. You would pull the depth of knowledge and information out of the publishing ring. And you would take the intrinsic interactivity of computers and put these three things together to get the sensory, rich, deep, interactive systems that today we call multimedia. The idea made sense 20 years ago . . . and even today it's a good way of summarizing what we do." The initial response to the Media Lab from within the academic world was largely skeptical, however, and Negroponte and his colleagues were sometimes dismissed as charlatans. The Lab was widely discussed in the media, with most major periodicals and television science programs doing pieces on the research that was taking shape there. Initial projects included a personalized newspaper that assembled content based on the user's interests, holographic models to aid in automobile design, and new musical instruments with the ability to adjust to the idiosyncracies of the player. Negroponte assembled a strong research team that included such luminaries of computer science as Marvin Minsky, a pioneer in the field of artificial intelligence, and the learning theorist Seymour Papert, who invented LOGO, a computer language for children. The Lab also employed photographers, musicians, typographers, and other artists. Describing a tour of the Lab, Thomas Bass wrote, "We tossed a ball to a virtual dog, created a personalized onscreen news service, and tickled the keys on a Bösendorfer piano converted into an electric sound machine. By the end of our tour I would have been hard-pressed to decide whether I wanted to invest in digital TV, holographic imaging, electronic publishing, or any of a hundred other nifty ideas."

Negroponte succeeded in securing numerous corporate sponsors for the Media Lab. He told Bass that because of a "no poaching" rule, he originally had to seek funding from sources not already supporting MIT. "We weren't allowed to go to the old friends of MIT—the IBMs and AT&Ts of corporate America—because they were already endowing the university. It would have been embarrassing to find myself in the lobby of the Ford Foundation sitting next to the president of MIT, both of us looking for an endowment." He continued, "At first the no-poaching rule seemed like a handicap, but it later turned out to be an asset. It forced us to make new friends, who turned out to be publishers. Time, Inc., Warner Communications—and other companies that make movies, books, and television programs—were the original sponsors of the Media Laboratory." Negroponte began attending the World Economic Forum, at Davos, Switzerland, in the mid-1980s. The forum, an annual meeting of CEOs from the world's premier companies, served as a means of establishing relations with foreign corporations in order to obtain sponsorships. By 1987 the Lab had raised nearly $60 million and could boast of 75 corporate sponsors, including ABC, NBC, Columbia Pictures, Paramount, IBM, Apple, Sony, Sanyo, and Hitachi, along with federal funding from the National Science Foundation and the Defense Department's Advanced Research Projects Agency (ARPA). The amount of interest from the private sector was remarkable, considering that the Lab emphasized the flow of new ideas rather than products. For their monetary contribution, companies were allowed to visit the Lab and send researchers for extended stays. Edward Dolnick, in a feature for the *New York Times Magazine* (August 23, 1987), quoted Jerome S. Rubin of the Times Mirror Company, the newspaper-publishing group, on why companies would continue to support research that did not necessarily lead to practical applications: "I'm sure there may be folks in the controller's department who wonder about it, but nobody at any senior level questions this kind of expenditure." Rubin explained that "being in touch with new ideas and being exposed to people having the new ideas is worth any investment we make. We don't expect any direct return." Michael

P. Schulhof, chairman of strategic planning for Sony Corporation of America, told Dolnick that "we couldn't even begin to look at the range of topics Negroponte looks at."

Some critics, mostly in academia and other areas of computer research, dismissed the Lab as more glitter than substance. Dolnick commented in his article that "the place seems designed to dazzle, to convince the constant stream of visitors that they're not in Kansas anymore." Many found Negroponte himself lacking in credibility because of his flamboyant claims about the future of the digital age. "Newspapers as we know them, won't exist," Negroponte told Dolnick. "The whole concept of newsworthiness will change. Newspapers will be printed for a readership of one." Negroponte predicted similar changes in television as well: "My view of the future of televison sets is that on these hand-held controllers you won't just have channel knobs, but you will have one button that says 'Tell me more' and another that says 'Tell me less.'"

In 1987 Negroponte tried to establish a Japanese version of the Media Lab, with Congressman Richard Gephardt spearheading the project. A $10-million endowment was obtained from a Japanese donor in return for a five-year agreement during which Negroponte and MIT would assist in building a research laboratory in Japan, and Japanese researchers would be allowed to visit the Media Lab. Critics at the time denounced the agreement as a sale of MIT expertise that could result in a threat to American competitiveness. The project gradually collapsed due to organizational difficulties and internal bickering, and in 1993 Negroponte resigned from the board of directors of the International Media Research Foundation, the organization trying to establish the Japanese lab.

Also in 1993 Negroponte began writing a monthly column for *Wired*. The magazine's founders, Louis Rossetto and Jane Metcalfe, approached Negroponte with a funding proposal for the publication, and Negroponte agreed to make a financial investment. Negroponte felt that the best way to protect his money was by helping out, so he offered to write a column. In his first piece he denounced the pursuit of high-definition television (HDTV) as irrelevant: "What is needed is innovation in programming, new kinds of delivery, and personalization of content." He continued, "It can be argued that today's TV set is, per cubic inch, the dumbest appliance in your home. As the television's intelligence increases, it will begin to select video and receive signals in 'unreal time.' For instance, an hour's worth of video—based on a consumer's profile or request—could be delivered over fiber to an intelligent TV in less than five seconds." Negroponte's columns became a popular success, and for a time his fame as a provocative essayist on the Information Age eclipsed his already-high profile as the director of the Media Lab. An amused Negroponte told Bass that when he gave public speeches, he was frequently introduced as a senior columnist from *Wired*, with only an occasional mention of MIT or the Lab. Negroponte also remarked to Bass, "It's unclear to me whether the back page of *Wired*, or the book that developed out of it, are in the best interest of the Media Lab. I've become a bit too public. I'm always going to be getting somebody pissed off, and among those somebodies will be sponsors of the lab, which now includes 105 companies. On several occasions, sponsors have told me they didn't like what I wrote. Nobody has withdrawn funding yet, but it's getting to the point where there is some tension. . . . There is a certain inconsistency in my roles: running a research laboratory with corporate sponsors and writing a snappy back page."

Based on the popularity of the column, Negroponte authored a book, *Being Digital*, a paean to the future of digital technology and the Information Age. The book was published in January of 1995, and by April it had reached number 11 on the *New York Times* best-seller list of nonfiction hardcover titles, having sold more than 100,000 copies. (Most serious nonfiction books, by comparison, sell somewhere between 8,000 and 12,000 copies.) The core of the book is Negroponte's argument that we are in the midst of a paradigm shift from a world view focused on the movement of atoms to an age in which the fundamental reality is the movement of bits. (A bit, as Negroponte explains, is the smallest unit of information, the name resulting from joining the words "binary" and "digit." Computers process these bits and transform them into text, sound, and images.)

In *Being Digital*, Negroponte maintains that the enhanced ability of machines to process bits of information will have unprecedented effects on our daily lives. He writes, as quoted by Simson L. Garfinkel in the *Christian Science Monitor* (March 15, 1995), that "the bits may be from one of a dozen sound tracks that enable you to watch a foreign movie in your own language. The bits may be the control data for a knob that allows you to change X-rated to R-rated to PG-rated (or the reverse). Today's TV set lets you control the brightness, volume, and channel. Tomorrow's will allow you to vary sex, violence, and political leaning." Negroponte envisions a host of such radical changes. By 2005, he predicts, Americans will be spending more time on the Internet than watching network television, video rental stores will be out of business as video-on-demand products dominate the market, and individuals will have private multimedia "butlers," programmed to screen our telephone calls, make our daily schedules, and personalize our entertainment.

Garfinkel wrote that "*Being Digital* is the finest, most understandable explanation of the digital revolution to date. Even better, Negroponte does it without jargon or plugging products. Being Digital is an evangelical and visionary work, written by one of this planet's masters of media." Garfinkel found fault with the book, however, for the scant space allotted to assessing the possible drawbacks

of the dawning digital age: "*Being Digital* devotes exactly one half of one sentence to the question of electronic privacy; the other half of the sentence is devoted to 'intellectual-property abuse'—the danger that big companies might have their digitized information stolen."

In 1995, the year *Being Digital* was published, the Media Lab shifted its focus from multimedia, which by that time had become widespread through the popularity of video games, CD-ROMs, and the Internet, to a new project entitled "Things That Think." The idea behind the project was to explore ways of implementing computer intelligence into everyday products—shoes that could calculate the time needed to reach a given location, a jacket that would adjust its thermal properties to different climates, and clothing that would relay a recovering patient's vital signs to a database in a doctor's office.

In December of 1998 Negroponte stopped writing monthly columns for *Wired*. In his final article he predicted that the digital world was headed for the same banality as plastics, another industry once heralded as revolutionary. Negroponte wrote that "the decades ahead will be a period of comprehending biotech, mastering nature, and realizing extraterrestrial travel, with DNA computers, microrobots, and nanotechnologies the main characters on the technological stage. Computers as we know them today will a) be boring, and b) disappear into things that are first and foremost something else: smart nails, self-cleaning shirts, driverless cars, therapeutic Barbie dolls, intelligent doorknobs that let the Federal Express man in and Fido out, but not 10 other dogs back in. Computers will be a sweeping yet invisible part of our everyday lives: We'll live in them, wear them, even eat them. A computer a day will keep the doctor away."

Negroponte is currently the Jerome B. Wiesner Professor of Media Technology at the Media Lab, although his busy schedule no longer allows time for teaching or performing research. Negroponte has appointed a new executive director, Walter Bender, to manage the day-to-day affairs of the Lab. Negroponte is now senior director and continues to raise funds and deliver speeches in countries around the world. Today the Lab has nearly 170 sponsors worldwide, and enrolls approximately 170 graduate students. Current research focuses on the intersection of computing and the arts. Specific areas of research include software agents; machine understanding; how children learn; human and machine vision; speech interfaces; wearable computers; advanced interface design; tangible media; object-oriented video; interactive cinema; and new approaches to spatial imaging, nanomedia, and nano-scale sensing. Negroponte also serves on the board of directors for Motorola Inc., and is a general partner in a venture capital firm specializing in digital technologies.—A. I. C.

Suggested Reading: *Business Week* p122 Feb. 10, 1992; *Christian Science Monitor* p14 Mar. 15, 1995; *Financial Times* p11 Apr. 10, 1995;

(London) *Guardian* p19 July 22, 1993; *New York Times* D p7 Oct. 18, 1993, C p17 Jan. 30, 1995, D p1 Apr. 24, 1995, D p6 May 15, 1995, G p1 Nov. 9, 2000; *New York Times Book Review* p10 Feb. 5, 1995; *New York Times Magazine* p30+ Aug. 23, 1987; *Time* p86+ June 19, 2000

Nelson, Ted

1937– Software developer; creator of Xanadu

In the 1960s, decades before the advent of the World Wide Web, the computer visionary Ted Nelson sought to create a vast repository of information, a "docuverse," as he called it, of electronic texts connected by links over a network of computers. He coined the terms "hypertext" and "hypermedia" to describe the tools that would enable a computer user to follow the connections from one text or fragment of text to another. These terms are familiar today to anyone who uses the World Wide Web—where someone reading a Web page can click on a link (usually a piece of text) with a computer mouse and be immediately shown another Web page. Rather than taking credit for anticipating the vastly popular World Wide Web, however, Nelson prefers to point out its shortcomings. "The World Wide Web is what we were trying to prevent: spaghetti hypertext and non-reusability," Nelson told Steve Ditlea for the *New York Times* (June 21, 1997, on-line). "The Web is intrinsically broken: the links go only one way, you can't link to spans of things, you can't link to parts of things, [and] you can't quote things." Nelson had his own vision of how computing should be done, and he spent decades trying to develop a text-publishing and information-storage system, called Xanadu, that avoided these flaws. The design was never completed, however, and in 1999 the code for Xanadu was placed in the public domain. Nevertheless, Xanadu has taken on a mythical status in the computing community, and Nelson—although regarded by many as an outsider because of his acerbically critical views and failure to deliver completed software—is frequently cited on lists of influential computer pioneers.

Theodor Holm Nelson was born in 1937 to show-business. His father, Ralph Nelson, directed 11 films, including *Soldier Blue* and the 1956 television production *Requiem for a Heavyweight*, for which he won an Emmy. His mother, Celeste Holm, was an actress. She starred in more than a dozen films and won an Academy Award as best supporting actress for her role in *Gentleman's Agreement* (1947). Nelson was raised primarily by his grandparents in the New York City neighborhood of Greenwich Village.

"When I was 12 years old, bang, here came this thing called television," Nelson recalled to William Saletan for the *Swarthmore Alumni Bulletin* (December 1998). "So the notion of one medium succeeding another was plain to me, as was the no-

tion of men at work in front of cathode ray tubes." Childhood trips to his father's studio had a formative effect. "I sat behind my father [in the studio]. These bright, intelligent guys sitting at screens with absolutely captive intensity in the control rooms—that seemed to me the way it ought to be." He also recalled an early obsession with the Japanese film *Rashômon*, directed by Akira Kurosawa, which he saw three times. The story, which is told from different perspectives, helped encourage Nelson in his view that information did not have to flow linearly, but could be assembled in "multiple parallel versions," as he told Saletan.

By the time Nelson enrolled at Swarthmore College, in Pennsylvania, his distrust of linear thinking and entrenched systems of thought was nearly complete. In addition to irking professors by citing the theories of Alfred Korzybski (a scientist and author with radical views on semantics and human development), he came into conflict with the dean by arguing for sexual freedom well before the Sexual Revolution of the 1960s. At Swarthmore, Nelson "majored in everything," as he told Owen Edwards for *Forbes* (August 25, 1997). In 1959 he received a B.A. in philosophy. "By the time I got out of college," Nelson told Tracey Logan for the *BBC News* (October 8, 2001, on-line), "I had already produced a long-playing record, written a book, had my own magazine, had my own newsletter, [and] written the world's first rock musical in 1957."

Although he briefly considered becoming a filmmaker, Nelson instead pursued graduate studies at Harvard University, in Cambridge, Massachusetts. During his first year there he took a computer course that focused his disparate thoughts around a single goal: the structure of information. As a writer, Nelson had for some time been frustrated with the limitations of paper documents. "The four walls of paper are like a prison," Nelson explained to Logan. "Every idea wants to spring out in all directions." As Nelson saw it, ideas and documents were connected in multiple dimensions, and to look at them as isolated or self contained was a distortion. Because paper documents come in a "finalized" form, a reader can't see the edits or changes that have been made in the process, nor the source material used in the preparation. To Nelson's mind, these various connected thoughts are a necessary part of any document. "There was no way, with paper, to represent the changes and structures and connections," he explained to William Saletan. "You can represent the changes with arrows, but after a certain point, you have to retype it."

The computer, a new medium of organizing and presenting information then still in its nascent stages, appeared to Nelson as the perfect opportunity to overcome the conventional thinking about documents. As a project for his computer course Nelson sought to create a "writing system" that would embody his ideas of an enhanced textual format. It was similar in design to today's word processors, allowing the user to enter text, edit it, and print it out. In 1960, however, word processing had not yet been invented, and when it did appear, to Nelson's dismay, it simply carried the idea of paper documents onto the computer screen. Nelson had something far more ambitious in mind. "Everything everyone was saying about computers was a lie," Nelson told Edwards. "It was up to me to design the literature of the future." Nelson's envisioned program would link each section of a new draft to the same section of previous drafts. The links would be traceable back to the original notes. Thus the "document" would be comprised of numerous parallel versions. Nelson's design called for two screen windows with visible lines connecting the various parts of text. He never finished the design for the program, but over the coming years he continued to develop his vision of linked texts. In 1963 Nelson graduated from Harvard in 1963 with a master's degree in sociology.

Nelson coined the term "hypertext" in a 1965 paper, "A File Structure for the Complex, the Changing and the Indeterminate", which he presented to a national conference of the Association for Computing Machinery. Nelson's concept of hypertext differed from the version that came to be used in the World Wide Web. On the Web, links go only one way, for example, but Nelson thought that all links should operate in both directions. Nelson also thought documents should be published "permanently"—making all versions of a document available. If a document's location was secure, the links into and out of the document would similarly be permanent—unlike the situation on the Web, where documents are constantly created and lost, and any changes can alter the system of linkages. Furthermore, Nelson felt that any user should be able to add links to a document, in order to append their own notes or commentary to a text. Nelson's ideas resemble a complex system of footnoting, wherein these linked notes would become the essence of the text. "[The] notion of hypertext," Nelson told Logan, "seemed to me immediately obvious because footnotes were already the ideas wriggling, struggling to get free, like a cat trying to get out of your arms."

Nelson named his vision Xanadu, a reference to the idyllic place mentioned in the poem *Kubla Khan* (originally published in 1816) by Samuel Taylor Coleridge. Xanadu represented "the magic place of literary memory where nothing is forgotten," as quoted on the official Xanadu Web site. An important feature of Xanadu was something Nelson called "transclusion." The Xanadu publishing system would contain only one copy of a document (a novel, for example). Anyone wanting to quote from that document, rather than type out or copy the section into their own document, would be able to "transclude" the desired section of the original. Transclusion, Nelson thought, would make it possible to have a universe of secure documents, where each connection between them would be traceable. One benefit, for example, would be that when viewing a piece of commentary, alongside it would be the original document, thus making it harder to take another writer's words out of context. Even more important for Nelson, transclusion seemed to solve the problem of copyrights. Whenever someone's text was referenced by another, a "micropayment" would be assessed electronically.

All of this proved notoriously difficult to implement. For most of Xanadu's history, computers have not had the memory or the computing power to handle the necessary amounts of data that Nelson's project demanded. Xanadu first started taking shape in 1970 when Nelson and other programmers developed a key part of the program that they called the "enfilade," a word referring to an interconnected group of rooms, usually in a row, with one opening into the next. Although the details were kept secret, the enfilade provided the data structures and algorithms that would be the basics of much of the later work. The first bout of programming for Xanadu occurred from 1970 to 1972, when the project was put on hold.

Taking a reprieve, Nelson wrote *Computer Lib/Dream Machines*, which he published himself in 1974. The volume was actually comprised of two books attached to each other, upside down and backwards. It was a chaotically organized screed, written in small print on 11-by-16-inch sheets, containing Nelson's ideas about the inevitable future of computing. (It was a notably prescient work, appearing months before the first widely available personal computers.) It also included, as Gary Wolf noted for *Wired* (June 1995), "whatever enraged or inspired Nelson during the months he wrote it, including population statistics, hacker psychology, the evils of IBM, holograms, musical notation, lists of places to rent a PDP-8 [an early general-purpose computer], Watergate, and how to program in Trac [a rudimentary computer language], among other topics." The book was immediately popular with the rapidly emerging cult of computer programmers. "Its tone—energetic, optimistic, inexhaustible, confused—matched theirs exactly," Wolf wrote. "Nelson managed to publish an insider's bible and highly intimate guide to hacker culture." The book sold steadily, if modestly, and was republished in 1987 by Microsoft Press.

In 1976 Nelson began teaching classes in interactive software and multimedia at Swarthmore College. The next major progress on Xanadu was made in the summer of 1979, which Wolf described as "Xanadu's Golden Age." Programmers from around the country joined Nelson that summer in a rented house and began to complete some of the coding. "We were pushing the envelope of practicality on every side," Nelson recalled to William Saletan. "We were writing a program that was bigger than compilers could handle." Eventually, however, the programmers ran out of money and the project again disbanded.

In 1983 Nelson formed the Xanadu Operating Company, (XOC) to carry out the design. Things proceeded slowly until 1988, when XOC was acquired by Autodesk, a pioneer in computer-aided design software. Autodesk's founder, John Walker, was very enthusiastic about the project. "In 1964," Walker announced, as quoted by Wolf, "Xanadu was a dream in a single mind. In 1980, it was the shared goal of a small group of brilliant technologists. By 1989, it will be a product. And by 1995, it will begin to change the world." Autodesk invested $5 million in developing Xanadu, only to drop the project in 1992 during a management reorganization.

A working model of Xanadu has never been completed. It has, however, had a profound influence on the computer industry at large. HyperCard, a text-linking software released by Apple Computer in 1987, followed Nelson's basic idea, but it allowed for links only between documents on a single computer, rather than a network of computers as Nelson had envisioned. Nelson was also an inspiration for Ray Ozzie, the creator of Lotus Notes, the leading software for collaborative work at the corporate level. "During the time that I was pulling my thoughts together for what would eventually become Notes, Ted's thinking was quite influential," Ozzie told Steve Ditlea for *MIT's Technology Review* (September/October 1998). "The concept of using the new and wonderfully 'personal' computer for shared thought and collaborative process augmentation was a bit antithetical. His work gave me confidence that thinking differently was actually an okay thing to do, even if I couldn't fully grasp where it was all going to end up." Thanks to Nelson, when Tim Berners-Lee introduced his idea for the World Wide Web, in 1990, hypertext and hypermedia were already familiar concepts in the computer world. A presentation Nelson made about Xanadu to the National Center for Supercomputing Applications (NCSA) eventually inspired Larry Smarr, the NCSA's director, to create a graphical interface for the Web called Mosaic.

In 1994 Nelson founded a research facility called the HyperLab in Sapporo, Japan, where he continued to develop his ideas. In 1996 he became a visiting professor of environmental information at the Shonan Fujisawa Campus of Keio University, in Fujisawa, Japan. When it began to appear to Nelson that a completed version of Xanadu was a distant reality, he opted to focus on certain aspects of the design that could be turned into commercial applications. In 1998 he released ZigZag, a software system for organizing personal and professional information. "[This is] the first software deliverable I've ever had," Nelson enthusiastically informed his audience at the 1998 International Conference on Wearable Computing, as quoted by Steve Ditlea for *MIT's Technology Review*. ZigZag is a cell-based spreadsheet designed to be more free-form and multidimensional than traditional spreadsheets.

In 1999 Nelson placed a majority of the almost-working code for Xanadu in the public domain. He retained the trademarked name Xanadu, and the open-source code was licensed under the name Udanax. Nelson continued to develop other Web-adapted applications using Xanadu ideas, including the idea of "micropayments" to collect royalties and the ability to "transcopyright" materials. "Everybody else thinks that payments will be on a huge level, like 10 cents," Nelson explained to Steve Ditlea for the *New York Times*. "I think if you charge more than a tenth of a cent for a picture, people just won't put up with it. The whole point is to have a mist of money in very small quantities and many-to-many micropayments instead of this notion of vendors and consumers." Nelson has adapted his designs to the World Wide Web with a certain degree of reluctance. "I don't think you can put wings on a child's wagon," he remarked to William Saletan. "To me, binding the whole thing together into an indivisible structure was always the center. Being a monist made it hard to break it down into tactical goals. And that's a fundamental failing that's left me where I am. If I were a company man or somebody able to do small things in a small way, it would have been much more effective."

Nelson is the recipient of the 1998 Yuri Rubinsky Insight Foundation lifetime achievement award. In 2001 he was knighted by the French Minister of Culture as an Officier des Arts et Lettres.—A. I. C.

Suggested Reading: *BBC News* (on-line) Oct. 8, 2001; *Economist* p108 Sep. 15, 1990, p37 Dec. 9, 2000; *Forbes* p134+ Aug. 25, 1997; *MIT's Technology Review* p44+ Sep./Oct. 1998; *New York Times* (on-line) June 21, 1997; *Swarthmore Alumni Bulletin* Dec. 1998; *Wired* p137+ June 1995

Newman, Maxwell Herman Alexander

Feb. 7, 1897–Feb. 22, 1984 Developer of computer technologies

One of the leading mathematicians of his time, M. H. A. Newman was a behind-the-scenes contributor to some of the major breakthroughs in computer technology that took place in England in the mid-20th century. While the engineers Alan Turing and Thomas Kilburn conceived the ideas that led to technological innovations, Newman gave them crucial support by offering theoretical advice, procuring the necessary equipment and personnel, and creating the type of atmosphere that they needed to work efficiently. Newman was a member of the team of scientists at Bletchley Park who developed the revolutionary Colossus machine, which was used to decipher Nazi codes during World War II. He also helped facilitate the construction of the Manchester Mark 1, the first computer with the ability to store in its memory the programs it needed in order to operate. Throughout his involvement with these projects, Newman continued to do research in topology, his primary field of interest, and his work brought a new understanding of the topic to mathematicians. As a faculty member of the University of Manchester for 19 years, Newman helped to establish the school as a cutting edge center for math and computer science.

The son of a German immigrant father, M. H. A. Newman was born Maxwell Herman Alexander Neumann on February 7, 1897 in the Chelsea section of London, England. From 1904 to 1908 he attended school in Dulwich, and he then continued his studies at the City of London School. In 1915 he entered Cambridge University on a scholarship to St. John's College. Newman was in residence there as a student until December 1916 (he changed his last name that same year) and spent the following three years in various forms of national service. During this time, he served as a paymaster in the British Army, and was briefly employed as a schoolmaster in Epping Forest. In the fall of 1919, Newman returned to Cambridge. In 1923 he was elected a fellow of St. John's and he spent the following year in Vienna, where he was strongly influenced by Reidemeister. From 1928 to 1929, he visited the United States where he was a Rockefeller Research Fellow at Princeton University, in Princeton, New Jersey.

Throughout his career, Newman was deeply interested in the study of combinatorial topology (topology is a branch of math that concerns certain properties of geometric configurations). Newman's early contributions to mathematics, however, were in the area of mathematical logic and this topic served as a bridge between topology, and his later interest in computer science. Perhaps his most significant contribution to topology was in developing and proving "the notion of a combinatorial move, designed to generate an equivalence relation between combinatorial manifolds." In 1939 Newman wrote his first and only book, entitled *Elements of the Topology of Plane Sets of Points*. Peter Hilton, writing in the *Bulletin of the London Mathematical Society* (1986) as quoted from the University of St. Andrews Web site, later applauded the work: "This is the only text in general topology which can be wholeheartedly recommended without qualification. It is beautifully written in the limpid style one would expect of one who combined clarity of thought, breadth of view, depth of understanding, and mastery of language. Newman saw, and presented, topology as part of the whole of mathematics, not as an isolated discipline: and many must wish he had written more."

In September 1942, during the height of World War II, Newman joined the Government Code and Cipher School at Bletchley Park, a government research compound. While he was there, he was in charge of the section of operations involving the development and use of machines that aided in deciphering German secret codes, and he worked alongside the distinguished mathematician Alan Turing. The machines that Newman and his colleagues used, the Bombe and the Colossus, were among the most innovative devices of the day and are considered forerunners of modern computers. Newman's contribution to the Bletchley Park initiative, which remained secret until long after the war, was primarily as a facilitator. For example, he made sure that those individuals in his section had the best possible conditions in which to work, free from distraction. Newman also had a talent for anticipating future needs for equipment and personnel, and in this respect, he helped ensure that no time or effort was wasted in the war movement.

After the war, Newman resigned from his positions at Cambridge to become the Fielden Professor of Mathematics at the University of Manchester, in 1945. With the help of the applied-mathematics professor Sydney Goldstein, Newman set about improving the university's math department, which already employed the noted inventors F. C. Williams and Thomas Kilburn. To round out the group, Newman hired his old colleague from Bletchley Park, Alan Turing, in 1948. Newman's self-appointed role at Manchester was similar to the one he played at Bletchley Park as well, namely, that of a gifted administrator whose efforts proved invaluable in helping his teams' projects become realities. His experience with the specialized code-breaking computers at Bletchley Park had aroused his interest in general-purpose computers. Realizing that a working computer was necessary in order to discover existing problems and make improvements, in his new position, Newman persuaded university authorities that a computer could be built on the premises. He then successfully commissioned Ferranti, Ltd., to build a computing machine called the Manchester Mark 1. Both Newman and Turning also lent their theoretical expertise to the computer's development.

The Manchester Mark 1, which successfully ran its first program on June 21, 1948, was a breakthrough machine in many respects. It was the first computer truly capable of storing programs, making it substantially more advanced than any other computers at the time, which were only able to perform calculations. Furthermore, although the Manchester Mark 1 was large enough to fill an entire room, it was much smaller, and faster, than any previous machine. Its success paved the way for future advancements in computer technology and put the city of Manchester on the map as a hub in the growing computer industry of the 1950s.

During this time, Newman maintained his involvement in mathematics. He was instrumental in the creation of one of that discipline's most vital institutions at that time, the British Mathematical Colloquium. The group's first meeting took place in Manchester, in 1949, and the colloquium stayed successful, largely because of Newman's round-up of support from his university department. In 1962 Newman was invited to give an address at the International Congress of Mathematicians in Stockholm, Sweden. The request was considered a particular honor because Newman, who was 65 years old at the time, had made his significant contributions to the field many years earlier.

During his tenure at the University of Manchester, Newman was adamant about running the mathematics department as efficiently as possible. He rigorously oversaw course curriculum and teaching assignments and he introduced a system that required the entire faculty of the department to carefully examine all proposed test questions, along with the corresponding model answers. Measures such as these won both Newman and his department a great deal of respect among his fellow scholars. Newman remained on the faculty at the University of Manchester until his retirement, in 1964.

After he gave up his post at the University of Manchester, Newman two years teaching at the Australian National University, and one year as a visiting professor at Rice University in Houston, Texas. In 1968 he was given an honorary D.Sc. degree by the University of Hull, and in 1973 he was elected to an honorary fellowship at St. John's College. Newman had married Lyn Irvine, a successful writer, in 1934, and they had two sons, Edward and William. She died in 1973, and later that same year Newman was remarried to Margaret Penrose. Maxwell Herman Alexander Newman died on February 22, 1984 at his home in Comberton near Cambridge, in Cambridgeshire, England.

Newman received numerous awards for the work he conducted in mathematics during his years at the University of Manchester, including the Sylvester Medal from the Royal Society in 1968. Newman was president of the London Mathematical Society from 1950 to 1952, and he was presented with the society's De Morgan Medal in 1962. In a tribute to Newman on that occasion, Society President Mary Cartwright said: "His early work on Combinatory Topology has exercised a decisive influence on the development of that subject." Newman was a fellow of the Royal Society from 1939 until his death. A noted researcher who published papers on the subject of mathematics throughout his life, Newman was also an accomplished pianist.—D. B.

Suggested Reading: *St. Andrew's University* (online); Lee, J. A. N., ed. *International Biographical Dictionary of Computer Pioneers*, 1995; *International Who's Who*, 1983–84; *Larousse Dictionary of Scientists*, vol. 1, 1994; *Who's Who in Science*, 1968

Noorda, Raymond

June 19, 1924– Computer-services executive; entrepreneur

During the course of turning Novell from a dying computer manufacturer into the most powerful network software company in the world, Raymond Noorda was instrumental in making local area networks a fixture of the business community. Noorda realized before most others that compatibility within and between computer systems was essential, and his vision of "co-opetition"—his term for working with competitors to establish standardization—helped make Novell's NetWare one of the most ubiquitous software packages in computing. Despite his success, Noorda presents a friendly, down-to-earth persona. For years, while his stocks skyrocketed, Noorda drove a pick-up truck to Novell's headquarters in Utah and avoided eating in restaurants because he considered it a waste of money. "Ray presents himself as a very down-home, fatherly, 'can I have a bite of your apple,' kind of guy," a business associate of Noorda's recalled to Lawrence M. Fisher for the *New York Times* (March 29, 1992), "but he's very smart, a true visionary." Beginning in the early 1990s, Noorda was one of the few willing to challenge the power of Bill Gates's Microsoft Corporation: In the name of maintaining competition in the computer world, Noorda challenged Gates repeatedly, including filing a lawsuit and providing crucial information for the federal government's investigation of Microsoft's business practices. Since leaving Novell in 1994, Noorda has continued to be active in funding and running new companies.

Raymond Noorda was born on June 19, 1924 in Ogden, Utah. His parents were Dutch immigrants who had settled in the American West in the 1890s; neither was educated beyond the fifth grade; his father had two jobs, as a stock clerk and a janitor, and normally worked 16 hours a day. Noorda served in the U.S. Navy during World War II, after which he earned a B.S. in electrical engineering. Around 1949 he went to work in the computer department of General Electric. Later, as an executive at Boschert Inc., a power-supply system manufacturer, Noorda helped improve the company financially before selling it in 1981.

Noorda's influential reign at the helm of Novell began in 1982. The ailing company, then known as Novell Data Systems, was unable to afford a booth at Comdex, the computer industry's major trade show, held in Las Vegas, Nevada; executives had instead rented a nearby hotel room to showcase their wares. Noorda dropped by, and he was impressed with Novell's fledgling network software, despite the fact that Novell was primarily a personal-computer hardware company. Soon Noorda signed on as the president of the firm. He immediately phased out the hardware department to focus on Novell's network software, which, he felt, offered the promise of great expansion. The network software was called NetWare, and it offered one of the first ways to hook together a group of personal computers in order to share peripheral devices, such as printers and hard drives. Thanks to Net-Ware, Novell began to grow, steadily acquiring other companies that might complement the larger goal of expanding into the field of computer networking. In November 1985 Novell bought Microsource to help distribute its products; in May 1986 it bought another distributor, Cache Data Products; in March 1987 Novell acquired CXI, which specialized in connecting IBM mainframes; in June 1988 it bought Dayna Communications, which specialized in Macintosh computer connections.

In 1989 Novell released NetWare 386, a new, more powerful version of NetWare that allowed users to incorporate not only IBM-compatible hardware into their networks, but also Apple's Macintosh OS and Unix, two operating systems that were becoming increasingly popular. NetWare 386 was a flexible way to control the flow of data between previously incompatible computers. Aware that his business depended on making the various parts of computer systems and networks work together, Noorda developed his practice of cooperating with competitors, or "co-opetition," as he called it. "Today the customers demand that everything has to work together," Noorda told Louise Kehoe and Geof Wheelwright for the *Financial Times* (September 11, 1993). "That means that everyone in the computer industry has to work together. We have tried to make a successful business out of working with companies who would otherwise be called our competitors."

One of the most important aspects of Noorda's strategy was employing a huge number of "value-added resellers" (VARs), or independent distributors, to whom Novell provided free instruction on installing and maintaining its products. Novell recruited more than 13,000 VARs. Noorda also worked with "original equipment manufacturers" (OEMs), who were licensed to repackage Novell's products under their own company names. Novell even purposely left holes in their product lines so that other companies would seize upon the opportunities to develop products compatible with Novell's and, in so doing, market Novell's products by extension. "To begin with," Noorda explained to Fisher, "our aim was NetWare somewhere—just get it sold. Then it was NetWare everywhere—distribute it broadly. Then we said it has to be Net-Ware anywhere, so we'll sell it through a lot of O.E.M.'s. Now we say it has to be almost invisible, so people buy it out of necessity—NetWare underwear."

For a while it seemed that even the computer software giant Microsoft might slip into NetWare underwear: Late in 1989 Microsoft's CEO, Bill Gates, contacted Noorda about a possible merger between Novell and Microsoft and floated a proposal to buy Novell for $2 billion. Then, in early 1990, Gates abruptly broke off negotiations. Microsoft had also entered into an agreement with IBM in 1989 to market an alternative to NetWare called LAN Manager, which worked in conjunction with

IBM's OS/2 operating system. Angry at the rebuff, Noorda suggested that Gates had proposed the merger only to extract networking secrets from Novell.

LAN Manager, however, failed to compete with NetWare. Noorda had succeeded in winning support for his flagship product by cultivating a host of unaffiliated companies dependent on NetWare for their businesses. Then, in 1991, Novell announced its decision to buy Digital Research Inc., a software company that produced an operating system called DR DOS. DR DOS was a competitor of Microsoft's popular MS-DOS operating system; two days later Gates approached Noorda to reinstate their merger plans. With a possible $15 billion now at stake, Noorda participated in the talks before backing out in March 1992, after he learned that Gates, without telling him, had made plans to buy the database maker Fox Software Inc.

Since 1989, the Federal Trade Commission (FTC) had been investigating Gates's empire as a possible monopoly. The investigation, however, did not become serious until 1992, when Novell began to supply the FTC with new evidence against Microsoft. Gates and Noorda became archenemies. Kehoe and Wheelwright quoted the two combatants in the *Financial Times*. Gates remarked: "[Noorda] has a tremendous vendetta against us. Novell has made a conscious decision to spread lies about us." "In my more than 40 years in the industry," Noorda said, "I have not met a bunch like [Microsoft executives]. They are possessive, aggressive, and strong challengers, but they are afraid of head-on competition and that is anathema to me."

Novell continued to compete well in the networking market. In fact, by 1993 it owned more than 70 percent of the world's networking software market. Noorda had acquired 15 smaller companies since taking over Novell, and the company's earnings had grown between 35 percent and 153 percent each year since going public in 1985. This did not prevent Noorda from maintaining his characteristic thriftiness. He continued to insist on flying stand-by in order to get his senior ticket discount, and, after his two sons began working at Novell, he dropped his own salary from $90,000 per year to $40,000. (Novell board members later insisted he raise his salary to $198,000 after some market analysts publicly questioned Noorda's commitment to the company based on his low salary.) Later in 1993, however, Noorda regretted his aggressive stance towards Microsoft, which unveiled a new operating system, Windows NT, that had built-in networking software similar in function and breadth of application to NetWare. Microsoft's position as the primary provider of PC operating systems meant that if they could get vendors to carry Windows NT, the need for NetWare might be circumvented.

Noorda bought Unix Systems Laboratories (USL) from AT&T in June 1993. Like Windows NT, Unix was a desktop operating system with built-in networking capabilities. Popular among scientists and academics, it had yet to become a huge commercial success, owing in part to issues with compatibility. In the interest of spreading the Unix technology, Noorda soon gave the rights to the Unix name to an industry consortium.

NetWare 4, the new version of NetWare, was released in the fall of 1993. It differed from the previous version in several respects, and many companies were reluctant to install the new software in their systems for fear that it would be too big of a modification. Reviewing the new software in *Info-World* (October 4, 1993), Les Kent wrote, "The advantage of 4's powerful new global naming service and wonderfully efficient mass-storage system are considerable. But to enjoy these and other benefits offered by NetWare 4, network managers will have to pay their dues through extensive planning plus saintly patience while the application developers catch up to Novell's innovations."

Noorda, at 69, began to have problems with memory loss. Sometimes he was unable to recognize people he had worked with at Novell for years, but he refused to step down from his post. "What's this word? Death? Retire? Expire?" Noorda told Kathy Rebello for *Business Week* (November 22, 1993). "I tell them I'll probably expire before I retire." In March 1994 Noorda orchestrated a major deal to buy the WordPerfect Corporation for $1.4 billion. As Don Clark wrote for *Wall Street Journal* (January 15, 1996, on-line) "Mr. Noorda's concept was to meld WordPerfect's popular word processor and other programs with Novell's operating systems, a business model similar to Microsoft's. It might have worked—if executed perfectly." But the combination of competition from Windows NT, the expenditure of acquiring USL and WordPerfect, and the unwieldiness of NetWare 4, began to take its toll on Novell. The stock plunged, and by the spring of 1994 Noorda's own holdings had dropped by 44 percent from more than $1 billion to about $568 million. Noorda stepped aside on April 5, 1994, naming Robert J. Frankenberg, a former Hewlett Packard executive, as the new CEO of Novell.

After leaving Novell, Noorda immediately embarked on a series of business ventures. The first was called Caldera Systems, the seed of which had been planted in 1993 when two Novell employees approached Noorda with a business plan for an operating system that incorporated the graphic interface of the Internet. In 2000 Caldera Systems went public, offering five million shares. Noorda also owns Caldera Inc., the home of the DR DOS operating system, which he acquired from Novell. In 1996 Caldera filed a lawsuit against Microsoft, claiming that the company entered into illegal licensing agreements with computer makers to use MS-DOS to the exclusion of DR DOS. The suit was settled out of court for a reported $275 million in January 2000, while Microsoft was also in the midst of an ongoing federal lawsuit.

In the summer of 1995 Noorda formed Canopy Technologies Inc., a company that provided aid to new computer start-ups. One of Noorda's most recent ventures, founded by his Canopy Group, is an e-business service provider called Center 7, which officially launched on June 12, 2000.

Noorda, a practicing Mormon, currently lives in Utah with his wife.—P. G .H.

Suggested Reading: *BusinessWeek* p28+ Jan. 11, 1993, with photo; p124+ Sep. 27, 1993, with photo; p93+ Nov. 22, 1993, with photos; *Computer Reseller News* p100 June 26, 2000; *Financial Times* p8 Sep. 11, 1993; *Forbes* p106+ Mar. 1, 1993; p376 Oct. 13, 1997; *InfoWorld* p57+ Oct. 4, 1993, with photo; *Network World* p1+ Dec. 11, 1989, with photo; *New York Times* III p1 Mar. 29, 1992, with photo, I p39 Nov. 13, 1993; *Wall Street Journal* B p5 June 20, 1995, A p3 Jan. 11, 2000, B p6 Mar. 9, 2000

Norton, Peter

1943– Computer-software pioneer

The computer programmer and entrepreneur Peter Norton is the creator of Norton Utilities, a series of software programs that improves the performance of personal computers (PCs). On the strength of his flagship program, UnErase, which permitted the restoration of deleted computer files, Norton founded his own company, Peter Norton Computing, in Santa Monica, California, in 1982. His programs, which were the first popular set of utilities for the PC, proved so helpful in overcoming the difficulties and frustrations that commonly arise through computer and human error that Norton came to be touted as "the quintessential good guy of personal computing," as Richard O'Reilly wrote for the *Los Angeles Times* (February 2, 1989).

Peter Norton was born in 1943 in Aberdeen, Washington. He grew up in Seattle, in "a real white-bread, white-picket fence, Ozzie-and-Harriet type of family," he told Bettijane Levine for the *Los Angeles Times* (June 12, 1994). His father was an insurance sales executive, and his mother was a homemaker. Norton was a lonely child with very few friends. He had a distant relationship with his brother, older by two years, who was athletic and popular—attributes Norton lacked. His favorite activities were reading science fiction and riding aimlessly on his bicycle for hours. In high school, he recalled to Kathleen K. Wiegner for *Forbes* (October 19, 1992), "I had my head stuck in a book. I was very self-absorbed."

Norton studied math and physics at Reed College in Portland, Oregon. During his college summers he worked for an actuarial firm, where he learned computer programming. "They showed me a new IBM 1620, threw the manual at me and said, 'Here it is,'" he recalled to Wiegner. "Luckily I took to it like a duck to water." The computer was from the "pre-interrupt generation of machines," Norton explained to David Owen for the *New Yorker* (January 30, 1995). "That means that when anything went wrong, the whole thing just stopped." Norton studied the problem and devised "a little program that would sneak itself into a part of memory that wasn't being used, and when the machine crashed, my program would track down the information that the programmer would otherwise have to figure out from the dials and the flashing lights, and print it out." Norton offered the helpful program to anyone who wanted it, and soon he was receiving letters of appreciation from as far away as Argentina.

Norton dropped out of college midway through his senior year and was subsequently hired by Boeing as a junior engineer. As Owen reported, Norton was drafted into the army at the time that the Vietnam War was escalating—as a conscientious objector; he trained as a noncombatant medical corpsman. The army had a shortage of medical instructors at the time, however, so he spent the remainder of his two-year service training new draftees in the skills he had just learned.

After his release he decided to finish his schooling and earned a bachelor's degree in math from the University of California at Berkeley in 1969. He subsequently drifted through several computer-related jobs, but feeling alone and spiritually unfulfilled, he entered a Zen Monastery in Northern California in 1971. Ultimately unsatisfied with the experience, he left the monastery after about five years and relocated to Los Angeles. He worked as a computer programmer in several venues over the next two years. He then treated himself to a year-long trip around the world, after which he returned to Los Angeles, wanting to work in computers but with no clear idea of the direction his career should take.

In 1981 when International Business Machines (IBM) unveiled a new PC, Norton bought one and wrote experimental programs for it, mostly for his own amusement. One of his creations was an early version of UnErase, the program that makes it possible to retrieve deleted files. UnErase works because a PC does not physically erase a file when it is deleted. Instead, the name of a file is erased from the directory, rendering the data inaccessible. Since the old file is stored physically on the disk—until a new file overwrites the old data—Norton's program could search the disk sector by sector to find it. "Erasing a file is somewhat like throwing valuables into a trash can," the UnErase user's manual explained, as quoted by Lawrence J. Magid for the *Los Angeles Times* (August 26, 1985). "If we're lucky, we can still find what we lost by digging through the trash."

Norton began by selling UnErase and other programs through word of mouth and through small ads in a newsletter he wrote and distributed for free. Things moved slowly at first but after a few years business began to pick up as the usefulness of Norton's programs became more widely known.

Also around that time Norton began writing guides for computer users, including *Inside the IBM PC* (1983) and *MS-DOS and PC DOS: User's Guide* (1984). His books bolstered his growing popularity, and "remain models of expository clarity," according to David Owen. Norton's marketing sense—and his awareness that new computer users were often intimidated and perplexed by their machines—contributed to his success. When naming his company he chose to avoid such "big, important-sounding" names as Oracle, which were "intended to hide the fact that this was really just two guys in a garage," as well the "sophomoric" names such as Intergalactic Digital Research, opting instead for the more modest and personable-sounding Peter Norton Computing Inc. On each of his products he placed a photograph of himself, looking hardworking and friendly—no jacket, loosened tie, arms crossed with the sleeves rolled up, and wearing a confident smile.

In addition to UnErase, the Norton Utilities package included such programs as DiskLook, which analyzed the configuration of data on a disk and presented the layout to the user; WipeDisk, which allowed privacy-concerned users to permanently erase files on a disk; and SpeedDisk, which reorganized the disk for greater efficiency, grouping similar files and data into one location. Another popular program that was developed later was the Norton Disk Doctor, which repaired malfunctions and fixed program glitches that might otherwise render a floppy or hard disk useless. The original Norton Utilities were developed to run on IBM PCs and compatible machines that used the Disk Operating System (DOS) but later programs were engineered to run on Macintosh and Unix systems as well.

Peter Norton Computing reported sales of $15 million for 1988 and that year was ranked 30th on a list of the 100 largest software companies. The escalating popularity of his programs had earned Norton a reputation as a "software saint," according to Carla Lazzareschi, writing for the *Los Angeles Times* (May 1, 1989). "His program established the category of what we now know as PC utility programs," the market analyst Steward Alsop told Lazzareschi. "These programs overcome the shortcomings of computers, and his overcomes the biggest shortcoming of them all: the loss of your work. . . . He is an enormously respected figure in the business."

Although Norton's company was successful and growing strong, he decided that it was time to ease himself out of the business. In April 1989 Ronald Posner became the new chief executive, and Norton assumed the role of company chairman. "I'm not an executive and never was," Norton told Lazzareschi. "My company has outgrown my management ability." With his personal wealth estimated at between $200 million and $400 million, Norton decided to call off "the money acquisition phase" of his life, as he explained to Levine.

In 1990 Symantec Corporation of Cupertino, California, acquired Peter Norton Computing for $70 million. Norton became Symantec's largest shareholder as a result of the deal, with 30 of the company's stock. His name and face remained in use on Norton products for several years, for which he received royalties.

Since that time, Norton and his wife, Eileen, whom he met when they both placed personal ads in the same issue of the singles magazine *Intro*, have devoted their energy and their wealth to various philanthropic causes. In addition to establishing the Norton Family Foundation to benefit cultural and humanitarian causes, they are significant collectors of contemporary American art. They are highly appreciated among the art community both for their large contributions to museums and art institutions—which have included a series of $50,000 grants to curators to expand their museums' permanent collections—as well as for their generous patronage of emerging avant-garde artists. "The Nortons are America's model millionaires," David Ross, director of the Whitney Museum of American Art in New York, told Levine. "If

this country had even a few more like them, we'd be in a better place." Although the Nortons are sometimes criticized for their lack of artistic taste, Norton explained to Levine that he remains unfazed: "I spent my life doing what I'm good at—computer science. It's more interesting to do what I'm not particularly good at, what I must struggle with and may even be incompetent at."

The Nortons live in Santa Monica, California, with their two children, Diana and Michael. He is a director of Acorn Technologies and serves on the board of directors of the California Institute for the Arts, Reed College, Crossroads School, Signature Theatre Company, the Los Angeles County Museum of Art, and the Museum of Modern Art. He occasionally uses his wealth for more personal interests—in 1996 he paid a six-figure sum to become the lord of William Shakespeare's hometown, Stratford-on-Avon, England.—A. I. C.

Suggested Reading: *Forbes* p272 Oct. 19, 1992; *Los Angeles Times* IV p3 Feb. 2, 1989, E p1 June 12, 1994, IV p3 Aug. 26, 1985, IV p1 May 1, 1989, with photo; *New Yorker* p36+ Jan. 30, 1995, with photo

Noyce, Robert

Dec. 12, 1927– June 3, 1990 Co-inventor of the integrated circuit

Throughout his life, Robert N. Noyce exhibited the kind of diverse talents which would earn him a reputation as a modern-day Renaissance man. He excelled in engineering, athletics, philanthropic activities, and made shrewd business decisions which earned him a personal fortune with the corporations he ran from the 1960s through the 1980s. For all of his eclectic achievements, however, there is one creation whose name will be forever linked with his own: the microchip. Using metal strips and silicon, Noyce was one of the first inventors to create an integrated circuit, later known as the microchip. He secured a patent for his creation in 1959 and in the process helped set the booming computer industry in motion with the miniaturization of electronics. In the course of the next two decades, once monstrous computing machines would be, with the help of Noyce's technology, reduced to the compact-size personal computers now used on a daily basis. Noyce's company, Intel, would further enhance computer capabilities with its work on data storage, and continues to build on the microchip's capabilities today.

The son of a minister, Robert Noyce was born in Burlington, Iowa, on December 12, 1927. He grew up in the small college town of Grinnell, Iowa, a curious boy with a penchant for conducting experiments with whatever sources he had available. He had his own workshop in his parents' basement, and he would often create new objects out of the

remains of discarded parts found in a local junkyard. One such invention involved the merging of his bicycle with the engine from an old washing machine. Another involved a primitive chemistry experiment that resulted in the creation of nitroglycerine.

By the time he entered high school, it was obvious to Noyce and his parents that he had a natural inclination toward math and the sciences. Grant Gale, a family friend who taught physics at nearby Grinnell College, was impressed by the young scientist's early interest in the subjects and invited him to take a freshman physics course at the college. After graduating from high school in 1945, Noyce decided to enroll at Grinnell full-time as a physics major. It was during these years as an undergraduate that Noyce began to display his true flair for engaging in diverse activities with an equal amount of passion and talent. In addition to thriving in his physics studies, he excelled as a diver on the college swim team, winning the Midwest Conference championship in 1947. He also dabbled in the arts and had an ongoing role on a radio soap opera. Noyce's passion for fun almost cost him his college career when, in the spring of 1948, he and another student stole a pig for a Hawaiian luau. The influence of Gale and Noyce's father, however, prevented the young collegian from spending any time in jail, but before he was permitted to graduate in 1949, he was forced to sit out a semester, during which time he worked as an actuary for Equitable Life in New York City.

College solidified Noyce's interest in electronics, and he continued working on his inventions. He was particularly captivated by the sight of one of the first transistors, which Gale brought into his classroom courtesy of his good friend John Bardeen, who had helped to invent the transistor in late 1947. Noyce began to perform experiments using transistors and even built his own solid-state transistor in 1948, but when he arrived at the Massachusetts Institute of Technology, in Cambridge, to pursue graduate work on the topic, he found to his dismay that there was no overwhelming student desire in transistor technology and no available courses in the subject. Not easily dissuaded, Noyce pursued the subject independently and was awarded his doctorate degree in physics, in 1953.

As the industry began to spark, Noyce found himself on the receiving end of a great number of job offers from electronics firms, including Bell Laboratories, RCA, and IBM. Because of its new semiconductor unit, he ultimately chose Philco, a company located in Philadelphia, Pennsylvania. He worked for the company's transistor division for almost three years but became disenchanted with Philco's lack of interest in his research work and sought other employment. His future opened up to him in the form of William Shockley, co-inventor of the transistor, who approached Noyce about coming to California to interview for his company. Shockley had just established a new firm to develop high performance transistors in an area that would later become known as Silicon Valley.

In January 1956 he joined the Shockley Semiconductor Laboratory as a research engineer, hoping to work in the development of silicon semiconductors. He soon realized however, that the trend of the day was toward the study of germanium-based semiconductors. He did not approve of Shockley's focus on these devices, which he felt were inferior to transistors as semiconductor devices. Noyce and a growing number of other employees also became dissatisfied with Shockley's searches for the sources of supposed "conspiracies," which delayed production. In the spring of 1957, a group of eight engineers, including Noyce, went to the company's financier and asked for Shockley to be removed from his management duties. When the financier balked at such a request (Shockley, along with Bardeen, had just won the Nobel Prize in Physics in 1956), the group of men, later dubbed the "traitorous eight" by Shockley, left their jobs and signed an agreement with Fairchild Camera and Instrument to finance a new company, Fairchild Semiconductor. The group unanimously chose the 29-year-old Noyce to head the team.

Fairchild Semiconductor opened its doors just 12 blocks away from the group's previous building of employment, and the competition accelerated between the only two semiconductor companies in Silicon Valley at the time. Tension also mounted with the presence of the space race. The successful Soviet launching of Sputnik occurred in 1957, and U.S. manufacturers began to crave smaller electronics, meaning fewer vacuum tubes and more transistors. In order to keep pace with the Soviets, the U.S. government began to significantly increase its funding for research projects. Specifically, the government needed computers small enough to fit on board rockets, and since a good deal of electronics was necessary to run these computers, those electronics had to be miniaturized.

Although Fairchild had been producing silicon transistors since 1958, there were still many kinks in the system. Transistors were made by having workers create a number of connections on a single wafer and then cutting that wafer into smaller pieces, which would eventually have to be rewired. This process was laden with errors and waste and limited any complexity that could be added to the circuits. In addition, the presence of any kind of substance, from dust to a small amount of gas, could cause the transistor to stop working. Fairchild solved this dilemma when an employee, Jean Hoerni, discovered that a layer of silicon oxide, applied to the top of the N-P-N chip, would cling to the silicon and protect it from contaminants. The company labeled it the "planar" process, and Noyce, after consulting attorneys about a patent, was encouraged to find other electronic uses for the new invention. It was during this time, in early 1959, that Noyce began to formulate what would later be called "the Monolithic Idea": the notion that if one transistor could be made by placing a few small wires on a tiny piece of silicon, then it might be possible to create a complete electronic system (including elements such as transistors and resistors) on that same small silicon chip. In this way, the problem of having to physically connect electronic circuitry could be eradicated, while lowering the cost to put together the necessary components for a computer system. In an interview with Robert Slater for his *Portraits in Silicon* (1987), Noyce said he wrote in his notebook, "It would be desirable to make multiple devices on a single piece of silicon, in order to be able to make interconnections between devices as part of the manufacturing process, and thus reduce size, weight, etc., as well as cost per active element." This idea would eventually evolve into a device called an integrated circuit (IC), the forerunner of the microchip, the component that helped revolutionize home computing.

The initial theology of the IC was formulated, but there were still obstacles to overcome, namely the connecting of big wires to the tiny regions of the N-P-N transistor. (N-P-N refers to the type of semiconductor materials and their electrical properties, in this case a P-type material sandwiched by N-type material.) Noyce hypothesized that the planer process could be utilized to make such precise connections. He concluded that by using Hoerni's oxide spread on top of the silicon, the large wires could be pushed through to their precise connection on the chip, with the oxide holding them in place. This idea led Noyce to discover that instead of wires, he could use tiny lines of metal in the oxide to connect separate areas of a transistor. Furthermore, two transistors, as well as other circuit components, could be placed on one piece of silicon using this method. When Noyce pieced together all of these conclusions, he essentially created the integrated circuit and paved the way for the miniaturization of electronics.

Noyce was not the first person to come up with the method destined to serve as the backbone technology of the IC, however. In July 1958 Jack Kilby, an engineer from Texas Instruments, wrote in his notebook the essential concepts behind the Monolithic Idea but employed germanium instead of silicon in his IC. Yet because not all of the problems had been worked out, Kilby's ICs were unmarketable until Noyce introduced the idea of using silicon, which gave the IC better conductivity. Neither man knew of the other's work on ICs at the time, and the two companies (Fairchild and Texas Instruments) would engage in a decade-long legal battle over patent rights. The case was settled in 1969, with a cross-licensing of the two companies' technologies, and with both men receiving credit as co-inventor. Still, the inventors' methods on the road to discovery were vastly different, and Noyce would later comment to Slater that Kilby's work was "really more of a brute-force approach, of taking a piece of semiconductor and shaping it so that there'd be the areas that were resistors and then putting wiring from one area to another, still doing a lot of hand wiring." Despite the court ruling, Noyce is often cited as the inventor behind the technology that makes up the modern integrated circuit.

Noyce's new chip, later coined the microchip, set off a revolution in electronics almost immediately after it was produced. Once hulking machines that took up the entire space of a room, computers could now be fitted with the first miniature electronic components, providing companies with simpler as well as more cost-effective systems. Noyce's invention caught the eye of NASA, which chose Fairchild's new technology for the spacecraft used in the Gemini astronaut program. Further strides were made when the first commercially sold integrated circuit was used in a hearing aid in 1964. Although Texas Instruments eventually became the largest microchip manufacturer, it was Noyce who was credited with jump-starting the industry. With product demand steadily increasing throughout the 1960s, Fairchild began to emerge as a $150 million a year business. The microchip itself also underwent renovation as technology expanded, with the chip Noyce invented in 1959 capable of holding 10 circuits by 1964 and 1,000 circuits only five years later. Fairchild's work during this period would have long-reaching effects on the computer industry, but Noyce would later comment that the company did not foresee the future impact of its work: "We were really working day to day to try to get a competitive edge on competitors, and not really looking out at the next decade, but rather the next year."

By 1968 Noyce was the owner of 12 separate integrated circuit and transistor patents. He had begun his career at Fairchild as director of research and development, and by 1959 had become vice president and general manager of the company. In ten years the firm grew from eight employees and revenues of only a few thousand dollars a year, to over 12,000 employees and revenues upwards of $130 million. In late 1968, however, with semiconductor spin-off companies continually popping up around him, Noyce decided to leave Fairchild and start his own business. Joined by Gordon Moore, another member of the "Traitorous Eight" who had defected to Fairchild, Noyce founded Intel Corporation. Noyce did not want to try to compete with Fairchild by focusing on semiconductors, so the company centered its attention on a little-explored area of computing: data storage. The decision to take on this new, challenging field of technology was, Noyce claims, a simple one to make. "It was a fertile field out in front of me, which wasn't being addressed in a very aggressive manner by Fairchild or anybody else," he once remarked.

In 1970 Intel produced the 1103 random access chip, which stored information on silicon and polysilicon, and which proved to be much more cost-effective than any chip previously manufactured. This new chip brought electronics to yet another level of miniaturization and became the core foundation of computer developments during the 1970s. During that time, the company also developed the world's first microprocessor, or a processor contained on an IC chip.

Noyce stated from an early age that he believed in simplifying tasks as much as possible, and he approached his research in the same manner. Inventors like himself, he once asserted, were essentially lazy people trying to find an easier way to do things. As he moved into managerial positions, first at Fairchild and then at Intel, this attitude was reflected in the style in which the companies were run. Simplicity and efficiency were the desired characteristics of his working atmosphere. Rather than having luxurious offices, executives were given cubbyholes, and Noyce walked around the building with a name tag like everyone else. It was, for many, a welcome departure from the highly divisional nature of big business, and it came to be known as the "Intel culture."

Intel's sales skyrocketed during the next decade, but Noyce turned over the day-to-day running of the company to Gordon Moore in 1974, deciding to take on diverse roles within the Silicon Valley area. He became the community's unofficial spokesperson, earning him the appreciative title Mayor of Silicon Valley, and served as the chairman of the Semiconductor Industry Association in the later part of the 1970s. Intel, meanwhile, of which Noyce became chairman of the board, continued to accrue millions in sales per annum, reaching $1.3 billion by 1985. Technology also blossomed, as the company's original chip, capable of holding 8,000 characters of information, developed only a decade later into a chip that could contain a quarter of a million characters.

In 1988, as the U.S. began to lose substantial chip market share to Japanese competitors, Noyce was named CEO of Sematech, a government-industry consortium of semiconductor firms designed to perform the research and development needed to advance U.S. competitiveness. He continued to promote public support of Silicon Valley's industry by making speeches and appearing before the U.S. International Trade Commission to discuss tariffs on the Japanese telecommunications industry. On June 3, 1990, at the age of 62, Robert Noyce died unexpectedly of a heart attack.

A slender man with a square jaw and curly hair, Robert N. Noyce was the recipient of numerous awards and honors during his distinguished career, including the National Medal of Science in 1980. He was inducted into the National Inventors Hall of Fame in 1983 and was given the National Medal of Technology by President Reagan in 1987. Noyce was married for 21 years to Elizabeth Bottomley, with whom he had four children, William, Pendred, Priscilla, and Margaret. He and Elizabeth divorced in 1974, and in 1975 he married Ann Bowers, Intel's former personnel director.

A strong believer in giving back to one's community, Noyce enjoyed many other roles outside the semiconductor industry. He served as a regent at the University of California, and in 1970 he and his wife (who would later live her life as a beloved philanthropist in Maine) formed a charitable organization called the Irving Foundation. Noyce's memory was preserved by his alma matter, Grinnell College, when it established the Robert N. Noyce Senior Student Award, which has been given annually since 1984 to students who make the greatest contribution to computer-based technology.—D. B.

Suggested Reading: *Byte* p135 Sep. 1995, with photo; *Electronics* p4 July 1990; *Fortune* p132+, with photo; *Portland Press Herald* Sep. 22, 1996; *Technology Review* p20+ Jan. 1988; *Virginia Polytechnic Institute and State University* (online); *Vital Speeches of the Day* p671+ Aug. 15, 1989; *Dictionary of Scientific Biography*, vol 13, 1976; *Larousse Dictionary of Scientists*, vol 1, 1994; Slater, Robert. *Portraits in Silicon*, 1987; *Who's Who in Science*, 1968

Nygaard, Kristen

Aug. 27, 1926–Aug. 9, 2002 Computer scientist; developer of Simula

The Norwegian computer scientist Kristen Nygaard developed SIMULA I and Simula 67, the first object-oriented computer languages. Created jointly by Nygaard and his colleague Ole-Johan Dahl at the Norwegian Computing Center in Oslo, Norway, during the 1960s, the two languages provided programmers with powerful new tools to model the behavior of complex systems. Although Simula itself was never widely adopted, it initiated the field of object-oriented programing (OOP), introducing such important concepts as classes, objects, and inheritance. In California, at Xerox's Palo Alto Research Center (PARC) during the 1970s, Alan Kay used Simula as a platform for the development of Smalltalk, the first computer language used to create a graphical user interface (GUI)—which was adopted with great success by both Macintosh operating system software and Microsoft Windows. C++, which is now the major commercial OOP language, was the result of incorporating key components of Simula into the C programming language. One of the most popularly known OOP languages is Java, developed by Sun Microsystems. Java is now widely used on Internet servers, although frequently presented to Web users as "Java applets," which refers to a Java programs that run from within a Web page.

Kristen Nygaard was born on August 27, 1926 in Oslo, Norway. He received his master's degree in mathematics from the University of Oslo in 1956.

Nygaard was employed at the Norwegian Defense Research Establishment (NDRE) from 1948 to 1960, working primarily on computers, programming, and operational research. He joined the Norwegian Computing Center in 1960, and in 1962 he became its director of research. His earlier work in operational research revealed the need for better tools to make computer simulations. In "The History of Simula" (1995), an article accessible on Nygaard's personal Web site, Jan Rune Holmevik explained that Nygaard was "encouraged by the promising prospects of computer-aided simulation, . . . [and] soon started to think conceptually about how he could formalize the procedures for systems description in a way that would allow standardized concepts to be easily processed by a computer." Nygaard had attained some familiarity with computer programming while at the NDRE before being assigned to operations research in 1952, but he realized that greater expertise would be required to implement his ideas. He initiated a series of discussions with a former acquaintance from NDRE, Ole-Johan Dahl, which led to the development of SIMULA I (SIMUlation LAnguage).

First proposed in 1962, SIMULA I was completed in January 1965; Simula 67 followed two years later. SIMULA I was primarily a simulation programming language, but Simula 67 was engineered as a general programming language. They were the first object-oriented programming languages, although the term "object-oriented" was actually first used by Alan Kay years later, when using Simula to develop his Smalltalk language.

OOP language improved upon procedural programming language because it allowed programmers to treat data structures—files, lists, data trees, tables, etc.—as "objects." As such they contained both the data and the information for processing that data, which meant that "classes" of objects could then be created. In a program to determine payroll, for example, a class could be designated Employee; individual employees (e.g., Mary or Joe) would be particular instances, or "objects," of that class. This feature is called "encapsulation." OOP also introduced the concept of "inheritance," which makes it possible to structure classes into hierarchies. In the example above, the Employee class could be divided into subclasses of Manager, Secretary, and Clerk. The class of Employee contains the data and processing that apply to all subclasses, and the subclasses contain only the information pertinent to that particular job. This arrangement greatly reduces the amount of programming required when adding new functions, as changes made at the top of a hierarchy modify all the subclasses, and new subclasses can be added that inherit the features of the existing classes.

Following his work on Simula 67, Nygaard did research for Norwegian trade unions on planning, control, and data processing to assist the objectives of organized labor. He was a professor at Aarhus University, in Denmark, during 1975–76, after which he returned to Norway to accept a professorship at the University of Oslo. He performed research on the social impact of computer technology and developed the general system description language DELTA and the programming language BETA. He was involved in committees on environmental protection and trade unions, and was long active in Norwegian politics. In the early 1990s he served as the chairman of Nei til EU (No to EU), an organization that led the opposition to Norway's European Union membership.

Nygaard was the recipient of numerous awards and honors. In 1992 *Computerworld* awarded him its honorary prize for "having made Norway known internationally in the information technology field," as quoted on Nygaard's personal Web site. The king of Norway awarded him the honorary title Commander of the Order of Saint Olav in August 2000. In 2001 he received, with Ole-Johan Dahl, the John von Neumann Medal from the Institute of Electrical and Electronic Engineers (IEEE), for "the introduction of the concepts underlying object-oriented programming through the design and implementation of Simula 67." Nygaard and Dahl also shared the 2001 A. M. Turing Award from the Association of Computing Machinery.

Nygaard was a professor emeritus at the University of Oslo, a consultant at the Norwegian Computer Center, and a visiting professor emeritus at the Simula Research Laboratory. He married his wife, Johanna, in 1951; they have three children and seven grandchildren. On August 9, 2002 Nygaard died of a heart attack in Oslo.—A. I. C.

Suggested Reading: Lee, J.A.N., ed. *International Biographical Dictionary of Computer Pioneers*, 1995; Waldrop, Mitchell M. *The Dream Machine: J. C. R. Licklider and the Revolution That Made Computing Personal*, 2001

Odhner, Willgodt Theophil

1845–1905 Inventor of the Odhner calculator

The Swedish engineer and industrialist Willgodt Theophil Odhner invented a mechanical calculator in the 1870s that made use of an innovative pinwheel mechanism. Odhner's design became very popular, eventually replacing the Arithmometer—which had been designed by Thomas de Colmar in the 1820s—as the dominant calculating machine of the time. Numerous manufacturers adopted Odhner's design, which continued to be produced well into the 20th century.

Odhner, who was born in 1845, built his contribution to calculating history on the foundations of earlier luminaries. The first widely noted mechanical adding machine was the Pascaline, built by the French mathematician Blaise Pascal in 1642. Housed in a brass rectangular box, the Pascaline had a set of wheels that were notched in such a way that a full rotation of one wheel moved the adjacent wheel one 10th of a rotation. The machine was built to perform addition; subtraction required a lengthy and complicated process. Although Pascal's invention attracted a lot of attention, it never came into common usage as it was expensive, unreliable, and somewhat difficult to operate. The 17th-century philosopher Gottfried Wilhelm von Leibniz improved upon Pascal's design in 1672 with a machine he called the Stepped Reckoner, which used a stepped-drum design and was able to perform the four basic arithmetic operations. Pascal and Leibniz's models provided the basis for most of the mechanical calculators built during the 18th century and well into the 19th. Calculators—which were considered an engineering sensation and were often prominently displayed in the houses of the wealthy—remained largely a curiosity, however, until 1820, when Charles Thomas de Colmar built the first commercially successful model, the Arithmometer (also known as the Thomas Machine). A desktop device with dials and a handle that used a modification of Leibniz's design, Thomas's Arithmometer sold well and continued to be manufactured until the 1920s, though early models tended to be erratic.

The first significant improvement upon Leibniz's design did not appear until 1874, when Willgodt Odhner—who was then working for Ludwig

Nobel (the brother of Alfred Nobel, who originated the Nobel Prize) in St. Petersburg, Russia—built a mechanical calculator that relied on a pinwheel mechanism rather than stepped drums. The pinwheel calculator consisted of a series of wheels, each containing nine radial pegs along its circumference that could be fully extended or retracted by the operator depending on what number was entered into the calculator. Numerous wheels were arranged along a central crank shaft; each wheel (with the appropriate number of pegs extended) represented a digit. The crank was then turned to rotate the wheels, causing them to turn counter wheels and produce the desired mathematical result. Since the wheels were thin (about a quarter of an inch thick), the device was relatively compact and easy to use.

Odhner patented his device in 1878. A few years earlier an American named Frank S. Baldwin, working independently, had arrived at a very similar design, which he had patented in 1875. Eventually, the names "Baldwin type" and "Odhner type" became synonymous for machines of this kind.

Odhner's company, W. T. Odhner, Maschinenfabrik & Metallgiesserei, started manufacturing calculators in about 1886, under the name "Original-Odhner." The company also manufactured other products, for use in World War I. In all, about 30,000 Odhner-type calculators were produced in Russia, about 20 percent of which were exported.

In 1892 Odhner sold his patent rights to Grimme, Natalis & Co. A.G., of Braunschweig, Germany, which sold Odhner calculators in Germany and neighboring countries under the name Brunsviga. The company later changed its name to Brunsviga, one of the most well-known brands of Odhner-type calculators. Machines based on Odhner's design were eventually sold under licence by numerous companies, including Triumphator, Marchant, Rapide, Dactyle, Britannic, Arrow, Éclair, and Vaucanson. Odhner-type calculators continued to be used worldwide until the mid-20th century.

Odhner died in 1905.—A. I. C.

Suggested Reading: Museum of HP Calculators Web site; X-Number World of Calculators Web site

---

Ohm, Georg Simon

Mar. 16, 1789–July 6, 1854 Physicist; mathematician; electrical pioneer

The physicist and mathematician Georg Simon Ohm was one of the first scientists to use experimental evidence to derive fundamental laws of electricity. His major work, written in 1827, postulated what is now known as Ohm's Law, an equation that describes the relationships between electrical current, voltage, and resistance. Ohm's work was initially derided and misunderstood, and he spent much of his life lamenting his inability to secure a prestigious university position, though by the end of his life he had received acknowledgment of the importance of his discoveries. In 1881 the International Congress of Electrical Engineers adopted standard units for measurable electrical properties, naming the unit of resistance the ohm. (The standard unit of current is the ampere, and that of electrical potential is the volt.) "Ohm's Law is still one of the building blocks of electrical power," noted a writer for *Electrical World* (January/February 2000).

The son of Johann Wolfgang Ohm, a locksmith, and Maria Elizabeth (Beck), Georg Simon Ohm was born in Erlangen, Bavaria (now Germany), on March 16, 1789. He was one of seven children, but only three—he, a brother, and a sister—survived into adulthood. As a child Ohm was educated in mathematics, physics, and other subjects by his father, who had achieved a high level of expertise through independent study. When Ohm entered the Erlangen Gymnasium at age 11, his mathematics teacher was extremely impressed with his command of the subject. In 1805 Ohm entered the University of Erlangen. It soon became evident that he was at least as interested in dancing, billiards, and ice skating as in his studies, and his father, angered at his son's squandering of an opportunity he had never had, ordered him to leave school and get a job. Ohm found a position teaching mathematics at a school in Gottstadt bei Nydau, Switzerland, in 1806 and also began studying on his own, reading works by such mathematicians as Euler, Laplace, and Lacroix. In 1809 he took a position as a private tutor in Neuchâtel, Switzerland, while continuing to study mathematics himself. Two years later, he returned to the University of Erlangen and, despite having completed only three semesters there previously, earned his doctorate in just six months. He was immediately given a post as an unpaid lecturer at the school; he taught there for three semesters, but lived in poverty. In 1813 the Bavarian government assigned him to teach math and physics in Bamberg. Though he was unhappy at the school, Ohm remained there until it closed in 1816.

In September 1817 Ohm accepted a teaching position at the Jesuit Gymnasium of Cologne, Germany, which gave him access to a well-equipped physics laboratory. When he wasn't lecturing, he spent time in the lab, often doing experiments to confirm the ideas of various scientists whom he was reading at the time. After he learned about Hans Christian Oersted's discovery of electromagnetism in 1820, Ohm grew particularly interested in the subject and conducted his own related experiments in the lab. By 1825 the standards of the Jesuit Gymnasium had, in Ohm's opinion, faltered. Still eager to gain a prestigious university post, he set about trying to publish some of his experimental findings. His first paper was published in 1825 and dealt with electromagnetic force passed through differing lengths of wire. Ohm found that the force decreased as the length of the wires increased. Allowed time off and half-pay by his school, he published two more related papers in 1826. Ohm was influenced by Jean Baptiste Joseph Fourier's study of heat conduction. Fourier had discovered that the conduction of heat between two points depended on the temperatures of each point and the level of heat conductivity of the connecting substance. Ohm hypothesized that electrical conductivity between two points would similarly depend on the electrical potential of the two points and the conductivity of the connecting material.

In 1827 Ohm published the findings of his now-famous electrical experiments under the title "The Galvanic Circuit Investigated Mathematically." By measuring a current (the rate of electron flow, designated as I) passed through a wire and noting the effect of the wire's resistance (R) and the electrical potential, or voltage (V) on it, Ohm found that current is directly proportional to the voltage and inversely proportional to the resistance. (In other words, he found that a higher current will pass through a wire that has low resistence, and that the same holds for a wire that connects two points of high relative electrical potential, or voltage.) A useful analogy: if a length of pipe connects two buckets of water, one higher than the other, then the amount of water flow corresponds to current, the thickness of the pipe corresponds to the resistence, and the degree at which the pipe is tilted corresponds to voltage. Ohm's law, which sums up the relationships of these factors, can be stated as I=V/R. The law applies to a variety of conductive materials and remains consistent over a very wide range of voltage and current.

As noted in the *Hutchinson Dictionary of Scientific Biography* (1999), "Ohm's derivation of a basic law of nature from experiment was a classic piece of scientific deduction. Together with the laws of electrodynamics discovered by André Ampère (1775–1836) at about the same time, Ohm's law marks the first theoretical investigation of electricity." However, at the time of its publication there was little positive response to "The Galvanic Circuit Investigated Mathematically," and Ohm was bitterly disappointed by its reception in the scientific community. It is likely that the complex mathematics of Ohm's paper were too advanced for many German physicists at the time, because mathematics was not considered integral to physics in Germany in 1827. He returned to teaching in Cologne.

In 1833 he found a position as a professor of physics at the Polytechnic Institute in Nuremberg, which was a significant advancement for him, though still far from the honor he coveted. Finally, in 1841, he was honored in Britain with the Copley Medal of the Royal Society; he became a foreign member of the society the following year. Recogni-

tion in Germany belatedly followed in 1849, when he became Extraordinary Professor of Physics at the University of Munich. He was appointed chair of the university's physics department in 1852. Two years later, on July 6, 1854, he died in Munich.

Ohm also did research on human hearing, defining the fundamental principles underlying our perception of complex combinations of tones, such as in a musical chord.—P. G. H.

Suggested Reading: *Electrical World* p45 Jan./Feb. 2000; Muir, Hazel, ed. *Larousse Dictionary of Scientists*, 1994; Millar, David, et al. *The Cambridge Dictionary of Scientists*, 1996; *Hutchinson Dictionary of Scientific Biography*, 1999; Simonis, Doris, ed. *Lives and Legacies: Scientists, Mathematicians, and Inventors*, 1999

Steve Liss/Getty Images

Olsen, Kenneth H.

Feb. 20, 1926– Founder of the Digital Equipment Corporation (DEC)

In a 1986 *Fortune* magazine article, the editors proclaimed Kenneth H. Olsen, the founder of the Digital Equipment Corporation (DEC), to be "arguably the most successful entrepreneur in the history of American business." At the time the article was written, DEC was the second-largest computer company—right behind IBM—with more than $7.6 billion in annual revenues. During his tenure as DEC's president and guiding spirit, Olsen fostered a climate of innovation, restructuring the company periodically from within, and with it, inevitably, the computer industry.

Kenneth Harry Olsen, the second of the four children of Oswald and Svea (Nordling) Olsen, was born in Bridgeport, Connecticut, on February 20, 1926. He grew up in Stratford, Connecticut, a machine-tool manufacturing center, in a working-class community among neighbors of Norwegian, Polish, and Italian descent. Influenced by the stern discipline and religious fundamentalism of his parents, Ken was pious and obedient. As a youngster he preferred technical manuals to comic books and, inspired by his father, a machine-tool designer who held several patents, spent much of his time in the basement tinkering, inventing gadgets, and repairing broken radios. Neighborhood residents called him "the local Edison." At the age of 14, with his younger brother Stanley, Olsen put together a radio station and broke in on local broadcasts with a humorous singing commercial about meatballs. After graduating from Stratford High School, Ken Olsen served during World War II in the United States Navy, from 1944 to 1946. There he obtained his first formal training in electrical engineering. Enrolling at the Massachusetts Institute of Technology (MIT), in Cambridge, in 1947, he raced through the curriculum and earned a B.S. degree in electrical engineering, in 1950.

While studying for a master's degree (which he earned in 1952) at MIT, Olsen was recruited to work on the transistor-driven Whirlwind computer, a breakthrough machine that the school was building for the Office of Naval Research and the Air Force. An anomaly in an era of giant machines used mainly for scientific calculations, the Whirlwind was to be used for flight simulation, with applications ranging from air-traffic control to guided-missile warfare. This work introduced Olsen to interactive computing, one of the Whirlwind's most innovative features, epitomized by the computer's immediate response—verging on dialogue—to instructions and incoming data.

In 1951, after the completion of the Whirlwind, the Air Defense Command assigned to MIT the development of the Semi-Automatic Ground Environment (SAGE) early-warning system. Olsen's immediate boss, Norman Taylor, asked him to design a small computer to test the memory device used in the Whirlwind for use in the SAGE. Olsen handled the project so well that when IBM won the contract for the actual manufacturing of the system, Taylor sent him to Poughkeepsie, New York, to oversee the project. In an interview with Katherine Davis Fishman for her book *The Computer Establishment* (1982), Taylor said, "Ken lived in Poughkeepsie for two and a half years, in the bowels of IBM. There was this whole new world called production that he didn't know anything about, but he was a bona fide engineer; if something didn't work he'd take his coat off and redo it himself. He could do anything." Olsen found IBM's production inefficiencies in those days "appalling" according to Taylor, and Olsen has been quoted as saying that his sojourn at IBM "was like going to a Communist state," because "they knew noth-

ing about the rest of the world, and the world knew nothing about what went on inside."

Back at MIT Olsen applied what he had learned at IBM to direct the building of the first transistorized research computer. He realized that the breakthroughs he and his colleagues were making and writing papers about were thought to be meaningless outside academia, and Olsen longed to have some practical effect on the rest of the world. He knew that such relatively simple computing jobs as tracking a scientific experiment or maintaining an inventory list did not require the expensive, room-sized mainframes produced by IBM. With an MIT associate, Harlan Anderson, he began to look for backing for his idea of a small general-purpose computer.

Olsen and Anderson prepared for the plunge into entrepreneurship by consulting Standard and Poor's financial data on other companies and reading books on management theory in the public library in Lexington, Massachusetts. (During this time Olsen served as the superintendent of Boston's Park Street Church Sunday School. The church pastor, Harold Ockenga, had been one of the first radio evangelists, and Olsen admired his use of a technological instrument to promote his religious values.)

In 1957 Olsen and Anderson presented their ideas about computing to executives of the American Research and Development company and its president, General Georges F. Doriot; they received $70,000 in seed money from him. Doriot advised them to make something other than computers, however, because he felt that it would be too difficult for a fledgling enterprise to compete with IBM, Burroughs, and RCA—companies that had already entered the relatively new and precarious computer business.

Opening the Digital Equipment Corporation in one corner of a woolen mill dating back to the Civil War era, Olsen and Anderson, who were joined by Olsen's brother Stan, took Doriot's advice and began producing the printed-circuit logic modules used by engineers to test equipment. Recalling the austerity of 1957, DEC's first year of operation, Olsen said in a *New York Times* article (January 14, 1979): "We did everything ourselves; we cleaned the johns and swept the floors. We did the photography in my basement; we made our printed circuit boards with real silk on wooden frames and etched them in aquarium tanks. Since I was the closest thing we had to a toolmaker, I made the tools." Some of DEC's first customers were other MIT alumni, and it was nine months before Olsen hired a full-time salesman.

Among the uncommon business policies Olsen implemented as DEC prospered in the years ahead were: no government funding for research, so that DEC's emphasis would remain on manufacturing for the marketplace; no mergers or acquisitions; no leasing (even of big machines) because a reluctance to allow a product that is still producing revenue to become obsolete can grind technical development to a halt; no commissions for salesmen (who were engineers, rather than business-school graduates), so that they would not be enticed into selling customers unnecessary equipment; and no dividends for shareholders, so that profits could be plowed back into development.

DEC's circuit modules, as Olsen had intended, became the building blocks of the company's first computer. It was marketed in 1960 and equipped for interactive computing with a CRT or cathode ray tube terminal similar to that of a television screen. Olsen called it the Programmed Data Processor or PDP-1, to help customers suspend their disbelief in a computer that sold for $120,000 instead of the then-standard $1 million, that was relatively small (the size of a compact refrigerator), and that could be installed anywhere. The device was well received by the engineers, scientists, and technicians at whom it was aimed. It was accepted as standard equipment after the International Telephone & Telegraph Corporation began buying it in great quantities for message-switching.

DEC's next coup came in 1963, when its PDP-4 began to attract a lucrative and previously unchartered market of original equipment manufacturers (OEMs), who added their own software to the powerful machines and resold them in new markets under new names. In that way, OEMs gradually became a kind of auxiliary sales force for DEC, while saving it the enormous expense of developing new lines of software for each new group of users.

DEC became known as an ideal employer for engineers in that period, because Olsen shunned any formal corporate structure in favor of a fluid, MIT–like atmosphere in which his engineers contributed to each project as their skills and ambitions dictated. Two of them, Edson de Castro and Gordon Bell, joined forces to oversee the development of the $27,000 PDP-5 and of the firm's breakthrough machine—the smaller, more powerful PDP-8, which was built using a new technology: tiny integrated circuits, which were relatively inexpensive and faster than individual transistors.

Launched in 1965, the PDP-8, generally thought to be the first true minicomputer, sold for an astonishingly low basic price of $18,000 and opened up entirely new markets for DEC. The PDP-8 gradually revolutionized the way in which industries conducted business, making it economical and practical for a technician to perform a computing job on the spot, instead of having to wait to take a turn on the company mainframe. As customized by OEMs and by DEC's other customers, many of whom wrote their own software, the PDP-8 could perform in a wide variety of environments, and it turned up in machines ranging from typesetters and medical scanners to the scoreboards at sports arenas. Hundreds of start-ups hurried to enter the market it created, but most found it difficult to compete with an already entrenched DEC.

As sales skyrocketed, the company outgrew its free-form structure. In 1966, the year in which DEC went public, Olsen decided to restructure the enterprise into product line groups—in effect, companies within the company, each studying and serving its own market and headed by a senior manager who worked as an entrepreneur, submitting an annual budget and product-line plan to a committee of his peers that, chaired by Olsen, functioned as a kind of internal venture-capital group. If his product line was deemed satisfactory, the manager proceeded with research and development and received services from DEC's still-centralized manufacturing and sales divisions. Olsen remained the company's binding force however, keeping committee meetings going and finding elegant solutions to complex business problems. The corporate culture thus created has been called both amazingly democratic and sternly patriarchal. It generated nearly two decades of 30 percent annual revenue and profit growth and made DEC one of the model companies regularly celebrated in business magazines and included on their "best managed" lists. The fruits of that success (and of going public) included takeover bids from the Xerox Corporation, Hewlett-Packard, and others. DEC also continued to battle its surviving start-up competitors, including Data Point and Data General (formed in 1968 by de Castro and other deserters from DEC).

The firm made a strong bid for a piece of the IBM–dominated mainframe market in 1967, when it launched its biggest machine, the PDP-10, a $400,000 computer designed for time sharing. In 1970 DEC reconquered the minicomputer industry with the 16-bit PDP-11, which became the most popular minicomputer line in history. Distributed processing networks using another innovation, DECnet software, to link PDP-11s with larger machines such as the PDP-10, became increasingly popular throughout the 1970s, monitoring such processes as the assembly of cars and the workings of oil refineries. IBM, by comparison, did not enter the mini market in earnest until late 1976.

Networking on a grand scale—through the linking of existing networks to each other as if they were individual computers—began for DEC with the Virtual Address Extension or VAX technology developed by Gordon Bell in 1974, the year in which its profits pushed DEC into the *Fortune* 500 category. VAX grew out of a realization by Bell and the company's other engineers that, to remain competitive, the PDP-11 needed more of the space that stores a computer's memory and determines the size and efficiency of the networks it can support. As drafted by Bell, the VAX line was to range from 32-bit computers—with twice the space of the 16-bit PDP-11—down to desktop-sized machines. More important, all were to have the same architecture, which would enable them to run the same software, share data bases, and communicate with ease.

The first supermini in the series, the VAX-11/780, was as powerful as the IBM 370 at a quarter of the price and was designed to accept each completed part of the VAX line as add-on equipment to make it even more powerful. Running the VMS operating system, which was developed at the same time, it had the potential of automating entire companies, and was immediately accepted as the standard against which all other minicomputers were to be measured. By 1979 the package had secured 40 percent of the worldwide minicomputer market for DEC.

Almost simultaneously with the triumph of the VAX-11/780 and the commitment of billions of DEC's dollars to the development of the rest of the VAX line, an explosion took place in the growth of the microcomputer industry at the low-priced end of the market. Attracting a horde of white-collar workers who lacked the technical expertise of DEC's traditional customers, these user-friendly micros took Olsen and his engineers by surprise and left them in a vulnerable position in a changing industry. The silicone chips at the core of the micros were soon so powerful that some of DEC's low-end customers were lured away, while some IBM mainframes dropped in price enough to entice buyers at the high end. Belatedly, in 1982, a year after IBM introduced its own best-selling micro, the PC, DEC offered a confusing selection of three such machines. Each had been built by a separate product line group of the "many-headed hydra" that, in the view of some journalists, Olsen's matrix management structure had become. Competing with established micros and with each other in an area where DEC had neither marketing expertise nor name recognition, the computers sold sluggishly at best.

On October 18, 1983 DEC's stock plunged 21 points. By the end of fiscal year 1983, the company's net earnings had dropped 32 percent. Industry analysts faulted the product line groups that had churned out the ill-fated micros and blamed Olsen's lack of foresight for DEC's fall. (It has been pointed out that Olsen, early in his career, expressed doubt about the need for home computers, making it ironic that the development of such machines had severe repercussions for his company.) Olsen was also chided, in an unsigned cover story in *BusinessWeek* (November 5, 1984), for a "seeming preoccupation with an illustrious past" that might lead to an "also-ran status in the industry" for DEC.

But, in fact, Olsen was once more engaged in restructuring his firm. He scrapped the product line groups—despite the consequent departure of several senior managers who prized their independence—to make the company a centralized market-driven operation.

Beginning with VAX clusters, in 1983, DEC marketed a series of computers "linked by a golden thread of connectivity," according to Glenn Rifkin, writing for *Computerworld* (September 24, 1986). The VAX 8600 (also called Venus), a small but mighty mainframe, appeared in October 1984. In May 1985 the MicroVAX II workstation, which put the classic VAX-780 on a thumbnail-sized silicon chip, was saluted as one of the most important new products since the IBM PC. During the next 18 months, seven new models in the 8000 series, in every size category, were produced by DEC. The cycle culminated in September 1986 with the Vaxmate, an IBM-compatible system with an all-in-one software package, which made it possible for IBM PC users to retrieve data instantly from any VAX computer. IBM itself was still struggling to develop a networking system to link even its own machines.

In 1986, during an industry-wide recession, DEC's procession of new machines—combined with a bonus plan for its top sales people—raised company profits by 38 percent to $617.4 million. In the *Los Angeles Times* (September 22, 1986), Oswald Johnston, proposing superior products as a solution to the United States trade deficit, wrote: "A growing number of economists believe Digital [as DEC is sometimes known] is doing what American business must do much more frequently if it is to survive against increasingly stiff worldwide competition. . . . The trouble is that the United States does not have enough Digitals. . . . Many of the companies with Digital's potential have not taken the steps to realize it."

In 1988 Olsen entered in a deal with Apple to have that company's Macintosh computers work with DEC's VAX mainframes, providing the market with an alternative to IBM. (Still, DEC made sure that IBM personal computers would be able to work on VAX networks as well.) John Sculley, then head of Apple Computer, said of the deal in *BusinessWeek* (February 1, 1988): "Ken Olsen has the vision to see where the industry is heading."

Despite Sculley's assertion, Olsen was sometimes less of a visionary. In 1988, for example, DEC offered its first reduced instruction set computing (RISC) design several years after IBM offered its version. (RISC involves microprocessors specifically designed to perform fewer types of computer instructions at a faster speed.) This late start was due in large part to Olsen's belief that RISC could not compete with Digital's VAX hardware. Olsen was also said to scoff at the move towards the popular Unix operating system.

By 1992, after several executive departures, layoffs, financial setbacks, and a general loss of direction at DEC, Olsen was asked by the board of directors to resign as head of the company he had co-founded. At the time, he gamely announced that he was leaving to allow the "next generation of management to assume leadership," but he has since been openly bitter about his resignation. "We grew faster and larger, with more profit, than any company in history," he told Laurence Zuckerman for the *New York Times* (September 25, 1995). "And I was always being beaten up for being stupid and backward. I was the stupidest, dumbest guy there ever was." (In 1998 DEC would be acquired by Compaq, which itself would later be merged with Hewlett-Packard.)

Almost immediately, at the end of 1992, Olsen founded a new company, Advanced Modular Solutions, to sell computers containing only a microprocessor and memory chips no disk drives. He reasoned that removing storage from desktop machines and using a server instead would decrease the cost and increase the manageability of desktop computing for the companies that purchased the units. Many observers marveled that Olsen, then in his 60s, wanted to keep working. He explained his decision to Rochelle Garner for *Computerworld* (September 29, 1997, on-line): "You do what seems important, and what's important is the most satisfying. I keep telling myself that I'm not doing this to prove something, but to explore something new and to show how something can be done."

Olsen did finally retire, in 2000, after more than four decades of involvement in the computer industry. His many honors include the Franklin Institute's 1980 Vermilye Medal and, in 1986, the first Institute of Electrical and Electronic Engineers (IEEE) Leadership Award and the first IEEE Computer Society Award. Kenneth H. Olsen married the former Eeva-Liisa Aulikki Valve on December 12, 1950; they have four children, Ava-Lisa, Eleanor, Glenn Charles, and James Jonathan.—C. M.

Suggested Reading: *BusinessWeek* p152+ Sep. 21, 1968, p58+ Apr. 26, 1976, p66+ May 2, 1983, p64+ Apr. 21, 1986, p83+ Feb. 1, 1988; *Computerworld* (on-line) Sep. 29, 1997; *Forbes* p22+ Sep. 1, 1973, p 41+ Jan. 7, 1991; *Fortune* p91+ May 3, 1982, p24+ Oct. 27, 1986; *New York Times*, D p1+ July 17, 1992, D p3 Sep. 15, 1992, D p3 Mar. 25, 1993, D p5 Sep. 25, 1995; *Washington Post* B p1+ July 17, 1992, H p1+ Aug. 8, 1993

Osborne, Adam

Feb. 6, 1939–Mar. 18, 2003 Founder of the Osborne Computer Corporation

Although Adam Osborne's success as a personal computer manufacturer was short-lived, he is widely credited with making two contributions that permanently changed the computer industry. Osborne, who founded the Osborne Computer Corporation, in 1980, is considered the father of portable, or laptop, computers. His first computer, the Osborne 1, combined such features as a disk drive, monitor, and keyboard into one unit. It weighed 24 pounds and folded neatly into a carrying case; for the first time, users could carry their computers to and from work or on trips. In another first for the computer industry, Osborne sold his machines with free software, including popular spreadsheet and word processing programs. After initial success, Osborne Computer succumbed to pressures created by increased competition and too-rapid growth. "When you become an entrepreneur you can go up awfully fast but you can go down just as fast," Osborne told Robert A. Mamis in *Inc.* (November 1983). "It's so ephemeral, like actors who end up committing suicide. One day they're famous, the next day nobody knows who the hell they are."

The son of British parents, Adam Osborne was born on February 6, 1939 in Bangkok, Thailand. His father taught Eastern religions and philosophy at the University of Bangkok. The Osborne family also lived in southern India before settling permanently in England in the early 1950s.

In 1961 Osborne graduated from the University of Birmingham, in England, with a degree in chemical engineering. He then immigrated to the United States, becoming an American citizen in 1967. A short time after his arrival, he was hired as a chemical engineer with the M. W. Kellogg Company, where his brash style often alienated his coworkers. "I quickly became the guy everyone wanted to watch slip on a banana skin," he recalled to Mamis. Osborne left the Kellogg company to return to school and, in 1968, he received a doctorate in chemical engineering from the University of Delaware, in Newark. He then joined the Shell Oil Company in California's San Francisco Bay Area.

After working at Shell for two years, Osborne realized that he was ill-suited to work in a large company. One of his managers told him that he would have only a mediocre career to look forward to at Shell. "That finally forced my hand," Osborne told Mamis. "That's when I said to myself, 'Don't go out and get another job with another company. Do it yourself.' Originally it came to me in a kind of negative way that I was a misfit. Then it occurred to me that maybe I wasn't a misfit after all. I was just at the wrong place."

During the early 1970s Osborne developed an interest in computers and used his mathematical skills to learn programming. He became a freelance consultant, specializing in microcomputer software and technical manuals. He also wrote an instruction manual, *An Introduction to Microcomputers* (1975), that, after receiving rejections from many publishers, he published and promoted himself. Later that year, ISMAI, a major computer manufacturer, began selling Osborne's book with its computers. *An Introduction to Microcomputers* eventually sold more than 300,000 copies and established Osborne as an expert on the computer industry.

This success led Osborne to create a publishing company, Osborne Books. By the end of the decade, the company had published more than 40 books, many written by Osborne himself. He also began writing a regular column, "From the Fountainhead," for the computer magazine *Interface Age* and later for *InfoWorld*. He frequently criticized the computer industry, asserting that, instead of competing to make their products unique, computer manufacturers should concentrate on driving down prices in order to make computers affordable to ordinary people.

In 1979 Osborne sold Osborne Books to the publishing conglomerate McGraw-Hill and, with the proceeds set out to follow his own advice, establishing a company to manufacture low-cost personal computers, the Osborne Computer Corporation. In his article for *Salon* (July 17, 1999, on-line), David Pescovitz noted that Osborne visited the Xerox company's Palo Alto Research Center (PARC), in California, in 1980 and was impressed by Notetaker, a small computer that could be taken to and from work. "Everyone was very open at PARC, and he [Osborne] saw all the drawings and asked a few questions and left not saying anything," Gwen Bell, a curator at the Computer Museum History Center in Mountain View, California, told Pescovitz.

In 1981 Osborne Computer introduced the Osborne 1, the first commercial portable computer. The machine resembled Xerox's Notetaker, but was unique in several ways. The screen, disk drives, and keyboard were all part of a single, portable machine that had 64 kilobytes of memory and could fit under an airplane seat. The Osborne 1 also came with two popular software applications—the word-processing program, WordStar, and the spreadsheet program, SuperCalc. While writing his computer column, Osborne had often heard people complain about the difficulty of assembling the various computer components. "One of the major gripes was that they said, 'How are you supposed to use this machine that comes in five boxes and is wired together like spaghetti?'" he told a *Washington Post* (August 12, 1984) reporter. "They were all using the computer for exactly the same thing, which was word processing or spread sheets, and it seemed obvious that what you do is make it convenient to use by shoving everything into one box and give them the spread sheet and word processor."

Priced at $1,795, the Osborne 1 was less expensive than other personal computers on the market and—with free software—was viewed by many as a bargain. It became an immediate hit with consumers and, by 1982, sales totaled over $100 million. The company successfully competed against other personal computer sellers, greatly expanded its workforce, and attracted investors. Osborne predicted that the company's sales would exceed $1 billion in 1984.

In September 1983, however, the company declared bankruptcy. Several factors contributed to its rapid downfall, including a recession in the computer industry and competition from other companies. Many computer manufacturers followed Osborne's lead by offering free software and introducing portable computers—some less expensive or more advanced than the Osborne 1. Perhaps most damaging to Osborne's market share was that,

in 1981, IBM had introduced a state-of-the-art personal computer, with which the Osborne machines were not compatible.

Osborne also made a tactical error. In the spring of 1982 he announced the Executive—billed as the next generation of personal computers—several months before the machine would actually be available in stores. Thinking that the Osborne 1 would soon become obsolete, many retailers stopped carrying it, and consumers waited for the new system. In the months before the Executive reached the market, revenues shrank. Osborne intended to take the company public in July 1983 to raise capital, but the announcement that it had $26 million in losses derailed the plan. In the fall of that year, the company's board of directors forced Osborne to resign as chief executive officer. Without him, Osborne Computer managed to survive, emerging as a marketer of personal computers manufactured by other firms. Osborne and John Dvorak co-wrote *Hypergrowth: The Rise and Fall of Osborne Computer Corporation* (1984), which offered Osborne's opinions on what had gone wrong with the company.

In 1984 Adam Osborne founded Paperback Software International, a company focused on developing inexpensive software packages. "What we're doing is structuring [the company] to try to avoid the various pitfalls and problems," he told the *Washington Post* reporter. "First of all, we want to have a lot of products. To do that, we're going out to small software companies and individuals out there with excellent products and no distribution. We're bringing them into our organization with a scheme that is designed to avoid the normal ripoffs that are prevalent in the software publishing business." In 1985 Paperback introduced its first major product, VP-Planner, a spreadsheet program priced at $100. Osborne boasted to John Eckhouse, a reporter for the *San Francisco Chronicle* (September 6, 1985), that "VP-Planner does everything that the $595 Lotus [1-2-3] does, and then some—and does it a hell of a lot easier."

In fact, VP-Planner was often described as a virtual clone of 1-2-3. In 1987 the Lotus Development Corporation filed a lawsuit against Paperback, alleging that it violated copyright laws because VP-Planner copied many of 1-2-3's features. Speaking to Lawrence Edelman, a reporter for the *Boston Globe* (February 4, 1990), Osborne admitted that VP-Planner's menu and command keys were similar to 1-2-3. However, he argued that building on existing systems was a common practice in software development as well as a benefit to users, who when using new software would not have to learn entirely new protocols. Some critics agreed with Osborne, and alleged that Lotus was using litigation to drive competition off the market. In an interview with William M. Bulkeley for the *Wall Street Journal* (February 6, 1990), Osborne said that the lawsuit's "effect on our business has been absolutely devastating. Everyone said they don't want to mess with a company that is litigating with a large company . . . because the big guy always wins." On June 28, 1990 a federal judge ruled that Paperback infringed on Lotus's copyright by duplicating some of its program's features. VP-Planner was withdrawn from the market, and Osborne resigned from Paperback a short time later.

In the early 1990s Osborne tried to make a comeback by founding another company, Noetics Software, but the venture never got off the ground. After the failure of Noetics, Osborne vanished from public view. In 1992 he reportedly suffered the first of what would be a series of small strokes and returned to India to live with his sister, Katya. On March 18, 2003 Osborne died in Kodiakanal, India, at the age of 64.

Adam Osborne's first marriage, to Cynthia Geddes, ended in divorce in 1981, after 19 years. He married again in 1983, to Barbara Zelnick, but that union also ended in divorce. Osborne is survived by three children: Alexandra, Paul, and Marc. —D. C.

Suggested Reading: *Boston Globe* A p1 Feb. 4, 1990, A p21 June. 29, 1990; *Business Week* p86+ Feb. 22, 1982; *Computerworld* p10+ Sep. 29, 1997; *Inc.* p21+ Nov. 1983, with photo; *New York Times* D p1+ Feb. 15, 1982, III p1+ Nov. 6, 1983; *Salon* (on-line) July 17, 1999; *San Francisco Chronicle* p33 Sep. 6, 1985; *Wall Street Journal* p1+ Oct. 12, 1984, p1+ July 20, 1987, B p1 Feb. 6, 1990; *Washington Post* F p2 Aug. 12, 1984, with photo

---

Oughtred, William

Mar. 5, 1575–June 30, 1660 Inventor of the slide rule

The English mathematician and scholar William Oughtred is credited with the invention of the slide rule, a mechanical calculating instrument used by scientists until the late 20th century when it was replaced by the electronic pocket calculator. In his most important work, *Clavis mathematicae* (*The Key to Mathematics*), published in 1631, Oughtred established a new system of symbols for mathematical equations, including the "x" symbol for multiplication and the "::" symbol to express a proportion. He also developed the abbreviations for sine, cosine, and tangent. In 1657 he wrote and published *Trigonometrie*, an important work that discussed plane and spherical triangles.

William Oughtred was born in Eaton, Buckinghamshire, England, on March 5, 1575. (Some sources use the date 1574.) His father was a scrivener who taught writing at Eton while teaching his son some arithmetic. Many scholars attribute Oughtred's clear writing to his father's influence. Young William Oughtred was a king's scholar at Eton until age 15, when he left to attend King's College at Cambridge University. During this time, although very little mathematics was taught at Eton and Cambridge, it became the subject in which Oughtred would be passionately interested for the rest of his life.

Oughtred became a fellow of Cambridge in 1595, graduated with his bachelor's degree in arts the following year, and earned his master's degree in 1600. While at Cambridge, around 1598, he wrote *Easy Way of Delineating Dials by Geometry*, which was not published until 1647. In 1603 he was ordained an Anglican priest, and a year later he became the vicar of Shalford, Surrey, a position he would hold until 1610, when he was named the rector of Albury, Surrey. He would remain rector of Albury for the rest of his life, receiving 100 pounds annually for his services.

Though very devoted to his parish and ecclesiastical duties, Oughtred began to tutor in mathematics in the 1620s and continued to do so free of charge until his death. Among his pupils were Seth Ward, Jonas More, Charles Scarborough, John Wallis, Christopher Wren, William Forster, and Robin Wood. He also produced inventions to aid in his study of mathematics, the most notable of which was the slide rule, consisting of graduated, relatively moveable scales that could make simple calculations mechanically. In 1617, some years before Oughtred began tutoring, John Napier, a Scottish nobleman and mathematician, created a set of numbering rods to ease calculations. The rods, known as "Napier's bones," were movable tables that simplified multiplication and division. In 1621 or 1622 Oughtred invented a circular slide rule he called "circles of proportion" that translated Napier's logarithms onto a set of rotating scales. (Today the invention is considered one of the first analog computing devices.) He later invented the rectilinear slide rule and a method of calculating logs. Beginning in 1628 he tutored Lord William Howard, the son of the earl of Arundel, who in turn became a staunch supporter of Oughtred's work and encouraged him to publish. While educating the duke's son in mathematics, he wrote a treatise on algebra and arithmetic entitled the *Clavis mathematicae* (key to mathematics).

Though only 100 pages long, the *Clavis mathematicae* significantly influenced Europe's scientific community when it was published in 1631, since it was a complete survey of the entire body of mathematics known in Oughtred's era. It included a lengthy section on algebra and descriptions of Hindu- Arabic notations, along with a large amount of new symbols for mathematics, including those for proportion and multiplication mentioned earlier. Though the writing is dense and many of the rules complex, *Clavis mathematicae* received high praise from many of Oughtred's contemporaries, including Oughtred's pupil, John Wallis, who remarked in his book *Algebra* (1695), as cited in the *Dictionary of Scientific Biography* (1974), "The *Clavis* doth in as little room deliver as much of the fundamental and useful parts of geometry (as well as of arithmetic and algebra) as any book I know." Later, Sir Isaac Newton, in a letter to Nathaniel Hawes dated May 25, 1694, also quoted in the *Dictionary of Scientific Biography*, called the priest "a man whose judgment (if any man's) may be relyed [sic] on."

Though Oughtred's work received enormous praise in Europe, Oughtred was bothered by the assertions of Richard Delamain, a respected mathematician and school teacher, who in his book *Grammelogie, or the Mathematicall Ring* (1630), claimed to have invented the circles of proportion and the horizontal quadrant, a type of sundial. Since Delamain was Oughtred's former student, the ensuing debate between them was personal. This initial dispute, which began around 1632, escalated into a war between the two men in which each accused the other of improper mathematical practice. Oughtred advocated pure theoretical study and believed that the comprehension of theory should precede the understanding of instruments. Delamain, however, believed that he could teach the practical use of instruments without theory. Scholars have long debated the merits of each mathematician's beliefs, and also the question of who invented the slide rule. While there are merits to each argument, most scholars now agree with Oughtred's former pupil William Forster, who translated Oughtred's *The Circles of Proportion and the Horizontal Instrument* (1632), which contains notes on the slide rule. Forster claimed that Delamain rushed into print his *Grammelogie* before Oughtred's work could be translated from Latin. (A similar modern "war" raged between John V. Atansoff and John Mauchly over ownership of the ENIAC computer patent. In the end, as in Oughtred's case, the professor won—Atansoff was granted the patent—almost 20 years after the machine was mothballed.)

Oughtred remained fiercely loyal to the British crown. However, during the 17th century, a rift was growing between the monarchy and Parliament. Both King James I and his son and successor Charles I vigorously defended their firm belief in the divine right of kings and a preference for the Anglican religion while persecuting all opponents, including those in Parliament. This division culminated in the English Civil War of 1642, in which the parliamentarians (led by Oliver Cromwell) defeated the royalists. Charles I was beheaded in 1649 by the parliamentarians, leading many royalists like Oughtred to fear for their lives. In fact, in 1646, the government sequestered Oughtred, but Sir Bulstrode Whitelocke, along with other influential people, persuaded Parliament to spare him. Oughtred continued to work and teach into his old age. In 1657 he published *Trigonometrie*, a 36-page work that dealt with both plane and spherical triangles and used abbreviations for sine ("sin"), cosine ("cos"), and tangent ("tan"). He died on June 30, 1660 in Albury, near Guildford, in Surrey, supposedly after hearing the joyous news that Charles II had ascended the throne of the reestablished British monarchy.—C. M.

Suggested Reading: *British Journal of the History of the Sciences* p253+ Sep. 1998; *Catalog of the Scientific Community* (on-line); Galileo Project Web site; Asimov, Isaac. *Asimov's Biographical Encyclopedia of Science and Technology*, 1982; *Columbia Encyclopedia*, 1993; *Dictionary of Scientific Biography*, 1974; *Larousse Dictionary of Scientists*, 1994

Packard, David

Sep. 7, 1912–Mar. 26, 1996 Co-founder of Hewlett-Packard

"We weren't interested in the idea of making any money," David Packard once said about the billion-dollar computer company he started with his college friend William Hewlett. "Our idea was if you couldn't find a job, you'd make one for yourself." In the process of making a job for himself, Packard also made himself a legend. Although he did not realize it when his company was launched in the garage of his home, the co-founder of Hewlett-Packard had created what would later become one of the most admired corporations in the history of industrialized society. With its extensive line of products and equipment related to almost all aspects of the electronics industry, Hewlett-Packard has become a household word for most of the world. Packard's legend extends beyond his company's notoriety however. His style of management, a technique of nonformality and trusting employees known as the HP Way, has been imitated by corporations around the globe and has been incorporated into most business textbooks. His philanthropic projects, for which he donated more than $500 million during his lifetime, and his dedication to the promotion of scientific education and support of universities earned him as much fame as his business, and he acquired a reputation as an unpretentious, yet outspoken family man. With his company's almost continual climb to the top of the computer hierarchy, David Packard carved himself a place among the great entrepreneurs in computer history, and with the widely implemented tactics of his HP Way so evident in corporations, will live on as one of the most influential pioneers of the electronics industry.

The son of a lawyer father and a mother who was a teacher, David Packard was born on September 7, 1912, in Pueblo, Colorado. As a young boy, Packard took an early interest in science and electricity, building his first radio while he was still in elementary school. By the age of 12, he was serving as secretary of the local amateur radio club. When he graduated high school, he decided to enroll at Stanford University, in California, as an electrical-engineering major. He was drawn to Stanford in part because it boasted professor Fred Terman who had written an important book on radio engineering. Packard soon became an honor student at Stanford, and one of Terman's prize students. A natural athlete who took pleasure in outdoor activities, Packard excelled in varsity sports such as football, basketball, and track. In addition to playing sports, Packard took part in many other extracurricular activities and was elected president of his fraternity. It was at Stanford that Packard met William Hewlett, another of Terman's students, and the two soon became good friends. While on a mountain-climbing trek in Colorado, the two agreed that someday they would go into business together, not realizing the profound impact their impromptu decision would eventually have on the world technology market.

In 1934 Packard graduated from Stanford with a B.A. in engineering, and after a few months of further work at the university, left for Schenectady, New York, to work in the vacuum tube engineering department of the General Electric Company. He stayed at the company only briefly, returning to Stanford in 1938 to study the theory of the vacuum tube and pursue a master's degree. While back at his alma mater, Packard caught up with his old friend Hewlett, who had gone to MIT for his master's degree, and who had developed an extensive knowledge of negative feedback circuits. The two began to talk again of starting a business together, and started to tinker around in the garage of Packard's Palo Alto home. They pooled together $538 in start-up capital and set up a laboratory in the garage, with Packard's college sweetheart and wife, Lucile, taking on the roles of secretary and bookkeeper. They decided to call their new venture Hewlett-Packard (HP), after the latter lost a coin toss to decide whose name would go first.

The company did not take off until Hewlett developed an audio oscillator, which he had been conceptualizing since his Stanford days. The device generates a controlled signal at a predetermined frequency in order to test sound equipment, such as amplifiers. HP's device was unique in that it worked with a broader set of conditions than any previous model and also cost significantly less: $55 instead of the $500 that was the common price for such equipment at the time. HP received its first significant order of business when Disney approached the company to supply eight audio oscillators (some of which provided sound effects) for the movie *Fantasia*. At the end of their first year in business, HP had produced a profit of $1,563, with sales of $5,369.

The company constructed its first official building in 1942 and soon introduced another device, the Vacuum-tube Voltmeter, which was used for electronics research as well as development in production processes, largely used because of its high sensitivity and ability to handle a wide range of frequencies. When World War II erupted, Hewlett was called away to the Army while Packard attempted to hold the company together. At the end of the war, business declined dramatically, and the company was forced to layoff employees. It would prove to be the only layoff ever carried out under Packard's direction in the next five decades.

By 1950 HP began to rebound from its slump, with sales of $2 million and more than 200 employees. The product lines soon evolved as well, dipping into the previously unexplored area of electronic measuring devices. Such products included a high-speed electronic counter and a calibrated laboratory oscilloscope. As it grew in size and scope, HP began to make acquisitions that would serve to further expand the boundaries of its inventions. In the early 1960s, it bought the Sanborn Company, which was a manufacturer of electrocardiographic equipment and supplier of recording instrumentation. HP then acquired the F&M Scientific Corporation, a producer of gas chromatographs. These acquisitions helped HP to broaden its selection of devices to include electronics in the fields of analytical chemistry and medicine. By 1958 Packard's company was involved in the production of 373 electronic test and measuring instruments and parts, and the following year it began expansion plans to Europe.

One of the company's most crucial moves came in its decision to begin marketing of data processing equipment. HP began to work on various forms of data processing technologies and by 1966 released its first processor, the Instrumentation Computer. This machine was intended to work in conjunction with other, earlier machines in order to provide computational support. HP's foray into data processing was successful on several levels. It was, most obviously, monetarily advantageous, contributing $68 million in revenues by 1972. But data processing also served to expand HP beyond what had been its sole customer base—engineers and scientists—and cemented the company as a premier player among its fellow Silicon Valley inhabitants.

As Packard's company progressed into the 1970s, it continued to develop revolutionary products. One such innovative product, which made its debut in 1970, was the laser interferometer. This device could measure a distance of up to 200 feet with an accuracy of a millionth of an inch. In 1972 HP came out with the first hand-held scientific calculator and introduced the HP 3000, a minicomputer system which supported many of the languages found on mainframes and could perform general computations. The machine was capable of doing multi-programming, online processing, batch processing or time-sharing. During the decade, HP continued to work out the bugs in this series and eventually created models that could hold up to two million bytes of storage and support remote teleprocessing. HP would also add an operating system and software capable of supporting as many as 63 terminals per configuration. It soon began to manufacture equipment in support of these systems, such as disk drives and printers. One of the company's biggest success stories, the LaserJet printer, emerged in 1984, while it continued to expand its computer base to include desktop computers.

As advanced as the HP product line was the company had built a reputation, over the decades, for more than just its equipment and sales figures. The corporation, one of the first to infiltrate the area that came to be known as Silicon Valley—(Packard's Palo Alto garage is now an official California landmark)—was a model of successful business practices based on the philosophy Hewlett and Packard shared of an egalitarian company. The partners shunned the then prevalent hierarchical system of other big corporations, promoting instead a relaxed, casual atmosphere in their buildings, without any large formal offices. Believing that management should stay close to workers—to hear their concerns or discuss new ideas—Packard would often roam the hallways of HP, intermingling with all of his employees. Dave, as he preferred to be called by his workers, was so familiar to HP's denizens that they jokingly awarded him a degree of M.B.W.A., Master By Walking Around. Packard expounded on this notion in his 1995 autobiography, The HP Way, explaining this principle as "management by walking around", or MBWA. According to Packard, interacting with workers allowed a manager to learn much more about his business and the people running that business than simply sitting behind a desk all day.

Packard also believed in displaying respect for and trust in his employees. His employee philosophy included profit sharing, cooperating on the meeting of goals, and sharing personal as well as professional development, creating what Packard viewed as a feeling of productive teamwork at HP. Packard went to great lengths to make sure that as his company grew (with employees reaching into the tens of thousands), areas of operation would be broken up when they reached more than 1,500 employees. Each division was split up according to product types and had its own engineering, marketing, manufacturing, and research groups. This kept a close-knit feeling akin to his "management by objectives" (MBO) technique which mandated that teams participate in creating goals and then determine how they can best attain those goals. Many of Packard's proteges at HP went to other, highly successful computer firms, and applied HP's business strategies, the most notable of them being Stephen Wozniak, co-founder of Apple Computer. Packard's methods are now taught as standard subjects in many business-management courses throughout the world.

Packard wrote The HP Way in order to share his knowledge and methods by which he turned his garage-size company into a computer powerhouse. In addition to his management techniques, Packard relayed a piece of advice that he himself was given in the early days of his career by a retired engineer. The man told him that "more businesses die from indigestion than starvation," words Pack-

ard held onto as he developed his own business philosophies. "I have observed the truth of that advice many times since then," he wrote in his book.

While Hewlett was generally considered the technological whiz of the company, David Packard occupied himself with the managerial end of Hewlett-Packard's operations. Packard served as the company's president until 1964, when he was elected chairman of the board and chief executive officer. In 1969, Packard, a longtime Republican, left the company in order to take a position in the administration of President Richard Nixon, as U.S. Deputy Secretary of Defense. As part of his agreement to come work for the government, Packard had to relinquish his annual million dollar salary in exchange for the $30,000 a year offerings of his new position. Also, to avoid conflicts of interest, Packard had to place his stock in Hewlett-Packard, which did nearly $100 million in business related to defense, in a trust fund, with all dividends and capital increases given to charities.

Packard resigned from his post in 1971 and was reelected chairman of the board at Hewlett-Packard. In his autobiography, Packard expressed his frustration dealing with Washington officials who did not warm up to his management style during his time in the Capital. "Working with the Washington bureaucracy was like pushing on one end of a 40-foot rope and trying to get the other end to do what you want," he wrote of the experience.

Throughout his career, Packard earned himself a reputation as a generous philanthropist. Packard once said that "you shouldn't gloat about anything you've done; you ought to keep going and find something better to do." He did exactly that and served for more than 30 years as president and chairman of the David and Lucile Packard Foundation, which he began in 1964 in an effort to support universities, community groups, youth organizations, and hospitals. Through this foundation, the Packard family donated an estimated $461 million to various activities for the foundation's first 30 years in operation. Packard also played a central role in the establishment of the Monterey Bay Aquarium, donating $55 million for its facilities. In addition, he was very involved with the theater community, serving as a director of the Wolf Trap Foundation, a performing arts organization in Virginia. Perhaps most evident in his philanthropic activities was Packard's devotion to higher education and the promotion of scientific research. He established numerous fellowships for science and engineering and was chairman of the Panel on the Health of U.S. Colleges and Universities convened by the White House. "The universities have been the prime source of new science from their work in basic research, and at the same time they are also the producers of scientific talent for the future," Packard once told the Christian Science Monitor (November 21, 1986).

Packard remained chairman of the board of HP until 1993. He and Hewlett had been planning to quietly phase themselves out of everyday operations in the late 1980s, but when the company began to take a nosedive in 1990, the partners stepped in and reasserted their power in an attempt to bring the company back from its slump. They accomplished exactly that, and by 1995, the multinational company was second in the industry, posting revenues of $31.5 billion and employing over 100,000 people worldwide. Packard, who continued to own significant amount of stock in the company, suddenly developed pneumonia in March 1996 and died from complications to the illness on March 26, 1996 at Stanford University Hospital. He is survived by his four children, David Woodley Packard, Nancy Ann Packard Burnett, Susan Packard Orr, and Julie Elizabeth Packard. His wife, Lucile Salter Packard, died in 1987.

David Packard, who was often described as "gracious" and "unpretentious", was an avid outdoorsman who enjoyed fishing and hunting. He was also known to enjoy working the land of his extensive cattle ranching operations of which he and Hewlett—who remained good friends for more than 60 years—had been co-owners. In his lifetime, Packard was the recipient of hundreds of awards, including the American Electronics Association Medal of Achievement "for significant contributions to the advancement of electronics," (1960); the Medal of Honor from the Electronic Industries Association (1974); the Founders Award from the National Academy of Engineering (1979); and the National Medal of Technology (1988). He was also the recipient of honorary degrees from six universities and colleges across the United States and was inducted into the Silicon Valley Engineering Hall of Fame in 1991.—D. B.

Suggested Reading: *Christian Science Monitor* p22+ Nov. 21, 1986; *Computer World* p32 Apr. 1, 1996; *Current Biography* June 1996; *Detroit News* Mar. 27, 1996; *Fortune* p143+ Mar. 14, 1988; *Hewlett Packard* (on-line) 1996; *Laser Focus World* (on-line) Aug. 1995; *New York Times* D p20 Mar. 27, 1996; *The Computer Paper* (on-line) May 1996; *U.S. News & World Report* p13 Apr. 8, 1996; *American Men and Women of Science*, vol 7, 1986; Lee, J. A. N., ed. *International Biographical Dictionary of Computer Pioneers*, 1995; Cortada, James W. *Historical Dictionary of Data Processing: Organizations*, 1987

Pajitnov, Alexey

1955(?)– Mathematician; computer programmer; creator of Tetris

The Russian-born mathematician and programmer Alexey Pajitnov is the creator of *Tetris*, one of the most popular video games of all time. Working at the Soviet Academy of Science's computer center in Moscow, Pajitnov wrote *Tetris* to test the center's new computers. Many of his colleagues found themselves immediately addicted to the game, in which the player has to arrange falling blocks into orderly rows. A short time later, illegal copies of *Tetris* were being used on nearly every personal computer in Moscow. Thinking that *Tetris* had potential to be commercially successful in the West, Pajitnov sought out an American publisher. The game reached the United States in 1988, released by Spectrum Holobyte, but became an international sensation in 1989, when versions for the arcade and Nintendo's popular Gameboy handheld video-game system reached the market. Although *Tetris* sold over 50 million copies, totaling more than $800 million in sales, Pajitnov never received any royalties at the height of its popularity because his employer, the Soviet Academy of Science, owned the rights to the game. Pajitnov emigrated to the United States in 1991 to work as a video-game designer and joined the Microsoft Corporation in 1996.

Alexey Pajitnov (sometimes spelled Pazhitnov) was born in about 1955 in Moscow, Russia. His father, a writer and philosopher, was among the growing number of political dissidents in the tightly governed communist country during the 1960s and 1970s. Alexey's mother worked as a journalist. As a child Alexey learned chess from his father and later developed an interest in mathematics, computers, puzzles, and strategy games. An excellent student, he received a master's degree in applied mathematics from the Moscow Institute of Aviation. After pursuing some postgraduate studies at the Soviet Academy of Sciences computer center in Moscow, he began working there as a programmer during the early 1980s, specializing in speech recognition, artificial intelligence, and computer-assisted design. "This was a very serious place, with very serious work," Pajitnov recalled to Charles Petit for the *San Francisco Chronicle* (January 18, 1990). The job paid him the equivalent of $30 a month.

Pajitnov began writing games to test the center's new computers. In 1984 he wrote *Tetris* in the Pascal computer language for the Electronica 60, a Soviet clone of the DEC Rainbow computer. Pajitnov based *Tetris* on Pentamino, an ancient Roman puzzle game where the player has to arrange 12 puzzle pieces, each a different shape, on a rectangular board. Pajitnov explained to Don Steinberg for *PC/Computing* (May 1990) that if the pieces in Pentamino are removed and mixed up, "it's a big problem to put them back."

In *Tetris* blocks of different shapes descend from the top of the screen. The player must correctly arrange the pieces into rows before they hit the bottom. The original version of *Tetris* was quite crude and lacked color or sound. "The field is dotted with asterisks," Pajitnov told Alex Pham for the *Los Angeles Times* (August 9, 2001). "The squares are created by using square brackets. Imagine working with *Tetris* in text mode only, where you're working only with letters and numbers." *Tetris* quickly became popular with Pajitnov's colleagues at the center, who played it for hours on end. Displeased that the game was distracting people from their work, Pajitnov's boss tried to ban *Tetris* from the center's computers but failed and eventually became addicted to the game himself.

Pajitnov realized that *Tetris* had commercial potential as a video game. He worked with Vadim Gerasimov, a 16-year-old programmer and hacker, to adapt it for the IBM PC. Unauthorized copies of the PC-version of *Tetris* were smuggled out of the center and distributed to other PC users. "In two weeks, the game like a fire was on every PC in Moscow," Pajitnov told Steinberg.

Tetris had gradually made its way to the United States by 1988. Steinberg reported that Victor Brjabrin, one of Pajitnov's colleagues, sent the game to a software company in Budapest, Hungary, to see if it could be marketed to the West. (Pajitnov, however, expressed doubts to Steinberg that Brjabrin played any role in the negotiations.) After acquiring the game, the Hungarian company forwarded *Tetris* to its agent in London, Andromeda Software, Ltd., which then licensed it to Spectrum Holobyte, a subsidiary of Sphere Inc., in Alameda, California. Although he had created *Tetris*, Pajitnov had no role in licensing the game. "The first version [of *Tetris*] came out without our permission," he told Steinberg. "We were not very experienced in this kind of negotiation."

Tetris became the first Soviet-made software application sold in the United States. The game, however, became a smash hit in 1989 when Sega Enterprise introduced an arcade version of *Tetris*, and Nintendo, the Japanese video-game maker, released a version for its highly popular Gameboy hand-held system. Pajitnov told Pham that the Gameboy version "was the best possible version of *Tetris*. It was very well balanced. The rules included everything I really wanted. The squares were soft-dropped, not hard-dropped so you could see the blocks as they fell. That was a pleasant small detail that makes the game more controllable." Millions of people became addicted to *Tetris*; it was "easy to learn, impossible to master," as Barbara Carson wrote for the *Boston Globe* (January 30, 1990). *Tetris*, which was also designed for other systems, eventually sold more 50 million copies, making it one of the most successful video games ever sold. (The IBM-PC version included a convenient feature that allowed addicted users at work to hit the escape key to switch to a Lotus 1-2-3 spreadsheet screen shot if their bosses walked by.) In 1989 the Software Publishers Association, the software equivalent of the Academy of Motion Picture Arts and Sciences, gave four awards to *Tetris*, including best original game achievement and best entertainment program of 1988. Speaking with Pham, Pajitnov offered several explanations for the international popularity of the game, asserting

"that it appeals to the human need to have order and harmony. You have a random, chaotic situation, and your mission is to create order. The other theory [is] that all your achievements, the blocks you arranged, disappear as soon as they're lined up. So what you have in front of your eyes is all your awful mistakes. It makes you want to fix it all the time."

Although the game made Alexey Pajitnov a global gaming celebrity, he received no royalties for *Tetris*, which generated about $800 million in total sales according to Susan Wloszczyna for *USA Today* (April 25, 1996). Under the Soviet Union's copyright laws, the Soviet Academy of Science owned the rights to the game. (The Academy rewarded Pajitnov by promising to buy him a new computer, an IBM-AT, which was already considered antiquated in the United States.) Pajitnov, however, never expressed any bitterness, saying that he preferred to design enjoyable puzzle games and help develop the Soviet Union's fledgling computer industry. Pajitnov received little attention for *Tetris* in his native country. "Nobody knows me there," he told Carton. In 1996 Pajitnov finally received the rights to *Tetris* and earned some small royalties.

Pajitnov toured the United States in 1990 to observe the computer industry. His trip included stops in Honolulu, Las Vegas, Seattle, San Francisco, Chicago, New York City, Boston, and at the Massachusetts Institute of Technology (MIT) in Cambridge. In 1991 he wrote two new games, *Welltris* and *Faces*. A sequel to *Tetris*, *Welltris* featured three-dimensional graphics. T. R. Reid wrote about the new game for the *Washington Post* (September 9, 1991): "The flying puzzle pieces now fall down a four-sided well and you have to steer and rotate them so they land in the right spot at the bottom of the well. It's fast, it's fun, and my only caveat is that playing one game of *Welltris* is like eating one potato chip; you just can't stop." Although it was not as commercially successful as *Tetris*, *Welltris* generated sales and fans. Like Pajitnov's other games, *Faces* was a moving jigsaw puzzle. Instead of manipulating blocks and other geometric shapes, players arranged pieces of the faces of such well-known figures as Soviet President Mikhail Gorbachev and former British Prime Minister Margaret Thatcher, or the faces from such famous paintings as the *Mona Lisa* or *Whistler's Mother*. "Every game is a very complicated product," Pajitnov explained to Pham. "For me, it's like a movie. The idea is the most important thing, what kind of mechanics are in the game. The second thing is the balance. It should have rules simple enough to be understandable, but the game should still be challenging."

Pajitnov and Vladimir Pokhilko, a psychologist and computer programmer, co-founded their own software company, Intec, in 1989. The two men formed a joint venture, AnimaTek, with Henk Rogers, the founder of Bullet-Proof Software in Redmond, Washington, who provided financial support. The company's first product was El-Fish, a technologically-advanced application that created life-like images of fish and underwater scenes. AnimaTek reached an agreement with the software company Maxis to market El-Fish in the United States. When it reached the market in 1993, El-Fish impressed many reviewers. "More than anything, [El-Fish is] an exploration of the computer's potential to simulate some of the characteristics and behaviors of living organisms . . . . it's a fascinating and unusual program that will captivate students and encourage both curiosity and computer literacy," Paul Fleisher wrote for *Technology and Learning* (October 1994).

In 1991 Pajitnov and his family moved to the United States, settling in Kirkland, Washington. AnimaTek, which opened an office in the San Francisco area, released two more programs, El-Dino and Arena. After acquiring the rights to *Tetris*, Pajitnov founded the Tetris Company in 1996 to license the game. "I am always working on new games and puzzles," he told Wloszczyna. "But I am not expecting a repeat success. Something like Tetris usually happens to a person only once in a lifetime."

In September 1996 the Microsoft Corporation hired Pajitnov as a game designer to develop a series of "mind teasers" and puzzle games. Pajitnov's first product for Microsoft, *Pandora's Box*, was unveiled in 1999. The game is an interconnected series of 10 puzzles, with more than 350 variations. In the game, seven tricksters have unleashed chaos in the world by scattering the pieces of Pandora's Box. (Pandora, according to Greek myth, was given a box by the gods and told never to open it. Her curiosity won out, and many types of plagues and despair escaped into the world from the open box.) The player must restore order in the world by solving puzzles, which leads to finding the pieces. "The puzzles in *Pandora's Box* are not like typical word and logic puzzles but instead take advantage of computer technology by challenging players' visual skills," Pajitnov explained in a press release on the Microsoft Web site (September 30, 1999). "While traveling the globe, players are treated to visually stunning puzzles that include fine art and famous landmarks from around the world."

In 2000 physics students at Brown University in Providence, Rhode Island, paid tribute to *Tetris* by constructing a 10-story version of the game on the side of the university's Sciences Library. The project occupied 30 students for four months and used thousands of Christmas lights. In an interview with the *Washington Post* (April 21, 2000), Pajitnov said he was "amazed" and "very grateful" to the students, adding that it "was my dream for maybe 10 years to have something like that."

Pajitnov's wife, Nina, is a teacher. They have two sons, Peter and Dmitri.—D. C.

Suggested Reading: *Boston Globe* p53 Jan. 30, 1990, with photo; *Los Angeles Times* A p19 Jun. 17, 1990, with photo, T p6 Aug. 9, 2001 with photo; *New York Times* p7 Sep. 16, 1999; *Omni* p22 Oct. 1990; *PC/Computing* p110 May 1990, with photos; *San Francisco Chronicle* B p3 Jan. 18, 1990; *Technology and Learning* p7 Oct. 1994, *USA Today* D p10 Apr. 25, 1996, with photo; *Washington Post* F p22 Sep. 9, 1991, E p11 Apr. 21, 2000; *Wired* (on-line) May/June 1993, May 1994

Courtesy of Seymour Papert

Papert, Seymour A.

Mar. 1, 1928– Inventor of Logo

As the inventor of Logo, an educational computer programming language for children, Seymour A. Papert has become highly regarded as an important thinker about the ways in which computers can aid in a child's learning. Papert was a post-doctoral mathematics fellow when he met the noted child psychologist Jean Piaget at the University of Geneva, in Switzerland. After studying under Piaget and absorbing his educational theories, Papert sought to find a way to use mathematics to understand better how children learn and think. In the early 1960s he joined Marvin L. Minsky's team at the Massachusetts Institute of Technology (MIT), in Cambridge, where the group was studying the viability of artificial intelligence. With Minsky he created Logo, a computer language, which, by enabling children to write their own programs, has aided thousands of youngsters in understanding mathematical concepts. Since that time Papert has dedicated himself to the task of bettering American education by encouraging the use of computers as a primary tool. He is the author of a number of books, including *Perceptrons* (1969), which he co-authored with Minsky, *Mindstorms* (1980), *The*

Children's Machine (1993), and *The Connected Family* (1996).

Seymour A. Papert was born on March 1, 1928 in Pretoria, South Africa, the son of an entomologist who, with his family in tow, moved around the eastern coast of Africa to study the tsetse fly. As Papert recalled to Betsy Carpenter for *U.S. News & World Report* (July 16, 1990), life in the family camp was basic: "Our food was hunted, and when a truck broke down we fixed it." When Papert was eight years old, his family settled in Johannesburg, and, for the first time in his life, he was confronted with the brutality of apartheid. Not understanding why the government would oppress people because of their color, as he toured the city during his first few days there, Papert began wondering how people's minds worked. As he entered high school, his fascination with the workings of the human mind increased. He studied at the University of Witwatersrand, in Johannesburg, and during that time he was active in the anti-apartheid movement. He received a bachelor of arts degree, in 1949, and then continued his studies at the school, earning a Ph.D. in mathematics, in 1952.

In 1954 Papert traveled to England as a Royal Command Research Scholar at St. John's College at Cambridge University, and for the next two years he was involved in postgraduate mathematical research. For the school year of 1956 to 1957, he worked as a mathematics researcher at the Henri Ponicare Institute at the University of Paris. His exposure to the theories that would influence him the most began in 1958, when he became a researcher in child development at the University of Geneva. There he studied under the renowned child psychologist Jean Piaget, who is noted for reversing the idea held by generations of teachers that postulated that children are merely "empty vessels" to be filled. Instead Piaget theorized that children were active builders of knowledge who attempted daily to comprehend the world by constantly creating and testing their own ideas about it. From this point onward, Papert devoted his life to seeing how mathematics, combined with Piaget's theories on how children think and learn, could better the learning experience. Papert worked with Piaget until 1963, although this work was temporarily interrupted by Papert's return to Cambridge to receive his second Ph.D., also in math, in 1959. That same year he became a senior fellow at the National Physics Laboratory in London, a position he held until 1961. He returned to Piaget and the University of Geneva in 1962, where he taught as an assistant lecturer in cybernetics for the next year.

In 1963 Papert became a research associate of electrical engineering at the Massachusetts Institute of Technology, where he worked with Marvin L. Minsky, another man who would greatly influence Papert's work. Minsky, an expert on artificial intelligence (AI), brought Papert to MIT so that they could pool their knowledge in the hopes of making "smart" computers. By 1967 Papert had become a professor of applied mathematics and co-director of the Artificial Intelligence Laboratory at MIT, which he founded with Minsky. In that same year, they completed their work on the computer programming language Logo, which was designed to help children learn math by writing programs that would draw geometric shapes and patterns and other pictures on their computer screens. Minsky and Papert intended Logo to be a learning tool for children, one they hoped would be so riveting that students would begin initiating their own learning. Studies have since proven Minsky and Papert's theories about the language: children who have used Logo unraveled basic mathematical concepts, such as the number of degrees in a circle, for example, with very little help from their teachers.

1969 saw the publication of Minsky and Papert's *Perceptrons: Introduction to Computational Geometry*, a seminal book on artificial intelligence and the first work to discuss thoroughly parallelism in computing. In parallel computer architecture, small amounts of information are transmitted simultaneously via many different circuits. This structure, according to the predominant theories, is analogous to the functioning of the human mind, in which billions of neurons, or brain cells, send and receive messages by way of electrochemical signals. In *Perceptrons*, Minsky and Papert conclude that intelligent computers could be created by simulating the brain using networks of neuron-like entities—devices that would receive, evaluate, and respond to signals electronically. However, through mathematical analysis, the authors also show the limitations of so-called thinking computers. Since the initial publication of *Perceptrons*, several new editions have been published in which the authors have commented on the latest developments in AI.

Papert's next major publication was *Mindstorms: Children, Computers, and Powerful Ideas* (1981), in which he describes his work with children using the Logo program at his lab at MIT. Throughout the course of the book, the author gives examples of how children are typically fascinated by the process of writing their own programs and become active initiators of their own learning, which allows them to progress faster than they would in a classroom. He suggests that having children teach themselves through the use of computers is a better way for them to learn than through traditional schooling, and postulates that it would be possible to buy every child in the United States his or her own computer for about five percent of the total cost of educating them by conventional means. Sarah Berman, writing for *Science Books and Films* (September/October 1981), noted, "Papert worked with Piaget for five years on how children become thinkers, and then he worked at MIT on how to make machines think. . . . His ideas are exciting. . . . This approach also encourages the development of positive attitudes toward difficult problems by substituting the concept of 'debugging' for the image of failure usually associated with incorrect answers." In his review of the book for the *New York Times Book Review* (November 23, 1980), Timothy Ferris wrote, "In his enthusiasm Mr. Papert occasionally verges on the utopian. . . . But he offers one of the most promising glimpses yet of how we might build towards an educational system in which we could take renewed pride."

Papert left the Artificial Intelligence Laboratory in 1981 to found the Media Lab at MIT, where his group developed educational video games and other computerized learning tools. The group was most interested in studying constructivism, the branch of theory that grew out of the work of Piaget. Financed in part by a $3-million-dollar grant from the video game manufacturer Nintendo Ltd., Papert and his team based their research on the belief that children learned best while building something, which led to an experiment with the plastic children's building blocks knows as Lego. The group developed motors and light and touch sensors that could be incorporated into structures built with Lego blocks. Connecting these devices to a computer enabled children to write programs in Logo to make the motors and sensors move windmills or cars the children had built. The system, known as Lego/Logo, has been used in schools worldwide, giving children a fun way to explore principals of math and physics by understanding the workings of simple machines. In 1989 Papert became the Lego Professor of Learning and Research at MIT.

In 1993 Papert published another influential volume, *The Children's Machine: Rethinking School in the Age of the Computer*. In it, he notes that while computers have become more common in the classroom, the technology available to educators has not changed the way children are taught. According to Papert, computers have not become learning tools but have instead been confined to computer labs as things to be studied. In order to compete more effectively in a global marketplace, Papert argues, students must control their education, and they can do that best through the use of computers. P. Anand, reviewing the book for *Choice* (November 1993), believed it to be "as inspiring and educationally relevant as the author's previous book, *Mindstorms: Children, Computers, and Powerful Ideas*." A critic for *Kirkus Reviews* (May 1, 1993) asserted, "Even those who resist Papert's belief that the foundation of modern schooling is faulty will agree with his central theme that the ability to learn new skills is the most critical skill of all—and that computers have a unique, accelerated role to play in developing that ability."

Papert's most recent book is *The Connected Family: Bridging the Digital Generation Gap*, published in 1996. In it he encourages parents and children to use computers jointly, to stimulate the children's minds through games, drawing programs, and even research projects using the Internet. He also suggests that because children generally master new computer skills more quickly than adults, parents tend to learn a great deal from their children by using computers together. Laverna Saunders praised the book in *Library Journal* (November 1, 1996), noting that "Papert addresses parents in a conversational and nontechnical style." However, Ann Hulbert, who had attempted to do some of the exercises suggested in *The Connected Family* with her own son, complained in her *New Republic* (November 3, 1997) review that "Papert's bedside manner can be trying, even for veterans of Spockian solicitude." While generally believing Papert's educational goals to be commendable, Hulbert concluded that his method of seeking them, via computers, is more difficult and complicated in practice than his book would have readers believe. Furthermore she felt that many of these goals were attainable by way of more traditional classroom techniques and ways in which families spend time together. Still, she wrote, "You [do not] have to feel that independence, idiosyncratic exploration, or creative interdependence between young and old are as woefully absent from home and school as Papert does to want to promote more of all three, and to applaud the use of computers to help."

In addition to being a professor of applied mathematics and the Lego professor of learning and research, Seymour A. Papert previously held the title of Cecil and Ida Green Professor of Education at MIT, from 1974 to 1981. He has received a number of awards for his work, including a Guggenheim Fellowship (1980–81) and a Marconi International Fellowship (1981). Now a professor emeritus at MIT, his recent projects include an educational program at the Maine Youth Center in South Portland, a rehabilitation center that houses 200 teens who have been convicted of crimes. By using the Lego/Logo program and developing other projects, such as building their own Web sites, many of the teens there are able to master difficult concepts and gain a more positive idea of their potential. Papert often quotes Albert Einstein's saying: "Love is a better teacher than duty."—C. M.

Suggested Reading: *Booklist* p1756 June 1–15, 1993; *Choice* p18 Mar. 1981, p511 Nov. 1993; *Issues in Science and Technology* p84+ Spring 1994; *Kirkus Reviews* May 1, 1993; *Library Journal* p105 Sep. 15, 1980, p99 Nov. 1, 1996; *New Republic* p38 Nov. 3, 1997; *New Scientist* p45 Nov. 6, 1993; *New York Times* C p1+ Aug. 16, 1988, B p15 Dec. 26, 1990, C p16 July 22, 1993; *New York Times Book Review* p16 Nov. 23, 1980, p14 Nov. 14, 1993; *Science Books and Films* p10 Sep./Oct. 1981, p263 Dec. 1993; *U.S. News and World Report* p56+ July 16, 1990; *American Men and Women of Science 1998–99*, 1998; Spencer, Donald D. *The Timetable of Computers*, 1997

Hulton Archive by Getty Images

Pascal, Blaise

June 19, 1623–Aug. 19, 1662 Mathematician; inventor of the Pascaline calculator

The mathematician and philosopher Blaise Pascal lived a brief, but highly influential life. A largely self-educated man, Pascal began exploring mathematics from an early age and eventually helped bring a fresh perspective to geometry. He is, however, most well known in the world of computers for his pioneering Pascaline calculator, which he developed in 1642. This machine, although primitive and prone to error, was a highly significant step for science. Pascal spent much of his life engaged in philosophical and religious pursuits rather than science, but his inventive contributions to math and science make him one of the earliest forefathers of the Information Age.

Born in Clermont, Auvergne, France, on June 19, 1623, Blaise Pascal was the third child of Etienne Pascal and Antoinette (Begon) Pascal. His mother died when he was three years old, and his father, a man of scientific background who worked as a local judge, raised his children by himself, moving Blaise, along with his sisters, Gilberte and Jacqueline, to Paris after he retired in 1631. Pascal's father, who held unconventional thoughts on schooling, refused to allow Pascal a formal education and instead taught him at home. Deciding that Pascal was not to study mathematics before he turned 15, he locked up all mathematical texts in the house and forbade Pascal to look at them. Natural curiosity and teenage rebelliousness ultimately led the young Pascal to defy his father, and at age 12 he began to work on geometry by himself. He soon figured out that the sum of the angles of a triangle are two right angles; when his father realized

he was powerless to halt his son's interest in mathematics, he began to lend his texts to his intellectually advanced offspring.

By the age of 14, Pascal began to participate with his father in Mersenne's Circle, a weekly discussion group held by scientists and mathematicians. Here Pascal was able to absorb new ideas and present his own in a forum built on constructive feedback. At 16 he presented his own theorems to the group, including his idea, in the field of projective geometry, for what is now referred to as the mystic hexagon, and received good reviews from everyone in the group. However, the following year, Pascal's father was involved in an argument with the French government and Cardinal Richelieu over lowering interest rates. He was forced into hiding until he could fall back into the good graces of the Cardinal, at which time he was sent to Rouen and given the job of tax collector. Pascal continued to communicate with the Mersenne's Circle in Paris, and it was during this period that he engaged in his most active writing in not only mathematics, but literature and philosophy as well. In 1640 Pascal sent his first published paper, "Essay on Conic Sections," to Paris in order for it to be included in one of the evening discussion groups of Mersenne's Circle. This paper, which included his previous "mystic hexagon" concept, contained a number of projective geometry theorems and was well received by the mathematicians in Paris.

Having witnessed the tedious nature of his father's daily tax work, Pascal became interested in finding a way to relieve the grind of adding up long columns of figures. At the age of 19 he designed one of the first calculating machines, which he called the Pascaline. Wilhelm Schickard had designed a calculating machine several years earlier, but Pascal's was completely different from this invention. He hired a group of local workman to build the machine from his drawings, but the men were more accustomed to building houses and farm equipment, and the intricate workings of Pascal's device proved too difficult for them. Pascal then decided to train himself as a mechanic and began experimenting with various gears made from ivory, wood, and copper in an attempt to find the best possible materials for his device.

Pascal's machine was completed in 1642 and was contained in a box small enough to fit on top of a desk or small table. The calculator's interface was made up of a row of toothed wheels, over which was a row of small windows designed to display the results of the calculations. Adding a number to the accumulator (the portion of the mechanism responsible for making the actual calculations) required simply inserting a small stylus into the toothed wheel at the position marked with whatever number was desired, and then rotating the wheel in a clockwise fashion until the stylus encountered the fixed stop. The windows to show the results were made up of two separate sections, an upper and lower section, with a brass slide to cover the section which was not in use at the time. The upper window section was used for addition, the lower for subtraction—which could be done only by using a somewhat complicated mathematical process. Pascal had to use this system because the internal construction of the machine made it impossible to turn the dials backward to perform direct subtraction.

Pascal had realized that using a single toothed gear would not work for a general carry mechanism (the mechanism for carrying a number from the ones column to the tens and hundreds and so on) because of the delicacy of the gears. In order to solve this problem, Pascal devised an entirely new mechanism that was based on the movement of falling weights instead of a long chain of gears. The internal workings of Pascal's machine were as follows: One wheel (X) was connected to the ones digit of the accumulator, and another wheel (Y) was connected to the tens digit. A carry could be propagated from one wheel to the other through a device that lay between the two wheels. As the X wheel was rotated, two pins projecting from it raised a weight. When the wheel rotated from 9 to 0, the pins slipped out from the weight, allowing it to fall. As a result, a small, spring-loaded foot would hit the pins sticking out of Y, driving it around one place. This carry mechanism (obviously assisted by the forces of gravity) was put between each pair of digits in the accumulator, and when a carry was made through several digits, it made a clunking noise all the way down the line of figures. By using this type of carry mechanism, Pascal was able to eliminate strain on the gears.

Interested in selling Pascalines for profit, Pascal had 50 more constructed. Each was slightly different, having different numbers of digits in the accumulator. Attempting to produce such a large amount of technical equipment in the 17th century was a bold move for Pascal, and his venture was ultimately unsuccessful. Part of the problem was that while Pascal's device was ingenious for his day, it was also prone to producing erroneous results. Many of his original machines have survived to the present day (seven of them in public or private collections), and mathematicians have observed that they do not work properly if not used with the utmost care. For instance, even lightly bumping into the machine will cause it to generate extra carries in certain digits of the accumulator. Problems in calculations also occurred for Pascal due to the design of French currency at the time. With 20 sols in a livre and 12 deniers in a sol, Pascal found himself working division problems with unwieldy numbers, which proved to be much more difficult than had the division required, for instance, 100 as a base figure.

Modern commentators have theorized that had Pascal continued to refine his device, he would have been able to solve the technical problems he encountered. However, by the time the last of his calculators had been produced in 1652, Pascal was already straying away from scientific study. In ad-

dition to his work with the calculator, he did perform scientific experiments in the late 1640s, focusing mostly on atmospheric pressure. In 1647 he proved, to his satisfaction, that a vacuum existed, but his views were hotly contested by René Descartes, who, after visiting Pascal to discuss the matter, wrote in a letter that the young mathematician had "too much vacuum in his head," as quoted by Dr. Charles Friel on his Web site at Sam Houston State University. After writing *New Experiments Concerning Vacuums* in October of that same year, Pascal found himself embroiled in further arguments with other scientists, who, like Descartes, did not believe in the existence of a vacuum. In 1653 Pascal wrote *Treatise on the Equilibrium of Liquids*, in which he explains his law of pressure. This treatise was described by D. Adamson in *Blaise Pascal: Mathematician, Physicist, and Thinker About God* (1995) as "a complete outline of a system of hydrostatics, the first in the history of science [which] embodies his most distinctive and important contribution to physical theory."

Pascal had begun to grow religious following his association with members of a religious sect who had cared for his father after he had injured his leg in 1646, an injury that eventually ended his life. For a time following his father's death, Pascal gave up both mathematics and science to instead focus on religious contemplation and philosophical writing, but he returned to science for a brief period during the years that he explored vacuums. Then, on November 23, 1654, Pascal was traveling in a four-horse carriage when the horses broke away; had their harness not broken at the last second, Pascal would have been thrown off the bridge at Neuilly. This life-threatening incident was taken as a miracle by Pascal and as a sign by God that he should return to a life of contemplation—which he did for the rest of his life. His most famous philosophical work, *Pensees*, which is a collection of personal thoughts on human suffering and faith in God, was started in 1656 and continually worked on throughout 1657–58. The work contains "Pascal's Wager," which claims to prove, using probabilistic and mathematical arguments, the rational nature of belief in God.

Toward the end of his life, Pascal once again began to contemplate mathematical problems; through deep concentration on these problems he was able to find some relief from intense pain caused by a malignant ulcer in his stomach. Riddled with various health problems since childhood, Pascal was often unable to sleep at night, and he would lay awake trying to figure out mathematical problems in order to forget his suffering. Described by Adamson as "a man of slight build with a loud voice and somewhat overbearing manner," he died of complications from his malignant ulcer on August 19, 1662 in Paris, at the age of 39.
—P. G. H.

Suggested Reading: University of St. Andrews School of Mathematics and Statistics Web site; Goldstine, Herman H. *The Computer From*

Pascal to von Neumann, 1972; *Dictionary of Scientific Biography*, vol. 13, 1976; Williams, Michael R. *A History of Computing Technology*, 1985; *Larousse Dictionary of Scientists*, vol. 1, 1994

Patterson, John H.

Dec. 13, 1844–May 7, 1922 Entrepreneur; industrialist

In 1882 John H. Patterson, the general manager of the Southern Ohio Coal and Iron Company in Coalton, Ohio, couldn't figure out why the company store kept losing money. After personally investigating the matter, he found that clerks at the store were giving away free goods in order to build a loyal following among customers. Patterson didn't have the time to personally supervise the store, but he had to find a way to keep the clerks honest. He heard that two brothers in Dayton were selling a machine that tabulated sales, and he decided to try out one of these new "cash registers." The store stopped losing money and, within one year, turned a profit. Thinking that cash registers had a promising future, Patterson and his brother Frank bought controlling stock in the National Manufacturing Company, which made the machines. They changed its name to the National Cash Register Company (NCR) and, by the end of the decade, turned it into one of the country's most successful corporations. The keys to NCR's success were Patterson's revolutionary sales strategies and advertising campaigns, which permanently changed the way American business was conducted. After Patterson's death, in 1922, NCR made the gradual transition to developing computer technology.

The grandson of a veteran of the Revolutionary War, John Henry Patterson was born near Dayton, Ohio, on December 13, 1844. He was the seventh of 11 children and grew up on his parents' farm. His mother often read him Washington Irving's accounts of his travels, telling John that if he worked hard and saved his money, he too could travel the world and meet people. Patterson grew up working on the farm, performing such tasks as tending the cows and chopping wood in between going to school. He graduated from Dayton's Central High School in 1862. Patterson enrolled at Miami University in Oxford, Ohio, but was forced to return to the farm when his father died to help take care of his family.

During the Civil War (1861–65), President Abraham Lincoln asked for volunteers to serve in the Union army for a period of 100 days. Patterson joined the 131st Ohio Volunteer Infantry. The unit reached as far as Baltimore, Maryland, but never saw combat. Patterson completed his service and was discharged in August 1864. The next year, he resumed his education, attending Dartmouth University, in New Hampshire.

Patterson's mother told him about Eliam Barney, a successful manufacturer of railroad cars in Dayton. Barney had acquired the skills to be a good manufacturer while teaching school. "I decided then that I would teach school as a way of becoming a good manufacturer," Patterson said, as quoted by Samuel Crowther in the book *John H. Patterson: Pioneer in Industrial Welfare* (1926). "I spent three months of my vacation teaching school. I left Dartmouth College and went up in back of the mountains. There I learned how to make everything simple and plain. I learned how to use small words and big ideas."

Patterson received his bachelor's degree in 1867. "What I learned [in college] mostly was what not to do," he said, as quoted by Crowther. "They gave me Greek and Latin and algebra and higher mathematics and Edwards on the Will—all useless." Unable to find a job after graduating from Dartmouth, Patterson returned home. He performed chores around the farm and worked at the family grist and saw mills and began managing the family store. At the store, Patterson had great difficulty keeping the books. "At that time we had no system of receipts," he recalled, as quoted by Crowther. "Our book of accounts was kept in a desk in the hall. We were always forgetting to make proper records of things given out, and our books very rarely agreed with the books of our employees." Patterson added that these mistakes always hurt the seller and not the buyer.

Patterson tired of working on the farm and decided to pursue his plans to be a manufacturer. Despite his college degree, he couldn't find a job. "It seemed that nobody had anything for a college man to do," he said, as quoted by Crowther. "College men were only fitted for certain thing—doctors of medicine, doctors of law, and doctors of theology. I didn't want any of these professions. I wanted to get into manufacturing, but I couldn't get anything to do." Patterson couldn't get an office job because he lacked administrative experience, but no one would hire him as a manual laborer because employers thought that he, as a college graduate, was unsuited for such work.

In 1868 Patterson finally found employment as a toll collector for the Miami and Erie Canals in Ohio. Although the position paid $800 per year, which was a lot of money back then, Patterson had to pay for his own office, room, supplies, and lighting, and the expenses left him with only $500 a year. (The job also required him to be on duty 24 hours a day, seven days a week.) As in the family store, the lack of precise financial records became a problem. Ships were charged specific tolls based on the type of cargo they carried. However, since each toll collector decided how to classify the goods, ships were often charged different tolls at different locations. Captains refused to pay a higher toll than the one they had paid at the previous station. Because precise records were not kept and circulated, some captains lied about what they previously paid. Much of Patterson's time was spent arguing with captains over their tolls. Since the revenue was often lower than expected, Patterson feared that his superiors would suspect him of embezzlement. To solve these problems, Patterson devised a system of receipts. Every ship that passed his station was given a receipt, which the captain had to show to the next toll collector for passage. Copies of the receipts were also sent to the other toll collectors and to the main office. "This system worked very well," Patterson said, as quoted by Crowther. "I had no disputes with the captains of any of the boats and no arguments with the home office as to the amount of money which I had taken in."

Although it provided a steady income, toll collecting was a dead-end job for John Patterson. He had no opportunities for advancement, and his salary would probably remain the same for years. Since his system of receipts went into effect and eliminated disputes, Patterson had more free time. He took the opportunity to start a sideline from the office. In 1868 he set up a coal and wood business, taking orders from friends. A coal yard was located nearby. After taking an order, Patterson went out, bought the coal or wood, and hired someone to deliver it. He used a slate to keep track of all transactions, but still had trouble with bookkeeping. Patterson's coal business gradually grew, thanks to his reputation for delivering what he promised. A short time later, Patterson's brother Steve joined the business, which was then renamed S. J. Patterson & Co. In a year the business was so successful that the Patterson brothers decided to become full-time coal merchants. John Patterson borrowed $250 from a local bank and purchased the coal yard, and his brother Frank joined the enterprise.

In 1881 the Patterson brothers went into business with John M. Corse, a former Civil War general who was president of a major railway. The Pattersons bought coal lands along the railway on behalf of Corse and then resold them to a corporation he owned. The brothers got one-third of the profits of each sale. With financial backing from Corse and other investors, the Pattersons bought 4,705 acres of land in Jackson County, Ohio, and set up the Southern Ohio and Iron Company, which they managed.

The company established a store for its employees. Despite relatively high prices and no competition, the store lost money year after year. One day Patterson went to investigate the matter personally. He discovered that the clerks were trying to win a cash award he had instituted for the clerk who sold the most merchandise. To lure customers and build a personal following, the clerks were giving away a lot of free goods. Patterson immediately fired the clerks and the superintendent of the store. Because his duties with the company kept him too busy to supervise the operation of the store himself, Patterson had to find a way to keep the clerks honest. He had heard that two brothers, John and James Ritty, the owners of the National Manufacturing Company, in Dayton, had invented a cash register, a machine that tabulated sales. The machine came in a wooden cabinet and had numbered keys that punched holes in a roll of paper. Patterson was the Rittys' first customer. He purchased two cash registers for $50 each. The register did not solve the store's problems immediately. Patterson recalled that the new superintendent "did not register all the sales, but at night counted the cash and credit sales and worked the register to balance the amount," as quoted by Crowther. This time, Patterson had the store's new superintendent watched closely and fired him when his dishonesty was discovered. After that the store finally began showing a profit.

Impressed by the cash register, John and Frank Patterson bought some stock in the National Manufacturing Company in 1882. Two years later, they bought controlling stock in the company from a group of businessmen and changed its name to the National Cash Register Company (NCR). After discovering that the company was losing money, the Patterson brothers offered the businessmen $2000 to get out of the deal, but the offer was refused. An article on the official NCR Web site quoted John Patterson as saying, "Very well. I am going into the cash register business, and I will make a success of it!"

To turn NCR around, John Patterson stressed advertising and selling. He immediately expanded the number of salesmen. At the time most salesmen used their own methods to sell goods, with little or no input from their companies. In 1886 Patterson called a meeting of NCR's sales representatives from New York City; Chicago; Washington, D.C.; Boston; and Denver at a hotel in Dayton to learn their sales techniques. Harry R. Blood, a salesman from Chicago, was NCR's most successful salesman. He told Patterson that he never even mentioned the cash register until he had made friends with the customer and the other employees who would use it. "All the rest of the men ought to know about this," Patterson said, as quoted by Crowther. Patterson also consulted with his brother-in-law, Joseph H. Crane, who was known as the best wallpaper salesman in Ohio and who eventually joined NCR. Crane said the customer must always be taken away from the store's distractions and be brought to a place where his complete attention would be focused on the register. (The salesmen always had demonstration models with them.) "The idea was simply this: I knew that a cash register was a good thing," Crane said, as quoted by Crowther. "I knew that retail merchants ought to have it, and if they knew this as well as I did, they would buy. My only duty was to explain all about it from beginning to end." Patterson gathered what he learned from Blood, Crane, and the other salesmen into *The NCR Primer*, a 450-word, 16-page instructional manual. Patterson expected the salesmen he hired to memorize the entire manual or be fired.

When the Patterson brothers acquired NCR, in 1884, the company had only 13 employees, including one full-time salesman. At first, Patterson marketed the cash register to saloon keepers. Within four years, NCR had over 1,000 employees, and by the end of the decade, salesmen were pitching the cash register to grocery stores, hotels, and numerous other businesses. Sales of cash registers increased each year.

Patterson held a meeting for the company's salesmen once a year, so they could exchange ideas and other important information. To keep in touch with his salesmen, or agents, as he called them, Patterson published a company newsletter, *The N.C.R.* In 1894 Patterson opened the NCR Hall of Industrial Education, a training school for salesmen. Crowther estimated that this was the first school for salesmen ever established. Patterson ordered all of NCR's salesmen around the country to enroll at the school, which was on the family farm, to sharpen their skills. The company paid for the students' travel and hotel expenses. The classes were taught by Crane, and *The NCR Primer* served as the main textbook.

In 1900 Patterson instituted a quota system, requiring his sales agents to sell a specific number of cash registers within one month. As an incentive, Patterson divided up the country into sales districts that were guaranteed to individual salesmen. No other corporation had ever guaranteed territories to its salesmen before. "The N.C.R. salesmen caught the spirit," Crowther wrote. "They sold. They sold according to the primer, and they sold according to their ingenuity when nothing in the primer seemed to fit."

Over the years NCR made several technological improvements to the cash register. A "detail adder" model displayed sales on counter wheels instead of a paper roll. In 1906 a young inventor named Charles F. Kettering added an electric motor to the cash register, which allowed it to open and close with speed and ease.

Aggressive advertising played an important role in NCR's success. Patterson had an illustrated, 300-page catalogue printed, which was given to the company's traveling salesmen. He also began direct advertising. A precursor to junk mail, hundreds of thousands of circulars were regularly sent to saloons, restaurants, grocery stores, and other retailers around the country. Each piece of literature also contained a business reply card. The circulars were so successful that they evolved into magazines, which offered advice and suggestions on how to run a store and improve business.

In 1894 Patterson was shocked when NCR's customers in England returned about $50,000 worth of registers to the company, asserting that they didn't work properly. He looked into the matter to see what was going wrong and concluded that many of his workers lacked motivation because of poor working conditions at the factory. "To go back, when we began business few employers considered workmen other than as people to be hired at the lowest possible wage, worked as hard as they could be worked, and then fired when anyone felt like firing them," Patterson said, as quoted by Crowther. "It did not make much difference then where or how the men or women worked, because it did not seem to have occurred to any one that in the shops who came in the morning and went home at night." Patterson initiated several reforms to improve conditions at the factory. He offered a free hot lunch to all female employees. They refused it, however, because they would not take charity. As a compromise, hot lunches were priced at five cents. In 1895 he installed a dining room for the female employees. Patterson also provided health care to his workers and established children's programs and an employee country club. He redesigned the factory, installing glass windows that stretched from the floor to the ceiling. The windows provided daylight and could be opened to let in fresh air. The employees were all given lockers, and showers were installed. He raised workers' wages and improved safety at the factory. "In fact, we did everything that we could discover to make the conditions of work as comfortable as possible," Patterson said, as quoted by Crowther. "Men and women work better when they have self-respect; the first step toward self-respect is decent living and working conditions. A man cannot come out of a hovel, have a dirty breakfast, go into a dark, noisome factory, and then do a good day's work; he can do neither himself nor his employer justice under such conditions." Patterson's fellow industrialists criticized his reforms, asserting that he was coddling his workers. Stung by the criticism, Patterson threatened to move the NCR factory out of the Dayton area in 1908, but never carried it out.

Despite Patterson's new reputation as a model employer, NCR's business practices attracted the scrutiny of the federal government, because by 1913 Patterson and his top executive, Thomas Watson Sr., had virtually eliminated all competition. The same year, Patterson, Watson, and 26 other NCR employees were convicted of violating the Sherman Anti-Trust Act, which was passed by Congress in 1890 to dissolve monopolies and punish corporations that used unfair competitive practices. Patterson was sentenced to one year in prison and fined $5,000. The Court of Appeals later reversed the conviction.

In 1913 a massive flood caused great devastation in Dayton. The NCR factory was spared because it was located on high ground. Patterson and Watson immediately organized a relief program, providing food, shelter, electricity, and health care to the victims. The factory was used to shelter many of those who were left homeless by the disaster. Under Patterson's supervision, relief supplies were shipped to the area from New York by train. His charitable efforts made him a folk hero to the people of Dayton. Before the Court of Appeals threw out Patterson's conviction, his supporters petitioned President Woodrow Wilson to pardon him. Patterson, however, said he would refuse a pardon and wished only "simple justice," as quoted by a reporter for the *New York Times* (May 8, 1922).

NCR served as a training ground for many people who became important executives and enjoyed distinguished careers with other corporations. At the time Crowther wrote his book, in 1926, he estimated that every large sales organization in the country employed at least one person who had worked under Patterson's tutelage. Alvan Macauley, the president of the Packard Motor Car Company; Henry Theobald, the president of the Toledo Scale Company; Harry Ford, the president of the Saxon Car Company; Jacob Oswald, the president of the Roto-Speed Company; and William Pflum, the president of the Burke Manufacturing Company, had all been employed by NCR in various capacities. Two other NCR employees, Charles F. Kettering and Edward A. Deeds, co-founded Delco, a scientific-research firm, in 1907. Kettering made important contributions to the improvement of the automobile such as developing the complete ignition system and the self-starter and became a well-known philanthropist. The employee who enjoyed the most success after leaving NCR, however, was Watson. A former piano salesman, he gradually climbed the NCR hierarchy, becoming second only to Patterson. After he left NCR, Watson became president of the Computing-Tabulating-Recording Company, which later changed its name to Industrial Business Machines (IBM). He employed many of the management practices that he had learned from Patterson and guided IBM into one of most successful corporations in American history.

NCR remained in business for the next few decades, branching out into other fields and making important contributions to the development of information processing. In 1938 NCR's electrical department produced a counting device using vacuum tubes, which was a precursor to computers. The company began producing digital computers in 1952. NCR also helped pioneer state-of-the-art technology such as MOS/LSI circuitry for computer terminals, optical scanner systems, encapsulation systems, and the tower—a combination hard drive and disk drive that has become the standard in most desktop machines. The company that John Patterson built is still in business today as the NCR Corporation, which is a subsidiary of AT&T, the telecommunications conglomerate.

John Patterson retired from NCR in 1921. His wife, the former Katherine Beck, died in 1894. One of the couple's two children, Frederick Beck Patterson, became an executive with NCR. After his retirement, Patterson traveled extensively. He died, from chronic heart disease, on May 7, 1922, aboard a train en route to Atlantic City, New Jersey, where he had planned to rest and recuperate.
—D. C.

Suggested Reading: NCR Web site; *New York Times* p17 May 8, 1922; Crowther, Samuel. *John H. Patterson: Pioneer in Industrial Welfare*, 1926

Rajchman, Jan Aleksander

Aug. 10, 1911–Apr. 1, 1989 Engineer; inventor

Although he has remained largely in the shadows of his fellow computer innovators, Jan Aleksander Rajchman stands as an important figure in the development of computing technology. His work on electron photomultipliers—vacuum tubes that direct light, often from dim sources, through both photoemission and secondary emission in order to produce enough electrons to generate a current—had a profound impact on their structure that is still evident 60 years after Rajchman's contribution to their development. The improvements he contributed include his use of electrostatic rather than magnetic focusing, and the elimination of the problem of dark currents. Using a unique rubber model, Rajchman also shed light on how electrons moved in fields of complex electrodes. After the United States entered World War II in 1941, Rajchman assisted the ongoing computer projects of the time by developing the Selectron, a memory system that, although technically complicated and unreliable, proved useful in the JOHNNIAC computer. During Rajchman's nearly 40 years as an engineer and researcher at the Radio Corporation of America (RCA), he helped lead the company into new areas of exploration, including data processing, for which it developed products during the 1950s. For all of these contributions, in addition to his work as a solo inventor, Rajchman is recognized as a significant force in the burgeoning technological era of the 1930s to 1950s.

Born in London on August 10, 1911, Jan Aleksander Rajchman remained in England, where his father was involved in medical research, until the age of seven. Rajchman then returned with his parents to their native country, Poland, before moving again, three years later, to Geneva, Switzerland. There, he attended the College de Geneve, graduating in 1930, and continuing on to the Swiss Federal Institute of Technology, in Zurich, from which he received a degree in electrical engineering in 1934. Four years later, Rajchman received his doctorate of science from the same institution.

Following his graduation, Rajchman decided that he wanted to do research in electronics and, realizing that his opportunities were limited in Europe, he moved to the United States. He had heard of the Russian inventor Vladimir Zworykin and his work in electronics, including his invention of the Kinescope, a cathode-ray-tube receiver that paved the way for the introduction of television. Upon his arrival in the U.S., Rajchman applied for a position at the Radio Corporation of America (RCA) in Camden, New Jersey, where Zworykin was employed. Rajchman did not get the job, and he decided to take a summer course at the Massachusetts Institute of Technology (MIT), in Cambridge, in order to strengthen his English. While at the school, Rajchman received word from one of his initial RCA job interviewers that there was a position opening up, and he jumped at the opportunity and made his way back to New Jersey.

Rajchman began his career at RCA in the company's factory. Stationed in the testing department, his job was to make sure the variable condensers for superheterodyne radio receivers to conformed to standards, making adjustments by bending plates by hand. He remained in that position only briefly, however, and his wish to work with Zworykin was answered as he was transferred into the television pioneer's laboratory. Rajchman began there as a researcher on January 1, 1936, and his first assignment was to assist Zworykin with work on electron photomultiplier tubes. In these tubes, electrons released by photoelectric emission are multiplied in successive stages by dynodes, electrodes that produce secondary emission of electrons. Rajchman's contribution to the project was to focus electrostatic rather than magnetic force. He would also later design an intricate system of dynodes in order to keep gas ions from feeding back to the cathode. These ions were the main causes of dark current—the darkest emissions that the photomultiplier tubes were able to detect which set the lower limit of light detection for the phototubes. In order for Rajchman to create this system of dynodes, however, the research team had to solve an equation that described the movement of electrons moved in fields of complex electrodes, a problem that was too difficult for the computational methods and devices available at the time.

Rajchman found a way to circumvent the difficult equation by building a model containing small steel ball bearings on rubber sheets which was intended to simulate the electron paths. In an interview for RCA conducted by Mark Heyer and Al Pinsky that appeared as part of the *RCA Engineers Collection* (July 11, 1975), Rajchman described his early research at RCA: "The multipliers had already been conceived. They were of a magnetically focus type that were [sic] complicated. They also suffered from large dark current; in other words, when there was no light there was still a fairly large output. There was a limit to how small light you can measure with [sic]. What I really did was to make them simpler by making them electrostatic and also discover the reasons for the dark current problem and try to avoid it. In order to do that you have to understand how electrons move in complex electrostatic fields . . . We did have to resort to a rubber model to do this, which is an analogy of motion of a little ball rolling in a stretched rubber membrane to electrons moving in a vacuum . . . I think that we were the first people to ever use this analogy as an actual tool in design."

Rajchman's designs for the electron photomultiplier were the basis of his doctoral thesis which he completed in 1938 for the Swiss Federal Institute of Technology, and they remain the basis for photomultipliers at the beginning of the 21st century. By 1939, World War II had broke out in Europe, and RCA become involved in U.S. government projects aimed at improving American antiaircraft fire control, which at the time was inferior to the German technology. Rajchman was one of the first individuals to get involved in this project, and his research group's first work on the matter involved assessing the effectiveness of analog devices that the military was then using. According to Rajchman, he soon recommended switching to digital devices because "it was so difficult to get the right accuracy on [the analog] devices." RCA gradually began collaborating with other research groups that were working on computational devices all with the aim of helping the war effort. One of these groups was centered at the Moore School of Engineering at the University of Pennsylvania, in Philadelphia, and it included the noted mathematicians John Mauchly and John von Neumann.

As the war progressed, Rajchman's group became aware that analog devices were well-suited for use in the field of battle, whereas digital devices could be used for computations that were necessary for the war, such as those used in compiling ballistics tables. Ballistics tables were required in order for the Army to determine where to fire its weapons and successfully strike the enemy. The U.S. Army was regularly receiving requests from its officers for new ballistics tables, and the calculations required to prepare them were tremendously complex and time-consuming. The best available computing equipment at the time, the differential analyzer, was not accurate or fast enough for the job. Mauchly had suggested that the Moore School engineers build an electric, high-speed vacuum-tube computer that would be better able to perform the necessary calculations. RCA, including Zworykin's and Rajchman's group, was asked to help undertake the building of this new machine, but they rejected the offer. According to Rajchman, Zworykin turned down the request to work on the computer, which was later successfully completed and dubbed the ENIAC, was that he did not wish to work with a machine that used so many vacuum tubes (over 20,000) and would therefore be both large and, because the tubes frequently burned out, unreliable. It was a decision that Rajchman admitted he regretted during his 1975 RCA interview. "I was very sorry by the way he did decline the offer because I thought it would be rather fun to do it, and we were by far the most able group, I think, in the country at the time to do it. In fact, we were asked to tell everything we knew to the Moore School, and I went to the Moore School many times."

Throughout the 1940s, Rajchman continued his engineering work at RCA, and it was during this period that he developed the core computer memory technology for which he would remain famous for the rest of his life. In 1946 John von Neumann asked RCA if it would like to assist in developing a memory system for the IAS computer which was being constructed at the Institute for Advanced Study (IAS) at Princeton University, in New Jersey. At the time, Rajchman was developing a storage tube that would eventually become known as the Selectron. The Selectron had a storage capacity of

256 bits and is considered the first truly digital, random-access high-speed memory system. The tube had two grids of equally spaced bars at right angles to each other and forming a great number of "windows." One window could be opened at a time through the application of proper voltage, and one electron beam was allowed to flow through the window to a screen where information could be read or written. The Selectron was first used in the Rand Corporation's first computer, the JOHN-NIAC. However, as it turned out, Rajchman's Selectron tube was not reliable enough to be incorporated into von Neumann's IAS computer, and with the emergence of F.C. Williams's more dependable "Williams" tube in Great Britain, workers on the IAS chose not to use Rajchman's invention.

In 1947 Rajchman began to design a memory system that he hoped would prove more reliable than the Selectron, while at the same time in Great Britain, similar research was being undertaken by Andrew D. Booth. Rajchman created a memory consisting of small, doughnut-shaped ferrite substances that could be used to represent positive or negative charges, the equivalent of "on" or "off" bits. However, after the IAS team chose to use the Williams tube for that computer's memory, RCA decided to return to its own projects, including building its own complete computer, and Rajchman's work on the improved memory system was not pursued by the company. He did manage to persuade RCA to conduct research in the area of word processing, which they explored in the 1950s, and Rajchman stayed with the company for many more years, becoming associate director of the systems laboratory in 1959, and director of the laboratory in 1961. He remained in that position until 1971, when he was made RCA's staff vice president of information sciences. RCA continued to move away from the area of computers however, and Rajchman left the company in 1976 in order to take a position as Mackay Professor at the University of California at Berkeley. After a year, he decided to become an independent industry consultant. He continued to conduct his own research and develop inventions, delving into such areas as non-impact printers, display units, and optical devices.

Rajchman died in Princeton on April 1, 1989 at the age of 77. During his long career with RCA, Rajchman was the recipient of numerous honors for his work, including the Levy Medal from the Franklin Institute in 1947, the Liebman Award from the Institute of Electrical and Electronics Engineers (IEEE) in 1960, and the Edison Medal, in 1974. He was also a member of the National Academy of Engineering and a fellow of the IEEE.—D. B.

Suggested Reading: *IEEE History* (on-line) July 11, 1975; Goldstine, Herman H. *The Computer from Pascal to von Neumann*, 1972; Lee, J. A. N., ed. *International Biographical Dictionary of Computer Pioneers*, 1995; Cortada, James W. *The Historical Dictionary of Data Processing: Biographies*, 1987; Williams, Michael R. *A History of Computing Technology*, 1985

Ramo, Simon

May 7, 1913– Co-founder of TRW

In 1953 the engineers Simon Ramo and Dean Wooldridge left their positions with the Hughes Aircraft Company, where they developed advanced electronic systems for combat aircraft, to start their own company, the Ramo-Wooldridge Corporation (R-W). A short time after the firm was established, the United States Air Force contracted R-W to supervise the development of Intercontinental Ballistic Missiles (ICBMs), which would carry nuclear warheads and serve as a deterrent to the Soviet Union's own nuclear missiles. After mankind entered the space age in 1957—with the Soviet launch of the Sputnik satellite—Ramo devoted more attention to developing space technologies. In 1959 R-W merged with Thompson Products to form Thompson Ramo Wooldridge (TRW), which soon expanded into a global conglomerate; by 1970 the company was employing two percent of all the nation's physicists. In 2002 Ramo helped orchestrate the merger of TRW with the Northrop Grumman Corporation.

The son of Lithuanian immigrants named Benjamin and Clara Ramo, Simon Ramo was born on May 7, 1913 in Salt Lake City, Utah. His father operated a clothing store. At the age of seven, Ramo began taking violin lessons and became proficient enough to perform at parties. "As a youngster I displayed talent in mathematics and in playing the violin, so everyone told me that I should be a scientist or a violinist," Ramo recalled in his memoirs, *The Business of Science: Winning and Losing in the High-Tech Age* (1988). When he was 12, Ramo attended a concert by the renowned violinist Jascha Heifetz. After concluding that he would never be as talented as Heifetz, Ramo decided to pursue a career in science. An excellent student, he skipped some grades and graduated from high school at the age of 15.

Despite his decision to pursue a career in science, Ramo did not abandon the violin entirely. He won first place in the violin category at the Intermountain High School Music Contest. The prize included a full scholarship to the University of Utah, in Salt Lake City, and a monthly stipend of $25.

Ramo studied engineering at the University of Utah. "I went on winning [musical] contests," he recalled to Thomas J. Murray for *Dun's Review* (May 1975). "I also had a job playing on weekends and became soloist and concert master for the university symphony." In 1933 Ramo graduated at the top of his class with a B.S. in engineering.

Because of the Great Depression, there were few engineering jobs available. Ramo, whose academic record earned him a graduate fellowship, decided to continue his education. He enrolled at the California Institute of Technology (Caltech), in Pasadena, to pursue graduate studies in electrical engineering. "I thought my study of science was behind me and what I needed was to become expert at applying science to the design of real-life electrical equipment," Ramo wrote in *The Business of Science*. "But when I began my courses at [Caltech] I thought I had a made a terrible mistake and come to the wrong place. At this institute, probing the scientific frontiers was the dominant endeavor. There were graduate courses listed under Electrical Engineering, but their main thrust was the science underlying the engineering. Physics, electrical engineering, and mathematics were all in one division. What I would be spending my time learning at [Caltech], I now realized, was science and the mathematical tools needed to deal with science." Ramo eventually realized the benefits of this approach. "My eyes were opened to a whole new concept of how to prepare for a career in the application of science," he wrote in his book. "Innovative engineering consists in part of brilliant inventing by creative engineers of new ways to put well-established scientific principles to work. But a large part of what engineering is also about, I came to see, is the exploiting of new scientific knowledge as soon as possible after it is uncovered." At Caltech, Ramo became acquainted with Dean Wooldridge, a fellow doctoral student who would become his partner in scientific research and business. In 1936 Ramo earned a doctorate in electrical engineering and physics.

In the spring of 1936, Maynard M. Boring, a recruiter from the General Electric Corporation (GE) in Schenectady, New York, spoke at Caltech. Boring told the audience of engineering students that although the company wasn't then hiring engineering graduates because of the economy, he would make an exception for any candidate who could make a contribution to the GE community beyond science. Since Ramo was known on campus as a talented violin player, Boring offered him a job with the expectation that he would also perform with the Schenectady Symphony Orchestra, which GE supported. Ramo's first assignment was working as a researcher in GE's General Engineering Laboratory. In 1937, after GE officials gave him permission to pursue a project of his own choosing, Ramo began conducting research into the transmission of microwaves. He was eventually promoted to section chief in GE's electronics laboratory and then to director of the physics laboratory. During World War II, GE served as an important producer of military equipment.

Ramo decided to leave GE after the war because he believed that the company lagged far behind in research-and-development efforts to produce new technologies. "The old-time companies in the East were interested primarily in getting back to their peacetime specialities [after the war ended]," Ramo told Walter McQuade for *Fortune* (November 1970). "But I was sure there was going to be a need for a very sophisticated development in physics and advanced electronics for weapon systems—and beyond weapons."

In 1946 Ramo accepted an offer from the Hughes Aircraft Company, in Culver City, California, to set up and run a research-and-development group in electronics. The company was founded by Howard Hughes (1905–1976), an eccentric pilot, industrialist, film producer, and billionaire. Among the scientific researchers that Ramo hired was his Caltech classmate Dean Wooldridge, who was working for Bell Telephone Laboratories in New York City. "Dean and I became partners in building up the new organization," Ramo wrote in *The Business of Science*. "We thought so much alike on management principles that either of us could handle a policy issue alone, confident that the other would have done it the same way. We divided between us the directing of the effort and constantly conferred about problems and progress. Our working relationship became a model for cooperation throughout the organization."

The United States Air Force awarded Hughes Aircraft several research contracts. Ramo and Wooldridge developed an electronic fire-control system that was later installed on the Lockheed F-94 interceptor aircraft. In 1950, after the Korean War broke out, the fire-control system became standard equipment for all interceptor aircraft. Ramo and Wooldridge also developed an electronic-guidance system and the Falcon air-to-air guided missile, which was widely used by U.S. aircraft during the Korean War. In 1950 Ramo and Wooldridge won an air force design competition for a navigational control system for the F-102 supersonic interceptor. The demand for electronic systems and military hardware created by the war turned Hughes Aircraft from a modest venture with about $400,000 in 1949 sales into a successful corporation and leading player in the electronics industry—with almost $200 million in sales in 1953 alone. In addition to their research, Ramo and Wooldridge assumed management positions with Hughes Aircraft; Ramo was named vice president of operations and Wooldridge served as vice president of the research-and-development laboratories.

Howard Hughes, who knew little about the fundamentals of aircraft technology, exercised limited control over the day-to-day operations of Hughes Aircraft, especially in the areas managed by Ramo and Wooldridge. Hughes occupied himself instead with his other holdings, including Transcontinental & West Airlines (later TWA) and the RKO Pictures film studio. Hughes's absence allowed Ramo and Wooldridge complete freedom in directing the company's research. "I liked Howard," Ramo told McQuade. "He never treated me the way he was famous for treating people: the middle-of-the-night phone calls, the hurried flights to and from the desert. The main difficulty in dealing with him, I think, is that he will only think of one thing at a time." As the company expanded, however, Hughes's hands-off style became problematic. An absentee CEO, Hughes was never available when Ramo and Wooldridge needed him to resolve disputes or approve the spending of millions of dollars on potential projects. Additionally, the billionaire's clashes with government regulators over his administration of TWA and RKO—which were both publicly traded companies—and his bizarre behavior and lifestyle, which were attracting public attention, alarmed officials at the Pentagon, who didn't want to exclusively depend on a company owned by such a person for important military technologies. On September 11, 1953, Ramo and Wooldridge officially resigned from Hughes Aircraft. Realizing that their departure would likely result in the loss of millions of dollars in government contracts, Hughes tried to persuade them to stay, to no avail.

Five days after severing their ties with Hughes Aircraft, Ramo and Wooldridge founded their own electronics company, the Ramo-Wooldridge Corporation (R-W), in Los Angeles. Because of their fine reputations in the industry, Ramo and Wooldridge received offers of financing from many prominent companies and individuals, including, somewhat ironically, Howard Hughes. After weighing the offers, the two engineers settled on Thompson Products, an automobile-parts manufacturer in Cleveland, Ohio, which had attempted to buy Hughes Aircraft a few years earlier. Thompson provided $400,000 in financing in exchange for 49 percent of the common stock and 87.5 percent of the preferred stock in R-W. They were inundated with job applications from engineers and scientists. Two weeks after it opened for business, R-W was awarded its first contract from the U. S. Air Force, to provide scientific and engineering analysis to back up the U.S. Department of Defense's strategic-missiles planning effort.

Drawing from their previous experiences with other companies, Ramo and Wooldridge tried to create the best environment possible for their scientists and engineers to conduct their research. "We were considered radical for creating a campus-like structure where engineers were given [spacious] rooms with walls," Ramo told Curt Schleier for Investor's Business Daily (December 20, 2000). "It cost us 2 percent more than if we'd done it the other way [with scientists and engineers working at desks in communal rooms], but we were able to get top people." Ramo and Wooldridge also shunned the "top-down" management structure that was common at many other companies. "I discovered that at typical meetings [at previous jobs], when anything came up, the elders typically said, 'This is how we do this,'" Ramo told Schleier. "It always occurred to me that what ought to be discussed was not how something was done in the past but how do we make it work best." Ramo and Wooldridge held frequent meetings with their employees to listen to their ideas and concerns and discuss ways to improve the management of the company.

During the early 1950s, the United States government feared that within the next decade the Soviet Union would successfully develop and deploy an Intercontinental Ballistic Missile (ICBM), which could carry a nuclear warhead and travel thousands of miles at high speed. Because the Soviet Union's successful development of an ICBM would make the United States vulnerable to a nuclear attack, the air force decided to accelerate its own ICBM effort and recruited R-W to lead and coordinate a crash program costing billions of dollars. Ramo recognized that the effort to build an ICBM required "marshaling the resources of industry, government, and science on a broader scale than had ever been previously attempted in peacetime," as quoted by Davis Dyer in TRW: Pioneering Technology and Innovation Since 1900 (1998). Ramo and Wooldridge assembled a team of scientists and aerospace engineers to solve the scientific problems associated with launching a missile thousands of miles and guiding it to its target. Ramo-Wooldridge expanded its operations to accommodate the demands of the ICBM project, hiring more than 3,000 people within four years of its founding. In addition to his duties at R-W, Ramo was named chief scientist of the United States Intercontinental Ballistic Missile Program. Ramo and Wooldridge contracted many firms to build the different components of the missiles, and the number of companies involved in the ICBM program quickly exceeded 200. After several failures, the Thor intermediate-range ballistic missile (IRBM), which could travel about 2,000 miles, was successfully tested and deployed in September 1958. The Thor was followed by the more powerful Atlas, Titan, and Minuteman ICBMs, which could travel more than 6,000 miles. "The American ICBM effort not only defeated the Russians in the race to a first operational force," Ramo observed in The Business of Science, "it also was remarkably free of most cost overruns, schedule slippages, waste, and fraud." (During the 1950s, the United States Army and Navy jointly pursued their own ballistic-missile research, which resulted in the development of the Jupiter intermediate-range class of missiles and then the Juno rockets. The Jupiter missile was deployed by the United States military in Europe, in 1958, a few months before the Thor. That same year, the Juno rocket carried the first American satellites into space.)

Although both the United States and the Soviet Union were focused on their ballistic-missile programs during the 1950s, both countries began devoting resources to space exploration. The air force directed R-W to conduct several studies for organizing and managing the space program; among the topics that R-W explored were landing vehicles on the moon, orbiting the planet Mars, and using nuclear propulsion for deep-space travel. On October 4, 1957 the Soviet Union beat the United States into space by successfully launching the Sputnik satellite. Embarrassed by the Soviet triumph, the United States intensified its efforts and established a new agency, the National Aeronautics and Space Administration (NASA), on October 1, 1958. At R-W, the company's Guided Missile Research Division was renamed Space Technologies Laboratories (STL), which operated as an autonomous entity with Ramo as its president. In January 1958 STL was awarded a contract to develop a lunar probe. On August 17, 1958, STL's first lunar probe, Able 1, exploded 77 seconds after its launch. On October 11, 1958, STL's second probe failed to achieve its goal of establishing an orbit around the moon and disintegrated in the Earth's atmosphere.

Although Ramo knew that R-W could not hope to compete with such computer giants as IBM or Remington Rand, the company's computer division manufactured machines for both military and commercial use; in 1957 it introduced the R-W 300, one of the first completely solid-state computers ever built. The R-W 300 could add a thousand numbers or conduct 350 multiplications within one second.

In 1958 Thompson Products merged with Ramo-Wooldridge to form a new company, Thompson Ramo Wooldridge Inc., which became more commonly known by its initials, TRW. In *TRW: Pioneering Technology and Innovation Since 1900* (1998), David Dyer wrote, "Through the end of 1964, TRW had participated in readying 218 of the 248 satellites orbited by the United States. . . ." In the late 1960s a TRW subsidiary developed the lunar excursion module descent engine (LEMDE), which was used by the Apollo 11 astronauts to land on the moon in 1969. By 1970 the company, which had been expanding and diversifying its businesses during the preceding decade, had sales in excess of $1 billion.

Dean Wooldridge retired from TRW on January 1, 1962. He later taught at Caltech and wrote several books. Ramo continued to exercise a leadership role with TRW, as the vice chairman of its board of directors, until his own retirement, in 1978. Over the decades, Simon Ramo's achievements and contributions have been recognized with many prestigious awards, including, in 1983, the Presidential Medal of Freedom, the nation's highest civilian honor. A member of numerous government committees, he is also the author of several books. Although most of these concern scientific topics, he also wrote *Extraordinary Tennis for the Ordinary Player: Winning Strategy for the Tennis Enthusiast Who Plays for Fun* (1970). In addition to his books, Ramo has written occasional editorial pieces decrying the state of science education and technological achievement in the U. S.

In 2002 TRW Inc. merged with the conglomerate Northrop Grumman Corporation. Several executives and directors with both companies told Peter Pae for the *Los Angeles Times* (July 30, 2002), that Simon Ramo, who was then 89 years old, played a key role behind the scenes in the merger. Although Ramo declined to discuss his exact role, he told Pae, "I know a lot of people in the industry. Many of them worked for me, so when they call and ask for advice, I give it to them."

Ramo married the former Virginia Smith on July 25, 1937; they have two sons.—D. C.

Suggested Reading: *Dun's Review* p70+ May 1975, with photo; *Forbes* p31+ Mar. 15, 1977; *Fortune* p116+ Feb. 1954, with photos, p105+ Nov. 1970, with photos, p298+ Apr. 25, 1988, with photos, p124+ May 9, 1988; *Investor's Business Daily* A p3+ Dec. 28, 2000; *Los Angeles Times* Business p1+ July 30, 2002, with photo; *Time* p84+ Apr. 29, 1957; Dyer, Davis. *TRW: Pioneering Technology and Innovation Since 1900*, 1998; Mettler, Ruben F. *The Little Brown Hen That Could: The Growth Story of TRW Inc.*, 1982; Ramo, Simon. *The Business of Science: Winning and Losing in the High-Tech Age*, 1988

Rand, James Henry, Jr.

Nov. 18, 1886–June 1968 President and general manager of Remington Rand

In the early 1950s, when new room-sized computers seemed like a risky venture to most businessmen, James Henry Rand Jr. of Remington Rand bought the financially unstable Eckert-Mauchly Computer Company and made their computer, the UNIVAC, a household word. The UNIVAC was the first commercially available digital computer that was sold in large quantities in the United States. It was also the first computer to be used for calculating figures for the U.S. Census and was the first to predict accurately the outcome of an American presidential election. Though Rand's company was never able to capitalize fully on the potential of such a machine and was eventually outpaced by IBM, Rand helped to make the computer a viable piece of commercial equipment with his steadfast faith in Mauchly and Eckert's UNIVAC. Today, Rand is recognized for his vision in expanding the market for office products, as well as his support for early electronic devices, including computers.

James Henry Rand Jr. was born on November 18, 1886 in the town of North Tonawanda, in New York State, the son of James Henry Rand Sr. and the former Mary Scribner. Rand's father had once been a bank clerk in Tonawanda who had been frustrated by the difficulties in retrieving documents from the late-19th-century filing systems. He subsequently developed a "visible" index system of vertical folders, with colored signal strips, tabs, and dividers. This system could locate documents three to four times faster than any system previously used and could also be expanded to contain more documents.

In 1898 Rand Sr. established the Rand Ledger Company, which, within 10 years, managed to dominate the record-keeping industry and had 40 branches in cities throughout the world. In the meantime, Rand Jr. attended high school in Newton, Massachusetts, and studied at Harvard University between 1904 and 1908. He joined his father's company upon his graduation and soon proved to be as inventive as his namesake. He created the Kardex System, a new card-based record-keeping system that permitted infinite expansion and almost instant retrieval. Between 1910 and 1914, while his father was recovering from an extended illness, Rand Jr. took control of the Rand Company.

However, after his father returned to work, Rand Jr. was bothered by his father's timidity in business. In 1915 Rand Jr. borrowed $10,000 and broke away from his father's company to establish the Kardex Company, which sold the system he had invented. He proved to be an even better entrepreneur than his father; he was soon able to pay off the initial loan, take out another for $50,000, and, within five years, expand his company to 90 branches across the United States, with 60 international offices and a plant in Germany. In all, he had over a 100,000 customers.

At the behest of his mother, Rand Jr. made peace with his father in 1925 and merged their two companies into the Rand Kardex Company. Though Rand Sr. was in his sixties and approaching retirement age, he remained at the company as chairman until his death in 1944, with Rand Jr. as president and general manager. Together they took out a loan for $25 million and sought to expand their company into a conglomerate by building the "greatest office supply company the world has ever seen." According to Martin Campbell-Kelly and William Aspray in their book *Computer: A History of the Information Machine* (1996), "The combined firm was by far the largest supplier of business record-keeping systems in the world, with 4,500 field representatives in 219 branch offices in the United States and 115 agencies in foreign countries."

Under Rand Jr.'s direction, the company began expanding through mergers and acquisitions. Soon the Library Bureau of Boston, the Dalton Adding Machine Company, the Baker-Vawter Company, the Kalamazoo Looseleaf Binder Company, the Safe-Cabinet Company, the Powers Tabulating Machine Company, and the Remington Accounting Machine Company were under Rand's umbrella. With the merger of the Remington Typewriter Company in 1927, the company official changed its name to Remington Rand. Until that time Remington had been the largest manufacturer of typewriters in America; after the merger, Remington Rand had more than $73 million in assets and was the undisputed leader in business machines.

After buying the Powers Tabulating Machine Company in 1927, Remington Rand directly challenged IBM's share of the punched card tabulator market. Thomas Watson Sr., then head of IBM, brought out an 80-column card to surpass the 45-column capacity of the cards both companies were then producing. As a result, through the 1930s and 1940s, the American government looked more to IBM to provide calculating machines, especially for such projects as Social Security registration or calculating materials for the war effort. IBM outpaced Remington Rand in the tabulator market until the early 1950s, when Rand bought a machine from John Mauchly and J. Prespert Eckert which

would ultimately lead to the demise of the tabulator. That machine was the UNIVAC.

Rand Jr. was one of the first business leaders in the United States to recognize the importance of such computers as the UNIVAC (Universal Automatic Computer). When it seemed likely that the Eckert-Mauchly Computer Corporation was about to go bankrupt in 1950, he seized the opportunity to take control of it. However, Mauchly and Eckert, who were respected for their development of the ENIAC (Electronic Numerical Integrator and Computer) and BINAC (Binary Automatic Computer), initially sought to sell their company to IBM in early 1950. They approached Thomas Watson Sr. and Jr., but the Watsons claimed that purchasing their company—one of IBM's few competitors—would violate antitrust laws. According to Campbell-Kelly and Aspray, "the Watsons must have surely judged that Eckert and Mauchly would bring very little to IBM that it did not already have under development; by 1950 the company had well over a hundred R & D workers engaged in electronics and computer research, an effort that comfortably matched that of Eckert and Mauchly's company."

The National Cash Register (NCR) and Remington Rand companies were both interested in the UNIVAC, and Eckert and Mauchly were willing to listen to any reasonable offer, since they were near bankruptcy. Remington Rand, spurred on by Rand's ambitious postwar expansion ideas, made the first bid. During World War II, Rand had seen firsthand how scientific instruments, especially electronics, had been crucial to the war effort, and he wanted his company to expand on that technology in everything from xerographic copiers and television systems to microfilm recorders and computers. In order to facilitate his company's transition from a wartime economy to a peacetime one, he hired General Leslie R. Groves, the administrative boss of the Manhattan Project, to head Remington Rand's research and development division in late 1947. Since Groves had had contact with the ENIAC during the Manhattan Project, he appreciated the importance of computers and could see how machines like Mauchly and Eckert's could be used for governmental and corporate purposes.

At his Florida retreat, Rand made Eckert and Mauchly an offer: he would pay off all of their company's debt, give Eckert, Mauchly, and their 134 employees $100,000 for the stock they owned, and retain the pair at an annual salary of $18,000 each. The duo readily accepted this modest offer in the hope that they would continue to work as senior executives in charge of the UNIVAC operation. Eckert remained at the company and eventually became a vice president; Mauchly initially had trouble clearing government security due to some previous connections with left- wing political groups and had to be transferred to the sales division.

Now firmly under the wing of Remington Rand and Groves' research and development division, Eckert and Mauchly's work continued uninterrupted in their Philadelphia-based facilities. However, the company had to intervene to shore up their financial problems. After an initial visit to the Philadelphia operation, Rand and Groves realized that the UNIVAC was being sold at about one-third of its true value. Rand decided to attempt contract renegotiations, starting with the agreement made with the U.S. Census Bureau. When the Census Bureau was unwilling to renegotiate, he threatened to cancel the contract, which in turn prompted the bureau to sue. Rand knew that the company could not make a profit from the UNIVAC if its price was anything less than $500,000 per machine, but they were forced to honor the original contract with the bureau for $300,000. Two other contracts, with Prudential and A. C. Nielsen, had to be canceled after much legal wrangling when Rand realized it was impossible to renegotiate those companies' $150,000 contracts.

By the spring of 1950, Eckert and Mauchly had nearly completed the first UNIVAC, which was subsequently delivered to the Census Bureau on March 31, 1951. It became the second computer ever to be produced for a commercial customer, the first having been the Mark I, which had been delivered to Manchester University in England a month earlier. Two more UNIVACs were shipped 18 months after the Census Bureau machine. A total of 46 UNIVACs were eventually installed by Remington Rand between 1951 and 1957. (In the latter year the company replaced the machine with the more advanced UNIVAC II.) Though bulky, with the earliest machine being 10 feet wide, 14 feet long, and 9 feet high, and containing more than 5,000 vacuum tubes, the UNIVAC proved to be the first large-scale computer successfully marketed by a company.

During the presidential election of November 1952, Remington Rand performed a publicity stunt which made the UNIVAC synonymous with the computer for the remainder of the decade. Rand had convinced the CBS television network to use the UNIVAC to predict the outcome of the election between Dwight D. Eisenhower and Adlai Stevenson. Mauchly, along with a statistician from the University of Pennsylvania, had months earlier developed a program that used early election returns from a few key states to predict the outcome of the entire election by comparing it to the voting patterns in those same states in 1944 and 1948. CBS set up its cameras in the company's Philadelphia headquarters while at the same time constructing a dummy UNIVAC in the CBS studio in New York City, behind anchorman Water Cronkite. (The dummy terminals were even built with a flickering console run by blinking Christmas tree lights.)

At around 8:30 on the night of the election, the UNIVAC used the few results that were then available to predict a landslide victory for Eisenhower, speculating that people would vote for the retired general at the rate of 100 to 1. CBS and Remington Rand officials were shocked by the results; only a day earlier Roper and Gallup polls had predicted a close race. They quickly decided not to publish those initial predictions but instead adjusted the parameters of the program to bring about the more-reliable results of something like eight to seven. As it became more and more clear during the course of the night that Eisenhower was winning by a landslide, a UNIVAC spokesman named Arthur Draper had to admit that they had not released the machine's original prediction, fearing that it was completely wrong. "When UNIVAC made its first prediction, we just didn't believe it. So we asked UNIVAC to forget a lot of the trend information, assuming it was wrong," Draper was quoted as saying in Joel Shurkin's Engines of the Mind (1996), "[but] as more votes came in, the odds came back, and it is now evident that we should have had enough nerve to believe the machine in the first place." UNIVAC ultimately proved to be off by only about 1 percent. Eisenhower had won 442 electoral votes to Stevenson's 89; the machine had predicted that Eisenhower would win 438 electoral votes to Stevenson's 93.

Though UNIVAC proved its complete reliability on national television, the Remington Rand Corporation suffered setbacks over the next two to three years that allowed IBM to overtake their position as the most dominant computer manufacturer in the country. Many factors contributed to this decline: the highly trained and dedicated IBM sales force; the fact that, unlike the UNIVAC, IBM computers were modular and could be constructed on site after being transported in standard size elevators; and finally, Remington Rand's general fear that computer sales might negatively affect sales of its more traditional office equipment products. Remington Rand also suffered from a great deal of infighting between its Minneapolis and Philadelphia factories. Minneapolis wanted to build computers with contemporary technology; Eckert and Mauchly in Philadelphia wanted to develop new technology. Shurkin noted in Engines of the Mind that, according to company legend, engineers spent "20 percent of their time working on computers, and 80 percent of their time working on each other." Such infighting helped the company lose good press as well. In The Supermen: The Story of Seymour Cray and the Technical Wizards Behind the Supercomputer (1997), Charles J. Murray tells of how a Time cover story about IBM might have been about Remington Rand instead—had the RR management been more cooperative. Rand himself was also unwilling to invest large sums of money in building and marketing computers, thereby preventing him from obtaining more UNIVAC customers. Strangely, he did this while at the same time expanding the computer division by buying the Minneapolis-based Engineering Research Associates, which created the UNIVAC 1103, the company's first scientific computer. The company continued through the 1960s in this fashion, producing very good computers but being unable to generate the kind of sales IBM had been achieving.

By the time Rand merged his company with Sperry Gyroscope in 1955 (and became Sperry Rand in the process), IBM had convinced the business community that their computers, salesmanship, and services were far superior. In that year orders for IBM's 700 series exceeded orders for UNIVACs for the first time. Within a year IBM had installed 66 of its computers, compared to Sperry Rand's installation of only 46 UNIVACs. The merger with Sperry did little for the computer division. Harry Vickers of Sperry became chief executive of Sperry Rand, with Rand as vice chairman until his death in 1968. Retired General Douglas MacArthur became chairman of the new company. However, the effects of this powerful new leadership at the top did not trickle down to middle management, where a series of incompetent presidents in both the research and development and the sales divisions presided over an ever-crumbling UNIVAC market. In 1964 J. Frank Forster, originally at Sperry, was put in charge of the UNIVAC operations and managed to streamline the division and make it financially solvent by 1966. Unfortunately, UNIVAC was never able to reclaim the mantle from IBM.

James Rand Jr. died in June 1968. In 1986 Sperry Rand merged with the Burroughs Corporation and subsequently changed its name to Unisys Corporation. Rand married twice, first in 1910 to Miriam Smith, who later died, and then in 1929 to Evelyn Greeley. He had three children, Miriam, Henry James, and Marcell, with his first wife.—C. M.

Suggested Reading: Campbell-Kelly, Martin and William Aspray. *Computer: A History of the Information Machine*, 1996; Shurkin, Joel. *Engines of the Mind*, 1996; Cortada, James W. *Historical Dictionary of Data Processing: Biographies*, 1987; Williams, Michael R. *A History of Computer Technology*, 1997; Spencer, Donald D. *The Timetable of Computers*, 1997; *Who's Who in Commerce and Industry*, 1953

Ratliff, C. Wayne

Dec. 10, 1946– Software engineer; creator of dBASE database computer software

C. Wayne Ratliff holds a unique place in computer science history as the father of dBASE, an innovative software program he created in 1978, which provides database capabilities for computers. The applications for dBASE are vast: Among other things, the program allows computer users to sort, cross-reference, and manipulate information from data stored within it, such as customer lists, personnel records, or accounts receivable. The original version of the software and its successors—which have been used by millions of consumers since the early 1980s—expanded common applications for the computer beyond simple spreadsheets or word processing, thus helping to pave the way for the personal-computer revolution of the 1980s.

The son of Cecil and Bonnie Jean Ratliff, Cecil Wayne Ratliff, known as Wayne, was born on December 10, 1946 in Ironton, Ohio. He spent much of his childhood in Ohio towns or in Germany. He attended college at the University of Colorado, in Boulder, where he soon became interested in engineering. At one point Ratliff began designing a two-seater, rear-engine car and decided to use an early CDC 6400 computer to assist in his project. As he explained in an interview with Susan Lammers for the *FoxPro History* (on-line), "I wanted to get into car design from a real engineering standpoint, instead of simply guessing how big an engine I could fit into my design. I wrote a number of small programs to help design suspensions, figure out the center of gravity, that sort of thing. It didn't take long until I started looking for other programs to write, because I was enjoying the programming more than I was enjoying building the car." Shortly before completing his degree in 1968, Ratliff took a job working as a "computer" for the Denver-based Martin Marietta Corporation (now called the Lockheed Martin Space Systems Company), an aeronautics firm that has been one of the main contractors for the National Aeronautics and Space Administration's (NASA) space exploration program since the mid-1950s. In the late 1960s, Ratliff performed administrative-type engineering tasks for Martin Marietta, such as computing portions of equations. As he told Lammers, "Other people have programmed computers, but I have been one."

Ratliff was drafted into the U.S. Army to serve in the Vietnam War, but because he had acquired specialized civilian skills at Martin Marietta, he avoided battle and was instead given a desk job programming for the army. From 1969 to 1971, he worked on the logistics war game, LOGEX, through which he primarily managed the ordering of equipment and supplies. After his release from the army, he finished his B.S. degree in 1973 at the Metropolitan State College of Denver. Ratliff, who had returned to Martin Marietta following his stint in the army, continued working as a group engineer and a participant in the historic Viking project—a 1976 space mission in which two unmanned spacecraft, Viking I and Viking II, landed on the surface of Mars. (Martin Marietta employees conducted the mission operations in conjunction with NASA.) Ratliff served as a member of the NASA Viking Flight Team and wrote the data-management program MFILE, which supported the Viking Lander. He also worked as a contractor at NASA's Jet Propulsion Laboratory (JPL) in Pasadena, California, analyzing the incoming data from the unmanned space probe.

Around the time of the Viking launch, Ratliff became interested in expanding his programming knowledge by using natural language, a user-friendly communication device used in computer design and development. To further his experimentation he purchased an IMSAI 8080 eight-bit computer kit—one of the earliest personal microcomputers—which he assembled himself. He recalled to Lammers, "Once I had put it together, all I had was a computer. Nothing was included except 1K of memory. You had to keep buying things, such as a keyboard. I had already spent $1,000 for the kit, then I had to spend another $159 for a keyboard. Eventually I ended up spending about $6,000." After nearly a year of assembling the computer, in 1978 Ratliff commenced the project that would lead to his development of the dBASE software. The concept, while in many ways ahead of its time, began in part because of Ratliff's participation in an office football pool. He explained to D. Powell for *PC Magazine* (February 7, 1984): "Four weeks into the season, my entire room had become covered with Monday morning newspapers containing the information I needed to make my final picks. I realized there must be a better way to assemble and analyze this information, so I started writing a computer program. But I wanted the program to do more than just analyze football pools. Within a week, the whole idea had grown into something very intelligent."

Ratliff quickly realized that any comprehensive software system must include database capabilities. For example, in the case of analyzing a football pool, a user must have a place to store a sizable amount of data before the numbers could be manipulated or sorted for information. Initially Ratliff began writing his software in IMSAI's assembly language; yet, as he told Powell, "By accident, I soon discovered a program at NASA's Jet Propulsion Laboratory called JPL DIS (JPL Display and Information System)." Ratliff became familiar with this program in his work with the Viking space probes. Inspired by the software's capabilities, which allowed technicians to use English commands to manipulate the stored data, Ratliff decided to re-create a similar system for his own use. Working in the evenings, he spent one year designing a complete database program, which upon completion featured such commands as *Create, List, Modify, Append, Copy, Count,* and *Display* to direct users. Of the 58 commands presented, Ratliff borrowed 33 of them from the JPL software. Nevertheless, he maintained that the two sets of software bore little further resemblance. For example, the JPL program had been written in the Fortran computer language for the display and information system, while Ratliff's was written in 8080 assembly language (and later translated into the C computer language) for the CP/M operating system. (The program was later moved over to an IBM personal computer.) In addition, many of Ratliff's commands had completely different meanings from the corresponding words in the JPL program. Ratliff

named his new software Vulcan, in honor of the popular *Star Trek* character Mr. Spock.

While still working at JPL, Ratliff began a second career in the evenings, marketing, selling, and making improvements to his new software. He began by advertising Vulcan in the October 1979 issue of *Byte* magazine; Ratliff personally handled all customer correspondence, copying and shipping of the product, and customer service problems. "I kept looking for easier ways to do things," he told Powell. "Vulcan itself helped. When I received Byte's response cards, I entered the names into a Vulcan database and printed personal replies. But even with that help, the workload got to be too much. I wrote a form letter and had a thousand copies printed. Eventually, even that got to be too much work. The interest in Vulcan kept rising." Yet, over a nine-month period in 1980 he sold only 60 copies of Vulcan and decided to seek outside help in marketing his software. After meeting with George Tate and Hal Lashlee, owners of the mail-order company Software Plus (which soon became Ashton-Tate on the advice of its advertising agency), Ratliff sold the team exclusive rights to the Vulcan product. In marketing Vulcan, Ashton-Tate took several risky measures. First, they decided to change the product's name to something more in fitting with computer language. The name dBASE II was chosen, Hal Pawluk, a member of Ashton-Tate's advertising team, explained to M. Lynch for PC Magazine (February 7, 1984) because "it was Britishy, and with the small 'd' and capital letters, it looked good in type." In addition, although there was never a "dBASE I," the presentation of dBASE II implied that there had been improvements upon an original product. Perhaps the boldest move came in the company's advertising campaign. In Ashton-Tate's first advertisement in a national magazine, the headline read, "dBASE II vs. The Bilge Pump," as quoted by Lynch. The ad continued: "We all know that bilge pumps suck, and by now, we have found out—the hard way—that a lot of software seems to work the same way." For Ratliff and Ashton-Tate, the marketing paid off: By 1984, the company had sold more than 280,000 copies of dBASE II and dBASE III, which was released in 1984; both packages retailed for about $700 each. The high traffic of the dBASE technology helped boost Ashton-Tate's sales up to nearly $40 million in 1983—the year the company went public with a common stock sale. Ratliff was considered one of the world's most prominent software developers and Ashton-Tate one of the fastest-growing software-publishing companies. In August 1983 Ratliff became chief scientist and vice president of new technology at Ashton-Tate. He sold the company all of his rights to dBASE II for an estimated $10 million, some of which took the form of common stock and a promissory note.

Ratliff remained at Ashton-Tate through September 1985; when he left the company he signed an agreement that prevented him from competing with the firm for one year. On September 2, 1986, he began working for a small software development company, Migent Software, in Incline Valley, Nevada. In his new position, he planned to oversee development of a database engine that could operate on the then-new 32-bit microcomputers, as well as all current 16-bit microcomputers. The new product was code-named "Emerald Bay" after a body of water located near Incline Valley. (Despite Ratliff's enthusiasm for the project, development of Emerald Bay slowed in 1987, when Ashton-Tate filed suit against him for breach of the non-competition contract and misappropriation of secret information relating to the dBASE software. The case was settled in March 1988, with Ratliff claiming that all allegations were groundless.) In the spring of 1988 Migent began shipping Emerald Bay, which retailed for $695 and ran on Microsoft's DOS operating platform. In addition, it was marketed as being able to funnel information through a multi-user network. The database engine was also accompanied by several add-on programs that would allow users to customize a computer to suit individual needs. Although the Emerald Bay package was highly awaited, it failed to generate the publicity of dBASE. After one year the company had sold less than 2,000 copies of the product, and Migent canceled its marketing license. Migent

went out of business in early 1989, after being forced into bankruptcy. Ratliff immediately filed suit to retain all rights to the Emerald Bay product from a Canadian company trying to acquire Migent and its assets. After winning the suit he began marketing and selling Emerald Bay himself, through his own company, Ratliff Software Production Inc. (RSPI), based in California. (Ratliff had founded RSPI in 1986, shortly after leaving Ashton-Tate.) Of supporting the project on his own, he told Daniel J. Lyons for *PC Week* (February 26, 1990), "I believe this is the best thing I've ever done." In 1991 he forged a nonexclusive agreement with SuccessWare90 Inc., a small third-party vendor that agreed to market and sell Emerald Bay.

Ratliff continues to work as a computer consultant and as president of RSPI. He is a member of the Association for Computing Machinery and the Institute of Electrical and Electronics Engineers. He resides in California with his second wife, Carolyn.— K. D.

Suggested Readings: *FoxPro History* (on-line); *Guardian* Oct. 1, 1987; *InfoWorld* p142 Nov. 13, 1989; *Los Angeles Times* 4 p1 May 10, 1987, with photo, D p1 Dec. 15, 1990, with photo; *PC Magazine* p131 Feb. 7, 1984; *PC Week* p61 Feb. 26, 1990; *PC–Computing* p102 Jan. 1991

Ritchie, Dennis

Sep. 9, 1941– Developer of the C programming language and Unix operating system

Dennis Ritchie, a computer programmer at Bell Laboratories, is the creator of the C programming language and the co-creator of the Unix operating system. C is a high-level computer language that has come to be widely used in application programming and system development, and has spawned the popular programming languages C++ and Java. C and Unix were developed in tandem in the late 1960s and early 1970s by Ritchie and one of his colleagues at Bell Labs, Kenneth Thompson. Their goal was largely a personal one: they hoped to develop a time-sharing operating system to support their own work. The result, however, was so efficient and easy to use that the Unix operating system surged in popularity. After Ritchie and Thompson published their first paper on Unix in *Communications of the Association of Computing Machinery* in 1974, close to 40 organizations requested copies of the operating system. Today Unix is widely used by Internet service providers and in large research-oriented institutions. One of the keys to Unix's success was that it was written in Ritchie's C language. This made Unix highly portable, which meant it could be easily adapted to different hardware systems, a unique achievement at the time. Together with his colleague Brian Kernighan, Ritchie authored *The C Programming*

Language (1978), which served as the guideline for use until 1983, when universal standards for the language were established.

Dennis M. Ritchie was born on September 9, 1941 in Bronxville, New York. In about 1950 the family moved to Summit, New Jersey. His father, Alistair E. Ritchie, went to work for the nearby Bell Laboratories, where he became a director of the Switching Systems Engineering Laboratory. Ritchie graduated from Harvard University, in Cambridge, Massachusetts, in 1963 with a degree in physics and stayed to pursue a Ph.D. in applied mathematics. His doctoral thesis was on the sub-recursive hierarchies of functions, which Richie described to Robert Slater for his book *Portraits in Silicon* (1987) as "sort of the mathematics of computation, the theory of what machines can possibly do." Despite five years spent in intensive doctoral study and writing his dissertation, which he completed, Ritchie never received his doctorate. "I was so bored, I never turned [my dissertation] in," he told Slater. His education did succeed in planting an interest in computers, however. "My undergraduate experience convinced me that I was not smart enough to be a physicist, and that computers were quite neat," Ritchie wrote in a brief autobiographical article posted on the Bell Labs Web site. "My graduate school experience convinced me that I was not smart enough to be an expert in the theory of algorithms and also that I liked procedural languages better than functional ones."

Ritchie joined Bell Labs in 1967, while still a graduate student. The following year he began working with Kenneth Thompson on the Multics project, a multiorganizational effort that brought together Bell Labs, the Massachusetts Institute of Technology (MIT), and General Electric (GE). Multics, which is short for "multiplexed information and computing services," was intended to be a panacea for the growing pains of the emerging community of computer users. Early mainframes could accommodate only one user at a time, a wasteful and frustrating process when many researchers were competing for the opportunity to run their programs. During the 1960s time-sharing operating systems that allowed for multiple simultaneous users were created. The organizations behind the development of Multics hoped to build an even more ambitious operating system, one that could accommodate up to 300 users simultaneously.

The costs and labor necessary to complete the project, however, grew unwieldy, and in 1969, after a four-year effort, Bell Labs withdrew from the project. "Multics," Ritchie would later explain, as quoted by Slater, "turned into an expensive morass for the labs, because it was sold as an answer to real computing needs, not as just a research project." In the meantime, however, Ritchie and a few other colleagues who were involved in the project—notably Thompson, Doug McIlroy, and J. F. Ossanna—had grown attached to the system, and were disappointed by the cancellation. Multics was never able to support 300 users, but it had succeeded in supporting these few. As Ritchie explained, quoted by Slater, "We had become used to interactive environments where you could actually type things on the machine and get instant responses. It is just more satisfying to work that way. This is as opposed to taking our deck of cards and handing it over a counter, and coming back in an hour, and getting a big pile of listings." In addition to these material benefits, the group enjoyed the sense of community that was fostered by such close communication. "We were among the last Bell Laboratories holdouts actually working on Multics, so we still felt some sort of stake in its success," Ritchie noted in "The Evolution of the Unix Time-sharing System," a paper he presented in 1979 at the Language Design and Programming Methodology Conference. "We didn't want to lose the pleasant niche we occupied, because no similar ones were available; even the time-sharing service that would later be offered under GE's operating system did not exist. What we wanted to preserve was not just a good environment in which to do programming, but a system around which a fellowship could form."

In 1969 the group began casting about for an alternative to Multics. They made several requests for hardware purchases that would allow them to develop a multiuser, time-sharing operating system. Bell Laboratories' management, still dealing with the failure of Multics, did not lend their support to the idea of another time-sharing user system. In answer to their request for new hardware Ritchie and Thompson were given an obsolete and underpowered Digital Equipment Corporation PDP-7 computer that their office had discarded. The limited memory (8K) and processing capacity of the machine required a spartan approach to programming. Ritchie and Thompson undertook the ambitious project of rewriting a flight-simulator game called *Space Travel*, which Thompson had developed for the Multics operating system, so that it could run on the very limited PDP-7. One of the key problems that they had to tackle was that of data storage. "We wrote the code for the manipulations that would run this file system," Ritchie told Robert Slater. "In the process it became evident that you needed various commands and software to test out the file system. . . . And so we wrote a small command interpreter that would be things you typed to the keyboard, a command to copy files and delete them, do the various operations that you need to work on files." The structure of the file system and the simple commands to access it were to become the hallmarks of Unix.

The PDP-7 initially contained no software, so Ritchie and Thompson had to write their programs on a large GE machine. They then transferred the programs to the PDP-7 by hand, using paper-tape output that the PDP-7 could read. By 1970 the system could process data without support from another computer. Thompson felt that a system programming language was needed, and began looking at BCPL, a computer language favored by those working on Multics that had been designed in the mid-1960s by Martin Richards at MIT. The constraints of the PDP-7 demanded a streamlined version of BCPL, and Thompson used Richards' language to develop his own, which he called B. As Ritchie wrote in an article titled "The Development of the C Language," which he presented at the Second History of Programming Languages conference in 1993, "B can be thought of as C without types; more accurately, it is BCPL squeezed into 8K bytes of memory and filtered through Thompson's brain."

Shortly thereafter, Ritchie and his colleagues succeeded in convincing the management at Bell Labs to purchase a more powerful computer, the PDP-11, by offering to create some word-processing software. Once they acquired the new machine, in the summer of 1970, Thompson's B language was moved to it. While they developed the promised word-processing software they also worked on the operating system. Around this time, Brian Kernighan, a colleague at Bell Labs, suggested that the operating system be called Unix, as a play on the name Multics. Ritchie began deriving a new programming language based on B, adding data types and new syntax. He called the new language C, and Unix was subsequently rewritten in C on the PDP-11. Ritchie's C language made the Unix operating system portable, allowing its implementation on almost any computer system with a minimum of code changes. In an interview with

Robert McMillan for *Linux Magazine*, Ritchie explained that "the portability realization came a little bit after C was in existence. C was moved to a variety of other environments; it was on the [IBM] 360 or 370; it was on our Honeywell machine. And it turned out that creating the C environment and the predecessor to the portable C library was really a pain. It was a pain to produce these semiportable programs because the libraries were hard to write. So the actual genesis of the notion of portability was, 'Instead of trying to rewrite the library to these various machines and systems, why not produce an operating system so you can take the whole system with you?'"

Ritchie's C was the first programming language to fully integrate elements of a high-level language with assembly language. A high-level programming language is one that allows a person to write programs without a detailed understanding of the bare workings of a computer. High-level languages often use words and phrases as commands and sometimes resemble spoken or written language. Commands in assembly language, by contrast, correspond directly to a computer's binary codes. They are generally more difficult to learn and install, but they are more efficient because they communicate more directly with the computer. According to the *Dictionary of Computer and Internet Terms* (1996), C is unique among high-level languages because, "unlike other general purpose languages, it gives the programmer complete access to the machine's internal (bit-by-bit) representation of all types of data. This makes it convenient to perform tasks that would ordinarily require assembly language, and to perform computations in the most efficient way of which the machine is capable." Unix also made use of "pipes," an innovative computing mechanism that allowed programs to run simultaneously and communicate data to solve larger problems. The inclusion of pipes allowed larger, more intricate programs to be broken down into smaller ones, with the output of one program becoming the input of another. The result was a remarkable gain in terms of time-sharing and multitasking capability.

The creation of Unix and C coincided with significant changes taking place within the computing industry at large. Centralized mainframes had fallen out of favor and were replaced by decentralized, smaller computers. Computer prices had dropped due to improvements in integrated-circuit electronics. Although the hardware was more affordable, there were few suitable operating systems available; Unix fit the need perfectly. Ritchie, as quoted by Martin Campbell-Kelly and William Aspray in their book *Computer: A History of the Information Machine* (1996), explained that "because they were starting afresh, and because manufacturers' software was, at best, unimaginative and often horrible, some adventuresome people were willing to take a chance on a new intriguing, even though unsupported, operating system." Bell Labs furthered the spread of Unix by adopting the practice

of licensing the system to universities and research departments for a small fee. The simplicity and accessibility of the system ensured its success in the world of academia as well as in industry. It has been estimated that by 1984 there were approximately 100,000 locations running Unix on various platforms. Today there are thought to be more than five million installations. Internet providers make extensive use of Unix to operate their servers. The system's portability made it possible for other programmers to build upon its foundations and develop their own versions, such as the Berkeley Software Distribution Unix (BSD), developed at the University of California, Berkeley.

During the 1990s Richie focused his attention on the development of distributed operating systems. The Plan 9 operating system, which derives its name from the 1958 cult film *Plan 9 from Outer Space*, was released in 1995. It incorporates networking and distributed computing technologies that were not included in Unix. The Inferno distributed operating system, developed in 1996, employed an innovative design that allowed it to stand alone as an operating system for many different processing chips, as well as run as an application under other operating systems, such as Windows 98.

Ritchie has received numerous honors and awards for his work. He received the 1982 Emmanuel Piore Award from the Computer Society of the Institute of Electrical and Electronics Engineers. In 1983 he received, in conjunction with Thompson, the Association of Computing Machinery's A. M. Turing Award, and he was made a Bell Laboratories Fellow. He has been a member of the U.S. National Academy of Engineering since 1988. In 1989 *PC Magazine* honored Ritchie with the Lifetime Achievement Award for Technical Excellence. He is also the recipient of the 1990 Hamming Medal, the 1994 Computer Pioneer Award, and the NEC C&C Foundation award. In 1998 President Bill Clinton awarded Ritchie and Thompson the National Medal of Technology for their contributions to computing.

Ritchie works in the Computing Sciences Research Center at Bell Labs in Murray Hill, New Jersey. He manages a small group that performs research on distributed operating systems, languages, and routing/switching hardware.—A. I. C.

Suggested Reading: Bell Labs Web site; *Computerworld* p76 May 24, 1999; *Linux Magazine* June 2001; Campbell-Kelly, Martin and William Aspray. *Computer: A History of the Information Machine*, 1996; Dowling, Douglas A., et al. *Dictionary of Computer and Internet Terms*, 1996; Slater, Robert. *Portraits in Silicon*, 1987

Roberts, H. Edward

Sep. 13, 1941– Maker of the Altair 8800

The appearance of Ed Roberts's Altair 8800 on the cover of the January 1975 *Popular Electronics* is considered by many to mark the birth of the personal-computer revolution. Selling for just under $400, the Altair 8800 brought the capabilities of traditional minicomputers—which typically sold for about $20,000 and were found only at large universities and laboratories—to the individual computer user. Although he could never have predicted the massive impact and popularity of the personal computer, Roberts told Steve Lohr for the *New York Times* (August 19, 2001) that he was guided by a simple vision: "If you give bright people computers, some amazing things are going to happen."

Henry Edward Roberts was born in Miami, Florida, on September 13, 1941. (Some sources list 1942.) His father was an appliance repairman, and his mother was a homemaker. As a teenager Roberts envisioned a medical career for himself, and he worked for a time as a scrub technician for heart surgeons at Jackson Memorial Hospital, in Florida. The first in his family to attend college, he studied at the University of Miami. There, in his preparations for medical school, he was exposed to computing. "We used a lot of electronics, and that's how I got into it," Roberts told Steve Lohr. Among other projects Roberts worked on at that time was a basic relay computer for a heart-lung machine.

Roberts had to drop out of college in his junior year when his wife, Joan, became pregnant with their first child. He joined the U.S. Air Force, which sent him to Oklahoma State University, in Stillwater, to study electrical engineering. Oklahoma State had an IBM 1620 mainframe computer and was one of the few universities to allow students to use it directly, rather than submit their programs to authorized operators. "This was a big machine with a lot of money invested into it," Roberts explained to an interviewer for *Historically Brewed* magazine (on-line). "It was open to engineering students and we would go down there and just put our name on a roster to use it. It was fantastic! And that had probably more impact on my feelings later on about computers than anything else."

Roberts graduated in 1968 with a degree in electrical engineering. He was subsequently commissioned as a second lieutenant and assigned to the weapons laboratory at Kirtland Air Force Base, in Albuquerque, New Mexico. In his spare time Roberts, along with other young engineers at the base, built radio-controlled rocket systems, which they would set off in the New Mexico desert. They soon started selling their remote-guidance designs to various magazines, including *Model Rocketry, Radio Electronics*, and *Popular Electronics*. In 1969 Roberts and three others—Forrest M. Mims III, Bob Zaller, and Stan Cagle—formed a company they named Micro Instrumentation and Telemetry Systems (MITS). One of their early products, the Opti-

com, an infrared voice communicator sold in kit form, was featured in the November 1970 *Popular Electronics*. The company failed to earn a profit, however, and the other founders of MITS soon sold their stock to Roberts, who was loathe to give up on the venture. Supporting his growing family on a lieutenant's salary was proving difficult, and he was determined to find an additional source of income.

At the lab Roberts used a Hewlett-Packard programmable scientific calculator—a tremendously useful piece of equipment, but at $1,000, not something many individuals could easily afford. Roberts wondered if it would be possible to develop a calculator in kit form and sell it through the hobbyist magazines. With the help of a few other engineers at the base, he succeeded in developing the first digital-calculator kit. The kits cost Roberts about $100 each to produce, and he sold them to customers for $179. The MITS 816—so named because it showed eight digits on the screen at a time and provided 16-digit output—was the cover story of the November 1971 *Popular Electronics*. Within days of the magazine's publication thousands of orders poured in. As demand increased Roberts moved the company several times to larger quarters. Realizing that he could sell more calculators if they were preassembled, he established a manufacturing line, with teams of assemblers working along a conveyor belt. By 1973 MITS employed more than 100 people.

By the end of 1973, however, MITS was being edged out of the market by larger electronics companies, including Texas Instruments. The advent of the integrated circuit made it possible to incorporate hundreds of transistors, resistors, capacitors, and diodes on a single, thin sheet of silicon, drastically reducing the cost of manufacturing electronic equipment. "It got really grim when [the prices of competitors' calculators] started dropping down to the $50 range," Roberts recalled to Jeffrey Young for *Forbes Greatest Technology Stories* (1998). "The American electronics industry took the small-scale integrated circuit technologies of the late sixties and just blew through to large-scale integration, with hundreds of components on a single wafer of silicon, much faster than anyone predicted." In response to his financial difficulties, Roberts took the company public, offering 500,000 shares at a dollar apiece. He succeeded in selling only half that amount, which allowed him to pay off his debts, but left him little working capital. He began pursuing other projects, including a digital clock and an integrated-circuit tester, but failed to develop any lucrative products.

For several years Robert had considered the possibility of building his own general-purpose computer. Other hobbyists had been making some headway; in 1974 a primitive model, using an Intel 8008 microprocessor, had been advertised in *Radio Electronics*. Intel was about to release the 8080, a new and more powerful microprocessor, and Roberts thought that with the new chip he would be able to build a superior machine—one that other hobbyists would want to own. When he did a marketing survey, however, he "couldn't find one person who thought it was a good idea," as he told Mike Hoffman for *Inc.* (May 16, 2000). Nevertheless, he decided to proceed. "I was bullheaded," he explained to Bo Emerson for the *Atlanta Journal-Constitution* (April 27, 1997). "My assumption was that there were a bunch of nuts out there like me that would like to have a computer. . . . To engineers and electronics people, it's the ultimate gadget."

Roberts was encouraged by his friend Les Solomon, then the technical editor for *Popular Electronics*. Roberts recalled to Jeffrey Young, "As soon as [the 8080] became available, as soon as I got the specs for that . . . I called up the publisher of *Popular Electronics* and told him what we were going to do. And I told him that this was going to be a no-compromise, full-blown, general-purpose minicomputer, that it would be able to do anything that a minicomputer could do. He said if we could do if for under $400, they would publish [an article about] it." (In modern terminology, the Altair was actually a microcomputer, or personal computer.)

The Intel 8080s were expensive—$360 apiece—but Roberts was able to negotiate a deal with Intel, ordering 1,000 of them for less than $100 each. At the urging of another *Popular Electronics* editor, the chip was then placed in a sleek, metal cabinet, to make it an attractive machine. The front panel was lined with lights and a series of toggle switches. Users entered programs in pure binary code by flipping the switches. The computer had only 256 bytes of RAM—minuscule by today's standards—no keyboard, no permanent memory, no monitor, and no software. The kits sold for $397 each, just under the $400 limit Roberts had been given by Solomon. The first working prototype of the machine was completed in October 1974.

Roberts shipped the prototype to the *Popular Electronics* offices in New York via Railway Express and flew there with the corresponding documentation. Due to a shipping error, the computer never arrived, and the engineers at MITS had to scramble to put together a non-functioning model to be used for the magazine's cover photo. Before the article ran, the *Popular Electronics* editors wanted to rename the computer, which Roberts had been calling the PE-8. The daughter of one editor suggested using Altair—the name of a star she had heard about on an episode of the television series *Star Trek*. They disliked the number 8080 and changed it to 8800. "I didn't care what they called it as long as it sold," Roberts told Young.

The cover of the January 1975 *Popular Electronics* heralded the Altair as the "World's First Minicomputer Kit to Rival Commercial Models," as quoted by T. R. Reid for the *Washington Post* (February 4, 1985). The response to the article was overwhelming, and the MITS office was flooded with orders. Roberts had planned to sell about 400 in the first year; according to one former employee,

by the end of the month MITS had sold more than 800. (Other sources claim that between 1,000 and 2,000 units were sold in the first few weeks.) This was especially surprising considering that the Altair, as packaged, didn't actually do anything useful. In order to achieve any complex results, other add-ons were necessary—such as a paper-tape interface card for storing information and a memory card to expand the working memory of the system. To accommodate additional hardware and features, Roberts devised the Altair bus. The bus allowed users to attach subsystems such as a memory card, a hard drive, or a floppy disk directly to the motherboard—the circuit board containing the microprocessor. One of the first add-ons that MITS released was a memory card that increased the system's memory from 256 to 1,000 bytes.

The Altair also lacked an efficient means of entering information. Entering binary code by flipping switches was a tedious, time-consuming process; Roberts realized that a simple programming language such as BASIC (Beginners All-purpose Symbolic Instruction Code), which had been developed about a decade earlier, would greatly improve the machine's functionality. The employees at MITS were too busy filling orders for the Altair and developing add-ons to tackle the problem, so Roberts advertised that he would buy a version of BASIC if it could be engineered to run on the Altair. In early 1975, just after the Altair had made its debut, Roberts received a call from Paul Allen, explaining that he and a fellow programmer, Bill Gates, had succeeded in compiling an Altair version of BASIC. Allen, who was 23 at the time, flew out to New Mexico to convince an incredulous Roberts. Roberts was impressed and hired Allen as his vice president of software. Gates, then still a student at Harvard University, in Cambridge, Massachusetts, started working for Roberts part-time that summer, for $10 an hour. Roberts recalled to Steve Lohr that Gates was "a very bright kid, but he was a constant headache at MITS. You couldn't reason with him. He did things his way or not at all."

The ownership of BASIC would later lead to a permanent rift between Roberts and Gates. Rather than sell BASIC to Roberts, the programmers had decided to license it to MITS on a royalty basis. As BASIC grew in popularity, Allen and Gates, calling their firm Micro-Soft (the company would later drop the hyphen), started selling the programming language to competitors—which Roberts claimed was a violation of their contract. Well after Roberts had left MITS the company filed a suit against Micro-Soft in an arbitration court, but the judge ruled in favor of Allen and Gates.

The friction with Micro-Soft was only one of several problems facing Roberts. To run BASIC on the Altair required more than 4,096 bytes of memory—16 times the amount provided. MITS developed a 4K memory card, but the company's designs were consistently plagued with functional difficulties. Before long another start-up company, Processor Technology, began releasing an Altair-compatible 4K memory card that worked well. Roberts was dismayed. He had been counting on sales of the MITS cards to bring in a profit for the company; the Altair machine itself was priced so low that sales revenue barely covered expenses. Roberts tried to retain customers by bundling BASIC with MITS boards. The plan backfired: hobbyists resorted to making copies of BASIC and distributing them for free, in what was to be the first wide-spread instance of software piracy.

MITS had arguably grown faster than prudent, and the quality of its products was suffering. Soon numerous other companies began to develop software, memory boards, and other add-ons for the Altair. Some companies, such as Processor Technology and IMSAI, began selling their own microcomputers. Two young entrepreneurs—Steve Jobs and Steve Wozniak—had examined an Altair at a meeting of the Homebrew Computer Club, a cadre of computer lovers who got together regularly to share ideas and discuss products. The Altair inspired them to build their own model using the new Mostek 6502 microprocessor. They called their computer the Apple and founded a company of the same name, which eventually became a major supplier of personal computers.

Roberts, struggling to keep MITS afloat, was angered by what he perceived as an intrusion on his business. He responded by trying to control the market; for example, in the small retail computer shops that had begun opening, he insisted that only MITS products be sold. This succeeded merely in alienating the retailers, however, since a large part of the ethos in the early days of the personal-computer movement involved the liberal exchange of information and freedom from traditional corporate controls. "I'd have been much better off to support them than to try and stop them," Roberts admitted to Young. "But I wasn't much of a businessman, and I didn't see it at the time."

By 1976 more than 10,000 Altairs had been sold, resulting in approximately $3 million in sales. MITS had more than 230 employees; a hardware-distribution office in Austin, Texas; and a software office in Atlanta, Georgia. In March 1976 MITS staged the first Altair Users Conference in Albuquerque. Thousands of computer users from across the country attended the event. The pressure from competitors continued to mount, however, and in 1977 Roberts sold MITS for $6.5 million to the Pertec Computer Corporation, which specialized in disk and tape drives for minicomputers and mainframes. Roberts received a reported $2 million from the sale. He stayed on as an employee, but under the new management MITS deteriorated rapidly, and he left shortly thereafter. Within a year of his departure MITS stopped producing the Altair, and within two years the company had closed.

As part of his separation agreement with Pertec, Roberts had signed a five-year non-competition clause. Weary from the trials of running the company, he was content with those terms. "When I left Albuquerque, I figured the only decision I wanted to make was whether to turn left or right at the end of the road," he told Lohr. With the proceeds from the sale, Roberts moved his family to a 1,200-acre farm in Wheeler County, Georgia. He planned to do some farming, but he soon decided to revive an earlier passion; in 1982 he enrolled in the medical school at Mercer University, in Macon. He received his medical degree in 1986.

In 1988 Roberts divorced Joan, with whom he had five sons and a daughter. He settled in Cochran, Georgia, where he worked as a doctor for Bleckley Memorial Hospital, specializing in internal medicine. "I ended up [in Cochran] sort of by default," Roberts told Emerson. "I was working at emergency rooms at 10 different hospitals around the state, and Cochran was the most under-served area." He remarried in 1991, to Donna Mauldin, a nurse at Bleckley.

Roberts is frequently asked if he regrets his decision to leave the computer business before it became a multibillion-dollar industry. "If I had everything to do over again, I'd do what I did," he told Samantha Miller and Gail Cameron Wecott for *People* (January 27, 1997). "Most of the time, I've been the only doctor on call here at night. That's mattered a lot to folks—and it's mattered to me."—A. I. C.

Suggested Reading: *Atlanta Journal-Constitution* M p1 Apr. 27, 1997; *Computers and Electronics* p58+ Jan. 1985; *Inc.* p71 May 16, 2000; *New Mexico Business Journal* p8 Dec. 1989; *New York Times* III p1 Aug. 19, 2001; People p97 Jan. 27, 1997; *Washington Post* p9 Feb. 4, 1985; Young, Jeffrey. *Forbes Greatest Technology Stories*, 1998

Roberts, Lawrence G.

Dec. 21, 1937– Project manager and lead architect of the ARPANET

Back in the early 1960s, when computers were still unattractive, bulky, and used only by specialists, the researcher Lawrence G. Roberts envisioned a scenario in which these machines would evolve to be more like their human creators. "The concept was that this was a major step for mankind also," Roberts recalled to John Papageorge in an interview for *Silicon Valley Radio* (1998, on-line). "Evolution has gone from language to the printing press and now we're where we've got to have computers do the same thing—they've got to be able to interact and communicate." As one of the principal developers of the ARPANET, a primitive computer network that was launched in 1969 and was the prototype for today's Internet, Roberts is regarded as an elder statesman of the Information Age. He also developed an early e-mail management program that is the model for today's systems. Though approaching the point at which many retire, Roberts is still working hard to make the Internet

Lawrence G. Roberts

faster, more supple and reliable; to effectively bring the early networking model into the 21st century.

Lawrence Roberts was born in Norwalk, Connecticut, on December 21, 1937, the son of Elliott John and Elizabeth (Gilman). He received his B.S., M.S., and Ph.D. degrees from the Massachusetts Institute of Technology (MIT), in Cambridge. After earning his doctorate, in 1963, he remained at MIT as a researcher in the Lincoln Laboratory. While he was still a graduate student there, in 1957, the Soviet Union stunned the world by launching Sputnik into orbit and thus beating the United States into space. Theoretically, America's cold war enemies could now launch missiles into space and drop them anywhere on earth. In *Internet for Historians*, an on-line history of the Internet, R. T. Griffiths, an economic and social historian at the University of Leiden, the Netherlands, describes the surprise Sputnik launch: "The effect in the United States was electrifying, since it seemed overnight to wipe out the feeling of invulnerability the country had enjoyed since the explosion of the first nuclear bomb thirteen years before. One of the immediate reactions was the creation of the Advanced Research Projects Agency."

The Advanced Research Projects Agency (ARPA), sometimes called the Defense Advanced Research Projects Agency (DARPA), was created by President Dwight D. Eisenhower in order to jump-start the research and technology programs in this country. Although it began under the guidance of the Defense Department, ARPA was intended to be a deliberate counterpoint to traditional thinking and conventional military structures. Its raison d'être was defense, with the initial focus

on space, ballistic missiles, and nuclear test monitoring, but from the beginning ARPA members were interested in communicating between their operational base, in Arlington, Virginia, and the various sub- contractors in research universities and private corporations across the country. It was this need to share information and data among ARPA researchers that led to the creation of a network of computers.

In 1962, ARPA initiated a computer-research program and appointed as its head the MIT scientist J. C. R. Licklider. Licklider had just published his first memorandum on a "Galactic network," a seemingly futuristic vision in which computers would be networked together and available to everyone. The University of California, Los Angeles (UCLA) researcher Leonard Kleinrock, who also worked for ARPA, had been developing a theory of sending information via computer by breaking it up into small packets, to be sent separately and then reassembled at their destination. Roberts was very interested in these ideas and, in 1965, co-published a paper with Thomas Marill called "Toward a Cooperative Network of Time-Shared Computers," in which he argued for the need for a "wide area network" to expand the computer community. He documented his experiments in linking computers at MIT and Berkeley University over a low-speed telephone line. His conclusion was that, while linked, or "networked," computers could in fact work well together—efficiently running programs and retrieving data—the circuit-switched telephone system was totally inadequate to facilitate this networking. Apart from being slow and expensive, the circuit switching of a conventional telephone system was unreliable. If any one link in the network failed, the overall connection would be lost, as in a string of Christmas lights: when one bulb burns out, the rest of the string fails to light. Packet-switching avoids this problem by dividing information into small, digital packets, usually about one kilobyte, or 1,000 characters in length, and then routing the packets along the fastest available routes.

The metaphor of traditional mail has frequently been invoked to explain packet-switching. Imagine that the contents of a 10-page document are written out on several postcards, each labeled with the recipient's address. The postcards could then be sent through whichever routes are available and most efficient. The receiving computer then reassembles the postcards—or packets—in the original order, and in so doing effectively recreates the original document. Although the packet-switching theory was disputed by nearly all communications experts during the 1960s, Roberts believed in its viability and perceived its benefits. In addition to increasing reliability and speed, packeting makes it harder to intercept, or "eavesdrop," on network communications.

Early discussions of the security benefits of packet-switching contributed to one of the most persistent myths about the Internet. While working at the RAND Corporation, a Cold War–era think tank, the computer scientist Paul Baran published a paper on packeting communications and security. Baran argued that distributed networks would help to maintain communications in the event of a nuclear attack. Fueled in part by the atmosphere of paranoia and hyperbole that permeated cold war culture, the rumor arose that the Internet was being clandestinely planned by the military as a form of emergency communications in the event of full-scale nuclear war. Baran was never able to secure funding for his project, but his data communications theories influenced Roberts's plans for the ARPANET. Roberts and his collaborators were primarily interested in sharing software and research via a computer network; as Roberts told Bruce Haring for *USA Today* (September 2, 1999, on-line), nuclear war "wasn't the reason we did anything. That story is just wrong."

In 1966 Roberts joined ARPA as the new head of computer research. With government funding and the resources of the research and development community now at his disposal, he was able to quickly produce a plan for a network system using packet-switching technology. When the ARPANET plan was published, it became evident that teams at MIT, the National Physics Laboratory, in England, and the RAND Corporation had all been independently pursuing the feasibility of wide area networks without the other's knowledge. The best ideas were incorporated into Roberts's ARPANET design for the government. At the time, the network was mainly thought of as a time- and cost-saving device. The only existing methods for sharing data were to mail computer punch cards or magnetic tapes, and separate software programs had to be purchased or built for each computer site. By linking all of ARPA's software and data, Roberts argued, scientists would be better able to perform their research. "I knew we couldn't grow a community, our information and so on, by having every computer separate," he told Papageorge. "We would never have been able to grow the information base or the literature base or the knowledge base or the use of the software." There was as yet no thought of using the network for e-mail, voice, video, or other forms of communication—these concepts were still to come.

In addition to being one of the network's main architects, Roberts was also its most vociferous promoter within research and government circles. He told Papageorge about that struggle. "It was a huge fight because the telephone industry was convinced that this was crazy and stupid and it would never work—that packet-switching was . . . just going to blow up in our face. . . . It was like any new thing that somebody is trying to make happen. We had to fight all our critics who said this was ridiculous. In fact, within my own community, within the computer community, nobody wanted to do it . . . a lot of universities and research labs didn't want anything to do with it because they wanted the computer all to themselves. They didn't want anybody else to get on it."

During the late 1960s Roberts refined his plan for ARPANET, working on network design, line optimization, and the selection of computer sites to be connected. Kleinrock and his team of UCLA graduate students were selected to perform the first test of a computer network. Roberts then designed the protocol that would allow special-purpose computers, called Interface Message Processors (IMPs), to send and receive messages and act as "translators" between the local host computer and the network. The task of building the IMPs was contracted out to a team of engineers at Bolt, Beranek & Newman (BBN).

In the fall of 1969, after the first man had walked on the moon and rock music had invaded Woodstock, New York, another, quieter revolution began at Kleinrock's laboratory when the first computer network was connected. Although the 30th anniversary of this event was celebrated with conferences and media events, at the time the participants didn't think of what they were doing as an historical event. "We didn't even have a camera," Kleinrock told the *USA Today* reporter. To create the first network, the IMP that Roberts had built was delivered to Kleinrock's laboratory. The refrigerator-size unit was too big for the elevator, and had to be hoisted through a third-floor window. It was then connected to a Sigma-7 host computer, and the first attempt was made to send a message to a computer housed at Stanford University, in Northern California. UCLA students had just typed an "l" and an "o" of the "log-on" command when they lost the first connection, making "lo" the Internet equivalent of Alexander Graham Bell's first telephone message: "Come here Watson, I need you." Within hours, the fledgling network was back up, and within months two more computers were added to it. Roberts described the incredible growth rate of Internet traffic in an article for *IEEE Computer* (December 1999), posted on the *Ziplink* Web site. "My grand plan for the network at that time was to connect 15 computers across the U.S. as an experiment. However, the experiment kept growing and we had connected 52 computers by the time I left ARPA in four years," he wrote. The Internet's surging popularity was due, in part, to Roberts's creation, in 1972, of an e-mail management program. The program allowed users to file, forward, and reply to incoming messages and is still the prototype for today's e-mail systems. From there, e-mail took off as the largest network application for the next decade, a harbinger of the enormous volume of person-to-person—rather than machine-to-machine—traffic that would eventually be generated over the Internet with the creation of the World Wide Web.

In his history of the Internet, Griffiths considers the legacy of this first computer network. "Since [the ARPANET] is . . . fairly basic, it is worth considering [that] the underlying principles have basically remained the same (even if they, mercifully, operate far faster and look much prettier)," he argued. Others have disputed whether or not this

1969 event marks the true beginning of the Internet, or merely a precursor. According to another Internet creation theory, the real beginning came with implementation of what is effectively the common language of the Internet, the Transmission Control Protocol (TCP) and Internet Protocol (IP), commonly known as TCP/IP. This program, which was co-designed by Roberts and Vinton Cerf (based on a 1974 plan by Cerf and Robert Kahn at Stanford) created a network with great flexibility and potential for growth, making it possible to link from any computer to any network. TCP/IP remains the Internet standard.

Roberts, Leonard Kleinrock, Vinton Cerf, and Robert Kahn were all invited to speak at a 1999 UCLA symposium celebrating the Internet's 30th anniversary, where they were each dubbed "co-founders." Still, there is some disagreement among them as to the Internet's true birth date. Cerf, who was present as a graduate student at the 1969 network connection, told the *USA Today* reporter that, although that was a significant step, it was not quite a "birth." "There were no other people to connect to. It was like being the first guy on the block with a telephone but nobody to talk to," he said. Kleinrock disagreed: "[The ARPANET computer] is the box out of which the magic genie of the Internet came," he said to the *USA Today* reporter. "This is where it all began." And, even though Roberts's personal Web site describes him as "the Founder of the Internet," he also acknowledges that controversy exists. "Everybody is claiming responsibility for everything at this point," he told Haring. Griffiths offers an historian's perspective, arguing that the Internet can best be described not as a single invention, but as a "series of innovations" that include the idea of decentralization, the common language (TCP/IP), and the efficient routing of data through packeting. According to this viewpoint, the Internet is a collective creation of government, academia, and industry, in itself fueled by the need to share information. What seems clear is that the Internet has become more revolutionary and widely used than any one of its developers imagined.

Having seen the first network become a reality, Roberts left DARPA, in 1973, to pursue his research in the private sector. He founded Telenet, a commercial version of ARPANET, and served as its CEO until 1980. By that point other scientific communities, including NASA and the Department of Energy, had developed networks along the ARPANET model, but until the adoption of the universal language, in 1982, electronic space was fairly chaotic and atomized, with each community working on its own sub- network. In 1989, with the development and subsequent release of the World Wide Web and its user-friendly searching and browsing capabilities, the Internet evolved from a specialized tool into a telecommunications revolution. By 1998 the number of hosts had reached almost 37 million, according to Griffiths.

Roberts has spent the last two decades trying to improve the performance and reliability of the Internet for this ever-increasing pool of users. By working to regulate the flow of information through networks, for example, he hopes to reduce delay and eventually to guarantee response times in accessing Web sites in a process he terms "explicit rate." He has worked at a variety of telecommunications companies, and is currently chairman and chief technical officer of Packetcom, based in Palo Alto, California. He foresees the Internet as necessarily becoming more responsive to its users. "The Internet will become the pervasive network for the world's telecom traffic," he told Haring. "Voice and video will transfer over to it in the next five to 10 years. Clearly, you're going to have video on demand, radio or TV, that can have millions of different sources or special subjects that [small numbers] care about."

Since Roberts was working for the government when he developed the ARPANET and e-mail management program, he was unable to patent his innovations. His work has been widely recognized, however, and he has received many awards, including the Secretary of Defense Meritorious Service Medal, the Harry Goode Memorial Award from the American Federation of Information Processing, the W. Wallace McDowell Award from the Institute of Electronics and Electronics Engineers, and the prestigious Ericsson Award for data communications research from the Swedish National Academy, the equivalent of a Nobel Prize in his field.

Roberts has also become interested in life extension and improvement. Back in the 1960s, he hoped to make computers more like humans; now, he hopes to make himself a little less so. "The thing I have concluded is that evolution really has tried to get rid of us after childbearing age," he told Papageorge. "It doesn't really need us around, given the old cavemen scenario, at that point. And therefore we have built-in mechanisms that kill us off, that don't need to be there." Roberts believes that, by taking supplements to counteract those aging processes, including some that help to increase the blood flow to his brain, he will be able to live longer, and remain at the forefront of the Internet revolution that he helped to create.—M. A. H.

Suggested Reading: *A Brief History of the Internet* (on-line); *IEEE Computer* Dec. 1999; *Internet for Historians* (on-line); *Silicon Valley Radio* (on-line), 1998; *USA Today* (on-line) Sep. 2, 1999, Nov. 23, 1999

Erik S. Lesser/Getty Images

Robertson, Michael

Apr. 4, 1966– Founder of MP3.com

The maverick Internet entrepreneur Michael Robertson is the founder of MP3.com, a Web site that allows computer users to download CD-quality digital music for free. Despite its inauspicious origins as a four-employee start-up in La Jolla, California, MP3.com was soon being trumpeted as the Internet's premier digital-music Web site, boasting more than 800,000 songs from more than 125,000 artists. Robertson, who was named one of the 100 most influential figures in the industry by the music magazine *BAM*, didn't invent the technology behind MP3s or devise an ingenious marketing campaign—the types of accomplishment usually associated with Internet pioneers. He simply caught sight of an emerging trend in music listening and distribution, realized that it held the potential to transform the $40-billion record industry, and positioned himself at the center of it.

Michael Robertson was born on April 4, 1966 in Redwood City, California. Robertson, his twin sister, and two younger sisters grew up mostly in Los Angeles and Orange Counties, raised primarily by their mother; Robertson's father, a handyman, reportedly drank heavily and was seldom around. Somewhat ironically, Robertson's only real musical experience growing up was playing the clarinet in his high-school band, in Huntington Beach, California; his religiously conservative mother discouraged him from listening to popular music. When he was 17 years old, Robertson moved in with a friend, hoping to make things financially easier on his family. He supported himself with a variety of jobs during his high-school years, including as a grocery-store boxboy and a delivery

boy. "I grew up poor. A lot of times when you grow up poor you have a high motivation not to be poor," he told Andrea Siedsma for the *San Diego Business Journal* (April 19, 1999).

In 1985 Robertson enrolled at the University of California, San Diego (UCSD); it was the only school he applied to. "It never occurred to me they wouldn't take me," he recalled to Siedsma. "It's the eternal optimist in me." Although he had intended to study political science, the conservative-leaning Robertson quickly became disillusioned by the liberal slant of the school's political-science department. He had an interest in computer science but did not want to study programming; he focused instead on cognitive science, an interdisciplinary field involving linguistics, artificial intelligence, philosophy, and psychology. While a student Robertson worked in the Super Computer Center on the UCSD campus—a job he credits for much of his technical knowledge—and he obtained an internship at Apple Computer.

After receiving his B.A. in cognitive science, in 1990, Robertson embarked on a series of entrepreneurial ventures, beginning with his own computer-consulting company, MR Mac Consulting. He next founded MR Mac Software, which provided networking and security tools. In September 1995 he founded Media Minds, a maker of digital-imaging software, but the company failed a year later.

Undeterred, in 1996 Robertson formed the Z Company to capitalize on the new search technology that was developing for the World Wide Web. The Z Company designed such Web sites as Filez.com, a search engine for downloadable files, and Websitez.com, a domain-name search engine. At that time, Robertson was mostly "throwing stuff at the wall, trying to see what stuck," as he admitted to Charles C. Mann for *Forbes* (April 2, 2001). Finding a workable product was becoming an imperative because, much to his wife's displeasure, the company's operations were financed in part by a $20,000 second mortgage on their home.

In October 1997 Roberts noticed that search engines such as Yahoo were receiving an impressively large number of inquiries about MP3s—short for MPEG audio layer 3, software that compresses digital music files by a factor of 10 or more, thus allowing computer users to download them over the Internet in a reasonable time. After sampling the software, he became convinced that the MP3 format held the potential to tap a large market. His first order of business was to purchase the MP3.com domain name for $1,000. (Its owner had been a man whose initials were M. P.) Along with a partner, Greg Flores, a former stockbroker, Robertson then launched MP3.com.

"We set the site up at 10 a.m., and before the day was over we had 10,000 people visit and advertisers calling us cold," Robertson told Chuck Philips for the *Los Angeles Times* (December 4, 1998). "We looked at each other and said, 'This is amazing. What have we stumbled onto here?'" The site initially offered news and links to other MP3 sites on the Web, but soon Robertson hit upon the idea that would make his company an Internet success story—the digital automatic music (DAM) label program. Musicians that signed up for the program would be allowed to place copies of their songs on the Web site; visitors to the site could then download the songs and listen to them for free. If a listener liked a song, he could buy a full CD of the artist's music. Using CD burners, Robertson would press the CDs and ship them to the buyer.

DAM represented a bold break with the traditional practices of the recording industry. In his research Robertson had been startled to find that musicians often received less than 10 percent of the retail price from a CD sale. Moreover, they were forced to sign long-term contracts and surrender ownership of their music. "The system is broken," Robertson told Jodi Mardesich for *Fortune* (May 10, 1999), "and we can fix it." At MP3.com, the artist set the price and received 50 percent of the sale, while retaining ownership of the music. Robertson fashioned himself as a music-industry Robin Hood—giving power back to the artist. "We're working for a higher purpose," he told Mardesich. "We're providing artists with an option besides the traditional industry route—an avenue in which they have control of their destiny and keep ownership of their work."

Soon thousands of independent artists began to post their music on the site. The service appealed to little-known bands, eager to reach a wider audience; it was especially popular with musicians working in genres such as trance and techno, which were traditionally ignored by the major record labels. Within a year the site was receiving an estimated 150,000 visitors daily; of those, about half were reportedly downloading a free song during each visit. Mainstream acts, including the Beastie Boys, Billy Idol, and Alanis Morissette, began expressing their support for a distribution alternative to the major labels. Tom Petty posted an MP3 of a new song on the site to promote his next album release (although Warner Music reportedly asked him to remove the song within a few days).

By the end of 1998, MP3.com was being heralded as the leader of what pundits were calling "the digital-music revolution," and Robertson was attracting attention with controversial denouncements of the record industry. "The rules of commerce are changing fast, and the record industry needs to wake up and deal with it," Robertson told Chuck Philips. "Fans are tired of paying $15 for a CD to get one good song. Artists are sick of signing their lives away and ending up in debt. That tired, old business model that the [record] companies have exploited for decades is not going to work in cyberspace. If the sleeping giants don't open their eyes pretty soon to the way things work on the Web, they are going to lose a huge, multibillion-dollar opportunity to upstarts like me." In January 1999 Sequoia Capital Partners, which financed such technology companies as Yahoo and Oracle,

invested $11 million in MP3.com, allowing the company—which had begun with just four employees working out of their homes—to move into a larger office in an aerospace park in La Jolla, near UCSD. By April MP3.com was employing more than 30 people; the Web site featured songs from an estimated 10,000 music artists and was receiving an average of 250,000 visitors a day. The company seized upon its growing reputation by having its initial public offering of stock in July 1999, turning Robertson, at least on paper, into a billionaire.

MP3.com's stock price wavered dramatically over the next six months, however, as Robertson tried to develop a viable business plan. Revenue continued to increase, but the company was operating at a net loss. Most of the revenue came from advertising, with only a small fraction from actual CD and merchandise sales. Despite the site's flourishing popularity with Internet users, the company faced growing criticism. "I do not see anything that MP3.com has or has built up that protects it from more recognizable music from people we know and trust," Mark Hardie, a senior market analyst told Alex Berenson for *TheStreet.com* (November 16, 1999). He likened the site's plentitude of unknown bands to a "flea market," adding that such a place "is not where most people shop on an regular basis. . . . In discussions around the music industry, I think there is very little support for MP3's model as the future of the music business." David Goldberg, a media executive, told Susan Karlin for *Upside* (December 1999), "They've done a fantastic job of building a pretty large audience around music that people don't really like. . . . The consumer probably would prefer Mariah Carey, Puff Daddy and Bruce Springsteen to 25,000 bands they've never heard of."

Robertson attempted to broaden the company's reach into more popular markets in January 2000, when he unveiled two new services—Beam-It and Instant Listening—as part of a feature called My.MP3.com. Beam-It allowed members to listen to music from the CDs they already owned, using the Internet. After users proved they owned a CD by inserting it into their computer, a copy of the music would be placed in their on-line music folder at My.MP3.com. They could then access the songs from any networked computer device—whether at home or the office—or by using a cell phone. Instant Listening allowed users who had purchased a CD over the Internet from one of MP3.com's retail partners to listen to it immediately, without having to wait for it to arrive in the mail.

Several major record companies pounced on Robertson, claiming the new services violated copyright laws. The songs in a user's on-line music folder, it turned out, were not actually recorded off the user's CD; they were instead copied from MP3.com's own collection of 45,000 albums—an important distinction that landed Robertson in court. Nine days after the new services debuted, 10 record labels, organized by the Recording Industry

Association of America (RIAA), sued MP3.com for copyright infringement, seeking between $750 to $150,000 per CD. In April U.S. District Judge Jed Rakoff ruled against MP3.com, and the company's stock fell to below $10 per share, from an earlier high of $66.

In an unexpected turn of events, Robertson found his pariah status in the music industry mitigated by the emergence of such peer-to-peer music-swapping technologies as Napster and Gnutella. In light of these immensely popular programs, which allow users to trade music files via the Internet for free, the record labels began to view Robertson as more of an ally than a threat. When the RIAA filed a motion for a preliminary injunction against Napster, the declaration included a statement of support from Robertson. "MP3.com has not authorized Napster or Napster users to distribute or copy the music of MP3.com artists," he said, as quoted by Benny Evangelista for the *San Francisco Chronicle* (June 14, 2000). "Any such distribution would cause potential detriment to both MP3.com and the artists who upload their music to the Web site."

The tide had shifted, and the major labels began to realize the necessity of revising their traditional business practices to accommodate the demands of Internet users. By August 2000 Robertson had reached settlements with four of the five major record labels suing MP3.com—BMG Entertainment, Warner Music Group, EMI Group, and Sony. The payoffs were expensive—reportedly $20 million in damages to each company—but the agreements granted MP3.com a license to run its Beam-It service using the labels' songs. One holdout, Universal Music Group, refused to settle, and in September Judge Rakoff issued a ruling calling for MP3.com to pay $25,000 for every Universal CD it had illegally copied. Universal put the number of copied CDs at 10,000—which would have amounted to $250 million in damages. Rather than use the ruling to drive MP3.com out of business, Universal, the world's largest record company, used it to form a partnership. In November the two companies reached a settlement in which MP3.com agreed to pay $53.4 million to Universal in exchange for access to its songs. In addition, Universal was granted warrants to purchase MP3.com stock, which at the time was languishing at around $4 a share.

Despite its legal troubles, MP3.com remained one of the Internet's most popular digital-music sites. By December 2000 it featured music from more than 125,000 artists; in that month alone, more than 50 million songs were downloaded by users. In May 2001 Vivendi, Universal's parent company, announced that it was acquiring MP3.com for $372 million. Robertson remained chairman and chief executive officer of the company until August of that year, when the acquisition was complete. After Robertson stepped down he continued to serve as an advisor to Vivendi's chairman and chief executive officer, Jean-Marie Messier.

While Robertson was winding up his tenure at MP3.com, he was quietly preparing for his next venture—an Internet start-up called Lindows.com. Founded in September with $4.5 million of Robertson's own money and $500,000 from an early MP3.com investor, the new company began work on a computer operating system intended to compete with Microsoft's market-dominating Windows. Based on Linux (a powerful, free, Unix-based computing platform), the Lindows operating system (LindowsOS) was built to run both Linux and Windows programs. At the time of publication, the venture's level of success remains to be seen; it does, however, have some factors in its favor. Whereas Microsoft's latest version, Windows XP, sells for $199, LindowsOS sells for $99. In addition, it can be installed on multiple PCs; Windows, on the other hand, requires an activation code to prevent multiple installations by the same user.

Considering Robertson's track record for inciting controversy, it perhaps came as no surprise when, in December 2001, Microsoft filed a lawsuit against Lindows.com, alleging that the name was too similar to Windows and could damage Microsoft's trademark. The trial is scheduled to take place late in 2003 in Seattle, Washington. In the interim, Microsoft requested an injunction barring Lindows from using the name, but a judge ruled against the request. Meanwhile, business prospects are beginning to pick up for Robertson; Lindows.com recently made a deal with Wal-Mart to offer its operating system on low-cost computers sold through the retail giant's Web site.

Michael Robertson is married to Leslie Burcham. As of April 1999, they had two sons, Samuel and Keith. He has been frequently praised by industry critics as a smart, opinionated, and risk-taking entrepreneur, yet he retains a different self-image. "Hey, I'm a hustler," he joked to Charles Mann. "Entrepreneur is just a fancy way of putting it."—A. I. C.

Suggested Reading: *Forbes* p35+ Apr. 2, 2001; *Fortune* p96 May 10, 1999; *Los Angeles Times* A p1 Dec. 4, 1998; *New York Times* III p2 Apr. 11, 1999; *San Diego Business Journal* p8 Apr. 19, 1999; *San Diego Union-Tribune* H p1 Feb. 24, 2002; *San Francisco Chronicle* C p1 June 14, 2000; *TheStreet.com* Nov. 16, 1999; *Upside* p106+ Dec. 1999; *USA Today* D p6 Jan. 27, 1999; *U.S. News and World Report* p36 July 3, 2000

Rohrer, Heinrich

June 6, 1933– Nobel Prize–winning physicist

Heinrich Rohrer is best known for his work with Gerd Binnig on the development of the scanning tunneling microscope, for which the two men won the 1986 Nobel Prize in Physics. The microscope has important applications for the study of biochemistry, chemical reactions on surfaces, biology, nanotechnology, and electrochemistry, as well as technological applications, such as the study of semiconductor surfaces and the development of small solid-state electronic devices. It is due to these latter applications that Rohrer and Binnig's microscope is important to computing, aiding in the development of smaller and smaller electronic components.

The Swiss physicist Heinrich Rohrer was born in the town of Buchs in eastern Switzerland to Hans Heinrich Rohrer, a distributor of manufactured goods, and the former Katharina Ganpenbein. As a young man he excelled in physics and chemistry and, although he found modern languages difficult, he showed an aptitude for Latin and Greek. After briefly considering advanced studies in classical languages, he enrolled at the Federal Institute of Technology in Zurich to study mathematics and physics. His doctoral research at the institute concerned pressure and volume effects in superconductivity, for which he obtained his Ph.D. in 1960.

Following a year of service in the Swiss army, Rohrer accepted a position as a postdoctoral fellow at Rutgers University, in New Brunswick, New Jersey, where he spent two years investigating superconducting phenomena. In 1963 he returned to Zurich to work at the research laboratory of International Business Machines(IBM). Except for the academic year 1974–75, which he spent studying nuclear magnetic resonance as a visiting scientist at the University of California, Santa Barbara, he has remained at the IBM laboratory.

While working at IBM, Rohrer became interested in types of solid-state physics other than superconductivity. He was particularly intrigued by the problems posed by the surfaces of materials, where chemical and other types of interactions between substances take place. There are methods for exploring the arrangement of atoms in the bulk, but surprisingly little was known about the very different behavior of surface atoms. The complexities involved in this behavior, which long thwarted advances in understanding it, once drove the theoretical physicist Wolfgang Pauli to exclaim, as quoted in *Nobel Prize Winners* (1987), "The surface was invented by the devil."

In 1978 Rohrer was joined in his efforts to understand surfaces by Gerd Binnig, who had just completed graduate studies at the University of Frankfurt. The two scientists soon hit upon a novel approach for probing surfaces by exploiting a quantum-mechanical effect called tunneling. The phenomenon is a direct consequence of the Heisenberg uncertainty principle (named for the German physicist Werner Heisenberg), which states that both the position and velocity of a subatomic particle cannot be known simultaneously. As a result, a particle such as an electron behaves not as a particle but as a diffuse "cloud" of matter. The cloudlike nature of a subatomic particle permits it to "tunnel," or diffuse, between two surfaces, even if they are not touching. Tunneling was verified experimentally by Ivar Giaever in 1960.

At the time of Rohrer and Binnig's work, tunneling was well known; other physicists had even used the effect to obtain gross data about interfaces between "sandwiches" of materials. The two IBM investigators took a different tack by trying to get electrons to tunnel through a vacuum. Their approach ultimately culminated in the invention of a new instrument called the scanning tunneling microscope. The basic idea underlying such a device is to scan the surface of a solid in a vacuum with a sharp needle tip; current models have tips that consist of just one atom, while earlier tips were several atoms wide. If a voltage is applied between the sample and the tip, and if the distance between the two is small enough, electrons will tunnel from one to the other. The flow of electrons can then be measured as a tunneling current. The amount of tunneling current depends on the distance between the sample and tip and is expressed as an exponential function of distance. By sweeping the tip over the sample and monitoring the current, it is possible to map the atomic-sized hills and valleys of the surface.

Despite the formidable technical difficulties they faced, Rohrer and Binnig were optimistic from the outset. As Rohrer later told a reporter for *Science* (November 14, 1986), "We were quite confident. Even at the beginning, we knew it would be a significant development. The surprising thing is that it went so fast." They conducted their first successful test of the scanning tunneling microscope in the spring of 1981; in collaboration with two other IBM workers, Christoph Gerber and Edmund Weibel, they distinguished irregularities only one-atom high on the surface of calcium-iridium-tin $(CaIrSn_4)$ crystals. Ironically, when they first submitted a paper reporting their results, a referee rejected it as "not interesting enough."

The biggest hurdle the IBM team faced was to eliminate all sources of vibrational noise. The dependence of the tunneling current on the distance between the sample surface and the scanning tip means that the vertical position of the tip must be controlled to within a fraction of the diameter of an atom. Without sufficient preventive measures, street noises and even footsteps can jar the delicate operation of the scanning tunneling microscope. Rohrer and Binnig initially sought to solve the problem by placing the microscope on a heavy stone table, which they insulated from external disturbances in the laboratory building with inflated rubber tires. The microscope itself was suspended over a bowl of superconducting lead with permanent magnets. To move the tip as precisely as possible, piezoelectric materials, which contract or expand upon the application of voltages, were used.

Since its rather primitive beginnings, the instrument has been refined considerably. By the mid-1980s, a scanning tunneling microscope (except for the vacuum chamber) fit in the palm of the hand, and by 1987, Rohrer and his IBM research team had developed a version the size of a fingertip. These microscopes can resolve vertical features as small as 0.1 angstrom (1 hundred-billionth of a meter), or roughly one-tenth the diameter of a hydrogen atom. Scanning tips only a few atoms in width permit lateral features to be resolved within 2 angstroms. By 1986, at least fifty scanning tunneling microscopes were being used in laboratories around the world, and two companies had begun making commercial versions. The instrument works in a variety of environments besides the vacuum, including air, water, and cryogenic fluids. It has been employed to study a variety of materials other than inorganic substances, including virus particles and deoxyribonucleic acid (DNA).

Rohrer and Binnig shared half of the 1986 Nobel Prize in Physics "for their design of the scanning tunneling microscope." The other half was awarded to Ernst Ruska for his contributions to the electron microscope. In awarding the prize to Rohrer and Binnig, the Royal Swedish Academy of Sciences stated, "The scanning tunneling microscope is completely new, and we have so far seen only the beginning of its development. It is, however, clear that entirely new fields are opening up for the study of the structure of matter. Binnig's and Rohrer's great achievement is that, starting from earlier works and ideas, they have succeeded in mastering the enormous experimental difficulties involved in building an instrument of the precision and stability required." It was perhaps these difficulties that Rohrer and Binnig's colleagues had in mind when they initially reacted to plans for the device. As Rohrer later told a writer for *BusinessWeek* (November 3, 1986), "They all said, 'You are completely crazy—but if it works, you'll get the Nobel Prize.'"

In 1961 Rohrer married Rose-Marie Eggar, with whom he has two daughters. When asked to comment about himself, Rohrer, who is known as an affable and modest man, once replied, "The ones who know me, understand me; for those who don't, it is hopeless."

In addition to the Nobel Prize, Rohrer and Binnig have shared other honors for their work. In 1984 they received the Hewlett-Packard Prize of the European Physical Society and the King Faisal International Prize in Science from the Saudi Arabian government for their efforts in scanning tunneling microscopy. Rohrer was made an IBM Fellow in 1986 and received the Cresson Medal from the Franklin Institute, in Philadelphia, in 1987. He was named to the National Inventors Hall of Fame, in Akron, Ohio, in 1994.

Heinrich Rohrer has also been distinguished by a number of universities for his work and has received honorary doctoral degrees from Rutgers University, in 1987; Marseille University, in 1988; Madrid University, in 1988; and Tsukuba University, in 1994. He is also a member of several scientific societies, including the Royal Microscopical Society, the Swiss Association of Engineering and Architecture, and the Zurich Physics Society.
—C. M.

Suggested Reading: *BusinessWeek* p134+ November 3, 1986; *New York Times* Oct. 16, 1986; *R & D Magazine* p47+ June 1998; *Science* Nov. 14, 1986; *Science News* Oct. 25, 1986; *American Men and Women of Science, 1998–99*, 1998; Millar, David and John and Margaret Ian. *Cambridge Dictionary of Scientists*, 1996

Ruska, Ernst

Dec. 25, 1906–May 27, 1988 Inventor of the electron microscope

The German physicist Ernst Ruska spent his life making advancements in electron optics, but it was his invention of the electron microscope in 1933 that garnered Ruska the most fame as a scientist. This instrument has proven to be a monument in the field of microscopy, allowing researchers to study in detail the structures of metals, viruses, and protein molecules. Ruska's invention had further impact when it eventually spun off the creation of the scanning tunneling microscope, a device that has been an invaluable help in detecting carbon and oxygen atoms in semiconductors for the computer industry. Sending reverberations through such varied areas of the scientific community has made Ruska a significant inventor in history, and earned him a share of the 1986 Nobel Prize in Physics.

Ernst August Friedrich Ruska was born in Heidelberg, Germany, on December 25, 1906, the fifth of seven children born to Julius Ferdinand Ruska and Elizabeth Merx Ruska. He began to train in the physical sciences at the Technical University of Munich in 1925, then transferred to the Technical University of Berlin in 1927. During this time, Ruska studied high voltage and vacuum methods, a background that would serve him well when he began work on electron optics. He went on to earn a degree as a certified engineer at the Technical University of Berlin in 1931 and spent the next two years working under Max Knoll in pursuit of a doctorate in electrical engineering.

Ruska and Knoll had constructed a microscope in 1928 that possessed a magnification of 17. At the time, the conventional light microscope was limited by the wavelength of visible light, which consists of about 5,000 angstroms (one half-millionth of a meter). By contrast, the width of an atom is only one angstrom (one ten-billionth of a meter), thereby making it impossible to build a light microscope powerful enough to focus on objects so small. It was well known by the mid-1920s that electromagnetic radiation exhibits particle-like properties, and could, if experimental conditions permitted, also act as waves. H. Busch had also discovered that a magnetic coil could focus a beam of electrons in the way that a convex lens could focus a light beam. In 1924 the French physicist Louis De Broglie had concluded that the greater the energy of an electron, the shorter its wavelength should be, making an electron with an energy level of 100 kiloelectron volts, for instance, possess a wavelength of about 0.1 angstrom. By 1927, Clinton J Davisson and Lester H. Germer of Bell Telephone had confirmed the wavelike properties of the electron. Ruska and Knoll's microscope was constructed using these theories.

By the time Ruska was working toward his doctorate, he was making even further advances that would ultimately lead him to the invention of the electron microscope—a microscope that would exploit electrons instead of light. His first discovery was that a magnetic coil could be used as a lens for electrons; then he expanded on that idea and built a magnetic lens with a focal length short enough that it could be used to obtain an image of an object irradiated with electrons. In 1931, with this newly discovered system, Ruska and Knoll built an early version of the electron microscope. Consisting of two magnetic coils in series, and with a magnification of 15, the device was significantly less powerful than other optical microscopes of the time. However, this instrument proved to be a breakthrough in electron optic technology and would provide the basic principle of electron microscopy. In 1933 Ruska built another, more advanced version of his microscope, which had the capability to examine features consisting of 500 atoms and had a magnification power of 12,000. The new instrument had the power to reveal details 10 times smaller than the most powerful light microscope was capable of examining.

After receiving his doctorate in electrical engineering in 1933, Ruska took on employment with the Fernseh Corporation in Berlin, where he began to work on television tube technology. Four years later, he decided to take a position with the Siemens Company in order to begin the development of the first commercially produced electron microscope. In 1939 the device made its debut. A huge improvement over any previous microscope of the time, the transmission electron microscope could resolve features as small as 100 angstroms. It operates by bombarding the material to be examined (in the form of a thin slice) with a narrow beam of electrons. As the electrons travel through the slice of material, they are deflected according to the material's structure and composition. Some electrons are absorbed or bounce off the specimen; others pass through and form a magnified image of the specimen. By recording where the electrons fall on a piece of photographic emulsion, the user of the microscope can obtain a magnified image of the material. The instrument Ruska invented was capable of studying metals, viruses, protein molecules, and other biological structures.

Unfortunately, however, Ruska was not able to secure the first patent for his invention. G. R. Rudenberg filed first, and his claim was upheld in a U.S. lawsuit, although it was not upheld in Germany. The Siemens Company continued to support Ruska's work during World War II, while he worked out of a converted bakery in Berlin. His work ceased when Russian troops looted his laboratory towards the end of the war.

Ruska's transmission electron microscope led to the development of many other forms of electron microscopes, including the scanning electron microscope (SEM). With this particular instrument, a sharply focused beam of electrons is aimed at the specimen, and instead of looking at the electrons that pass through it, one looks at the electrons that are scattered off it. Magnetic coils are used to sweep the incident beam over the surface in much the same manner that the electron beam in a television tube is swept across its surface. Through recordings of the variations in the emission of the scattered electrons, an image with a large depth of focus—in contrast to the sectional image of the transmission microscope—is obtained. Scanning electron microscopes have the ability to magnify objects 100,000 times or more. Since the resolution of the scanning electron microscope is lower than that of the transmission electron microscope, the two types complement each other.

Ruska's initial work also helped in the creation of the scanning tunneling microscope (STM), which was created by Gerd Binnig and Heinrich Rohrer of IBM in 1978. The scanning tunneling microscope uses an ultra sharp tip at a high voltage to explore conducting surfaces, thereby making it a valuable tool for the study of metal surfaces, with a resolution capable of reaching atomic size. Some of these metal surfaces, such as silicon, are key components of computer systems, and with the emergence of this microscope, computer developers suddenly had the ability to detect if carbon or oxygen atoms were present in semiconductors. Ruska's primitive invention in 1933 would therefore have lasting effects on a wide variety of scientific areas, including the computer industry.

Ruska continued to work for Siemens until 1955, and in 1949, he took on the additional duties of a privatdocent (an unsalaried lecturer) at the Technical University of Berlin. That same year, he was named an honorary professor at the Free University of Berlin. Five years later, he became a member of the Max Planck Society, which appointed Ruska to the position of director for its Institute of Electron Microscopy in 1957. In 1959 he took on a concurrent position as professor of electron optics and electron microscopy at the Technical University of Berlin. Ruska decided to retire in 1972, but his pioneering work in electron optics earned him half of the 1986 Nobel Prize in Physics. He received the award in recognition for his "fundamental work in electron optics and for the design of the first electron microscope." The other half of the award was given to Binnig and Rohrer for their contributions to the scanning tunneling microscope. In presenting the award to Ruska, the Royal Swedish Academy of Sciences stated: "The significance of the electron microscope in different fields of science, such as biology and medicine, is now fully established: it is one of the most important inventions of the century. . . . Electron microscopy has developed extremely over the past few decades, with technical improvements and entirely new designs. . . . Its importance can scarcely be exaggerated, and, against this background, the importance of the earliest, fundamental work becomes increasingly evident. While many researchers were involved, Ruska's contributions clearly predominate. His electron-optical investigations and the building of the first true electron microscope were crucial for future development."

Ruska married Irmela Ruth Geigis in 1937. The couple had two sons and a daughter and lived in Berlin until Ruska's death, in May 1988. He received many awards and distinctions, in addition to his Nobel Prize for Physics. He was given the Senckenberg Prize of the University of Frankfurt in 1939, the Leibniz Silver Medal of the Prussian Academy of Sciences in 1941, and the Duddell Medal and Prize of the Institute of Physics in London in 1975. Ruska also received numerous honorary degrees from universities such as the University of Kiev, the Free University of Berlin, and the University of Toronto.—D. B.

Suggested Reading: *Albany Times-Union* A p10 Oct. 16, 1986; *Biography* (on-line) 1994; *Nobel Prize Internet Archive* (on-line) 1995; *St. Louis Post-Dispatch* A p10 May 31, 1988; *Dictionary of Scientists*, 1996; *International Who's Who*, 1987–1988; *Larousse Dictionary of Scientists*, vol 1, 1994; *Nobel Prize Winners*, 1987

Hulton Archive by Getty Images

Russell, Bertrand

May 18, 1872–Feb. 2, 1970 Philosopher; mathematician; educator; author

"The outstanding feature of [Bertrand] Russell's work as a philosopher," wrote H. W. Leggett in *Bertrand Russell* (1950), "is his attitude of 'methodological doubt' applied to every stage of philosophic enquiry, and above all, to the actual language of philosophy itself." By perfecting mathematical logic as a technique for investigating empirical knowledge—particularly in his three-volume *Prin-*

cipia Mathematica (1910–13), which made waves throughout the sciences—he has shown that "a great deal of what had passed in previous ages for philosophy (particularly metaphysical speculation) was based entirely on grammatical or linguistic misunderstanding." Russell, the British mathematician, philosopher, and activist, is generally regarded as one of the 20th century's greatest thinkers for his major contributions to mathematical philosophy and symbolic logic. At the same time, the breadth of his interests, ranging from history, politics, and economics to education, morals, and various societal problems, and the scope of his writings in over 40 volumes, have assured his wide-ranging influence in numerous fields. The winner of the 1950 Nobel Prize in Literature, he was a small, slim, hawk-faced man with a shock of white hair—pedantic in speech, with a whinnying laugh, but with immense charm of manner. As Sidney Hook once wrote in the *New York Times Book Review*, "he was without peer as a brilliant conversationalist. There was an unfailing play of common sense, profundity and puckish wit in his treatment of the most diverse themes. Others could have made careers out of the crumbs of his table talk."

Bertrand Arthur William Russell was born on May 18, 1872 at Ravenscroft, near Trelleck, in Monmouthshire, England, the second of the three children of John Russell, the viscount of Amberley, and Katharine (Stanley) Russell. The Russell family had been prominent in English history since the early 16th century. Russell's grandfather, Lord John Russell, twice served as Liberal prime minister, introduced the Reform Bill in 1832, and was created the first Earl Russell by Queen Victoria in 1861. Russell's mother was the daughter of Baron Stanley of Alderley. Both of Russell's parents were disciples of John Stuart Mill, a 19th-century En-

474   Leaders of the Information Age

glish philosopher and economist, and held views that were radical for their time. They were early advocates of birth control and "free love." When Russell was two years old his mother and sister died, and his father died some 20 months later. The Russells had arranged for their sons to be adopted by agnostic friends, but the court set aside that provision, and in 1876 Russell and his older brother went to live in Richmond Park, where they were given a Christian upbringing by their grandmother, Countess Russell. Though politically radical, she was a strict and joyless Presbyterian, known in some quarters as Deadly Nightshade. Russell received his early education from German and Swiss governesses and English tutors.

The rest of Russell's long life has been widely perceived as a search for certainty—for some irreducible bedrock of truth. At the age of 11, he thought he had found it when his brother, Frank, introduced him to Euclidean geometry. "I had not imagined that there was anything so delicious in the world. . . . (It was) as dazzling as first love," Russell later recalled, as quoted by Thomas Filbin in the *Virginia Quarterly Review* (Autumn 1997). He was grief-stricken, however, when he discovered that Euclid's unassailable theorems depended on axioms that must be taken on trust. By the time he was 18 he had abandoned all belief in Christianity. In 1890 Russell went with a small scholarship to Trinity College at Cambridge University. His brilliance was soon recognized, earning him membership in an exclusive society known as "The Apostles," the forerunners of the "Bloomsbury Group," which included such writers and critics as E. M. Forster, John Maynard Keynes, Virginia Woolf, Aldous Huxley, and T. S. Eliot. At Trinity his friend J. M. E. McTaggart introduced him to German Idealism and the writings of 19th-century philosopher Georg W. F. Hegel. After obtaining a First Class degree in both mathematics (1893) and moral sciences (1894), he was elected a fellow of his college in 1895. His fellowship dissertation was *An Essay on the Foundations of Geometry* (1897).

Meanwhile, Russell had already left Cambridge in the summer of 1894 and for several months served as honorary attaché at the British Embassy in Paris, France. He quit the post in December 1894 to marry, against his family's wishes, Alys Whitall Pearsall Smith, sister of the essayist Logan Pearsall Smith. The couple went to Berlin, Germany, where Russell spent most of 1895 studying economics and collecting material for his first book, *German Social Democracy* (1896). After visiting the United States for three months in 1896, the couple returned to England, to live in a small cottage in Sussex. Russell's next book, *A Critical Exposition of the Philosophy of Leibniz* (1900), grew out of his lectures on Leibniz at Cambridge, where he was asked to substitute for McTaggart in 1898. It was during this time that he abandoned the idealist philosophy of Hegel for the metaphysical realism of his friend G. E. Moore.

Of utmost importance in Russell's intellectual life was the year 1900. In that year, together with Alfred North Whitehead, then a lecturer on mathematics at Trinity, he attended the International Congress of Philosophy in Paris, where he was particularly impressed by the work of Giuseppe Peano, one of the originators of symbolic logic. Proceeding to develop and extend the investigations of Peano and Gottlob Frege, he wrote the first book to win him widespread intellectual attention, *The Principles of Mathematics* (1903), in which he outlined the view that mathematics and formal logic were identical and that the whole of mathematics could be deduced from a few logical concepts and axioms.

Collaborating with Whitehead, he spent the following 10 years working out the detailed demonstration of this thesis, which was published as *Principia Mathematica* in three volumes between 1910 and 1913. Although the book did not solve quite all of the problems it set itself, as David R. Bell wrote in his *Bertrand Russell* (1972), it "caused a deep and lasting intellectual revolution, as important in its way as the *Principia* of Newton." Much disputed, it remains "a work of novelty and genius" and "the focal point and stimulus to extensive investigations and extensions of both logic and mathematics." The book popularized modern mathematical logic and demonstrated the power of the modern idea of a formal system, which, as described on the Britannica Web site, "provides an ideal language by means of which to abstract and analyze the deductive structure of thought apart from specific meanings." The book has exerted an influence in fields such as philosophy, mathematics, linguistics, economics, and computer science.

The intensity of Russell's concentration on *Principia* had been profoundly exhausting—he claimed that his intellect never fully recovered, and he never again worked intensively in mathematics. Nevertheless, the range of his other activities during those years was remarkable. He applied his tools of logical analysis to a variety of concerns, including causation, perception, knowledge, truth, and the nature of philosophy itself. He called his philosophical method "logical atomism," because it aimed to analyze language down to irreducible "atoms" of meaning that are grounded in the sensory experience of reality. He had previously been, for a short period, a "neutral monist," before working out his theory of logical atomism. According to A. J. Ayer in *Bertrand Russell* (1972), "there is no philosopher of our time (with the possible exception of [Ludwig] Wittgenstein) who has made such a large difference, not only to the treatment of particular philosophical problems, but to the way in which the whole subject is pursued."

Russell also became an active convert to pacifism, campaigned for free trade, and in 1907 stood unsuccessfully for Parliament as a candidate for the National Union of Women's Suffrage Societies. He became a Fellow of the Royal Society in 1908.

Over the next few years Russell came to believe that inherited money was immoral, and gave most of his away to his university. In 1910 he was very low on funds—partially because he may have secretly paid off Whitehead's debts—and was glad to accept a Trinity lectureship in 1910. The same year, the Liberals rejected him as a Parliamentary candidate because of his agnostic views.

Russell held a complex attitude towards religion, expressed in *Why I Am Not a Christian* (1927) and other books. He thought that all organized religions are the residue of the barbaric past, dwindled to hypocritical superstitions that have no basis in reality and do terrible harm. On the other hand, he had personally been deeply affected by mystical experiences. As a scientist who was also a passionate humanist, he professed "cosmic piety" and sought to live "in the vision of the good." His daughter Katharine Tait, a missionary, shrewdly suggested in *My Father, Bertrand Russell* (1976) that he was essentially a religious man whose whole philosophic career had been a "search for God."

The strains of his work on *Principia* had been exacerbated by his realization, in 1902, that he no longer loved his wife. They lived painfully together for nine years, until Russell began a lengthy, hectic, and essentially unhappy affair with the literary hostess Lady Ottoline Morrell. (He told her in a letter that "loving you is like loving a red-hot poker.") Other liaisons followed, between or during subsequent marriages, earning Russell a notoriety to equal his philosophical fame. In *Marriage and Morals* (1929) and elsewhere, Russell outraged many by writing as freely about his sexual morality as he did about his agnosticism. Russell believed that human beings are not naturally monogamous and cannot be one another's property. Exclusive fidelity to a single partner, he maintained, is not to be required of either sex.

In 1911 Russell became president of the Aristotelian Society. Four years later Harvard University, in Cambridge, Massachusetts, invited him to deliver the Lowell lectures, which were published as *Our Knowledge of the External World as a Field for Scientific Method in Philosophy* (1914). On his return to England, he plunged vigorously into the antiwar movement through his connection with the No Conscription Fellowship, a pacifist organization. "I could not feel that the victory of either side would solve any problem," he explained. Both his pacifist stand and his books designed for the general reader, such as *Principles of Social Reconstruction* (1916; entitled *Why Men Fight* in the United States), *Justice in War-Time* (1916), *Political Ideals* (1917), and *Roads to Freedom* (1918), first made him a public figure outside academic circles. He was fined in June 1916 for writing a pamphlet in protest against the sentencing of a conscientious objector. The following month Trinity removed him from his lectureship. Offered a post at Harvard, he was refused a passport. In February 1918 he was prosecuted for a *Tribunal* article allegedly

casting aspersions on the American army, and sentenced to four months in prison, which he spent writing *Introduction to Mathematical Philosophy* (1919).

After the war Russell found it impossible to return to a purely academic life. Instead, he spent five weeks in Russia in 1920, where he talked with Marxist revolutionaries Vladimir Lenin and Leon Trotsky and socialist author Maxim Gorky. Although sympathetic to the general aims of socialism, he disliked the Soviet regime and said so frankly in *The Practice and Theory of Bolshevism* (1920). He then visited the Far East from 1920 to 1921 as professor of philosophy at the National University in Peking, China, and expressed his great admiration for Chinese civilization in *The Problems of China* (1922). While in China, he nearly died of bronchitis; his death was erroneously reported in one missionary journal. A former student of Russell's, Dora Black, went with him to China. They were married on their return to England on September 27, 1921, after which Russell bought houses in Cornwall and in Chelsea, where he was an unsuccessful Labour candidate in 1922 and 1923. He supported himself by journalism, writing such books as *The ABC of Atoms* (1923) and *The ABC of Relativity* (1925), and making lecture tours to the United States in 1924, 1927, 1929, and 1931. With the birth of his two children, John Conrad (Viscount Amberley) and Katharine Jane, he became greatly interested in the problems of education, and in 1927 he and Dora opened an experimental school for young children near Petersfield. Russell's educational theories are summarized in *On Education* (1926) and *Education and the Social Order* (1932).

After the death of his elder brother in 1931, the philosopher became the third Earl Russell of Kingston Russell. During this period he directed his chief attention to world affairs in such books as *Freedom and Organization, 1814–1914* (1934), *Which Way to Peace?* (1936), and *Power: A New Social Analysis* (1938). He married for the third time, on January 18, 1936, to Patricia Helen Spence, his former secretary, with whom he had a son, Conrad Sebastian Robert. Although he had opposed any steps that might have led to war, Russell publicly announced his support of the war and the cause of the democracies soon after Hitler's invasion of Poland. In 1938 he came to the United States to serve as visiting professor of philosophy at the University of Chicago, in Illinois, and the next academic year he taught at the University of California at Los Angeles.

When it was announced in February 1940 that Russell had been appointed professor of philosophy at the City College of New York, a storm of protest immediately arose from among the clergy, several religious organizations, a section of the press, and the city council, denouncing him as "an enemy of religion and morality." A taxpayer's suit brought into the courts by a Brooklyn housewife resulted in a judicial order to rescind the appointment on March 30. Russell's appeal was denied, and the appointment remained invalidated. Unsuccessful attempts were also made to oust him from Harvard, where he gave the William James lectures in the fall of 1940. The substance of Russell's courses during his residence in the United States was published in *An Inquiry into Meaning and Truth* (1940). In October 1940 Russell signed a five-year contract to lecture at the Barnes Foundation, in Merion, Pennsylvania. Upon his dismissal from this post at the end of 1942, he sued for breach of contract and was awarded $20,000 in damages the following year. The lectures designed and partly delivered at the foundation were published in *A History of Western Philosophy* (1945).

In 1944 he returned to Cambridge as a Fellow of his old college, Trinity. He was by then 72, but his intellectual agility and strong opinions made him a star of *The Brains Trust,* a popular BBC radio show. Throughout the 1940's his preoccupation with philosophical questions became dominant again, culminating in his book *Human Knowledge: Its Scope and Limits* (1948). In 1948 and 1949 he delivered the first Reith lectures, an endowed series of broadcasts over the BBC, which formed the basis for *Authority and the Individual* (1949). That year he was also admitted by King George VI to the Order of Merit. It was during a month's lecture tour of the United States that Russell learned on November 10, 1950 that he had won the 1950 Nobel Prize in Literature. In presenting Russell the $30,000 award a month later in Stockholm, the permanent secretary of the Swedish Academy hailed him as "one of our time's most brilliant spokesmen of rationality and humanity and a fearless champion of free speech and free thought in the West."

Russell's marriage to Patricia Spence had ended in 1949, and in 1952 he married an American, Edith Finch, with whom he lived happily for the rest of his life. In 1955 they settled permanently at Penrhyndeudraeth, in North Wales. Although content, Russell was by no means ready to fade peacefully into history. By the mid-1950s, he had come to believe that atomic weapons posed the greatest contemporary threat to human survival. He wanted the British government to lead the way to general disarmament, arguing his case in *Common Sense and Nuclear Warfare* (1959) and *Has Man A Future?* (1961). In 1958 he became president of the Campaign for Nuclear Disarmament (CND), and in 1960 he split the CND to set up the militant Committee of 100. After two mass demonstrations in 1961, he and his wife were charged with incitement to breach of the peace. They were sentenced to two months' imprisonment, reduced on medical grounds to seven days; thus, Russell returned to Brixton Prison after 40-odd years.

He continued to campaign for nuclear disarmament after serving his sentence, and in 1964 established the Bertrand Russell Peace Foundation, selling his archives to McMasters University, in Ontario, to finance it. He also intervened in the Cuban missile crisis of 1962, supported the Jews in Russia

and the Arabs in Palestine, condemned the Vietnam War, and involved himself in innumerable other causes. Although some derided him as "England's wisest fool," he was a hero to many all over the world, especially the idealistic young.

Russell died of influenza at the age of 97 on February 2, 1970 at his residence in North Wales. As David R. Bell claimed, "Bertrand Russell is now commonly believed to be one of the great minds of the twentieth century." Throughout his intellectual endeavors, Russell brought an unflagging determination to his quest for truth. When asked by a journalist in the last week of his life what he would say to God if he found himself before Him, he replied, "I should reproach him for not giving us enough evidence."—P. G. H.

Suggested Reading: *American Scholar* p123+ Winter 1994; New Leader p3+ Dec. 16, 1996; *New Republic* p37+ Aug. 13, 1992, p46+ Dec. 2, 1996; *New Yorker* p104+ Dec. 9, 1996; New York Times Book Review p7 Oct. 31, 1993, p5 Dec. 29, 1996; *Smithsonian* p128+ May 1993; *Virginia Quarterly Review* Autumn 1997; Leggett, H. W. *Bertrand Russell,* 1950; Ayer, A. J. *Bertrand Russell,* 1972; Bell, D. R. *Bertrand Russell,* 1972; Tait, K. *My Father, Bertrand Russell,* 1976; Clark, R. W. *Bertrand Russell and His World,* 1981; Winchester, I. and Blackwell, K. *Antinomies and Paradoxes: Studies in Russell's Early Philosophy,* 1989; Hylton, P. *Russell, Idealism and the Emergence of Analytic Philosophy,* 1990; Tiles, M. *Mathematics and the Image of Reason,* 1991; Rodriguez-Consuegra, F. A. *The Mathematical Philosophy of Bertrand Russell,* 1991; Irvine, A. D. and Wedeking, G. A. *Russell and Analytic Philosophy,* 1993; Patterson, W. A. *Bertrand Russell's Philosophy of Logical Atomism,* 1993

Sammet, Jean E.

Mar. 23, 1928– Computer programmer; developer of COBOL (with Grace Hopper) and FORMAC

Jean E. Sammet has been recognized for her accomplishments in the field of computer languages, particularly for her work on COBOL with Grace Hopper, and for her own development of FORMAC, a computer language used with nonnumerical mathematical expressions, such as those common in algebra. These high-level programming languages were utilized widely in a variety of functions by the U.S. government as well as the private sector. Sammet was one of the earliest female programmers, computers being a field that was dominated by men until the 1960s and beyond. An expert on the history of computing languages, she wrote *Programming Languages: History and Fundamentals* (1969), which is considered a cornerstone of the field. In addition to teaching and lecturing, Sammet was a programmer for IBM for 27 years and a president of the Association for Computing Machinery.

Jean E. Sammet was born in New York City on March 23, 1928. The daughter of Harry and Ruth Sammet, she was educated at Mount Holyoke College, in South Hadley, Massachusetts, where she received a bachelor's degree in mathematics in 1948, graduating magna cum laude and Phi Beta Kappa. She completed her master's degree in mathematics a year later at the University of Illinois.

After finishing her education, Sammet was initially drawn to the teaching profession and was a teaching assistant in math at the University of Illinois from 1948 to 1951. She left teaching for a year, from 1951 to 1952, and joined the staff at the Metropolitan Life Insurance Company, working as a dividend technician. In 1952 she joined the mathematics department at Barnard College and Columbia University, located on adjacent campuses in New York City. Sammet left full-time teaching in 1953 to become an engineer at the Sperry Gyroscope Company in Great Neck, New York. She worked in that capacity for two years, until 1955, when she was charged with developing and directing the first scientific programming group for the company, a job in which she remained through 1958.

However, Sammet's first truly significant contribution to computer programming came in 1959, when she joined the Committee on Data Systems Languages (CODASYL), a group assembled with the goal of perfecting computer business languages. As a member of CODASYL, Sammet worked with Grace Hopper, the developer of the FLOWMATIC language, to create a compiler that would enable such languages to run on all types of computers. (A compiler is a type of program that translates an entire set of high-level instructions—written in another programming language, for example—into machine language, in which form the instructions are then ready to be carried out by the computer.) Three months after the group had begun their work, their efforts produced the Common Business Oriented Language, better known as CO-BOL, the world's first computer language designed for business applications. In addition to its other merits, COBOL served as an answer to the U.S. Defense Department's demand for a computer language that could be used by all of the government's suppliers. As a charter member of CODASYL, as well as chairman of the group's Statement Language Task Group and its Editing Committee, Sammet was an essential figure in the development of COBOL. She remained a member of the committee until the group was disbanded, in 1964.

Since COBOL could run on many types of computers and was adopted as the standard computer language for the U.S. government, its popularity as a business application grew almost overnight. In 1960 COBOL was installed on the RCA 501 and the UNIVAC II computers, which eliminated the need for programming to be done separately on each brand of computer. Later that same year the U.S. Department of Defense mandated that all its computers be capable of compiling COBOL.

Sammet was next employed by Sylvania Electric products as a staff consultant for programming research, a position she held from 1958 to 1961. In the latter year she joined the Boston Advanced Programming Center, part of the data systems division of IBM. There, Sammet organized and managed the advanced stages of programming development. While she initiated and guided the work on a number of programming languages, her major contribution in this period was the conceptualization and development of the Formula Manipulation Compiler (FORMAC), the first widely used computer language that could handle nonnumeric algebraic expressions. For her work on FORMAC, she received the 1965 IBM Outstanding Contribution Award.

In that same year Sammet became programming language technology manager in the IBM systems development division. As part of that job, Sammet was able to write a book on the history and basics of computer languages. Entitled *Programming Languages: History and Fundamentals*, the book was published in 1969 by Prentice-Hall. In 1989, in recognition of her work on computer languages, Sammet received the Augusta Ada Lovelace Award, named for Ada Lovelace, the 19th-century British mathematician who is credited as the first computer programmer for her work on Charles Babbage's Difference Engine. The award citation particularly noted Sammet's book, calling it "the best history of programming languages." In *Computer Pioneers*, J. A. N. Lee quoted sources that described the book as "the standard work on programming languages," and an "instant computer classic."

In all, Sammet spent 27 years working for IBM. Between 1968 and 1978, she held a number of posts in IBM's federal systems division, and her responsibilities included lecturing on programming languages and internal consulting and planning. In 1978 she became the divisional program manager for Ada, a computer programming language named for Augusta Ada Lovelace. Sammet's work entailed coordinating the federal systems division's steps for initiating the use of Ada. Three years later she was put in charge of IBM's efforts to standardize Ada. (By 1984 Ada had become the standard language for the U.S. Department of Defense.)

In 1979 Sammet became software technology manager for the federal system division. In this capacity she managed a department that appraised software technology for the division and advised on its use. She also continued to oversee the general development of computer languages, including Ada. Four years later she returned to her previous position as programming technology manager so she could resume her focus on the development of such languages. In 1986 she was appointed senior technical staff member, a title she kept until she retired from IBM, in 1988. Since that time Sammet has continued to do consulting work, give lectures, and write articles, and she has also worked on the second edition of *Programming Languages*. She lives in Bethesda, Maryland.

In addition to her work at IBM, Sammet has been a highly active member of the Association for Computing Machinery (ACM). From 1965 to 1968, she was the first chairman and chief organizer of the ACM Special Interest Committee on Symbolic and Algebraic Manipulation (SICSAM). In 1966 she was elected the Northeast regional representative, which made her an ACM council member, and she remained in those roles until 1968. She was a lecturer for the organization from 1967 to 1968, and again in 1972. From August 1968 to September 1970 she was chair of the ACM Committee on Special Interest Groups and Committees, and through that position coordinated the activities of 26 technical committees. A year later she became the chair of the ACM Special Interest Group on Programming Languages. In 1972 she was elected ACM vice president, a position she held until 1974, when she became ACM president. In these latter two positions Sammet greatly aided the organization by helping to bring about its financial stability. Her work on the ACM Awards Committee and the Fellowship Investigation subcommittee, which began in 1976 after she completed her term as president, was noteworthy for her conception and development of the highly successful ACM SIGPLAN History of Programming Languages Conference in 1978.

From 1979 to 1987 Sammet was the editor in chief of the *ACM Guide to Computing Literature* and ACM's *Computing Reviews*. As a member of the American Federation of Information Processing Societies, she helped to establish that group's journal, *Annals of the History of Computing* in 1978. She has remained fascinated with computer history and keeps scores of historical files dating back to the mid-1950s on programming languages. She carried that interest into the development of the Computer Museum in Boston, where she was on the board of directors from 1983 to 1993.—C. M.

Suggested Reading: *Association for Women in Computing* (on-line); *American Men and Women of Science 1998–1999*, 1998; Lee, J. A. N., ed. *International Biographical Dictionary of Computer Pioneers*, 1995; Spencer, Donald D. *The Timetable of Computers*, 1997; *Who's Who in America*, 2000

Sarnoff, David

Feb. 27, 1891–Dec. 12, 1971 CEO of RCA and founder of NBC

David Sarnoff, despite humble beginnings, is a pivotal figure in the history of the communications industry. A Russian immigrant who was forced to leave school after the eighth grade to support his family, Sarnoff started his career in 1906 as an office boy with the American subsidiary of the Marconi Wireless Company, in New York City. One of the first to see the commercial possibilities of radio, Sarnoff eventually attained the presidency of the Radio Corporation of America (RCA). He went on to found the National Broadcasting Company (NBC), which began as a network of radio stations and then branched into the fledgling field of television. "Not money, but the opportunity to express the forces within me is my motivation, and will be till I die," Sarnoff once said, as quoted by a reporter for the *New York Times* (December 13, 1971). "Whether a man is a plumber or an artist, a musician or an industrialist, his mission on Earth is to express the creative forces within himself."

David Sarnoff was born on February 27, 1891 in Uzlian, a small town in the province of Minsk, in Russia. In his book *David Sarnoff: A Biography* (1966), Eugene Lyons noted that Uzlian, which was inhabited by several hundred Jewish families, "was the kind of forsaken corner described by the great Yiddish storyteller Sholem Aleichem: a ragged remnant of the Middle Ages steeped in poverty and piety." David's father, Abraham, worked as a painter and paperhanger. On his mother's side, David was descended from a long line of chief rab-

Alfred Eisenstaedt/Getty Images

bis. As a child, David spoke Yiddish and studied the Talmud with the hope of becoming a rabbi himself.

In 1896 Abraham Sarnoff immigrated to the United States. (At that time many Jews were fleeing poverty and anti-Semitic persecution by the czarist monarchy in Russia for a better life in the United States.) Abraham hoped to quickly earn enough money to send for his family. In the meantime David was sent to live with his grandparents in Korme, a small town in the Borisov region, where he continued his Judaic studies under his grandfather.

Within four years Abraham Sarnoff had saved enough money to bring his family to the United States. After a long voyage at sea, they arrived in New York City, on July 2, 1900. They settled in the Lower East Side section of the city. David helped support his family by selling Yiddish newspapers for one cent a copy. The newspapers were dropped at the East Broadway train station early in the morning. "I schooled myself to awaken at the first sound of the approaching train," Sarnoff recalled, as quoted by Kenneth Bilby in *The General: David Sarnoff and the Rise of the Communications Industry* (1986). "I'd throw on my pants and shirt and shoes and get to the street about the same time the bundle landed. Then I'd deliver them by running up and down the stairs of the various tenement buildings. It was great for the appetite."

In September 1900 David Sarnoff enrolled in an English language course for immigrants and became fluent within several months. He broadened his knowledge of English by reading newspapers he found discarded in trash cans. Sarnoff took night classes at the Educational Alliance, an organization for immigrants that operated out of a settlement house in New York's East Side. Sarnoff eventually began running his own newsstand, which employed other newsboys, including two of his younger brothers. He supplemented his income by singing in a synagogue choir.

When he was 16, Sarnoff graduated from eighth grade. Although he was an excellent student who had adapted quickly to his American studies, he was forced to abandon plans for high school and work full time to help support his family. Sarnoff dreamed of being a newspaper reporter, and in 1906 he decided to apply for a job at the *Herald*. By mistake, he walked into the office of the Commercial Cable Company, which was a tenant in the *Herald* building on 35th Street and Broadway. Sarnoff was offered a job as a messenger boy, which paid him a salary of five dollars a week—and ten cents for every hour of overtime he worked. Sarnoff accepted and studied electronics and Morse code during his free time.

Several months later the company fired Sarnoff after he requested three days off so he could sing in his local synagogue for the Jewish High Holy Days. In September 1906, he got a job as an office boy with the American subsidiary of Marconi's Wireless Telegraph Company in New York City. Headquartered in London, England, the parent company was founded by the Italian scientist Guglielmo Marconi (1874–1937) to market his invention, the radio transmitter, which sent and received signals through the air without the need of connecting wires. Sarnoff introduced himself to Marconi, who sometimes worked in the New York City office, and occasionally served as his personal assistant. "I carried his bag, delivered candy and

flowers to his girlfriends," Sarnoff told a reporter for *Time* (July 23, 1951). "I admired the simplicity of his approach to problems."

Starting in the late 1890s, radio stations that could transmit signals over great distances were being built in the United States, Canada, and Europe. The wireless, as Marconi's invention was frequently called, was used primarily by ships at sea and newspaper correspondents who needed to file dispatches. In 1907 Sarnoff was promoted to junior wireless operator: one of his first postings was as the wireless officer aboard the steamship *S.S. New York*, which crossed the Atlantic Ocean from New York to Southampton, England. A year later Sarnoff was sent to work at the remote Marconi station at Siasconset, on the Massachusetts island of Nantucket, where he rose from assistant telegraph operator to full operator. In 1909 he was named the night manager of the Sea Gate wireless station in Coney Island, located in the New York City borough of Brooklyn. The job allowed him to take courses in electrical engineering at the nearby Pratt Institute. In 1910 Sarnoff became the manager and operator of the wireless station on top of Wanamaker's Manhattan-based department store, which was one of the most powerful transmitters in the country. After brief stints as the wireless operator aboard the *S.S. Beothic*, a seal-hunting ship that traveled to the frozen waters of the Arctic Ocean, and the *S.S. Harvard*, which traveled between New York City and Boston, Sarnoff went back to work at Wanamaker's.

Sarnoff was on duty at Wanamaker's on the night of April 12, 1912 when he received this message from the *S.S. Olympic*, a ship in the middle of the Atlantic Ocean: "S.S. Titanic ran into iceberg. Sinking fast," as quoted by Lyons. According to several accounts Sarnoff remained at his post, without eating or sleeping, for the next 72 hours, receiving information about the disaster (including the names of survivors), which he, in turn, relayed to members of the press and anguished relatives who gathered at the store to hear any news. In his book, Bilby asserts that the story of the heroic young operator working for 72 hours straight was slightly embellished over the subsequent decades and became widely accepted as part of the David Sarnoff legend. In response to the tragedy, the U.S. Congress passed legislation requiring all ships with more than 50 passengers to install a wireless and maintain a constant watch at sea.

Over the next several years, Sarnoff acquired additional responsibilities within the Marconi company. By the end of 1912, he had been promoted to radio-station inspector, and he also instructed new wireless operators at the Marconi Institute. In 1913 he was named chief radio inspector and assistant engineer. In January 1914 Sarnoff conducted a successful test of radio equipment aboard a moving train, sending the first communication between trains on the Erie Lackawanna line between Binghamton, New York, and Scranton, Pennsylvania. In the same month, at the Marconi station in Belmar, New Jersey, Sarnoff allowed Edwin Armstrong, an electrical engineer, to test his invention, the regenerative circuit, which greatly improved the ability of the radio transmitter to receive signals from long distances. Armstrong's circuit, which represented an important contribution in the development of radio, allowed Sarnoff to hear messages from stations as far away as Ireland, Germany, and Hawaii. In a letter dated February 2, 1914 to F. M. Sammis, the Marconi company's chief engineer, Sarnoff wrote, "I would state that the results obtained with Mr. Armstrong's receiver are sufficiently convincing to warrant our most careful investigation of his patents and circuits, etc., for I believe that his device has tremendous advantages, and unless there be other systems of equal merits, which are unknown to me, I am of the opinion that this is the most remarkable receiving system in existence," as republished in *Looking Ahead: The Papers of David Sarnoff* (1968). Sir Godfrey Isaacs, the managing director of the Marconi company in London, was reportedly outraged to learn that Sarnoff had spent the company's money to test the invention without permission and considered firing him. Despite that, Sarnoff remained with the company, earning a promotion to contract manager in 1914 and to assistant traffic manager in 1915.

A short time after the 1914 outbreak of World War I in Europe, President Woodrow Wilson imposed strict regulations on all radio stations operating in the United States. Thus, the timing was poor when on September 30, 1915, Sarnoff submitted a memorandum to Edward J. Nally, the vice president and general manager of Marconi's Wireless Telegraph Company of America. In it he sketched out the details of a plan to market the wireless or radio, in hopes of making it as common a household item as a piano or phonograph. He proposed building new radio stations, with ranges of 25 to 50 miles, that would broadcast music, sports, lectures, and events of national importance as they happened. "The receiver can be designed in the form of a simple 'Radio Music Box' and arranged for several different wavelengths, which should be changeable with the throwing of a single switch or pressing of a single button," Sarnoff wrote, as republished in *Looking Ahead*. "The 'Radio Music Box' can be supplied with amplifying tubes and a [loudspeaker], all of which can be neatly mounted in one box. The box can be placed on a table in the parlor or living room, the switch set accordingly, and the transmitted music received." Sarnoff observed that thousands of families within the radius of a single station could enjoy its programs. "This proposition would be especially interesting to farmers and others living in outlying districts removed from cities," he added. "By the purchase of a 'Radio Music Box,' they could enjoy concerts, lectures, music, recitals, etc., which might be going on in the nearest city within their radius." Sarnoff estimated that the Radio Music Box would be priced at $75, noting that "there are

about 15 million families in the United States alone, and if only one million, or seven percent of the total families, thought well of the idea, it would, at the figure mentioned, mean a gross business of about $75 million, which should yield considerable revenue." Because Nally's attention was focused on complying with the government's regulations and other demands, he turned down Sarnoff's ambitious proposal.

In 1917 the United States entered the war. Eager to serve his adopted country in uniform, Sarnoff applied for a commission in the navy, but he was refused. According to Bilby, Sarnoff suspected that he was rejected because he was Jewish and attempted to enlist the army. His local draft board granted him an exemption, however, since his services as a civilian were deemed essential to the war effort. Bilby wrote that during the war, Sarnoff commuted frequently to Washington, D.C., "negotiating contracts at naval bases and providing expert advice on communications to congressional committees and government bureaus."

The war demonstrated the inarguable importance of radio. Several of the involved powers used the radio to communicate with their forces and one another after undersea cables were cut by enemies. After the war, the navy sought legislation that would give it control of all radio stations in the United States. At a congressional hearing Sarnoff testified against the proposed legislation, which never made it out of committee. In order to prevent a foreign company from dominating the entire industry, the navy brokered a deal that resulted in the establishment of a privately held radio monopoly in the United States. In 1919 the navy approached the General Electric Corporation (GE), which owned the rights to a high-frequency alternator that was expected to revolutionize radio communications, about setting up a new subsidiary by acquiring American Marconi from its parent company in London. As an incentive, the navy offered to share its lucrative radio patents with the new company. Thinking that American Marconi would eventually founder under the weight of a government-favored competitor, the parent company agreed to sell its subsidiary to GE for $3.5 million. On October 17, 1919 the new, privately owned company came into existence as the Radio Corporation of America (RCA). Owen Young, the GE general counsel who had negotiated the deal with British Marconi, was named chairman of RCA's board of directors. Edward J. Nally became president of the new company, and David Sarnoff was appointed as the commercial manager. Sarnoff also advised Young on emerging radio technologies. (Westinghouse later purchased 20.6 percent of RCA's stock and exercised some influence over the direction of the company.)

In his new position—and without the distraction of the war—Sarnoff renewed his efforts to market a radio music box. After receiving Young's approval, in January 1920 Sarnoff outlined his proposals in a memorandum to E. W. Rice Jr., the president of GE. Rice forwarded Sarnoff's proposal to RCA's board of directors, which allocated $2,500 to research the idea. Sarnoff then recruited Alfred Goldsmith, RCA's director of research, to build the prototype of a radio receiver, which would be about the size of a breadbox. Goldsmith successfully completed the prototype, which he named "Radiola."

Sarnoff knew that he needed to create consumer interest in RCA's radios by demonstrating their practical benefits to the ordinary person. He decided that the highly anticipated world heavyweight championship boxing match between Jack Dempsey, the U.S. champion, and Georges Carpentier, the French champion, on July 2, 1921 at Boyle's Thirty Acres, in Jersey City, New Jersey, was the ideal event to broadcast live. After Sarnoff secured permission from Tex Rickard, the fight's promoter, to broadcast the bout, RCA engineers installed a microphone at ringside, as well as various other equipment at the venue, which accommodated about 90,000 spectators. To ensure as wide an audience as possible, Sarnoff had radio receivers with amplifying speakers placed in many clubs, school auditoriums, dance halls, and movie theaters. Sarnoff sat at ringside with Andrew J. White, the editor of RCA's internal magazine, *Wireless Age*, and a boxing enthusiast, who provided the blow-by-blow account of the fight, in which Dempsey knocked out Carpentier in the fourth round. (According to Bilby, listeners actually heard J. O. Smith, an RCA technician, who relayed White's descriptions.) The broadcast, the first ever of a major sports event, was a huge success for Sarnoff and RCA, drawing an estimated 300,000 listeners. In 1922 Sarnoff was promoted to vice president and general manager at RCA.

During the early 1920s, the radio became a national sensation. From 1922 to 1924 RCA's revenues from radio sales doubled each year, totaling over $85 million and exceeding Sarnoff's estimate. In an address to the Electrical Jobbers Convention on May 26, 1922, Sarnoff boasted that radio broadcasting was a permanent industry and would overcome any mechanical and economic obstacles. "When you provide an institution of this kind, when you make it possible for men and women and children to sit in their homes and listen to opera and jazz, if you please, and lectures and political debates and market reports and all kinds of information of value," Sarnoff said, as republished in *Looking Ahead*, "it seems to me that you have provided something which collectively represents a sufficient answer to the question of whether radio broadcasting is here to stay."

Despite radio's popularity with millions of people, Sarnoff thought that the quality of broadcasts would eventually be one of the most important factors that affected sales. In a letter to Rice dated June 17, 1922, Sarnoff proposed that RCA establish a subsidiary that would own and operate a national network of radio stations that offered high-quality broadcasts. In September 1926 RCA established

the National Broadcasting Corporation (NBC). In 1927 NBC set up two divisions, the Red Network and the Blue Network, which brought news, sports, music, and entertainment into the homes of tens of millions of people each day. (The main source of NBC's revenue came from companies that advertised their products and services on the air.) In 1927 the Columbia Broadcasting System (CBS), a rival radio network, went on the air.

Concerned that the company owned the majority of radio stations in the country and was unfairly dominating the broadcast industry, in 1941 the Federal Communications Commission (FCC) ordered NBC to divest itself of one its networks. NBC sought a reversal of the decision, but the U.S. Supreme Court upheld the FCC. In 1943 NBC sold the Blue Network to Edward J. Noble, whose company made Lifesavers candy. A few years later, Noble changed the name of the network to the American Broadcasting Company (ABC).

Seeing radio as a means that brought culture to ordinary people, Sarnoff established the *Music Appreciation Hour* program on NBC. In 1937 he scored a personal triumph when he persuaded the renowned Italian conductor Arturo Toscanini (1867–1957) to head up the NBC Symphony Orchestra, which performed on the air and toured extensively.

Although he was pleased with the commercial success of the radio, Sarnoff continually pushed for the development of new products and looked for opportunities to expand RCA's interests. In 1922, for example, he encouraged Goldsmith to build a "radiolette," a portable, battery-powered radio with a light source. In 1929 Sarnoff was named executive vice president of RCA and in that capacity pursued several other notable ventures. After the General Motors Corporation (GM) successfully devised a technique to install radio receivers in the dashboards of automobiles, Sarnoff negotiated an agreement with GM that created a joint-owned company that manufactured car radios from the automaker's plant in Dayton, Ohio. RCA engineers next developed the photophone, a device that added sound to motion pictures. In exchange for 65 percent ownership, Sarnoff offered the rights to the photophone to Joseph P. Kennedy, the millionaire and Kennedy-family patriarch, who controlled the Keith-Albee-Orpheum movie-theater chain, the FPO Productions film studio, and the Pathé film studio. Kennedy, who wanted to branch into talking films, agreed, and the merger resulted in Radio-Keith-Orpheum (RKO) Pictures, which made numerous classic films, including *King Kong* (1933) and *Citizen Kane* (1941). RCA then acquired a controlling interest in the Victor Talking Machine Company, which manufactured phonographs. Sarnoff's decision shocked many observers, including several executives at RCA, because the phonograph was widely seen as radio's chief competitor in the home-entertainment market. In response to the criticism, Sarnoff proposed combining the radio and the phonograph in the same set, thus giving birth to the modern stereo system.

In 1929 Sarnoff formed a partnership with the theater owner and promoter Samuel "Roxy" Rothafel (1882–1936) and the philanthropist John D. Rockefeller Jr. (1874–1960) to build a new theater, which they envisioned as an important cultural venue, in New York City. At the time, Rockefeller was developing a new complex of office buildings in midtown Manhattan on property he leased from Columbia University. Sarnoff eventually moved both RCA and NBC into the complex, which became known as Rockefeller Center. The 6,200-seat theater, one of the largest in the country, was opened in 1932. Sarnoff and Rothafel named the theater Radio City Music Hall.

In 1930 David Sarnoff was elected president of RCA. It was a difficult decade: revenues were dropping precipitously because of the Great Depression, and the federal government initiated an antitrust action, forcing GE and Westinghouse to divest themselves from RCA. Although the action resulted in RCA's independence, which Sarnoff had long desired, the company was forced to pay nearly $18 million in debt to GE and Westinghouse.

Despite the need to cut costs, Sarnoff pressed for the development of the then-experimental medium of television. In a memorandum to RCA's board of directors dated April 5, 1923, Sarnoff made a prediction: "I believe that television, which is the technical name for seeing instead of hearing by radio, will come to pass in due course," he wrote, as republished in Looking Ahead. "It is not too much to expect that in the near future, when news is telegraphed by radio—say, to the United States—of important events in Europe, South America, or the Orient, a picture of the event will likewise be sent over radio and both will arrive simultaneously. Thus, it may well be expected that radio development will provide a situation whereby we shall be able actually to see as well as read in New York, within an hour or so, the event taking place in London, Buenos Aires, or Tokyo." In 1929 Vladimir Zworykin (1889–1982), a Russian-born engineer met with Sarnoff to seek RCA's support for his television research. Zworykin, who had previously worked at Westinghouse, developed the iconoscope, the television camera's electronic eye, and the kinescope, a cathode ray tube that acted as the receiver of the television signal. When he had demonstrated his primitive television system in 1924 for Westinghouse executives, they expressed little interest in it. Zworykin estimated that he needed $100,000 to perfect his all-electric television system. Sarnoff hired the engineer, appointing him as the director of RCA's electronic-research laboratory. "The Sarnoff-Zworkin encounter proved to be one of the most decisive in industrial annals," Bilby observed. "It brought together television's leading inventor and the executive who would guide its development. Their spirt of kinship, perhaps forged out of a Russian cradle, would endure for Sarnoff's life, and would lead to a fundamental alteration in the direction of technology and its management." Zworykin's estimate turned out to be too low. Over the next 20 years, RCA would invest about $50 million in television research. Despite the costs, Zworkin and RCA's engineers made substantial progress throughout the 1930s, gradually improving television's picture quality and range of reception. By the end of the decade, Sarnoff concluded that he was ready to unveil television to the public.

On April 20, 1939 David Sarnoff demonstrated television at that year's World's Fair, in Flushing Meadows-Corona Park, in the New York City borough of Queens. "A new art and a new industry, which eventually will provide entertainment and information for millions and new employment for large numbers of men and women, are here," he said, as republished in Looking Ahead. "And now we add radio sight to sound. It is with a feeling of humbleness that I come to this moment of announcing the birth in this country of a new art so important in its implications that it is bound to affect all society." The broadcast was watched by approximately 2,000 people, most on screens set up at RCA headquarters or around the fairgrounds.

On April 30, 1939 NBC made its first telecast, broadcasting President Franklin Roosevelt's remarks on the opening of the World's Fair. "The initial NBC schedule varied from eight to twelve hours weekly, blending dramas and variety shows with sports and feature films and round-table discussions," Bilby wrote. "From a live baseball telecast of the New York Giants and Brooklyn Dodgers at Ebbets Field and from boxing at Madison Square Garden the schedule ranged to a nighttime dramatization of Treasure Island and a seventy-minute feature film, Young and Beautiful." On June 1, 1941, the NBC-owned WNBT, the nation's first commercial television station, went on the air.

The United States's involvement in World War II delayed the progress of television, as RCA devoted its resources to the war effort. Zworykin, for example, developed the "Sniperscope," an infrared, night-vision device that was used by American soldiers. Sarnoff, who was commissioned a lieutenant colonel in the U.S. Army reserve in 1924, was called to active duty, serving for several months in 1942 with the Army Signal Corps. In March 1944 he was activated again and sent to Europe, where he served as a communications consultant for General Dwight Eisenhower, the Supreme Commander of Allied Forces. Sarnoff developed and implemented electronic news-coverage systems for the Allied D-Day invasion of Europe, which began on June 6, 1944, and the liberation of Paris on August 25, 1944. For his wartime service, Sarnoff was honored with the Legion of Merit medal and promoted to brigadier general. After returning to civilian life, Sarnoff's employees, friends, and even his children, addressed him as "General."

In 1947 Sarnoff became the chief executive officer (CEO) of RCA and the chairman of its board of directors. After several decades of research and development, television was finally sweeping the United States. More and more families purchased black-and-white television sets each year to watch the many programs offered by the four major networks, NBC, ABC, CBS, and DuMont (which folded in 1956), and various local stations. The number of television sets in the United States went from several thousand in the mid-1940s to tens of millions by the early 1950s. RCA, which manufactured and sold television sets, earned its $50 million investment in television development back within three years. The television craze, which paralleled the rapidly spreading popularity of radio in the 1920s, eventually swept Europe and the rest of the world. Although some critics scoffed that television was only a fad, the medium became a powerful force in society, impacting popular culture and even politics; it endures today as one of the most popular forms of entertainment and sources of information. When the quality of television programs was assailed—as it often was, even then—Sarnoff generally replied that broadcasters were simply catering to the wishes of viewers. "A lot of people would rather listen to swing than to Toscanini," he observed, as quoted by a reporter for the New York Times (December 13, 1971). "Those are the facts of life. Of course we have a certain responsibility for creating programs, but basically we're the delivery boys."

In 1950 Sarnoff lost a major battle when the FCC adopted the color-television system developed by CBS as the industry standard. CBS's system, however, could not accommodate black-and-white broadcasts. "We have lost a battle but we'll win the war," he assured the press, as quoted by the New York Times (December 13, 1971). Sarnoff pushed his engineers at RCA Laboratories, in Princeton, New Jersey, to develop a superior color system that was compatible with black-and-white. RCA spent $150 million and three years to develop such a system. In 1953 Sarnoff persuaded the FCC to reverse its decision and adopt RCA's color system as the industry standard. (The television industry, however, made a gradual transition to color in the mid-1960s.)

Under Sarnoff's leadership, RCA continued to expand into a global conglomerate. By 1970 its product line included ferrite cores for computers and radar for tracking satellites and missiles. RCA and its many subsidiaries employed tens of thousands of people around the world and total annual sales exceeded $3 billion.

In 1966 Sarnoff stepped down as RCA's CEO. Two years later, a mastoid infection forced him into total retirement. Sarnoff and his French-born wife, the former Lizette Hermant, lived in a 30-room townhouse in New York City. The couple had three sons: Robert, Thomas, and Edward. Over the decades, Sarnoff received honorary degrees from 27 colleges. His most prized certificate, however, was said to be the honorary high-school diploma he received in 1958 from the prestigious Stuyvesant High School, in New York City.

David Sarnoff died on December 12, 1971. His obituary in the New York Times (December 13, 1971) noted his accomplishments: "He was not an inventor, nor was he a scientist. But he was a man of astounding vision who was able to see with remarkable clarity the possibilities of harnessing the electron, a minute particle of electrical energy that is one of the basic components of all matter, to the uses of man."

RCA went into gradual decline after Sarnoff's death. In 1985 GE acquired NBC. A year later, GE purchased RCA as well, but sold it in 1987 to Thomson Consumer Electronics. RCA endures today as a Thomson subsidiary. In 1951 RCA Laboratories was renamed the David Sarnoff Research Center, which now operates as the Sarnoff Corporation, a computer-technology company. The David Sarnoff Library, in Princeton, houses Sarnoff's papers and keeps his legacy alive.—D. C.

Suggested Reading: David Sarnoff Library Web site; Fortune p62+ Jan. 1938, with photos; NBC Web site; New York Times p1+ Dec. 13, 1971, with photos; New York Times Magazine p7+ Feb. 25, 1941, with photos; RCA Web site; Time p47+ July 15, 1929, p74+ July 23, 1951, with photos; Bilby, Kenneth. The General: David Sarnoff and the Rise of the Communications Industry, 1986; Looking Ahead: The Papers of David Sarnoff, 1968; Lyons, Eugene. David Sarnoff: A Biography, 1966

Scheutz, Georg

Sep. 23, 1785–May 22, 1873 Builder of the first operational Difference Engine

The Swede Pehr Georg Scheutz was a respected publisher and translator who also made a name for himself in the history of science. In 1834 he read an article about the recent attempts of his contemporary Charles Babbage to build a machine called a Difference Engine—an early calculating device that was intended to produce mathematical tables for use in such fields as navigation and astronomy. Babbage had tinkered on his machine for about a decade, but abandoned it to pursue a new idea for an Analytic Engine. Scheutz, however, was intrigued with Babbage's design and undertook the arduous project of constructing his own device—despite having few financial resources and minimal knowledge of the mathematics and engineering involved. With great determination and perseverance, as well as the help of his son Edvard, he spent the next two decades working intermittently on the machine, and in 1853 the Scheutzes unveiled the world's first commercially available, fully operational Difference Engine.

Pehr Georg Scheutz was born on September 23, 1785 in Jonkoping, Sweden. He grew up with a wide array of interests, ranging from science to literature. He had planned on becoming a mining engineer, but upon attending Lund University he discovered that the school did not offer the courses he needed to fulfill the degree requirements. Instead, he studied law, receiving his degree in 1805. After graduation Scheutz worked as a probationer for six years, before moving on to a succession of jobs in law and actuarial work.

In 1816 Scheutz found himself the recipient of a large inheritance, which he used to set himself up as a newspaper publisher. He began publishing and editing *Anmärkaren* (The Swedish), and soon other journals and trade publications followed. By the 1820s *Anmärkaren* had earned a reputation as Sweden's most important political newspaper.

Scheutz kept abreast of contemporary scientific achievements. In 1834 he published a small book about a device that was an improved form of Napier's bones. (Napier's bones, invented by the Scottish mathematician John Napier in the early 1600s, was a mechanical device consisting of a series of rods, often made from bone, used for multiplication and division.) Later that same year, Scheutz translated into Swedish an article by Dionysus Lardner that had appeared in the *Edinburgh Review*, describing the recent attempts of the English mathematician Charles Babbage to build a calculating machine. Between 1822 and 1832 Babbage had built a series of prototypes of a mechanical device, which he called a Difference Engine, that would calculate logarithmic tables. In the early-19th century, the rise of science and the ferment of the industrial revolution led to a vast increase in the need for accurate and convenient numerical calculations. Mathematical tables were widely consulted in fields such as banking, navigation, engineering, astronomy, and architecture—any area where calculations were required. These tables were often very lengthy, with some tables on a single subject occupying several volumes of books. The tables were produced by highly trained mathematicians, but the computations involved were long, tedious, and complex, resulting in frequent errors. Babbage's Difference Engine was designed to compute these tables mechanically, preventing errors and reducing the need for human labor.

The name Difference Engine was a reference to a mathematical method, known as the "method of differences," that can be used to simplify multiplication and division problems by reducing them to a series of additions and subtractions. It is used to calculate polynomials, which are mathematical expressions involving a variable raised to a certain power, such as x to the second power. (This is called a second-order polynomial. A third-order polynomial would be raised to the third power, and so on.) The method of differences can be used to tabulate the results of x to the second power as follows: the series of numbers {1, 2, 3, 4, and 5} has the series of squares {1, 4, 9, 16, and 25}. Subtracting a square from the square that follows it {4 - 1, 9 - 4, 16 - 9, 25 - 16} gives the series of numbers {3, 5, 7, and 9}, which are called the "first differences." Subtracting one of the numbers in this se-

ries from the number that follows it {5 - 3, 7 - 5, 9 - 7} gives the series of numbers {2, 2, and 2}, which are called the "second differences." The second difference, 2, is always constant. Thus it is possible, by doing successive additions, to calculate backwards from the second differences to determine a series of squares. This basic formula can therefore be used to solve higher-order polynomial equations. Babbage's prototype operated on six-digit numbers and second-order differences. The completed Difference Engine, which was to be room-sized, was projected to operate both on sixth-order differences with 20-digit numbers, and third-order differences with 30-digit numbers.

Lardner's article offered only a general description of Babbage's device and its operation and contained no drawings. Sheutz, however, was enthralled with the concept and decided to build his own Difference Engine based on what little information he had. Later that year he completed a small prototype, made with wood, but responsibilities at work drew him away from the project and forced him to set aside the construction of a fully operational machine.

In the summer of 1837, Scheutz's son Edvard returned from the Royal Institute of Technology, in Stockholm, where he was studying engineering. Inspired by his father's prototype, Edvard joined him in constructing a working Difference Engine made from metal. By October of that year, the Scheutzes realized that building such a machine was beyond their financial means, and they appealed to the Swedish government for a grant. The government refused, but the Scheutzes carried on, contributing what time and money they could afford.

By 1840 the duo had assembled a small Difference Engine that operated from only the first difference, with each of two registers capable of holding a five-digit number. By 1842 the inventors had extended the machine's capabilities so that it could handle three orders of difference. In 1843 a printing mechanism was added, and the Scheutzes presented their machine to the Royal Swedish Academy of Science for approval. The Academy praised the device and issued a certificate recommending it for commercial use, but to the Scheutzes' dismay, no orders were forthcoming. They let their plans to build a full-scale machine languish for the next seven years.

In 1851 Scheutz again approached the Swedish government and requested money for the construction of a full-size, working Difference Engine. After an initial refusal, the parliament eventually decided to supply the Scheutzes with a conditional grant, payable only after the Swedish king had examined the completed machine and judged it a success. The Scheutzes maneuvered to obtain the money in advance, and the government finally relented, on the condition that a number of the Scheutz family's friends guarantee to repay the money if the machine was not finished to the king's satisfaction by 1853.

With sufficient resources now at their disposal, the father and son team set to work on their new Difference Engine, which was completed in October 1853. They made several improvements on their original design, such as enabling computations in the sexagesimal scale (based on increments of 60, and therefore of use in calculating time tables and angle-related tables) as well as the decimal scale (increments of 10). The king approved of their work, and at the urging of the Royal Academy, was generous enough to provide a second grant, equal to the first, to help compensate the Scheutzes for the large out-of-pocket expenses they had sustained.

The construction of the Scheutzes' Difference Engine was similar to the way Babbage had envisioned it. It was composed of five horizontal rows, each consisting of 15 silvered brass wheels. The wheels rotated around 15 vertical steel axles. Each horizontal row or register could accommodate a 15-digit number. Four rows were for the four orders of difference and one for the final result. The Scheutzes' machine also employed a sequential carrying mechanism (the mechanism for carrying a number from the ones column to the tens and hundreds and so on).

The printing feature worked by punching stereotype plates, or duplicate plates, with all digits of a number being impressed simultaneously. The machine prepared only a single column of tabular values, and the page layout was made up manually from these strips of numbers. It was capable of producing 120 lines of a table per hour. In one recorded test, the device was able to generate logarithms of the numbers from one to 10,000 in under 80 hours.

In 1954 the Scheutzes took their device, which they called a Tabulating Machine, to London, England, where they demonstrated it to Babbage and other members of the scientific community. Scheutz had begun to correspond with Babbage via mail in the early 1950s, and Babbage, who had abandoned the idea of constructing his own Difference Engine to begin work on his Analytical Engine, often gave the Scheutzes advice during the construction process. Upon his review of the Tabulating Machine, Babbage applauded the Scheutzes' achievement, later writing of the occasion, "Mr. Scheutz . . . had far greater difficulties to encounter [than myself]. The construction of mechanism, as well as the mathematical part of the question was entirely new to him. He however undertook to make a machine having four differences and fourteen places of figures, and capable of printing its own Tables," as quoted by Herman H. Goldstine in *The Computer from Pascal to von Neumann* (1972).

The Scheutzes remained in London for almost a year, hoping to find a buyer. In 1855 they shipped the Difference Engine to Paris to enter it in the Paris Exhibition being held there. It received much acclaim, and a panel of jurors from all over Europe unanimously awarded the Scheutzes' machine the Exhibition's Gold Medal. This attracted the attention of B. A. Gould, of the Dudley Observatory, in Albany, New York, who purchased the machine for $5,000 in 1856. The machine was used briefly by the Observatory, but then sold to the inventor of the comptometer, Dorr E. Felt (of the Felt and Tarrant Manufacturing Company, of Chicago), who added it to his private collection of calculating devices. Before it was retired from use, the Scheutzes' machine was employed in various projects, including a series of calculations for an 1856 publication called *Specimen Tables*, which consisted of tables of five-figure logarithms of the integers from one to 1,000. Today the Tabulating Machine is kept at the Smithsonian Institution, in Washington D.C.

In about 1858 a copy of the device was produced by Bryan Donkin & Co. for the General Register Office in England. This version of the Sheutzes' machine was also used to calculate tables, including the volume *Mountain Barometer Tables*, used for assessing heights on mountains and depths in mines from simultaneous observations of barometric pressure and temperature, and the *English Life Tables* (1864), a new set of tables for the insurance industry. During its lifetime the English machine was put to use in computing and stereotyping more than 600 different kinds of tables. Its utility was limited, however, due to several significant flaws. William Farr, editor of the *English Life Tables*, commented on the machine's shortcomings in *Tables of Lifetimes, Annuities and Premiums* (1864), as quoted by Michael Williams in *A History of Computing Technology* (1985): "The machine required incessant attention. The differences had to be inserted at the proper terms of the various series, checking was required, and when the mechanism got out of order it had to be set right. . . . Its work had to be watched with anxiety, and its arithmetical music had to be elicited by frequent tuning and skillful handling, in the quiet most congenial to such productions." This second machine was eventually donated to the South Kensington Science Museum, in England, where it currently remains.

Neither model of the Scheutzes' machine proved very useful in the final analysis, and both were in operation for only a brief period of time. Performing calculations was a slow process, mostly because of an awkward carry propagation mechanism. In addition, the design depended on friction alone to keep the figure wheels in their correct position when a number was stored, as opposed to the locking mechanisms Babbage had intended. As a result, the figure wheels became easily displaced from their correct position, leading calculations astray. These errors were detectable and therefore correctable, but nevertheless time-consuming and frustrating for the operator. The printing mechanism may also have been unreliable, producing largely undetectable errors. Both of the models required a great deal of skill to operate and were therefore unsuitable for routine use in calculating tables.

The Scheutzes' Difference Engine is notable, however, for demonstrating that the method of differences could be implemented mechanically, with successful results. Although Babbage conceived of the engine, he never completed a fully functioning machine. Scheutz, despite having limited experience in the area, was able to make Babbage's idea a reality, providing inspiration for many others who were seeking new mechanical means of simplifying calculations. In 1856 Scheutz was knighted by the king of Sweden for his achievement and accepted into the Swedish Academy.

The Scheutzes' invention, despite its popularity in scientific circles, did not bring the family the expected financial returns, and Scheutz died nearly bankrupt on May 22, 1873. During his life, Scheutz was highly esteemed for his translations into Swedish of the works of such authors as Shakespeare, Boccaccio, and Walter Scott. He received substantial honors and awards for this work, including a prize from the government for his translations of Shakespeare. The citation made reference to Scheutz's scientific accomplishment; it read in part, as quoted by R. C. Archibald in the journal *Mathematical Tables and Other Aids to Computation* (vol. 2, 1947): "Georg Scheutz, the first who successfully clothed Shakespeare in Swedish costume, and for whom literature, even though as author, an occupation, comprehensive and pursued to the evening of a long life, has in addition for a long period had a connection which has not been effaced by the fact that the man of letters has also acquired a respected name for himself in a field which lies beyond the boundaries of belles lettres."—A. I. C.

Suggested Reading: Goldstine, Herman H. *The Computer From Pascal to von Neumann*, 1972; Williams, Michael R. *A History of Computing Technology*, 1985; Cortada, James W. *The Historical Dictionary of Data Processing—Biographies*, 1987; Aspray, William. *Computing Before Computers*, 1990; *Larousse Dictionary of Scientists*, vol. 1, 1994; Lee, J. A. N., ed. *International Biographical Dictionary of Computer Pioneers*, 1995

Schickard, Wilhelm

Apr. 22, 1592–Oct. 23, 1635 Astronomer; mathematician

Although his accomplishments were often overlooked during his lifetime, Wilhelm Schickard was a pioneering figure in the history of computing. Because of his wide range of interests and his superior intellect, he has invited comparisons to Leonard da Vinci (1452–1519). Schickard devoted much of his time to astronomy, mathematics, linguistics, religion, engraving, and painting; yet, despite his valuable contributions to these areas, he did not gain widespread acclaim until more than 300 years after his death. Only then, when a professor researching the works of astronomer Johannes Kepler (1571–1630) discovered Schickard's rough sketches of a mechanical calculating machine, did the world take greater notice of this 17th-century German academic. Although efforts to find any original models of Schickard's machine have proved fruitless, an approximate duplicate of it was constructed in the 1970s, which served to illuminate the functions and capabilities of the primitive machine. Its mechanisms were simplistic in nature, but the machine itself was much more sophisticated than anything similarly designed during the early 17th century. It included a carry function of up to six digits, with a provision for numbers larger than 999,999. The reconstruction of the mechanical calculator, which was one of the first such instruments in Europe to incorporate a carry function, proved the significance of Schickard's mathematical work, establishing him as a forefather in the field of computing.

Born on April 22, 1592 in Herrenberg, near Tübingen in Württemberg (what is now Germany), Schickard was educated at the University of Tübingen, where he received his B.A. degree in 1609 and his M.A. in 1611. A brilliant student, Schickard studied a diverse collection of subjects, including mathematics, astronomy, geography, Hebrew, Oriental languages (many of which he taught himself), meteorology, optics, and cartography. In addition he was a skilled mechanic, engraver, and painter. He even constructed his own astronomical instruments and in about 1618 was invited by the famed astronomer Johannes Kepler—who formulated three laws of planetary motion—to make some of the copper plates used to illustrate Kepler's famous book, Hermonices Mundi (Harmony of the World), published in 1619.

After leaving the university, Schickard continued to pursue the study of theology and Oriental languages until 1613; during this time he wrote several treatises on Semitic studies. A religious man, he then decided to explore his Lutheran faith by becoming the pastor for several nearby towns. He remained in this capacity until 1619, at which time he took a position as professor of Hebrew at the University of Tübingen. In 1631 he changed his area of specialty to astronomy and was appointed a professor of that subject at the university.

Although he possessed an inquiring mind and explored a wide variety of intellectual subjects, little is known about the extent of Schickard's research beyond his work in mathematics. In this discipline, he was considered a highly influential man of his day, and many of his mathematical findings remained in popular use until well into the 19th century. However, Schickard was also one of the earliest explorers of calculating machines, even inventing his own device as early as 1623. Information about this aspect of Schickard's work did not come to light until centuries after his death, when a group of scholars was attempting to compile a complete collection of Kepler's work. While investigating the library of the Pulkovo Observatory (near Leningrad), they discovered an original drawing of Schickard's machine, which he had evidently mailed to his friend Kepler; the drawing was found inside a copy of Kepler's Rudolphine Tables, where it had apparently been used as a bookmark. The sketch provided a visual, detailed model of the machine that Schickard had described in two previously discovered letters to Kepler, thus proving that Schickard had, in fact, invented a workable form of calculating machine—one of the first such machines in existence in Europe.

It is known that Schickard and Kepler, who was also a native of Herrenberg and had an association with Tübingen University, enjoyed an ongoing friendship and collaborated together on several projects. As early as 1617 Schickard and Kepler were discussing Napier's bones—a set of multiplication tables inscribed on strips of wood or bone, which were produced in the early 1600s by the Scottish mathematician John Napier (sometimes referred to as Laird of Merchiston), who also invented logarithms. Kepler and Schickard met often, with Kepler sharing many of his findings using Napier's bones. This transference of information between the two scientists is believed to have inspired the young Schickard to begin designing a machine that could incorporate both a set of Napier's bones and a mechanism to add up the partial products they produced. He was interested in finding a mechanical means of solving mathematical problems—an invention that was then sorely needed, particularly in the field of astronomy. In 1957, Franz Hammer, who was then the assistant curator of Kepler's papers, discovered two letters providing evidence that Schickard had in fact completed his machine and that it was in working order. In the first letter, dated September 20, 1623, as quoted by William Aspray for Computing Before Computers (1990), Schickard wrote, "What you have done in a logistical way (i.e., by calculation), I have just tried to do by mechanics. I have constructed a machine consisting of eleven complete and six incomplete (actually 'mutilated') sprocket wheels which can calculate. You would burst out laughing if you were present to see how it carries by itself from one column of tens to the next or borrows from them during subtraction." Schickard went on to speak specifically of the machine's functions and capabilities, writing that it "immediately computes the given numbers automatically, adds subtracts, multiplies, and divides. Surely you will beam when you see how [it] accumulates left carries of tens and hundreds by itself or while subtracting takes something away from them," as quoted by Herman H. Goldstine in The Computer from Pascal to von Neumann (1972).

Evidently, Kepler was interested in the direction of Schickard's work, for in the other letter retrieved from Kepler's papers, it is apparent that he had previously requested that a copy of Schickard's machine be provided for his own use. In this letter, dated February 25, 1624, Schickard included a description of the machine and several drawings, as well as news of a second machine built exclusively for Kepler, which had been destroyed in a fire at a hired workman's house. According to Goldstine, Schickard wrote, "I had placed an order with a local man, Johann Pfister, for the construction of a machine for you; but when half finished, this machine, together with some other things of mine, especially several metal plates, fell victim to a fire which broke out unseen during the night. . . . I take the loss very hard, now especially, since the mechanic does not have the time to produce a replacement soon."

From these letters and drawings, researchers determined that Schickard had constructed his mechanical calculating machine—and had begun work on a copy of that machine—at some point between 1622 and 1625. The next step was to recreate the machine in its original form from the drawings, which proved a difficult task given the lack of details in the 350-year-old sketches. Still, with the aid of the descriptions in Schickard's letters, Professor Bruno Baron von Freytag Löringhoff, a mathematics professor at the University of Tübingen, and his team of engineers in the 1960s began work on such a reconstruction. When it was completed, the machine (as depicted in a 1971 commemorative stamp issued by West Germany to mark the 350th year of the invention) was set to show the number 100,722 being multiplied by 4 in the upper portion of its body, with the resulting answer added to the accumulator in the lower portion of the machine. The upper part (where the number was being multiplied) was actually a set of Napier's bones, or multiplication tables, drawn on cylinders so that any single bone could be selected with the turn of a small dial. In turn, the horizontal slides would move to expose different sections of the bones, thus showing any single-digit multiple of the selected number. On the other hand, on the bottom of the machine, a person could make any number appear through the windows simply by turning the small knobs—a feature that eliminated the need to have pen, ink, and paper nearby to record intermediate results in the problem-solving process.

The device used to actually move one digit to the next was relatively simple in design, with Schickard employing three accumulator wheels: When the first wheel went through a complete rotation, a single tooth would latch onto an intermediate wheel, turning it, and thus causing the next highest digit to increase, or carry over, on the third wheel. Perhaps the most difficult aspect of the mechanism was in getting the single tooth to join into the teeth of the intermediate wheel and rotate it 36 degrees, then exit the teeth, all while simultaneously rotating only 36 degrees itself. The solution lay in making the intermediate wheel consist of two separate "gears"—one with long teeth and one with short teeth—and a spring device (similar to the pointer mechanism used on large spinning wheels) that would make the gears stop in only specific locations. While von Freytag Löringhoff never ascertained whether this mechanism was actually employed by Schickard, the device worked well in his recreation of the machine.

The "carry over" mechanism, however, did have its drawbacks. Due in large part to the weak building materials available during Schickard's time period, his machine could only carry calculations through six digits. If an individual wanted to perform the addition operation of 999,999 +1, the result would be a carry that was extended right through each digit of the accumulator. To do this the force would have to be so great that it would likely result in significant damage to the gears on the units digit. Schickard overcame this flaw with an ingenious additional device. In order to accommodate larger numbers, he created a set of brass rings which could be slipped over each finger on the operator's hands every time a carry had exceeded six digits. A small bell would ring each time such an "overflow" occurred, in order to remind the operator to slide another ring on his finger.

Technically, Schickard's machine was capable only of addition and subtraction, but by using Napier's bones, all multiplication and division problems could be reduced to additions and subtractions. It was a reliable machine, and if it had been reproduced, could have possibly had a significant influence on the work of future inventors and mathematicians, such as Blaise Pascal and Gottfried Wilhelm von Leibniz. However, no trace of Schickard's machine, a copy of that machine, or his original sketches have ever been located, and it is believed that they were destroyed in Europe's Thirty Years War (1618–48). Schickard and his entire family were also victims of this war; they all died of the resulting plague that swept through the German states during the 1630s. Schickard himself is believed to have died from the disease on October 23, 1635 at his home in Tübingen.

Wilhelm Schickard's work extended well beyond one mechanical calculating machine. His expertise in a wide variety of subjects caused him to experiment and perform successful research in other areas. In cartography, for example, he proved how contemporary developments in the field could produce more accurate maps than the ones then being constructed. He also made significant contributions to the world of astronomy, including observations on the comets of 1618 and descriptions of unusual phenomena of the cosmos, such as meteors. His other mechanical inventions consisted of, among other things, a machine used to calculate astronomical dates and a mechanism for Hebrew grammar. Due to the ravaged conditions of Schickard's homeland that resulted from war and disease, as well as the highly advanced nature of his inventions, few of his contemporaries took notice or interest in his work. One obvious exception is Kepler, who once said of his friend, as quoted by Goldstine, "[He is] a fine mind and a great friend of mathematics; . . . he is a very diligent mechanic and at the same time an expert on oriental languages."

With his many talents for invention and discovery in a wide array of topics, Wilhelm Schickard was undoubtedly ahead of his time, and he was a progenitor of the calculating machines that slowly began to emerge after his death.—D. B., K. D.

Suggested Reading: Goldstine, Herman H. *The Computer From Pascal to von Neumann*, 1972; *Dictionary of Scientific Biography*, vol. 13, 1976; Williams, Michael R. *A History of Computing Technology*, 1985; Ritchie, David. *The Computer Pioneers*, 1986

Schultz, Peter C.

Dec. 3, 1942– Ceramics engineer; co-inventor of telecommunications optical fibers

The explosive growth of telecommunications over the last quarter century—both via the telephone and the Internet—would not have been possible without the creation of optical fiber in 1970 by the scientists Peter C. Schultz, Robert D. Maurer, and Donald B. Keck. The trio's invention enhanced the speed and efficiency by which telecommunication signals are transmitted across long distances. Today, more than 90 percent of all long-distance calls (including Internet usage) in the United States are carried via optical fiber; more than 145 million miles of the fiber stretches across the world. As telecommunications improve in the coming decades, including advances in the cable television industry, this significant invention is expected to have even greater applications.

Peter C. Schultz was born on December 3, 1942 in the New York City borough of Brooklyn, the elder of two children of Arthur Schultz and Agnes Kincelik. During Schultz's early childhood, his father was in the military, though he was able to avoid service in World War II due to a back injury. Later, Arthur became a bookkeeper with the Chubb Insurance Company, while Agnes worked as a legal secretary. As Schultz recalled to Kathy L. Woodard for the *American Ceramic Society Bulletin* (September 2000), his family was fairly close while he was growing up and often visited with relatives around New York. "It was a typical family, typical childhood," he said, "in the sense that we would do things together, make do with the little money we had."

As a young child Schultz performed well in school, but by the time he reached junior high school he had become more interested in his image than in academics. "I sort of got lazy—actually almost flunked algebra," he told Woodard. "I was not quite a hood, but the stereotypical cool guy, had the Elvis look." Once he reached high school, however, his freshman-year algebra teacher challenged him to change, encouraging him to improve his grades and maximize his education. Schultz took the advice to heart and began to study diligently, excelling in such subjects as chemistry and physics. In addition, he participated in numerous after-school activities including playing trumpet in the school band and serving as team captain for the soccer team. As he approached his senior year, he began to give serious consideration to college—a goal that his parents greatly supported, as he would be the first in his family to attend. "Here we were, going from blue collar to gray collar to developing into white collar," Schultz recalled to Woodard. "At the time, I really didn't know what to think. I really had no role model, but in my junior year, my father encouraged me to meet a fellow in the neighborhood they called the professor. An engineer for Westinghouse, he told me a bit about what it was like and encouraged me." After performing well on his college entrance exams and obtaining scholarships from the Chubb Foundation and the state of New Jersey, Schultz decided to attend Rutgers University, in New Jersey. He entered college determined to become an engineer, partly because of his neighbor's influence but also due to his own interest in space. (He enrolled at Rutgers just prior to the "space race" of the 1960s, when scientists were working to build and improve rockets.) An inherent insecurity about his academic abilities motivated Schultz to dedicate all his time to studying. A traumatic event during his freshman year—the sudden death of his mother the week before Christmas—helped further his determination to succeed. "[My mother] died of a stroke," he told Woodard. "But she was so proud of me for going to school, and that provided more of a stimulation."

During his second year of college, Schultz decided to specialize in the engineering discipline of ceramics, although his true interest was in creating high-temperature materials that could be used in rocket nozzles and missile cones. The summer before his senior year, he was hired to work as a laboratory assistant to C. J. Phillips, who taught glass technology. As part of his duties, Schultz helped conduct many of the department's experiments, gaining experience measuring properties of glass, including its thermal characteristics, electrical resistance, and transmission. "That summer was the turning point of my career," he told Woodard. Schultz finished his undergraduate work in 1964, earning a B.S. degree in ceramic engineering. As a member of the Reserve Officers Training Corps (ROTC), he was expecting to serve in the military after graduating, especially in light of the escalation of the Vietnam conflict; he had even enrolled in a helicopter training program with the U.S. Army. In a twist of fate, however, Schultz was deemed to have high blood pressure and was there-

fore discharged from military duty. This turn of events allowed him to return to the Rutgers laboratories.

Another of Schultz's mentors, John Koenig, chair of Rutgers' ceramics department, helped Schultz to secure a National Science Foundation fellowship that allowed him to continue at Rutgers in pursuit of his Ph.D., without requiring a master's degree. The intense three-year program enabled Schultz to continue his experimental work on glass technology; but his thesis advisor, Norbert Kreidl, also pushed him to expand his skills in other directions. "He took me under his wing," Schultz explained to Woodard, "coached me, encouraged me and saw things I never saw in myself. What he saw was not only that I had the ability to do well as a scientist, but that I would be apt to go quickly into a management role. That was going to be the biggest challenge, going into management but still having time to be a good scientist." While completing his thesis, Schultz developed his first patent—a glass-ceramic that could be used to create crystalline ferrites more economically than through current processes. (Ferrites, heavy mixtures of iron oxide with another metal—such as zinc or nickel—were then being used in magnetic memory cores.) But shortly after Schultz's discovery, other engineers developed integrated circuitry, immediately outmoding his find. Ultimately, his first patent failed to produce any business. Nevertheless, in 1968 Schultz completed his Ph.D. in ceramics science.

Even before earning his doctorate, Schultz had accepted a position as a senior research scientist in the department of glass chemistry at Corning Glass Works. He began researching new uses for fused-silica glass, a component created through flame hydrolysis (which was developed in the 1940s by Frank Hyde, who also invented silicone). Fused-silica glass was then being used mainly in space telescopes or in optical delay lines. Schultz was assigned to investigate new applications for the glass, as well as to try to create other types of glass with the same technique. After experimenting with various types of glass over the next year, Schultz was asked to join the research team of Robert D. Maurer, a senior physicist at Corning. Maurer's team was then striving to improve telecommunications systems. Throughout the 1960s researchers had been trying to boost the quality of telephone signals. At that time, telephone traffic was transmitted through copper cable systems, which were bulky and inefficient; each wire could handle only two dozen conversations at once. Engineers began increasing the frequency of the electrical waves carrying the signal—in the hopes of sending more information over the wires—but found that the signal deteriorated into static. Any attempts to increase bandwidth in the copper system required expensive, signal-boosting devices to be installed every few thousand feet. As more and more telephone calls began to flood the copper system, telecommunications officials worried that the existing copper wires would not be able to support future traffic. Laying new lines into the ground was not a feasible solution, as city streets were already stuffed with communication cables, electrical wires, steam pipes, water pipes, and subways.

Faced with the limitations of the copper system, Maurer and his team of researchers set out to test a different medium for communication: optical fiber. With the creation of the first working laser in 1960, scientists had determined that optical frequencies were billions of times faster than those of electrical frequencies. The difficulty, however, came in steering light through the air. As early as 1880 Alexander Graham Bell had tried—and failed—to transmit light through pipes equipped with lenses and mirrors. By the 1930s engineers had found they could transmit images through crude fibers of solid glass or quartz, thus providing applications for internal medicine. However, they had not developed a method for carrying voice traffic more than a few feet through cables on wavelengths of light. When Schultz joined Maurer's team, he began applying his previous experimental work developing new types of glass to the project at hand. Working with a third scientist, Donald B. Keck, Schultz and Maurer spent the next two years designing and developing an appropriate fiber that could deliver telephone signals with small losses in sound quality. In 1970 the team achieved its goal: They created a unique glass-in-glass fiber—employing two separate kinds of the material—that was one million times more transparent than the clearest known glass. In the core, where the light would be carried, they used a thin silica glass—essentially a sand melted into glass strands so thin that a few dozen could fit inside a human hair—fused with titanium atoms to make the glass less pure and thus prevent it from absorbing light. The outer glass was made of an ultrapure "cladding" glass, which acted as a cylindrical mirror. As light traveled through the tube, it ricocheted off the outer layer and back into the core, helping to ensure that the least amount of information was lost.

Keck made the initial breakthrough working alone on a Friday night in 1970. The team named this discovery *optical waveguide fibers*. While Keck's experiment proved the theory of optical fiber (which had first been proposed by the scientist Charles Kao), the fiber that the team was then using proved to be difficult to manufacture. As Schultz explained to Woodard, special heat treatments were required in order to produce the low optical losses, but these treatments weakened the fiber. Schultz continued to research the process and made an important step in June 1972: He created a new fiber made of fused-silica (with tiny impurities of germanium, called "germania-doped") that did not require any heat treatments. "This was not discovered by chance," he told Woodard. "I was methodically looking for better glasses that would have better optical performance. We tested a variety of formulations and found this one was the best."

Over the next decade Schultz, Maurer, and Keck continued to refine their work on optical fiber. From early on it became apparent that this patented process would dramatically change telecommunication; major telephone companies were soon ordering large amounts of the fiber. Since the first major order from MCI, more than 140 million miles of optical fiber have been installed around the globe, even across oceans. Through the optical system, one fiber can carry up to 80,000 telephone calls using just one infrared wavelength of light—that is, 65,000 times more information than through a conventional copper wire. As of 2002, more than 90 percent of long-distance telephone calls in the U.S. were carried via optical fiber. With the advent of the Internet in the mid-1990s, application for the team's discovery expanded in ways that Schultz, Maurer, and Keck had never conceived. "It is exciting, frankly, to look back now and see how it all really did work," Schultz told Woodard. "The big surprise to most of us was that we could not have dreamed of the Internet being one of the driving forces behind the demand for more bandwidth. Without that, optical fiber communications—the Internet as we know it today—could not exist."

In 1983, while he was still working at Corning, Schultz was sent by the company to attend Sloan Business School at the Massachusetts Institute of Technology. As he recalled to Woodard, being outside of the laboratory for an extended period helped him to realize the possibilities of doing other things. In 1984 he left Corning to become vice president of technology at SpecTran Corporation, a company that produced fiber optics. He left SpecTran in 1986, accepting a position as vice president of technology at Galileo ElectroOptics. Two years later he relocated to Atlanta, Georgia, this time to become president of Heraeus Amersil., the U.S. subsidiary of a German company that manufactures fused silica and other technical glass for fiber optics and semiconductors. Since Schultz became president, Heraeus Amersil has increased its annual sales from $20 million to more than $200 million. He currently sits on the boards of two southeastern U.S. technology companies, Peachtree Fiberoptics and Geltech.

Now approaching his retirement years, Schultz told Woodard that although he is looking forward to relinquishing his leadership roles in private enterprise—although he is not yet ready to retreat from research. He is currently working with a group of Russian scientists to develop new applications for fiber optics. "One would be to noninvasively measure blood glucose levels for diabetes so you don't have to prick the finger," he explained to Woodard. "When I retire, I would like to be more actively involved in that work. We probably are a year away from a practical solution, but getting back closer to the research bench is one thing I would like to do."

Schultz has been recognized with a number of awards, including the International Glass Science Weyl Award (1977), the Society of Photo Industrial Engineers Technology Achievement Award (1981), the American Society of Metals Engineering Materials Achievement Award (1983), the Outstanding Alumnus Award from Rutgers University (1983), the Scholes Award from Alfred University (1986), the first-ever American Innovator Award from the U.S. Department of Commerce (1995), and the MacLaren Award from the New Jersey Ceramic Association (1999). In 1993, Schultz was inducted into the National Inventors Hall of Fame, in Akron, Ohio, along with his fellow inventors, Maurer and Keck; in 2000 President Bill Clinton honored the trio with the National Medal of Technology, the nation's highest recognition for a technological achievement. Schultz has professional memberships in the American Ceramic Society, the Optical Society of America, Keramos (Ceramics Honor Society), Tau Beta Pi (Engineering Honor Society), and Sigma Xi. He holds 26 patents and has published nearly 30 research papers.

Peter C. Schultz currently resides in Atlanta, Georgia, with his wife, Mary Anne, whom he married in 1990. The couple has a second home in St. Thomas, U.S. Virgin Islands. From his first marriage, which ended in divorce in 1983, Schultz has two adult children, Melissa and David. Schultz enjoys sailing in the Caribbean and mountain climbing in the Adirondacks of upstate New York.
—K. D.

Suggested Reading: *American Ceramic Society Bulletin* p38+ Sep. 2000, with photo; *Atlanta Journal-Constitution* H p1 Mar. 26, 1993; *Los Angeles Times* D p7 Aug. 23, 1993; (Cleveland) *Plain Dealer* B p2 Apr. 20, 1993; *Washington Post* H p1 Nov. 10, 1999

Shannon, Claude E.

Apr. 30, 1916–Feb. 24, 2001 Information theorist; mathematician; artificial-intelligence pioneer

Claude E. Shannon, while also at the forefront of the field of artificial intelligence, is often referred to as the father of information theory, a scientific study of the communication process. The appellation, however, barely describes his historic contributions to the Information Age. "In its simplest [terms]," Robert X. Cringely wrote for the PBS Web site (March 1, 2001), "he made possible the leap from telephones to computers." James Gleick wrote in a *New York Times* (December 30, 2001) tribute: "Halfway through the last century, information became a thing. It became a commodity, a force—a quantity to be measured and analyzed. It's what our world runs on. Information is the gold and the fuel. We measure it in bits. That's largely because of Claude Shannon."

Claude Elwood Shannon was born on April 30, 1916 in Gaylord, Michigan. His father was an attorney and a probate judge. Shannon's mother, a foreign-languages teacher, later became principal of the Gaylord High School. As a child Shannon often spent his free time putting together model planes and radio circuits, and he even managed to construct a telegraph system between his house and a friend's. As a teenager he repaired radios for a local department store. After graduating from high school, in 1932, he entered the University of Michigan, in Ann Arbor, as an electrical-engineering major. He loved mathematics and took as many classes on the subject as he could fit into his schedule. In 1936 he received his B.S. degree.

Shannon continued his study of mathematics and science at the Massachusetts Institute of Technology (MIT), in Cambridge. One day, while passing a university bulletin board, he came across a want ad for a graduate student to run the MIT differential analyzer. The machine—built by Vannevar Bush, then vice president and dean of students at MIT—was widely regarded as one of the most sophisticated analog computers available in the 1930s.

In his new position Shannon received differential equations from MIT scientists and figured out how to punch those equations into the analyzer to be solved. Unfortunately, he also spent a great deal of time just trying to keep the machine in working order. As mechanical failures continued to pile up, he looked for ways to improve the machine's complex relay circuit, which consisted of 100 separate relays and controlled the operation of the analyzer. He hoped to find a mathematical process that would both describe and analyze the behavior of relay circuits. Ultimately he concluded that Boolean algebra would be the best way to attack the problem. Shannon later commented, as quoted in Robert Slater's *Portraits in Silicon* (1987), "I observed that this branch of mathematics . . . was very closely related to what happens in a switching circuit."

Shannon's 1937 thesis, "A Symbolic Analysis of Relay and Switching Circuits", was based on his studies of the differential analyzer. A relay is made up of three parts: an electromagnet, a moveable electrical contact, and a spring. When the electromagnet draws the moveable contact into the stationary contact, an electrical circuit is completed. However, if you remove the energy from the electromagnet, then the movable contact is pulled away from the stationary one by the spring and the circuit is broken. Therefore, relays only have two states, on and off. Similarly, in Boole's system of logic, decisions are reduced to two possibilities, either yes or no, true or false. Seizing upon this analogy, he hypothesized that the circuits could be assigned corresponding values of one and zero for their states of open and closed. He concluded that contacts in series correspond to the logical operator AND, while contacts in parallel correspond to OR. Broken contacts correspond to the logical operator NOT. As Shannon wrote in his thesis, as quoted in Slater's book, "It is possible to perform complex mathematical operations by means of relay circuits. Numbers may be represented by the positions of relays and stepping switches. Interconnections between sets of relays can be made to represent various mathematical operations." Therefore, Shannon concluded, relays could be arranged so as to carry out AND, OR, and NOT operations. Shannon's master's thesis became a cornerstone of early computer development, not only in that it proved computers could handle a variety of tasks—addition, subtraction, multiplication, division—but also that they could use logic to draw conclusions.

After completing his master's degree, in 1937, Shannon began to pursue a doctorate in mathematics on the advice of Vannevar Bush. He conceptualized his doctoral thesis during the summer of 1939 while working at Cold Spring Harbor, in New York. Bush had just then been appointed president of the Carnegie Institution, in Washington, D.C., and suggested that Shannon visit the institution's branch in Cold Spring Harbor. Bush felt Shannon's theories might be of use to Barbara Burks, a scientist working on genetics there. Bush's intuition turned out to be correct. Shannon's doctoral dissertation, "An Algebra for Theoretical Genetics", completed in the spring of 1940, greatly aided in the organization of genetics, just as his master's thesis had helped to organize switching circuits.

After receiving his Ph.D. in mathematics, Shannon accepted an employment offer from Bell Laboratories. During the summer of 1940, he performed research on switching circuits and designed a new method to reduce the number of contacts needed to synthesize complex switching functions. He later published a paper on his findings, "The Synthesis of Two-Terminal Switching Circuits."

After working briefly under Herman Weyl at the Institute for Advanced Study at Princeton University, in New Jersey, on a National Research Fellowship, Shannon returned to Bell Labs in the spring of 1941. During World War II, Bell, like so many other American companies, shifted its focus from domestic to military products. Shannon aided the company's efforts in designing fire-control systems for antiaircraft use and helped in devising machines that would track enemy planes and rockets and then compute the aim for counter missiles.

Over the next decade at Bell Labs, Shannon pursed research in the electronic communication of messages, a field of study that had been encouraged by Bell's management. In 1948 (some sources say 1949), he published *Mathematical Theory of Communications*, which supplied a set of theorems suggesting how to achieve efficient transmission of messages over noisy media. He effectively demonstrated that any message could be transmit-

ted with tremendous reliability once the right codes were devised. His paper provides insight on how data can be altered as a system "drops" or distorts bits and illustrates how aspects of communications, such as redundancy and noise, can be quantified and therefore measured. As a result of his theorems, a major program was created to achieve reliable communications with a minimum of error, and thus was born what is now known as information theory. As James W. Cortada wrote in *The Historical Dictionary of Data Processing: Biographies* (1987), "The significance of this field of study cannot be overemphasized since work on this subject has contributed to the design of circuits up to the present time. It also influenced the architecture and technologies embedded in computers and telecommunications equipment. By the 1980s, his ideas were even being applied to the study of biology, psychology, phonetics, semantics, and literature."

In 1948 Shannon published an important monograph, *Programming a Computer for Playing Chess*, one of the first papers on the subject of computer gaming. The publication has been credited with influencing computer-game designers for years after its debut. In 1950, using an erector set he had received for Christmas, he built a maze-solving mechanized "mouse," one of the first scientific attempts to build a machine with some learning capabilities. He called the mouse Theseus, after the Greek mythological hero. Controlled by a relay circuit, the unit was capable of moving around a maze containing 25 squares. Its brain held more than 100 relays, and its muscles were a pair of motors driving an electromagnet, which through magnetic action moved the mouse through the maze. Underneath the mouse were relays that "remembered" which way the mouse had left the square the last time. The maze could be changed, and the mouse appeared to be learning, as it would search through the passageways until it found a known position, moving toward the goal and adding the new information to its memory. Theseus is believed to be the first device built with these capabilities.

In 1953 Shannon wrote another important paper, "Computers and Automata," in which he posed a list of questions. Could machines be organized into hierarchies, similar to the human brain, with learning progressing up through these levels? Could digital computers be designed and programmed so that eventually 99 percent of all of their instructions would be created by the machines themselves? The paper is widely considered to be a groundbreaking work in the field of artificial intelligence.

In 1956 Shannon left Bell Labs and became a visiting professor at MIT. He spent the following year at the Center for Advanced Study in the Behavioral Sciences, in Palo Alto, California, where he continued his research on information theory. In 1958 he accepted a full-time position at MIT as the Donner Professor of Science, teaching both mathematics and electrical engineering. Shannon retained a position as consultant to Bell Labs until 1972. In 1978 he retired from his post at MIT, becoming a professor emeritus.

A recipient of the Morris Liebman Memorial Award (1949), the Stuart Ballantine Medal (1955), the Institute of Electrical and Electronic Engineers (IEEE) Medal of Honor (1966), and the National Medal of Science (1966), Shannon was also a fellow of the IEEE and a member of the American Academy of Arts and Sciences. He received the Kyoto Prize in Basic Science in 1985. He has received several honorary degrees.

In 1949 Claude Shannon married Mary Elizabeth Moore; the couple had four children, Robert, James, Andrew, and Margarita. Shannon exhibited a lifelong interest in unicycles, often riding down the halls of Bell Labs or MIT on one. He enjoyed spending his free time working on mechanical inventions, including a chess machine with a mechanical arm and juggling automata. Shannon died on February 24, 2001 after a long battle with Alzheimer's disease. Marvin Minsky, a fellow MIT scientist, told George Johnson for the *New York Times* (February 27, 2001), "[As the Alzheimer's progressed], something inside him was getting lost. Yet none of us miss him the way you'd expect—for the image of that great stream of ideas still persists in everyone his mind ever touched."—D. B., C. M.

Suggested Reading: *Electronic Design* p214 Oct. 2002; InfoNation Web site; *New York Times* VI p48 Dec. 30, 2001; PBS Web site; Slater, Robert. *Portraits in Silicon*, 1987

Alfred Eisenstaedt/Getty Images

Shockley, William

Feb. 13, 1910–Aug. 12, 1989 Co-inventor of the transistor

Arguably the most controversial figure in the history of computing, William Shockley is the co-inventor of one of the 20th century's most vital technological innovations. A physicist, Shockley worked at Bell Laboratories, studying solid-state physics and attempting to discover an alternative to an unreliable and costly device, the vacuum tube, which was used to amplify current at that time. His breakthrough came in the form of the transistor, a small device using a germanium base and gold wires that, improved over the years, would revolutionize technology. With the emergence of the transistor, miniaturization became possible, and the computer industry soared to new heights as machines became smaller, faster, and more reliable. Present in an enormous number of modern products, from cameras and cellular phones to jets and satellites, the transistor is considered by many to be the single most important invention of the 20th century. Shockley is also credited with helping launch the semiconductor industry in the area of California that later became known as Silicon Valley, where he founded his own company in Palo Alto, in the late 1950s. Shockley was also a professor at Stanford University and a prominent consultant at Bell Labs. Although the controversial theories on race and genetics that he developed later in his life cast a dark cloud over his reputation, his work as an inventor provided immense contributions to society.

William Bradford Shockley was born in London, England, on February 13, 1910 to William Hillman, a mining engineer, and May (Bradford) Shockley, a mineral surveyor. His parents, who were American citizens, decided to move back to the United States when Shockley was three. Shockley's parents did not enroll him in school until he turned eight, believing that they could offer him a better education at home, where they taught their son mathematics and encouraged his early interest in science. Upon returning to the United States, the family settled in Palo Alto, California, where Shockley was soon influenced by a neighbor, Perley A. Ross, a professor of physics at Stanford University who often invited Shockley over to play with his children. While at the professor's house, Shockley learned about the inner workings of radios and the principle of wave coupling, lessons that, as he later acknowledged, remained with him for the rest of his life.

Shockley attended the Palo Alto Military Academy for two years before enrolling at Hollywood High School in Los Angeles. After graduating, he entered the University of California, Los Angeles, where he studied for one year before transferring to the California Institute of Technology, in Pasadena. He graduated with a bachelor of science degree in physics in 1932. Shockley accepted a teaching fellowship at the Massachusetts Institute of Technology (MIT), in Cambridge, and while there, he worked on his Ph.D.; his dissertation was entitled "Calculations of Wave Functions for Electrons in Sodium Chloride Crystals." The paper involved intensive research into the area of solid-state physics, work that was later of significant use in the development of the transistor. Shockley obtained his doctorate from MIT in 1936 and promptly received several job offers, among them one from General Electric. He accepted a position at Bell Telephone Laboratories in Murray Hill, New Jersey, largely because of his desire to work with C. J. Davisson, a Nobel Prize winner who had done extensive work on electron diffraction. At Bell Labs, Shockley worked directly with Davisson, in the company's vacuum tube department.

Shockley's first experiments at Bell were motivated by the desire to make semiconductors, which were already known to possess the ability to rectify electric current, able to amplify current as well. Rectifying is the transforming of an alternate current into a direct one, a process which had, in early crystal radio sets, been accomplished by a piece of galena, a material whose ability to conduct electricity falls between that of a conductor, such as copper, and an insulator, such as rubber, with a crystal diode. Thus, it is a semiconductor and it rectifies current. Galena was discarded by radio manufacturers in favor of the vacuum tube, which could both amplify and rectify current. However, when it became apparent that vacuum tubes failed to rectify extremely high-frequency radar signals, the use of semiconductors was revived, despite the fact that no one had yet found a means to give them the ability to amplify, a fact which Shockley strove to alter through work in solid-state physics.

World War II interrupted Shockley's work and he took a leave of absence from Bell Labs to take a position as director of research for the U.S. Navy's antisubmarine Warfare Operations Research Group. He served in this position for two years and then as an expert consultant for the Office of the Secretary of War in 1944 and 1945. In the latter job, Shockley's work largely involved radar in B-29 bomber aircraft, and his efforts were rewarded with the Medal of Merit, the highest decoration the government awarded to civilians during that time period.

After the war, Shockley returned to Bell Labs and continued his efforts to find an alternative to vacuum tubes, which in addition to their other limitations were fragile as well as costly to manufacture and use. Companies were becoming increasingly frustrated with the large glass tubes, which gave off a great deal of heat and burned out easily. Due to new advances in quantum physics, there was a better understanding of atomic structure, which in turn led to a better general understanding of the properties of solids. In light of this new knowledge, Shockley became convinced that solid-state physics was the key to a new method of amplification. While examining electrical conduction in semiconductors (a topic that had been explored by Bell staff member Russell S. Ohl in the early 1940s) Shockley came to the conclusion that it was possible to control the supply of movable electrons inside a semiconductor with an electric field imposed from the outside. This theory served as the backbone of the technology involved in creating the transistor, although initial attempts to build such a device were not successful. In an interview that appeared in *Fortune* (March 1953), Shockley explained the process. "John Bardeen (also of Bell Labs) . . . proposed a theory involving surface traps to explain why the device didn't work. You see, we started with a device idea, then got a physics idea. This led to more physics experiments to learn more about surface states."

One of the central experiments, conducted by Bardeen, a theoretical physicist, and Walter Brattain, an experimental physicist, involved a germanium diode immersed in an electrolyte and connected to a source of direct current. According to the two men, the experiment "led to the concept that a portion of the current was being carried by holes flowing near the surface. Upon replacing the electrolyte with a metal contact, transistor action was discovered." Bardeen concluded that an amplifier could be made by placing two wire electrodes close together on a germanium crystal. Shockley's team of researchers then attached two small gold wires, one-two-thousandth of an inch apart, on one side of a piece of germanium, which served as the semiconductor. On December 23, 1947 an electrical signal was given to the germanium via the wires, and the transistor was demonstrated for the first time by amplifying a human voice. A series of transistors had the power to amplify the small amount of current in a microphone into enough current to power a loudspeaker.

The transistor was a small device that required only one-fiftieth of the space of a vacuum tube and just a millionth the power, and performed most of the tubes' functions. John R. Pierce, an electrical engineer at Bell Labs, named the new invention, deriving the word "transistor" from its property of transfer resistance, or the transfer of current from a low-resistance input to a high-resistance output. Because the gold wire points were in contact with the germanium semiconductor base, the first transistor was called a point of contact transistor.

There were roughly 10 individuals involved in the creation of the first transistor and among them, Shockley is often considered the most influential. His theories and personality served to inspire the other researchers, among whom he was highly regarded, and as a result, he shared credit for the invention. Bardeen and Brattain obtained a patent for the transistor, and in June 1948, the group published their results to little fanfare. Few foresaw the long-term consequences of the transistor; initially the high hopes that the device would replace vacuum tubes was dashed by technical glitches. The primary problem was that no two transistors worked identically, and it was doubtful that they could be sold commercially.

Shockley quickly began to formulate ideas as to how to build a better transistor and the new model, which he called a junction transistor, was capable of being mass produced. Shockley took out a patent on the new transistor in 1948, and in 1950 he wrote a book entitled *Electrons and Holes in Semiconductors,* which included his theory on junction transistors. In 1951 the first reliable transistor was constructed by a research team led by Shockley, and the device gradually began to permeate industries, enabling the development of technologies that were previously unthinkable. With its powerful amplification abilities, the transistor could perform fast on-off switching, sending signals along controlled paths in semiconductor circuits, a capability which made it a highly valuable component of computers. The transistor was also hailed for its durability. Unlike a vacuum tube, the device needed no time to warmup and it would not burn out or break. In addition, whereas the vacuum tube needed one full watt of power to operate, the transistor used only one-millionth of a watt.

In 1953 transistors were used by the public for the first time as amplifiers for hearing aids, and in the following year, the first transistor radios were built. In around 1957 UNIVAC and Philco began selling the first commercial computers using transistors, and Shockley made a prediction that dollar sales volume in the semiconductor industry would reach $300 million by 1960. In fact, by the time 1960 rolled around, sales of semiconductors were upwards of $500 million. By the transistor's tenth anniversary, 30 million had been produced worldwide, and their price dropped from $20 a piece to $1.50.

Shockley was named director of transistor physics research at Bell Labs in 1954, and in 1955 he began serving as a visiting professor at the California Institute of Technology and as deputy director of the Weapons Systems Evaluation Group for the U.S. government's department of defense. Perhaps the ultimate recognition came in 1956, when Shockley, along with Bardeen and Brattain, were awarded the Nobel Prize in Physics for their work on the transistor.

By this time, Shockley's career was beginning to turn in a new direction. He left Bell Labs in 1955 to found his own company, the Shockley Semiconductor Laboratory, near Palo Alto, California. The firm began as a research and development venture and was the first semiconductor company in the area, which would later be dubbed "Silicon Valley" due to its high number of computer firms. Shockley began the company with the hope of capitalizing on his extensive knowledge of solid-state physics, and he brought with him a group of top engineers, calling them his "Ph.D. production line." The firm's main product, a transistor with a solid-state switch (one which works within a material that is a semiconductor) that performed a function previously requiring five components, looked promising. Shockley however, proved to be much less successful at business management than he was at inventing. He was consumed by fears of employee secrets, and when there were production delays, he suspected sabotage. He unsuccessfully tried to promote honesty through posting everyone's salaries, and he asked that his employees regularly rate each other's job performance. Many of his employees resented these practices which they deemed intrusive and they also questioned Shockley's focus on producing a four-layer germanium diode. This type of semiconductor diode uses a pellet of germanium as the rectifying element, but its characteristics are unpredictable and vary with temperature. The engineers viewed this product as unmarketable and they felt that research should instead be directed toward silicon transistors, which, in their view, were more predictable and commercially promising. In 1957 eight of Shockley's researchers (including Robert Noyce, who would later enjoy great success as the founder of Intel, which dominated the micro-processor industry in the late 20th century) demanded a change in management. When the company's financier refused, the engineers, whom Shockley dubbed the traitorous eight, left the company and started their own, 12 blocks away from Shockley's firm. Later, Noyce praised Shockley as a "marvelous intuitive problem solver" and a "tremendous generator of ideas" but also opined that his managerial tactics were "oppressive" and that he "didn't have trust and faith in other individuals."

Shockley's firm immediately felt the impact of losing its top employees. There had already been production delays due to Shockley's management style, and with its workforce depleted, the company could not keep its head above water. It was purchased by Clevite Transistor in the spring of 1960; Shockley stayed on as a consultant. While his business venture did not reap the benefits he had predicted, Shockley's firm served the spark that ignited the "entrepreneurial chain-reaction that launched the semiconductor industry" in what became the Silicon Valley area. Shockley had begun lecturing at Stanford University, in California, in 1958, and in 1963 he returned to Bell Labs as a part-time consultant. In February 1975, he retired from Bell Labs, and during the fall of that year he also retired from Stanford.

Shockley became a controversial figure during the 1970s and early 1980s, when he began to direct his attention to a subject he called dysgenics, or the "retrogressive evolution caused by the excessive reproduction of the genetically disadvantaged." Shockley theorized that "a major cause of American Negroes' intellectual and social deficit is hereditary and racially genetic" and "not remediable to a major degree by practical improvement in environment," (*New York Times*, October 23, 1994). Shockley also suggested that private institutions offer money to hemophiliacs, epileptics, and those with low IQS, if they agreed to be sterilized in an effort to stop what he termed "the brutal elimination mechanism of evolution." His views on this subject resulted in anti-Shockley demonstrations on the Stanford campus during the 1970s. In June 1982 Shockley announced plans to run in the Republican primary for the U.S. Senate, basing his campaign on the one issue of dysgenics. He lost, coming in eighth, but he continued to focus on the subject exclusively throughout the rest of his life, and his views, which were widely condemned as racist, came to overshadow the importance of his earlier inventions in the eyes of many. On August 12, 1989 he died from prostate cancer at his home on the Stanford campus, at the age of 79.

William Shockley was an expert mountain climber and sailor throughout his life. He married a teacher, Jean Bailey, in 1933, and had three children, William, Richard, and Alison. In addition to his Nobel Prize in Physics, Shockley received the Morris Liebmann Award of the Institute of Radio Engineers in 1952 and the Oliver E. Buckley Solid State Physics Prize of the American Physical Society in 1953. Although Shockley's reputation was severely tarnished during the latter part of his life, his early contributions to science have stood the test of time. In the last 50 years, transistors have emerged as a fundamental building block for al-most all of modern technology, and they are currently mass-produced for use in items such as watches, televisions, toys, and even cars. They allowed the notion of the personal computer to become a reality, igniting the wave of miniaturization of electronics that has continued into the 21st century. During his Nobel Prize acceptance speech, Shockley acknowledged his desire to perform research that would be of lasting scientific value. "Frequently, I have been asked if an experiment I have planned is pure or applied research; to me it is more important to know if the experiment will yield new and probably enduring knowledge about nature," he said, as quoted in *Portraits in Silicon*. "If it is likely to yield such knowledge, it is, in my opinion, good fundamental research; and this is more important than whether the motivation is purely aesthetic satisfaction on the part of the experimenter."—D. B.

Suggested Reading: *Fortune* p47 Mar. 1953; *Microelectronics Design* (on-line); *National Inventors Hall of Fame* (on-line); *New York Times* D p15 Oct. 23, 1994, C p1 Feb. 4, 1997; *The University of Passau* (on-line); *Current Biography Yearbook* p569+ 1953, with photo; *American Men and Women of Science*, vol 7, 1986; Lee, J. A. N., ed. *International Biographical Dictionary of Computer Pioneers*, 1995; Slater, Robert. *Portraits in Silicon*, 1987

Shugart, Alan F.

Sep. 27, 1930– Disk-drive innovator

Alan F. Shugart, the co-founder of Seagate Technology, Inc., is a dedicated entrepreneur who has survived the ups and downs of the technology industry for decades. Shugart was one of the pioneers of the first disk drive, which was developed at International Business Machines (IBM) in the early 1950s. He worked at IBM for 18 years, then moved to Memorex, where he served as vice president of product development. In 1973 Shugart left Memorex to found Shugart Associates, the company that innovated the floppy disk. He founded Seagate Technology, in Scotts Valley, California, in 1979, and spent two decades building the company into the single largest independent manufacturer of disk drives in the world. In an unexpected and widely criticized move, the Seagate board of directors fired Shugart, in 1998. Unfazed, he established Al Shugart International, a venture capital firm with an emphasis on ethics, where he is currently the president, chairman, and CEO.

Alan Shugart was born in Los Angeles, California, on September 27, 1930. He was raised in Chino, a farming town east of Los Angeles, by a single mother who worked as a schoolteacher. He attended the University of Redlands, in Redlands, California, where—after switching majors several times—he received a B.S., in engineering physics, in 1951. On the day after graduation, he went to work for IBM, in Santa Monica, California, as a customer engineer. In 1955 IBM offered him a position at its new research facility, in San Jose, California. Shugart described his first impressions of the facility in a keynote address on December 14, 1998 at Santa Clara University, as published in *DataStorage* (April 1999, on-line). "I can still see Don Johnson, one of the pioneers in disk development, pouring iron oxide paint from a Dixie cup onto a rotating, 24-inch-diameter disk. There was no cleanroom, and the equipment was so crude that the Dixie cup didn't look out of place at all," he recalled. "I certainly had no idea I was walking into a product development program that would have such a profound impact upon the computer industry." Shugart served as the product manager for IBM's Random Access Memory (RAM) products. One of his early projects, known as Random Access Method of Accounting, or RAMAC, was to develop a machine that could read disks instead of punch cards. His work formed an integral part in the development of the world's first disk drive—the Advanced Disk File, which later became the IBM 1301. (The drive is the device that rotates disks so that they can read and record data.)

In 1969 Shugart became the director of engineering for the systems development division and transferred to Harrison, New York. He was lured away—after only two weeks—to become the vice president of product development at the Memorex Corporation, in San Jose, California. When he left IBM for Memorex, nearly 200 of his IBM colleagues followed. Shugart left Memorex a few years later, along with another longtime colleague, Finis Conner. According to Conner, Shugart attracted a loyal following because of his managerial skill. "His management style is the style technical people like," noted Conner, as quoted by John Longwell in *Computer Reseller News* (November 16, 1997), "and that is basically hands-off. He's not combative or confrontational."

In 1973 Shugart and Conner launched a company, Shugart Associates, to develop floppy-disk storage capability. Although Shugart Associates successfully introduced the 5.25-inch floppy disk for microcomputers (now called personal computers), Shugart's tenure at the company proved short-lived. By 1974 the initial venture funding was exhausted, and the company did not yet have a viable product. Following a disagreement with his backers, Shugart left the company. "There's an argument about that," Shugart told Longwell. "I say I got fired, and they say I quit." Shugart Associates was eventually sold to Xerox.

Shugart took a short detour from his career path, working as a commercial fisherman and also purchasing a bar. He maintained his ties to the computer industry by working as a private consultant. In 1979 Shugart and Conner regrouped and founded Shugart Technology, which would later change its name to Seagate Technology. Seagate Technology became the first manufacturer to introduce a hard-disk drive that could fit into the 5.25-inch space used by floppy-disk drives. (Hard-disk drives, commonly called hard drives, are the central information storehouses for most computers. The hard disk has provided today's computer user with highly reliable and efficient storage media for everything from financial records to video on demand and has made unwieldy paper tape and punch cards unnecessary.) With Shugart as chairman, operations ran smoothly, and the company was soon able to demonstrate its first hard-disk drive. After another 16 months the company had an initial public offering (IPO) and by 1984 sales had reached $344 million. Seagate encountered financial trouble, in 1985, when IBM—its largest customer by far—demanded lower purchasing prices. That same year, Shugart and Conner had a dispute, and Conner left the company. Conner founded Conner Peripherals, which then became Seagate's top competitor.

Seagate survived the loss in business by moving its manufacturing plants to Singapore and Bangkok. While the moves significantly cut production costs, they also entailed laying off hundreds of employees at the Scotts Valley headquarters. "We got a lot of bad press for that," Shugart told Julie Pitta in *Forbes* (July 8, 1991). "But if we hadn't done it we would have lost the company." Shugart also sought to reduce Seagate's dependence on any single customer. The company began selling low-cost disk drives to computer resellers, who installed them in stripped-down personal computers obtained from other companies. Shugart also introduced several new products, including a 2.5-inch drive for laptop computers. In 1986 Seagate reported a 50 percent growth in sales over the previous year.

Meanwhile, Conner Peripherals had leap-frogged ahead of Seagate in the development of new technologies. It shipped the first 2.5-inch disk drives five months ahead of Seagate, and it led the release of 3.5-inch disk drives by almost a year. According to Shugart, Seagate had been operating under a business model that needed to be retooled. "Seagate has never been that interested in getting products out of the lab first," he remarked to Pitta. "We wait until we've squeezed every penny of cost out of a product before we bring it to market. But the product cycles are getting shorter and shorter. Now, we can't afford to wait."

By 1991 Seagate was again in trouble; personal computer sales had declined, and inventories were piling up. In September of 1991 David Mitchell stepped down as president and CEO, and Shugart, then chairman, filled the position. Shugart redesigned the business model to focus on bringing leading-edge technologies to the marketplace. He diversified the company by acquiring other hardware and software companies, including Crystal of Canada, Palindrome, Dragon Systems, Frye Computer Systems, and Holistic Systems, Ltd. In 1996 Seagate purchased Conner Peripherals for $1.1 billion in stock. This put Seagate in control of 30 percent of the independent disk-drive market, which provides drives to such companies as Compaq and Dell, as well as to individual computer users seeking to increase their machine's storage capacity. Seagate became the single largest independent disk-drive manufacturer in the world, employing more than 100,000 people world-wide. In July 1998, after two decades of navigating Seagate through the treacherous waters of the computer economy, Shugart was fired by the board of directors—a move that surprised many in the industry. "They didn't give me a reason," Shugart told Tom Diederich in *Computerworld* (July 27, 1998). "The only thing I got was, 'It's time for a change, and you won't retire, so therefore, you're fired.' . . . I didn't think [retiring] was the right thing to do. I thought we were doing a real good job." Shugart told Diederich that "one of our competitors [IBM's Jim Vanderslice] called me to say he thought I got a raw deal, which I thought showed a lot of class. Then [former Walt Disney Co. President] Michael Ovitz, who got booted out of Disney, called me and later shot me a fax that said, 'Dear Al: Been there, done that, it's not too bad. Their loss. . . . Don't get mad, get even.'"

Shugart founded Al Shugart International (ASI) in 1998. Two employees followed him from Seagate: Judy Plummer, who became ASI's vice president of communications, and Karen Seifer, who became its vice president of administration. Headquartered in Santa Cruz, California, ASI is a venture capital firm that offers guidance, resources, and public relations services to early-stage start-up companies. In founding the company, Shugart hoped to support socially responsible companies and to emphasize ethical business practices. One of ASI's clients, Orange Guard, of Carmel Valley, California, manufactures an organic and environmentally friendly insecticide made of orange-peel extract, for example. ASI also promotes trust by refusing to create formal contracts with its clients. "We [at ASI] hate contracts," Shugart told Gina Fraone in *Electronic Business* (April 1999). "[At ASI] we don't keep any documentation." If clients do not like this approach, Shugart said, "then we don't have a deal."

Shugart believes that corporate litigation has a crippling effect on business. During his days as CEO of Seagate, he was the defendant in several shareholder lawsuits. In an interview for *Computer Technology Review* (Fall 1997), Mark C. Ferelli asked Shugart about litigation used to gain a competitive or financial advantage. "I think the U.S. has the world's worst system for resolving such matters," Shugart said. "I think the patent system is crazy. I think we could save a lot of money in this country and be more productive if we took all the money that supports the patent system and spend it somewhere else. Most litigation is a waste of time and resources for the company and the country. I'm a strong believer in cross licensing everything we've got from a patent standpoint. . . . I really want to compete on the shipping dock and not in the courtroom." Shugart acted on these beliefs, albeit in an unusual manner. In 1995 he funded a campaign for Ernest, his 110-pound Bernese mountain dog, to run for the congressional seat in California's 17th district. "This is my way of protesting how politicians and lawyers have really screwed up our government, which is stifling productivity, economic growth, and employment," he is quoted as saying on DigitalCentury.com, the *Jones Telecommunications and Multimedia Encyclopedia* Web site. (Shugart had considered a run for Congress himself, in 1992, but decided against it when he realized that members of Congress could not hold other jobs.) Although Shugart succeeded in obtaining a campaign number for Ernest, shortly thereafter the Federal Election Committee discovered that Ernest was a dog and ruled him to be an illegitimate candidate. In 1997 Shugart founded Friends of Ernest (FOE), an activist group dedicated to educating the public about the political process, and, in 1998, he formed the Friends of Ernest Political Action Committee (FOEPAC) to promote the "None of the above" ballot initiative for the state of California. This unsuccessful initiative would have given voters the opportunity to register their opposition to all contenders for a particular office by selecting "None of the above" on statewide and presidential election ballots. Nevada is currently the only state with this option. In

1998 Shugart published a book about Ernest and his campaign, *Ernest Goes to Washington (Well, Not Exactly): A True Story About the Dog Who Ran for Congress*. He self-published another book, *Fandango: The Story of Two Guys Who Wanted to Own a Restaurant—Fortunately, One Knew What He Was Doing*, about his experience operating a restaurant in Palo Alto, California.

Shugart has been honored numerous times for his achievements. For six consecutive years, from 1993 through 1998, he received the *DataStorage* Award for the most admired industry executive. In 1997 he received the Reynold B. Johnson Information Storage Award from the Institute of Electrical and Electronics Engineers (IEEE). In that same year he was inducted into the Computer Museum and *Computer Reseller News* Industry Hall of Fame. In 1997 and 1998 he was included in the *Forbes* list of Corporate America's Most Powerful People and, in 2000, *Electronics Business Magazine* named him one of the Top 25 Executives of the Past 25 Years. He is a member of the National Academy of Engineering and the American Electronics Association.—A. I. C.

Suggested Reading: *BusinessWeek* p94 Mar. 16, 1987; *Computer Reseller News* p114 June 1, 1997, p89+ Nov. 16, 1997; *Computer Technology Review* p32+ Fall 1997; *Computerworld* p8 July 27, 1998; *DataStorage* (on-line) Apr. 1999; *Electronic Business* p40 April 1999, p42+ Oct. 15, 2000; *Forbes* p94+ July 8, 1991; *Jones Telecommunications and Multimedia Encyclopedia* (on-line)

Simon, Herbert Alexander

June 15, 1916– Pioneer in the field of artificial intelligence; economist

On the surface, Herbert A. Simon might appear to be a dilettante: he has studied administration, economics, psychology, philosophy and computer science, among other topics. Upon deeper inspection, however, one can find a solid link between all of his interests—the human ability to solve problems and make decisions. In awarding Simon the Nobel Prize in Economic Science in 1978, the members of the Swedish Academy of Sciences cited "his pioneering research into the decision-making process within economic organizations" and acknowledged that "modern business economics and administrative research are largely based on Simon's ideas." In the 1950s Simon applied his interest in decision making to the realm of artificial intelligence (AI); with the computer scientist Allen Newell, he developed a method of computer problem solving based on the human model. Simon also helped write the list-processing languages and programs necessary to implement the method. (Simon and Newell formulated a theory of "list structure," which realized the importance of lists in symbolic processing. By way of example—If X happens, then Y and Z will follow.) In the decades since then Simon has worked tirelessly to further simulate human cognitive functions in computers for the benefit of humanity.

Herbert Alexander Simon was born to Arthur and Edna (Merkel) Simon in Milwaukee, Wisconsin, on June 15, 1916. He has one older brother, born five years earlier. Simon discussed his parents, whom he describes as nurturing and involved, in an autobiographical statement posted on the Nobel e-Museum Web site: "My father, an electrical engineer, had come to the United States in 1903 after earning his engineering diploma at the Technische Hochschule of Darmstadt, Germany. He was an inventor and designer of electronic control gear, later also a patent attorney. . . . My mother, an accomplished pianist, was a third generation American, her forebears having been '48ers who immigrated from Prague and Köhn." As a child Simon developed an avid interest in books and learning, as well as a fascination with music and outdoor activity.

Simon's parents taught him that curiosity is the beginning of all science, and their household was run on that conviction. If there was a question or phenomenon the Simons failed to understand, they immediately set out to investigate the topic further. Simon attended Milwaukee's public schools, which he has maintained provided him with an excellent general education, which he supplemented with frequent trips to the local library.

When he entered the University of Chicago, in 1933, Simon had already decided to apply the same rigorous methodology to social science that is employed in the so-called hard sciences. He discussed the matter in his Nobel e-Museum autobiography: "I would prepare myself to become a mathematical social scientist. By a combination of formal training and self study, the later continuing systemically well into the 1940s, I was able to gain a broad base of knowledge in economics and political science, together with reasonable skills in advanced mathematics, symbolic logic, and mathematical statistics." His career specialization was more sharply defined when he made an undergraduate field study of the administration of Milwaukee's recreation department, which focused his attention on the process of decision making in organizations.

After receiving a bachelor's degree in political science, in 1936, Simon became an assistant to Clarence E. Ridley of the International City Managers' Association. In that post he carried out investigations in the field of municipal administration, and from 1939 to 1942 he engaged in similar work as director of administrative measurement studies in the Bureau of Public Administration of the University of California at Berkeley. In 1942 he joined the political science faculty at the Illinois Institute of Technology, where he remained for seven years. In 1943 Simon received a doctoral degree in political science from the University of Chicago.

His doctoral dissertation, with some modifications and additions, was published in 1947 under the title *Administrative Behavior: A Study of Decision-Making Processes in Administrative Organization*. In that seminal study, Simon sharply attacked the sterility of existing administrative theory, primarily in public administration, but not neglecting commercial, industrial, military, and private nonprofit organizations. As Chester I. Barnard explained in his foreword to the book, Simon's objective was to construct a set of concepts and a vocabulary suitable for describing an organization and the way it works. "If any 'theory' is involved," Simon himself pointed out, "it is that decision-making is the heart of administration, and that the vocabulary of administrative theory must be derived from the logic and psychology of human choice."

Building upon his belief in the centrality of the decision-making process in administration, Simon accomplished some of his most influential work over the next decade. In 1949 he became a professor of administration at the Carnegie Institute of Technology's (now Carnegie-Mellon University's) newly established Graduate School of Business Administration, in Pittsburgh, Pennsylvania. There Simon and his associates, aided by Ford Foundation grants, conducted field studies of the decision-making processes in several companies and ran laboratory tests to observe the same processes under controlled experimental conditions.

By the mid-1950s Simon had come to the conclusion that in complex modern organizations, individuals could not possibly process or even obtain all of the information relating to the decisions they must make. He therefore maintained that instead of seeking the most advantageous possible decisions, companies merely try to set goals that represent reasonable achievement levels or minimally acceptable targets—a course of action he called "satisficing" behavior. In the second edition of *Administrative Behavior* (1957), Simon spelled out the theoretical implications of his conclusions, noting that classical economic theory subscribes to the belief that the decision maker, known as "economic man," is omniscient and therefore capable of making decisions that maximize profits. Rejecting this construct as unrealistic, he offered in its stead what he referred to as "administrative man," who "satisfices" or looks for a course of action that is simply satisfactory or "good enough." Though many economists balked at his controversial conclusions, some specializing in business operations gave his ideas considerably more credence. As a result, his work has greatly influenced teaching methods in business schools.

During the mid-1950s Simon's work took a crucial turn: he realized that the understanding of administrative decisions required a more adequate theory of problem solving. He began collaborating with Allen Newell in 1954. After mutually concluding that the right way to study problem solving in human beings was to simulate it with computer programs, the duo began working with human subjects in order to chart cognitive processes for building such a program. In their research, they posed a well-structured problem in logic that required fundamental reasoning processes for its solution to a volunteer. The volunteer was asked to verbalize his or her reasoning while solving the problem, after which the basic elements of that reasoning were coded onto a program for computer simulation. The program made no specific reference to the subject matter of the problem; its objective was to enable the computer to solve any problem stated in a certain general form. In effect Simon and Newell were trying to make the computer simulate intelligent, adaptive thought rather than merely perform rote procedures involving no discrimination. Since computers record their own steps, success would provide valuable insight into the human thought processes. In 1955 Simon and Newell created an AI programming language known as the Information Processing Language (IPL). IPL was developed specifically for use in computer programs capable of resolving mathematical logic programs. By the end of the year they had created the Logic Theorist—a program that used recursive search methods to solve mathematical equations.

Simon regards December 15, 1955 as the most exciting day of his career. "We were working on a logic theorist program, and we finally got it running," he told Jeffrey Zaslow for the *Pittsburgher* (February 1979). "It was then that we knew we had a program that could solve problems in a humanoid fashion." Using general reasoning processes, the computer had solved the same problem as a human volunteer. That successful experiment was the first example of what was only later termed "artificial intelligence."

Through the 1950s Simon worked with Newell to produce programs that enabled computers to replicate more complex forms of human thinking. While perfecting the Logic Theorist, in 1956 the pair developed IPL II, an updated version of their list-processing language, and a heuristic technique through which they are able to prove theorems in logic. (A heuristic technique involves trial-and-error or other self-educating methods.) In the summer of that year they were invited to a conference at Dartmouth College, in New Hampshire, with a number of their peers to discuss ways in which to develop true AI and possible applications in the field. Among the noted guests were John McCarthy, who organized the conference and is credited with coining the term artificial intelligence. However, Simon and Newell were widely acknowledged as the highlight of the conference in that they were the only attendees able to display a working model of AI in the form of their Logic Theorist.

In 1957 Simon and Newell, along with John Clifford Shaw, a scientist with whom they had previously worked closely, wrote the General Problem Solver program. By using means-end analysis, the program was able to come up with solutions to problems it hadn't been specifically programmed to solve. In one widely cited example, the computer was asked how a man could get from his office to the airport. The General Problem Solver looked for solutions by asking itself how one gets from where one is to where one wants to be. Then it began to process the tools by which to cover that distance by selecting from a number of choices—from biking to taking a taxi. In an interview with Doug Stewart for *Omni* (June 1994), Simon elaborated the program's abilities: "Every time you set up a problem, it thinks of some method or tool already stored in memory that can remove the difference between where it is and where it wants to be. Each tool required that certain conditions be met before that tool can be applied, so it then searches its memory for a tool for doing that. Eventually, it finds one it can apply: You call the taxi, it comes, and the first thing you know you're delivered to the airport." He continued, "Note [the program] doesn't try everything—not walking or a helicopter. It knows all sorts of things about walking or helicopters that help it decide that they don't work in this situation."

By the 1960s Simon pushed the existing boundaries of AI even further. He realized that the way to best simulate human thought processes was to focus AI programs on tasks that must be done using general knowledge. One such program was the Elementary Perceiver and Memorizer (EPAM), which Simon created with Edward A. Feigenbaum, Lee W. Gregg, and Howard B. Richman. According to the *International Biographical Dictionary of Computer Pioneers* (1995): "The work on EPAM has . . . [produced] a system that simulates human behavior over a wide range of the perceptual, learning, and concept induction tasks that have been studied in the psychological laboratory, thereby constituting a theory of unmatched generality in this domain."

Since the 1970s Simon has had a hand in developing a number of other AI programs. One of the most notable among them is the Understand program, which he developed with John R. Hayes. Understand had the ability to read task descriptions in ordinary language and then build representations of the task appropriate to use as inputs in the General Problem Solver. Another AI program Simon worked on in the 1970s was called BACON, named after Sir Francis Bacon. That program, using raw data, was able to rediscover Kepler's Third Law of Motion by using the same numbers Kepler had used in the 17th century to determine the distance of the planets from the sun and their periods of revolution. BACON figured out the pattern to the numbers in three attempts; it had taken Kepler ten years.

After achieving his initial programming success in the 1950s, Simon continued to investigate the artificial simulation of human thought processes. As a result, his work fell primarily within the academic disciplines of psychology and computer science, although his fundamental intellectual concern remained the area of decision making. Official recognition of that fact came in 1966, when he became Richard King Mellon University Professor of Computer Science and Psychology at Carnegie-Mellon University.

Convinced that psychological research can be greatly advanced by studying how computers simulate human thinking, Simon has reached certain basic conclusions about thought processes. The ability to create artificial intelligence, he argues, demonstrates that the mind is an information-processing machine. "My mind works according to laws and mechanisms, not some mysterious mind fluid," Simon told a writer for *Time* (October 30, 1978). Furthermore, he contends, the ability of computers to solve problems using no more than the known, simple elements of human thinking demonstrates that subconscious thought follows the same principles as conscious thought. On the practical plane, Simon contends that by using the information gained about thought through charting the workings of artificial intelligence, people can be taught to be more efficient problem solvers.

His experience with AI gave Simon the reputation of being what he called a "technological radical" in the computer-science field. John Kobler quoted him in the *Saturday Evening Post* (May 4, 1968) as saying that "in our time a computer will do anything a man can do. They can already read, think, learn, create." He and his associates have programmed computers to play chess, prove 38 out of 52 theorems from Bertrand Russell's *Principia Mathematica*, and discriminate between geometrical shapes. In the revised edition of his book *The New Science of Management Decision* (1977), Simon wrote that "we should avoid the simple assumption that the higher-status occupations, and those requiring the most education, are going to be the least automated. There are perhaps as good prospects technically and economically for automating the job of a physician (but not a surgeon), a corporate vice president, or a college teacher as for automating the job of the person who operates a piece of earth-moving equipment."

As one of the most celebrated faculty members at Carnegie-Mellon University, Simon has helped shape the teaching methods at its internationally renowned Graduate School of Industrial Administration. Carnegie-Mellon has challenged the Harvard Graduate School of Business Administration's case study approach with an attempt to provide businessmen with the basic tools they need to learn on their own, an approach that reflects Simon's interest in enhancing the efficiency of overall problem-solving ability. He told a writer for *Business Week* (December 5, 1970) that "if we could somehow teach . . . [the] capacity to learn independently, we wouldn't have to teach the manager anything else." Carnegie-Mellon was one of the earliest advocates of management's use of the computer, and Simon was one of the founders of the university's computer center.

Simon's extraordinary intellectual versatility and curiosity are demonstrated by the variety of courses he has taught at the school. They include political science, economics, psychology, and computer science, as well as an undergraduate history course on the French Revolution. Simon has more than 15 books and 500 scholarly articles to his credit and has received honorary degrees from several prestigious universities.

In addition to winning the Nobel Prize in Economic Science in 1978, Simon has received numerous other honors; these include the Distinguished Science Contribution Award from the American Psychological Association in 1969 and the A. M. Turing Award from the Association for Computing Machinery in 1975. He is the recipient of the James Madison Award (1984), the National Medal of Science (1986), the John von Neumann Theory Award (1988), and the Dwight Waldo Award (1995). He served as chairman of the National Research Council's Division of Behavioral Sciences from 1968 to 1970 and was a member of the President's Science Advisory Committee from 1968 to 1972.

Herbert A. Simon married the former Dorothea Pye, who was a research associate in Carnegie-Mellon University's psychology department, on December 25, 1937. They have three children: Kathie, Peter, and Barbara.—C. M.

Suggested Reading: Carnegie-Mellon University Web site; *New York Times* III p5 Nov. 26, 1978; Nobel e-Museum Web site; *Omni* p70+ June 1994; Public Administration Review v55 July/Aug. 1995; Lee, J. A. N., ed. *International Biographical Dictionary of Computer Pioneers*, 1995

Simonyi, Charles

1948–Computer programmer; chief architect at Microsoft Research

As a computer programmer and software developer, Charles Simonyi has helped to launch the era of personal computing. Through his work on some of the earliest personal computer applications at Xerox's Palo Alto Research Center (PARC), in California, and at Microsoft, Simonyi has literally changed the "face" of computing by designing the applications that shape the way information is organized and displayed on personal computers. He is credited with helping to develop many of the features—such as windows, icons, pull-down menus, and the mouse—that have made computers easier to learn and to use. In 1997 Simonyi was granted membership in the National Academy of Engineering for his work in creating widely used desktop productivity software. As chief architect of Microsoft Research since 1991, Simonyi has been working to develop a more sophisticated method of programming that, he believes, will pro-

Charles Simonyi

Paul Schofield/Getty Images

duce better and more specialized computer applications.

Charles Simonyi was born in 1948 in Budapest, Hungary. Through his father, who was a professor of electrical engineering, Simonyi gained access to computers while still a teenager, as he told John Brockman in an interview for the on-line technology magazine *Edge* (June 25, 2000). "I've been incredibly lucky, in a strange way," Simonyi explained. "In the U.S., computers that operated with vacuum tubes were obsolete in the late 1950's, whereas in Hungary, where I grew up, they were in use. . . . When the personal computer revolution came about much later, the people in the U.S. that had worked with tube computers were long retired, if not dead, while I was really in the prime of my career." When Simonyi graduated from high school at age 17, he was too young to be drafted by the military, and was therefore given permission to work for one year at a computer research facility in Copenhagen, Denmark. As Simonyi explained to Brockman, this was an act of subterfuge in order to emigrate from Hungary: "I got out legally; but it was illegal not to return." Simonyi explained that he and his father had planned his defection, although it created problems both for his father in Hungary and for Simonyi when he arrived in the United States, at age 18, to attend the University of California, Berkeley. "Basically, I had a lot of problems with the immigration people," he told Brockman, "because nobody had been shooting at me at the Hungarian border. I was just a normal student, except a student whose passport seemed to expire every minute." Simonyi's move from what he calls the "time-warp" of Communist-controlled Hungary in 1965, to Denmark the following year, and

then to Berkeley in 1967—just as personal computing technology was heating up—gave him an overview of technological development. "In a period of three years I traversed three generations of computers," Simonyi told Brockman.

At Berkeley Simonyi studied engineering and mathematics. As a foreigner, he was not eligible for scholarships; to support himself he worked at the University's computer center, where he met a group of professors who had recently founded the Berkeley Computer Corporation. He was invited to join the computer company and was even awarded a stock option. In his interview with Brockman, Simonyi related how this extra-curricular activity took time away from school and made his grades fluctuate, prompting a university dean to become concerned. "'Mr. Simonyi,'" he recalled the dean as saying, "'you were doing so well and are now doing so poorly; what's the reason? Can we help you? You can share anything with us, tell us what it is. Is it drugs, is it grass, acid, or mescaline?' I smiled at him and said, 'I think it's a stock option.' He said, 'Well in that case we can't help you.'"

Although the stock option ultimately proved worthless, Simonyi's involvement with the Berkeley Computer Corporation led to a job at Xerox's PARC. Xerox established PARC in 1969 to expand on their copier business, which was facing strong competition from Japanese manufacturers, according to Martin Campbell-Kelly and William Aspray in *Computer: A History of the Information Machine* (1996). Xerox put about half of the PARC money into computer science research, specifically into creating personal computers, then called "microcomputers," for use in what they imagined would be the "office of the future," according to Campbell-Kelly and Aspray. Along with some of the Berkeley professors, Simonyi was recruited to work at PARC as a researcher in 1972, as he was finishing his bachelor's degree. Simonyi was made part of a team that was developing the "Alto," Xerox's first personal computer. Meant to serve as a convincing prototype for a new method of computer use, the Alto was designed to sit on a desktop with a specially constructed monitor that could display a standard sheet of "paper."

Simonyi worked to create a text editor for the Alto. By this time, he had finished his B.S. at Berkeley and had enrolled at Stanford University, in Stanford, California, earning a Ph. D. in 1976. He decided to incorporate the text editor project into his dissertation research, and built BRAVO, the first WYSIWYG (What You See Is What You Get) text editor, in 1975. In his interview with Brockman, Simonyi explained his text editor's curious appellation: "Once the Bravo editor and the other component of the 'office of the future' were operational, it created a fair amount of attention, and a lot of VIPs came to look at what PARC was coming up with." His research team demonstrated BRAVO on the Alto's computer screen, displaying the Xerox logo in a specific size and font. They printed out what was on the screen onto transparent slide stock, and when held up to the screen, the transparent stock was identical. According to Simonyi, one of the visitors then remarked "'I see, what you see is what you get'," which was, as he told Brockman, a tag-line from *Laugh-In*, a popular television show from the period. WYSIWYG (pronounced *wizzie-wig*), became the standard term to describe the technology of being able to print out documents as they appear on a computer screen. Prior to WYSIWYG word processing, a typesetter who was formatting a page would see only unformatted lines of type and coding on the screen and would have to hope that the copy emerged properly printed. In addition to guaranteeing results, the WYSIWYG text editor allowed users to make changes, such as adding text, moving blocks of text, deleting text, and incorporating graphics into a document.

In order to make the Alto even more user-friendly, Simonyi's team evolved a graphical user interface (GUI). Using the metaphor of an actual office environment, and building on research that had begun with Doug Engelbart and the Human Factors Research Center, the PARC team designed the computer screen as an idealized desktop, on which graphics and icons would represent folders, documents, and other office tools. The GUI was a great improvement over earlier operating systems, such as the Digital Operating System (DOS), in which users had to type precise lines of instruction to perform simple tasks. According to Campbell-Kelly and Aspray, for the ordinary user this system was "rather like having to understand a carburetor in order to be able to drive an automobile." By comparison, Campbell-Kelly and Aspray praise the GUI as "a natural and intuitive way of using a computer that could be learned in minutes rather than days," and, in an introduction to his interview with Simonyi, Brockman describes the BRAVO text editor and its GUI as revolutionary—"a fundamental departure from the way information was previously organized and displayed," one that "ultimately led to personal computing."

Simonyi told Brockman that he immediately grasped the commercial and technological potential of the Alto computer, but feared that not everyone at Xerox shared his vision: "The most interesting thing: when you see a capability that kind of blows you away, and you know that this is going to be the biggest thing, but then some people don't see it. I thought Xerox suffered from a disease we call 'biggerism,' which is the bigger-the-better type of engineering mentality," one that makes it difficult to discern what the market really demands, he explained. Indeed, though many of the early computer innovations, such as GUI, laser printers, and the personal computer itself, were discovered at PARC, the company never successfully marketed these innovations, according to the *ComputerUser* Web site. The commercial version of the Alto computer, the Xerox star workstation, was too expensive to attract a sizeable market, although its format represented an unmistakable "glimpse of the future."

Simonyi found someone who shared his vision for personal computing when, in 1980, he met Bill Gates, founder of a fledgling venture called Microsoft. Simonyi was very impressed by what he told Brockman the young Gates's "extraordinary vision" for the future of personal computers, which included the potential for Microsoft to become the "leading producer of microcomputer software, worldwide." At the time, Microsoft had only 32 employees and annual sales of about $8 million. Simonyi joined the company in 1981 and was put in charge of developing software applications. One of his first tasks was to hire and manage the programming teams, who would be responsible for writing the thousands of lines of code. "It was interesting to look at a company like Xerox, with a hundred thousand people and billions of dollars, and realize that the success of your project depends on having the right two people that you want to hire," Simonyi told Brockman. "Bill just said, 'hire two people, or hire five people. What do you need? Do you need rooms? Do you need chairs? Yeah! We can do that.'"

When Simonyi joined Microsoft, the company had already produced a DOS platform for IBM-compatible machines, but was working on a newer, more accessible operating system along the lines of Xerox's GUI concept. There was a huge financial incentive to do so, since whatever company produced the new operating system would have a significant advantage in marketing their software products. The software wars of the 1980s were launched, with hundreds of companies competing to produce the new operating systems and applications. Simonyi, who described himself to Brockman as being "the messenger RNA of the PARC virus," brought his knowledge of user-friendly software with him from Xerox to Microsoft. He claims to have relished the race to develop software, having once written in *Byte* magazine (January 1989) that "the health of the microcomputer industry is built on the myriad of developments and controversies that emerge, interact, and compete in a never-ending pattern." Throughout the 1980s, Simonyi managed the teams that created the phenomenally successful Microsoft Word word-processing program, the Excel spreadsheet program, and other applications. As Microsoft's researchers worked to develop the Windows operating system, the company was financially supported by profits from Simonyi's application programs. During the 1980s, Microsoft experienced phenomenal growth, due in part to its software applications.

A computer programmer decides what a particular program needs to do, develops the logic of how to do it, and writes instructions for the computer in a programming language that the computer can then translate into its own language and execute. As chief architect of Microsoft Research since 1991, Simonyi has been working to develop what he sees as the next evolutionary step in computer software—a concept he calls "Intentional Programming." Intentional Programming, Simonyi explained in a 1995 technical paper for Microsoft, shifts emphasis away from codes and languages and toward the specific ideas behind the program. Ideally, Intentional Programming would make a program completely self-describing, so that programmer's idea will be embedded in the program code itself. This will make programming easier and more creative, create increased diversity and competition among programmers, and make altogether "more shareable software artifacts," as Simonyi told Brockman.

Simonyi's long career at Microsoft has made him wealthy, with assets totaling about $1.5 billion, according to *Forbes* (October 11, 1999). Simonyi has spent millions to endow chairs at Stanford University, Oxford University, and the Institute for Advanced Study in Princeton, New Jersey. In the *New York Times* (November 12,

1990), John Markoff wrote that Simonyi enjoys taking visitors to the machine shop in the basement of his home, complete with lathe and drill press. "'In Hungary,'" Simonyi told Markoff, "'they told us that the workers would never own the means of production.'" Simonyi's glass-and-steel home on the shores of Lake Washington, outside Seattle, also has a helipad and a state-of-the-art computer laboratory. Simonyi collects paintings by the 20th-century artists Roy Lichtenstein and Victor Vasarely. These artists, Simonyi explained to the *Forbes* reporter, "had premonitions of the digital age."—M. A. H.

Byte p 343+ Jan. 1989; *Edge* June 25, 2000 (online); *Forbes* p81 Oct. 6, 1997, Oct. 11, 1999 (online); Campbell-Kelly, Martin and William Aspray. *Computer: A History of the Information Machine*, 1996

Hulton Archive by Getty Images

Sinclair, Clive

July 30, 1940– Inventor; founder of Sinclair Research

Some would say that Sir Clive Sinclair embodies a longstanding stereotype of brilliant inventors—he has had the ingenuity to come up with several clever products, but has lacked the business acumen to successfully market them. Sinclair invented the miniature radio amplifier, the pocket calculator, and the digital watch; his greatest achievement has arguably been sparking the computer revolution in the United Kingdom by developing several inexpensive computers that ordinary people

could afford. His computers, the ZX 80, ZX 81, and the Spectrum, while not very sophisticated, sold hundreds of thousands of units within a few years of their introduction. As other manufacturers began to offer similar products, however, Sinclair's business suffered; although he is a wealthy man by most standards, Sinclair Research, as his current enterprise is named, lacks the name recognition and revenues of many of his competitors.

The son of an industrial-equipment salesman, Clive Marples Sinclair was born on July 30, 1940 in London, England. As a child he displayed early acumen by tinkering with his wind- up cars in order to make them go faster. Although mathematics and physics fascinated him, Sinclair found himself frequently bored by school and often worked on his own projects in his spare time. During his teenage years he designed a calculating machine that he programmed with a numerical language of his own device consisting exclusively of 1s and 0s. Unfortunately, the numerical language, popularly known as the binary system, had already been developed. For a classroom assignment Sinclair designed a miniature radio and figured out how much it would cost to manufacture 1,000 of them. "I always wanted to be an inventor," Sinclair told Mike Anderiesz for the *Scotsman* (June 29, 1999). "I was always making things at school, solving problems, finding different ways to do simple things."

Because his parents moved frequently, Sinclair attended 13 different schools, some of dubious quality, and he abandoned his education, in 1957, to make his mark in the real world. That year he applied for a summer job at Mullard, an electrical engineering company. To impress the company's personnel officer during his job interview, Sinclair brought a miniature radio amplifier he had invented with him. The personnel officer, however, told Sinclair that his amplifier would never work and turned down his request for a job. Despite this setback, Sinclair found a job writing for *Practical Wireless*, a technical magazine that he would eventually edit. He also wrote numerous radio manuals for Burns Publications.

In 1962 Clive Sinclair founded his own company, Sinclair Radionics. The first products that he sold were radio kits, which were based on his previous design for a miniature radio amplifier. Sinclair advertised the radio kits, which could be purchased via mail order, in hobby magazines. Sinclair also purchased 1,000 transistors that had not worked in the computers for which they had been made, but that he was certain would be useful for other purposes. Mail-order sales of the transistors were brisk, and Sinclair realized a 700 percent profit. Sinclair Radionics remained profitable during the 1960s, eventually adding high-fidelity systems and electronic instruments to its product line.

In 1971 Sinclair designed the world's first pocket calculator. "It was almost impossible to get anyone in retail to support it," Sinclair recalled to Anderiesz. "We launched it first by mail order because if you don't get an idea out to the public you will always find it hard to get a new concept across." Sinclair Radionics began selling its pocket calculator, the Sinclair Executive, in 1972. Costing about $174, the Sinclair Executive performed basic mathematical functions. In an interview with Tom Standage for the London *Daily Telegraph* (December 17, 1996), Sinclair explained that supply created its own demand for the item: "Take the pocket calculator: no one was going around saying that they needed one, but once they'd got it they needed it. It's finding something that will be useful to people and change the world in a small way." The Sinclair Executive was instantly popular with consumers, and profits from sales were considerable. The next year, Sinclair Radionics released a more advanced pocket calculator, the Sinclair Executive Memory.

The success of the Sinclair Executive calculators was short-lived. Within a few years American and Japanese firms were selling their own pocket calculators, which were less expensive and more technologically advanced than Sinclair's models. Sinclair attempted to keep his company competitive by releasing other products, such as a compact radio and a plastic digital watch. Production problems delayed the release of Sinclair's digital "Black Watch," as it was advertised, for 18 months. When it finally reached the market, in 1975, Black Watch sold poorly. The few people who actually bought the watch discovered that it stopped working in cold weather. The commercial failure of the Black Watch and the resources Sinclair was spending to develop a pocket-sized television brought financial troubles for the small company. The inventor sought backing from London's financial community, but failed to attract any investors. In 1976 Sinclair formed a partnership with the National Enterprise Board (NEB), a government-funded organization that provided financial backing for high-risk ventures. Although support from the NEB kept Sinclair Radionics afloat, he and the organization often clashed about the direction of the company. Sinclair told *Fortune* that "the NEB had a view of me as a mad inventor who couldn't run anything," as quoted by David Remnick for the *Washington Post* (October 17, 1984). The partnership was dissolved, in 1979, and Sinclair Radionics went out of business. Sinclair was given $22,000 as a part of the dissolution agreement; the venture had cost the NEB $17 million. "The message has come through loud and clear that Sinclair is a good designer, but he is no good at running a business," Richard Harwood, a financial analyst with the London-based brokerage firm of Scott, Goff, Hancock & Company, told Elizabeth Bailey for the *New York Times* (April 12, 1981).

Clive Sinclair bounced back after this failure by founding a new company, Sinclair Research, in 1979. The inventor embarked on another high-risk venture, developing computers that most people could use and afford. In 1980 Sinclair Research unveiled its first home computer, the ZX 80. Priced at about $200 and compact in size, the ZX 80 was hooked up to a televison and stored data on cassettes. Although it was less powerful than the computers sold by Apple and Tandy, the ZX 80's low price made it attractive to customers. According to Bailey, more than 50,000 units of the ZX 80 computer were sold in the first nine months of 1980. By the next year, Sinclair was manufacturing ZX 80s at the rate of 10,000 per month.

In 1981 Sinclair Research issued a more advanced model, the ZX 81, which outsold its predecessor. "The ZX 81 was a better machine—more powerful, more elegant—but we priced it less and everyone said we were crazy," Sinclair told Michael Schrage for the *Washington Post* (October 25, 1982). The inventor's strategy worked. In his article for the *New York Times Magazine* (May 19, 1985), Barnaby Feder estimated that the ZX 81 eventually sold more than 500,000 units.

In 1982 Sinclair signed an agreement with the Timex Corporation, the well-known watchmaker, to market the ZX 81 in the United States. The American version of the machine was sold as the Timex Sinclair ZX 81. Although it generated some consumer interest in the United States, it failed to displace the popularity of the Commodore 64 or computers sold by Apple, IBM, and Tandy. Sinclair, however, continued to dominate the British computer market. He released two new products, Microvision, a miniature, flat-screen televison, and a technologically advanced computer, the Spectrum, which offered eight-color graphics capability, a micro-floppy disk drive, and communications modems. His success as a businessman and accomplishments as an inventor earned him a knighthood from Queen Elizabeth II, in 1983.

As they did in the previous decade, Sir Clive Sinclair's fortunes soured quickly. His more expensive and advanced QL personal computer, which he designed to compete directly with Apple and IBM, failed to meet sales expectations. A recession in the computer industry in 1984 and 1985 also hurt Sinclair Research's revenues. Sinclair helped set the stage for his own downfall by pursuing what many considered a foolish project. In early 1985 he introduced the C5, a compact vehicle powered by electricity. Resembling a small golf cart and priced at $450, the C5 could carry only one passenger and stood on three wheels, which led many to describe it as an "electric tricycle." The C5's top speed was 15 miles per hour, and its battery had to be recharged every 20 miles. Because it was powered by electricity and not pollution-causing fossil fuels, Sinclair believed the C5 would appeal to environmentally conscious consumers. He envisioned it as the first in a series of electric vehicles. The C5, however, generated little consumer interest and was often the subject of ridicule in the British press. Several owners reported that their C5s could not go up hills and left them stranded when the battery died. The British Safety Council claimed that the vehicle was unsafe, an allegation frequently repeated by the media. Despite his prediction that the C5 would sell 100,000 units in 1985, Sinclair abandoned the project by the end of that year.

Sinclair then decided to abandon business and focus solely on inventing new products. In 1986 he sold Sinclair Research's computer division to Amstrad Consumer Electronics, a computer manufacturer in the United Kingdom. After fading from the public spotlight for several years, Sinclair reemerged, in 1992, with the Zike, an electric bicycle. Although less ambitious than the much-ridiculed C5,

the Zike also failed to meet Sinclair's sales expectations. In 1994 the inventor found some success with the Zeta (zero-emission transport accessory), an electric motor that people attached to the back wheels of their bicycles to make them operate without pedaling. "It is about putting the fun back into cycling and providing a viable, convenient alternative for the many thousands of short car journeys carried out each day," Sinclair told Roger Trapp for the London *Independent* (July 20, 1997). In 1997 Sinclair unveiled the X1, an inexpensive, button-sized radio that fit in a person's ear and sometime later developed the Z1, an even smaller model. According to some reports, he is currently working on a jet pack.

Sir Clive Sinclair has been the subject of two books, Ian Adamson's and Richard Kennedy's *The Sinclair Story* (1985) and Rodney Dale's *Sinclair and the Sunrise Technology: The Deconstruction of a Myth* (1986). Sinclair's first marriage ended in divorce, in 1985, after 22 years.—D. C.

Suggested Reading: *Computergram International* (on-line) May 5, 1999; (London) *Daily Telegraph* p3 Dec. 17, 1996; *Guardian* p25 Mar. 28, 1992, with photos; (London) *Independent* p10 Oct. 10, 1996; *New York Times* III p6 Apr. 12, 1981; *New York Times Magazine* p101+ May 19, 1985, with photos; *Scotsman* p4+ June 29, 1999; *Washington Post* p31+ Oct. 25, 1982, with photo, D p1+ Oct. 17, 1984, with photo; Adamson, Ian and Richard Kennedy. *The Sinclair Story*, 1985; Dale, Rodney. *Sinclair and the Sunrise Technology: The Deconstruction of a Myth*, 1986

Sperry, Elmer Ambrose

Oct. 12, 1860–June 16, 1930 Inventor; pioneer in the field of gyroscopic technology

The prolific inventor Elmer Ambrose Sperry held more than 350 patents during his lifetime; these covered a wide range of areas, including electric light and power, mining machinery, electric railways, electric automobiles, batteries, and electro-chemistry. Today he is perhaps best known for his seminal contributions to the field of gyroscopic technology—his gyrocompasses and gyrostabilizers that were used in both ships and aircraft. He also developed the first gyro-controlled autopilot system, which was used in ships and played an important role in the development of the aerial torpedo. These systems and others that Sperry pioneered utilized complex feedback controls—a method of operation wherein the output of the system and its actions becomes the input for the system. Accordingly, Sperry's work laid the foundations for modern control theory, cybernetics, and automation.

Elmer Ambrose Sperry was born on October 12, 1860 (some sources say October 21) in Cortland, New York. His father, Stephen Decatur Sperry, was a farmer. His mother, Mary (Borst) Sperry, was a schoolteacher who died shortly after he was born. As a child Sperry was keenly interested in the technological advancements of the age—batteries, doorbells, and telegraphs, among them. As a high-school student, he built an electric supply system for a local church. He attended the State Normal School, in Cortland, until 1880. He then informally attended lectures at Cornell University, in Ithaca, New York, and developed his first invention—a generator suitable for arc lighting (arc lamps were a precursor to incandescent lamps and were becoming a common source of outdoor lighting at the time).

In 1883 Sperry moved to Chicago, Illinois, where he founded a company to manufacture his patented generator. The managerial and administrative aspects of the work weighed heavily on him, however, and he wrote in a letter at the time that he feared he would "break down . . . between work and worry," as quoted by Thomas P. Hughes in *American Genesis: A Century of Invention and*

Technological Enthusiasm, 1870– 1970 (1989). He solved the problem in 1888, when he established the Elmer A. Sperry Company of Chicago—which would today be considered a research-and-development company and laboratory. The enterprise allowed him to focus on bringing patents—his own and others—to fruition. He next founded a mining-machinery company. In 1893 he moved to Cleveland, Ohio, where he developed improvements for streetcars.

In 1907 Sperry moved to the New York City borough of Brooklyn, and began working with gyroscopes. A gyroscope is a rapidly spinning disk mounted on a base in such a way that it can spin freely along both the X and Y axis. Accordingly, the position of the disk will remain stable regardless of the movement of the base. The first recorded construction of a gyroscope is generally attributed to C. A. Bohnenberger, in 1810. The instrument remained a mere curiosity, however, until 1890, when G. M. Hopkins developed the first electrically driven model. The practical relevance of this invention was not lost on Sperry. At the time, seafaring ships were increasingly built using steel, which rendered a standard magnetic compass unreliable. A properly calibrated gyroscope, however, allows the gyro to settle towards true north. This is due to a feature of gyroscopic behavior called precession. Following the natural laws of motion and inertia, if the spindle is moved in one direction it will respond by forcing the spindle to move at right angles to the original direction of motion. Accordingly, a gyrocompass responds to the force of gravity by precessing until the axis of rotation of the spinning wheel is parallel to the axis of rotation of the earth.

In 1908 Sperry patented his gyrocompass and founded the Sperry Gyroscope Company to manufacture the instrument. In 1911 the U.S. Navy began using Sperry's gyrocompass in its ships. After World War I merchant ships began using another of Sperry's inventions, Metal Mike—the first gyroscope-guided autopilot steering system.

While Sperry was developing his gyrocompass, he was also working on another invention, the gyrostabilizer. He was inspired by the German naval engineer and inventor Ernst Otto Schlick, who had recently used a gyro to stabilize a ship, and the Englishman Louis Brennan, who had stabilized a monorail car. The gyrostabilizer made use of the same basic of features of gyroscopic movement as the gyrocompass, but was mounted to a vehicle in such a way so as to counteract unwanted motion. Sperry's first gyrostabilizer was for a wheelbarrow used by a circus clown on a tightrope. He soon patented a gyrostabilizer for automobiles, which in that era frequently overturned on rough roads. Sperry also considered installing gyrostabilizers on passenger ships to reduce the roll and thereby ameliorate seasickness. However, he had a difficult time selling his stabilizers on the commercial market.

Again, the U.S. Navy expressed interest in Sperry's invention; a stabilized ship could offer greater shooting accuracy than a rolling ship. In 1912, a five-ton Sperry gyro was installed aboard the U.S.S. *Worden*, a 433-ton destroyer. The gyro reportedly reduced a total roll of 30 degrees to about six degrees. The mechanism was not largely adopted, however, because of the strains it placed on the structure of the ship. After the war, a simpler stabilizer came into use, which employed gyro-controlled stabilizer fins extending from bow of the ship.

Sperry also designed gyrostabilizers for use in aircraft. His son Lawrence aided him in the development of the aircraft stabilizer, completing by 1914 a version that used four gyros mounted together on a single stable platform (an arrangement that became the industry standard). In June 1914 Lawrence demonstrated the mechanism when flying near Paris, France. A French mechanic named

Courtesy of the Computer Museum of America

A Sperry invention

Emile Cachin walked out on the wing of the small Curtiss airplane, while Lawrence raised his hands in the cockpit to show that the plane was being operated by the gyrostabilizer.

From this development came another military contribution for which Sperry is well known—the aerial torpedo. The aerial torpedo was the first of its kind, preceding by two decades the German V-1 flying bomb of World War II. Developed by the Sperry Gyroscope Company, the torpedo was a specially built Curtiss pilotless airplane intended to deliver a 1,000-pound load of explosives to a target up to 100 miles away. Thomas P. Hughes explained the workings of the mechanism in *American Genesis*: "The gyrostabilizer would maintain the plane in level flight, as Lawrence had demonstrated [during the flight of 1914]; the automatic steering gyro would hold the airplane on pre-set course; an altitude barometer would activate controls to level the airplane after its initial climb and to maintain elevation; and a simple engine revolution counter would cut off power and dive the aerial torpedo at its target after a predetermined distance." Despite a successful test run in March 1918, further tests were less successful, and the project was gradually abandoned. Nevertheless, Hughes wrote, "The aerial-torpedo project was a milestone in the history of automatic feedback controls."

Sperry died in Brooklyn, New York, on June 16, 1930. Zula Goodman, his wife since 1887, had died a few months before. Upon Sperry's death, Secretary of the Navy Charles Francis Adams said, as quoted in the *New York Times* (June 16, 1930), "It is safe to say that no one American has contributed so much to our naval technical progress." The U.S.S. *Sperry* was named in his honor. During his life Sperry received numerous awards for his inventions, including two Franklin Institute medals (1914 and 1929), two Collier Trophies (1915 and 1916), the grand prize at the 1915 Panama Exposition, the Holley Medal (1927), the John Fritz Medal (1927), and the Albert Gary Medal (1929). Sperry received two decorations from Nicholas II, the last czar of Russia, and two decorations from the Emperor of Japan—the Order of the Rising Sun and the Order of the Sacred Treasure. He was awarded honorary degrees from Northwestern University, in Chicago, Illinois, and Lehigh University, in Bethlehem, Pennsylvania.

Sperry was a founder and charter member of the American Institute of Electrical Engineers and of the American Electro-Chemical Society. He was a member of the American Association for the Advancement of Science, the American Physical Society, the American Society of Mechanical Engineers, and the Society of Naval Architects and Marine Engineers, among others.—A. I. C.

Suggested Reading: *New York Times* June 16, 1930, June 17, 1930; Hughes, Thomas P. *American Genesis: A Century of Invention and Technological Enthusiasm, 1870–1970*, 1989

Stanhope, Charles, third earl of Stanhope

Aug. 3, 1753–Dec. 15, 1816 Inventor of the Stanhope Demonstrator

The British statesman and scientist Charles, third earl of Stanhope, is best remembered for his invention of the Stanhope Demonstrator, the first real logic machine. Known as Lord Mahon until he inherited the earldom, in 1786, Stanhope was an avid experimenter, as well as a colorful and active political figure. In addition to the Demonstrator, he invented a hand-operated printing press—the first to be made entirely of iron—that contributed to the development of high-speed presses in the 19th century. He developed a process of stereotyping—a process by which a whole page of type is cast in a single mold—that was acquired by the Clarendon Press, in Oxford, in 1805. He fashioned a powerful microscope lens that bears his name and invented a monochord for tuning musical instruments. He also patented steam vessels, in 1790 and 1807, that were adopted by the Admiralty.

Charles, third earl of Stanhope, was born on August 3, 1753 in London, England. The eldest surviving son of Philip, second earl of Stanhope, he was educated at Eton College, a boys' school in Eton, England. He completed his education in Geneva, where his parents moved when he was 10. At 19 he was elected to the Royal Society, a prestigious scientific academy. In 1774 he married Lady Hester Pitt, sister of William Pitt, the Younger, a controversial prime minister of England during the late 18th and early 19th centuries. Stanhope developed two calculating machines, in 1775 and 1777, that could multiply and divide through repeated additions and subtractions. Although similar machines had existed previously, Stanhope's calculators were more solidly constructed. His most significant contribution to computing was what he called the Demonstrator, a device capable of solving logical problems. The Stanhope Demonstrator could solve both traditional and numerical syllogisms, as well as problems of probability. It was a small mahogany box with a brass plate mounted on one face, in the center of which was a small window. A panel of gray wood could be inserted from the left side to cover some or all of the window; a second panel, of transparent red glass, could be inserted from the right side of the box to cover some or all of the window, and slide over the gray panel in the case of overlap. The system of logic Stanhope used in designing his Demonstrator relies on the assumption that any proposition could be interpreted as a statement of identity; when the two panels overlap in the window, an identity is established. To solve a syllogism, the box would take two propositions, or premises, for example "all men are mortal," and "Socrates is mortal." The problem for the logic machine to solve would be whether or not it is possible, based on these premises, to conclude that Socrates is a man. The window, in this case, would represent all mortals. The first premise, "all men are mortal," indicates that the group of "all men" is equal to a portion of the group of all mortal things (since not all mortals are men). The gray panel, representing "all men," is inserted to partially cover the window (to leave room for things that are mortal, but not men). The red panel, inserted on the other side, represents Socrates. Socrates is a mortal, but not all mortals are Socrates, so this panel also covers only a portion of the window. The two panels would therefore not overlap. This means that an identity has not been established, or, in other words, it can not be said for certain that Socrates is a man. Stanhope never published his speculations on logic or any details about the workings of the machine. He planned to do so, and printed, on his own press, early chapters of an unfinished work titled *The Science of Reasoning Clearly Explained Upon New Principles*. He was protective of his invention, and feared that an imitation might appear before his own work could be published. After his death, the Demonstrator lingered in obscurity for over 60 years, until Reverend Robert Harley discovered the device, along with some of Stanhope's notes. Harley studied the notes and wrote an article, "The Stanhope Demonstrator," which appeared in April 1879 in the British journal *Mind*. During his lifetime, Stanhope was better known for his radical political opinions than his inventions. He was a member of the House of Commons, from 1780 to 1786, and then succeeded to the House of Lords. A champion of democratic ideals, he vociferously opposed the war with the American colonies. He became chairman of the Revolution Society (founded in 1788), which sought to make Parliament more democratic— measures also advocated by his brother-in-law,

William Pitt. Stanhope later broke with Pitt over the French Revolution. Calling himself "Citizen Stanhope," he advocated friendship with the French Republic and opposed the British government's war with Revolutionary France. His audacious proposals for reform were nearly always overwhelmingly defeated. As a result, he became known as the "minority of one," and was caricatured in political cartoons of the day. He opposed the suspension of the Habeas Corpus Act, the union with Ireland, and the slave trade in British overseas possessions. He published his opinions on various subjects, including *Considerations on the Means of Preventing Fraudulent Practices on the Gold Coin* (1775), *On the Principles of Electricity, Containing Devices New Theories and Experiments, together with an Analysis of the Superior Advantage of High and Pointed Conductors* (1779), and *A Letter to Burke, Containing a Short Answer to His Late Speech on the French Revolution* (1790). He died in Chevening, Kent, on December 15, 1816.—A. I. C.

Suggested Reading: Gardner, Martin. *Logic Machines and Diagrams*, 1958; Goldstine, Herman H. *The Computer: from Pascal to von Neumann*, 1972

Steinmetz, Charles Proteus

Apr. 9, 1865–Oct. 26, 1923 Electrical engineer; inventor

Charles Proteus Steinmetz was one of the most prominent electrical engineers of the early 20th century. John M. Staudenmaier, in the *American Historical Review* (December 1993), called him an "engineer's engineer" who came to "rival [Thomas] Edison's mythic importance in the early 1920s." Standing about four feet three inches, with a hunchback and an enlarged head, he never let his physical limitations hinder his success. The prolific scientist wrote 14 books and about 260 articles and was issued more than 200 patents. His work on the mathematics of alternating current (AC) greatly simplified the design and calculation of AC circuits and machines for all subsequent electrical engineers, as did his formula for calculating hysteresis loss—the loss of efficiency in an electric device due to alternating magnetism.

Carl August Rudolph Steinmetz—who later Americanized his first name and added Proteus, a college nickname— was born in Breslau, Germany, on April 9, 1865. His paternal grandmother raised him after his mother died when he was still a young boy. Steinmetz was initially a poor student; at the age of eight he had trouble mastering his multiplication tables. Two years later he had worked his way to the head of his class, and in 1882 he was the only student to graduate with honors from St. John's Gymnasium, where he studied

Latin, Greek, Hebrew, French, Polish, chemistry, philosophy, and mathematics.

Steinmetz identified as a socialist for most of his life, but some reports say that he joined the socialist club at the University of Breslau because of the rollicking nature of its parties. He qualified to receive his doctorate in philosophy from the university, in 1888, but he left the country before accepting his degree because he feared his socialist student activities might get him in trouble with the German government. (Some sources theorize that unpaid tuition bills and tension with his father contributed to the move, as well.) For a year he attended the Swiss Polytechnic Institute, in Zurich, where he studied mechanical engineering, before he moved to the United States with a friend, Oscar Asmussen. (Asmussen's father bankrolled the trip.) On July 1, 1889 an immigration official in New York City hesitated to allow the diminutive, deformed, and penniless Steinmetz into the country, but Asmussen swore that his friend was a brilliant, wealthy scientist, and the official was swayed by the partial fabrication.

After being rejected by the Edison Machine Works, Steinmetz found a position in the drafting department at the Osterheld and Eichenmeyer Company, in Yonkers, New York. One of the first things he was asked to do was design an alternating-current motor. (The first AC motor had been invented by Nikola Tesla in the early 1880s.) Electrical engineers working with AC motors had been struggling with losses in efficiency caused by alternating magnetism, the phenomenon known as hysteresis. Steinmetz, in the course of designing his motor, mathematically derived the law of hysteresis, which was subsequently termed the Steinmetz law. In 1892 he delivered a paper on hysteresis before the Electrical Engineering Institute. His discovery allowed engineers everywhere to improve the efficiency of AC motors.

The Osterheld and Eichenmeyer Company was bought by General Electric (GE) the year Steinmetz delivered his paper, and Steinmetz joined the staff of the calculating department at a branch in Lynn, Massachusetts. Continuing his study of AC motors, Steinmetz soon discovered the mathematical principles underlying AC theory. Using complex numbers, he derived a method for calculating the mathematics of AC circuits and machines. The discovery greatly facilitated the design of all subsequent AC systems. Steinmetz presented his findings to the International Electrical Congress, in 1893. "He found himself in an unapproachable intellectual solitude, however," according to the GE Web site, "for practically no one could understand his theory or use his method. Through the publication of several textbooks, he ultimately brought about a clear understanding of his symbolic method, which is now universally used in alternating-current calculation."

Among Steinmetz's text books are *Theoretical Elements of Electrical Engineering* (1901) and *Theory and Calculation of Transient Phenomena and Oscillations* (1909), the latter of which dealt with surges in AC circuits and machines. Steinmetz considered the book to be one of his greatest accomplishments, and it is still acknowledged as a seminal work. In 1894 Steinmetz was transferred to GE's main branch in Schenectady, New York, where he continued to be one of the company's most valued and visible employees. (By 1900 he was GE's chief consulting engineer.) In 1902 he began his career in education, becoming the part-time head of the electrical engineering department at Union College, in Schenectady. He was a dedicated and well-loved professor who never put his own research interests above his students. "He always began with simple concepts and then proceeded step-by-step to the more difficult and involved ideas," one Union College colleague said of Steinmetz, as quoted in *Union College Magazine* (fall 1998, on-line). "Like many another brilliant man, he had trouble realizing that all of his students could not immediately see how logical the steps were. But unlike some other brilliant lecturers, he had great patience in answering students' questions at the breaks and at the end of his lectures, and even at his home in the evening. His willingness to help students with their work was almost a fault. This warmth toward students was reciprocated when members of Phi Gamma Delta fraternity invited him to become a brother."

Steinmetz's prominence in Schenectady and elsewhere stemmed not only from his work with GE and at Union, but also from his activity in the political arena. He was appointed by James Lunn, the city's socialist mayor, to the board of education in 1912 and was voted president of the board at his first meeting. As president Steinmetz helped raise $800,000 in bond issues to build three schools and enlarge three others. He was instrumental in instituting special classes for the learning disabled and new immigrants, and he made sure there were ample meals provided during the school day for undernourished pupils. Each Christmas every orphan in Schenectady received a gift paid for by Steinmetz. In 1913 he was elected president of the city's board of parks and city planning, and he succeeded in building several new parks.

Steinmetz was also known for his unceasing social activities. An enthusiastic cook, he regularly held large dinner parties, though he always asked his guests to do the dishes and even saved up dirty dishes for days beforehand. Guests delighted in his strange assortment of pets, including his owls, alligators, raccoon, crows, and gila monster. Poker was another favorite activity of Steinmetz's, and he formed a poker club called the Society for the Adjustment of Salaries. He grew exotic cacti in his home conservatory and was rarely seen without a panatela cigar.

Beginning in about 1907 Steinmetz began conducting extensive research on lightning. On stage before an audience, he produced a lightning bolt 50 feet long. In 1916 his generator came the closest to approximating the estimated actual power of a real lightning bolt. Newspapers referred to him as "The Thunderer" and a "Modern Jove." According to the *Union College Magazine*, his research on lightning "helped electrical corporations create efficient, cost-effective devices that harnessed electricity for industrial use."

Steinmetz continued to do research and patent new inventions in the field of electrical engineering until his death. In 1920 he started the Steinmetz Electric Motor Car Co., and in 1922 his company's first electric-powered truck was produced. (As a publicity stunt it was driven up a hill in Brooklyn.) The firm was dissolved after Steinmetz's death when a shareholder accused it of overstating the number of vehicles it had manufactured. On October 26, 1923, after doing a series of successful lectures on the West Coast, Steinmetz died of heart failure.

Steinmetz received an honorary master's degree from Harvard University, in Cambridge, Massachusetts, in 1911 and an honorary doctorate in philosophy from Union College in 1903. He was named president of the American Institute of Electrical Engineers in 1902 and also served as president of the Illuminating Engineer Society. In 1977 he was inducted into the U.S. Patent Office Inventor's Hall of Fame. A stamp bearing his image was minted in 1983.—P. G. H.

Suggested Reading: *American Historical Review* p1693 Dec. 1993; *Lighting Design and Application* p6+ Feb. 2000; *San Francisco Chronicle* p6 Sep. 7, 1986; *Union College Magazine* (on-line) fall 1998

Stibitz, George Robert

Apr. 30, 1904–Jan. 31, 1995 Creator of the complex-number calculator

George Stibitz is widely considered to be the father of the modern digital computer. One weekend while working for Bell Labs in New York, Stibitz took his work home and came up with the idea for a binary adder using telephone relays. His idea led to the development of the complex-number calculator, which made its official debut in 1939. Soon afterward, at a mathematics meeting, Stibitz made another remarkable breakthrough, when he demonstrated the operation of his new machine via remote control (at a distance of 250 miles), thereby introducing remote computing to the world. During World War II Stibitz worked for the National Defense Research Committee, where he came up with the programmable Model 2 computer, which provided a faster, more reliable way for gunners to shoot at enemy planes. This machine led to a series of other computers, each of which in turn solved increasingly complex problems. After the war Stibitz worked as a consultant in government and industry before taking a position with Dartmouth College, where, as a member of the faculty for more than 20 years, he made significant contributions to biomedical technology. He was professor emeritus when he died, in 1995, at the age of 90.

George Robert Stibitz was born on April 30, 1904 in York, Pennsylvania, and grew up in Dayton, Ohio. His father, George, was a clergyman with the German Reformed Church; he later taught ancient languages at a theological seminary. Young Stibitz attended the experimental Moraine Park School, in Dayton, which had a flexible curriculum and small classes that were designed to promote intellectual investigation and exploration. While at Moraine Stibitz developed a strong interest in mathematics and physics. He got the opportunity to pursue these areas more fully at Denison University, in Granville, Ohio, which he attended on a full scholarship. At Denison, where he majored in mathematics, Stibitz discovered a love for English language and literature; this interest became a lifelong passion. He graduated from Denison in 1926, with an A.B. degree, and then attended Union College, in Schenectady, New York, where he received an M.S. degree in physics, in 1927.

After completing his master's, Stibitz took a position with General Electric (GE). Working in a farmhouse deep in the country, he studied the propagation of radio waves. In an example of his inventiveness, he and his co-worker created a remote-control system that enabled them to warm up their workplace before they arrived on cold mornings. After working for GE for a year, Stibitz enrolled in the doctoral program in physics at Cornell University, in Ithaca, New York. He received a Ph.D. from Cornell in 1930.

Stibitz next accepted a job as a mathematical engineer at Bell Telephone Laboratories in New York City. In one of his projects he investigated the design of telephone relays, which are metal devices that click open and shut and control electrical circuits. Stibitz noticed a similarity between the on/off operation of the relays and the binary-number system, which he had learned about in college. He realized that the relays could be used to represent the mathematical operations of addition and subtraction and thus multiplication and division as well.

Stibitz soon got the idea of building a binary adder, based on relays, that could function like a desk calculator. He began to experiment, bringing home relays from the scrap pile at work and spreading out the parts on his kitchen table. One weekend in November 1937, Stibitz cut strips from a tin tobacco can and nailed them to a piece of wood, thereby creating a primitive on/off switch. He fastened two relays to the wood and wired them together, to form a circuit. Then he added two dry-cell batteries and a few flashlight bulbs, which served as an output device. This invention, according to an on-line obituary of Stibitz produced for the Computer History Association of California, "could add two bits and display the result." According to an on-line biography of Stibitz, it was "the prototype binary adder circuit—an electromechanical circuit that controlled binary addition." "It was just fun seeing what could be done with very simple things," Stibitz later said. His wife named the new invention the "K-model," the *K* referring to their kitchen.

When Stibitz showed the device to his fellow workers at Bell Labs, most of them were more amused than impressed. They laughed at his suggestion that an entire calculator could be built using such equipment. "Unfortunately, there were no fireworks, no champagne," Stibitz later remarked. But workers at Bell Labs routinely had to perform long, complicated calculations that involved complex numbers (that is, numbers in the form x + yi, where x and y are real numbers and i is the square root of minus 1), and Thorton Fry, head of the mathematical section at the laboratory, decided that Stibitz's line of investigation was worth pursuing. Stibitz then began to design binary circuits for complex-number calculations. Samuel I. Williams, a Bell Labs engineer, assisted him. Their efforts to build the calculator got underway in September 1938, and by the spring of 1939, Stibitz and Williams had completed the design. Soon afterward mechanical engineers began assembling what would become the Bell Telephone Laboratories Model I complex calculator.

The engineers decided on a 10-key board setup, which was simple to use but, compared to Stibitz's original design, required more memory and was therefore much more expensive. The board also required extra keys for mathematical operations as well as keys for positive and negative values of the imaginary number I. In a signal innovation, Stibitz created a mixed binary-decimal system that enabled the calculator to convert the decimal numbers being input by a human operator into the one-and-zero binary notation with which the machine executed its computations. On January 8, 1940 the complex-number calculator became fully operational—that is, capable of adding, subtracting, multiplying, and dividing complex numbers. Containing 450 standard telephone relays and 10 crossbar switches, among other components, the calculator could find the quotient of two eight-place complex numbers in about 30 seconds (about 100 times faster than a human operating a mechanical desk calculator). For Stibitz, seeing his machine perform was, in his words, a "spine-tingling experience."

Moreover, the calculator could aid not merely a single operator, but operators at different locations. At Bell Labs' main office, in Manhattan, Stibitz and others set up three operating stations, each with a standard teletype. The operator at any of the stations would type in an arithmetical problem, which would be relayed to the calculator; moments later, the answer would print out on the same teletype machine. The calculator could handle only one problem at a time; a mechanism in the system alerted an operator as to the availability of the calculator, much as a busy signal does on a phone line.

On September 11, 1940 Stibitz demonstrated the effectiveness of his calculator at a meeting of the American Mathematical Society in Dartmouth, New Hampshire, which was attended by such renowned mathematicians as Norbert Wiener and John Mauchly. Using a teletype machine at the site, Stibitz sent a problem to the complex-number calculator in New York, 250 miles away. In what is recognized as the first instance of remote-access computing—and, as it is also referred to, remote job entry—the answer arrived within seconds.

That same year, with the approval of Bell Labs, Stibitz began developing plans for a general-purpose automatic computational device. He worked on circuit designs that provided for interchangeable taped programs and also on an assembly language and an error-detection representation code. But after Bell Labs' upper managers saw the bill for the Model I—$20,000 (almost $235,000 in 1999 dollars)—they decided that the company would not build more computers. The federal government, however, felt a need for automatic computing machines, because of the involvement of the United States in World War II, and the National Defense Research Committee (NDRC) asked Stibitz to help develop such machines. Stibitz took a leave of absence from Bell Labs and went to work for the NDRC. He served as a technical aide in the division that dealt with antiaircraft gun directors (AA directors).

AA directors are analog devices that help aim guns at enemy aircraft. The devices do their job by predicting the flight path of a moving enemy plane. When Stibitz arrived at the NDRC, the AA directors worked effectively only at close range; new technology was needed for long-range firing. Duncan Stewart, an NDRC employee and a good friend of Stibitz's, came up with an analog device, called the "dynamic tester," to test new AA directors. However, this machine was expensive to manufacture and operated too slowly. Stibitz conceived of another design, the punch-tape dynamic tester, which was both fast (it could take 10 readings of the tape per second) and accurate (it could follow a target to within a few thousandths of a second, which is comparable, in the case of a marksman, to targeting the fuzz of a falling peach at 50 paces). According to Stibitz, the tester's speed and accuracy were attributable to its ability to switch "from mechanical to electrical data storage, from decimal to binary representations, and from continuous to digital data handling."

To ensure reliability, Stibitz turned once again to telephone relays. He and his fellow NDRC workers placed relays inside another invention— the relay interpolator computer, called the Model 2 computer, to perform what mathematicians call iterative operations, in which small, simple operations are performed repeatedly until a final answer is obtained. The Model 2, which possessed 493 relays and stood five feet tall and four feet wide, was installed at Bell Labs in late 1943. The relays, which Stibitz once dubbed "awesomely reliable," were so steadfast that the computer continued to work in that same room, all day, every day, for years, requiring "human attention for only a few hours a week, when someone put problems into it." The Model 2 computer was revolutionary not only because it was one of the first programmable computers, but also because it contained features that were unique at the time (and would later become standard parts of microcomputers). One such feature was an error-detection system; the system would shut down the computer after detecting an error.

Stibitz later helped create the Model 3 computer, which was a larger and more versatile machine than the Model 2, with more relays and the ability to "hunt" for information that was requested. The Model 3 could simultaneously solve a problem and search for information, and it also possessed the ability to carry out multiplication problems directly, without having to break down the numbers into strings of addition, as the Model 2 did when it performed iterative operations.

After the Model 3, Stibitz assisted with the building of the Model 4 computer, which had the added feature of being able to solve some trigonometric functions. This machine was succeeded by the Model 5, an even larger computer, which could handle extremely complex problems with a high degree of reliability. The Model 5 was the first computer to implement floating-point arithmetic. Two Model 5s were built, one for the National Advisory Committee for Aeronautics (NACA) and one for U.S. Army ballisticians at the Aberdeen Proving Grounds, in Maryland. Model 6, which dealt with numbers containing up to 10 digits rather than seven, was completed in 1946 along with the

Model 5s, the last in the series of relay computers built by Bell Labs. (Stibitz was not involved in the design of the 5s.)

At the end of the war, Stibitz did not return to Bell Labs. Instead, he established himself as a private consultant to government and industry. One of his projects, for Barber-Coleman, the president of which was Duncan Stewart, was the design of a desk-size electronic digital computer for use in business. Stibitz helped make two working prototypes for a Barber-Coleman computer, but the project was eventually abandoned for financial reasons. In 1964 Stibitz accepted a position as a research associate in the Department of Physiology at Dartmouth Medical School, in Hanover, New Hampshire. For the next 20 years, he worked on various biophysical problems. His achievements include the creation of a computer display of brain-cell anatomy and a mathematical model of capillary-transport phenomena. He often used computers to teach students about complex medical problems, such as the tracking of oxygen movement in the lungs. Although Stibitz officially retired from the university in 1974, he remained an active consultant to the medical school until the mid 1980s.

On January 31, 1995, after a year of failing health, Stibitz died of natural causes at his home in Hanover. He had been married since 1930 to Dorothea Lamson Stibitz, with whom he had two daughters, Mary Stibitz Pacifici and Martha Stibitz Banerjee. In addition to the devices he created for Bell Labs, Stibitz was awarded 38 patents, for inventions ranging from computer systems to a stereophonic organ. He won the 1965 Harry Goode Award from the American Federation of Information Processing Societies, and the 1982 Computer Pioneer Award from the Institute of Electrical and Electronics Engineers. He received honorary degrees from Denison University, Keene State College, and Dartmouth College.—D. B.

Suggested Reading: National Inventors Hall of Fame Web site; *New York Times* B p11 Feb. 2, 1995; *San Francisco Chronicle* D p5 Feb. 3, 1995; *St. Louis Post-Dispatch* Feb. 3, 1995; Cortada, James W. *The Historical Dictionary of Data Processing*, 1987; *Dictionary of Scientific Biography* vol. 13, 1976; Williams, Michael R. *A History of Computing Technology*, 1985

Strachey, Christopher

Nov. 16, 1916–May 18, 1975 Computer designer and programmer

In 1952 Christopher Strachey abandoned a successful career in teaching to work in Great Britain's fledgling computer industry. With no formal training, he learned how computers operated and how to write programs for them. As a technical officer with the National Research and Development Corporation (NRDC) computer unit and later as a freelance consultant during the 1950s and 1960s, Strachey made important contributions to the design of several computers, including the Elliott 402, Elliott 502, the Pegasus, and the Emidec 2400. In a research paper, Strachey explained how a time-sharing system could allow a single computer to run several programs at the same time, accommodating the growing number of programmers. In 1965 he established the Programming Research Group (PRG) at Oxford University, which expanded into one of the most prominent computer laboratories in the world. Strachey's greatest contribution is pioneering denotational semantics, a computer-science field that explains the meanings of computer programs and languages in mathematical terms. Christopher Strachey died tragically, in 1975, at the height of his professional career.

Christopher Strachey was born into a prominent family on November 16, 1916 in London, England. His father, Oliver, worked as a cryptographer for the War Office Code and Cypher School. Strachey's mother, Ray, was a writer, broadcaster, feminist activist, and one-time parliamentary secretary to Lady Nancy Astor, the first woman elected to the House of Commons. "Christopher was a complete Strachey, all sensitivity and intellect, who was heard explaining to his nurse at the age of five what a gradient of one in four meant, and who used to insist in playing imaginary three-dimensional noughts and crosses [tic tac toe] in his mother's bed in the early morning," his sister, Barbara, recalled in 1980, as quoted by Martin Campbell-Kelly in his article for the *Annals of the History of Computing* (January 1985). Shortly after Christopher's birth the family moved to Gordon Square, in the Bloomsbury district of the city. Their neighbors included some of the most celebrated intellectuals of the day: Clive and Vanessa Bell, Virginia Woolf, and John Maynard Keynes, among them. Christopher and Barbara grew up in an environment in which music and literature were highly prized. (Christopher also inherited the family's well-known passion for puzzles and games.)

After failing to distinguish himself academically at Gresham's School, in Norfolk, in 1935 Strachey enrolled at King's College, in Cambridge. He neglected his studies and soon switched his major from mathematics to physics, which he considered less demanding. He led an active social life, however, joining many of the school's intellectual societies. Strachey met Alan Turing (1912–1954), a brilliant young mathematician and junior research fellow at King's College, who later made substantial contributions to the development of computers and the field of artificial intelligence (AI). In his third year, Strachey suffered a mental breakdown and took a leave of absence from the college. His sister speculated that the breakdown may have been caused by Christopher's struggles with his homosexuality. After he recovered, Strachey resumed his studies. In 1938 he graduated from King's College with a mediocre "lower second" in the Natural Science Tripos. The poor results frustrated his hopes of obtaining a research fellowship.

Strachey then went to work as a physicist with Standard Telephones and Cables Limited (STC). In August 1939, one month before World War II broke out in Europe, he was assigned to STC's Valve Development Laboratories, in London. (In Britain, a valve is the equivalent of a vacuum tube.) Several months later German air raids forced the facility to move to Somerset. Strachey worked with a research team led by J. H. Fremlin that investigated the theoretical design of centimetric radar waves. "Strachey's particular contribution was the derivation of analytical formulas for valve parameters and their experimental verification," Campbell-Kelly explained. "His mathematical work involved the integration of differential equations, some of which proved particularly intractable, and so, with a colleague, P. J. Wallis, he began to obtain numerical solutions using a differential analyzer." According to Campbell-Kelly, Strachey later regarded his use of a differential analyzer, an early analog computer, as the turning point in his career. He began reading literature on computing and assisted his colleagues with computing tasks. In July 1944 Strachey was transferred to STC's Radio Division, in London. The work, which involved electrical and mechanical design, bored him, however.

In October 1945 Strachey left the STC for a teaching position at St. Edmund's, a school in Canterbury. In addition to teaching physics and mathematics, he revived many of the school's clubs and societies, which had been disrupted by the war. In 1949 Strachey began teaching at the Harrow School, one of London's most prestigious public schools.

In January 1951 Strachey visited the National Physical Laboratory (NPL), which was then building the Pilot Ace computer. Strachey spent a whole day learning everything he could about the machine, and, after returning to Harrow, he began writing a program that allowed the computer to play checkers. Several months later he learned that Manchester University had installed a Ferranti Mark I computer. Strachey obtained a copy of the computer's manual, which was written by his old acquaintance at King's College, Alan Turing. (Turing was then serving as the assistant director of the Manchester University Computing Machine Laboratory.) In June 1951 Strachey visited the university to see the computer. He talked with Turing, who was impressed with his ideas for a checkers program. Turing suggested that Strachey might find it interesting to write a complex "trace program" that would make the computer simulate itself. Strachey took up the challenge, and his program, which contained over 1,000 instructions, was at the time the longest one ever written for the Mark I. The program ran on his first attempt. As Campbell-Kelly

observed, 'This was a considerable tour-de-force: an unknown amateur, he had got the longest program yet written for the machine working in a single session; his reputation was established overnight."

In November 1951 Lord Halsbury, the managing director of the NRDC, offered Strachey a job as a technical officer in its computer section. After finishing the academic year at Harrow, he began working at the NRDC on June 3, 1952. With little to do in his first few months, Strachey continued working on the programs he had begun for the Mark I—including one that produced love letters by randomly selecting words and phrases. In September Strachey traveled to Canada to attend the second annual Association for Computing Machinery (ACM) National Conference at the University of Toronto. There he delivered a paper, "Logical or Non-Mathematical Programmes," which described his checkers program and illustrated a typical game with a set of slides. The conference coincided with the installation of the Ferranti Mark I, which was called FERUT, at the university's Computation Centre. Strachey remained in Canada for several months. The NRDC assigned him to the University of Toronto to assist with programming the calculations for the St. Lawrence Seaway project. (The seaway, which links the Atlantic Ocean with the Great Lakes, is one of the world's most complex inland navigation systems. Currently, more than 50-million tons of freight are transported annually through the its canals and locks.) Strachey also visited several research laboratories in the United States, studying the instruction sets of different computers.

After returning to Great Britain, in 1953, the NRDC asked Strachey to evaluate the prototype of the Elliott 401 computer at Cambridge University. Strachey, who was assisted by Donald B. Gillies, produced a report that resulted in the complete redesign of the computer's order code and multiplier. Their recommendations were later included with the construction of the Elliott 402 computer. As a consultant for the NDRC, Strachey also influenced the logical design of the Ferranti company's Pegasus computer and helped test the prototype. (Campbell-Kelly described the Pegasus as "the most elegant British machine of its generation.") During the late 1950s and early 1960s, 36 Pegasus machines were sold.

Nationally recognized as an expert, Strachey was often invited to deliver lectures and speeches on computer-related subjects. Once, during a meeting of employees in NDRC's computer section, Strachey complained that he was unable to find an appropriate technical journal in which to publish one of his research papers. This inspired Lord Halsbury to organize the British Computer Society (BCS), which began publishing the *Computer Journal* in 1957. Strachey served on several of the BCS's technical committees, but declined to take on any administrative or public roles with the organization.

Despite the many technological advances that were being made in both Great Britain and the United States, the only available computers were large, expensive mainframe systems, which only universities, research laboratories, corporations, and government agencies could afford. Strachey recognized that the relatively small number of existing computers, running only one program at a time, could not accommodate the needs of the growing number of programmers. In a paper, "Time Sharing in Large Fast Computers," he presented to the United Nations Educational Scientific and Cultural Organization (UNESCO) Conference on Information Processing in Paris, France in July 1959, Strachey outlined the details of an early time-sharing system that would allow a single computer to run multiple programs at the same time and accommodate more users. He envisioned a large computer equipped with six consoles or terminals with input/output devices and hand switches. In 1961 Fernando Corbató, a professor at the Massachusetts Institute of Technology (MIT), in Cambridge, successfully developed the Compatible Time-Sharing System (CTSS). Corbató generously (and honestly) credited Strachey with originating the concept of time-sharing. "'Time Sharing in Large Fast Computers' was probably the first paper to discuss time-sharing and multi-programming as we know them," Strachey reflected in 1971, as quoted by Campbell-Kelly. "It is a matter of history that the time-sharing idea became extremely fashionable in the middle [1960s] and dominated much of the work on computing at the time. When I wrote the paper in 1959 I, in common with everyone else, had no idea of the difficulties which would arise in writing the software to control either the time-sharing or multi-programming. If I had I should not have been so enthusiastic about them."

In 1959 Strachey left the NRDC to work as a private computer consultant, a position that was just beginning to appear in England. He commanded large fees for working on computer design, programming, and applications for such clients as Ferranti, EMI, and the NRDC.

During the early 1960s, Strachey's outspoken views attracted public attention. Although the ALGOL computer language enjoyed a loyal and devoted following, Strachey considered it deficient. In 1961 Strachey and Maurice Wilkes co-wrote a controversial paper that suggested ways to improve ALGOL, which displeased many of the language's devotees. Strachey additionally alleged that Great Britain had fallen far behind the United States in the field of programming. He attributed this trend to insufficient spending on university research and to his belief that British computers were smaller than their American counterparts and could not implement new applications based on revolutionary new languages such as LISP, which had been developed by John McCarthy.

In June 1962 Strachey accepted an invitation from Maurice Wilkes to participate in the effort to create a new language and compiler for the Titan computer at Cambridge University's Mathematical Laboratory. In the fall the project became a joint effort with London University's Computing Unit, which wanted the language to run on its Atlas computer. In 1963 Strachey and his colleagues collaborated on a paper published in the *Computer Journal* that described the broad specifications of the Combined Programming Language (CPL). Development of the CPL, however, was slowed after Strachey became preoccupied with describing the language's semantics. Strachey sketched out some preliminary ideas in his paper, "Toward a Formal Semantics," which he submitted to the International Federation for Information Processing (IFIP) Technical Committee, which met in Vienna, Austria, in 1965. A year later, Strachey's paper was published in the book, *Formal Language Description*.

Another result of Strachey's work on the CPL was his General Purpose Macrogenerator (GPM), a string processor he described in an article for the *Computing Journal* (October 1965). Although Strachey subsequently dismissed it as a waste of time, computer researchers in many countries found the GPM a useful programming tool.

By 1963 Strachey was ready to leave the CPL project and head up a university research group in programming theory. He applied for the chairmanship of the Computing Science department at Imperial College, on the University of London campus, but was turned down.

In July 1965 the Department of Scientific and Industrial Research (DSIR) provided funding to establish the Programming Research Group (PRG) at Oxford University. After a short stint as a visiting lecturer at MIT, in April 1966 Strachey began working at Oxford University. He resumed work on CPL, collaborating with David Park, who left Cambridge to join the PRG to edit the final version of the language's reference manual. About 150 copies of the reference manual were privately circulated as the "CPL Working Papers." Although the CPL project was never completed and was abandoned in 1967, the work provided Strachey and his colleagues with several insights into the design of programming languages. Strachey and his research assistant, Joseph E. Stoy, developed a successful single-user operating system, OS1, for the CTL Model 1 minicomputer, which the PRG acquired in 1969. (Strachey and Stoy upgraded the operating system several times.)

For the remainder of his career, Strachey devoted his attention to formal semantics, an area that fascinated him. In 1969 Strachey met Dana Scott, a mathematical logician on leave from Princeton University in New Jersey. According to Campbell-Kelly, Scott provided a sound mathematical basis for Strachey's theories. The collaboration with Scott led Strachey to conclude that the ideas he previously articulated in his paper "Toward a Formal Semantics" lacked a solid mathematical foundation. In 1971 Strachey and Scott discussed their findings in a paper titled "Toward a Mathematical Semantics for Computer Languages," which they presented to the Symposium on Computers and Automation at the Polytechnic Institute of Brooklyn in New York City. Strachey and Scott thus gave birth to denotational semantics, a new field in computer science.

By the 1970s Christopher Strachey was enjoying significant recognition in Great Britain as a computer expert. In 1971 Oxford University appointed him a personal chair. The same year he was named a Distinguished Fellow of the British Computing Society. Strachey, however, was not content with those laurels and sought admission to the Royal Society, which is considered one of the most prestigious honors for scientists in Great Britain. In 1972 Lord Halsbury nominated him for membership, but his candidacy was rejected because he hadn't published enough and the value of his most recent work was still being proven at the time.

To enhance his professional standing, Strachey competed for Cambridge University's Adams Prize, an honor that established the reputations of many British mathematicians. Strachey and Robert E. Milne, a research student at Cambridge, collaborated on a paper, "A Theory of Programming Language Semantics," which exceeded 500 pages. Although some sections of the paper were not completed, the authors managed to submit the essay for consideration by the December 1974 deadline. As they waited for the results during the spring months in 1975, Strachey and Milne began revising their essay for publication in book form.

The work on the original essay exhausted Strachey and impacted his health. Although he took several weeks off to rest, he became stricken with jaundice after going back to work. On May 18, 1975, several weeks before the winner of the Adams Prize was announced, Christopher Strachey died from infectious hepatitis. (The winners were D. Barton and J. P. Fitch for a treatise on algebraic manipulation programs.)

In 1976, with Strachey listed as a joint author, Milne published *A Theory of Programming Language Semantics* in two volumes. A year later, Joseph E. Stoy, Strachey's protégé, published *Denotational Semantics: The Scott-Strachey Approach to Programming Language Theory*. Today, the PRG is internationally recognized as one of the most prominent computer research laboratories in the world. The National Cataloguing Unit for the Archives of Contemporary Scientists (NCUACS) at the University of Bath in the United Kingdom presently holds Christopher Strachey's papers.—D. C.

Suggested Reading: *Annals of the History of Computing* p19+ Jan. 1985, with photos; Milne, Robert E. *A Theory of Programming Language Semantics*, 1976; Stoy, Joseph E. *Denotational Semantics*, 1977

Svoboda, Antonin

Oct. 14, 1907–May 18, 1980 Computer scientist; engineer; inventor

A computer pioneer in Eastern Europe, Antonin Svoboda helped usher in a technological revolution in his home country of Czechoslovakia during the late 1950s. Although most historical accounts of early computer exploration focus on the American and Western contributors to the field, Svoboda holds a distinct place in computer history: After spending time in Western Europe and the United States for portions of his career, he returned to Czechoslovakia after World War II determined to elevate his nation's role in the computer industry. Svoboda first turned his sights to developing punch card equipment for a well-known Prague-based manufacturer, the National Enterprise Aritma; he constructed several keypunch and punch card devices, the most recognized of which went on to become the centerpiece of Aritma's system in the 1950s. In 1950 he started his own laboratory, which later developed into the Research Institute of Mathematical Machines and, in association with the Czechoslovakian Academy of Sciences, grew to become the center for computer science research in Eastern Europe. During his tenure there, Svoboda led his research team in creating an innovative computer known as the Samočinný Počítač (SAPO), a relay machine with a magnetic drum that became the country's first electronic computer. Svoboda and his staff later made improvements upon the SAPO device in a second electronic computer, the EPOS, which utilized vacuum-tube technology, germanium diode logic units, delay-line registers, and ferrite core memory. In the early 1960s, as the political situation within Czechoslovakia was becoming increasingly anti-Western, Svoboda fled the country for the U.S., where he joined the faculty at the University of California, Los Angeles (UCLA). Svoboda, who died on May 18, 1980, was honored posthumously with the 1996 Institute of Electrical and Electronics Engineers (IEEE) Computer Society Computer Pioneer Award.

Antonin Svoboda was born on October 14, 1907 in Prague, Czechoslovakia, where his father worked as a professor of Czech language and literature. He attended the Czech Institute of Technology and completed his undergraduate studies in electrical engineering in 1931. After submitting his doctoral thesis on the application of tensor calculus to electric power distribution, Svoboda received a Doctor of Technical Sciences degree, equivalent to a Ph.D., from the Institute of Technology in 1936; he also did graduate work in physics at Prague's Charles University, where he met his wife, Miluna Joanelli. (They married in 1936.) During this period, he participated in a wide array of extracurricular activities. A successful musician, he was the pianist for the Prague Wind Quartet and also performed occasionally as a percussionist with the Czech Philharmonic Orchestra. In addition, he published a book, *New Theory of Bridge,* in which he outlined a scientific approach to bidding in the card game of bridge.

While Svoboda intended to pursue a career in scientific research and teaching, his plans were abruptly altered when he was drafted into the Czech army in the fall of 1936; he spent much of his time in the service working on antiaircraft fire-control devices. (Czechoslovakia at the time was becoming increasingly threatened by its neighbor, Germany, then ruled by the Nazis.) After completing his military service in 1938, Svoboda returned to the Institute of Technology as an assistant professor of mathematics. However, he did not remain at his alma mater for long: In March 1939, when the German army began its occupation of Czechoslovakia, many former officials in the Czechoslovak Ministry of Defense encouraged Svoboda to flee the country for Paris, France, for what was officially declared a prolonged scientific visit. He brought Czechoslovakia's most advanced fire-control equipment with him to France, and he promptly shared the technology with the Allied forces. In Paris Svoboda also constructed his first analog computer, which was designed for use with the fire-control equipment. When Paris fell to the German army in June 1940, Svoboda set out for the United States, arriving in January 1941. There he continued his work developing anti-aircraft defenses and in 1943 joined the staff at the Massachusetts Institute of Technology's (MIT) Radiation Laboratory, in Cambridge, Massachusetts, which was then conducting secret research on military-related radar devices. During his tenure at MIT, Svoboda refined his own computational devices; he summarized his research in his 1946 book, *Computing Mechanisms and Linkages.* For his contributions to the war effort, the U.S. government honored Svoboda with the Naval Ordinance Development Award in 1948.

In 1946, following the end of World War II, Svoboda returned to his native Czechoslovakia with the hope of establishing a thriving computer industry there. His dream was for Czechoslovakia to develop expertise in computers, just as Switzerland was then known for its superiority in watchmaking. After having witnessed a multitude of computing projects in Western Europe and the U.S., he felt that digital computers were ultimately more useful than either analog or electromechanical calculators. To begin his research, Svoboda established a laboratory in Prague in which he could develop computer equipment. He also entered into a contractual agreement with a Prague-based manufacturer of keypunch and punch card equipment. (The company eventually became known as the na-

tionalized business National Enterprise Aritma.) Svoboda built several programmable devices for Aritma; his most valued project was a piece known as a "calculating punch," which was essentially a relay computer that employed card input and output and was programmed with the use of a plugboard. The piece became a fundamental component of Aritma's equipment and systems in the 1950s, and several hundred models were constructed.

In 1950 Svoboda joined the newly established Central Institute of Mathematics in Prague, where he founded a department of Mathematical Machines, which eventually became the Research Institute of Mathematical Machines associated with the Czechoslovakian Academy of Sciences. This laboratory quickly developed into Czechoslovakia's center of computer research, even offering a Ph.D. in computer science. The institute began producing an annual publication, *Information Processing Machines*, in 1952; it later grew into a well-known computer journal. By the time Svoboda departed the institute in 1964—after serving first as executive director, director of research, and finally as a member of the scientific board—the organization housed more than 900 employees or students, distinguishing it as one of the largest computer research facilities in all of Eastern Europe. Under Svoboda's direction, the group explored diverse research projects in areas such as numerical analysis, arithmetic codes and algorithms, switching theory, and cybernetics. Yet, its most important contribution to computer history was the construction of two major computational devices: SAPO and EPOS.

SAPO, built between 1950 and 1956, is recognized as the first large automatic digital computer constructed in Czechoslovakia. It was a classic relay computer supplied with a magnetic drum memory that made it similar to the Harvard Mark III—American computer pioneer Howard Hathaway Aiken's third computer version, completed in 1949—which ran from a stored program. While the Harvard Mark III provided the means for a program to receive data from an address stored in a register, Svoboda's SAPO offered even greater stored-program capabilities through its five-address instructions. In addition, it had a unique design feature of fault-tolerant characteristics, which ensured that the machine would not break down. For example, SAPO was equipped with three central processing units (CPUs) that worked simultaneously on each problem and compared the results for utmost accuracy. The units then "voted" on the correct solution, with the majority vote providing the final answer. This design concept remains common today.

Nevertheless, Svoboda's research team realized the shortcomings of a relay computer and from 1958 to 1963 set about developing a vacuum-tube–based machine, similar to those then being developed in the United States. The result, EPOS, was also equipped with germanium diode logics, delay-line registers, and ferrite core memory—all components that made the machine considerably more reliable than SAPO. (Yet, like SAPO, it was built with fault-tolerant capabilities.) EPOS also relied on transistor technology and was capable of managing multiple tasks at various stages of the computation. For example, the machine could concurrently handle printing the results from one problem while engaging in calculations on another. Finally, EPOS was designed to be more compact than SAPO and in fact resembled today's smaller computing machines, as compared to SAPO's wall-length, metal-box design.

In the early 1960s, the political atmosphere in Czechoslovakia was becoming increasingly suspicious of Western technologies. The Czech government began restricting Svoboda's appearances at international conferences. As research on his machines grew more difficult, he decided to leave Czechoslovakia for a second time—this time to settle permanently in the U.S. Together with his family and several friends, Svoboda arrived in the United States in 1965; the following year he joined the staff of UCLA, where he taught courses in logic design, computer architecture, and computer arithmetic. He became a full professor in 1968, the same year he received the IEEE Fellow Award for "his contributions in logic design, mechanical design,

and his fundamental work on residue class number system," as quoted in a 1980 In Memoriam press release from the University of California (on-line). In addition to teaching, Svoboda remained active in his research on logic design for computers. He published some of his later work in his second book, *Advanced Logical Circuit Design Techniques* (1979), written with his student Donnamaie E. White.

Antonin Svoboda retired from UCLA in 1977 as professor emeritus. After moving to Oregon to live with his son, Tomas Svoboda, a gifted composer and professor of music at Portland State University, Svoboda died at his home on May 18, 1980. On October 28, 1999, the 81st anniversary of Czechoslovakia's foundation in 1918, Svoboda was posthumously decorated by Czech President Vaclav Havel for his "excellent academic achievement," as reported by the CTK National News Wire (October 28, 1999).—K. D.

Suggested Reading: Goldstine, Herman H. *The Computer From Pascal to von Neumann*, 1972; Cortada, James W. *The Historical Dictionary of Data Processing; Biographies*, 1987; Aspray, William. *Computing Before Computers*, 1990; Lee, J. A. N., ed. *International Biographical Dictionary of Computer Pioneers*, 1995

Tanenbaum, Andrew S.

1944– Creator of the Minix operating system

Andrew S. Tanenbaum is best known for his pioneering work in the field of computer operating systems, particularly for his design of the Minix system, which greatly simplified and streamlined the popular Unix system, then unavailable for use with personal computers (PCs). Years later he was the principal designer for Amoeba, a distributed operating system for Sun, Vax, and other workstation computers, as well as the chief designer for the Amsterdam Compiler Kit, a compiler-producing system used on some 10 different types of machines to translate between high-level computer languages and machine code. In addition to his work on operating systems, Tanenbaum has written several popular computer books about computer networks, operating systems, and organization.

Andrew S. Tanenbaum was born in the New York City borough of the Bronx, in 1944. His paternal grandfather was born in Chorostkow, Poland (in present-day Ukraine), which was then under Hungarian control. He immigrated to the United States in 1914. Tanenbaum, in his early childhood, moved with his family to Westchester County. He remarked in an interview with *Leaders of the Information Age*, "When I was eight, the city of New York decided to build a freeway though the building I was living in, so my family had to move. We moved up north to Westchester County [White

Courtesy of Andy Tanenbaum

Plains]. I did fourth grade through high school there. I liked White Plains and was active in many activities at White Plains High School, including the math club, chess club, but especially the stage crew. I was also photographer for the school newspaper. I have always liked photography."

Tanenbaum's interest in electronics and computing began early in high school. (While in high school he entered a county science fair, submitting a hardware device that played tic-tac-toe.) His love of computers increased during his college years. "I went to college at MIT [Massachusetts Institute of Technology], where I stumbled on a [Digital Equipment Corporation] PDP-1 computer," he recalled for *Leaders*. "It was love at first sight. I taught myself to program it and spent thousands of hours playing with it during the next four years." He also worked at IBM one summer during college, but the company's corporate environment did not suit him. "One day I wore a shirt that wasn't the right shade of white," he explained on his Web site. "My coworkers informed me of my transgression and made suggestions for improving matters. In great detail. That's when I figured out that maybe the industrial experience was not for me."

After receiving a bachelor of science degree from MIT, in 1965, Tanenbaum earned his Ph.D. at the University of California at Berkeley, in 1971. In September 1971 he accepted a postdoctoral fellowship in Amsterdam, in the Netherlands, where he came into contact with a computer that helped set him on his ultimate career path. As he told *Leaders of the Information Age,* "Our department had just bought a PDP-11 computer, one of the successors of my beloved PDP-1. The operating system it came with was dreadful, so I decided to write my own [TSS-11]. Before it was finished, Unix came along, and it was clear Unix was far more developed, so the TSS-11 project was abandoned and I installed Unix on the PDP-11. I think we were one of the first two or three Unix sites in Europe."

Unix is a computer operating system developed in 1969 by Kenneth Thompson and Dennis Ritchie at Bell Laboratories. The system was originally designed to run on minicomputers (intermediate in size between mainframe and personal computers), but by 1980, when the Microsoft Corporation licensed Unix, the plan was to create a personal-computer version. Microsoft's personal-computer version, XENIX, never made a dent in the computer market. Neither did AT&T's Unix PC, introduced in 1985, which used model 68000 microchips and sold for $5,600. AT&T's machine failed in part because the company charged businesses thousands of dollars for the source code to Unix but gave the same code to schools and universities for free. After Unix finally became popular with business users (many of whom, like Tanenbaum, had learned the system in school), AT&T decided to prevent the Unix source code from being used in classrooms. Tanenbaum responded to this in 1987 by introducing a completely new Unix-style operating system, Minix, which resembled Unix but did not share any of its source code.

Tanenbaum explained his development of Minix to *Leaders of the Information Age*: "John Lions, a professor in Australia, wrote a book about Unix shortly after it appeared. Many professors all over the world used it to teach students. Unfortunately, AT&T, which owned Unix, didn't like this and forbid professors from teaching Unix. I decided to write a Unix clone so that I could teach. It took me about three years, but I succeeded. That was Minix. Within three months, an Internet newsgroup with 40,000 people was formed about Minix. Some of them contributed software and help relating to Minix. A lot of them wanted to add more and more features to Minix, but I wanted to keep it simple enough so my poor students could still understand it. After several years of my saying no, one of the Minix users, a Finnish student named Linus Torvalds got tired of all those 'No's' and decided to write a Minix clone using Minix as his development system. His system became Linux, which is now quite popular. But Minix is alive and well and used by many universities for teaching."

In the late 1980s Minix was hugely popular among students and computer afficionados, who found Tanenbaum's operating system to be more accessible and better-structured than Unix. The Minix system was also easier to teach. Perhaps most importantly, Minix, unlike Unix, could be used with PCs instead of just mainframes and minicomputers.

As advanced as Minix was, like most operating systems of the era it could only control the operations of a single processor. In the 1960s and '70s, large mainframes and minicomputers were shared by many users. The personal computers of the 1980s eliminated the need for sharing. At the start of the 1990s, Tanenbaum, along with other researchers, was searching for a way to create a distributed system, which would give individual PC users the ability to access the power of many computers at one time. Tanenbaum's answer was Amoeba. As he explained to *Leaders of the Information Age,* "Amoeba was a research project at the Vrije Universiteit where I work. What I wanted to do was connect dozens of computers over a local area network and have them act like a single computer. The user could issue a command and the system, Amoeba, would figure out how and where to execute it. Amoeba was one of the first distributed systems in the world. Unlike TSS-11, which was never finished, Amoeba was fully implemented and put into use. We wrote many articles for technical journals about it." Amoeba was used by the European Space Agency to control dozens of experiments aboard the Columbia space station.

In addition to his work on Minix and Amoeba, Tanenbaum was also the chief designer of the Amsterdam Compiler Kit, a system that created compilers for six different languages on 10 different types of computers. He has also been involved in a number of other recent projects. The Paramecium operating system, as he explained to *Leaders of the Information Age,* was "dreamed up by one of my graduate students, Leendert van Doorn. He wanted a tiny little operating system that would be so small that it would actually work all the time and never crash (unlike, say, Windows, which crashes quite a bit). He also put a lot of effort into security, so it would be very safe." Tanenbaum is currently working on the Globe Project, which, like Amoeba, is a distributed system. He told *Leaders of the Information Age*, "Amoeba was about connecting dozens of computers over a local area network. Globe is the next step. It is about taking billions of computers all over the world connected by the Internet and making them work together in a single integrated system. It is pretty advanced stuff, but we are making a lot of progress."

Tanenbaum has published several influential computer-related books. In 1981 he published *Computer Networks*, which covered the networking of PCs to mainframes. In a review of the second edition (published in 1989) for *InfoWorld* (February 6, 1989), Sharon Fisher wrote: "In general, this book is a great resource for anyone who wants to learn the theoretical basis behind networks today. It won't help a person figure out which OS/2 network operating system to buy or how to set up a network, but it will help that person learn how the network is put together and what principles all networks follow." (Additional editions of *Computer Networks* were published in 1996 and 2003.) In 1987 Tanenbaum published *Operating Systems: Design and Implementation*, which is considered to be one of the central texts for designing and building computer operating systems.

Andrew S. Tanenbaum is presently a professor of computer science at the Vrije Universiteit, in Amsterdam. He also serves as the dean of the Advanced School for Computing and Imaging, an inter-university graduate school that conducts research in the fields of distributed, imaging, and advanced parallel systems. Tanenbaum has received numerous awards and recognitions for his work: he is a fellow of the Institute of Electrical and Electronics Engineers (IEEE), a fellow of the Association for Computing Machinery (ACM), and a member of the Royal Netherlands Academy of Arts and Science. In 1994 he was the recipient of the ACM Karl V. Karlstrom Outstanding Educator Award; three years later he received the ACM/SIGCSE Award for outstanding contributions to computer-science education.

Tanenbaum continues to work on new computer programs. As he told *Leaders of the Information Age*, "In the past year I have become more and more concerned about security. Computers are unreliable and companies and the government can find out far too much about people. I am starting to work on making computer systems more secure." He is forthright about his approach to designing such computer programs. "I guess my motto is KISS: Keep It Simple, Stupid," Tanenbaum explained to *Leaders of the Information Age*. "Don't make things more complicated. Features are bad. They should be avoided. I like programs that do one thing and do it well. I don't like programs that try to do many things. For example, Microsoft Word is a program for producing printed docu-

ments. It now has the ability to include links to Web pages so if you click on them it starts up a browser. Printed documents do not need links to Web pages. This is an example of a bad idea. The problem with adding lots of features is that it makes the software big, slow, and full of bugs."

Tanenbaum is hesitant to speculate about the future of computing, but noted to *Leaders of the Information Age*: "I think the main difference between computers and systems in a generation and now is that they will be largely invisible. If you ask someone how many motors do they own, most people will say zero. But they probably own dozens of them. A CD player probably has two or three and a car probably has dozens. Computers are going to be like that. The average person will own dozens of computers, in their appliances, watch, and everything else that is electrical. My camera already has three computers in it—in the body, the lens, and the flash. Buildings will be loaded with computers. They will be everywhere. They will all communicate over wireless networks, and the operating systems will be designed for this environment."—C. M.

Suggested Reading: Andrew S. Tanenbaum Web site; *Computers Today* p87 Aug. 15, 2001; *Dr. Dobb's Journal of Software Tools* p139 May 1992; *InfoWorld* S p 15 Feb. 6, 1989; (London) *Guardian* May 28, 1987; *New York Times* D p9 Oct. 17, 1990; *Unix Review's Performance Computing* p55 Dec. 1, 1999

Taylor, Robert W.

Feb. 10, 1932– Computer administrator

Robert W. Taylor has led three of the most significant computer-research laboratories in history. As an administrator of the Advanced Research Projects Agency (ARPA) of the United States Department of Defense in the late 1960s, he spearheaded the push for the forerunner of today's Internet—the Advanced Research Projects Agency Network, better known as the ARPANET. At Xerox's Palo Alto Research Center (PARC) in the 1970s, he led the creation of graphical-user interfaces, the Ethernet, and Local Area Network (LAN) connections. During the 1980s and 1990s he oversaw the development of modern computer workstations and electronic books—among other innovations—at the Digital Equipment Corporation (DEC). For his pioneering vision he received the 1999 National Medal of Technology.

Robert William Taylor was born on February 10, 1932 in Dallas, Texas. His father was a Methodist minister who traveled from parish to parish throughout Taylor's childhood. Despite changing schools often, Taylor remained a good student and began taking courses at Southern Methodist University, in Dallas, at age 16. His studies, however, were interrupted by a tour of duty in the navy during the Korean War (1950–1953). After returning home, he entered the University of Texas in Austin under the G.I. Bill, a program by which veterans were granted tuition funds. In 1957 Taylor received a bachelor's degree in experimental psychology, with minors in mathematics, English, philosophy, and religion. In 1964 he received a master's degree in experimental psychology from the same institution.

Between 1955 and 1959 Taylor worked as a research scientist at the Defense Research Laboratory at the University of Texas. In 1959 he left the university to teach mathematics and coach basketball at a co-ed prep school in Florida. The position was short lived. "I had a wonderful time but was very poor, with a second child—which turned out to be twins—on the way," he explained in an interview with Marion Softky for the *Almanac* (October 11, 2000, on-line). In order to make more money, he took a series of engineering jobs, first at the Martin Company, in Florida (1960–1961), then at ACF Electronics, in Maryland (1961–1962). After writing a proposal to the National Aeronautics and Space Administration (NASA) for a flight-control simulation display, he was offered a position there at the Office of Advanced Research and Technology.

Taylor had become fascinated by computers after reading a seminal paper on the subject in an Institute of Electrical and Electronics Engineers (IEEE) journal in 1960. The paper, titled "Man-Computer Symbiosis," was written by J. C. R. Licklider; it proposed that computers would ultimately prove to be a conduit for the exchange of human knowledge—instead of the bulky punched card-driven computational mammoths then in use. Taylor was already familiar with Licklider's work; he had written a thesis paper on psycho-acoustics, a subject for which Licklider was world renowned.

Taylor came into personal contact with Licklider in late 1962, after Licklider had become the director of ARPA. (ARPA, which later became known as DARPA, had been established in 1958 in response to the Soviet Union's successful launching of Sputnik, the world's first satellite.) As Taylor explained to John Markoff for the *New York Times* (December 20, 1999): "Licklider, shortly after he took over at ARPA, organized an informal committee of people in the government who were supporting computer research. He invited me to come over and join the committee. I walked into his office and right away he started talking to me about my thesis. It blew me completely away. How would he know anything about my thesis? I was a no-name nobody graduate student. He wowed me from Day 1."

Licklider had been given approximately $10 million in funding to direct the newly formed Information Processing Techniques Office (IPTO) at ARPA. The IPTO's mission was to develop a revolutionary networking system in which individual computers would not merely do their own work, but would link up, communicate with one another, and share resources; to that end he began distributing the money to several universities to create computer-science programs and do research in time-sharing and other areas.

In July 1964, after a two-year tenure, Licklider left the IPTO. He was replaced by Ivan Sutherland, another of his devotees. During Sutherland's tenure, in 1965, Taylor left NASA for ARPA, and he replaced Sutherland as head of the agency in 1966. In Taylor's office at the Pentagon were three terminals: one connected to a time-sharing computer at the Massachusetts Institute of Technology (MIT), one connected to a computer at the University of California at Berkeley, and one connected to the Systems Development Corporation in Santa Monica. This situation proved cumbersome. As Taylor explained to Marion Softky, "To talk to MIT I had to sit at the MIT terminal. To bring in someone from Berkeley, I had to change chairs to another terminal. I wished I could connect someone at MIT directly with someone at Berkeley. Out of that came the idea: Why not have one terminal that connects all of them?"

The ARPANET, a government-contracted computer network, developed from this idea. The network, which could be used to communicate in the event of a nuclear attack, would be beneficial to the military, but would also allow scientists and researchers to share information more easily. In order to help develop the project, Taylor contacted Larry Roberts, a rising MIT–educated networking expert. ARPA contracted with Bolt, Beranek & Newman (now known as BBN Technologies) to build the physical network and persuaded numerous universities and computer centers to install stations and test the system.

The project posed three immediate problems: physically connecting the time-sharing systems, economizing on the use of expensive high-speed connections between computers, and linking together systems built by different manufacturers that used different operating systems. The first two problems were addressed by the concept of "store-and-forward packet-switching," which had been independently developed during the 1960s by the computer scientists Paul Baran and Donald Davies. Packet-switching involved breaking down information into smaller chunks, sending the chunks through the network separately, then reassembling them when they reached their destination. As Martin Campbell-Kelly and William Aspray explained in *Computer: A History of the Information Machine* (1996), the network itself would be based on the old telegraph system: "Instead of having every computer connected to every other, store-and-forward technology would be used to route messages through the network; there would be a single 'backbone' communications line that connected the computers together, with other connections being added as the need arose. Packet-switching technology [thus] addressed the problem of making economic use of the high-speed communication lines." Larry Roberts solved the third problem facing the network. Instead of modifying existing software, he reasoned, a separate minicomputer called an Interface Message Processor (IMP) would be connected to each node (switching station) on the ARPANET to translate and handle all the traffic.

Concurrently, ARPA was funding the studies of Douglas Engelbart at the Stanford Research Institute, whose work included the development of the mouse and remote computing. At a 1968 public demonstration in San Francisco, Engelbart amazed his audience by using a mouse to remotely manipulate a computer in Menlo Park. "It was stunning," Taylor told Marion Softky. "It really waked a lot of people up to a whole new way of thinking about computers—not just as number crunchers."

In the late 1960s Taylor was asked by the White House to aid in the war effort in Vietnam. He was given the honorary rank of brigadier general (so that he could deal with senior officers) and was sent to Vietnam to straighten out conflicting reports that had been sent to Washington. Taylor revised conflicting protocols and set up a computer center near Saigon.

Returning from Vietnam, Taylor discovered that Congress was pushing ARPA to focus more intently on military objectives, rather than on the fluid combination of university and government projects it had previously undertaken. In 1969 Taylor left the agency, concerned that its new direction impeded his personal mission to spread computer-communication technology to a wide range of people. He was quickly hired by the University of Utah to direct its Information Research Laboratory. While there, in 1970, he received a phone call from George Pake, a physicist at Xerox. As Taylor explained to John Markoff: "He told me that Xerox was going to have a research lab here in Palo Alto and part of it was going to be devoted to computer research. The research group was going to develop technologies that would be used as S.D.S., a computer company that Xerox had recently purchased. I said, 'Oh, that's too bad.' He said, 'What do you mean?' 'Well, you won't be able to get anyone who's any good to come work here because there's absolutely no respect for S.D.S. among the best computer folks.' They were floored. They said, 'What do you think we ought to do?' I replied, 'You ought to computerize the office; everything that happens in [an] office can be put on the computer.'"

Taylor was hired as chief scientist and associate manager of the new PARC. True to his vision, he set about developing the computerized office of the future. Taylor nurtured a freewheeling environment of young computer geniuses—who often clashed with the more-staid Xerox management. Despite such confrontations, the engineers and scientists at PARC laid the groundwork for modern computing. Although Xerox's management has been derided for not taking full advantage of the groundbreaking work, some of the technologies created at PARC included: the Xerox Alto and Dorado personal computers, which employed the

graphical user interfaces (GUI) ultimately used in the Macintosh; the laser printer and the graphics programs that formed the basis for the Adobe Systems; a revolutionary word-processing program based on the idea that "what you see is what you get" (WYSIWYG), which formed the basis of Microsoft Word; and the evolution of the Ethernet, a local computer network.

Xerox's corporate management did take advantage of the laser printer, which became a billion-dollar business for the company, but by 1983 Taylor was too discouraged to continue there. "Xerox continued to ignore our work," he told Softky. "I got fed up and left, and about 15 people came and joined me at DEC."

At DEC's Systems Research Center, Taylor continued to spearhead pioneering computer work. Under his leadership the center produced such innovations as high-performance workstations, advanced networking and storage capacities, a computer language that formed the basis for Java, and electronic books—handheld devices with the ability to load text or pictures.

Though he remains a consultant for DEC, which was eventually acquired by Compaq, Taylor retired from the company in 1996. Settled in Woodside, California, he enjoys gardening, cooking, listening to music, and reading. Perhaps ironically, he doesn't own a cellular phone, fax machine, scanner, or copier. (He does admit to an interest in computer games.) He dislikes traveling—so much so that he refused in 1999 to attend the presentation ceremony in Washington, D.C., at which President Bill Clinton awarded him the National Medal of Technology.—C. M.

Suggested Reading: *Almanac* (on-line) Oct. 11, 2000; Information Sciences Hall of Fame Web site; *New York Times* F p1 Oct. 12, 1999, C p38 Dec. 20, 1999; Campbell-Kelly, Martin and William Aspray. *Computer: A History of the Information Machine*, 1996

Teal, Gordon K.

Jan. 10, 1907– Germanium and silicon crystal developer

While William Shockley and his team of scientists at Bell Laboratories created the first transistor—the basic building block of all solid-state electronics—another crucial and little-known contributor to this most important invention was Gordon K. Teal. Teal pioneered the technique for growing single, pure crystals of the semiconductors germanium and silicon. Without his germanium crystals, Shockley's transistor, introduced in 1950, would not have been possible. Teal's technique for growing silicon crystals, perfected in 1954 while he was working at Texas Instruments, led directly to the development of the first silicon transistors, which are more reliable and inexpensive than germanium transistors and are still the main type of semiconductor transistors used today.

The son of Olin Allison Teal and Azelia (Kidd) Teal, Gordon Teal was born on January 10, 1907 in Dallas, Texas. In 1927 he earned his A.B. in math and chemistry, with honors, from Baylor University, in Waco, Texas. He received his master's (1928) and doctoral (1931) degrees in chemistry—first as a Marston Scholar and then as a Metcalf Fellow—from Brown University, in Providence, Rhode Island.

While at Brown Teal had studied the semiconductor germanium, and in 1930, when he was hired as a researcher for Bell Labs, he cultivated his "continuing personal sentimental attachment for germanium," as he was quoted in the *Brown Alumni Magazine* (November/December 2000, on-line). Teal was not directly involved in the transistor research conducted at Bell Labs in the 1930s, although he was on occasion asked to grow crystals for the effort. The reason for the research was that vacuum tubes, which were used to amplify and regulate electric currents, consumed too much power, had a tendency to overheat, and were unreliable. Some alternative to the tubes was needed, though researchers did not yet know what it would be.

In late 1947 Bell Lab's Walter Brattain and John Bardeen invented the point-contact transistor, which was made of strips of gold foil put in contact with a layer of germanium. However, the point-contact transistor was still not reliable enough. In early 1948 Shockley conceived of—but did not yet build—the junction transistor, a semiconductor "sandwich" that consisted of two layers of semiconductor surrounding a third layer of a different form of semiconductor. It was soon discovered that in order for the sandwich to work, the middle layer had to be extremely thin. Teal suggested growing a single thin crystal of germanium, but Shockley's team decided to cut a sliver of germanium from a larger ingot of crystals. Nevertheless, Teal continued to develop the method for growing single crystals. When the Shockley team's method proved ineffective (because the gaps between the separate crystals allowed for erratic electron movement), Teal was able to provide the single germanium crystals that were necessary for the first working junction transistor, which was produced in April 1950.

That same year Teal began working on growing silicon crystals, partly because germanium transistors had several flaws, the most important of which was that they were less reliable at high temperatures because germanium releases electrons when heated. Silicon was less susceptible to heat, and as one of the earth's most plentiful substances, it was inexpensive. In 1952 Teal left Bell Labs and was hired to direct materials research at the newly christened Texas Instruments company, in Dallas, Texas, where he continued to work with silicon. Only two years later, on April 14, 1954, Teal succeeded in growing single silicon crystals and produced the first functional silicon transistor.

He was given the honor of presenting a paper on his findings, "Some New and Recent Developments in Silicon and Germanium," at the National Conference on Airborne Electronics, in Dayton, Ohio, on May 10, 1954. Teal was the second to last speaker, and while many of the other presenters outlined the faults of germanium transistors, none expected a working silicon transistor for several years. Teal took the podium, pulled three small objects from his pocket, and said, "Contrary to what my colleagues have told you about the bleak prospects for silicon transistors, I happen to have a few of them here in my pocket," as quoted on PBS's *Transistorized* Web site. The audience rushed over to a Texas Instruments employee handing out literature on the silicon transistors, leaving the final speaker without an audience. Teal had moved transistor technology a big leap forward, and he had helped send Texas Instruments along its road to success.

Teal remained at Texas Instruments for the rest of his career, helping the company pioneer numerous semiconductor technologies. In 1972 he retired as chief scientist and became a consultant for the company. His honors include the Inventor of the Year award from George Washington University, in 1966; the Golden Plate award from the Academy of Academic Achievement, in 1967; a Medal of Honor (1968) and Centennial Medal (1984) from the Institute of Electrical and Electronics Engineers (IEEE); a Creative Invention award from the American Chemistry Society, in 1970; and the Semy award from the Semiconductor Equipment and Materials Institute, in 1984. He is a member of the National Academy of Engineering, the IEEE, the American Physics Association, the American Chemistry Association, the American Institute of Chemists, and the American Association for the Advancement of Science.

Teal's 1969 induction into the National Academy of Sciences citation reads, "In recognition of his pioneering research on single crystals of germanium and silicon and his coinvention and reduction to practice of the single crystal grown junction transistor, contributions which must be ranked among the most critical and essential to the development of the semiconductor industry and electronics."

Teal is married to Lyda Louise (Smith), with whom he had three children: Robert, Donald, and Stephen (now deceased).—P. G. H.

Suggested Reading: *Brown Alumni Magazine* (on-line) Nov./Dec. 2000; *Proceedings of the IEEE* p922+ May 1999

Hulton Archive by Getty Images

Tesla, Nikola

July 10, 1856–Jan. 7, 1943 Inventor of alternating current

Though in the 1880s the inventor Nikola Tesla gave us the technology that still forms the basis for all of our electrical power, he died penniless and largely estranged from the scientific community, in 1943. Tesla invented alternating current (AC), making possible the affordable long-distance transmission of electrical power—a critical improvement over Thomas Edison's strictly local direct current (DC) technology. Tesla also invented the high-frequency coil, or Tesla coil, which, as Bill Lawren stated in *Omni* (March 1988), "helped lay the groundwork for every broadcasting system from radio to radar." Tesla was a bold thinker whose many inventions—only a small proportion of which he ever bothered to patent—included the first remote-controlled boat and an immense transmitter capable of emitting 135-foot electrical bolts. Hugo Gernsback, a science journalist and contemporary of Tesla's, once wrote of him, as quoted by James P. Rybak in *Popular Electronics* (November 1999), "Without a shade of doubt, Nikola Tesla is the world's greatest inventor, not only at present but in all history. . . . His basic as well as revolutionary discoveries, for sheer audacity, have no equals in the annals of the intellectual world."

Tesla was an extremely eccentric man. He insisted on having exactly 18 napkins on the table at every meal, refused to shake hands with anyone or be in the same room with women wearing pearl earrings, and complained that vivid images produced by his photographic memory frequently blotted out his vision. He believed it possible to photograph thoughts on the surface of the retina, control the weather, and communicate with alien intelligence, and claimed to have received messages from Mars. Famous for sheathing himself in a glowing two-million-volt electric field, his much sought-after public appearances often resembled carnival acts as much as scientific demonstrations. By the time of his death, Tesla's idiosyncrasies had nearly overshadowed his achievements.

Nikola Tesla was born on July 10, 1856 in Smiljan, Croatia, which was then part of the Austro-Hungarian Empire. His father was a priest in the Serbian Orthodox church, and it was expected that Tesla would also become a priest. Tesla, however, was far more interested in being an inventor. He often maintained that his gifts as an inventor came from his mother, a homemaker. In a series of essays collected after his death in the book *My Inventions; The Autobiography of Nikola Tesla* (1982), Tesla wrote of his mother, "She was a truly great woman, of rare skill, courage and fortitude. . . . [She] was an inventor of the first order and would, I believe, have achieved great things had she not been so remote from modern life and its manifold opportunities."

Tesla, who attended the Real Gymnasium, in Karlovac (in present-day Croatia), excelled in school, learned several languages, and showed a particular aptitude for mathematics. He went on to study engineering at the Technical University, in Graz, Austria. At the university Tesla learned about DC motors and, despite his teacher's skepticism, became convinced that a better type of electrical motor could be produced. Before he could devote much time to developing a new type of motor, his father died, forcing him, in 1881, to drop out of the University of Prague, in which he had enrolled after leaving the Technical University.

Tesla was capable of working out complex mathematical problems and visualizing mechanical devices in his head and rarely drew up blueprints for his inventions. "When I get an idea I start at once building it up in my imagination," Tesla wrote in *My Inventions*. "I change the construction, make improvements and operate the device in my mind. It is absolutely immaterial to me whether I run my turbine in thought or test it in my shop. *I even note if it is out of balance.* There is no difference whatever, the results are the same. In this way I am able to rapidly develop and perfect a conception without touching anything. When I have gone so far as to embody in the invention every possible improvement I can think of and see no fault anywhere, I put into concrete form this final product of my brain. Invariably my device works as I conceived that it should, and the experiment comes out exactly as I planned it." Tesla's rare talent would continue to serve him throughout his life, particularly because he often lacked the financial resources to build many of his inventions.

In 1881 a friend of Tesla's found him a job in Budapest as an engineer for a telephone company. He was quickly put in charge of the operation, but as had recurrently happened to him as a young man, he grew very ill, which forced him to leave the company. By the time he had fully recovered, in 1882, Tesla felt confident that he had solved the puzzle of how to build an AC motor. Others had tried to build electric motors using only one circuit, but Tesla envisioned two circuits, to each of which he would apply out-of-phase currents of identical frequency. This would produce a continuously rotating magnetic field to turn the rotor of the engine. This, at least, was the theory, though Tesla did not yet possess the resources to test it.

The Budapest telephone company where Tesla had worked before falling ill had closed down; with the help of his friend, Tesla, in 1882, found a job with the Continental Edison Company branch in Paris. While working on an assignment in Germany, in 1883, Tesla found the time to build his AC motor and AC generator, both of which functioned as he had foreseen. Still, he was unable to interest any investors in his invention. Upon returning to Paris, he grew exasperated with his immediate supervisors, who had failed to provide him with a promised bonus, and he resigned.

Despite Tesla's disagreements with his supervisors, the manager of Continental Edison, Charles Batchelor, was impressed with Tesla and promised to introduce him to Thomas Edison in New York. Tesla jumped at the opportunity. Armed with a letter from Batchelor and a little money from the sale of his possessions, Tesla went to New York and met the esteemed inventor, who offered him a position. At first, Tesla had a favorable impression of Edison. "I was amazed at this wonderful man who without early advantage or scientific training had accomplished so much," Tesla said, as quoted in *Wired* (October 1988, on-line). "But after working with him day in and day out, I became frustrated. If Edison needed to find a needle in a haystack, he would not stop to reason where the needle might be, but rather would examine every straw, straw after straw like a diligent bee until he found the object of his search." Tesla vowed to improve the efficiency of the DC dynamos, or generators, that Edison's company produced, and reportedly was promised a $50,000 bonus if he could do so. Several months later, by the spring of 1885, Tesla had invented 24 types of new, more efficient DC dynamos. However, when he asked Edison for his bonus, he was told that the offer had been a joke. Tesla immediately quit.

Unable to find an engineering job, Tesla was forced to work as a general laborer. By 1887 his abilities had attracted the attention of his foreman, who introduced Tesla to A. K. Brown, of the Western Union Telegraph Company. Based on Tesla's plans for his AC generator, Brown and a friend agreed to finance the "Tesla Electric Company," in April 1887, enabling Tesla to build his AC generator and motor as well as some other devices he had designed in his mind. In 1888 he was granted basic patents for his AC inventions. After delivering a speech about his new technologies before the American Institute of Electrical Engineers (AIEE),

Tesla was introduced to George Westinghouse, the prominent inventor and manufacturer, who offered Tesla $1 million for his patents (half of which went to Brown and his co-investor), as well as a lucrative position as a consultant for Westinghouse's company.

Edison, meanwhile, mounted a campaign against AC technology, which he rightly saw as a threat to his DC systems. To demonstrate the risk of sustaining electric shock when using an AC system, as opposed to the safer DC systems, Edison publicly electrocuted dogs, cattle, and other animals before horrified audiences. He told audiences that the unfortunate creatures had been "Westinghoused." But because of the inherent advantages of AC, Edison's propaganda proved ineffectual. In 1893 Westinghouse won a contract to employ AC technology in building an electrical plant at Niagara Falls, in New York. A DC system would not be able to serve Buffalo, which was 22 miles away, while an AC generator could easily supply the city. By 1895 Westinghouse's system was lighting up Buffalo, providing a highly visible demonstration of the power of Tesla's invention.

By this time Tesla's fame was widespread. Beginning in 1888 he had turned his attention to high-frequency electrical systems. In 1890 he invented the revolutionary hollow-core transformer, or Tesla coil, which was capable of generating electric sparks and transmitting and receiving very high-frequency radio signals. Tesla also realized that high-frequency AC current travels over the surface of the human body rather than through it and could be used for therapeutic purposes, a process known as diathermy. He amazed the world in 1891, when in a public demonstration he passed some two million volts of high-frequency AC current over his skin and produced seemingly magical electrical sparks from his fingertips. He also induced Geissler tubes (sealed tubes of gas) to glow, without wires, by discharging electrical pulses from across the stage. Audiences clamored to see the eccentric inventor wreathed in electric flame and emitting sparks from his body. Tesla became a celebrity and clearly enjoyed the attention; in later years he referred to the 1890s as the happiest years of his life.

In 1893, in St. Louis, Missouri, Tesla gave another influential public presentation, during which he demonstrated one of the earliest forms of wireless technology using his Tesla coil. Tesla's "transmitter" was a tuned circuit that consisted of a capacitor and a power distribution transformer connected to a spark gap, and hooked to a vertical wire to serve as an antenna. The "receiver" was an identically tuned circuit connected to a Geissler tube that, to the amazement of the audience, lit when a signal was sent. This demonstration of the wireless transmission of high-frequency radiation occurred two years before Guglielmo Marconi, who is often credited with inventing radio, began his critical experiments.

Throughout the 1890s Tesla continued to experiment with the wireless transmission of electrical energy over greater and greater distances. In his laboratory, in 1894, he built a transmitter and a portable receiver, but in 1895, before he could do a public demonstration of his work, his laboratory burned down. Tesla lost virtually all of his records and equipment, in which he had invested most of his money. None of it was insured. It was a devastating blow, but he persisted. Tesla, as quoted in *Wired*, believed that man's greatest purpose in life was "to concentrate all his energies on one single great effort. Let him perceive a single truth, even though he'll be consumed by the sacred fire, and millions of less gifted men can easily follow him. Let him toil day and night with a small chance of achieving and yet be unflinching."

With borrowed funds Tesla began the laborious process of rebuilding his laboratory and his equipment. In the spring of 1897 he took his receiver out in a boat along the Hudson River, in New York, and succeeded in transmitting a signal over a distance of 25 miles. Even with the setback of the fire, he was well ahead of Marconi, who, in May 1897, sent messages across the Bristol Channel, a distance of less than nine miles. Tesla was issued two patents for wireless technology in September 1897. In September 1898 he dazzled an audience at New York City's Madison Square Garden with his "mind-powered" boat, a three-foot remote-controlled vessel that employed his wireless technology. To prove the simplicity of his device, he even allowed members of the audience to control the boat. Tesla, who abhorred war, proposed to the U.S. Navy that a remote-controlled submarine might save lives if used in the Spanish-American war, but the Navy expressed no interest. His attempts to use the media to pressure the Navy backfired, and some began to view him as a boastful eccentric.

Tesla was interested in using his wireless technology not only as a communications device but also as a way of transmitting large amounts of power around the world without wires. Using borrowed money, he assembled in his New York laboratory a large Tesla coil capable of generating four million volts. It soon became apparent that he needed more space for his experiments, and in 1899 he secured a $30,000 loan to build a lab in Colorado Springs, Colorado. Granted a free source of electricity from the town's generator, he built another huge Tesla coil, which he called his "magnifying transmitter," capable of producing 135-foot lightning bolts. Tesla had two plans for transmitting the energy—either through the earth's ionosphere (the uppermost, electrically conductive layer of the atmosphere), or in the form of low-frequency radiation, through the earth's core. Before he could get very far on either of these theories, Tesla managed to short out Colorado Springs' power and destroy the city's generator in one of his experiments. He was informed that power would be returned to his laboratory only if he fixed the city's generator.

On January 7, 1900 Tesla left Colorado Springs and returned to New York. His credibility was beginning to suffer. He had done little to publicize his pioneering work with wireless technology, yet just before leaving Colorado he received some strange transmissions on his receiver and announced, to much ridicule, that he had gotten a message from Mars. Nevertheless, he convinced the affluent industrialist J. P. Morgan to provide $150,000 for a new 187-foot transmitter in Long Island, New York, which he called the Wardencliffe Tower. The plan was to set up a wireless communication system and power transmission station that could span the globe. Instead, Tesla's grandiose and immensely complex plans bogged down in financial and design difficulties. Toward the end of 1901, Marconi sent a radio signal 2,100 miles across the Atlantic Ocean, a highly publicized event that made him a household name. Tesla, as Lawren quoted him in *Omni*, reportedly said, "Let him continue. He is using seventeen of my patents." Marconi did indeed continue. His Wireless Telegraph and Signal Company became the world's primary radio company, and in 1909 he won, with Carl Ferdinand Braun, the Nobel Prize for physics. By this time Wardencliffe Tower was still not completed, and in 1915 Tesla lost the laboratory to creditors.

In November 1915 it was announced in the press that for the first time Americans would be awarded a Nobel Prize: the prize in physics was to go to Tesla and Edison. However, the award was never issued, and it was rumored that the two scientists, still fuming from their feud years before, refused to share the honor jointly. Two years later, Tesla initially refused the Edison Medal awarded him by the AIEE and only agreed to accept it after much pleading from an AIEE official. Tesla continued to contrive new inventions, but he rarely had the money to implement them. He had gotten himself into insurmountable debt, and though he would have been a billionaire from the royalties for his AC power technologies, he had torn up his contract with Westinghouse in a gesture of friendship years before.

Many of Tesla's inventions in his latter years seemed fantastic and far-fetched. He conceived of a machine to capture the energy of cosmic rays. He spoke of designing a particle-beam that could destroy 10,000 enemy aircraft from 250 miles away. He claimed he knew a way to control the weather. Toward the end of his life, Tesla eschewed food and sleep, considering them a waste of time. Instead, he tried to replenish his energy by routinely applying a vibrating electrified plate to his body. Tesla had predicted that he would live to be 140, but on January 7, 1943, he died in a small hotel room in New York City. His closest associates were the pigeons he habitually fed and nursed.

Many of Tesla's inventions have only recently been rediscovered or recognized. For example, he outlined a system for detecting ships at sea, which later formed the basis for radar, and he designed a

"bladeless turbine" that is still being investigated for its potentially improved efficiency over that of regular turbines. He was also an early outspoken advocate of solar energy. In 1943 the U.S. Supreme Court overturned Marconi's patent No. 7777, which had given him a virtual monopoly on radio transmissions. The court ruled that Nikola Tesla, along with Sir Oliver Lodge and John Stone, had also contributed to the development of the patented technologies. In 1974 Tesla was voted into the hall of fame of the Institute of Electrical and Electronics Engineers (IEEE), and his reputation as a brilliant inventor has been largely restored.
—P. G. H.

Suggested Reading: *Electrical World* p42+ Jan./Feb. 2000; *MIT's Technology Review* p66+ Nov./Dec. 1997; *Omni* p65+ Mar. 1988; *Popular Electronics* p40+ Nov. 1999; *Wired* (on-line) Oct. 1998; Johnston, Ben. ed. *My Inventions; The Autobiography of Nikola Tesla*, 1982

Thomas de Colmar, Charles Xavier

1785–1870 Inventor of the Arithmometer

The inventor Charles Xavier Thomas de Colmar created the first commercially successful calculating machine in 1820. The Arithmometer, as he named it, was also known as the Thomas Machine; it was a desktop device capable of performing addition, subtraction, multiplication, and division. During the latter half of the 19th century it was the most popular device of its kind, and its design spawned numerous imitations. Versions of the machine continued to be sold until World War I, almost 100 years after its original patent.

Charles Xavier Thomas de Colmar was born in 1785 in Colmar, in the Alsace region of France. In 1820, while serving in the French Army, he submitted a patent for a calculating device he had built, called an Arithmometer. The machine was based on the same design as the Stepped Reckoner, an earlier calculator built by the 17th-century philosopher and mathematician Gottfried Wilhelm von Leibniz. Leibniz's calculator used a stepped-drum mechanism, also known as the Leibniz Wheel, which was a long cylinder with nine bar-shaped teeth of different lengths running parallel to the cylinder's axis. When a crank was turned, the drum rotated, in turn causing other ten-toothed wheels placed adjacent to the cylinder to rotate. (The Stepped Reckoner was able to perform the four basic arithmetic functions, as well as calculate square roots.)

While the Leibniz design was the basis for most mechanical calculators built during the 18th and 19th centuries, Thomas's Arithmometer was the first to be widely used. This was in part due to an increased demand for accurate, labor-saving, calculating methods as industry and science made tremendous advances during the 19th century. In addition, the Arithmometer was better constructed and more reliable than previous calculating machines. The gears, for example, were produced using improved manufacturing techniques. Springs and other mechanisms were installed to eliminate the momentum of moving parts, preventing them from rotating beyond the intended point. (This was a major source of error in earlier machines.) The Arithmometer was also easy to use, employed an efficient automatic carrying function, and was encased in a 24-by-7.5-by-5-inch wooden box, with a hinged bottom to allow it to be inclined for work. Some versions of the Arithmometer were large enough to cover a desk and required two men to move.

Thomas's prototype was subject to frequent errors, but over the next several decades, he continued to revise the design and improve its accuracy. Although it became one of the best machines available, it apparently drew mixed responses, as noted by a writer for *Scientific American* (1849), who is quoted on the Computer Museum of America Web site: "M. Colmar, a French gentleman who invented a calculating machine about 20 years ago, has improved it in such a wonderful manner that it is said to be one of the most astonishing pieces of mechanism that has ever been invented, but to our view, its complexity shows its defectability." Thomas eventually demonstrated the machine to the French Academy of Sciences, a prestigious institution whose approval bolstered the Arithmometer's commercial success. In addition, in 1850 Thomas gave an Arithmometer as a gift to the King of Portugal. Its popularity continued to grow, but the considerable expense of the machine, combined with a lack of advertising, contributed to slow sales during the 1850s and '60s. The device was included in the Paris Exhibition of 1867, where it was highly praised by judges and critics; it was soon widely adopted for use in business and scientific calculations.

Thomas had produced several machines individually before he founded a company to manufacture them, the Compagnie d'Assurance le Soleil. Based in Paris, it was the first company to manufacture mechanical devices to aid in calculation, and it had produced about 800 units by 1870. The Arithmometer inspired numerous copies made by other manufacturers, and the term Arithmometer soon became synonymous with any four-function calculating machines. Although its market dominance was eclipsed at the turn of the century by the Odhner Calculator, built by the Swedish engineer Willgodt T. Odhner, versions of the Arithmometer continued to be sold through the early part of the 20th century.

By the end of his life, Thomas was an acknowledged leader in the field of mechanical calculators, and in recognition of his achievement he was awarded the Chevalier of the Legion of Honor, a tribute founded by Napoleon Bonaparte to recognize eminent service to the Republic of France. Thomas was also an insurance entrepreneur, and he founded the companies Phénix and Eagle in Paris. He was married to an Italian woman, the Duchess of Bojano, with whom he had a son, Thomas de Bojano. He died in Paris in 1870. —A. I. C.

Suggested Reading: Computer Museum of America Web site; The History of Computing Project (THOCP) Web site; Museum of HP Calculators (on-line); Williams, Michael R. *A History of Computing Technology*, 1997

Thompson, Kenneth

Feb. 4, 1943– Developer of Unix

Kenneth Thompson, an icon in the computer world, got his start as a programmer at Bell Labs in the late 1960s. Thompson, along with his fellow programmer Dennis Ritchie, developed the Unix operating system, which is now regarded by some as one of the design masterpieces of computing history. The story of Unix's development has become legendary within the field, and it has become commonplace to refer to Thompson simply as Ken (often uncapitalized, since in the early days of Unix it served as a file name and a log-in) on Usenet and other discussion boards. While working on an early version of Unix, Thompson developed the B programming language, which became the foundation for Ritchie's C language. Thompson then rewrote the Unix operating system in C. The result was a system that not only broke new ground in time-sharing and multitasking ability, but was more portable than other operating systems. At a time when computer users were increasingly interested in working on smaller machines, the portability of Unix made it the operating system of choice, and Unix became a phenomenal success. Today Unix is widely used in businesses and research institutions. It also forms an important part of the infrastructure of the Internet, as it is used by many Internet providers to operate their servers.

Kenneth Lane Thompson was born in New Orleans, Louisiana, on February 4, 1943. The family moved frequently from place to place because Thompson's father was in the navy. Interested in electronics, he enrolled at the University of California, Berkeley, where he studied electrical engineering, receiving a B.A. in 1965 and an M.S. in 1966. Thompson then joined the Bell Labs Computing Research Department, the research and development arm of Lucent Technologies. In 1968 Thompson began working with Dennis Ritchie on the Multics project, a huge multiorganizational endeavor. The goal of Multics, which is short for "multiplexed information and computing service," was to create a dependable time-sharing operating system for large mainframe computers that would support hundreds of users. The drive to create time-sharing systems had been around since the early sixties, as part of a continuing effort to over-

come the bottlenecks that researchers faced as numerous users vied for time to run their programs on a single computer. The Multics system was the most ambitious attempt to date, with the goal of supporting 300 users simultaneously.

Thompson's other achievements include the creation of Belle, a champion chess-playing computer; the Plan 9 operating system, released in 1995; and the Inferno operating system, released in 1996. Thompson has received numerous honors and awards for his work. In 1982 the Computer Society of the Institute of Electrical and Electronics Engineers (IEEE) awarded him the Emmanuel R. Priore Award. In 1994 Thompson received the Computer Pioneer Award from the IEEE Computer Society. In 1998 Thompson received, with Ritchie, the National Medal of Technology for the development of Unix. In 1999 he received the Tsutomu Kanai Award from the IEEE, recognizing his contributions in the area of distributed computing systems. He has been a member of the U.S. National Academy of Science since his induction, in 1980.

The effort proved unsuccessful, however, and in 1969 Bell Labs withdrew from the project. In a paper he presented in 1979 at the Language Design and Programming Methodology Conference, "The Evolution of the Unix Time-sharing System," Dennis Ritchie explains that the cancellation was a disappointment for those few who were still involved in the project, notably Thompson, Doug McIlroy, J. F. Ossanna, and himself: "We were among the last Bell Laboratories holdouts actually working on Multics, so we still felt some sort of stake in its success. More important, the convenient interactive computing service that Multics had promised to the entire community was in fact available to our limited group. . . . Even though Multics could not then support many users, it could support us, albeit at exorbitant cost." This time-sharing opportunity was highly valued by the group, most importantly because of the form of community it fostered: "We knew from experience that the essence of communal computing, as supplied by remote-access, time-shared machines, is not just to type programs into a terminal instead of a keypunch, but to encourage close communication."

Accordingly, Thompson and Ritchie decided to pursue the idea of a system that would enable multiple simultaneous users to share a computer file system. Bell Labs allowed its employees a significant degree of freedom in order to foster inventiveness and creativity, and Thompson and Ritchie benefitted from that open environment. Unfortunately, still smarting from the failure of Multics, Bell Labs was unwilling to supply them with the requested hardware. Thompson and Ritchie had to settle for a discarded and obsolete computer, the PDP-7, manufactured by the Digital Equipment Corporation. The PDP-7 was a small computer with only a fraction of the storage and processing capabilities of a mainframe, and this necessitated a more simplistic approach to the Multics problem. In a telling bit of computing history, one of the key steps toward the development of Unix turned out to involve a computer game called Space Travel. The game was a flight simulation, originally written for Multics and adapted to run on a different operating system. Thompson and Ritchie rewrote the game to run on the PDP-7, and this proved to be instrumental in learning how to prepare programs for the machine. Then, in 1970, Thompson took a computer language called BCPL from Martin Richards at the Massachusetts Institute of Technology, in Cambridge, and adapted it to work on the PDP-7. The result was a significantly different language, which Thompson called B.

Eventually it became imperative that a more powerful computer be obtained. After several unsuccessful requests, an opportunity presented itself when Thompson and Ritchie discovered that Bell Labs was considering developing a word processing system. The duo wrote a proposal to write the system themselves, and a new PDP-11 was purchased for them. Ritchie later acknowledged that this was a slightly underhanded ploy on their part. "There was a scam going on," he was quoted as saying in *Byte* magazine (September 1995). "We'd promised a word processing system, not an operating system. But by the time the full computer had arrived in the summer of 1970, work was moving at full steam on both." Around this time, Brian Kernighan, a Bell colleague, suggested the name Unix, as a play on the name Multics. After Unix was rewritten in PDP-11 assembly, it was possible to export it to several internal Bell telephone applications, where it could be used to gather reports and monitor cables.

With the new computer, Ritchie took the B language developed by Thompson and developed C. (C, in turn, spawned C++ and Java.) Unix was subsequently rewritten in C, and it was this synthesis that was responsible for the power and elegance of the Unix operating system. C made the operating system portable, meaning it could be implemented on almost any computer system with a minimum of code changes. It also meant that the operating system could be upgraded easily, and that newer versions could be easily grafted upon the existing foundations. According to the *Dictionary of Computer and Internet Terms* (1996), C is unique among high-level languages because, "unlike other general purpose languages, it gives the programmer complete access to the machine's internal (bit-by-bit) representation of all types of data. This makes it convenient to perform tasks that would ordinarily require assembly language, and to perform computations in the most efficient way of which the machine is capable." Another major innovation of the Unix system was the use of "pipes," which were incorporated into the operating system between 1972 and 1973, at the urging of Doug McIlroy. Pipes made it possible to break down longer programs into smaller units, with the output of one program becoming the input of another. The smaller programs could run concurrently and communicate data to each other, thus reduc-

ing the complexity of the overall system, as well as the likelihood of errors. The Unix system, augmented by Ritchie's C language and McIlroy's pipes, was an unprecedented achievement in terms of time-sharing and multitasking capability.

The Unix operating system, like Thompson's later work, depended upon simple, yet powerful, abstractions. In an interview for *Computer* (May 1999, on-line), Scott Hamilton asked Thompson how he had arrived at such elegant solutions to such complex problems. Thompson replied, "It is the way I think. I am a very bottom-up thinker. If you give me the right kind of Tinker Toys, I can imagine the building. I can sit there and see primitives and recognize their power to build structures a half mile high, if only I had just one more to make it functionally complete."

The timing of Unix proved to be auspicious. In the early 1970s computer users were becoming increasingly frustrated with depending on a centralized mainframe, and there was a desire to move to decentralized computers. The cost of computers had fallen drastically between 1965 and 1975, due to the development of integrated circuit electronics. Manufacturers were able to meet the demand for smaller machines, but there were few operating systems available for them. Unix, because of its portability, fit the niche. In his interview with Hamilton, Thompson commented on the serendipity of the release of Unix: "It was a massive change in the way people used computers, from mainframes to minis; we crossed a monetary threshold where computers became cheaper. People used them in smaller groups, and it was the beginning of the demise of the monster comp center, where the bureaucracy hidden behind the guise of a multimillion dollar machine would dictate the way computing ran." AT&T, as a government-regulated monopoly, could not legally sell the software, but they adopted the practice of licensing Unix to colleges and universities at a low cost. The simplicity and accessibility of the design was a success in the academic world and research laboratories. The use of the system spread, and soon businesses realized its utility. Once Unix was out of the laboratory and in practical use, other computer programmers began developing their own programs for the system.

From 1975 to 1976 Thompson worked as a visiting professor at the University of California, where he made further contributions to the Unix system. Thompson's next major project, a collaborative effort with Joseph Condon, was the creation of Belle, a chess-playing computer. In 1980, Belle won the U.S. and World Computing Chess Championships. (Thompson's subsequent work caused a stir in the chess world, when in 1986 he created a program that used retrograde analysis to produce a list of all possible chess positions in which one side can force a win.)

In 1983 Thompson and Ritchie jointly received the prestigious ACM Turing Award. As quoted by Martin Campbell-Kelly and William Aspray in *Computer: A History of the Information Machine*

(1996), the award stated: "The genius of the Unix system is its framework, which enables programmers to stand on the work of others." Thompson, in a paper presented to the ACM on the occasion of the award, as reprinted on the organization's Web site, commented on his relationship with Ritchie: "Our collaboration has been a thing of beauty. In the ten years that we have worked together, I can recall only one case of miscoordination of work. On that occasion, I discovered that we both had written the same 20-line assembly language program. I compared the sources and was astounded to find that they matched character-for-character. The result of our work together has been far greater than the work that we each contributed."

In the 1990s Thompson worked on the Plan 9 and Inferno distributed operating systems, and also became involved in the collection of digital music. He reported to a writer for *Computer* (online) in May 1999 that he had already collected about 20,000 songs: "My collection is not generally available because of the legal aspects. I went to legal and told them I was collecting a lot of music, but I don't think they realized what I mean by 'a lot.' Anyway, they said that in the case of research there's something similar to fair use and that they'd back me, but wouldn't go to jail for me. So I can't release it generally. But it's pretty impressive. It's split-screen like a Web browser; you can walk down lists, years, or weeks."

When asked for his thoughts on the future of computer science, Thompson told the *Computer* writer that his advice to his son was to get into biology, where developments like gene therapy are on the forefront of scientific research. "Computer science is coming into its middle age," Thompson remarked. "It's turning into a commodity. People don't know about Carnot cycles for refrigerators, yet they buy refrigerators. It's happening in computing too. Who knows about compilers? [People] buy computers to play games and balance their checkbooks. . . . I think that computing is a finite field and it's reaching its apex and we will be on a wane after this. I am sorry to say that, but that's the way I feel." One difficulty Thompson points to is the baggage that operating systems have to carry: "Today, if you're going to do something that will have any impact, you have to compete with Microsoft, and to do that you have to carry the weight of all the browsers, Word, Office, and everything else. Even if you write a better operating system, nobody who actually uses computers today knows what an operating system interface is; their interface is the browser or Office." He does not, however, preclude the possibility of another paradigm shift in computing like the one he experienced: "Anything new will have to come along with the type of revolution that came along with Unix. Nothing was going to topple IBM until something came along that made them irrelevant. I'm sure they have the mainframe market locked up, but that's just irrelevant. And the same thing with Microsoft: Until something

comes along that makes them irrelevant, the entry fee is too difficult and they won't be displaced."

Thompson is still a researcher at Bell Labs, in Murray Hill, New Jersey. His more recent work includes the development of Lucent's PathStar Access Server, which allows for low-cost, high-quality voice and data communications over the Internet.—A. I. C.

Suggested Reading: Bell Labs Web site; *Byte* p133+ Sep. 1995, with photo; *Computer* (on-line) May 1999; *Current Biography* Mar. 1999; Campbell-Kelly, Martin and William Aspray. *Computer: A History of the Information Machine,* 1996

Titus, Jonathan

Nov. 24, 1945– Creator of the Mark-8 computer

Jonathan Titus is the creator of the Mark-8, one of the first microprocessor-based personal computers. In July 1974 Titus's computer was featured on the cover of *Radio Electronics* magazine. The accompanying article, written by Titus, contained instructions for computer hobbyists to build their own model. The Mark-8 was essentially a scaled-down version of the minicomputers in use at that time, but whereas those computers were relatively large and expensive, the Mark-8, which used the recently released Intel 8008 microprocessor, put an unprecedented amount of computing power into the hands of individual computer users. Although it was soon eclipsed in popularity by the 1975 appearance of the Altair 8800 computer kit, the Mark-8 is still remembered as an important first step in the personal-computer revolution.

Jonathan A. Titus was born on November 24, 1945 in Washington, D.C. He received his B.S. in chemistry from Worcester Polytechnic Institute, in Massachusetts, in 1967 and his M.S. in the same subject from the Rensselaer Polytechnic Institute, in Troy, New York, in 1969. He received his Ph.D. in chemistry from the Virginia Polytechnic Institute and State University (Virginia Tech), in Blacksburg, in 1978.

While pursuing his degree at Virginia Tech, Titus belonged to a research group that used minicomputers to control chemical instruments and experiments and analyze the data. He had been interested in computers since high school, when he built some simple adding machines and other computing devices. Now that he was able to work with the school's powerful minicomputer, a Digital Equipment Corporation PDP-8/L, Titus found himself increasingly drawn to computers and electronics. Using the PDP-8/L he taught himself how to program a computer using assembly language. Like many computer enthusiasts of the period, he wanted to have a computer of his own, but the available minicomputers, although smaller and less powerful than mainframes, were nevertheless too expensive for individual hobbyists to afford. The PDP-8/L, for example, sold for $8,500 when it was originally released in the late 1960s. By the early 1970s it was available for $5,000, but that was still well beyond reach. In an article titled "The Mark-8 Minicomputer," posted on a Web site run by a computer enthusiast named John Lewczyk, Titus noted that some members of the Amateur Computer Society, of which he was a member, had made attempts to build a copy of the PDP-8/L. "I can't recall whether or not they had any success," he wrote. "In those days, although some functions were available on small-scale integrated circuits, the biggest roadblock was the memory. The minicomputers of the time used core memory, which took quite a bit of external circuitry to properly drive the individual magnetic cores which actually stored information. Thus, memory was out of reach for almost all amateur computer enthusiasts, and so were computers themselves."

In 1972 Intel Corporation introduced the 8008 chip, the first commercial 8-bit microprocessor. (The term 8-bit refers to the amount of data the central processing unit can compute at one time.) The 8008 was able to access 16 kilobytes (Kb) of memory. This technological advancement led to the first microprocessor-based computers, the earliest of which was the Micral, built in France in 1973. The Micral, priced at $1,750, did not sell well in the U.S., but the term "microcomputer" first appeared in print in reference to that computer in June 1973. In that same year, the Scelbi Computer Company, of Milford, Connecticut, introduced the Scelbi-8H microcomputer, also based on the Intel 8008 chip. (The company name was an acronym for scientific, electronic, and biological.) The Scelbi was the first microprocessor-based computer that sold as a kit. (The Micral was sold fully assembled.) The Scelbi was advertized for $565 and came with 1Kb of programmable memory. An additional 15Kb of memory was available for $2,760.

When the Intel 8008 first appeared Titus spent months studying the chip architecture and an accompanying databook provided by Intel. In his online article, Titus wrote, "While driving to Canada for a vacation in 1973, I resolved to adapt a demonstration circuit that Intel published in its book and use it as the basis of my own computer. I wrote to Intel and asked for some sample devices because the 8008 chips sold for $125 each from distributors." Even if cost had not been a factor, the availability of the chips was limited. "Not many distributors carried them, because they didn't know what sort of market there was for them," he noted.

Although Titus used the basic Intel circuit, he made several modifications to exploit the chip's memory capabilities. Titus then gave his computer a set of front-panel controls and indicators, similar to those found on the PDP-8/L. Short programs could be entered in binary code using the switches. He connected the computer to a TV Typewriter (a popular keyboard designed by Don Lancaster in 1973), a digital-to-analog converter (DAC), and an oscilloscope. Titus called his computer the Mark-8; the number 8 referred to the number of bits the computer used, and the term Mark, according to Titus, was simply a spur-of-the-moment choice.

After thoroughly testing the prototype, Titus contacted Larry Steckler at Radio Electronics magazine to discuss publishing information about the Mark-8 as a construction project. (Titus had also approached Popular Electronics, but the magazine had shown no interest.) Steckler, after verifying that the Mark-8 worked as described, put it on the cover of the 1974 July issue, with the headline "Build the Mark-8: Your Personal Minicomputer." Titus wrote the accompanying article, plus a more detailed explanation of the computer that Radio Electronics published in a separate 50-page booklet, which sold for $5.

The Mark-8 carries the distinction of being the first personal computer to have its plans published in a major magazine. Unlike the Micral, which was sold as a completed unit, or the Scelbi, which was available in kit form, the Mark-8 had to be assembled by hobbyists with their own materials, using the circuit-board layouts and assembly information published by Radio Electronics. The computer could be built for about $350. In 1974, when few hobbyists had their own computers, this was an inexpensive and attractive option. According to Titus, Radio Electronics sold about 7,500 of the $5 booklets about the Mark-8. Titus contracted with Techniques, a circuit-board company in New Jersey, to sell sets of circuit boards for about $50. Titus recalled that approximately 400 of these sets were sold. Besides his fee for writing the Radio Electronics article, Titus received royalties on the boards and on the booklets. Although he never got rich from his invention, this was a fair amount of money for a graduate student, and Titus used the proceeds to buy a top-of-the-line IBM Selectric III typewriter.

The Mark-8 caused a considerable stir in the computing world. Numerous user groups sprouted up across the country to share ideas and construction tips. The Mark-8 also inspired some of the earliest hobbyist newsletters, including Hal Singer's Micro-8 Newsletter and Hal Chamberlin's Computer Hobbyist magazine. The first issue of Creative Computing, a magazine that became an important source of information for hobbyists, appeared in September 1974. The cover of the January 1975 issue of Popular Electronics featured the Altair 8800, an inexpensive computer kit sold by Micro Instrumentation and Telemetry Systems (MITS), a company co-founded by Ed Roberts. The Altair, which was based on Intel's advanced new 8080 chip and which MITS sold in kit form for less than $400, became a startling commercial success. Although the Altair suffered from design flaws, it rode the wave of hobbyist enthusiasm that the Mark-8 had helped to create and quickly surpassed its predecessor in popularity.

In 1974 Titus co-founded the Blacksburg Group, a small company that developed educational electronic equipment and published books about electronics and computers. In 1984 he left the Blacksburg Group to join the staff of *EDN*, an electronics and technology magazine, where he worked until 1993. From 1993 to 2002 Titus was an editorial director at *Test and Measurement World* magazine, covering the electronics-testing industry. Since 2002 he has been a self-employed technical writer and computer consultant. He lives in Milford, Massachusetts.

Titus is a member of the National Association of Science Writers. In 2002 he received the George R. Stibitz Computer & Communications Pioneer Award, presented by the American Computer Museum in conjunction with the Computer Science Department of Montana State University. The orig-inal Mark-8 computer now resides in the permanent Information Age exhibit in the Smithsonian Institution's National Museum of American History.

"I still run into people who remember the Mark-8 or who have used some of the books I wrote and edited in the 70s and 80s," Titus recalled in an e-mail that is posted on-line on the Classic Computing Web site. "That makes me feel very proud, and it's a feeling that money can't buy. So I didn't become rich in dollars from the Mark-8, but it was a rich and rewarding experience. That's plenty."—A. I. C.

Suggested Reading: Classic Computing Web site; Computer Museum of America Web site; John Lewczyk Web site; Maxfield and Montrose Interactive Web site

---

Tomlinson, Ray

April 23, 1941– Electronic-mail pioneer

A handful of inventions have revolutionized the way human beings communicate—Johannes Gutenberg's printing press, Samuel Morse's telegraph, and Alexander Graham Bell's telephone among the most prominent. In the aforementioned cases, the men behind the inventions have become famous, their names forever linked with their achievements in the public consciousness. This is not so in the case of electronic mail. Ray Tomlinson, who designed and implemented the first network-wide e-mail system in 1971, is generally known only in computing circles, not by the general public. (He is sometimes celebrated in such circles as the creator of the now-ubiquitous @ sign in e-mail addresses.) It is widely acknowledged among computer users that Tomlinson's invention is on a par with those of Morse or Bell and that without e-mail the Internet might never have become such a popularly used medium.

Ray Tomlinson was born on April 23, 1941 in Amsterdam, New York. In an interview with *Leaders of the Informationa Age*, Tomlinson recalled how his interest in technology first developed: "I think the seminal event was the wiring of our garage by my dad, uncles, and grandfather when I was about six or seven. My grandfather explained to me about wires conducting electricity and how switches worked. He called it juice and I had a vivid picture of orange juice flowing through the wires. As far back as I can remember, I seemed to be interested in how things worked. If something was broken, I would try to take it apart, figure out how out should work, why it wasn't working as it should, and maybe fix it. I was pretty good at taking it apart, frustrated at not knowing how it should work. It took a while before I could do the 'fixing it' part. A number of clocks, radios and such met their doom. Finally, I got a electronic circuit kit for Christmas."

In 1963 Tomlinson received a B. S. from Rensselaer Polytechnic Institute, in Troy, New York. (In 2001 he was inducted into the school's Alumni Hall of Fame.) In 1965 he earned a master's degree in electrical engineering from the Massachusetts Institute of Technology (MIT), in Cambridge, and he spent the next two years working on a doctorate. He was then hired by Bolt, Beranek & Newman Technologies (BBN), a company founded in 1948 and based in Cambridge. BBN had a government contract to help develop the ARPANET, the forerunner to the modern Internet, which had been intended to link computer systems all over the country in case of a nuclear attack. BBN's work on the ARPANET began in the late 1960s, when the U.S. Department of Defense Advanced Research Projects Agency, most commonly known as ARPA (or sometimes DARPA), commissioned the company to build a network of Interface Message Processors (IMPs), or nodes, at various sites. Tomlinson explained to *Leaders of the Information Age*: "Our company, BBN, was building the nodes for the network, but only four IMPs were delivered the first year. Our [own] IMP was built in the second year, but it was installed in a different building from where our computer was located so we had to wait for special hardware to be built." The network had expanded to 23 sites by 1972.

When Tomlinson began work at BBN, the company was in the process of developing a time-sharing computer-operating system called TENEX, as well as an electronic-message program named SNDMSG. Electronic-message programs were not unheard of at the time; in the mid-1960s an e-mail system of sorts was created at MIT, but because it was only able to send mail to people who were logged onto the MIT computer, it never provided more than a little-used alternative to the campus's regular mail system. Computer mailboxes were fairly primitive in those days; changes to text could not be made by overwriting, but had to be appended to the end of the mailbox. During the summer and fall of 1971, Tomlinson was, in addition to his work on TENEX and SNDMSG, developing an experimental file-exchange system called CYPNET (referred to in some sources as CPYNET.) that would allow users to transfer files across the ARPANET. As Tomlinson explained in an on-line interview for *SAP Info* (April 15, 2002), "CYPNET could send and receive files, but, unlike SNDMSG, could not write any material onto the end of the mailbox. Therefore, the idea occurred to me to incorporate the CYPNET code into the SNDMSG code so as to enable it to direct messages through a network connection to remote mailboxes in addition to appending messages to local mailboxes." In a profile posted on the BBN Web site, he admitted, "Adding the missing piece [to the protocol] was a no-brainer—just a minor addition." In order to distinguish local mail from network mail, Tomlinson looked for a symbol that wasn't a digit and didn't occur naturally in someone's name. He hit upon the @ sign, which had previously been used predominately for indicating unit price, as in a grocery receipt reading "four apples @ 20 cents each." He noted in his BBN profile, "[It] seemed to make sense. . . . I used the @ sign to indicate that the user was 'at' some other host rather than being local."

Tomlinson sent the first e-mail message to himself using two Digital Equipment Corporation PDP-10 computers, standing side-by-side but unconnected except for their link to the ARPANET. "The test messages were entirely forgettable and I have, therefore, forgotten them," he quipped in his BBN profile. He has theorized that one of the first was most likely QWERTYUIOP, composed by dragging his fingers over the first row of letters on the computer keyboard. Satisfied that his system worked, he sent another message to his colleagues via e-mail to inform them about the new feature and to demonstrate how it worked. "The first use of network mail," Tomlinson explained in his profile, "announced its own existence."

Initially, Tomlinson was hesitant to reveal the existence of e-mail because he wasn't supposed to be working on such a project. However, his worries quickly faded when Larry Roberts, an ARPA director, began conducting all of his own correspondence using the system. Electronic mail began to spread dramatically across the ARPANET. Within two years an estimated 75 percent of all ARPANET traffic was attributable to e-mail. To its early users, the system seemed much more like a natural outgrowth of the work they had been doing than an entirely new technological approach to communications. The style of e-mail—terse, direct, and unpolished—appealed to engineers who were used to communicating in such a manner anyway. According to a 1978 paper (published by the Institute of Electrical and Electronic Engineers) by J. C. R. Licklider and Albert Vezza, two of the architects of the ARPANET, the popularity of e-mail was not surprising. As quoted in a 1998 article by Todd Campbell for *PreText Magazine* (on-line), Licklider and Vezza noted: "One of the advantages of the message systems over letter mail was that, in an ARPANET message, one could write tersely and type imperfectly, even to an older person in a superior position and even to a person one did not know very well, and the recipient took no offense. . . . Among the advantages of the network message services over the telephone were the fact that one could proceed immediately to the point without having to engage in small talk first, that the message services produced a preservable record, and that the sender and receiver did not have to be available at the same time."

Tomlinson told *Leaders of the Information Age*, "E-mail was immediately popular among those who had the facilities to use it. The problem was that very few people had access to a computer connected to the network. I would estimate that number at a few hundred individuals. More computers and more network access were needed. Computers were expensive — $100,000 for a computer with less memory than a modern PDA [personal digital assistant], and so were network connections. E-mail was right there near the top of the list for consumers of network bandwidth and just about everyone with access to a network-connected computer used e-mail. It was only a question of reducing the cost and that took time."

By 1975 there were 1,000 registered users of e-mail on the ARPANET, and demand was growing quickly, beginning with universities who wanted their own computer network with a messaging system. One of the first of these new networks was Usenet, formed in 1978 by colleges not included on the ARPANET. Usenet even allowed users to subscribe to news groups where people could discuss issues. By 1991, 20 years after Tomlinson sent the first e-mail to himself, there were millions of newsgroup subscribers and 35,000 nodes on the Usenet system.

The driving force behind the expansion of these networks—and of the Internet itself—was unquestionably electronic mail. E-mail allowed important messages to cross the country within a matter of minutes, instead of the days it would take for conventional mail; it all but eliminated the problems of communicating between different time zones. In businesses, face-to-face meetings were reduced because important messages could be sent to everyone without the need for a meeting; even long-distance phone calls were reduced, as e-mail proved to be cheaper and more efficient.

As with every revolutionary development, unintended problems arose with Tomlinson's brainchild. The speed of the system is such that responses are often hasty or ill conceived. The general terseness of the messages sometimes appears rude to those unused to the conventions of the medium. Some bemoan that traditional grammar and punctuation are being lost. Perhaps most seriously, there is the unending problem of junk e-mail or "spam"—mass mailings selling everything from real estate to sexually explicit photographs that the networks have been unable to staunch effectively thus far. Tomlinson remains proud of his discovery, despite the problems. When asked by *Leaders of the Information Age* if he ever thinks about the immense significance of his invention, Tomlinson joked, "If I stop thinking about it, somebody is sure to come along and remind me." He continued, "Certainly I think about it and it is gratifying to have done something that has affected so many people. My favorite example is of a librarian at the National Institute of Standards and Technology who interviewed me for a newsletter. She asked the same sort of questions that you are asking and wrote her article. A few months later, I received a message from her thanking me profusely. Her reason was that after she spoke to me, her brother had been diagnosed with a neural disorder, and she and her sister-in-law were understandably upset. But, they discovered others in a similar situation and through e-mail formed a kind of support group where they discussed the disease, its prognosis, ways of coping, and so on. This brought home to me the nature of what I had done."

Ray Tomlinson, who continues to work as a principal engineer at BBN, is a member of Tau Beta Pi and Eta Kappa Nu and has published a score of papers on distributed architecture, networking protocols, processor hardware design, speech synthesis, and time-sharing computers. In 2000 he was awarded the George R. Stibitz Computer Pioneer Award from the American Computer Museum, and in 2001 he was honored for his work by the International Academy of Digital Arts and Sciences, which presented him with its first Lifetime Achievement Award.—C. M.

Suggested Reading: BBN Technologies Web site; *Darwin* (on-line) Jan. 2002; *Forbes* (on-line) Oct. 5, 1998; *PreText Magazine* (on-line) 1998; *SAP Info* (on-line) Apr. 15, 2002

Torres y Quevedo, Leonardo

Dec. 28, 1852–Dec. 18, 1936 Engineer; mathematician

One of the earliest explorers of digital computational devices, Leonardo Torres y Quevedo was a pioneer in the field of Spanish science research. Trained as an engineer and mathematician, Torres y Quevedo was instrumental in the construction of many railways throughout Spain, and contributed significantly to the study of remote-control systems. His work with computational devices is less well known, because the few papers he did write never made it beyond his Spanish and French audience. Still, he was a man ahead of his time, expounding on the ideas put forth by Charles Babbage in the early 1800s, and proving that automated computing machines could be successfully built. Resources for his work (which he did not promote for commercial use but as a physical means of proving his theories) were limited at the time in his country, and as a result, his ideas received little attention outside of Spain until after his death. Had he been more widely acknowledged, and had there been a more pressing need, it is believed that Torres y Quevedo could have invented the first digital computer decades before it was unveiled in the United States.

Leonardo Torres y Quevedo was born in Santa Cruz de Iguna, Santander, Spain, on December 28, 1852. He was born into a family of technicians and as a result, he studied civil engineering for the first part of his life. For a while, he drew plans for railroad lines in southern Spain and went on to be a member of the French Academy of Science and president of the Academy of Science of Madrid. He was, however, primarily interested in the construction of machines that performed functions automatically. He would spend his entire life working on the theoretics behind these "automatics," as he called them, but he rarely built any of his inventions, as there was no overwhelming need or desire for such machines during his lifetime. He was also a victim of the mechanical and engineering limitations affecting his country's technological growth during his day. Even more problematic to his work was his disinterest in writing, which he once called a "form of martyrdom." As a result, there are few documented reports from his hands, and historians have had to rely on information from the few papers he did write, as well as from the patents he obtained during his lifetime. Still, most scientists have categorically agreed that Torres y Quevedo's work, although limited, was ahead of its time and, had it been pursued, could have led to the creation of a much earlier version of the digital computer.

As early as 1893, Torres y Quevedo proposed an electromechanical application for the ideas and theories expressed by Charles Babbage in the 1820s and 1830s. This early exploration of digital computational devices was a significant step toward advancing existing technology, which mostly consisted of punched-card, input/output adding machines. One of Torres y Quevedo's earliest inventions was a mechanical analog device used to perform mathematical calculations. In 1906 he built a model boat that was radio controlled and demonstrated it before the king of Spain, commanding it by radio to adjust rudder and speed. He later applied this same technology to a torpedo project.

Eager to take advantage of emerging electromechanical methods, Torres y Quevedo touted the energy source of radio as a radical new way of solving mathematical operations. Problems mathematicians struggled with for the previous 300 years could, he argued, be worked out through the application of electricity. He suggested that electrically driven machines could be able to be instructed to "do certain things which depend on certain conditions." He also suggested that preestablished arbitrary rules used to control the behavior of machines would make the use of electricity an ideal energy source for calculations. This theory can be said to be one of the earliest definitions of a programmable machine, decades before they would be constructed.

Torres y Quevedo was specifically interested in the building of machines capable of computation and data processing. Algebraic machines were the focus of his inaugural lecture to the Royal Academy of Sciences in 1901, in which he combined mechanical and electromechanical means to theorize a machine that would solve algebraic equations of any degree. The central component of the machine was an endless spindle that was made to add the construction of one monomial with that of another, automatically working out the formula $y = \log(10^x+1)$. Torres y Quevedo later developed Telekino, a remote control system using Hertzian waves (electromagnetic waves produced by the oscillation of electricity in a conductor), in 1906, using it as a tool for carrying out various experiments.

Torres y Quesdao's most noted work emerged in 1911, when he unveiled a machine (the first of two) that could automatically play chess. It was the first such machine in history, electronically sensing the pieces on the board and then moving them via a mechanical arm. In 1922 he invented another chess machine, this one using magnets (placed under the chess board) to move the pieces. This later device is still fully operational today. From what other researchers have conjectured, Torres y Quevedo was interested in challenging society's accepted notions regarding the limitations of machines, and his main motivation behind these chess sets was to exploit, to its fullest capacity, the new proficiencies that the electromechanical techniques offered. *Scientific American* offered an observation of the chess machine and its inventor: "There is no claim that (the chess player) will think or accomplish things where thought is necessary, but its inventor claims that the limits within which thought is really necessary need to be better defined, and that an automation can do many things that are popularly classed with thought. It will do certain things which depend upon certain conditions, and these according to arbitrary rules selected in advance."

In 1913, Torres y Quevedo published a paper titled "Essais sur l'Automatique" (Essays on Automatics), which would later be considered a significant contribution to the history of computing. In the paper the inventive pioneer explored his work with computational devices and his ideas on computing in general. He further developed his argument that electromechanical methods be applied to the construction of analytical devices. He also extended acknowledgment to Charles Babbage's work on constructing a mechanical Difference Engine and Analytical Engine, placing it within the context of the developments in calculators that had occurred near the time of the paper's publication. Most significantly, in the paper, Torres y Quevedo described a complete design for a machine capable of calculating the value of the formula $a^x(y-z)^2$ for a sequence of sets of values of the variables involved. The machine would be able to store decimal digits, perform arithmetic operations using built-in function tables, and compare the values of two quantities. He further suggested that the program be controlled by a read-only program. In addition, this ground breaking paper also provides what many believe to be the first proposal of the notion of floating-point arithmetic. Looking back, many scientists believe that, if finances and practical need had been present, Torres y Quevedo would have constructed a general purpose electromechanical computer more than 20 years before one was invented.

Outside of his innovative work with computers, Torres y Quevedo was responsible for several engineering feats. He built the 280-meter-long funicular railway on Mount Ulia in San Sebastian and he helped construct the cable-car line at Niagra Falls, Ontario, which was 580 meters long and installed on February 10, 1916. The line was made by suspending the cable car by several cables. The cables' tensions were made to be independent of the weight of the car through counterweights which were maintained at the ends of each cable. The result of Torres y Quevedo's system was that safety could be ensured because if one cable broke there would be no increase in the load carried by the others, and therefore there would be no danger. The Spanish Aero Car, as it was named, remains a popular tourist attraction at Niagra Falls to this day.

In 1920 Torres y Quevedo actually carried out some of his automatic computation device theories, through the construction of a series of prototypes. He first produced a demonstration machine with the ability to evaluate the value of p x q-b. He then impressed the attendees of a Paris conference with a machine consisting of an arithmetic unit connected to a typewriter on which commands could be typed and the results printed automatically. By all accounts, Torres y Quevedo had no intention of producing the machine for commercial use, but rather as merely a means by which to demonstrate his theories. As a result, the machine, called an electromechanical arithmometer, was never fully completed, but it did solidify Torres y Quevedo's claim that such machines could be built and become fully operational "automatics."

Torres y Quevedo died in Madrid on December 18, 1936, at the start of the Spanish civil war. With his death, a void was left in the Spanish scientific community, and serious research did not take hold again in Spain until the late 1950s. Despite the significance of his early work, the writings of Torres y Quevedo had almost no bearing on developments in computer engineering during the next three decades. He is highly revered in his native country of Spain however, where a laboratory was named after him and where several books have been written about him. Many of his primitive machines, some of which are still in working order, remain on exhibition at the Colegio di Ingenieros do Caminos, Canales, y Puertos, in Madrid.—D. B.

Suggested Reading: *World Who's Who in Science*, 1968; *Dictionary of Scientific Biography* vol. 13, 1976; Lee, J. A. N., ed. *International Biographical Dictionary of Computer Pioneers*, 1995

Torvalds, Linus

1969– Creator of the Linux operating system

As a 21-year-old student at the University of Helsinki, the Finnish programmer Linus Torvalds grew fed up with Microsoft operating systems, but he could not afford to buy the more powerful Unix operating system. (Operating systems, such as Unix and Microsoft Windows, are the master control programs that run a computer.) In an act of programming braggadocio, he wrote his own operating system, called Linux (pronounced *lee-nucks* or *lih-nucks*). Since then Linux has been maintained and updated by Torvalds and a loose-knit group of hackers who, driven by their love of programming, communicate over the Internet and never copyright their results—an approach to software development known as the open-source model. One would not normally think that a product that originated as little more than a hobby could seriously challenge another developed by armies of well-paid software programmers. Yet many people believe that Linux—which currently has more than 10 million users worldwide and is steadily gaining more adherents—may be the David that topples Microsoft's Goliath-like dominance of the operating-systems market. Some industry analysts have even predicted that the growing popularity of Linux may signal the eventual triumph of the open-source movement, turning the capitalist orthodoxy of proprietary ownership on its head.

Unlike Microsoft's operating systems, the code of the Linux operating system is not kept secret. Anyone—from a teenage computer enthusiast to the most knowledgeable computer programmer—can go into Linux, tinker with its code, and suggest a change to Torvalds, who, for the past decade, has functioned as the nerve center of this sprawling Linux community. Already users have contributed thousands of ideas that have made Linux better. In fact, the number of lines of code that Torvalds himself has written is now minuscule. As he explained to Amy Harmon for the *New York Times Magazine* (February 21, 1999), "The kernel [the most vital code of the operating system] is 1 percent of the entire program. Of that 1 percent, I've written between 5 and 10 percent. I think the most important part is that I got it started."

The unlikely Information Age folk hero was born in Finland into a family of journalists in 1969, the year that Unix was being developed by Dennis Ritchie and Kenneth Thompson at Bell Labs. His parents named him for both the chemist Linus Pauling and the cartoonist Charles Schultz's *Peanuts* character Linus. Torvalds got interested in programming when he was 10, after his grandfather bought a Commodore VIC-20. Young Torvalds used the computer to program his own games.

Torvalds attended the University of Helsinki, where he studied computer science. During this time he came to the conclusion that, from a technical standpoint, Microsoft's operating systems were unsatisfactory. Unix was better, he believed, but it was designed primarily for computer workstations, not personal computers, and at the time it cost several thousand dollars, far more than Torvalds could afford. Buoyed by his youthful sense that he "was the best programmer in the world," as he told a reporter for the on-line magazine *boot*, he decided to write his own operating system for his personal computer. "A lot of people have told me that you need to be good," he explained, "but you also need to be bad enough because if you knew beforehand how much work it would have been to do, nobody sane would have even started it."

After completing a bare-bones version of Linux, Torvalds thought that he would be the only person who would actually use it. But after he put it on an FTP (file-transfer protocol) site to make it available to others over the Internet, several people expressed interest in it. "What happened almost immediately was that people started commenting on the missing features that I didn't need personally," he told a reporter for *Computerworld* (August 17, 1998, on-line). The Linux community began to grow, with more and more people offering their advice and help.

With the collective IQ of computer hackers from around the world continually nourishing Linux, many managers maintain that Linux is technically superior to Microsoft's operating systems, which are notorious for their frequent crashes. Users of Microsoft's Windows NT, for example, have grown to fear the nasty surprise referred to as the "blue screen of death." By contrast, computers using Linux have been known to operate for months without crashing, freezing, or requiring a single reboot. The reliability and efficiency of Linux—not to mention the fact that it can be downloaded for free from the Internet—have won it numerous converts. Linux-driven computers have done everything from generating the special effects in the movie *Titanic* to simulating atomic shock waves at the U.S. Department of Energy's Los Alamos National Laboratory, in New Mexico.

The advocacy of some Linux users resembles the fierceness of a religious crusade. To many of those adherents, Microsoft is an evil empire and Linux their savior. Torvalds doesn't share that view. "I don't mind Microsoft making money," he told Amy Harmon. "I mind them having a bad operating system." Although Microsoft is frequently berated by critics like Torvalds, its systems have certain undeniable advantages that have led to its market dominance. Its ease of use for computer neophytes is one of its major selling points. Another is the wide variety of Microsoft-compatible applications, ranging from word processing to spreadsheet arrangements to publishing. But in some ways, Microsoft's advantages, according to Torvalds and others, can become disadvantages. Revising a bug in the operating system, for example, can potentially make unusable the hundreds of applications and related programs designed for use with the system. With Linux, Torvalds has argued, the process of revising the program is much simpler and more meritocratic: the best code wins.

Originally, Torvalds placed a very restrictive license on Linux; for example, because he didn't want people selling the program to others, he made it impossible to transfer the operating system to a disk. In 1992 he changed his philosophy and registered it under a General Public License (GPL) with the Free Software Foundation (FSF). Under the GPL's copyright (or "copyleft," as the FSF calls it), the source code for Linux was made public. Other developers were free to modify it and make improvements, which they could then market without paying Torvalds a commission. But there was a catch: They too would have to make any changes in the source code available to the public. Torvalds also ensured that he could not personally profit from Linux in the future. "So even if I turn to the dark side [by trying to benefit financially from Linux], nobody can take it over," he explained to Amy Harmon.

Allowing the code to be freely distributed contradicted the development model on which Bill Gates, the co-founder and head of Microsoft, had made his fortune. In "Open Letter to Hobbyists," a now-famous memo that he wrote in 1976, Gates contended that sharing software, which in early computer culture was common, was preventing "good software from being written," as quoted by Nick Langley in *Computer Weekly* (January 25, 2001). "What hobbyist can put three man years into programming, finding all bugs, documenting his product, and distribute for free?" Gates asked rhetorically. There were several programmers, however, who espoused doing just that, most notably Richard Stallman, who founded the FSF in 1984, and is considered by many to be one of the fathers of the open-source movement. Stallman had developed a free operating system, called GNU (a recursive acronym for *Gnu's Not Unix*), and later made fundamental contributions to Linux. By the time Torvalds was putting together Linux, the open-source model had found success in several areas, such as the Berkeley Software Distribution Unix (BSD), developed by Bill Joy at the University of California at Berkeley. Other open-source products that have been successful in the IT (information technology) business are Perl, Python, Apache, and Samba.

Torvalds has called his decision to get a GPL copyright and use open source his single best decision in the development of Linux. "There are lots of advantages in a free system, the obvious one being that it allows more developers to work on it, and extend it," he told the on-line journal *First Monday* (1998). "However, even more important than that is the fact that it in one fell swoop also gave me a lot of people who *used* it and thus both tested it for bugs and tested it for usability. The 'usability' part comes from the fact that a single person (or even a group of persons sharing some technical goal) doesn't even think of all the uses a large user community would have for a general-purpose system."

Dealing with suggestions for improvements has consumed a significant amount of Torvalds's time. "On average I almost have to read E-mail for two hours a day just to keep up," he told *Computerworld*. "On top of those two hours for just reading E-mail, [I spend an additional] two or three hours to actually do something about it." The University of Helsinki helped Torvalds devote himself to Linux by allotting some of his work-study time to the project (in addition to his required teaching and research). He wrote his master's thesis on "porting" Linux. (Porting refers to the changes made to a program to allow it to run in a different computer environment, such as different hardware.)

Linux use blossomed during the heady "dot-com" era of the late 1990s, as countless Internet start-ups sought ways to get on-line quickly and cheaply. Since Linux could be easily installed on whatever low-end hardware was lying around, technology officers were able to solve their technical problems without going through the process of purchase orders, getting approvals, and buying expensive new hardware. As a result, Linux was widely adopted for use on Web servers, file servers, and print servers. According to some industry estimates, Linux today can be found on about 30 percent of computer servers—the computers that function as the hub on a network.

When Torvalds began building Linux in 1991, however, he did not have servers on his mind. He was looking to create a Unix-like operating system that would work on his own Intel 386 personal computer. The Internet and business communities appropriated the technology for their networking needs, and it has only been within the last few years that Linux has begun to make headway as a desktop operating system for personal computers. What was missing before was a user-friendly graphical interface, such as the familiar screen with windows and icons found in Microsoft Windows or the Macintosh operating system. In the early days of Linux, instead of pointing and clicking, one had to know arcane Unix-like command strings to run programs and add software, ensuring that Linux remained an operating system for the technically proficient.

This drawback has recently been overcome with the appearance of at least a dozen different graphical interfaces, the most popular of which are KDE and GNOME. Numerous software applications are now available as well, including word-processing programs and graphics programs, such as GIMP. Linux currently commands only a tiny fraction of the desktop business, but analysts predict that its low cost and enhanced reliability of Linux and its software applications could lead to strong growth, especially in the corporate world. "I absolutely believe in a Linux desktop," Torvalds told Steve Lohr for the *New York Times* (November 4, 2002). "I think the way it will happen is through corporate desktops, where Windows maintenance and licensing costs are just going to eventually cause more and more corporations to realize they just don't need the headaches of Windows anymore." This possibility, although for the moment mostly speculation, has spawned worried memos within Microsoft and accordingly transformed Torvalds into one of the most popular figures in the computing world.

In explaining why he has been willing to work on Linux without compensation, Torvalds has said that, more than money, bragging rights and the sheer fun of programming motivate programmers like himself. "If you're good, it's easy to get paid," Torvalds explained to *Forbes* (August 10, 1998). "Good programmers are rare enough that people pay them well. A big part of personal satisfaction is having your work recognized by your peers. That's fundamental in any psyche." Creating Linux has led to other benefits. As the person most closely associated with Linux, Torvalds received many job offers. In 1997 he accepted one from Transmeta, a secretive Silicon Valley start-up that is partially funded by Paul Allen, who co-founded Microsoft with Gates. Transmeta manufactures microprocessors, such as the power-saving Crusoe processor, and is not involved with Linux development in any way. Torvalds has said that he purposely chose a job unrelated to Linux so that his decisions about Linux would be made from a technical—rather than a marketing—perspective. (Torvalds blames the Microsoft system's technical problems on the company's emphasis on sales.)

Unlike Windows and Mac, which have only one or two current versions, Linux is available in several different "distributions" for users to choose from. As the demand for Linux grew rapidly in the late 1990s, companies such as Red Hat and Turbolinux began selling a packaged version of the operating system, including user guides and free tech support. These packages made it possible for those who were less tech-savvy to make an easy transition to Linux, rather than go through the process of downloading Linux and piecing it together themselves. Gaining ground on Windows, Linux soon became the fastest-growing server operating system. In 2000 Windows accounted for 42 percent of server operating-system shipments and Linux accounted for 27 percent. Also in 2000, in light of the proliferation of Linux brands, such as Caldera, Slackware, Mandrake, and SuSE, the Linux Standard Base was formed to establish compatibility standards to ensure that applications are able to run on any distribution.

The collapse of the dot-com market has been as difficult on Linux as it has been on the rest of the industry. Red Hat and the hardware maker VA Linux both had spectacular initial public offerings (IPOs) in 1999, with VA Linux setting the year's record for opening price, at $299 a share. By August 2000, shares of VA Linux were down more than 70 percent, and by February 2002 it was trading at $1 a share.

Nevertheless, the interest in Linux products has remained solid, perhaps in part because the sluggish economy has compelled managers to seek out inexpensive options. Major corporations have come out in support of Linux: International Business Machines (IBM) has invested heavily in bringing the operating system into the mainstream, and Compaq and Hewlett-Packard have been strong advocates, incorporating the operating system on several of their server product lines. Red Hat now claims such major clients as Amazon.com, and the Linux purveyor Lindows.com has released a personal computer preloaded with Linux that sells for $200 at Wal-Mart. Linux is also increasingly being used in high-performance scientific and research projects, such as in supercomputers for oil and gas exploration as well as medical and drug research.

The popularity of Linux has been strong enough to cause Microsoft CEO Steve Ballmer to identify Linux in 2001 as the number-one threat to Windows in the market for server software. Since Microsoft derives most of its desktop revenue not from its Windows operating system but from its Microsoft Office software applications, some analysts predict that it may eventually back off from the operating-system competition and focus on its other software development. Torvalds, for his part, has said that he is not particularly concerned about the looming battle. "They've had a lot of enemies in their time," Torvalds told Paula Rooney in an interview for *Computer Reseller News* (January 29, 2001). "Let them fight one enemy that doesn't care for a change."

In January 2001 Torvalds released the long-awaited version 2.4 Linux kernel, with a wealth of new features and add-ons. He is still the sole overseer of the kernel, which means that, although he does not profit from it, he must sign off on any changes developers wish to make. This is a job that Torvalds enjoys (his approvals are usually sent in casual E-mails), and an arrangement that most of the Linux community accepts as a given. Those who have worked with him say that he can be headstrong at times, but that he is ready to discard his own work whenever something better comes along and has made a practice of responding to submissions promptly, courteously, and patiently. "Torvalds' decisions are not ones you'd quickly throw out the window," Bob Shimp, a marketing director at Oracle, which contributed to version 2.4, told Paula Rooney. "When he's ready to release the final version, that's when distributors package it up. Having a little bit of control like that is a good thing. . . . When Linus says it's ready to go, that's the release people tend to pick up and focus on." With the market for Linux rapidly expanding, however, some industry observers have suggested that Torvalds may come to be seen more as a bottleneck than a facilitator. Moreover, with large blue-chip corporations now investing heavily in Linux development, Torvalds will face increased pressure to meet deadlines (version 2.4 suffered some delays, as Torvalds worked out a few "finishing touches") and give companies more influence over the final product. Some vendors contend that a "Linux Board" should be formed, with full-time engineers devoted to testing new code, finalizing it, and releasing it as quickly as possible. Torvalds, however, has as yet no interest in relinquishing his post, and does not see an advisory board as being a real improvement. "Delays are kind of inevitable in this business," Torvalds told Paula Rooney. "Of course, because I never really had any hard deadlines that I set for myself—my only criterion was really, 'when I'm happy with it'—I probably didn't get as hung up about the release as an 'official' body would have. And maybe a 'Linux Board'

would have held people to stricter deadlines. Who knows? At the same time, I think 2.4x happened when it was ready—not before, and not later."

Fluent in Swedish (his native language), Finnish, and English, Torvalds currently lives in Santa Clara, California. He and his wife, Tove, who is a six-time karate champion of Finland, have two daughters, Patricia and Daniela. The programmer is fond of penguins and chose the image of one as the logo for Linux. He has been described as humble and self-effacing, albeit proud of his programming achievements. "He is easygoing in a lot of ways. He is modest, almost shy, but strong-willed when it comes to technical issues," John "Mad Dog" Hall, the executive director of Linux International, told Charlene O'Hanlon for *Computer Reseller News* (November 12, 2001). "That has put him in a leadership role."—A. I. C.

Suggested Reading: *Computer Reseller News* Jan. 29, 2001; *Computer Weekly* p28 Jan. 25, 2001; *Computerworld* (on-line) Aug. 17, 1998; *Forbes* Aug. 10, 1998; *New York Times* G p1+ Oct. 8, 1998, C p1 Nov. 4, 2002; *New York Times Magazine* p34+ Feb. 21, 1999, with photo; *Technology Review* p36+ Jan./Feb. 1999, with photos; *Time Digital* (on-line) Apr. 12, 1999, with photo; *Washington Post* F p15 May 22, 1995, with photo

---

Tramiel, Jack

1928– Entrepreneur; computer-industry executive

Jack Tramiel survived both a Nazi death camp in his native Poland and a business scandal in Canada to become one of the major figures in the personal-computer revolution. He successfully expanded his company, Commodore Business Machines, from selling typewriters into manufacturing personal computers. Tramiel was determined to get computers into the homes of ordinary people. He frequently declared war on his competitors, slashing his prices constantly. In 1982 he released the Commodore 64, which eventually became the best-selling computer of all time. The Commodore 64 and its companion devices enabled users to play games, write programs, create documents, and communicate through commercially available on-line services. After a dispute with a major stockholder, Tramiel resigned from Commodore at the height of its success. For the next 12 years he tried to resurrect Atari, the troubled video-game company that had previously dominated the market. Despite his efforts, Atari was unable to compete with rival game-makers Nintendo, Sega, and Sony, and Atari's line of personal computers, while popular, eventually lost users to IBM-compatible PCs. When he piloted Commodore, however, Jack Tramiel paved the way for such companies as Apple, IBM, Microsoft, Dell, and Compaq to become a daily part of ordinary people's lives.

Jack Tramiel was born Idek Tramielski in 1928 in the city of Lodz, in Poland. When Germany invaded Poland on September 1, 1939, starting World War II, the young Tramiel looked upon the arriving tanks, planes, and weapons with a child's fascination. "It was a fantastic thing," he recalled to Carol J. Loomis for *Fortune* (April 13, 1998). Soon, however, the Nazis began to segregate the city's population. The Tramielskis, who were Jewish, were confined to a ghetto along with Lodz's 200,000 other Jewish residents. For the next five years, Tramiel and his parents struggled to survive in the Lodz ghetto, living together in a single room. Tramiel's father made a meager living as a shoemaker. Tramiel, who was an only child, worked in a pants factory.

In August 1944 the Nazis deported the Tramielskis to the notorious Auschwitz death camp, where over one million Jews were exterminated, in Poland. The men and women were separated, and Tramiel lost track of his mother. Tramiel and his father were examined by Dr. Josef Mengele, the infamous Nazi scientist who conducted barbaric medical experiments on many prisoners. Mengele concluded that they were strong enough to work; others less fortunate were sent to the gas chambers. Tramiel and his father were assigned to work in a concentration camp near Hanover, Germany. Tramiel's mother remained behind.

In Germany, father and son endured cold weather and a poor diet. In December 1944 Tramiel's father, suffering from malnutrition, was sent to the camp's infirmary, where he died. Tramiel later learned that the Nazis had fatally poisoned him by injecting his veins with gasoline. Tramiel continued to work until the spring of 1945, when the Third Reich collapsed and U.S. troops liberated the camp. For the next two years, he lived among the ruins of post-war Europe. He supported himself by working at odd jobs and for a U.S. Army kitchen. For a brief time Tramiel had himself admitted to a sanitarium, even though he was perfectly sane, in order to have food.

Tramiel learned that his mother had survived Auschwitz and had returned to Lodz. In 1947 he married Helen Goldgrub, a woman he had met in a concentration camp. In November of the same year, he left Europe for the United States. "I figured I could handle just about anything," he told Loomis. His wife joined him a short time later.

Tramiel settled in New York City. He found a job working as a handyman for a lamp store and learned to speak English by watching films. He eventually adopted the name Jack Tramiel and shed his Polish accent.

In 1948 Tramiel enlisted in the U.S. Army, where he learned to repair office equipment. After his release, in 1952, he went to work as a typewriter repairman. He had soon saved enough money to open his own typewriter repair shop in the New York City borough of the Bronx. He began buying old typewriters, fixing them up, and reselling them. His most important client was Fordham University, a well-known Bronx college.

Tramiel wanted to expand his business by importing Italian typewriters. The U.S. import regulations were too restrictive, so in 1955 Tramiel moved to Toronto, Canada, where he established Commodore Business Machines. (He chose the term Commodore—a navy rank—because he wanted to give his company a name with a "military ring"; his first ideas, General and Admiral, had already been taken.) Along with foreign and domestic typewriters, Commodore sold adding machines.

Commodore held a public offering of stock in 1962, an action that eventually embroiled Jack Tramiel in a financial scandal. According to an article by Subrata N. Chakravarty in *Forbes* (January 17, 1983), Tramiel accepted substantial loans from C. Powell Morgan, the president and controlling stockholder of the Atlantic Acceptance Corporation. Morgan also served as Commodore's chairman and held huge amounts of stock in the company. A report by Ontario Supreme Court Justice Samuel H. S. Hughes, as cited by Chakravarty, stated that heavy insider trading of Commodore stock took place in order to inflate share prices. The report also accused Commodore of issuing "misleading financial statements and letters to shareholders." Tramiel denied any wrongdoing, claiming that he acted on Morgan's instructions. Tramiel

was never indicted, and in subsequent interviews over the past few decades, he has declined to discuss the scandal. Canada's financial community shunned him, however, and he was compelled in the late 1960s to return to the United States, setting up Commodore's headquarters in California's Silicon Valley, a region that was then distinguishing itself as a major center of electronic-systems manufacturing.

In the early 1970s Commodore introduced a series of innovative and popular handheld electronic calculators, built using semiconductor chips manufactured by Texas Instruments. When Texas Instruments began selling its own electronic calculators, however, they were able to undercut Commodore's sales with lower prices, threatening to put Tramiel's company out of business. Vowing never to be at the mercy of another supplier, Tramiel purchased MOS Technology, a Pennsylvania-based computer-chip manufacturer, in 1976. Tramiel was unaware at the time that MOS had developed a new computer chip, the 6502 microprocessor. Charles Peddle, an engineer at MOS, informed Tramiel that the chip could be used to build small computers for personal use in the home. Peddle believed that these personal computers would have a profitable future. Intrigued, Tramiel instructed Peddle and his son, Leonard, who was nearing the completion of his studies at Columbia University, in New York City, to build a prototype of a small computer, to be demonstrated six months later at the Comdex electronic show. The prototype was a success, and in 1977, after securing a $3 million loan from Irving Gould, a wealthy Canadian investor, Commodore Business Machines entered the personal-computer market. The company's first computer was the Personal Electronic Transactor (PET). The machine was priced at $795. Tramiel, unsure if the PET would sell enough units to make a profit, attracted attention by purchasing advertisements in newspapers and magazines. Within the first few months the PET had generated $3 million in sales.

As soon as PET hit the market, Commodore found itself competing against Apple Computers and the Tandy Corporation, which began selling their own personal computers the same year. Tramiel initiated a price war, gradually slashing PET's retail cost to attract customers. "Business is war," Tramiel explained to Loomis. "I don't believe in compromising. I believe in winning." Tramiel also began offering schools the opportunity to buy two PET computers for the price of one, in a bid to gain control of the large education market. He quickly became known as a fierce competitor. At one point he ran several full-page newspaper advertisements boasting that "Commodore ate the Apple," as quoted by Frederic Golden in *Time* (January 3, 1983). Tramiel also developed a reputation for being very difficult to work for. His authoritarian style of management, while making Commodore successful, did not always earn the appreciation of the executives and employees who served under him.

In 1980 Commodore unveiled the VIC-20, the first affordable color computer, priced at less than $300. It was primarily a video-game system; its use for business applications was limited, since it could display only 22 characters of text per line. A stunning commercial success, the VIC-20 was the first computer to sell more than one million units, with production up to 9,000 units per day. (The Apple II, which had been on the market since 1977, reached the one million mark a few months later.) A contributing factor to the VIC-20's success was Tramiel's decision to sell the computer in mainstream retail outlets instead of only obscure computer stores and via mail order.

In 1982 Tramiel introduced the Commodore 64 to the public. In many respects a new and improved version of the VIC-20, it had 64KB of memory and sold for about $600. (The comparable Apple II Plus offered only 48KB of memory and sold for twice as much.) The Commodore 64 had color graphics and was the first personal computer with an audio synthesizer chip. It was easy to operate and offered such add-ons as a disk drive, tape recorder, color monitor, modem, and printer. A large number of software programs were available, including games, spreadsheets, word processors, databases, personal organizers, and financial planners. For several years most of the programs came in three different formats: on disk, tape, and in the form of cartridges that were placed in a slot behind the computer. Having programs in three different formats gave customers different price options. Although slower than disk drives, tape drives were less expensive. As more people purchased disk drives, which gradually became less expensive, fewer programs were sold in the tape and cartridge formats.

The Commodore 64 introduced millions of people to the world of personal computing. Students used it to write term papers for school. Small-business owners used the computer to keep books and other records. Many others simply enjoyed the numerous games that were available from different software companies. Users with modems were able to log on to the Commodore Information Network, an on-line user forum hosted by CompuServe, one of the first pay-for-use on-line services. Users could access news and discussion forums, as well as send electronic mail and chat live with fellow computer users across the country.

In 1983 Commodore recorded about $700 million in sales and $88 million in profits. Sales for the following year exceeded $1 billion. The Commodore 64 eventually became the best-selling computer of all time, with between 17 and 22 million units sold overall. Commodore's success with low-priced, high-quality machines forced such rival companies as Timex, the internationally known watchmaker, and Coleco, a leader in the video-game industry, to abandon their attempts to break into the personal-computer market. In 1984 Commodore purchased personal-computer maker Amiga Corporation and made

plans to unveil the Commodore Amiga, a computer with revolutionary technology, in 1985.

At the height of Commodore's success, however, Jack Tramiel stepped down as president on January 13, 1984. In a statement issued to the media, Tramiel said, "Personal reasons prevent my continuing on a full-time basis with Commodore," as quoted by Andrew Pollack in the *New York Times* (January 14, 1984). Although exact details about Tramiel's resignation were never made clear, the press speculated that he had a major disagreement with Irving Gould, Commodore's chairman and chief financial backer.

Despite this setback, Jack Tramiel did not fade from public view. In July 1984 he made headlines by purchasing the home video-game division of Atari Corporation from Warner Communications. (Warner retained the coin-operated games division and Ataritel, the telecommunications division.) Atari, after dominating the video-game market for several years, had encountered serious economic difficulties in late 1982, due to a sudden drop in consumer demand for video-game products. Atari's sales plummeted as it faced strong competition from rival companies, primarily Commodore. Tramiel was able to acquire the company by granting Warner $240 million in promissory notes and warrants for a 32 percent interest in Tramiel's new venture. As part of the deal, Tramiel also invested about $30 million of his own money in Warner stock and took out a loan for about $45 million. "Warner essentially gave away the company, in hopes Tramiel could make something happen," one analyst told David E. Sanger for the *New York Times* (July 3, 1984). Other observers told the press that Jack Tramiel was the one person who could turn Atari around.

Tramiel moved quickly to make Atari profitable again. He reduced Atari's workforce from 5,000 employees worldwide to 1,500. Tramiel appointed his three sons, Leonard, Sam, and Garry, to key executive positions and hired 25 former Commodore employees. "We are keeping it very simple," he told Christine Winter for the *Chicago Tribune* (February 5, 1985). "We've reduced the staff to only what we need to run the company. When we have more transactions, not just more money, we will hire more people and build accordingly." To cut costs further, Tramiel attempted to cancel expensive contracts signed before he took over the company, such as a $6 million advertising campaign that was scheduled to run during the Olympics in the summer of 1984 and a $10 million agreement with popular actor Alan Alda, who was hired to promote Atari's new products in television commercials and print advertisements for the next several years.

Tramiel's chief strategy for resurrecting Atari centered on shifting the company's focus from selling video games to manufacturing personal computers. He hoped Atari could successfully compete against IBM, Apple, Compaq, and even Commodore. Shortly before the Christmas shopping season in 1984, Tramiel increased sales by cutting the price of the Atari 800XL computer from $180 to $120. In 1985 he unveiled several new computers that were both inexpensive and technologically advanced, such as the Atari ST personal computer. Although his plans to reap $1 billion in sales in 1985 proved too ambitious, Tramiel managed to double Atari's profits in 1985 to $120 million.

Atari held an initial public offering of stock in 1986, raising enough money to pay off the remaining $36 million debt with Warner. Under Tramiel's firm hand, Atari boasted its first profit in several years, $57 million from $492 million in revenues. Several newspaper articles credited Tramiel's leadership abilities with bringing the company back from the dead. In 1987 Tramiel even lured Nolan Bushnell, who founded Atari in 1972, back to the company to design video games.

Atari's comeback was short-lived. In 1987 Tramiel made a decision that helped set the stage for the company's downfall. Atari acquired the Federated Group, which owned a chain of electronics retailers, for $67.3 million. Tramiel hoped Federated's stores would help boost sales, by making Atari's computers and products more available and visible to consumers. However, Federated, operating as a subsidiary of Atari, began losing money in 1988. Several cost-cutting measures, including the closing of 25 stores by the next year, failed to stop Federated's slide. In 1989 two former Federated executives who were fired by Tramiel sued Atari, alleging that Tramiel refused to pay them the benefits and severance pay they were promised. According to Eric Lichtblau in the *Los Angeles Times* (August 16, 1989), Atari claimed during the trial that Federated's executives had inflated the firm's value at the time of the acquisition and also concealed several outstanding financial commitments. The two executives won their suit against Atari. Meanwhile, Atari was forced to close and sell off the remaining Federated stores in 1990. The Federated disaster cost Atari tens of millions of dollars.

Meanwhile, sales of Atari's popular ST series of personal computers began to decline in both the United States and Europe, where Tramiel had previously found a lucrative and receptive market. In 1989 Atari attempted to reestablish itself in the video-game market, releasing the Lynx, the first handheld video-game system with color. Although the Lynx featured excellent graphics, only a handful of games were available. By contrast, Nintendo's Gameboy, while having only black-and-white graphics, offered a wide library of games, many from high-profile game developers. The Gameboy, which was also smaller, cheaper, and used less battery power, quickly became the leader in the handheld market.

At the same time, Atari was losing ground in the home video-game console market, which was now controlled primarily by Nintendo and Sega. In 1993 Tramiel sought to recapture Atari's past success with the release a new product, Jaguar, the first 64-bit home video-game system. The techni-cally advanced Jaguar generated considerable consumer interest at first, but sales proved disappointing.

After nearly 20 years in the computer industry, Jack Tramiel decided to retire. In August 1996 he sold Atari to JTS, a disk-drive manufacturer. In 1998 JTS sold Atari's extensive video-game library to HIACXI Corporation, a subsidiary of Hasbro Interactive, for $5 million. Commodore went out of business in 1994.

Jack Tramiel is a supporter of numerous charitable organizations, including those that commemorate the Holocaust.—D. C.

Suggested Reading: *BusinessWeek* p106 Dec. 15, 1986, p50 June 20, 1988; *Byte* p252 Aug. 1994; *Chicago Tribune* III p14 Feb. 5, 1985, with photo; *Forbes* p47+ Jan. 17, 1983, with photo, p52 Aug. 3, 1992; *Fortune* p64+ Apr. 13, 1998, with photos; *Los Angeles Times* IV p1 Aug. 25, 1987, IV p3 Aug. 16, 1989; *Maclean's* p25 Jan. 25, 1988, with photo; *New York Times* I p27 Jan. 14, 1984, D p1 Jul. 3, 1984, III p1 Feb. 10, 1985, with photos; *Time* p28+ Jan. 3, 1983, with photos

---

Turing, Alan M.

June 23, 1912–June 7, 1954 Developer of the Turing machine

The visionary British mathematician Alan Mathison Turing is hailed as a pioneer of computer technology and one of the most influential thinkers of the 20th century. Although he never built a computer, his design for a multifunctional computing device, called the Turing machine, paved the way for today's computers. In much of his work, Turing attempted to link nature and technology, and he is credited with being a forerunner in the field of artificial intelligence. He played a key role in the fight against Germany during World War II, by helping to crack German military codes. Turing's later work involved the nature of biological growth, or morphogenesis; a thesis he wrote on the subject is considered a founding paper in nonlinear theory. An openly gay man, Turing was arrested and convicted in 1952 for violating British decency statutes. In 1954, two weeks before his 42d birthday, he committed suicide, apparently as a result of a crippling depression brought on by the hormone treatments he was forced to undergo as punishment. In part because of the circumstances surrounding his death, his huge contributions in computer science, mathematics, and other areas have gained wide recognition only recently.

The second son of Julius Mathison Turing and Ethel Sara Turing, Alan Mathison Turing was born on June 23, 1912 in Paddington, a section of London. His father worked in India for the Indian Civil Service, and as a result Alan, along with his brother, John, spent most of his childhood in foster

An Enigma Machine   Courtesy of the Computer Museum of America

homes. Despite the less-than-supportive attitude of his foster parents, who did not encourage, but actively discouraged, originality and individuality, Turing displayed a strong scientific bent at an early age. He read with excitement such books as *Natural Wonders Every Child Should Know* and performed rudimentary chemistry experiments. In 1926, when he was 14, Turing's parents returned from India. At about this time Turing was admitted to the Sherborne School, a very strict boarding facility. He did not strive for high grades and took no pains to hide his lack of interest in any subjects other than math or science—behavior that irritated his teachers and school administrators.

Moreover, Turing did not get along well with the other boys at Sherborne, and he found himself socially segregated. He spent most of 1928 privately contemplating the concept of relativity. His situation changed dramatically that same year, after he met Christopher Morcom, a student one year ahead of him. The two became intellectual companions, spending many extracurricular hours together discussing math and astronomy, and they developed a strong emotional bond. Turing and Morcom both hoped to attend King's College, Cambridge University. After taking the entrance examination, Morcom was offered a scholarship, but Turing was not. Then, in 1930, Morcom died from tuberculosis. Devastated, Turing began pondering questions about the human mind and soul and about whether death might release them from the body. These questions, which he posed in letters to Morcom's mother, later led him to studies in physics and quantum-mechanical theory and their connections to mind and matter.

Meanwhile, Turing focused on obtaining a scholarship to King's College—partly to serve as a sort of proxy for Morcom—and he accomplished that goal in 1931. As a Cambridge undergraduate he delved deeply into logic and quantum mechanics and became increasingly interested in work by the mathematician John Von Neumann on the logical foundations of quantum mechanics. Other works that reportedly exerted a powerful influence on him were the books *Introduction to Mathematical Philosophy*, by Bertrand Russell, and *Principia Mathematica*, by Russell and Alfred North Whitehead, a classic work on mathematical logic and the foundations of mathematics that proposed that mathematics is in some significant sense reducible to logic.

Turing excelled at King's College, where he felt free to express his ideas. He remained there after earning his bachelor's degree, in 1934. He received a master's degree in 1935 and, on the strength of his thesis on the so-called Gaussian error function, was elected a fellow of the college. In 1936 he won a Smith's Prize for his work on probability theory. By that time Turing had conceived the idea for what became known as the Turing machine. His idea grew out of his ruminations about the problem of computable numbers, which are numbers that can be described in finite terms, and the problem of decidability, which among mathematicians is commonly referred to by the German word *Entscheidungsproblem*. In a Web site devoted to Turing, Andrew Hodges, the author of *Alan Turing: The Enigma* (1984), phrased the decidability problem this way: "Could there exist, at least in principle, any definite method or process by which all mathematical questions could be decided?" According to the MacTutor History of Mathematics

Archives (on-line), "In one sense 'decidability' was a simple question, namely, given a mathematical proposition, could one find an algorithm which would decide if the proposition was true or false. For many propositions it was easy to find such an algorithm. The real difficulty arose in proving that for certain propositions, no such algorithm existed. When given an algorithm to solve a problem it was clear that it was indeed an algorithm, yet there was no definition of an algorithm which was rigorous enough to allow one to prove that none existed."

In thinking about decidability, Turing imagined a computational process that would rely on mechanics. He introduced that concept, which is embodied in the Turing machine, in his paper "On Computable Numbers, with an Application to the Entscheidungsproblem," which was published in the *Proceedings of the London Mathematical Society* in 1937. As the *Stanford Encyclopedia of Philosophy* (on-line) explains, "A Turing machine is an abstract representation of a computing device," and it is "more like a computer program (software) than a computer (hardware)." The components of the Turing machine are a storage tape (which may be limitless), a read/write head, and a unit to control the action of the head. Essentially, the machine would work by reading the tape, on which a series of ones and zeros would describe the steps needed to solve a particular problem. The machine would read each of the steps and carry them out in order, and it would thereby come up with the proper solution for the specific problem or task.

The Turing machine may be thought of as an extremely sophisticated sort of tape player. At any moment, the machine is in a given "state," or "functional state." The tape is marked off in squares, with each square containing the numeral one or zero. According to the *Stanford Encyclopedia of Philosophy*, "Computation begins with the machine, in a given 'state,' scanning a square. It erases what it finds there, prints a 0 or 1, moves to an adjacent square, and goes into a new state. This behavior is completely determined by three parameters: (1) the state the machine is in, (2) the number on the square it is scanning, and (3) a table of instructions. The table of instructions specifies, for each state and binary input, what the machine should write, which direction it should move in, and which state it should go into. (E.g., 'If in State 1 scanning a 0: print 1, move left, and go into State 3.') The table can list only finitely many states, each of which becomes implicitly defined by the role it plays in the table of instructions." The power of the machine lay with its tape storage capabilities. With infinite extendability, the machine could utilize an unlimited external storage space as "rough paper" for calculations and was also able to produce an output of unlimited size. Therefore, the Turing machine's tape possessed three functions: that of a holder of input for the machine, a storage for partial results during execution of a problem, and a medium for the output of the machine.

Turing expanded on this idea with his "universal" Turing machine, which theoretically could calculate any number and function if given the appropriate instructions—that is, a machine that could do virtually anything if properly programmed. Even more revolutionary was Turing's link between the technical and the natural. Assuming that, for human beings, there is a finite number of possible states of mind, the Turing machine, he argued, could perform tasks as well as the human brain. It is widely speculated that Turing's work helped satisfy his obsession with questions of mind and matter. Andrew Hodges, quoting from his biography of Turing, wrote, "As in so many aspects of his life, Turing made a bridge between the logical and physical worlds, thought and action, which crossed conventional boundaries." At about the time that Turing submitted his groundbreaking paper to the London Mathematical Society, in 1936, the *American Journal of Mathematics* published a paper by the American logician and mathematician Alonzo Church bearing on the question of decidability in arithmetic. Like Turing, Church, who died in 1995, is considered a major contributor to the foundations of computer science. The appearance of Church's paper delayed the publication of Turing's, which refers to Church's work. According to Hodges, the earlier publication of Church's "parallel conclusion" "robbed" Turing of "the full reward for his originality."

Turing studied under Church at Princeton University, in New Jersey, which he entered in 1936 to pursue a doctoral degree. While at Princeton he wrote papers on logic, algebra, and number theory. He completed the requirements for his Ph.D. in 1938; his dissertation focused on ordinal logics and the realm of the uncomputable. Rejecting Princeton's offer of a temporary post, he returned to King's College, which renewed his fellowship. Soon after his arrival he began to construct gearwheel parts to be used in making a mechanical computing device for investigating an unsolved mathematical problem known as the Riemann hypothesis.

Turing's work was interrupted when, in 1939, the British government recruited him to join a high-security code-breaking team at the wartime cryptanalytic headquarters, called the Government Code and Cypher School, in Bletchley Park, in Buckinghamshire. The team's mission was to decipher Germany's constantly changing military codes, called the Enigma codes because they were generated by the German military's Enigma machines. By 1940 Turing and his colleague W. G. Welchman had designed a new machine, the Bombe, which successfully read Enigma messages sent by the German air force. Messages sent by the German navy proved far more difficult to decipher, and in early 1942 a further complication in the German code made the messages impossible to read. The previous month Turing had traveled to the United States to share critical aspects of his country's cryptanalytic progress. He met with American intelligence officials and assisted with several war-related scientific projects. During this time Turing learned a great deal about electronics, in part during visits with engineers at Bell Laboratories in New York.

By the time he returned to Great Britain, in March 1943, the German naval Enigma code had been broken, and the battle in the Atlantic was being won by the Allies. Turing stayed on at Bletchley as a consultant, working with a selected staff (there were more than 10,000 people employed on various projects at Bletchley Park) on the cracking of the highly sophisticated "Fish" cipher-text, used in top-level German communications. Breaking this code involved, for the first time, the full-scale use of electronic switching technology. This technology was employed in so-called Colossus machines, whose design Turing helped oversee. The Colossus helped paved the way for large-scale digital electronic technology and was in essence the forerunner of digital computers.

Quoting another source, the MacTutor History of Mathematics Archives reported that the years that Turing spent at Bletchley Park were "perhaps the happiest of his life," because the work gave him "full scope for his inventiveness, a mild routine to shape the day, and a congenial set of fellow-workers." At Bletchley he became known as an eccentric, fun-loving, amazingly brilliant, shabbily dressed "prof" who had a passion for chess and long-distance running. He bicycled everywhere, sometimes peddling 20 or 30 miles to get to meetings. Among the many anecdotes told about him is one from a local constable, who once encountered Turing riding his bicycle with a gas mask on his face. When the constable asked him why he was wearing the mask, the young mathematician replied that doing so helped alleviate his hay fever.

In 1945 Turing joined the staff at the National Physical Laboratory (NPL) in London, with the title of principal scientific officer and the assignment of designing a computer. His plans for the machine, officially known as the Automatic Computing Engine (ACE), called for programming rather than electronic components to perform arithmetical functions, and 4K bytes of storage, an amount that the NPL regarded as unrealistically large. According to Andrew Hodges, "Turing proposed building a computer that would switch at will from numerical work to algebra, codebreaking, file handling, or chess-playing." His highly innovative ideas also included the construction of "a national computer center with remote terminals, and the prospect of the machine in time taking over programming work." Turing proceeded to design so-called abbreviated code instructions in 1947, but no parts of the ACE had yet been constructed, and Turing, for the most part excluded from the engineering facet of the project, became frustrated. With the permission or, as Hodges has suggested, encouragement of the NPL, for several months beginning in October 1947, Turing studied neurology and physiology at Cambridge University. He produced a paper, not published until after his death, on what came to be labeled neural nets, in which, as Hodges put it, he "amplif[ied] his earlier suggestions that a sufficiently complex mechanical system could exhibit learning ability."

In 1948 a team guided by M. H. A. "Max" Newman (with whom Turing had worked at Princeton and Cambridge) at Manchester University, in England, produced the Manchester Mark I, a machine that is recognized as the world's first working electronic realization of Turing's ideas. Having lost the competition to produce the first such device, Turing turned his attention to a different type of race. After the war he had become a strong runner, and now he began to participate in marathons and other types of long-distance running in addition to daily treks across town. He placed consistently well in the races, and, had it not been for an injury, he probably would have competed for Great Britain in the 1948 Olympic Games.

In May 1948 Turing accepted the posts of reader and deputy director of the Computing Laboratory at Manchester University, where MADAM, the Manchester Automatic Digital Machine, was being constructed. Turing had very little control over the project, and its importance diminished after the British government decided that an atomic-bomb project took precedence. While at Manchester Turing wrote a journal article called "Computing Machinery and Intelligence," in which he asked the question "Can machines think?" and discussed "building a brain," an idea that has evolved into the concept of artificial intelligence (AI). In his paper he described the Turing Test, which was intended to show that the operations of a computer could resemble that of a human brain. The test involved having someone "talk" to a computer by means of typed messages and then seeing if the computer could determine whether the messages were coming from a human or a computer. Among the most comprehensive of the papers in which he detailed his philosophy linking mind and machine, "Computing Machinery and Intelligence" was published in the philosophical and psychological journal *Mind* in 1950. It had far-reaching effects and has continued to influence thinkers in the philosophical community to this day.

Also in 1950 Turing bought a house in Wilmslow, near Manchester, and, with a garden for inspiration, he began to form a theory of biological growth and form, a process he termed the mathematical theory of morphogenesis. While various observers thought that he was moving in an entirely new direction, his work was essentially a return to the sort of wonders that had fascinated him in his childhood. Moreover, again merging the natural with the technical, he began using a computer (the Ferranti Manchester Mark I) for hands-on mathematical research, thus becoming the first person to do so. Turing's research focused on specific biological phenomena, and he suggested, by means of a mathematical formula, that biological forms mirror patterns in concentrations of hypothetical chemicals, called morphens. Starting with a uniform distribution of morphens, under precisely controlled conditions, the reaction of these chemicals and the diffusion of their reaction products would lead to the formation of distinctive patterns. According to Hodges, Turing "concentrated on the idea that non-linearity could account for the way that an initially homogeneous mixture of chemicals could come to take shape in an asymmetrical way." This research is associated with the later-emerging specialty of nonlinear systems. As recently as 1992, scientists realized that Turing's theory is a key to understanding the mechanism that produces patterns of spots and stripes on animals. Turing's 1951 paper *The Chemical Basis of Morphogenesis* contains his conclusions on morphogenesis.

Turing lived an active homosexual lifestyle, and at least since his college years, he had never attempted to hide his sexual preference. In 1952, after he reported to the police that he was being blackmailed, the police discovered that he had had a sexual liaison with a young Manchester man. Performing homosexual acts was illegal in Great Britain until the 1990s, and Turing was arrested for what was termed "gross indecency." At his trial he maintained that he had done nothing wrong, but he was found guilty. Given a choice of a prison sentence or treatment with psychoanalysis and estrogens to reduce his libido—what Hodges termed "chemical castration"—he chose the latter. Unbeknownst to most of his associates, after the end of World War II Turing had worked for the government organization that succeeded the setup at Bletchley Park. After his arrest Turing was stripped of his security clearance and his government assignments ceased.

Turing continued to work on his morphogenetic theory, but according to people who knew him, he began to act oddly; various sources have suggested that the hormone treatments, administered in the form of painful injections, had triggered a severe depression. On June 7, 1954 he apparently took his own life while alone in his house; a half-eaten apple that had been dipped in cyanide was found next to his body. While his mother insisted that his death was an accident—he had been performing experiments with cyanide—the coroner's office ruled it a suicide. Hodges has suggested that Turing intentionally staged his death so that his mother would be spared the thought that he had killed himself.

In 1950 Turing was honored with an Order of the British Empire for his cryptographic work during World War II. In 1994 the city of Manchester honored him by naming part of an inner-city road after him, and in 1998 English Heritage, which preserves buildings and other monuments of historic significance, affixed a commemorative plaque on the building where Turing was born.—D. B.

Suggested Reading: *AI Magazine* p92+ Summer 1992, with photo; *Alan Turing Home Page* (online); *Datamation* p152+ Dec. 1983, with photo; *Mathematical Intelligencer* p22+ Fall 1991; *New Scientist* p789+ Sep. 15, 1983, with photo; *Scientific American* p98+ Apr. 1999; *Time* p147+ Mar. 29, 1999, with photo; Greene, Laura. *Computer Pioneers*, 1985; Hodges, Andrew. *Alan Turing: The Enigma*, 1994; Miller, Neil. *Out of the Past: Gay and Lesbian History from 1869 to the Present*, 1995; Spencer, Donald D. *Great Men and Women of Computing*, 1996

---

von Kempelen, Wolfgang

1734–1804 Inventor

A consummate inventor, the 18th-century Austrian scientist Wolfgang von Kempelen may best be known for his construction of a chess-playing automaton known as "the Turk," which debuted in the Viennese imperial court in 1770. As the Turk toured Europe and America over the next several decades, crowds were awed by von Kempelen's invention of a machine that could seemingly comprehend a complex game such as chess. A self-taught scholar of the emerging sciences of physics, hydraulics, and mechanical engineering, von Kempelen designed bridges, experimented with steam engines, and devised a pressurized water supply system. His most notable—and most influential—invention, however, was his construction, in 1791, of the first "speaking machine" that could produce whole words and sentences. (The 18th-century Russian professor Christian Kratzenstein had built an earlier speaking machine in 1779, but it could replicate only some speech sounds.) Von Kempelen has been called the first experimental phonetician and a mechanical genius; his speaking machine marked one of the first major innovations in the field of speech synthesis.

Wolfgang von Kempelen was born in 1734 in Bratislava, then the capital of Hungary. (Hungary was then under the rule of Austria's Hapsburg dynasty.) By 1769 he was working in Vienna as a senior civil servant to Maria Theresa, the empress of the Austrian Empire. That year a French lecturer named Monsieur Pelletier visited the empress's court to stage a display of experiments, automata, and conjuring tricks. In a moment of boldness, von Kempelen told Maria Theresa that he could build a machine more revolutionary than anything she had seen from Pelletier. The empress accepted the offer and allowed von Kempelen six months leave from his duties. In early 1770 he unveiled his invention: a life-size wooden figure, adorned in a robe and turban, who was seemingly capable of playing chess. The Turk, as it was called, was seated behind a large cabinet—four feet long, three feet high and two and a half feet deep—on top of which sat the chess board. When von Kempelen exhibited his chess-playing device, he would dramatically open the cabinet doors to reveal the innards, consisting of cogs, levers, wheels, and clockwork machinery; using a candle for light, he would pan the inside to show the audience that a human figure could not fit inside the cabinet. After winding up the device with a large key, he invited a chess player to come forward for competition. Once the game began the Turk would pause before each move, while components inside the machine began clicking and whirring. The noise was used to conceal any sounds from the human chess master who was, in fact, hiding in a secret compartment inside. The device swivelled its head and rolled its eyes to evaluate the pieces, then used its elaborate mechanical arm to move them. To viewers, it seemed that the Turk was capable not only of maneuvering the chess board but also of analyzing and comprehending the complex game. The hidden human was actually examining his opponent's moves by use of an ingenious magnetic board on the underside of the cabinet. Of von Kempelen's decision to clothe his machine as a Turk, chess scholars have suggested it was because the game was known to be an Eastern invention; in addition, in this period of Europe's Age of Enlightenment, the Turk represented the mystery of the East. As Tom Standage, author of *The Life and Times of the Famous Eighteenth-Century Chess-Playing Machine* (2002), explained to Robert Siegel for National Public Radio's *All Things Considered* (April 13, 2002), the Turk was an "instant success." "It was the talk of Vienna literally the day after it made its debut," he noted. "The reason it was such a big hit was that it took the popular technology of the day, automata, which are machines that imitate living things, to its logical conclusion. So people were used to seeing machines that could play instruments or mechanical animals and that sort of thing. But here was the ultimate automaton, because it appeared to be able to think."

Although von Kempelen quickly shelved his creation to commence other projects, Emperor Joseph II (Maria Theresa's son) later convinced him to resuscitate the device to entertain a Russian grand duke. In 1776 the Turk was sent on a tour of Russia, and in 1783 it visited Europe, where the American statesman Benjamin Franklin studied it during a demonstration in Paris. The machine rarely lost a match and generated controversy wherever it appeared. From the beginning, a number of skeptics branded the device a hoax, theorizing correctly that a human hand was actually controlling its moves. Among the Turk's most outspoken critics was the American writer Edgar Allan Poe, who viewed the machine in the United States in the 1830s; he wrote a celebrated exposé for the *Southern Literary Messenger* in 1836. Nevertheless, many onlookers found the machine intriguing and even inspirational. As Standage described in his book, as quoted by Matthew Price for the *Chicago Tribune* (April 21, 2002), these curious observers viewed the Turk as "a mechanical puzzle to be solved, rather than a fraud to be uncovered." Indeed, the Turk is said to have inspired such historic inventors as the clergyman Edmund Cartwright to begin building the first power weaving loom,

and Charles Babbage (who was entranced by the device as a boy) to commence his own research on technology and machine intelligence. Toward the end of his life, von Kempelen became tired of being overshadowed by the Turk and dismantled his invention for good. Yet, after his death in 1804, his son sold the Turk to Johann N. Maelzel, himself a mechanical genius who is thought to have invented a metronome used by Beethoven. With debts to pay, Maelzel exploited the Turk's fame, arranging a match with Napoleon Bonaparte in 1809—a match that the emperor famously lost—and taking the chess player through Europe, on and off, for several years. In 1826 Maelzel was again having trouble with creditors and took the Turk to the United States, exhibiting it through cities up and down the East Coast. Maelzel died in 1838 on a return trip from Cuba; the Turk was destroyed in 1854 after a great fire swept through Philadelphia, where it was then being housed in a museum. While von Kempelen's invention offered few concrete technological advancements, many computer scientists recognize it as a precursor to the creation of thinking machines. In addition, historians of magic widely regard it as one of the first cabinet illusions.

Von Kempelen's most significant contribution to the Information Age was not the Turk; rather, it was his invention of the speaking machine. Although Kratzenstein had produced his speaking machine in 1779—some 12 years before von Kempelen completed his—the latter inventor had in fact begun his research first, in 1769. After more than 20 years of studying human speech production, in 1791 von Kempelen introduced his "Acoustic Mechanical Speech Machine." He also published the book *Mechanismus der menschlichen Sprache nebst Beschreibung einer sprechenden Maschine* ("Mechanism of Human Speech with the Description of a Speaking Machine"), in which he discusses the origin and nature of language and provides a detailed description of its construction so that others could build it themselves and improve upon his design. (Despite all of his work, von Kempelen still did not consider his invention complete.)

Von Kempelen had theorized that the vocal tract, or the cavity between the vocal cords and the lips, was actually the main source for speech delivery. (Prior to this, the larynx had been considered the center of acoustic production.) He also believed that no more than one vocal tract could be used to make continuous speech. His device featured a bellows, or pressure chamber, which simulated the lungs and was controlled by a large forearm. (A bellows is an instrument that alternately expands and contracts, drawing in air through an opening and expelling it through a tube.) In addition, it included a "wind box," which was operated with levers, a "mouth" made of rubber, and a "nose" that had two nostrils, both of which would be covered with fingers during operation unless a nasal sound was to be produced. The speech-production apparatus, which had to be controlled by a human operator, was contained within a small box with holes for the hands, and additional holes on top. Air was sent through the machine by way of an oscillating reed and then through a narrow leather shunting tube. Manipulation of the leather tube affected air pressure within the mouth cavity, allowing the machine to produce different vowel sounds. Consonant sounds were created by the operator using his or her fingers to control four separate constricted passages. The vocal cords, which were imitated with an ivory reed, could be varied in length, thus affecting the tone of the speech. However, this could not be done during speech synthesis, so the machine spoke in only one tone.

Von Kempelen's machine was considered a success and proved to have a significant impact on the field of speech synthesis. In 1835 the English physicist Charles Wheatstone presented his version of von Kempelen's machine in Dublin, Ireland; his design varied mainly in its complexity and was better able to produce vowel and consonant sounds. In the late 1800s Alexander Graham Bell, inspired by Wheatstone's device, began working on his own speaking machine. Later experimentation with mechanical and semielectrical analogs of vocal systems led to the development of telegraphs, sound spectrographs, and other computer technology. Von Kempelen's machine is currently housed at the Detaches Museum, in Munich, Germany.

In addition to being an inventor, Wolfgang von Kempelen was an accomplished dramatist and artist. His landscape engravings earned him membership at Vienna's Royal Academy of Fine Arts. His excellence in a number of fields is undisputed, as is his place in technological history. As Slalomír Ondrejovič noted in his essay "Wolfgang von Kempelen and His Mechanism of Human Speech," translated from Slovak and posted on the Institute for Linguistics's Wolfgang von Kempelen page, "Whether we agree . . . that W. von Kempelen was a founder of experimental phonetics . . ., whether we consider him the real founder of logopaedia as a science [logopedics is the study and treatment of defective speech] and of practical cybernetics or not, we cannot deprive this Bratislava native of a significant position in history of all mentioned branches. In any case the *Mechanism of Human Speech* remains undoubtedly the peak of all [that] people knew about speech sound formation 250 years ago."—K. D.

Suggested Reading: *All Things Considered* Apr. 13, 2002; *Chicago Tribune* C p1 Apr. 21, 2002; *Los Angeles Times* R p5 July 14, 2002; Stockholm University Institute for Linguistics Web site; *Washington Post* C p9 Feb. 25, 1996

---

von Klitzing, Klaus

June 28, 1943– Physicist; discoverer of the quantum Hall effect

In 1985 the German physicist Klaus von Klitzing won the Nobel Prize in Physics for his discovery of the quantum Hall effect, which has provided scientists with the basis for a new absolute standard for the unit of electrical resistance, the ohm. Klitzing's finding enabled scientists to measure electrical resistance more precisely and allowed them to test more accurately theories about the movement of electrons within atoms. According to the Royal Swedish Academy of Sciences, as quoted on the Nobel Foundation Web site, Klitzing's work "opened up a new research field of great importance and relevance." The academy went on to add that "we are dealing here with a new phenomenon in quantum physics, and one whose characteristics are still only partially understood." The discovery is particularly relevant to the study of semiconductor electronics, a field that is important to computer science. However, its importance extends beyond semiconductors, the type of material in which the effect was observed by von Klitzing, holding implications for many areas of physics. In addition, while quantum theory is commonly applicable only on the level of individual particles, such as electrons, the quantum Hall effect is one of few instances in which the theory's effects can be observed on a larger scale. Klitzing has been the director of the Max Planck Institute for Solid State Research, in Stuttgart, Germany, since 1985, where he heads the department named in his honor.

Klaus-Olaf von Klitzing was born during World War II, on June 28, 1943 in the town of Schroda, which was then in a part of Germany close to the Polish border. He was the third of four children of Bogislav von Klitzing, a forestry official, and the former Anny Ulbrich. Soon after Klaus was born, it became apparent that as the German military position deteriorated, the Soviet army would reach the region of Posen (now Poznań) in which his family lived. Fleeing west, they eventually resettled in Lutten in April 1945, shortly before the end of the war. The family moved again, in 1948, to Oldenburg and then settled in Essen in 1951. Klaus's secondary education at the Artland Gymnasium in Quakenbrück prepared him for specialization in physics at the Technical University of Braunschweig in 1962.

At Braunschweig, Klitzing was first introduced to the problems of the physics of semiconductors. Although he had taken an interest in X-ray spectroscopy (and had traveled to Darmstadt to take a course in computer programming with this topic in mind), it was the technique of luminescence measurement that seized his attention. He used this method to determine the lifetimes of carriers in the semiconductor indium antimonide and reported this work in a thesis written under the guidance of F. R. Kessler in 1969. He then moved to the University of Würzburg where, after briefly teaching laboratory physics to premedical students, he spent the next decade honing his skills in semiconductor research. Klitzing spent 1975 at Oxford University, in England, where at that time the finest superconducting magnets were manufactured. They were of particular interest to Klitzing because strong, homogeneous magnetic fields are an essential tool for the study of electrons in semiconductors.

Seeking still stronger magnetic fields, Klitzing left Würzburg in 1979 to work at the high-field laboratory in Grenoble. In 1980 he took a new position as professor at the Technical University of Munich, where he remained until 1985. The combination of low temperatures and strong magnetic fields to which he gained access at Grenoble played an important role in his discoveries concerning the Hall effect. This phenomenon, first observed in 1880 by the American physicist Edwin H. Hall, had previously been considered as only a rough means of measuring the concentration of electrons in semiconductors. In Hall-effect measurements, an electric current is passed through a sample in the presence of a magnetic field applied in a perpendicular direction. A voltage then appears across the sample at right angles to both the current and the magnetic field. This Hall voltage is generally proportional to the magnetic field and inversely proportional to the concentration of electrons. Uncertainties of the order of 10 percent are typical in the interpretation of these results, as a consequence of a variety of interactions between the electrons and the atoms forming the crystalline lattice of the semiconductor.

At Grenoble, working in collaboration with Michael Pepper of the Cavendish Laboratory at Cambridge University and with Gerhard Dorda of the Siemens Corporation research laboratories in Munich, Klitzing conducted an experiment that differed from traditional measurements, primarily in the nature of the sample he used. The silicon that he studied formed part of a transistor in which the mobile electrons were confined to a thin layer near one of the surfaces of the device. The electrons were then able to move in only two dimensions rather than the three dimensions available in a uniform sample. Constrained in this way by the voltage applied to the device, the electrons behaved in a markedly different way from their behavior in bulk material.

The most startling aspect of Klitzing's measurement was the departure of the Hall voltage from its normal smooth variation with the applied magnetic field and electron concentration. As the number of electrons in the two-dimensional layer was steadily increased, the Hall voltage at first dropped smoothly, then held constant for a while until dropping to another plateau, here it again remained steady before repeating its drop to a new level. The Hall voltages at these plateaus were then divided by the current passing through the sample

to give a set of numbers with the dimensions of an electrical resistance. When the numbers were compared, they were found to be simple fractions of a very special resistance, namely 25,813 ohms. This resistance is the ratio of two fundamental constants of nature—Planck's constant, which governs all quantum-mechanical behavior, and the square of the electrical charge on the electron.

The important feature of this result was the great precision with which the relationship was obeyed. In repeated experiments using not only differently shaped samples but also devices made from different materials, the same numbers have been observed with a precision of one part in 10 million. The results immediately led Klitzing to suggest that the phenomenon, now known as the quantum Hall effect, could form the basis for a new absolute standard of electrical resistance. Klitzing and his colleagues reported their findings in August 1980 in the journal *Physical Review Letters*.

The work that Klitzing published in 1980 was remarkable in at least three ways. First, it showed the effects of the quantum theory, which most commonly is relevant only to the behavior of microscopic entities, such as single electrons, in a measurement of a laboratory-scale electric current. Second, it was totally unexpected by theoretical physicists who had been studying semiconductors for decades. And third, it yielded reproducible measurements of such great precision that they immediately suggested themselves as a new international standard for the unit of electrical resistance, the ohm. For his discovery of the quantum Hall effect, Klitzing was awarded the 1985 Nobel Prize in Physics.

The precision and reproducibility with which the quantum Hall effect can be measured give the phenomenon an importance that extends far beyond the realm of either metrology or the physics of semiconductor devices. Because the measured unit of resistance appears to be determined only by the most fundamental constants of nature, the result has implications for many other areas of physics. The fine structure in the emission spectra of hot gases, for example, is governed by the same combination of fundamental constants found by the quantum Hall effect. As a result, the measured Hall resistance has provided a verification of the long, difficult calculations that predict the fine-structure constant of atomic spectroscopy.

In some ways, Klitzing's discovery of the quantum Hall effect can be compared with the prediction two decades earlier by Brian D. Josephson of the phenomenon of superconductive tunneling. Both effects demonstrate in a laboratory-scale experiment the quantum-mechanical behavior normally limited to systems of atomic size. Both have led to new absolute standards for electrical quantities—the volt in the case of the Josephson theory and the ohm in the case of the quantum Hall effect. The particular importance of Klitzing's work lies, perhaps, in the stimulus it has given to the study of electrons effectively confined to two dimensions. The wealth of new phenomena that have been found and new questions raised in the physics of electron layers owe much to the remarkable observations made by Klitzing in 1980.

In 1971 Klitzing married Renate Falkenberg, with whom he has two sons and a daughter. He has received, in addition to the Nobel Prize, the Walter-Schottky Prize for Solid-State Physics of the German Physical Society (1981) and the Hewlett-Packard Prize of the European Physical Society (1982).—C. M.

Suggested Reading: Max Planck Institute Stuttgart Web site; *New York Times* Oct.17, 1985; Nobel Prize Internet Archive Web site; *Physics Today* Dec. 1985; *Science* Feb. 21, 1986

---

von Neumann, John

Dec. 28, 1903–Feb. 8, 1957 Mathematician; computing innovator

John von Neumann was a child prodigy who developed into one of the most gifted mathematicians in the world, particularly influencing the study of quantum theory and economics with his "game theory." He became a lecturer at Princeton University after emigrating from Hungary in 1930, and he began working with the atomic bomb project at Los Alamos, New Mexico, during World War II, helping to develop a detonation device. After the war, von Neumann dedicated his time to improving the speed of computers, and he is credited with being the first person to publicly endorse the creation of a computer that would have a memory capable of storing programs. He then spent five years working on his own computer, the IAS, which was the fastest electronic calculator ever built at the time. A man of profound intelligence who was highly respected, von Neumann spent his later years working on the development of nuclear power and weapons and was appointed to the Atomic Energy Commission three years before his death from cancer in 1957.

The eldest of three sons, John von Neumann was born Johann (later changed to John) von Neumann in Budapest, Hungary, on December 28, 1903. His mother, Margaret Kann von Neumann, and father, a successful Jewish banker named Max von Neumann, were from an upper-class background, and were forced to flee Hungary after the Communist regime took control of the government in 1919. The von Neumanns became aware of John's unusual intellectual ability before he reached school age. By the time he was six years old, von Neumann could divide eight-digit numbers in his head and joked effortlessly with his father in ancient Greek. Both von Neumann's parents and his teachers realized that the boy exhibited traits of a genius, and it was therefore suggested that a private tutor be hired for his education. From 1911 to 1916 he attended the Lutheran gymnasium in Budapest, becoming easi-

ly its best mathematician. In 1921 he enrolled at the University of Budapest, completing his first paper under the tutelage of M. Fekete, but he spent the majority of his time at other institutions of higher learning in Europe. From 1921 to 1923 von Neumann studied chemistry at the University of Berlin, where he could hear lectures by Albert Einstein. He then moved on to the Swiss Federal Institute of Technology in Zurich, from which he received a degree in chemical engineering in 1925. A year later, at the age of 22, von Neumann received his doctorate in mathematics from the University of Budapest, where he also minored in chemistry and experimental physics. He began studying as a Rockefeller Fellow at the University of Gottingen in 1927, where he met J. Robert Oppenheimer, who went on to become a key figure in nuclear research at Los Alamos, New Mexico.

From 1927 to 1930 von Neumann took a post as a lecturer in mathematics at the University of Berlin, a rare appointment for someone so young. Von Neumann immediately proved adept at his position and published five papers in his first year at the university, three of which would prove to be tremendous contributions to the field of quantum theory. He produced his most significant mathematics from the years 1925 to 1940, working on many aspects of logic and analysis as well as mathematical physics. The main topics he explored and made contributions to were logic and set theory, measure theory, lie groups and rings of operators. Thus, although he was not yet 30 years old when he began publishing, by the late 1920s, von Neumann was coming to be recognized as one of the world's premier mathematicians.

Von Neumann spent the spring of 1929 in Hamburg, and during this time he was invited to teach at Princeton University in New Jersey, as a visiting lecturer. Von Neumann accepted and came to the United States in 1930; after serving as a lecturer of quantum statistics for a year, he was made a tenured professor. For the next two years, von Neumann lectured on mathematical hydrodynamics and in 1933 he was made one of the six original professors at the university's newly formed School of Mathematics, part of its Institute for Advanced Study.

Von Neumann became a U.S. citizen through the sponsorship of Oskar Morganstern in 1937, in time to receive wartime security clearance and begin working for the U.S. government. His expertise in a vast array of topics, from hydrodynamics, to ballistics, to metrology and statistics, was utilized in a variety of projects during the war. Early on in his work, von Neumann toyed with the idea of using machines to perform computations and by the later war years he was serving as an executive management consultant, working with several committees, and acting as a liaison for scientists who were separated from each other for reasons of war secrecy. In the early 1940s von Neumann was invited to go to Los Alamos, New Mexico, where scientists were in the process of building the first atomic bomb. Meeting up once again with J. Robert Oppenheimer, towards the end of 1943, von Neumann was persuaded to become a mathematical consultant for the Manhattan Project, as the group involved in designing the bomb was called. Viewing the bomb as the key to winning the war, researchers looked to von Neumann for his expertise in calculations and background in the areas of shock and detonation waves. His assistance was most notable in determining the method used to detonate the bomb. Other scientists on the project dismissed the "implosion method," but von Neumann was certain that this method would work, and he successfully convinced the others to employ this technique. Von Neumann and other scientists then developed the implosive lens, which generates a strong spherical shock wave that implodes or compresses a ball of plutonium or uranium isotope. When a critical point is reached, a chain reaction is set off. After this method of detonation was proven effective in preliminary tests, it was utilized when the atomic bomb was dropped over the city of Nagasaki, Japan.

By 1944 von Neumann's ideas about using machines to perform computations more quickly were beginning to take form. He took a keen interest in the work others were doing on the subject at that time, and he corresponded with Howard Aiken about his Harvard Mark I calculator and with George Stibitz about his work on early computer technology at Bell Labs. Then, in June 1944, von Neumann met Herman Goldstine by chance on a railroad platform in Aberdeen, Maryland. Goldstine was a mathematician and army officer who worked as a liaison between the Ballistics Research Laboratory and the Moore School of Electrical Engineering at the University of Pennsylvania, in Philadelphia, where researchers were building a computer. Goldstine told von Neumann about the Moore School's project, which was being called the Electronic Numerical Integrator and Computer (ENIAC) and which could perform 333 multiplications a second. Von Neumann took an interest in the project and received clearance to visit the Moore School in September 1944. The ENIAC had been widely criticized as a misdirection of government funds, but upon von Neumann's arrival, the project quickly gained esteem in the scientific community. Von Neumann was impressed by the machine, although he was already beginning to envision computers that would out perform the ENIAC, which, while faster than any other machine of its day, had no memory capabilities. He stayed on as a consultant for the ENIAC project and the team of researchers, which included John Mauchly and J. Prespert Eckert, began to formulate plans for an improved machine called the Electronic Discrete Variable Automatic Computer (EDVAC).

Von Neumann's time at the Moore School caused one of the biggest controversies to ever inhabit the computer industry. Based on his experiences working with the ENIAC team, von Neumann published a 101-page report, the "First Draft of a Report on the EDVAC," which arrived at the Moore School in June 1945. In the paper, von Neumann described the theory and design of the EDVAC machine, stating that it would be a "very high speed automatic digital computing system," with a memory that enabled it to store data and programs. The report was copied and circulated by Goldstine to Moore School members, as well as to other American and British scientists, making it known on a wide scale to outsiders that the school had plans for a stored-program computer. Perhaps because of the report, von Neumann was largely perceived as the chief motivator behind the EDVAC project, leaving Mauchly and Eckert out in the cold in terms of receiving proper credit, despite the fact that Eckert had written a memo detailing plans for a stored-program computer six months prior to von Neumann learning of ENIAC. Goldstine maintained that von Neumann was the driving force behind the group's work and later, in his book *The Computer from Pascal to von Neumann* (1972), wrote that von Neumann, "by writing his report, crystallized thinking in the field of computers as no other person ever did. He was, among all members of the group at the Moore School, the indispensable one . . . only von Neumann was essential to the entire task." Von Neumann and Goldstine applied to the Pentagon's legal branch for a patent for EDVAC on March 22, 1946, but were refused on April 3, 1947 due to a stipulation that required patents to be filed within a year after the appearance of published evidence.

Von Neumann had been inundated with offers of academic positions at prestigious institutions after the end of World War II but he decided to remain at Princeton in the hopes of building his own computer. Von Neumann theorized that a computer could have a simple, fixed structure and still be able to compute any type of problem as long as there was a properly programmed central-control system that didn't require hardware modification. In developing this theory, he contributed to a new understanding of how computers that were both practical and fast could be planned and constructed. His ideas, the realization of which became known as the stored-program computers, would eventually be adopted universally and become a fundamental characteristic of high-speed digital computers. Ironically, the computer that von Neumann envisioned was almost not to be. The members of Princeton's Institute for Advanced Study were hesitant at first, not wanting their facilities to become a laboratory-cum-garage where researchers would be dissecting mechanical parts. However, von Neumann convinced them otherwise, and set out to construct his own fully automatic, digital, electronic calculating machine. The IAS computer, named after the Institute for Advanced Study, was intended for scientific research and not commercial use, and was completed in 1951, five years after work on it began. In 1952, von Neumann designed a high-speed computer called the MANIAC I, which used a flexible stored program.

Working with Norbert Wiener in 1948, von Neumann published a groundbreaking book entitled *Cybernetics: Or Control and Communication in the Animal and the Machine*. The publication was instrumental in putting forth the notion that electronic "brains" could take over human tasks.

Von Neumann's talents extended well beyond the field of computer science. In 1944 he and his friend Oskar Morganstern, published a book titled *Theory of Games and Economic Behavior*, in which the duo analyzed games such as poker in order to demonstrate that a "best possible" method of play existed and, moreover, was mathematically determinable. Their "game theory," as it came to be known, provided ideas and techniques that could also be applied to economic and social problems. This union of mathematics and economics demonstrated that "the typical problems of economic behavior become strictly identical with the mathematical notions of suitable games of strategy" (*Current Biography Yearbook*, 1955).

Von Neumann also developed a theory of automata, which by definition, is a machine or control mechanism designed to follow automatically a predetermined sequence of operations or to respond to encoded instructions. By the early 1940s, Von Neumann knew there was a close connection between mathematical logic and automata, and he spoke of a "logical theory of automata" (*Brunel University* on-line). He conceived a systematic theory that would be both mathematical and logical in form and that furthered the understanding of natural systems, also known as natural automata, as well as analog and digital computers, or artificial automata. Later, von Neumann became interested in more complicated automata, such as the human nervous system and the enormously large computer systems he predicted would eventually be constructed, and he also invented the idea of self-replicating automata. Specifically, he sought a way to overcome the limitations posed by the lack of sufficiently reliable components on the complexity of the automata humans were able to build; only such highly complex automata, he believed, would be able to self-reproduce.

In the 1950s von Neuman served as a consultant reviewing technology projects for IBM and in 1954 he was appointed a member of the Atomic Energy Commission (AEC) which dealt with the development and stockpiling of nuclear weapons. He was confirmed by the U.S. Senate in March 1955, and he and his wife relocated to the Washington, D.C., area. In his new appointment, von Neumann became a key advisor about nuclear power and nuclear weapons. Due to his early negative experiences with communism in Hungary, von Neumann's political views were distinctly right-wing, and he supported the escalation of the nuclear arms race with the Soviet Union. In an article in *Life* magazine (February 25, 1957), von Neumann declared, "If you say why not bomb them tomorrow, I say why not today. If you say today at five o'clock, I say why not one o'clock."

During the summer of 1954 von Neumann injured his shoulder, and when the pain persisted, surgery revealed the presence of bone cancer. Later research has led some to speculate that von Neumann's cancer may have been caused by his exposure to nuclear radiation during his extensive stays at Los Alamos. Although von Neumann grew weaker as the cancer progressed, he continued to attend three AEC meetings a week and remained a member of the Scientific Advisory Board of the U.S. Air Force. As he neared death, meetings were held from von Neumann's bedside, in Walter Reed Hospital in Washington, D.C., during which the ailing mathematician was surrounded by such high profile figures as the secretary of defense and the secretaries of the army, navy, and air force. On February 8, 1957, von Neumann died from cancer, at the age of 53.

John von Neumann was a man who in many ways exemplified the stereotype of a quirky, absent-minded professor; he wrecked automobiles on a regular basis due to careless driving, and loved to hold parties at his Princeton home and tell racy stories and limericks. The short, heavy-set mathematician was both well liked and highly respected among his peers, who were at times dumbfounded by his uncanny ability to analyze and memorize. A noted mathematician once spent a whole night trying to solve a problem using a calculator, only to have von Neumann solve the same problem in six minutes the next morning. Another time, his friend Herman Goldstine tried to test von Neumann's astounding memory by asking him to recall the beginning of Charles Dickens's *A Tale of Two Cities*. Although he had read the book years earlier, von Neumann proceeded to recite the entire first chapter, verbatim. The Johnniac computer, built in 1953 by the Rand Corporation in California, was named in his honor.

Von Neumann married Marietta Kovesi in January 1930, and the couple had one daughter, Marina, before divorcing in 1937. In December 1938 he married Klara Dan, and the two lived in the Washington, D.C. suburb of Georgetown with their dog, Inverse, until von Neumann's death. Among the many accolades von Neumann received during his lifetime were the Medal of Merit Presidential Award in 1947, the Distinguished Civilian Service Award in 1947 and the Medal of Freedom Presidential Award in 1956. Von Neumann also received honorary doctoral degrees from Harvard University, the University of Istanbul, the University of Pennsylvania, and the University of Maryland.—D. B.

Suggested Reading: *Biography* (on-line) 1994; *Brunel University* (on-line); *Computers From the Past to the Present* (on-line); *Current Biography Yearbook* p624+ 1955, with photo, obituary p570 1957; *San Francisco State University* (on-line); *St. Andrews University* (on-line); *Virginia Polytechnic Institute and State University* (on-line); Goldstine, Herman. *The Computer from Pascal to von Neumann*, 1972

Courtesy of Gateway Inc.

Waitt, Ted

Jan. 18, 1963– Chairman, CEO, and co-founder of Gateway

Ted Waitt is the chairman, chief executive officer and co-founder of Gateway, the mail-order personal-computer (PC) company that has grown from a two-person start-up in an Iowa farmhouse to a multibillion-dollar concern. By selling products directly to consumers over the telephone, Gateway was able to eliminate the expensive middleman, and thereby keep their prices relatively low. Moreover, Gateway built computers to a customer's specifications, allowing the company to keep inventory low and avoid being left with a warehouse of obsolete, overpriced equipment. At Gateway, sales representatives take the orders, and within about five days the system is built and shipped—packed in the company's trademark cartons, which are strewn with distinctive dairy-cow spots. The logo was inspired by the Holsteins on Waitt's family farm where Gateway first started its operations, and it became an important part of Gateway's image as a Midwestern company built on heartland values—"hard work, honesty, friendliness, quality—and putting people first," as quoted on the Gateway Web site. During the firm's heyday it was ranked the nation's fourth-largest personal-computer maker, employing approximately 25,000 people. The U.S. economic slump and a decline in global PC sales hurt Gateway considerably, yet Waitt—who returned to the company in 2001 after a year-long hiatus—believes that a recent restructuring will get the company back on its feet. "It's not like the game is over yet," Waitt told David Whitford for *Fortune* (February 1, 2002, on-line). "There's still a tremendous opportunity if you're

smart enough to find it and good enough to be able to execute it."

Theodore William Waitt was born on January 18, 1963, in Sioux City, Iowa. As the son of a fourth-generation cattle farmer, Waitt might have been expected to take the reigns of the family business, but it became clear he had other entrepreneurial interests. One early job he took was selling time-share holidays at a vacation resort. He made $1,500 the first week, but he quit when he discovered that the enterprise involved fraud. After graduating from Sioux City North High School, Waitt attended the University of Iowa, in Iowa City, where he studied marketing. One weekend in 1984, while accompanying his housemates, members of a rockabilly band, on a gig in Des Moines, he met Mike Hammond. Hammond worked for the retailer Radio Shack. The business sounded interesting to Waitt, and, reasoning that he could learn more and make more money if he got an actual job, he dropped out of school and went to work for Radio Shack as a clerk the following Monday.

There was one feature of the retail business that particularly impressed Waitt. "I was fascinated to see that if you knew what you were doing, you could sell a $3,000 computer system over the phone," Waitt told Joshua Hyatt for *Inc.* (December 1991). "Everybody seemed to be looking at those sales as just gravy." Waitt thought otherwise; the following year, he and Hammond devised a plan go into business for themselves—selling PCs to consumers directly over the phone. While working at Radio Shack Waitt had spotted a niche: the computer company Texas Instruments (TI) had sold a lot of personal computers but had stopped releasing software upgrades, and owners were seeking add-on devices that would enable them to run programs written for IBM's PC. Waitt and Hammond decided to start a TI user's club; charging a membership fee of $20, they published a newsletter cataloguing all the add-on products available, which they then sold at a slight markup. They figured that once they had enough members, they would be able to negotiate with manufacturers to build products to order and effectively corner the market.

Waitt needed $10,000 to get the business started, but he had trouble getting banks to lend him the money. He persuaded his grandmother, Mildred Smith, to put up a certificate of deposit as collateral. In August 1985 Waitt and Hammond launched TIPC Network, using a barn on the Waitt family farm as an office. They lived on the upper level of the barn with their two dogs; they frequently woke to the sound of phones ringing with orders. With such low overhead, Waitt and Hammond could undercut competitors' prices significantly. In the first four months, sales reached $100,000. In early 1986 Waitt hired his older brother, Norman Waitt Jr., to handle the company's finances. (Waitt himself has expressed an aversion to banking matters.) Norman agreed to join, in exchange for part ownership of the company.

In 1987 the firm—rechristened Gateway Corporation—entered the PC market, spurred on by a deal Texas Instruments was offering at the time wherein TI computer owners could trade in their old machine and, for an additional $3,500, get an IBM-compatible one. "We figured we could do the same thing for $1,500," Waitt told Hyatt. Hammond and Waitt searched computer publications to find the best deals on computer components, which they ordered and assembled themselves. Waitt, as Gateway's chief executive officer, decided what to build. He was guided by what he refers to as the value equation—offering consumers the most value at the best price. As Waitt saw it, other PC companies were either offering cheap computers that were so basic nobody wanted them or computers with so many high-technology additions that they were unaffordable. He thought it would be best to pursue the middle ground: "not to add technology for the sake of adding technology, but to go after it when it offers the best value for consumers," he explained to Hyatt.

Gateway's first computer was priced at $1,995—comparable to other PCs—but it offered two floppy-disk drives instead of one, a color monitor (then still a deluxe feature), and a larger-than-usual memory capacity. "We gave people more for their money," Waitt told Hyatt. "We didn't do a whole lot of market research on it. A lot of it was instinctive," Waitt added. "The first question would always be, Would I buy it?" Waitt's instincts proved correct; sales grew from $1.5 million in 1987 to $12 million in 1988.

In spite of his sizeable revenues, Waitt remained determined to keep operating costs low. The company moved into Sioux City's Livestock Exchange Building, where they paid $350 a month for 5,000 square feet and endured the wafting odor of their bovine neighbors. The low cost of living in the area allowed Gateway to pay employees $5.50 an hour, which Waitt began supplementing with a cash bonus based on profits. For the first five years Waitt paid himself only $200 a week. "Getting paid less didn't bother me because I thought it was right to reinvest as much as I could in the business. I knew it would come back to me in the end," Waitt told Brian Dumaine and Jacqueline Graves for *Fortune* (March 21, 1994). In 1990 the company changed its name to Gateway 2000 and moved to North Sioux City, in South Dakota, where there is no corporate or personal income tax. By that time there were approximately 185 employees, shipping 225 PCs a day.

An important component of Gateway's success was its advertising. Waitt had learned from his retailing days that consumers were more willing to purchase computers from a company they believed would be in existence for a long time; publications such as *Computer Shopper* featured hundreds of machines from numerous firms, many of which proved short lived in the rapidly changing market. Waitt realized he could capitalize on his company's location and rural beginnings, and he market-ed Gateway as a product of America's homeland—an honest name consumers could trust. Gateway's first ads featured a picture of his father's cows and the Sioux City water tower beneath the self-deprecating headline "Computers from Iowa?" Many of the ads didn't even include a picture of the product—they often featured Gateway employees, including Waitt and his brother, in such odd scenarios as playing poker or acting out movie spoofs. "We get horrible marks from the marketing-guru types," Waitt told Hyatt. "But it seems to work." The company's black-and-white-spotted boxes have become a nationally recognized logo—the exterior of the company's building was even painted with the Holstein pattern.

Gateway's sales crossed the billion-dollar mark in 1992. Unlike its competitor Dell—the pioneer of the mail-order computer business—Gateway has avoided spending a lot of money on research and development. Waitt disagrees with industry analysts who maintain that a company must have some technological edge to remain competitive. "There are too many people out there doing too good of a job. You run the risk of not always having the best if you rely only on your own staff to develop things," Waitt told Peter H. Lewis for the *New York Times* (January 3, 1993). By keeping their options open Gateway was able to stay at the forefront of the computer industry, frequently offering high-quality features before their competitors did. Gateway was the first company to make EGA color monitors standard on all its systems, the first company to make Microsoft Windows standard, and in 1994 it was the first to make the Pentium chip and CD-ROMs standard. Gateway was also the first to sell computers to customers directly over the Internet.

Gateway 2000 had its initial public offering of stock in 1993, with shares selling for $15 each. Waitt told Michael Warshaw for *Success* (March 1997) that going public "was the right thing to do, to bring the company to the next level of financial stability." In that year Gateway opened up a marketing and manufacturing plant in Dublin, Ireland, through which they were able to sell to France and Germany and gain a foothold in the European market.

Gateway soon began recruiting top executives from such firms as Digital Equipment Corporation and TI, but the influx of new, corporate-minded personnel altered the company's down-home culture. Waitt sought to stave off the change by writing down a list of company values, which the employees learned by heart: respect, caring, teamwork, common sense, aggressiveness, honesty, efficiency, and fun. "These values provide our boundaries along the path to prosperity," Waitt wrote, as quoted by Warshaw. The memo also counseled employees to "relax. Nothing is the end of the world. There is a solution to everything. We must never, ever, take ourselves too seriously."

By 1996 Gateway's sales reached $5 billion—almost equal to that of Dell's $5.3 billion. That year the company introduced Destination, a new product that combined a Pentium PC with a 35-inch television set. Although it failed to sell well, it was the first of its kind. In 1997, in addition to opening a $28 million site in Hampton, Virginia, Gateway 2000 shortened its name to Gateway Inc., as part of a larger attempt to retool the company's image to attract more interest from the corporate market. Later that year Gateway released the industry's first NetPC—a specialty computer designed for big companies. Despite the low price—under $1,000—the response from corporate consumers was tepid.

In 1998 Waitt, hoping to improve recruiting, made the controversial decision to relocate the corporate headquarters to San Diego, California. Several members of the company were unhappy with the decision, and some of the management team refused to make the move. In addition to hiring 10 new top executives—culled from Toshiba, Kraft Foods, American Express, and Pizza Hut—Waitt hired a new president, Jeff Weitzen—the former head of AT&T's $24 billion business-markets division—to groom as his successor. Initially the two worked well together. They signed an $800 million deal with America Online to run Gateway.net, an Internet access site. As part of a newly hatched expansion strategy, Gateway began offering such services as Internet training and financing plans and started including add-ons— such as printers, software, and digital music—with the company's PCs. In addition, Gateway opened up more than 100 outlets nationwide, where customers could sample products and place orders. By the end of 1999 sales had grown by more than a third, and net income had nearly tripled.

On December 31, 1999 Waitt relinquished the position of CEO to Weitzen. Acting as chairman of the board, Waitt largely removed himself from day-to-day business operations, preferring to give Weitzen his freedom. "I wanted to take a little bit of time off, clear my head, and look at other opportunities," Waitt told David Whitford for Fortune (February 1, 2002). He set up his own philanthropic organization, the Waitt Family Foundation, to donate computers to the needy; served on the board of digital music company MP3.com; and considered buying a pro basketball team.

Meanwhile, Weitzen's management style was alienating many employees. Whereas Waitt had been a familiar face around the company—he would frequently drop in on the sales department to field customer phone calls, for example— Weitzen restricted his interactions to a circle of hand-picked executives. Long-time employees were further demoralized by a series of restrictive policies and procedures imposed by Weitzen. Among the most unpopular was a policy that limited customer-service calls to 13 minutes; representatives who spent longer on the phone would lose their monthly bonuses. This lead sales representa-

tives to rush calls, and Gateway's reputation for quality customer service deteriorated.

Waitt grew increasingly distressed at the direction his company was taking without him. Following a serious drop in sales during Thanksgiving of 2000—30 lower than the same period the previous year—Waitt began taking a more active role in Gateway's affairs. Weitzen reportedly didn't appreciate the interference, and the two clashed in January 2001. They were unable to resolve their differences; Weitzen left the company, and Waitt assumed the role of CEO. He dismissed six of Weitzen's eight top managers and rehired many Gateway veterans who had left under Weitzen's tenure. "I'm putting the band back together," he told one friend and former executive, as quoted by Katrina Booker for Fortune (April 30, 2001).

Waitt promptly abrogated dozens of policies that Weitzen had put in place and vowed to refocus on the basics. "We're in retrenchment mode," Waitt told Katrina Booker. He closed down Gateway's foreign sales and manufacturing (which had by that time expanded beyond Europe to include Japan, Australia, New Zealand, Singapore, and Malaysia), and reduced the workforce by more than 25 percent.

Although sales fell drastically, resulting in a $1 billion loss in 2001, and Gateway stock went from a high of $80 to $8 by the end of that year, Waitt retains high hopes for the future. "We're going to succeed—it's just a matter of how soon and how much," Waitt told David Kirkpatrick for Fortune (May 1, 2002, on-line). "We are NOT going to go under. There is NO WAY. I can't craft a scenario where we go out of business."

Waitt is married with four children. He lives in San Diego.—A. I. C.

Suggested Reading: Fortune p115+ Sep. 23, 1991, p34+ Mar. 21, 1994, p94+ Apr. 30, 2001; Fortune (on-line) Feb. 1, 2002, May 1, 2002; Inc. p36+ Dec. 1991; New York Times III p8 Jan. 3, 1993; Success p28+ Mar. 1997; USA Today B p1 Apr. 9, 2001

Wang, An

Feb. 7, 1920– Mar. 24, 1990 Founder of Wang Laboratories

During his 40-year career in computers, An Wang was referred to as "the Doctor," "the data bank," and "the guru of gizmos." His reputation as the intellectual force behind the computer boom of the 1970s prompted a reporter to declare that during his lifetime An Wang's name "was to word processing what Kleenex is to facial tissue." His first major breakthrough was his design for a magnetic core component, a small ring of metal that would eventually become the basic element of computer memory until the microchip was invented in the 1960s. After founding his own company, Wang

Laboratories, Wang went on to invent the first electronic scientific desk calculator, as well as the first machines to combine data-processing and word-processing features. Wang led the company to substantial growth in the 1970s and early 1980s, making it a billion-dollar leader in the industry. Despite hefty accolades, his amassed fame and fortune, and his complicated computer designs, the quiet, small-framed Wang earned his renown because of a basic belief that technology should simply solve people's problems.

The oldest of the five children born to Yin Lu and Zen Wan (Chien) Wang, An Wang was born in Shanghai, China, on February 7, 1920, during the "Age of Confusion," one of the most turbulent time periods in China's history, when Japanese invasions often resulted in massive bloodshed. Wang's father was employed as an English teacher in a private school located in Kun San, but he often had to abandon his teaching and turn to the practice of traditional Chinese medicine when fighting disrupted school. Wang learned English from his father, starting when he was four years old. By the age of 16, he was enrolled at Chiao Tung University, in Shanghai, considered by many to be the "MIT of China," but by 1937 war had broken out. Wang lost both his parents and one sister to the civil wars in his homeland.

To escape the horrors of the conflict around him, Wang immersed himself in the study of electrical engineering. With an emphasis on communications in his field, he worked as an editor for a scientific publication, translating articles from American magazines such as *Popular Science* and *Popular Mechanics*, into Chinese. He graduated from Chiao Tung with a B.S. degree, in 1940, and was hired by the university as a teaching assistant in electrical engineering. During the summer of 1941, he volunteered for a project that involved designing and building transmitters and radios for the government troops of China. He then became an engineer for the Central Radio Works in Kweilin. As World War II escalated, Wang and his fellow workers often found themselves waiting in a cave during Japanese bombing raids.

In 1945 Wang participated in a program sponsored by the Nationalist government in which he, along with several hundred other engineers, traveled to the U.S. as technical observers. The excursion was only meant to last two years, but while he was there, Wang decided to enroll in the graduate program at Harvard University, in Cambridge, Massachusetts. With his previous experience, Wang maneuvered easily through Harvard and received his M.S. degree in 1946. He spent the next several months in Ottawa, Canada, where he worked in a largely clerical position for the Chinese government.

Wang returned to Harvard to enter the school's Ph.D. program in applied physics, in February 1947. Keeping abreast of the political situation in his home country, Wang became aware of the growing presence of Communism in China, and when he realized that Mao Tse-tung and the Communist forces would defeat the Chinese Nationalists, he decided not to return home. In his autobiography, *Lessons*, Wang explained, "I knew myself well enough to know that I could not thrive under a totalitarian Communist system. I had long been independent, and I wanted to continue to make my own decisions about my life."

In 1948 Wang took a position as a research fellow in the Harvard Computation Laboratory working under Howard Aiken, creator of the Harvard Mark I, the first electric binary computer. Aiken immediately set Wang to work on a problem involving data storage. According to Wang, his task was to "find a way to record and read magnetically stored information without mechanical motion" within the computer. It had already been discovered that information could be stored without mechanical motion in the form of a magnetic flux through the process of magnetizing material in either a positive or negative magnetic direction. Reading text in this manner, however, reversed the direction of the flux, thereby destroying the information that it had stored. It did not take Wang long to develop the solution to this problem, as he explained in Lessons: "It did not matter whether or not I destroyed the information while reading it. . . . I could simply rewrite the data immediately afterward. Moreover, since magnetic flux could be changed in a few thousandths of a second, I could do this without any real sacrifice of speed." Wang then devised a combination of materials consisting of metal composites, called ferrites, to make his design work.

Wang patented his invention and continued to work with Aiken on projects, most notably the Mark IV, but he left the Harvard lab when the university began to phase basic computer research out of its curriculum. Striking out on his own, Wang decided to seek contracts for special projects relating to the manufacture of memory cores. With a start-up capital of $600, Wang rented a 200-square-foot loft in Boston, and he opened the doors to Wang Laboratories on June 30, 1951. For his first day of business, Wang had no contracts and only one part-time staff member working in his office.

Wang focused his business on diverse, small-scale commercial needs; one of his earliest success stories was the new electronic scoreboard put in place at Shea Stadium in New York City. Business slowly picked up, and as a result, Wang relocated to nearby Cambridge, Massachusetts, in 1954. Exactly four years after the business had opened its doors, Wang Labs officially became a corporation, with Wang serving as the company's first president and treasurer. Building up his company was not always an easy road for the young entrepreneur: in addition to the problems normally associated with any new business, Wang had to battle an American mistrust of Asians that still lingered after World War II. In 1956, however, Wang's steadfast determination paid off when, after heavy negotiations, Wang sold his memory-core patent to IBM for a then-unheard of $400,000 and suddenly found himself a wealthy businessman. He moved the company once again, to Tewksbury, near Lowell, Massachusetts, and the firm took on a variety of projects, including electronic counters, machine-tool controls, block-type readers, and encoders. Wang was personally involved in almost every facet of his business, and he helped design most of the company's offerings.

LINASEC, designed by Wang in 1962 and thereafter one of Wang Labs' biggest money-makers, was the first electronic justifying typesetter system, a device that would prove invaluable to newspaper producers across the country. Wang's truly breakthrough invention, however, came out in 1964. The Logarithmic Calculating Instrument (LOCI), the world's first electronic scientific desk calculator and a precursor to today's modern desktop calculator, could not only perform the basic functions of math (addition, subtraction, multiplication, division, and computer roots), but could also produce exponential values with the touch of a single button. The product's first model gained prestige among scientists and engineers, its popularity in part due to its easier operation and lower cost ($6,500) than the standard computer of the day. Wang further developed this concept and a year later produced the Model 300 desktop calculator, which was even easier to use than the previous model and sold for one-quarter the price.

Over the next few years, Wang Labs came to dominate the calculator market, and sales skyrocketed, reaching $6.9 million by the end of the 1967 fiscal year. That same year the company—after it had established international offices in the United Kingdom, Belgium, and Taiwan—went public, its stock jumping from $12 to $37 in the first day alone.

Wang's next project marked his company's first entry into the data-processing market. Using magnetic core memory for storage in a programmable calculator, Wang created a general-purpose minicomputer. In addition, Wang Labs became the first company to purchase semiconductor-based Random Access Memory (RAM) chips from Robert Noyce's Intel Corporation, which Wang Labs installed in its 600 series of calculators.

As Wang's company entered the 1970s, the man who had earned the nickname "Doctor," accurately diagnosed a need for businesses to incorporate both data processing (which is the process by which structured data can be manipulated) and word processing (a machine's ability to create and edit documents). In pursuing this combination, Wang set his sights on a market that was, at the time, largely dominated by IBM. In 1972 Wang produced his company's first entry into this vast, new arena: the 1200 Word Processing System, a "thinking typewriter" that used an electronically controlled dual cassette. By 1975 Wang Labs was rolling out its Wang Computer System (WCS) series of computers, priced well below IBM's machines. The following year Wang further revolutionized

the industry by creating the WPS, a word-processing system that used cathode ray tubes, which allowed the user to manipulate text by moving words on a television-size screen. After this machine hit the desks of businesses across the country, Wang Labs secured its place in the *Fortune* 1,000 list and earned a new reputation as "the word processing company."

The innovations to emerge from Wang Labs did not cease with the WPS series. In 1977 the company developed the VS line of minicomputers, which could run programs previously used with larger mainframe computers. In 1979 Wang once again saw into the future of the information age and identified a market for a machine that could not only link word processing and data processing, but could also be upgraded to suit the individual needs of a user. After launching this Office Information Systems (OIS) series, Wang continued to work on developing office-related technology, focusing on image processing, audio processing, and networking functions. In 1981 the company produced Alliance, part of the OIS series that united all the major technologies, and WangNet, a broad-band–based local network allowing transmission of all text, voice, and video information within an office. By 1981 the company appeared unstoppable, posting $100 million in revenues for the fiscal year and reporting five years of solid, 55-percent annual growth.

With his company's fame and fortune steadily on the rise, Wang, a quiet man who shied away from publicity, continued to go head-to-head with IBM, even going so far as to predict that his company would overtake the computer giant by the mid-1990s. By 1982 Wang's company employed 24,800 workers, and while many corporate executives choose to take a hands-off approach to their businesses, Wang strove to remain an integral part of all operations. He continually immersed himself in all of the firm's designs and earned a loyal following for his easy accessibility. Through Wang Labs' continued success, the insightful electronics wizard revealed himself as not only a technological master but an artful businessman who could successfully juggle all aspects of his operations. As one former engineer told *Business Month* reporter Daniel Cohen (February 1990), "The Doctor had a whim of iron. He was into everything. He would come into the engineering department, head to the blackboard of a first-level engineer, and sketch out what he wanted."

In 1981 Wang decided to cede part of his extensive control over Wang Labs to a management committee that included his son and vice president, Frederick A. Wang, and John F. Cunningham, Wang's favorite marketing man and loyal employee, whom Wang's wife referred to as "our American son." Despite the momentum of producing three decades of vital computer and word-processing technology, Wang's hold on the market began to slip in the early 1980s as companies such as IBM, Hewlett-Packard, and AT&T staked claims in the office automation market. In 1982 IBM's Personal Computer quickly surpassed the Wang Professional Computer, which was introduced that year. During 1983 the company had delivery problems with 14 new products but maintained its place in the industry and earned publicity as one of *Business Month*'s (October 1984) "five best-managed companies of 1984." The year 1985, however, saw a significant fall, as earnings plummeted from $210 million in 1984 to $15.5 million, resulting in a company layoff of 1,600 workers. At the same time, Cunningham resigned, and in June 1985, Wang came out of semiretirement to run the company as president of day-to-day operations. The following year, although it continued to struggle, Wang Labs introduced innovations in the VS line, and after acquiring InteCom, a communications switching manufacturer, it produced a tele-workstation called Keystone.

The company's continual decline was a result of several intermingling factors, most notably a general recession in the economy and an industry-wide computer slump. Another key to Wang Labs' problems lay with the company's slow response to the lightning-fast changes and upgrades that had begun to rock the computer industry, but further damage was inflicted by product delays and servicing glitches that annoyed big customers and sent them running to competitors.

In November 1986 Wang named Frederick Wang as Wang Labs' new president, a controversial move that led many, both inside and outside the company, to wonder if the inexperienced son could adequately fill his father's shoes as the charismatic leader with an almost religious following among his workers. Wang, though, wished to follow a strict Chinese tradition of keeping business in the family, and he spent 14 years grooming his son to take over his post as president. His critics' predictions were proven true as the company continued to sink among the giants in the industry. In 1989 the company lost an unprecedented $424 million, and Wang was forced to fire his son as president. That same year it was discovered that Wang had esophageal cancer, and he underwent an operation to remove a tumor, in July, 1989. He developed complications, however, and died at Massachusetts General Hospital on March 24, 1990, at the age of 70. Wang was survived by his wife of more than 40 years, Lorraine Chiu, and their three children, Frederick, Courtney, and Juliette.

While Wang's company continued to suffer after his death (Wang Laboratories filed for bankruptcy in August 1992), his reputation lives on in the many contributions that he made during his extensive career. A versatile man with a passion for tennis, Wang managed to accumulate the authorship of more than 40 patents during his lifetime, some of which (such as his patent for a mark on the handle or strings of a tennis racket) lie completely outside his professional focus of computer engineering. Wang also believed strongly in the philosophy that, as his son, Frederick, summed up, "you

should return more to the community than you took from it," and he contributed a great deal of money during his lifetime to various causes in the fields of education, medicine, and the arts. One of his most notable legacies can be found in the form of the Wang Center for the Performing Arts, in Boston, which Wang rescued in 1983.—D. B.

Suggested Reading: *Business Month* p24+ Feb. 1990, with photos; *Christian Science Monitor* p12 Jan. 7, 1981, B p6 Mar. 10, 1981, with photos, p17+ Sep. 23, 1985, with photos; *Computer World* p67+ Feb. 17, 1992, with photo; *Fortune* p327 Apr. 25, 1988, with photo; *St. Louis Post-Dispatch* D p12 Mar. 25, 1990, with photo, E p1 Aug. 23, 1992, with photo; *American Men and Women of Science, 1986*; *Current Biography Yearbook*, p586+ 1987, with photo

---

Courtesy of Adobe Systems

Warnock, John

Oct. 6, 1940–Chairman and CEO of Adobe Systems

"If you walk into a magazine store, or look at the packages on the shelf of a grocery store, or see the catalogs that you get in the mail every day, or the billboards that you see on the highway or on the sides of trucks, probably our technology is used in every one of those pieces of information," John Warnock, the chairman and chief executive officer (CEO) of Adobe Systems, told Robert Holleyman in an interview for the Business Software Alliance Web site. Warnock's PostScript software, along with the emergence of personal computers and affordable laser printers, helped to launch the desktop-publishing revolution in the early 1980s. Together with a colleague from Xerox's Palo Alto Research Center (PARC), in California, Warnock founded Adobe Systems in 1982; since then the company has developed a stream of pioneering software products for graphics design, publishing, and electronic-document technology. Adobe has grown to become the third-largest personal-computer software provider in the country. Warnock, who was trained as a programmer and holds six patents for his software designs, has said that his company's transformation from a think-tank idea to a billion-dollar industry leader was "serendipitous," the result of different technologies coming together at the right time and producing a shift in the way businesses create and produce documents. Warnock is now helping to parlay Adobe's document-design expertise into the paperless realm of the World Wide Web. Already, according to a *Forbes* reporter (October 2, 2000, online), 91 percent of all Web sites use Photoshop, one of Adobe's signature programs. "What I try to do is factor in how people use computers, what people's problems are, and how these technologies can get applied to those problems," Warnock told Jill Wolfson and Denise Cobb for *The Tech* Web site.

John Warnock was born on October 6, 1940 in Salt Lake City, Utah. Like Einstein, Warnock failed algebra in the ninth grade. After taking an aptitude test, he was told that he was not college material. Luckily, a brilliant math teacher sparked Warnock's intellect, and he went on to college at the University of Utah, in Salt Lake City, to study mathematics and philosophy. He was then accepted into the school's graduate program in mathematics—albeit on probation due to his mediocre grades. Soon his reputation and his fortunes changed, when he solved a difficult math problem that had never been solved. He was subsequently nominated to the mathematics honorary fraternity. His plan was to become a professor of mathematics.

In 1963 Warnock took a summer job recapping tires at a Firestone rubber plant, but the grueling work and sweltering summer heat were too much for him. "The terrible nature of this job pushed me into applying for a job at IBM," Warnock told Michael P. McHugh for *Innerview* (March/April 1996). In the air-conditioned environs of IBM, Warnock learned about punched-card technology and eventually mastered programming. In 1964 he finished his master's degree and began teaching mathematics at the University of Utah. After getting married, in 1965, he decided that his teaching salary was inadequate and moved from the math department to the computer-science department, where his technical skills were in demand. In 1969 he earned his doctorate in electrical engineering and launched his career in the nascent computer industry.

Warnock's first job after completing his Ph.D. was with a start-up company called Computime Canada Ltd., in Vancouver. After the company failed, in 1970, Warnock went to work for the Computer Sciences Corporation in Toronto. He then moved with the company to Maryland to work under the auspices of the Goddard Space Flight Center. In 1972 Warnock moved with his family to California to work at the Ames Research Center, where he developed operating systems and real-time flight simulators. In 1978, having followed a path through academia, industry, and government, Warnock landed a job working with some of the best technology innovators at Xerox's PARC, which he once described as "the world's greatest sandbox," according to McHugh.

Hired by PARC's Charles Geschke to develop graphics systems, Warnock began by trying to solve long-standing software-related problems in document printing. At the time, software developers had to use different print commands for each printer and include a library of different sizes for each font. There was also a language barrier between computers and printers, making it difficult to gauge how an electronic document would actually look on paper. Because of this difficulty, changes to page layouts and additions of graphic images were typically made by graphic artists, who physically cut and pasted documents together after printing and sent the pasted-up pages to a commercial printer. Warnock and his colleague Martin Newell co-wrote a language aimed at solving such problems, calling it "JaM," after "John and Martin." Although Xerox adopted the JaM language as an in-house standard, the company decided not to market the technology to the public. Frustrated by Xerox's inactivity, Warnock and Getschke started their own company. "I was concerned that here was technology that was state of the art," Getschke told Lee Pender for *Computer Reseller News* (November 15, 1998). "Technology is like fish: If you don't cook it, it spoils."

With modest funding, Warnock and Getschke founded Adobe Systems in 1982, naming it after a river that ran behind their homes. Their goal was to re-create the creative environment at PARC while also maintaining a focus on developing viable products, not just new technologies. Warnock redeveloped the JaM language from its conceptual phase and renamed it PostScript. A "page-description language," the PostScript software tells a printer how to reproduce an electronic document on paper and ensures that users are able to print exactly what they see on the computer screen. It is "device-independent," meaning that it can be used across any platform and with any printer. Having worked for both the government and big industry, Warnock imagined that PostScript could be used in those arenas to solve "heavy-duty, industrial-strength publishing problems," as he told Holleyman. He was therefore surprised when, in 1983, his software attracted the interest of Steve Jobs, chairman of Apple Computer, who at the time was testing prototypes for the Macintosh personal computer. Realizing that the Post-Script software would make the use of personal computers and laser printers easier, Jobs invested $1.5 million in Adobe to bring the software to market. Jobs's interest in Adobe "was like a gift from God," Warnock told Katherine M. Hafner for *Business Week* (October 5, 1987). Around this time, Warnock heard from his friend Paul Brainerd, who was starting up the Aldus Corporation and, as Warnock told Holleyman, was "thinking about making a piece of software to help people design church flyers more easily." "We happened to hit the timing exactly right," Warnock told Pender. "There were three of four things coming together at exactly the right time: There was the graphical user interface from Apple on a low-cost machine—Macintosh. There was Canon's first low-cost laser printer. There was our development of PostScript, and there was Paul Brainerd putting together Page-Maker on the Macintosh." These technologies working together had the potential to replace the complicated and inefficient equipment used for typesetting and publishing. Warnock and his collaborators developed a marketing strategy to promote the newly emerging technology of "desktop publishing."

In 1985 the new Apple laser printer came equipped with Adobe PostScript. Other manufacturers followed suit, and PostScript soon became the industry standard. Because PostScript describes text mathematically, in outline form rather than as a library of fonts and sizes, it allows the text to be easily manipulated—and to appear as white on black, shaded, mirrored, or a range of other styles. In *Forbes* (June 5, 1995) Owen Edwards credited Warnock and his PostScript software with setting "graphics-imaging standards" and noted that "Human printed communication has always been guided by style as well as content. The beauty of calligraphy, manuscript illuminations, and type have been central to the way we receive information." As the husband of a graphic artist, Warnock is well aware of the importance of graphics and the changes it has undergone in recent years. In a speech at the 1997 Seybold Conference, as archived on the Seybold Seminars Publications and Consulting Web site, Warnock described how he used to help his wife with design projects: "The creation process was manual and labor intensive. My wife . . . used to give me two weeks' notice on a project, and we would amass all of the Exacto knives and everything and put things together." Since the advent of desktop publishing, Warnock noted, the creative process has become easier, faster, and cheaper, and the number of graphic artists has grown dramatically. In his interview with Holleyman, Warnock offered one example: In 1965 Sears, Roebuck, and Co. produced an annual catalog of several hundred pages that took a full-time staff an entire year to complete. By the mid-1990s Macy's department store was using desktop publishing to annually distribute almost 200 separate catalogs—each aimed at a different market—in the Western half of the United States alone.

As desktop publishing transformed the business world, Adobe's fortunes rose—which came as a great surprise to Warnock. "When you start a company you do all kinds of contingency planning for failure events. You never do much planning for success," he told McHugh. Warnock once made a statement that Adobe would never have more than 50 employees; the company now has thousands around the world. After taking his company public in 1986, Warnock decided that Adobe needed to develop more than just the PostScript product. In 1987 the company released Adobe Illustrator, a software package for professional graphic artists. In 1988 Adobe Photoshop debuted. An image-editing program, Photoshop made it possible to manipulate the size, color, and style of images and to work with extensive libraries of typefaces. It is used, for example, in the production of art catalogs, for which great pains are taken to reproduce the precise coloration and shadings of paintings. Extremely popular with illustrators and graphic artists, it is the company's greatest moneymaker. Warnock estimated that Photoshop garners 90 percent of the professional desktop-imaging market, as cited by Bob Weibel for *Photo District News* (February 1999).

In 1990 Warnock wrote a paper called "The Project," in which he discussed how a subset of the PostScript software could be used to create electronic documents that could be viewed and printed by many different machines and operating systems. In 1993 Adobe released Acrobat, which was based on that insight. The software can convert a DOS, Windows, Unix, or Macintosh document into "Portable Document Format" (PDF), which can then be displayed on any computer with an Acrobat reader. Though Warnock had the idea for the software before the appearance of the World Wide Web, his invention turned out to be ideally suited for on-line interactions. "Few companies have been so accidentally well-prepared for the Web as San Jose-based Adobe Systems," one *Forbes* (October 2, 2000, on-line) reporter observed. "John has good gut instincts on where technology is going. . . ." Charles Geschke, Warnock's colleague, told Deborah Gage for *Computer Reseller News* (November 6, 1995). "He knew strategically that Acrobat was the right thing to do. He understood by gut instinct, as opposed to foreknowledge, that the Internet would hit us and we'd need this technology." After initially struggling to make Acrobat catch on, Adobe began giving away the software for reading PDF documents for free, in 1994. As people began making the transition from paper to electronic information, Acrobat proved to be a key program. To meet President Clinton's directive to reduce paperwork, 120 government agencies adopted the Acrobat technology. The Center for Disease Control began to issue its weekly reports on-line using the Acrobat technology, and the IRS began to post tax forms in PDF format on the Web. Acrobat made it possible to disseminate highly formatted or graphics-laden documents on-line and across many different platforms. Newer versions of the software can be used in conjunction with multimedia technologies such as video and audio. By 2000 Acrobat had become the company's second-biggest moneymaker.

While Photoshop and Illustrator programs were marketed mainly for professional use, Adobe also began producing tools designed for the average user. "We're going to make it very easy for anyone to have his own Web site," Warnock said at the Seybold Conference in 1995, as quoted by Gage. "There is nothing intrinsically difficult about it. And the more people get access to this, the more people have a voice. It helps with government, general communications, literacy—all kinds of things." Adobe now has a full line of products for use in both print and electronic publishing, including Web-publishing products, print-publishing tools, Acrobat software, and special-effects and video-editing software.

At a conference in the summer of 2000, Warnock demonstrated some of Adobe's latest technologies, including new software for creating 3D and scalable graphics. "The Web is at the intersection of community, commerce, multimedia and 2D and 3D content. Consumers will want to interact within a visually-rich and realistic setting and virtually 'walk on the web' in real-time," Warnock said, as quoted in an Adobe press release.

Warnock is the recipient of many honors, including a Lifetime Achievement Award for Technical Excellence from *PC Magazine*, the Association for Computing Machinery (ACM) Software Systems Award, and the first Rhode Island School of Design Distinguished Service to Art and Design International Award. He was inducted into the Computer Industry's hall of fame in 1998.

Regarded as a quiet intellectual in an industry dominated by forceful personalities, Warnock lives in a Silicon Valley home built in 1922. He collects rare, first-edition books that, in his opinion, have changed the "direction of mankind," as he told McHugh. He owns Galileo's *Sidereus nuncius* (Starry Messenger, 1610), in which the astronomer recorded his telescopic observations, and Newton's *Principia* (1687), in which the scientist laid out the laws of gravity and motion. "These are time machines back into history," Warnock told Erika Brown for *Forbes* (October 9, 2000). "I could never sell any of these. I'll pass them down to my children. They will be in the family for generations." Warnock and his wife have three grown children.—M. A. H.

Computer Reseller News p138 Nov. 6, 1995, with photo, p49+ Nov. 15, 1996, with photo; *Forbes* (on-line) Oct. 2, 2000; *Innerview* (on-line) Mar./Apr. 1996; *Photo District News* p29+ Feb. 1999; *The Tech* (on-line)

Warren, James

1936– Co-founder of the West Coast Computer Faire; journalist; publisher; computer consultant; political activist

In 1964 Jim Warren, a Texas native, moved to California's Bay Area with the hope of finding a more exciting and rewarding life. He wasn't disappointed. A short time after his arrival, the counterculture swept through the region (and shortly thereafter to the rest of the nation). Warren became a hippie and, like many people at the time, participated in political demonstrations against the Vietnam War. Warren had learned computer skills back in Texas, and to support himself, he worked as a programmer and computer consultant. On the eve of the personal-computer revolution, in the mid-1970s, Warren often attended meetings of local computer clubs, sharing information and trading software programs with other hobbyists and users. He decided to organize a computer convention, hoping to bring together thousands of people with the many computer and software companies that were springing up in California and throughout the country at the time. The first West Coast Computer Faire, which was held at the San Francisco Civic Auditorium in April 1977, was an enormous success. Nearly 13,000 people paid admission to see

the many exhibitors; these included Commodore Business Machines and the fledgling Apple Computer Corporation, which used the event to promote its revolutionary Apple II personal computer. The convention's success encouraged Warren and his partners to make the West Coast Computer Faire an annual event in California. By the early 1980s, it had grown into one of the personal-computer industry's most important trade shows, attracting tens of thousands of people and hundreds of exhibitors. After buying out his partners and selling the rights to the Faire for $3 million, in 1983, Warren devoted himself to several projects, including publishing and editing computer periodicals, writing extensively about computer-related topics, lobbying for on-line access to government records, and championing on-line privacy and freedom of expression in cyberspace.

James Warren, referred to in the media most often as Jim, was born in 1936 in San Antonio, Texas. After his parents divorced, Warren lived with his mother. "Mom was a really good entrepreneur and pretty much a failure as a human being—very personable when she was wanting something from someone," Warren recalled to Robert Levering, Michael Katz, and Milton Moskowitz, the authors of *The Computer Entrepreneurs: Who's Making It Big and How in America's Upstart Industry* (1984). "I had a lot of problems with her and eventually moved out." Warren's father worked as a door-to-door salesman, a gas-station attendant, and an office manager for a small welding-supply company. "Dad was an exact opposite to Mom," he told Levering, Katz, and Moskowitz. "As a business person, he was an absolute flop, but as a human being, just a delightful man. A sincere, concerned, gentle man."

Warren enrolled at San Antonio Junior College, in Texas, planning to major in chemical engineering. He changed his major twice, however. "Thanks to having an incredibly awful freshman college chem instructor . . . I decided to switch to electrical engineering," he explained to *Leaders of the Information Age*. "Thanks to having a rather abysmal freshman physics teacher . . . I thought yet again. I realized that I'd always enjoyed math, realized that—unlike the real world—logic and mathematics were, almost by definition, intellectually clean, consistent, unambiguous."

Warren transferred to Southwest Texas State University in San Marcos, Texas. He dropped out, however, in 1957, during his senior year. Although he did not have an undergraduate degree, Warren was able to find work as a high-school mathematics teacher in San Antonio, because the city was experiencing a shortage of teachers at that time. Explaining to *Leaders of the Information Age* why he chose teaching, Warren replied that he "liked the notion of being my own boss, teachers are the nearest things to independent contractors in 'employee' positions. I liked the hours and the annual schedule. . . . Also, in my heart and my thoughts, I really liked the vague, ill-understood notion . . . that I was doing something worthwhile." He continued, "Within a few years, I had more consciously characterized this as something that I have, ever since then, preached, and hopefully practiced, as being an all-important life principle: We must put more into our culture and society than we take out. To the extent that we take more than we return, our society and culture are degraded and shrivel; to the extent that we 'invest' more than we 'withdraw' from our society, our culture and our collective futures are enhanced." In addition to teaching, Warren resumed his education, taking night classes at Southwest Texas State University. He earned a B.S. in mathematics, in 1959; he then earned a master's degree in mathematics and statistics from the University of Texas at Austin, in 1964.

Warren's first experience with a computer had been in 1961 when he took a programming course at the Lackland Air Force Base in San Antonio. "We were doing machine coding," Warren explained to *Leaders of the Information Age*, "and later assembler coding on the [IBM] 650—which was a 2,000 word magnetic-drum-memory computer where no more than six to eight people could be in the same room with the machine; it had a separate building just for its air conditioner." Two years later, he took a course in the FORTRAN computer language as part of his work for his master's degree at the University of Texas at Austin. Ex-

plaining to *Leaders of the Information Age* what fascinated him about the machines, Warren said: "Like math, they were clean and orderly and completely predictable—well, at least they were when they weren't malfunctioning. They did exactly what I told them to do, even if it was wrong."

A short time after receiving his master's degree, Warren decided to move to California's Bay Area. "I loved teaching," he explained to *Leaders of the Information Age*, "but despised most of the racist, chauvinistic, sexist, age-ist, conformist, jock-ist, narrow-minded 'society' of Texass." (He notes that he always spells the state's name that way, as a matter of "truth in labeling.") A lesbian friend from college who had moved to the region told Warren that he might like the Bay Area and its more-liberal attitudes. "Having nothing better to do," Warren told *Leaders of the Information Age*, "but a string of professional successes and 'honors' . . . and my shiny new master's degree (which meant somethin' in the hicksland of Texass), and having minimal financial needs, I decided to hitch up my house trailer and go west, as a young man."

Warren joined the faculty of the College of Notre Dame, a small Catholic women's college in Belmont, California, as the chairman of the mathematics department. He purchased a home in La Honda, a city a short distance from the Pacific Ocean. The mid-1960s witnessed the birth of both the counter-culture—which challenged society's prevailing attitudes toward morality, sex, and other matters—and the student-protest movement against the Vietnam War. Warren enthusiastically embraced the counterculture and participated in anti-war rallies organized by the Free Speech Movement, a group of student activists at the University of California at Berkeley. "It was . . . challenging and questioning everything—authority, rules, traditions, educational programs, and 'standards,' and most especially our misbegotten business, educational, and political 'leaders,'" Warren explained to *Leaders of the Information Age*. He quipped, "It was a time when we 'knew' we were going to change the world—even if it took a year or two."

A couple whom Warren had met at a nudist camp told him about a nude beach only ten miles from his home. Warren told *Leaders of the Information Age* that he enjoyed "not only the two-mile-long, cliff-locked beach, but also the variety of couples, families, and singles—mostly university folks plus some families—whom I met as I strolled, stark-naked, from one end to the other." Warren invited many of the people he met back to his home for a party. "Without any of us expecting a 'nude party' in any way, we ended up having one," Warren recalled to *Leaders of the Information Age*. "All were delighted—most of all me. I promptly started throwin' [more] such parties—mostly, but never entirely, nude. 'Nudity' was not a requirement. That would have been as oppressive as the traditional oppression of mandated clothing. [The gatherings were] never overtly sexual [and were marked by] great fun, great joy, good friendships."

Warren's nude parties immediately became famous, attracting many people over the next few years. The Berkeley, California, *Barb*, a radical newspaper; *Playboy* magazine; and the *San Francisco Chronicle* all published stories about the parties, and a camera crew from BBC Television in the United Kingdom filmed one for a program on California life. Although Warren was never identified by name, rumors that he was the chief organizer of the gatherings filtered back to the College of Notre Dame administration. When questioned by the president of the college, a Catholic nun, Warren admitted that the rumors were true and agreed in 1967 to resign, since such behavior was deemed, as he put it to *Leaders of the Information Age*, "rather incompatible with the philosophy of a Catholic girls' college."

After resigning from the College of Notre Dame, Warren began teaching on a volunteer basis at the Mid-Peninsula Free University, an alternative institution of higher learning set up in Palo Alto, California, by local activists. To supplement his income, he became a computer programmer at the Stanford Medical Center, in Palo Alto. He used a PDP-8 minicomputer to support the center's biomedical research. "It was also great fun to program in data-acquisition and process-control applications—where the computer was presenting tests to test subjects (animal and human), recording their responses, and giving response-driven feedback," Warren elaborated to *Leaders of the Information Age*. "The research itself was interesting—single-cell mapping of the visual cortex, effects of minimally toxic agents . . . on subjects, control and imaging of and from electron microprobes and microscopes." Warren also taught computing and programming on a part-time basis at various schools, including Stanford University, San Francisco State University, and San Jose State University. In 1968 he founded Frelan Associates, a computer consulting firm.

During the 1970s, Warren returned to school as a student. In 1974 he earned a master's degree in medical information science from the University of California Medical Center, in San Francisco. To broaden his knowledge of computers, he enrolled as a graduate student at Stanford University, receiving his third master's degree, this one in computer engineering, in 1977. Warren remained at Stanford to pursue a doctorate in computer engineering. His first dissertation advisor and research supervisor was Vinton G. Cerf, an assistant professor of computer science who played a major role in the development of the ARPANET, the precursor to the Internet. (Cerf went on to achieve international recognition for co-developing with Robert E. Kahn the TCP/IP protocol, which served as the foundation of the modern-day Internet.) Warren told *Leaders of the Information Age* that after his first year in the program, he switched to another advisor because Cerf had failed to provide him with any guidance on possible topics for his dissertation. Warren eventually withdrew from the doc-

toral program, and the resume he provided to *Leaders of the Information Age* lists "Abd" for "all but dissertation" in regard to his doctoral studies.

During the mid-1970s, Warren attended meetings of the Homebrew Computer Club, an informal group of computer hobbyists who met in Menlo Park, California, to trade software and share information. Warren also became involved with the People's Computer Center (PCC), a nonprofit company that was co-founded by Bob Albrecht and Dennis Allison. Also based in Menlo Park, the PCC promoted the use of personal computers and allowed computer enthusiasts to exchange information and software. Allison wrote Tiny BASIC, a smaller version of the BASIC computer language, which made it easier for people to create programs for the Altair 8800 microcomputer, which reached the market in 1975.

Albrecht and Allison recruited Warren to serve as the founding editor for a computer newsletter, *Dr. Dobb's Journal of Computer Calisthenics and Orthodontia* (later shortened to *Dr. Dobb's Journal*). "[Allison] told me they needed a technically competent sucker to edit the thing and asked me how much I needed to live on," Warren recalled to Hal Plotkin for the San Francisco *Metro* (August 24, 1995, on-line). "I figured I could get by on $350 a month." *Dr. Dobb's Journal* eventually evolved into a professionally published magazine that is still in business today. Warren, who edited the periodical until 1978, explained to *Leaders of the Information Age* that it "was definitely not for a lay audience. It was for computer professionals and computer hobbyists—but people who were technically knowledgeable, either self-taught or formally educated therein. It was the first magazine to focus on software for microcomputers."

In August 1976 Warren attended the Personal Computing Festival, in Atlantic City, New Jersey. About 3,500 people braved the searing heat to peruse the exhibition booths, many of which were set up by fledgling computer companies; share information; and display their self-built computers and programs. The success of the festival inspired Warren to organize a similar event in California. "My myopic contention was that all of this good stuff was happening on the wrong coast," he told Paul Freiberger and Michael Swaine for *Fire in the Valley: The Making of the Personal Computer* (second edition, 1999). Warren planned to hold the convention at Stanford University, but the hall he wanted wasn't available. The only available venue that could accommodate a convention with thousands of people was the San Francisco Civic Auditorium, which cost $13,000 a day to rent. Since Warren made less than $5,000 a year at the time, Albrecht agreed to put up the $1,200 deposit to reserve the auditorium. Warren and Albrecht figured that they could break even if enough exhibitors rented booths (which cost between $300 and $500) and if at least 6,000 people payed between $5 and $8 each for admission. Warren aggressively publicized the convention, telling all of his friends in the area about it. He named the event the West Coast Computer Faire, to evoke the popular Renaissance Faires that often played across the country. He even had himself identified in the event's program as the "Faire Chaire." The West Coast Computer Faire ran for three days—from April 15–17 in 1977—and greatly exceeded Warren's and Albrecht's expectations by attracting nearly 13,000 people and making a substantial profit. "Once inside, attendees found themselves in computer heaven," Freiberger and Swaine wrote in their book. "Rows and rows of festively decorated booths touted the latest advances in personal computing. An inquiring hobbyist could find him—or herself chatting up with the very person who had designed some innovative product." Among the exhibitors were Steve Jobs and Steve Wozniak, the co-founders of the Apple Computer Corporation, who impressed patrons with their revolutionary Apple II personal computer. The Faire gave the Apple II a major boost, and by 1980 it had sold more than 50,000 units. Jobs and Wozniak helped spark the personal-computer revolution in the late 1970s, and, in 1982, Apple Computer's annual sales exceeded a phenomenal $1 billion.

The success of the first West Coast Computer Faire led Warren, with the financial backing and assistance of several partners, to organize subsequent Faires once a year in different cities in California. The Faire grew each passing year, attracting more attendees and exhibitors. Warren personally supervised the events, often using a pair of roller skates to move around on the convention floor to make sure everything went well. Within a few years, the West Coast Computer Faire had become one of the largest and most important computer trade shows in the country. The 1983 Faire, the last organized by Warren, attracted more than 47,000 people and 800 exhibitors.

Despite this success, Warren grew tired of organizing the Faire. "I was gaining eight pounds per Faire," he told Plotkin, "and eventually I told my crew that I had to get out. There were lots of people who wanted to buy the Faire, and by 1983, I was ready to sell." That year, Warren bought out his partners and sold the rights to the West Coast Computer Faire to the Prentice-Hall publishing company for $3 million. (Although the Faires continued, they gradually experienced a decline in popularity. The last Faire took place in 1990.)

In addition to editing *Dr. Dobb's Journal*, Jim Warren pursued several other ventures. From 1977 to 1986 he published and edited the *Silicon Gulch Gazette*, a free tabloid newsletter. (When discussing the publication's quality, Warren often quipped that readers got what they paid for.) In 1978 Warren founded the *Intelligent Machines Journal*, which he sold a year later to Patrick McGovern, the founder and chief executive officer of the International Data Group (IDG) and publisher of the popular *Computerworld* magazine. In 1980 *Intelligent Machines Journal* changed its name to *InfoWorld*; it is still a leading computer magazine

today. During the 1981–82 season Warren served as the founding host for the PBS series *Computer Chronicles*. In 1982 he began publishing *DataCast* magazine, which offered tutorials for popular software programs, but it folded a year later. From 1982 to 1984 Warren also produced several instructional videos on computer-related topics with his company, Video Initiative.

Warren used the money he had made from the West Coast Computer Faires to purchase land in the mountains of San Mateo County, in Woodside, California. He built a three-story house that served as a commune for himself and his friends. He turned his attention to local politics. In 1985 he was elected as one of five trustees of the San Mateo County Community College District in California, which is responsible for overseeing three colleges, a budget of more than $60 million, and more than 12,000 students. Warren told *Leaders of the Information Age* that he ran for the position in order "to give something back" to the community and because he believed that the board "needed to have at least one member who was technically knowledgeable." A year later he ran against the president of San Mateo County's Board of Supervisors, but lost. "My platform was local control over local community issues—and I knew, going in, that I didn't have a chance of winning," Warren explained to *Leaders of the Information Age*. "But I damn-well wasn't going to let [the incumbent] seek re-election unopposed."

In 1990 Warren joined *MicroTimes* magazine as a contributing editor and "Technology & Public Policy" columnist. As a journalist and frequent speaker at conferences, Warren argued that public access to government information and records, which citizens were already allowed to obtain in writing under the law, could be facilitated in an easy and inexpensive way by posting them on-line. In 1993 Warren backed a bill introduced by Assemblywoman Debra Bowen that required the California state legislature to post information, including the text of bills, committee reports, votes by members, transcripts of debates, and other legislative activities, on-line on a daily basis. After learning that it had little chance of passing, Warren used the Internet, which was still in its infancy, and numerous on-line Bulletin Board Systems to rally support for Bowen's bill. Within a few days, Bowen's office received many letters and faxes supporting her legislation. Several journalists, political activists, talk-show hosts, such organizations as the League of Women Voters and the Sierra Club, and businesses—including Apple Computer—backed the bill, greatly increasing its chances for passage. According to Graeme Browning's book *Electronic Democracy: Using the Internet to Influence American Politics* (1996), Warren closely monitored the bill's progress in the state legislature and helped keep supporters informed of hearings, proposed changes, and votes. Warren and other supporters successfully mobilized opposition to an amendment to the legislation that would have required users to pay fees to download information for commercial purposes. In September 1993 both houses of the legislature passed the bill, and, one month later, it was signed into law by Governor Pete Wilson.

From 1993 to 1996 Warren frequently wrote about these topics as the "Public Access" columnist for *Government Technology* magazine, which is read by state and local officials in California, and the "Government Access" columnist for *Board-Watch* magazine, which is read by information systems' operators and users. In 1997 the California State Senate appointed Warren to the Electronic Access to Public Records Task Force.

Warren also lobbied for legislation that would make records of campaign contributions to candidates available on-line free of charge. In 1995 the California Secretary of State appointed him as a member and co-chairman of the Electronic Filings Advisory Panel, which studied the issue and submitted a report in 1997 to the California legislature. In 1998 California began posting records of political campaign contributions on-line. As Internet usage exploded during the 1990s, more and more states began making public records available through the Internet. When asked by *Leaders of the Information Age* how on-line access to government records would affect the political and legislative process, Warren replied: "Knowledge is power. But knowledge depends on information. Thus, personal political power depends on timely access to adequate information on which to base knowledgeable decisions, as responsible participants in the process of our own governance."

During the 1990s Warren turned his attention to on-line privacy and censorship. In 1991 he served as the founding chairman of the First Conference on Computers, Freedom, and Privacy. He frequently warned that government censorship would undermine freedom of expression and destroy the Internet as a means of communication. In 1995 he vocally opposed the federal Communications Decency Act, which restricted the on-line transmission of obscene material. (Although it was approved by Congress and signed into law by President Bill Clinton in 1996, the act was struck down by the Supreme Court in 1997.) Also, in 1995, Warren criticized government efforts to exclusively control computer-encryption technology. Warren argued that the technology would thwart hackers and enhance computer privacy if it were widely available. The same year, the United States Attorney's office in San Jose, California, subpoenaed Warren to testify at the grand jury hearing on Philip Zimmermann, who developed the Pretty Good Privacy (PGP) encryption program, for allegedly allowing its export overseas through the Internet without a license. (In January 1996 the government ended its investigation of Zimmermann without filing any charges, which pleased many on-line privacy activists.)

Over the years, Jim Warren's activism has been recognized several times. In 1992 he received the Electronic Frontier Foundation's first annual Electronic Frontier Pioneer Award. In 1994 the Northern California chapter of the Society of Professional Journalists presented Warren with the James Madison Freedom of Information Award. The same year, the Playboy Foundation honored him with the Hugh M. Hefner First Amendment Award. In 1995 Warren earned the John Dvorak Lifetime Achievement Award.

Jim Warren continues to write and work as a computer consultant. He and his wife live in Woodside, California.—D. C.

Suggested Reading: *Dr. Dobb's Journal* p96+ Jan. 1991; *Forbes* p82 Aug. 1, 1983; San Francisco *Metro* (on-line) Aug. 24, 1995, with photos; *New York Times* G p6 Feb. 24, 2000, with photo; Levering, Robert, Michael Katz, and Milton Moskowitz. *The Computer Entrepreneurs: Who's Making It Big and How in America's Upstart Industry*, 1984; Browning, Graeme. *Electronic Democracy: Using the Internet to Influence American Politics*, 1996; Freiberger, Paul and Michael Swaine. *Fire in the Valley: The Making of the Personal Computer* (second edition), 1999

Watson, Thomas J., Jr.

Jan. 8, 1914–Dec. 31, 1993 Longtime head of IBM

Thomas J. Watson Jr., who in 1952 succeeded his father as president of the International Business Machines (IBM), is widely credited with fomenting the computer revolution by offering adaptable mainframe computers to the private sector—in addition to the government agencies and large research facilities that had previously constituted the market. Over the course of his tenure Watson made IBM almost synonymous with technological advancement and established it as the world's leader in the computer industry—a position the firm has yet to relinquish.

Thomas John Watson Jr. was born in Dayton, Ohio, on January 8, 1914, the eldest son of Thomas John and Jeannette (Kittredge) Watson. His mother was the daughter of an Ohio industrialist. Thomas Watson Sr., formerly a sales executive for the National Cash Register Company, moved the family to New York shortly after the boy's birth, to assume the presidency of the Computing-Tabulating-Recording Company. Because of its expanded business activity, the firm's name was changed in 1924 to International Business Machines Corporation, universally recognized by the famous acronym, IBM. The senior Watson's accomplishments were an impetus to the youngster, who at five years of age was taken on a tour of a company factory and at age nine joined his father in an inspection of European plants. Watson Jr. told a reporter for the *New York Herald Tribune* (August 31, 1950), "I

Courtesy of the Computer Museum of America

Thomas J. Watson Jr.

take real pride in being a great man's son. My father has set a fine example for me. Because he is who he is, I realize that nearly every act of mine will be scrutinized very closely."

Thomas Watson Jr. attended private grammar schools in Short Hills, New Jersey, where the family lived, then the Hun Preparatory School, in Princeton. Following his 1937 graduation from Brown University, in Providence, Rhode Island, with a B.A., he joined IBM as a junior salesman. He was assigned to New York's Wall Street area, traditionally a difficult selling district for the company. In this capacity he not only met his quota, but produced a fabulous record by selling two and a half times more than the previous salesman. Even by his father's strict standards, he had made his mark. "That was the only right way," the elder Watson told a reporter for *Time* (March 28, 1955). "He had to make his own records. Otherwise, people might feel that he had some special help, which he did not haveDD

The younger Watson met all of his quotas consistently and even became a member of IBM's prestigious 100 Percent Club (the requirements of which were to achieve 100 percent of one's quota). He was equally busy after hours, enthusiastically patronizing Manhattan night clubs.

This changed in 1940, when Watson Jr. enlisted as a private in the U.S. Air Force. He was trained as a pilot and commissioned a second lieutenant later in the same year, and was reportedly one of the first to participate in the lend-lease ferry route between Alaska and Russia. During his years in the service he flew DC-3s and B-24s on dangerous supply route missions between Russia and the Middle East, as well as missions to India and China. In ear-

ly 1946 he was discharged as a lieutenant-colonel, having earned his senior pilot's wings, won the U.S. Air Medal, and accumulated 2,000 hours of flying time.

Upon his return to IBM, in January 1946, he was named assistant to the vice president in charge of sales, becoming the vice president in June and a member of the board of directors in October. Undoubtedly, his quick rise in the company was due in part to his father's influence but also to his earnest desire to prove himself the elder man's peer. Three years later he was appointed executive vice-president, and in January 1952 he became IBM's president. (His father retained his position as chairman of the board.) In other business affiliations Watson Jr. was the director of Bankers Trust and Mutual Life Insurance Company, among others.

Father and son worked together for a sometimes-tumultuous decade. Watson Sr. had always seen computers as something with little mass-market appeal. Watson Jr., by contrast, saw great opportunity in the new machines then being created and realized that corporations would be interested in such devices to improve their productivity. Watson Jr. continually pressured his reluctant father to make changes—doubling the research and development budget, for example, and hiring hundreds of electronic engineers. Watson Sr. retired in 1956 and died shortly afterwards, after more than 40 years with IBM.

In 1952 Watson Jr. had fought off the first U.S. government antitrust suit against IBM, for monopolizing the card-processing industry. He accomplished this by signing a consent decree with the government that loosened IBM's grip on the industry. Watson had seen the writing on the wall long before the antitrust suit, however, and quickly began replacing the punched-card–processing portion of the business with computer manufacturing.

One of Watson's first decisions as president, in 1952, was to manufacture the IBM 701 computer, the first large computer based on small, easily replaceable vacuum tubes. It could execute 17,000 instructions per second; though the model was initially intended for governmental use and scientific research, private industry quickly took notice of its merits. Its speed made it useful for inventory control, payroll, and billing, among other functions.

Under the younger Watson's direction, IBM took the lead in the automation field. IBM sold or rented $461,000,000 worth of its machines in 1954; its sales increased 19 percent each year between 1952 and 1956. By the end of the same period, the company held more than 1,500 patents, employed 34,000 workers at six plants across the United States, and made 5,960 different models of business machines. (IBM overseas offices, known as the World Trade Corporation, were run by Arthur Watson, the younger brother of Tom Jr.)

In February 1955 IBM introduced an electronic machine similar to a master switchboard that could control as many as 40 tasks—as simple as switching lights on or off or as complicated as starting and stopping machinery of an assembly line. After seeing a demonstration, a reporter for the *Christian Science Monitor* (April 22, 1955) wrote: "Mechanical 'brains' are accomplishing feats today that defy the imagination. . . . Requiring only a few trained technicians to feed them directions and 'problems,' the machines do the work and produce solutions in minutes that would often take hundreds of persons as much as decades to achieve."

In a March 28, 1955 article in *Time*, a reporter noted that "IBM's success in office automation was built on machines of cogs and gears. . . . But in the last few years there has been a profound change in the business. The mechanical cogs and gears have given way to electronic circuits, cathode-ray tubes and transistors. . . . Tom Watson, Jr., fought his ideas through [and] persuaded everyone that IBM had to learn to make electronic circuits do the work of old-fashioned cogs and gears."

IBM's list of "firsts" grew. The company was the first to use transistors in its computers; the IBM 7090 was the first fully transistorized mainframe. It could perform 229,000 calculations a second. Like many of IBM's other early computer systems, the 7090 was initially used by the U.S. government—in this case to run the Ballistic Missile Early Warning System—and only later by private industry. In 1964 American Airlines used two 7090 mainframes to link ticket sales desks in 65 cities.

Watson was especially proud of model 702, installed at the Monsanto Chemical Company in April 1955. Besides preparing financial statements, the machine handled cost control and sales analysis, sales forecasting, property records, wage rolls, and amortization issues, as well as other engineering problems. The computer's calculations were instantly transmitted in the form of punched cards to Monsanto's field offices. That same year, IBM had orders for 14 model 702 computers, which rented for $20,000 a month.

Other machines pioneered by IBM during this period were the 705, devised to record and calculate the earnings of those 119,000,000 Americans then holding Social Security cards; the 305, which worked on inventory data for the Department of Defense and private manufacturing concerns; and machines built for specific activities, including the IBM card checks that were used by banks to mechanize the check-sorting process and the computer that kept a complete inventory of reservations for airline flights, pilot schedules, and freight deliveries. In addition, the Ohio Turnpike calculated its toll charges by weighing the vehicle and measuring the distance driven with the assistance of IBM machines equipped with photoelectric eyes. In 1955 the U.S. Air Force ordered IBM computers to be used to detect approaching enemy planes.

In 1956 and 1957, IBM generated two developments that would have a lasting impact on computing: RAMAC and FORTRAN. RAMAC, which stands for Random Access Method of Accounting and Control, was the world's first computer-disk storage system. As part of the IBM 305, RAMAC's "random access" arm was able to retrieve information stored on one of 50 spinning disks in less than a second. In 1958 the system was exhibited at the World's Fair in Brussels, where it answered questions on world history in ten languages. FORTRAN, an abbreviation of the name Formula Translation, was a computer language based on grammar, algebra, and syntax rules. As the need for computer languages grew, FORTRAN's popularity soared.

Perhaps the greatest achievement of Watson's tenure came in 1964 with the release of the IBM Series/360 line of mainframe computers, which the company hoped would make all its previous machines obsolete. The Series/360 was the first set of machines that gave customers the ability to add or change software and hardware as needs changed—instead of scrapping the system for an entirely new one. Any of the Series/360 software or peripheral equipment could work interchangeably on different sized processors. It gave the consumer a variety of options, including 19 combinations of speed, power, and memory as well as a choice of five processors. For this system IBM engineers developed Solid Logic Technology (SLT), a new technology composed of half-inch ceramic modules containing circuits that were more reliable, faster, and denser than any previous transistors. Because the series proved to be highly adaptable to a company's particular needs, the private sector embraced it like no other machines IBM had previously produced. IBM shipped thousands of these machines and a number of their features would become industry standards for mainframe computers. With this series, IBM fully launched the modern computer era and helped usher in the concept of office computers. (At the time, ironically, *Fortune* referred to the system as "IBM's $5 billion gamble.")

Other innovations soon followed, including the one-transistor memory cell, in 1966, and cache memory, in 1968, but Watson's next great stride came not in product development but in the area of marketing. In 1969, as IBM mainframe computers dominated the market, Watson took the bold step of changing the way his company sold its technology. Instead of offering hardware, software, and service in packages, he unbundled the various components and sold them separately. By doing this, he effectively created the modern software and service industries.

In 1971, after years of high-stress executive life, Watson suffered a heart attack. In response, he stepped down as CEO of the company, turning the reigns over to T. Vincent Learson, who had risen through the ranks of IBM since being hired in 1935. By the time Watson stepped down, he had seen the company expand to 270,000 employees; its gross revenue had topped $8 billion.

Although no longer CEO, Watson continued to serve the company as chair of the executive committee until 1979, when he accepted the post of ambassador to the Soviet Union from President Jimmy Carter. He served in that position until 1981. He had previously been a member of several presidential committees, including ones on Labor-Management Policy (1961–69), Troop Information and Education (1962), the Task Force on the War Against Poverty (1964–68), the Income Maintenance Programs (1968–70), and the American Committee on the East-West Accord (1975–78). He was also a chairman of a U.S. Arms Control Commission and gave speeches across America calling for nuclear disarmament. Watson was president of the Greater New York Council of the Boy Scouts of America, director of the New York chapter of the American Red Cross, and a member of the board of managers of Memorial Hospital for Cancer and Allied Diseases. In February 1955 he was elected as a trustee of the American Museum of Natural History, in New York City; he was also a trustee of Brown University and a member of the steering committee of the United Negro College Fund. In 1949 he served as chairman of United Nations Week.

An avid pilot, Watson occasionally flew the company plane during business trips, and after his retirement from IBM he piloted everything from jets to helicopters to stunt planes. An accomplished sailor, Watson often sailed his yawl, Palawan (named after an island in the Philippines he had visited between combat flights in World War II), in Newport-to-Bermuda races, and he navigated the Antarctic and Hudson Bay. He once won the Blue Water Medal, considered "yachting's Noble Prize." *Fortune* (November 22, 1999) deemed him one of the most important businessmen of the century, and the magazine's tribute read in part, "Watson not only knew how to run a business—he had a life." Watson wrote a memoir, *Father, Son & Co.: My Life at IBM and Beyond*, which is still in print.

Thomas J. Watson Jr. married Olive Field Cawley on December 15, 1941. They had five children: Thomas III, Jeannette, Olive, Lucinda, and Susan. Watson died on December 31, 1993, from complications following a stroke.—C. M.

Suggested Reading: *Christian Science Monitor* Oct. 26, 1955; *Fortune* p220+ Nov. 8, 1999, p108+ Nov. 22, 1999; IBM Web site; *Time* p81+ Mar. 28, 1955

Watson, Thomas J., Sr.

Feb. 17, 1874–June 19, 1956 First president and CEO of IBM

During the first half of the 20th century, Thomas J. Watson Sr. became a towering figure in American business as he shaped the Computing-Tabulating-Recording Company, a struggling, 235-employee firm, into International Business Machines (IBM), a major American corporation that for many years was the world's dominant manufacturer of business machines and—from roughly the 1950s through the 1980s—computers. Although Watson's son Thomas J. Watson Jr. took the helm of IBM in 1956, it was Watson Sr. who built the organizational foundation that enabled IBM to emerge as a leader in the computer industry. Watson Sr. himself didn't believe that computers would ever become mass-market products; he is famous for stating, in around 1949, his belief that "There is a world market for maybe five computers," as quoted in the *Dictionary of Computer Quotations* (1997). However, he did oversee and initiate IBM's development of the Harvard Mark I calculating machine; the Selective Sequence Electronic Calculator, which was the world's first computer with memory; and the IBM 700 series, which generated commercial interest in computers and helped to establish IBM as a leading developer of technology. Though not a computer scientist, Watson had an ability to perceive what businesses wanted and how to sell it to them, and through that insight, he helped advance computer technology at its earliest stages of development.

Courtesy of the Computer Museum of America
Thomas J. Watson Sr.

Under Watson's firm direction, IBM was said to have been a striking example of "one-man rule in business," according to the *Saturday Evening Post* (May 24, 1941). According to a source quoted in a profile of Watson in *Current Biography 1940*, Watson's "personality and force have saturated IBM until now the personality of the man and the personality of the corporation are so closely identified as to be practically one and the same." The personality that Watson shaped for his company was one of the most respected and envied corporate cultures anywhere, fostering employee loyalty and "esprit de corps," as Donald Spencer put it in *Great Men and Women of Computing* (1999). Under Watson, IBM helped set a new standard for the model American corporation, and this is one of the contributions for which he is best remembered.

A gifted manager and salesman, Watson motivated his highly trained staff with pep talks and slogans such as "THINK," a motto that at one point could be found mounted on a wall in nearly every room of every IBM building. He stressed the importance of preparation in order for a sales staff to achieve maximum effectiveness and established an IBM training school for both mechanics and salesmen at the company's Endicott facilities, where the latter learned how to install, operate, and repair the IBM products as a necessary step in learning how to sell them. Watson worked out the details of the three basic steps in the selling technique taught at Endicott—the approach, the demonstration, and the closing. During his more than 40-year tenure as IBM chief, Watson continually emphasized that the keynote of the IBM salesman's argument was that the company sold not machines, but service. He made a practice of visiting Endicott's training school frequently, addressing the "graduating classes" of the sales school.

In addition to receiving excellent training, IBM employees were compensated very well in return for their service. Laurence Bell, in an article in a 1948 issue of *Forbes*, declared that Watson had created "the nearest to ideal working conditions in the company." He granted his employees competitive salaries and excellent employee welfare benefits, including health insurance that paid full salary for a maximum of six months, life insurance, and retirement pay, the latter three of which were all unusual at the time Watson instated the policies. The company even maintained a country club for all employees at their Endicott, New York, center of operations. Watson also initiated IBM's exclusive 100 Percent Club, for sales representatives who consistently achieved their full quotas.

On February 17, 1874 Thomas John Watson was born in rural Campbell, New York, located southwest of the Finger Lakes, the son of Thomas and Jane (White) Watson. The elder Thomas Watson, a lumber dealer and strict Methodist, urged his son to study law after the latter's graduation from the Addison Academy, in New York. Young Watson, however, eager to begin "paying his own way," took a year-long course at the Elmira School of Commerce, in the nearby town of Elmira. He then found a job in the neighboring community of Painted Post, at a store that sold pianos, sewing machines, and organs, and he replaced its haphazard bookkeeping methods with the ledger system.

At the age of 19, Watson entered the business machine field as a salesman for the National Cash Register Company (NCR). One anecdote of Watson's early days there, as related in the *Saturday Evening Post* (May 24, 1941), tells how, after being discouraged by his initial lack of success in selling, Watson was "fortified with certain tried and true homilies" by his manager. To this incident is attributed the future IBM chief's faith in maxims as a means of stimulating employees. Watson would later install on IBM's factory and office walls many framed recommendations such as "Aim High," "Sell and Serve," and, most famously, "THINK." Within a few years Watson progressed to be sales manager of the Rochester branch of NCR, then special representative, and eventually general sales manager. His contact with John Henry Patterson, the company's president, impressed upon him the philosophy of the "company spirit," of which Patterson has been called the "original apostle." Wat-

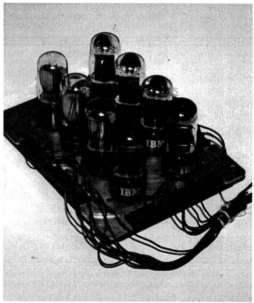

Courtesy of the Computer Museum of America
Early IBM vacuum tubes

son's employment at NCR ended in 1913 due to a disagreement with Patterson over an antitrust law issue.

Upon leaving NCR the 39-year-old Watson became president of the Computing-Tabulating-Recording Company. It had been formed in 1911 as a holding company controlling four business-machines manufacturers: the Bundy Manufacturing Company and the International Time Recording Company (both makers of time clocks), the Computing Scale Company of America, and the Tabulating Machine Company, the last of which had been founded in 1896 by Herman Hollerith, a pioneer in punched-card tabulating machines. One of Watson's first steps as president was to obtain loans large enough to finance expansion. The increase in the company's gross sales from two million in 1914 to more than 33.25 million by 1949 was largely attributed to the president's "ingenuity in creating new markets, perfecting of educational-sales technique, and stubborn strength for hard work," as quoted from the *Saturday Evening Post*. The personnel in the same period increased from 235 to 12,000. In 1924 Watson became president and CEO and changed the company's name to the International Business Machines Corporation, better known as IBM.

That same year IBM introduced the Carroll Press, which, according to Donald D. Spencer in his book *The Timetable of Computers* (1997), was "a printing cylinder that [was] used to manufacture punched cards commercially at high speed." Punched cards were used to feed instructions to the tabulating machines, like those sold by IBM, that were being used increasingly by businesses to perform accounting. As the market for punched cards and their accompanying equipment grew, the Carroll Press enabled IBM to meet the demand. A year later the company began selling punch card equipment to Japan. Also in 1925, IBM began manufacturing its 080 card sorter, which had the ability to sort and process more than 400 punched cards a minute.

In 1933 Watson expanded the company by purchasing Electromatic Typewriters Inc., and IBM soon became the industry's leading manufacturer of such machines. With a product line now including the electric typewriter, the key punch, the card sorter, and a variety of other accounting machines— devices for which it held approximately 1,400 patents as of 1941— IBM assumed a near monopoly in their field. The company's foreign sales increased 340 percent between 1938 and 1948, largely due to Watson's energetic pursuit of international trade, and by 1950 it had added to its roster of machines an electric Chinese language typewriter, which could type 5400 characters either vertically or horizontally. Around this time the company also produced a manual calculator that could perform higher mathematical computations.

During this period, Watson began traveling the globe to build trade relations between IBM and other countries. In 1937, for instance, he took a five-month tour of Europe during which he was received by a number of the heads of state, including King Leopold of Belgium, Benito Mussolini of Italy, and Adolf Hitler of Germany. He also spoke with world financial leaders, and was decorated in Sweden, Yugoslavia, Italy, and France for his efforts to promote trade. On that same trip, Watson was presented with the Merit Cross of the German Eagle by Hitler, who assured him that there would be no war in Europe. Returning from that trip, Watson declared that "it is important to think in terms of moving goods, not armies, across borders," as noted in *Current Biography 1940*. Throughout his tenure at IBM, Watson was a strong proponent of international commerce as a key to world peace; "World Peace through World Trade" was an IBM slogan coined by Watson. Some months after war

broke out in Europe in September 1939, he sent his medal back to Hitler, "because the present policies of [the German] government are contrary to the causes for which I have been working and for which I received the decoration," as Watson was quoted in *Current Biography 1940*. In response, Hitler forbid Watson from ever setting foot in Germany. After the war, while visiting the border city of Basel, Switzerland, Watson walked across the bridge to Germany and back.

When the United States entered World War II in December 1941, Watson put all IBM facilities at the disposal of the American government. Throughout the war, more than 5,000 IBM accounting machines were used in Washington, D.C., to keep track of men and materials moving across the various theaters of conflict, and additional machines were sent overseas as part of mobile units. Like most American companies during World War II, IBM used their assembly lines to manufacture military equipment needed for the war, including Browning automatic rifles, .30-caliber carbines, bombsights, naval and aircraft fire control instruments, and aircraft supercharger impellers. At the same time Watson's company continued to produce new products, including the IBM 040 unit, which was the first machine that could convert telegraph paper tape directly into punched cards.

Perhaps the most significant event of the war years for IBM began in 1939, when the company agreed to build the Mark I, a calculating machine designed by Howard Aiken, for Harvard University, in Cambridge, Massachusetts. Known officially inside IBM as the Automatic Sequence Controlled Calculator (ASCC), the machine was to be the realization of 19th-century British inventor Charles Babbage's never-completed Difference Engine, with 20th-century modifications provided by Aiken, some of which were based on Herman Hollerith's punched card machinery. The Mark I would be an improvement over its predecessors in that it would be fully automatic, would be able to handle both positive and negative numbers, would use "transcendental functions," such as those in trigonometry and probability, and would be able to compute lines instead of columns. This last capability would facilitate the solution of differential equations, in which the computation of a value often depends on values obtained in the preceding steps.

Though Aiken had developed the idea for the Mark I, it was up to three IBM engineers, Clair D. Lake, Francis E. (Frank) Hamilton, and Benjamin Durfee, to build an operational machine. Problems immediately arose between the theoretically minded Aiken and the more practical IBM engineers. According to the *International Biographical Dictionary of Computer Pioneers* (1995), "Aiken often tended to think of this IBM trio as mere mechanics, supergadgeteers, clever in their work but in no possible sense his peers. They, in turn, considered 'their machine' to be their invention, admitting only that Aiken had supplied the initial broad outlines and the occasion for the project. Naturally, these men (and everyone else at IBM) would resent any later move by Aiken to present himself as principal inventor, on a different and more fundamental level of creativity than Lake, Hamilton, and Durfee."

In January 1943 the Mark I was completed and ran a test problem at IBM's North Street Laboratory, in Endicott, New York, where the company's main factory and training facilities were also located. After a demonstration for Harvard faculty members in December, the machine was disassembled and shipped to the university for unveiling in August 1944. The Harvard News Office, in association with Aiken, released a statement to the press identifying Aiken as the sole inventor and with no mention that IBM had constructed the machine. After reading the news release, Watson, who was known throughout his life for his hot temper, was so furious that he initially planned to skip the dedication ceremonies altogether. Aiken and James Bryant Conant, Harvard's president, succeeded in pacifying Watson, and he did attend the ceremonies, which took place the following day. However, he reportedly held a lifelong grudge against Aiken due to the news release, which Watson perceived as a snubbing of IBM, and of Lake, Hamilton, and Durfee's essential contributions to the project. Though today the Mark I is most closely associated with Aiken, it is doubtful whether the machine would have proved successful without the participation of IBM and its engineers.

The Mark I is memorable for several reasons: first, it could run 24 hours a day, seven days a week, and produce highly reliable results, as opposed to comparable machines of the day, which required "downtime"; second, it continued to serve the Harvard research community until it was retired in 1958; and finally, it proved that it was possible to build complex calculating machines—i.e. computers—that would work dependably, and Watson sought to capitalize on that knowledge.

In 1945 Watson ordered IBM engineers in Endicott to develop a successor to the Mark I, and in 1947 the company unveiled the Scientific Sequence Electronic Calculator (SSEC). Watson had the machine installed in the lobby of IBM's New York City offices, where scientists, as well as the general public, could use it free of charge. The SSEC consisted of more than 21,000 electromechanical relays and 12,000 vacuum tubes and was the first stored-program computer, meaning that it was the first machine with a built-in memory that was able to store basic programming instructions. (Before the SSEC, operators of such calculating machines had to program a computer's every function. Once a function was completed, the machine had to be reset for the next calculation.) Billed as the world's fastest calculator, the SSEC was far more powerful than anything built previously, marking significant improvements over the Mark I, and it provided the basis for future IBM computers. Despite the machine's success, the SSEC became

the target of cartoonists and filmmakers, who mocked the enormous machine with its flashing lights and buttons as ridiculous.

In 1948 IBM developed the first "replaceable unit" in the history of the computer industry, consisting of an assemblage of electronic parts in the new IBM 604 multiplying punch machine. Before the creation of such a unit, an entire computer had to be disassembled for servicing or, in the case of a more serious malfunction, scrapped and replaced. With the advent of the replaceable unit, engineers could simply take out the faulty unit and put in a new one. The IBM 604 was also the first multiplying punch machine to incorporate vacuum tube technology. In September 1949 a single wholly owned subsidiary company was formed of IBM international branches—IBM World Trade Corporation—and Watson was named chairman of its board. At the same time he became chairman of the board of directors of the parent company.

In 1950, at the beginning of the Korean War, Watson announced that IBM would build a "defense calculator" to aid in the war effort. That machine, which was later designated the 701 computer, was one-quarter the size of the SSEC and 25 times faster, with the ability to perform 21,000 calculations in a second. The 701 proved to be a huge success and was followed by the IBM 650 and the IBM 704, in 1954; the IBM 702, in 1955; and the IBM 705, in 1956. Thanks largely to this series of machines, as the decade progressed, IBM emerged as the world leader in the computer industry.

Watson, however, while aware of the computer's importance to the scientific community, did not believe that computers would prove to be of much use to average people and initially did not want to push IBM into the computer industry. It was at the insistence of his son, Thomas J. Watson, Jr., that the company continued to expand its efforts to develop and market computers. In 1946 after serving as a pilot in World War II, the younger Watson, who had previously held a sales position with his father's company, rejoined IBM determined to prove himself his father's equal. In 1952 Watson Sr. turned over the IBM presidency to his son while keeping the position of chairman and chief executive. They worked together for 10 years, with the elder Watson instilling his business acumen in the younger while vocally protesting many of the decisions his son was making. Computers were one of their most hotly contested issues. Watson Jr. believed that IBM was being directly threatened when businesses began buying computers like the Univac, invented by John Presper Eckert and John Mauchly and manufactured by Remington Rand, which had bought out the company started by the two inventors. In response to such competition, Watson Jr. strove to convince his father to commit more of IBM's resources to developing new computer technology. By the time the father stepped down as CEO of the company on May 8, 1956, Watson Jr. was overseeing most of the decisions regarding IBM's computers, including the

700 series. On June 19, about six weeks after retiring, Thomas J. Watson died of a heart attack in New York City at the age of 82. At the time of his death, IBM had 60,000 employees, 200 U.S. offices, and factories throughout the world.

Although Watson Sr. was called "Salesman Number 1," according to a source quoted in *Current Biography 1940*, when he began to speak he was "the kind of slightly bashful, dignified gentleman who would be the last person on earth to try and sell you anything." Apparently this was part of the key to his success; the writer for *Current Biography 1940* went on to say that "What happens is that those who talk to him forget their sales resistance and only when they leave discover the size of the order they have given." Another source quoted in that volume described Watson's style of dress, noting his "relentless conservatism—a dark suit of expensive worsted relieved by a timid stripe, a decorous tie of moiré knotted perfectly in a dazzling collar." Dress code was one of the many ways in which Watson's taste pervaded IBM's corporate culture, and his employees made a strong impression with their grooming and attire. Through the end of the century, the company's de facto dress code remained a conservative dark suit and white shirt. During Watson's tenure, IBM employees wore suits even on service calls, "to the amazement of customers," according to Donald Spencer's *Great Men and Women of Computing.*

The Captain Robert Dollar Memorial Award for 1940 was presented to Watson for his contribution to the advancement of American foreign trade, and that year he was cited during Court of Peace ceremonies at the New York World's Fair "for his important contributions to the laying of a solid foundation" for future world peace. For meritorious service during World War II the IBM chairman was given the United States Medal of Merit. Watson was a member of the American Friendship Committee, the Foreign Policy Association, Council on Foreign Relations, and a director of the American Association of the United Nations. In 1950 he was given the American Arbitration Association award. In addition to his work at IBM, he served on the boards of directors of a number of banks and insurance and real estate companies.

Among Watson's numerous other pursuits was his patronage of art. A longtime collector, he was especially supportive of American artists. The industrialist's interests also extended to the medical field, in which he encouraged the development of the eye bank and research in arthritis; to religious education, in Sunday school and Bible class movements, Protestant welfare measures, the Salvation Army, and Christian-Jewish cooperation; to education, in the United Negro College fund, support of the Merchant Marine Library Association, aid in financing the development of the Massachusetts Institute of Technology, and serving as trustee of a number of universities and colleges; and to young people's groups, such as the YMCA, YWCA, and the Boy and Girl Scouts.

Thomas J. Watson married Jeannette M. Kittredge on April 17, 1913. They had four children: Thomas John, Arthur Kittredge, Jane, and Helen Mary.—C. M.

Suggested Reading: *Christian Science Monitor* p15 May 24, 1940; *Forbes* p18 May 15, 1948; *Fortune* p36 Jan. 1940, p108+ Nov. 22, 1999; *Newsweek* p5 Nov. 22, 1937, p41 June 17, 1940; *Saturday Evening Post* p10 May 24, 1941, p22 May 31, 1941; *Time* p73 Apr. 20, 1936, p57 June 17, 1940; *Business Executives of America*, 1950

Courtesy of Gerald M. Weinberg

Weinberg, Gerald M.

Oct. 27, 1933– Computer scientist; author

Gerald M. Weinberg has made an indelible mark on the computer industry through his extensive collection of books and essays, most notably his 1971 classic *The Psychology of Computer Programming*, which is widely recognized as one of the most influential books about computer programming ever written. In this work Weinberg proposed the innovative idea that software engineering can actually be studied as an extension of human behavior. The book has remained almost continually in print for more than three decades; the Silver Anniversary Edition was released in 1998. According to J. J. Herschfelder, writing for *Computing Reviews*, as quoted on Weinberg's Web site, "*The Psychology of Computer Programming . . .* was the first major book to address programming as an individual and team effort, and became a classic in the field. . . . Despite, or perhaps because of, the perspective of 1971, this book remains a must-read for all software development managers." Throughout his technical career as a software developer and researcher, Weinberg, who is called Jerry by his friends and admirers, has authored and co-authored more than 30 books and several hundred articles on such topics as programming, computer systems, consulting, technical leadership, and management. He is also a dynamic lecturer and teacher, and he has operated the consulting/training firm Weinberg & Weinberg since 1980. Garry Ray, writing for *PC Week* (October 3, 1988), described Weinberg as a "stark, raving, dyed-in-the-wool humanist. He's a 'systems thinker' who considers human systems equally important to computer systems." Weinberg was inducted into the Computer Hall of Fame in 1997.

Gerald Marvin Weinberg was born in Chicago, Illinois, on October 27, 1933. After reading about computers at age 11, he determined that he wanted to study math and physics because, as he noted on his Web site, "my guidance counselor told me that computers 'had something to do with electronics.'" Weinberg attended the University of Nebraska and graduated in 1955 with a B.S. in physics and math with highest distinction. The following year he received a master's degree in physics from the University of California, Berkeley. From 1956 to 1958 he worked at the IBM Corporation. He then took a position as manager of supervisory programming for Project Mercury, the first U.S. program of manned space flights. He returned to IBM, however, in 1960, and he remained there in various capacities until 1969. During that time Weinberg studied for his Ph.D. in communication science at the University of Michigan. He earned his doctoral degree in 1965, with a thesis entitled *Experiments in Problem Solving*.

In 1969 Weinberg began teaching at the School of Advanced Technology at the State University of New York at Binghamton, where he stayed until 1975. From 1972 to 1980 he also worked as a chief scientist at Ethnotech, a small technical company based in Binghamton. Weinberg began publishing several technical books, including *Computer Programming Fundamentals* (1961) with H. D. Leeds, *PL/I Programming Primer* (1966), *Computer Programming Fundamentals—Based on the IBM System 360* (1970) with Leeds, and *PL/I Programming—A Manual of Style* (1970); nevertheless, it remained a struggle for him to obtain a publisher for *The Psychology of Computer Programming*, which he had completed on an eight-week vacation in Italy in 1969, largely because the book explored computer programming from such a vastly new perspective. It was ultimately published by Van Nostrand Reinhold.

In the book Weinberg examines programming from four sides: programming as human performance, programming as a social activity, programming as an individual activity, and programming tools. He theorizes that programming should be an "egoless" activity, which he later described in an interview for the *Dorset House Quarterly* (on-line,

1998) as "the practice of turning the developer's attention away from ego-defense and toward the production of a quality product, whatever that takes." He continued, "One of the things it takes is an acceptance that none of us is perfect, and that pretending to be perfect just conceals errors until they hurt the most." Weinberg also emphasizes teamwork and quality management as vital to programming. He points out that when an entire team—including the program's own author—checks a software program for defects, rather than the author simply trying to defend his work as perfect, everyone ends up learning something. In a review of the silver anniversary edition, Michael Schrage wrote for *Computerworld* (November 23, 1998), as quoted on Weinberg's Web site, "Weinberg clearly believed in managing teams more than managing technology. Even more, he believed in managing dysfunctional teams. He understood that managing people's weaknesses and flaws is as important as managing their strengths."

In the 1990s Van Nostrand sold the rights to *The Psychology of Computer Programming*, along with all of its other computer volumes, to another publisher, who let the book go out of stock for months. After a lengthy battle to reacquire the rights to his work, Weinberg published the Silver Anniversary Edition in 1998 with his new publisher, Dorset House Publishing. As he noted in his preface to this edition, he wanted to release a new edition for several reasons: "1. to make the original book available to a new generation of software people 2. to offer a historical perspective that is usually lacking in our young field [and] 3. to take advantage of a once-in-a-lifetime opportunity—the chance to comment on an industry's development and to revisit what I thought might have been." One effort that Weinberg did not undertake in the anniversary edition was to rewrite his earlier material; instead, he added a fresh perspective with the inclusion of new commentaries in each chapter. Despite some outdated technological information, he left the original text unchanged. As Sue Petersen noted for *Visual Developer* magazine (March–April 1999), as quoted on Weinberg's Web site, "*Psychology* is valuable as history in a field that is all too ready to repeat the errors of its past. Read *Psychology* as a picture of where we've been, where we are now, and where we need to go next. Read it as an index to the thinking of one of the most influential figures in our field."

Throughout the 1970s Weinberg continued publishing influential books on technology and programming, including *Are Your Lights On? How to Figure Out What the Problem Really Is* (1972) with Donald C. Gause (rereleased in 1982 and 1990), *Introduction to General Systems Thinking* (1975; Silver Anniversary Edition, 2001), *Humanized Input* (1976) with Daniel Freedman, and *Handbook of Walkthroughs, Inspections, and Technical Reviews: Evaluation Programs, Projects and Products* (1977), which has since been through four separate editions, the last published in 1990. In 1980 he and his wife, Daniela, launched their own Lincoln, Nebraska–based training and consulting firm, Weinberg & Weinberg. Weinberg released several notable books over the next decade, including *Understanding the Professional Programmer* (1982), *The Secrets of Consulting* (1985)—which became a best-seller, popularizing Weinberg's theory that all problems, at the root, are "people-problems." His other books include *Becoming a Technical Leader: An Organic Problem-Solving Approach* (1986), *General Principles of Systems Design* (1988) with Daniela Weinberg, *Rethinking Systems Analysis & Design* (1988), and *Exploring Requirements: Quality Before Design* (1989). In the 1990s he published the four-volume series *Quality Software Management*, which consisted of *Systems Thinking* (1992), *First-Order Measurement* (1993), *Congruent Action* (1994), and *Anticipating Change* (1997).

As Weinberg built his reputation as one of the most respected writers critiquing the computer industry, he also became known for his leadership workshops, such as System Effectiveness Management, Problem Solving Leadership, the Congruent Leadership Change-Shop, and Software Engineering Management Development Group. From 1984 to 1985 he served on the advisory board for the Western Institute of Software Engineering, and from 1982 to 1987 he was the president of the Warnier Prize Foundation. Weinberg has been the keynote speaker at numerous prestigious conferences, and he has been an adjunct professor of computer science at the University of Nebraska since 1982.

In 2000 Weinberg coedited a collection of essays, *Amplifying Your Effectiveness*, with James Bach and Naomi Karten. He then launched the annual AYE (Amplifying Your Effectiveness) Conference, designed to help individuals who work in arenas where problem solving is a key skill. Weinberg has also established a subscription-only Internet forum called Software as a Human Activity Practiced Effectively, or SHAPE, through which members can discuss a number of technical and professional issues. With James Bullock and Marie Benesh, Weinberg edited *Roundtable on Project Management: A SHAPE Forum Dialogue* (2001) and *Roundtable on Technical Leadership: A SHAPE Forum Dialogue* (2002). His most recent book, *More Secrets of Consulting: The Consultant's Tool Kit* (2002), is the much-awaited sequel to his 1985 best-selling classic. Throughout his lengthy career, Weinberg has also published hundreds of articles in professional journals.

Gerald Weinberg resides in Lincoln, Nebraska, with his wife and partner, Daniela Weinberg. He has four adult children from a previous marriage. In 2000 he received the Stevens Award for outstanding contributions to the literature and practice of software-development methods. Of his contribution to the computing industry, Weinberg once said, as quoted on the Dorset House Publishing Web site: "I think that my special skills are empathy and the ability to see the big picture in complex situations. I want to further develop my understanding of human beings when they are not acting up to their full potential. My special vision is to bring computing technology to better serve the world, especially by working with the leaders in this field. I like to think of my profession as restoring human works of art."—K. D.

Suggested Reading: *Computerworld* p25 Sep. 24, 1984; Dorset House Publishing Web site; *PC Week* p58 Oct. 3, 1988

Weizenbaum, Joseph

Jan. 8, 1923– Artificial-intelligence pioneer; creator of ELIZA

Joseph Weizenbaum is widely credited with making an important contribution to the development of artificial intelligence (AI), a branch of computer science that seeks to create machines that can simulate human intelligence. In 1965 Weizenbaum, who taught computer science at the Massachusetts Institute of Technology (MIT), in Cambridge, completed work on ELIZA, a computer program that allowed people to converse with it. ELIZA simulated a psychotherapist interviewing a patient. People used a computer keyboard to submit a question or a statement, and ELIZA then provided a response. ELIZA had no conceptual understanding, but "talked" by incorporating a word or fragment from the user's input in formulating a reply. The continued interaction between ELIZA and the user resulted in a simple, but realistic conversation between a computer and a human being. ELIZA impressed many people and helped illustrate the potential of computers to perform complicated tasks normally associated with human beings. Weizenbaum, however, was stunned by how many people quickly became obsessed with ELIZA, wrongly thinking that the program actually understood them.

Troubled by society's growing dependence on computers and the involvement of many scientists and computer experts in the weapons industry, Weizenbaum came to fear that computers could enslave—and possibly destroy—humanity. Weizenbaum's best-selling book, *Computer Power and Human Reason: From Judgment to Calculation* (1976), attracted considerable attention because it strongly criticized computer scientists and AI experts for making extravagant claims about the potential of computers and ignoring ethical concerns about their work.

The son of Jewish parents, Joseph Weizenbaum was born on January 8, 1923 in Berlin, Germany. His father, Jechiel, worked as a furrier. Weizenbaum was affected by the sight of crippled veterans from World War I. "In Berlin, one could see the cripples, who survived the war, terribly mutilated," he told Benjamin Weinthal for the German-Jewish newspaper *Aufbau* (January 9, 2003, online). "It shocked me." In January 1933 the Nazi Party, led by Adolf Hitler, took power in Germany and began persecuting the Jewish population. After the 1935 enactment of the Nuremberg Laws, which stripped German Jews of their citizenship and civil rights, Weizenbaum was expelled from his school, the Luisenstädtische Real-Gymnasium. He then enrolled in the J"udische Knabenschule, a Jewish school for boys. "Very rarely did a tiny group of the Hitler Youth bother me," he recalled to Weinthal. "The fact that I was kicked out of the Gymnasium was not a tragedy." At his new school Weizenbaum encountered East European Jews, known as the *Ostjuden*, many of whom lived in poverty. He told Weinthal, "I think it stamped me for the rest of my life. For the first time I really saw poverty first hand, and I do not know if hate is the right word, but certainly the distance, the rejection [by others] of these people." Weizenbaum added that his encounter with the *Ostjuden* "changed me most particularly . . . in the direction of recognizing the underdog and preferring them to the overdog."

In 1936 Weizenbaum and his family fled Nazi Germany and immigrated to the United States. The family settled in Detroit, Michigan, near an aunt who had obtained visas for them. After graduating from high school Weizenbaum enrolled at Wayne University (later Wayne State University), in Detroit. He majored in mathematics. After completing one year, he was drafted by the army for service in World War II. "One of the things the Army did was give us an intelligence test," Weizenbaum told Weinthal. "I was one of the few who could add fractions and that put me in the genius class. The man told me I could choose whatever I liked. I chose cryptography because that is mathematical. He then said, 'That is the one thing you cannot chose, because you are an enemy alien.' So I chose meterology." After the war, Weizenbaum learned that many of his relatives who had stayed behind in Germany were killed by the Nazis. Weizenbaum's family responded to the Holocaust by turning against their German heritage. "We did not continue to talk or read in German," he told Weinthal. "My family did things like not playing German music. Wagner was out." Weizenbaum, however, eventually re-embraced his German heritage, thinking it was a positive influence in his life.

After leaving the army, Weizenbaum resumed his education at Wayne University, graduating in 1948 with a B.S. He continued his education there and in 1950 received a master's degree. Weizenbaum then went to work as a computer technician at a naval base that developed cruise missiles. He told Weinthal that the "Cold War was a mistake," and that he was deceived by propaganda of the U.S. government, which alleged that the Soviet Union had more missiles than the United States.

In 1955 Weizenbaum was hired by the General Electric (GE) Corporation's Computer Development Laboratory. There he participated in the development of the Electronic Recording Machine and Accounting (ERMA) system, which computerized such tasks as check processing, deposit accounting, and bookkeeping for the Bank of America, which was the largest banking firm in the United States at the time. "It was a very hard job," Weizenbaum told Diana ben-Aaron for an MIT student newspaper, the *Tech* (April 9, 1985, on-line), "to design a machine that would handle paper checks of various sizes, some of which might have been crumpled in a person's pockets and so on, to handle those the way punch cards are handled in a punch card machine and so on. There were many very hard technical problems. It was . . . a lot of fun attacking those hard problems, and it never occurred to me at the time that I was cooperating in a technological venture which had certain social side effects which I might come to regret [such as the centralization of the banking industry]." The success of ERMA eventually led to the computerization of the entire banking industry and opened the door for other industries to adopt computers.

In 1963 Weizenbaum accepted an invitation to join the faculty at MIT. "I was like a little boy interested in electrical trains and things like that," Weizenbaum explained to Weinthal. "And somebody asked me to come to a place where there are hundreds of electrical trains and if you need some more, they will be there. It is a paradise of technology. Who would say no to that?"

One of Weizenbaum's first accomplishments was the creation of SLIP, a list-processing computer language. As a member of the computer-science faculty, Weizenbaum had a computer terminal installed in his home. He used the computer to create a simple program that answered questions such as "Is this April?" and "Is today Thursday?" According to Pamela McCorduck's book *Machines Who Think* (1979), the success of the program led Weizenbaum to ask if he could create a more complex question and answer program.

Weizenbaum spent 1964 to 1965 developing a natural-language analysis program that could simulate a conversation between a person and a computer. He named the program, ELIZA, after the character of Eliza Doolittle in George Bernard Shaw's play, *Pygmalion* (1916), in which a linguistics professor teaches Eliza, a lowly flower girl with a thick Cockney accent, how to speak and act properly to pass as a member of London's aristocratic classes. Weizenbaum wrote ELIZA for the IBM 7094 computer, which operated on MIT's time-sharing system. A person used the computer terminal to ask or say something to ELIZA and then received a response. "The gross procedure of the program is quite simple; the text is read and inspected for the presence of a *keyword*," Weizenbaum explained in his paper on ELIZA for the *Communications of the ACM* (January 1966). "If such a word is found, the sentence is transformed according to a *rule* associated with the keyword, if not a content-free remark or, under certain conditions, an earlier transformation is retrieved. The text so computed or retrieved is then printed out." Weizenbaum stressed that ELIZA had no conceptual understanding of what the user entered into the program. ELIZA analyzed the user's input and incorporated a word or a fragment from it in formulating a response. "Because conversations must be about something, that is because they must take place within some context, the program was constructed in a two-tier arrangement, the first tier consisting of the language analyzer and the second of a script," Weizenbaum elaborated in *Computer Power and Human Reason: From Judgment to Calculation.* "The script is a set of rules rather like those that might be given to an actor who is to use them to improvise around a certain theme. Thus ELIZA could be given a script to enable it to maintain a conversation about cooking eggs or about managing a bank checking account, and so on. Each specific script thus enabled ELIZA to play a specific conversational role." Weizenbaum added that he "gave ELIZA a script designed to permit it to play (I should really say parody) the role of a Rogerian psychotherapist engaged in an initial interview with a patient. The Rogerian psychotherapist is relatively easy to imitate because much of his technique consists of drawing his patient out by reflecting the patient's statements back to him." (The interview technique was developed and popularized by the late psychologist Carl Rogers.)

In his paper, Weizenbaum recalled that a typical conservation between a person and ELIZA was as follows (with ELIZA's responses presented in capital letters):

Men are all alike.
IN WHAT WAY
They're always bugging us about something or other.
CAN YOU THINK OF A SPECIFIC EXAMPLE
Well, my boyfriend made me come here.
YOUR BOYFRIEND MADE YOU COME
He says I'm depressed much of the time.
I AM SORRY TO HEAR YOU ARE DEPRESSED
It's true. I am unhappy.
DO YOU THINK COMING HERE WILL HELP YOU NOT TO BE UNHAPPY
I need some help, that much seems certain.
WHAT WOULD IT MEAN TO YOU IF YOU GOT SOME HELP
Perhaps I could learn to get along with my mother.
TELL ME MORE ABOUT YOUR FAMILY

Weizenbaum became dismayed by the powerful effect that ELIZA had on many people who tried it, especially those with little or no knowledge of how computers worked. "People who knew very well that they were conversing with a machine soon forgot that fact," Weizenbaum wrote in *Computing Power and Human Reason.* "They would often demand to be permitted to converse with the system in private, and would, after conversing with it for a time, insist, in spite of my explanations, that the machine really understood them."

While at MIT, Weizenbaum was introduced to Kenneth Colby, a psychiatrist who was examining whether computers could help devise new therapies and provide insights into neurosis. Weizenbaum helped Colby develop DOCTOR, a program closely based on ELIZA. Colby and several other psychiatrists believed that DOCTOR could serve as the basis for computer programs that would provide automated therapy to patients in mental institutions and hospitals that had a shortage of human professionals.

Weizenbaum strongly disagreed with Colby's views, believing that computer therapy raised several ethical questions. "I had thought it essential, as a prerequisite to the very possibility that one person might help another learn to cope with his emotional problems, that the helper himself might participate in the other's experience of those problems and, in large part by way of his own empathic recognition of them, himself come to understand them," Weizenbaum observed in his book. "There are undoubtedly many techniques to facilitate the therapist's imaginative projection into the patient's inner life. But that it was possible for even one practicing psychiatrist to advocate that this crucial component of the therapeutic process be entirely supplanted by pure technique *that* I had not imagined! What must a psychiatrist who makes such a suggestion think he is doing while treating a patient, that he can view the simplest mechanical parody of a single interviewing technique as having captured anything of the essence of the human encounter?" He continued, "What can the psychiatrist's image of his patient be when he sees himself, as therapist, not as an engaged human being acting as a healer, but as an information processor following rules, etc.?" Colby subsequently hailed DOCTOR's potential as a therapeutic tool in several publications and addresses, but failed to give Weizenbaum the proper credit for his role in developing the program, further straining relations between the two men.

In *Computing Power and Human Reason,* Weizenbaum recalled that DOCTOR, because of its ease, was frequently used at MIT to demonstrate to visitors the information-processing power of computers. Copies of the program, based on Weizenbaum's public descriptions on it, soon appeared on computers at other institutions in the United States. Like ELIZA, DOCTOR had a hypnotic effect on many users. "I knew of course that people form all sorts of emotional bonds to machines, for example, to musical instruments, motorcycles, and cars," he wrote in his book. "And I knew from long experience that the strong emotional ties many programmers have to their computers are often formed after only short exposures to their machines. What I had not realized is that extremely short exposures to a relatively simple computer program could induce powerful delusional thinking in quite normal people. This insight led me to attach new importance to questions of the relationship between the individual and the computer, and hence to resolve to think about them."

ELIZA and DOCTOR were seen as major contributions to the field of artificial intelligence (AI). During the 1970s, however, Weizenbaum vocally distanced himself from his colleagues in AI, including John McCarthy, Herbert Simon, Allen Newell, Roger Schank, and Kenneth Colby. Weizenbaum believed that many of them were greatly exaggerating AI's potential and practical benefits. Weizenbaum also objected to AI on philosophical and ethical grounds. "The human is unique by virtue of the fact that he must necessarily confront problems that arise from his unique biological and emotional needs," he wrote in *Computer Power and Human Reason*. "The human individual is in constant state of becoming. The maintenance of that state, of his humanity, indeed, of his survival, depends crucially on his seeing himself, and on his being seen by other human beings, as a human being. No other organism, and certainly no computer, can be made to confront genuine human problems in human terms. And, since the domain of human intelligence is, except for a small set of formal problems, determined by man's humanity, every other intelligence, however great, must necessarily be alien to the human domain." Although Weizenbaum agreed that it was possible that computers could eventually be programmed with enough knowledge to make psychiatric judgments and even judicial decisions in courtrooms, he insisted that they should not be given such power. "They may even be able to arrive at 'correct' decisions in some cases—but always and necessarily on bases no human being should be willing to accept," Weizenbaum wrote in his book.

Computer Power and Human Reason: From Judgment to Calculation, which included several essays explaining for the lay reader how computers and programs actually worked and what they could and could not do, became a best-seller and received substantial attention in the mainstream media and in the AI community. "Weizenbaum has written a superb study of the place of the digital computer in . . . our society," Theodore Roszak wrote in his review for *The Nation* (May 1, 1976). "The book surveys the social vices of the computer establishment, its role in servicing the military-industrial complex, and its contribution to the technocratic ethos of contemporary capitalism." Roszak added that "Weizenbaum is commendably skeptical that human 'progress' is really dependent on having quite so much information technology around" and concluded that the book would be read "with a profound sense of moral pleasure." By contrast, John McCarthy faulted the book in a review that appeared, in 1976, in an internal newsletter published by the Artificial Intelligence Laboratory at Stanford University, in California. McCarthy described the book as incoherent, polemical, and excessively moralistic, asserting that Weizenbaum failed to articulate his positions clearly and frequently confused the reader by "making extreme statements which are later qualified by contradictory statements." According to

McCorduck, several AI experts believed Weizenbaum was attacking their work because he was no longer making any scientific contributions.

In addition to teaching, Joseph Weizenbaum has frequently spoken out on issues that concern him. A passionate anti-war activist and advocate for nuclear disarmament, he frequently accused scientists and computer experts, in both the West and in the Soviet bloc, of neglecting their moral responsibilities by helping the military develop technologically advanced weapons systems. "None of the weapons systems that threaten genocide and whose design, manufacture, and sale condemn countless people to poverty and starvation could be developed without the earnest, even enthusiastic, cooperation of computer scientists and technicians," Weizenbaum wrote in an article for *Technology Review* (January 1987). "Without our help, the arms race could not advance another step." Weizenbaum co-founded Computer Professionals Against the ABM, an advocacy group that opposed the deployment of the anti-ballistic missile (ABM), which was designed as a defense against incoming nuclear missiles. In 1981 Weizenbaum co-founded Computer Professionals for Social Responsibility (CPSR), a national advocacy organization that vocally opposed the arms race between the United States and the Soviet Union and warned of the dangers and limitations of using technology for military purposes. In 1988 the CPSR recognized Weizenbaum's achievements in science and social activism by presenting him with its Norbert Wiener Award for Professional and Social Responsibility.

During the 1980s Weizenbaum expressed reservations about introducing computers in schools. He argued that students should first learn how to read, write, and master language before being taught how to use computers. "As for the computer itself, I think it inhibits children's creativity," Weizenbaum told Franz-Olivier Giesbert for the French newspaper *Le Nouvel Observateur*, as republished in *Harper's* (March 1984). "In most cases, the computer programs kids and not the other way around. Once they have started a program, the computer may leave them a few degrees of freedom, to be sure, but on the whole it will tell them what to do and when to do it."

Weizenbaum has also been unimpressed by the World Wide Web. "The Internet is like one of those garbage dumps outside of Bombay," he observed to Katie Hafner for the *New York Times* (April 1, 1999). "There are people, most unfortunately, crawling all over it, and maybe they find a bit of aluminum, or perhaps something they call sell. But mainly it's garbage."

In 1988 Joseph Weizenbaum retired from MIT. In 1997 he returned to his native Germany, where he was invited to deliver lectures at several universities. Weizenbaum, who lives in Berlin, is married and the father of four children.—D. C.

Suggested Reading: *Aufbau* (on-line) Jan. 9, 2003; *Communications of the ACM* p36+ Jan. 1966; CPSR Web site; *Harper's* p22 Mar. 1984; John

McCarthy Home Page; New York Times G p7 Apr. 1, 1999; *Tech* p2 Apr. 9, 1985; *Technology Review* p22 Jan. 1987; McCorduck, Pamela. *Machines Who Think*, 1979

Wetzel, Don

1929– Inventor of the ATM

In 1968 Don Wetzel originated the idea for the automated teller machine, or ATM, and over the course of the next three years he helped make his idea a reality. This breakthrough invention marks a key moment in the development of the information age in that it is one of the earliest examples of computers having a direct impact on people's daily lives. In addition to his work on the ATM, Wetzel was an employee of IBM during the 1950s and '60s, a period during which the company shifted its focus to electronic computers.

Don Wetzel was born in 1929 in New Orleans, Louisiana, where he was raised and received his education. He enrolled at the University of Loyola in New Orleans in 1947 and pursued a bachelor's degree in foreign trade.

While attending college, Wetzel spent three years playing minor league baseball in the New York Giants farm system. He passionately wanted to become a professional ballplayer, but after three years playing shortstop, he came to the disappointing conclusion that he would probably never make it to the major leagues. Nevertheless, Wetzel learned several valuable lessons from his time in the minors, as he explained in a 1995 interview for the *National Museum of American History* (NMAH) (on-line): "I met a lot of people that I would never have met and was able to interact with them. So I learned about . . . people, and how they feel, and how they react under situations that sometimes are a little pressing and trying. The other thing I learned was how to live away from home."

Wetzel graduated from Loyola in 1951. The dean of the university's business school, whom Wetzel had gotten to know quite well, helped him obtain a job interview with IBM, and Wetzel was soon hired as a machine operator at IBM's Service Bureau Corporation in New Orleans, where he processed payroll forms, accounts receivable, sales analyses, and other such materials for businesses that did not own their own IBM machines. At the time, computers were not yet commonly used; the equipment Wetzel operated was strictly mechanical, relying on punched cards containing instructions and information that the machines were able to "read." After some time, Wetzel was promoted to a supervisory position.

After five years at the Service Bureau Corporation in New Orleans, IBM transferred Wetzel to the Service Bureau branch in Fort Worth, Texas, where he was made branch manager. "I was very pleased to be working for IBM," Wetzel said in his NMAH interview. "IBM was a company that treated its employees extremely well, paid us very well, expected good things from us. . . . They taught responsibility and rewarded you for what you did." Wetzel's duties in Fort Worth were similar to those he had performed in New Orleans, except that as manager he was also involved with sales, which proved to be a major development in Wetzel's career. He continued in this vein for IBM, transferring in 1957 to the Denver, Colorado, branch of the Service Bureau, where he also served as manager.

"The only problem with the Service Bureau," Wetzel recalled in his NMAH interview, "was that we worked long, long hours, many, many weekends, and we were on call any time there was a need for something. . . . I was really getting burned out." Wetzel asked for a different position in the company, and IBM decided to increase his involvement in sales. They sent him to San Antonio, Texas, where he worked as a systems engineer, serving in a "sales support" capacity. His responsibilities including inspecting hardware before it was shipped out to customers. Shortly after his arrival in San Antonio, IBM began getting involved in the manufacture and sale of computers, and Wetzel became one of their first programmers.

In 1958 Wetzel officially transferred to IBM's sales department in San Antonio, where he supplied computers to businesses, specializing in sales to financial institutions, such as savings and loan companies, credit unions and, most importantly, banks. Wetzel was charged with weaning banking institutions off the traditional methods of handling data manually and introducing them to the advantages of the emerging computer technology. At the time, most banks were extremely conservative when it came to managing their operations and thus were hesitant to purchase computing equipment. Also impeding Wetzel's efforts was the fact that bank accounts at that time were identified using the name of the account holder, rather than an account number, thus making them difficult for a computer to manage.

Wetzel moved up the ranks in sales, and in 1960 IBM made him a special representative. In this capacity he worked with IBM offices in Texas, Louisiana, and New Mexico, supervising sales of computer equipment to banks. During the three years Wetzel spent as special representative, computers became more common in the business world and, as they did, the banking industry began to recognize the potential of the new technology. The computers of this era were quite large, equipped with air-conditioning units and requiring false flooring to allow for wires to be run underneath the machines.

In 1963 Wetzel was made a special sales manager in charge of sales to financial, insurance, communications, utilities, and transportation companies. For five years, he based his operations in Houston, Texas, until, in 1968, IBM asked him to transfer his headquarters to Armonk, New York. When Wetzel balked at the idea of having to relocate once more, IBM instead offered to make him a salesman again. Wetzel, however, opted to end his employment with IBM and took a position as vice president of product planning for Docutel, a new company based in Dallas.

Not long after moving to Docutel, Wetzel stumbled upon the idea for which he is most remembered. While waiting in line at a bank, it suddenly occurred to him that it might be possible for a machine to do much of a bank teller's work. He reported his idea to his colleagues at Docutel, and Wetzel and his fellow vice presidents, along with the company president, began having weekly meetings to discuss the logistics of manufacturing such a machine and also conducted extensive market research. At that time Docutel was planning to place the machines only in banks.

Once they had determined that an automated teller machine, or ATM, was a financially feasible concept, Wetzel and his associates had to determine exactly what form the machine would take. At the time, almost all business computers were off-line, meaning that they were not connected to a host computer that coordinated their actions. Therefore, the ATM would have to be designed to be completely self-sufficient. Built-in security was an issue to be dealt with, because an off-line machine had no way of determining if the funds required to cover a specific withdrawal were actually in the customer's account.

Further, it was agreed upon that the "activating device" for the ATM would be a plastic card with a magnetic strip that would hold such data as the customer's account number and the bank's routing number. The idea was relatively new, as not even credit cards had magnetic strips at the time, and finding a company that could manufacture the cards proved to be a major obstacle. The project went into high gear after a nationwide Docutel survey revealed that bank customers, particularly younger ones, were generally receptive to the idea of an ATM. A card manufacturer was found, and by the start of 1969 Wetzel and his colleagues were given the official go-ahead to produce a prototype.

Convincing banks of the ATM's viability was another problem altogether. Contrary to Docutel's marketing survey, banking organizations seemed convinced that an automated machine would not appeal to their customers, who would prefer the personal service a teller provides. Banks were also afraid that the ATM, by reducing the human interaction involved in banking, would hurt their chances of cross-selling services to their customers. But as Wetzel put it in his NMAH interview, "The customers did not agree with the bankers. . . . The tellers never cross-sold to anybody. Their mentality was: 'You have a check, I'm going to give you some money, and I hope you go away. And that way, if you move fast, I'll get to the next person and everybody will be happy.'" Once Wetzel and company persuaded bankers that customers were first and foremost interested in speed and convenience, they were able to move forward with their project.

Docutel went to work developing the components of the ATM, such as a card reader, a cash dispensing unit, and a printer that would make dual copies of a transaction record, one each for the customer and bank office. Over the course of time, several glitches with these various devices were worked out, and a functional prototype was completed. Security was a major concern for bankers, as this would be the first time cash would be available to the customer with no bank employee present. To reassure their potential clients, Docutel housed the machine in a stainless steel casing that was five-eighths of an inch thick.

At first, the prototype was developed without the benefit of computer technology, using a completely hard-wired, or electronically based, structure. However, this proved insurmountably complicated. Fortunately for Wetzel and Docutel, the mini-computer was invented at around this time, and that technology was quickly incorporated into the ATM. Once the design was realized, it was Wetzel's job to pitch the machine to prospective buyers. Using the contacts he had established in the industry over the years, he set up meetings across the nation with bank executives, utilizing a cardboard replica of the prototype as a demonstration prop.

The first automated teller machine was installed at a Long Island branch of Chemical Bank in September 1969. The following year, Docutel filed for a patent on the machine, although, due to several legal complications, the official patent was not issued until 1973. As Wetzel gradually convinced bankers of the ATM's efficiency, many other banking institutions became Docutel customers. Wetzel stressed the importance of making bank patrons aware of the new service; as more and more customers began using the ATM, bank managers could view firsthand the machine's success. "And then the selling job became a lot easier," said Wetzel in his interview, "when you have one installed and a banker can talk to another banker, not to the salesman who's saying all these neat things." Over time, Docutel developed the ATM from a simple cash dispenser into a computerized machine that could perform all the basic functions of a teller. This revised version, often known as the "total teller," helped sell the remaining holdout banks on the ATM concept.

In 1970, with his brainchild finally hitting its stride, Wetzel suffered a tragic loss when his wife died of cancer. Wetzel remarried, to a widow, in 1972, and the new couple wound up with a total of 12 children between the two of them from their previous marriages. From that point on, the heavy traveling that had been such an integral part of Wetzel's job became increasingly difficult due to his family responsibilities. As a result, he resigned from Docutel in 1973 and started his own company, Financial Systems and Equipment. Feeling that he had had enough of computers during his years at IBM and Docutel, Wetzel decided that his company would sell noncomputerized bank equipment, such as vault doors and safe deposit boxes.

Five years after starting Financial Systems and Equipment, while still in charge of that company, Wetzel established his second business, Electronic Banking Systems. This brought him back into the ATM industry in the role of a consultant to banks that were adjusting to the new technology. Electronic Banking Systems was the first company to put ATMs in locations other than banks, beginning with supermarkets, and the company became so profitable by doing this that in 1984 it was bought by Docutel, Wetzel's former employer.

Having left Electronic Banking Systems, Wetzel's attentions focused chiefly on Autosig Systems, a third company he had started in 1979 that marketed signature verification systems to the financial community. He retired from active duty in 1989 but remained chairman of the board of that company as of his 1995 interview. "I think the ATM was the first instance where a person had the opportunity to interface with a piece of machinery," commented Wetzel in his interview, "and that allowed that person then to be comfortable with interfacing to other pieces that came out since then—like PCs, as an example." Thus Wetzel's ATM helped prepare the way for the computer revolution that was to take place in the decades to come. By the start of the 21st century, ATM machines have become ubiquitous, particularly in major American cities, where, for many people, they have virtually done away with the need for human bank tellers.—B. S.

Suggested Reading: *Money* p138+ Oct. 1992; Smithsonian Institute Web site

Hulton Archive by Getty Images

Whitehead, Alfred North

Feb. 15, 1861–Dec. 30, 1947 Mathematician; philosopher

In his obituary in the *New York Times* (December 31, 1947), the British mathematician and philosopher Alfred North Whitehead was called "a supreme adventurer in the realm of the mind" and "an Englishman who evolved from [a] mathematician into one of the world's most important philosophers and educators." Whitehead is perhaps best known for the historic three-volume work *Principia Mathematica* (1910–13), which he composed with his former student Bertrand Russell. In it Whitehead and Russell set forth evidence showing that mathematics could be deduced from formal logic. As he moved into studies of moral philosophy, Whitehead explored the foundations of natural science, producing three major works: *An Enquiry Concerning the Principles of Knowledge* (1919), *The Concept of Nature* (1920), and *The Principle of Relativity, with Applications to Physical Science* (1922). In the final phase of his career, he turned to metaphysics, a division of philosophy that contemplates the essential nature of reality and being; one of his most important works from this period is *Process and Reality* (1929). Although Whitehead's philosophical works are often praised for their brilliance, they are also known for their difficulty. (The philosopher often created entirely new vocabularies to express his ideas.) A professor throughout his career—at Trinity College of Cambridge University, in England; the University of London; and Harvard University, in Cambridge, Massachusetts—Whitehead remained an outspoken proponent for educational reform. He presented his views on the topic in the 1916 lecture "The Aims of Education: A Plan for Reform," in which he criticized Britain's system of educating only a select faction of the upper class. He encouraged making education more accessible to the wider population, including to artisans, people from all social classes, and women.

Alfred North Whitehead was born on February 15, 1861 in Ramsgate, the Isle of Thanet, in East Kent, England. He was the fourth and last child of Reverend Alfred Whitehead, a clergyman with the Church of England, and Maria Sarah Buckmaster. Because of his small size, Whitehead was thought to be of delicate health and was therefore schooled at home by his father until the age of 14. (Whitehead's father had been a schoolmaster in Ramsgate for many years before becoming ordained in 1860.) His lessons included both Latin and Greek, and he proved to be a quick learner. For most of his childhood, Whitehead lived with his family in the vicarage of St. Peter's-in-Thanet. He often accompanied his father on parochial visits to parishioners homes and was greatly influenced by the elder White-head's powerful sermons. Aside from his lessons, Whitehead spent much of his time outdoors, and throughout his early years he developed strong connections to his physical surroundings—much of which were steeped in history. At age 14 Whitehead was sent to Sherborne, a reputable private school in Somerset, where he continued his studies in Latin and Greek and also pursued courses in history and mathematics. At Sherborne, Whitehead distinguished himself as an exceptional scholar, as well as a well-rounded young man. In addition to being named head prefect (a student monitor responsible for discipline outside the classroom) in his final year, he was active in sports, particularly rugby.

By the time Whitehead enrolled at Trinity College (to which he was awarded a scholarship in October 1880), he had decided to devote his studies entirely to mathematics. Trinity was the largest of Cambridge University's 16 colleges and was widely considered the most prestigious. While the university had dozens of extracurricular societies, Whitehead made few commitments outside of his field, instead focusing rigorously on his mathematics coursework. He satiated his other interests, which included politics, religion, philosophy, and literature, by reading extensively and engaging in lengthy discussions with friends and young dons. He was elected to an elite discussion club known as the "Apostles." After three years of attending lectures, Whitehead performed well on the Mathematical Tripos, the demanding examinations that determined whether he would earn a mathematics degree. Soon after receiving his B.A., in 1884, he was elected a fellow of Trinity College and appointed assistant lecturer in mathematics. Whitehead was promoted to lecturer in math in 1888, before rising to senior lecturer in 1903. He earned his D.Sc. degree (the equivalent of a Ph.D.) in 1905.

On December 16, 1890, while still at Trinity College, Whitehead married Evelyn Willoughby Wade, a young Irish woman who had been educated in France and come to England at the age of 17. In the *Dictionary of American Biography*, Supplement 4: 1946–1950 (1974), Victor Lowe described Evelyn as "witty, with passionate likes and dislikes, a great sense of drama, and—what was entirely lacking in [Whitehead's] parents' household—a keen aesthetic sense." Whitehead fell intensely in love with Evelyn, who despite being what Lowe called "unacademic" remained his close companion throughout his life. The couple had three children: Thomas North, Eric, and Jessie Marie. "She always had the energy to rule the family, take youngsters with problems under her wing, make friends, be useful, and shield her husband from financial anxiety," Lowe said of Evelyn Whitehead. Throughout his life Whitehead attributed much of his happiness to his wife, who he said taught him that "beauty, moral and aesthetic, is the aim of existence," as quoted by Norman Pittenger in *Makers of Contemporary Theology*

(1969). Until shortly before he married Evelyn, Whitehead had considered joining the Roman Catholic Church. Though he was under the personal influence of Cardinal John Henry Newman, he ultimately decided against joining the church and sold all his theological books. Whitehead remained agnostic for most of his life, abandoning religion even more after the death of his second son, Eric, in World War I.

By 1898 Whitehead had published few papers in mathematics, yet in that year he issued his first book, *A Treatise on Universal Algebra*, in which he investigated systems of symbolic logic and Boolean algebra. The work was recognized as highly original and earned Whitehead election to the Royal Society in 1903. He was most interested in studying the newer branches of mathematics, which challenged notions of what math really was, particularly as a system of logical reasoning.

In July 1900 Whitehead invited his former student Bertrand Russell to attend the First International Congress of Philosophy, which was being held in Paris, France. (Whitehead had taught Russell at Trinity College in 1890 and immediately recognized the younger man's talents. The two eventually became friends.) At the congress Whitehead and Russell became interested in the work of the Italian mathematician Giuseppe Peano, who had recently invented a new set of symbols for use in symbolic logic. Russell expanded on many of Peano's methods in his important work *Principles of Mathematics* (1903), the first draft of which he composed toward the end of 1900. Whitehead readily agreed with the thesis of Russell's work—the idea that mathematics is a part of logic—and in early 1901 began collaborating on a second volume of Russell's *Principles*.

The founding father of modern logic is generally thought to be the German mathematician Gottlob Frege. With their knowledge of Frege's work, Whitehead and Russell set out to derive the foundations of mathematics. They intended to deduce mathematical principles from those of logic, using symbolic reasoning. As the project became more complicated, Whitehead and Russell agreed that their findings should be issued separately from Russell's earlier book. After nearly a decade of collaboration, the duo published their monumental, three-volume *Principia Mathamatica*. The book was extremely technical, and while it has not gained universal support, it is still regarded as a major landmark in the history of logic. Despite some early attempts by scholars to give Russell the majority of credit for the work, Russell always insisted that the project had been a true collaboration. It is generally thought that Russell handled matters of logical theory, while Whitehead led discussions on mathematics. Without Russell's assistance, Whitehead next undertook the writing of a fourth volume of *Principia Mathematica*— covering the theory of geometry—but he soon abandoned the effort as his academic interests expanded beyond pure mathematics.

In 1910 Whitehead resigned his lectureship at Trinity College and moved to London. At first he focused mainly on writing; his well-regarded book *An Introduction to Mathematics* was published in 1911. Soon he resumed teaching, at the University College of the University of London, where he began lecturing on applied mathematics and mechanics and later became a reader in geometry. In 1914 he became professor of applied mathematics at the Imperial College of Science and Technology, in Kensington, where he remained until 1924. During his years in London, Whitehead served on the governing bodies of several technical schools and was the only scientist appointed by the British prime minister to serve on a committee investigating the role of classics in education. He contributed to the University of London's administration, serving as a member of the senate, dean of the faculty of science, and chairman of the Academic Council. From 1919 to 1924 he was chairman of the group that governed the teacher's college, Goldsmith's College. These experiences helped Whitehead formulate his own ideas on the state of Britain's educational system. He presented his criticisms throughout several lectures, the most famous of which, "The Aims of Education: A Plea for Reform," he delivered to the Mathematical Association in 1916. In this address Whitehead lamented the tendency of teachers to impart "inert ideas," according to Lowe. He insisted, "Culture is activity of thought, and receptiveness to beauty and humane feeling. Scraps of information have nothing to do with it."

During these years Whitehead's interests began to shift from pure mathematics to the philosophy of natural science. While he never completed his exploration of geometric theory (which he considered to be a foundational theory of natural science), Whitehead returned to the topic for his next three major works, each of which dissected the roots of natural science: *An Enquiry Concerning the Principles of Natural Knowledge* (1919), *The Concept of Nature* (1920), and *The Principle of Relativity, with Applications to Physical Science* (1922).

In 1924 Whitehead accepted a five-year appointment to Harvard University to serve as a professor of philosophy. At 63, Whitehead was approaching the mandatory retirement age at the Imperial College, a fact that made the move to Harvard particularly opportune. In addition, he was excited by the prospect of teaching philosophy. This professional transition coincided with a shift in Whitehead's written work. While he had made a point of leaving metaphysical discussions out of his works on natural science, Whitehead now felt he could assume a metaphysical position to explore his beliefs on value and existence. Some of his earliest books on the topic—including *Science and the Modern World* (1925), *Religion in the Making* (1926), and *Symbolism: Its Meaning and Effect* (1927)— examine aspects of natural science in conjunction with moral and aesthetic values, religious feeling, and theology. As noted by the Harvard Faculty of Arts and Sciences as quoted on the Harvard Square Library Web site, "Whitehead would restore to us that world of our first intuitions of reality which had been lost sight of when the one world of the natural man was separated into the finite, sensible, and sinful world of sense-perception and the good, the beautiful and really true, which were sent off to live in Plato's Heaven."

Whitehead's most ambitious work from this period was *Process and Reality: An Essay in Cosmology* (1929), in which he set forth his overall structure of speculative philosophy, which he called cosmology. Because of its complexity and Whitehead's practice of inventing new terminology to articulate his principles, this work has been called one of the most difficult to read in the history of philosophy. As Lowe described, "[Whitehead] developed the thesis that an experience [of an event] is fundamentally a process of absorbing the past and making ourselves different by actualizing some value-potentialities and rejecting others." Whitehead also incorporated his concepts of theism and his original definition of God. *Process and Reality* is widely considered one of the most important works in the history of metaphysics. TXT=In the remainder of his books, Whitehead presented his views on metaphysics in more accessible terms. His *Adventures of Ideas* (1933) explores the humanistic and sociological aspects of his philosophy, focusing on the course of Western civilization. He defines what he considers the essential qualities of civilized life: art, beauty, truth, and peace, the last of which he understood in a religious context. The book is highly regarded for what Lowe called its "solid wisdom." Whitehead's additional works include *Nature and Life* (1934) and *Modes of Thought* (1938).

Although Whitehead was initially contracted to stay at Harvard for only five years, he remained at the university for 13, retiring in 1937. He remained professor emeritus of philosophy at Harvard until his death on December 30, 1947. Whitehead died at his home in Massachusetts, four days after suffering a paralytic stroke. (At his request, his wife destroyed all of his unpublished writings and correspondence upon his death.) Throughout his years at Harvard, Whitehead became somewhat of an academic celebrity, enjoying wide popularity among his students. He was known to entertain students at his home on Sunday nights, often leading well-attended discussions on a number of topics. As Pittenger described in 1969, "Those who studied under him tell of his charm of manner, his sly humour, his profound knowledge, his ability to illuminate difficult points with telling illustrations of a homely sort; but above all they speak of the fascination they felt as his lecturer or their seminar leader did his own thinking aloud in their presence and with their help." During his first 10 years in the United States, Whitehead gave numerous lectures around the country. After his retirement, he lived the remainder of his years in Cambridge, Massachusetts, rather than returning to England.

Although he always considered himself an Englishman, Whitehead had "[fallen] in love with America," as his son Thomas North told William Ernest Hocking for *Alfred North Whitehead: Essays on His Philosophy* (1963). Whitehead found Americans full of energy and open to new ideas. He was also pleased to see that many of the educational reforms for which he had been working in England were already being realized in the United States. His son recalled, "My father not only did not regret crossing the Atlantic. He thought it one of the best things he ever did; he genuinely loved this country and believed in it."

Throughout his accomplished career, Alfred North Whitehead received significant recognition for his work. In addition to earning six honorary doctorates, he was elected a fellow of the Royal Society (of the U.K. National Academy of Science) and held the society's Sylvester Medal. He also served as president of the Mathematical Association of Great Britain. In 1945 he received the Order of Merit from the British Crown for his contributions to mathematics, philosophy, and education.—K. D.

Suggested Reading: *American Scholar* p515+ Fall 1978; *Great Thinkers of the Western World* p441+ 1999; Kline, George L. ed. *Alfred North Whitehead: Essays on His Philosophy*, 1964; Lowe, Victor. *Alfred North Whitehead: The Man and His Work* vol. 1, 1861–1910, 1985

Wiener, Norbert

Nov. 26, 1894–Mar. 18, 1964 Originator of cybernetics

The brilliant mathematician Norbert Wiener helped to explain the meaning of computers by showing how they related to human beings. In his book *Cybernetics, or Control and Communication in the Animal and the Machine* (1948), he discussed the link between the functions of the human nervous system and the automatic functions of machinery, believing that one could apply statistical methods of control to both and achieve similar results. Since the 1940s, cybernetics has developed into an interdisciplinary field with implications for everything from neuropsychology, to biomechanical regulation, to computer-programming design. By better understanding the complex electrical systems that exist in both animals and machines, Wiener argued, people could build machines that would liberate them from drudgery and give them more time to devote to creativity. Though he claimed that there was no real distinction between organic and inorganic entities, Wiener did caution against human beings becoming too dependent on machines and spent the last decades of his life warning people about the implications of the coming age of automation.

Norbert Wiener was born to Leo and Bertha (Kahn) Wiener on November 26, 1894 in Columbia, Missouri. His father was a Russian Jewish immigrant who later became a professor of Slavic languages and literature at Harvard University. Leo Wiener was a forceful man who took charge of his son's early education and influenced his development well into his adulthood. Noted for his precocity and made the subject of several newspaper articles during his childhood, Norbert Wiener was a child prodigy: he began reading at the age of four and at seven was reading the psychiatric writings of Jean Charot and the works of Charles Darwin. The family moved to a farm in the town of Harvard when Norbert was an infant. At nine he began his first formal education at the Ayer Public High School in Massachusetts, from which he graduated two years later.

Wiener received his bachelor of arts degree from Tufts College in Medford, Massachusetts, in 1909, at the age of 14. A mathematics and classics major at Tufts, he subsequently told Harry M. Davis for the *New York Times Book Review*, as quoted in *Current Biography* (1950), "I got my classical education from my father, who was professor of Slavic languages at Harvard. My scientific education I got for myself. I had four years of Greek, seven years of Latin, four years of German, a year of French, some Spanish, and a little Chinese." Yet by the time he graduated from Tufts he was so fascinated with the biological sciences that he went to Harvard University to study zoology in 1909. He remained there for only one year because he found he had a great deal of trouble with laboratory work. On the advice of his father, he studied philosophy at Cornell University in Ithaca, New York, during the academic year 1910–11. Unhappy with his chosen subject at Cornell, he returned to Harvard for the 1911–13 terms and produced a dissertation that looked at the boundary between mathematics and philosophy. He received his master's degree from Harvard in 1912 and the following year received the Bowdoin Prize and his doctorate for his work in mathematical logic.

Under the terms of Harvard's Sheldon Traveling Fellowship, Wiener studied at Cambridge University in England from 1913 to 1915, where he became a student of the noted mathematician and philosopher Bertrand Russell and Godfrey H. Hardy, the English mathematical theorist. As Wiener's chief mentor at Cambridge, Russell asked his student to study more mathematics. (Wiener had already published his first paper in the journal *Messenger of Mathematics* in 1913 with great success.) In 1914 he studied at Göttingen University in Germany under David Hilbert, one of the most celebrated mathematicians of the time. From Hilbert he received similar advice—concentrate on mathematics. Wiener, however, did not take his mentors' advice and after studying at Columbia University in New York, in 1915, began a very shiftless period of his life.

Wiener attempted to enlist in the U.S. army during World War I but was rejected because of bad eyesight. (He was eventually able to work for the military as a civilian computational expert in 1918 at the Government Proving Ground in Aberdeen, Maryland, and later was made an army private.) Harvard retained Wiener as a docent lecturer in mathematics for the academic year 1915–16. He later joined the staff of the University of Maine as a math instructor for 1916–17 but was very unhappy there. He then tried his hand at writing. "I made my living for a year as a hack writer for the *Encyclopedia Americana*," Wiener said of his occupation in 1917 and 1918, as quoted in *Current Biography*, "and I worked on a newspaper." The latter reference is to the *Boston Herald*, where he was employed in 1919.

In 1919 Wiener accepted an instructorship in mathematics at the Massachusetts Institute of Technology (MIT), in Cambridge. This turned out to be a fortuitous move for the young scientist, since at that time MIT had not yet distinguished itself in the mathematics community and had no tradition of research or scholarship. Here Wiener, having just entered a very productive period, was able to shine. He remained an instructor until 1924, when he received a promotion to assistant professor. Four years later he was made an associate professor and, in 1932, full professor, a title he held until his retirement in 1960. Over the course of his career at MIT he became one of the institute's most famous faculty members.

Wiener completed some of his greatest early mathematical work during his first years at MIT. He later claimed that his interest in modern mathematics was rekindled in 1918 after he encountered ideas on integration, differential equations, and functionals in the books of a fellow Harvard student who had died. During this same period he met I. A. Barnett, who suggested to Wiener that he focus on integration in function spaces. This encouragement led to Wiener's work on some of his most important mathematical problems, starting with differential space. According to Hans Freudenthal in the *Dictionary of Scientific Biography* (1976), "It was already characteristic of Wiener's openness of mind that, rather than being satisfied with a general integration theory, he looked for physical embodiments to test the theory. The first he tried, turbulence, was a failure; but the next, Brownian motion (1921), studied earlier by Einstein, was a success. Wiener conceived a measure in the space of one-dimensional paths that leads to the application of probability concepts in that space." (Brownian motion is, according to the *Encyclopaedia Britannica* [on-line], the construction of an exact mathematical description of a physical process that consists of random change.) Between 1923 and 1925 Wiener published papers on Dirichlet's Theo-

rem concerning prime numbers, which widely influenced future theories in that subject. After completing his work on Brownian motion, he studied more general random processes involving probability or chance. Because of its relation to the mathematical needs of MIT's engineering department, he devoted the next five years of his life to this study. The work concluded in 1930 with a long paper on generalized harmonic analysis—the study of functions into periodic parts and the generalizations derived from that study. Three years later Wiener was elected to the National Academy of Science but soon resigned his post, angered by the institutionalized science practiced at the academy. That same year he won the Bocher Prize, an award offered every five years by the American Mathematical Society, and was asked to present the society's Colloquium Lectures.

Wiener's personal life was changing at this time. After a courtship of several years, he married Margaret Engemann in 1926. The couple would later have two daughters, Barbara and Margaret. Wiener traveled extensively with his family over the next decade. Aided by a Guggenheim fellowship, he pursued his research at Göttingen and Copenhagen in 1926. He was an exchange professor at Brown University in 1929–30, then returned to Cambridge, this time in the dual capacity of lecturer and student for the 1931–32 year. During 1935 and 1936 he held the post of visiting professor at Tsing Hua University in Peiping, China. He also paid a number of visits to Germany in the years between the two world wars.

During World War II, Wiener worked for the American government, researching guided missiles and constructing predictors. His main area of study was gunfire control, essentially trying to solve the problem of shooting a moving target. He worked on mathematical equations which would aid antiaircraft artillery in predicting the location of a moving target at a certain time, thereby increasing the chances of hitting the target more than once every 2,500 times. (This statistic was derived from the average score of antiaircraft artillery that were attempting to shoot down German planes in southern England during World War II.) Wiener eventually developed the M-9 Predictor, which, according to a contributor to *Scientific American* (August 1998), "used feedback from radar data to help forecast where the enemy would be up in the sky when the next shell arrived. On that basis, his invention directed how the gun should be pointed." At the end of the war, Wiener announced that he would no longer contribute to military research. In an open letter published in the *Atlantic* (January 1947), Wiener elaborated his position: "The interchange of ideas which is one of the great traditions of science," he wrote, "must of course receive certain limitations when the scientist becomes an arbiter of life or death. . . . I realize of course that I am acting as the censor of my own ideas and it may sound arbitrary. . . . If I do not desire to participate in the bombing of defenseless people—and I most certainly do not—I must take serious responsibility as to those to whom I disclose my scientific ideas." Wiener also spent the remainder of his life warning people about the dangers of automation. In the *Dictionary of Computer Quotations* (1997), Donald D. Spencer quotes Wiener as stating, "Render unto man the things which are man's and unto the computer the things which are the computer's."

Wiener next turned his attention to the "handling of information" in highly involved machines, such as automatic computers, radar devices, and servomechanisms, an interest piqued by his work during the war. From the two basic elements of these devices—the feedback principal exemplified by the thermostat and "a preoccupation with accuracy rather than efficiency"—it became evident to Wiener and his fellow workers in the field—physicists, psychologists, electronics engineers, and researchers from almost every other division of the sciences—that a similarity existed between such mechanisms and the operations of the human brain and nervous system. Wiener considered his first book on the new science, *Cybernetics* (1948), an invasion of "the no-man's land between the established fields." Half a century after the book's publication, cybernetics is a field of study in its own right, influencing everything from automation theory to computer programs that aid people by reducing time-consuming work. "I made up the word 'cybernetics' from the Greek for 'steersman,'" Wiener explained, as quoted in *Current Biography*. "As the book says, it refers to control and communication in the animal and the machine. The typical example is the governor of a steam engine, which senses mechanically when the engine is going too fast and reduces the supply of steam." Cybernetics is an interdisciplinary field based on the common relationship between automatic functions exhibited by human beings and machines. According to an entry in the *International Biographical Dictionary of Computer Pioneers* (1995), "In cybernetics [Wiener] sought to discover the degree to which the human nervous system is a mechanized process as it carries stimuli to the brain—in other words, how much in a human is unconsciously a machine." Such questioning led him to think about how *human* a machine could become if both shared certain automatic functions.

Originally published in Paris, within six weeks of the first American printing of *Cybernetics*, three more printings were necessary due to an unprecedented demand from readers of all types. Reviews of *Cybernetics* in the American press were almost unanimously laudatory. Churchill Eisenhart of the National Bureau of Standards wrote in *Science* (April 22, 1949) that Wiener "has been remarkably successful in pointing out the similarities and equivalences (from a mathematical standpoint) of many diverse phenomena of man, animal, machine, and society. . . . The introduction ends with a pessimistic view of the future of human society and a note of discouragement concerning the possibility of developing an exact science of economics or sociology." To John B. Thurston of the *Saturday Review of Literature* it appeared "impossible for anyone seriously interested in our civilization to ignore this book. . . . It is a beautifully written book, lucid, direct and, despite its complexity, as readable by the layman as the trained scientist." Anthony Standen, reviewing the work for *Commonweal*, observed, "The tremendous difference between men and machines Professor Wiener does not pretend to discuss, contenting himself in this book with pointing out these extraordinarily suggestive resemblances between machines and the human brain and nervous system. . . . A machine, when 'instructed' to carry out a certain computation, will carry out that computation, except in the case of mechanical 'failure.' A man, if instructed to carry out a computation, may carry it out. . . . The man . . . may refuse to . . . for laziness or for any other good reason. And that is one immense superiority of the man over the machine."

In his more than 100 contributions to mathematical, philosophical, and scientific journals, Wiener has discussed the postulate theory, the foundations of mathematics, assemblages and functions of a real variable, probability theory, analysis, Tauberian theorems, mathematical logic, trigonometric expansions, potential theory, relativity, epistemology, and electrical networks. Some of his published essays include "Dirac Equations and Einstein Theory" for the June 22, 1929 issue of *Nature*; with D. J. Struik, "Fifth Dimension in Relativistic Quantum Theory" for the March 1928 *National Academy of Science Proceedings*; with Manuel S. Vallarta, "On the Spherically Symmetrical Statical Field in Einstein's Unified Theory of Electricity and Gravitation" (same publication, April 1949); and with Arturo Rosenblueth, "Role of Models in Science," for the October 1945 issue of *Philosophical Science*. He also authored several books. In *The Human Use of Human Beings* (1954), he described how automation could liberate people from repetitious, mind-numbing work—like that of assembly lines—and give them more time for creative endeavors. He also wrote two volumes of his autobiography *Ex-Prodigy—My Childhood and Youth* (1953) and *I Am A Mathematician—the Later Life of a Prodigy* (1956), as well as *God and Golem, Inc.: A Comment on Certain Points Where Cybernetics Impinges on Religion* (1964). Finally, he wrote a number of mathematical texts that include *The Fourier Integral, and Certain of Its Applications* (1933) and *Nonlinear Problems in Random Theory* (1958), among others.

Norbert Wiener received the Bocher Prize of the American Mathematical Society in 1933 and the Lord and Taylor $1,000 American Design Award in 1949. He was a consultant for the American Mathematical Society and was its president from 1935 to 1937. He was also a member of the Mathematike Verein, the Societe Mathematique de France, the London Mathematical Society, and the National

Academy of Sciences, the latter called by *Scientific American* "the highest earned honor in American science." In 1964 Wiener was presented with the National Medal of Science by President Lyndon B. Johnson. A few weeks later, on March 18, 1964, while on a speaking tour in Stockholm, Sweden, Wiener died.—C. M.

Suggested Reading: *Scientific American* p115 Sep. 1934, p102+ Aug. 1998; *Time* p28 Sep. 19, 1938; *American Men of Science*, 1949; Asimov, Isaac. *Asimov's Biographical Dictionary of Science and Technology*, 1982; Lee, J. A. N., ed. *International Biographical Dictionary of Computer Pioneers*, 1995; Spencer, Donald D. *The Timetable of Computers*, 1997

Wilkes, Maurice Vincent

June 26, 1913– Designer of the Electronic Delay Storage Automatic Calculator (EDSAC)

The British mathematician and computer scientist Maurice V. Wilkes, from 1945 to 1980 the director of the Mathematical Laboratory (later renamed the Computer Laboratory) at Cambridge University, in England, designed and built the Electronic Delay Storage Automatic Calculator (EDSAC), one of the world's first digital stored-program computers. Wilkes approached the construction of the machine pragmatically, emphasizing its rapid construction, rather than investing in innovative hardware. As a result, the EDSAC was completed before the Electronic Discrete Variable Automatic Computer (EDVAC)—the computer whose conceptual plans had initially inspired Wilkes to build a stored-program computer. The EDSAC, which ran its first program in May 1949, proved to be one of Britain's most influential postwar computing projects. Wilkes' other achievements include the development of the EDSAC 2, which used magnetic storage in place of mercury delay lines, and Titan, which used an early form of time-sharing technology. In addition to heading the Mathematical Laboratory, Wilkes educated generations of computer scientists as a professor of computer technology at St. John's College, Cambridge University, from 1965 to 1980. He has written several notable books, including *Memoirs of a Computer Pioneer* (1985), an autobiographical account of his years as the director of the prestigious lab. More recently, he served as a consultant to AT&T Laboratories in Cambridge before the lab's dissolution in 2002, and he continues to publish papers on a variety of scientific topics.

Maurice Vincent Wilkes was born on June 26, 1913 in Dudley, Straffordshire, England. He studied mathematics and physics at St. John's College of Cambridge University, earning his degree in 1934. He received his Ph.D. in 1936, after writing a thesis on the propagation of very long radio waves in the ionosphere. The following year he was hired for a junior faculty position at Cambridge, an appointment made in connection with the establishment, in 1937, of a computer laboratory at the school. The Mathematical Laboratory, as it was called, was equipped with differential analyzers (analog computers that solve differential equations), a Mallock Machine (an analog device built in 1933 to solve linear simultaneous equations), and an array of desk calculators. John Lennard-Jones, the Plummer Professor of Theoretical Chemistry at Cambridge, was appointed as the part-time director of the laboratory, and Wilkes was named a university demonstrator (similar to assistant professor in the United States). Wilkes' first assignment was to visit Manchester University to study its differential analyzer, and then supervise the construction of a new differential analyzer at the laboratory in Cambridge.

Like many of his fellow physicists, Wilkes was called away from his duties at Cambridge during World War II. During the war, he took on many projects dealing with radar and operational research, and made important contributions to the fields. In September 1945 he returned to Cambridge and was appointed to the post of director of the Mathematical Laboratory. In May 1946 he received a visit from Leslie Comrie, a New Zealand computer enthusiast. Comrie had brought a copy of John von Neumann's *First Draft of a Report on the EDVAC*, an influential paper outlining an innovative stored-program concept that was to be incorporated into the EDVAC, which was soon to begin construction at the Moore School of Engineering at the University of Pennsylvania, in Philadelphia. Unable to make a copy of the entire paper, Wilkes had one night to read and assimilate the contents of the report before Comrie departed the next day. That brief exposure was enough to convince him of the potential of the stored-program computer architecture, which greatly reduced the need for more clumsy methods of programming, such as punched paper tape. "[I] recognized this at once as the real thing, and from that time on never had any doubt as to the way computer development would go," Wilkes later recalled, as quoted by J. A. N. Lee in *Computer Pioneers* (1995).

Soon after, Wilkes received an invitation to attend a series of lectures that were being held at the Moore School. The highly anticipated lectures, held July 8 to August 31, 1946, were titled "Theory and Techniques for Design of Electronic Digital Computers" and they drew hundreds of scientists from the United States and Great Britain. While in Philadelphia Wilkes met several luminaries in computer research and design, including Howard Aiken, Herman Goldstine, John Mauchly, and J. Presper Eckert. Mauchly and Eckert, of the Moore School, had recently completed construction of the ENIAC (Electronic Numerical Integrator And Computer), the world's first electronic digital computer. Wilkes later described the ENIAC—a gigantic, 60,000-pound machine thousands of times faster than its predecessors—as the focus of "the big bang" that led to the explosive growth of computing technology in the postwar years. It was also Mauchly and Eckert who first proposed the stored-program concept of which von Neumann had written, and many of their discussions that summer revolved around the plans for building the EDVAC.

When Wilkes returned to Cambridge in October 1946, he was determined to build a stored-program computer at the Mathematical Laboratory. Pragmatic in his approach, he opted to rely on the technology at hand, rather than invest in research and new development. This would allow him to get his computer built and operational in as little time as possible. His intention was not to extend the frontiers of computer hardware, but to have a functioning computer that could be used to work on programming issues. "Building the machine was only the start of the project," Wilkes later explained, as quoted by David Ritchie in *The Computer Pioneers* (1986). Much remained to be learned about "how to use the machine for numerical analysis, numerical calculation, and all the rest of it."

The completed computer, named the EDSAC, contained 3,000 vacuum tubes arranged on 12 racks—larger than expected, but an improvement over the ENIAC, which, by comparison, contained 18,000 vacuum tubes. (Vacuum tubes are electronic devices that control the flow of electrons in a vacuum; they function as on/off switches, allowing computers to carry out digital calculations.) The EDSAC could execute a modest 650 instructions per second. Programs were input using punched paper tape, and results were passed to a teleprinter. To store information the EDSAC used delay lines— mercury-filled tubes about 1.5 meters in length. An electrical signal to the tube generated a pressure pulse that was transmitted through the mercury to the other end, where it was converted back into an electrical impulse. By incorporating numerous tubes and suitable amplification, an electrical signal could be stored indefinitely, an essential requirement of computer memory. The EDSAC contained 16 such tubes, which stored 32 words of 17 bits each.

The EDSAC was first officially demonstrated in May 1949. The computer that had inspired it, the EDVAC, was not completed until 1952, largely because Eckert and Mauchley had taken time off to pursue other projects. The EDSAC's claim to being the world's first digital stored-program computer was undermined, however, by the Manchester Mark I. The Mark I, built by Tom Kilburn at the University of Manchester, England, had completed its first successful test run almost a year before the EDSAC debut. Unlike the Manchester machine, however, the EDSAC was not simply a prototype but a working machine that could solve realistic problems, and for this reason it is still considered by many to be the first full-scale operational electronic digital stored-program computer. Whereas other machines were often retained by their engineers for experimental use and development, the EDSAC went into regular use as a service machine

for the university about eight months after it ran its first program, and it remained operational until 1956. It was used to solve problems in such fields as theoretical chemistry, X-ray molecular biology, numerical analysis, atmospheric oscillations, and radioastronomy.

Programming on the EDSAC was not easy, but Wilkes quickly initiated a project to develop a set of subroutines which made it possible to do realistic work on the machine. (A subroutine is a sequence of computer instructions for performing a specified task that can be used repeatedly.) Originally, subroutines were simply strung together on the input tape, to be executed one after another. One of Wilkes' graduate students, David J. Wheeler, devised a method in which the program would jump to the subroutine, execute it, and, when required, return to the original program. This programming technique, which became known as the Wheeler Jump, greatly improved the efficiency of the machine. It was rapidly adopted by other computer makers and forms the basis for how programs are written today. Wheeler also developed the idea of the "bootstrap," a program that is run every time the computer is turned on. The bootstrap loaded the programs to be executed, and allowed programs to be relocated to different parts of the memory, thus freeing up space. Wilkes, Wheeler, and another graduate student, Stan Gill, wrote a textbook explaining these innovative procedures, *The Preparation of Programs for an Electrical Digital Computer* (1951), which became one of the most influential textbooks of the period.

After the EDSAC Wilkes began the construction of a more advanced model, the EDSAC 2, which became fully operational in 1958. Built with funding from the Nuffield Foundation, a British charitable trust, the EDSAC 2 used magnetic core memory in place of the delay lines used in its predecessor. It was the first computer to possess a microprogrammed control unit. Microprogramming allowed for frequently used machine-level commands to be housed in the computer, so they did not have to be loaded each time a particular program was executed. The EDSAC 2 played a prominent role in several notable scientific projects, including that of the chemist John C. Kendrew, who earned a Nobel Prize for Chemistry in 1962 for his work on the molecular structure of myoglobin. Kendrew had used the machine to analyze 10,000 X-ray diffraction patterns. The astronomer Sir Martin Ryle later used the EDSAC 2 in the development of his radio telescope, for which he was awarded the Nobel Prize for Physics in 1974.

During the 1960s the Cambridge laboratory collaborated with Ferranti Ltd., a computer hardware company, to build Titan, a reduced-scale version of the Atlas machine, which had been a joint effort between Ferranti and Manchester University. The Atlas was a large, expensive machine; scientists hope to create a less costly, but relatively compatible computer. Titan was in the midst of development when Wilkes learned of the Compatible

Time-Sharing System (CTSS), which was in development at the Massachusetts Institute of Technology (MIT), in Cambridge, Massachusetts. Time-sharing operating systems had come into high demand during the 1960s, as a means of overcoming the bottlenecks that researchers faced as numerous users vied for time to run their programs on a single computer. Realizing the growing importance of time-share technology, Wilkes recast the development plans for Titan to incorporate the concept. Upon completion, Titan had a user base of several hundred people and 73 terminals, 26 of which could be used simultaneously. The machine, which was in conventional service at the university until 1973, was also notable as the first computer to employ a cache memory, as well as one of the first machines to use a one-way function to protect its password file.

By the mid-1960s Wilkes had become a leading figure in the field of computer development and design. Although still interested in research, he began to assume more leadership roles. In the late 1950s he had been elected the first president of the British Computer Society, a post he held for three years. In 1965 he was appointed chairman of the Computer Advisory Committee of the Agricultural Research Council, a position he held for 10 years. When he reached the mandatory retirement age at Cambridge in 1980, he moved to Maynard, Massachusetts, and became a staff consultant for the Digital Equipment Corporation and an adjunct professor at MIT. He returned to England in 1986 and became a founding member of the esteemed Olivetti Research Laboratory (ORL) at Cambridge. (ORL later joined with Oracle to become the Olivetti and Oracle Research Laboratory.) In 1999 the lab was acquired by AT&T, but in 2002 financial restructuring forced the telecommunications company to discontinue its funding.

Among his numerous awards and distinctions, Wilkes received the Association for Computing Machinery (ACM) Alan M. Turing Award (1967), the ACM/Institute of Electrical and Electronics Engineers (IEEE) Eckert-Mauchly Award (1980) and the McDowell Award from the IEEE Computer Society (1981). In 1992 Wilkes was honored with the Kyoto Prize for Advanced Technology for his "enormous contribution to the research and development of computers for practical use," according to the Kyoto Prize Web site, sponsored by the Inamori Foundation. He is a distinguished fellow of the British Computer Society, a fellow of the Royal Society, and a fellow of the Royal Academy of Engineering. He is a foreign associate of both the U.S. National Academy of Sciences and the U.S. National Academy of Engineering. He is also a foreign honorary member of the American Academy of Arts and Sciences. He has written several noted books, including *Memoirs of a Computer Pioneer* (1985) and *Computing Perspectives* (1995). Among his recent papers are "The Memory Gap and the Future of High Performance Memories" (2001) and "A Personal Revisitation of Neural Nets" (2002).

Wilkes married Nina Twyman in 1947. They have three children: Margaret, Helen, and Anthony.—A. I. C.

Suggested Reading: Aspray, William. *Computing Before Computers*, 1990; Lee, J. A. N., ed. *International Biographical Dictionary of Computer Pioneers*, 1995; Ritchie, David. *The Computer Pioneers*, 1986

Williams, Frederic Calland

June 26, 1911–Aug. 11, 1977 Inventor of the Williams Tube

Partially responsible for putting Manchester on the map of computer development in the 1940s and 1950s, Frederic Calland Williams was one of the premier inventors of modern times. His ingenuity filtered over several fields including computers, as he pioneered the Williams tube, a revolutionary piece of equipment that allowed quick, random access to data and would replace the slower mercury delay lines, which ran serially. For years, Williams's Manchester Mark 1 was viewed as the most progressive piece of computation equipment to date, although in actuality, it was just the starting point for an entire technological revolution that would claim the city of Manchester as its headquarters. Although his CRT storage system would eventually be replaced by a more advanced method of data storage, it was incredibly advanced for its time. Even after losing interest in computers, Williams's ingenuity would show itself when he designed one of the first automatic transmissions for cars.

Frederic Calland Williams was born on June 26, 1911 in Romiley, Cheshire, England. He was the only son of Frederic Williams, a locomotive draftsman, and Ethel Alice Smith Williams. During his childhood, Williams was educated at the Stockport Grammar School. By 1929 Williams had entered the school of engineering at the University of Manchester on a scholarship. In 1932 he graduated with honors and the following year, he earned his Master of Science degree and joined Metropolitan-Vickers for a brief period as an apprentice, before entering Oxford University's Magdalen College in 1934. He enrolled on a scholarship given to him by the Institute of Electrical and Electronics Engineers (IEEE) and performed research in the study of circuit and valve noise. He remained at Oxford for two years, where he would spend his recreational time as a coxswain, or steersman, in the eight-man boating races on the Thames River. Williams received his Doctor of Philosophy degree from Oxford in 1936, and he decided to return to Manchester to work as an assistant lecturer in the school of engineering. During this period, Williams offered a course called Electro-Technics, which, with its combination of physics and electrical engineering, was unique for that time.

By 1939 Williams had garnered himself a solid reputation among his peers as an insightful and innovative researcher. With more than 20 published papers under his belt, Williams was rewarded for his work with a Doctorate in Science from the University of Manchester. In 1938 Williams married Gladys Ward, and they subsequently had two children, a daughter, and a son who would go on to become a professor of civil engineering.

As World War II escalated, Williams asked to participate in the field of radar research, first at Bawdsey and then at the Telecommunications Research Establishment (TRE). One of Williams's first projects in his new position involved the IFF (Identification Friend or Foe) system. He also developed detailed coding procedures that allowed aircraft to disguise themselves electronically, so as not to alert enemy radar. Taking into account single-seat aircraft, Williams helped design a fully automatic radar system that required little pilot attention. When a target was located, the system would filter out the distracting ground echoes (as well as echoes from other planes) using electronic identification signals, which enabled it to identify the direction of the target as well as its range. This technological breakthrough made it possible for the military to perform accurate bombing despite heavy cloud cover and for pilots to navigate their planes by radio at night, during bad weather, or other difficult conditions when the crew was unable to use the stars or other geographical landmarks.

Williams went on to do further research for TRE and during his time there was described by others as "prolific, enthusiastic, and unselfish" (*Computer Pioneers*, 1995). As the war neared an end, Williams became involved in a project for the Radiation Laboratory at the Massachusetts Institute of Technology (MIT). The university was putting together a 24-volume publication designed to cover all aspects of electrical engineering. Williams came aboard as an editor and contributor to volumes 19 and 20 and visited the Radiation Laboratory, where he learned of the innovative work that was being performed there (as well as at the Moore School of Engineering) on cathode-ray tubes (CRTs) working as data storage instruments. The project was a lengthy one, but one that Williams deemed essential for use at the TRE, for according to Williams, with the end of the war, the lack of clear objective or urgent need for equipment "left many scientists and engineers at TRE searching for new projects to occupy themselves" (*Computer Pioneers*, 1995). Furthermore, the new technology was greatly needed at the time. In order for electronic computers to process data, they needed some method of storing and accessing instructions in their memory in order to perform operations on data in a systematic way. Previously, the method of stored memory in electronic computers was mercury delay lines, which were difficult to manufacture. In addition, mercury delay lines were highly sensitive and could store data only serially, which meant that for a computer to read a single instruction in the middle of an instruction set, it would have to read from the beginning all the way through to the middle to get to the one instruction it needed, an extremely slow process.

When Williams returned to Manchester from MIT in July 1946, he began to study CRTs in order to solve this storage problem. Only three months later, Williams, with the help of Tom Kilburn, was able to demonstrate how a CRT could store a single, binary digit in spots on the tube. Storing spots on a CRT was difficult, however, because the spots would fade away quickly. Williams devised a way to overcome this obstacle by developing electronic circuits for the purpose of refreshing the spots on the tube, so that it could be stored indefinitely.

When word of Williams's successful work in CRT storage reached the National Physical Laboratory (NPL) Mathematics Division, Sir Charles Darwin, director of the NPL, requested to see the tube (later called the Williams tube) demonstrated at TRE. After his visit, the subject was brought up at an NPL meeting during which members pressured TRE to agree to perform most of the electronic development work required to build the Automatic Computing Engine (ACE) being designed by pioneering mathematician Alan Turing. However, Williams, considered one of NPL's biggest assets, was about to leave TRE in order to join Manchester University after being offered the position of Chairman of Electro-Technics. The lab persisted in trying to persuade Williams to devote his energy toward incorporating CRT storage systems into the ACE project, going so far as to entice him with a strict contract, but he refused, opting to work with TRE under the sponsorship of Manchester University.

After Williams moved into his new position at Manchester, Kilburn followed, and the two continued to work on CRT storage systems. They spent 1947 perfecting their new CRT memory unit and were joined by researchers A. A. Robertson and G. C. Toothill. By the fall of 1947, the CRT storage tube was able to store 2,048 bits.

The next phase of the project involved the construction of a computer to use the new improved Williams tube. For the first time, separate divisions of research joined together for this common goal, with the renowned M. H. A. Newman's mathematics team providing advice to the Electro-Technics engineers. Less than a year later, the research group had built the Manchester Mark 1 "Baby" machine.

The Manchester Mark 1, which utilized Williams's CRT storage system, was a breakthrough machine for several reasons. The machine possessed a random-access memory (RAM) of 32 locations, or "words," and each word in turn consisted of 32 bits, thereby giving the Manchester Mark 1 a total memory of 1,024 bits (stored on one Williams tube) and making it the world's first electronic stored-memory computer. The only input device was a series of switches, and output was read directly from the Williams tube. The Manchester Mark 1 failed on its first operating attempts but finally sparked to life on June 21, 1948, when Kilburn's Highest Factor Positive program was executed in 52 minutes. Williams would later comment on the turbulent road the team took to get the program to work: "A program was laboriously inserted and the start switch pressed. Immediately the spots on the display tube entered a mad dance. In early trials it was a dance of death leading to no useful result, and what was even worse, without yielding any clue as to what was wrong. But one day it stopped, and there, shining brightly in the expected place, was the expected answer. It was a moment to remember. This was in June 1948, and nothing was ever the same again" (*University of Manchester*, on-line).

Sir Ben Lockspeiser, chief scientist from the Ministry of Supply, took an interest in the Manchester Mark 1 as part of his goal to open up opportunities in defense research and to support industry, which was declining in the post-war era. Lockspeiser then decided that the company Ferranti Ltd. would make a good industrial partner for the Manchester machine, and a contract was drawn up for the production of "an electronic calculating machine to the instructions of Professor F. C. Williams."

By the fall of 1948, work began on a larger, commercial prototype computer version of the Manchester Mark 1. Eventually 20 of these computers would be installed in Britain as well as other countries across the globe. The Williams tube took computing into a whole new direction as suddenly, the whole process was free of wires, dust, or messy operations, and every problem could be quickly and reliably solved.

Despite the enormous success of the Manchester Mark 1 and his own Williams tube, F. C. Williams lost interest in the engineering of computers and turned his attention to motors. Later in his career, Williams built one of the earliest automatic transmissions for cars. He continued to work until his death on August 11, 1977 in Manchester, England.

Throughout his lifetime, F. C. Williams was highly honored in his country. He was named a Commander of the British Empire in 1961 and was knighted in 1976. He was also the recipient of a wealth of awards in both Britain and the United States for his work on computers. He was given the Benjamin Franklin Medal from the Royal Society of Arts in 1957 and the John Scott Award from the city of Philadelphia in 1960 and was elected a Fellow of the Royal Society in 1950.

Richard H. Bigelow, an American researcher, complimenting Williams's ability to improvise, described him as a good example of "British 'string and sealing wax' inventive genius."—D. B.

Suggested Reading: Manchester University Web site; Lee, J. A. N., ed. *International Biographical Dictionary of Computer Pioneers*, 1995

Wirth, Niklaus

Feb. 15, 1934– Developer of the Pascal computer language

The Swiss computer scientist Niklaus Wirth is perhaps best known for developing the Pascal computer language in the late 1960s. Pascal reflected Wirth's philosophy that computer languages should be simple and elegant. He named the language after Blaise Pascal (1623–62), the French mathematician. During the 1970s and 1980s, it became popular with programmers around the world who found it a powerful and effective tool that greatly reduced the number of errors in their work.

Niklaus E. Wirth was born on February 15, 1934 in Winterthur, Switzerland. His father, Walter, was a geography professor. Growing up in rural Switzerland, Niklaus enjoyed making model airplanes. His experience repairing them taught him the importance of simplicity. "If you have to pay out of your own pocket money, you learn not to make the fixes overly complicated," he observed to Jonathan B. Levine, for *BusinessWeek* (June 15, 1990).

In 1954 Wirth enrolled at the Eidenössische Technische Hochschule (ETH), the Swiss Federal Institute of Technology, in Zürich, Switzerland. At the time, the only course in computers that the school offered was an elective taught by Ambros P. Speiser, who developed the legendary ERMETH computer. (Some sources spell the teacher's name *Ambrose*.) In 1959, according to his curriculum vitae, Wirth graduated with a degree in electronics engineering.

As a graduate student at Laval University, in Quebec, Canada, Wirth took a course in numerical analysis. Since the university's Alwac III E computer wasn't working most of the time, he performed programming exercises on paper. After earning a master's degree in 1960, Wirth headed to the University of California, Berkeley (UC Berkeley), to pursue a doctorate. "At Berkeley, I was confronted with Harry Huskey's pet machine, the Bendix G-15 computer," Wirth recalled in his article for the *Communications of the ACM*, as quoted in the book *The School of Niklaus Wirth: The Art of Simplicity* (2000). "Although the Bendix G-15 provided some feeling of success by producing results, the gist of the programming art appeared to be the clever allocation of instructions on the drum. If you ignored the art, your programs could well run slower by a factor of one hundred. But the educational benefit was clear: You can not afford to ignore the least little detail. There was no way to cover up deficiencies in your design by simply buying more memory. In retrospect, the most attractive feature was that every detail of the machine was visible and could be understood. Nothing was hidden in complex circuitry, silicon, or a magic operating system."

During his graduate-school years, Wirth abandoned hardware design in favor of studying how to use computers more elegantly and efficiently. He joined a research group that was developing a compiler for the IBM 704 computer. The result was the NELIAC programming language, which Wirth described as a *dialect* of the ALGOL 58 language. In his article Wirth concluded that "programs should be designed according to the same principles as electronic circuits, that is, clearly subdivided into parts with only a few wires going across the boundaries. Only by understanding one part at a time would there be hope of finally understanding the whole." For his dissertation, Wirth defined Euler, a language based on ALGOL 60. Wirth named the language after Leonhard Euler (1707–83), a Swiss mathematician. "The result was academic elegance, but not much of practical utility—almost an antithesis of the later data-typed and structured programming languages," Wirth recalled in his article. "But it did create a basis for the systemic design of compilers that, so was the hope, could be extended without loss of clarity to accommodate further facilities."

Wirth received his doctorate in 1963. He then joined the faculty of Stanford University, in California, as an assistant professor of computer science. Wirth's development of Euler led to an invitation to join the International Federation for Information Processing (IFIP) Working Group 2.1, a team of computer scientists who were exploring ways to enhance ALGOL 60. Wirth's proposal to develop an adequate extension of the language was voted down by members who had more ambitious plans. Wirth, however, collaborated with Tony Hoare, a member of the Working Group, to improve his original proposal. The result was ALGOL-W, which ran on the IBM 360 computer. ALGOL-W was used at several universities for teaching purposes.

At Stanford, Wirth also developed PL360, an algorithmic language for the IBM 360 computer. "The experiment of describing the compiling algorithm in PL360 itself proved to be the most effective test on the usefulness and appropriateness of the language and it influenced the subsequent development of the language considerably," Wirth wrote for the *Journal of the ACM* (1968), as quoted in *The School of Niklaus Wirth*. "During the process, several features which seemed desirable were added to the language, and many were dropped again after having proved to be either dubious in value, inconsistent with the design criteria, or too involved and leading to misconceptions. The leading principle and guideline was to produce a [conceptually] simple language and to keep the number of features and facilities minimal." Although it was developed only to serve Wirth's immediate needs, PL360 became an effective tool for many programmers.

In 1967 Wirth left California to return to his native Switzerland. After teaching for about a year at the University of Zürich, Wirth returned to his alma mater, ETH, where he co-founded its computer-science department. In 1969 Wirth and three assistants began working on the language that would become known as Pascal. "Confronted with the duty to teach programming, I had been faced with the dire options of [FORTRAN] and ALGOL," Wirth explained in his article "Pascal and its Successors" (September 25, 2002), as posted on the Swiss Delphi Center Web site. "The former did not appeal to my taste as a scientist, the latter not to those of the practical engineer. I liberated myself from this jail by designing Pascal, convinced that an elegant style and an effective implementation were not mutually exclusive. I felt strongly—and still do—that a language used in teaching must display some style, elegance, consistency, while at the same time also reflecting the needs (but not necessarily the bad habits) of practice. I wanted to design a language for both my classroom and my 'software factory.'" Wirth added that "the general idea dominating the design of Pascal was to provide a language appealing to systematic thinking, mirroring conventional mathematical notation, satisfying the needs of practical programming, and encouraging a structured approach. The rules governing the language should be intuitive and simple, and freely combinable." Wirth and his assistants completed Pascal in 1970. "At ETH, we introduced Pascal in programming classes in 1972, in fact against considerable opposition," Wirth once wrote, as quoted in *The School of Niklaus Wirth*. "It turned out to be a success because it allowed the teacher to concentrate more heavily on structures and concepts than features and peculiarities, that is, on principles rather than techniques."

Pascal gradually caught the attention of other programmers, who requested that the language be implemented on their own machines. Wirth developed Pascal-P (for *portable*), a compiler version of the language that could generate code on other machines. "Pascal-P proved enormously successful in spreading the language among many users," Wirth wrote, as quoted in *The School of Niklaus Wirth*. "But Pascal gained widespread recognition only after Ken Bowles [a professor and computer scientist] in San Diego recognized that the P-system could well be implemented on the novel microcomputers [which were powered by microprocessors]. His efforts to develop a suitable environment with integrated compiler, filer, editor, and debugger caused a breakthrough: Pascal became available to thousands of new computer users who were not burdened with acquired habits or stifled by the urge to stay compatible with software of the past." Pascal became one of the most popular programming languages of all time. Many programmers found that Pascal's rigorous and simple structure forced them to write high-quality programs with fewer errors than before. During the 1980s, Pascal got a major boost when Philippe Kahn, one of Wirth's former students at ETH and the founder of the software manufacturer Borland International, developed Turbo Pascal, a best-selling version of the language for the personal computer.

Wirth next developed the Modula computer language. "The attempt to distill concrete rules for a multiprogramming discipline quickly led me to formulate them in terms of a small set programming facilities," Wirth explained, as quoted in *The School of Niklaus Wirth*. "In order to put the rules to a genuine test, I embedded them in a fragmentary language, whose name was coined after my principal aim: modularity in program systems. The module later turned out to be the principal asset of this language; it gave the abstract concept of information hiding a concrete form and incorporated a method as significant in [uni-programming] as in multiprogramming. Also, [the language] Modula contained facilities to express concurrent processes and their synchronization." Wirth implemented Modula on the PDP-11 microcomputer.

In 1976 Wirth took a leave of absence from ETH to spend a year at the Xerox Palo Alto Research Center (PARC), in California. There, he discovered the personal workstation, a high-performance computer for a single user. "The most elating sensation was that after 16 years of working for computers, the computer now seemed to work for me," he recalled, as quoted by *The School of Niklaus Wirth*. "For the first time, I did my daily correspondence and report writing with the aid of a computer, instead of planning new languages, compilers, and programs for others to use. . . . These new working conditions were so many orders of magnitude above what I had experienced at home that I decided to establish such an environment there as well." After returning to ETH, Wirth embarked on ambitious project to develop a revolutionary workstation with an operating system and a programming language. Wirth and a large team of assistants completed the project in three years, far ahead of schedule, resulting in the workstation Lilith, the operating system Medos, and the programming language Modula-2. The entire project is widely considered an important milestone in Niklaus Wirth's career as a computer scientist. The first Liliths were being used at ETH by 1980, years before similar systems became available commercially.

Wirth spent another year, 1984–1985, at PARC, where he observed the Cedar Operating System, which was developed for the personal workstation. Although powerful and revolutionary, Cedar's complexity and size often created problems for users. After returning to ETH, Wirth and a colleague, Jürg Gutknecht, began work on Project Oberon, an effort to create an operating system based on Cedar's principles, but smaller and more manageable. The effort produced both the Oberon operating system and the Oberon language. In his article, Jonathan B. Levine described Oberon as "a warehouse of reusable software modules" that "gives programmers mix-and-match building blocks from which they can create complex programs faster—and with fewer bugs." Some of Wirth's other contributions include the Venus time-sharing system, which he developed in 1970 for ETH's CDC 6000 mainframe; a high-speed laser printer; and an Oberon-based system that controls the flight path of model helicopters.

Niklaus Wirth has written many papers and books on programming languages and computer hardware. Throughout his career, his contributions to the field of computer science have been recognized many times. His honors include the 1983 Emanuel R. Piore Award for achievement, the 1984 A. M. Turing Award, the 1987 IEEE Computer Pioneer Award, the 1991 Marcel Benoit Prize, and the 2002 Eduard-Rhein Technology Prize, among others. Wirth has also received honorary doctorates from several universities around the world.

Although Niklaus Wirth retired from teaching in 1999, he has continued his computer research. Wirth and his wife, the former Nani Tucker, are the parents of three children: Carolyn, Christian, and Tina. The couple make their home in Zürich, Switzerland.—D. C.

Suggested Reading: *BusinessWeek* p136 June 15, 1990, with photo; Niklaus Wirth Faculty Page; Swiss Delphi Center Web site; Böszörményi, László, Gutknecht, Jürg, and Pomberger, Gustav. eds. *The School of Niklaus Wirth: The Art of Simplicity*, 2000

Wozniak, Stephen

(WOZ-nee-ak)

Aug. 11, 1950– Co-founder of Apple Computer

In the early 1970s Stephen Wozniak, then in his early 20s, had the idea of creating an inexpensive computer that would be easy for nontechnical people to use. While working as an engineer at Hewlett-Packard, Wozniak built a circuit board for such a system in his spare time, but he could not interest his superiors in pursuing the project. Wozniak's friend, Steve Jobs, saw the potential of Wozniak's minicomputer, and the two men started Apple Computer in 1976. Working out of Jobs's garage, they built the Apple I computer, a pre-assembled circuit board that could be attached to a TV monitor and a keyboard. The Apple I was a hobbyist's computer, but its successor, the Apple II, which debuted in 1977, became a huge success beyond the confines of computer lovers. Apple became one of the fastest-growing companies in history, generating over $1 billion in stock sales when it went public in 1980. Wozniak, a multimillionaire by age 30, grew increasingly disenchanted with the corporate mentality at Apple, and he left the firm in 1985 to pursue a variety of philanthropic interests, including donating hundreds of computers to public schools, and teaching children and teachers how to use them.

Of Polish and German ancestry, Stephen Gary Wozniak was born on August 11, 1950 in San Jose, California, to Margaret Wozniak, a homemaker, and Jerry Wozniak, an electrical engineer who designed satellites for the Lockheed Corporation. From an early age Wozniak, who grew up in the Silicon Valley town of Sunnyvale with his two younger siblings, showed great acumen in mathematics and electronics. In the sixth grade he earned his ham radio operator's license, after which he built his own radio transmitter and receiver. At age 13 Wozniak won the blue ribbon at a science fair for building a 10-bit parallel digital computer, using his own design for an integrated circuit. In high school he scored a perfect 800 on the math portion of the Scholastic Aptitude Test. Wozniak's other main interest was staging practical jokes, such as building devices to set off fire alarms or interfere with TV reception. "I knew my son would either be rich or wind up in jail," his mother was quoted as saying in *People* (May 30, 1983).

Fascinated by computers as a teenager, he spent many hours reading technical manuals. Bored by his school's electronics class, he was permitted to spend that class period at a large electronics company nearby, where he learned computer programming. "In high school, I could never afford to go near a computer," he recalled to John Hubner for the *Chicago Tribune* (January 2, 1985). "I'd sit down with a mini-computer manual and I'd redesign it. I'd get books on better chips that had just come out, and I'd redesign my favorite computers for them. If a computer used 20 chips, I'd try to use 10. If another system used 10, I'd try to use four. It was an intellectual exercise, something I did because it was neat. I did it over and over until I just sort of developed a technique for looking at things in a new way."

After graduating from Sunnyvale's Homestead High School in 1968, Wozniak enrolled at the University of Colorado, in Boulder. Unable to afford the high out-of-state tuition, he left after his freshman year, and spent a year at a community college near his parents' home. He took a leave of absence the following year to work at a small start-up company that was developing a new computer. When the company failed and he was laid off, he enrolled at the University of California, Berkeley, which had an excellent engineering program. Wozniak, however, was soon more involved in his personal projects than in his engineering courses. One of these was the now-famous "blue box"—an illegal device that allowed the user to make phone calls for free—which he built with the help of a friend, Steve Jobs, who was five years younger than Wozniak but shared his passion for electronics and computers.

Again low on funds, and with side interests occupying more and more of his attention, Wozniak decided to quit Berkeley after his junior year. "I didn't really drop out," he told Hubner. "I already knew everything they were teaching in computer classes. Suddenly, ROMs [read-only memories] and microprocessors had become very inexpensive. I realized that, for the first time in my life, I could afford a computer. I took a year off to work on it. My one year turned into 10." (Wozniak even-

tually returned to Berkeley and graduated in 1986 with a B.S. degree in engineering. Famous and wealthy by then, he studied under the pseudonym Rocky Clark "to avoid scaring the students and professors," as he once put it.)

In 1973 Wozniak accepted a position as an engineer at Hewlett-Packard (HP) in Cupertino, California, where he designed calculators. HP was a dream job for Wozniak: the company was unconventional and tried to foster creativity by allowing employees to vary their schedules to suit their needs, and formal business attire was not required. Provided that they fulfilled their responsibilities, employees could use the company facilities in their spare time for their own projects, a provision Wozniak capitalized on, spending many late nights developing his own computer games and graphics programs. (At HP he acquired his lasting nickname, Woz.)

Meanwhile, in 1975, Wozniak became involved with a group of young computer aficionados who met in Palo Alto, California, and called themselves the Homebrew Computer Club. "A friend told me that a club was starting—if he had said it was a microprocessor club, I would have been too shy to attend," Wozniak explained in an interview with Hamish Mackintosh for the *Guardian* (October 11, 2001, on-line). "But he said it was for people who had terminals. I had just designed and built a TV terminal, so I went to the first meeting. I saw there the excitement of affordable computers based on eight-bit microprocessors. I studied them and found that they were just like the minicomputers that I had taught myself to design and program while at high school. I was hooked and knew that I would have my dream computer capable of running a language, soon."

At one of the club meetings, Wozniak got his first look at an Altair, the first commercially available microprocessor-based minicomputer. Designed by Ed Roberts, the Altair was a rudimentary, low-cost (although out of reach for Wozniak) computer that hobbyists could order through the mail and assemble themselves. The Altair was an inspiration to Wozniak, who had been working on designs for a minicomputer since 1970, when he and a friend constructed a simplistic machine, without a microprocessor, using mainly discarded parts. (They named it the "Cream Soda Computer" as a tribute to the cream soda they drank as they worked.)

Wozniak began designing schematics for a new computer, which he often brought to the club to discuss with members. The Altair used an Intel 8080 computer chip, and the unassembled computer cost about $370, which was too expensive for him to use. Motorola's 6800 chip interested Wozniak—and was available to him at a discount through HP—but he decided to build his computer using the recently released Mostek 6502 chip, which was available for only $25. He also opted to use dynamic RAM (random access memory, a function of a group of memory chips that act as the computer's primary workspace), whereas nearly all other hobbyists were building computers using static RAM, which was easier to engineer but required four times as many computer chips. (Today dynamic RAM is far more common than static RAM.) To make his computer easier to use, he attached a keyboard to it, rather than a panel of switches like that of the Altair.

The Altair also used a computer programming language called Beginners All-purpose Symbolic Instruction Code (BASIC). Wozniak had never used BASIC—in fact, he had never taken a course on computer language—but he was convinced that this language was the key to building an efficient low-cost computer. He obtained a BASIC manual at HP, studied it thoroughly, and spent several weeks developing a version of BASIC to run on his computer.

Steve Jobs, who was then working as a video-game salesman for Atari, was impressed with Wozniak's computer. Jobs had heard that Ed Roberts was overwhelmed with orders for his Altair, and he believed that even more people would be interested in a computer they didn't have to assemble themselves. A born entrepreneur, Jobs suggested in 1976 to Wozniak, then 26, that they start their own computer company. Wozniak, content with his job at HP, was reluctant to leave. He first took his computer to his managers at HP, to see if they would be interested in producing it, but they didn't see a market for personal computers at the time, so Wozniak agreed to go into business with Jobs. "We never expected to make any money," Wozniak remarked in the 1983 *People* article. "But it was a chance to have a business for once in our lives." Jobs named the company Apple, in memory of a happy summer he had spent as an orchard worker in Oregon, as well as a tribute the Beatles' record label of the same name.

Working in the Palo Alto home of Jobs's parents, Wozniak perfected the design of what became the Apple I—a preassembled circuit board with on-line ROM to receive data from an external source and a built-in video interface. (It had no case, graphics, or sound. Wozniak used a TV monitor as a screen.) To finance the production of a prototype, Wozniak sold his HP programmable calculator and Jobs sold his Volkswagen van, netting about $1,500. In April 1976, they demonstrated the computer at the Homebrew Computer Club, and in May, they received their first order, from the Byte Shop in Mountain View, California, for 100 computers at $500 each. "When I heard the number $50,000 for our first sale, I couldn't believe it," Wozniak told *People* (February 14, 1994). Jobs used the order as leverage for credit, and he and Wozniak built 50 Apple I circuit boards in the garage. The computer store supplied the cabinets, transformers for power supply, and keyboards. (Customers had to supply their own monitors.) Two months later, the Apple I board was advertised for sale to hobbyists and electronics enthusiasts, at a price of $666.66. "I was into repeating dig-

its," Wozniak explained to Mackintosh, dispelling rumors that the figure had a superstitious significance. "Otherwise it might have been $650 or $667."

In January 1977 Mike Markkula, a venture capitalist, invested $250,000 in the new firm, became a partner, and set up a management team; Apple moved from Jobs's garage to a building in Cupertino. Wozniak had been working on improving the design of the Apple I, and he eventually figured out a way to replace the clumsy magnetic tape that all small computers had used for information storage with an easy-to-use floppy disk. The Apple II was unveiled at the West Coast Computer Faire in April 1977 and was met with enthusiasm. The new machine was housed in a professional-looking plastic case, with built-in power supply and circuitry allowing it to interface directly to a video monitor or TV set. It was also the first personal computer with color graphics. (It did not, however, have a graphical user interface, or GUI, the familiar screen with windows, menus, and icons that later became synonymous with personal computers. It still made use of the command-line feature of early PCs, requiring users to enter instructions in arcane computer language. Apple first used a GUI in the Lisa computer in 1983, and in the more successful 1984 model, the Macintosh.)

Wozniak later reflected on his achievement: "Designing a computer is the hardest work you could ever do in your life," he told Hubner. "It's so difficult, you've got to concentrate on so many hundreds of little things and how they interplay with each other. You've got to keep so many really tiny details in your head, it's like solving the hardest puzzle there ever was. It's very rare that individuals go out and build something that is so incredibly great. Usually it's done by corporations. Corporations invest the money, the time, the manpower. They end up owning the product, and you never hear of the people who developed it. One reason why the Apple myth is so strong is that we did it on our own."

The Apple II was the first personal computer to become popular with people who weren't computer hobbyists. It sold for about $1,300, and within three years generated sales of $139 million. Its technology set the standard at that time for personal computers, and it spawned the so-called PC revolution, in part by prompting IBM, in 1980, to "wake up," as one writer put it, and introduce its own PC. Apple, to raise the capital to expand and stay ahead of the competition, went public in December 1980, offering 4.6 million shares at $22 per share. Within minutes of going on sale, every share was purchased. The result was a windfall for Apple's co-founders: Wozniak found himself in possession of stock valued at about $100 million.

In early 1981, Wozniak, who had divorced his first wife, Alice Robertson, in 1980, became engaged to Candi Clark, a financial analyst at Apple and former Olympic kayaker. In February 1981, Wozniak was piloting his private plane, with Clark and two friends on board, when he crashed on takeoff. He suffered a concussion and had amnesia for five weeks afterward. After he recovered, he took a leave of absence from Apple. The company had by that time become a major corporation, employing more than 1,000 people. "[Apple] had become a big business, and I missed tinkering," he explained in the 1983 *People* article. "I just wanted to be an engineer."

While on leave, Wozniak founded Unuson (Unite us in song), a music-promotion company that organized festivals in San Bernardino, California, in 1982 and 1983. Both events drew a huge audience, but because of the high fees for such major headliners as David Bowie and Eddie Van Halen, Wozniak lost money. (In 1987, Wozniak sponsored the first joint U.S./U.S.S.R. stadium rock concert, featuring a high-tech satellite connection that allowed for live performances at one stadium to be projected on a big screen at the other—a pioneering use of technology to help establish cultural connections between the two Cold War rivals.)

Wozniak returned to Apple in late 1983 to work as an engineer, without executive responsibilities. But soon afterward, he realized that he had made a mistake. "I can't join the corporate world," he remarked to Hubner. "The one project here I could have worked on since the [Apple] II was the Macintosh, and even that was too bureaucratic." Wozniak resigned from active participation in the company in 1985, although he continued to receive a nominal salary as an "Apple fellow." The last computer to bear his mark was the Apple IIGS, which had *the Woz* printed on the front of the CPU cover of some models.

By the mid-1980s Apple had serious financial problems, which grew worse over the next decade. Jobs had made a critical mistake by not allowing other computer manufacturers to build machines that could run Apple's operating system software. Another company, Microsoft, had developed rival operating systems such as DOS and, later, Windows that ran on various systems, which increased competition in the hardware market and drove prices down. As a result, although customers were impressed by Apple's technology, many turned away from the company's expensive hardware and bought cheaper clones from such companies as IBM. Apple had also created its own incompatibilities by introducing the Apple III (which was plagued by snags), the Lisa (a high-tech model with a high price that was eventually withdrawn from the market), and the Macintosh (a less expensive Lisa spinoff that, after a rocky start, became a big success) without standardizing the operating software. (That meant that an Apple III user could not easily transfer a floppy-disk file to a Lisa or Macintosh computer, for example.)

Wozniak had started a new company, CL9 (short for Cloud Nine), to produce a remote-control device for home electronics. He found the work overly consuming and missed time with his family. Although the prototype was completed, Wozniak withdrew from the business around 1990 and passed the design of the device on to a friend. Since then, he has devoted much of his time to instructing schoolchildren and teachers to use Macintosh computers. He began by installing hundreds of Macs in elementary classrooms in the public-school systems of the San Francisco suburbs. He has donated laptops, helped schools develop computer networking plans, provided computer maintenance and support, and set up free America Online accounts for students.

In 1995 Wozniak created his own Web site at woz.org. The site includes a link to the Woz Cam, a live video feed from his office at Unuson, which has become a music foundation dedicated to educational pursuits. Through Unuson Wozniak has been conducting computer classes twice a week for teachers in the Los Gatos Unified School District, in California. His ultimate goal is "to put a Woz Cam in every classroom," as he told Steve Ditlea for the *Cybertimes* section of the *New York Times* (May 2, 1996, on-line).

After years focused on philanthropy, Wozniak re-entered the computer business in January 2002, when he announced that he was founding a new company, Wheels of Zeus (wOz). The company will develop wireless products using the latest global-positioning technology. "I'm doing it for the entrepreneurial thrill," he told Ann E. Marimow for the San Jose *Mercury News* (January 27, 2002).

Wozniak, a legendary figure in the history of computers, has received numerous awards for his achievements. President Ronald Reagan honored him and his Apple partner, Steve Jobs, with the National Medal of Technology in 1985. In 2000 the Computer Museum of American inducted him into the Computer Industry Hall of Fame, and the following year he received the Heinz Award, which confers $250,000 in honor of humanitarian work.

Wozniak lives in Los Gatos with his third wife, Suzanne Mulkern, a lawyer and mother of three, whom he married in 1990, after his divorce from Candi Clark. From his marriage to Clark, he has two sons, Jesse and Gary, and a daughter, Sara.
—A. I. C.

Suggested Reading: *Chicago Tribune* II p1+ Jan. 2, 1985, with photos, II p1+ May 25, 1986, with photos; *Guardian* (on-line) Oct. 11, 2001; San Jose *Mercury News* B p1 Jan. 27, 2002; *People* p89+ May 30, 1983, with photos, p61+ Feb. 14, 1994, with photos; *New York Times Cybertimes* (on-line), May 2, 1996, with photos; Kendall, Martha E. *Steve Wozniak: Inventor of the Apple Computer*, 1994

Yourdon, Ed

1944– Computer consultant; writer

Ed Yourdon, active in the computer industry since the 1960s, has written numerous books and technical manuals, as well as hundreds of articles that have appeared in major computer journals. His books include *Decline and Fall of the American Programmer* (1992), *Object-Oriented Systems Development: An Integrated Approach* (1994), *Mainstream Objects* (1995), *Rise and Resurrection of the American Programmer* (1996), *Death March: Managing "Mission Impossible" Projects* (1997), *Managing High-Intensity Internet Projects* (2001), and *Byte Wars: The Impact of September 11 on Information Technology* (2002). Much of his work has been translated into Japanese, Russian, Spanish, Portuguese, Dutch, French, German, Polish, and other languages. In *Crosstalk: The Journal of Defense Software Engineering* (December 1999) he was named one of the 10 people who have most influenced the software world.

Edward Nash Yourdon was born in 1944. He received a B.S. in applied mathematics from the Massachusetts Institute of Technology (MIT), in Cambridge. He did graduate work at MIT and at the Polytechnic Institute of New York—"an experience which convinced him that politics are far nastier in academia than in private industry," according to a biography posted on his official Web site. In 1964, as an undergraduate, Yourdon was hired by the Digital Equipment Corporation (DEC) to write the FORTRAN math library for the PDP-5 and the assembler for the PDP-8 minicomputer. He was next hired by General Electric (GE). In 1967, while working there, Yourdon published his first book, *Real-Time Systems Design*, a collection of technical papers that he had edited. His subsequent writings included several books on structured programming; a crime novel about computer hackers, *Silent Witness* (1982); a book for the general public exploring the impact of computers on society, *Nations at Risk* (1986); and two books co-written with Peter Coad about object-oriented analysis.

After working for a time at a consulting firm, Yourdon struck out on his own and founded his own company, Yourdon Inc., to provide educational, publishing, and consulting services in state-of-the-art software-engineering technology and project-management techniques. With Yourdon as CEO, the company grew over the next decade, eventually employing more than 150 people, with offices throughout North America and Europe. Yourdon Inc., was sold in 1986 and eventually became part of CGI, a French software company that is now part of IBM. Yourdon Press, the publishing arm of the company, is now part of Prentice Hall. The division has published more than 150 technical books, many of which are used as texts in university-level computer-science courses.

In *Decline and Fall of the American Programmer*, Yourdon argued that American programming groups are increasingly likely to fall behind their foreign competitors. "The American programmer is about to share the fate of the dodo bird," Yourdon wrote, as quoted by Michael Zielenziger for the *Toronto Star* (December 26, 1992). In India, for example, as Yourdon noted, a college-educated programmer received a salary of 15 to 20 percent that of an American programmer. He also observed that American software projects frequently contain far more errors than those of other countries. The book contained Yourdon's prescriptions for reversing the trend. James E. Gauntt Jr., in a review for the *Journal of Information Systems* (fall 1992) wrote that *Decline and Fall of the American Programmer* could be used "as a resource for anyone developing information systems or teaching information systems courses. [It contains] the most comprehensive reading list this reviewer has seen, and the individual chapters offer overviews of several topics that are not commonly discussed in information systems texts—but probably should be."

Over the next several years, Yourdon reversed his view of the future of American programming, which led him to write *Rise and Resurrection of the American Programmer*. Although Yourdon noted that the lower cost of software production in other countries was still a threat, he argued that it was limited to commodity jobs—well-defined projects that require big programming teams and don't vary tremendously from one project to the next. In the rapidly evolving software market, however, Americans, according to Yourdon, had a better likelihood of keeping on top of the trends, due to their familiarity with consumer technology, knowledge of the language, better access to customers, and insight into cultural preferences. Yourdon also pointed to the American ethos of "good enough" software, in which a certain number of defects are tolerated in a product in exchange for timely completion and a wider array of features. "There is much food for thought in this book, as in all of Yourdon's work," Paul Gray wrote for *Information Systems Management* (spring 1997). "The argument that he presents for his change of mind is compelling but could be made crisper by a suitable summary that reiterates and crystallizes his various ideas. Nonetheless, [*Rise and Resurrection*] is well written and easy to read."

Yourdon's next book, *Death March: Managing "Mission Impossible" Projects*, was a survival guide for software developers and project managers. Kathleen Melymuka, writing for *Computerworld* (March 31, 1997), called the book a "long, hard, funny and practical look at this all-too-common reality." Yourdon, in an interview with Melymuka, explained that there were four categories of "death-march" projects: the "Mission Impossible project," in which the risks involved are outweighed by strong morale and a high possibility of success; the "ugly project," in which success is likely but morale is low and workers suffer; the "kamikaze project," in which everyone knows the project will fail but feels good about the effort nonetheless; and the "suicide project," in which everyone knows the project will fail and feels miserable about it. To assess the degree of hopelessness in a death-march project, Yourdon joked about what he termed the "Inverse Dilbert Correlation"—"You look at how many Dilbert cartoons are on the bulletin board to get a sense of how jaded and cynical the project team has become."

In *Time Bomb 2000: What the Year 2000 Computer Crisis Means to You!*, which Yourdon co-wrote with his daughter Jennifer, he sounded the alarm about the possibility of a large-scale computer malfunction on the eve of the new millennium. Yourdon was one of many computer experts who feared that a shortcut commonly used by early computer programmers to write the date with two digits instead of four (98, for example, instead of 1998) would lead to widespread disaster in 2000 (which was often referred to as Y2K). The book became a *New York Times* best-seller. Numerous companies were created to ensure that large computer systems were Y2K-compatible, and many people began stocking up on canned food and bottled water in case of a crisis. Yourdon moved out of New York City, where he had lived for close to three decades, and resettled in Taos, New Mexico, believing that "there's enough of a chance that the disruptions might make major cities like New York totally unlivable for a year," as he told a reporter for the Charleston *Sunday Gazette Mail* (November 29, 1998). The predicted disaster failed to materialize. Yourdon afterwards remarked to Dennis Duggan for *Newsday* (January 4, 2000), "Boy, do I feel stupid . . . does anyone want to buy tuna fish?"

Yourdon's next book, *Managing High-Intensity Internet Projects*, treated such topics as business-process re-engineering and the development of an e-business strategy. In it Yourdon also discussed the negotiations and politics of Internet projects and risk-minimizing strategies. *Byte Wars: The Impact of September 11 on Information Technology*, Yourdon's most recent book, examined the effect that the terrorist attacks of September 11, 2001, have had on the Internet community, particularly in regards to security and privacy issues.

Yourdon is a frequent keynote speaker at major computer conferences around the world, and he has lectured at numerous colleges, including MIT and Harvard University, in Cambridge, Massachusetts; the University of California, Los Angeles; and the University of California, Berkeley. He has served on the board of directors of iGate, Mascot Systems, and the Requisite Corporation. In 1997 he was inducted into the Computer Hall of Fame. He now divides his time between New York and New Mexico. He and his wife have three grown children. According to the biography posted on his Web site, "He is kind to children, dogs, and little old ladies; and on good days, he firmly believes the Force is with him."—A. I. C.

Suggested Reading: *Computerworld* p77+ Mar. 31, 1997; Ed Yourdon's Home Page; *Information Systems Management* p83+ Spring 1997; *Journal of Information Systems* p182 Fall 1992; *Software Magazine* p68+ Jan. 1997; (Charleston) *Sunday Gazette Mail* B p7 Nov. 29, 1998; *Toronto Star* D p6 Dec. 26, 1992

Zimmermann, Philip R.

1954– Founder of PGP Inc.; privacy activist

As the creator of the computer program Pretty Good Privacy (PGP), Philip R. Zimmermann has become known as a pioneer in e-mail encryption software. During the 1980s Zimmermann realized that governments were becoming increasingly adept at spying on citizens through electronic means—telephone wiretaps, video surveillance, and hacking into personal e-mail and other computer documents—while at the same time becoming more secretive themselves through the development of sophisticated encryption software. He envisioned giving individual citizens the same sort of protection for their electronic documents that governments used, and as a result he developed PGP, which remains the world's most widely used software of its type. As Zimmermann noted in the PGP user's guide posted on his personal Web site, "There's nothing wrong with asserting your privacy. Privacy is as apple-pie as the Constitution."

An only child, Philip R. Zimmermann was born in Camden, New Jersey, in 1954 and was raised in Miami, Florida. His father was a cement-truck driver; his mother was a housewife. He was an avid fan of science fiction and enjoyed solving all sorts of puzzles and codes; when his friends sent away for secret decoders to unscramble the messages shown on a local television program, Zimmermann figured out the code entirely by himself. One friend refused to believe he had cracked the code on his own and wrote Zimmermann a long, coded message and dared him to solve it. "I brought it back in with the plain text the next day," Zimmermann told John Schwartz for the *Washington Post* (April 3, 1995). "He was amazed—but kids were pretty easily amazed."

When Zimmermann enrolled at Florida Atlantic University, in Boca Raton, he had intended to study physics and ultimately become an astronomer. Once at the university, however, he discovered computer science and switched his major. His early interest in decoding messages was further inspired when he stumbled across an article in *Scientific American* on a recent advancement in cryptology: the public key. As John Schwartz wrote, "It addressed one of the biggest problems with sending coded messages: The person you send the message to needs a 'key' to unscramble the message, which can weaken the sender's own security. But

Courtesy of Phil Zimmermann and Associates LLC

Philip R. Zimmermann

in public key encryption, every user has two keys: a 'private key' and a 'public key.' Anyone can use a recipient's public key to send a protected message to that person. But no one—not even the original sender—can unscramble the message. That's what the private key is for."

Upon receiving his bachelor's degree in 1978, Zimmermann began working as a computer-software engineer. He discovered that a number of companies were developing cryptology software that would allow businesses and wealthy individuals to maintain electronic security—something that only governments had been able to do up until that point. Zimmermann and his wife were dedicated members of the peace movement and participated in the Nuclear Weapons Freeze Campaign, a growing grassroots effort. He quickly realized that privacy protection cryptology could be useful to the cause. "The peace movement in the mid-'80s was in an adversarial relationship with the White House," Zimmermann explained to Marcia Savage for *CRN* (on-line), "and I felt grassroots political organizations needed a way to protect their data."

Zimmermann was once arrested at a test site in Nevada, for protesting nuclear-weapons testing, along with such notable figures as the actor Martin Sheen and the author Carl Sagan. "[The arrest] gave me my perspective that it is sometimes better to take direct action to change unjust laws, which helped guide me in developing PGP," he told Savage.

Zimmermann began work on PGP, or Pretty Good Privacy, in 1986. The U.S. National Security Agency had a virtual stranglehold on encryption technology, and over the next four years Zimmermann worked on the program in his spare time,

slowly writing it while gathering whatever information he could. In 1990 he decided to allow himself six months to finish the PGP program once and for all. With two young children to support (a son born in 1980 and a daughter born in 1985) and a mortgage to pay, the effort greatly strained his finances.

By the middle of 1991, however, Zimmermann's PGP was ready. He planned to upload the program and its source code—free of charge—onto the Internet. In June he sent version 1.0 to a pair of friends electronically. One of these friends posted it to Peacenet, which had links to various peace organizations around the world. The other uploaded it to a Usenet news group, which distributed source code. The Usenet posting was marked "U.S. only" at Zimmermann's request. Soon, however, PGP was being uploaded to computers all over the world.

When the federal government discovered Zimmermann's program, in 1993, they launched a full-scale criminal investigation into his activities, arguing that he had violated federal encryption export laws when he uploaded PGP to the Internet. Ironically, the fervent peace activist faced the threat of indictment for exporting munitions to foreign powers; encryption technology had been considered as such since World War II, when the first primitive computers were used to encrypt national secrets and break such enemy codes as the Enigma system, used by the Nazis. Zimmermann argued in his defense that he was merely trying to make cryptology available to the average man and woman before the government made it illegal to do so.

That possibility seemed likely: in 1991 a proposed Senate bill had included a measure that would force the manufacturers of secure communication systems to insert a special "trap door" in their encryption software to allow any government agency to read someone's private e-mail. The bill was defeated when members of the computer industry and civil libertarians balked at the idea, but that didn't prevent a similar bill from passing the Senate three years later. The 1994 Communications Assistance for Law Enforcement Act (CALEA) required phone companies to build remote wiretapping ports into their central switching stations, thereby allowing federal agents to monitor conversations right from their desks rather going through the effort of literally tapping into phone lines.

The Federal Bureau of Investigation (FBI) went even further when they disclosed plans to require phone companies to build into their infrastructure the ability to tap one percent of all the phone calls in the United States simultaneously, which would have precipitated a serious increase in the monitoring of ordinary citizens. The plan was defeated in Congress after a massive public outcry, but Zimmermann found the fact that the agency had even attempted to broaden its powers to such an extent frightening.

Perhaps most significantly, in 1993 the Clinton administration announced a sweeping new encryption initiative when it asked to place a government-designed encryption device, the Clipper chip, into every single secure communication product. The chip was loaded with its own "backdoor" key that allowed the government to listen in on a conversation at any time "when duly authorized by law." The Clipper chip controversy sparked another public outcry, and its suggested use was ultimately abandoned.

PGP spread through the computer world like wildfire, despite the fact that Zimmermann had no funding and no paid staff to aid him in its distribution. In January 1996 the Justice Department abruptly dropped its case against him without giving its reasons for doing so. Many observers suspected that the Justice Department had no alternative, as there was little legal precedent as to whether or not placing encryption software on the Internet actually violated export law. Others have suggested that the fact that it was an election year and that the statute of limitations on the matter was due to run out were the deciding factors.

In 1996 Zimmermann founded PGP Inc. and took up the posts of chairman and chief technology officer of the company. On June 26, 1996 he addressed the Senate Subcommittee on Science, Technology and Space, speaking of his fight against the United States government and the need for strong encryption software for the general public. As quoted on his personal Web site, he stated, "Advances in technology will not permit the maintenance of the status quo, as far as privacy is concerned. The status quo is unstable. If we do nothing, new technologies will give the government new automatic surveillance capabilities that [Soviet dictator Josef] Stalin could never have dreamed of. The only way to hold the line on privacy in the information age is strong cryptography. Cryptography strong enough to keep out major governments."

In December 1997 PGP was sold to Network Associates, and Zimmermann became a senior fellow at the new company. In 2000 the Clinton administration reversed itself and relaxed the rules governing the export of strong cryptography. Zimmermann remained with Network Associates until January 2001, when new senior management decided to reduce the amount of PGP source code they would publish. Disagreeing with this position, he resigned his post and turned his attention to new ventures. In early 2001 he became the chief cryptographer at Hush Communication, a provider of managed security solutions and encryption technology. He also joined the board of directors at Veridis, a provider of information-clearing technology. He next launched the OpenPGP Consortium, dedicated to making his protocol available as an industry-wide standard for other implementers of crypto products. (The consortium will also guide the future development of the OpenPGP standard.)

Zimmermann has vowed to continue to fight for better encryption in order to protect personal privacy. In an age of spy satellites and video surveillance, he knows he can make only a small contribution to these efforts. "I know how to fix e-mail. I can secure e-mail. I know how to encrypt data," he remarked to Savage. "I don't know how to solve the other problems, but I'll work on the ones I know how to solve."

Philip R. Zimmermann lives in the San Francisco Bay area of California. He has received numerous awards and accolades for his work. In 1995 he was named one of the 50 most influential people on the Internet by *Time*. That same year he won the Pioneer Award from the Electronic Frontier Foundation. In 1996 he won the *PC Week* IT Excellence Award, the Network Computing Well-Connected Award for best security product, and the Norbert Weiner Award from Computing Professionals for Social Responsibility. He is the recipient of the 1999 Louis Brandeis Award from Privacy International, and he has been a fellow of the Stanford Law School Center for Internet and Society. In 2000 *InfoWorld* named him one of the Top Ten Innovators in electronic business. In 2001 he was inducted into the *CRN* Industry Hall of Fame.—C. M.

Suggested Reading: *Business Wire* Feb. 20, 2001; *CRN* (on-line); *eWeek* (on-line) Aug. 19, 2002; *New York Times* D p6 Apr. 10, 1995, D p1+ Jan. 12, 1996; *Washington Post* A p1+ Apr. 3, 1995

Zuse, Konrad

June 22, 1910–Dec. 18, 1995 Creator of the first binary digital computer

Although his pioneering work with computers went largely unrecognized for years, Konrad Zuse was perhaps one of the most original inventors of his day. Without the benefit of exposure to other computer projects or designs, Zuse created the first binary digital computer in the world, the Z1, and the first fully functional, program-controlled, electromechanical digital computer in the world, the Z3. Because his work was performed under severe conditions in war- ravaged Germany, both of these machines were destroyed before they had received any degree of recognition. The one Zuse machine to survive the war, the Z4, which was a more sophisticated version of the Z3, is a testament to his talents as an inventor and to the computing concepts he engineered almost singlehandedly.

While others, such as John Atanasoff in the United States, were on the threshold of making significant contributions to computer technology, Zuse was already several steps ahead of them, building fully automatic calculating machines while the rest of the world relied on manual programming. His machines, though they lacked the advantage of the expensive vacuum tube technology, were nevertheless advanced for their time. Unfortunately, the German government offered little support for Zuse's efforts, and, while the United States took some interest in his work for a time, Zuse was not eager to communicate with the same Allied forces that had destroyed all of his previous work during World War II. Only years later did Zuse receive recognition for being one of the most inventive computer engineers of the 20th century.

Konrad Zuse was born on June 22, 1910 in Berlin-Wilmersdorf, Germany, and was raised in East Prussia, where his family moved shortly after his birth. His father worked as a postal administrator, and although his income was small, he wanted his son to have a good education. Zuse first attended school in Braunsberg, where his conservative education consisted of reading the classics and learning Latin. When he was a teenager, he decided to act on his childhood dreams of designing great cities and moon rockets, and at the age of 18 he began studying architecture with the intention of becoming a designer. After he enrolled at the University of Berlin's Technische Hochschule (Technical Institute), Zuse found himself drawn to the tedious and time-consuming process of solving equations, which is often required of civil engineers. As a result, Zuse decided to pursue engineering rather than architectural design.

While in school, Zuse was faced with learning the theory of static indeterminate structures, which was based on a part of algebra known as linear equations and was necessary for determining the potential behavior of the structures of buildings. The process of solving the equations turned out to be highly impractical given the limitations of existing calculators. For example, with the average calculator capable of doing no more than six equations with six unknowns, the calculations required to engineer the design of a large roof could take months. It was during this time that Zuse began to formulate ways in which calculations could be made more efficiently. In particular, he began to make plans for a mechanical calculator that would prove to be significantly faster than any of its predecessors.

In 1935 Zuse graduated from the Technische Hochschule with a degree in civil engineering, and he began working as an engineer and designer in the aircraft industry, taking a position as a stress analyst with the Henschel aircraft factory in Berlin. His job entailed solving long calculations necessary in the designing of aircraft and, "out of laziness," his thoughts turned to creating a machine to facilitate this process. By 1936, he was ready to begin building his own calculating machine, and he decided to build it based on the binary system, a notion that would not occur to John Atanasoff until a year later. Zuse chose the binary system because of his desire for a speedy computer, and because he felt the electromagnetic relay was a good tool for expressing a binary digit. In a binary numbering system, data is represented as either a one or a zero. Although Zuse's use of the system would mark a profound change from the past, binary language

was far from an original concept. Gottfried Wilhelm von Leibniz had written about the use of binary systems in making calculations as early as 1680, and Zuse was familiar with the earlier man's writings, going so far as to title one of his reports on his first computer "Hommage to Leibniz." By the late 20th century, the influence of such men as Leibniz and Zuse was evident in the makeup of computer systems throughout the world, all of which use binary mathematics for calculations.

Zuse's initial quest was to build a machine that possessed both a calculator and a mechanical keyboard, which would solve the problem of recording and transferring intermediate results from calculations. Zuse's idea was essentially a recreation of the system first envisioned by the British inventor Charles Babbage during the 1820s and 1830s, although Zuse did not learn of Babbage until 1939. In fact, Zuse's work is considered by some to be all the more impressive because Zuse had not been exposed to the ideas of others, unlike his contemporary Howard Aiken, for example, an American computer scientist who was well acquainted with Babbage's work. Zuse was not able to copy or attempt to improve on the inventions of Babbage or others, because Zuse was simply unaware of the existence of computing machines similar to the one he intended to build himself. Zuse was largely untrained and unskilled as a computer designer, although he did possess talent for mechanics and as a draftsman. He was also therefore unburdened by the potential limitations imposed by conventional ideas on the subject, and later in life he acknowledged his belief that his lack of education in electrical engineering had been a blessing. "Thus—unprejudiced—I could go new ways," he said (*The Computer Pioneers*, 1986).

Zuse's first dilemma—that of keeping track of the results of each intermediate calculation—was solved through a step by step process. First, he designed a series of special forms that contained preprinted boxes in which the numbers from the calculations could be written. Boxes that were horizontally adjacent would have their contents multiplied together, while those vertically adjacent would have their contents added. Zuse next began to figure out a way in which a device, which would possess a mechanical arm capable of moving over the surface of a table, could be used to read numbers from and write numbers into the various boxes in his design, using punched cards to represent the sums involved. In this plan, the arithmetic would be performed by a mechanical calculator, while the arm would be moved via a mechanism that would follow a series of coded instructions for the series of calculations to be performed.

After formulating this plan, Zuse came to the realization that there was no longer a need for the special forms at all, as they were essentially nothing more than a series of boxes acting like a computer memory. In order for his machine to be capable of doing all types of equations, Zuse envisioned a calculating unit that had a memory; a control unit that would govern the movement of numbers and instructions; a device that could read data and instructions from the punched cards; and input and output units, in order give instructions to the computer and display the results. Thus, by 1934, Zuse had come to the conclusion that his automatic calculating machine required only a few basic components, the same components that would prove to essential to computers for years to come.

Zuse soon began to build his machine, which he named the V1, with the V standing for *Versuchsmodell* (or Experimental Model). It was later renamed the Z1 so as to avoid confusion with the German rocket bombs the V1 and V2. The computer was constructed in a makeshift workshop Zuse set up in a corner of his parents' living room in their home in Berlin. The machine's memory system consisted of a metal plate that, similar to Babbage's idea, stored numbers, using the position of pins in slots to represent single digits. One side of the plate represented the number one and the other side of the plate represented zero, thereby creating the binary system. A second plate, which was positioned against the first plate, could sense the placement of the pins, and could therefore "read" the numbers. A third plate, which was positioned perpendicular to the first two plates, was responsible for the reading and writing functions. This memory system was capable of holding 16 binary digits, which was the equivalent of between four and five decimal digits.

Creating the computer's arithmetic unit, or the portion of the machine used to compute calculations, was a more difficult task for Zuse. With the binary system, multiplication was a simple process. What was challenging however, was expressing other arithmetic functions in binary form so that the computer could understand them. Zuse began to work out a set of notations in order to describe arithmetic functions in terms that would be relevant to a binary device. Thus, everything had to be designed so that answers to calculations could be given as either yes or no, on or off, 1 or 0. In the end, the results of machine's calculations were expressed in statements, consisting of the words *and*, *or*, and *not*. Zuse decided to feed instructions to his computer through the use of strips of old movie film, an inexpensive material that could be perforated, or hole-punched, and thereby "read." In 1938, he connected the arithmetic unit to the memory, and the Z1 was born.

The Z1 measured 2 meters by 1.5 meters as was a completely mechanical machine, with 1,000 thin, slotted plates. The arithmetic unit did not work consistently however, and the parts did not allow for computations that took longer than a few minutes. Nevertheless, Zuse applied for a patent claim with the U.S. Patent Office in 1938, but was refused on grounds that he was not precise enough in describing the nature of his computer's hardware. Zuse would later claim that he was denied a patent for the Z1 was because the patent authorities believed incorrectly that his machine was derived directly from the work of Charles Babbage.

Before the Z1 was completed, Zuse had already begun planning an improved version, the Z2, and after speaking with Helmut Schreyer on the benefits of using electricity in a computational device, Zuse decided to make his next computer an electromechanical machine. Schreyer, a close friend of Zuse's, was working as an engineer, and he suggested that Zuse use vacuum tubes in his new machine—an idea that, according to Zuse, seemed quite fantastic at the time. "At first I thought it was one of his student pranks. . . . But after thinking about it, we decided that his idea was definitely worth a try. . . . [Vacuum tubes] could switch a million times faster than elements burdened with mechanical and inductive inertia" (*Computer Pioneers*, 1995).

Zuse and Schreyer hoped to fill the new computer with 2,000 tubes, a number that would seem comparatively small only a few years later. In a later speech, Zuse related the reaction their plan received: "We cautiously told some friends about the possibilities. The reaction was anything from extremely skeptical to spontaneously enthusiastic. Interestingly enough, most criticism came from Schreyer's colleagues, who worked with tubes virtually all the time. They were doubtful that an apparatus with 2,000 tubes would work reliably" (*Computer Pioneers*, 1995). Zuse and his colleagues would later learn of the ENIAC computer, which held nearly 18,000 vacuum tubes, and as he recalled, "We could only shake our heads. What on earth were all the tubes for?" (*Computer Pioneers*, 1995).

Zuse's plans were temporarily put on hold when World War II broke out and he was drafted into military service. Unlike other countries such as the United States and Great Britain, where scientists were utilized in developing technology to aid in the war effort, in Germany Zuse was made into a standard soldier. In fact, Zuse's talents as an inventor garnered absolutely no support from the German government. A calculator maker, who had helped finance Zuse's initial forays into computing, approached Zuse's superior officer to inquire whether Zuse might be spared from his military duties in order to build a machine of great importance. This machine, he and Zuse said, would be of assistance to the German air force, because it would greatly speed up the calculations required for aircraft design. The officer refused to listen to the arguments of the calculator manufacturer, and replied simply that he considered the German air force infallible and in no need of further assistance. When told that the building of such a machine would be a two year project, the officer asked, "And just how long do you think it will take us to win the war?" (*Computer Pioneers*, 1995). Zuse was not released from the military until six months later, and he was then assigned to an engineering project with the Henschel aircraft factory.

While Zuse was away, Schreyer continued to perform research aimed at developing electric counterparts to Zuse's Z1 equipment, attempting to duplicate its memory system. After he was released from the army, Zuse once again immersed himself in finishing the construction of the Z2, using his own money to purchase the necessary parts, which were expensive during the war years. Vacuum tubes in particular were hard to come by, and thus the idea of using them was abandoned. However, rather than use the mechanical parts that had comprised the Z1's arithmetic unit, Zuse decided to use secondhand telephone relays. The relays had several advantages over the mechanical parts, allowing the arithmetic unit to carry and borrow numbers when performing subtraction, and since they could turn on and off hundreds of times per minute, they also sped up the computer's operations.

Zuse and Schreyer quickly went to work on getting the relay-based arithmetic and control units up and running, before putting them together with the mechanical memory. Once this was done, Zuse demonstrated his machine at the Deutsche Versuchanstalt für Luftfahrt (German Aeronautical Research Institute), or DVL. Although the Z2 performed well for the demonstration, problems with the relays made it largely unreliable. Nevertheless, the DVL expressed an interest in the machine, due to their difficulties in overcoming the problem of flutter, a shivering of aircraft wings. The DVL felt the computer could possibly speed up the extensive calculations required in order to solve the problem, and therefore the organization decided to fund the design and construction of a new model, the Z3. As a result of this decision, Zuse became the only German allowed to develop computers during the war, and he led a largely isolated life, with few of his friends or colleagues understanding the need or intended goals behind his work.

While Zuse's place of employment, the Henschel aircraft factory, was supportive of his work, they were seeking a special purpose computer to solve their immediate problem of flutter. Although the young inventor's true goal was to design a computer with broader applications, he was encouraged by the opportunity and resolved to build a computer that would not only solve wing flutter equations but also a wide variety of other problems. The factory set up a 15 man staff for the building of the machine, which was completed in 1941. The Z3, finished a full two years before work on the ENIAC began in the United States, was the first fully functional, programmable, general-purpose digital computer. The machine, which like its two predecessors was built in Zuse's parents' living room, contained 2,600 relays, 1,800 of which were dedicated to memory, 600 to the arithmetic unit, and the remaining 200 to the control of the input and output devices. It could perform floating-point arithmetic, and was capable of multiplying, dividing, or extracting a square root in three seconds. (By comparison, it took six seconds for Howard Aiken's Mark I computer to perform multiplication.) In addition, it was an electromechanical machine and possessed all of the conventional characteristics of a computer, including a memory system and the ability to be programmed. Zuse also designed an advanced programming notation for the machine, using the symbols $\geq$ to indicate *greater than or equal to*, and $\leq$ to indicate *less than or equal to*.

The Z3 was completed at roughly the same time as John Atanasoff's ABC, which is considered by many to be the first American computer, and like the Z3 was both automatic and programmable. In many ways, however, the Z3 was technologically superior to the ABC. Unlike the Z3, the ABC was not fully functional, was limited in the types of calculations it could do, and was a more manual machine. Almost every step of the ABC's operation had to be controlled by a human technician, who had to press buttons and turn knobs as well as insert and extract punched cards. The Z3, on the other hand, was a far more intricate machine, with a sophisticated push-button control panel that allowed the user to carry out operations by simply lifting a finger. The Z3 could convert decimal numbers into binary with a single keystroke, and with another stroke turn them back again. The Z3 therefore represented a major turning point in technology, for it was the first computer to automatically solve equations.

Unfortunately for Zuse, few individuals had the chance to view the Z3 before it was completely destroyed in an Allied air raid that struck the Zuses' apartment in 1944. By 1943 he had built two more special-purpose computers for the Henschel aircraft factory, the S1 and S2, that were used in the making of glider bombs, the most feared aerial weapons the Germans possessed. However, after seeing firsthand in his Z3 the power of a general purpose computer, Zuse began work on the Z4. Progress was slow in the making, as the war was drawing to a close and Allied bombing was growing more intense. Zuse had to frequently stop his work and move his equipment to a new location before the Z4 was completed, in 1945. The Z4 relied more extensively on relays than the Z3 had, and had more capacity, going from 22 to 32 binary digits. Its memory was larger as well, with the ability to store 512 numbers, making it eight times the size of that of the Z3.

Fearing impending bombing, in early 1945 Zuse decided to transport his machine via wagon to the town of Gottingen. He was soon ordered by the German government to take the Z4 into underground factories near Northheim, but after visiting there and seeing the concentration camps for the first time, Zuse decided he could not bring his machine there. He still feared it would be destroyed by the advancing Allied forces however, and decided to move it once again, to a small Alpine village called Hinterstein, where he hid the Z4 in a barn. It was a move that would ultimately have a detrimental effect on the young inventor's career; Gottingen, a town where Zuse's work would likely have won attention, was left undamaged by the war, and in the obscure locale of Hinterstein, his research was ignored outside of Germany until many years after the war.

After the fall of the Third Reich, Zuse remained in a small house in Hinterstein, alone, with his computer hidden in the cellar. Soon rumors began to circulate about the nature of Zuse's device. Local villagers feared the machine would explode, killing them all, and in a panic sought help from the Allies. Two intelligence officers were sent out to inspect the machine and interview Zuse. It might have been the ideal opportunity for Zuse to garner outside attention for his work, and possibly receive the recognition he deserved. Because the Allies bombed his first computers, however, and because he supported the German war efforts so staunchly, Zuse did not cooperate with the investigators. Furthermore, the Allies, mistakenly assuming the Z4 was no more than a simple machine, dismissed Zuse's work with the comment, "It's only a calculator . . . it's of no interest to us" (*Breakthrough to the Computer Age*, 1982).

Leaving Hinterstein, Zuse settled in another Alpine village, Hopferau, where he remained for three years. Here Zuse began to turn his thoughts toward computer programming and he developed a prototype programming language called Plankalkul. He believed that this language could be utilized for more than mathematical problems enabling a computer to play chess, for instance. However, no one displayed any interest in Zuse's language, and he abandoned the project.

The Z4 eventually went on to perform routine work for the Federal Technical Institute at Zurich in 1950, bringing long-awaited attention to Zuse and his prewar work. As a result Zuse established his own company, Zuse KG, which developed and marketed computers, one of the first being the Z5. Subsequent models, including fully electronic computers, were constructed by the company until the mid-1950s. Zuse eventually found himself in financial difficulty; he could not raise sufficient capital to support the company's research and development costs. In the early 1960s, his company was taken over by the Siemens Company, which remained a successful European computing firm throughout the later part of the century. After the takeover, Zuse continued to pursue theoretical research and began writing about his earlier computer work. Nearly 40 years after he first built the Z1, which like the Z3 was destroyed in the war, Zuse managed to recreate his machine from memory. He remained a consultant to the Siemens Company for many years after his retirement, but spent the majority of his time pursuing his lifelong hobby of painting, signing many of his works with the pseudonym of "Kone See." Konrad Zuse died from a heart attack on December 18, 1995 at age 85, at his home, near Fulda, Germany.

Konrad Zuse could, in the opinion of many, be correctly credited as the father of the modern computer. His work on the Z1 and Z3 was particularly significant in that he built highly advanced machines virtually on his own, with little outside influence. Many in the industry have speculated that had he been given access to more advanced parts, such as vacuum tubes, Zuse would have constructed the world's first programmable, high-speed, all-electronic computer, years before any similar work was completed in the U.S. Scholars have also been left to consider the frightening thought of how different World War II might have been had the German military used Zuse's talents more thoroughly. A man of talent and ingenuity, Konrad Zuse developed computing devices that were significantly more advanced than those of his contemporaries, and he was clearly one of the most gifted inventors of the 20th century.

Because Zuse's work never received the recognition it deserved, his early machines had little impact on the technological revolution that occurred in the U.S. and Britain. He did, however, receive accolades in his native Germany, including a wealth of honorary degrees from institutions of higher learning. By the 1970s, his writings had been translated into English, and he began to receive proper acknowledgment from around the world, often earning the title of "inventor of the computer." When asked about this distinction, Zuse replied, "It took many inventors besides me to develop the computer as we know it nowadays. I wish the following generation all the best for their work with the computer. May this instrument help you solving the problems which we old folks have left behind" (*RT-Distribution* on-line).—D. B.

Suggested Reading: *Washington Post* D p5 Dec. 20, 1995; Wulforst, Harry. *Breakthrough to the Computer Age*, 1982; Greene, Laura. *Computer Pioneers*, 1985; Lee, J. A. N., ed. *International Biographical Dictionary of Computer Pioneers*, 1995

Zworykin, Vladimir Kosma

July 30, 1889–July 29,1982 Inventor of the cathode-ray tube

A Russian physicist who immigrated to America after World War I, Vladimir Kosma Zworykin brought with him ideas for technology that would be instrumental in the development of television over the course of the next 40 years. Using concepts born under the tutelage of the famed physicist Boris von Rosing, Zworykin worked toward developing ways in which sound waves could be utilized for images. His work on television, using iconoscopes and then kinescopes, paved the way for modern color television; it made television sets easier and more practical to build and operate and garnered him with the label of "father of television." His efforts to create images on a screen by use of light waves and electronic scanning were also instrumental in the evolution of computer monitors. In this respect, Zworykin was truly an elemental part of the computer age, and he can be credited with having a significant impact on the industry as it further developed his initial tube technology.

Vladimir Kosma Zworykin was born to Kosma and Elaine Zworykin in Mourom, Russia, 200 miles east of Moscow, on July 30, 1889. He attended the Mourom Gymnasium, and at the age of nine, began to spend summers as an apprentice aboard the boats his father ran on the Oka River. The water held little interest for the young Zworykin, however, and he spent most of his time during those summers repairing electrical equipment on the boats. After graduating from Mourom in 1906, Zworykin left to attend the St. Petersburg Institute of Technology. He received his degree in electrical engineering from St. Petersburg in 1912 but stayed on at the Institute a short while afterwards in order to perform research work under Professor Boris von Rosing, who was attempting to transmit pictures by wire. Among the pair's work was an experimentation with a primitive version of a cathode-ray tube, which had been developed in Germany by Karl Ferdinand Braun.

With an interest in theoretical physics, Zworykin made his way to Paris, where he enrolled at the Collège de France in 1912. He stayed at the university for two years, performing x-ray experiments under the guidance of the famous physicist Professor Paul Langevin. With the onset of World War I, Zworykin returned to Russia to serve in the Russian Army Signal Corps as a radio officer. After the armistice, he traveled the world twice before settling on America as his new home. He took a job as a bookkeeper for the financial agent of the Russian Embassy upon his arrival in 1919, but by 1920 was invited by Westinghouse Electric and Manufacturing Company to come and work for the company on the development of radio tubes and photoelectric cells. When he wasn't working at his new house of employment, Zworykin studied for his Ph.D., which he received from the University of Pittsburgh in 1926. Reflecting on his work at Westinghouse, his dissertation was titled "The Study of Photoelectric Cells and Their Improvement", but his true passion remained in television. In 1923 he reproduced an image from a screen by dividing it into a large number of insulated photoelectric cells, which held an electrical charge proportionate to the light that fell on them. An electric beam that was scanning the screen then discharged the cells, giving them an electrical signal. Zworykin filed a patent application for his invention, his first television camera tube, which he called an iconoscope. In 1924 he demonstrated his work for the executives at Westinghouse and, as he told *American Magazine* (August 1949) felt "terribly excited and proud" but was told several days later that it would be better for the company if he would spend his time "on something a little more useful."

Zworykin's next project was the kinescope, a cathode-ray tube receiver in which a beam of electrons "paints" the picture it receives on a flat-screen surface. The cathode-ray tube could produce focused spots on its screen by using electric and magnetic fields. When the beam scanned the screen the intensity of the spot varied in conjunction with the electrical signal and could therefore reproduce the images from his first invention. In an interview with Mark Heyer and Al Pinsky for the *RCA Engineers Collection* (July 4, 1975) Zworykin explained the process and origin of the kinescope: "We used a cathode-ray tube and a fluorescent screen with the respondent amplitude of the cathode-ray tube intensity in the light, and deflected the beam magnetically or electrostatically by the signals we received from an iconoscope through the proper amplifier. This type of combination of the iconoscope and receiving tube we called *Kinescope*, from two Greek words. *Kine* is movement and *scope* is target." The result of Zworykin's new creation was a television transmitting and receiving system. Zworykin obtained a patent for this invention in 1924, demonstrating it at a convention of radio engineers on November 18, 1929. The invention served as the first all-electronic television system, and it would later render the previous television process (which used a scanning disk) obsolete.

That same year, Zworykin left Westinghouse and joined the Radio Corporation of America (RCA) in Camden, New Jersey. Serving as director of the company's Electronic Research Laboratory, Zworykin sought to improve on his television system. He filed his first color television patent later that year but also spent time working on secondary emission multipliers and image tubes, including the Image Orthican Tube. In 1930 Zworykin began work on an infrared image tube, which converts infrared rays into visible light allowing people to have clear vision in the dark. This invention, which provided the technology for the "Sniperscope" and "Snooperscope," proved valuable during World War II, when these two instruments were used by snipers, drivers, and reconnaissance patrols.

Zworykin would continue to work on a wide variety of inventions over the next decade. In later interviews, Zworykin would say that he spent almost 10 years trying to reproduce the human eye electronically in the form of the iconoscope; in 1933 he invented one of the earlier forms of what became known as the "electric eye." In 1934 he created plans for an airborne television system for use in guiding radio-controlled flying torpedoes and also served as senior author on a book entitled *Photocells and Their Application*.

By 1937 Zworykin began to act on his long-founded belief that, as he once said, "a scientist always is tempted to find other uses for a new discovery" (*Current Biography Yearbook*, 1949), and he applied his television tube to microscopy, a move that ultimately resulted in the invention of the electron microscope. Zworykin realized that visible light, which consists of a long wavelength, made it impossible to magnify anything more than

2,500 times life size, and that details had to be larger than one-half the wavelength to be visible under magnification. Instead of using light, Zworykin and his scientists decided to use a wavelength focused by electromagnetic fields instead of glass lenses, which was 100,000 times shorter than a visible light wavelength. This electron microscope, which originally occupied the space of two rooms, was continually redesigned and improved, so that by 1942 it was condensed into a portable 16-inch model, which, only seven years later, could magnify objects up to 200,000 times its size.

With the onset of World War II, Zworykin became a member of the scientific advisory board to Air Force Commanding General H. H. Arnold and the Ordinance advisory committee on guided missiles. He also directed research in areas such as aircraft gunnery control, television guided missiles, storage tubes, and his previously discovered infrared image tubes for Sniperscopes and Snooperscopes. During this time, he also worked with noted scientist John von Neumann on a weather control project. The two came to the conclusion that forecasting and future control of the weather could be accomplished through the development of a calculating machine, which could quickly and accurately analyze information it was given. In January 1946 Zworykin and von Neumann presented their plans for such a calculator, capable of computing 100,000 equations a minute and of doing a multiplication problem in 11 millionths of a second. The machine was also able to perform operations in 400 stages, far exceeding any other calculator of the day, the most advanced of which could perform with a memory of 12 stages.

Zworykin worked on several other inventions during the mid-1940s, including a clock without any moving parts and an electronic diffraction camera. Zworykin also helped create an electronic reading device for the blind, which consisted of a stylus, which, when passed over the text of a printed page, reflected the shape of each letter to a phototube, which then returned it as a distinctive sound. In addition Zworykin continued in his television research and developed the idea for reversible television receivers for accurate and instantaneous public-opinion polls.

In May 1947 Zworykin and RCA demonstrated color television, a concept that was continually improved upon and eventually made its way on to the commercial market, a move that would revolutionize the industry. When then-president of RCA David Sarnoff asked him how much it would cost to perfect his system in 1929, Zworykin gave him the then-unheard-of sum of $100,000. By the end of a 20-year devotion to the project, RCA had spent more than $50 million on the development of television. Zworykin faced great opposition to the extensive work he put into his television research, and many questioned the purpose of such a device. Zworykin responded with an unintentional prediction, saying to his detractors, "You can see the opposite side of the moon if someone sends a rocket there with a television camera." Zworykin's statement of defense would prove to be true 30 years later as millions watched the first man land on the moon from the comfort of their homes on color television.

In 1954 Zworykin retired from RCA and took a position as the director of the Medical Electronics Center of the Rockefeller Institute for Medical Research, a post he retained until 1962. He continued in his role as consultant to RCA until 1978, but most of his later research focused on medical electronics, a move which he reasoned to Heyer and Pinsky was because "I don't play golf; therefore I have to do something."

Over the decades, Zworykin would come to realize that his inventions had their negative side, and in his interview with Heyer and Pinsky, he spoke out about the dangerous effects of commercial, ratings driven television programming. "They put in a lot of broadcasted violence and murder . . . Ratings systems are not good for the population, the younger population in general. It also makes us look bad abroad," he said. "I feel very guilty for [sending such bad programming] even indirectly, having a part in it."

Even as he neared the age of 86, Zworykin kept one eye toward future technology and made another prediction similar to his prophecy for moon exploration in the 1930s. When speaking to Heyer and Pinsky about the future of universal television and video, he spoke of "cheap discs" which "will be done by anybody who wants to record like they record music now." Zworykin described a visual library that could be used for a variety of educational and recreational purposes. This universal system, spoken of in 1975, was visualized by Zworykin several years before the onset of home VCRs and almost two decades before the explosive popularity of CD-ROMs. Zworykin died on July 29, 1982 in Princeton, New Jersey.
—D. B.

Suggested Reading: *American Magazine* Aug. 1949; *Current Biography Yearbook* p654+ 1949; *National Inventors Hall of Fame* (on-line); *RCA Engineers Collection* (on-line) July 4, 1975; *American Men and Women of Science*, vol 7, 1986

Leaders of the Information Age Timeline

1300–1310

• Ramon Llull becomes the first person to create a mechanical device for proving logical theorems.

1450–1460

• Johannes Gutenberg invents the movable-type printing press.

1600–1610

• Galileo Galilei invents the telescope.

• Johannes Kepler publishes his first two laws of planetary motion.

1610–1620

• John Napier invents logarithms and a calculating device called Napier's rods.

• Henry Briggs collaborates with Napier and publishes new logarithm tables.

1620–1630

• Wilhelm Schickard designs an early calculating device based on Napier's rods.

• William Oughtred invents a slide rule calculator.

1640–1650

• Blaise Pascal invents a rotary-type adding machine called the Pascaline.

1660–1670

• Samuel Morland invents several mechanical adding machines.

1670–1680

• René Grillet invents a mechanical adding machine.

• Gottfried Leibniz creates a cylindrical calculating device called the Stepped Reckoner.

1700-1710

• Pierre Jacquet-Droz builds mechanical androids.

1710–1720

• Jacob Leupold adapts Leibniz's design and creates a circular calculator.

1770–1780

• Charles Stanhope invents the Stanhope Demonstrator, an early logic machine.

1790–1800

• Wolfgang von Kempelen creates the first machine to produce speech sounds, words, and sentences.

1820–1830

• Georg Simon Ohm postulates one of the fundamental laws of electricity, known as Ohm's Law.

• Charles Thomas de Colmar creates the Arithmometer, the first commercially successful calculator.

• Charles Babbage begins developing the Difference Engine, a mechanical calculating device.

1830–1840

• Charles Babbage begins work on his Analytical Engine, an early computational machine.

• Augusta Ada Lovelace collaborates with Charles Babbage on programming the Analytical Engine.

• Louis Jacques Daguerre discovers early photographic processes and invents the daguerreotype.

• Samuel Morse creates the first successful electric telegraph network.

1840–1850

• Mathew Brady makes advances in photography.

1850–1860

• George Boole combines logical reasoning and mathematics to form Boolean Algebra.

• D. D. Parmalee is awarded the first U.S. patent for a key-driven adding machine.

• Georg Scheutz unveils the first commercially available, fully operational Difference Engine.

• Giovanni Caselli invents the pantelegraph, precursor to the modern fax machine.

1870–1880

• Frank Stephen Baldwin is awarded a U.S. patent for the earliest American-made calculator.

• Willgodt Odhner invents a pinwheel-based mechanical calculator.

• Jean-Maurice-Émile Baudot creates a telegraph code replacing Morse code as the standard.

• Alexander Graham Bell develops the first telephone system.

• Emile Berliner improves telephone communication by inventing a microphone transmitter.

• George Barnard Grant builds a working calculator based on Charles Babbage's machines.

• William Stanley Jevons invents an early logic machine, called the Logical Abacus.

• Thomas Edison improves telegraphy and the telephone, invents the phonograph, and pioneers electric lighting.

• Ramon Verea receives a patent for the first calculator that can multiply and divide directly.

1880–1890

• Dorr E. Felt introduces his key-driven mechanical calculator, called the comptometer.

• William S. Burroughs builds the first mechanical adding machines with printing capabilities.

• Albert Blake Dick invents the mimeograph with the help of Thomas Edison.

• George Eastman makes advances in photographic technology.

• Heinrich Hertz demonstrates the existence of electromagnetic waves.

• Allan Marquand conceives of an electrically powered logic machine.

• John H. Patterson and his brother Frank establish the National Cash Register Company.

• Oberlin Smith publishes new ideas about magnetic storage.

• Otto Steigler builds an automated version of Gottfried Leibniz's machine.

• Nikola Tesla pioneers alternating current (AC) and invents a high-frequency transformer called a Tesla coil.

• Herman Hollerith invents an electromechanical statistical tabulating device that uses punched cards.

1890–1900

• Léon Bollée creates an early calculating machine called the calculer that can multiply directly.

• John K. Gore builds an improved punched-card sorter.

• Guglielmo Marconi invents the wireless telegraph.

• Charles P. Steinmetz improves the efficiency of alternating-current (AC) systems.

1900–1910

• Valdemar Poulsen demonstrates the Telegraphone, a magnetic sound-recording device.

• Vilhelm Bjerknes pioneers weather forecasting using numerical analysis.

• Joseph E. Boyer becomes the third president of the American Arithmometer Company, which he renames the Burroughs Adding Machine Company.

• John Ambrose Fleming invents a two-electrode radio rectifier known as the thermionic valve or Fleming valve.

• Marie Curie receives the Nobel Prize for pioneering work in radioactivity.

• Leonardo Torres y Quevedo invents a radio-controlled machine called the Telekino.

• Lee de Forest creates the Audion triode vacuum tube.

• George W. Fairchild founds the International Time Recording Company, which later becomes part of the Computing-Tabulating-Recording Company (C-T-R).

• Percy Ludgate publishes a design for an analytical engine similar to that of Charles Babbage.

• Elmer Ambrose Sperry pioneers gyroscopic technology.

• Albert Einstein publishes discoveries on Brownian motion, the photoelectric effect, and the special theory of relativity.

• Ernst F. W. Alexanderson improves radio communication with a high-frequency alternator.

1910–1920

• Charles Ranlett Flint merges companies to form C-T-R, which later becomes International Business Machines (IBM).

• W. H. Eccles and F. W. Jordan design the first electronic flip-flop circuit, known as the Eccles-Jordan trigger circuit.

• Thomas J. Watson Sr. becomes general manager of C-T-R, which he later renames IBM.

• William F. Friedman pioneers American cryptology.

• Irving Langmuir invents the gas-filled light bulb and a high-vacuum radio tube.

• Bertrand Russell and Alfred North Whitehead publish the *Principia Mathematica*.

• Edwin H. Armstrong improves wireless radio communication with the regenerative circuit.

• Leonardo Torres y Quevedo invents a chess-playing analog computer and conceives of an electromechanical computer.

1920–1930

• Philo Taylor Farnsworth develops the first television.

• Ernst F. W. Alexanderson demonstrates the first transatlantic facsimile and the first home television receiver.

• David Sarnoff becomes general manager of RCA, creates the first sports broadcast, and founds the NBC radio network.

• Edwin H. Armstrong develops the frequency modulation (FM) radio broadcasting system.

• Vannevar Bush builds the differential analyzer at the Massachusetts Institute of Technology (MIT).

• Vladimir Kosma Zworykin develops the first all-electronic television system.

• James Ware Bryce and Clair D. Lake develop punched-card technology at IBM.

1930–1940

• Ernst Ruska and Max Knott develop the electron microscope.

• Alan Turing devises a theoretical computer known as the Turing machine.

• Leslie John Comrie founds the Scientific Computing Service in Britain.

• Konrad Zuse builds the Z1, a binary mechanical computer.

• Claude Shannon completes his master's thesis on Boolean algebra.

• Edwin Land founds the Polaroid Corporation.

• George Philbrick develops an electronic analog computer.

• Jan Rajchman contributes to the development of the electron photomultiplier.

• Louis Couffignal publishes a dissertation on binary mechanical calculators.

• Chester F. Carlson invents xerography, or electrophotography, which leads to the first photocopier machine.

• James Hillier and Albertus Prebus develop the first commercial electron microscope.

• George R. Stibitz and Ernest G. Andrews build the Bell Labs Model I relay computer.

• William Hewlett and David Packard found Hewlett-Packard.

• David Sarnoff pioneers commercial television broadcasting in the U.S.

1940–1950

• Alan Turing begins working with the British government to crack Germany's Enigma codes.

• John Atanasoff and Clifford Berry build the Atanasoff-Berry Computer (ABC).

• George Antheil and Hedy Lamarr invent frequency hopping, which is used in modern cell phones.

• Marvin Camras pioneers new technology for magnetic recording.

• Konrad Zuse builds the Z3, a binary electromechanical programmable digital computer.

• Leslie R. Groves becomes director of the Manhattan Project, the U.S. program to build an atomic bomb.

• Donald A. Flanders heads the computing unit at Los Alamos for the Manhattan Project.

• Ernest G. Andrews develops relay computers at Bell Labs that use binary code.

• Howard Aiken designs the Automatic Sequence Control Calculator, also known as the Harvard Mark I.

• Clair D. Lake at IBM builds Howard Aiken's Mark I computer.

• Tommy Flowers develops the Colossus, a special-purpose electronic computer used to crack German codes.

• Antonin Svoboda joins the MIT Radiation Lab.

• Vannevar Bush publishes his article "As We May Think," about a theoretical machine called a memex.

• J. Presper Eckert and John Mauchly build the Electronic Numeric Integrator and Computer (ENIAC).

• John G. Brainerd serves as the project administrator for the ENIAC.

- Derrick Lehmer and Herman H. Goldstine contribute to the ENIAC.

- Douglas R. Hartree, a co-founder of Britain's National Physical Laboratory (NPL), advocates greater use of computers for scientific advancement.

- Harry D. Huskey contributes to the ENIAC and SWAC.

- Grace M. Hopper becomes the first person to "debug" a computer.

- J. Presper Eckert and John Mauchly begin work on the Electronic Discrete Variable Automatic Computer (EDVAC).

- John von Neumann, a consultant for the ENIAC and the EDVAC, publishes his "First Draft of a Report on the EDVAC."

- Jan Rajchman makes advances in core computer memory technology.

- Arthur W. Burks makes contributions to the ENIAC and the EDVAC.

- Frederic Calland Williams and Thomas Kilburn develop an improved cathode-ray tube, called the Williams tube.

- William Shockley, John Bardeen, and Walter Houser Brattain discover the transistor effect.

- John von Neumann designs the IAS computer at Princeton University's Institute for Advanced Study (IAS).

- Julian Bigelow serves as the chief engineer of the IAS computer.

- Herman H. Goldstine contributes to the development of the IAS computer.

- Maurice V. Wilkes develops the Electronic Delay Storage Automatic Computer (EDSAC).

- Richard Hamming creates programs, called Hamming Codes, to correct errors in computer code.

- George Dantzig invents the "simplex" method of linear programming.

- Herbert Mataré invents a transistor component in France.

• Edwin Land at Polaroid introduces the first instant camera.

• Alan Turing designs the Pilot ACE (Automatic Computing Engine).

• Harry D. Huskey builds the prototype of the Pilot ACE.

• Stanley Gill contributes to the Pilot ACE and the EDSAC.

• Thomas Kilburn and Frederic Calland Williams design the Manchester Mark 1 computer in Britain.

• Maxwell Newman makes contributions to combinatory topology, Boolean algebra, and logic.

• Claude Shannon publishes *A Mathematical Theory of Communication*.

• Norbert Wiener publishes *Cybernetics, or Control and Communication in the Animal and Machine*.

• J. Presper Eckert and John Mauchly begin work on the Universal Automatic Computer (UNIVAC).

• An Wang makes advances in ferrite core memory.

• Sergie A. Lebedev pioneers digital computing in the Soviet Union with the MESM and BESM computers.

1950–1960

• James Henry Rand Jr., president of Remington Rand, introduces the 409, the first business computer.

• Remington Rand buys the Eckert-Mauchly Computer Corporation and begins selling the UNIVAC.

• Alan Turing proposes the "Turing Test," a theory of machine intelligence.

• Antonin Svoboda founds the Research Institute of Mathematical Machines in Prague.

• Maurice V. Wilkes et al. publish *The Preparation of Programs for an Electrical Digital Computer*.

• Jay Wright Forrester invents magnetic core memory.

• Nicholas C. Metropolis develops the Mathematical Numerical Integrator and Computer (MANIAC).

• John Diebold publishes *Automation.*

• Andrew Kay founds Non-Linear Systems (NLS) and develops the first digital voltmeter (DVM).

• Grace M. Hopper writes the first compiler program.

• Cuthbert C. Hurd, director of IBM's Applied Science Division, develops the IBM 701 and the IBM 650.

• Simon Ramo co-founds Ramo-Wooldridge, which later becomes Thompson Ramo-Wooldridge (TRW).

• Gordon Teal builds the first silicon-based junction transistor.

• Reynold B. Johnson invents the RAMAC disk drive at IBM.

• John Backus develops the FORTRAN programming language.

• Herbert A. Simon, Allen Newell, and J. C. Shaw create an artificial-intelligence program called the Logic Theorist and the General Problem Solver (GPS) algorithm.

• Edsger Dijkstra discovers the shortest-path Algorithm, also known as Dijkstra's Algorithm.

• John McCarthy coins the phrase "artificial intelligence" (AI) and organizes the first AI conference.

• The "Fairchild Eight" establish the Fairchild Semiconductor Corporation.

• Grace M. Hopper develops an improved compiler, called Flow-matic, which proved instrumental in the development of the COBOL programming language.

• Herbert Kroemer pioneers the use of heterostructures for semiconductor transistors.

• John Bardeen, Leon Cooper, and John Schrieffer develop a theory of superconductivity known as the BCS theory.

• Seymour Cray co-founds the Control Data Corporation and develops the CDC 1604, 6600, and 7600 systems.

• Kenneth Olsen founds the Digital Equipment Corporation (DEC).

• John McCarthy co-founds MIT's Artificial Intelligence Laboratory and develops the LISP programming language.

• Marvin Minsky co-founds and becomes director of MIT's Artificial Intelligence Laboratory.

• Jack Kilby develops the first germanium-based integrated circuit, also known as a microchip.

• Jean Hoerni, co-founder of the Fairchild Semiconductor Corporation, develops the planar transistor.

• John Backus develops Backus Normal Form, also known as Backus/Naur Form (BNF), and helps develop the ALGOL 60 programming language.

• Robert Noyce, co-founder of the Fairchild Semiconductor Corporation, develops a silicon-based integrated circuit.

• Peter Naur contributes to the development of ALGOL 60 and John Backus's BNF.

• Edsger Dijkstra contributes to ALGOL 60.

1960–1970

• Jean E. Sammet contributes to COBOL and creates the FORMAC programming language.

• J. C. R. Licklider publishes *Man-Computer Symbiosis.*

• Fernando Corbató develops the Compatible Time-Sharing System (CTSS) at MIT.

• Paul Baran develops distributed networks and a packet-switching theory.

• J. C. R. Licklider becomes the first director of IPTO (Information Processing Techniques Office) at the U.S. Department of Defense Advanced Research Projects Agency (ARPA).

• Robert Hall invents the semiconductor laser.

• Herbert Kroemer and Zhores Alferov discover a method to produce a semiconductor-based laser.

• Wesley Clark builds the Laboratory Instrument Computer (LINC) at MIT's Lincoln Laboratory.

• Brian D. Josephson theorizes the properties of superconductors known as the Josephson effects.

• H. Ross Perot founds Electronic Data Systems (EDS).

• Ivan Sutherland develops Sketchpad, the first computer-graphics program.

• Leonard Kleinrock publishes *Communication Nets.*

• John Kemeny and Thomas Kurtz create BASIC (Beginners All-purpose Symbolic Instruction Code).

• Ivan Sutherland becomes the second director of IPTO at ARPA.

• An Wang, the founder of Wang Labs, unveils the LOCI (Logarithmic Calculating Instrument), an electronic scientific desktop calculator.

• Joseph Weizenbaum creates ELIZA, an artificial-intelligence computer program.

• Roy Ash and Charles Thornton manage Litton Industries.

• Robert Moog creates a modular analog synthesizer called the Moog synthesizer.

• Donald Davies develops a packet-switching theory.

• Edward Feigenbaum develops the Dendritic Algorithm (DENDRAL) computer program, the first "expert system."

• Ted Nelson coins the term "hypertext" and conceives of the Xanadu text-publishing system.

• Robert Taylor becomes the third director of IPTO at ARPA, where he oversees the development of the ARPANET.

• Gordon Bell designs the PDP-4, PDP-5, and PDP-6 computers.

• Edson deCastro designs the PDP-8.

• Robert Dennard invents Dynamic Random Access Memory (DRAM).

• Kristen Nygaard develops the object-oriented programming languages SIMULA 1 and Simula 67.

• Lawrence G. Roberts becomes chief developer of the ARPANET.

• Douglas Engelbart develops NLS (oNLine System), the mouse, and the graphical user interface (GUI).

• Seymour Papert and Marvin Minsky create the LOGO computer programming language for children.

• Hewlett-Packard introduces the first desktop scientific calculator, the HP 9100A.

• Christopher Strachey becomes the first director of the Programming Research Group (PRG) at the Oxford University Computing Laboratory.

• Frederick P. Brooks Jr. leads the development of the IBM 360 family of computers.

• Gordon Moore, Robert Noyce, and Andy Grove found Intel.

• Gordon Moore postulates Moore's Law.

• Arthur C. Clarke and Stanley Kubrick write the screenplay for *2001: A Space Odyssey*.

• Frank Heart manages the team at Bolt, Beranek & Newman (BBN) that builds the ARPANET components.

• William R. Crowther at BBN works on Interface Message Processors (IMPs) for the ARPANET.

• Severo M. Ornstein at BBN works on IMPs for the ARPANET.

• J. C. R. Licklider and Robert Taylor write *The Computer as a Communication Device*.

• Donald Knuth publishes the first volume of *The Art of Computer Programming*.

• Charles H. Moore invents Forth, a high-level programming language used by NASA.

• Alan Shugart invents the 8-inch floppy disk.

• Donald Wetzel invents the automated teller machine (ATM).

• Kenneth Thompson and Dennis Ritchie develop the Unix operating system.

• Dennis Ritchie creates the C programming language.

• Donald Keck, Peter Schultz, and Robert Maurer invent a low-loss optical fiber.

• Norm Abramson creates ALOHANET, a wireless data network.

• Marcian E. (Ted) Hoff Jr. creates the Intel 4004 microprocessor.

• Stanley Mazor contributes to the software and design of the Intel 4004 microprocessor.

• Federico Faggin contributes to the silicon design of the Intel 4004 microprocessor.

• Ray Tomlinson creates the first network electronic-mail (e-mail) program.

• Niklaus Wirth creates the Pascal programming language.

• John Blankenbaker develops the Kenbak-1 personal computer.

• Seymour Cray founds Cray Research Inc. and develops the line of Cray supercomputers.

• Gerald M. Weinberg publishes *The Psychology of Computer Programming*.

• Nolan Bushnell creates the popular video game *PONG* and founds the Atari Corporation.

• Alan Kay develops Smalltalk, an object-oriented programming language, and pioneers the graphical user interface (GUI).

• André Thi Truong, founder of the French company R2E, develops the Micral, a microprocessor-based personal computer.

• Philippe Kahn writes the software for the Micral.

• Robert Metcalfe invents the Ethernet and founds the 3Com Corporation.

• Raymond Kurzweil founds the Kurzweil Computer Corporation and creates the first optical character recognition (OCR) technology.

- Jonathan Titus creates the Mark-8, a microprocessor-based personal-computer kit.

- Vinton Cerf and Robert Kahn develop TCP/IP (Transmission Control Protocol/Internet Protocol).

- The Alto desktop computer is developed at the Xerox Palo Alto Research Center (PARC).

- Ed Roberts founds MITS (Micro Instrumentation and Telemetry Systems) and develops the Altair 8800 personal-computer kit.

- Gordon French and Fred Moore hold the first meeting of the Homebrew Computer Club.

- Bill Gates and Paul Allen write a version of BASIC (Beginner's All-purpose Symbolic Instruction Code) for the Altair 8800 and found the Microsoft Corporation.

- Gene Amdahl founds the Amdahl Corporation and releases the first IBM-compatible mainframe computer.

- Victor Glushkov works on the MIR series of computers and the ES-1766.

- Gary Kildall writes the CP/M operating system and founds Intergalactic Digital Research Inc. (later renamed Digital Research Inc., or DRI).

- Charles Simonyi develops BRAVO, the first WYSIWYG (What You See Is What You Get) word processor, for the Alto.

- Whitfield Diffie and Martin Hellman invent public key cryptography.

- William Mensch co-develops the Motorola 6800 chip and the MOS 6502 microprocessor.

- Frederick P. Brooks Jr. publishes *The Mythical Man-Month: Essays in Software Engineering*.

- Jim Warren becomes the original editor of *Dr. Dobb's Journal*.

- Steve Jobs and Steve Wozniak found Apple Computer.

- Steve Wozniak designs the Apple I and Apple II computers.

- Alan Shugart creates the 5.25-inch floppy disk, which is used in IBM's first PC, in 1981.

- Michael Schrayer creates the Electric Pencil, a word processor.

• Raymond Kurzweil develops the Kurzweil Reading Machine.

• Edward Yourdon pioneers structured systems analysis/design and co-develops object-oriented analysis.

• Bill Joy leads the development of Berkeley Software Distribution (BSD) Unix.

• Lawrence Ellison founds the Oracle Corporation.

• Jim Warren founds the West Coast Computer Faire.

• Raymond Damadian Magnetic develops magnetic resonance imaging (MRI) scans.

• Arthur Rock serves as a key financial backer for such companies as Intel and Apple Computer.

• James Martin publishes *The Wired Society*.

• C. Wayne Ratliff creates dBASE, a database software program.

• John Cocke develops the Reduced Instruction Set Computer (RISC) technology at IBM.

• Dan Bricklin and Bob Frankston found Software Arts and create the VisiCalc spreadsheet program.

• Seymour Rubinstein creates WordStar, a word processor.

• Alan Shugart founds Shugart Technology, which becomes Seagate Technology.

1980–1990

• Steve Ballmer joins Microsoft as business manager.

• Klaus von Klitzing et al. publish findings on the quantum Hall effect.

• Clive Sinclair founds Sinclair Research and releases the ZX 80 and ZX 81 low-cost computers.

• Microsoft releases MS-DOS.

• Adam Osborne founds the Osborne Computer Corporation and introduces the Osborne 1 portable computer.

• Commodore Business Machines, founded by Jack Tramiel, releases the VIC-20 color computer.

• Larry Tesler leaves Xerox PARC to become Apple's chief scientist.

• Vinod Khosla founds Daisy Systems.

• Philip "Don" Estridge leads the team that develops the first IBM PC.

• Gerd Karl Binnig and Heinrich Rohrer invent the scanning tunneling microscope (STM)

• Charles Simonyi joins Microsoft, where he leads the development of Microsoft Word.

• Rod Canion, James Harris, and William Murto found the Compaq Computer Corporation.

• Commodore releases the Commodore 64 computer.

• John Warnock and Charles Geschke found Adobe Systems, a pioneering desktop-publishing firm.

• Andrew Kay, the founder of the Kaypro Corporation (formerly NLS), introduces the Kaypro II personal computer.

• Sid Meier co-founds MicroProse Software and designs such computer games as *F-15 Strike Eagle*.

• Vinod Khosla, Andy Bechtolsheim, Scott McNealy, and Bill Joy found Sun Microsystems.

• Mitchell Kapor and Jonathan Sachs found the Lotus Development Corporation and release Lotus 1-2-3.

• James Clark founds Silicon Graphics.

• Benoit Mandelbrot publishes *The Fractal Geometry of Nature*.

• Ray Noorda becomes president of Novell.

• Peter Norton founds Peter Norton Computing and develops utilities software for the PC.

• Steve Jobs manages the development of the Apple's Macintosh computer.

• Jef Raskin designs the Macintosh.

• Bill Atkinson develops MacPaint and QuickDraw for the Macintosh.

• Philippe Kahn founds Borland International Inc. and creates Turbo Pascal.

• Bjarne Stroustrup at Bell Labs develops the C++ programming language.

• Apple introduces the Macintosh.

• Sandy Lerner and Leonard Bosack found Cisco Systems.

• William Gibson publishes *Neuromancer.*

• Raymond Kurzweil creates the Kurzweil 250 synthesizer.

• James Martin co-develops CASE (computer-aided software engineering).

• Broderbund Software, founded by Doug Carlston, pioneers educational software with such releases as *Where in the World is Carmen Sandiego?*

• Jay Miner develops the Amiga computer.

• Nicholas Negroponte founds MIT's Media Lab.

• Alexey Pazhitnov creates *Tetris*, the popular computer game.

• Stewart Brand and Larry Brilliant found the WELL (Whole Earth 'Lectronic Link), an on-line discussion forum.

• Steve Case helps found Quantum Computer Services, which later becomes AOL.

• Steve Jobs founds NeXT Software Inc. to develop the NeXTSTEP operating system.

• Bill Atkinson develops HyperCard.

• Andrew Tanenbaum creates the Minix operating system, based on Unix.

• Steve Jobs introduces the NeXT Cube.

• Steven Hawking publishes *A Brief History of Time.*

• Ray Ozzie creates Lotus Notes.

1990–2000

• Linus Torvalds develops the Linux operating system.

• Tim Berners-Lee leads the development of HTML, HTTP, and the World Wide Web at CERN, the European Organization for Nuclear Research, in Switzerland.

• Mitchell Kapor and John Perry Barlow found the Electronic Frontier Foundation (EFF).

• James Gosling and Bill Joy lead the development of Java (then called Oak).

• Philip R. Zimmermann develops Pretty Good Privacy (PGP), an e-mail encryption software program.

• John Kilcullen publishes *DOS for Dummies,* the first in the series of "for Dummies" books.

• Steve Case becomes CEO of AOL.

• Halsey Minor founds CNET: The Computer Network.

• Johan Helsingius creates anon.penet.fi, a "remailer," which allows for anonymous e-mail.

• Marc Andreessen develops the Mosaic Internet browser.

• Francis Collins becomes director of the National Human Genome Research Institute (NHGRI).

• Anita Jones becomes director of research and engineering at the U.S. Department of Defense.

• Marc Andreessen and James Clark found the Netscape Communications Corporation and unveil Netscape Navigator, an Internet browser.

• Jerry Yang and David Filo found Yahoo!.

• Ari Patrinos becomes director of the Human Genome Program for the U.S. Department of Energy.